WORLD OF INFORMATION

AFRICA REVIEW

2003/04

Twenty-fifth edition

Published by
Walden Publishing Ltd

2 Market Street
Saffron Walden
Essex CB10 1HZ, England
Tel: +44 (0)1799 521150
Fax: +44 (0)1799 524805
E-mail: Asiapacificreview@worldinformation.com
Website: www.worldinformation.com

In association with
Kogan Page Ltd
120 Pentonville Road
London N1 9JN
Tel: +44 (0) 20 7278 0433
Fax: +44 (0) 20 7837 6348
E-mail: info@kogan-page.co.uk
Website: www.kogan-page.co.uk

Publisher: Sue Hewitt
Managing Director: Anthony Axon
Managing Editor: Daniel Brett

First published in 1980

Publishers note
Every possible effort has been made to ensure that the information contained in this book is accurate at the time of going to press. The Publishers cannot accept responsibility for any errors or omissions, however caused.

ISBN 07494 40651 (Kogan Page Ltd)
ISBN 1 86217 037-1 (Walden Publishing Ltd)
ISSN 0269 3844

ICC
The world business organization
www.iccwbo.org

AFRICA
SEYCHELLES
Victoria
Algiers
Tunis
Rabat
MOROCCO
TUNISIA
Tripoli
WESTERN SAHARA
Cairo
ALGERIA
LIBYA
EGYPT
Nouakchott
MAURITANIA
Dakar
SENEGAL
MALI
NIGER
Banjul
THE GAMBIA
ERITREA
Khartoum
Asmara
Bissau
Bamako
BURKINA FASO
Niamey
CHAD
SUDAN
GUINEA BISSAU
GUINEA
Ouagadougou
Djibouti
DJIBOUTI
Conakry
Freetown
N'Djamena
COTE D'IVOIRE
BENIN
NIGERIA
SIERRA LEONE
TOGO
Addis Ababa
Monrovia
Abuja
ETHIOPIA
GHANA
LIBERIA
CENTRAL AFRICAN REPUBLIC
Yamoussoukro
Accra
Lomé
Cotonou
CAMEROON
Bangui
SOMALIA
Malabo
Yaoundé
Mogadishu
EQUATORIAL GUINEA
UGANDA
KENYA
Kampala
SAO TOME & PRINCIPE
CONGO
Libreville
GABON
Nairobi
RWANDA
Kigali
Bujumbura
BURUNDI
Brazzaville
Kinshasa
DEMOCRATIC REPUBLIC OF CONGO
TANZANIA
Dar es Salaam
Luanda
CAPE VERDE ISLANDS
COMOROS
Moroni
ANGOLA
MALAWI
Lilongwe
ZAMBIA
Lusaka
Praia
Harare
MOZAMBIQUE
ZIMBABWE
Antananarivo
Windhoek
MADAGASCAR
NAMIBIA
BOTSWANA
Gaborone
Pretoria
Maputo
Mbabane
SWAZILAND
Maseru
SOUTH AFRICA
LESOTHO
MAURITIUS
Port Louis
REUNION
0 Miles 1,000
0 Km 1,600

Contents

Countries

Key indicators – Africa 2000/01

	Population (m)	Area ('000 sq km)	GDP per capita (US$)	Inflation (%)	GDP real growth (%)	Balance of trade (US$m)
Algeria	31.29	2,381.7	1,401 (*)	4.1	3.6	12,300
Angola	13.13	1,246.7	330 (*)	152.6	3.2	4,300 (*)
Benin	6.23	112.6	373	3.8	5.8	-207
Botswana	1.63	582.0	3,369 (*)	7.2	7.1	347 (*)
Burkina Faso	11.90	274.0	185	4.9	5.7	-320
Burundi	6.61	27.8	126	8.0	3.3	-59
Cameroon	15.40	475.4	593	2.8	5.3	586
Cape Verde	0.43	4.0	1,297	3.7	3.0	-236
Central African Republic	3.72	623.0	268	3.8	-0.3	2
Chad	7.89	1,284.0	182	12.4	8.9	-62
Comoros	0.71	2.2	238	5.0	1.9	-58
Congo	3.02	342.0	927	-0.5	3.3	1,900 (*)
DR of Congo (ex-Zaíre)	50.95	2,345.4	452	299.0	-4.0	-275
Côte d'Ivoire	16.40	322.5	573	4.4	-0.9	1,500(*)
Djibouti	0.64	23.2	873	1.8	2.0	-200
Egypt	66.70	1,001.5	1,274	3.3	2.4	-8,300
Equatorial Guinea	0.46	28.1	3,478	12.0	46.5	597
Eritrea	4.00	125.0	191	15.1	6.4	-436
Ethiopia	63.49	1,251.3	99	-7.2	7.9	-645
Gabon	1.21	267.7	3,451	2.5	1.7	1,700 (*)
The Gambia	1.39	11.3	312	4.0	5.8	-69
Ghana	20.15	239.5	261 (*)	32.9	4.0	-800 (*)
Guinea	8.15	245.9	380	6.8	2.9	140
Guinea-Bissau	1.12	36.1	196	6.4	7.8	-18
Kenya	29.30	582.7	310 (*)	0.8	1.1	-1,400 (*)
Lesotho	2.16	30.4	458	6.5 (*)	2.9	-17
Liberia	2.92	111.4	176 (*)	9.9	15.0 (*)	–
Libya	5.29	1,775.5	6,260 (*)	12.0 (*)	5.6 (*)	6,300
Madagascar	15.97	592.0	243	5.0	6.7	-165 (*)
Malawi	11.31	118.5	142 (*)	27.2	2.8	-169
Mali	11.22	1,241.2	223	5.0	6.2	-400 (*)
Mauritania	2.67	1,030.7	322	4.7	4.6	16
Mauritius	1.18	1.9	4,194 (*)	4.4	6.7	-426 (*)
Morocco	29.00	711.0	1,156 (*)	0.5	6.3	-3,200
Mozambique	17.69	799.4	282	9.0	6.3	-609 (*)
Namibia	1.74	824.3	1,839 (*)	9.2	2.7	-200 (*)
Niger	10.83	1,267.0	167	4.0	5.1	-45
Nigeria	111.50	923.8	321	18.9	4.0	6,500
Rwanda	7.62	26.3	231	3.5	6.2	-153
São Tomé & Príncipe	0.16	1.0	350	9.3	4.0	-25
Senegal	9.52	196.2	462	3.0	5.7	-300 (*)
Seychelles	0.08	0.5	7,453	6.2	-1.0	-223
Sierra Leone	4.82	72.3	133	-0.9	5.4	-86
Somalia	9.28	738.0	140	100.0 (*)	-3.2 (1)	–
South Africa	44.70	1,127.2	2,645 (*)	5.7	2.2	4,100
Sudan	31.00	2,505.8	465 (*)	5.0	5.3	607
Swaziland	1.01	17.4	230 (*)	7.5	1.6	-111
Tanzania	33.64	945.1	267 (*)	5.3 (*)	5.1	-864 (*)
Terres Australes	0.00 (a)	439.8	–	–	–	–
Togo	4.63	56.6	283	1.4	2.5 (*)	-60
Tunisia	9.57	164.2	2,071 (*)	1.9	5.0	-2,200
Uganda	22.19	236.0	251 (*)	4.6 (*)	4.9	-906 (*)
Zambia	10.72	752.6	346 (*)	22.5	5.0	-243 (*)
Zimbabwe	12.63	391.1	748 (*)	76.7	-8.4	500 (*)

(*) estimated figure; (a) 100 people; (1) 1999

Currencies (units per US$)

	Unit	Jan 1998	Jan 1999	Jan 2000	Jan 2001	Jan 2002
Algeria	Algerian dinar	58.50	61.62	68.15	72.03	76.35
Angola	Readjusted kwanza	257,128.00	257,128.00	5.57 (a)	17.68	32.12
Benin	CFA franc	611.95	565.97	637.54	691.39	733.16
Botswana	Pula	3.84	4.63	4.59	5.46	7.02
Burkina Faso	CFA franc	611.95	565.97	637.54	691.39	733.16
Burundi	Burundi franc	415.50	505.73	623.27	790.09	863.96
Cameroon	CFA franc	611.95	565.97	637.54	691.39	733.16
Cape Verde	Cape Verde escudo	97.93	94.71	106.26	116.01	119.80
Central African Republic	CFA franc	611.95	565.97	637.54	691.39	733.16
Chad	CFA franc	611.95	565.97	637.54	691.39	733.16
Comoros	Comoros franc	459.11	491.97	472.20	515.35	548.06
Congo	CFA franc	611.95	565.97	637.54	691.39	733.16
Côte d'Ivoire	CFA franc	611.95	565.97	637.54	691.39	733.16
Democratic Republic of Congo	Congolese franc	137,500.00	137,500.00 (b)	4.50	4.50	313.00
Djibouti	Djibouti franc	177.72	177.72	172.25	175.40	170.00
Egypt	Egyptian pound	3.41	3.41	3.43	3.86	4.58 (c)
Equatorial Guinea	CFA franc	611.95	565.97	637.54	691.39	733.16
Eritrea	Nakfa	6.71	6.99	7.97	8.24	8.47
Ethiopia	Ethiopian birr	6.71	6.99	7.97	8.24	8.47
Gabon	CFA franc	611.95	565.97	637.54	691.39	733.16
The Gambia	Dalasi	10.10	11.10	11.61	15.58	17.48
Ghana	Cedi	2,265.00	2,355.00	3,530.00	7,175.00	7,402.50
Guinea	Guinean franc	1,000.00	1,286.00	1,367.25	1,855.00	1,965.00
Guinea-Bissau	CFA franc	28,412.10 (*)	565.97	637.54	691.39	733.16
Kenya	Kenya shilling	59.75	61.45	72.70	78.60	78.82
Lesotho	Maloti	4.97	6.12	6.05	7.84	12.09
Liberia	Liberian dollar	1.00	1.00	1.00	1.00	1.00
Libya	Libyan dinar	0.38	0.45	0.46	0.54	0.64
Madagascar	Franc Malgache	5,000.00	5,220.00	6,415.00	6,491.00	6,364.00
Malawi	Kwacha	21.43	43.50	46.25	80.25	67.00
Mali	CFA franc	611.95	565.97	637.54	691.39	733.16
Mauritania	Ouguiya	169.66	204.91	223.39	247.15	264.01
Mauritius	Mauritian rupee	22.52	24.73	25.40	27.83	30.25
Morocco	Moroccan dirham	9.85	9.32	9.97	10.55	11.46
Mozambique	Metical	11,495.00	12,374.00	13,260.00	17,191.50	22,885.00
Namibia	Namibian dollar	4.97	6.11	6.05	7.84	12.09
Niger	CFA franc	611.95	565.97	637.54	691.39	733.16
Nigeria	Naira	22.00 (o)	21.89 (o)	21.89 (o)	110.70 (m)	115.75
Rwanda	Rwanda franc	348.49	320.63	336.06	359.03	454.00
São Tomé & Príncipe	Dobra	2,390.00	2,390.00	2,318.63	2,390.00	8,937.20
Senegal	CFA franc	611.95	565.97	637.54	691.39	733.16
Seychelles	Seychelles rupee	5.21	5.45	5.30	6.35	5.62
Sierra Leone	Leone	900.00	1,630.50	1,913.00	2,036.08	2,241.00
Somalia	Somali shilling	2,620.00	2,620.00	2,555.16	2,620.00	2,620.00
South Africa	Rand	4.97	6.11	6.05	7.84	12.09
Sudan	Sudanese dinar	161.29	196.00	256.00	258.70	258.70
Swaziland	Lilangeni	4.97	6.11	6.05	7.84	12.09
Tanzania	Tanzania shilling	622.50	676.08	794.50	803.00	918.00
Togo	CFA franc	611.95	565.97	637.54	691.39	733.16
Tunisia	Tunisian dinar	1.17	1.11	1.23	1.36	1.46
Uganda	Ugandan shilling	1,145.00	1,371.50	1,510.00	1,855.00	1,730.00
Zambia	Kwacha	1,482.50	2,620.00	2,800.00	4,650.00	3,820.00
Zimbabwe	Zimbabwe dollar	19.25	43.20	38.23	55.13	55.45

(a) Angolan kwanza readjusted 13 Dec 1999;
(b) Congolese franc introduced 30 Jun 1998; (c) central bank devalued the Egyptian pound to LE4.5 per US$; (m) market rate;
(o) official rate

Contributors

Philip Alexander writes on Commonwealth development, European Union enlargement and the Middle East peace process. He has contributed to *Jane's Sentinel* political risk pointers and *Emerging Markets Online.*

Andrew Allimadi is a development economist currently working as a consultant in Uganda. He previously taught the political economy of Africa at London University's School of Oriental and African Studies.

Guy Arnold is a freelance writer who specialises in north-south relations and African affairs. His most recent publications include *A Third World Handbook, Wars in the Third World Since 1945* and *The End of the Third World.*

Nick Awde is the editor of *Caucasus World* and a development journalist specialising in the Middle East, Horn of Africa, Caucasus and Central Asia.

Daniel Brett is a managing editor at World of Information. He specialises in the politics and economics of developing countries. He is also a columnist for the *Accra Daily Mail* and the Zimbabwean *Standard.*

Desmond Davies is editor of the London-based *West Africa* magazine. The Sierra Leonean-born journalist has been writing and commenting on African affairs for almost 30 years.

Jonathan Derrick is a journalist and historian specialising in African affairs and contemporary history. He has worked on the editorial staff of West Africa and Africa magazines and as an editor of the reference books *Africa Today, Africa Who's Who* and *Makers of Modern Africa*

Michael Fishpool is an analyst at World of Information who specialises in international politics and security with a particular focus on Western Europe and the Balkans.

Alvise Forcellini studied politics with an emphasis on African social development and urban poverty, at Brussels University.

Vincent Foucher is a graduate from the Institut d'Etudes Politiques de Paris and University of London's School of Oriental and African Studies; he is finishing a PhD on Casamançais nationalism. He is a regular contributor for *Jane's* and *Mondes Rebelles*.

Nicole Goldin is an international development consultant and has lived and worked in Africa and Asia. She is currently a PhD candidate at the School of Oriental and African Studies (SOAS), University of London.

Fred J Hill is a development journalist specialising in the Caucasus, Central Asia and Latin America.

Marybeth McKeever has worked for the UN as a consultant on development programmes, and is pursuing her career in international development management.

Nils P Mork is a management consultant specialising in the humanitarian and development sectors and is currently involved in researching the African arms trade.

Anita Parameswaran is a business analyst for a leading insurance company working on corporate strategy.

Falguni Patel is a development consultant and has worked for Christian Aid on west and central Africa projects and in the Jubilee 2000 Secretariate during the campaign for debt relief for heavily indebted poor countries.

Dominique Rakotomalala studied political science and international relations in Heidelberg, Saarbrucken, Vienna and Madrid. He is currently working with a German foundation in Antananarivo, Madagascar.

Alex Vatanka has lived in Iran and Denmark and is a London-based political risk analyst and a contributor to *Keesings Record of World Events*. He specialises in the Middle East, Central Asia and energy issues.

Anver Versi is the editor of the UK based *African Business* magazine. His articles have appeared in a variety of international publications including *Newsweek, The Wall Street Journal, The Times, The Guardian* and *The Independent*.

Africa

Africa experienced strong growth in 2002, despite the decline of the global economy. The level of growth was broadly determined by international commodity markets, agricultural output, domestic economic policy and internal conflict. GDP growth for sub-Saharan Africa was 3.7 per cent in 2002, a repeat performance of the previous year. For Africa as a whole, growth fell marginally from 3.0 per cent in 2001 to 2.9 per cent in 2002, due to North Africa's mediocre 1.9 per cent growth. The best performers included Angola, Chad, Equatorial Guinea and Mozambique, which all enjoyed growth rates of over 10 per cent. This was largely due to an influx of foreign investment in economies with a low level of economic development. Countries recording negative growth rates were Côte d'Ivoire, Guinea-Bissau, Nigeria and Zimbabwe, which all experienced social unrest or internal conflict as well as drought.

'The best performers included Angola, Chad, Equatorial Guinea and Mozambique, which all enjoyed growth rates of over 10 per cent ... largely due to an influx of foreign investment in economies with a low level of economic development.'

Peace efforts in Angola, the Democratic Republic of Congo (DRC), Sierra Leone and Sudan have all helped to lift the growth levels of these countries, particularly Angola which is the focus of a regional oil rush. This will have a positive impact on neighbouring countries, which have suffered the spillover of political instability. West Africa is still plagued by a number of low-level conflicts and instability, particularly in Liberia where the government of President Charles Taylor has sought to undermine neighbouring states in its war against rebel armies.

Oil leads growth

Oil exporting nations such as Algeria, Angola, Cameroon, Nigeria, Libya and Sudan enjoyed strong growth in 2001 on the back of high oil prices. However, in most African states in 2002 economic activity declined due to the global slowdown, lower oil prices and production cuts in Opec states. The exceptions were the non-Opec states of Angola and Sudan, which saw an increase in production which far outweighed the fall in prices. GDP growth in the Opec states was modest, ranging from -0.9 per cent for Nigeria and 0.8 per cent for Libya to 4.8 per cent for Cameroon.

Crude oil prices did not fall below US$20 per barrel in the first half of 2002 and rose to over US$25 in the second half of 2002, reaching US$30 by the end of the year due to fears of war in the Middle East and to political instability in Venezuela. In Africa's non-oil producing countries primary commodity prices failed to rise as fast as oil on the international markets and continued to face deteriorating terms of trade. Soft commodities, such as coffee and cotton, as well as many metals, had experienced a decline in prices during the first half of 2002, but experienced something of a come-back in the second half. An upturn in copper, silver and gold prices provided some relief for ore producers such as South Africa, Ghana and Zambia, although they continued to experience the adverse effects of consolidation and risk-aversion within the mining sector. The effects of rising prices of agro-exports were boosted by bumper crops in some countries. Uganda and Tanzania experienced highly favourable climatic conditions and saw GDP growth increase as a result. On the whole, countries dependant on agro-exports suffered drought, which severely hampered their ability to take advantage of favourable conditions.

Hunger stalks Africa

Drought also meant hunger for millions of Africans. By the end of 2002, more than 38 million people in Southern Africa and the Horn of Africa faced severe food shortages and possible starvation. Famine was also spreading to West and Central Africa, in what the director of the UN's World Food Programme (WFP), James Morris, called 'an unprecedented crisis'.

Drought revealed the underlying structural problems which lie behind the problem of food scarcity in Africa. A variety of factors contributed to the crisis in 2002: drought, floods, the impact of HIV/AIDS, armed conflict, political instability and unsuitable economic policies. The worst hit country in Southern Africa was Zimbabwe, where around seven million people were affected by food shortages due to a cereal grain deficit of 1.5 million tonnes. While drought was an immediate cause of Zimbabwe's problems, the contentious land reform programme and the distribution of food on the basis of political affiliation helped fuel the crisis. Food assistance was also needed in Angola. By the end of 2002 the WFP was feeding around 1.8 million people in Angola, up from 1.0 million at the beginning of the year. This put a great burden on the agency, which only managed to receive a third of the money needed to continue its relief work in southern Africa.

'The worst hit country in Southern Africa was Zimbabwe, where around seven million people were affected by food shortages due to a cereal grain deficit of 1.5 million tonnes.'

In the Horn of Africa, Eritrea and Ethiopia continued to struggle with the effects of the war between them which ended in 2000. Around a quarter of Eritrea's 4.2 million population and 13 million Ethiopians faced famine and were living in conditions which the US's Famine Early Warning System (FEWS) claimed was worse than the famine of the mid-1980s when eight million faced starvation. Commercial imports of food have been hampered by high levels of external debt in Ethiopia, which made over US$160 million of debt service payments in 2002. In Eritrea, there was total crop failure in the main crop-growing region of Barentu.

As well as debt, war has played a significant part in food insecurity. In Sudan, around 2.9 million people were dependent on food aid in 2002. In Central and West Africa, a large number of internally displaced people and refugees have increased demand for relief aid due to conflicts that have swept these regions.

Outlook

Economic growth for Africa as a whole is set to grow by 4 per cent in 2003, due to an expectedly rapid growth in the continent's largest economies and the rise in oil prices, which will lift growth in the North. However, this is contingent on political stabilisation, conflict resolution, a continuing rise of non-oil commodity prices on international markets and improved agricultural output. The conflict in Côte d'Ivoire and the strong possibility of instability surrounding the Nigerian election, scheduled for April 2003, could have serious repercussions for growth in West Africa. Some Sahelian countries, such as Mali and Burkina Faso, which rely on Côte d'Ivoire for access to ports on the Atlantic coast will be particularly vulnerable. Nevertheless, Ghana is expected to show strong growth, on the back of rising gold and cocoa prices. In East Africa, Kenya is likely to become the star performer following the election of Mwai Kibaki as president. The defeat of Kanu, Kenya's ruling party since independence, in the elections removed the main obstacle to the anti-corruption legislation demanded by international donors. This should revive investor sentiment and lead to a resumption of donor support. In Southern Africa, the South African economy should stabilise after a difficult year which saw growth and inflation hit by a volatile rand. Zimbabwe's deepening political and economic crisis could drag the region down. This will be partly offset by the economic boom in Angola and Mozambique, spurred on by investment in their respective oil and aluminium sectors.

The African Union: false dawn for Africa?

The creation of the African Union (AU), officially launched in June 2002, was seen as an antidote to Africa's cycle of violence and poverty. Developing a consensus on issues such as political reform and economic integration is, however, proving to be an onerous and almost impossible task. Modelling the AU on the European Union (EU) has numerous problems, particularly given the continent's diverse range of political systems and uneven economic development. The controversies surrounding the EU's expansion and economic integration are amplified in Africa. Mistrust, conflict and vested interests tend to take precedence over the principles of pan-Africanism.

Ideological divisions

Even before its launch, the AU was divided along ideological grounds with a fierce debate over the direction of African unity should take. The AU is supposed to overcome the shortcomings of its predecessor, the Organisation for African Unity (OAU) which was often dubbed a 'dictators' club'. Its founding document, the Constitutive Act, enables it to intervene in member states where there is evidence of serious human rights violations (unlike its predecessor). Yet, from its inception, the AU appears to be beset with the same problems that affected the OAU: lack of commitment among member states, lack of money and a failure to agree on any principles beyond weak platitudes about unity and integration.

> 'Mistrust, conflict and vested interests tend to take precedence over the principles of pan-Africanism.'

The organisation is divided between the economic liberalisers, including South Africa, Nigeria and Senegal, and protectionists, including Libya and Zimbabwe. The approach of the liberalisers is enshrined in the New Partnership for Africa's Development (Nepad), which commits African states to democracy and free market reform, in return for assistance from the Group of Eight (G8) leading industrialised nations. The African leaders pioneering Nepad believe it is the continent's best bet to secure US$64 billion and plug a resource gap of around 12 per cent of African GDP. Libya's Colonel Muammar Al-Qadafi denounced the programme, claiming its neo-liberal stance constituted a new form of colonialism. Qadafi also has a different view on the promotion of democratic institutions outlined in the AU's Constitutive Act, claiming that Libya and other African states are entitled to their own interpretation of democracy and should resist the imposition of Western political systems. His position won the sympathy of those African political elites who have much to fear from open markets, greater transparency and democratisation. Without a consensus on the interpretation of the Constitutive Act, the whole process of peer review promoted by South Africa is more or less redundant.

Regional building blocks for union

African states have not entirely dismissed the notion of free trade and economic co-operation, regardless of the ideological divisions that have already beset the AU. The development of regional economic communities (RECs) is seen as the first step towards the continent's economic and monetary union. Africa has 14 RECs, the most significant of which are the Economic Community of West African States (Ecowas), the Union du Maghreb Arabe (UMA) (Arab Maghreb Union), the Central Africa Economic and Monetary Community (CEMAC), Union Economique et Monetaire Ouest Africaine (UEMOA) (West African Economic and Monetary Union), the Common Market for Eastern and Southern Africa (Comesa) and the Southern African Development Community (SADC). Most countries belong to two or more sub-regional trading blocks; the Democratic Republic of Congo (DRC) belongs to four RECs.

The stated aim of the African Economic Community (AEC), which is headed by the AU, is to absorb all the RECs, which will form the basis of a single African currency and central bank. This is the AU's ultimate aim, with the AU Secretariat presiding over the integration of the AEC. Yet, the six-stage process, lasting up to 40 years, faces almost insurmountable obstacles in the form of political resistance and economic barriers.

Barriers to integration

The fact that political frictions exist between many states comes as no surprise in a continent racked by war and where democratic standards vary wildly. The development of the RECs has been hindered by open warfare and alliances between governments and guerrilla groups. Regional economic integration can only occur when there is good faith between governments, a rare commodity in a continent where few countries have avoided war since the end of colonial rule. And governments led by vested interests often fail to make the short-term sacrifices necessary for the long-term goals of regional economic integration. Consequently, time-tables for opening up markets and reducing tariff barriers are often broken or ignored, leading to chaos and mistrust among participants.

The main administrative problem for Africa's economic integration is merging the large array of RECs which encompass a diverse range of economies integrating at different speeds. The speed of integration is often dictated by the amount of tangible benefits. For many countries, the RECs have not delivered on their ambitious goals for growth, while trade remains dependent on the markets of the developed world. Tanzania's withdrawal from Comesa in 2000, two months ahead of the organisation's inauguration, highlighted the problems of opening up countries to free markets. Tanzania's industrial sector cannot compete with more efficient foreign rivals, such as Kenya and South Africa, causing the government to fear that free trade would lead to deindustrialisation. States such as Tanzania earn a large amount of money through import tariffs; to lift tariffs would lead to a financial shortfall which in turn would risk higher levels of debt and painful fiscal adjustment. As the AU's Constitutive Act does not compel states to join a REC, let alone lift trade barriers, states like Tanzania are able to drop out of the process of economic integration, or at least make more tentative steps towards free trade than envisaged by the AEC.

Single currency blues

As efforts towards economic integration are stepped up, tensions between African countries with varying levels of development and differences in trade patterns are likely to intensify. The chances are that a single African currency would reflect the value of trade associated with the main exports of larger, more developed economies, such as Nigeria and South Africa. In the EU, such disparities in development have been evened out through structural funding in which funds are transferred from richer states such as Germany and the UK and targetted at poorer countries and regions, such as Ireland and Portugal. Africa does not have the kind of wealth needed to undertake a redistribution programme that could bridge the gap between the dynamic but highly localised industrial sectors and the under-developed semi-subsistent agricultural sectors, from which most Africans derive their income. Consequently, a single currency determined by capital-intensive sectors producing value added exports will distort the African economy, potentially damaging labour-intensive sectors such as agriculture. A move towards a single currency could therefore be detrimental to development, a fact that has created friction among those West African states seeking to create a single currency for the region.

West African disharmony

Creating a free-floating African currency would require economic convergence. Economic policy harmonisation is fundamental to the creation of a monetary union, in order to keep inflation low and stabilise the exchange rate. The difficulties involved in harmonising economic policy are evident in the efforts to create the West African Monetary Union (Wamu), which envisages the merger of UEMOA, formed by Benin, Burkina Faso, Côte d'Ivoire, Guinea Bissau, Mali, Niger, Senegal and Togo, and the West African Monetary Zone (WAMZ) (Ghana, Nigeria, Sierra Leone, Gambia and Guinea).

The WAMZ was initiated in 2000 and was expected to be fully established by 2003. It was envisaged that the WAMZ would create a common central bank with a single currency, the Eco, being in circulation in 2003. In November 2002, the launch of the Eco was postponed until July 2005 after none of the WAMZ states managed to meet all four convergence criteria. The criteria included maintaining single digit inflation, a low budget deficit of not more than 3 per cent of GDP in 2002, foreign reserves of at least three months' import cover and central bank financing that does not exceed 10 per cent of the revenue earned in the previous year. The failure of the WAMZ states to meet their economic targets for 2003, as well as failing to meet the convergence criteria, will set back Wamu's launch and the introduction of the Ecoi, the currency of the merged UEMOA and WAMZ which was due to replace the Eco in 2004.

The problems of economic convergence are not simply due to a lack of political commitment to fiscal discipline. The basis of the new monetary regime in West Africa is also in dispute. Nigeria is resisting the adoption of a fixed euro peg, such as the one currently used by the CFA franc (currency of the UEMOA countries), arguing that it would affect competitiveness and the flexibility of regional monetary policy. As an oil producer, Nigeria would prefer a US dollar peg; oil is traded in US dollars on the international markets. In contrast, countries with a close trading relationship with the EU are keen to hold on to the fixed euro peg, or at least introduce a crawling peg that would take account of differentials in inflation and shifts in terms of trade.

> 'Economic integration will happen at its own pace and when governments deem it in their best interest; it will not happen through coercion.'

An alternative union

The divisions between African states are unlikely to be overcome, even within the lengthy time-table set by the Abuja Treaty. Yet, what some proponents of African unification fail to grasp is that the AU need not be modelled on the EU. Africa is a different continent with different problems and so requires different institutions and economic processes. Summits are wasted trying to agree on creating farcical structures such as the African parliament or promoting fanciful dreams such as a single currency. The RECs have emerged more or less organically, without the need for protocols from the OAU or the AU. Economic integration will happen at its own pace and when governments deem it in their best interest; it will not happen through coercion.

Instead, the AU should seek to provide a political forum for conflict resolution and prevention, something which the OAU failed to achieve and which the UN has completely avoided. Poverty has gone hand-in-hand with conflict in Africa. Some of the continent's most impoverished states are its most war-racked, a fact that emphasises the need to place conflict resolution above economic integration. The most notable example is the DRC, which saw governments and rebel groups take the opportunity to invade and pillage with impunity for the sake of profit. Up to three million people died and millions of others were impoverished and displaced in what has been called 'Africa's World War'. A common rule of law needs to be developed and enforced in the AU, which defines the relationship between the AU, member states and civil society. This requires more than a peer review body, but structures that are effective, respected and independent. Only then can the AU distinguish itself from its predecessor and improve the wellbeing of all Africans.

Africa and trade: globalisation or marginalisation?

African farmers are exasperated. In recent years, they have endured the rigours of free market reform, which has involved an end to subsidies and guaranteed prices. The liberalisation of the agricultural sector was largely at the behest of the IMF, World Bank and Western governments, which tied aid to reform. The moves have exposed African farming to a highly unequal global market, where agricultural produce from rich nations has been dumped on world markets, often at below cost price.

The World Trade Organisation's (WTO) Doha round of talks held in November 2001 set an agenda which heavily protected agricultural producers in the developed world found hard to reject in fear of being seen as hypocritical. For the first time in the history of international trade summits, Doha touched on the issue of agricultural liberalisation, compelling developed markets to open up to African imports. Yet Africa still faces an uphill task to persuade the US and the EU to drop protectionist measures and risk the wrath of their powerful farming lobbies. In 2002, the governments of the developed world continued to deal out farming subsidies worth US$300 billion per year, more than six times the amount of aid given to the developing world. Instead of improving efficiency, this trade liberalisation has rewarded the inefficient and heavily subsidised farmers of the developed world. On the issue of trade liberalisation, it was a case of do what I say, not do as I do.

> 'For the first time in the history of international trade summits, Doha touched on the issue of agricultural liberalisation, compelling developed markets to open up to African imports.'

Sugar leaves Africa bitter

African farms are more productive than their European and US counter-parts in several key commodities. Sugar is a prime example of African efficiency, with raw cane sugar produced at a fraction of the cost of sugar beet in the EU. Yet the world sugar market remains highly regulated with major tariff and non-tariff barriers impeding Africa's ability to trade. The EU's sugar market is particularly distorted, due to a variety of protectionist measures, ranging from high tariffs to large subsidies, designed to maintain inefficient and costly sugar beet production. Action for Southern Africa (ACTSA), a UK-based campaigning organisation, pointed out that 'it is cheaper for Cadburys to produce chocolate bars in their factory in Birmingham and export them to South Africa, than produce them using local sugar at their South African plant in Port Elizabeth'.

The EU's sugar market is complex and regulation is uneven. For instance, the EU Sugar Protocol and Special Preferential Sugar (SPS) arrangement gives some African sugar producers duty-free access to markets at fixed quotas to sell unrefined sugar, but countries such as South Africa, the region's largest producer, are denied such access. However, value-added produce, such as confectionary, faces stiff EU tariffs which are intended to stifle competition from Africa. In doing so, the EU has pushed African sugar producers and manufacturers out of production by dumping surplus sugar on world markets.

A reduction in subsidies and trade barriers would stimulate trade, delivering much-needed foreign exchange to efficient sugar producers such as Swaziland, where sugar accounts for 67 per cent of agricultural production and more than 20 per cent of GDP. However, according to ACTSA, in recent years EU dumping has led to the loss of 16,000 jobs in the Swazi sugar industry and 20,000 jobs in sugar associated industries. The liberalisation of sugar markets would lead to a rise in economic growth in many southern African countries and provide a boost to the manufacturing sector. Some estimates indicate that reduced market intervention, particularly in the EU, would cause international raw sugar prices to rise by up to 41 per cent by 2005. Already, more than 680,000 people are employed in sugar production throughout southern Africa, which exports half its sugar to the EU. Market liberalisation would create thousands more jobs in the sugar and related industries, such as confectionary.

An element of sugar market liberalisation has taken place in the EU. The UN-backed Everything But Arms (EBA) initiative and the EU's Cotonou Agreement with the developing nations of Africa, the Caribbean and the Pacific (ACP), which were both implemented in 2001, have given preferential access to sugar exports. Nevertheless, the market distortions persist, with some African states receiving unlimited access to EU markets, while others face high restrictions. It is clear that the current patchwork of agreements designed as a compromise between the EU's domestic demands and the interests of African development cannot meet the demands of the WTO's Doha round. The problems confronting the African sugar industry demonstrate that if trade is to be equitable and Africa is to thrive in a globalised market, the liberalisation of agriculture is an imperative.

Doha and beyond

The Doha Development Agenda, agreed in November 2001, was intended to reduce the trade barriers which had acted against African farmers. WTO director general, Mike Moore hailed the Doha round of negotiations as 'a watershed for the WTO', but as 2002 progressed the project rapidly became a farce. Developing countries hoping for an end to market-distorting protectionism by developed countries were badly let down as the EU and the US battled over the issue of subsidies. The debate over agricultural trade liberalisation is polarised between the US and the Cairns Group of 17 agricultural exporting countries (which includes just one African state, South Africa), which advocates deep and speedy cuts in import tariffs, and the EU, which has called for cuts in subsidies. The EU itself has stumbled on developing a single negotiating position. It is split between countries such as the UK, whose agricultural sector mainly consists of internationally competitive large farms, and France, which has a long history of heavily subsidised smallholdings which are often the focus of the rural economy.

Hopes of resolving the dispute and correcting the imbalances in the world market were dashed by the US government's decision in May 2002 to increase subsidies to its farmers by up to 80 per cent with an extra US$180 billion of pay-outs over the next 10 years. The US appeared to be moving away from the objectives of the Doha round. In contrast, in July 2002 the EU seemed to have accepted the need for reform of the CAP with the European Commission (EC) pledging to sever the link between farm subsidies and output in a process dubbed 'decoupling', reducing minimum prices for cereals and imposing a ceiling of 300,000 (US$275,000) on subsidies to large farms. Under the plan, direct payment would be made dependent on observing environmental and food safety laws. CAP spending will increase by 1 per cent per year between 2006 and 2012. The move was more in response to the enlargement of the EU than a commitment to the Doha agreement, but it received a cautious welcome from developing nations.

'It is unlikely that the move from subsidies to direct aid will solve the problem of market distortions, which allow inefficient EU farmers to sell at a lower price than African competitors. '

Nevertheless, it did not meet the needs of many African states for a comprehensive dismantling of trade restrictions and subsidies. The level of subsidies will not be reduced, simply redirected. This is not a genuine commitment to Doha, it is simply exploiting a loop-hole which allows the EU to continue financial backing for rich farmers without appearing to subsidise their produce. It is unlikely that the move from subsidies to direct aid will solve the problem of market distortions, which allow inefficient EU farmers to sell at a lower price than African competitors. Moreover, the EU reforms are not expected to be introduced until 2007, after the current CAP regime expires. This long period of delay leaves the door open for a climb down by the EU, particularly if the French government insists on blocking any reform that could raise the hackles of the militant French farming lobby. An agreement between the French and Germans to stall a decision on the more contentious issues of policy until some time in the distant future may ultimately threaten African interests and break with the whole basis of the Doha round. The prevarication over the CAP will ultimately undermine the timing of the EU's negotiating mandate at the WTO and dash European prospects of securing a moral victory against the US.

Trade imperialism at an end

The unequal trading relations between African and developed markets is a hang-over of colonialism. Globalisation and free trade have so far worked in favour of the developed world, keeping Africa in a position of subservience in international trade. The WTO is slowly but surely changing this and eventually everyone will have to live by the same rules. Unlike the UN, the WTO's members all have an equal vote, giving developing nations the chance to push their agenda. Doha truly was a watershed and sooner or later the EU and the US will have to match their own free market rhetoric with deeds. Western chickens have finally come home to roost.

AIDS defines the future

The HIV/AIDS pandemic will define the future of Africa. Around 30 million Africans had HIV/AIDS in 2002, amounting to 70 per cent of all cases world-wide. The disease is no longer seen as a medical issue and instead is being treated as a major impediment to economic development and growth. Donor countries have begun to tackle the problem head on, helping to reinforce national strategies designed to fight the spread of HIV/AIDS.

In January 2003, the US pledged US$15 billion over five years to combat the disease in a number of AIDS-hit countries, mostly in Africa. US President George W Bush claimed the money would prevent seven million new HIV infections and treat two million people with life-extending anti-retroviral (ARV) drugs. Although the money was welcomed by recipient states, it represented only a fraction of the US$25 billion per month the US earmarked for a war with Iraq in 2003, leading to criticism that the developed world was not taking the issue seriously.

> 'The disease is no longer seen as a medical issue and instead is being treated as a major impediment to economic development and growth.'

Millions will perish

Despite increasing international attention on the effects of HIV/AIDS, infection rates in most African countries have not abated. The continent is sharply divided between the predominantly Arab north, where adult HIV prevalence rates are under 0.5 per cent of the population, and sub-Saharan Africa, where the rate averages 9 per cent. In July 2002, it was revealed that west Africa, where rates were thought to have stabilised at below 5 per cent, HIV/AIDS infection had reached 6.5 per in Nigeria and 9.7 per cent in Cameroon.

The worst-hit region is southern Africa, where HIV prevalence stands at between 15–40 per cent of the population. In Botswana, Lesotho, Swaziland and Zimbabwe, at least one in three people are HIV positive. Consequently, life expectancy at birth has plummeted from above 60 years in 1990, to under 40 years by 2002, causing population growth to stagnate or even turn negative in many countries.

Nearly 80 per cent of those infected with HIV are aged between 15–45 years, which is the prime age for work and bringing up children. The young are particularly vulnerable. In 2001 alone, half a million children below the age of 15 died of AIDS in sub-Saharan Africa, mostly as a result of HIV infection during pregnancy. Children represent around a fifth of all African AIDS deaths every year. Another aspect of the epidemic is the large number of orphans. Since the beginning of the epidemic in the 1980s, more than 13 million children have lost their mother or both their parents to AIDS. Many children in households affected by HIV/AIDS are taken out of school and made to work to maintain the household. They are more likely to be illiterate and suffer a higher incidence of malnutrition. The consequences of the HIV/AIDS epidemic will therefore be felt for decades to come, even if the rate of HIV infection is reduced.

Assessing the economic impact

Many claim that the nature of AIDS, which can be contracted years after HIV infection, is a demographic time-bomb waiting to go off. The famine of 2002 indicated that the crisis may have already exploded. In southern Africa, AIDS has joined forces with other factors such as droughts, floods and poor support for farmers, to cause a dramatic fall in agricultural output. Estimates suggest that AIDS-related deaths in a farming household can cause productivity to drop by up to 60 per cent. At current rates of infection, the UN's Food and Agriculture Organisation (FAO) estimates that 16 million African agricultural workers, or a quarter of the sector's workforce, will die between 2002 and 2020. This will affect both subsistence farming and cash crops, leading to a drop in food consumption and to malnutrition.

The structure of agriculture is likely to change. As rural families struggle to pay for food due to falling incomes and rising prices, production is being directed towards subsistence farming and away from cash crops, with a preference for less labour-intensive crops. The death of women, who form a majority of Africans with HIV, has a particularly strong impact on farm output, since women are traditionally responsible for maintaining soil fertility and irrigation as well as transporting produce. Women also produce 60–80 per cent of sub-Saharan Africa's food supply.

Other structural economic problems are magnified by the HIV/AIDS epidemic. Most African governments are struggling with unsustainable debt and in recent years have undertaken structural adjustment which has cut expenditure and increased direct taxation. The decline in the labour force will erode revenue from individuals and private sector firms, while the costs associated with HIV/AIDS are likely to increase leading to pressure on expenditure. With a deteriorating fiscal position, governments will be forced to borrow and redirect expenditure to the healthcare and social services, particularly the care of orphaned children.

New economic problems are also likely to emerge that will severely undermine Africa's international competitiveness and ultimately deter foreign direct investment. Labour shortages have never been a significant problem in Africa, which has a burgeoning informal sector. The UN's International Labour Organisation (ILO) predicts that by 2020 the labour force in African countries with an HIV prevalence rate of over 10 per cent in 2002 will be 10–22 per cent smaller due to AIDS deaths. This will reduce the number of skilled as well as unskilled workers. Firms which rely on skilled labour, particularly professional workers, will be hardest hit. According to an ILO survey in South Africa, more than 60 per cent of firms thought they would have significant problems replacing skilled workers who had died of AIDS. Estimates reveal that southern African countries will lose between a quarter and a third of their skilled and professional population in coming years. Human capital losses, caused by the loss of skilled labour and the lack of schooling for children, will be a major impediment to future sustainable development. The ILO forecasts that productivity could decline by as much as 50 per cent by 2010, resulting in large losses for the private sector, an increase in costs for the public sector and a reduction in the quality of public services.

Medicine the best investment

The first decade of the new millennium will be the worst decade ever in terms of AIDS deaths, according to UNAIDS. The development of an AIDS vaccine is unlikely to help Africa. Most of the US$300–600 million spent on research and development of a vaccine is focused on strains of the virus normally seen in the developed world, which promises the most profitable markets for pharmaceutical corporations. It is unlikely that any AIDS vaccine, if it is ever developed, will be effective or affordable in Africa. Moreover, if a vaccine is discovered it will take up to five years before it can be put on the market.

Only the widespread use of ARVs can prevent the deaths of millions of HIV infected people. Yet, currently these drugs are expensive. Estimates reveal that it will cost US$370 per person per year to provide basic treatment to AIDS patients, including testing, counselling, education and pain relief. Intermediate care, including the provision of ARV drugs to pregnant HIV positive women and the treatment of associated infections, will cost a further US$500, while advanced care for infected adults, including the provision of highly active ARV therapies (HAARTs) which are available in the developed world, will cost over US$3,000 per year.

The World Health Organisation (WHO) has set a target of three million HIV positive Africans to be on ARV therapy by 2005, up from 30,000 in 2002. But Africa cannot afford the costs of such a dramatic increase in ARV therapies without a massive reduction in drug costs. Current per capita healthcare expenditure in the vast majority of African countries does not cover even basic treatment, let alone the cost of life-extending ARVs. Much of the continent's population lives on less than US$1 per day and the cost of basic care surpasses many countries' GDP per capita levels. According to one study, AIDS-related government expenditure in South Africa will reach about 5 per cent of GDP by 2010, a cost which without foreign aid will ultimately reduce spending on other sectors essential to economic development, such as infrastructure. This explained the reluctance of the South African government to promote ARVs. It took a high court ruling in 2002 to force the government to provide ARVs to HIV-positive pregnant women and their babies.

Even when ARVs are freely available, they are not necessarily taken up by HIV/AIDS patients. In Botswana, a government programme begun in 2001 to distribute ARV drugs to all HIV/AIDS victims has made limited progress. By end-2002, only 4 per cent of the estimated 110,000 people eligible for therapy took up the offer of free treatment. A major impediment to seeking help is the stigma and denial which prevents people from participating in therapy programmes. Governments also face an uphill challenge trying to change the attitudes of many men and sex workers towards using condoms and therapy. The problems are not helped by resistence from religious organisations, particularly the Catholic Church which proscribes the use of all contraception. Prejudice and fear also prevent people from seeking an HIV test. In Tanzania, surveys show that 50 per cent of women know where they could be tested for HIV, but only 6 per cent have been tested. Millions do not know they have HIV/AIDS and are doing nothing to protect themselves from it.

Even if there was unlimited funding for ARV drugs and ignorance was not a problem, it is not certain whether all HIV/AIDS patients would have access to this medicine. The healthcare infrastructure needs to be in place, including trained nurses, doctors and counsellors, to ensure effective use of medicine. Therapies are often complex and require constant supervision to ensure the correct dosage, particularly with the use of a combination of drugs. In Africa, healthcare provision is poor and distinctly lacking in rural areas while health workers are also succumbing to the disease. The deterioration in public services and the increase in malnourishment are also likely to increase the incidence of diseases not associated with HIV/AIDS, such as diarrhoea and cholera, which are an underlying problem in Africa. On top of this is the ever-present problem of malaria, which consumes 40 per cent of Africa's health budget and kills one million people a year and places a major burden on healthcare services.

'A small number of *sangomas* have perpetuated the belief that having sex with virgins will cure AIDS. In a climate of ignorance, this myth has led to a disturbing and dramatic rise in the rape of young girls and babies.'

The failure to distribute adequate medicines is leading to despair, violence and moral decline. Many of those without access to adequate medicines to treat HIV/AIDS are turning to traditional healers or *sangomas* for remedies. A small number of *sangomas* have perpetuated the belief that having sex with virgins will cure AIDS. In a climate of ignorance, this myth has led to a disturbing and dramatic rise in the rape of young girls and babies. In South Africa, there are 20,000 reported cases of child rape every year, with thousands more left unreported.

Future may be brighter

Governments will have a greater ability to absorb the impact of the epidemic if the cost of ARVs is brought down to Uganda's levels. The signs are encouraging. The relaxation of patenting rules, agreed at the Doha summit of the World Trade Organisation (WTO) in mid-2002, will pave the way for the supply of cheaper generic drugs. The new rules allow African countries either to produce generic drugs or to arrange a licence with companies in countries such as India or Brazil to supply cheap ARVs. In January 2003, six multi-national drug manufacturers pledged to increase the supply of ARVs to Africa, in fear of losing out in the event of a boom in generic ARVs. One of the NGOs leading the campaign against HIV/AIDS in Africa, Médecins sans Frontières (MSF), estimates that by 2004 the cost of treating a patient with ARVs will have dropped to between US$50–80 per year. This will enable African states, many of which started drawing up HIV/AIDS strategies only in the late 1990s, to combat the disease more effectively.

Long-term economic issues are being over-looked in the drive to encourage condom use and the supply of ARVs. The structural adjustment measures advanced by the IMF, and which form the basis of many governments' economic policies, need a radical rethink. Continuing policies such as privatisation at a time when HIV/AIDS is hitting labour productivity and capital formation will exacerbate Africa's problems. International financial institutions, governments, donors and businesses will need to combine their efforts to minimise the potential for economic collapse caused by HIV/AIDS, particularly in the public sector and farming. Unless the international community engages in a radical rethink of economic policy and the basis of donor support, much of Africa will waste away.

Algeria

Jonathan Derrick

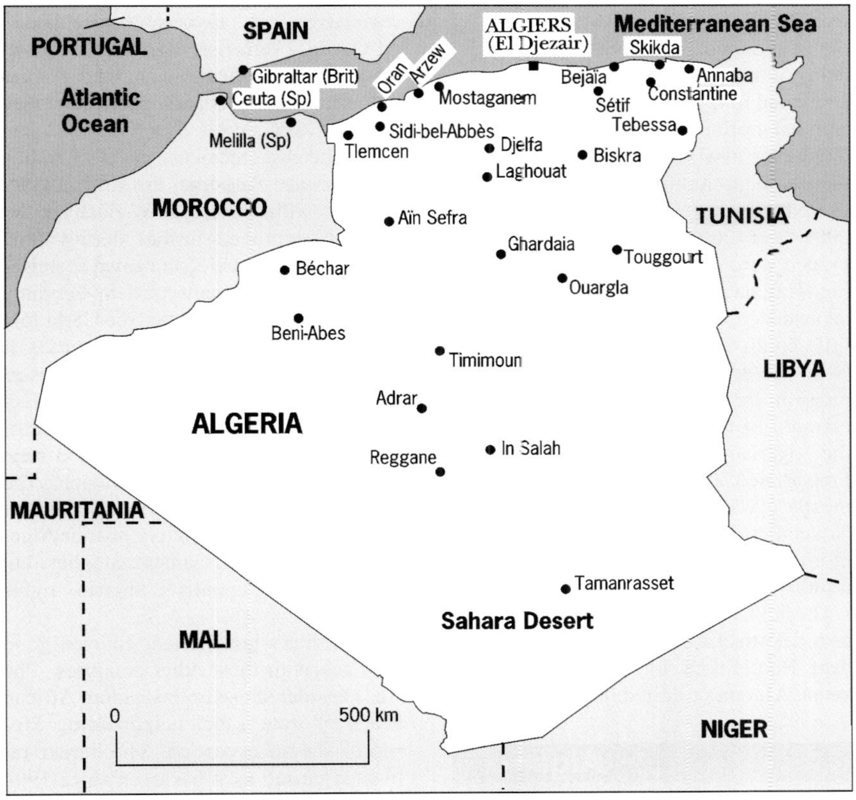

Algeria's civil war continued in 2001 and 2002, but at a reduced intensity. Deaths due to the war were about 200 per month on average in 2001. Between 1992–2001, it was estimated that over 150,000 people were killed in the violence. The deadline for members of armed groups to come forward and claim amnesty theoretically passed on 13 January 2001. This amnesty offer followed the cease-fire with the Front Islamique du Salut (FIS) (Islamic Salvation Front), although the ban on the FIS was maintained. Having rejected the cease-fire, the Groupement Islamique Armé (GIA) (Armed Islamic Group) and a less well-known group, the Groupe Salafiste pour la Prédication et le Combat (GSPC) (Salafist Group for Preaching and Combat), continued to fight against the overwhelmingly stronger army. In November 2002, nine soldiers were killed in a gun and bomb attack by Islamic militants in northern Algeria. The government had blamed the GIA for the deaths of 26 people in western Algeria three months earlier.

Berber unrest during election

Tensions between the Berber minority and Algerian authorities were high after the death of a young Berber in police custody in April 2001. For months afterwards, protesters demonstrated, rioted and created a near-breakdown of authority in Kabylie, as the grievances of many decades boiled over.

These descendants of Algeria's original inhabitants mainly protested about the status of their language (Tamazight) and culture. 'Berber-ness' (*amazighité*) was recognised as part of the 'Algerian personality' in the 1996 constitution, but only Arabic was recognised as an official

KEY FACTS

Official name: Al-Jumhuriya Al-Jazairiya Ad-Dimucratiya Ash-Shabiya (Democratic and Popular Republic of Algeria)

Head of State: President Abdelaziz Bouteflika (elected Apr 1999)

Head of government: Prime Minister Ali Benflis (leader of FLN) (appointed Aug 2000; re-appointed Jun 2002)

Ruling party: Front de Libération Nationale (FLN) (National Liberation Front) (results of 30 May 2002 elections: FLN won 199 seats out of 380, the Rassemblement Nationale Démocratique (RND) (National Democratic Rally) 48, the Mouvement pour la Réforme Nationale (MRN) (Movement for National Reform) 43, the Mouvement de la Société pour la Paix (MSP) (Social Movement for Peace) 38 and the Parti du Travail (PT) (Workers' Party) 21; turnout was 46.1 per cent.

Area: 2,381,741 square km

Population: 30.70 million (2001)

Capital: Algiers

Official language: Arabic and Tamazight (the Berber language)

Currency: Algerian dinar (AD) = 100 centimes

Exchange rate: AD78.93 per US$ (Jan 2003)

GDP per capita: US$1,789 (2001); US$1,918 (2002)*

GDP real growth: 1.70% (2001); 3.0% (2002)*

Unemployment: 28.50% (2001); 27.8% (2002)*

Inflation: 3.40% (2001); 4.5% (2002)*

Oil production: 1.56 million (2001)

Balance of trade: US$9.33 billion (2001)

Foreign debt: US$22.50 billion (2001)

Annual FDI: US$10.00 million (2000)

* estimated figure

For the latest Key Facts, go to www.worldinformation.com

language. The Berber movement, represented mainly by the Rassemblement Culturel et Démocratique (RCD) (Rally for Culture and Democracy), had demanded more recognition of the minority culture. Eventually, on 3 October 2001, President Bouteflika announced that Tamazight would be an official language and there would be constitutional amendments dealing with state institutions.

Despite Bouteflika's concessions, over 2,000 youths rioted over unemployment in Tizi Ouzou, the main town in the Berber-speaking region of Kabylie, during the parliamentary election on 30 May 2002. Only 175 out of 880 polling centres in Tizi Ouzou were opened.

The electorate were generally apathetic during the election, as most Algerians feel that the government cannot be held accountable by parliament and that the military hold the real power. Turnout during the election was low at 46.1 per cent. The Front de Libération Nationale (FLN) (National Liberation Front) emerged as the largest party, winning 199 seats in the 380-member Al-Majlis Al-Sha'abi Al-Watani/Assemblé Populaire Nationale (National People's Assembly). The Rassemblement Nationale Démocratique (RND) (National Democratic Rally), which had 156 seats in the 1997 election, won only 48 seats. The Mouvement pour la Réforme Nationale (MRN) (Movement for National Reform) won 43 seats, the Mouvement de la Société pour la Paix (MSP) (Social Movement for Peace) 38 and the Parti du Travail (PT) (Workers' Party) 21. The FLN's Ali Benflis was re-appointed prime minister in June 2002.

La sale guerre

A new book published in France in 2001, *La Sale Guerre* by Habib Souaidia, a former soldier of the Algerian army, described atrocities by that army in the civil war. While few outside Algeria doubted the government forces' responsibility for many of the worst crimes, the government continued to deny French and other international criticisms. French protests following the new book came when France's then foreign minister, Hubert Védrine, visited Algiers in February. Relations in 2001 and 2002 between Algeria and France were generally good and improving. Traumatic memories of the war of independence were a factor, but there was little controversy when President Chirac (who served in Algeria) attended a ceremony in Paris on 25 September 2001 in memory of the Harkis. The Harkis were the Algerian soldiers who fought on the French side. Over 200,000 Harkis died, mostly massacred after independence. In November 2002, Chirac unveiled a memorial in Paris to the Harkis and French military personnel who died in the war.

The impact of the 11 September 2001 terrorist attacks in the US affected President Bouteflika's foreign relations. For years, Algeria protested that the West did not support it in its 'struggle against terrorism', accusing the UK in particular of harbouring Islamist suspects. As police in many Western countries began arresting Islamist terrorist suspects, including several Algerians, the Algerian government gained more acceptance as an ally in the US-led 'war against terror'. In November 2002, the Algerian authorities claimed that they had killed the North African representative of Osama bin Laden's Al-Qaeda terrorist network, Emad Abdelwahid Ahmed Alwan, who was involved in training Islamic guerrilla groups like the GSPC.

Despite disagreements over US policy on Libya and Palestine, the government's relations with the George W Bush administration improved further during 2001 and 2002. There were joint naval exercises held off the Algerian coast in February 2001 and Bouteflika visited the US in July and November 2001. In December 2001, Bouteflika visited NATO's headquarters in Belgium for talks on Algeria's involvement in NATO's Mediterranean Dialogue, which attempts to encourage good relations in the Mediterranean region. The Bush administration confirmed that in late 2002 that it would probably honour Algeria's requests for armament supplies, but criticised the country's human rights records.

Bouteflika's government enjoyed good relations with most other countries – he was considered one of the leading African heads of state – but neighbouring Morocco was an exception. The border remained closed as it has been since 1994 and efforts to improve relations still came up against the problem of the Western Sahara and Algeria's backing for the Sahrawi Republic.

KEY INDICATORS — Algeria

	Unit	1996	1997	1998	1999	2000
Population	m	28.57	29.05	29.80	30.77	31.29
Gross domestic product (GDP)	US$bn	46.90	47.80	47.40	47.90	39.67
GDP per capita	US$	1,640	1,647	1,589	1,556	1,725
GDP real growth	%	3.8	1.3	3.9	3.2	2.4
GNP per capita	US$	0	0	1,630	0	0
Inflation	%	18.7	8.4	2.3	2.7	0.3
Unemployment	%	28.0	26.4	27.1	28.0	28.0
Oil output	'000 bpd	1,380.0	1,410.0	1,385.0	1,340.0	1,580.0
Natural gas output	bn cu m	61.1	70.4	75.4	82.2	89.3
Exports (fob) (goods)	US$m	13,210.0	13,820.0	13,300.0	11,940.0	21,700.0
Imports (fob) (goods)	US$m	9,090.0	8,130.0	9,100.0	9,000.0	9,200.0
Balance of trade	US$m	4,120.0	5,690.0	4,200.0	3,300.0	12,300.0
Current account	US$m	1,250.0	3,460.0	1,700.0	-2,000.0	9,000.0
Foreign debt	US$bn	39.5	30.1	32.4	28.2	25.0
Total reserves minus gold	US$m	4,235.0	8,047.0	6,846.0	4,526.0	12,024.0
Foreign exchange	US$m	4,230.0	8,046.0	6,844.0	4,407.0	11,910.0
Exchange rate	per US$	54.75	57.71	58.74	66.57	75.26

Economic developments

Serious floods hit Algiers on 10 November 2001; 764 people were killed and 23,000 houses were destroyed. While due essentially to exceptional falls of rain, the disaster exposed the shortages and poor quality of housing in Algeria. The housing crisis was one aspect of the general hardship of the majority, which included several millions – an estimated 25–30 per cent of the total population – living below the poverty line; unemployment was estimated at 28.5 per cent of the working-age population in 2001. In August 2002, the World Bank announced a US$89 million loan to help Algeria protect its cities from floods, earthquakes and other disasters.

To make a start in meeting basic needs, Bouteflika announced a three-year

US$1.6 billion recovery plan on 26 April 2001. The plan proposed to start with two deprived wilayas, Djelfa and M'Sila. About 40 per cent of the money was allocated to infrastructure, a little over 20 per cent to local development; there would be a special fund for 13 southern wilayas. Part of the programme, which emphasised job creation, was already included in the 2001 budget. The government hoped to create 750,000 jobs in three years. It was in a position to spend more on basic needs because of the exceptionally good year for oil earnings in 2000, when exports – largely oil and gas – rose in value by 76 per cent to US$21.7 billion.

The year 2001 was less successful as far as the current account went. After registering a surplus of 17 per cent of GDP in 2000, the current account surplus fell to 12 per cent of GDP as exports slowed to approximately 3 per cent. Official reserves increased in 2001 from US$12.02 billion in 2000 to US$17.9 billion in 2001.

An IMF Article IV Consultation report on Algeria in October 2001 noted the improved situation – GDP rose by 2.4 per cent in 2000, for example, and inflation was down to 0.3 per cent – and approved the three-year recovery plan. However, the IMF noted that high economic growth was needed to reduce unemployment and improve living standards, and stressed the importance of promoting private investment and pursuing privatisation and restructuring of public enterprises, as well as banking reform and an end to remaining price controls (subsidies for electricity, gas and oil products cost about US$2.4 billion per year). In 2001, GDP grew by only 1.7 per cent while inflation increased to 3.4 per cent. There was an improvement to GDP growth in 2002 with a 3 per cent rise, although inflation rose to 4.5 per cent.

The Benflis government was already committed to extending the role of private enterprise. During 2001, it worked on new investment rules; plans were reported to include a 'one-stop shop'. The government announced in early 2001 plans to privatise 184 state enterprises as part of its 2001–04 economic plan.

Oil and gas

While the IMF report urged diversification of export and revenue bases, both still depended heavily (60 per cent of revenue) on oil and gas. Algeria remained vulnerable to oil price fluctuations and the two boom years ended in the latter months of 2001. The government based the supplementary budget of mid-2001 on an oil price of US$22 per barrel and retained this for the 2002 budget, despite the Organisation of the Petroleum Exporting Countries (Opec) price remaining between US$25–US$26 per barrel for most of 2002. As a result, this should provide Algeria with extra revenue, allowing it to cover the 2002 finance bill. The 2003 finance bill is based on an oil price of US$19 per barrel. Oil production at the end of 2001 was over 810,000 barrels per day (bpd), above the Opec's then quota of 740,000bpd. Exploration and development continued. On 11 August 2001, a US$2.5 billion contract was signed with BP for the development of seven gas fields at In Salah, with BP providing 65 per cent of the finance and the state corporation Sonatrach 35 per cent. In October, five companies were awarded exploration blocks in the Berkine basin, and in November, Sonatrach opened its first open licensing round for development of oil and gas fields.

The giant Sonatrach increased its turnover by nearly 70 per cent to US$22 billion in 2000. During 2001, major reforms were under discussion. The energy and mines minister, Chakib Khelil, hopes to liberalise the oil and gas sector by 2005, but has ruled out Sonatrach's privatisation. New legislation to end the Sonatrach monopoly in the domestic oil market and open the upstream, downstream and transport sectors to national and foreign investors was reported to be planned during 2001, but progress was not forthcoming in 2002 due to opposition from trade unions and even in government circles.

After years of negotiations an EU-Algeria Association Agreement was signed on 19 December 2001, during a visit to Belgium by Bouteflika. It provides for gradual removal of duties on imports of EU industrial products over 12 years and for immediate liberalisation, after entry into force of the agreement, of a number of Algerian agricultural exports to the EU export quotas on some sensitive categories of products. As part of the agreement, Algeria will reciprocate with substantial cuts in tariffs on farm imports from the EU. Thus, the basic grievance of Maghrebian states about farm exports to the EU is hardly, if at all, satisfied in Algeria's case, while the likely effect of unrestricted industrial imports from Europe will be, as in Morocco and Tunisia, the closure of many local industries – if they are not closed anyway under a deregulation programme. Announcing a US$15.9 million programme for upgrading of small- and medium-scale industries in September 2001, the industry minister, Abdelmadjid Menasra, said such businesses were unaware of the threat from the EU agreement and World Trade Organisation (WTO) entry (on which negotiations were well advanced by late 2001).

The EU agreement, which incorporates a 'political dialogue' as well as a regular 'economic dialogue', has clauses relating to justice and home affairs, but it does not deal with Algerians' demand for easier migration to Europe (France, the principal country of Algerian emigration, has retained a highly restrictive visa policy). The agreement provides for new aid. In December 2001 a new National Indicative Programme for 2002–04, to be aided by the EU, was approved, to concentrate on economic reforms and the market economy, infrastructure, human resources development, and the rule of law and good governance.

Outlook

Following consultations with the IMF, Bouteflika is making it his main priority to develop Algeria's economy and is already committed to carrying out further economic reforms, such as privatisation. While economic performance has improved, more will need to be done to remove Algeria's vulnerability to the energy markets to aid the country's economic performance in the long-term. The EU-Algerian Association Agreement could be the key to this diversification.

Risk assessment

Economic	Satisfactory
Political	Improving
Regional stability	Satisfactory
Stock market	Improving

COUNTRY PROFILE

Historical profile

In the seventh century, Arab culture and Islam came to the predominantly Berber peoples of what is now Algeria.

In the sixteenth century, Ottoman proconsuls ruled Mediterranean towns, including Algiers. The Berbers kept control of the interior.

1830 France attacked Algiers. Opposition to the French was led by Abdelkader, who effectively established a separate state in western and central Algeria.

1839–44 A French campaign against Abdelkader led to his defeat at Isly near Oujda. Abdelkader surrendered in 1846.

1871 France controlled the whole country and set about removing the local cultural and religious identity. Land was also appropriated by European settlers.

1954 The Algerian war of independence began on 31 October in the Aures mountains, east of Algiers. Opposition to the French was led by the Front de Libération Nationale (FLN) (National Liberation Front). The fighting killed at least one million Algerians.
1961 Militant settlers formed the underground Organisation de l'Armée Secrète (OAS) (Secret Army Organisation) and began a violent campaign of reprisals against the nationalists, resulting in extensive destruction of Algeria's economic and social infrastructure.
1962 A referendum on the question of independence for Algeria resulted in a vote of six million in favour and 16,000 against. Ahmed ben Bella of the FLN was designated Algeria's first president; the FLN was the sole legal party.
1965 Ahmed ben Bella was ousted by Colonel Houari Boumédienne who introduced a programme of industrialisation.
1978 After the death of President Boumédienne, the FLN candidate, Colonel Chadli Benjedid, was elected president of the Republic for a five-year term. He was re-elected in 1984 for a second term and in 1989 for a further term.
1990 The Front Islamique du Salut (FIS) (Islamic Salvation Front) performed well in local elections, defeating the ruling FLN.
1991 In the first round of the parliamentary election in December, the FIS won 55.4 per cent of the vote.
1992 President Chadli resigned. Outbreaks of violence followed the cancellation of the December 1991 parliamentary elections which the FIS was poised to win. The five-member Haut Conseil d'Etat (HCE) (High Council of State), instituted after the resignation of President Chadli Bendjedid, was led by Ali Kafi, who was then succeeded by President Mohammed Boudiaf in 1992. The decision to cancel the elections had already been taken before the appointment of President Boudiaf. The FIS was banned.
1995 Liamine Zeroual was elected head of state in the first multi-party democratic elections.
1998 By early 1998, an estimated 28,000 people had been killed in the campaign of guerrilla warfare against the government conducted by the Armée Islamique du Salut (AIS) (Islamic Salvation Army), the military wing of the banned FIS.
1999 President Zeroual stood down as head of state (one year early). Abdelaziz Bouteflika won the April presidential elections with 73.8 per cent of the vote. President Bouteflika appointed Ali Benflis prime minister on 26 Aug 2000, replacing Ahmed Benbitour.
2001 There were 60 deaths when young Algerians rioted in Kabylie, the Berber-speaking region, in May. The Berbers continued their protest against the Algerian government in June. After two years of drought, a month's rain fell in 24 hours in November. Over 600 people died in the floods and thousands lost their homes.
2002 The first parliamentary elections since 1997, and the second since December 1991, took place on 30 May. Berber activists in the Kabylie region and several opposition parties elsewhere boycotted the polls. Election results: Prime Minister Ali Benflis' Front de Libération Nationale (FLN) (National Liberation Front) won 199 seats out of 389, the Rassemblement Nationale Démocratique (RND) (National Democratic Rally) 48, the El Islah (Movement for National Reform) 43, the Mouvement de la Société pour la Paix (MSP) (Social Movement for Peace) 38 and the Parti du Travail (PT) (Workers' Party) 21; turnout was 46.1 per cent.

Political structure

Constitution

The 1976 constitution has been amended three times. As part of an amendment to constitution in 1997, the government imposed a law restricting the formation of political parties. All political parties must hold a founding conference attended by 400–500 new delegates elected by 25,000 supporters from 25 of the country's 48 provinces. This policy is intended to limit the number of political parties in Algeria and placed a severe disadvantage on those parties with lower funds – particularly those, such as the Front Islamique du Salut (FIS) (Islamic Salvation Front), without access to state funds. The law also banned religion-based parties.

Form of state

Republic

The executive

The head of state is the president, elected by universal suffrage for five years. He appoints a prime minister, who in turn appoints a government.
The president has the power to dissolve the government and request elections.

National legislature

The parliament is composed of the 380-member Al-Majlis Al-Sha'abi Al-Watani/Assemblé Populaire Nationale (National People's Assembly) and the 144-member Al-Majlis Al-Umma/Conseil de la Nation (National Council). Members of the National People's Assembly, which holds legislative power, are elected for five years by universal suffrage. Members of the National Council (the lower house) are elected by communal councils and the president.

Legal system

The legal system is based on French and Islamic law. The judicial system consists of 183 courts and 31 appeal courts organised on a regional basis. There are three special criminal courts in Oran, Constantine and Algiers, which deal with economic crimes against the state (against which there is no appeal) – the Court of State Security which is composed of judges and army officers, the court of audit and the Supreme Court in Algiers, which is the ultimate judicial authority. Algeria has not accepted International Court of Justice (ICJ) jurisdiction.

Last elections

30 May 2002 (parliamentary) (the first since 1997 and the second since December 1991); 15 April 1999 (presidential).

Next elections

2004 (presidential); 2007 (parliamentary).

Political parties

A law was passed in 1997 imposing restrictions on forming political parties.

Ruling party

Results of 30 May 2002 parliamentary elections: the Front de Libération Nationale (FLN) (National Liberation Front) won 199 seats out of 380, the Rassemblement Nationale Démocratique (RND) (National Democratic Rally) 48, the Mouvement pour la Réforme Nationale (MRN) (Movement for National Reform) 43, the Mouvement de la Société pour la Paix (MSP) (Social Movement for Peace) 38 and the Parti du Travail (PT) (Workers' Party) 21; turnout was 46.1 per cent.

Main opposition party

Four opposition parties, including the leading Front des Forces Socialistes (FFS) (Socialist Forces Front) and the Rassemblement pour la Culture et la Démocratie (RCD) (Rally for Culture and Democracy), boycotted the May 2002 elections.

Population

31.29 million (2000).
The annual population growth rate was 2.6 per cent between 1992–98, and is projected to drop to 1.7 per cent per annum between 1999–2015. Nearly 60 per cent of the population is under the age of 25 and approximately 38 per cent of the total population is under the age of 14. The population density is 12 inhabitants per square km, with an urban population of 59.6 per cent.

Ethnic make-up

The majority of Algerians are of Berber descent. The other significant ethnic group is Arab, although as a result of centuries of integration the two ethnic groups have become increasingly indistinguishable. The distinct Berber culture and language is best preserved in the northern regions of Algeria.
The European population has declined from over one million before independence in 1962 to less than 50,000 in 2001, most of whom are French.

Religions

Islam is the official religion Approximately 99 per cent of the population is Sunni Muslim, while Christians make up about one per cent.

Main cities

Algiers (capital, estimated population 2.5 million in 1998), Oran (1.2 million), Constantine (1 million), Annaba (800,000).

Languages spoken

French is often used in government, business and diplomacy. In 1998, an Arabisation law came into force, making the use of Arabic compulsory for all official businesses.

Official language

Arabic and Tamazight (the Berber language).

Media

The 1990 media law bans visual or written media that contravene Islamic moral principles or national values or that encourage racism, fanaticism or treason. Journalists and editors are obliged to reveal sources to the authorities for articles regarding economic or defence 'secrets'. The law allows the formation of privately owned newspapers, radio and television stations, all of which have been state-owned in the past. Any new non-Arabic publication must first be approved by the independent Information Council.

The law guarantees freedom of access to information and freedom of expression in accordance with the constitution. However, it also makes it a criminal offence to publish or broadcast 'wrong or tendentious information harmful to state security or national unity'. Penalties for this range from five to 10 years in jail.

Media regulation and monitoring is delegated to a 12-member council, composed of three members appointed by the president, three appointed by the national assembly and six elected by journalists.

Press

Algeria has some 35 daily newspapers, most of which are in private ownership. The official press agency is the *Algérie Presse Service*.

Dailies: Algeria has some 35 daily newspapers, most of which are in private ownership. The main national papers include *El Khabar*, *Le Matin* and *El Watan*.

Other leading national dailies in Arabic, French and English include *El Alam Essyassi* (Arabic), *El Moudjahid* (French and Arabic), *El Massa* (Arabic and French), *L'Authentique* (French), *Liberté*, *Latribune* (both in French), *Horizons* (English section) and *Ech-Chaab* (Arabic).

The main provincial dailies include *An Nasr* (Arabic) and *Al Joumhouria* (Arabic).

Weeklies: Weeklies include *Azul de Kabylie* on tourism and employment news and *Echibek* covers sports.

Business: The monthly business periodical *L'Actuel Revue Economique* is useful for investors and financers.

Periodicals: *Le jeune indépendant* has 300 issues yearly. *Le Matin* covers current affairs.

Broadcasting

Broadcasting is controlled by the government through Radiodiffusion Télévision Algérienne (RTA).

Radio: Radio services are in Arabic, French and Tamazight.

Television: Television services are in Arabic and French. The network is operated by the state-run RTA.

Advertising

Although advertising is allowed and adverting agencies operate in Algeria, the impact of advertising is limited to basic consumer products. The market is underdeveloped and the foremost form of advertising is through print media and the RTA.

Economy

Algeria's political and geographical divisions are reflected by the economic outputs – and problems – of the different regions. The north is densely populated, with high levels of unemployment. The centre of the country has relatively low levels of industrial, service and manufacturing output. The south is rich in oil and natural gas, the exploitation of which is dominated by the state-owned Sonatrach company, and has been the foremost generator of government revenue for decades, contributing as much as 60 per cent of budgetary revenues.

Real GDP growth is estimated to have been 3.6 per cent in 2001, compared to 2.4 per cent in 2000, although this figure will be dependent on the development of oil prices. Low oil prices in 2001 should affect Algeria's current account balance and foreign reserves. Oil and gas account for over 90 per cent of exports and the country's economic performance is directly linked to the international market price for oil. The non-oil sector of the economy declined in the 1990s; each year its contribution to GDP diminished between 1–4 per cent. The civil conflict together with financial restraints on the government and a dated infrastructure resulted in significant cuts in production in the industrial and manufacturing sectors during this period.

Inflation, which was as high as 30 per cent in 1995, has largely been brought under control and is estimated to have been 0.30 per cent in 2000 was 1.5 per cent in 2001. The country continues to suffer from high unemployment with an official estimate of 27.9 per cent in 2001. Realistically, the government underestimates the unemployment rate with unofficial estimates placing it higher at 50 per cent in 2001.

Algeria is heavily dependent on its oil income and if economic prospects are to improve in the long-term, then GDP growth needs to be accelerated in order to reduce the country's high levels of unemployment, foster private investment and raise living standards throughout the country. The country's geographic proximity to the massive EU market holds tremendous potential for the development of Algeria's rich natural resources sector.

External trade

The strict control of imports combined with broadening of hydrocarbons exports traditionally produces a balance of trade surplus. Exports are heavily dependent on oil and gas.

The government introduced a series of measures designed to boost non-hydrocarbon exports, while cutting imports of consumer goods.

The invisible account remains heavily in deficit owing to high loan repayments.

Algeria belongs to the Union du Maghreb Arabe (UMA) (Arab Maghreb Union), together with Libya, Morocco, Mauritania and Tunisia.

In December 2001, Algeria signed an association agreement with the EU. The agreement will provide for the gradual removal of import duties on industrial products over 12 years and the liberalisation of Algeria's agricultural export market.

Exports

Principal exports are hydrocarbons (total around 96–98 per cent) (of which natural gas 25 per cent, condensates 25 per cent, crude petroleum 24 per cent, petroleum products 20 per cent); wine, tobacco, foodstuffs.

Main destinations: Italy (22.9 per cent of 2000 total), USA (12.4 per cent), Spain (12.4 per cent), France (10.5 per cent), Brazil (7.5 per cent).

Imports

Principal imports are capital goods (typically around 24–26 per cent of total), semi-finished goods (24–26 per cent), food and tobacco (20 per cent), consumer goods (15–17 per cent), transport equipment (14–16 per cent), raw materials (5–8 per cent).

Main sources: France (30.8 per cent of 2000 total), USA (9.5 per cent), Italy (8.6 per cent), Germany (6.1 per cent), Spain (5.5 per cent).

Agriculture

The sector employs about a quarter of the labour force and contributes around 13 per cent to GDP.

Around 30 per cent of total area is potentially cultivable with irrigation, with about 5 per cent currently under cultivation, mostly in the northern coastal strip.
Despite extensive irrigation programmes and the dividing of state holdings into smaller units, agricultural output has failed to keep pace with the rate of population growth. Imports still provide around 25 per cent of domestic food requirements.
Underlying constraints to growth include soil erosion, desert encroachment, inefficient management in the state sector, poor marketing, recurrent droughts and rebel activities.
The government plans to increase output and reduce dependence on imports by a series of measures including investing in new technology, financial incentives for state and private sector farms to buy equipment, encouraging foreign investment, less interference in the private sector and tree planting to arrest desertification.
Main cash crops are grapes, oranges, olives, dates, tobacco, sugar beet and tomatoes. Hard and soft wheat and barley are grown for the home market, as are vegetables, pulses and citrus fruit.
Livestock farming takes place mainly in the north-east.

Fishing

Commercial fishing is marginal in Algeria, making up only some 3 per cent of agricultural output. Fishing is centred on sardines, anchovies, sprats, tuna and shellfish.

Industry and manufacturing

Industry represents 50 per cent of GDP and employs 23 per cent of the labour force. Algeria's industrial sector, which grew by 1.3 per cent in the first half of 2001, is dominated by large, inefficient state-owned companies that have largely survived only due to the credit extended them by the country's state-owned banks.
Government attempts to privatise these industries have been frustrated by a lack of investor interest and the fear that the possible mass redundancies which may result will cause further social instability.
The largest company in Algeria is the state-owned hydrocarbons concern, Société Nationale pour la Recherche, la Production, le Transport, la Transformation et la Commercialisation des Hydrocarbures (Sonatrach).
Production is dominated by heavy industries such as steel, petrochemicals, fertilisers and cement, but the focus of development is changing to light industry.
Traditional agro-allied industries are also important, particularly textiles, food processing and tobacco and cigarette processing, which are being expanded, and public companies are now allowed to set prices and invest profits. Industry is opening up to more foreign involvement, particularly in large-scale projects such as motor vehicle assembly.
Main constraints to development are shortages of vital inputs and skilled labour, high production and transport costs and maintenance problems. Industrial development is centralised in the northern coastal strip, but plans exist to extend industry to the high plateaux in the south.

Mining

The mining and hydrocarbons sector employs 4 per cent of the labour force and contributes 40 per cent to GDP.
Algeria is rich in minerals, including iron ore, uranium, zinc, phosphates, gold, antimony, bituminous coal, tungsten, manganese, lead, mercury and salt. The mining of iron ore and phosphate for feedstocks (for local steel and fertiliser production, respectively) and for export are the most important.
Also located near the Moroccan border are iron-ore reserves estimated at two billion tonnes. The remote location and the Western Sahara/Morocco conflict have so far prevented exploitation.

Hydrocarbons

The oil and gas sector is of fundamental importance and accounts for about 95 per cent of foreign exchange, 23 per cent of government revenues and 90 per cent of total export revenues. The country has proven oil reserves of 9.2 billion barrels, and an oil production capacity of 1.5 million barrels per day (bpd). By the end of 2001, however, Algeria was producing 810,000bpd, above Opec's production quota of 740,000bpd.
Up to 70 per cent of the country's oil reserves are found in the Hassi Messaoud field. Algeria's natural gas reserves stand at 159.7 trillion cubic feet, and the fuel is exported via pipeline to Tunisia, Italy, Portugal, Spain and Slovenia. The country's hydrocarbons are administered by the Société Nationale pour la Recherche, la Production, le Transport, la Transformation et la Commercialisation des Hydrocarbons (Sonatrach), the state oil company, which is the world's fourth largest exporter of natural gas and the second largest exporter of liquefied petroleum gas (LPG).
Unlike most members of Opec, Algeria's hydrocarbons sector is relatively diversified and thus partially protected from world price shifts. Another difference from the Opec trend is that Algeria's oil sector has been open to foreign investors since the 1980s, leading to extensive participation by international firms.

Energy

Algerian power demand has been increasing by 5 per cent per annum. As a result, the state-owned power company, Sonelgaz, invested US$15.5 billion during the period 1996–2001 to develop and expand electricity production and distribution throughout Algeria. There are plans to build Algeria's first independent power plant by 2006 at a cost of US$12 billion.
In late 2001, a number of agreements were signed with EU countries, to increase Algeria's electricity supply. In Novermber 2001, Sonelgaz signed an agreement with Spain's Red Electrica de Espana to build an underwater power line between Algeria and Spain. In December 2001, Sonelgaz signed an agreement with Italy's power grid manager GRTN to develop a similar power line to export electricity to Italy via Europe. Sonelgaz has also formed a joint company in March 2001 with the state oil company Sonatrach to export electricity to countries such as Morocco, with which Algeria already has two links to its electricity grid.

Financial markets

Stock exchange

In July 1999 the Algiers stock exchange (Bourse d'Alger) was formally opened and was scheduled to hold trading sessions once a week. The pharmaceutical company Saidal was the first company to be listed. It was a small but significant step towards a more normal economic climate. However, by mid-2000 the stock exchange had only four listed companies including the food company Eriad Setif, the El-Aurassi hotel chain and Sonatrach, which issued bonds on the exchange.
The government's privatisation programme could be a major provider of vitality over the short- to medium-term. However, many companies believe that the slow privatisation progress has significantly reduced investor interest and therefore damaged the prospects of Algerian firms establishing a viable position in the financial markets of the region.

Banking

Central bank

Banque d'Algérie.

Time

GMT plus one hour.

Geography

Algeria is the second largest country in Africa, and within its 2.38 million square km comprises three distinct regions – a narrow coastal plain, which has the most fertile soils and houses the majority of the country's population, agriculture and industry; the uplands of the Atlas mountain chain, which tend to be semi-arid steppe in the valleys; and the vast sandy desert to the south. Algeria has borders with

Morocco to the west, Tunisia and Libya to the east and Niger, Mali and Mauritania to the south.

Climate

The coastal region has a temperate Mediterranean climate, averaging 13 degrees Celsius (C) to 24 degrees C throughout the year and rising to a daytime high of 32 degrees C during the summer (June to September). The rainy season is October to May, with rains especially heavy from November to February. The desert is constantly inhospitable, with temperatures rising to 45 degrees C during the day, falling to 10 degrees C at night, and with very little rainfall.

Dress codes

Western-style dress is acceptable, although lightweight or safari suits are recommended in summer. Women should not wear revealing clothes.

Entry requirements

Passports

Required by all

Visa

Required by most nationals – check with embassy. Visas cannot be issued at the border. Extensions can be obtained from the Service des Etrangers. Entry visas are usually valid for 90 days.

Prohibited entry

Nationals of Israel

Currency advice/regulations

Visitors entering the country must change a fixed sum (AD1,000) of foreign exchange into Algerian dinars at the point of entry. Unlimited amounts of foreign currency may be imported but must be declared. Foreign exchange receipts must be repatriated within 120 days.

To enable re-export of any unchanged foreign currency, declaration forms issued on arrival should be kept, used at each successive currency change and surrendered on departure. Failure to comply with these regulations may mean visitors are liable to forfeit the currency. Export of local currency is prohibited. It can sometimes be difficult to reconvert dinars to foreign currency.

Health (for visitors)

Mandatory precautions

A yellow fever and/or cholera vaccination certificate is required if arriving from infected or endemic areas.

Advisable precautions

Hepatitis 'A', typhoid, tetanus and polio vaccinations are advisable. There is risk of malaria in some areas, therefore prophylaxis is recommended. There is also a rabies risk. Water precautions should be taken throughout the country. Bottled water is often hard to find, particularly in southern parts of the country.

Hotels

Hotels are classified from one to five star. Major hotels in the business centres tend to be expensive, but are generally of a reasonable standard. It is advisable to book well in advance as accommodation in Algiers is difficult to obtain. The service charge is usually 15 per cent.

Credit cards

The use of credit cards is restricted to Mastercard and American Express and only in top hotels.

Public holidays

Fixed dates

1 Jan (New Year's Day), 1 May (Labour Day), 19 Jun (Historic Readjustment Day), 5 Jul (Independence Day), 1 Nov (Anniversary of the Revolution).

Variable dates

Eid Al-Fitr (two days, end of Ramadan), Eid Al-Adha (end of pilgrimage to Mecca), Moharram (Muslim New Year), Ashura (Charity Day), Prophet's Birthday.

Working hours

The Muslim weekend is Thursday afternoon and Friday, but many industries close all day Thursday.

Banking

Sun–Thur: 0900–1530.

Business

Sat–Tue: 0800–1200 and 1300–1700;
Wed 0800–1200 and 1300–1600.

Government

Sat–Wed: 0800–1200 and 1400–1730;
Thur 0800–1200.

Shops

Sat–Wed 0800–1230 and 1430–1800;
Thu: 0800–1300.

Telecommunications

Telephone/fax

Algeria is linked to the international telephone network and public telephones are plentiful in cities. The Algerian government tendered about US$1.3 billion worth of contracts in the telecom sector between 1997–2000. Over this period, pilot fibre-optics have been installed by a variety of firms, including Italtel, Siemens, NEC and Fujitsu.

In August 2001, the Ministry of Posts and Telecommunications (PTT) created a new company, Algerie Telecom, to oversee the development of the country's telecommunications sector. Algerie Telecom will oversee all of Algeria's telephone, telex, telegraph and facsimile networks, maritime radio service, mobile telephone system and public data communications network.

Installed telephone lines total an estimated 1.8 million. About 80 per cent of the national telecommunications network uses digital technology.

Postal services

All business correspondence should be sent air mail and marked 'Documentation Technique – Sans Valeur Commerciale'. Advisable to rent a post box.

Courier services

DHL has been operating a courier service in Algiers since 1994. The company has offices at Annaba, Arzew, Constantine, Hassi Messaoud, Oran, and Skikda.

Mobile phones

The expansion of the mobile phone network is expected to result in a significant rise in accessibility and ownership of mobile phones over the short-to-medium term. It is expected that there will be 10 million mobile telephone users in Algeria by 2015. There are efforts to meet this estimated demand. In July 2001, a new GSM license was granted to Egypt's Orascom Telecom (OT) for US$737 million.

Internet/e-mail

There were 28 Internet service providers (ISPs) in Algeria by end-2000. While it is expected that further providers will enter the market, the development of the sector is likely to be slow given the cost of telecommunications and the limited availability of personal computers (an estimated 50 per 10,000 people).

Electricity supply

Electricity supply varies from 127–220V. All types of plug fittings in use.

Social customs/useful tips

Business appointments should be made in advance. Business cards are exchanged after introductions. French-style courtesy should be adopted by visitors. Hospitality is regarded as very important, as it is throughout the Arab world.

Wives often do not accompany their husbands to business meetings or social engagements outside the home.

Security

Extreme caution must be used when visiting the country; check with your government's foreign affairs department before travelling to Algeria. Violence has been endemic since 1991. Economic hardship and unemployment have led to massive discontent and a rise in Islamic extremism. Some 15,000 troops are stationed in and around Algiers. Many expatriates have left the country, and strict security measures have been put in place for those who remain.

Getting there

Air

National airline: Air Algérie (Compagnie Générale de Transports Aériens) (state-owned).

Main airport: Algiers-Houari Boumédienne (ALG), 20km from city. Airport facilities

include duty-free shop, restaurant, buffet, bank, post office, shops, car hire.
Other main airports are Annaba-Les Salines (AAE), 12km from city (restaurant, buffet, bank, post office, shops, car hire); Constantine-Ain El-Bey (CZL), 9km from city (restaurant); Oran-Es Senia (ORN), 10km from city (bank, car hire, buffet).
Airport tax: None
Surface
The National Travel and Transport Company (SNTV) operates bus services linking Libya, Niger, Morocco and Tunisia with Algeria. Road access also possible from Mali by one of the trans-Saharan highways. A daily train service (the TransMaghreb) links Tunis with Algiers and Oran.
Road: The National Travel and Transport Company (SNTV) operates bus services linking Libya, Niger, Morocco and Tunisia with Algeria. Road access is also possible from Mali by one of the trans-Saharan highways.
Rail: A daily train service (the TransMaghreb) links Tunis with Algiers and Oran.
Water: Regular ferry services connect Algiers with Marseilles and other Mediterranean ports.
Main ports: Algiers, Annaba, Arzew, Bejaia, Oran.

Getting about

National transport
Air: There are frequent services from Algiers to Annaba, Constantine and Oran which are operated by Inter Air Services (internal branch of Air Algérie). Regular flights also link these towns with other principal centres. In mid-2000, Khalifa Airways began providing daily services from Algiers to Batna and Tiaret. Fares are generally low for domestic flights but overbooking can occur, especially in summer.
Road: Main roads are in good condition generally, but desert routes are rarely maintained.
Buses: Long-distance coach services are operated by SNTV and Altour. Bookings for long trips should be made well in advance.
Rail: The service is operated by SNTF. There are two classes; some services are air-conditioned and/or have couchettes.
City transport
Taxis: Taxis are widely available in main centres; they are radio-controlled in Algiers. Taxis are identified by a local colour code. They are supposed to be metered, but owing to demand, usually operate without a meter and use a minimum fare system instead. A surcharge is imposed after dark. Tips are usually 10 per cent of fare.
Buses/trams: A state-owned service operates in Algiers, which can be overcrowded during rush hours. Daily and longer duration tickets are available.
Car hire
Car hire is available in most main towns and at airports. An international driving licence and third-party insurance are required. The maximum speed limit is 50kph in towns and 100kph on main roads.

BUSINESS DIRECTORY

Telephone area codes

The international dialling code (IDD) for Algeria is + 213 followed by the area code, which changed from 15 December 2000:

Algiers	21
Annaba	38
Béchar	49
Blida	25
Boumerdes	24
Constantine	31
Ghardaia	29
Oran	41
Sétif	36
Tiemcen	43
Tindouf	49

Useful telephone numbers

Directory enquiries: 19
Telegrams: 13
Police: 17

Chambers of Commerce

Chambre Nationale de Commerce, 6 Boulevard Amilcar Cabral, Place des Martyrs, Algiers (tel: 574-397; fax: 577-025).

Algiers Chamber of Commerce, 11 Chemin Doudou Mokhlar Ben Aknoun (tel: 792-323).

Constantine Chamber of Commerce, 6 Rue de 24 Novembre 1954 (tel: 935-923).

Oran Chamber of Commerce, 8 Boulevard de la Soummam (tel: 391-299; fax: 396-312).

Banking

Arab Banking Corporation Algérie (ABC), 54 Avenue des Trois Frères Bouadou, Bir Mourad Rais, Algiers (tel: 540-345; fax: 541-604; e-mail: abcbank@wissal.dz).

Banque Al Baraka d'Algérie, 9 Rue Emir El Khettabi, Algiers (tel: 632-526, 643-665/67; fax: 632-713, 643-679).

Banque de l'Agriculture et du Développement Rural (BADR), 17 Boulevard Colonel Amirouche, Algiers (tel: 743-273; fax: 743-367).

Banque Algérienne de Développement (BAD), 21 Boulevard Zighout Youcef, Algiers (tel: 739-904; fax: 737-638).

Banque Commerciale et Industrielle d'Algérie (BCIA), 4 Chemin Doudou Mokhtar, Algiers (tel: 911-504; 912-915).

Banque de Développement Local (BDL), 5 Rue Gaci Amar, Staouéli, Algiers (tel: 393-755; fax: 393-757).

Banque Extérieure d'Algérie (BEA), 3 Rue de Docteur Lucien Reynaud, Algiers (tel: 239-330; fax: 239-099); bea@algerianetwork.net).

Banque Nationale d'Algérie (BNA), 8 Boulevard Che Guevara, Algiers (tel: 713-519; fax: 712-424).

Caisse d'Epargne et de Prévoyance (CNEP Banque), 42 Rue Khelifa Boukhalfa, Algiers (tel: 713-395; fax: 714-131).

Crédit Populaire d'Algérie (CPA), 2 Boulevard Colonel Amirouche, Algiers (tel: 719-081; fax: 719-219).

El Khalifa Bank, 27 Blvd Zighout Youcef, Alger Centre, Algiers (tel: 739-798, 739-778; fax: 739-778).

El Mouna Bank, 22 Rue Boudjellal Ahmed, Haï El Moudjahidine, Oran (tel: 411-590; fax: 411-808).

Natexis Bank, 62 Chemin Drareni, Algiers (tel: 694-042; fax: 534-407).

Société Générale Algérie, 75 Rue Cheikh Bachir Ibrahimi, El Biar, Algiers (tel: 922-181; fax: 922-182).

Union Bank, 5 bis Chemin El Bakri, 16 030 Algiers (tel: 914-552: fax: 914-548).

Central bank
Banque d'Algérie, 38 Avenue Franklin Roosevelt, Algiers (tel: 230-023; e-mail: BAcom@ist.cerist.dz).

Travel information

Air Algérie, 1 Place Audin, Algiers (tel: 642-428, 644-822; fax: 610-533).

National tourist organisation offices
Office National du Tourisme (ONAT), 126A Rue Didouche Mourad, Algiers (tel: 742-985; fax: 747-049; e-mail: onat@ist.cerist.dz).

Ministries

Prime Minister's Office, Rue Docteur Saadane, Algiers (tel: 732-340; fax: 717-927).

Ministry of Agriculture, 4 Route des Quatre Canons, Algiers (tel: 711-712; fax: 615-739).

Ministry of Commerce, Rue Docteur Saadane, Algiers (tel: 732-340; fax: 735-478).

Ministry of Communications and Culture, Palais de la Culture, Les Annasers, Algiers (tel: 679-420; fax: 684-041).

Ministry of Defence, Les Tagarins, El-Biar, Algiers (tel: 711-515).

Ministry of Education, 8 Avenue de Pékin, Algiers (tel: 605-761; fax: 606-757).

Ministry of Energy and Mines, 80 Avenue Ahmed Ghermoul, Algiers (tel: 673-300; fax: 650-997).

Ministry of Finance, Immeuble Mauretania, Place du Pérou, Algiers (tel: 711-366; fax: 731-959).

Ministry of Foreign Affairs, Place Med Seddik Ben Yahia, El-Mouradia, Algiers (tel: 692-333; fax: 691-164).

Ministry of Health and Population, 125 Rue Abderahmane Laala, Algiers (tel: 615-315; fax: 653-646).

Ministry of Higher Education and Scientific Research, 11 Rue Doudou Mokhtar, Algiers (tel: 912-323; fax: 911-197).

Ministry of Housing, 137 Rue due Caire, Kouba, Algiers (tel: 689-500; fax: 585-638).

Ministry of Industry and Construction, Immeuble le Colisée, 4 Rue Ahmed Bey, Algiers (tel: 601-466; fax: 692-501).

Ministry of the Interior and Local Communities, Place du Gouvernement, Algiers (tel: 732-340; fax: 734-367).

Ministry of Justice, 8 Place Bir Hakem, El Biar, Algiers (tel: 924-183; fax: 921-243).

Ministry of Labour and Social Protection, 44 Rue Med Belouizded, Belcourt, Algiers (tel: 683-366; fax: 675-777).

Ministry of National Solidarity, Rue Docteur Saadane, Algiers (tel: 732-340; fax: 717-927).

Ministry of Participation and Reforms Co-ordination (MPCR), Chemin Ibn Badis el Mouiz, El Biar, Algiers (tel: 929-885/93, 929-874; fax: 921-755, 926-282; e-mail: ABIDKN@hotmail.com).

Ministry of Post and Telecommunications, 4 bis Boulevard Krim Belkacem, Algiers (tel: 711-220; fax: 719-217).

Ministry of Religious Affairs, 4 Rue de Timgad, Algiers (tel: 608-555; fax: 600-936).

Ministry of Small and Medium Enterprises, Immeuble le Colisée, 4 Rue Ahmed Bey, Algiers (tel: 601-326; fax: 605-559).

Ministry of Tourism and Handicraft, Rue des Frères Ziata, El Mouradia, Algiers (tel: 605-202; fax: 590-664).

Ministry of Transport, 119 rue Didouche Mourad, Algiers (tel: 740-699; fax: 646-637).

Ministry of Vocational Training, 44 Rue Med Belouizded, Belcourt, Algiers (tel: 683-366; fax: 675-777).

Ministry of War Veterans, 2 Avenue du Lt. Med Bearfa, El-Biar, Algiers (tel: 922-355; fax: 923-516).

Ministry of Youth and Sports, 3 Rue des Frères Belouizdad, Place du 1er Mai, Algiers (tel: 683-350; fax: 657-778).

Other useful addresses

Algerian Embassy (US), 2118 Kalorama Road, NW, Washington DC 20008 (tel: 265-2800; fax: 667-2174; e-mail: embalgus@cais.com).

Algero-European Financial Participation Company (FINALEP), Route Nationale 11, Staoueli, Wilaya de Tipaza (tel: 393-494/6; fax: 392-020).

British Embassy, Résidence Cassiopée, 7 Chemin des Glycines, Algiers (tel: 230-068; fax: 230-067).

Entreprise Nationale de Commerce 6-9 Rue Belhaffat-Ghazali, Hussein Dey, Algiers (tel: 774-320).

Entreprise Nationale d'Génie Civil et de Développement des Industries Legères, 50 Rue Khelifa Boukhalfa, BP 1140, Algiers (tel: 663-390).

Entreprise Nationale d'Engineering Petrolier, 2 Boulevard Mohamed V, Algiers (tel: 630-892).

Entreprise Nationale de Raffinage et de Distribution des Produits Petroliers, Avenue Ahmed Ghermoul, Algiers.

Office Algérien Interprofessionel des Céréales, Rue Ferhat Bousaad, Algiers.

Office Nationale des Statistiques, 8 Rue des Moussebilines, Algiers (tel: 639-974; fax: 637-955; e-mail: ons@onssiege.ons.dz).

Privatisation and Foreign Investment Organisation (APSI), Boulevard du 11 Décembre 1960, El-Biar, Algiers (tel: 925-127; fax: 923-762).

Radiodiffusion Télévision Algérienne (RTA), 21 Boulevard des Martyrs, Algiers (tel: 602-300).

Service des Etrangers, Boulevard Zeroud Yousef 19A, Algiers.

SNTF (rail company), 21 Boulevard Mohamed V, Algiers (tel: 611-510).

Société Algerienne des Foires et Expositions (SAFEX), Palais des Expositions, Pins Maritimes El-Mohamedia, Algiers (tel: 210-123; fax: 210-639).

Société Centrale pour l'Equipement du Territoire, Rue Sergent Addoun, Algiers.

Société Nationale d'Edition et de Diffusion, Boulevard Zeroud Yousef, Algiers (deals with books, stationery, advertising).

Société Nationale de Constructions Mécaniques, Route Nationale, Bukhadem, Algiers (deals with vehicles, agricultural equipment etc).

Société Nationale de Gestion et de Développement des Industries Alimentaires, Avenue Mustapha El Ouali Sayed, Algiers.

Société Nationale des Matériaux de Construction, Rue Didouche Mourad, Algiers.

Société Nationale d'Etudes de Gestion, de Réalisations et d'Exploitations Industrielles, Rue Khélifa Boukhalfa, Algiers.

Société Nationale pour la Rechereche, la Production, le Transport, la Transformation et la Commercialisation des Hydrocarbures (Sonatrach), 10 Rue du Sahara, Hydra, Algiers (tel: 609-022; fax: 601-949).

US Embassy, 4 Chemin Cheikh Bachir El-Ibrahimi, Algiers (tel: 691-255; fax: 693-979; e-mail: embalgus@cais.com).

Internet sites

Africa Business Network: http://www.ifc.org/abn

AllAfrica.com: http://allafrica.com

African Development Bank: http://www.afdb.org

Algeria Interface: http://www.algeria-interface.com

Algeria News Agency: http://www.aps.dz

Algeria On-Line: http://www.djazaironline.net

Mbendi AfroPaedia: http://www.mbendi.co.za

Angola

Daniel Brett

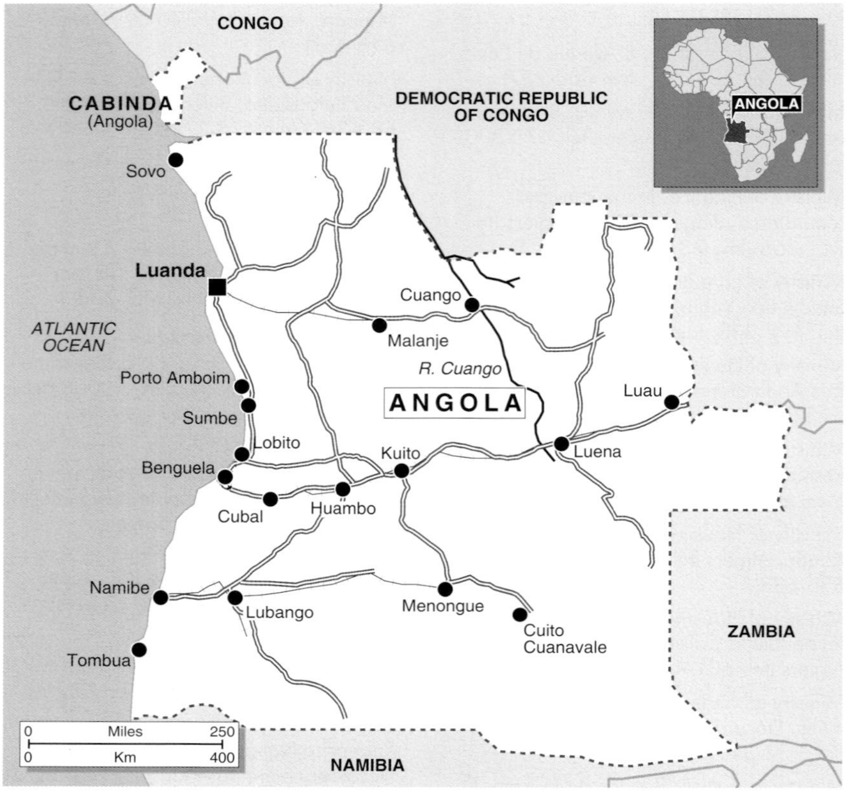

KEY FACTS

Official name: Republica de Angola (Republic of Angola)

Head of State: President José Eduardo dos Santos

Head of government: Prime Minister Fernando da Piedade Dias dos Santos (from 5 Dec 2002)

Ruling party: Government of Unity and National Reconciliation (GURN); dominated by Movimento Popular de Libertação de Angola (MPLA) (Popular Movement for the Liberation of Angola)

Area: 1,246,700 square km

Population: 13.13 million (2001)

Capital: Luanda

Official language: Portuguese

Currency: Kwanza (Kz) = 100 Lwei

Exchange rate: Kz58.86 per US$ (Jan 2003)

GDP per capita: US$310 (2001); US$359 (2002)*

GDP real growth: 3.30% (2001); 10.5% (2002)*

Labour force: 5.10 million (2001); 5.3 million (2002)*

Unemployment: 50.00% (2000)

Inflation: 152.60% (2001); 125.0% (2002)*

Oil production: 731,000 bpd (2001)

Balance of trade: US$3.44 billion (2001)

Foreign debt: US$9.25 billion (2001)

Annual FDI: US$1.35 billion (2001)

* estimated figure

For the latest Key Facts, go to www.worldinformation.com

Angola's apparently ceaseless civil war ended in 2002, with both the government and the rebels signing a peace agreement in April. It took the death of the rebel leader, Jonas Savimbi, and his deputy, Antonio Dembo, at the hands of the army to pave the way for a truce between the two sides. By mid-2002, the voluntary demobilisation of large numbers of former fighters of the União Nacional de Independencia Total de Angola (Unita) (National Union for the Total Independence of Angola) suggested many combatants were war weary and wanted an end to conflict.

The war had served to deflect criticisms of corruption and mismanagement by the ruling Movimento Popular de Libertação de Angola (MPLA) (Popular Movement for the Liberation of Angola). The truce with Unita has led to renewed pressure on the MPLA to reform itself and choose a new leader in order to gain the confidence and support of the international community. With a large proportion of the population facing starvation in a land renowned for its fertility, the importance of foreign aid and the expansion of the oil and mining sectors will be dominant themes in post-war reconstruction.

Dos Santos not standing

In August 2001, President José Eduardo dos Santos indicated that he would not stand for re-election in the next presidential elections. Dos Santos claimed Unita's inevitable defeat on the battlefield would enable the MPLA to debate openly his likely successor, without fear that this would undermine national security.

Although some in the MPLA were startled by this shock announcement, many find it hard to believe that he will quit Angolan politics. There is no obvious successor within the MPLA hierarchy and with dates for fresh elections yet to be announced, it is unclear when dos Santos' present term in office will end. Following the announcement, one MPLA politician said: 'He personally said he was not interested, but he will certainly be confronted by the wishes of the party leadership and the party members'. This implied that many in the MPLA still believe that dos Santos will stand for re-election.

Life after death

Savimbi's death in February 2002 removed the largest obstacle to peace, which became a reality for the first time since Angola achieved independence from Portugal in 1975. The conflict had begun as a Cold War confrontation, with the MPLA one-party government backed by Cuba and the Soviet Union and Unita rebels supported by apartheid South Africa and the US. Ideological differences diminished in the 1980s and 1990s and the civil war evolved into a scramble for control of the country's two main commodities, with the MPLA controlling the oil-rich areas and Unita fighting for the diamond mines.

Agreements between the two sides in 1991 and 1994 never achieved permanent peace. The results of the first multi-party elections in 1992, which were won by the MPLA and described by UN observers as free and fair, were dismissed by Unita. The rebel group feared the threat peace posed to its large war chest, which amounted to hundreds of millions of US dollars mostly earned from the diamond trade. In 1998, civil war broke out again, but by 2001 Unita had retreated on the battlefield. Its hungry guerrillas left devastation in their wake, looting farms in the south and east of Angola and across the border in neighbouring Namibia. Unita was brought to the brink of defeat by the drying up of arms supplies and international sanctions against so-called 'blood diamonds'.

Savimbi's death enabled Unita to exit the war with a small amount of dignity. The commanders left in charge of the fragmented and broken rebel armies realised that a continuation of the war would have eventually led to Unita's political annihilation as well as its military defeat. The peace agreement of April 2002 reiterated the Lusaka peace agreement of 1994, which recognised Unita as a legitimate political force in return for demobilisation of its guerrillas or their integration into the Angolan army.

Unita's troop demobilisation following the truce was far larger than the government had expected. Although more than 85,000 people flocked to the demobilisation camps, the UN claimed that most were not Unita soldiers and estimated that in reality Unita had only 10,000 troops by the end of the war. Most were non-combatants who had turned themselves in as Unita soldiers in the hope of getting access to food and health facilities. This appeared to be borne out by the fact that the number of weapons handed in varied between 10–25 per cent of the number of soldiers' in the camps. In addition, more than 250,000 civilians, mostly relatives of Unita fighters, moved into camps surrounding the centres in search of food and medical care.

A worrying security problem following the peace agreement is the lack of information on the number of weapons held by Unita at the end of the war. The dissolution of Unita as a military force does not necessarily entail nationwide stability. There is a medium-term danger of localised security problems and banditry by disbanded Unita units retaining their arms, fuelled by the lack of food, medicines and other assistance. Most security experts agree that even if many Unita soldiers retain their weapons, the rebels have little chance of re-igniting the civil war.

The government hopes that by 2003 it will have relocated demobilised Unita combatants and their families and incorporated around 5,000 Unita soldiers into the Angolan army. However, there is a distinct possibility that the demobilisation camps will become permanent settlements exclusively for Unita supporters, thereby perpetuating the country's political polarisation.

Peace and poverty

The civilian population has suffered years of mass murder, looting and dislocation at the hands of Unita and government forces. Meanwhile, the government has diverted vital resources to the armed forces and away from social services. The IMF estimated that defence spending was around 40 per cent of total expenditure, while spending on social services was less than 10 per cent by 2000.

The World Bank has noted that years of war have increased income inequality and the IMF estimates that some 69 per cent of the population lives in 'absolute poverty'. A report by the UK-based Save the Children Fund, released in November 2001, estimated that nearly one in three Angolan children died before the age of five and 42 per cent of Angolan children were underweight. The organisation claimed that 'years of under-investment in health, coupled with decades of conflict, have been debilitating to the public health services. Just 5.7 per cent of the annual budget was directed towards health and sanitation [in 2001]. Effectively, the government delegates its responsibilities for providing these services to humanitarian agencies.'

War has also severely disrupted food production and supply. The UN estimated that at least four million people were vulnerable to famine in mid-2002, half of

KEY INDICATORS — Angola

	Unit	1996	1997	1998	1999	2000
Population	m	11.70	12.05	12.40	12.76	13.13
Gross domestic product (GDP)	US$bn	6.50	7.70	6.40	3.30	4.00
GDP per capita	US$	576	657	537	267	314
GDP real growth	%	7.7	6.2	6.9	3.4	3.0
Inflation	%	4,145.1	219.2	107.3	248.2	325.0
Consumer prices	1995=100	4,245.2	13,550.1	25,327.3	97,807.0	415,713.0
Unemployment	%	2.9	*3.2	50.0	50.0	50.0
Oil output	'000 bpd	715.0	740.0	760.0	780.0	736.0
Exports (fob) (goods)	US$m	5,095.0	5,006.0	3,542.9	5,165.5	7,802.0
Imports (fob) (goods)	US$m	2,040.5	2,597.0	2,079.4	3,109.1	3,430.0
Balance of trade	US$m	3,054.5	2,409.8	1,463.5	2,047.4	4,372.0
Current account	US$m	3,266.4	-872.1	-1,857.6	-1,702.1	-4.0
Total reserves minus gold	US$m	551.6	396.4	203.5	496.1	1,198.2
Foreign exchange	US$m	551.5	396.3	203.3	495.9	1,198.0
Exchange rate	per US$	0.13	0.23	0.39	2.79	10.04

* estimated figure

whom were dependent on some kind of international assistance for their survival. The total number of internally displaced persons (IDPs) was estimated at around 4.3 million or a third of the population in early 2002. The UN claimed that Angola would need just under 19,000 tonnes of food assistance every month along with agricultural inputs, such as seeds and tools, in order to prevent mass starvation and bring farmland back into production.

Neglecting the poor

The government appears to be well aware of the desperate needs of the Angolan population. In his speech to a rally in Luanda in November 2001, President dos Santos stated that 'normalising life throughout the national territory implies that the government must review its strategy for solving the problem of displaced people'. However, following the truce between the government and the rebels in April 2002, the government was overwhelmingly focussed on the needs of demobilised Unita troops as part of the peace process. This diverted attention from the crisis in the rest of Angola. In June 2002, the aid organisation Médecins Sans Frontières (MSF), one of the few organisations active in Unita-controlled areas during the war, condemned the UN and the Angolan government for their 'shamefully slow and shockingly insufficient' response to the growing famine in Angola. It claimed that 'thousands of Angolans have died and hundreds of thousands more face starvation from a catastrophic man-made nutritional crisis unless the Angolan government and the UN drastically increase their efforts to meet the needs of the civilian population'. The Angolan authorities were accused of a 'chronic criminal neglect of their own people'.

The UN agencies denied they were neglecting the civilian population and claimed they were overstretched due to a lack of resources and a failure of foreign donors to respond to their appeals for funds. By July 2002, the UN Consolidated Inter-Agency Appeal reported that it had received only a third of its US$232.8 million target from international donors. The situation was becoming so desperate that the World Food Programme (WFP) warned that unless donors got their act together, food stocks would run out by September 2002, with at least one million people starving as a result.

Development dreams

The end of the war has the potential to unlock Angola's enormous economic potential. After Nigeria, Angola is the second largest producer of oil in sub-Saharan Africa and the world's fourth largest producer of diamonds by value. Angola's oil production is projected to double by 2005, which could make it the biggest oil exporter in Africa. The sector is projected to receive investment totalling US$23 billion in the period 2002–07. With oil contributing between 80–90 per cent of government revenues, the state stands to receive massive gains from the expansion of this sector.

Angola's offshore oil fields have attracted considerable international attention since the mid-1990s. With fighting taking place hundreds of miles inland from the coast, there was little danger of the offshore oil sector being disrupted by the civil war. In January 2002, crude oil production reached 820,000 barrels per day (bpd), according to the International Energy Agency (IEA). Output is expected to exceed 900,000bpd in 2003, with production reaching capacity in the deepwater Girassol field and its satellite Jasmim. The Sociedade Nacional de Combustiveis de Angola (Sonangol), the state-owned oil concessionaire, expects output to hit 1.8 million bpd by 2010.

Unita's defeat means the government will have control of the diamond mines which were located in Unita territory. The disbanding of Unita's military forces will lead to the lifting of international sanctions against the Angolan diamond trade, which was worth US$600 million annually before the ban which was imposed in 1999.

Despite its potential in mining and hydrocarbons, Angola has pressing problems with its poor macroeconomic fundamentals. Retarded by the effects of the recent bout of civil war, GDP growth rose marginally from 3 per cent in 2000 to 3.2 per cent in 2001. Meanwhile, the government's perennial fiscal deficit, which was estimated at around 7 per cent of GDP in 2001, has helped fuel inflation. Although inflation fell from 325 per cent in 2000 to 152.6 per cent in 2001, more effort will be needed to strengthen the government's fiscal position. This will involve greater transparency and accountability in spending, which could mean tackling the thorny issue of corruption.

Oil and corruption

Endemic corruption has led to large amounts of government revenue accrued through the expansion of the oil sector going straight into the pockets of top officials and ministers. Up to US$1.4 billion out of a total of US$4 billion of government expenditure was not properly accounted for in 2001. Missing funds since 1997 are estimated at over US$1 billion per annum, up to a third of state income. The failure of the Angolan authorities to account properly for revenue and expenditure has raised concerns over corruption among international financial institutions such as the IMF as well as investors and foreign governments. In June 2001, the IMF, ceased lending to Angola due to the country's opaque accounting and corruption by officials.

During the civil war, the government and Sonangol bypassed the ministry of finance and the central bank to mortgage future oil revenue in return for oil-backed loans to help fund arms purchases. Oil-backed loans represented up to a third of Angola's US$10.4 billion debt in 2001. These loans, which have repayment terms of three years or less, were obtained at high interest rates and channelled through foreign banking facilities.

In March 2002, Global Witness issued a ground-breaking report entitled *All the President's Men*, which alleged that 'highest level individuals connected to the presidency – Angola's 'oligarchy' – loot cash from oil revenues and oil-backed international loans off the back of arms trafficking and the military procurement process'. It added that 'most international oil companies in Angola are complicit in state looting because they refuse to release any public information about payments to the state, making it impossible for civil society to hold the Angolan government to account over the misappropriation of money from their resources'.

Many oil companies are concerned that by adopting a more transparent approach, they will lose their production-sharing agreements (PSAs) with Sonangol. In February 2001, Sonangol threatened to end BP-Amoco's PSA after the UK-based oil company pledged to reveal publicly all its payments to the Angolan authorities. However, BP-Amoco managed to hold on to its shareholding in Angola's Block 17, which commenced commercial operations in December 2001.

Outlook

With civil war at an end, the issue of the government's mismanagement of oil revenues is generating growing national and international condemnation. In the past, the government has suppressed public criticism and clamped down on the media, while the international community has turned a blind eye to the MPLA's activities. The end of Unita's insurgency will focus attention on government corruption. Many donors are beginning to ask why they should be expected to give large amounts of aid when leading figures are misappropriating funds generated by the country's natural resources. Foreign governments are also likely to step up pressure on the government to clean up its act and could threaten to freeze the assets of leading political figures if it fails to meet the basic requirements of fiscal transparency and accountability. An anti-corruption campaign coupled with an end to conflict could have far-reaching implications for Angola's political and economic situation. Civil society would be strengthened, putting the MPLA under greater public scrutiny. This opens the way for new political actors in Angola and the possibility of real political change led from the grassroots.

Risk assessment

Economic	Poor
Political	Improving
Regional stability	Poor

COUNTRY PROFILE

Historical profile

1482 The Portuguese settlement began in Angola.
1575 The Portuguese founded Luanda. The country became a major source of slaves, who were transported to Brazil.
1836 The slave trade was abolished.
1951 Angola's status changed from a colony to an overseas territory.
1956 The Movimento Popular de Libertação de Angola (MPLA) (Popular Movement for the Liberation of Angola) was founded as a guerrilla force fighting against Portuguese rule.
1957 The Frente Nacional para a Libertacao de Angola (FNLA) (National Front for the Liberation of Angola) was formed.
1966 The União Nacional de Independencia Total de Angola (Unita) (National Union for the Total Independence of Angola) was formed.
1975 Independence from Portugal. Elections were scheduled to be held. However, (MPLA took power without an election, and Unita and the FNLA retreated.
1979 José dos Santos became president and enjoyed the backing of the Soviet Union and Cuba. There followed a long period of civil war between the MPLA and Unita, which gained the support of the US and South Africa.
1991 The MPLA introduced multi-party democracy. Talks with Unita began and the Cuban troops withdrew. The Bicesse accords were signed in May.
1992 The first multi-party elections were held. A coalition government was formed by the MPLA-PT, but the newly- legalised Unita rejected the election results and returned to the battlefield to fight on.
1994 A cease-fire peace agreement, the Lusaka Protocol, was signed on 20 November between the government and Unita.
1997 On 11 April, Unita joined the ruling MPLA in a power-sharing government of national unity.
1998 Renewed hostilities between MPLA and Unita broke out.
2001 President José dos Santos announced in August that he would not stand in presidential elections, although he did not set a date for the elections. A treaty establishing the Gulf of Guinea Commisssion was signed by five of the seven member states in July (Gabon, Congo, São Tomé and Príncipe, Nigeria and Angola).
2002 Jonas Savimbi, the leader of Unita, was killed in February. In March, the Angolan government stopped all offensives against the Unita rebels and offered an amnesty for guerrillas who surrendered. On 4 April, a cease-fire was signed, ending the civil war.

Political structure

Constitution
The constitution was agreed in 1992 following the signing of the Angolan Peace Accords in May 1991. It recognises fundamental rights and duties, based on the principles of the major international treaties on human rights to which Angola is a signatory. It also established multi-party politics, enabling elections to be held in September 1992.

Form of state
Unitary republic

The executive
The head of state is the president, elected by direct universal suffrage.

National legislature
Unicameral legislature elected for a four-year term.

Legal system
The constitution defines the judiciary as an independent body that is nominated by the National Assembly on the decision of two-thirds of those casting their votes. The Judicial Proctorate is appointed for a four-year term of office and may be re-appointed for another four-year term.

Last elections
29/30 September 1992 (parliamentary and presidential)

Next elections
No date set

Political parties

Ruling party
Government of Unity and National Reconciliation (GURN); dominated by Movimento Popular de Libertação de Angola (MPLA) (Popular Movement for the Liberation of Angola).

Main opposition party
União Nacional de Independencia Total de Angola (Unita) (National Union for the Total Independence of Angola)

Population

13.13 million (2000)
Annual population growth: 3 per cent (1994–2000). The projected annual growth rate for 1999–2015 is 2.7 per cent. An estimated 48 per cent of the total population is under 14 years.
Population density: 10 inhabitants per square km. Urban population: 34 per cent (1994–2000).

Ethnic make-up
Main ethnic groups include: Ovimbundu (37 per cent), Mbundu (25 per cent) and Bakongo (13 per cent).

Religions
Traditional beliefs (47 per cent), Christianity (38 per cent), mainly Roman Catholic.

Education

Estimates show that 50 per cent and 70 per cent of men and women are illiterate respectively. Primary school enrolment has steadily declined and in 1997 was at 35 per cent, which was below the average of 56 per cent for Sub-Saharan Africa. Education expenditure amounted to only 5.8 per cent of the 2001 national budget.

Health

Decades of conflict have debilitated access to primary healthcare, while most people find it difficult to pay for private treatment. In many places healthcare support has been left to non-governmental organisations and churches. It is estimated that 5.7 per cent of the annual budget is typically directed towards health and sanitation.
The national HIV rate is estimated to be 3–5 per cent in the adult population aged 15–49 years (2000).

Welfare

Around 4.3 million people were internally displaced persons (IDPs) in early 2002. At least four million people were vulnerable to famine in 2002, according to the UN. About 69 per cent of the population are living in 'absolute poverty', according to the IMF. As Luanda and provincial capitals have to cope with the refugee crisis, thousands also sought shelter in western Zambia and northern Namibia . The high concentration of landmines, estimated to be between nine and 15 million, make rehabilitation of the refugees even more difficult.

Main cities

Luanda, capital (population 2.2 million), Huambo (120,000), Lobito, Benguela, Lubango, Soyo, Malanje.

Languages spoken

Local languages: principally Ovimbundu, Kimbundu (the language of the Mbundu), Bakongo and Chokwe.

Official language/s

Portuguese

Media

Press

Angola's only national daily newspaper is *O Jornal de Angola (JA)*. *Diário da República* (government news sheet) is published daily. Regional newspapers are published in several towns. *El Moujahid* is also circulated here. *Correio da Semana* is the Sunday newspaper.

Broadcasting

Radio: National radio service with broadcasts in Portuguese, English, French, Spanish and vernacular languages, operated by the state-owned Radio Nacional de Angola. The Black Cock of Unita is also permitted to operate.

Television: Limited TV service operated by Televisão Popular de Angola (TPA).

Economy

The Angolan economy is highly dependent on its offshore oil sector. Positive growth rates are attributable to the regional oil boom which is centred on developing Angola's large oil reserves. However, ordinary Angolans languish in poverty with one of the lowest GDP per capita rates in the world while oil revenues have been ploughed into fighting the Unita rebels in the south and east of the country.

The war brought a number of macroeconomic problems, namely triple-digit inflation and supply bottlenecks. Government policy is generally haphazard, reflecting the kind of political pressure it was under in pursuing a war with the Unita rebels. Expenditure is out of control, with a large proportion spent without authorisation by the treasury. Around a third of government expenditure went 'missing' in 1997–2001, suggesting widespread corruption within the government. The period of civil war in 1998–2002 saw military expenditure soar to 40 per cent of total government expenditure, or 22 per cent of GDP. Meanwhile, social spending stayed level and was less than 10 per cent of government spending.

Currency depreciation has increased the cost of imports, although this was partly offset by a reduction in import tariffs since 2000. This has satisfied multilateral agencies such as the IMF which had cut off financing due to the government's deepening and unremitting external debts. Although the change in utility prices and the realignment of the exchange rate satisfied the IMF, many of Angola's poor were deeply upset that the country's enormous oil wealth was being plunged into a fruitless war while they had to bear the brunt of the painful stabilisation and structural adjustment policies imposed by international financial institutions (IFIs). The process of stabilisation and adjustment is unlikely to let up in 2002 as public utility and fuel price subsidies are gradually scrapped.

External trade

Exports

Principal exports are crude oil, gas and derivatives (typically 92 per cent of total), diamonds (8 per cent) (before being banned by the De Beers diamond corporation in 2000 following international sanctions against diamond sales used to fund armed groups), coffee. Also small quantities of cement, fishmeal, marble and timber.

Main destinations: US (44.6 per cent of 2000 total), China (22.7 per cent), Republic of Korea (8.1 per cent), Belgium (7.7 per cent), France (4.6 per cent).

Imports

Principal imports are oil equipment, vehicles and machinery, foodstuffs, textiles, consumer goods and arms.

Main sources: Portugal (17.4 per cent of 2000 total), South Africa (15.9 per cent), US (11.3 per cent), France (6.1 per cent), UK (5.9 per cent).

Agriculture

The agricultural sector fell from 13 per cent of GDP in 1998 to 6.7 per cent in 2000 as a result of falling agricultural output and the increasing importance of the oil sector. A fall in production has led to widespread food insecurity and malnutrition, with around four million people facing severe food shortages by mid-2002.

At least 75 per cent of national food requirements are imported and this is likely to continue until the government succeeds in stabilising the currency, freeing farmgate prices and providing rural areas with farm inputs, basic transport and essential commodities. The advent of peace in 2002 is likely to make a programme of agricultural rehabilitation more likely.

Of the major crops, only coffee is produced in exportable volumes, while the cultivation of sisal and cotton has virtually ceased. Several overseas companies are reportedly interested in rehabilitating sugar, cotton and sisal estates.

Livestock farming has been disrupted by insecurity, the neglect of veterinary services and recurrent droughts which have affected much of the south and centre of Angola.

Fishing

The fishing sector represents less than 5 per cent of GDP. The war disrupted the fishing industry. Foreign trawlers, particularly Spanish ones, were quick to capitalise on the lack of local competition and poor regulation and over-fished the country's waters, leading to a substantial depletion of fish stocks. Government policy is aimed at increasing the amount of foreign fishing operations in Angolan waters in order to increase foreign investment in the sector.

Industry and manufacturing

The industrial sector, including diamond mining, oil refining and other ancillary services, accounted for approximately 70 per cent of GDP in 2000 compared to 53 per cent of GDP in 1998 and employs around 12 per cent of the workforce.

The manufacturing sector includes food processing, brewing, sugar, textiles and tobacco products. Also important are light manufacture, electrical goods (eg radio production), construction materials, steel production, motor vehicles, detergents, bicycles and chemicals.

Activity is concentrated in Luanda, Lobito and Huambo. Output has been sluggish due to shortages of foreign exchange, poor management and a low-paid labour force. About 60 per cent of total production is accounted for by nationalised industries. The government proposed a privatisation programme involving some 200 state-owned enterprises in a variety of industrial sectors. However, civil war in 1998–2002 disrupted the programme and much of the non-oil industrial sector remains in state hands.

Tourism

Angola has considerable natural beauty, ranging from its tropical beaches to mountains and lakes inland. The end of war in 2002 is likely to lead to an increase in the number and quality of Angola's hotels as the country begins to attract more tourists.

Mining

The mining and hydrocarbons sectors together typically account for around 55 per cent of GDP and employ 4 per cent of the workforce. Prior to the civil war, Angola was a major producer of iron ore, gold and copper. However, the major disruptions to the country's infrastructure and economy throughout the war has meant that the country's considerable base metal and gold potential have been barely exploited.

After a campaign was launched by European human rights organisations to stop the use of diamond sales to finance rebel armies, De Beers announced that it would no longer buy Angolan diamonds and the UK government joined the campaign to block unofficial trade. However, with diamond smuggling rife throughout Africa, these moves were merely gestures by the international community which continues to permit a flow of arms into Angola.

Diamonds (mostly of gemstone quality) were the country's second-largest foreign exchange earner – as well as providing a source of revenue for the rebel Unita armies until all purchases of Angolan diamonds were banned by De Beers. Before this, Angola was the fourth-largest diamond producer in the world, producing some US$600 million of rough diamonds per year. The government controlled only 20 per cent of the trade, bringing in only US$12 million to government coffers every month. Diamond exports were severely reduced by lower production and, especially, by smuggling, with revenue going to Unita to finance arms purchases. According to unofficial estimates, Unita made around US$100 million from illegal diamond mining in 2000.

Aside from diamonds, there are also deposits of phosphates (Cabinda site, estimated 100 million tonnes: Kindonakasi, estimated 50 million tonnes), gold (at Cassinga and Lombige), copper, lead and zinc (in Tetelo and Alto Zambeze). There are deposits of marble and black granite (in southern Angola).

Hydrocarbons

Oil

Angola's economic performance is largely determined by the level of oil production which accounts for over 90 per cent of exports. Production was estimated to have reached 820,000 barrels per day (bpd) by early 2002. The government estimates that Angola could contain at least 12 billion barrels of oil, making it one of the largest oil reserves in Africa. Most of the oil is located offshore, with the largest reserves found off the shore of the Cabinda enclave, which is jointly operated by Cabinda Gulf Oil and Sonangol, the state-owned concessionaire. The remaining offshore area is divided into 13 blocks, eight of which are allocated to foreign operators.

There is considerable international interest in Angolan oil, with companies such as Agip, Chevron and Texaco investing more than US$8 billion in the sector. In July 2001, BP Amoco announced that it would invest US$7 billion between 2001–11. The group's chief executive remarked that Angola was 'one of the most important places' for BP Amoco in the world. The company had already invested around US$1 billion in offshore exploration.

Although the offshore oil industry has been immune to the civil war, the downstream sector has remained small due to the war-ravaged infrastructure. The country's only refinery, owned by Fina Petroleos de Angola (a consortium of Sonangol (36 per cent), TotalFinaElf (61 per cent) and private investors (3 per cent)), is decrepit and has a capacity of just 36,000bpd. An upgrading and expansion of refining facilities in Angola would give considerable added value to the country's oil exports.

By June 2001, 12 oil discoveries had been found in Block 15, which has seen intense activity since exploration began in 1998. The concession owned by Esso (40 per cent), BP Amoco (26.67 per cent), Agip (20 per cent) and Statoil (13.33 per cent) and lies over 300km northwest of Luanda. Analysts believe the block has reserves in excess of 3.5 billion barrels. The first oil is scheduled to come on stream in 2004.

In the same month, BP Amoco and Sonangol announced that they had discovered two new wells in Block 18, 200km off the coast. The wells have an estimated output of 5,000bpd. The first three wells discovered in the block have total estimated reserves of 700 million barrels BP Amoco believes that the block's total reserves could be over 1 billion barrels. Royal Dutch/Shell holds a 50 per cent stake in the concession.

Sonangol and Namibia's National Petroleum Corporation (Namcor) announced in 2001 that they would co-operate in finding tenders for concessions in the Namibe Basin, which straddles the two countries' maritime borders. At the time, a consortium including US-based Vanco (88 per cent), Namcor (9 per cent) and a local black empowerment group Pamue (3 per cent) held the only exploration licence in Namibe.

Gas

Gas reserves are estimated at 700 billion cubic metres. In mid-2001, Sonangol and Texaco announced that they were progressing onto the second phase of the construction of a liquefied natural gas (LNG) facility in Luanda. The first consignment of LNG is due to be delivered in mid-2005.

Energy

The state-owned Empresa Nacional de Electricidade (ENE) is responsible for the generation and supply of electricity in Angola. The country's total electricity generating capacity is estimated at 596MW. Half of this is provided by thermal generation and half through hydroelectric dams. Only 15 per cent of the population has access to electricity. Much of the country's electricity generation and transmission infrastructure has been damaged during the civil war. The government estimates it will need US$500 million to recover electricity capacity. Around US$200 million has already been allocated to Angola's six dams, only three of which are working. The Matala and Cambambe dams were undergoing rehabilitation in 2001 and 2002. Foreign investors are becoming involved in the construction of new dams. Angola's hydroelectric potential means it stands to become an exporter of electricity in the future. In 2000, the Angolan and Namibian governments agreed on bilateral co-operation on the development of a hydroelectric facility on the Cunene River. In October 2001, the two governments signed a memorandum of understanding to evaluate the feasibility of the project.

In 2001, the Russian Alrosa diamond company proposed a hydroelectric project on the Chicapa River to provide a source of power for its planned US$40 million investment in diamond mining infrastructure in Angola.

Banking

Central bank

Banco Nacional de Angola (BNA) started functioning in late-1996 as the central bank, ceasing its commercial activities, as part of the government's financial reforms.

Main financial centre

Luanda

Time

GMT plus one hour

Geography

The Republic of Angola lies on the west coast of Africa.The Cabinda district is separated from the rest of the country by the estuary of the River Congo (formerly known as the River Zaïre under President Mobutu and as the River Congo in the Republic of Congo), and Democratic Republic of Congo (DRC) territory, with the Republic of Congo lying to its north. Angola is bordered by the DRC to the north, Zambia to the east and Namibia to the south.

Climate

In Luanda and northern regions, October–April is hot and humid with usual temperatures ranging from 28–32 degrees Celsius (C) with a maximum of 34 degrees C. April–September is hot but less humid with daytime temperatures ranging from 25–30 degrees C and cool evenings. Southern regions are more temperate and rainfall can be frequent and heavy, particularly in April.

Dress codes

Informal dress is suitable for most occasions. Lightweight suits are recommended for business meetings. Visitors to the central and southern plateux will need warm clothes at night, as will visitors to the coastal region during May to September.

Entry requirements

Passports

Required by all. Passport must be valid for three months.

Visa

Required by all (except certain transit passengers). Exit permit also required.

A business visitor requires sponsorship from a local Angolan company or state entity. Visas can be obtained in Luanda via the inviting company or government agency or from an Angolan embassy.

Currency advice/regulations

There are no restrictions on the amount of money that can be taken in and out of the country. However, visitors are required to declare all their foreign currency to the Banco Nacional de Angola (BNA) within 24 hours of entering the country. All foreign exchange transactions must be arranged through the BNA.

Customs

No goods can be imported without the prior permission of the government.

Health (for visitors)

Mandatory precautions

Yellow fever vaccination certificate is required if travelling from an infected area.

Advisable precautions

Yellow fever, hepatitis A, typhoid, tetanus and polio vaccinations are recommended. Malaria prophylaxis is essential.

Hotels

Accommodation shortages in the capital have intensified in the post-war atmosphere but a programme of hotel privatisation may help relieve the problem.

Credit cards

American Express accepted at Presidente and Tivoli hotels. Generally, credit cards are not accepted.

Public holidays

Fixed dates

1 Jan (New Year's Day), 4 Feb (Anniversary of Start of Independence War), 1 May (May Day), 17 Sep (National Heroes' Day), 2 Nov (Remembrance Day), 11 Nov (Independence Day), 25 Dec (Christmas Day).

Variable dates

Good Friday, Easter Day.

Working hours

Banking

Mon–Fri: 0800–1100, 1400–1500.

Business

0830–1230, 1430–1800. (Exceptions: Sat 0830–1230, Sun closed.)

Government

Mon–Fri: 0730–1230, 1430–1830.

Telecommunications

Telephone/fax

Telephone dialling for Angola: IDD access code + 244 followed by area code (2 for Luanda) followed by subscriber's number. There are satellite links with Lisbon.

Electricity supply

220V AC, 50 cycles.

Social customs/useful tips

Travel permits may be required for travel outside Luanda province. Visitors are advised to carry spare passport photographs. Visitors should not attempt to photograph any public building, infrastructure or security forces. Visitors should carry indentity documents at all times.

Security

Angola has endured a civil war for many years and security procedures are tight. Non-essential travel should be avoided. Crime levels are high even in the capital Luanda and the period after dusk is extremely dangerous. Armed hold-ups are common, including on the road from the airport to the city.

Getting there

Air

National airline: TAAG (Linhas Aéreas de Angola).

International airport/s: Luanda-4 de Fevereiro (Code: LAD), 4km from city, restaurant.

Airport tax: None.

Surface

Road: Road travel is not generally practicable though access is now possible across the Namibian frontier to the south. Some 3,000 bridges were damaged during the war though a reconstruction programme has commenced.

Rail: Rail travel to Angola is difficult in the extreme due to regional conflict and war damage which has destroyed railways and bridges.

Main port/s: Cabinda, Lobito, Luanda, Namibe. Lobito and Luanda are being repaired. Namibe port was rehabilitated during 1996 with a World Bank grant of US$3million.

Getting about

National transport

Air: TAAG operates domestic flights connecting main centres – can be unreliable. Separate helicopter/plane services to Cabinda enclave. It is no longer necessary to carry a document authorising you to leave the city of Luanda (Guia de Marcha).

Road: The 7,500km network of well made, major roads is still in relatively good condition and traffic is now free to travel at will along the main roads between provincial capitals. Identity papers should be carried.

Buses: There are buses throughout the country but the service is poor and the buses are generally very crowded.

Rail: Service operated by PCFT and CFB. The railway system is under repair, since the damage caused during the civil war. There is a regular passenger route from Lobito and Benguela to Luaubut unless you are travelling first class this is very basic, no sleeping cars or air-conditioning.

City transport

Taxis: Restricted service operated by state company. No service operated from airport to Luanda.

BUSINESS DIRECTORY

Telephone area codes

Telephone direct dialling code for Angola is +244 followed by area code (Lobito 711, Luanda 2, Namibe 64), followed by subscriber's number. Operator Services:155.

Chambers of Commerce

Angolan Chamber of Commerce and Industry, Largo do Kinaxixi 14, 1o Andar, CP No 92 (tel: 344-506; fax: 370-804, 344-629).

Banking

Banco de Comercio e Industria SARL, PO Box 1395, 86 Avenida 4 de Fevereiro, Luanda (tel: 333-684, 333-748; fax: 333-823).

Banco Comercial Angolano SARL, PO Box 6900, 83A Avenida Comandante Valódia, CP 6900 Luanda (tel: 349-548, 349-517; fax: 349-516).

Banco Africano de Investimentos SA, 34 Rua Major Kanhangulo, Luanda (tel: 337-369; fax: 335-486).

Banco de Poupança e Crédito (BPC), CP 1343, Luanda (tel: 233-9158, 239-014).

Banco Totta e Açores SA (Angola), CP 1231, Luanda (tel: 233-4257).

Banque Paribas (Angola), CP 1385, Luanda (tel: 239-0877).

Central bank

Banco Nacional de Angola (BNA), (National Bank of Angola), Rua 4 de Fevereiro 151, CP 1243 (fax: 335-943; e-mail: bnagab@ebonet).

Travel information

Direcção de Emigração e Fronteiras de Angola (visa queries), Defa, Luanda (tel: 330-314, 330-019).

TAAG-Angola Airlines (Linhas Aéreas de Angola), Rua da Missão 123, CP 179, Luanda (tel: 332-485; fax: 393-548).

Ministry of tourism

Ministerio do Comercio e Turismo (Ministry of Commerce and Tourism), Largo 4 de Fevereiro 3, Luanda (tel: 338-741).

Ministries

Ministry of Agriculture and Rural Development, 2 Avenida Comandante Gika, CP 527 Luanda (tel: 322-694; fax: 323-217).

Ministry of Defence, Rua 17 de Setembro, Luanda (tel: 337-530; fax: 392-635).

Ministry of Education and Culture, Avenida Comandante Gika, CP 1281 Luanda (tel: 322-797; fax: 321-592).

Ministry of Energy and Water, 105 Avenida 4 de Fevereiro, CP 2229 Luanda (tel: 393-681; fax: 393-687).

Ministry of Ex-Servicemen and War Veterans, 2 Avenida Comandante Gika, CP 5466 Luanda (tel: 321-117; fax: 323-561).

Ministry of Family and Women's Advancement, Edifício Palácio de Vidro, Largo 4 de Fevereiro, 1242 Luanda (tel: 338-745; fax: 330-028).

Ministry of Finance, 127 Avenida 4 de Fevereiro, CP 592 Luanda (tel: 332-122; fax: 332-069).

Ministry of Fisheries and Environment, Edifício Atlantico, Avenida 4 de Fevereiro, CP 83 Luanda (tel: 390-690; fax: 333-814).

Ministry of Foreign Affairs, 8 Avenida Comandante Gika, CP 1500 Luanda (tel: 323-250; fax: 393-246).

Ministry of Geology and Mines, Avenida Comandante Gika, CP 1260 Luanda (tel: 326-724; fax: 321-655).

Ministry of Health, Rua 17 de Setembro, CP 1201 Luanda (tel: 322-797; fax: 321-592).

Ministry of Hotels and Tourism, Edifício Palácio de Vidro, Largo 4 de Fevereiro, CP 1242 Luanda (tel: 331-323; fax: 338-211).

Ministry of Industry, 25 Rua Cerqueira Lukoki, CP 594 Luanda (tel: 397-070; fax: 334-700).

Ministry of Information, 1 Avenida Comandante Valódia, CP 2608 Luanda (tel: 342-818; fax: 343-495).

Ministry of the Interior, 204 Avenida 4 de Fevereiro, CP 2723 Luanda (tel: 391-049; fax: 395-133).

Ministry of Justice, Rua 17 de Setembro, CP 2250 Luanda (tel: 330-327).

Ministry of Petroleum, Avenida 4 de Fevereiro, CP 1279 Luanda (tel: 337-440; fax: 372-373).

Ministry of Planning, Largo 17 de Setembro, Luanda (tel: 390-722; fax: 339-586).

Ministry of Posts and Telecommunications, 42 Avenida 4 de Fevereiro, CP 1459 Luanda (tel: 337-799; fax: 330-776).

Ministry of Public Administration, Employment and Social Security, 32 Rua 17 de Setembro, CP 1986 Luanda (tel: 338-654).

Ministry of Public Works and Town Planning, Rua Ed Mutamba, CP 1061 Luanda (tel: 336-717; fax: 333-814).

Ministry of Science and Technology, 25 Rua Cerqueira Lukoki, CP 1288 Luanda (tel: 338-987).

Ministry of Social Assistance and Reintegration, 117 Avenida dos Massacres, CP 102 Luanda (tel: 340-370; fax: 342-988).

Ministry of Territorial Administration, 8 Avenida Comandante Gika, Luanda (tel: 320-638; fax: 323-238).

Ministry of Trade, Edifício Palácio de Vidro, Largo 4 de Fevereiro, CP 1242 Luanda (tel: 338-737; fax: 370-804).

Ministry of Transport, 42 Avenida 4 de Fevereiro, Luanda (tel: 337-744; fax: 337-687).

Ministry of Youth and Sports, Avenida Comandante Gika, CP 5466 Luanda (tel: 321-117; fax: 323-561).

Other useful addresses

Angolan Embassy (USA), 2100-2108 16th Street, NW, Washington DC 20009 (tel: 785-1156; fax: 785-1258; e-mail: angola@angola.org).

ANGOP (news agency), CP 2181 Luanda (tel: 334-945).

Associação Comercial de Luanda, CP 1275, Edificio Palácio de Comércio, le Andar, Luanda (tel: 322-453).

DHL International Ltd, Avenida Che Guevara 52–52a, CP 1545 (tel: 390-326, 390-376, 392-082).

Direcção dos Servicos de Comércio, CP 1337, Largo Diogo Cão, Luanda.

Direcção dos Servicos de Estatistica (statistical agency), CP 1215, Luanda.

Direcção da Aviacao Civil (National Civil Aviation Directorate), Rua Frederich Engels, 92-6 andar, CP 569, Luanda (tel: 339-412, 338-196, 338-596).

Direcção dos Caminhos de Ferro (National Railways Directorate), Rua Major Kanhangulo, CP 1250, Luanda (tel: 370-061).

Direcção Nacional de Correios e Telecomunicacoes (National Posts and Telecommunications Directorate), Rua Frederich Engels, CP 1459, Luanda (tel: 339-750).

Direcção Nacional da Marinha Mercante e Portos (National Merchant Navy and Ports Directorate), Rua Rainha Ginga, 74-4 andar, Luanda (tel: 332-032, 339-847, 339-848).

Direcção Nacional dos Transportes Rodoviarios (National Road Transport Directorate), Rua Rainha Ginga, 74-1 andar, Luanda (tel: 339-390).

Empresa Nacional de Construcão de Obrtas Industrials (National construction Company for Industrial Projects), Bairro do Cazenga, 5 Avenida Zona Industrial, CP 18612, Luanda (tel: 390-087, 391-478).

Empresa Nacional de Diamantes de Angola (Endiama-Angolan Diamond Company), Avenida Rainha Ginga, 73-3 andar, CP 1247, Luanda (tel: 393-336).

Empresa Nacional de Electricidada (ENE - National Electricity Company), Edeficio de Geologia e Minas 7, CP 772, Luanda (tel: 323-382, 337-498, 323-568, 321-498, 321-499).

Importang (state import agency), Calçada do Município 10, CP 1003, Luanda (tel: 392-787).

Institute Foreign Investment, Rue Serqueira Lukoki 25 (tel: 334-700).

Instituto Nacional do Cafe de Angola (INCA – National Coffee Institute of Angola), Rua Dr Alves Maciel 17-1D, Luanda (tel: 370-386).

Instituto Nacional de Estradas de Angola (National Roads Institute), Rua Amilcar Cabral 35-4, Caixa Postal 5667, Luanda (tel: 332-828, 391-536; fax: 335-754).

Radio Nacional de Angola, CP 1389, Luanda.

Sociedade Nacional de Combustiveis (SONANGOL-Angola National Fuels Company), Rua I Congresso do MPLA, Caixa Postal 1316, Luanda (tel: 334-143/9; fax: 333-542/6, 391-782).

Televisão Popular de Angola (TPA), CP 2002, Luanda.

Internet sites

Africa Business Network: http://www.ifc.org/abn

AllAfrica.com: http://www.allafrica.com

African Development Bank: http://www.afdb.org

Africa Online: http://www.africaonline.com

Angola News: http://www.ourworld.compuserve.com/homepages/anginfolon/

Information on Angola including government, business and economics: http://www.angola.org/

Jornal de Angola (JA): http://www.ebonet.net/jornaldeangola

Benin

Jonathan Derrick

KEY FACTS

Official name: République du Bénin (Republic of Benin)

Head of State: President Mathieu Kérékou (since Mar 1996; re-elected Mar 2001 for his last five-year term)

Head of government: President Mathieu Kérékou (since May 1998)

Ruling party: Coalition government in which Parti du Renouveau Démocratique (PRD) (Party of Democratic Renewal) is the dominant party (parliamentary election 30 Mar 2003)

Area: 112,622 square km

Population: 6.40 million (2001)

Capital: Porto-Novo (administrative); Cotonou (seat of government)

Official language: French

Currency: CFA franc (CFAf) = 100 centimes (Communauté Financière Africaine (African Financial Community) franc)

Exchange rate: CFAf629.73 per US$ (Jan 2003); CFAf655.95 per euro (pegged from Jan 1999)

GDP per capita: US$375 (2001)

GDP real growth: 5.00% (2001)

Inflation: 4.00% (2001); -0.1% (year-on-year, Feb 2002)

Balance of trade: -US$451.00 million (2001)

Foreign debt: US$1.36 billion (2001)

Annual FDI: US$48.00 million (2001)

For the latest Key Facts, go to www.worldinformation.com

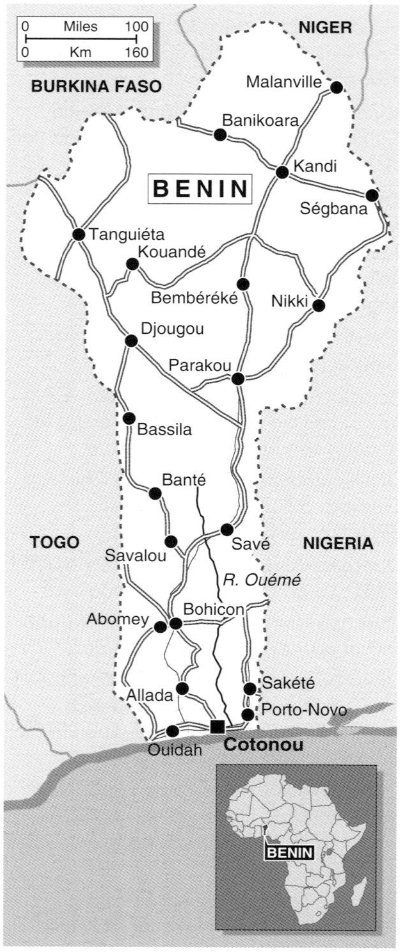

While the circumstances of President Kérékou's re-election in March 2001 – when leading opposition candidates withdrew from the second round of voting and there were calls for a boycott – were controversial with widespread and detailed reports of rigging, he remained in power and the country remained at peace. Benin also remained one of the most deprived countries of Africa; extensive poverty was one cause of the widespread crime wave that burst into world headlines in 2001 with the sale of Beninese children into virtual slavery to other African countries, notably Gabon.

Easy win?

Kérékou's victory in the March 2001 presidential elections with 84 per cent of the vote was marred after the opposition parties declared a 'national day of mourning'. Both Kérékou's presidential opponents, the former president, Nicéphore Soglo, and the former prime minister, Adrien Houngbédji, decided to boycott the election, alleging irregularities in the voting. Nine members of the National Electoral Commission (NEC) resigned after it had been criticised for giving out false results. Despite the alleged irregularities, voter turn-out was poor and most observers had expected Kérékou to win, whether or not Soglo and Houngbédji had stood for election. Following his victory, Kérékou reshuffled his government in May, introducing eight new ministers. Bruno Amoussou, the only person to stand against Kérékou in the presidential election and who won about 15.9 per cent of the vote, remained in the government as minister in charge of government co-ordination for future planning and development.

Children for sale

The trafficking in children has been widespread for some years. It may have had a basis in the common African custom of sending children from the village to do domestic work in the cities as well as the Benin tradition of *vidomegon* ('child confined to someone' in the Fon language). However, the rackets have gone far beyond the norms of such traditions. Poverty-stricken families were paid to let children be taken to domestic work elsewhere, which turned out to involve commonly harsh exploitation and abuse. In April 2001, there were reports that a ship named *Etireno* was carrying a number of child slaves. Reports of the numbers varied and there was some mystery about the whole affair, but Benin's social protection minister, Ramatou Baba Moussa, appealed for help in tracking down the ship, which called at Libreville and Douala in Cameroon before docking at Cotonou. Some unaccompanied children were found aboard, resulting in an investigation being launched.

Improving relations

In the course of continued good relations with neighbouring states, Benin signed an agreement with Niger in June 2001 to refer the two countries' dispute over the Lete Islands in the Niger river to the International Court of Justice (ICJ). Relations between the two countries improved dramatically. In November 2001, the two countries held joint military exercises in Togo.

IMF aid for the economy

The IMF released in November 2001 a further tranche of US$5 million under the Poverty Reduction and Growth Facility (PRGF). An IMF statement in November 2001 had praised 'the satisfactory macroeconomic performance' achieved under the first-year programme aided by the PRGF, noting that 'real GDP growth remained robust and well above the population growth rate, inflation continued to be moderate, and fiscal performance remained strong. All qualitative performance criteria were observed, and the structural benchmark on the creation of a unified database for the civil service was implemented.'

The IMF noted that there had been delays in implementation of some 'important structural measures'. The IMF noted the importance of maintaining 'a stable macroeconomic environment' in view of the uncertainties in the world economic situation in general after the 11 September 2001 terrorist attacks in the US and in the world cotton market in particular, which accounts for 80 per cent of Benin's export earnings. The 'structural measures' on which the IMF wanted faster action included privatisation of a number of companies, including the Société Nationale pour la Promotion Agricole (Sonapra), the parastatal responsible for the marketing and ginning of cotton. The World Bank announced a new loan package for Benin in early 2002 to finance reform of the cotton sector. The World Bank committed over US$148.2 million for over nine projects.

In July 2002, the IMF approved an additional US$5 million as part of its Heavily Indebted Poor Countries (HIPC) initiative. The IMF reiterated what it reported in November 2001, but stressed that poverty alleviation was too slow and the government should reallocated some its public expenditure to basic social welfare spending.

Budget approved

The IMF's continued help and approval ensured that Benin could continue to receive aid, which it needed to do to balance its budget. The 2002 budget provided for expenditure of CFAf462.9 billion (US$623 million) and total revenue, nominally, of the same amount, although about a third of the total revenue – CFAf137.7 billion (US$185 million) – was to come from external resources. Domestic revenue amounted to only CFAf325.1 billion (US$437 million) which was higher than the CFAf281.3 billion (US$378 million) collected in 2001. When parliament failed to agree on the budget, the president applied a budget by decree, increasing revenue and expenditure to CFAf478.7 billion (US$644 million). The budget forecast economic growth of 6 per cent in 2001, confirming the IMF's optimism Actual GDP growth in 2001 was lower than forecast at 5 per cent while inflation was 4 per cent. In 2002, GDP growth was 6 per cent and inflation fell back to 3.3 per cent.

Developing key sectors

Benin's oil production has remained too small to make a noticeable difference to its income. Prospects of an assured natural gas supply have moved ahead as work on laying the West African Gas Pipeline linking Nigeria's gas fields with Benin, Togo and Ghana is expected to start during 2002–03, after many years of study and planning. The first phase to be built by the West African Gas Pipeline Company (WAPCo) – a consortium headed by Chevron Nigeria Ltd and including the Shell Petroleum Development Corporation and the national oil companies of Nigeria, Benin, Togo and Ghana – will produce daily delivery of 160 million cubic feet. In Benin, the gas could fuel power generation to supplement the supply from the Volta Dam in Ghana, which had fallen to critically low levels in 1998. The project is still under attack from environmental campaigners at the Nigerian end, in the turbulent Niger Delta.

Development of a modern telecommunications network proceeded in 2001. Libercom, the country's first mobile phone network, announced in May the completion of a 400km fibre optics line linking Cotonou and Parakou by the Benin Posts and Telecommunications Board (OPT) and the Titan group of the US. These companies, and France's Alcatel, set up a joint venture to install new telephone systems, under a US$60 million contract between Alcatel and Afronetworks, a joint affiliate of the OPT and Titan. This will involve full digitalisation and combined GSM-type mobile phones and fixed equipment through state of the art switchboards. The GSM network will be gradually extended from Cotonou and the coastal area inland, and new exchanges and GSM coverage will be extended northwards as far as Kandi and Malanville.

Outlook

Following his presidential election victory in March 2001, Kérékou appears to have cemented his position as Benin's leader. He faces very few opponents to his rule until at least 2006 when he will be 70 years old and too old legally to govern the country. In the meantime, Benin's economy appears to be greatly improving, although economic reforms need to be implemented in the long-term. Foreign investment and aid will still be needed to improve the economy in 2003, along with

KEY INDICATORS — Benin

	Unit	1996	1997	1998	1999	2000
Population	m	5.59	5.83	6.04	6.06	6.23
Gross domestic product (GDP)	US$bn	2.21	2.14	2.31	2.26	2.30
GDP per capita	US$	395	367	382	373	373
GDP real growth	%	5.6	5.6	4.4	5.0	5.0
Inflation	%	4.9	3.5	5.8	0.3	4.2
Consumer prices	1995=100	104.9	108.6	114.8	115.2	120.0
Exports (fob) (goods)	US$m	527.7	424.0	414.3	385.3	246.0
Imports (fob) (goods)	US$m	559.7	576.9	572.6	673.2	453.0
Balance of trade	US$m	-32.0	-152.9	-158.3	-288.0	-207.0
Current account	US$m	-57.4	-169.9	-151.5	-141.0	-172.0
Total reserves minus gold	US$m	261.8	253.1	261.5	400.0	458.1
Foreign exchange	US$m	258.4	250.1	258.4	396.8	455.2
Exchange rate	per US$	511.55	583.67	589.95	615.70	711.98

structural reforms to Benin's important cotton industry.

Risk assessment

Economic	Improving
Political	Good
Regional stability	Good

COUNTRY PROFILE

Historical profile

Much of the area now comprising Benin belonged to the ancient kingdom of Dahomey, which gave up its independence to France in 1893.

1960 Gained independence from France as the Republic of Dahomey. Hubert Maga was elected president.

1963 Maga was overthrown by the army.

1970–72 Triumvirate leadership including Hubert Maga until the army intervened.

1974 Major Mathieu Kérékou seized power.

1975 The Republic of Dahomey was renamed Republic of Benin.

1990 With the country bankrupt and on the brink of social collapse, President Kérékou handed power to a national conference. The government abandoned Marxism-Leninism and committed itself to political reform.

1991 Nicéphore Soglo became president.

1995 Legislative elections were held on 28 March; parties opposed to the president won a majority in the National Assembly. However, the results in 13 constituencies were invalidated and fresh polls were ordered.

1996 After elections held in March, Kérékou took office again and Adrien Houngbédji, leader of the Parti du Renouveau Démocratique (PRD) (Party of Democratic Renewal) assumed the role of prime minister from April 1996.

1998 Houngbédji resigned in May. As the constitution made no provision for a prime minister, on 15 May a new government was formed without one.

1999 The March legislative election results were published in May. Former president Nicéphore Soglo's Parti de la Renaissance du Benin (PRB) (Benin Renaissance Party) emerged as the largest single opposition party in the National Assembly. Adrien Houngbédji (PRD) was elected president of the new Assembly.

2001 President Kérékou was re-elected in March, with 84 per cent of the vote. This is his last five-year term since in 2006. He will be over the age limit of 70 years for presidential candidates.

Political structure

Constitution

In December 1990, a new constitution was given approval by a referendum. It allows for multi-party politics and a president to be directly elected by popular vote.

Form of state

Republic.

The executive

The president is directly elected by popular vote for a five-year term. The age limit for presidential candidates is 70 years. No provision is made for a prime minister with the president the head of government.

National legislature

Benin has a directly elected legislature, the 83-member Assemblée Nationale (National Assembly), with a maximum life of four years.

Last elections

30 March 1999 (parliamentary); March 2001 (presidential).

Next elections

March 2006 (presidential).

Political parties

There are over 100 registered parties in Benin, but only a handful are represented in parliament. The last parliamentary elections were held in March 1999. Former president Nicéphore Soglo's Parti de la Renaissance du Bénin (PRB) (Benin Renaissance Party) won 27 seats; ; Parti Social-Démocrate (PSD) (Social Democrat Party) (nine seats); Mouvement pour l'Engagement et le Réveil du Citoyen (MADEP) (African Movement for Democracy and Progress) (six seats); Impulsion au Progrès et la Démocratie (IPD) (Impulse to Progress and Democracy) (four seats); Alliance Etoile (Etoile) (Star Alliance) (four seats); Car DUNYA (DUNYA) (three seats); Mouvement pour l'Engagement et le Réveil du Citoyen (MERCI) (Movement for Citizens' Commitment and Awakening) (two seats); others (seven seats).

Ruling party

Coalition government in which Parti du Renouveau Démocratique (PRD) (Party of Democratic Renewal) is the dominant party.

Main opposition party

Parti de la Renaissance du Bénin (PRB) (Benin Renaissance Party)

Population

6.23 million (2000)

Annual population growth: 2.8 per cent (1994–2000). Approximately 46 per cent of the total population is under 15 years. Population density: 51 inhabitants per square km. Urban population: 42 per cent (1994–2000).

Ethnic make-up

African (99 per cent) (42 ethnic groups, most important being Fon, Adja, Yoruba, Bariba), European (1 per cent).

Religions

Animists (70 per cent), Christians (15 per cent) and Muslims (15 per cent).

Health

Life expectancy: 53 years. Infant mortality rate: 87 per 1,000 live births. About 29 per cent of children were malnourished (1992–2001).

There are an estimated 70,000 people living with HIV/AIDS in Benin – 3,000 are under the age of 15 (2000). Little over 1 per cent of the population is infected. With around half of sex workers testing positive, there is a chance that the pandemic could cause future problems if issues of contraception use are not addressed.

Main cities

Cotonou (estimated population 850,000 in 1998, seat of government), Porto-Novo (180,000, administrative capital), Parakou (68,000), Ouidah (60,000), Abomey (57,000), Natitingou (39,000).

Languages spoken

African languages (Yoruba, Bariba and Fon) are widely used in everyday life.

Official language

French (Fon, Yoruba, Bariba widely spoken).

Media

Press

Dailies: The government information bureau publishes the daily *Le Nation*. *Ehuzu* is the other widely read national daily. *Le Matinal En Ligne* is a French language daily.

Weeklies: The Chamber of Commerce publishes a weekly bulletin. *La Gazette du Golfe* is a weekly sport publication.

Periodicals: Periodicals include a fortnightly publication of the government information bureau *Journal Officiel de la République du Benin*.

Broadcasting

The state-owned Office de Radiodiffusion et de Télévision du Bénin broadcasts radio services in French, English and 18 local languages and television transmissions for eight hours weekly.

Advertising

Advertising is available in the press, on radio, in Benin's seven cinemas and on hoardings and trains.

Economy

Subsistence farming and cotton production dominate Benin's economy. By the end of the 1990s, the country had achieved price stability, with inflation in single figures. Rapid population growth has offset the effects of economic growth and Benin remains one of the poorest countries in West Africa. The economy also suffers from fuel shortages and is overshadowed by neighbouring Nigeria, the hub of the regional economy.

The country has been 30 per cent dependent on foreign aid, although creditors have eased the debt burden on Benin.

However, donors have pressed for further action to privatise state enterprises and scale down the bloated civil service.
The International Development Association (IDA) and IMF agreed to support debt relief for Benin under the enhanced Heavily Indebted Poor Countries (HIPC) initiative in 2000. This was expected to reduce the country's debt servicing burden from 218 per cent of export earnings in 1998 to 150 per cent. The IDA will provide debt service relief amounting to US$124.3 million over 15 years, while the IMF will provide debt relief worth US$24.3 and bilateral creditors US$77 million. The programme will reach completion with the final disbursment of debt relief after Benin fulfills several conditions including the implementation of a poverty reduction strategy paper, the maintenance of a satisfactory macroeconomic framework, and the introduction of structural and social reforms impacting on poverty reduction, school enrolment, governance and other areas.

External trade

Exports

Principal exports are fuel, palm products, cotton, coffee and cocoa.

Main destinations: Portugal (typically 14 per cent of total), Morocco (14 per cent), USA (10 per cent), Italy (8 per cent).

Imports

Principal imports are food, capital goods, fuel and energy.

Main sources: France (typically 20 per cent of total), Thailand (11per cent), China (7 per cent), Netherlands (6per cent).

Agriculture

The agricultural sector is the most important economic sector. It accounts for about 38 per cent of GDP and employs 56 per cent of the workforce.
Productivity is low. Subsistence farming (mainly collectivised) and animal husbandry form the cornerstone of the economy and the country is virtually self-sufficient in food. Livestock farming is particularly important in the north. Principal food crops are yams, cassava, sorghum, beans, millet, maize and rice. The main export crops, cotton and palm oil, are farmed mainly on large industrial plantations. Other cash crops include coffee, sugar, cocoa, karité nuts and tobacco.
Fishing is confined mainly to inland waters and augments local food supplies.
There is a heavy dependence on cotton. Production was estimated at 340,000 tonnes of cottonseed in 2000/01.

Industry and manufacturing

The industrial sector is small-scale, contributing 8.4 per cent to GDP and employing 6 per cent of the workforce.
Manufacturing activity is centred on processing primary products (palm oil, fats, sugar, beverages, cotton) for export, and the manufacture of consumer goods and construction materials for home consumption. Cement production and oil refining are the main heavy industries.
The government is encouraging foreign investment in canning, paper processing units, glass manufacturing, salt processing units, agribusiness, pharmaceuticals, clothing, palm oil, building materials and chemicals.
In 2000 the cottonseed oil plant at Bohicon was extended and modernised, raising capacity to 12,000 tonnes of oil, and a sugar-producing enterprise which has been closed since 1990 was reopened.

Mining

The mining sector accounts for 5.5 per cent of GDP and employs 3 per cent of the workforce.
Activity is confined to extraction of limestone for the local cement industry, and marble There is a limestone quarry at Onigbolo. There are known reserves of phosphate, chromite, uranium, low grade iron ore, marble and gold. The government has awarded a number of gold exploration licenses to foreign investors. Under Beninese law, all mineral resources belong to the state, which grants exclusive rights for exploration, development and mining activities.

Hydrocarbons

The US$260 million West African Gas Pipeline (WAGP) will supply natural gas from Nigeria's Escravos field to Benin, Togo and Ghana. In November 2000, an agreement was reached between the US company, Chevron, Anglo-Dutch Shell and the participating governments on shareholding arrangements.
Oil production is on a very small scale. There are an estimated 5.5 billion barrels of reserves in the coastal sedimentary basin. Production has declined slightly since 1999 due to the closure of Sèmè off-shore oil field which produced 8,000 barrels per day (bpd) from two wells. However, the Zetah Oil Company has been given a license and has been undertaking feasibility studies at redeveloping the oil field.
The downstream oil industry is dependent on refined petroleum products imported from neighbouring Nigeria. An oil terminal with a capacity of 55,000 cubic metres of crude was opened at Cotonou at the end of 1999. From 2000, it serves Benin, Niger, Burkina Faso and Mali. Importation, distribution and marketing is carried out by Sonacop, which was privatised in 1999.
There are proven gas reserves offshore. Natural gas output is 90 billion cu cm a year.

Energy

Benin produces about 25 million kilowatt-hours of electricity each year. Traditional fuels account for over 70 per cent of total energy consumption. The rest comprises mainly of hydroelectric power, which endures erratic supply.
Electricity is imported from the hydroelectric Akosombo Dam in Ghana. The Akosombo and Nkong hydroelectric dams generate about 1,072MW annually.
A joint hydroelectric power project with Togo on the river Mono has been in full operation since 1988 since the building of the Nangbeto Dam. To improve Benin's energy position, in 1998 the Akpakpa and Bohicon thermal power stations were rehabilitated and 17 generators purchased, and a gas turbine built at Cotonou by Toutelectric of France, was commissioned in 1998.

Banking

Central bank

Banque Centrale des États de l'Afrique de l'Ouest

Main financial centre

Cotonou and Parakou.

Time

GMT minus one hour

Geography

Benin is a narrow stretch of territory in West Africa. The country has an Atlantic coastline of about 100km, flanked by Nigeria to the east and Togo to the west. In the north it is bordered by Burkina Faso and Niger.

Climate

Equatorial in the south with average daytime temperatures reaching 30–38 degrees Celsius (C). Main dry season from January–March. Rainy season from May–July and from September–December. Very humid in coastal areas. The north is tropical with more extreme temperatures, and single dry and rainy seasons. Length of rainy season varies with location but it is generally very wet from July–October.

Entry requirements

Passports

Required by all except nationals of certain African countries.

Visa

Required by all except for an unlimited stay by nationals of Algeria, Burkina Faso, Central African Republic, Congo, Cuba and Romania.
Visas are not required for a stay up to 90 days by nationals of Organization of African Unity (OAU) countries, Denmark and Germany.

Currency advice/regulations
There are no restrictions on import of local or foreign currency, but amounts of foreign currency must be declared on arrival.
Foreign currency exports are allowed up to the equivalent of Ff500.

Health (for visitors)
Mandatory precautions
A yellow fever vaccination certificate is required by all.
Advisable precautions
Hepatitis A, typhoid, tetanus and polio vaccinations.
Malaria prophylaxis should be taken.
Water precautions are necessary, especially outside towns.
There is a rabies risk.

Hotels
Available in all main towns. Accommodation in Cotonou is limited. Advance booking essential. Service charge usually included in bill, otherwise 10 per cent tip.

Credit cards
Access/Mastercard/Visa accepted by hotels, etc.

Public holidays
Fixed dates
1 Jan, 1 Apr (Youth Day), 1 May, 1 Aug (National Day), 15 Aug (Assumption), 25 Dec, 31 Dec (Harvest Day).
Variable dates
Eid Al-Fitr, Eid Al-Adha (Tabaski), Good Friday, Ascension Day, Whit Monday.

Working hours
Banking
Mon–Fri: 0800–1130, 1500–1630.
Business
Mon–Fri: 0800/0830–1230, 1500–1830.
Government
Mon–Fri: 0800/0830–1230, 1500–1830.
Shops
Mon–Sat: 0830–1300, 1600–1930; (Sun) 0800–1200. Shops that open Sun mainly close Mon am.

Telecommunications
Telephone/fax
Dialling code for Benin: IDD access code + 229, followed by subscriber's number. There are no area codes.

Electricity supply
Electricity supply 220V AC 50 cycles.

Getting there
Air
Main airport: Cotonou Cadjehoun (COO), 5 km west of Cotonou.
Airport tax: There is no airport tax.

Surface
There are routes from Burkina Faso, Togo, Nigeria and Niger.
Main ports: Cotonou.

Getting about
National transport
Air: Regular government-run services between Cotonou, Parakou, Natitingou, Kandi and Djougou.
Rail: The railway line from Cotonou to Porto Novo, closed since 1990, was reopened in January 1999.
City transport
Taxis: Fixed charge within towns, but advisable to negotiate fares in advance. Tipping is optional.
Car hire
Available in Cotonou. Chauffeur-driven services are recommended. Insurance/liability position should be checked. International driving licence required.

BUSINESS DIRECTORY

Telephone area codes
Dialling code for Benin: IDD access code +229, followed by subscriber's number.There are no area codes.

Chambers of Commerce
Chambre de Commerce et d'Industrie du Bénin, BP 31, Cotonou (tel: 313-299).

Banking
Bank of Africa Bénin (BOA), BP 08-0879, Ave Pape Jean Paul II, Cotonou (tel: 313-228; fax: 313-117).

Banque Centrale des Etats de l'Afrique de l'Ouest, BP 325, Ave Jean Paul II, Cotonou (tel: 312-466/7; fax: 312-465).

Banque Internationale du Bénin (BIBE) BP 03-2098, Carrefour des 3 Banques, Cotonou (315-549, 315-621; fax: 312-365, 312-707).

Continental Bank Bénin, 01 BP, Avenue Pape Jean-Paul II, 2020 Cotonou (tel: 312-424, 313-393; fax: 315177).

Ecobank Bénin, BP 1280, Rue du Gouverneur Bayol, 01 Cotonou (tel: 314-023, 313-069; fax: 313-385, 313-718).

Financial Bank Bénin (FBB), BP 2700, Rue du Commandant Decoeur, Cotonou (tel: 313-100, 313-103, 313-104; fax: 313-102).

Central bank
Banque Centrale des États de l'Afrique de l'Ouest, PO Box 3108, Avenue Abdoulaye Fadiga, Dakar, Senegal (tel: 390-500; fax: 239-335).

Travel information
Transports Aériens du Bénin (tel: 314-797).

Ministries
Ministry of Public Service, Labour and Administrative Reform (tel: 313-112).

Ministry of Public Works and Transport, PO Box 16, Cotonou, Benin (tel: 313-380).

State Ministry of Government Coordination, Planning, Development and Employment Promotion (tel: 301-553).

Other useful addresses
Agence Bénin-Presse, BP 120, Cotonou.

Import/Export Alimentation de Bénin, BP 53, Cotonou.

Institut National de la Statistique et de L'Analyse Economique, BP 323, Cotonou (tel: 314-101/103).

Mission de Co-opération et d'Action Culturelle, BP 476, Cotonou (tel: 300-824).

Mission Permanente d'Aide et de Co-opération, BP 476, Cotonou (administers aid from France).

Organisation Commune Benin-Niger des Chemins de fer et des Transports (OCBN) (Benin Railways), PO Box 16, Cotonou, Benin (tel: 313-380).

Société Nationale d'Equipement, BP 2042, Cotonou (deals with capital goods).

Société Nationale de Commercialisation et d'Exportation du Bénin (Sonaceb), BP 933, Cotonou (tel: 312-822).

Société Nationale de Commercialisation des Produits Pétroliers (Sonacop), BP 245, Cotonou (tel: 312-290).

Société Nationale d'Importation du Bénin, BP 2042, Cotonou.

Syndicat National des Commerçants et Industriels Africains du Bénin, BP 367, Cotonou.

Internet sites
Africa Business Network: http://www.ifc.org/abn

AllAfrica.com: http://www.allafrica.com

African Development Bank: http://www.afdb.org

Africa Online: http://www.africaonline.com

Benin: http://www.guide-benin.

Harambee Afrika (UK business club for traders with east, central and southern Africa; includes annotated web resource list): http://www.harambee.co.uk

Mbendi AfroPaedia (information on companies, countries, industries and stock exchanges in Africa): http://mbendi.co.za

Botswana

Daniel Brett

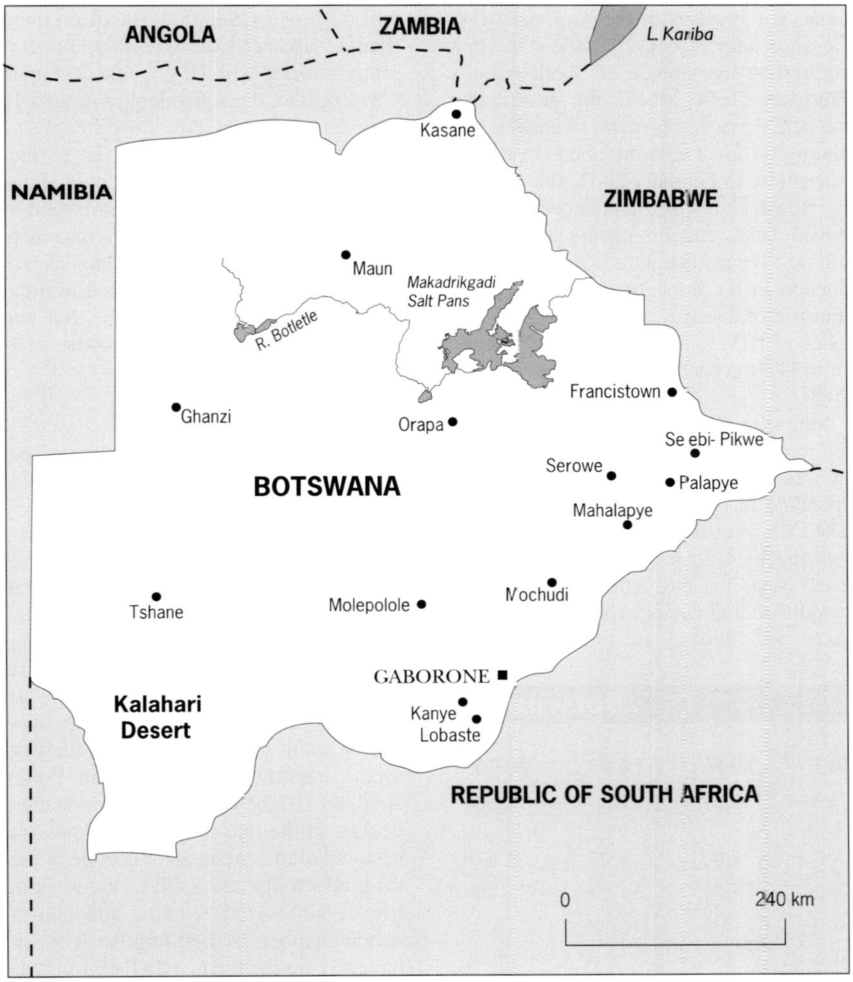

Decades of diamond-fuelled prosperity look likely to come to an end as Botswana faces the withering effects of the AIDS epidemic. Botswana has the highest recorded HIV prevalence rate in the world, leading to dramatically diminishing life expectancy and undermining economic growth. Between one-third to one-half of the working population in 2001 is expected to have died by 2010 due to the AIDS epidemic. In June 2001, the IMF released a lengthy report on the impact of HIV/AIDS on Botswana. It compared the pandemic to the outbreak of the bubonic plague in fourteenth century Europe and concluded that 'the unfolding disaster now overshadows what should otherwise be seen as an African success story'.

Meanwhile, the ruling Botswana Democratic Party (BDP) continues to dominate the country's stable, if elitist, democracy. Vice President Ian Khama's quest to succeed President Festus Mogae is generating ethnic tensions within Botswana that threaten to tear apart the BDP. The opposition Botswana National Front (BNF) stands to gain from BDP in-fighting having settled its own internal squabbles following the election of a new leader in November 2001.

KEY FACTS

Official name: The Republic of Botswana

Head of State: President Festus Mogae (since Apr 1998)

Head of government: President Festus Mogae

Ruling party: Botswanan Democratic Party (BDP) (since 1965; re-elected Oct 1999)

Area: 582,000 square km

Population: 1.70 million (2001)

Capital: Gaborone

Official language: English (official); Setswana (national)

Currency: Pula (P) = 100 thebe

Exchange rate: P5.40 per US$ (Jan 2003)

GDP per capita: US$3,315 (2001); US$3,202 (2002)*

GDP real growth: 4.30% (2001); 4.5% (2002)*

Unemployment: 21.00% (2001) (official); 40.0% (2001) (unofficial)

Inflation: 500.00% (2001); 6.1% (2002)*

Balance of trade: US$468.08 million (2001)

Foreign debt: US$365.00 million (2001)

* estimated figure

For the latest Key Facts, go to www.worldinformation.com

War on AIDS

Botswana is sitting on a time-bomb. More than a third of the population aged between 14 and 49 is infected with HIV, with infection rates reaching 50 per cent in the 25 to 34 age group. By 2010, life expectancy is expected to plummet to under 30 years compared to 60 in 1990. The death rate per thousand population climbed from 15 in 1990 to 30 in 2000 and is projected to reach 45 by 2007. Surveys suggest that in the absence of AIDS, the death rate would have steadily declined to around 11 per thousand in this period. Demographic trends indicate that by 2004, the total population and labour force will begin shrinking as a direct result of AIDS. International agencies forecast that by 2010, 40 per cent of children will be orphans as a result of AIDS, putting extra financial burdens on the state. Botswana is seeing a relentless procession of coffins containing mostly young people, who represent the country's future workforce, paraded through its streets. Meanwhile, hospitals are on the brink of collapse, with over 60 per cent of beds being occupied by AIDS patients, denying care to those suffering from other diseases.

The government has been slow to act, despite its relative advantage over most other African states in terms of financial resources. This has led to harsh criticism from development agencies and non-governmental organisations, who have urged the government to adopt a more proactive approach. In an effort to turn back the tide of disapproval against his government's handling of the tragedy, President Mogae declared the epidemic a national crisis in 1999, calling for a war against the disease. The first comprehensive national programme to combat the spread of infection was launched in 2000 under the auspices of the National AIDS Co-ordinating Agency (NACA). In stark contrast to the attitude of South Africa's President Thabo Mbeki, the government has begun a campaign to boost condom use and break down cultural taboos over contraception. In February 2002, Health Minister Joy Phumaphi announced that the government's condom campaign was seeing positive results, with a 70 per cent reduction in the infection rates of sexually transmitted diseases and a fall in the prevalence of HIV found among blood donors, from 11.9 per cent in 1996 to 7.9 per cent in 2000.

Mogae's crusade against HIV/AIDS has led to a sharp increase in health expenditure, from 5.2 per cent of total government spending in 1998 to 7.6 per cent in 2001. The IMF forecasts that public expenditure will rise by at least 5 per cent of GDP by 2010 due to the spiralling costs of healthcare and social services. However, there are doubts as to whether the government can keep up with the demands placed on it by AIDS. The Harvard AIDS Institute estimated that it will cost US$370 per person per year to provide basic treatment to AIDS patients, including testing, counselling, education and pain relief. Intermediate care, including the provision of anti-retroviral drugs to pregnant HIV-infected women, will cost a further US$500, while advanced care for infected adults will cost over US$3,000. Based on these figures, advanced care for all adults currently infected with HIV would cost up to US$1 billion, the equivalent of around 18 per cent of annual GDP.

As Botswana is classified as a middle-income country, it is low down on the priorities of international donors and is struggling to find external funds to combat HIV/AIDS. The government claims it will need more than US$290 million in order to sustain its AIDS programme, but will be unable to finance this unless the international community steps in.

KEY INDICATORS — Botswana

	Unit	1996	1997	1998	1999	2000
Population	m	1.50	1.53	1.57	1.61	1.63
Gross domestic product (GDP)	US$bn	4.41	4.70	4.83	5.03	5.57
GDP per capita	US$	2,768	3,065	3,079	3,124	3,420
GDP real growth	%	7.0	6.9	4.8	7.7	5.8
Inflation	%	10.1	8.6	6.7	7.4	8.5
Consumer prices	1995=100	100.1	119.6	127.6	136.6	149.4
Unemployment	%	22.0	21.8	19.6	*17.0	15.8
Exports (fob) (goods)	US$m	2,217.5	2,819.8	2,060.6	2,671.0	2,690.0
Imports (fob) (goods)	US$m	1,467.7	1,924.4	1,983.1	1,996.5	2,040.0
Balance of trade	US$m	749.8	895.4	77.5	674.5	657.0
Current account	US$m	495.0	721.5	170.1	516.8	449.0
Foreign debt	US$bn	0.7	0.6	0.6	0.5	0.4
Total reserves minus gold	US$m	5,027.7	5,675.0	5,940.7	6,298.7	6,318.2
Foreign exchange	US$m	4,957.8	5,609.6	5,856.2	6,229.2	6,256.2
Foreign direct investment (FDI)	US$bn	0.1	0.1	0.1	0.1	0.0
Bank rate	%	13.0	12.5	12.5	13.3	0.0
Exchange rate	per US$	3.32	3.65	4.23	4.62	5.10

* estimated figure

End of the African dream?

With annual GDP growth averaging 7 per cent since independence in 1966, Botswana has been cited as an African success story. The country has thrived on a booming mining sector, with diamonds accounting for more than a third of GDP and 70 per cent of total exports. But the impact of the AIDS epidemic on the economy is likely to be devastating, with labour productivity and the quality of human capital suffering large blows.

As a result of the AIDS crisis, the Botswana Institute of Development Policy Analysis (BIDPA) forecasts a permanent decline in the rate of capital inflows and accumulation, a permanent decline in factor productivity and a fall in the working life of both AIDS victims and non-infected members of their families who will have to care for them. The IMF forecasts that the AIDS crisis will result in GDP growth slowing by between 3 to 4 per cent per year between 2001–11.

Botswana cannot rely solely on mining production, which has virtually reached full capacity, as a major source of growth to see it through the AIDS crisis. Meanwhile, according to IMF models, growth in the non-mining economy is likely to shrink from 3.2 per cent in 2001 to 1.4 per cent by 2010, averaging 2.4 per cent across the decade. This contrasts with its no-AIDS scenario which forecasts average growth rate of 5.7 per cent between 2000–10.

Botswana already suffers from a severe skills shortage which is deterring foreign investment. The situation is exacerbated by a ten-fold increase in the death of school teachers between 1994 and 2001 due to AIDS. A shortage of teachers and high death rates among young people can only hamper efforts to replace much-needed skilled labour. This will dent the government's hopes of diversifying the economy away from diamond mining. Investment, particularly in the non-mining sector, is also likely to suffer a major setback as the AIDS crisis heightens. The agricultural sector, dominated by livestock rearing, will be the hardest hit. Family farms will be put under immense strain as young members succumb to AIDS and become dependent on older relatives for care.

Tribal tensions

Despite President Mogae's call for national unity behind his Total Mobilisation Campaign (TMC) against AIDS, ethnic tensions are mounting, particularly within the ruling BDP. Vice President Ian Khama is determined to use his position in the Ngwato royal family to secure his place as Mogae's heir. The emergence of the 'Ngwato factor', a group of tribalists loyal to Khama, has opened up a rift within the BDP. They have stepped up pressure on Mogae not to contest the 2004 presidential elections and drawn up a 'hit-list' of dissidents they are determined to silence or force out of the party.

The aggressive mobilisation of pro-Khama supporters began backfiring in 2001. BDP members of parliament opposed to Khama began talking openly of moving a motion that would bar any automatic succession of the vice president to the presidency if the president dies or retires. Khama's divisive bid for the party leadership also failed after Mogae and other leading party members succeeded in persuading him not to challenge Ponatshego Kedikilwe for the chairmanship 'for the sake of party unity'. Mogae also turned on some of his own cabinet ministers who had engaged in a hostile war of words with the party's parliamentary backbenchers. However, many of Kedikilwe's supporters had hoped Khama would stand, confident that the vice president would lose. One party insider said that a defeat for Khama would 'explode the myth that he is invincible' and bring him back in line.

The emergence of the Ngwato factor and Khama's use of tribal politics encouraged ethnic tensions within some quarters of Botswanan society during 2001 and into 2002. The opposition has been quick to condemn the growth of tribalism, which has threatened to become violent. As a number of ethnic-based organisations began to emerge by late 2001, the country's opposition parties criticised Mogae for his 'deafening silence' over tribal outbursts. In an open letter to Mogae in October 2001, Mokgweetsi Kgosipula, secretary general of the Botswana Congress Party (BCP), wrote 'you have elected to only lament the dangers of tribalism without offering concrete proposals on how to promote ethnic equality in this country'. He added: 'Tribalism is dangerous. It will destroy us as a nation, even faster than the scourge that is currently ravaging our people – HIV/AIDS.' The BNF has echoed these sentiments, calling on the various ethnic groups to restore calm, open up dialogue and respect the nation's democratic values.

The opposition's call for peace and dialogue was followed up by a conference held in October 2001 organised by the human rights group Ditshwanelo, which brought together the two main rival ethnic organisations – Pitso Ya Batswana (a Setswana promoting group) and the Society for the Promotion of the Ikalanda Language (SPIL). Passionate pleas for national unity and tolerance by academics, politicians and businessmen attending the conference appeared to quell the tensions between the groups.

Opposition re-alignment

The decision by opposition groups to reject tribal politics and Khama's failure to use his ethnic background to launch his presidential career illustrates that ethnic tensions are not a strong political rallying point in Botswana. The country's fragmented opposition continues to find it hard to mobilise the largely apathetic electorate and shake the BDP's hold over the political system. Instead of uniting under a common banner of unity to overthrow the BDP, the opposition has continued to fragment and parties have become riven with internal rivalries.

However, the situation improved in 2001 and 2002 as the BNF settled its in-fighting by electing a new leadership. The resignation of BNF leader Kenneth Koma helped seal a rift that had emerged in the party, which holds six seats in the 47-seat National Assembly. The tensions within the party had become so great that rival factions began fighting in the streets. Otsweletse Moupo and his Concerned faction won a resounding victory at the BNF's congress, held in November 2001. Moupo won the contest for the party leadership, defeating his long-standing rival Peter Woto, the candidate Koma had picked to succeed him. The Concerned faction, regarded as representing the majority of the BNF rank-and-file, also triumphed over Woto's Party Line faction in the election of the central committee, winning all 26 positions. In his acceptance speech, Moupo pledged to revive the party's structures, which had become defunct under Koma's repressive leadership, and instil discipline in the party. With the Party Line group completely trounced in the elections, Moupo will have the legitimacy he needs to unify the party behind him ahead of the 2004 election. Even the usually bellicose Koma called for the party to rally behind Moupo, his old adversary, following the announcement of the results.

Moupo's victory could lead to further consolidation within the opposition, perhaps siphoning off support from rival opposition parties. However, he has rejected proposals to merge the BNF with the BCP, which was originally formed by BNF supporters who had become dissatisfied with Koma's autocratic leadership style. Although it holds only one seat in the National Assembly, the BCP has a stronger standing in municipal government and has attracted a lot of disenchanted BNF supporters in recent years. Shortly before his election as party leader, Moupo stated that 'people need to understand that before a merger can take place, there must first be a unity of purpose', adding that the BNF needed to spend much of 2002 repositioning and reconstituting itself before considering an alliance with other parties.

The BCP rank-and-file also resisted merger talks with other parties in 2001. However, at the BCP's conference in July 2001, the leadership called for the party to disband and form a new party with the Botswana Alliance Movement (BAM). Nevertheless, BAM, which commanded just 4 per cent of the vote in the 1999 elections and failed to win a single seat, is united in its resolve to merge with the BCP. A BCP–BAM merger may pose a significant threat to the BNF, although some within the BCP believe it is 'opportunistic posturing' and would lead to the capitulation of many BCP supporters to the BNF and BDP.

Outlook

The general population and the ruling elite have only just woken up to the fact that Botswana is faced with a crisis of breath-taking proportions. The only way Botswana can tackle the AIDS crisis is through a spirit of national unity. The threat of tribalism and social disorder appears to have diminished as political leaders from all sides seek reconciliation among ethnic adversaries. However, the problem is likely to return as parliament considers the controversial recommendations by the Balopi Commission, which include giving ethnically neutral names to local districts. Social turmoil generated by tribalism will do nothing to allay investor sentiment as the country braces itself for the economic fall-out from AIDS.

Risk assessment

Economic	Deteriorating
Political	Good
Regional stability	Poor

COUNTRY PROFILE

Historical profile

1885 Britain declared the country a protectorate and called it Bechuanaland.
1966 Independence for Botswana came a year after the territory's first election which was won by Seretse Khama and his Democratic Party.
1980 On his death, Khama was succeeded by his vice president, Quett Masire.
1984 and 1989 The ruling Botswana Democratic Party (BDP) easily won elections but was tainted by allegations of corruption.
1994 In the election, the opposition party, Botswana National Front (BNF), took 13 seats and unseated three ministers.
1998 President Sir Quett Ketumile Masire retired from the presidency in March and was succeeded by Festus Mogae of the BDP.
1999 The October legislative election was won by the BDP. The National Assembly chose Festus Mogae as President.

Political structure

Constitution
Botswana has a code of human rights enshrined in the 1966 constitution.
The approval of a 15-member House of Chiefs is needed for some measures, but it cannot veto legislation.
Form of state
Multi-party democratic republic
The executive
The National Assembly elects a president who has executive power for a renewable five-year term. He appoints a vice president and the cabinet, over which he presides. The president is an ex-officio member of the Assembly.
National legislature
The legislature is the 47-member National Assembly, 40 of whom are elected for five years by universal adult suffrage and seven members are ex-officio members appointed by the president. The attorney-general is also appointed by the president.
A 15-member House of Chiefs advises on tribal matters.
Legal system
Roman-Dutch law. Rural areas have customary courts.
Last elections
16 October 1999 (legislative)
Next elections
2004 (legislative and presidential)

Political parties

Ruling party
Botswanan Democratic Party (BDP) (since 1965; re-elected Oct 1999).
Main opposition party
Botswana National Front (BNF)

Population

1.63 million (2000)
Annual population growth – 1.9 per cent between 1994 and 2000 – is forecast to decline to 0.6 per cent during 1999–2015.
Approximately 43 per cent of the total population is under 14 years.
Population density: three inhabitants per square km. Urban population: 50 per cent (1994–2000). Seventy-five per cent of the population live in the eastern 10 per cent of the country.
Ethnic make-up
The Batswana, of which the largest group is the Bamangwato, comprise 95 per cent of the total population. The Kalanga, Basarwa and Kgalagadi make up 4 per cent.
Religions
The majority of the population are Christians (about 49 per cent); other religions include various traditional beliefs, including animism, mostly in rural areas (50 per cent), and a small Muslim population.

Education

Attendance at primary level rose from 91 per cent of the relevant age group in 1980 to 108 per cent in 1996; secondary level from 19 per cent in 1980 to 65 per cent in 1996, and tertiary level from 1 per cent in 1980 to 6 per cent in 1996.

Health

The infant mortality rate was 62 per 1,000 live births in 1998, and approximately 27 per cent of children were malnourished in the period 1992–97. About 70 per cent of the total population have access to safe water.
HIV/AIDS prevalence was estimated at 35.8 per cent of the adult population in 2000. Projections by UNAIDS shows that the impact of HIV on firms could equal 4.9 per cent of their total wage bill between 1996–2004.
Government spending on health amounted to 7.6 per cent of total expenditure in 2001. There are 1.6 hospital beds per 1,000 of the population.

Main cities

Gaborone, capital (estimated population 213,000 in 2000), Francistown (102,000), Selebi-Phikwe (49,000), Lobatse (25,992), Orapa (8,853), Jwaneng (11,199), Sowa (2,220).

Languages spoken

Setswana (national)
Official language
English (official)

Media

Press
Dailies: *Botswana Daily News* is owned by the government. *Daily News Online* (http://www.gov.bw/cgi-bin/news.cgi) is a news service provided by the Botswana Press Agency.
Weeklies: Weekly publications are *Botswana Guardian*, *Gazette* and the *Midweek Sun*. *Mmegi wa dikgeng/the Reporter* with on-line edition (http://www.mmegi.bw/) is an independent weekly.
Business: *Business Gazette* covers financial and business interests.
Periodicals: *Marung* is a monthly periodical and *The Voice* is an irregular publication from Francistown.
Broadcasting
Radio: National service in Setswana and English operated by Radio Botswana, based in Gaborone.
Television: South African and Bophuthatswana transmissions can be received.

Economy

The mining sector, particularly diamonds, dominates Botswana's economy. In recent years, the government has initiated strategies to diversify export markets and has invested heavily in communications and water. As part of its plans to boost the economy in 1997–2002, the government is moving toward privatisation of state-owned industries. However, diamonds are still a motor for the economy providing 70 per cent of export earnings and increasing the country's wealth – a further 10 per cent is provided by nickel and copper production.
Export markets have remained healthy with the pula's depreciation of 6 per cent against the euro and 14 per cent against the US$ in 2001, securing the competitiveness of Botswana's exports. The government's exchange rate policy, which pegs the pula to the rand and the SDR, has largely served the country well while giving the central bank latitude over monetary policy.
Despite the economy's health, the IMF's directors have warned of the AIDS time bomb that is likely to hit the country's workforce in coming years. Although the

government has led a concerted and largely successful AIDS campaign, the IMF is concerned about the wider costs of the disease which has infected nearly 36 per cent of the adult population. The growing macroeconomic impact of AIDS-related problems is likely to coincide with a decline in the value of diamond exports – the IMF believes diamond revenues have reached a plateau. The IMF has also criticised the government's poor statistical collation performance which it believes could trip the country up with the implementation of macroeconomic policies that lagged behind economic conditions. The government has begun to rectify the situation by publishing quarterly national accounts and strengthening fiscal data collection.

External trade

The balance of payments depends heavily on earnings from diamonds, which have risen considerably since the early 1980s.

Exports

Principal exports are diamonds and copper/nickel (typically 80 per cent of total), soda ash, textiles, meat and meat products, animals, hides and skins.

Main destinations: Europe and Southern African Customs Union.

Imports

Principal imports are food, machinery and electrical goods, transport equipment, chemical and rubber products, wood and paper products, textiles, footwear, metals and metal products, beverages and tobacco.

Main sources: Southern African Customs Union, other African countries, mainly Zimbabwe.

Agriculture

The agricultural sector contributes around 3.5 per cent to GDP and employs 60 per cent of the workforce.

Production is divided between small, traditional farms and around 360 large-scale commercial units (including Pandamantenga, Barolong Farms and Tuli Block).

The climate and poor soil are suitable for extensive ranching, with the result that livestock produce accounts for about 80 per cent of marketed output. In the past, rearing of livestock has been hampered by frequent outbreaks of foot-and-mouth disease – now largely controlled – and more recently by drought. However, the livestock sector has predominated in the sector due to a lack of cultivatable land – only 5 per cent of the land is suitable for arable production – in a country which is mostly arid and contributes around 80 per cent of agriculture's share of GDP. Beef is one of the country's main exports and the Botswana Meat Commission (BMC) operates three abattoirs with a combined capacity of up to 2,000 head of cattle and smaller stock every day.

Government aims for self-sufficiency in basic foodstuffs, such as maize, millet, beans and sorghum are far from being realised.

Industry and manufacturing

The industrial sector as a whole contributes around 5 per cent to GDP and employs 10 per cent of the workforce.

The manufacturing sector is underdeveloped. There is a wide range of consumer products manufactured by a relatively small number of enterprises. There is also a large number of village industries, mainly producing handicrafts. The main industrial base depends on the livestock sector. Beverages, chemicals, paper, plastics and electrical goods are also produced.

The small domestic market has hampered attempts to stimulate production. Therefore, emphasis is on expansion of the export market for traditional products, such as textiles, leather goods, processed meat and import substitution.

The manufacturing sector's future was adversely affected by several textile firms closing down in 1998 due to difficulties in securing sales in Zimbabwe and the collapse of the Motor Company of Botswana (MCB) car assembly operation in 1999 due to cash flow problems caused by a fall in demand on the South African market. However, Hyundai and Scania continue to have vehicle assembly operations in Botswana.

The government is pushing for increased value-added on the country's primary goods production. The soda ash industry has helped develop the local manufacture of detergents, potash and fertilisers. The country also produces electrical components which utilise copper and nickel production.

The government has set up the Botswana Development Corporation (BDC) in an effort to promote industrial development, particularly in sugar refining, furniture, clothing, milling, brewing, packaging and handicrafts.

Tourism

The tourism industry contributes about 3 per cent of GDP. The government is committed to improving tourism awareness and developing skilled human resources in the area of hotel inspection and grading, languages and computer skills. Botswana has benefited from improved political stability in Southern Africa.

The Tourism Development Unit (TDU) emphasises the role of joint ventures between local firms and foreign investors. Of the total land area, 17 per cent has been designated as game reserves and a further 23 per cent as wildlife management areas.

The town of Maun is the gateway to the tourist destination of Okavango.

Mining

Exploitation of rich mineral reserves, notably diamonds, provided the key to Botswana's rapid economic growth, with the mining sector accounting for up to 50 per cent of GDP and employing 7 per cent of the workforce.

Diamonds, together with copper and nickel production, account for around 80 per cent of Botswana's foreign exchange revenue and a third of GDP. They remain the main focus of prospecting activities. Botswana is the second-largest producer of gem diamonds in the world, after Russia.

All diamond mining is carried out by De Beers Botswana Mining Company (Debswana), a company jointly owned by the government and De Beers of South Africa. In 2001, Debswana's total revenue increased by 6 per cent over the previous year to P10.7 billion (US$1.6 billion), compared to a projection of P11.6 billion (US$1.7 billion). Depreciation of the pula has meant that in US dollar terms revenue fell by up to 13 per cent. The terrorist attacks on the US in 2001 combined with the global slowdown helped depress world diamond prices and squeeze profits. During the course of the year, Debswana participated in the buy-out of De Beers. Debswana's total diamond sales, including mine output and stockpile releases, amounted to 25.24 billion carats in 2001 compared with 25.74 billion in the previous year.

Estimated reserves of copper/nickel total 93 million tonnes. The Selebi-Pikwe copper/nickel mine and the Sua Pan salt/soda ash facility are the main export earners after the diamond mines. There is also some production of gold.

Debswana completed the Orapa 2000 project during 2000. Capacity at the Orapa mine has increased to 12 million carats per year, and Debswana's overall production (including the Jwaneng and the small Letlhakane mines) is higher by about a quarter, at 24 million carats annually.

Hydrocarbons

Botswana has the largest known coal reserves in Africa: proven reserves are 17 billion tonnes, total reserves are estimated at about 50 billion tonnes, although of low quality.

Coal output from the Morupule coal mine, which is mainly used in power stations, has increased to around 900,000 tonnes.

There are no known domestic oil reserves; all petroleum products are sourced via South Africa.

Energy

Total installed electricity generating capacity (all thermal) is 220MW. Consumption per capita is estimated at 874kWh and only 22 per cent of the population have access to electricity. Electricity prices are the highest in Southern Africa and consequently demand is falling. There is potential for hydroelectric generation and solar power. Half of total primary energy requirements is met by fuelwood.

Financial markets

Stock exchange

Botswana Stock Exchange (BSE) was launched in 1989 and became a fully-fledged stock market in 1995. The Contributory Funded Pension Scheme was launched in 2000. The BSE is dominated by Barclays and Standard Chartered and is widely seen as a small but vibrant market.

Banking

Of the established commercial banks, the largest is Barclays Bank of Botswana, which was launched in 1950 and has approximately 42 branches and agencies. It has 19.6 per cent local equity with the rest held by the UK's Barclays Bank. Standard Chartered Bank of Botswana has been operating in the country since 1897 and has 14 branches and four agences.

Central bank

Bank of Botswana

Main financial centre

Gaborone

Time

GMT plus two hours

Geography

Botswana is a landlocked country in southern Africa, with South Africa to the south and east, Zimbabwe to the north-east and Namibia to the west and north. A short section of the northern frontier adjoins Zambia.

Climate

Sub-tropical, with hot summers and dry winters. Temperatures range from about 5–23 degrees Celsius (C) in July to 18–31 degrees C in January.

Entry requirements

Passports

Required by all. Passports should be valid for six months from the date of arrival.

Visa

Required by all except Commonwealth citizens (not including Ghana, India, Mauritius, Nigeria and Sri Lanka), EU citizens and US citizens for stays up to 90 days. Visas for nationals of Ghana, India, Mauritius, Nigeria and Sri Lanka take two to three weeks to issue from the date of application. Visitors are not permitted to work or seek employment.

Currency advice/regulations

Import of local and foreign currency is unlimited, provided it is declared on arrival. Export of local currency is restricted to P10,000. Botswana is not part of the Rand area. Export of foreign currency is allowed up to the amount imported and declared.

Customs

Member of Southern African Customs Union, therefore virtually no restrictions on movement of goods from South Africa, Namibia, Lesotho and Swaziland.

Health (for visitors)

Mandatory precautions

Cholera inoculation certificate if arriving within six days of travelling from an infected area. No other compulsory vaccinations.

Advisable precautions

Hepatitis A, polio, tetanus and typhoid immunisations are advisable. Anti-malarial prophylaxis is necessary for visitors to northern game reserves.

An examination is advisable within 10 days if bitten by insects, in case of sleeping sickness.

AIDS infection rates are high in Francistown and Gaborone.

Hotels

First-class hotels available in all main towns. Generally advisable to book in advance – essential at weekends and during public holidays.

Credit cards

American Express, Access/MasterCard, Barclaycard/Visa, Diners.

Public holidays

Fixed dates

1–3 Jan (New Year), 1 Jul (Sir Seretse Khama Day), 18–19 Jul (President's Day), 30 Sep–1 Oct (Botswana Day), 25–27 Dec (Christmas).

Variable dates

Good Friday, Easter Monday, Ascension Day.

Working hours

Banking

Mon–Fri: 0815–1245; Sat: 0815–1045.

Business

Mon–Fri, Apr–Oct: 0800–1300, 1400–1700; Mon–Fri, Oct–Apr: 0730–1630.

Government

Mon–Fri: 0730–1230, 1345–1630.

Shops

Mon–Fri: 0830–1300, 1400–1700; Sat: 0830–1300.

Telecommunications

The liberalisation of telecommunications service began during 1998, and tenders were awarded to two companies for the provision of cellular telephones.

Telephone/fax

Landlines connect the 12 main towns by microwave links. With the completion of the Gantsi-Mamuno microwave radio link in 1998, Botswana is directly connected to South Africa, Zimbabwe, Zambia and Namibia.

Social customs/useful tips

The noun for the people of Botswana is: singular, Motswana; plural, Batswana.

Getting there

Air

National airline: Air Botswana.

Main airport: The Sir Seretse Khama airport (GBE) is 14km from Gabarone's centre. Francistown (FRW) and Kasane (BBK) also have international flights.

Airport tax: There is no airport tax.

Surface

Road: Bitumised roads link Botswana with South Africa in the south, and Zambia and Zimbabwe in the north.

The Trans-Kalahari highway was completed in 1998. It provides a shorter all-tarred road link between Namibia and South Africa's Gauteng province, crossing south-west Botswana, via Kanye and Ghanzi.

There are bus services from Zimbabwe and South Africa.

Botswanan border posts are at Ngoma Bridge and Shakawe. The road from Namibia, via Shakawe border post, is paved all the way to Maun.

Rail: Botswana has rail links with South Africa and Zimbabwe.

Getting about

National transport

Air: Air travel is the best way to get around Botswana.

Regular flights operated by Air Botswana connect Gaborone, Francistown, Maun and Selebi-Pikwe. Air Botswana also provides direct charter flights to other airstrips throughout country.

Road: There are over 13,000km of well-developed roads, of which some 1,900km are tarred and a further 1,000km gravelled. They carry 92 per cent of vehicle traffic. The network of bitumised roads extends along the populated eastern side of the country.

Most major towns are connected by good roads. Travellers to Okavango should note that the road to Maun is tarred, but it is impossible to travel further without use of an overland vehicle.

Rail: Botswana's railway system consists of 641km of main line plus three branch lines – between Morupule and Palapye, Selebi-Phikwe and Serule, and between Sua Pan and Francistown.

The main Cape Town (South Africa)–Bulawayo (Zimbabwe) railway runs for over 700km through Botswana, linking several towns. This section is operated by Botswana Railways, along with freight-only lines to Selebi-Phikwe and Sua Pan. Botswana Railways has lost a great deal of freight business to road transporters. It has established the Gaborone Container Terminal (Gabcon), a dry port facility acting as a container terminal, specifically for locally based importers and exporters.

City transport

Taxis: Taxis are available in the capital. Tips are not common; if offered, 10 per cent would be acceptable.

Car hire

Foreign or international driving licence is required. Speed limits: 120kph on main roads, 60kph in built-up areas. Seat-belts must be worn. Facilities are available to hire Avis car in South Africa and deposit it in Botswana, or vice versa. Hire cars are only available for driving from Botswana to Zimbabwe or Zambia by special prior arrangement.

BUSINESS DIRECTORY

Telephone area codes

The international direct dialling (IDD) code for Botswana is +267, followed by the local area code:

Francistown	210
Gaborone	310
Lobatse	330
Kanye	340
Jwaneng	380

Chambers of Commerce

Botswana National Chamber of Commerce and Industry, PO Box 20344, Gaborone (tel: 352-677).

Francistown Chamber of Commerce and Industry, PO Box 196, Francistown (tel: 212-149).

Gaborone Chamber of Commerce and Industry, PO Box 1402, Gaborone (tel: 353-721).

Banking

Barclays Bank of Botswana, PO Box 478, Barclays House, Plot 8842 Khama Crescent, Gaborone (tel: 352-041; fax: 313-672).

National Development Bank, PO Box 225, Development House, Plot 1123, The Mall, Gaborone (tel: 352-801; fax: 374-446).

Standard Chartered Bank Botswana Ltd, PO Box 496, 5th Floor, Standard House, The Mall, Gaborone (tel: 360-1500, 353-111; fax: 372-933, 353-446).

Central bank

Bank of Botswana, Private Bag 154, Gaborone (tel: 360-6000; fax: 301-100, 313-890, 371-231, 313-862).

Travel information

Air Botswana, Sir Seretse Khama Airport, PO Box 92, Gaborone (tel: 352-812; fax: 374-802).

Botswana National Parks Reservations, Maun (tel: 661-265; fax: 661-264).

Ministry of tourism

Department of Tourism, 2nd Floor, Standard House, Main Mall, Private Bag 0047, Gaborone (tel: 353-024, 313-314; fax: 308-675; e-mail: botswanatourism@gov.bw; internet site: http://www.botswanatourism.org)

Ministries

Ministry of Agriculture, Private Bag 003, Gaborone (tel: 350-500, fax: 356-027).

Ministry of Commerce and Industry, Private Bag 004, Gaborone (tel: 360-1200; fax: 371-539).

Ministry of External Affairs, Private Bag 00368, Gaborone (tel: 360-0700; fax: 313-366).

Ministry of Finance and Development Planning, Private Bag 008, Gaborone (tel: 350-100, 355-272; fax: 356-086).

Ministry of Mineral Resources and Water Affairs, Private Bag 0018, Gaborone (tel; 352-452; fax: 372-733).

Ministry of Works, Transport and Communications, Private Bag 007, Gaborone (tel: 358-500, 355-563, 355-303; fax: 358-500, 313-303).

Office of the President, Private Bag 001, Gaborone (tel: 350-800).

Other useful addresses

Botswana Confederation of Commerce, Industry and Manpower, Botsalano House, PO Box 432, Gaborone.

Botswana Development Corporation Ltd, Private Bag 160, Gaborone (tel: 351-790; fax: 305-375).

Botswana Diamond Company (Pty) Ltd, Debswana House, The Mall, Gaborone (tel: 351-131; fax; 356-110).

Botswana Embassy (USA), 1531-3 New Hampshire Avenue, NW. Washington DC 20036 (tel: 244-4990; fax: 244-4164).

Botswana Enterprise Development Unit (promotes industrial & rural development), PO Box 0014, Gaborone.

Botswana Meat Commission, Private Bag 4, Lobatse (tel: 330-321; fax: 330-530).

Botswana Power Corporation, Motlakase House, Macheng Way, PO Box 48, Gaborone (tel: 360-300; fax: 373-563).

Botswana Telecommunications Corporation, PO Box 700, Gaborone (tel: 358-000).

Debswana Diamond Company, Gaborone (tel: 351-131; fax: 356-110).

Department of Geological Survey, Private Bag 14, Lobatse (tel: 330-0327; fax: 332-013).

Department of Information and Broadcasting, Private Bag 0060, Gaborone (tel: 365-8000, 365-3081; fax: 357-138, 301-675; e-mail: ib.publicity@info.bw).

Department of Mines, Private Bag 0049, Gaborone (tel: 352-641; fax: 352-141).

Department of Trade and Investment Promotion (TIPA), Private Bag 004, Gaborone (tel: 351-790; fax: 305-375).

Office of the President, Private Bag 001, Gaborone (tel: 350-800).

Stockbrokers Botswana Ltd, Ground Floor, Barclays House, Khama Crescent, Post Bag 00417, Gaborone (tel: 357-900; fax: 357-901).

Water Utilities Corporation, Private Bag 00276, Gaborone (tel: 352-521).

Internet sites

Africa Business Network: http://www.ifc.org/abn

AllAfrica.com: http://www.allafrica.com

African Development Bank: http://www.afdb.org

Africa Online: http://www.africaonline.com

Bank of Botswana: http://www.bankofbotswana.bw/

Harambee Afrika (UK business club for traders with east, central and southern Africa; includes annotated web resource list): http://www.harambee.co.uk

Mbendi AfroPaedia (information on companies, countries, industries and stock exchanges in Africa): http://mbendi.co.za

Burkina Faso

Falguni Patel

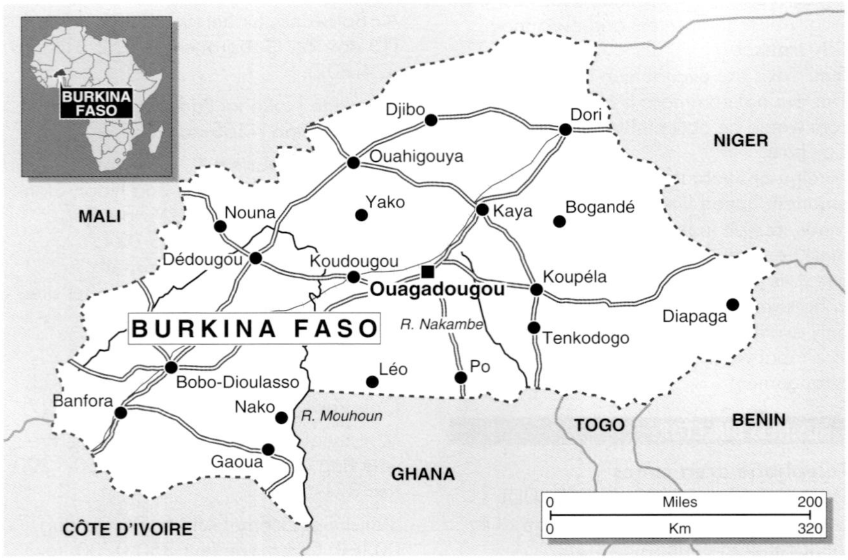

KEY FACTS

Official name: République Démocratique Populaire de Burkina Faso (The Popular Democratic Republic of Burkina Faso)

Head of State: President Captain Blaise Compaoré (since 1987)

Head of government: Prime Minister Paramanga Ernest Yonli (from Nov 2000)

Ruling party: Coalition led by Congrès pour la Démocratie et le Progrès (CDP) (Congress for Democracy and Progress) (Prime Minister Yonli appointed government, 10 Jun 2002)

Area: 274,000 square km

Population: 11.90 million (2001)

Capital: Ouagadougou

Official language: French

Currency: CFA franc (CFAf) = 100 centimes (Communauté Financière Africaine (African Financial Community) franc)

Exchange rate: CFAf629.73 per US$ (Jan 2003); CFAf655.95 per euro (pegged from Jan 1999)

GDP per capita: US$193 (2001)

GDP real growth: 5.70% (2001)

Inflation: 4.90% (2001); 2.4% (year-on-year, Feb 2002)

Balance of trade: -US$280.00 million (2001)

Foreign debt: US$1.74 billion (2001)

Annual FDI: US$8.00 million (2001)

For the latest Key Facts, go to www.worldinformation.com

In 2001 and 2002, a number of positive political gestures by the country's leadership helped counter increasing concerns over human rights abuses and Burkina Faso's role in fuelling conflict in West Africa. If these gestures are genuine, the future looks somewhat brighter for the Burkinabe people and West Africa. Staying in the good books of the IMF and World Bank resulted in a sizeable financial disbursement.

Elections to the Assemblée National (National Assembly) take place on 5 May 2002. President Blaise Compaoré's Congrès pour la Démocratie et le Progrès (CDP) (Congress for Democracy and Progress) saw its presence in the National Assembly fall from 103 seats to 57 seats after winning only 49.5 per cent of the vote. Of the other coalition government parties, the Alliance pour la Démocratie et la Féderation-Rassemblement Démocratique Africain (ADF-RDA) (Alliance for Democracy and Federation-African Democratic Rally) came second with 12.7 per cent of the vote and 17 seats.

Slow progress

Popular concern over human rights abuses and political tensions since the murder of Burkinabe journalist, Norbert Zongo, in December 1998 generated growing opposition to President Compaoré's regime during 2001 and 2002. It is now well established that Zongo was killed purely for carrying out investigative journalism, the findings of which were politically sensitive. The authorities have been extremely reluctant to find and convict his murderers. In February 2001, Marcel Kafando, former head of the presidential guard, was charged with Zongo's murder, an important step in meeting growing public concern.

Public scepticism about the leadership's commitment to human rights was, by now, too deep-rooted to be easily washed away. In an attempt at reconciliation, President Compaoré declared 30 March 2001 'Journée National du Pardon' (National Forgiveness Day) and, in a public address, apologised for human rights abuses perpetrated against the Burkinabe people.

In November 2001, a National Human Rights Commission was set up by the Compaoré government to demonstrate its commitment to improving the country's human rights record. Yet it failed one of the first significant tests of this newly declared political commitment. In February 2002, Amnesty International urged the authorities to investigate allegations made by the Burkina Faso Human and Peoples' Rights Movement that security forces had committed extra-judicial killings during the course of an anti-banditry campaign launched by the government in 2001. In response, the country's security minister leapt to the defence of his forces and the authorities categorically denied the allegations without further investigation.

Regional involvement

In December 2000, a UN panel of experts presented the UN Security Council with investigative evidence that Burkina Faso, together with Charles Taylor's Liberia, had played a significantly destabilising role in the West Africa sub-region. The country was accused of fuelling two civil wars in the region by knowingly circumventing UN arms and diamond bans aimed at anti-government forces in Angola and Sierra Leone. Consequently, Burkina Faso was faced with the very real threat of UN sanctions. In response, the Burkina Faso government set up the High Control Authority on Arms Imports and Use, which is responsible for informing the UN Security Council of new arms purchases, the weapons' final destinations, and the types and points of origin of weaponry already used by the country's security services. The government also allowed the UN supervisory power over the High Control Authority.

The events of 2001 showed that the country is attempting to build political bridges with its neighbours. In July 2001, President Compaoré met with Laurent Gbagbo, his counterpart in Côte d'Ivoire. The two leaders agreed to forge economic and cultural ties between their countries, and to end the bilateral tension caused by accusations of Burkina Faso involvement in efforts to destabilise Gbagbo's government. By October 2002, relations appeared to have deteriorated when Burkina Faso warned Côte d'Ivoire of serious consequences if it failed to protect its 2 million Burkinabe immigrants, many of whom have been attacked by the ethnic population. The Côte d'Ivoire government had accused the immigrants of supporting rebel forces, although Burkina Faso denied the allegation.

In December 2001, President Compaoré and the leaders of the CDP met with a delegation from the Liberian opposition and agreed that Burkina Faso will help the Liberian opposition work towards democracy in Liberia. Given Burkina Faso's previously strong alliance with Liberia's warring President Taylor, this indicated a deliberate attempt to distance itself from Taylor's government, bringing its own stance more in line with that of its fellow members of the Economic Community of West African States (Ecowas).

Parched prospects

Burkina Faso remained one of the poorest countries in the world in 2001 and 2002, with weak levels of foreign investment. In 2001, GDP remained at the robust level of 5.7 per cent, although the rate fell to 5.6 per cent in 2002.

The country continued with its successful privatisation programme, begun in 1991 as part of the structural adjustment deal it struck with the IMF and the World Bank. In December 2001, the IMF and the World Bank showed satisfaction with the progress of economic reforms and announced their final approval of the fourth review under the Poverty Reduction and Growth Facility (PRGF), leading to the immediate release of a US$7 million disbursement. A second US$7 million disbursement was agreed by the IMF in November 2002.

Although 2001 harvests were better than the year before, Burkina Faso still suffered the effects of previous food crises, with an estimated national cereal deficit of 80,000 tonnes. While there have been no reports of major food shortages in the country since November 2001, it was expected that there would be a food shortfall in 2002 due to severe nation-wide water shortages. In an effort to combat grain deficits, the government launched an irrigation project in December 2001, with the aim of exploiting all available water for use in out-of-season farming. There is tentative optimism that, in some areas of the country, this project will enable three crops a year to be harvested rather than just the one.

One of the most serious potential threats to Burkina Faso's social and economic development is the HIV/AIDS epidemic, with more than 7 per cent of the country's adult population thought to be HIV positive. In June 2001, international donors pledged US$85 million to Burkina Faso for a five-year programme to fight the epidemic and its effects.

Outlook

With the Burkinabe leadership making some effort to restore the faith of its people, of Ecowas and of the UN in its 'good global citizen' credentials, there is reason to believe that a more positive political climate will slowly emerge. Assuming that the government continues to profit from the sale of inefficient state companies, manages to attract more foreign investment and remains committed to addressing the country's food deficit and HIV/AIDS epidemic, it looks likely that Burkina Faso will continue on its slow, modest economic upswing. The year 2003 is unlikely to produce dramatic economic improvements for the poverty-ridden Burkinabe people.

Risk assessment

Economic	Poor
Political	Stable
Regional stability	Improving

COUNTRY PROFILE

Historical profile

Formerly an ancient African kingdom, the area was taken over by France in the nineteenth century.
1960 Granted full independence from France as Upper Volta.

KEY INDICATORS Burkina Faso

	Unit	1996	1997	1998	1999	2000
Population	m	10.78	11.09	10.68	11.62	11.90
Gross domestic product (GDP)	US$bn	2.57	2.38	2.63	2.50	2.20
GDP per capita	US$	253	223	245	215	185
GDP real growth	%	6.0	4.8	6.2	5.5	2.2
Inflation	%	6.2	2.3	5.1	-1.1	-0.2
Consumer prices	1995=100	106.2	108.6	114.2	112.9	112.5
Exports (fob) (goods)	US$m	232.5	229.5	311.4	313.3	210.0
Imports (fob) (goods)	US$m	562.4	0.0	572.0	637.6	530.0
Balance of trade	US$m	-330.0	-282.0	-261.0	-324.0	-320.0
Current account	US$m	-372.3	-332.4	-317.4	-396.5	-149.0
Foreign debt	US$bn	1.6	1.3	1.4	1.5	1.5
Total reserves minus gold	US$m	338.6	344.8	373.3	295.0	243.6
Foreign exchange	US$m	325.6	332.9	362.4	284.3	233.8
Exchange rate	per US$	511.55	583.67	598.95	615.70	711.98

1980–82 The first president, Maurice Yameogo, was ousted by Colonel Sangoule Lamizama.
1983 Captain Thomas Sankara took over as president and changed Upper Volta's name.
1987 Sankara was assassinated. Captain Blaise Compaoré seized power on 15 October.
1991 Compaoré was elected president in November.
1992 Legislative elections postponed from January took place on 24 May, when the Organisation pour la Démocratie Populaire-Mouvement du Travail (ODP-MT) (Compaoré's party) won.
1998 Compaoré won 87.53 per cent of the votes in the November presidential elections which were boycotted by opposition parties.
1999 Prime Minister Ouédraogo and his cabinet resigned on 8 January but were reinstated by presidential decree on 11 January.
2000 The IMF and World Bank agreed US$400 million in debt relief under the enhanced Heavily Indebted Poor Countries (HIPC) initiative.
2001 In June, international donors agreed to fund a US$85 million programme to combat the AIDS epidemic.

Political structure

Constitution
Military rule ended on 2 June 1991 and a constitution was adopted allowing for multi-party politics.
Constitutional changes were adopted by the National Assembly in January 1997. These included the abolition of the limit of two seven-year terms for the president, and an increase in the number of seats in the legislature from 107 to 111.

Form of state
Unitary and secular state

The executive
Executive power is vested in the head of state (the president), who is elected by universal suffrage for a seven-year term, and in the government, which is elected by the president.

National legislature
Multi-party Assemblée des Députés Populaires (ADP) (National Assembly) with 111 members, elected by universal suffrage for a four-year term.

Last elections
15 November 1998 (presidential); May 1997 (legislative).

Next elections
5 May 2002 (parliamentary, delayed); 2005 (presidential).

Political parties

Ruling party
Coalition led by Congrès pour la Démocratie et le Progrès (CDP) (Congress for Democracy and Progress)

Main opposition party
Parti pour la Démocratie et le Progrès (PDP) (Party for Democracy and Progress)

Population

11.90 million (2000)
The annual population growth was 2.4 per cent in the period 1994–2000. Approximately 46 per cent of the population is under 15 years.
Population density: 39 inhabitants per square km. Urban population: 19 per cent (1994–2000).
An estimated two million Burkinabes live in neighbouring Côte d'Ivoire.

Ethnic make-up
There are a number of ethnic groups, the most numerous of whom are the Mossi in the north (49 per cent), the Gourma in the east and the Bobo in the south-west. Other sizeable groups include the Fulani, the Hausa, the nomadic Tuareg with their Bella domestic serfs in the north-west and the Lobi in the south.

Religions
Animist (55 per cent), Muslim (40 per cent), Catholic (5 per cent).

Education

Three in five children are unable to go to school, since more children apply for schools than there are places. Although most children will not have heard any French at home, it is used in teaching. School fees are charged although payment can be put off until after harvest. About 10 per cent of schools are run outside the state system. Oxfam estimates that 49 per cent of children age 6–11 will enrol for school in 2015.

Health

Life expectancy: 44 years (1998). Infant mortality rate: 104 per 1,000 live births (1998). About 33 per cent of children were malnourished (1992–98).
Around 7 per cent of the population are infected. With over 70 per cent of sex workers testing positive, there is a distinct chance that the pandemic will hit the country badly in coming years. According to studies by UNAIDS, the economic impact is being felt at the household level with AIDS expenditures double the GDP per capita income. This is exacerbated by the decline in agricultural incomes caused by AIDS deaths in the agricultural sector. The UN-affiliated organisation claims that there is a serious shortfall in public expenditure on scaled-up care and preventative measures. Moreover, it states that the loss in GDP per capita income is likely to be 0.8 per cent by 2010.
In June 2001, international donors pledged US$85 million to Burkina Faso for a five-year programme to fight the epidemic and its effects.

Main cities

Ouagadougou (estimated population 900,000 in 1998), Bobo Dioulasso (250,000), Koudougou (50,000).

Languages spoken

French is the universal medium for documentation. African languages include More, Dioula, Gourmantche and Peul.

Official language
French

Media

Press
Dailies: The main national dailies are *Sidwaya* (government-controlled), *Le Pays*, *l'Observateur* (Burkinabe daily newspaper) and *24 Heures*, published from May 2000 by the *Journal du Jeudi* media group.
Weeklies: Weeklies published from Ouagadougou include *Indépendent*, *Intrus Journal du Jeudi*, *Observateur* and *Le Journal du Soir*.
Periodicals: Several periodicals mainly economic and industrial are published.

Broadcasting
Radio: Radio Burkina broadcasts in French and 13 African languages. Also private FM stereo radio (Horizon FM).
Television: Télévision Nationale du Burkina provides transmissions seven days a week to Ouagadougou and Bobo Dioulasso, Koudougou and Ouahigouya, in French and African languages.

Economy

The government is heavily in arrears on domestic and foreign debts and depends on foreign aid. More than 80 per cent of the population is engaged in subsistence agriculture and nomadic livestock rearing. The government has implemented a series of economic reforms under the auspices of the IMF. Although GDP growth has improved in recent years, particularly after the devaluation of the currency in the mid-1990s, the economy is fragile and there has been little headway in reducing poverty.

External trade

Exports
Main exports include cotton, gold, live animals, hides and skins and manufactures.
Main destinations: China, France, Italy, Ghana, Côte d'Ivoire, UK, Japan.

Imports
Main imports are food, fuel and energy and capital goods.
Main sources: France, Côte d'Ivoire, Italy, US, Ghana, the Netherlands.

Agriculture

The agricultural sector accounts for around a third of GDP and employs three-quarters of the workforce. It accounts for around 50 per cent of export earnings. Over 90 per cent of the

population is engaged in subsistence farming and nomadic stock raising. Principal food crops are sorghum, millet, yams, maize, rice and beans.
Burkina Faso is prone to drought and has poor soil. Only 10 per cent of the total land area is cultivated. There are plans to mechanise farming and open up new areas for development.
Cotton is the main cash crop; others are sheanuts, sesame and sugar cane.
Livestock production is concentrated in the north, mainly for export to Côte d'Ivoire (which has severely restricted its Burkinabe beef imports in recent years) and Ghana.

Industry and manufacturing

The industrial sector as a whole contributes around 28 per cent to GDP and employs 10 per cent of the workforce; manufacturing contributes over 20 per cent.
Production is centred on the processing of agricultural commodities (flour milling, sugar refining, manufacture of cotton yarn and textiles) and production of consumer goods including moped/bicycle assembly, footwear and soap manufacture.
Foreign investment is minimal and development remains handicapped by the chronic shortages of raw materials and spares.

Tourism

The tourism sector employs around 10,000 people directly, and more than 20,000 indirectly.

Mining

The sector contributes around 7 per cent to GDP and employs 2 per cent of the workforce.
Activity is confined to extraction of gold-bearing quartz at Poura (reserves estimated at 30 tonnes), marble and antimony.
There are viable deposits of zinc and silver at Perkoa, and some 15 million tonnes of manganese deposits at Tambao, as well as known reserves of limestone, bauxite, nickel, phosphates and lead.
Exploitation of resources is hindered by weak infrastructure.

Hydrocarbons

Burkina Faso has no known hydrocrabons reserves and its downstream industry entirely relies on imported refined oil.

Energy

The rural population relies on wood as a fuel for cooking, which is causing problems of deforestation and desertification in some areas.
Electricity supply is overseen by the Societé Nationale Burkinabe d'Electricité (Sonabel). Installed generation capacity is estimated at around 90MW. Only 7 per cent of the country has access to electricity and there is no national electricity grid. Thermal power generators supply 60 per cent of electricity.
Government policy is directed towards reducing Sonabel's production costs, thereby reducing its extortionate prices. Moreover, electricity development is regarded as crucial to the country's development and the government is keen to extend transmission lines and improve supply to meet growing demand.

Financial markets

Burkina Faso has no stock exchange.

Banking

The banking sector has undergone liberalisation in recent years, with the government restricting its involvement to around a quarter of the sector.

Central bank

Banque Centrale des Etats de l'Afrique de l'Ouest (central banking authority for the members of the West African Monetary Union)

Main financial centre

Ouagadougou

Time

GMT

Geography

Burkina Faso is a landlocked country in West Africa, bordered by Mali to the west and north, by Niger to the east, and by Benin, Togo, Ghana and Côte d' voire to the south.

Climate

The climate is tropical. The dry season runs from November–March, when the Harmattan wind blows keeping the humidity low. Temperatures in Ouagadougou range from 14 degrees C at night to over 35 degrees C during the day. The main rainy season is from June–October. The highest rainfall is in the south, lowest in the far north where an arid desert climate prevails.

Entry requirements

Passports

Required by all except holders of national identity cards issued to nationals of Benin, Central African Republic, Côte d'Ivoire, Guinea, Mali, Mauritania, Niger, Senegal and Togo.
Passports must be valid for six months after departure.

Visa

Required by all except nationals of Benin, Cape Verde, Côte d'Ivoire, The Gambia, Ghana, Guinea, Guinea-Bissau, Liberia, Mali, Mauritania, Niger, Nigeria, Senegal, Sierra Leone and Togo.
An onward or return ticket is also required.

Currency advice/regulations

There are no restrictions on the import/export of foreign currency or local currency.

Health (for visitors)

Mandatory precautions

Yellow fever vaccination certificate.

Advisable precautions

Typhoid, tetanus, hepatitis A and polio vaccinations are recommended. Malaria prophylaxis should be taken as risk exists throughout the country.

Hotels

Hotels are available in Ouagadougou and Bobo Dioulasso with limited availability elsewhere.

Public holidays

Fixed dates

1 January, 8 March, 1 May, 4 August (National Day), 15 October, 1 November (All Saints' Day), 1 December, 25 December.

Variable dates

Easter Monday, Ascension, Whit Monday, Eid al-Fitr, Eid al-Adha, Ashura, Prophet's Birthday, Al Hijra.

Working hours

Banking

Mon–Fri: 0830–1130 and 1530–1630.

Business

Mon–Fri: 0730–1230 and 1500–1730.

Government

Mon–Fri: 0730–1230 and 1500–1730.

Shops

(Mon–Sat) 0800–1300 and 1500–1900; (Sun) 0800–1200.

Telecommunications

Telephone/fax

Dialling code for Burkina Faso: IDD access code + 226 followed by subscriber's number (there are no area codes).

Electricity supply

220/380V AC, 50 cycles.

Getting there

Air

National airline: Air Burkina

Surface

Road: Most practical during dry seasons – from Mali (Bamako) and Niger (Niamey), when buses operate on these routes. The road from Ghana is being improved. Land journeys are also possible from Côte d'Ivoire, Benin and Togo.
Rail: Daily express service from Abidjan (Côte d'Ivoire) to Bobo Dioulasso and Ouagadougou. Sleeping and dining cars.

Getting about

National transport

Air: Air Burkina serves Ouagadougou, Bobo Dioulasso and other main centres. Light aircraft can be chartered from Air Burkina. The airline also operates flights to surrounding countries, Mali, Togo, Benin, Côte d'Ivoire and Niger.

City transport

Taxis: Unmetered and available in main centres. A 10 per cent tip is usually given.

Car hire
National licence plus permit or international driving licence required. Use of chauffeur-driven cars advised.

BUSINESS DIRECTORY

Telephone area codes
The international direct dialling code (IDD) for Burkina Faso is +226 followed by subscriber's number (there are no area codes).

Useful telephone numbers
Police: 17
Fire: 18
Ambulance: 3066-43/44/45

Hotel reservations
For a list of international hotel reservation details, see the end of this Review.

Chambers of Commerce
Chambre de Commerce, d'Industrie et d'Artisanat du Burkina, BP 502, Ouagadougou (tel: 306-114/115, 301-266/267; fax: 306-116).

Banking
Bank of Africa-Burkina Faso, BP 1319, Avenue de la résistance du 17 mai 770, Ouagadougou 01 (tel: 308-870/73; fax: 308-874).

Banque Internationale du Burkina, BP 1336, Av Nelson Mandela 800, Ouagadougou 01 (tel: 307-888, 307-878; fax: 310628).

Banque Internationale du Burkina SA, BP 362, Rue de la Chance, Ouagadougou 01 (tel: 306-170, 306-171; fax: 300-171, 310-094).

Banque Internationale pour le Commerce, l'Industrie et l'Agriculture du Burkina SA, BP 8, Avenue Dr Kwamé N ' Krumah 479, Ouagadougou 01 (tel: 306-226/8, 306-227; fax: 311-955).

Caisse Nationale de Crédit Agricole du Burkina (CNCAB), BP 1644, Avenue Gamal Abdel Naser 2, Ouagadougou 01 (tel: 333-333).

Ecobank-Burkina, BP 145, Rue Maurice Bishop 633, Espace Fadima, Ouagadougou 01 (tel: 318-975, 318-980; fax: 318-981, 318-982).

Société Générale de Banque au Burkina (SGBB), BP 585, Rue du Marché 4, Ouagadougou 01 (tel: 323-232; fax: 310-561).

Central bank
Banque Centrale des Etats de l'Afrique de l'Ouest (central banking authority for members of the West African Monetary Union), BP 356, Ave Gamal Abdel Nasser, Ouagadougou (tel: 336-716; fax: 310-122).

Travel information
Air Burkina, Siège Sociale, avenue Loudun, BP 1459, Ouagadougou 307676 (tel: 306-144; fax: 310-268).

Division du Tourisme et de l'Hôtellerie, BP 624, Ouagadougou (tel: 332-448).

Ministry of tourism
Ministry of Transport and Tourism, 03 BP 7068, Ouagadougou 03 (tel: 306-211).

National tourist organisation offices
Faso Tours (national travel agency), BP 1318, Ouagadougou (tel: 335-350).

Ministries
Ministry of Agriculture, 03 BP 7005, Ouagadougou 03 (tel: 324-114).

Ministry of Administration, 03 BP 7034, Ouagadougou 03 (tel: 324-833).

Ministry of Commerce and Industry, 01 BP 365 Ouagadougou 01 (tel: 324-786).

Ministry of Communications, 03 BP 7045, Ouagadougou 03 (tel: 324-833).

Ministry of Defence, 01 BP 496, Ouagadougou 01 (tel: 307-214).

Ministry of Education, 03 BP 7032, Ouagadougou 03 (tel: 324-870).

Ministry of Employment and Social Security, 03 BP 7016, Ouga 03 (tel: 310-960).

Ministry of Energy and Mines, 01 BP 3922 Ouagadougou 01 (tel: 324-786).

Ministry of the Environment and Water, 03 BP 7044 Ouagadougou 01 (tel: 324-074).

Ministry of the Family, 01 BP 515, Ouagadougou 01 (tel: 310-960).

Ministry of Finance and Economy, 03 BP 7012, Ouagadougou 03 (tel: 306-995).

Ministry of Foreign Affairs, 03 BP 7038, Ouagadougou 03 (tel: 324-733).

Ministry of Health, 03 P 7009 Ouagadougou (tel: 324-158).

Ministry of Higher Education and Scientific Research, 03 BP 7047, Ouagadougou 03 (tel: 324-567).

Ministry of Integration and African Affairs, 01 BP 6943, Ouagadougou 01 (tel: 324-833).

Ministry of the Interior, 03 BP 7011, Ouagadougou 03 (tel: 324-905).

Ministry of Justice, 01 BP 526, Ouagadougou 01 (tel: 324-833).

Ministry of Public Relations and Modernisation of Administration, 03 BP 7006, Ouagadougou 03 (tel: 306-995).

Ministry of Transport and Tourism, 03 BP 7068, Ouagadougou 03 (tel: 306-211).

Ministry of Youth and Sports, 03 BP 7035, Ouagadougou 03 (tel: 324-786).

Other useful addresses
Burkina Faso Embassy (USA), 2340 Massachusetts Avenue, NW, Washington DC 20008 (tel: 332-5577; fax: 667-1882; e-mail: ambawdc@rcn.com).

Groupement des Petits Commerçants, BP 952, Ouagadougou.

Institut de la Statistique et de la Démographie, BP 374, Ouagadougou (tel: 335-537).

Office National de Commerce Extérieur, BP 389, Ouagadougou (tel: 336-225).

Société de Commercialisation, BP 531, Ouagadougou (tel: 333-007); BP 375, Bobo-Dioulasso (tel: 390-423).

Syndicat des Entrepreneurs et Industriels, BP 446, Ouagadougou.

Télévision Nationale du Burkina, BP 7029, Ouagadougou (tel: 336-801).

West African Economic Community, BP 643, Ouagadougou.

Internet sites
Africa Business Network: http://www.ifc.org/abn

AllAfrica.com: http://www.allafrica.com

African Development Bank: http://www.afdb.org

Africa Online: http://www.africaonline.com

Burkina Faso: http://www.fasobusiness.com

Harambee Afrika (UK business club for traders with east, central and southern Africa; includes annotated web resource list): http://www.harambee.co.uk

Mbendi AfroPaedia (information on companies, countries, industries and stock exchanges in Africa): http://mbendi.co.za

Burundi

Guy Arnold

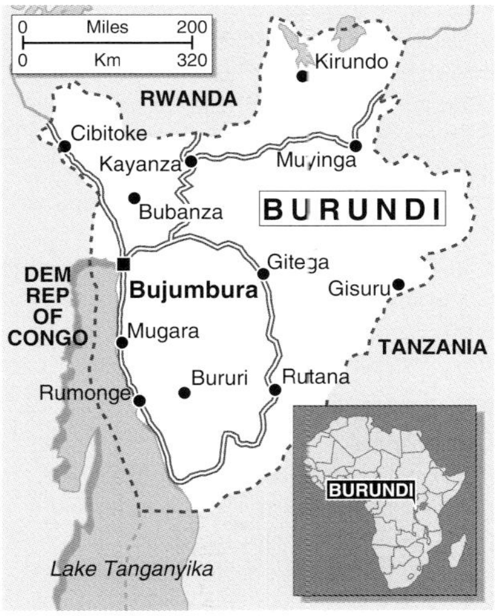

The search for peace in Burundi was the main preoccupation throughout 2001 and 2002 in a country that has seen more than 200,000 of its citizens killed since the late 1990s. The efforts of outsiders to achieve a lasting settlement of Hutu-Tutsi differences often seem greater and more sincere than those of Burundi's own people whose deep rooted suspicions of each other cannot easily or quickly be overcome.

Ongoing fighting

Fighting between government forces and Hutu rebels continued throughout 2001 and 2002 with both sides claiming they had inflicted heavy casualties on their opponents. Serious clashes occurred round the capital Bujumbura in February 2001. In March, members of the Hutu Forces Nationales de Libération (FNL) (National Liberation Forces) opposed to President Buyoya's government intensified large-scale attacks in the northern suburbs of Bujumbura, causing high numbers of refugees. In November 2002, an attack was launched in the Buganza province in south-west Burundi by the Forces pour la Défense de la Democratie (FDD) (Forces for the Defence of Democracy). This forced 20,000 civilians to flee the province while hundreds of others were killed.

Buyoya's government managed to quash two coup attempts during 2001. On 18 April, a group of soldiers led by Lieutenant Pasteur Ntarubimana attempted to stage a coup to topple Buyoya's government. There was a second attempt to topple Buyoya over 22/23 July, although this too failed. In November 2002, the former president, Jean-Baptiste Bagaza, was arrested and the authorities claimed that he was planning to topple the government.

Looking for peace

African attempts to find a solution to the conflict have been difficult. A peace agreement in 2000 failed to be signed by all parties, leading to an escalation of hostilities. In January 2001, 13 political parties agreed to the composition of a new parliament. People of Hutu origin (85 per cent of the population) were to have 60 per cent of the seats, while the Tutsi (16 per cent of the population) were to have the remaining 40 per cent.

A new peace agreement was signed in South Africa in July 2001. Chaired by the former South African president, Nelson Mandela, all the parties signed the agreement, except for the FNL and the FDD, which vowed to continue hostilities. The agreement allowed Buyoya to remain as president for the first 18 months of a three-year transitional term from November 2001, while the Hutu leader Domitien Ndayizeye would serve as the vice president. The two men would change places on 1 May 2003. The agreement also established a new government, which took power in November 2001. The Hutu-dominated Front pour la Démocratie au Burundi (Frodebu) (Front for Democracy in Burundi) holds 14 ministerial posts in the new 26-member government while the Tutsi-dominated Union pour le Progrès National (Uprona) (Union for National Progress) holds the other 12 posts.

Many African nations, including South Africa and Nigeria, deployed a peace-keeping force in late 2001. A cease-fire was signed by all the sides on 30 December 2002, but it is unlikely to be implemented until early 2003.

Burundi and the Congo

Throughout the tensions of 2001–02, the government remained deeply implicated

KEY FACTS

Official name: Republika y'Uburundi (The Republic of Burundi)

Head of State: President Major Pierre Buyoya (Tutsi); Vice President Domitien Ndayizeye (Hutu) (from Nov 2001) (the presidency will be assumed by Ndayizeye after 18 months)

Head of government: President Major Pierre Buyoya

Ruling party: Three-year Transitional Government of National Unity (installed 1 Nov 2001; the cabinet is almost equally split between Tutsi and Hutu).

Area: 27,834 square km

Population: 6.50 million (2001)

Capital: Bujumbura

Official language: Kirundi and French

Currency: Burundi franc (Buf) = 100 centimes

Exchange rate: Buf1,070.00 per US$ (Jan 2003)

GDP per capita: US$97 (2001)

GDP real growth: 2.00% (2001)

Inflation: 9.20% (2001)

Balance of trade: -US$109.00 million (2001)

Foreign debt: US$1.06 billion (2001)

For the latest Key Facts, go to www.worldinformation.com

in the rape of resources from its troubled neighbour, the Democratic Republic of Congo (DRC), according to a UN report which was issued following a detailed investigation. The report accused Uganda, Rwanda and Burundi of raping DRC resources in the eastern regions. Burundi does not produce gold, diamonds, copper, cobalt or other base metals yet it has been exporting such minerals as though they had been produced in Burundi. As in the cases of Uganda and Rwanda, Burundi's exports of diamonds coincide with its 1998 occupation of the eastern Congo.

Outlook

Despite the creation of a multi-ethnic transitional government, there has been no solution to the war in Burundi. The Hutu rebel groups have rejected the creation of a multi-ethnic transitional government and emphasised their stand by attacks upon civilians and raids upon schools . Given this ongoing violence and Burundi's illegal seizures of resources from the DRC to sustain its economy, the outlook for peace and a return to normality is at best fragile.

Risk assessment

Economy	Poor
Politics	Poor
Regional stability	Poor

COUNTRY PROFILE

Historical profile

1899 Burundi and its neighbour, Rwanda, were incorporated into German East Africa.
1916–23 Belgium occupied the area, which was named Ruanda-Urundi, and was allowed by the League of Nations to administer the country from 1923.
1962 Burundi received independence from Belgium as a kingdom.
1965 Tutsi-Hutu coalitions ruled, but a Hutu prime minister was killed and replaced by a Tutsi prince. The Hutus attemped a coup and failed. Instead, the Tutsis massacred the Hutu elite.
1966 After the king was deposed by his son, who was deposed by the army, Burundi was declared a republic.
1972 After another abortive coup attempt, between 200,000 and 400,000 Hutus were killed.
1976–87 The government of Tutsi Colonel Jean-Baptiste Bagaza was notorious for its violations of human rights.
1992 The constitution was adopted by referendum on 9 March.
1993 Tutsi Major Pierre Buyoya ousted Bagaza and permitted Burundi's first multi-party election. Melchior Ndadaye, who was committed to reforming the Tutsi-dominated army, became president in July. However, Ndadaye was assassinated in October, leading to civil war between the Tutsi-led army and Hutu rebels.
1994 Cyprien Ntaryamira, a Hutu, was elected president by the National Assembly. He was killed in a plane crash on 6 April, together with the Hutu president of Rwanda. Sylvestre Ntibantuganya, a Hutu, took over the presidency.
1995 A coalition government was formed under Antoine Nduwayu, a Tutsi.
1996 Major Pierre Buyoya seized power in a coup on 25 July.
1997 President Buyoya banned political parties and dissolved the National Assembly.
1999 Regional sanctions were suspended in January. By December, it was estimated that more than 250,000 Burundians had been killed in the ethnic conflict.
2000 President Pierre Buyoya and 13 political parties signed a peace deal on 28 August.
2001 An attempted coup in April failed. In July, the country's 19 political parties in talks chaired by Nelson Mandela agreed that Pierre Buyoya, a Tutsi, should remain president for the first 18 months of a new three-year transitional government. A Hutu would be vice president and half-way through the term their roles would be reversed. There was an attempted coup in July by 100 soldiers, who later gave themselves up. South Africa sent a peace-keeping force to Burundi in October. A three-year Transitional Government of National Unity as agreed in July, was installed on 1 November.

Political structure

Constitution
A transitional constitution replaced the 1992 constitution in 1998. Under the terms of the Transitional Constitutional Act in 1998, the position of prime minister was replaced by two vice presidents, although executive power remains with the president. The July 2001 peace plan introduced a new three-year transitional government in November 2001 with a rotating presidency.

Form of state
Burundi became a republic after a military coup in 1966.

The executive
The constitution vests executive power in a directly elected president who normally serves a five-year term. Following the July 2001 peace plan, part of a three-year transitional government will include a rotating presidency which will serve for 18 month stretches.

National legislature
Legislative power is vested in the Assemblée Nationale (National Assembly), normally elected for a five-year term by universal suffrage.

Legal system
Burundi law is based on Belgian and German law. The legal system is composed of a Supreme Court, Constitutional Court and a Courts of Appeal.

Last elections
June 1993.

Political parties

Ruling party
Three-year Transitional Government of National Unity (installed 1 Nov 2001; the cabinet is almost equally split between Tutsi and Hutu).

Main opposition party
Inama y'Igihugu Igwanira Demokarasi/ Conseil National pour la Défense de la

KEY INDICATORS — Burundi

	Unit	1996	1997	1998	1999	2000
Population	m	6.09	6.19	6.30	6.48	6.61
Gross domestic product (GDP)	US$bn	0.88	0.98	0.90	0.82	0.83
GDP per capita	US$	144	159	143	125	126
GDP real growth	%	-8.4	0.4	4.5	-1.0	1.8
Inflation	%	26.4	31.0	12.5	26.0	22.0
Consumer prices	1995=100	126.4	165.8	186.5	192.8	239.7
Exports (fob) (goods)	US$m	40.1	87.3	49.0	554.9	49.1
Imports (fob) (goods)	US$m	100.0	97.9	129.0	117.7	107.9
Balance of trade	US$m	-59.9	-10.6	-80.0	-62.7	-58.8
Current account	US$m	-40.3	4.0	-45.0	-27.0	-48.8
Foreign debt	US$bn	1.1	1.1	1.1	1.1	1.1
Total reserves minus gold	US$m	139.6	113.0	65.5	48.0	32.9
Foreign exchange	US$m	131.1	105.1	57.2	39.8	25.2
Exchange rate	per US$	302.75	252.35	447.77	563.56	720.67

Démocratie (National Council for the Defence of the Democracy)

Population
6.61 million (2000)
Annual population growth 2 per cent in 1994–2000. Approximately 46 per cent of the total population is under 15 years. Population density: 250 inhabitants per square km. Urban population: 9 per cent (1994–2000).

Ethnic make-up
The Hutu people are believed to comprise 85 per cent of the population, the Tutsi 14 per cent and the Twa 1 per cent, but there have never been any census statistics on ethnic groups.

Religions
Christianity (over 60 per cent), 32 per cent traditional beliefs.

Main cities
Bujumbura (estimated population 310,000 in 1997), Gitega (30,000), Rumonge (15,000).

Languages spoken
Kirundi is the official language, French the administrative language; KiSwahili is used commercially. English is compulsory in secondary education and there are broadcasts in English.

Official language
Kirundi and French

Media
Press
Dailies: The main government controlled daily newspaper in French is *Le Renouveau du Burundi*.
Weeklies: Weeklies include *Ubumwe* (Kirundi weekly) that is government-controlled and *l'Indépendant*.
Periodicals: Periodicals include *Carrefour des Idées*, *Le Citoyen* (twice monthly), *l'Aube de la Démocratie* (published twice monthly by the Frodebu party), *Intahe*, *Burakeyei* and *Kanura*.

Broadcasting
Radio: Radio service in Kirundi, KiSwahili, French and English operated by the state broadcasting station *Voix de la Révolution*.
Television: State-owned La Radiodiffusion et Télévision Nationale de Burundi (RTNB).

Economy
The instability experienced since 1996, coupled with sanctions imposed by seven African nations against the government of President Buyoya, caused immense damage to the economy. The period of sanctions (although widely flouted by Kenya, South Africa and Zambia) prevented Burundi from exporting as much coffee and tea as normal. While civil disturbance continues, the country will be unable to develop due to persistent disruptions in production. Despite peace plans being signed during 2001, the country is likely to undergo a long and perhaps painful period of adjustment.

External trade
There is a persistent trade deficit owing to depressed world coffee prices. However, Burundi may benefit from a global coffee retention plan which began in early 2001. Implemented under the auspices of the Association of Coffee Producing Countries (ACPC), it involves a 20 per cent production holdback by ACPC members to boost prices in a market depressed by a supply glut. Although Burundi is not a full member of the ACPC, it is likely to gain from an expected rise in world prices.
Economic sanctions were imposed by seven African nations in 1996 in protest at the violence used by President Buyoya's Tutsi army. Landlocked, reliant on imports of fuel and exports of coffee and tea for foreign exchange, the blockade hit the economy hard. The sanctions were lifted in January 1999.

Exports
Principal exports are coffee (normally 75 per cent of total), manufactures, tea (5 per cent), cotton fabrics (3 per cent).
Main destinations: UK (25.7 per cent of 2000 total), Switzerland (24.9 per cent), Kenya (12.4 per cent), Netherlands (8.1 per cent), Rwanda (4.1 per cent).

Imports
Principal imports are machinery and equipment (normally 18 per cent of total), petroleum products (15 per cent), food (10 per cent).
Main sources: France (13.3 per cent of 2000 total), Saudi Arabia (12.1 per cent), Tanzania (8.2 per cent), Kenya (5.4 per cent), Japan (5.2 per cent).

Agriculture
The agriculture sector is the mainstay of the economy. It typically employs around 90 per cent of the population and contributes around 50 per cent of GDP. However, the civil war, pressures on land and ecological damage have caused a 25 per cent contraction of the subsistence economy in recent years. Although Burundi is potentially self-sufficient in food, large numbers of internally displaced people rely on food parcels given by humanitarian organisations.
Most land under cultivation is devoted to subsistence crops – mainly cassava, bananas, sweet potatoes, pulses, maize and sorghum.
Cattle rearing is also an important source of food, as is fishing on Lake Tanganyika. The main cash crop is coffee, which accounts for up to three quarters of the country's exports. More than 90 per cent of coffee production is arabica, which is being encouraged with higher producer prices. Other cash crops include tea, cotton, palm oil and tobacco.
The Nile Basin Initiative (NBI) (signed by Egypt, Sudan, Tanzania, Kenya, Rwanda, Burundi, Uganda and Democratic Republic of Congo) launched seven feasibility studies backed by US$140 million granted by the World Bank and donor governments in June 2001. It will also develop a parallel legal framework for shared water management. Ethiopia refused to sign.

Industry and manufacturing
The industrial sector, which is based on import substitution, typically accounts for between 15–20 per cent of national output. Production is based almost entirely in Bujumbura and includes beer, soft drinks, cigarettes, glass, textiles, insecticides, cement, oxygen and coffee processing. Civil war has discouraged foreign investment and high import costs have hampered development of industrial capital.

Mining
Gold mining resumed in 1984.
Tungsten is also mined.
Substantial nickel reserves (up to 5 per cent of world total) have been found, but low world prices and an inadequate infrastructure mean extraction is not economically viable.
Deposits of vanadium and uranium are being surveyed.
Phosphates and limestone are used for cement production.

Hydrocarbons
Reliance on imported petroleum. Petroleum reserves have been located under the Ruzizi Plain and under Lake Tanganyika.

Energy
Wood is the main source of energy, providing 95 per cent of the subsistence sector needs.
Burundi has three power stations.
Large peat deposits are also being developed.

Banking
Central bank
Banque de la République du Burundi.

Main financial centre
Bujumbura.

Time
GMT plus two hours

Geography
Burundi is a landlocked country lying on the eastern shore of Lake Tanganyika, in central Africa, a little south of the Equator. It is bordered by Rwanda to the north, Tanzania to the south and east, and by the Democratic Republic of Congo to the west.

Climate
Equatorial around Lake Tanganyika (including Bujumbura); hot and humid with frequent winds with temperatures between 23–33 degrees Celsius (C). Temperate elsewhere with average temperature 20 degrees C. Rainy season from October–May (except brief dry period December–January), long dry season from June–September.

Entry requirements
Passports
Required by all.
Visa
Required by all.
Currency advice/regulations
No restrictions.

Health (for visitors)
Mandatory precautions
Yellow fever vaccination certificate if arriving from an infected area.
Advisable precautions
Yellow fever vaccination is considered essential. Vaccinations for hepatitis A, polio, tetanus and typhoid are recommended. Malaria prophylaxis should be taken as risk exists throughout the country.

Hotels
Advisable to book in advance. Very little accommodation available outside Bujumbura. A 10 per cent tip is usual.

Public holidays
Fixed dates
1 Jan, 5 Feb, 1 May, 1 Jul, 15 Aug, 13 Oct, 21 Oct, 1 Nov, 25 Dec.
Variable dates
Ascension Day, Easter Monday.

Working hours
Banking
Mon–Fri: 0800–1130; 1500–1600.
Business
Mon–Fri: 0730–1200, 1400–1730.
Government
Mon–Fri: 0730–1200, 1400–1730.
Shops
Mon–Fri: 0830–1200, 1500–1800. Sat: 0830–1230.

Electricity supply
220V AC.

Getting there
Air
National airline: Air Burundi (state-owned).
Main airport: Bujumbura.
Airport tax: No departure tax.
Surface
There are good roads from Bukavu (Democratic Republic of Congo) and Kigali (Rwanda) to Bujumbura. Roads from Tanzania are generally in poor condition. Main port: Bujumbura (on Lake Tanganyika). Ferries operate from Kigoma (Tanzania), Kalenjie (DRC) and Mpulungu (Zambia). Dar es Salaam is the nearest sea port.

Getting about
National transport
Air: Air Burundi operates internal flights linking Bujumbura with Kinundo; aircraft can be chartered at Bujumbura.
Road: Most of the roads leading to provincial towns are surfaced. Unsurfaced roads elsewhere can be difficult in rainy season.
City transport
Taxis: Available in Bujumbura.
Car hire
Local firms only. International driving licence is required.

BUSINESS DIRECTORY

Telephone area codes
The international direct dialling (IDD) code for Burundi is +257, followed by area code (2 for Bujumbura), followed by subscriber's number.

Useful telephone numbers
Police: 18, 19.

Chambers of Commerce
Chambre de Commerce et de l'Industrie du Burundi, BP 313, Bujumbura (tel: 22-280).

Banking
Banque Commerciale du Burundi, PO Box 990, Libere Ndabakwaje, Bujumbura (tel: 22-317; fax: 21-018).

Banque de Crédit de Bujumbura, PO Box 300, Avenue Patrice Emery Lumumba, Bujumbura (tel: 22-091; fax: 23-007).

Central bank
Banque de la République du Burundi, PO Box 705, Bujumbura, Burundi (tel: 25-142 fax: 23-128).

Travel information
Air Burundi, BP 2460, Avenue du Commerce, Bujumbura (tel: 23-460; fax: 23-452).

Bujumbura International Airport, PO Box 694, Bujumbura (tel: 23-707; 23-797; fax: 23-428).

National tourist organisation offices
Office National du Tourisme, 2 Avenue des Euphorbes, BP 902, Bujumbura (tel: 22-202, 22-023).

Ministries
Ministry of Agriculture, Bujumbura (tel: 10-342; fax: 22-873).

Ministry of Commerce, Industry and Tourism, Bumjumbura (tel: 17-775; fax: 25-595).

Ministry of Communication with the Government, Bumjumbura (tel: 12-601; fax: 16-318).

Ministry of Community Development, Bumjumbura (tel: 13-098; fax: 24-678).

Ministry of Defence, Bumjumbura (tel: 19-994; fax: 25-686).

Ministry of Education, Bumjumbura (tel: 17-776; fax: 26-839).

Ministry of Energy and Mines, Bumjumbura (tel: 18-586; fax: 23-337).

Ministry of the Environment, Bumjumbura (tel: 21-649; fax: 28-902).

Ministry of Finance, Bumjumbura (tel: 17-918; fax: 23-827).

Ministry of Foreign Affairs and Co-operation, Bumjumbura (tel: 17-595; fax: 26-313).

Ministry of Health, Bumjumbura (tel: 18-200; fax: 29-916).

Ministry of Human Rights, Law Reforms and Relations with the National Assembly, Bumjumbura (tel: 17-365; fax: 13-847).

Ministry of the Interior, Bumjumbura (tel: 12-480; fax: 23-904).

Ministry of Justice, Bumjumbura (tel: 10-595; fax: 22-148).

Ministry of Labour, Public Office and Professional Education, Bumjumbura (tel: 17-928; fax: 24-079).

Ministry of Peace Process, Bumjumbura (tel: 19-457; fax: 19-459).

Ministry of Planning, Development and Reconstruction, Bumjumbura (tel: 19-079; fax: 24-193).

Ministry of Public Works and Equipment, Bumjumbura (tel: 19-646; fax: 26-840).

Ministry of Repatriation of Displaced Persons, Bumjumbura (tel: 18-184; fax: 18-201).

Ministry of Social Action and Promotion of Women, Bumjumbura (tel: 10-376; fax: 16-102).

Ministry of Transport, Post and Telecommunications, Bumjumbura (tel: 10-462; fax: 26-900).

Ministry of Youth Sport and Culture, Bumjumbura (tel: 16-729; fax: 26-231).

Office of the President, Bumjumbura (tel: 17-806; fax: 26-424).

Internet sites
Africa Business Network: http://www.ifc.org/abn

AllAfrica.com: http://www.allafrica.com

African Development Bank: http://www.afdb.org

Africa Online: http://www.africaonline.com

Harambee Afrika (UK business club for traders with east, central and southern Africa: http://www.harambee.co.uk

Mbendi AfroPaedia (information on companies, countries, industries and stock exchanges in Africa): http://mbendi.co.za

Cameroon

Jonathan Derrick

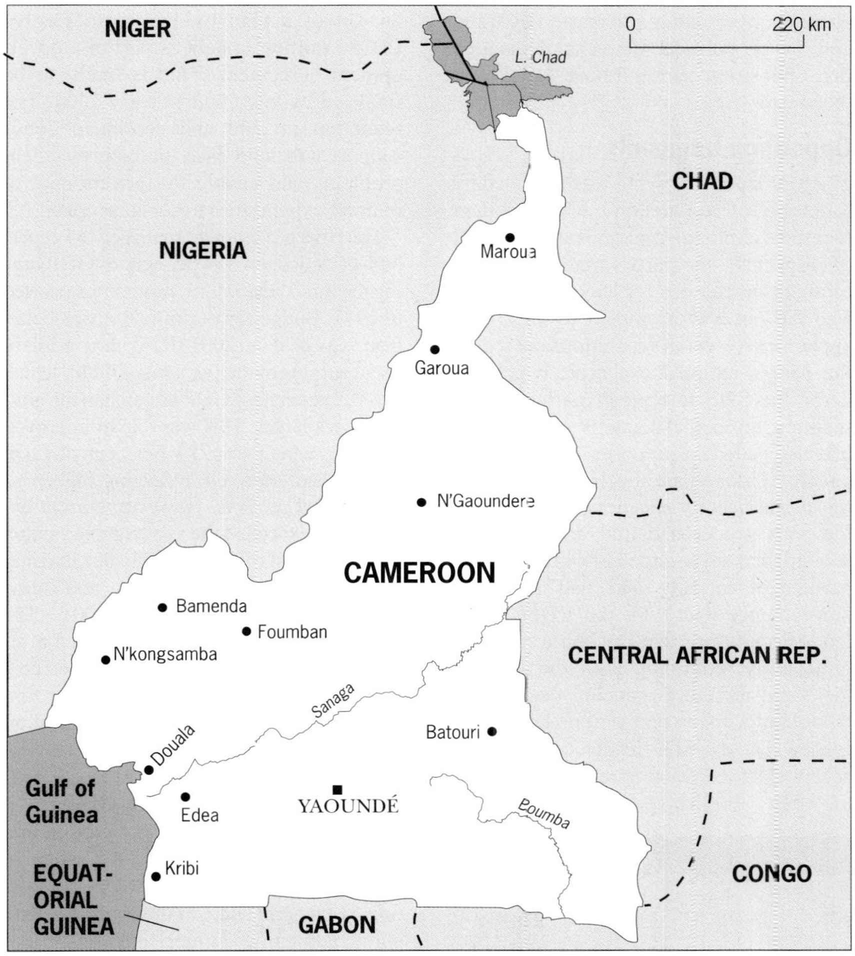

Cameroon's traditionally quiet and stable political situation began to deteriorate in 2001 and 2002 as a new wave of political militancy sprung up in opposition to the rule of President Paul Biya. Discontent between Anglophones and Francophones continued to simmer.

In October 2001, the Southern Cameroons National Council (SCNC) organised a series of mass demonstrations, which often turned violent, to co-incide with celebrations of the reunification of former British Southern Cameroons with the former French Cameroun. For over a decade, discontent has grown among the Anglophones of the ex-British territory, who widely feel themselves to be a distinctive minority suffering discrimination and marginalisation and resent centralised control from Yaoundé. Many have called for a return to the federal system, which existed from 1961–1972, led by the SCNC)

The SCNC organised demonstrations on the fortieth anniversary of reunification at Kumbo, which led to several people being killed by the police. Calls for outright independence were repeated. The self-proclaimed 'president' of Southern Cameroons, Frederick Ebong Alobwede, who had been in exile since being released from prison in March 2001, formed a breakaway 'government' in July.

KEY FACTS

Official name: République du Cameroun (Republic of Cameroon)

Head of State: President Paul Biya (re-elected 12 Oct 1997)

Head of government: Prime Minister Peter Mafany Musonge (since Sep 1996)

Ruling party: Coalition: Rassemblement Démocratique du Peuple Camerounais (RDPC) (Cameroon People's Democratic Movement) and Union Nationale pour la Démocratie et le Progrès (UNDP) (National Union for Democracy and Progress)

Area: 475,442 square km

Population: 15.20 million (2001)

Capital: Yaoundé

Official language: French, English

Currency: CFA franc (CFAf) = 100 centimes (Communauté Financière Africaine (African Financial Community) franc)

Exchange rate: CFAf629.73 per US$ (Jan 2003); CFAf655.95 per euro (pegged from Jan 1999)

GDP per capita: US$559 (2001)

GDP real growth: 5.30% (2001)

Inflation: 4.50% (2001)

Oil production: 80,000 bpd (2001)

Balance of trade: US$512.00 million (2001)

Foreign debt: US$6.58 billion (2001)

Annual FDI: US$102.00 million (2001)

Nota

The elections of 30 June 2002 saw the Rassemblement Démocratique du Peuple Camerounais (PDPC) (Cameroon People's Democratic Movement), the leading party in the coalition government, increase its share of parliamentary seats. The Supreme Court ordered fresh elections in nine constituencies due to irregularities

Election debates reform

Calls for independence for Cameroon's two English-speaking provinces has raised the issue of political reform, with many French-speakers joining in calls for greater regional autonomy. The main opposition party, the Social Democratic Front/Front Social-Démocratique (SDF), led by Anglophone John Fru Ndi, led calls for devolution and won support in Douala, the country's biggest city, and some other Francophone areas. The growing tide of public support for federalism has come on the back of public discontent with what is widely seen as a corrupt and authoritarian political system. However, these feelings were not translated into a rise in support for the opposition.

The elections of June 2002 saw the ruling Rassemblement Démocratique du Peuple Camerounais (RDPC) (Cameroon People's Democratic Rally) increase its number of seats in the national assembly, while the SDF retained less than half the seats it had won in 1997. The Supreme Court ordered fresh elections for 17 seats due to electoral irregularities. The re-elections, in which the RDPC won 16 of the seats and the SDF just one, saw the ruling party's total number of seats increase to 149, compared to 116 five years before.

The SDF was reduced to just 22 seats, while the Union Démocratique du Cameroun (UDC) (Democratic Union of Cameroon) and the Union des Populations du Cameroun (UPC) (Cameroon Peoples' Union) secured five and three seats respectively. The Union Nationale pour la Démocratie et le Progrès (UNDP) (National Union for Democracy and Progress), a moderate Islamic party, won just one seat, down from 13 in 1997. The main reason for the UNDP's decline was its continuing alliance with the RDPC, which has made it deeply unpopular. The elections were boycotted by the SCNC, allowing the SDF to take 19 seats in the Anglophone regions. Opposition parties and international observers claimed the elections were unfair and marred by fraud and many political activists demanded that opposition parties refuse to take up their seats.

Opposition fragments

The SDF's poor showing was followed by a number of resignations, with dissident members citing internal divisions and lack of respect for the party's manifesto commitments as reasons for leaving the party. The fall-out was prompted by Fru Ndi's apparent betrayal of resolutions passed by the party's national executive which ordered the SDF to boycott parliamentary seats and municipal councils it had won. It had also called on supporters to take to the streets to 'denounce the irregularities' at the parliamentary elections. In contrast, the party leader had told councillors to take up their seats, ended a brief boycott of parliament in July and had signed a non-violence pact with the RDPC. This led to accusations that Fru Ndi was acting unilaterally, colluding with the government and therefore reducing the SDF to the role of a 'token opposition'. Dissidents argued that the SDF leader continued to accept electoral fraud in return for control of the English-speaking Northwest province, making it a parochial rump with no national representation.

KEY INDICATORS — Cameroon

	Unit	1996	1997	1998	1999	2000
Population	m	13.55	13.92	14.31	14.69	15.40
Gross domestic product (GDP)	US$bn	8.52	8.51	9.01	9.20	8.90
GDP per capita	US$	620	620	630	626	593
GDP real growth	%	5.0	5.1	4.8	4.4	4.2
Inflation	%	4.7	1.0	0.1	3.1	0.8
Oil output	'000 bpd	110.0	125.0	105.0	95.0	88.0
Exports (fob) (goods)	US$m	1,760.0	1,970.0	1,870.0	1,780.0	2,124.0
Imports (fob) (goods)	US$m	1,200.0	1,350.0	1,500.0	1,500.0	1,538.0
Balance of trade	US$m	700.0	621.0	370.0	280.0	586.0
Current account	US$m	-217.0	-121.0	-218.0	-393.0	-153.0
Foreign debt	US$bn	9.5	9.3	9.6	9.1	9.9
Total reserves minus gold	US$m	2.8	0.9	1.3	4.4	212.0
Foreign exchange	US$m	2.1	0.3	0.6	1.1	203.6
Exchange rate	per US$	511.55	583.67	589.95	615.70	711.98

A debt-ridden economy

In September 2002, the IMF granted a disbursement of around US$21 million under the PRGF arrangement, while the Belgian government cancelled US$62.8 million of debt and rescheduled another US$15.5 million for a period of 40 years. This came on top of a plan by France to forgive US$80 million in debt as part of a development agreement. This is likely to be finalised by late 2003 or early 2004. The reduction in debt and continued donor support will help ease the country's debt problems and enable the government to redirect expenditure to social services.

The Biya government managed to keep its budget deficits to 3–4 per cent of GDP during the three year reform programme started in 1997. Budgetary performance was better than expected in 2001/02, with a primary fiscal surplus of 4.8 per cent of GDP, which was 0.2 per cent of GDP larger than the government's target. This was due to improved revenue, which was 0.3 per cent of GDP higher than expected, reflecting higher oil and non-oil receipts. However, current expenditure exceeded the government's target by 0.2 per cent of GDP, mainly due to rising wage costs and higher transfers and subsidies during July–September 2001. The 2002/03 fiscal programme envisaged a reduction in oil revenue from 4.9 per cent GDP in 2001/02 to 3.3 per cent, due to a modest fall in oil prices and a decline in oil production caused by the depletion of reserves. Non-oil government revenue is projected at 16 per cent of non-oil GDP.

Cameroon's privatisation programme got a significant boost in 2002 when in February, the government sold a controlling 51 per cent stake in the country's state phone company, Camtel, to a consortium of two Tunisian operators, Tunisie Telecoms and Sotetel, which are both owned by the Tunisian government. Camtel's privatisation had been stalled in 2001 due to protracted and ultimately fruitless negotiations with a consortium led by South Africa's Telecel. In July 2002, the World Bank pledged US$21.39 million to support the privatisation of Cameroon's railways. The privatisation of Cameroon Airlines was abandoned in July 2001 after investors refused to take on the company's debt, which had amounted to CFAf58 billion (US$78 million).

In the long-term, the government hopes to significantly increase non-oil revenues by reforming a number of areas within fiscal policy. One of these is the taxation system. With the technical assistance of the IMF and the EU, the authorities intend to broaden the tax base, universally enforce tax provisions and obligations, rationalise controls, simplify procedures and improve assistance to taxpayers. This will involve an increased allocation of staff and the adoption of a new code on tax procedures. Other areas which will be reformed are forestry licensing and customs procedures. In order to promote transparency and efficiency, the government plans to prepare comprehensive quarterly reports on the financial and physical operations of key ministries.

Tight fiscal policy is set to remain the focus of government macroeconomic policies for the foreseeable future. The fact that major international creditors such as the World Bank and IMF are offering Cameroon guidelines within which to frame its fiscal policy helps add a greater degree of legitimacy to difficult policy decisions. The government's commitment to widening the tax base, improving tax revenues and promoting greater transparency in public sector accounts are all positive moves which are likely to be rewarded by sounder public accounts in 2003.

Pipe dreams become reality

In June 2001, arrangements for financing of the Chad-Cameroon pipeline were completed, with large loans granted by the World Bank. This ensured that the 1,050km pipeline, subjected to delays and controversy for years, would be built from Chad's Doba oilfields to a terminal at Kribi in Cameroon. The project, due to be completed in 2003, will add 3 per cent to annual budget revenue.

The combined cost of the pipeline construction and the field development is expected to reach US$3.5 billion, although these costs are likely to be easily recovered if the 300 planned wells come to produce the one billion barrels of crude which the consortium is hoping for. Cameroon estimates that it will make US$0.46 from every barrel of oil which transits the pipeline. The project aims to pump oil from Doba in southern Chad to offshore facilities in Cameroon and is likely to begin production by 2004. It is expected that Cameroon will receive US$500 million in pipeline transit fees, taxes and dividends and another US$400 million in economic activity.

Following widespread criticism of the pipeline's effect on the environment, the project was adjusted to take account of public concerns. The pipeline, most of which will be on Cameroonian territory, will be buried. It will also not make any resettlement necessary and farmers' access to their land will only be interrupted briefly. Compensation will be given for fruit trees destroyed during construction and any lost income.

Outlook

Although President Biya's domination of Cameroon's political scene during the past two decades has contributed to a relatively stable political and economic environment, pressures are building on the government to facilitate further political reform. Biya's ability to temper his repression in dealing with English-speaking secessionists in the south and his willingness to incorporate a greater degree of transparency in the political process will be closely watched by opposition groups and international observers alike. However, continued economic growth is likely to lend legitimacy to the policies of the president and his ruling party, and the inability of many opposition parties to present themselves as viable political alternatives rather than opportunistic groupings with primarily economic interests suggests that political change is unlikely to be dramatic in 2003.

Risk assessment

Economic	Improving
Political	Poor
Regional stability	Improving

COUNTRY PROFILE

Historical profile

1470s Portuguese mariners arrived and gave Cameroon its name. Having found what they thought to be shrimps ('camaroes') in the main river, they named it *Rio dos Camaroes*.
1884 Germany established the protectorate of Kamerun.
1916 The German governor was ousted by the Allies in the First World War.
The post-war League of Nations gave mandates for four-fifths of the territory to France, and the remainder to Britain. After the Second World War the League of Nations mandates were converted to United Nations (UN) trust territories.
1960 French East Cameroon gained its independence.
1961 British West Cameroon gained its independence.
1972 A unified state was formed, with the Union Nationale Camerounaise (UNC) (Cameroonian National Union) dominating both the executive and legislative branches.
1982 Prime Minister Paul Biya became President after the resignation of President Ahidjo.
1985 Biya renamed the ruling party the Rassemblement Démocratique du Peuple Camerounais (RDPC) (Cameroon People's Democratic Movement), and introduced a number of political reforms which were largely viewed as cosmetic.
1990 A multi-party political system was legalised. Although this change marked the gradual opening of the Cameroonian political system, subsequent elections were marred by irregularities and accusations of electoral fraud.
1997 President Paul Biya was re-elected. The elections were boycotted by the three main opposition parties after their complaints about the handling of voter registration were ignored, allowing Biya to win with 92 per cent of the vote.
1999 English-speaking secessionists in the south announced a breakaway republic.
2000 Judge Frederick Ebong Alobwede was appointed 'president' of the self-proclaimed Federal Republic of Southern Cameroon. Several secessionists were arrested.
2001 Demonstrations calling for decentralisation of power were banned and several southern Cameroon separatists were killed.
2002 Results of 30 Jun 2002 elections: the ruling RDPC increased its seats from 116 to 133; Front Social-Démocratique (FSD) (Social Democratic Front) won 21 seats, down from 43; the Union Démocratique du Cameroun (UDC) (Democratic Union of Cameroon) retained its five seats; the Union Nationale pour la Démocratie et le Progrès (UNDP) (National Union for Democracy and Progress) won only one seat, down from 68 in 1997. Although the Supreme Court ordered fresh legislative elections in nine constituencies because of irregularities, to be held within two months, the 163 other legislators are to take up their seats on 30 July when the 2002–07 parliament holds its first session.

Political structure

Constitution

The constitution was promulgated in 1972 and revised in 1975 and 1996. The main provisions of the 1996 revision were for a more decentralised government, the creation of a unicameral national assembly (Assemblée Nationale), and the extension of the president's term of office from five years to seven, at the same time allowing him to run for a fourth consecutive term of office in 1997.

Form of state

Unitary republic

The executive

Executive power is vested in the president, who appoints a cabinet. The president serves a seven-year term. A prime minister, who acts as head of government, is appointed by the president. The president names and dismisses cabinet members and judges, ratifies treaties, heads the armed forces, controls legislation and can rule by decree.

National legislature
Legislative power is held by the 180-member unicameral Assemblée Nationale (National Assembly), elected for a five-year term.

Legal system
Cameroon's legal system is based on French civil law with common law influences. The country has a Supreme Court, the judges of which are appointed by the president. Provisions in the 1996 constitution for judicial independence have not been put into force. Cameroon does not accept the compulsory jurisdiction of the International Court of Justice, but does belong to the International Court of Arbitration of the International Chamber of Commerce.

Last elections
30 June 2002 (parliamentary); October 1997 (presidential)

Next elections
2004 (presidential)

Political parties

Ruling party
Coalition: Rassemblement Démocratique du Peuple Camerounais (RDPC) (Cameroon People's Democratic Movement) and Union Nationale pour la Démocratie et le Progrès (UNDP) (National Union for Democracy and Progress).

Main opposition party
Front Social-Démocratique/Social Democratic Front (SDF); Union Démocratique du Cameroun (UDC) (Democratic Union of Cameroon); Union Nationale pour la Démocratie et le Progrès (UNDP) (National Union for Democracy and Progress).

Population

15.4 million (2000)
The population growth rate was 2.7 per cent annually between 1994–2000, with projected annual growth at 2.1 per cent between 1998–2015.
Population density: 29 inhabitants per square km. Urban population: 49 per cent (1994–2000).

Ethnic make-up
Cameroon has a highly diversified population comprising some 200 ethnic groups, including Cameroon Highlanders (31 per cent), Equatorial Bantu (19 per cent) and Kirdi (11 per cent). There are about 200,000 Europeans in the country, mainly French speakers.

Religions
Indigenous beliefs are practiced by 40 per cent of the population, another 40 per cent are Christian, and 20 per cent are Muslim.

Education

The percentage of the school-age population in primary school enrollment was 78 per cent in 1997, compared to 27 per cent for secondary school and only 4 per cent for tertiary education. The adult illiteracy rate was 26 per cent in 1999.

Health

Life expectancy in Cameroon in 2000 was 51 years, and the infant mortality rate was 77 per 1,000 live births. Child malnutrition (proportion of children under 5) was 22 per cent in the period 1994–2000. There were 26 hospital beds and one physician per 10,000 people in 1998. Total expenditure on healthcare was 5.0 per cent of GDP in 1998, of which only 1 per cent was public expenditure. The total fertility rate was estimated at 4.88 children per woman in 2000. Cameroon has a high incidence of HIV cases, with 4.89 per cent of adults HIV positive in 1997.

Welfare

Cameroon's social insurance system provides cover for old-age pension, disability pension, sickness and maternity benefits, work injuries and family allowances.

Main cities

Douala (commercial centre, population 1.3 million), Yaoundé (capital, one million), Edea (80,000), Garoua (100,000), Buea (21,000), Limbe (formerly Victoria, 60,000), Nkongsamba, Bamenda, Bafoussam, Marona, Ebolowa, Kribi, Ngaoundere

Languages spoken

French and English are the official languages. 24 major African language groups including Bamileke, Ewondo, Bassa and Bamoun are spoken. Around 80 per cent of the population speak French as a second language (francophone Cameroon) and 20 per cent speak English as a second language (anglophone – formerly British West Cameroon).

Official language/s
French, English

Media

Press
Dailies: Privatisation of the media has steadily increased the size of the press over the years, as no authorisation is needed to start a newspaper. The official state-owned daily paper *Cameroon Tribune* (French) is also published in English twice weekly. Other English and French-language dailies include *Le Messager, Cameroun Today, Camnet Actualites* and *Wagne*.
Weeklies: Weeklies include *Socialist Chronicle, Star Headlines, Weekly Post, Temps, Perspectives hebdo, Le Phare, Politiks, Cameroon Post, Cigale, Héraut* and *Generation*.
Business: Business news is carried by a bi-weekly publication *La Dépeche économique*.
Periodicals: Monthly periodicals include *L'Aube des temps nouveaux, Contact magazine, La Démocrate, Dikalo, Effets du septennat, La Foi qui sauve, Le Météo, Le Devoir, Le Journal de Douala, Le Proces, Reforme, Revelation* and *Le Météo*.

Broadcasting
From Yaoundé, Cameroon Radio and Television Corporation (CRTV) operates a radio service in French, English and local languages (there are independent stations in all provincial centres), and the television network covers most of the country. Service is financed mainly by commercial advertising with some state input.

Advertising
There is a wide range of mediums for advertising in Cameroon. Radio and television airtime is available from state broadcasters, as well as on Gabon's 'Africa Number One' radio station. Cinema audiences in Yaoundé, Douala and Bafoussa can also be reached. Billboard space, once a state monopoly, has been liberalised. The Cameroonian chamber of commerce organises an annual trade fair, and the thriving independent press offers an alternative to advertising in the official newspapers.

Economy

The government's economic policy is guided by the three-year poverty reduction and growth facility (PRGF), agreed with the IMF in December 2000. This programme called for reforms to the government budget process, the privatisation of state enterprises and a reorganisation of Cameroon's inefficient port system. As a result of having satisfied the principal criteria, Cameroon was awarded debt service relief by the IMF and the World Bank's International Development Association (IDA). The reduced annual debt service obligations are freeing some US$100 million per year between 2000–03 for expenditure on health care, primary education, HIV prevention and other critical social services.
A number of factors may potentially hamper growth. The domestic market is still fragile due to relatively weak purchasing power and internal demand. Domestic companies are uncompetitive and investment has been sluggish. Other principal shortcomings are the country's top-heavy civil service and endemic corruption.

External trade

Exports
Cameroon's export earnings have slumped in recent years. This is due to

both a reduction in demand and weak world prices for Cameroon's principal commodities. Crude oil and petroleum products represent Cameroon's principal export commodity, accounting for a quarter of export earnings. Other goods include lumber, cocoa beans, aluminium, coffee, cotton and bananas.
Main destinations: The country's export destinations include Italy (typically 25 per cent of the total), Spain (20 per cent), France (16 per cent), the Netherlands (7 per cent) and Germany (6 per cent).

Imports

Cameroonian imports consist mainly of semi-processed products and industrial outputs, machinery and food products. There is also some importing of light crude oil for the country's refineries. Imports consist principally of machines and electrical equipment, transport equipment, fuel and food. Import volume has been constrained because of the strong growth of domestic industries (especially in food processing) which are offering cheaper alternatives to expensive imported goods.
Main sources: France (typically 28 per cent of the total), Nigeria (8 per cent), Italy, (7 per cent), the Benelux countries (7 per cent), the USA (8 per cent) and Germany (6 per cent).

Agriculture

In order to broaden the country's economic base and increase the value added of domestic production, the Cameroonian government is encouraging development of its full agricultural potential. Agricultural production as a percentage of GDP has been steadily increasing over the last 20 years reaching around 45 per cent of national output in 2001. Some 70 per cent of Cameroon's labour force is employed in the agricultural sector, although only 2 per cent of Cameroon's land area is used for permanent crops. Principal crops include cocoa, coffee, bananas, cotton and oil palms. Virtually all food requirements are met by local production. Most agricultural production is in the hands of smallholders, with the exception of rubber and palm, which are run under the plantation system.

Forestry

Around 70 per cent of Cameroon's land area is covered by trees. About 6 per cent of forests are officially protected. In 1990–2000, forest cover declined by an average of 222,000 hectares per year, or 0.9 per cent. Cameroon is one of Africa's leading producers and exporters of tropical logs and sawn timber. Cameroon also produces and exports veneer and plywood. Wood is an important fuel source in Cameroon.

Industry and manufacturing

The industrial sector accounts for around a fifth of GDP, a proportion which has been in steady decline since the late 1980s, contracting by an average of 3 per cent per year since 1990. The sector employs around 10 per cent of the workforce. Industrial output accounts for 25 per cent of Cameroon's exports.
The government is a major participant in the industrial sector, mainly through the Société Nationale d'Investissement (SNI) (National Investment Agency). The emphasis of policy is on reducing the sector's dependence on imports, decentralisation away from Yaoundé and Douala, increased local participation in small- and medium-sized enterprises (SMEs) and privatisation. The Technical Commission for the Rehabilitation of Public Enterprises oversees privatisation and restructuring of all state-owned companies.

Tourism

There is huge potential for tourism in Cameroon although development has been slow due to expensive air fares, the high cost of tourist visas, limited tourist infrastructure and the relatively high prices of hotels. A Tourist Development Plan is being undertaken in co-operation with the World Tourism Organisation (WTO). The government has devised a special investment code to encourage private investors. The deregulation of air traffic should help reduce air fares.

Environment

Cameroon's tropical forest is the second largest in the world but it is being exploited at a faster rate than is sustainable. Concessions to exploit the forests are awarded through a bidding system, with companies winning by offering high inducements to the officials. There is little monitoring of forest management. As the forests have become more accessible, poachers are shooting antelope, chimpanzees and gorillas, and selling them.

Mining

The mining sector accounts for around 10 per cent of GDP and employs 2 per cent of the workforce. Bauxite deposits of some 1,100 million tonnes at Adamaoua Province have been identified but remain unexploited, although the upturn in world aluminium prices has encouraged Société des Bauxitese de Cameroun to begin mining operations. There are deposits of iron ore at Kribi (reserves estimated at 197 million tonnes), and potential reserves of gold, diamonds, uranium, rutile, industrial clays and low-grade nickel and cobalt. Tin is mined on a very small scale. Investment by large mining companies is needed to exploit underground riches.

Hydrocarbons

Oil

Cameroon is sub-Saharan Africa's fifth-largest oil producer with crude oil production of up to 100,000 barrels per day (bpd). The Société Nationale des Hydrocarbures (SNH), Cameroon's national oil company formed in 1980, manages Cameroon's oil sector. Petroleum exploration began in the 1950s, and a number of important reserves were found in the Rio Del Rey basin in the 1970s. The Bakassi peninsula, located in the Gulf of Guinea, is thought to contain significant oil reserves, and is at the centre of political tension between Cameroon, Nigeria and Equatorial Guinea, all of which claim a right to explore the area.
The 1,050km Chad-Cameroon pipeline, the construction of which is scheduled for completion by the end of 2003, is the most important recent development in the sector. The combined cost of the pipeline construction and the field development is expected to reach US$3.5 billion, although these costs are likely to be easily recovered if the 300 planned wells come to produce the one billion barrels of crude which the consortium is hoping for. Cameroon estimates that it will make US$0.46 from every barrel of oil which transits the pipeline. There has, however, been strong opposition to the building of the pipeline from environmental and human rights groups, and the World Bank has set stringent conditions for its part of the financing.
Cameroon has recently revised its laws concerning oil and gas exploration in order to attract more investors. These changes include a fixed division of profits for joint venture projects (with 40 per cent going to the outside contractor), as well as tax breaks and other incentives for the further exploration and development of marginal and deepwater offshore fields.

Gas

Cameroon's estimated gas reserves are of 109.2 billion cubic metres (3.9 trillion cubic feet), although thus far the sector is only at the early stages of development. The largest project to date involves the Canadian firm Ocelot Energy, which is developing offshore gas fields in an agreement with the Société Nationale des Hydrocarbures.

Energy

Cameroon's total electricity generation capacity is estimated at 817MW, nearly 90 per cent of which is hydroelectric. The country has massive hydroelectric potential. Production from the Edéa Dam complex, Lagdo near Garoua, and Song-Loulou generates enough to meet 85 per cent of needs. All electricity is produced by the state-owned Société Nationale d'Electricité (SONEL).

Banking

The banking sector comprises nine banks, all privately owned. The sector is overcoming a period of crisis and the government has instituted reforms to bolster the viability of the country's banks.

Central bank

Banque des Etats de l'Afrique Centrale

Main financial centre

Douala

Time

GMT plus one hour

Geography

Cameroon lies on the west coast of Africa, with Nigeria to the west, Chad and the Central African Republic to the east, and the Republic of Congo, Equatorial Guinea and Gabon to the south. The country can be divided into four main regions. The coastal plain is tropical but tempered by the effects of the sea. The tropical plateau in the south is heavily forested and cut through by a number of rivers flowing west into the Bight of Biafra or south-east to join the River Zaire. The Adamawa and Bamenda highlands rise to 2,500 metres and are drier and cooler than the forest areas. The highlands are volcanic in origin, and include Mount Cameroon (4,070 metres).The savannah grasslands to the north lie between Nigeria and Chad, and stretch northwards to Lake Chad.

Climate

In the north the single wet season is between April and September, and there is a dry season during the rest of the year.
It is tropical in the south with fairly constant average temperatures throughout the year, ranging between 18 degrees Celsius (C) at night and 30–32 degrees C during the day. In the south rainfall is distributed throughout the year with two wet seasons and two dry seasons.

Dress codes

Tropical clothes are advised, with warmer clothes required for the higher altitudes. Lightweight raincoats are recommended for the rainy season.

Entry requirements

Passports

Passports are required by all and should be valid for at least six months upon arrival.

Visa

Visas, which are required by all visitors except nationals of the Central African Republic, Chad, Congo, Equatorial Guinea and Gabon, act as temporary entry permits. Exit permits are required by all. In addition to a visa, entry into Cameroon requires a return ticket. Travellers arriving without a visa may be asked to take the next available flight from the country if their country of origin has a Cameroonian embassy. Airport visas are generally available to citizens of states without diplomatic relations with Cameroon.

Currency advice/regulations

Foreign currency import is unlimited, but amounts must be declared. Local currency import is also unlimited, but export is limited to CFAf20,000 (approximately US$30) without official authorisation. Traveller's cheques are accepted on a limited basis.

Prohibited imports

Pornographic materials, illegal drugs, weapons and ammunitions may not be brought into Cameroon. Alcohol and other spirits (maximum 30 bottles) should be sent separately.
An invoice must accompany all furniture and electrical appliances to prove that they are more than six months old. Newer items are subject to customs duties and taxes. Home computers do not qualify as personal effects, and are subject to customs duties and taxes.

Health (for visitors)

Mandatory precautions

Visitors require an international certificate of vaccination against yellow fever, dated within the last 10 years, as well as cholera immunisation. Pets entering Cameroon need a health certificate from a veterinarian.

Advisable precautions

The principal health hazards for visitors to Cameroon are malaria and HIV. Rabies and bilharzia also occur, and the necessary precautions against these diseases should be taken. Vaccination against tetanus, typhoid, polio, meningitis, and hepatitis 'A' and 'B' are all advisable. Swimming in fresh water should be avoided, but well chlorinated swimming pools should be safe. Bottled water is readily available. Milk is unpasteurised and should be boiled; vegetables should be cooked and fruit should be peeled. Medical care is adequate, but can be expensive.

Hotels

Good hotel accommodation is available in main centres. Advisable to book in advance, and confirmation should be obtained from the selected hotel in writing. Service charges usually added to bill.

Credit cards

There is limited acceptance of the major credit cards only.

Public holidays

Fixed dates

1 Jan, 11 Feb (Youth Day), 1 May (Labour Day), 20 May (National Day), 15 Aug (Assumption), 25 Dec (Christmas Day).

Variable dates

Good Friday, Easter Monday, Ascension, Eid al-Fitr, Eid al-Adha.

Working hours

Different hours are kept in the French-speaking (including Yaoundé and Douala) and English-speaking areas (south-west and north-west frontier areas) of Cameroon.

Banking

French-speaking areas: 0800–1200 and 1515–1630 (Mon–Fri).
English-speaking areas: 1800–1330 (Mon–Fri).

Business

French-speaking areas:0730–1200 and 1430–1800 (Mon–Fri).
English-speaking areas: 0730–1500 (Mon–Fri); 1730–1200 (Sat).

Government

French-speaking areas: 0730–1200 and 1430–1800 (Mon–Fri).
English-speaking areas: 0730–1500 (Mon–Fri); 1730–1200 (Sat).

Shops

French-speaking areas: 0700/0800–1230 and 1430/1500–1830/1900 (Mon–Sat).
English-speaking areas: 0700/0800–1200 and 1430/1530–1830/1900 (Mon–Sat).

Post offices:

French-speaking areas: 0800–1200 and 1400–1700 (Mon–Fri); 0800–1200 (Sat)
English-speaking areas: 0800–1200 and 1430–1700 (Mon–Fri).

Telecommunications

Telephone/fax

Dialling code for Cameroon: IDD access code + 237 followed by subscriber's number. There are no area codes.
The modernisation of the telecommunications sector is under way with cellular telephone, satellite communications and digital telephone fronts. The national network extended throughout the country.

Postal services

Airmail service can take two or more weeks. Surface mail is irregular and slow. Mail to businesses, government offices and individuals is generally sent to a *boîte postale* (post office box). Many businesses and international organisations resort to express couriers such as DHL and Federal Express.

Mobile phones

Mobile phone communications are improving; French and South African companies set up cellular telephone businesses in 1999.
MTN Cameroun Ltd went live on a GSM 900 network in February 2000, and covers principally Youndé and Douala. The Société Camerounaise de Mobiles, also on a GSM 900 network, went live in January 2000, and has roaming agreements with the French networks SFR, France Telecom and Bouygues Telecom, as well as with Swisscom from Switzerland and SIM of the Ivory Coast.

Internet/e-mail
Camtel, the state telephone company, began providing internet services in 1997. There are now several other internet service providers in the market. There are Internet cafes in Yaoundé and Douala, linked via Africa's PDM network to the World-Wide-Web. However, in January 2000 there were only five Internet hosts under the Cameroonian (.cm) domain.

Electricity supply
220V AC, 50 cycles; plugs are of the two-pin round type.

Social customs/useful tips
Handshaking is the customary form of greeting. Business is conducted primarily in English and French.
If there is no service charge included in a bill, gratuities in hotels and restaurants are up to 10 per cent.
Care should be taken to respect Islamic and other local religious practices and conventions, and visitors should be aware of restrictions on food and drink in Muslim areas, particularly during the Islamic fasting period of Ramadan.
Visitors should take care when photographing. It is considered polite to ask permission to photograph traditional dances, and it is not advisable to take pictures of official buildings or military installations.

Security
Muggings and pickpocketing have increased in recent years, mainly in the large cities, and it is unwise to carry valuables or large amounts of cash in the street. Bandit attacks are known to occur along the N1 highway which runs through Cameroon's Far North Province between Nigeria and Chad. Care should also be taken at the international airports, where there is an abundance of unofficial 'porters'.

Getting there
Air
National airline: Cameroon Airlines (Camair)
International airport/s: Douala International (DLA), is 5km from the city and has a duty-free shop, bar, restaurant, buffet, bank, post office and shops.
Other airport/s: Yaoundé (YAO), 4km from the capital city, and Garoua International (GOU), 6km from the city, also accept international flights.
Airport tax: None.
Surface
Road: Road access is possible from Nigeria, Chad, Gabon, Equatorial Guinea and the Central African Republic. However, these routes are considered rough and may become impassable during rainy seasons. Bush taxis and minibuses are available. There have been many bandit attacks along the N1 highway which runs through Cameroon Far North Province between Nigeria and Chad.
Rail: Rail access is available from N'Gaoundal and Belabo in the Central African Republic.
Water: There are two boats a day from Nigeria (Calabar) across the Cross River to Cameroon (Oron), and from Ikang (Nigeria) there are speedboats to Ekonco Titi. Douala offers more freights links with Europe than other Central African ports. Cameroon Shipping Lines (Camshiplines) maintains an office in Paris.
Main port/s: Cameroon's main port is Douala. Other ports are at Limbe, Kribi and Garoua (on the River Bénoué, which handle river trade during the dry season.

Getting about
National transport
Air: Cameroon airlines operates domestic services between the main cities, including several daily flights between Yaoundé and Douala. Early arrival at the airport terminal is advisable, as overbookings are common. However, air services are generally efficient and certainly the fastest means of travelling within Cameroon.
Road: Cameroon's road network totals 31,800km of roads. Surfaced roads run between main centres although there are no tarmac road links between Yaoundé and Ngaoundéré. Major routes are from Douala to Limbé, Buea, Bafoussam, Sangmelima, Bamenda and Yaoundé (all-weather road). Most other roads are unsurfaced and are often impassable during rainy season.
Buses: There are few fixed schedules and routes outside main centres are subject to suspension in the rainy season.
Rail: The track network extends 1,168km. Regifercam (Cameroon Railways) links Kumba, Douala, Yaoundé and Ngaoundéré. An overnight service runs from Yaoundé to Ngaoundéré (12 hours). Second-class travel is cheap but uncomfortable. Sleeping facilities are available on some trains. There is an express three-hour service between Yaoundé and Douala with good facilities.
City transport
Taxis: Taxis are not metered but have a minimum fare and fixed prices; long journeys and daily hire should be negotiated; a 10 per cent tip is optional. There are taxis from the airport to Douala city centre.
Car hire
Chauffeur- or self-driven cars are available in Yaoundé and Douala, but can be expensive. An international driving licence is required.

BUSINESS DIRECTORY

Telephone area codes
The international direct dialling code (IDD) for Cameroon is +237 followed by the subscriber's number.

Useful telephone numbers
Police: 17.
Fire: 18.
Ambulance: 23-40-20.

Chambers of Commerce
Chambre d'Agriculture, d'Elevage et des Forêts du Cameroun, Parc Repiquet, BP 287, Yaoundé (tel: 223-885).

Chambre de Commerce, d'Industrie et des Mines: BP 4011, place du Gouvernement, Douala (tel: 424-888, 423-690); BP 36, Yaoundé (tel: 224-776); BP 59, Garoua (tel: 271-177); BP 211, Limbe (tel: 334-230); BP 944, Bafoussam (tel: 441-344); BP 551, Bamenda (tel: 361-820).

Banking
Amity Bank Cameroon, PO Box 2705, Douala (tel: 432-055; fax: 432-046).

Banque Internationale pour le Commerce et l'Industrie du Cameroun (BICIC), PO Box 1925, Avenue du Général-de-Gaulle, Douala (tel: 428-431, 420-001; fax: 424-184, 424-116).

Commercial Bank of Cameroon, PO Box 4004, Douala (tel: 420-202; fax: 433-802).

First Investment Bank; PO Box 13276, Douala (tel: 431-304; fax: 428-423).

International Bank of Africa-Cameroon, PO Box 3300, Douala (tel: 428-422; fax: 428-423).

Société Générale de Banques au Cameroun, PO Box 4042, 78 Rue Joss, Douala (tel: 427-010, 427-004; fax: 430-353).

Standard Chartered Bank Cameroon, PO Box 1784, Boulevard de la Liberté, Douala (tel: 424-191; fax: 422-789).

Central bank
Banque des États de l'Afrique Centrale, PO Box 1917, Rue du Docteur Jamot, Yaounde, Cameroun (tel: 234-030, 234-060; fax: 233-329).

Travel information

Cameroon Airlines, Littoral BP 4092, 3 Avenue General de Gaulle, Douala (tel: 422-525, 424-949; fax: 422-487, 423-459).

Douala International Airport, BP 3131, Douala (tel: 423-630, 423-577; fax: 423-758).

Société Camerounaise de Tourisme (Socatour), BP 7138, Yaoundé (tel: 233-219).

Ministries

Ministry of Agriculture, Yaoundé (tel: 234-085, 225-166, 231-190).

Ministry of Communications, Yaoundé (tel: 234-075; 223-155, 233-974).

Ministry of External relations, Yaoundé (tel: 220-133).

Ministry of Economy and Finance, BP 18, Yaoundé (tel: 234-000, 232-299).

Ministry of Environment and Forestry, BP 14276, Yaoundé (tel: 229-483, 221-225).

Ministry of Industrial and Commercial Development, Yaoundé (tel: 234-040, 225-085).

Ministry of Culture, Yaoundé (tel: 223-155, 233-974).

Ministry of Livestock, Fisheries and Animal Industries, Yaoundé (tel: 223-311, 220-443).

Ministry of Mines, Water and Energy, Yaoundé (tel: 233-404).

Ministry of Post and Telecommunications, Yaoundé (tel: 234-016; fax: 223-497).

Ministry of Public Works and Transport, Yaoundé (tel: 232-236).

Ministry of Tourism, Yaoundé (tel: 223-353, 235-258; fax: 221-295).

Other useful addresses

British Embassy, Avenue Winston Churchill, BP 547, Yaoundé (tel: 220-545, 220-796; fax: 220-148).

Cameroon Development Corporation (CDC), BP 28, Bota, Limbe (tel: 332-251).

Cameroon Embassy (USA), 2349 Massachusetts Avenue, NW, Washington DC 20008 (tel: 265-8790; fax: 387-3826; e-mail: info@ambacam-usa.org).

Cameroon Press and Publishing Co, BP 1218, Yaoundé (tel: 234-012).

Cameroon Telecommunications, BP 1571, Yaoundé (tel: 234-065; fax: 230-303).

Commission Technique de la Mission de Réhabilitation des Entreprises due Secteur Public et Parapublic, SNI Building, 9th Floor, Yaoundé (tel: 239-750; fax: 235-108).

Centre National d'Assistance aux Petites et Moyennes Entreprises, BP 1377, Douala (tel: 425-858).

Centre National du Commerce Exterieur (CNCE), BP 2461, Douala (tel: 421-685).

Department of Statistics, BP 25, Yaoundé (tel: 220-788).

EU Delegate, BP 847, Yaoundé (tel: 221-387, 222-149).

FEICOM (Special Equipment and Intercommunity Intervention Fund), BP 718 Yaoundé (tel/fax: 231-759).

National Tenders Board, Mballa II, 4th Floor, PO Box 6604, Yaoundé (tel: 201-803; fax: 206-042; e-mail: DGTC@GCNET.CM).

Office National du Café et du Cacao (ONCC), BP 378, Douala (tel: 426-776, 425-088) – sole marketing agency for cocoa, coffee, cotton, groundnuts, palm kernels.

Office de Radiodiffusion-Télévision Camerounaise (CRTV), BP 1634, Yaoundé (tel: 234-088).

Regifercam, BP 304, Douala (tel: 407-159; fax: 423-205).

Société Camerounaise des Depots Petroliers, Siège Social BP 2271, Douala (tel: 405-445; fax: 404-796).

Société de Développement du Cacao SODECAO), BP 1651, Yaoundé (tel: 220-991).

Société de Développement du Coton, Headquarters, BP 302, Garoua (tel: 271-556; fax: 272-068).

Société Nationale des Eaux du Cameroun, BP 157 Douala (tel: 433-066, 430-067; fax: 422-945).

Société Nationale de Raffinage, Cape Limboh, PO Box 365, Limbe (tel: 423-815, 423-817; fax: 423-444, 424-199).

Société Nationale d'Investissement, BP 423, Place de la Poste, Yaoundé (tel: 224-499, 224-422).

Société de Recouvrement des Créances du Cameroun, BP 11991, Yaoundé (tel: 223-739, 220-911, 230-067; fax: 233-833).

Sydicate of Wood Producers and Exporters (SPEBC), BP 2064, Douala (tel/fax: 428-617).

Syndicat des Commerçants, Importateurs et Exportateurs du Cameroun (SCIEC), BP 562, Douala (tel: 420-304).

Syndicat des Industriels du Cameroun, BP 1516, Yaoundé (tel: 222-468; BP 673, Douala (tel: 423-058).

Technical Committee for Privatisation and Liquidations, SNI Building, 9th Floro, Yaoundé (tel: 239-750; fax: 235-108).

US Embassy, rue Nachtigal, BP 817, Yaoundé (tel: 234-014).

Internet sites

Africa Business Network: http://www.ifc.org/abn

AllAfrica.com: http://allafrica.com

African Development Bank: http://www.afdb.org

Africa Online: http://www.africaonline.com

Harambee Afrika (UK business club for traders with east, central and southern Africa; includes annotated web resource list): http://www.harambee.co.uk

Mbendi AfroPaedia (information on companies, countries, industries and stock exchanges in Africa): http://mbendi.co.za

Federal Republic of Southern Cameroons: http://www.southerncameroons.org/

Cape Verde

Nicholas Awde & Fred J Hill

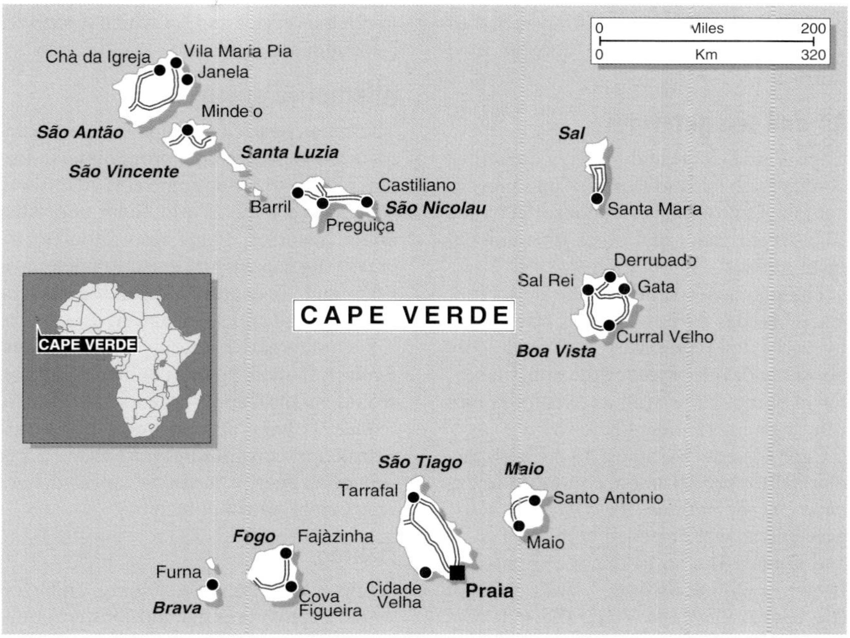

The start of 2001 saw closely fought elections and a change of government, a good example of the sturdiness of the democratic process in Cape Verde, which had gained independence from Portugal in 1975. In elections to the Asembleia Nacional (National Assembly), which took place on 14 January, the main opposition party, the socialist Partido Africano da Independência de Cabo Verde (PAICV) (African Party of Independence of Cape Verde) returned to power after ousting the Movimento Para a Democracia (MPD) (Movement for Democracy) which had been in power since 1991.

The PAICV won 40 out of the Asembleia's 72 seats, compared to the MPD's 30. Of the remaining parties in the contest, only the Democratic Alliance for Change (ADM) managed to win any seats – two in all.

The real drama, however, came with the presidential elections, which ended in near stalemate between the two principal candidates: Pedro Pires of the PAICV and former prime minister Carlos Veiga of the MPD. In the first round held on 11 February, Pires won 46 per cent compared to Veiga's 45 per cent of the vote. In the second round of presidential elections held on 25 February Pires scraped through with a majority of 164 votes.

Recounts narrowed the margin to a mere 17 votes. Veiga lodged a number of appeals in the Supreme Court citing electoral fraud, while Pires responded with his own assertions of foul play. Incredibly, the majority was further narrowed to 12 votes, but despite objecting right to the end, Veiga finally conceded defeat. Pires subsequently appointed José Mária Neves as his prime minister.

Economy on track

As 2001 drew to a close, Cape Verde convinced the IMF and other financial institutions that its economic reforms were back on track. During the previous year an economic and financial programme to restore financial stability, begun in 1998 and backed by a Stand-By-Arrangement, faltered after drought devastated the country's 1998/99 harvest and the government failed to address the resulting social hardships.

KEY FACTS

Official name: República de Cabo Verde (The Republic of Cape Verde)

Head of State: President Pedro Verona Rodrigues Pires (PAICV) (from Mar 2001)

Head of government: Prime Minister José Mária Neves (PAICV) (from Feb 2001)

Ruling party: Partido Africano da Independência de Cabo Verde (PAICV) (African Party of Independence of Cape Verde) (40 seats from Jan 2001)

Area: 4,033 square km (nine islands and 10 islets)

Population: 450,000 (2001)

Capital: Praia

Official language: Portuguese and Creole (national language)

Currency: Cape Verde escudo (CVEsc) = 100 centavos

Exchange rate: CVEsc108.95 per US$ (Jan 2003) (pegged CVEsc110.27 per euro)

GDP per capita: US$1,311 (2001)

GDP real growth: 3.00% (2001)

Inflation: 3.70% (2001)

Balance of trade: -US$205.00 million (2001)

Foreign debt: US$301.00 million (2001)

Visitor numbers: 145,000 (2000)

Annual FDI: US$23.00 million (2001)

For the latest Key Facts, go to www.worldinformation.com

The new government responded by implementing initial measures to improve the situation and tighten fiscal policy. In April 2002, the IMF agreed to provide Cape Verde with a US$1.5 million loan under its Poverty Reduction and Growth Facility (PRGF). A further US$1.65 million disbursement was approved by the IMF during a first review of the country's economic programme. To help Cape Verde restructure its debt and continue its economic reforms, Portugal also signed agreements totalling nearly US$40 million in mid-2001.

After recording several years of strong economic growth, GDP growth fell from 6.7 per cent in 2000 to 3 per cent in 2001. There is growing talk of Cape Verde joining the West Africa Economic and Monetary Union (WAEMU), but the government has expressed its satisfaction that the escudo was stable and will continue to maintain parity with the euro, to which it was pegged in 1999.

A key aim of PAICV's budget for 2002 was to achieve macroeconomic stability and to reduce deficit spending. Progress had already been made in 2001, which saw around 8 per cent reduction in the budget deficit (to around 10 per cent of GDP) compared to the previous year. Priority was given to the fishing, agriculture, health and education sectors. The government was optimistic that it would create more than 20,000 new jobs as part of its public investment programme. Nevertheless, while the PAICV's majority enabled it to push the budget through parliament, it was vociferously opposed by the MPD, with all the indications that the government would face tough times ahead.

Food aid deal

Cape Verde was also set to receive substantial aid from the US to meet its food requirements. With little agriculture, accounting for only 10 per cent of GDP in 2000 and beset by adverse conditions and a scarcity of water, Cape Verde imports most of its food. In a deal signed in December 2001, the US earmarked a food aid package worth US$14.5 million as part of a five-year programme to combat food shortages.

Air and sea gateways

Cape Verde's port and airways capacities continued to expand as part of ongoing development programmes, sponsored by the EU, World Bank and other international institutions.

The planned opening of the new Francisco Mendes Airport at Praia, São Tiago, by early 2003 promises to considerably boost the development of the tourism sector in particular as well as expand Praia's role as an international gateway.

Cape Verde Airlines (TACV), earmarked for privatisation, continued to expand its operations. In October 2001, agreements were reached between TACV and Guinea-Bissau to operate flights between Guinea-Bissau and Brazil (Fortaleza) via Cape Verde (Sal). TACV also signed an agreement with Mozambique airlines LAM and Angola's TAAG that would enable it to resume flights to Boston, USA, as from March 2002.

Cape Verde's most important sector is tourism. Increased airport capacity has been a major step in boosting the industry and it remains the sector with the most potential for development. In December 2001, Portugal announced it would make available substantial funds for projects to develop tourism.

Meanwhile, the archipelago will benefit from improved sea communications after the launch, in November 2001, of a ferry service operating from Ilha Brava to Fogo and Ilha de Santiago five times a week. The operating company Cabo Verde Nautica struck a deal with the government to run the service and for which it receives government subsidies.

Alternative energy boost

The state electricity company, Electra announced an investment programme in October 2001, totalling some US$70 million, supported by the World Bank and other donor agencies. Plans were afoot to increase the capacity of existing power stations and to explore alternative sources such as wind and solar power.

Such alternative energy resources, particularly suited to the country's climate, would enable Cape Verde to substantially reduce its huge dependency on imported petroleum, constituting more than 95 per cent of its energy needs, as well as the obvious environmental benefits.

Fishing

While Cape Verde's fishing industry, which centres on tuna and lobster, is under-exploited, it is a key industry. It was therefore encouraging news that exports would resume within the first half of 2002 with the lifting of an EU ban imposed in 1999. The government announced in December 2001 that it had addressed most of the EU's demands governing the import of fish products.

Employment prospects looked potentially grim for thousands of Cape Verde seamen working on international ships. Cape Verde's failure to fulfil the requirements of conventions laid down by the International Maritime Organisation (IMO) could leave its nationals without valid documentation and therefore without jobs, bringing economic hardship to those at home who depend on remittances. In 2002, Cape Verde was looking to Portugal for help in overcoming the problem.

Outlook

The MPD's defeat in the elections came amid growing dissatisfaction over its liberal policies and inability to tackle high unemployment and poverty. Although the new PAICV government tends towards greater state economic control, it appeared that the economic reform set out under IMF guidelines and the pattern of strong

KEY INDICATORS — Cape Verde

	Unit	1996	1997	1998	1999	2000
Population	m	0.40	0.41	0.41	0.42	0.43
Gross domestic product (GDP)	US$bn	0.43	0.48	0.50	0.47	0.56
GDP per capita	US$	1,065	1,170	1,000	1,114	1,297
GDP real growth	%	4.3	5.2	5.0	7.9	6.7
Inflation	%	6.0	8.6	4.4	4.3	-2.5
Exports (fob) (goods)	US$m	23.9	43.2	32.7	8.0	24.0
Imports (fob) (goods)	US$m	207.5	215.1	218.3	244.0	260.0
Balance of trade	US$m	-183.6	-171.9	-185.6	-236.0	-236.0
Current account	US$m	-35.0	-29.7	-58.0	-93.0	-75.0
Total reserves minus gold	US$m	51.8	41.8	37.1	60.4	28.2
Foreign exchange	US$m	51.7	41.7	37.1	60.4	28.1
Exchange rate	per US$	82.59	93.18	98.16	102.70	115.88

economic growth would continue. Nevertheless, the government needs to tread cautiously, balancing reforms and the expectations of the electorate. The PAICV also faces a formidable opposition in the form of the MPD whose forceful criticism of the budget was a clear foretaste of many battles to come.

Risk assessment

Economic	Improving
Political	Good
Regional stability	Satisfactory
Stock market	Improving

COUNTRY PROFILE

Historical profile

1462 The previously uninhabited islands were colonised by the Portuguese and became one of the most important slaving stations in West Africa.
1961 The movement for independence gathered strength, adopting guerrilla tactics against the Portuguese.
1975 Gained independence in July after the fall of the dictatorship in Portugal.
1975–80 Moves to unite Cape Verde and Guinea-Bissau were made, but came to nothing following the overthrow of President Luiz Cabral in Guinea-Bissau.
1980 The constitution was adopted in September.
1981 A revision to the constitution was passed.
1990 A multi-party system was introduced.
1991 Cape Verde's first free multi-party elections were won by the Movimento para a Democracia (MPD) (Movement for Democracy), and a government under Carlos Veiga was formed.
1992 A new constitution was adopted.
1995 The MPD secured an absolute majority in the December elections to the National Assembly.
1996 President Antonio Mascarenhas Monteiro (MPD) was re-elected on 18 February; no other parties put up candidates.
2001 In the January legislative elections, MPD was ousted by Partido Africano da Independência de Cabo Verde (PAICV) (African Party of Independence of Cape Verde). Pedro Pires was elected President and José Mária Neves was appointed prime minister.

Political structure

The president is elected by universal suffrage for a five-year term.
There are 17 municipios (administrative districts).

Constitution
A new constitution was adopted in 1992.

Form of state
Cape Verde is a unitary republic.

The executive
Executive power rests with the prime minister and his appointed Council of Ministers.

National legislature
The legislative unicameral parliament, the Assembléia Nacional (National Assembly), has 66 deputies elected in Cape Verde by universal suffrage, under a system of proportional representation, and six deputies elected by Cape Verdeans living abroad (two each for Africa, the Americas and the rest of the world).

Last elections
December 2000 (legislative); February 2001 (presidential).

Next elections
2005 (legislative); 2006 (presidential.

Political parties

There are six registered political parties.

Ruling party
Partido Africano da Independência de Cabo Verde (PAICV) (African Party of Independence of Cape Verde) (40 seats from Jan 2001)

Main opposition party
Movimento para a Democracia (MPD) (Movement for Democracy) (30 seats in the January 2001 elections)

Population

431,660 (2000)
Cape Verde's population is estimated to reach 700,000 by 2025.
Annual population growth rate: 0.92 per cent (2001). Approximately 43 per cent of the total population is under 15 years. Thirty per cent of the population lived below the national poverty line (1992–98). Population density: 237 inhabitants per square km. Urban population: 62 per cent (2001). It is estimated that 53 per cent of the population live in the country's three main cities, exerting great pressure on social services.
Beside the Cape Verdians resident on the islands, there are some 500,000 living abroad, many in the US. The government of Cape Verde encourages emigration.

Ethnic make-up
Creole (71 per cent), African (28 per cent), European (1 per cent).

Religions
Constitutional separation of church and state allows for freedom of religion. Christian (97 per cent Roman Catholic).

Education

Illiteracy is estimated at 26 per cent of the adult population. The National Development Plan of 2002–06 aims to increase vocational training and job creation and reduce illiteracy in an effort to generate foreign investment and therefore increase employment. US$3.5 million has been offered by the United National Population Fund (UNPF) to aid Cape Verde with its development objectives. It has been estimated by Oxfam that 100 per cent of children age 6–11 will enrol for school in 2015.

Health

Life expectancy at birth is 68 years and infant mortality is 55 per 1,000 births. In 2000, 775 people had the Aids virus. The government has a National Aids programme in place for the period 2001–04, financed by the World Bank.

Welfare

Around a third of the population live under the poverty line with around 14 per cent living in absolute poverty. Unemployment is estimated at 25 per cent, while underemployment is far higher. Poverty is worse in rural areas where employment opportunities are poor and incomes are declining. As a result, there is a steady migration to urban areas, creating pockets of extreme poverty within the cities and towns.

Main cities

Praia, on Santiago Island (estimated population 80,000), is the national capital; Mindelo, on São Vicente (51,000), is the commercial centre.

Languages spoken

Portuguese is the official language, although most inhabitants speak Creole, as their mother tongue.
In July 1996 Portugal and six of its former colonies (Angola, Brazil, Cape Verde, Guinea-Bissau, Mozambique and São Tomé) launched the Community of Portuguese Speaking Countries (CPLP) to protect their common language.

Official language
Portuguese and Creole (national language)

Media

Press
Dailies: The new authorities in Cape Verde suspended the country's sole daily newspaper *Horizonte* in 2001, emphasising the need to develop a new information policy. *Horizonte*, which was established in 1998 as a weekly, went daily in November 2000.
Weeklies: Weeklies are *Novo Jornal Cabo Verde*, (a government publication) and the *A Semana*.
Periodicals: Periodicals include *Terra Nova* the Catholic Church monthly publication, *Opinião*, *Noticias* (independent publication) and *Agaviva*.

Broadcasting
Programmes in Portuguese and Creole by Radio Nacional de Cabo Verde. A television service, TNCV, broadcasts in the evening.

Radio: The two main radio stations are Radio Nova and Radio Nacional de Cabo Verde (National Radio of Cape Verde).

Economy
Cape Verde has a subsistence economy due to limited natural resources.
Nine habitable out of 10 comparatively large islands and eight islets form the Cape Verde archipelago, of which only 20 per cent of the land can be used for agriculture because of the rugged volcanic nature of the landscape, erosion and persistent periods of severe drought. In 2001, the overall food situation was stable following two good harvests.
The islands continue to remain heavily dependent upon external donor assistance and food aid: half of the country's development expenses are funded by foreign aid. Basic products (cereals, cooking oil, milk) make up 20 per cent of Public Development Aid. Much aid is now also aimed at transforming the country into a self-sustainable economy.
There is a high rate of unskilled workers – 30–40 per cent of the population – and foreign investors are able take advantage of low wage rates.
In July 2001, Cape Verde signed two financial agreements with Portugal. Under the terms, Portugal will provide Cape Verde with US$40 million to support economic reform and aid debt restructuring. In 2001, Cape Verde owed Portugal US$25 million.
Luxembourg has financed educational and health infrastructure in Cape Verde over the last decade and in 2002, it provided 6,000 tonnes of wheat as supplementary food aid.
In 2001, Cape Verde will concentrate on the fishing, agriculture, health and education sectors. The government also aims to create about 20,000 jobs.

External trade
The trade deficit is partly offset by income from ship servicing, workers' remittances from abroad and substantial aid flows.
Exports
Principal exports are frozen, canned and fresh fish, bananas, garments, livestock produce, salt and entrepôt trade.
Main destinations: Portugal (typically 45 per cent of the total), Germany (15 per cent), UK (5 per cent), Malaysia (5 per cent).
Imports
Principal imports are foodstuffs such as rice, wheat and maize, cooking oil and milk; also livestock, fuel and energy, small quantities of manufactures, machinery and textiles.
Main sources: Portugal (typically 50 per cent of total), France (9 per cent), Netherlands (5 per cent), UK (4 per cent).

Agriculture
The agricultural sector forms the backbone of the economy, with 48 per cent of the population engaged in subsistence farming. It accounted for 13 per cent of GDP in 2000 and employed around 25 per cent of the labour force.
Approximately 20 per cent of total area is cultivable; most arable land is on the island of São Tiago.
Recurrent drought, interrupted by torrential rains and floods, soil erosion, disease and a weak infrastructure have reduced agricultural production considerably, but there are schemes for water conservation and irrigation.
Beans and maize are the staple foodstuffs. Maize covers 25 to 80 per cent of cultivated land according to rainfall. Only 10 per cent of food is produced locally.
Other crops include bananas, sweet potatoes, yams, manioc, pumpkins, sugar-cane, coffee and groundnuts.
About 90 per cent of food requirements are met by imports, largely in the form of food aid.
Fishing (shellfish and tunny) has been of growing importance, supporting some 20,000 people, and accounting for over 60 per cent of export revenues. Fishing accounts for about 4 per cent of GDP.

Industry and manufacturing
The industrial sector accounts for around 19 per cent of GDP and employs 15 per cent of the workforce.
Manufacturing is primarily in the agro-food industry (production of beer), and desalination plants (factories in Mindelo and Sal).
Less than 10 per cent of commercial goods are produced locally.
Other industries include ship repair and fuelling, construction, fish processing and canning, flour milling, soft drinks, cigar manufacture and garment making. Construction and civil engineering industries contribute about 10 per cent of GDP and is primarily related to the development of the tourism sector.
Two zones have been set up with industrial parks: Lazareto on São Vicente and Achada Grande Tras in Praia.
Construction of a fishing port in Mindelo on São Vicente was completed in 2001. Japan supplied the overall investment of US$12.5 million.

Tourism
The majority of visitors come from Portugal, France, Germany, Netherlands and Italy.
The tourism sector employs around 1,700 people. It was estimated that between 2000 and 2011, the increase in the rooms available, combined with more business visitors from European and American firms, will contribute to the creation of 11,000 direct jobs and more than 14,000 indirect jobs.
In 2000 tourist arrivals totalled 145,000, three times the 1998 figure. Tourism will be the focus in 2002 and is expected to be an important area of economic growth.

Environment
Cape Verde faces serious environmental problems, particularly concerning water management. Serious drought caused by global warming and the country's geographical location has undermined agriculture as well as plant cover. The government has drawn upon the Global Environment Facility (GEF) to help protect biodiversity and is supported by the UN's Food and Agriculture Organisation (FAO) in a forestry action plan.

Mining
The mining sector employs about 1 per cent of the workforce.
Activity is largely confined to exploitation of pozzolana (volcanic derivative) at São Antão, gypsum at Maio and production of salt on Sal and in Mindelo by evaporation method.

Hydrocarbons
Cape Verde has no oil or gas reserves and most energy requirements are imported from Portugal. The downstream industry is regulated by Direcão Geral da Energia. Around 96 per cent of energy needs come from oil derived products.

Energy
Dependence on imported petroleum and products.

Banking
Central bank
Banco de Cabo Verde
Main financial centre
Praia

Time
GMT minus one hour

Geography
Cape Verde is an archipelago of 10 islands and five islets in the North Atlantic Ocean, about 500km (300 miles) west of Dakar, Senegal.

Climate
Hot with very little rainfall. Temperatures range from around 20 degrees Celsius (C) at night to 32 degrees C during the day. Hottest months are July, August and September and rain most likely from August–September.

Entry requirements
Passports
Required by all. Passport must be valid for duration of stay.

Visa
Required by all except people born in Cape Verde, former nationals of Cape Verde and their spouses and children, provided they hold proof thereof. Nationals of Angola, South Africa and members of the Economic Community of West African States (ECOWAS) do not need a visa.
Currency advice/regulations
Import and export of local currency prohibited.
No restriction on import of foreign currency, but amounts must be declared. Export of foreign currency is limited to equivalent of CVEsc20,000 unless a higher amount is declared on arrival.

Health (for visitors)
Mandatory precautions
Yellow fever certificates if arriving from countries having notified cases in the last six years.
Advisable precautions
Typhoid, tetanus, hepatitis A and polio vaccinations. Malaria limited risk exists September to November in Sao Tiago Island. Water precautions should be taken. There is a rabies risk. There is a slight risk of cholera. Milk is unpasteurised and should be boiled. Dairy products should be avoided.

Hotels
Accommodation is available in all islands but the best establishments are situated in Fogo, Sal, Santiago, São Vicente.

Credit cards
Credit cards are only accepted in the bigger hotels.

Public holidays
Fixed dates
1 Jan (New Year's Day), 20 Jan (National Heroes' Day), 1 May (Labour Day), 5 Jul (Independence Day), 15 Aug (Assumption Day), 1 Nov (All Saints' Day), 25 Dec (Christmas).

Working hours
Banking
Mon–Fri: 0800–1400.
Business
Mon–Fri: 0800–1230, 1430–1800.
Shops
Mon–Fri: 0800–1300, 1500–1900.
Sat: 0900–1300. Closed all day Sunday.

Telecommunications
Telephone/fax
Major privatisation occurred in 1995 with the sale of 40 per cent of the shares of Cabo Verde Telecommunications (CVT) to Portugal Telecommunications. The network underwent extensive modernisation in 1996–2000. Also mobile phones, paging, videotext and video conferencing to be introduced as well as teleport services established.

Electricity supply
220V AC

Weights and measures
The metric system is in use.

Getting there
Air
National airline: Transportes Aéreos de Cabo Verde (TACV) – guarantees daily inter-island flights and weekly flights. There are flights to several European cities. South African Airlines, TAP Air Portugal and Tower Airlines also service Cape Verde
Main airport: Amilcar Cabral is the main airport, 2km south of Espargos. Another airport, the Francisco Mendes Airport in Praia, Santiago, opened in 2001.
Airport tax: There is no airport tax.

Getting about
National transport
Air: Transportes Aéreos de Cabo Verde (TACV) flies daily to all islands except Brava and Santo Antâo. The Cape Verde Airpass from TACV offers discounts to frequent flyers.
Flights from West African coast use San Pedro regional airport, near Praia on Santiago.
City transport
Taxis: Available on main islands. Taxis are available from Sal Amilcar Cabral International Airport to city centre.

BUSINESS DIRECTORY

Telephone area codes
Dialling code for Cape Verde Islands – IDD access code +238 followed by subscriber's number. There are no area codes.

Useful telephone numbers
Praia, Santiago
Airport docks: 615-821, 615-646
Electricity Board: 611-909
Fire brigade: 612-727
Ambulance: 612-462
Police: 613-637

Banking
Banco Insular (IFI), PO Box 556, Conjunto Residencial Comunidades, Lote Oito- Bloco D Fracção Oitava, Achada Santo Antonio-Praia (e-mail:bancoinsular@mail.cvtelecom.cv).

Banco Comercial do Atlantico, PO Box 474, Avenida Amílcar Cabral, Praia (tel: 614-953; fax: 613-235).

Banco Interatlântico, Avenida Cidade de Lisboa 131-A, Praia (tel: 614-008, 613-829, 614-425; fax: 614-712, 614-752).

Caixa Económica de Cabo Verde SARL, PO Box 199, Avenida Cidade de Lisboa, Praia (tel: 615-561; fax: 615-560).

Central bank
Banco de Cabo Verde, PO Box 101, Av. Amilcar Cabral, Praia (tel: 607-000, 607-080/1, 607-180; fax: 6

14-447, 611-914, 607-095; e-mail: bcv@mail.cvtelecom.cv; bcv-ealves-ca@mail.cvtelecom.cv).

Travel information
CABETUR (tourist agency), 4 Rua Serpa Pinto, CP 318, Praia, Santiago (tel: 615-551; fax: 615-553).

Intertur, Sal (tel: 411-580; fax: 411-590).

Praiatur, Av Amilcar Cabral, CP 100, Praia, Santiago (tel: 615-746/7; fax: 614-500).

Sal Amilcar Cabral International Airport, ASA-Empresa Nacional de Aeroportos E Seguranca Aerea-EP, PB 50, Ilha do Sal (tel: 411-135, 411-394, 411-468; fax: 411-570, 411-323; e-mail: asacv@milton.cvtelecom.cv).

Transportes Aéreos de Cabo Verde (TACV), Av Amilcar Cabral, CP 1, Praia, Santiago (tel: 615-813; fax: 615-905).

Other useful addresses
Associação Commercial e Agricola de Sotavento de Cabo Verde, CP 78, Praia (tel: 612-991).

Associação Comercial Barlavento, CP 62, Mindelo, S Vicente (tel: 313-281).

Cabo Verde Motors, SARL, CP 51-B, Praia (tel: 612-345; fax: 612-612).

Ceris, Sociedade Caboverdiana de Cerveja e Refrigerantes (beer and refrigeration), CP 320, Praia (tel: 615-575; fax: 614-488).

Direcção-Geral das Alfandegas (customs body), CP 98, Praia (tel: 613-835, 613-026).

Direcção-Geral do Comércio (trade body), CP 105, Praia (tel: 614-159).

Direcção-Geral de Estatistica (Statistics Department of the Ministry of Economic Co-ordination), Avenida Amilcar Cabral, Praia (fax: 611-922).

Direcção-Geral das Pescas (national fisheries authority), Praia (tel: 612-976).

Direcção-Geral do Plano (Planning Department of the Ministry of Economic Co-ordination), Avenida Amilcar Cabral, Praia (fax: 611-922).

Embassy of Portugal, Achada de S António, Praia, Santiago (tel: 615-602).

EMPA (state trading organisation), CP 107, Praia (tel: 249).

Empresa Caboverdeana das Infraestructuras de Pescas (fisheries infrastructure corporation), CP 59, Mindelo, S Vicente (tel: 2434).

Empresa Nacional de Aeroportos e Segurança Aérea, Aeroporto Amilcar Cabral, Ilha do Sal (tel: 411-394).

Empresa Nacional de Combustivels (national combustibles corporation), CP 1, Mindelo, S Vicente (tel: 313-659).

Garantia (insurance company) (tel: 615-661, 615-662; fax: 313-221, 313-470).

Ministry of Agriculture, Alimentation and Environment, Praia (tel: 615-716; fax: 614-717).

Ministry of Defence, Praia (tel: 610-372; fax: 611-286).

Ministry of Economic Coordination, Avenue Amilcar Cabral, Praia (tel: 613-210; fax: 611-922).

Ministry of Education, Science and Culture, Praia (tel: 610-507; fax: 612-764).

Ministry of Foreign Affairs, Praia (tel: 614-773; fax: 611-960).

Ministry of Health and Social Promotion, Praia (tel: 615-721; fax: 613-991).

Ministry of Justice and Internal Administration, Praia (tel: 615-687; fax: 611-396).

Ministry of Sea, Praia (tel: 616-662; fax: 611-770).

Ministry of Transport and Infrastructure, Praia (tel: 615-709; fax: 614-822).

National Statistical Service, Largo Pinheiro Chagas, Avenida 12 Setembro, Praia.

Prime Ministers Office, Palacio do Governo, Praia (tel: 610-513; fax: 612-288).

PROMEX, CP 89, Praia (tel: 622-621, 622-736, 622-741; fax: 622-737).

Radio Nacional de Cabo Verde, CP 26, Praia (tel: 613-729).

Shell Cabo Verde, Sarl, CP 4, S Vicente (tel: 314-470; fax: 314-755).

US Embassy, R Abilio Macedo, Praia, Santiago (tel: 615-616).

Internet sites

Africa Business Network: http://www.ifc.org/abn

African Development Bank: http://www.afdb.org

Africa Online: http://www.africaonline.com

Allafrica.com: http://allafrica.com

Mbendi AfroPaedia (information on companies, countries, industries and stock exchanges in Africa): http://mbendi.co.za

Central African Republic

Nils P Mork

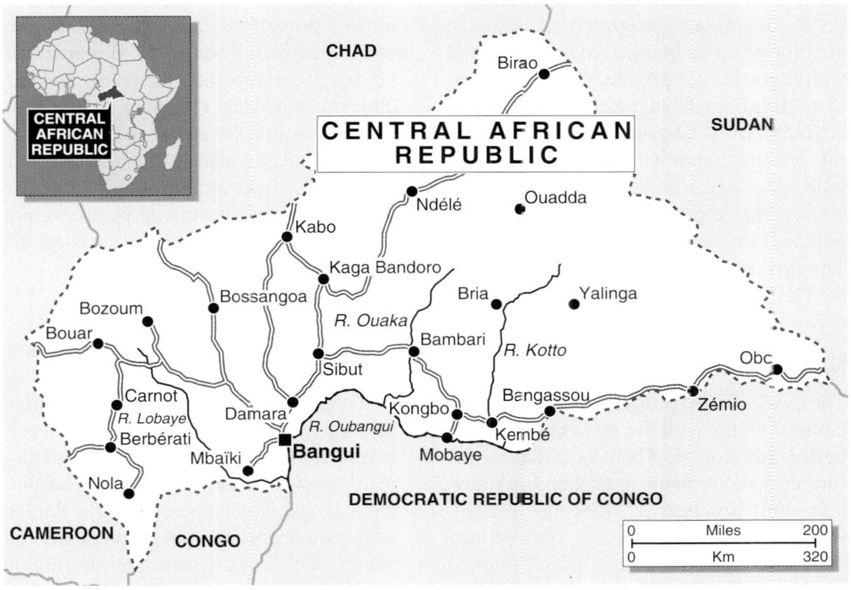

The Central African Republic (CAR) is a country of unlikely optimism. Having endured yet more destructive rebellions in May and November 2001, against a familiar backdrop of endemic corruption, unpaid salaries, regular strikes and stalled economic growth, Centrafricaines seem committed to improving their country's dire economic outlook. The government announced sweeping economic reforms in co-operation with the IMF and the UN Development Programme (UNDP) in April 2002. There are also plans to further develop the country's substantial mineral wealth. The question is if CAR will enjoy the political stability necessary to safeguard such developments.

Centrafricaine catch-22

In May 2001, following months of strikes in protest at unpaid salaries, CAR once again faced an attempted coup by its armed forces. The democratically elected president, Ange-Félix Patassé, was 'asked to resign' by his predecessor, General André Kolingba. After fierce fighting, President Patassé's reduced forces were assisted by a contingent of Libyan troops to quell the coup. Claims that a withdrawal of the remaining Libyan troops would lead to another coup gained resonance in November 2001 when ex-army chief of staff, François Bozize, refused arrest for assisting in the coup and launched five days of fighting in Bangui before fleeing to Chad. Once more, Libya weighed decisively on President Patassé's side. Libya's presence has raised scepticism as to what agenda it has towards its poorer southern neighbour, although Patassé appears to need Libya's support against the rebels. In October 2002, Libyan military aircraft provided air support to government forces in northern CAR and bombed rebels loyal to Bozize.

The attempted coup resulted from years of discontent with the Patassé regime's record of human rights abuses, corruption and economic mismanagement. Most important is the government's repeated failure to pay its civil service and military personnel. Unfortunately, the coup exacerbated the potential for ameliorating such grievances, forcing the government to slash the budget by one-third in September 2001. The coup also led to a near-standstill in economic activity while the government failed to meet performance criteria under the IMF-led Poverty Reduction and Growth Facility (PRGF). In short, political unrest is both the cause and effect of poor economic performance

KEY FACTS

Official name: République Centrafricaine (The Central African Republic)

Head of State: President Ange-Félix Patassé (MLPC) (re-elected Sep 1999)

Head of government: Prime Minister Martin Ziguélé (appointed by the president, Apr 2001)

Ruling party: Mouvement pour la Libération du Peuple Centrafricain (MLPC) (Central African People's Liberation Movement) (from Nov 1999)

Area: 622,984 square km

Population: 3.80 million (2001)

Capital: Bangui

Official language: French

Currency: CFA franc (CFAf) = 100 centimes (Communauté Financière Africaine (African Financial Community) franc)

Exchange rate: CFAf629.73 per US$ (Jan 2003); CFAf655.95 per euro (pegged from Jan 1999)

GDP per capita: US$258 (2001)

GDP real growth: 1.50% (2001)

Inflation: 1.40% (2001)

Balance of trade: US$9.00 million (2001)

Foreign debt: US$822.00 million (2001)

For the latest Key Facts, go to www.worldinformation.com

and it is hard to imagine any solution to the country's economic predicament without lasting political stability.

This socio-political catch-22 led the UN secretary general, Kofi Annan, to ask the international community for increased assistance to CAR in June 2002, before the 'social truce' signed between the government and its unions expired in July. The central point in a joint communiqué between the government and unions was the renewed commitment to ensure regular payment of salaries.

In July 2001, the Patassé regime's commitment to human rights was further questioned as international human rights non-governmental organisations (NGOs) claimed that the government had instigated 'witch-hunts' towards General Kolingba's ethnic group, the Yakoma. This sparked fears of escalating ethnic conflict and national division, further contributing to the wholesale desertion of Yakoma elements from the armed forces.

The attempted coup also led to increased tensions with Chad, as President Idriss Deby of Chad announced that Bozize had been given 'humanitarian asylum' in his country. Adding to the tension was the concurrent raiding of southern Chad by Chadian rebels based on CAR territory. In April 2002, the situation appeared to be resolved peacefully by presidential consultations.

The fallout from the coup had major political consequences. In August 2001, Patassé sacked several ministers, including defence minister, Jean-Jacques Demafouth. Approximately 69 people were tried in August 2002, including Demafouth, for their part in the coup. Demafouth was acquitted of any involvement in the coup, but those sentenced to death included CAR's former military dictator, General André Kolingba, who was not present at the trial.

Sweeping reforms

In response to these problems, the government launched a set of sweeping economic and political reforms in April 2002. The plans included improvements to the public services, extended decentralisation, good-governance programmes and the creation of an economic environment that would encourage private sector development. It is hoped that these reforms should enable CAR to take advantage of its natural resource endowments of diamonds, gold, uranium, iron, and potential oil deposits. The reforms are a continuation of policies that were interrupted by the coup. The government also hopes to re-qualify for IMF financial assistance, although this seems unlikely.

Natural resources

The CAR is heavily dependent on the agricultural sector with the main export crops coffee and cotton. There is potential for further developments in timber, but transport infrastructure is lacking. Indeed, infrastructural bottlenecks undermined the 2002 cotton harvest which looked likely to fall below half the 2001 production level. This led the government, with World Bank assistance, to establish a new cotton transport agency in May 2002.

The mining sector generates 40 per cent of the country's export earnings. There is considerable scope for expanding gold and diamond revenue. The diamond sector suffers from colossal amounts of smuggling. Traders smuggle diamonds both out from the CAR to avoid taxes and in from other war-torn African countries such as the Democratic Republic of the Congo (DRC) to avoid UN-imposed embargoes.

A January 2001 attempt to stop the large share of diamonds that were being smuggled held the prospect of doubling tax revenues from the sector. The political unrest of 2001 and 2002 damaged such hopes.

Nevertheless, international interest in CAR's mineral wealth holds the potential for a more prosperous future: Canadian company, Vaaldiam Resources Ltd, started surveying for kimberlite diamonds in May 2002 and Canadian company Axmin completed an optimistic survey of gold deposits in the Bandas Archean greenstone belt in June 2002. However, any significant international investment would depend on a minimum of political stability and such stability has been absent since May 2001.

Outlook

The CAR needs to perform a strenuous balancing act if its official optimism is to be coupled with harsh realities. Political discontent needs to be countered with economic stability and growth and a natural place to start would be the delayed payment of salaries. It is a task that the Patassé government, or any government for that matter, will find difficult, considering the present economic quandary. If managed successfully, the future for the CAR could see mineral-induced growth rates unparalleled in its troubled history.

Risk assessment

Economic	Poor
Political	Poor
Regional stability	Satisfactory

KEY INDICATORS — Central African Republic

	Unit	1996	1997	1998	1999	2000
Population	m	3.43	3.25	3.56	3.65	3.72
Gross domestic product (GDP)	US$bn	1.07	1.00	1.05	1.10	0.97
GDP per capita	US$	310	320	300	301	268
GDP real growth	%	-4.9	3.9	5.5	3.5	2.6
Inflation	%	3.7	1.6	-1.9	-1.5	3.1
Exports (fob) (goods)	US$m	146.0	155.0	138.0	136.0	142.0
Imports (fob) (goods)	US$m	126.0	145.0	150.0	139.0	140.0
Balance of trade	US$m	20.0	10.0	-12.0	-3.0	2.0
Foreign debt	US$bn	0.8	0.9	0.9	0.9	0.9
Total reserves minus gold	US$m	232.2	178.6	145.7	136.3	133.3
Foreign exchange	US$m	232.1	178.4	145.6	136.1	133.1
Exchange rate	per US$	511.55	583.67	589.95	615.70	711.98

COUNTRY PROFILE

Historical profile

1889 The French established themselves at Bangui, founding the colony of Oubangi-Shari (named after two main rivers) in 1907.
1958 The country was proclaimed a republic.
1960 Became independent under the presidency of David Dacko.
1966 President Dacko's cousin, Jean-Bedel Bokassa, an army commander, seized power, declaring himself life-president in 1972.
1977 Bokassa crowned himself emperor – the coronation consumed about one-quarter of the country's income.
1979 Bokassa's repressive regime was forced from office when French troops reinstated David Dacko.
1981 Dacko was ousted by the army chief of staff, General André Kolingba.

1986 Kolingba established a one-party state.
1990 Opposition groups united and forced the government to adopt a multi-party system.
1992 Elections were held after the government accepted the principle of multi-party democracy. The results were nullified after several groups boycotted the poll.
1993 A transitional government was appointed in May, before elections in August in which Kolingba was defeated. Ange-Félix Patassé became president.
1995 A democratic constitution was adopted in January.
1996 In May, France used its military presence of 1,600 troops to quell an army mutiny; 10,000 demonstrators opposed the intervention. In June, Patassé appointed Jean-Paul Ngoupandé (previously ambassador to France) to lead a government of national unity.
1997 Ngoupandé was in turn replaced by Michel Gbezera-Bira in January at the head of an 11-party coalition government. It included parties led by ex-presidents Dacko and Kolingba and the veteran politician Abel Goumba (chairman of the group).
1998 The parliamentary elections held in November/December were indecisive.
1999 Some deputies defected to Patassé MLPC and by September it had a slight majority. Presidential elections on 19 September confirmed support for President Patassé, who re-appointed Prime Minister Dologuélé to lead the government.
2001 In April, Dologuélé was sacked by Patassé and Martin Ziguélé was appointed prime minister. In May, soldiers rebelled against the president but failed to overthrow him. Libya sent troops to protect the Patassé government.
2002 In July, the finance minister, Eric Sorongope-Zoumandji was arrested and accused of embezzling public funds. His arrest was part of the government's ongoing campaign to fight corruption.

Political structure

Constitution

Following a referendum in December 1994, a democratic constitution was adopted on 7 January 1995 allowing the president to stand for re-election once. It provides for directly elected regional assemblies.

Form of state

Republic

The executive

The president serves for six years.

National legislature

The National Assembly has a five-year mandate.

Last elections

19 September 1999 (presidential); November/December 1998 (parliamentary).

Next elections

2003 (parliamentary); 2005 (presidential).

Political parties

Ruling party

Mouvement pour la Libération du Peuple Centrafricain (MLPC) (Central African People's Liberation Movement) (from Nov 1999)

Main opposition party

Mouvement pour la Démocratie et le Developpement (MDD) (Movement for Democracy and Development); Rassemblement Démocratique Centrafricaine (RDC) (Central African Democratic Rally); Front Patriotique pour le Progrès (FPP) (Patriotic Front for Progress); Alliance pour la Démocratie et le Progrès (ADP) (Alliance for Democracy and Progress).

Population

3.72 million (2000)
Annual population growth rate: 1.3 per cent (1994–2000). Approximately 43 per cent of the total population is under 15 years.
Population density: five inhabitants per square km. Urban population: 41 per cent (1994–2000).
It is estimated that 63 per cent of the total population and 75 per cent of the rural population lives below the poverty line.

Ethnic make-up

Bayas (34 per cent), Bandas (27 per cent), Manzas (21 per cent), Saras (10 per cent), Mbums (4 per cent), Mbakas (4 per cent)

Religions

About 24 per cent of the population hold traditional beliefs; 25 per cent Protestants; 25 per cent Catholics; 15 per cent Muslims.

Education

The UN estimates that adult illiteracy rates for men and women aged 15 years or over stands at 40.2 per cent and 65.1 per cent respectively. Education is compulsory between the ages of six and 14, although only 60 per cent of eligible children receive education. Basic education lasts for 10 years divided into six years' basic first stage and four years' basic second stage. General secondary school lasts for three years, which gives access to higher education. Only 10 per cent of secondary school-aged children are enrolled due to limited resources. Technical education at the secondary level is offered at two levels. School instruction is primarily in French, but the government has sought to promote Sango literacy and encourages its use in schools.
Higher education is offered at the Université de Bangui (1970), which also has a teacher training college.

Health

World Bank estimates during the period 1994–2000 showed that the average life expectancy was 44 years and the infant mortality rate stood at 98 per 1,000 live births. It is estimated that 23 per cent of children under the age of five were malnourished in the same period. The fertility rate shows that 4.7 children are born per adult woman. Estimates show that 15 per cent of adult women use contraceptives. The maternal mortality rate is typically 1,100 deaths per 100,000 live births. World Bank estimates in 2000 showed that 60 per cent and 31 per cent of the population had access to improved water and sanitation facilities respectively. There are 0.1 physicians and 0.9 hospital beds typically available for 1,000 people. The HIV rate is 13.84 per cent among adults. Modern healthcare facilities exist only in Bangui (with only one major hospital) and a few other towns. According to World Bank estimates, government expenditure on healthcare averaged 3 per cent of GDP including 2 per cent of GDP which was public expenditure between 1990–1998. Expenditure on private healthcare (such as private household expenditure and insurance) averaged 1 per cent of GDP over the same period.

Welfare

Amnesty International reports that some 30,000 mostly Yakoma civilians and members of the armed forces had escaped to the neighbouring Democratic Republic of the Congo (DRC) and northern Republic of the Congo following the coup attempt in May 2001. Most refugees survived without basic humanitarian assistance and were prone to malnutrition for more than six months. The government started preparations to repatriate refugees from the DRC in December 2001, although efforts to stabilise the situation could falter without the support of international donors. The country is in deep poverty, with two out of three people earning less than US$1 a day. All social security programmes are administered by the Central African Social Security Office.
In the first half of 2002, the UN's World Food Programme (WFP) provided assistance to 6,000 internally displaced people mostly in Batangafo and Kabo for a period of three months. The WFP is expected to provide food rations until the end of the year despite drastic cuts in its food stock.

Main cities

Bangui (population about 600,000 in 2002), Berbérati (38,000), Bossangoa (35,000).

Languages spoken

French is the official language. Sango, Banda, Baye and Zanda are widely spoken.

Official language/s

French

Media

Press

Dailies: The print media is relatively free from arbitrary government interference. There are some independent newspapers in circulation, although their influence remains limited. These include *Le Citoyen*, *L'Echo de Centrafrique*, *Le Novateur*, *L'Hirondelle* and *Le Démocrate*. The Sango-language *E Le Songo* is another daily published in Bangui.

Periodicals: A few periodicals are also published in Bangui, including *Journal Officiel de la République Centrafricaine*.

Broadcasting

Radio: The state-owned Radiodiffusion-Télévision Centrafrique broadcasts in Sango and French. The UN-sponsored Radio Ndeke Luka in Bangui rebroadcasts international news. Other radio services include Radio Centrafrique, Radio Notre-Dame, Radio Nostalgie, Africa No 1 and Radio France Internationale.

Economy

The economy is vulnerable to the adverse effects of drought and of domestic and regional political strife.

The Central African Republic's (CAR) landlocked position and relative isolation provide considerable problems in exploiting economic potential and foreign technical and financial assistance will remain necessary for some time.

It is estimated that two-thirds of the population live on less than US$1 a day. The CAR has one of the highest rates of urban poverty in Africa, at 51.3 per cent.

The economy would be enhanced by improved transport facilities, a recovery in international commodity prices and domestic reforms by the government. There is need for serious economic reform. The economy is dominated by subsistence agriculture.

External trade

Exports

Principal exports are diamonds, coffee, timber, cotton, tobacco, leather, rubber, gold, wax.

Main destinations: Belgium/Luxembourg (typically 59 per cent of total), Taiwan (16 per cent), France (3 per cent), Spain (5 per cent).

Imports

Principal imports are food products, fuel and energy, capital goods.

Main sources: France (typically 17 per cent of total), Cameroon (7 per cent), Belgium/Luxembourg (2 per cent), Germany (2 per cent), Japan (2 per cent).

Agriculture

Agriculture and forestry are the mainstay of the economy. The sector accounts for around 55 per cent of GDP and employs 66 per cent of workforce.

Around 12 per cent of the total land is arable; much of the rest is savannah. Forest covers 75 per cent of the country. There is significant forestry potential, including over 60 species of commercially viable trees, but it is under exploited because of poor transport infrastructure. Timber is the third-largest export earner.

Most agricultural activities include subsistence farming and animal husbandry.

Main crops are millet, sorghum, cassava, groundnuts, maize, sesame and rice. The main export crop is coffee.

Production is hampered by soil erosion, widespread drought and underdeveloped marketing and infrastructure.

Industry and manufacturing

The industrial sector typically accounts for around 18 per cent of GDP and employs 9 per cent of the workforce. Manufacturing accounts for around 9 per cent of GDP.

Manufacturing is relatively small-scale and is concentrated in the brewing, tanning, food processing, soap manufacture and textile sectors. There are also import substitution industries such as motor cycle and bicycle assembly.

The main industrial centre is the Bangui district.

Mining

The mining sector officially accounts for around 4 per cent of GDP, employs 3 per cent of the workforce and generates 40 per cent of the country's export earnings. Smuggling is endemic and production and trade is likely to be far higher than official estimates.

Around 80,000 autonomous artisinal miners are engaged in mining production, mostly of diamonds and gold. Diamond output is around 500,000 carats per year, over half of which are gem quality. Other mineral deposits include uranium, limestone, iron ore, copper and manganese.

Asquith Resources has discovered a potentially massive iron deposit in Bambari, with yields in excess of 66 per cent iron.

Hydrocarbons

There are no significant oil or gas reserves.

Energy

There is a strong dependence on imported fuels.

Around 80 per cent of electricity production is generated at the country's two hydro-stations: Boali and M'Bali, a joint project with the Democratic Republic of Congo (formerly Zaïre).

Banking

Central bank

Banque des Etats de l'Afrique Centrale

Main financial centre

Bangui

Time

GMT plus one hour

Geography

The Central African Republic is a landlocked country in the heart of equatorial Africa. It is bounded by Chad to the north, and Sudan to the east, by the Republic of Congo and the Democratic Republic of Congo to the south and Cameroon to the west.

Climate

Hot all year with temperatures up to 36 degrees Celsius. The dry season runs from November–February with cooler nights. The rainy season runs from May–October.

Entry requirements

Passports

Required by all except certain African and French document holders.

Visa

Required by all except nationals of certain African countries (including most West African nations).

An onward or return ticket is generally required.

Currency advice/regulations

No restrictions on import of foreign currency, but amount must be declared; export up to declared amount allowed. Unlimited import of local currency; export limited to CFAf75,000.

Health (for visitors)

Mandatory precautions

Yellow fever vaccination certificate required by all.

Advisable precautions

Typhoid, tetanus, hepatitis A and polio vaccinations are recommended. Malaria prophylaxis should be taken as risk exists throughout country. There is a rabies risk. Water precautions are necessary – bilharzia risk in some areas. AIDS risk.

Hotels

Good standard hotels are available in Bangui – limited accommodation elsewhere. Where service charge is not included in bill a 10 per cent tip is usual.

Public holidays

Fixed dates

1 Jan, 29 Mar (President Boganda's Remembrance), 1 May, 30 Jun (National Day for Prayer), 13 Aug (Independence), 15 Aug (Assumption), 1 Nov (All Saints'), 1 Dec (National Day), 25 Dec.

Variable dates

Easter Monday, Ascension Day, Whit Monday.

Working hours

Banking

Mon–Fri: 0730–1130.

Business

Mon–Fri: 0730–1530.

Government
Mon–Fri: 0700–1200, 1430–1700; Sat: 0700–1200.
Shops
(Mon–Sat) 0800–1200; 1600–1900.

Telecommunications
Telephone/fax
Dialling code for Central African Republic: IDD access code + 236 followed by area code (61 for Bangui) followed by subscriber's number.

Electricity supply
220/380V AC, 50 cycles

Weights and measures
The metric system is used.

Getting there
Air
Air Afrique (Central African Republic is a shareholder), Air France and Sudan Airways serve CAR.
National airline: Air Afrique (Central African Republic is a shareholder). Air France and Sudan Airways serve CAR.
International airport/s: Bangui-M'Poko (Code: BGF), 4km from city, restaurant, post office, shops, car hire.

Getting about
National transport
Air: Small light aircraft can be chartered from Air Afrique.
Road: Eight main roads run from Bangui to the main towns and those that are surfaced are toll roads. The Trans-African Lagos-Mombasa highway passes through the Central African Republic. Most other roads can become impassable during rainy season. NB Spare parts and petrol stations tend to be sparse outside Bangui.
Buses: Limited coach service operates between Bangui and Bangassou.
Water: Large volume of freight carried on rivers. The principal trading route is on the Oubangui River south of the capital Bangui which runs into the River Congo, connecting Bangui to the former Zaïre and the Congo (including Brazzaville, from where railway runs to Pointe-Noire). Also services from Salo on the Sangha River.
City transport
Taxis: Available in Bangui; fares by negotiation.
Car hire
Self- or chauffeur-driven cars available. International driving licence required.

BUSINESS DIRECTORY

Telephone area codes
Dialling code for Central African Republic: IDD access code +236 followed by area code (61 for Bangui).

Chambers of Commerce
Chambre de Commerce, BP 813, Bangui (tel: 614-255).

Chambre de Commerce, d'Industrie et de l'Artisanat, BP 252 ET 813, Bangui (tel: 614-255, 611-668).

Banking
Banque de Crédit Agricole et de Développement, BP 801, Place de la République, Bangui (tel: 613-200).

Banque Internationale pour le Centrafrique, BP 910, Place de la République, Bangui (tel: 610-042; fax: 616-136, 613-438).

Banque Populaire Maroco-Centrafricaine, BP 844, Rue Guerlliot, Bangui (tel: 613-190, 611-290; fax: 616-230).

Caisse Nationale d'Epargne, BP 839, Siège social, Bangui (tel: 612-296).

Commercial Bank Centrafrique SA, BP 839, Rue de Brazza, Bangui (tel: 612-990; fax: 613-454).

Central bank
Banque des États de l'Afrique Centrale, PO Box 1917, Rue du Docteur Jamot, Yaounde, Cameroun (tel 234-030, 234-060; fax: 233-329)

Travel information
Inter-RCA, BP 1413, Bangui.

Ministry of Water, Forests, Wildlife, Fisheries and Tourism, Bangui.

Office Centrafricain de Tourisme (OCATOUR), BP 655, Bangui (tel: 614-566).

Ministries
Ministry of Economy and Finance, Planning and International Co-operation, Bangui (tel: 610-811).

Ministry of Energy, Mines, Geology and Water Resources, Bangui.

Ministry of Posts and Telecommunications, Bangui (tel: 612-946).

Ministry of Rural Development, Bangui (tel: 612-800).

Ministry of Trade, Industry and Small- and Medium-scale Enterprises, Bangui (tel: 614-488).

Ministry of Transport and Civil Aviation, Bangui (tel: 612-307).

Other useful addresses
Central African Republic Embassy (USA), 1618 22nd Street, NW, Washington DC 20008 (tel: 483-7800; fax: 332-9893).

European Development Fund, BP 1298, Bangui (tel: 613-053, 610-113).

Office of the President, Palais de la Renaissance, Bangui (tel: 610-323).

Société Centrafricaine de Développement Agricole (SOCADA), ave David Dacko, BP 997, Bangui (tel: 613-033).

Internet sites
Africa Business Network: http://www.ifc.org/abn

AllAfrica.com: http://allafrica.com

African Development Bank: http://www.afdb.org

Africa Online: http://www.africaonline.com

Harambee Afrika (UK business club for traders with east, central and southern Africa; includes annotated web resource list): http://www.harambee.co.uk

Mbendi AfroPaedia (information on companies, countries, industries and stock exchanges in Africa): http://mbendi.co.za

Chad

Nils P Mork

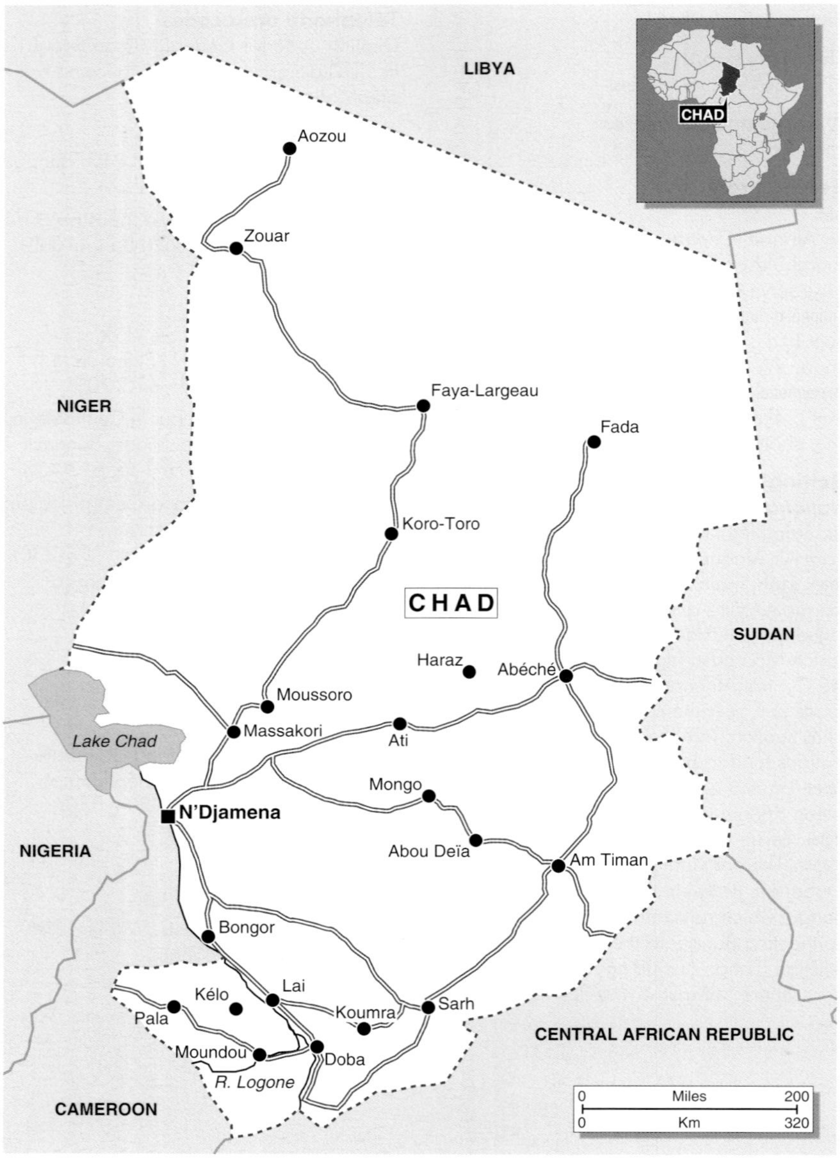

KEY FACTS

Official name: Republic of Chad

Head of State: President Colonel Idriss Déby (MPS) (since 1990; re-elected May 2001)

Head of government: Prime Minister Haroun Kabadi (appointed by the president on 12 Jun 2002)

Ruling party: Mouvement Patriotique du Salut (MPS) (Patriotic Movement for Salvation) (re-elected Apr 2002)

Area: 1,284,000 square km

Population: 7.90 million (2001)

Capital: N'Djamena

Official language: French and Arabic

Currency: CFA franc (CFAf) = 100 centimes (Communauté Financière Africaine (African Financial Community) franc)

Exchange rate: CFAf629.73 per US$ (Jan 2003); CFAf655.95 per euro (pegged from Jan 1999)

GDP per capita: US$202 (2001)

GDP real growth: 8.50% (2001)

Inflation: 12.40% (2001)

Balance of trade: -US$369.00 million (2001)

Chad is a country of lost opportunities. Despite its gold, uranium and oil, it is one of the world's poorest countries, ranking a gloomy 155th out of 175 in the 2001 UN Human Development Indicator. Chad's history since independence in 1960 is plagued with innumerable variations on the recurring themes of civil war, human rights violations, regional conflicts, economic mismanagement and rampant corruption. These have almost invariably coexisted with a multitude of peace-building efforts, development projects and international aid programmes. This ambiguous trend of cautious hopes and crushing disappointments was confirmed yet again by the failure of the May 2002 peace negotiations between the government and the rebel group Mouvement pour la Démccratie et la Justice au Tchad (MDJT) (Movement for Democracy and Justice in Chad). It remains to be seen if what has been heralded as 'the last, best hope for development in Chad', the Doba oil project, will suffer the same fate.

Democracy and peace?

The presidential elections of May 2001 – although considerably fairer than the 1996 poll that gave President Idriss Déby his first civilian mandate – were fraught with accusations of cheating, repression and unlawful arrests of opponents. Some observers, notably the Organisation for African Unity (OAU) (now the African Union), gave the green light for the proceedings, but international organisations responded in October 2001 by publishing a catalogue of politically motivated human rights abuses in Chad.

Having secured his next five-year term in office, Déby seems intent on improving his international reputation, especially as the financing for the Doba oil project is conditional on a minimum of good governance.

It seems likely that the need to safeguard the black gold also served as a contributing reason for the government's renewed efforts to reach a peace deal with the MDJT. These efforts resulted in a comprehensive and inclusive peace agreement being signed in Libya in January 2002. Youssef Togoimi, the leader of the MDJT and former defence minister, agreed to terms including a general amnesty, political representation and the integration of MDJT forces into the Chadian armed forces.

Hopes of peace were confounded when fractions of the MDJT resumed fighting in May 2002. Togoimi – who was later said to have lost both legs in a mine accident in August 2002 – reportedly leads a faction of hardliners that refuse to accept the terms of the peace deal, even though some elements of the MDJT appear to have defected to the government. Déby is asking that negotiations be resumed under the original framework and the situation currently seems to be at a deadlock. The joker in this game of political violence is the Libyan leader, Muammar Al-Qadafi, who has a thinly veiled hand in the conflict, helping the Muslim MDJT with supplies and the use of Libyan territory.

Relations with the Central African Republic (CAR) deteriorated in November 2001 when former CAR army commander, General François Bozize, was granted 'humanitarian asylum' in Chad having fled his country following a failed coup. Adding to the tension was the concurrent raiding of southern Chad by Chadian rebels based in CAR territory. CAR president, Ange-Félix Fatassé, was assisted by Libyan troops to avert the coup. Tensions between CAR and Chad remained high during 2002 In August 2002, Chad alleged that rebels launched attacks form CAR against Chadian troops. There was movement towards reducing tension between the two countries with talks in October 2002, when Chad agreed to extradite Bozize to France. The CAR responded by agreeing to send the Chadian rebel, Colonel Abdoulaye Miskine, to Togo. Chad alleged that Miskine had been behind the massacre of 150 Chadian nationals in November 2002.

Rags or riches

The most significant economic development in recent Chadian history is the decision to drill for oil in the Doba basin. Drilling commenced in January 2002 by Exxon Mobil. Chad has estimated that it could earn between US$2.5 billion and US$5 billion until 2030 from the project. The oil is to be transported to the Atlantic coast of Cameroon by a 1,080km pipeline. Construction of the pipeline began in December 2001 and the first Chadian oil is expected to be sold in 2004. The project is groundbreaking in its composition; in order to avoid the problems of environmental degradation and political corruption faced by other oil-rich African states, a complex four-way agreement was reached between Exxon Mobil, the African states involved, the World Bank and various non-governmental organisations (NGOs).

The World Bank has been able to use its power of conditionality to control the Déby government's use of early oil-related disbursements. Despite this, Chad's 2002 budget showed a worrying 34 per cent rise in expenditure, maintaining a substantial deficit. Déby's commitment to his pledge of spending 80 per cent of oil revenue on improvement of social and human capital, rather than lining his own pockets with it, will not be fully proven until the oil flows through Cameroon – at which point the World Bank loses much of its leverage.

Chad is in desperate need of a long and sustained boom to pull it out of its wretched poverty. The Doba pipeline may – if properly managed – be the lifeline it has been looking for.

In 2001 and 2002, the Chadian economy seemed to be on its way to recovery after successive decades of depression. GDP growth rose from 1.0 per cent in 2000 to 8.9 per cent in 2001 and 10.6 per cent in 2002. However, in a country so heavily leaning towards the rural sector – 80 per cent of the population eke out a living in the agro-pastoral sector – any oil-induced boom must be coupled with maintained agricultural growth so that the boom effects the whole national economy.

Chad's progress towards debt relief under the IMF's Heavily Indebted Poor Country (HIPC) initiative, first announced in May 2001, seemed to be on track. Eligibility is conditional on the construction and implementation of a Poverty Reduction Strategy (PRS), as well as a number of good governance criteria. In January 2002, the IMF approved a US$6.8 million disbursement under a three-year Poverty Reduction and Growth Facility (PRGF)

KEY INDICATORS — Chad

	Unit	1996	1997	1998	1999	2000
Population	m	6.95	7.17	7.40	7.64	7.89
Gross domestic product (GDP)	US$bn	1.61	1.57	1.71	1.60	1.40
GDP per capita	US$	210	230	230	209	182
GDP real growth	%	3.1	4.2	7.7	2.3	-0.3
Inflation	%	11.3	5.6	4.3	-8.4	3.7
Consumer prices	1995=100	112.4	118.7	133.1	124.1	128.8
Exports (fob) (goods)	US$m	262.1	246.4	250.5	188.0	181.0
Imports (fob) (goods)	US$m	248.3	241.5	253.2	246.0	243.0
Balance of trade	US$m	13.8	4.9	-2.7	-58.0	-62.0
Foreign debt	US$bn	1.1	1.1	1.1	1.1	1.1
Total reserves minus gold	US$m	164.5	135.8	120.1	95.0	110.7
Foreign exchange	US$m	163.8	135.4	119.7	94.6	110.3
Exchange rate	per US$	511.55	583.67	589.90	615.70	711.98

arrangement to address the effect on Chad's economy from declining global cotton prices. Another US$3 million disbursement was agreed in April 2002, meaning that the IMF had made a total of US$106 million available to Chad since it joined the PRGF in 2000. As of April 2002, Chad had drawn on approximately US$37 million. The prospect of oil-induced economic growth has created a favourable lending environment for Chad, leading to the EU announcing an extended aid programme in February 2002.

Outlook

Chad is at what must seem for its citizens to be a familiar impasse: the future holds the potential for lasting peace and economic development, but the country's past may well prevent it from happening. President Déby's renewed term in office should bring continued structural economic reforms and also pose questions over the country's path towards democratic stability. The development of the southern Doba oil fields gives reasons for cautious optimism, but may well provide a new set of grievances for northern rebels who are cut off from the black gold. Indeed, the major obstacle towards continued Chadian development is its endemic internal conflict, of which the MDJT is no more than the latest chapter. Peaceful dialogue is the only constructive way forward, requiring constraint and compromise from all parties, but promising substantial rewards if they manage to do so.

Risk assessment

Economic	Improving
Political	Poor
Regional stability	Improving

COUNTRY PROFILE

Historical profile

1900s France defeated the local ruler, Rabeh Zubeit, at a battle in Kousseri and formed the territory in 1916.
1929 A northern, Saharan, segment was added.
1946 Chad was granted status as a French overseas territory and gained its own regional assembly.
1960 Chad was granted independence. A one-party regime was imposed under President Francois Tombalbaye. A series of rebellions against Tombalbaye's rule were repressed.
1975 Tombalbaye was killed in a coup and replaced by Colonel Félix Malloum. Malloum agreed to share power with a rebel leader, Hissène Habré.
1979 Habré forced Malloum out of N'Djamena after a violent power struggle.
1980 A new alliance was formed between Habré and Goukouni Oueddei, which lasted until 1980 when Libya sided with Goukouni and Habré fled. Libyan troops and Chadian factions defeated Habré, at which point France intervened and the invading force was driven back from N'Djamena, leaving Habré in nominal control of the country.
1987 After several years of stalemate, an effort was made to resolve the conflict by President Mitterand of France and Colonel Al-Qadafi of Libya who both agreed to withdraw their forces from Chad. The French troops withdrew but those of Libya did not. The French returned and pushed Libya back across the Chad-Libya border.
1989–90 A rebellion was launched by Idriss Déby, an army commander. Habré fled to Senegal and Déby proclaimed himself president.
1996 Chad's first multi-party presidential elections were held in June in which Idriss Déby was elected to remain as Chad's president with 69.09 per cent of votes against 30.91 per cent for Wadal Abdelkader Kamougue.
1997 Legislative elections held in January and February saw the Mouvement Patriotique du Salut (MPS) (Patriotic Movement for Salvation) win 63 of the 125 seats, the Union pour le Rénouveau et la Democratie (URD) (Union for Renewal and Democracy) led by Kamougue won 29 and the Union Nationale pour la Démocratie et la Renouvellement (UNDR) (National Union for Democracy and Renewal) won 15.
2001 President Déby was re-elected on 20 May with 67 per cent of the vote. In December, a peace agreement was signed in Libya between the Chadian government and the northern rebel movement, Mouvement pour la Démocratie et la Justice au Tchad (MDJT) (Movement for Democracy and Justice in Chad).
2002 Results of the 21 April parliamentary election: MPS won 112 seats out of 155; Rassemblement pour la Démocratie et le Progrès (RDP) (Rally for Democracy and Progress) 10 seats and Front des Forces d'Action pour la République (FAR) (Front of Action Forces for the Republic) nine seats. Haroun Kabadi was appointed prime minister by the President on 12 June after the resignation of Nagoum Yamassoum.

Political structure

Constitution
A referendum in March 1996 passed a constitution based on the French model providing for a unitary state with 61.46 per cent of votes.

Form of state
Republic.

Last elections
21 April 2002 (legislative); 20 May 2001 (presidential)

Next elections
2006 (presidential)

Political parties

Ruling party
Mouvement Patriotique du Salut (MPS) (Patriotic Movement for Salvation) (re-elected Apr 2002)

Main opposition party
Rassemblement pour la Démocratie et le Progrès (RDP) (Rally for Democracy and Progress).

Population

7.89 million (2000)
Annual population growth rate: 2.9 per cent (1994–2000). Approximately 43 per cent of the total population is under 15 years.
Population density: six inhabitants per square km. Urban population: 24 per cent (1994–2000).

Ethnic make-up
There are more than 200 distinct groups.

Religions
Muslim (44 per cent), traditional beliefs, Christians (33 per cent)

Education

As reform in the education sector has been slow following from the period of disturbances, local communities continue to play a greater role in financing and operating their schools. To rebuild the education system, the government of Chad developed an Education-Training-Employment strategy for 1990–2000 with the help of the International Labour Organisation, and other UN development agencies.
Five national programmes were developed including basic, secondary, higher education and research, vocational training and literacy. Estimates show that the programme has trained some 2,400 teachers and 1,000 classrooms have been built.
However, enrolment in schools is poor with four out of 10 children remaining outside school and seven out of 10 adults are illiterate. Roughly half the workforce has no jobs.
French is the primary language of instruction in most higher education institutions. The University of N'Djamena is the country's main university, comprised of three faculties.

Health

World Bank estimates during the period 1994 and 2000 showed that the average life expectancy was 48 years and the infant mortality rate stood at 99 per 1,000 live births. It is estimated that 40 per cent of children under the age of five were malnourished in the same period. The total fertility rate shows that 6.3 children are born per woman while the rate of contraception practices is estimated at 4 per cent among women aged 15–49. The maternal mortality rate is typically 830 deaths per 100,000 live births. World Bank estimates in 2000 showed that 24 per cent and 29 per cent of the population had access to improved water and sanitation facilities respectively. There are less than 0.05 physicians and 0.7 hospital beds typically available for 1,000 people. The HIV rate is as high as 2.69 per cent among adults.

According to World Bank estimates, government expenditure on healthcare averaged 2.9 per cent of GDP of which 2.3 per cent was public expenditure between 1990 and 1998. Expenditure on private healthcare (such as private household expenditure and insurance) averaged 0.6 per cent of GDP over the same period.

Welfare

A 30-year civil war, which ended in 1990, caused many civilians to flee their own country in the early eighties. The repatriation began in 1995, following an agreement between UN refugee agency (UNHCR) Chad and the Central African Republic. A total of 14,000 refugees have been repatriated since then. A few hundred have chosen to remain in Central Africa, whose cases are pending to be resolved.

The International Monetary Fund (IMF) has a three-year arrangement for Chad under the Poverty Reduction and Growth Facility (PRGF) equivalent to about US$49.9 million to support the government's 1999–2002 economic programme.

Violence and societal discrimination against women remain common. Female genital mutilation (FGM) and child labour are widespread.

Main cities

N'Djamena (capital, formerly Fort Lamy, estimated population 550,000), Sarh (106,500), Moundou (95,800), Abéché (77,200), Faya-Largeau (17,600)

Languages spoken

French is the official and the business language. The language group in Chad is Afro-Asiatic; Arabic is spoken by most of the population and there are more than 50 African dialects.

Official language/s

French and Arabic

Media

Press

There are some independent newspapers that circulate freely in the capital, N'Djamena, but have little impact among the largely rural and illiterate population. Weeklies include *Le Progrès*, *N'Djamena Hebdo* (independent), *Le Contact* (bi-weekly) and *Le Temps*. A few newspapers and periodicals are published, including *Info-Tchad* (a daily news bulletin) and *Journal Officiel de la République du Tchad*. *L'Observateur* is an independent bi-monthly publication.

Broadcasting

Radio: The state primarily controls the broadcast media, although radio is the primary medium of mass communication. Government radio station, Radio Diffusion Nationale Tchadienne, broadcasts from N'Djamena, with stations at Moundou, Sarh and Abéché. Private commercial radio hardly exists due to high licensing fees. The Catholic Church owns one private radio station.

Television: The only television station, Télé-Chad is state-owned and its coverage favours the government. Télé-Chad has transmitted since December 1987 in French and Arabic.

Economy

Chad is the fifth poorest country in the world. Drought, civil war and permanent instability have crippled the economy.

The economy is highly dependent on cotton exports, the value of which vary considerably with price fluctuations on the world market and climatic changes. The construction of the Doba oil project is under way and analysts predict that it will double Chad's GDP by 2004, as well as doubling the government's budget. However, despite production predicted to peak at 250,000 barrels per day (bpd), the country will remain dependent on oil imports as it will not be refining any of the oil it produces.

The agricultural sector, which accounts for the bulk of GDP, employment and export earnings, was hit by adverse weather conditions in 2001.

The economy is undergoing a programme of liberalisation under the auspices of the IMF. This has been coupled with debt service relief under the enhanced Heavily Indebted Poor Countries (HIPC) initiative. In April 2001, the IMF completed the evaluation of Chad's performance under the Poverty Reduction and Growth Facility (PRGF) arrangement and allowed the country to draw on a US$3 million loan. The IMF originally approved a three-year arrangement for Chad under the PRGF in 2000, worth around US$49.9 million, to support the government's 1999–2002 economic programme.

Under the regime of liberalisation, the government has privatised public enterprises, aimed to secure macroeconomic stability and strengthened its fiscal position, and brought inflation down.

In terms of broad indicators, the programme has brought mixed success. Between 1996–2000, inflation fell from 11.3 per cent to 3.7 per cent, but rose again to 12.4 per cent in 2001. This is well above its 1983–92 average of 2.4 per cent. Meanwhile, real GDP has not shown particularly strong growth, averaging 2.9 per cent in 1996–2000 (-0.3 per cent in 2000) compared to 6.3 per cent in 1983–92. However, the IMF predicts that with the expansion of the oil industry, GDP will rise considerably, possibly making Chad one of the fastest growing economies in the world. In 2001, the first signs of Chad's economic growth was demonstrated when GDP growth rose to 9.7 per cent.

Chad's terms of trade are deteriorating due to rising world oil prices and falling cotton prices. In 2000, terms of trade fell by 2.5 per cent, but recovered to 12.0 per cent in 2001. The unsteady nature of the country's terms of trade poses significant problems for resolving the country's external imbalances, particularly with drought threatening agricultural productivity. Excluding official transfers, Chad's current account deficit represented an estimated 42.4 per cent of GDP in 2001, compared to 16 per cent of GDP in 2000. This is likely to worsen as the country's oil industry develops, which will involve importing capital goods such as machinery. The IMF predicts the deficit could get as high as 46.5 per cent by end-2003. This is likely to be met by increased capital investment flows into the country, although there is no guarantee that this will offset the effects of a yawning current account deficit.

External trade

Exports

Principal exports are raw cotton (typically 48 per cent of total), textiles, fish, meat and live animals, hides and skins, natron, gums and resins.

Main destinations: Portugal, Germany, France, Spain.

Imports

Principal imports are basic foods, petroleum products, machinery and transport equipment.

Main sources: France, US, Cameroon, Italy.

Agriculture

The agricultural sector forms the mainstay of the economy, accounts for around 40 per cent of GDP and 60 per cent of employment. Around 20 per cent of land is arable, and most of this is the southern flood plains of the Logone and Chari Rivers. About 1 per cent of arable land is farmed.

Rice is produced on the irrigated land along the banks of the Oubangi river north of Lake Chad. Subsistence farming and livestock predominate in the north.

The country's main food crops are sorghum, millet, dry beans, sesame, potatoes, rice and maize. Cash crops include oil seeds (groundnuts and sesame), sugar-cane and tobacco. However, cotton is the most important agricultural product, accounting for between 40–60 per cent of export earnings, depending on world prices and output. Annual production can vary between 150–200,000 tonnes. The cotton and cattle production sectors are under government control.
Cattle farming involves nearly 40 per cent of the population. It contributes 39 per cent to total agricultural production and 20 per cent to Chad's GDP. About 90 per cent of beef production is exported to Nigeria.

Industry and manufacturing
The industrial sector contributed 12.2 per cent to GDP in 1998 and employed 10 per cent of the workforce.
The industrial sector is small-scale and underdeveloped. Activity is centred in N'Djamena, Moundou and Sarh and is based on agriculture, particularly food processing, textiles, brewing, tobacco processing, leather and construction materials.

Mining
Mining contributes less than 3 per cent to GDP. The only minerals extracted in any quantities are soda and rock salt (which are exported mainly to Nigeria) and natron from Lake Chad (used in preservation of meat and in tanning).
Known deposits of chromium, tungsten, titanium, iron, wolfram, gold, uranium and tin remain unexploited.
Other mineral deposits are thought to lie in the disputed Aouzou Strip along the Libyan border.

Hydrocarbons
The development of Chad's oil industry is the subject of intense debate, although it could hold the key to the country's development. Chad has proven oil reserves of one billion barrels, most of which is located in the Doba basin.
In November 1996, a consortium (Exxon Mobil (40 per cent), Royal Dutch/Shell (40 per cent), Elf Aquitaine (20 per cent)) signed a memorandum of understanding (MOU) with the government to develop the Doba fields and the construction of a 1,050km pipeline to offshore facilities in Cameroon. The development was estimated to cost a total of US$3.5 billion. In April 2000, Chevron and Petronas replaced TotalFinaElf and Royal Dutch/Shell in the consortium.
Development of the project began in October 2000 with the industry set to come on-line by 2003. In June 2001, ABN Amro completed arrangements for a US$600 million project financing agreement to enable the work to begin on the pipeline. However, both the development of the oil fields and the construction of the pipeline have been the subject of political wrangling. While politicians squabble over oil revenues, organisations involved in environmental protection and human rights have attacked the Chad-Cameroon pipeline. Although the World Bank (which is providing 3 per cent of the project financing) has hailed the project as a model of poverty alleviation in Africa, according to its critics, the Doba development will increase regional problems, particularly in relation to conflict and corruption.
Problems began in 2000, when President Déby used a cash advance of US$4 million from Chevron and Petronas to buy arms ostensibly to provide security for the oil corporations. Aside from further militarisation of Chad, the project will also involve widespread deforestation and the forced migration of the indigenous population. In light of the ongoing problems, the European Parliament has advised the European Investment Bank (EIB) – which pledged a US$124 million loan to Chad, Cameroon and the oil consortium – not to approve funding unless Chad keeps to an agreement to safeguard the environment and human rights. Exxon finally began drilling in January 2002.

Energy
Chad has an installed electricity generation capacity of 29MW with electricity generation of 90 million kWh. Only 2 per cent of the population have access to electricity. The electricity supply is provided by two power stations in N'Djamena and plants in Moundou, Sarh and Abéché. Imports from Nigeria and Cameroon provide most of Chad's power requirements.
The Société Tchadienne d'Eau et d'Électricité (STEE) is the company responsible for electricity generation and supply in Chad. STEE is slated for privatisation under the terms of the country's IMF structural adjustment programme.

Banking
Central bank
Banque des Etats de l'Afrique Centrale.
Main financial centre
N'Djamena.

Time
GMT plus one hour

Geography
Chad is a landlocked country in north central Africa, bordered to the north by Libya, to the south by the Central African Republic, to the west by Niger and Cameroon and to the east by Sudan.

Climate
Hot and arid in northern desert regions, and wet and tropical in the south. Southern rainy season from May to October, central rainy season from June to September with temperatures ranging from 20 degrees Celsius (C) at night to as high as 40 degrees C during the day. Dry season throughout the rest of the year, lower evening temperatures.

Entry requirements
Passports
Required by all except nationals of certain African countries. Passports must be valid for three months.
Visa
Required by all except nationals of Nigeria and certain other African countries. A return or onward ticket is also required. All visitors must register with authorities on arrival. Exit permits must also be obtained before leaving.
Currency advice/regulations
No restriction on import of foreign currency, but amounts must be declared; export limited to declared amount.
Unlimited import of local currency which must also be declared.

Health (for visitors)
Mandatory precautions
Yellow fever vaccination certificate required if arriving from an infected area.
Advisable precautions
Hepatitis A, tetanus, typhoid and polio vaccinations. Malaria prophylaxis recommended as risk exists throughout the country. There is a rabies risk. Water precautions necessary outside the capital.

Hotels
Reservations should be made well in advance of visit. If service charge is not included in bill a 10 per cent tip is usual. Limited availability outside of N'Djamena.

Public holidays
Fixed dates
1 Jan (New Year's Day), 1 May, 25 May, 11 Aug (Independence), 1 Nov, 28 Nov, 25 Dec (Christmas).
Variable dates
Easter Sunday, Easter Monday, Eid al-Fitr, Eid al-Adha, Maulid al-Nabi, Whit Monday.

Working hours
Banking
Mon–Thu and Sat: 0700–1100; Fri: 0700–1030.
Business
Mon–Sat: 0900–1230, 1600–1930.
Government
Mon–Thu and Sat: 0700–1400; Fri: 0700–1200. Specific times vary within this period.

Telecommunications
Telephone/fax
Dialling code for Chad: IDD access code + 235, followed by the subscriber's number. There are no area codes.

Electricity supply
220V AC, 50 cycles

Getting there
Air
National airline: Air Tchad (98 per cent government-owned).
International airport/s: N'Djamena (NDJ), 4km from city. Post office, bank, refreshments, bar and duty-free.
Limited flights from surrounding countries and Paris, France.
Airport tax: Security tax for domestic departures CFAf1,200 and international departures CFAf7,500. Tourist tax for international departures CFAf3,000 for nationals and CFAf5,000 for non-nationals.
Surface
Road: Access is possible by road from Bangui (Central African Republic), from Maroua (Cameroon), Niger and Sudan. Road conditions are variable and access can be very difficult, especially in the rainy season.
Water: The main overland points of entry are by ferry across the Chari River to N'Djamena from Cameroon, or from Maiduguri (Nigeria), via Cameroon.

Getting about
National transport
Air: Restricted domestic service operated by Air Tchad. Scheduled services occasionally commandeered by armed forces.
Road: There are surfaced roads around N'Djamena; most other roads are not in good condition and are often impassable during rainy season (Jun–Oct). Permits and four-wheel drive vehicles required for all travel outside N'Djamena.
City transport
Taxis: Available in N'Djamena and the principal towns – Sarh and Mouncou; set-fare system in operation; 10 per cent tip is usual; can be hired on a time basis or by the day.
Car hire
Limited availablity in N'Djamena. French or international driving licence is required.

BUSINESS DIRECTORY

Telephone area codes
The international dialling code (IDD) for Chad is + 235 followed by the customer number.

Banking
Banque Agricole du Soudan au Tchad, BP 1727, 1727 NDjamena (tel: 519041, 519042 fax: 519040).

Banque Commerciale du Chari Tchad, BP 757, NDjamena (tel: 515958, 515231 fax: 5 6249).

Banque de Développement du Tchad, BP 19, NDjamena (tel: 522829, 523284 fax: 523318).

Banque Internationale pour l'Afrique au Tchad, BP 87, Ave Charles de Gaulle, NDjamena (tel: 525684. 52432 fax: 523053, 522345).

Banque Tchadienne de Crédit et de Dépôts, BP 461, NDjamena (tel: 524203, 522801, 524195 fax: 523713).

Financial Bank, BP 804, NDjamena (tel: 523389, 522660 fax: 522905).

Central bank
Banque des États de l'Afrique Centrale, PO Box 1917, Rue du Docteur Jamot, Yaounde, Cameroun (tel: +237 234030, 234060 Fax: +237 233329).

Travel information
Air Tchad, 27 Avenue du Président Tombalbaye, BP 168, N'Djamena (tel: 515-090, 513-581, 514-564).

Direction du Tourisme, BP 86, N'Djamena (tel: 515-032, 512-303, 512-305).

Ethiopian Airlines, BP 989, N'Djamena (tel: 513-027, 513-143).

Sudan Airways, BP 167, N'Djamena (tel: 515-148).

Other useful addresses
Chad Embassy (USA), 2002 R Street, NW, Washington DC 20009 (tel: 462-4009; fax: 265-1937; e-mail: info@chadembassy.org).

Chambre Consulaire du Tchad, BP 458, N'Djamena (tel: 515-264).

Commission for Trade and Industry, BP 453, N'Djamena (tel: 515-656).

European Development Fund, BP 532, N'Djamena (tel: 515-977, 512-276).

Office National des Céréales (ONC), BP 21, N'Djamena (tel: 513-731, 574-014).

Internet sites
Africa Business Network: http://www.ifc.org/abn

AllAfrica.com: http://allafrica.com

African Development Bank: http://www.afdb.org

Africa Online: http://www.africaonline.com

Chad: http://www.tchadrepertoire.com

Mbendi AfroPaedia (information on companies, countries, industries and stock exchanges in Africa): http://mbendi.co.za

KEY FACTS

Official name: Udzima wa Komori (L'Union des Comores) (Union of Comoro) (from Jan 2002)

Head of State: President Azali Assoumani (from 8 May 2002)

Head of government: Interim Prime Minister Hamada Madi Bolero (appointed prime minister Nov 2000; interim prime minister from 21 Jan 2002)

Ruling party: Government formed by the president, 7 Jun 2002

Area: 2,171 square km

Population: 727,000 (2001)

Capital: Moroni

Official language: Arabic and French

Currency: Comoros franc (Cf) = 100 centimes

Exchange rate: Cf470.36 per US$ (Jan 2003) (pegged Cf491.97 per euro)

GDP per capita: US$269 (2001)

GDP real growth: 1.00% (2001)

Inflation: 3.50% (2001)

Balance of trade: -US$35.00 million (2001)

Foreign debt: US$227.00 million (2001)

For the latest Key Facts, go to www.worldinformation.com

Comoros

Daniel Brett

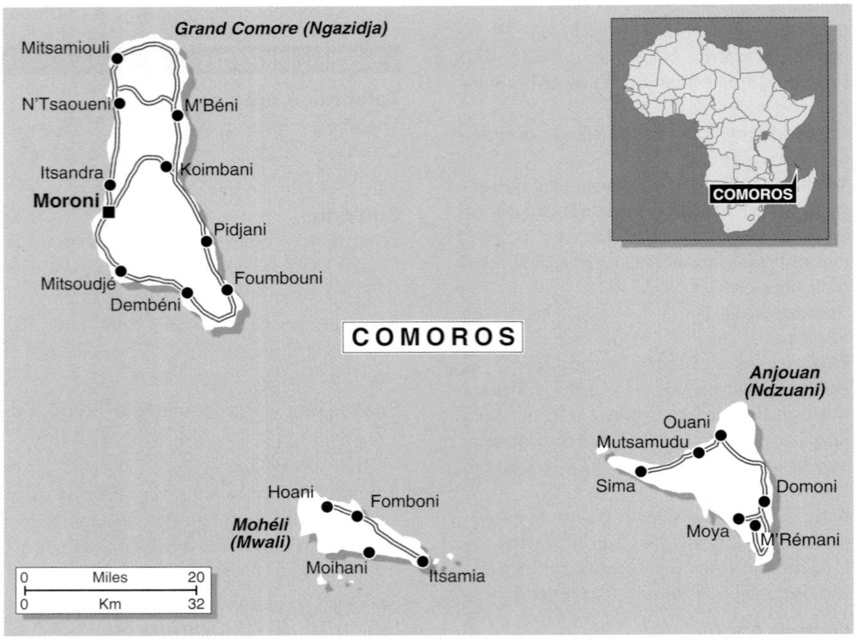

Since its independence from France in 1975, Comoros has been rocked by a succession of coups and secessionist movements led by an assortment of military officers, drug traffickers, mercenaries and chancers. The declaration of independence by the islands of Anjouan and Mohéli from Grande Comore, the largest island in the group, in 1997 prompted intervention by the then Organisation of African Unity (OAU). Years of OAU-sponsored peace talks and diplomatic isolation appeared to have succeeded when, in December 2001, a referendum showed strong popular support for re-uniting the islands. Yet, the new constitutional arrangement failed to demarcate departmental responsibilities and a potentially destabilising row broke out between the federal government and the president of Grande Comore.

The failure of the OAU to enforce stability on the islands, maintain the country's unity and introduce democracy in one of Africa's smallest states has proved to be a major embarrassment to the architects of African unity.

Paradise lost and found

The biggest problem the OAU faces is the country's political culture – or lack of it. It appears that any small reckless group of lightly armed men with limited foresight has a chance of seizing power in any one of Comoros' islands. Many Comorians, and indeed some foreigners, with some political sway have learnt that to pursue their interests, no matter how narrow, they simply have to land a boat and storm the local police station. The OAU's quest to change the political culture has been tough, although 2001 saw some breakthrough.

In February 2001, the country's leaders signed the Framework Agreement on Reconciliation, known as the Fomboni agreement, which was aimed at formally reinstating Comoros as a single, federal state and ending three years of secessionist conflict. It built on the Antananarivo agreement, brokered by the OAU and signed in Madagascar in 1999, which had been rejected by Anjouan's ruling junta and by a referendum held on the island in February 2000. The OAU had not recognised the results of the referendum, citing reports of intimidation, and it stepped up its campaign to prevent Anjouan secession, fearing that it could set a precedent for similar movements throughout Africa. The Fomboni agreement was hailed as a success by the OAU and claimed it vindicated its campaign of sanctions and threats of a naval blockade led by South Africa. Moreover, while the new unity agreement involved granting greater island autonomy, it included the democratic values embodied in the OAU charter.

The deal set up a transitional government headed by Colonel Azzali Assoumani, the army chief of staff who deposed Comoros President Tadjidine Ben Said Massoundi in a bloodless coup in 1999. The purpose of the transitional government was to oversee the installation of new institutions under the Fomboni agreement. A nationwide referendum was planned for December 2001 to ratify the new constitution, after which elections would be held to appoint a president for each island. The three islands would have their own separate constitution and president, ratified by a further round of referenda. The elected federal presidency would rotate on a four-year basis between the islands, starting with Grande Comore.

No rest for the wicked

The Fomboni agreement was never genuinely backed by the junta in Anjouan. The island's military rulers were effectively forced into accepting a new constitution which threatened their power base as well as their financial interests. Since he seized power in Anjouan with the unilateral declaration of independence in 1997, Colonel Abderemane Said Abeid, a French citizen, had operated an international crime syndicate which principally relied on drug trafficking and gun-running. The new constitution would force the Anjouanese authorities to be internationally accountable for the crime-based economy, thereby eroding Abeid's lucrative income.

Chaos reigned throughout 2001 as Anjouan was gripped by political turmoil as Abeid sought ways of strengthening his hold. In August, he was overthrown by Major Mohamed Bacar following growing public discontent over his authoritarian regime. In November, ahead of the referendum, Abeid launched a counter-attack from the nearby French island of Mayotte in an attempt to seize power and rip up the Fomboni agreement. However, forces loyal to Bacar thwarted Abeid's challenge and even some of those parties opposed to the Fomboni agreement condemned him. It seemed that on Anjouan, the vast majority were no longer willing to see the return of a corrupt and authoritarian figure like Abeid, no matter what their opinion on Comorian re-unification.

A similar attempt to sabotage the Fomboni agreement was seen in December 2001 when a 13-strong group of mercenaries, who had all served in the French army, tried to seize power. Acting on behalf of Achirafi Said Hachim, a former Comoran interior minister living in France, the raiders had meant to land on Grande Comore, but their boat sprang a fuel leak and they were forced to land on Mohéli. They roamed around the island in panic, looking for fuel and weapons, attacking the gendamerie and army base and taking civilians hostage. In an effort to appease the locals, the mercenaries claimed they were US soldiers hunting down Al-Qaeda terrorists fleeing from Afghanistan and accused President Assoumani of having links with Osama Bin Laden. Four mercenaries were killed by the Comoran army, two were lynched by the local population and the rest gave themselves up, fearing that they too would die at the hands of angry Mohélian islanders.

Grande catastrophe

The results of the Comoros referendum in December 2001 gave resounding support for re-unification and the federal constitution. Three-quarters of those who voted backed the Fomboni agreement in a 75 per cent turnout. This paved the way to another referendum in March 2002 on new constitutions for each island and elections in April. Assoumani announced he would stand for election as federal president and resigned as president of the transitional government, in accordance with the Fomboni agreement. This made the way for a government of national unity led by Prime Minister Hamada Madi that would govern the islands until the installation of a new government.

The whole process was thrown into turmoil as elections approached. The day before a referendum on the constitution in Grande Comore scheduled for 10 March, eight of the nine candidates for the island's presidency pulled out of the primary elections, citing massive electoral fraud. This delayed the referendum for a week. The result of the referendum delivered another shock to the transition process when a majority of voters rejected the proposed constitution for Grande Comore. This was in stark contrast to the overwhelming vote in favour of new constitutions for Anjouan and Mohéli.

In early April 2002, all three islands participated in elections, but turnout was low: 44.4 per cent in Grande Comore, 33.4 per cent in Anjouan and 35.0 per cent in Mohéli. Bacar won the election in Anjouan with over 70 per cent of the votes. Mohamed Said Fazul, the Governor of Mohéli and leader of the Union Comoran pour le Progrès (UCP) (Comoran Union for Progress), became president of Mohéli with 55 per cent of the votes. In a set-back for Assoumani, opposition leader Abdou Soule Elbak won the presidential election in Grande Comore with 63 per cent of the votes in a run-off election held in May.

The federal presidential election also took place on Grande Comore. The

KEY INDICATORS — Comoros

	Unit	1996	1997	1998	1999	2000
Population	m	0.63	0.65	0.67	0.69	0.71
Gross domestic product (GDP)	US$bn	0.21	0.19	0.20	0.19	0.17
GDP per capita	US$	338	298	294	297	238
GDP real growth	%	-1.2	4.2	1.2	1.9	-1.1
Inflation	%	2.0	3.0	3.5	3.5	4.5
Exports (fob) (goods)	US$m	0.0	15.0	17.0	18.0	20.0
Imports (fob) (goods)	US$m	0.0	0.0	0.0	73.0	78.0
Imports (cif)	US$m	0.0	68.0	70.0	0.0	0.0
Balance of trade	US$m	0.0	-53.0	-53.0	-55.0	-58.0
Current account	US$m	0.0	-24.0	-25.0	-9.0	-1.0
Total reserves minus gold	US$m	50.5	40.5	39.1	37.1	43.2
Foreign exchange	US$m	49.7	39.6	38.4	36.2	42.3
Exchange rate	per US$	383.66	437.75	442.46	461.77	533.98

election was marked by violence and the withdrawal of Assoumani's two rivals, Mahamoud Mradadi and Said Ali Kemal, who stormed polling stations with their supporters, destroyed ballot boxes and alleged that the electoral roll was fraudulent. Riots broke out in the capital Moroni after Assoumani was declared the winner, with just over 75 per cent of the vote. The offices of the UN Development Programme (UNDP), which had been giving technical assistance to the election authorities, were attacked by arsonists. The attack occurred after independent observers from La Francophonie (an organisation of French-speaking nations), the OAU and the Arab League confirmed that the elections had been carried out correctly. In contrast, the Comoros National Electoral Commission (NEC) claimed the elections were not free or fair because of incidents of violence and the small number of votes cast. The NEC appeared incapable of reaching a final judgement on whether to validate the election result, with the NEC's validation committee at odds with the general assembly.

The results prompted a national constitutional crisis, with Elbak and Assoumani engaged in a power struggle. Confusion over the delineation of administrative control between government departments and separation of the roles of the federal and island governments heightened tensions. Elbak called for equal control between local and federal government over Grande Comore's financial sector as the struggle focussed on who controlled the island's finances, particularly the issue of who has responsibility for the income from customs and taxes.

Perfume hides bad odour

The turmoil that began in 1997 has hindered economic development. All economic fundamentals have shown a sharp decline. The economy stagnated in 2001 due to a decline in donor support and investment combined with major electricity black-outs. The country's main exports – vanilla, cloves and the perfume ylang-ylang – were hit by falling output and problems accessing markets, although the price of ylang-ylang has been rising strongly in recent years on strong international demand. After a rise of 54.6 per cent in 2000, exports were projected to decline by 22.5 per cent in 2001 due to falling commodity prices, while imports were expected to rise by 14.9 per cent. The current account deficit was projected to increase to over 9 per cent of GDP by end-2001, although this was expected to be largely offset by higher foreign assistance and a decline in debt repayments. The decline in exports in 2001 has eroded the country's international reserves, which fell from 8.0 months of import cover in 2000 to an estimated 7.3 months in 2001, although this was still relatively high.

Economic decline has undermined the central government's fiscal position, not least because the economy was fractured by the secession of Anjouan and Mohéli. Nevertheless, the IMF praised the government's move to adopt fiscal restraint, although the overall fiscal deficit (including grants) was around 4 per cent of GDP in 2001 compared to 2 per cent in 2000. Debt-service obligations had risen to 4.3 per cent of GDP by 2001 and the government had generated significant arrears to suppliers as well as wage arrears which had risen to 8.1 per cent of GDP. Nevertheless, economic stability was still secure, even in the adverse economic conditions and political uncertainty. This was helped by single-figure inflation and exchange rate stability secured by the Comoros franc's fixed peg to the euro.

In July 2001, the Comoros government agreed to a one-year IMF staff monitored programme (SMP). This was designed to begin a process of economic rehabilitation to encourage further external donor support. The government committed itself to restraining the wage bill and scaling down the size of the public sector.

The constitutional crisis that occurred in April 2002 has put the economic programme on the back-burner. The transitional government is unable to make any long-term economic plans and donors are holding back their funding to see if the country can establish a stable government.

Outlook

The situation in Comoros is unlikely to get easier in the medium-term. Grande Comore will need to face the crisis created by the lack of properly defined areas of government. The impasse is likely to be overcome following the parliamentary elections of March 2003. Nevertheless, the longer the constitutional crisis contrinues, the stronger the popular discontent and the further economic turmoil will disrupt life on the islands. This can only heighten separatist sentiment on the other two islands as the constitutional crisis continues.

Risk assessment

Economic	Poor
Political	Poor
Regional stability	Poor

COUNTRY PROFILE

Historical profile

1843 The Comoros was ceded to France by Portugal.
1947 Formerly attached to Madagascar, the Comoros became a separate French Overseas Territory.
1961 It achieved internal self-government in December.
1972 Elections in December produced a large majority for parties advocating independence and Ahmed Abdallah became president of the government council.
1973 In June, Abdallah was restyled president of the government.
1975 The Federal Islamic Republic of the Comoros gained independence from France, except for Mayotte, which was the only island in the archipelago that voted to retain its link with France.
1978 A constitution was approved in a referendum.
1982 Constitutional amendments adopted in October increased the president's power by reducing that of each island's governor.
1985 In January, the constitution was amended to abolish the position of prime minister.
1989 A constitutional amendment permitting President Abdallah to remain in office for a third six-year term was approved in a referendum. In November, Abdallah was assassinated by members of his own 650-strong presidential guard. Said Djohar was appointed interim head of state.
1990 Djohar was elected president.
1992 A new constitution was approved.
1995 A coup toppled President Said Djohar and his government. Caabi el Yachroutou Mohammed declared himself interim president and prime minister. He appointed a government of national unity.
1996 Mohammed Taki Abdoul-Karim won the March presidential election with two-thirds of the vote in the second round run-off. The first round of legislative elections were held under military surveillance. They were boycotted by the opposition, Front pour le Redressment Nationale (FRN) (Front for National Redress), which wanted a neutral electoral commission, revised electoral roll and elections for constituent assembly. The ruling Rassemblement National pour le Développment (RND) (National Rally for Development) secured 32 of 37 seats in the first round and four of six seats in the second round. Tajidine Ben Said Massonde resigned as prime minister following the legislative elections and the President appointed Ahmed Abdou.
1997 The island of Anjouan (Ndzuani) set up its own administration on 3 August and declared independence from the

Comoros, expressing sentiments for reintegration with France due to a collapse in living standards since independence. The Moroni government led an unsuccessful invasion of the island in September.
1998 President Mohammed Taki Abdoul-Karim died in November. The interim president, Tajidine Ben Said Massonde, from Anjouan, failed to organise new presidential elections.
1999 On 30 April, the Comoran armed forces chief of staff, Colonel Azali Assoumani, seized power in a bloodless coup. He was sworn in as president in May. In legislative elections on Anjouan held on 15 and 22 August, the hardline secessionists won every seat.
2000 Negotiations between Anjouan and the Comoran government led to the signing of an accord in August, which aimed to create a loose federation. This was rejected by the Organisation of African Unity (OAU) which brokered the discussions. The Anjouan parliament was dissolved by the local military ruler and replaced by an unelected legislative council. Hamada Madi Bolero was appointed prime minister of Comoros in November.
2001 A national reconciliation agreement, known as the Fomboni agreement, was signed between the Comoros government and the secessionist island of Anjouan in February. On 9 August, soldiers ousted Lieutenant Colonel Said Abeid Abderemane, the leader of the junta in power on Anjouan since 1999. In the 23 December referendum on the Comoros draft constitution, 77 per cent voted for removing the federal structure of government and replacing it with a decentralised Comoran Union of three autonomous islands: Anjouan, Mohéli and Grand Comoros.
2002 The country's name was changed to Union des Comores (Union of Comoros) in January. Colonel Azali Assoumani was elected president of the Union of Comoros on 14 April with about three-quarters of the vote, however, the electoral commission declared the poll invalid. The two opposition candidates and most voters of Anjouan, boycotted the vote. On 8 May, Azali Assoumani was declared president-elect of the Union.
In Mohéli, Mohamed Said Fazul was elected president. Mohamed Bacar was elected president of Anjouan.
In presidential elections on Grande Comore on 12 May, Mze Abdou Soule won 17.1 per cent of the vote, Bakari Abdallah Boina 14.6 per cent and Kamar Ezamane Mohamed ben Charaf 10.9 per cent. Turnout was 70.1 per cent. A run-off was due by mid-2002.

Political structure

Constitution

The Constitution of 1992 was suspended after the 1999 military coup.
To provide political stability and to quell the secessionists on Anjouan and Moheli, a referendum on the Comoros draft constitution was held on 23 December 2001, in which 75 per cent voted for removing the federal structure of government.
The new constitution created a federation – the Union of Comoros – with greater autonomy for each of the three islands. Each island has its own legislature, constitution and budget. Foreign relations, defence and currency is the responsibility of the Union.

Form of state

Federal Islamic republic

The executive

Under the federal constitution, a president, who heads the Union of Comoros and the central government, is elected for a four-year term.

National legislature

The national constitution ratified in January 2002 established a 33-member legislature for the Union with 15 members appointed by the three island legislatures (five each) and 18 elected through direct universal suffrage. Each island has its own assembly.

Last elections

31 March 2002 (general); 14 April 2002 (presidential)

Political parties

Chuma Parti (CP) (Chuma Party), Mouvement pour la démocratie et le progrès (MDP) (Movement for Democracy and Progress), Forum National De Rétablissement (FNR) (National Recovery Forum), Union Comoran pour le Progrès (UCP) (Comoran Union for Progress)

Population

710,000 (2000)
The annual population growth rate was 2.5 per cent between 1994–2000. Approximately 48 per cent of the population is under 15 years of age.
Population density: 244 per square km.
Urban population: 32 per cent (1994–2000). Anjouan is overpopulated, with 650 inhabitants per square km, while Mohéli (Mwali) has a population density of 100 per square km.

Ethnic make-up

Antalote, Cafre, Makao, Oimatsaha, Sakalava.

Religions

Sunni Muslim 86 per cent (official religion), Roman Catholic 14 per cent.

Education

In 2000, the adult illiteracy rate was estimated at 33.5 per cent and 47.2 per cent for men and women respectively. UN Children's Fund (Unicef) estimates in early 2002 showed that the net school enrolment rate dropped from 64 per cent in 1994 to 60 per cent in 2000 due to insufficient classrooms and qualified teachers among other infrastructural inadequacies. Education suffers also from poor performance and quality. The Unicef sponsored humanitarian action plan for Comoros in 2002 will provide US$122,000 towards basic education of children.

Health

World Bank estimates between 1994 and 2000 show that life expectancy is 60 years. The proportion of children fully vaccinated in 2000 dropped to 66 per cent due to several problems. Acute and severe malnutrition affected between 3 per cent and 13 per cent of children with the island of Moheli being most affected. Infant mortality is 64 per 1,000 live births whereas under-five mortality is 86 per 1,000. The maternal mortality rate is estimated at 500 per 100,000 live births. A health survey in 2000 shows that only 63 per cent of births are attended by trained health personnel. The same survey shows that only 46 per cent of pregnant women are immunised against tetanus. Just under half the population has access to improved water sources.
HIV infection is low, with only 400 adults (0.12 per cent of the adult population) suffering from HIV/AIDS in 2000. While over 60 per cent of sex workers in Moroni are tested as positive, prostitution is relatively rare.
A Unicef-sponsored humanitarian action plan for Comoros in 2002 has a health budget of US$266,000 targeting up to 30,000 children and 1,800 pregnant women.

Welfare

There is no minimum wage, there are no laws prohibiting bonded or forced labour and no protection for anti-union practices by employers. The labour code allows for one day off per week and one month of paid leave per year, although the government generally does not enforce the law due to a lack of provision.
There is discrimination against Christians in Comoros, which is predominantly Muslim. Islamic clerics have been involved in unofficial campaigns against Christians, but despite threats and harassment there are no reports of widespread violence against them. The new constitution provides for equality to all citizens regardless of sex, origin, race, religion, belief or ideology.

Main cities

Moroni (on Grand Comore (Ngazidja), estimated population 60,000 in 1998), Mutsamudu (on Anjouan (Ndzuani),

(14,000), Fomboni (on Mohéli (Mwali), (7,000).

Languages spoken

Shikomor, French, Arabic and numerous African languages are spoken. English is rarely encountered.

Official language/s

Arabic and French

Media

Press

The semi-official weekly *Al-Watwan* and several private newspapers are published in the capital Moroni. *La Gazette de Comores* and the weekly *L'Archipel* are sharply critical of the government. The Afrol Comoros News Archive carries news articles and features published about Comoros in afrol.com (http://www.afrol.Com/Countries/Comoros/news_comoros.htm).

Broadcasting

Radio: Radio Comoros broadcasts in Comoran, French, Arabic and Swahili. A few private television and radio stations operate without overt governmental interference. Transmissions from French-controlled Mayotte are easily received and some people have access to satellite and other international broadcasting.

Television: There is no national television.

Economy

Between 1999–2001, the Comoran economy showed some improvement in its macroeconomic indicators, following a protracted recession. Part of the country's success is due to the pegging of the Comoran franc to the euro, which has ensured exchange rate stability while depreciating the currency's parity with the US dollar, making its exports generally more attractive on the world markets. The economy has also benefitted from the rising international prices of its main cash crops, ylang-ylang and cloves.

If the country succeeds in ensuring political stability in its transition to democracy, then relations with donors are likely to be fully restored and Comoros will receive much-needed credit. The distribution of wealth between the islands is likely to be a sore issue. Recent growth in economic activity has focussed on the clove output, which is mainly located in the breakaway Anjouan island. If the federation holds together in 2002, the other two islands will demand a greater share in the income from clove exports. This might not be forthcoming if clove prices decline again in the event of an increase in world supply.

Whatever direction external markets take, Comoros will need to embark on a process of economic diversification. The key to this is likely to come in the form of tourism, which has been traditionally small on the islands and fell back in the wake of the 1999 coup. The islands are idyllic and contain considerable biodiversity and rare flora and fauna. International financial institutions and bilateral donors are pressuring the government to increase revenues, liberalise trade, accelerate privatisation and remove the Labour Code in an effort to increase competitiveness and attract foreign investment. Structural adjustment is unlikely to bring many benefits, other than an increase in donor assistance and debt rescheduling.

External trade

Comoros runs annual deficits on its trade account, largely because of a limited export base. The IMF has urged better customs control as customs revenue represents over half of state financial receipts.

Exports

Principal exports are vanilla (typically 65 per cent of total), cloves (18.5 per cent), perfumes (ylang-ylang) (12.5 per cent), coffee and copra.

Main destinations: France (31 per cent of 2000 total), US (19.3 per cent), Singapore (18.4 per cent), Netherlands (9.5 per cent), Germany (5.2 per cent).

Imports

Principal imports are fuels, rice, vehicles.

Main sources: France (25.9 per cent of 2000 total), South Africa (16.3 per cent), United Arab Emirates (7.5 per cent), Kenya (7.3 per cent), Australia (5.8 per cent).

Agriculture

The agriculture sector is the principal source of export earnings. It contributes around 40 per cent to GDP and employs 65 per cent of the workforce.

Although as much as 50 per cent of the total land area is cultivated, the agricultural sector remains underdeveloped (due to poor soil, adverse weather conditions and inadequate facilities) and over 50 per cent of the country's food requirements (notably rice) have to be imported.

Major food crops grown are cassava, sweet potatoes, rice and bananas; yams and coconuts are also produced, while main cash crops are cocoa, ylang-ylang (perfumes), vanilla and cloves.

Fishing is unexploited, with tuna being the main catch. The fishing sector has received considerable aid from Japan and the EU.

Deforestation, caused by clearing for the cultivation of the ylang-ylang crop, is an increasing ecological problem.

Industry and manufacturing

The industrial sector contributes around 13 per cent to GDP and employs 5 per cent of the workforce; manufacturing contributes 5.4 per cent. The sector is underdeveloped, with activity confined to distillation of essences and perfumes (particularly from ylang-ylang), vanilla processing, soft drinks, plastics and woodwork.

Tourism

With investment, the number of tourists could expand from around 15,000 to 40,000 by 2006, increasing GDP by 15–20 per cent. Tourists have been deterred by political instability and social turmoil, although there are no reports of attacks on foreigners – apart from those who arrive heavily armed.

Mining

There is no mining activity.

Hydrocarbons

There are no known oil or gas reserves and the country relies on imports of refined oil for its energy needs. However, consumption is low. There is only one oil company in Comoros, the Société Comorienne des Hydrocarbures (SCH), which owns two storage depots.

Energy

There is heavy dependence on imports for all fuel requirements. The electricity generating infrastructure is poor and there are frequent blackouts, partly due to generator breakdowns and partly due to a lack of fuel. Electricity is provided by the parastatal utility Electricite et Eaux des Comores (EEDC).

Banking

The Banking sector is composed of the Banque Centrale des Comores (BCC), the central bank, the Banque de Développement des Comores (BDC), which focuses on development lending, and the Banque pour l'Industrie et le Commerce des Comores (BIC). The BIC is linked to France's BNP–Paribas and provides full international trade finance as well as local personal and business banking services.

Central bank

Banque Centrale des Comores (BCC)

Main financial centre

Moroni

Time

GMT plus three hours

Geography

The Comoros is an archipelago in the Mozambique Channel, between the island of Madagascar and the east coast of the African mainland. The group comprises four main islands – Grand Comore, Anjouan, Mohéli and Mayotte, and numerous islets and coral reefs. Mayotte is a French overseas territory, politically separate from the Comoros.

Climate

Tropical. Dry season May to October with average temperature 24 degrees Celsius (C). Rainy season from November to April with temperature 27–35 degrees C. Very hot and humid on coasts, cooler on inner highlands.

Entry requirements
Passports
Required by all.
Visa
Required by all; can be bought on arrival at airport. Onward ticket and exit permit also needed.
Currency advice/regulations
No restrictions.
Prohibited imports
Weapons, ammunition and radio transmission equipment, plants and soil.

Health (for visitors)
Mandatory precautions
Yellow fever vaccination certificates requested from visitors arriving from infected areas.
Advisable precautions
Typhoid, hepatitis A, tetanus and polio vaccinations recommended. Malaria prophylaxis advisable as risk exists throughout the country. Water precautions should be taken. There is a rabies risk. Seek further advice with regard to vaccinations for diphtheria, hepatitis B, meningitis and tuberculosis.

Hotels
Advisable to book in advance. Limited first-class accommodation available on Grande Comore, Anjouan and Mayotte (Maore), but several high-quality resort hotels have been built.

Public holidays
Fixed dates
6 Jul (Fête de l'Indépendance 75), 1 May (Labour Day), 25 May (Fête de l'OUA), 12 Nov (Fête Admission Comores á l'ONU).
Variable dates
Eid al-Fitr (after Ramadan), Eid al-Adha (Fête des Pélerins á la Mecque), Islamic New Year, Prophet's Birthday.

Working hours
Banking
Mon–Thu: 0800–1400; Fri: 0800–1100.
Business
Mon–Thu: 0730–1430; Fri: 0730–1100, Sat: 0730–1200.
Government
Mon–Thu: 0730–1200 and 1500–1730, Fri: 0730–1100, Sat: 0730–1200.
Shops
Closed daily between 1200–1500.

Telecommunications
Telephone/fax
Dialling code for Comoro Islands: IDD access code + 269, followed arec code (71 for Anjouan, 72 for Mohali, 73 for Moroni), followed by subscriber's number.
Internet/e-mail

Electricity supply
220V AC

Getting there
Air
There is an international airport on Grande Comore. Air Mauritius, Air France and South African Airways are the principal airlines that fly to the island.
National airline: Air Comores (state-owned).
International airport/s: International Prince Said Ibrahim (Code: HAH), 25km north of Moroni, on Ngazidja.
Airport tax: None.
Surface
Main port/s: Moroni (Grand Comore) and Fomboni (Anjouan): both have offshore anchorage for larger vessels.

Getting about
National transport
Air: Each island is served by Air Comores. There are regular flights between the islands.
Road: Surfaced roads on Grande Comore and Anjouan; other islands' roads can be difficult in rainy season. Mohéli has only very basic tracks.
Water: Small boats, which can be hired, ply between islands.
City transport
Taxis: Service is provided by taxi-brousse (bush taxis) on each island. The journey from the International Airport to the city centre takes 30 minutes.
Car hire
International driving licence required.

BUSINESS DIRECTORY

Telephone area codes
Dialling code for Comoro Islands: IDD access code +269, followed arec code (71 for Anjouan, 72 for Mohali, 73 for Moroni), followed by subscriber's number.

Useful telephone numbers
Emergency services: 744-890

Chambers of Commerce
Chambre de Commerce, d'Industries et d'Agriculture, BP 763, Moroni (tel: 732-116).

Banking
Banque de Development des Comores, Place de France, BP-298 Moroni (tel: 730154, 730818 fax: 730397, e-mail: bdc@snpt.km).

Banque pour l'Industrie et le Commerce - Comores, BP 175, Place de France, Moroni (tel: 730243, 730225, 730289 fax: 731229).

Central bank
Banque Centrale des Comores, BP 405, Place de France, Moroni (tel: 731814, 731002 fax: 730349).

Travel information
Comorian Association of Tourism (ACT) (tel: 732-847, 731-942; fax: 732-846).

Société Comorienne de Tourisme et d'Hotellerie (COMOTEL), Itsandra Hotel, Ngazidja (tel: 732-365).

International Prince Said Ibrahim Airport, BP 1003, Moroni (tel: 731-593, 732-452, 732-135; fax: 731-468).

Ministries
Ministry of Foreign Affairs and Co-operation, BP 428, Moroni (tel: 732-306).

Ministry of Transport, Tourism, Post and Telecommunications, Moroni (tel: 734-242; fax: 734-241).

Other useful addresses
British Honorary Consulate, BP 986, Moroni (tel/fax: 733-182).

Comoros Embassy (USA), East 50th Street, New York, NY 10022 (tel: 972-8010; fax: 983-4712; e-mail: comun@undp.org).

Société Internationale des Comores, BP 175, Moroni (tel: 730-243).

Internet sites
Africa Business Network: http://www.ifc.org/abn

AllAfrica.com: http://allafrica.com

African Development Bank: http://www.afdb.org

Africa Online: http://www.africaonline.com

Harambee Afrika (UK business club for traders with east, central and southern Africa; includes annotated web resource list): http://www.harambee.co.uk

Mbendi AfroPaedia (information on companies, countries, industries and stock exchanges in Africa): http://mbendi.co.za

Congo

Daniel Brett

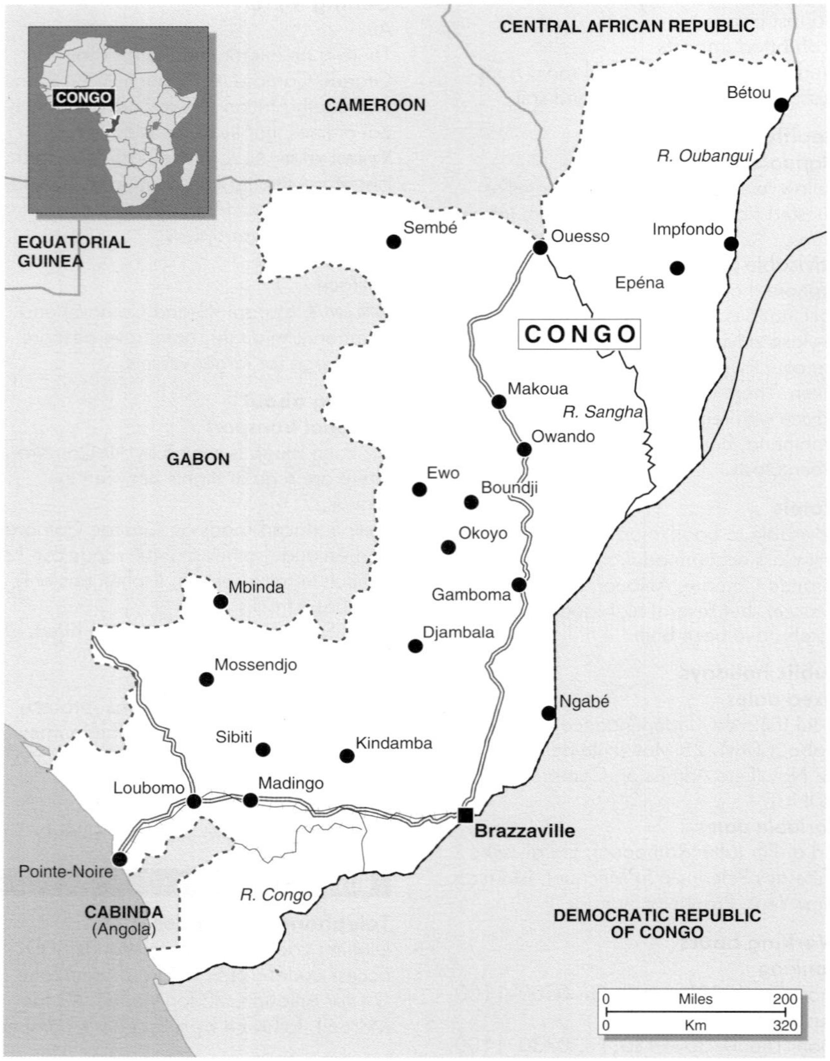

KEY FACTS

Official name: République du Congo (The Republic of Congo)

Head of State: President Denis Sassou-Nguessou (PCT) (since 1997; elected 10 Mar 2002 with 89.4 per cent of the vote)

Head of government: President Denis Sassou-Nguessou

Ruling party: Coalition of Parti Congolais du Travail (PCT) (Congolese Workers' Party), Forces Démocratiques Unies (FDU) (United Democratic Forces) and independents (a total of 83 seats out of 137)

Area: 342,000 square km

Population: 3.10 million (2001)

Capital: Brazzaville (political); Pointe-Noire (economic)

Official language: French

Currency: CFA franc (CFAf) = 100 centimes (Communauté Financière Africaine (African Financial Community) franc)

Exchange rate: CFAf629.73 per US$ (Jan 2003); CFAf655.95 per euro (pegged from Jan 1999)

GDP per capita: US$903 (2001)

GDP real growth: 2.90% (2001)

Inflation: -0.10% (2001)

Oil production: 271,000 bpd (2001)

Balance of trade: US$1.03 billion (2001)

Foreign debt: US$5.46 billion (2001)

Annual FDI: US$160.00 million (2001)

For the latest Key Facts, go to www.worldinformation.com

Hundreds of guns were melted down in April 2002 after a peace conference between the warring militias of rival political parties agreed on a new constitution. This development ignited fresh hope that Congo-Brazzaville had turned its back on five years of civil war which had killed 20,000 and displaced a third of the population. Although a new constitution, which came out of the peace conference, was approved by a majority of the electorate in a referendum held in January 2002, protests erupted over electoral fraud. A renewed outbreak of violence in and around the capital Brazzaville following the March presidential elections indicated that the country was still in a precarious state.

Finding peace

Despite a spate of coups since independence from France in 1960, the Republic of Congo was, until the mid-1990s, a relatively peaceful country. The first bouts of fighting began in 1993, after disputed parliamentary elections prompted ethnic factions to begin fighting. A ceasefire agreement, which saw members of the opposition join the government, held until 1997 when ethnic and political tensions erupted.

The democratically-elected President Pascal Lissouba and his prime minister, Bernard Kolelas, were overthrown in 1997 by Denis Sassou-Nguesso, prompting civil war. Ethnic-based factions were organised by regional warlords competing for the country's considerable offshore oil wealth. The army fragmented and the country was split between northern *Cobra* militias loyal to President Sassou-Nguesso and southern rebels – the Cocoyes, loyal to Lissouba and operating in *the* Bouenza, Niari and Lekoumou regions, and the *Ninjas*, led by the Reverend Frederic Bitsangou, alias Pasteur Ntoumi, who backed Kolelas and operated in the Pool region.

During the civil war, Sassou-Nguesso won the backing of Rwandan Hutu militiamen and the Angolan government, which sent troops to fight on the government's side. Sassou-Nguesso was also favoured by the French government. France had been angered by Lissouba's policies in the oil sector which had threatened the interests of France-based Elf, which enjoyed protected monopoly status in Congo-Brazzaville. Between 1997 and 2002, the country was ruled by the unelected 75-member Conseil National de Transition (CNT) (National Transition Council), which was appointed by President Sassou-Nguesso, who effectively ruled by decree.

A succession of military defeats forced the rebels to sign a ceasefire accord in 1999, which included a peace conference on reconciliation, the demilitarisation of political parties and the reform of the army to include ex-rebel combat units. This culminated in the 2001 peace agreement, which included a new constitution. The *Ninjas* were not signatories to the agreement, making it only a partial success.

Sassou-Nguesso's determination to maintain power by any means necessary, including his refusal to establish an independent electoral body, opened old wounds. Lissouba and Kolelas, both living in exile after being convicted *in absentia* for crimes committed during the civil war, were barred from standing for the presidency under the new constitution, which stipulated that a candidate had to have lived in the country for at least two years prior to the election. This removed two of Sassou-Nguesso's most credible challengers before the election contest even started. It also undermined the spirit of the peace conference's agreement to a 'national dialogue without exclusion' and fuelled resentment and distrust towards the government among rebel groups, who were still armed and dangerous.

Former prime minister André Milongo, Sassou-Nguesso's main rival and leader of the Union pour la Démocratie et la République (UDR) (Union for Democracy and the Republic), pulled out of the election race two days before the presidential election held on 10 March. He claimed there were significant electoral irregularities which made it impossible for him to mount a viable election campaign. He urged his supporters to boycott the elections, but cautioned against resorting to violence. The withdrawal of the UDR followed similar moves by five other political parties, which had lost faith in the electoral process. This assured the incumbent president a comfortable victory with 89.4 per cent of the vote over his six other opponents.

EU approval misplaced?

The EU, which had an election observer mission in the country, stated that it 'deplored the low level of participation by opposition parties throughout the electoral process and the withdrawal of several candidates in the days preceding the poll'. It criticised 'certain shortcomings ... in the organisation and conduct of the presidential election', which included administrative errors and the electorate's limited exposure to political campaigning. However, the EU claimed the election 'reflected the desires of the population' and gave Sassou-Nguesso its stamp of approval. Many observers could not help wondering whether the EU's favourable treatment of the election had been influenced by France. The French government had reportedly persuaded the EU to play down Sassou-Nguesso's brutality in the interests of 'stability' — this was in apparent conflict with the EU's policy towards the Zimbabwean elections which were held in the same month.

The EU commendation of the government was in marked contrast to the US State Department's report on human rights in Congo-Brazzaville, released in March 2002. It stated that the government's human rights record is poor and catalogued a large number of extrajudicial killings 'as well as summary executions, rapes, beatings, physical abuse of detainees and the civilian population, arbitrary arrest and detention, looting and solicitation of bribes'. The climate is such that citizens 'do not have the right to change their government peacefully', despite the peace accords and the implementation of the new 'democratic' constitution.

The EU's stance that the presidential elections were free and fair seems erroneous given the government control of the media, the continuation of state terror tactics and the alienation of opposition parties in the political process. Many exasperated Congolese civilians were not interested in the way the election was run or who was elected, so long as there was a return to peace. However, they were quickly disappointed as the elections only renewed conflict.

Return to war?

Doubts over the legitimacy of the presidential election results led to a fresh

KEY INDICATORS — Congo

	Unit	1996	1997	1998	1999	2000
Population	m	2.68	2.76	2.85	2.93	3.02
Gross domestic product (GDP)	US$bn	2.53	2.30	1.96	2.20	2.80
GDP per capita	US$	894	824	703	750	927
GDP real growth	%	4.3	-0.6	3.7	-3.0	7.9
Inflation	%	10.2	13.2	1.8	3.1	0.4
Oil output	'000 bpd	210.0	235.0	275.0	295.0	275.0
Exports (fob) (goods)	US$m	1,555.0	1,744.0	1,163.0	1,563.0	2,559.0
Imports (fob) (goods)	US$m	1,361.0	803.0	751.0	955.0	966.0
Balance of trade	US$m	194.0	941.0	412.0	608.0	1,593.0
Total reserves minus gold	US$m	91.0	59.9	0.8	39.4	222.0
Foreign exchange	US$m	90.2	59.2	0.1	38.5	221.3
Exchange rate	per US$	511.55	583.67	589.95	615.70	711.98

outbreak of violence. Fighting between the *Ninjas* and government troops in the Pool region resumed in late March 2002, although it was unclear which side was responsible for the resumption of the conflict. According to the UN's Office for the Co-ordination of Humanitarian Affairs (OCHA), the truce between the *Ninjas* and the government 'appeared to have been broken when hundreds of government troops arrived in the village of Vindza, near the base of [the] *Ninja* leader' on 27 March.

Civilians soon got caught up in the hostilities. The government used attack helicopters armed with bombs, rockets and heavy machine guns to attack villages believed to be controlled by the *Ninjas* in what was termed 'a wanton disregard for civilian lives' by the UN's Humanitarian Co-ordinator in Brazzaville. A UN team also reported that soldiers were gang-raping women and abducting young men fleeing the town of Kindamba, which became a battleground between the two sides.

By July 2002, more than 100,000 people had been displaced by the renewal of hostilities, which had reached the southern suburbs of Brazzaville. Soldiers were reported to have used the instability in the south of the capital to go on the rampage, looting shops and houses abandoned by local residents who had fled to safety. Despite the growing humanitarian crisis, the government closed off the Pool region to aid agencies in April. Opposition parties alleged that the army was recruiting mercenaries and forming death squads in Pool to fight the *Ninjas*. Despite the concerns of humanitarian agencies over the renewal of hostilities and a return to war, the EU refused to send any envoys to Congo-Brazzaville and the international community ignored the dangerous escalation in violence. The *Ninjas* mostly ignored Sassou-Nguesso's offers of amnesty if the rebels turned themselves in as the government continued to refuse a dialogue with the rebels, who they regarded as terrorists. Sassou-Nguesso gave the rebels a deadline of 18 December, when the amnesty offer was to end.

The turmoil delayed parliamentary elections, with the first round held at the end of May and the second round held at the end of June, concurrent with local and municipal elections. Following the elections, the PCT, the Forces Démocratiques Unies (FDU) (United Democratic Forces) and a number of independents formed a pro-Sessou-Nguesso coalition in parliament with a total of 83 seats in the 135-seat National Assembly. This confirmed parliament's position as a rubber-stamping chamber under the thumb of the president, thereby further alienating Sassou-Nguesso's opponents.

Dealing with debt

One of the main factors that fuelled Congo-Brazzaville's civil war — oil — is ironically the country's best hope for economic development. If the country can avert a return to full-scale civil war in 2002 and 2003, the economy is likely to boom. Economic recovery was already evident in 2000 and 2001 following a truce and the eventual peace agreement between the government and rebels. In 2001, non-oil real GDP growth reached 9 per cent, stimulated by high levels of construction activity as well as an expansion in the forestry sector, transportation and trade. The IMF reported that overall GDP growth was around 3.3 per cent, down from 7.9 per cent in 2000 due to declining oil output. An improvement in rail and sea port infrastructure improved the supply of goods, helping to stabilise prices, with inflation at -0.5 per cent compared to 0.4 per cent in 2000.

The first step of the newly-elected Sassou-Nguesso government will be to arrange a three-year Poverty Reduction and Growth Facility (PRGF) programme with the IMF, which could lead to the country getting access to debt reduction through the enhanced Highly Indebted Poor Countries (HIPC) initiative run by the World Bank and the IMF. Debt reduction is highly important as Congo-Brazzaville has been unable to meet its external debt-service payments since mid-2000. The rescheduling of the external debt, estimated at 186 per cent of GDP (half of which is payment arrears), will be a necessary requisite of Congo-Brazzaville's post-war recovery. If the country can overcome the fighting seen in the first half of 2001 and become more politically stable, there is a good chance of an improvement in relations with bilateral and multilateral donors.

Outlook

Achieving political stability is an important first step towards economic development. As Africa's fourth-largest oil producer, Congo-Brazzaville has a lot of potential. Oil is also a politically divisive factor. Until armed groups feel they have a stake in the new political order, they will continue to battle with the Sessou-Nguesso government over control of the nation's lucrative resources. The president's track record so far, which has included widespread human rights abuses against the civilian population and a move towards centralised presidential rule, does not bode well for future reconciliation and stability. Given the eruption of violence following the March 2002 presidential election, armed groups loyal to exiled dissidents do not seem to have much faith in a political system which is seen as too closely tied to the personality of the Sessou-Nguesso. Unless the government can convince combatants to disarm, either by giving them a financial incentive or through some form of political agreement, there is a strong likelihood that Congo-Brazzaville will be plagued by bouts of fighting in coming years.

Risk assessment

Economic	Poor
Political	Poor
Regional stability	Poor

COUNTRY PROFILE

Historical profile

From the fifteenth century, the Bakongo, Bateke and Sanga began settling what is now the Republic of Congo.

1482 Portuguese explorer Diogo Cao mapped the coastline.

1880s The colonisation of what is now Congo, began in the late nineteenth century after the French explorer Pierre Savorgnan de Brazza signed a treaty with the Chief of the Batekes to establish a French protectorate over the north bank of the Congo river.

1910 Middle Congo, as the country was then known, became a colony of French Equatorial Africa.

1928 Africans revolted over forced labour which was used to build the Congo railway. More than 17,000 Africans died in the revolt.

1946 Congo was granted a territorial assembly by the French and representation in the French parliament.

1960 Congo became independent with a catholic priest, Abbé Fulbert Youlou, as president.

1963 Abbé Fulbert Youlou was succeeded by Alfonse Massamba-Debat. Pascal Lissouba became prime minister. The country became a one-party socialist state.

1968 Massamba-Debat was forced from office in a coup by Captain Marien Ngouabi, who became president in January 1969. The Parti Congolais du Travail (PCT) (Congolese Workers' Party) became the only legal party and continued the previous government's commitment to socialism.

1970 Ngouabi proclaimed Congo as a Marxist state.
1977 Ngouabi was assassinated by forces loyal to Massamba-Debat. Massamba-Debat was executed for treason. Joachim Yhombi-Opango of the Comité Militaire du Parti (CMP) (Party of the Military Committee) became president.
1979 After a brief presidency under Yhombi-Opango, Colonel Denis Sassou-Nguesso took over in 1979, and remained in power under one-party PCT rule until 1992.
1981 Congo signed a treaty of friendship and co-operation with the Soviet Union.
1990 The PCT abandoned Marxism.
1991 After 21 years of a one-party government, in February, a national conference was inaugurated to formulate the country's future political system.
1992 A referendum held on 15 March approved the new constitution. Multi-party legislative and municipal elections took place in June at which the Union Panafricaine pour la Démocratie Sociale (UPADS) (Pan-African Union for Social Development), led by Pascal Lissouba, won 39 of the 125 assembly seats. In August Lissouba was elected president, defeating Sassou-Nguesso.
1993 Political unrest during 1992/93 forced new elections in May–June, which were won by UPADS. Civil war broke out over disputes over the elections.
1994 A peace agreement saw members of the opposition join the government.
1997 After the government attempted to disarm supporters of Sassou-Nguesso in June, civil war broke out in which thousands were killed and tens of thousands forced from their homes. Elections scheduled for July were postponed. After several months of fighting, Sassou-Nguesso succeeded in overthrowing the government of Pascal Lissouba in October. Sassou-Nguesso assumed the presidency at the head of a National Transitional Council.
1999 The militiamen of Bernard Kolelas and Lissouba entered into negotiations with the government and signed a peace accord on 16 November.
2001 In April, a peace conference adopted a new constitution. A treaty establishing the Gulf of Guinea Commisssion was signed by five of the seven member states in July (Gabon, Congo, São Tomé and Príncipe, Nigeria and Angola). In September, the new constitution was endorsed by the transitional government and 15,000 militia were demobilised through financial incentives. In December, Lissouba was convicted *in absentia* of treason and corruption and sentenced to 30 years hard labour.
2002 In January, a referendum showed that 80 per cent were in favour of the new constitution, revised by the transitional government to strengthen the power of the president. President Sassou-Nguesso was elected for a seven-year term on 10 March with 89.4 per cent of the vote. The legislative elections held in May and June led to the creation of a pro-Sassou-Nguesso coalition consisting of the PCT, the Forces Démocratiques Unies (FDU) (United Democratic Forces) and a number of independents. Disputes surrounding the elections led to intense fighting between government forces and the *Ninjas* in the south, which reached Brazzaville by July.

Political structure

Constitution
A new constitution was agreed in April 2001 as a result of dialogue between the government and rebel forces. This was later revised by the transitional government to bolster presidential powers. The amendments were approved in a referendum held in January 2002.

Form of state
Republic

The executive
Executive authority is vested in the directly elected president, who serves a seven-year term. The prime minister is appointed from the majority party or coalition in the legislature.

National legislature
Parliament consists of the National Assembly and the Senate. Parliament does not have the power to impeach the president.

Legal system
Based on French civil law system and customary law

Last elections
9 June 2002 (second round, legislative); 12 May 2002 (first round, legislative); 10 March 2002 (presidential).

Next elections
2009 (presidential)

Political parties

Ruling party
Coalition of Parti Congolais du Travail (PCT) (Congolese Workers' Party), Forces Démocratiques Unies (FDU) (United Democratic Forces) and independents (a total of 83 seats out of 137).

Main opposition party
Union Panafricaine pour la Démocratie Sociale (UPADS) (Pan-African Union for Social Development); Union pour la Démocratie et la République (UDR) (Union for Democracy and Republic).

Population
3.02 million (2000)
Annual population growth rate: 2.7 per cent (1994–2000).
Population density: 7.6 inhabitants per square km. Urban population: 63 per cent (1994–2000) – the highest urbanisation rate in Africa. Two-thirds live within 510km of the Congo-Océan Railway, which links Pointe-Noire on the Atlantic coast with Brazzaville, the national capital, in the interior. The government is anxious to discourage the present urban drift.

Ethnic make-up
Kongo (48 per cent), Sangha (17 per cent), Teke (17 per cent).

Religions
Traditional beliefs (over 50 per cent), Christianity (about 40 per cent, mainly Roman Catholic, some Protestant).

Education
In 2000, the UN estimated that adult illiteracy rates for men and women aged 15 years or over stood at 12.5 per cent and 25.6 per cent respectively. Primary education is compulsory between the ages of six and 12. World Bank estimates show that the total primary school enrolment of the relevant age group typically stood at 120 per cent for boys and 109 per cent for girls (including repetition rates) between 1994 and 2000. The number of pupils per primary school teacher is typically 70. Primary education is followed by seven years of secondary school which is divided into a four-year first cycle (ages 12 to 16) and a three-year second cycle (ages 16 to 19). In the second cycle, students can opt between general or technical education. Higher education is provided by the Université Marien-Ngouabi, which is largely state subsidised. It has a yearly enrolment of about 12,000 students.
Public expenditure on education typically amount to 6.1 per cent of annual gross national income between 1994 and 1997 according to the latest World Bank report.

Health
World Bank estimates during the period 1994 and 2000 showed that average life expectancy was 48 years and the infant mortality rate stood at 89 per 1,000 live births. It is estimated that 24 per cent of children under the age of five were malnourished in the same period. The United Nations International Children's Emergency Fund reported in October 2000 that some 70 per cent of internally displaced people were severely malnourished at the height of the emergency in Congo. The fertility rate shows that 5.9 children are born per adult woman. World Bank estimates in 2000 showed that 51 per cent of the population had access to improved water facilities. There are 0.3 physicians and 3.4 hospital beds typically available for 1,000 people. The HIV rate is as high as 6.43 per cent among adults. Government expenditure on healthcare averaged 5.8 per cent of GDP of which 2 per cent was public expenditure between 1990 and 1998, according to World Bank estimates. Expenditure on private healthcare (such as private household

expenditure and insurance) averaged 3.8 per cent of GDP over the same period.

Welfare

In 2000, the IMF approved a credit of about US$14 million to support the government's reconstruction and economic recovery programme in the aftermath of the 1998–99 armed conflict. A three-year programme supported by the IMF's Poverty Reduction and Growth Facility (PRGF) was initiated to allow relief on its external debt under the Initiative for the Heavily Indebted Poor Countries (HIPC) initiative. Efforts in this area remain high as economic reforms are undertaken following the referendum in January 2002.

In June 2002, UN agencies in Congo reported that at least 20,000 people were in urgent need of humanitarian aid particularly in the inaccessible areas of the troubled Pool region. Despite the looming political troubles, the United Nations International Children's Emergency Fund's has launched a national polio immunisation campaign targeting 650,000 Congolese children. The campaign is estimated to cost 1.2 million dollars.

The World Food Programme distributed a total of 646 tonnes of food in May 2002. Some 9,700 internally displaced people from the Pool region received food aid.

Main cities

Brazzaville (political capital, estimated population one million), Pointe-Noire (economic capital, 350,000), Dolisie, Loubomo, Madingou.

Languages spoken

French is the language for all business documentation. Numerous African languages are also spoken, including Lingala and Kikongo.

Official language/s

French

Media

Press

Main newspapers include *Semaine Africaine* (Catholic), the government-owned *Mweti* (four times a week), *Agence Congolaise d'Information* (official bulletin), *Soleil*, *La Madu Kutsekele*, *Le Pays*, *Choc* and *Aujourd'hui*. Several journals and periodicals, including *Etumba* and *Le Stade*.

Broadcasting

Radio and television are state-run. The fighting in the country has affected the communications, and radio and television can only be received in Brazzaville and environs (February 2000).

Radio: Radiodiffusion-Télévision Nationale Congolaise broadcasts programmes in French, Lingala and Kikongo.

Television: Broadcasts 80 hrs/week

Economy

The largest sectors of the economy are oil and forestry. The agricultural sector is the country's largest employer.

The government's main fiscal policy is to increase revenue to pay for the country's post-war reconstruction and meet IMF fiscal targets. Soon after seizing power in 1997, Sassou-Nguesso reduced the previous administration's production-sharing agreement (PSA) quota from 30 per cent to 20 per cent, largely at the insistence of the French. This fall in government oil allocations, which form a large part of revenue, has restricted Congo-Brazzaville's ability to raise expenditure. Production is not expected to increase until 2004 when new oil fields come online at Libondo, Tchibeli, Litanzi and Yanga-Sud. Therefore, the government will have to broaden the tax base and improve revenue collection. Oil price rises would also buoy up state revenues as will the resumption of the privatisation programme, which has been stalled since 1999 due to a lack of foreign interest.

External trade

There is a regular large trade surplus from oil export earnings, but invisibles and debt payments keep the current account in deficit.

Exports

Principal exports are crude petroleum (typically 85 per cent of total), timber (10 per cent).

Main destinations: US (typically 37 per cent of total), Italy (25 per cent), France (13 per cent), Belgium/Luxembourg (10 per cent).

Imports

Principal imports are machinery and transport equipment, metals and products, food.

Main sources: France (typically 42 per cent of total), US (14 per cent), Italy (10 per cent), Cameroon (4 per cent), Democratic Republic of Congo (formerly Zaïre).

Agriculture

The agricultural sector contributes around a quarter of GDP and employs a third of the workforce. Agriculture has been overshadowed by development of the petroleum industry.

An estimated 2 per cent of the total land area is under cultivation (mainly in the alluvial Niari Valley). Farming is small-scale with output concentrated on subsistence crops such as plantains, cassava, yams, groundnuts, manioc, potatoes, wheat, maize, beans and paddy rice. Despite some growth in food production, Congo relies heavily on food imports from the Democratic Republic of Congo.

The main cash crops are coffee, cocoa, tobacco and sugar. Attempts to expand production of other cash crops include the rehabilitation of oil palm estates and a major new cocoa project.

Fishing

Fishing is underdeveloped but is practised commercially on a small scale.

Forestry

The main agricultural export is timber, mostly Okoumé logs (of which Congo is a major world supplier). About half the total timber output is used for wood processing. Approximately 60 per cent of the country is covered by woodlands and forests, much of it unsuitable for commercial exploitation. There are large eucalyptus (fast growing) plantations near Pointe-Noire.

Industry and manufacturing

The industrial sector contributes over 10 per cent to GDP and employs a fifth of the workforce. The manufacturing sector is largely underdeveloped, contributing less than 5 per cent to GDP. Construction contributes a further 5 per cent, although this figure could grow rapidly if political stability is restored and reconstruction efforts begin.

Most manufacturing enterprises operate in the Brazzaville and Pointe-Noire districts and in the Niari Valley. Activity is centred on agro-food and timber processing, textiles and oil refining.

There are also a few small-scale import substitution industries (footwear, soft drinks, metal working, chemicals) and a cement plant.

Structure and ownership of parastatals is being reformed and the privatisation programme is expected to be renewed after years of delay. Emphasis is on joint-venture enterprises, particularly in pulp/paper and light manufacturing.

Mining

The mining sector, including hydrocarbons, contributes around a third of GDP and employs 5 per cent of the workforce. Gold, lead and copper are extracted in small quantities. Deposits of high-grade iron ore, phosphates, copper, potash and bauxite are known to exist.

Canada's Magnesium Alloy Corporation (MagAlloy) is owner and operator of the Kouilou magnesium deposit. Kouilou could be operating by 2005, producing 60,000 tonnes per year (tpy) of magnesium at around US$1 per kg. The plant is likely to be powered by the INGA hydroelectric project on the Congo river, which is to be expanded by Germany's Siemans.

Hydrocarbons

Oil

Congo Brazzaville has proven oil reserves of 1.5 billion barrels and production of around 271,000 barrels per day (bpd) (2001). Net oil exports amounted to 255,000bpd. Western Europe and North

America are Congo's dominant markets, although there is hope of expanding into Asian markets.
Congo is sub-Saharan Africa's fourth largest oil producer. TotalFinaElf still plays a dominant role in oil production, although it has recently lost its monopoly status to other foreign companies, especially Agip.

Gas

The country contains natural gas reserves of up to 90.5 billion cubic metres, most of which is oil-associated. A lack of infrastructure and investment means that most gas is vented or flared. There are plans to utilise gas for electricity production in the future.

Energy

Installed generating capacity is 89MW, although generating potential is estimated at 3,000MW. Most electricity is produced by the 74MW Bouenza and the 15MW Djoué hydroelectric plants. Around a quarter of the country's electricity requirements are imported from the Democratic Republic of Congo (DRC). The development of the postponed US$925 million Sounda Gorge hydroelectric project could increase capacity by 1,000MW and turn the country into a net electricity exporter. In 2001, a feasibility study was launched into the project. In November 2001, Congo and two Chinese companies signed a US$220 million contract to build a 120-MW hydroelectric power plant on the Congo River. When the plant is completed in 2006, it is expected to double Congo's power generating capacity.

Banking

Central bank

Banque des Etats de l'Afrique Centrale

Main financial centre

Brazzaville

Time

GMT plus one hour

Geography

The Republic of Congo is an equatorial country on the west coast of Africa. It has a coastline of about 170km on the Atlantic Ocean, from which the country extends northward to Cameroon and the Central African Republic. It is bordered by Gabon in the west, with the Democratic Republic of Congo to the east. In the south there is a short frontier with the Cabinda enclave of Angola.

Climate

Equatorial or sub-equatorial. Main dry season from June–September with average temperatures ranging from 15 degrees Celsius (C) at night to 32 degrees C during the day. Rainy season from October–May with higher average temperatures and high humidity. Generally hotter and more humid in Congo Basin, drier and cooler in highlands.

Entry requirements

Passports

Passports are required by all.

Visa

Required by all except tourists from Gabon.

Currency advice/regulations

There is no limit to the amount of foreign currency or CFA francs which can be taken into the country but receipts must be provided. The amount of local currency that can be exported in notes is limited to CFAf25,000.

Health (for visitors)

Medical and dental facilities are inadequate.

Mandatory precautions

A yellow fever vaccination certificate is required by all.

Advisable precautions

Typhoid, polio, hepatitis A and tetanus vaccinations are recommended. Malaria prophylaxis should be taken as a risk exists throughout the country. Water precautions should be taken. Visitors should avoid uncooked fruit and vegetables. There is an AIDS risk and a risk of rabies. There was an outbreak of ebola in January 2002.

Hotels

Good hotels are available in Brazzaville, Pointe-Noire and Loubomo; few elsewhere. Advisable to book well in advance. Ten per cent tip is usual. Brazzaville suffered considerable infrastructural damage during the 1997 conflict.

Credit cards

International credit cards are accepted at some establishments eg Meridien Hotel, PLM Mbamou Palace Hotel, Hotel Olympic Palace, Hotel Cosmos, Pullman and Marina Residence.

Public holidays

Fixed dates

1 Jan, 1 May (Labour Day), 15 Aug (National Day), 1 Nov (All Saints' Day), 25 Dec (Children's Day), 31 Dec (Foundation Day).

Variable dates

Good Friday, Easter Monday.

Working hours

Banking

Mon–Fri: 0630–1300. Counters close at 1130.

Business

Mon–Fri: 0800–1200 and 1430–1730, Sat: 0800–1200.

Government

Mon–Fri: 0700–1400, Sat: 0700–1200.

Shops

Mon–Fri: 0800–1200 and 1530–1800. Sat: 0800–1200 and 1530–1800/1900. Some shops close on Mon afternoons; a few open Sun mornings.

Telecommunications

Telephone/fax

Dialling code for Congo: IDD access code + 242 followed by subscriber's six-digit number (Brazzaville numbers begin 81, 82 or 83).
Caisse Française de Développement provided CFAf1 billion in 1999 for a new telephone network.

Electricity supply

220V AC 50 cycles; the voltage varies erratically.

Weights and measures

The metric system is used.

Getting there

Air

International airport/s: Brazzaville-Maya Maya (Code: BZV), 4km from city; restaurant. Pointe-Noire (Code: PNR), 6km from city.
Airport tax: None.

Surface

Road: There is a road from Lambaréné, in Gabon, to Loubomo and Brazzaville; this is not surfaced all the way. Entry from Cameroon is only practicable in the dry season. There is a surfaced road from the Cabinda enclave of Angola.
Water: A ferry service across the River Congo is operational daily from 0800–1200 and 1400–1700 between Kinshasa (Democratic Republic of Congo) and Brazzaville. Cars can be carried. The ferry takes about half an hour. There is also a vedette service for passengers only, which takes 15 minutes. Both services are liable to short-notice cancellation or delay.
Main port/s: Pointe-Noire. Brazzaville is the inland river port.

Getting about

National transport

Air: Internal air service operated by Lina Congo to Pointe-Noire (two or three times daily) and the main provincial towns.
Road: There are 243km of tarred roads; other routes are mainly tracks which can be impassable when wet.
There are very few metalled roads outside Brazzaville and Pointe-Noire, while the roads within the towns are generally poor. The main route from Pointe-Noire, through Brazzaville to Ouesso, is not uniform in quality; the section from Loubomo to Pointe-Noire is liable to become impassable in the rainy season.
Rail: The principal railway line is the Chemin de Fer Congo-Océan from Pointe-Noire to Brazzaville – 520km, which is part of the parastatal organisation Agence Transcongolaise de Communications. The service has been improved,

but the journey can take 10 hours or more.

About half-way between Brazzaville and Point-Noire, the Congo-Océan railway is joined by the Comilog railway from Mbinda on the Congo/Gabon border – 280km. This line is used mainly for the carriage of manganese ore produced by Comilog, but the company which runs the Congo-Océan line is responsible for passengers and general freight.

The railways are suffering from lack of maintenance and general upkeep.

Water: The ferries on the rivers Congo and Oubangui are a principal form of transport.

City transport

Taxis: Freely available in Brazzaville and Pointe-Noire; tipping is not usual. Can be hired by the hour or day. Fares should be negotiated in advance of journey.

Car hire

Available from main hotels in Brazzaville and Pointe-Noire. International or national driving licence accepted. Traffic drives on the right.

BUSINESS DIRECTORY

Telephone area codes

The international dialling code (IDD) for Congo is + 242 followed by the customer number.

Useful telephone numbers

Fire: 18.

Police: 17.

Ambulance: 822-365/368.

Chambers of Commerce

Chambre Nationale de Commerce, d'Industrie et Agriculture, BP 1438, Brazzaville (tel: 832-956).

Chambre de Commerce, d'Agriculture et d'Industrie de Kouilou, BP 665, Pointe-Noire (tel: 940-430, 941-280).

Chambre de Commerce, d'Agriculture et d'Industrie de Loubomo, BP 78, Loubomo.

Banking

Banque de Développement des Etats de l'Afrique Centrale, PO Box 1177, Brazzaville (tel: 811885, 811761 fax: 811880).

Banque des États de l'Afrique Centrale, PO Box 126, Brazzaville (tel: 832814/5, 833626, 833362 fax: 836342).

Banque Internationale du Congo, PO Box 33, Avenue Amilcar Cabral, Brazzaville (tel: 830308, 831411 fax: 815092, 835382).

Crédit pour l'Agriculture, l'Industrie et le Commerce (CAIC), PO Box 2889, Brazzaville (tel: 810978, 814050 fax: 810977, 835352).

Mutuelle Congolaise d'Epargne et de Crédit, PO Box 13237, Brazzaville (tel: 837001 fax: 837930).

Union Congolaise de Banques; PO Box 147, Avenue Amilcar Cabral, Brazzaville (tel: 83 3000 fax: 83 6845).

Central bank

Banque des États de l'Afrique Centrale, PO Box 1917, Rue du Docteur Jamot, Yaounde, Cameroun (tel: 234030, 234060 fax: 233329).

Travel information

Afri-Congo, Brazzaville. Direction Générale du Tourisme, BP 456, Brazzaville (tel: 830-953).

Ministries

Ministry of Construction and Urban Development, BP 1218, Brazzaville.

Ministry of Decentralisation and Regional Development, BP 630, Brazzaville.

Ministry of Defence, BP 1219, Brazzaville.

Ministry of the Economy, BP 2120, Brazzaville.

Ministry of Finance and the Budget, BP 64, Brazzaville (tel: 411-266; fax: 814-145).

Ministry of Foreign Affairs, BP 2070, Brazzaville.

Ministry of Industry, Fisheries and Crafts, Palais du Peuple, Brazzaville (tel: 835-130).

Ministry of the Interior and of Security, BP 64, Brazzaville.

Ministry of Trade and Small- and Medium-sized Enterprises, Brazzaville (tel: 831-827).

Ministry of Transport and Civil Aviation, BP 2146, Brazzaville.

Other useful addresses

Agence Congolaise d'Information (ACI), BP 2144, Brazzaville.

Bureau pour le Développement de la Production Agricole, BP 2222, Brazzaville.

Direction de la Statistique, BP 2031, Brazzaville (tel: 834-324).

Institut de Développement Economique de la République Populaire du Congo, c/o The Presidency, Brazzaville.

Office du Café et du Cacao (OCC), BP 2488, Brazzaville (tel: 831-902).

Office Congolais des Bois (OCB), BP 1229, Pointe-Noire (tel: 948-248).

Office Congolais de l'Entretien Routier (OCER), BP 2073, Brazzaville.

Office National du Commerce (ONC), BP 2305, Brazzaville (tel: 834-399).

Republic of Congo Embassy (USA), 4891 Colorado Avenue, NW, Washington DC 20011 (tel: 726-5500; fax: 726-1860; e-mail: info@embassyofcongo.org).

Société Nationale de Recherche et d'Exploitation Pétrolières (Hydro Congo), BP 2008, Brazzaville (tel: 833-560).

Syndicat des Commerçants, Importateurs et Exportateurs de l'Afrique Equatoriale (Sycomimpex), BP 84, Brazzaville.

Internet sites

Africa Business Network: http://www.ifc.org/abn

AllAfrica.com: http://allafrica.com

African Development Bank: http://www.afdb.org

Africa Online: http://www.africaonline.com

Congo-Brazzaville (French only, Actualité dossier): http://www.solcongolais.net/

Mbendi AfroPaedia (information on companies, countries, industries and stock exchanges in Africa): http://mbendi.co.za

Democratic Republic of Congo

Andrew Allimadi

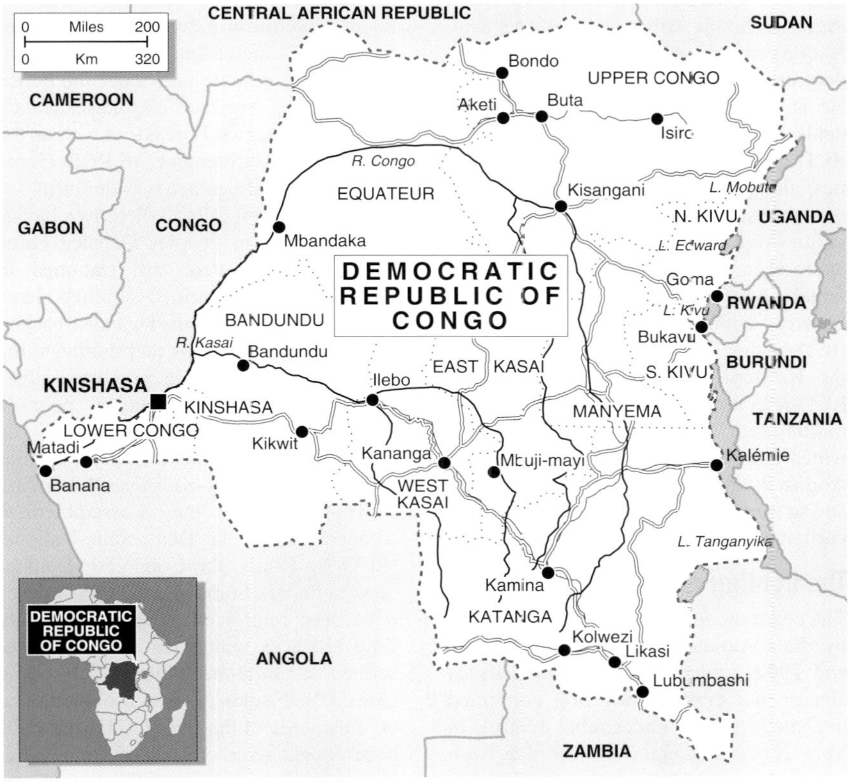

Governing the Democratic Republic of Congo (DRC) remains a huge challenge for the Kinshasa-based government and the rebel armies that control over one-third of the country's territory. The Lusaka peace accord of 1999 became the basis of a cease-fire, which is being observed by the major armies in the DRC conflict, but sporadic fighting and gross human rights abuses still plague areas under rebel control. By end-2002, the inter-Congolese dialogue, the peace process between the government, armed opposition and civil society organisations, appeared to achieve a major breakthrough, with the signing of a power-sharing accord in Pretoria, South Africa. Under the deal, Kabila will remain in office until elections are held, due by end-2004.

Inter-Congolese dialogue

In April 2002, the UN and the South African government convened the inter-Congolese dialogue to try and find a political solution to the conflict in the DRC. The dialogue was attended by over 350 delegates, which included the Congolese government, political parties, civil society organisations and armed groups. The dialogue resulted in the adoption of more than 30 resolutions on political and legal issues; economy and finance; defence and security; humanitarian, social and cultural issues; and peace and reconciliation.

Participants were unable to reach an all-inclusive agreement, especially on the key issue of power-sharing during the transition to democracy. Separately, the government and the Mouvement pour la Libération Congolaise (MLC) (Movement for Congolese Liberation) concluded a bilateral power-sharing agreement on the sidelines of the dialogue and then invited other delegations to sign the document. Over half the delegations agreed to the proposals, with the key exception the

KEY FACTS

Official name: République Démocratique du Congo (Democratic Republic of Congo) (DRC) (name changed from Zaïre, 19 May 1997)

Head of State: Interim President Major General Joseph Kabila (appointed 25 Jan 2001) (in Dec 2002, the DRC government signed a peace deal with the two main rebel groups: Joseph Kabila is to remain as president; elections in two years)

Head of government: Interim President Major General Joseph Kabila

Ruling party: Alliance des Forces Démocratiques pour La Libération (AFDL) (Alliance of the Democratic Forces for Liberation)

Area: 2,345,409 square km

Population: 53.00 million (2001)

Capital: Kinshasa

Official language: French

Currency: Congolese franc (Cf)

Exchange rate: Cf360.00 per US$ (Jan 2003) (currency floated 28 May 2001)

GDP per capita: US$138 (2001)

GDP real growth: -4.40% (2001)

Inflation: 358.00% (2001)

Balance of trade: US$238.00 million (2001)

Foreign debt: US$12.88 billion (2001)

Annual FDI: US$83.00 million (2001)

For the latest Key Facts, go to www.worldinformation.com

Rassemblement Congolais pour la Démocratie-Goma (RCD-Goma) (Rally for Congolese Democracy-Goma), the Rwandan-backed armed group which controls most of eastern DRC. The deal appeared to be a ploy to isolate RCD-Goma, which already faced increasing opposition from within its own ranks and widespread civilian hostility in the areas under its control.

The agreement between the Congolese government and MLC stipulates a 30-month transitional period leading up to the country's first democratic elections in over 40 years, although no specific date was set for the elections. Under the agreement, Joseph Kabila will keep his job as the interim president while Jean-Pierre Bemba, the leader of the MLC, will become interim prime minister.

The MLC-government agreement soon fell apart after Bemba called for the issue of the presidency to be re-opened for discussion, reacting to Kabila's call for new negotiations to reach an all-inclusive agreement. The government also abandoned its pledge to give Bemba the post of prime minister, arguing that an agreement was first needed with the RCD-Goma and its political allies, the Union pour la Démocratie et la Progrès Social (UDPS) (Union for Democracy and Social Progress). Bemba maintained this played into the hands of Rwanda and suggested that President Kabila was preparing to give the Rwandan authorities control of the North and South Kivu provinces in eastern DRC.

The government's proposals for an all-inclusive agreement include the appointment of four vice-presidents, representing the four main groups. The MLC claimed this would dilute its influence within the government and the deal 'did not respond to the principle of equilibrium, which was indispensable in the search for a non-conflictual solution and an efficient handling of state affairs'. The MLC also issued a veiled threat indicating that it may return to war against the DRC government.

In December 2002, the government, RCD-Goma, the MLC and the civilian opposition signed a power-sharing accord in Pretoria, South Africa. Under the deal, Kabila remains in office as interim president until elections are held in late 2004. He is to be assisted by four vice presidents, representing the government, RCD-Goma, the MLC and unarmed parties, along with 36 ministers and 25 deputy ministers, who will represent the various signatories to the accord. The legislature is to consist of a 500-member National Assembly and a 120-member Senate, with seats allocated to the RCD-Goma, MLC, political opposition, the Kinshasa government, civil society, RCD-ML, the pro-government *Mayi-Mayi* militia and RCD-Nationale. The UPC, which has been in control of Bunia since August 2002, failed to sign the agreement and so is not represented in the transitional parliament or government.

The fighting continues

The peace manoeuvres were accompanied by the continuation of fighting. In 2001 and 2002, violence, gross human rights abuses and civilian suffering continued unabated in areas under rebel control. In May 2002, Kisangani witnessed a fresh outbreak of violence that claimed the lives of at least 150 people. The crisis began in May with an apparent mutiny, when dissident RCD-Goma soldiers seized the local radio station and called upon the population to rise up against the 'Rwandan invaders'. Loyal RCD-Goma forces quickly regained control of the radio station and meted out summary justice on the mutineers and their alleged accomplices.

In South Kivu, fighting continued between RCD-Goma troops and forces led by a former RCD-Goma officer, Commandant Patrick Masunzu. In Bukavu, Uvira, Kalemie and Pweto, there were reports of increasing defections of RCD-Goma military personnel and police to the Forces Armées Congolaises (FAC) (Congolese Armed Forces), as well as the preventive disarmament of RCD-Goma troops whose allegiance was doubtful.

In northeastern DRC, where two battalions of Ugandan Peoples Defence Force (UPDF) troops were still stationed in mid-2002, violent armed conflicts have primarily been among the Ugandan-backed Congolese rebel groups that dominate the northeast – MLC and its purported allies, the Rassemblement Congolais pour la Démocratie-Kisangani/Mouvement de Libération (RCD-K/ML) (Rally for Congolese Democracy-Kisangani/Liberation Movement) and the Rassemblement Congolais pour la Démocratie-National (RCD-N) (Rally for Congolese Democracy-National). Some of these rebel armies have been reinforced at times by highly fluid alliances with what have been described as *Mayi-Mayi* fighters. In some cases, UPDF soldiers have also intervened on either side of the fighting. Battles have been fought over control of Buta, Isiro, Watsa, Bafwasende and Bunia, all endowed in varying degrees with deposits of gold, diamonds, coltan or cassiterite as well as stands of timber. Butembo, a major import and distribution centre where the country's second largest customs post is located, was repeatedly attacked.

Economic mess

Excessive taxes, revenue siphoning, seizure of local resources, forced requisitioning of assets and deepening control over general trade by foreign and local military, with or without the collusion of commercial operators, have paralysed local economies in the DRC. As a result, very few commercial enterprises operate and conditions in some towns are increasingly similar to those that might result from a trade embargo.

On the positive side, the government successfully implemented a 10-month stabilisation programme covering June 2001–March 2002. The vicious cycle of hyperinflation and currency depreciation

KEY INDICATORS — Democratic Republic of Congo

	Unit	1996	1997	1998	1999	2000
Population	m	46.12	47.33	48.39	49.58	50.95
Gross domestic product (GDP)	US$bn	5.90	5.40	11.80	17.50	23.00
GDP per capita	US$	127	115	244	353	452
GDP real growth	%	-1.0	-5.6	-1.6	-10.4	-7.0
Inflation	%	617.0	107.0	107.0	270.0	553.7
Exports (fob) (goods)	US$m	592.0	1,396.0	1,660.0	933.0	760.0
Imports (fob) (goods)	US$m	0.0	0.0	0.0	1,108.0	1,035.0
Imports (cif)	US$m	424.0	1,022.0	1,500.0	0.0	0.0
Balance of trade	US$m	168.0	374.0	160.0	175.0	-275.0
Foreign debt	US$bn	14.0	0.0	15.2	12.0	11.4
Exchange rate	per US$	0.50	1.31	*1.61	4.02	21.82

* estimated figure

appeared to have been broken, the rehabilitation of public finances has progressed steadily, major economic distortions have been eliminated and fundamental improvements in the judiciary and in the regulatory environment are being made.

The DRC has emerged from years of international financial isolation after paying its arrears with the IMF and reaching an agreement with the African Development Bank (AfDB) on mechanisms for clearing US$800 million of arrears with that institution.

In June 2002, the IMF also approved a three-year Poverty Reduction and Growth Facility (PRGF) for the DRC worth about US$750 million. The IMF pointed out that even if all policy initiatives are successfully implemented and yield the expected results, it will be several years before the impact is sufficient to reverse the continuing depreciation of the nation's human and physical capital.

The rapid improvements to fiscal policy since 2001 have meant a resumption of foreign aid and the granting of debt relief by the Paris Club of international creditors, the IMF and the World Bank. Grants, including relief aid, were expected to total 1.2 per cent of GDP in 2002, rising to around 5 per cent in 2003. In September 2002, the Paris Club agreed to the immediate cancellation of US$4.46 billion in external debt. The IMF estimates that total external public debt will fall from US$12.9 billion in 2001 to US$8.9 billion in 2002 as a result of debt relief and the clearance of arrears.

The government is also continuing with efforts to reform the mining sector and the state mining corporation, Gécamines. A draft mining code was prepared with the help of Congolese and international legal and tax experts. The major innovations introduced in the new mining code, effective from September 2002, include: (i) a change in the government's role from mining operator to mining regulator; (ii) the creation of a single mining regime without investment agreements negotiated on a case-by-case basis; (iii) the introduction of a special tax regime for the mining sector, which is fair and equitable; and (iv) the option, under a clear and straightforward system, of issuing mining titles on a first-come-first-served basis and managed transparently.

Telecommunications

With few fixed telephone lines, mobile operators are stepping into the void. The DRC's largest mobile operator in 2002 was Celtel, but it will face stiff competition from new entrants to the market, particularly Vodacom. Vodacom, Africa's largest mobile telephone operator, launched its Congolese service in May 2000. The company planned to invest US$370 million in its first year of operation in the DRC, believed to be the largest non-mining investment in the country's history. Company executives expect the number of mobile phone users to jump from 150,000 (in 2001) to over 600,000 by 2005. Vodacom is half owned by South Africa's state-controlled telecoms utility, Telkom The UK's Vodafone owns 31.5 per cent, the South African group VenFin holds 13.5 per cent and the investment holding company Hosken Consolidated Investments owns the remaining 5.0 per cent.

Plundering Congolese resources

In 2001, the UN set up yet another panel to investigate allegations that the belligerents in the DRC conflict are plundering the country's natural wealth. The panel was set up after two previous UN reports led to complaints, principally by Uganda and Rwanda, that the reports unfairly targeted and misrepresented their positions. In May 2002, the panel issued an interim report which confirmed that illegal exploitation of Congolese resources was continuing and was being consolidated in many areas. These activities include poaching for ivory, game meat and rare species, logging and mining for coltan, gold and diamonds. Criminal gangs from outside the region are also allegedly using DRC's resources for money laundering and trafficking in guns.

Outlook

The accord signed in Pretoria in December 2002 provided the DRC with its best chance yet for peace. Drawing together almost all the combatant factions along with civil society groups, the deal appears to have gained acceptance and is likely to hold together in 2003. Nevertheless, the DRC has seen a number of attempts at peace and power-sharing in the past and all have fallen apart due to a resumption of fighting on the ground and the ambitions of the top-level of command. RCD-Goma, which spent most of 2002 in retreat, is likely to hold firm to the agreement in order to retain its number of seats in parliament and the cabinet, which match those of its MLC rivals and the Kinshasa government.

There remains a danger that the MLC, which was strengthened militarily in 2002, will seek to withdraw from the agreement. The sticking point in any further dialogue will be the unification of combatant groups and the reorganisation of national defence, issues which could see the MLC lose territory and political influence. In the past, MLC leader Jean-Pierre Bemba has broken agreements when he has felt it has eroded his power base and there is little reason to suggest he will not do the same with the Pretoria accord. Whether he then chooses to resume the conflict will depend on the backing of Uganda, which serves as the MLC's main source of weapons. He will also need to convince local MLC commanders and combatants to give him support, which is by no means automatic.

Smaller groups represented in the transitional government and parliament – the RCD-ML, *Mayi-Mayi* and RCD-N – are harder to judge, due to their tendency to shift alliances radically, according to the situation on the battlefield. They have little support among the civilian population and their presence in government is mainly due to the amount of territory their control. Therefore they are highly likely to resume fighting if the MLC quits the Pretoria accord, if only to maintain their political presence.

Even if the signatories to the Pretoria accord remain within the interim administration, there are a number of local war-lords and smaller guerrilla groups that remain outside of the power-sharing deal. This could introduce an element of uncertainty and distrust within the power-sharing government. While the MLC and RCD-Goma may not officially stray from the deal, they may choose to employ other guerrilla groups to act as proxy armies. One particular threat to peace comes from the UPC, which continues to fight RCD-Goma forces for control of Bunia. The MLC may choose to employ the UPC, which also enjoys Ugandan support, to drive back the RCD-Goma forces, thereby increasing its future influence in government.

It is therefore clear that the DRC will need a speedy long-term resolution which sees political power allocated through the ballot box rather than the battlefield. This will mean a step-up in the demobilisation of combatant groups and irregular armies and the creation of a non-political military command. Progress towards this end will depend on compromise among warring groups, something which the DRC has found hard to resolve.

Risk assessment

Economic	Improving
Political	Poor
Regional stability	Poor

COUNTRY PROFILE

Historical profile

The thirteenth century saw the rise of the Kongo empire, which covered northern Angola and western Congo.

1482 Portuguese navigator Diogo Cao became the first European to visit the Congo. The Portuguese subsequently formed ties with the Kongo empire. During the sixteenth and seventeenth centuries, the British, Dutch, Portuguese and French bought slaves from the Kongo empire.

1870 King Leopold II of Belgium decided to colonise the Kongo empire.

1879–87 British explorer Henry Stanley established Belgian authority over the Congo basin.

1884–85 European governments recognised Leopold's claim to the Congo basin.

1885 Leopold established the Congo Free State.

1891–92 Belgium conquered Katanga.

1892–94 Belgium conquered eastern Congo, which was controlled by Arab and east African merchants.

1908 The Belgian state annexed Congo.

1959 A nationalist uprising based in Leopoldville (now Kinshasa) began the disintegration of Belgian colonial authority.

1960 Congo gained independence. The Belgian community fled and there were few professionals left to run the government. Chaos ensued as the diamond and copper mining province of Katanga attempted to secede under the leadership of Joseph Tshombe.

1961 Prime Minister Patrice Lumumba was deposed and murdered, allegedly by Katangan separatists. Marshal Joseph Mobutu was appointed prime minister by President Kasavuba. UN soldiers began disarming the Katangese soldiers on behalf of the Kasavuba government.

1963 Tshombe agreed to end the Katangan separatist war.

1964 Kasavuba dismissed Mobutu and appointed Tshombe as prime minister.

1965 Mobutu seized power after a coup.

1971 Congo was renamed Zaire. Joseph Mobutu renamed himself Mobutu Sese Seko.

1973–74 Mobutu nationalised foreign firms and forced foreign investors out of the country.

1977 French, Belgian and Moroccan troops fought an attack on Katanga by Angolan rebels.

1989 Zaire defaulted on its debt servicing to Belgium, leading to a suspension of development programmes.

1990 Mobutu ended the ban on political parties and appointed a transitional government, the High Council of the Republic (HCR).

1991 From March President Mobutu presided over a series of short-lived governments, edging towards a national conference and multi-party elections.

1993 Rival pro and anti Mobutu governments were formed

1994 The National Assembly and the HCR were reconstituted as a single body, known as the High Council of the Republic-Parliament of Transition (HCR-PT) (730 members). On 8 April the HCR-PT endorsed a Transitional Constitutional Act, which defined regulations between the government and president, and which entrusted the HCR-PT with the task of overseeing the government's activities.

1995 The general elections scheduled for July were postponed and the transition period was extended for a further two years.

1997 President Mobutu fled to Togo when Laurent-Désiré Kabila's Alliance des Forces Démocratiques pour la Libération (AFDL) (Alliance of Democratic Forces for Liberation) seized Kinshasa in May after a seven-month campaign against Mobutu's rule. Kabila was backed by Tutsi rebels and the Rwandan government. Zaire was renamed the Democratic Republic of Congo (DRC). Kabila declared himself president, giving himself wide powers. All government institutions were dissolved; Kabila announced that the HCR-PT was to be replaced by a constituent assembly, to draft a new constitution. Mobutu Sese Seko died in September in Morocco.

1998 The Rassemblement Congolais pour la Démocratie (RCD) (Congolese Democratic Coalition) was formed, with the support of Tutsi leaders in Rwanda and Burundi along with the Ugandan government, with the aim of overthrowing Kabila. A full-scale civil war broke out in August. Zimbabwe, Namibia and Angola came to the aid of the Kabila government. Peace talks began in Zambia's capital Lusaka, but broke down in October.

1999 In May, Ernest Wamba dia Wamba led a breakaway from the RCD, forming the Mouvement pour la Libération Congolaise (MLC) (Movement for Congolese Liberation). In July, the governments involved in the war signed a cease-fire followed by the MLC and the RCD in August. In October, Wamba announced the creation of his own government in the north-eastern city of Bunia. In the following month, renewed fighting broke out between the DRC government forces and the RCD and MLC rebel groups in the north-west, although all parties still claimed to be committed to the cease-fire.

2000 In February, the UN Security Council authorised a 5,500-strong UN force to monitor the cease-fire. On 1 July, Kabila appointed a Legislative and Constituent Assembly-Transitional Parliament (LCA-TP) and in October, he said UN peace monitors could be deployed in the country. In December, the DRC government and rebel groups signed an agreement in Harare, Zimbabwe, to withdraw their troops from frontline positions. Foreign governments involved in the conflict agreed to withdraw their forces.

2001 In January, President Laurent Kabila was assassinated by one of his bodyguards. His son, Major General Joseph Kabila, was appointed interim president by parliament on 25 January.

2002 Mount Nyiragongo erupted in January, pouring lava through the town of Goma. Uganda sent troop reinforcements to the DRC in February to quell ethnic fighting. In April, the government signed a power-sharing deal with the MLC, but the most powerful RCD faction refused to sign.

Political structure

Constitution

A draft constitution was approved in November 1998, but was still awaiting ratification by national referendum in 2002.

Form of state

Presidential republic

The executive

Personal rule of President Joseph Kabila since January 2001 following the assassination of his father, Laurent Kabila. There is no formal delineation of the power of the executive and power is exercised through military chiefs.

National legislature

The 730-member High Council of the Republic-Parliament of Transition (HCR-PT) was suspended indefinitely pending elections. However on 1 July 2000, the president appointed a Legislative and Constituent Assembly-Transitional Parliament (LCA-TP), naming 240 of the 300 members, with 60 to be appointed later.

Legal system

The civil code is based on the Belgian system, including the structure of the Supreme Court. Legal issues at the local level are usually dealt with according to tribal law.

Last elections

1987

Next elections

Multi-party elections were promised in May 1999, but have been postponed indefinitely.

Political parties

President Joseph Kabila lifted restrictions on political parties on 17 May 2001.

Ruling party

Alliance des Forces Démocratiques pour La Libération (AFDL) (Alliance of the Democratic Forces of Liberation)

Main opposition party

Mouvement Populaire de la Revolution (MPR) (Popular Movement of the Revolution)

Population
50.95 million (2000)
Annual population growth rate: 3 per cent (1994–2000); projected at 2.9 per cent (1998–2015).
Population density: 20 inhabitants per square km. Urban population: 30 per cent.

Ethnic make-up
There are over 200 ethnic groups in DRC. The largest is the Kongo, which predominates in Bandundu province. The Mongo are mainly found in the heavily forested north and north-west. The Luba predominate in the two Kasai provinces and the Shabans and Bemba live mainly in Katanga (formerly Shaba) province. Other large ethnic groups include the Zande, the Bwaka, the Lulua and the Songe. There are a large number of people of Nilotic origin, mainly concentrated in the eastern North Kivu province.

Religions
Some 50 per cent of the population adhere to animist beliefs. The remainder are mostly Christian, of which a majority are Roman Catholic. Muslims make up some 10 per cent of the population, residing mainly in North Kivu province.

Labour market and unemployment
The informal economy accounts for around 80 per cent of economic activity. A meaningful unemployment rate is therefore very difficult to measure. The projected growth rate is 2.9 per cent (1997–2010). Approximately 44 per cent of the labour force is female.

Education
School is compulsory for children between the ages of six and 11, but attendance is estimated at below 75 per cent and of these only about 40 per cent graduate. Secondary education, which is not compulsory, begins at the age of 12 and also lasts for six years. Enrolment in secondary school is less than 25 per cent of the relevant age group. There are three universities – at Kinshasa, Kisangani and Lubumbashi. The literacy rate is estimated at 75 per cent, but is thought to be much lower outside urban areas.

Health
Life expectancy is 51 years with an infant mortality rate of 92 per 1,000 live births. Child malnutrition affects 34 per cent of children under five (1992–98).
The Mobutu government had placed a low priority on standards of health and welfare, and continuing civil war has inhibited improvement. Health expenditure in the period 1990–97 was just 0.2 per cent of GDP. One-third of the population, mostly those in the larger cities, has access to local health care.
There are more than 900 hospitals with a total capacity of over 75,000 beds, but many of these are not operating due to a lack of resources and unpaid staff. There are an estimated 1,900 physicians working in the DRC.
It is estimated that between 5–10 per cent of the population aged 15–49 years have HIV. Tuberculosis incidence is about 260 per 100,000 population.

Welfare
Several active UN agencies and non-government organisations through a diverse range of activities manage the welfare situation in the DRC. While the western provinces of the country show stability, the eastern provinces featuring unrivalled poverty and insecurity are gripped by a humanitarian emergency. As many as 2.5 million people are estimated to have been killed or died as a result of the war to overthrow the DRC government which started in August 1998. Although a political settlement is necessary, the complex humanitarian crisis in the DRC is being reviewed by the 2002 Common Humanitarian Action Plan (CHAP) initiated by the UN. The action plan concentrates both on life saving operations and economic recovery.
UN estimates show that the eastern part of the country has most of the 2.4 million internally displaced people, with 16 million people requiring emergency food aid. As front line fighting between government and rebel held areas continues, UN World Food Programme (WFP), in June 2002, resumed its emergency airlift operation providing aid to an estimated 24,000 people in the northern Katanga province. WFP continues to assist 1.4 million people in the DRC.
The United Nations Development Programme (UNDP) data suggests that less than one-half of Congolese have access to safe water and only one in five has adequate sanitary facilities (1998 estimates).
The high level of insecurity has forced several international agencies to withdraw aid, including at least seven separate evacuations of humanitarian teams in March and April 2002. The slow response from the donor community to the 2002 UN Consolidated Appeal has made relief operations even more difficult.

Main cities
Kinshasa (capital, estimated population six million in 2000), Mbuji-Mayi (1.5 million), Kinsangani, Matadi, Bandundu, Mbandaka, Bukavu, Lubumbashi, Kananga, Goma, Kindu.

Languages spoken
Among the many African languages spoken, Lingala, KiSwahili, Tshiluba and Kikongo are the most prominent in DRC.

Official language/s
French

Media
Press
The press is able to criticise government bodies and some publications serve as mouthpieces for opposition parties, despite the fact that these were suspended shortly after Laurent Kabila became president in 1997. Journalists are often harassed, prompting many to exercise self-censorship.
Dailies: The former official daily, *Salongo* now appears weekly. Daily publications include *Umoja*, *L'Analyste*, *Boyoma*, *Société*, *Elima* (evening daily) and *Mjumbe*.
Weeklies: Weeklies include *Alarme*, *L'Avenir*, *Changement*, the French language *La Semaine*, *Compatriote*, *Demain le Congo*, *Libérateur*, *Forum des as Le Soft* and La Vérité.
Business: The main business publication is the French language *Soft de Finance*.
Periodicals: Monthly publications include *L'Emissaire*, *Le Potentiel* and *Tribune du peuple*.

Broadcasting
Radio: There is a domestic radio service broadcast in French and four African languages (KiSwahili, Lingala, Kiluba and Kikongo). Educational programmes are broadcast by Radio Candip.
Television: There is a limited television service broadcast by the government-owned commercial station.

Economy
Since the rebellion against Kabila began in August 1998, the economy of the DRC has been in chaos. In the north and east of the country which is occupied by rebels and foreign armies, much of the country's wealth is being siphoned off by foreign governments.
With its huge mineral wealth of cobalt, copper, gold, diamonds and uranium, its rivers with abundant hydroelectric potential, its fertile land and its virgin forests, the country should have become Africa's economic powerhouse. In the north and east of the country, much of the country's wealth was siphoned off by foreign governments throughout the civil war. Uganda and Rwanda have looted mines and smuggled out commodities such as diamonds and coffee.
However, the slow implementation of the UN-sponsored peace agreement, with a cease-fire holding from early 2001, has begun to stabilise the economy, particularly in government-controlled areas. In June 2002, the IMF approved a US$750

million arrangement under the Poverty Reduction and Growth Facility (PRGF) for the DRC. The DRC can draw up to US$543 million immediately with the rest drawn in six equal installments following performance reviews. The PRGF follows a staff-monitored programme (SMP) from June 2001 to March 2002 which the IMF claims helped break the 'vicious cycle of hyperinflation and currency depreciation'. The improved relations with the IMF came about after the government cleared its arrears with the Fund. The government ended exchange controls and shored up the fiscal regime with greater budgetary control.

External trade

The narrow export base, concentrated mainly on minerals, with some agricultural cash crops, has made the DRC's balance of trade susceptible to the vagaries of world commodity markets. Under-investment and regular strikes have further weakened the mining industry.

Exports

Principal exports are copper (typically 60 per cent of total), diamonds (14 per cent), cobalt (11 per cent), crude petroleum (9 per cent), coffee (6 per cent).

Main destinations: Belgium (58.9 per cent of 2000 total), US (18.5 per cent), Finland (16.5 per cent), India (3.8 per cent), Netherlands (2.8 per cent).

Imports

Principal imports are manufactured goods (typically, 37 per cent of total), raw materials (15 per cent), food (14 per cent), fuel and energy.

Main sources: Belgium (18.7 per cent of 2000 total), South Africa (18 per cent), Nigeria (10.6 per cent), France (5.7 per cent), Kenya (5.1 per cent).

Agriculture

Agriculture contributes around 50 per cent of GDP. Only about half of this is derived from subsistence farming even though it provides the livelihood of 57 per cent of the population.

Despite enormous agricultural potential, the sector has been handicapped above all by transport problems, occasional drought, smuggling and inflexible pricing policies. The government is developing the forestry sector with multilateral financial assistance.

Main food crops are cassava, maize, rice and plantain. Production is insufficient to meet demand, and poor transport restricts supplies to the urban areas. Main cash/export crops are plantation-grown coffee, cocoa, oil palm, rubber, tea, cotton, sugar and tobacco.

The Nile Basin Initiative (NBI) (signed by Egypt, Sudan, Tanzania, Kenya, Rwanda, Burundi, Uganda and Democratic Republic of Congo) is launching seven feasibility studies backed by US$140 million granted by the World Bank and donor governments in June 2001. A shared vision programme (SVP), including several regional and sub-regional projects, was agreed in February 2002 and is scheduled to begin by the end of 2002.

Fishing

Although the DRC only has a narrow coastline, the fisheries sector is based evenly on inland and coastal resources. Around 150,000 artisanal fisherman operate in the DRC, providing 90 per cent of the total national catch. By 2002, only three fishing vessels were operating under the DRC flag. Excluding subsistence production, inland fishing in the many rivers and lakes produce around 150,000 tonnes, compared to 160,000 for seafood production. The country a substantial net importer of seafood and freshwater fish. In 2002, the FAO began organising and funding a rehabilitation of the fisheries sector. The US$1.8 million programme aims to provide 20,000 fishing households with nets and other fishing gear, while 18,000 families will be provided with essential basic tools and supplies to engage in fish farming.

Forestry

DRC has 125 million hectares of tropical forest, roughly half the timber resources of the African continent. The first industrial exploitation started in 1930 at Mayumbe, but the sector is vastly under-exploited and holds out much potential, particularly in terms of export revenue. From 1970 onwards, the focus of activity shifted from Mayumbe to Cuvette region. Forrest cover fell by 532,000 hectares or 0.4 per cent per annum in 1990–2000. The DRC produces significant volumes of sawnwood, as well as plywood and veneer. Tropical hardwood logs and sawnwood are the principal exports. The country consumes large quantities of wood fuel.

Industry and manufacturing

The industrial sector contributes around 17 per cent to GDP and employs around 10 per cent of the workforce. Approximately three-quarters of production is centred around Kinshasa or in Shaba province, owing to the availability of electricity and adequate transport facilities in these areas.

In an environment of political instability, endemic corruption and poor regulation, few manufacturing industries have developed. They have also been hindered by a lack of technical and management expertise, the comparatively poor transport infrastructure and a chronic decline in domestic purchasing power eroded by inflation and lack of foreign exchange to purchase essential manufacturing inputs. Output is geared towards the domestic market and is mainly concentrated on brewing, food processing, textiles, consumer goods, construction industry inputs and transport equipment.

Mismanagement and shortages of spare parts and materials have led to cut-backs in production with most firms operating at below half capacity. The government is attempting to increase production by encouraging foreign investment and offering substantial tax incentives.

Tourism

The moves towards peace have opened up new prospects for tourism in the DRC. With its immense rainforests and rich bio-diversity coupled with incredible natural beauty, a peaceful DRC could become a focus of scientific expeditions as well as providing a destination for the more adventurous eco-tourist. War has led to a significant deterioration in infrastructure and this will prove to be a major impediment to growth in the sector.

Mining

The country is rich in mineral resources and is potentially one of Africa's richest countries. DRC's copper reserves are estimated at 75 million tonnes with iron at one billion tonnes, 240 million carats of diamonds and over 600 tonnes of gold. In the past, mining contributed around a third of GDP and employed 5 per cent of the workforce. In the 1980s, the DRC was the world's biggest producer of cobalt and the second-largest producer of industrial diamonds, but although output remains high, it fluctuated severely during the 1990s owing to political instability. Moves towards peace in 2001 and 2002 will lead to a resumption of investment in the mining sector, backed by planned new mining and investment codes. Mining is likely to be the driving force of the economy over the medium-term.

Diamonds are mined on a commercial scale by the Société Minière de Bakwanga (Miba) at Bakwanga in Kasai Oriental, but artisanal diggers account for almost three-quarters of total output. In August 2001, President Kabila sacked Miba director Jean Charles Okoto for corruption. Gold production has been erratic and has fallen to record lows during the years of war. However, renewed investor interest in 2002 is likely to increase production.

There is tin mining and small-scale mining of cadmium, cassiterite and wolframite. Activity is concentrated in the copper-rich Shaba province. Twangiza gold deposits are estimated at 4.1 million tonnes of ore. With the exception of diamonds, these minerals have been hit by weak world demand in recent years.

Katanga Province is part of the Central African Copperbelt, which extends from

Angola through the DRC into Zambia. The state-run Gécamines (Génerale des Carrieres et des Mines) has holdings containing the biggest concentrations of copper and cobalt in the world. It has experienced hard times since the last years of the Mobutu dictatorship. It has attempted to encourage foreign investment in its ailing mines, but production has stagnated with total output in 2001 around 10 per cent of former levels. Gécamines' troubles are rooted in long-term problems of corruption and mismanagement. Its misfortune is exacerbated by the civil war, which has led to foreign partners scaling down or pulling out of joint ventures. As a result, copper output at Gécamines dropped from 476,000 tonnes in 1996 to under 80,000 tonnes in 2000.

Australia's Anvil Mining plans to open a new copper and silver mine in Katanga province in the third-quarter of 2002. The mine is estimated to have reserves totalling , with reserves totalling 1.7 million tonnes. The mine is likely to have a lifespan of eight years.

Hydrocarbons
Some 140 million barrels of oil reserves are located off the Atlantic coastline and in the River Congo estuary The DRC is believed to have substantial onshore oil and gas reserves. A cease-fire and peace agreement in 2001 and 2002 is likely to open the way for renewed interest in exploration.

Energy
The huge River Congo has enormous hydroelectricity potential. There is a major plant at Inga, near the port of Matadi at the mouth of the river, which supplies the copper mines in Shaba, and produces two-thirds of the country's 2,400MW installed capacity.

Energy in rural areas is mainly derived from charcoal and wood.

The DRC imports most of its oil requirements, due to the inability of its own oil refinery to process the very heavy domestic crude.

Banking
The banking system is virtually non-existent as persistent hyperinflation has led to the collapse of all the country's banks.

Central bank

Central Bank of Congo.

Main financial centre

Kinshasa

Time
GMT plus one hour in Kinshasa and the western provinces; GMT plus two hours elsewhere.

Geography
The Democratic Republic of Congo (DRC) is a large and diverse country, straddling the equator. Much of the interior is covered by dense forest, with a large number of rivers flowing into the Congo river (formerly known as the Zaïre river under President Mobutu and as the Congo river in the People's Republic of Congo), which provides a major transport system. The land is highest in the east, along the border with Uganda, Rwanda and Burundi, and falls gradually to a very narrow Atlantic coastline. The southern part of the country is savannah grassland.

Most of the population is concentrated in areas with the best communications: near Kinshasa in the far west, along the Congo River and other main rivers, and in the southern and eastern border regions.

Climate
The climate varies widely owing to the size of the country. The lowlands in the western region are hot and humid. Temperatures range from 27–30 degrees Celsius (C). On the central plateau, the likely temperature range is 18–20 degrees C. Eastern DRC has a Mediterranean type climate. In Kinshasa rain is concentrated in the period from November to March. Temperatures are high in Kinshasa, reaching up to 32 degrees C in the hottest month, January, with 26 degrees C in the coolest month, June. In the south and the eastern province of Kivu the climate is slightly cooler, particularly in the winter months.

Dress codes
There are no particular restrictions on dress. Lightweight clothing is essential, especially if visiting during the rainy season.

Entry requirements
Visitors are advised to contact embassy representatives in advance to ascertain current entry requirements. Visitors are also advised to register their presence in DRC with their local embassy representative.

Passports

Required by all. All passports must be revalidated two months prior to expiry date and all documents must be issued in French.

Visa

Required by all except certain nationals of Congo or re-entry permit holders. Business visitors require a letter of invitation from a DRC company. Travel regulations should be studied carefully before visit.

Prohibited entry

Those with visas/entry/exit stamps for Rwanda, Burundi or Uganda are likely to be refused entry.

Currency advice/regulations

The import or export of local currency is prohibited. Foreign currency import is limited to declared amount. Currency declaration forms must be kept and all currency exchanges should be recorded.

Customs

Visitors are advised not to take in any equipment which may arouse suspicion, such as cameras, binoculars, maps or any kind of tools or military equipment.

Health (for visitors)
Mandatory precautions

Yellow fever vaccination certificate is required if arriving from an infected area.

Advisable precautions

Visitors should take precautions against all tropical diseases. Anti-malaria tablets are essential, and AIDS is widespread among both men and women. Dysentery, typhoid and typhus are also prevalent, especially outside Kinshasa. Bubonic plague exists in the Bunia region.

Tap water must be treated as unsafe unless boiled and filtered (bottled water is available in the main cities).

Outside Kinshasa and Lubumbashi, it is not advisable to eat raw vegetables or ice cubes.

There was an outbreak of ebola in December 2001.

Hotels
Several major hotels in main cities. Most tend to be expensive and are often heavily booked. A service charge is usually added to bill and further tipping is optional.

Public holidays
Fixed dates

1 Jan, 4 Jan, 1 May, 24 Jun, 30 Jun, 1 Aug, 14 Oct, 27 Oct, 17 Nov, 24 Nov, 25 Dec.

Working hours
Banking

Mon–Fri: 0800–1130.

Business

Mon–Fri: 0730–1200, 1430–1700; Sat: 0730–12.00.

Government

Mon–Fri: 0730–1500; Sat: 0730–1200, although it is normal practice for ministers and senior officials to work from 0830–1300 and from 1600–2000.

Shops

Mon–Fri: 0800–1200, 1500–1700; Sat: 0800–1200.

Telecommunications
Telephone/fax

Dialling code for Democratic Republic of Congo: IDD access code + 243 followed by area code (12 for Kinshasa, 2 for Lubumbashi) followed by subscriber's number.

The DRC is linked to the international satellite communications system via an earth station near Kinshasa. The state of the telephone network is poor and it can take days or even weeks to place an overseas call. Development of the internal network has been slow, with less than one line per 1,000 people in 1997. There was only one fax per 10,000 people in 1996.

Mobile phones

Faced with telephones that do not work, wealthy civilians have used mobile phones since the 1980s, although total usage remains negligible. Telecel, Comcell and Trans Global Telecommunication offer mobile phone services.

Electricity supply

220V AC.

Social customs/useful tips

With its vast range of ethnic groups and huge land area, there are many different traditions, according to the locality. The most recent, the campaign of Zaïreanisation introduced by President Mobutu in the 1970s, was officially abandoned in 1990 as part of sweeping political changes. As a result of this campaign, conventional 'Christian' names were changed to African names, public sector employees abandoned the wearing of jackets and ties in favour of a tailored jacket known as an abacost, women wearing Western clothing were frowned on, and local people addressed each other as Citoyen and Citoyenne (Citizen). Since 1990, however, Monsieur and Madame have been acceptable forms of address.

As in most French-speaking African countries, business etiquette when visiting government and (to a lesser degree) private commercial offices is more formal than in English-speaking Africa.

Do not openly criticise the government or attempt to photograph public buildings. Military installations are also best avoided if possible.

Security

The security situation in DRC since late 1998 has been volatile. Street crime is rife, especially in Kinshasa. Visitors are advised not to wear expensive jewellery or watches or to carry cameras conspicuously. To achieve anything expect to pay *katamulomo* tips, especially to soldiers (both genuine and fake), who are seldom paid and who man the roadblocks. Visitors should beware of unofficial 'porters' at N'djili airport. Those visiting for the first time should try to arrange for a local business associate or friend to meet them at the airport. Visitors are advised to stay in their hotels after dark. They should avoid public transport altogether and use hire cars rather than taxis whenever possible. The DRC is undergoing profound political change which means that any official efforts which may be made to protect foreign visitors are unlikely to be effective outside Kinshasa. The best advice is to contact embassy representatives in advance in order to check the safety of the region to which you wish to travel.

Getting there

Air

Scibe Air Lift flies from Brussels to Lubumbashi and Kinshasa. Charter facilities are available.

National airline: Congo Airlines.

International airport/s: Kinshasa-N'djili International airport (FIH) is 25km from central Kinshasa. As N'djili is located a long way from the city, it is advisable to pre-arrange transport either with a hotel or local car hire firm such as Hertz (office within the shopping gallery at the Inter-Continental Hotel) or to arrange for a business or social contact to meet first-time visitors to the country at the airport.

Other airport/s: Lubumbashi-Luano (Code: FBM), 6.5km from city; Gbadolite (BDT).

Airport tax: None.

Surface

Road: There are 2,400km of asphalted roads leading to most major cities, including those linking Lubumbashi with Kolwezi and the Zambian border. Most roads from neighbouring countries are in a bad state of repair.

Rail: The three main lines into DRC are the Voie Nationale running from Matadi port to Kinshasa (366km); the eastern route entering from Tanzania at Kalemie and the northern route entering from the Sudan at Mungbere. There are also links to southern African states via Zambia.

An end to Angola's civil war would allow reconstruction of the Benguela line from Shaba to Lobito port in Angola, but this could take several years.

Main port/s: The main port is Matadi, about 150km inland on the Congo River. Kinshasa is the main inland river port and the ferry crossing point from Brazzaville.

Getting about

National transport

Air: Scibe Air Lift provides domestic services, as well as Lubumbashi and Kinshasa to Brussels. Charter facilities are available. Other domestic airlines include ACS, Shaba Air and Blue Airline.

Road: Over 140,000km of roads, but outside main population centres these tend to be of poor quality and some parts have become impassable through lack of maintenance. Main routes link Kinshasa with Matadi and Kikwit, and Lubumbashi with Kolwezi and the Zambian border.

Buses: Very irregular, crowded and infrequent service.

Rail: A network of over 5,000km is operated by Société Nationale des Chemins de Fer Zaïroise (SNCZ), but some parts are inoperable. Four classes – 'deluxe' and first-class is advisable.

Water: Inland navigation is important, particularly for freight on the Congo River between Kinshasa and Kisangani and the Kasai River from Ilebo to the Congo River north of Kinshasa. However, all routes around Kisangani have been disrupted by the civil war. When available, passenger services run on all major rivers and lakes. It is advisable to travel luxury or first class.

City transport

Taxis: Volatile inflation rates and political instability mean it is virtually impossible to keep track of taxi fares in local currency. If resorting to a local taxi, it is absolutely essential to negotiate a fixed fare before starting the journey.

Ferry: In Kinshasa there is a regular ferry service to Brazzaville.

Car hire

Self-drive cars available in Kinshasa and at airport. A deposit is required unless an acceptable credit card can be produced. International driving licence required. Traffic drives on the right.

BUSINESS DIRECTORY

Telephone area codes

The international direct dialling (IDD) code for DRC is +243, followed by the area code:

Cellular network	88
Kinshasa	12
Lubumbashi	2

Chambers of Commerce

Chambre de Commerce et d'Industrie de Kinshasa, BP 7247, Kinshasa (tel: 24-623).

Banking

Banque Commerciale du Congo SARL, BP 2798, Boulevard du 30 Juin, Kinshasa/Gombe (tel: 21773, 21776, fax: 12 21770).

Banque Continentale Africaine (Zaire) SZARL, 4 Avenue de la Justice, Kinshasa/Gombe (tel: 28006, 28537 fax: 25243).

Banque Internationale de Credit SARL, 191 Ave de l'Equateur, Kinshasa/Gombe (tel: 8820404, 8841940, 8845631, 8843159, 8843790, 8801487 fax: 8801125, 3779790034).

Citibank NA Congo, BP 9999, Citibank Building, Coin des Avenues Colonel Lukusa et Ngongo Lutete, Kinshasa/Gombe 1 (tel: 20555/57 Fax: 40015).

Fransabank (Congo) SARL, BP 9497, Avenue du Port, 14/16 Immeuble Zaïre-Shell, Kin. 1, Kinshasa/Gombe (tel:12 20119, 20121/2/3/4 fax: 12 20199).

Nouvelle Banque de Kinshasa, 1 Place du Marché, Kinshasa/Gombe 1 (tel: 12 20562-5, 1 20459-60, 1 23461-63 fax: 12 581-496180043).

Stanbic Bank Congo sarl, 12 Avenue de la Mongala, Kinshasa/Gombe (tel: 88 48445, 88 41984, 88 43453, 88 43419, 88 04512 fax: 88 46216).

Union de Banques SARL, BP 197, Coin des Avenues de la Nation et des Aviateurs, Kinshasa/Gombe (tel: 88 4133, 88 43620, 88 44887 fax: 88 46628).

Central bank

Banque du Congo, 513 Boulevard Tshatshi, Kinshasa/Gombe. Congo (Democratic Republic of) (tel: 8846015 fax: 3769605, 3769606, 3769607).

Travel information

Air Zaïre, BP 10120, Airport de N'Djili, Kinshasa (tel: 20-939; fax: 20-940).

N'Djili International Airport, BP 10124, Kinshasa 24 (tel: 23-570).

Office National de Tourisme, boulevard du 30 Juin, BP 9502, Kinshasa.

SNCZ Railways, BP 597, Kinshasa.

Ministries

Civil Service Ministry, Avenue des Ambassadeurs, BP 3, Kinshasa-Gombe.

Ministry of Agriculture, Boulevard du 30 Juin, Building Sozacom, 3e Etage, BP 8722 KIN I, Kinshasa-Gombe.

Ministry of Economy, Industry and Commerce, Boulevard du 30 Juin, Building ONATRA, BP 8500 KIN I, Kinshasa-Gombe.

Ministry of Energy, 239 Avenue de la Justice, Building SNEL, BP 5137 KIN I, Kinshasa-Gombe.

Ministry of Environment and Tourism, 15 Avenue des Cliniques, BP 12348 KIN I, Kinshasa-Gombe.

Ministry of Finance, Boulevard du 30 Juin, BP 12998 KIN I, Kinshasa-Gombe.

Ministry of Foreign Affairs, Place de l'Indépendance, BP 7100, Kinshasa-Gombe.

Ministry of Health, Boulevard du 30 Juin, BP 3088 KIN I, Kinshasa-Gombe.

Ministry of Home Affairs, Kinshasa-Gombe.

Ministry of Information and Cultural Affairs, Avenue du 24 Novembre, BP 3171 KIN I, Kinshasa-Kabinda.

Ministry of International Co-Operation, Avenue de la Justice, Enceinte SNEL, Kinshasa-Gombe.

Ministry of Justice, 228 Avenue des 3 Z, Kinshasa-Gombe.

Ministry of Mines, 239 Avenue de la Justice, Building SNEL, BP 5137 KIN I, Kinshasa-Gombe.

Ministry of National Education, Enceinte de l'Institut de la Gombe, BP 3163, Kinshasa-Gombe.

Ministry of Planning and Development, 4155 Avenue des Coteaux, BP 9378 KIN I, Kinshasa-Gombe.

Ministry of Post and Telecommunications, 4484 Avenue des Huiles, Building KILOU, BP 800 KIN I, Kinshasa-Gombe.

Ministry of Public Works, Building TRAVAUX PUBLICS, Kinshasa-Gombe.

Ministry of Reconstruction, Boulevard Colonel Tshatshi, Building TRAVAUX PUBLICS, BP 26, Kinshasa-Gombe.

Ministry of Transport, Boulevard du 30 Juin, Building ONATRA, BP 3304, Kinshasa-Gombe.

Ministry of Youth and Sports, 77 Avenue de la Justice, BP 8541 KIN I, Kinshasa-Gombe.

Other useful addresses

Democratic Republic of Congo Embassy (USA), 1800 New Hampshire Avenue, NW, Washington DC 20009 (tel: 234-7690; fax: 237-0748).

Foire Internationale de Kinshasa, BP 1397, Kinshasa (annual international fair in July).

Internet sites

Africa Business Network: http://www.ifc.org/abn

AllAfrica.com: http://allafrica.com

African Development Bank: http://www.afdb.org

Africa Online: http://www.africaonline.com

Demorcratic Republic of Congo (French only): http://www.congonline.com

Harambee Afrika (UK business club for traders with east, central and southern Africa; includes annotated web resource list): http://www.harambee.co.uk

Mbendi AfroPaedia (information on companies, countries, industries and stock exchanges in Africa): http://mbendi.co.za

Côte d'Ivoire

Nicole Goldin

KEY FACTS

Official name: République de Côte d'Ivoire (Republic of Côte d'Ivoire)

Head of State: President Laurent Gbagbo (FPI) (since Oct 2000)

Head of government: Prime Minister Seydou Diarra (appointed by the president, 25 Jan 2003; sworn in, 10 Feb 2003)

Ruling party: Coalition government of national unity: Front Populaire Ivorienne (FPI) (Ivorian Popular Front), Parti Democratique de la Côte d'Ivoire-Rassemblement Democratique Africain (PDCI-RDA) (Democratic Party of Côte d'Ivoire-Democratic African Rally) and Rassemblement des Républicains (RDR) (Rally of Republicans) (since August 2002)

Area: 3,224,630 square km

Population: 16.70 million (2001)

Capital: Yamoussoukro (administrative capital); Abidjan (economic centre)

Official language: French

Currency: CFA franc (CFAf) = 100 centimes (Communauté Financière Africaine (African Financial Community) franc)

Exchange rate: CFAf629.73 per US$ (Jan 2003); CFAf655.96 per euro (pegged Jan 1999)

GDP per capita: US$634 (2001)

GDP real growth: -0.90% (2001)

Inflation: 4.30% (2001); 0.0% (year-on-year, Feb 2002)

Balance of trade: US$1.02 billion (2001)

Foreign debt: US$9.65 billion (2001)

Annual FDI: US$138.00 million (2001)

Conflict erupted in Côte d'Ivoire in late 2002 after a mutiny led to the capture of the key town of Bouake and the economically important cocoa-growing region. For most of its post-independence history, Côte d'Ivoire has been an island of stability and calm, but since a coup d'état in 1999, the country has suffered rising social and political tensions. By the end of 2002, Côte d'Ivoire was the focus of regional peace efforts alongside French military engagement on behalf of the Economic Community of West African States (Ecowas). The chaos is threatening to undo progress on a return to multi-party politics, decentralisation, economic stabilisation and favourable commodity prices and yields. The conflict affecting the cocoa-growing areas at a crucial time in the farming season is particularly damaging and Côte d'Ivoire is likely to experience enormous difficulties in 2003.

Tentative return to stability

Following the coup d'etat in December 1999 and the 2000 presidential and legislative elections marred by violence during which over 300 persons died, the relative success of the March 2001 municipal poll set Côte d'Ivoire on the road back to the political stability for which it had once been considered a beacon of promise in West Africa. After having been prohibited from running in the 2000 contests, the full electoral participation of former prime minister Alassane Ouattara's opposition Rassemblement des Républicains (RDR) (Rally of Republicans) party at the municipal level was significant in sparking the transition to both political and economic normalcy. The showing of President Laurent Gbagbo s ruling Front Populaire Ivorienne (FPI) (Ivorian Popular Front) party is also an important measure of his support following his win over the military rule of Robert Guei. Furthermore, a national reconciliation process commenced in 2001, culminating in a meeting between Gbagbo, Bédié (president before Guei's coup), Guei and Ouattara in the capital Yamoussoukro in January 2002. However, tensions flared up again as the July 2002 local elections for general councils and district leaders approached. Amid a bitter campaign, long-standing ethnic tensions between the Muslim north (Ouattara's stronghold) and the south (Gbagbo's stronghold) have degenerated into violence in Daloa, an important cocoa area. Arson, looting, and clashes have forced farmers and civilians – including many immigrants from Mali, Guinea, or the north of Côte d'Ivoire – to flee, potentially putting the crop yield at risk.

Optimism that the Constitutional Court's June 2002 confirmation of Ouattara's Ivorian citizenship would ease tensions soon fell away as Côte d'Ivoire entered a new crisis in September. Around 800 soldiers mutinied over the issue of their demobilisation from the military, most of whom had joined the army during the military transition led by Guei. Interior Minister Emile Boga Doudou, Guei and his wife were killed in the uprising, while Oauttara sought refuge in the French embassy before fleeing to Gabon in late November. Both Guei and Ouattara were accused of masterminding the uprising by the Ivorian authorities. The rebels named themselves the Mouvement Patriotique de Côte d'Ivoire (MPCI) (Patriotic Movement of Côte d'Ivoire) and included some civilians in an effort to gain legitimacy and negotiating power. A truce brokered by Senegal was agreed by the government and the rebels in October and was monitored by French troops ahead of a deployment of an Ecowas force comprsing around 1,300 soldiers from Benin, Ghana, Niger, Senegal and Togo Peace talks organised by Togo were set up by Ecowas to resolve the crisis and led to an agreement from both sides not to recruit mercenaries, enrol children or violate the cease-fire. However, by end-2002, little progress was made, with the MPCI demanding Gbagbo's resignation and fresh elections, while the government insisted the rebels disarm.

Return of the donors

The uprising was a set-back for Côte d'Ivoire's economic development, particularly as the country has begun to win back donors. Culminating in a US$200 million credit from the World Bank approved in June 2002, a steady stream of international donors re-commenced aid to and co-operation with the nation. Once the darling of the aid community, flows had halted following the military takeover and subsequent 'hiatus' from democracy. The credit will support the Economic Recovery Project which emphasises need for reform in the economy and its administration via the creation of 'conditions for renewed broad-based growth driven by the rural economy and a private sector that is more confident about its future'.

On 21 May 2002, US President George W Bush designated Côte d Ivoire as a beneficiary of the US's African Growth and Opportunity Act (AGOA), which allows exports of certain products to the US on a tariff-free basis. This move followed the signing one month earlier of a trade pact between the US and the Union Economique et Monetaire Ouestafricain (UEMOA) (West African Economic and Monetary Union), of which Côte d'Ivoire is a member. Also in May, the French Development Agency (AFD) re-engaged by granting a structural adjustment loan worth CFAf120 billion (US$174 million) at an interest rate of 0.41 per cent and 10 year repayment period. The EU had resumed macroeconomic support in June 2001, and announced in March 2002 an increase to CFAf56 million (US$53.2 million) for the coming year as part of a CFAf264 million (US$251.8 million) commitment through 2007.

Setting the trend in February 2002, the World Bank announced its return to continue already approved disbursements and consider new credits. Following the Bank's lead, the IMF approved, in principle, a US$418 million loan to fight poverty and promote economic growth.

The last major institution to return to Ivorian lending, was the African Development Bank, based in Abidjan, Côte d'Ivoire's own economic capital. As part of the Initiative for Highly Indebted Poor Countries (HIPC), a loan of CFAf160 billion (US$223 million) was awarded on 4 April 2002, the aim of which is to ease debt handling and budget pressures.

Perhaps the most significant of all these moves was that of the Paris Club, which, on 10 April 2002, cancelled Ivorian foreign debt valued at US$911 million and rescheduled outstanding credits to a 40-year repayment period with 16 years grace and interest rates at least as favourable as the original concessionary rates. Paramount to mitigating the lingering effects of the financial disaster, the relief is expected to reduce service payments between 1 April 2002 and 31 December 2004 from approximately US$2.26 billion to US$750 million.

New budget, new hopes

The 2002 budget, approved by the Ivorian parliament on 14 March 2002, was called a 'cleaning up budget', the aim of which is

KEY INDICATORS — Côte d'Ivoire

	Unit	1996	1997	1998	1999	2000
Population	m	14.78	15.04	15.37	15.69	16.40
Gross domestic product (GDP)	US$bn	9.78	9.44	10.34	11.10	9.40
GDP per capita	US$	662	710	710	707	573
GDP real growth	%	7.7	5.7	4.8	1.6	-2.3
Inflation	%	2.7	4.2	4.5	0.7	2.5
Industrial production	1995=100	113.3	126.8	141.0	145.0	133.6
Exports (fob) (goods)	US$m	4,446.0	4,299.0	4,575.0	4,661.1	3,972.9
Imports (fob) (goods)	US$m	2,622.0	2,480.0	2,705.0	2,766.1	2,175.5
Balance of trade	US$m	1,824.0	1,819.0	1,870.0	1,895.2	1,797.4
Current account	US$m	-313.4	-241.7	-312.6	-120.5	-12.9
Foreign debt	US$bn	16.9	15.6	14.3	14.8	14.0
Total reserves minus gold	US$m	605.8	618.4	855.5	630.4	667.8
Foreign exchange	US$m	604.4	618.1	855.0	626.6	666.2
Exchange rate	per US$	511.55	583.67	589.95	615.70	711.98

to support the economic recovery by levelling state expenditures and revenues following years of credit financing. The budget balances revenue and expenditure at CFAf1,948.6 billion (US$2.76 billion), where revenues comprise interior intake of CFAf1,373.3 billion (US$1.98 billion) and exterior income of CFAf572.3 billion (US$82.8 million) – including World Bank and EU credits. In line with IMF and other donor programmes and guidance, the socialist-oriented government gives priority to the social sectors, with agriculture, the HIV fight, health, basic infrastructure, security and regional administration accounting for 16.9 per cent of the total budget. Education is also considered an important measure in the attack on poverty, with free access seen as a fundamental building block of future growth. Government investment will utilise CFAf372.6 billion (US$54 million). Another CFAf770.1 billion (US$1.11 billion) will go towards the public debt, and a balance of CFAf779.3 billion (US$1.12 billion) for other programmes and state expenditures.

Cocoa prices soar

Although progress has been made to diversify agricultural exports to include tropical woods, petroleum, cotton, bananas, pineapples, palm oil, and fish, cocoa is Côte d'Ivoire's principal export, constituting 33 per cent of total exports. Together, cocoa and coffee account for 40 per cent of GDP. Due to estimates of a 160,000 tonne global shortage of cocoa supply for 2001/02 (crop year October–September), and an even greater supply deficit forecast for the 2002/03 year, the Ivorian economy is getting an intense boost as prices have leapt to 14-year highs. Prices jumped nearly 70 per cent between September 2001 and March 2002 and were reportedly trading at US$1,697 per metric ton (mt) in June 2002. Cumulative arrivals to December 2001 were 670,000mt, 50,000mt higher than at the same point in the previous harvest. The key reason for the increase is the smuggling of beans from nearby Ghana, where prices are around 30 per cent lower. Smuggling was estimated at around 20,000mt of Ghana's production during the first quarter of the 2001/02 season. In other cocoa developments, the International Cocoa Organisation announced its May 2002 decision to relocate its headquarters to Abidjan, the nation's administrative and commercial capital, another sign of renewed international confidence.

Ongoing coffee decline

After cocoa, coffee is Côte D'Ivoire's second export. In January 2000, robustas were fetching just over US$53 per pound. By January 2001, prices dropped to US$32.40, and by January 2002, they hit a low of US$22.80 – a two-year price loss of 57 per cent. Although rising slowly to a 2002 mid-year price of US$28, crop analysts do not predict a recovery to the 2000 highs. Ivorian production for the crop year beginning 2001 is estimated to be 41 million bags, up from the 2000/01 harvest of 39.74 million bags, but still below the 1999/2000 five-year high of nearly 59 million bags. Similarly, exports between June 2000 and May 2001 totalled 5,039,764 60lbs bag; however 2001/02 exports reached only 3,950,498 – a drop of 27.5 per cent.

Recovery thwarted

The government originally forecast 3 per cent GDP growth and 3 per cent inflation in 2002, with a current account deficit of 2 per cent of GDP. This was based on an increase in the export of cocoa and processed goods and an increase in the investment rate to 13.5 per cent of GDP, up from 9.9 per cent in 2001.

The political turbulence in the aftermath of the September 2002 army mutiny and continuing social unrest threaten to derail Côte d'Ivoire's economic recovery. Although the uprising dramatically increased the value of cocoa futures, it also threatened the cocoa harvest, as much of the fighting centred on cocoa-growing areas, particularly Daloa. This could adversely affect the 2002/03 harvest, particularly if farm workers do not return to their homes. Therefore, growth in 2003 will be determined by the resumption of peace and security, particularly for the thousands of immigrant labourers who have fled for safety following attacks on foreigners. If Côte d'Ivoire does manage to achieve political stability and a long-lasting settlement with rebels, then the country's economy is likely to continue its recovery in 2003, although probably not at the 4.5 per cent growth rate predicted by the IMF before the uprising took place.

Outlook

Côte d'Ivoire's crisis will be a major problem for West Africa. It makes up around 40 per cent of the GDP of the entire UEMOA, employs millions of migrant workers and serves as an important trading route for many Sahelian countries, particularly Burkina Faso. It will be essential for Ecowas to find a solution or else the country is destined to become engulfed in a regionalised conflict on a par with the civil wars that affected Sierra Leone and the Democratic Republic of Congo in the late 1990s.

Risk assessment

Economic	Improving
Political	Fair
Regional stability	Poor
Stock market	Poor

COUNTRY PROFILE

Historical profile

1960 Côte d'Ivoire gained independence from France in August. Felix Houphouet-Boigny, selected by French colonial rulers as the most promising successor to their rule, established a benevolent authoritarian regime which tended towards paternalism. Politics were based around oligarchs who gained power through government position, ran state-owned companies or gained positions in the ruling party, the Parti Démocratique de la Côte d'Ivoire (PDCI) (Democratic Party of Côte d'Ivoire.

1970s–1980s Economic decline increased the pressure for political reform. Laurent Gbagbo, a lecturer and long term dissident emerged as Côte d'Ivoire's main opposition leader. He went into exile in 1982.

1988 Gbagbo returned from exile and founded the Front Populaire d'Ivoirie (FPI) (Ivorian Popular Front) to campaign for multiparty democracy.

1990 Houphouet-Boigny was forced to call elections. Gbagbo's opposition coalition consisted of Bernard Zadi's Union des Sociaux-Democrates (USD) (Union of Social Democrats), Francis Wodie's Parti Ivoirien des Travailleurs (PIT) (Ivorian Workers' Party) and Morifere Bamba's Parti Socialiste Ivoirien (PSI) (Ivorian Socialist Party). The PDCI convincingly won, taking 163 of 175 seats, the FPI nine and the PIT one. In the presidential election Houphouet-Boigny polled 81.7 per cent and Gbagbo 18.3 per cent.

1993 President Felix Houphouet-Boigny died in December after 30 years in power. The presidency passed provisionally to the former Speaker of Parliament and leader of the ruling PDCI, Henri Konan-Bédié. Under the constitution he held the position of President of the National Assembly until the autumn 1995 election.

1995 Legislative and presidential elections were convincingly won by Konan-Bédié and the PDCI party.

1999 President Bédié was toppled in a military coup. General Robert Guéi seized the presidency.

2000 Gbagbo declared himself president following controversial elections which saw a boycott by one of the leading political parties.
2001 There was an unsuccessful armed coup by rebel soldiers in January.
2002 In June, the constitutional court granted the main opposition leader Alassane Ouattara citizenship. Ouattarra was banned from participation in legislative and presidential elections in 2000 due to doubts over his nationality.

Political structure

Constitution

A multi-party system is enshrined in the constitution, but in practice no party other than Parti Démocratique de la Côte d'Ivoire (PDCI) (Democratic Party of Côte d'Ivoire) was allowed to operate until May 1990 when the government legalised party political activity.
A 1990 constitutional amendment allowed for the appointment of a prime minister, with the speaker of the National Assembly empowered to assume the office of president of the republic prior to a presidential election in the event of a sudden presidential vacancy.
The constitution was suspended following a military takeover in December 1999. In 2000, the constitution was revised, stipulating that presidential candidates must be of Ivorian origin, born of parents who are not naturalised Ivorians, should not have dual nationality and must have lived in Côte d'Ivoire for a minimum and uninterrupted period of five years. Those with at least 21 years of Ivorian citizenship are eligible to vote.

Form of state

Republic

The executive

Executive power rests with the president (elected by universal suffrage for a five-year term) who appoints the cabinet. The president can veto legislation, but his veto can in theory be overridden by a two-thirds vote of the National Assembly.

National legislature

The 175-member National Assembly was dissolved in December 1999 and replaced by an appointed National Council for Public Salvation formed by the military junta. This was dissolved following elections to a new 225-seat assembly in December 2000 and January 2001. From time to time, the president also summons an informal grass-roots body known as the National Council for Consultations on Controversial Issues.

Legal system

All civil, criminal, commercial and administrative cases come under the jurisdiction of the tribunaux de première instance (magistrates' courts), the assize courts and the court of appeal.

Last elections

22 October 2000 (presidential); 10 December 2000 (parliamentary).

Next elections

2005 (parliamentary and presidential)

Political parties

Ruling party

Front Populaire Ivorienne (FPI) (Ivorian Popular Front)

Main opposition party

Rassemblement des Républicains (RDR) (Rally of Republicans); Parti Démocratique de la Côte d'Ivoire (PDCI) (Democratic Party of Côte d'Ivoire).

Population

16.40 million (2000)
Annual population growth rate: 2.8 per cent (1994–2000). It is estimated that the population will increase 1.7 per cent per annum during the period 1997–2015.
More than a quarter of the population is under the age of 20; 18 per cent is under nine and only 2 per cent over the age of 60.
Population density: 44 inhabitants per square km. Urban population: 51 per cent (1994–2000).

Ethnic make-up

Akan (the Baoule subgroup accounts for 23 per cent of the population), Kru (the Bete subgroup accounts for 18 per cent), Senoufo 15 per cent, Malinke 11 per cent, Agni, Mande. There are nearly three million foreign Africans (mainly from Burkina Faso and Mali) and an estimated 130,000–330,000 non-Africans (French 30,000 and Lebanese 100,000–300,000).

Religions

Islam (60 per cent), Christianity (mainly Roman Catholic) (22 per cent), traditional animist beliefs (18 per cent) (some of these are also numbered among the Christians and Muslims).

Labour market and unemployment

The labour force, of which approximately 33 per cent is female, increased 3.3 per cent per annum between 1994 and 2000. The adult literacy rate is around 40 per cent. The workforce is well educated by regional standards; although labour costs are high.

Education

Education is provided free of charge. Primary education lasts for six years from the age of six. Secondary education lasts for up to seven years from the age of 13. There are universities at Abidjan and Yamoussoukro, but many students attend French universities.

Health

World Bank estimates during the period 1994 and 2000 showed that the average life expectancy was 54 years and the infant mortality rate stood at 88 per 1,000 live births. It is estimated that 24 per cent of children under the age of five were malnourished in the same period. The total fertility rate is around 4.9 children born per woman while the rate of contraception practices is estimated at 15 per cent among women aged 15–49. The maternal mortality rate is typically 600 deaths per 100,000 live births. World Bank estimates in 2000 showed that 63 per cent of the population had access to improved water sources. There are 0.1 physicians and 0.8 hospital beds typically available for 1,000 people.
According to World Bank estimates, government expenditure on healthcare averaged 3.8 per cent of GDP of which 1.2 per cent was public expenditure between 1990 and 1998. Expenditure on private healthcare (such as private household expenditure and insurance) averaged 2.6 per cent of GDP over the same period.
The HIV rate is as high as 10.76 per cent among adults. UN surveys in 1997 (according to available reports in 2000) showed that patients with AIDS-related illness occupied 41 per cent of all hospital beds in Abidjan. AIDS-related costs typically absorb 11 per cent of the total public health budget.

Welfare

An employer must declare each worker employed to the Caisse National de Prevoyance Sociale (CNPS), the national social security fund. The employer is responsible for deducting social security contributions paid by the worker. Large firms are also expected to provide in-house medical care.
Social security is divided into three areas: family allowances, retirement pensions, medical care and compensation payments in case of accident at work. There are no payments for illness unconnected to work.
Social security contributions are paid every quarter by firms employing fewer than 20 people and each month for those employing 20 or more. The CNPS budget is separate from the main budget.
The social security system does not cover unemployment. The labour exchange pays a monthly allowance to the registered unemployed. This is financed by a national solidarity contribution of 1 per cent of salary, which is levied on each employee's wages.
In July 2002, the African Development Bank (ADB) approved a loan of about US$20.4 million to finance a rural development project in eastern Cote d'Ivoire to cope with unemployment.

Main cities

Abidjan (economic centre and site of embassies, estimated population 3.3 million in 2002), Yamoussoukro (political capital since 1983, 130,000), Bouaké (600,000), Daloa (100,000), Man (75,000), Korhogo (60,000), Gagnoa (60,000), San Pedro (55,000).

Languages spoken

French and approximately 60 local African languages are spoken, including Dioula, Baoule, Akan, Kru and Bete.

Official language/s

French

Media

Press

At independence in August 1960, Côte d'Ivoire had only two publications, *Fraternité* and *Abidjan-Matin*, and one radio station, Radio-Abidjan. The two official newspapers were merged in 1964 into the daily *Fraternité Matin*. Other official newspapers include *Ivoire Soir* (Mon–Fri) *Fraternité-Hebdo* and the PDCI party weekly. Other publications include *Abidjan 7 Jours*, *Le Griot* and *Le Guido*, a guide to movies, television and restaurants.

Broadcasting

The government gradually created its own information network founding the Ivorian news agency, Agence Ivoirienne de Presse, in 1961, taking full control of the radio station in 1962 and setting up a television station in 1963. On two channels, Télévision Ivoirienne broadcasts in French from stations in many parts of the country, several hours a day. Colour television was introduced in 1973.

Radio: Radiodiffusion Ivoirienne, the government radio station, broadcasts in French, English and 13 African languages. It has 13 transmitters which cover 85 per cent of the country. A ground station at Akakro, near Abidjan, allows Côte d'Ivoire to receive television pictures by satellite from around the world. The commercial service is known as Radio Abidjan-Inter.

Television: Transmissions (including colour) for several hours a day with stations in many parts of the country.

Economy

Although Côte d'Ivoire is classified by the World Bank as a low income country, in the good times, it has been sub-Saharan Africa's second most developed economy behind South Africa. Despite Côte d'Ivoire's dependence on a limited range of traditional exports, it is one of Africa's most diversified economies.

Apart from coffee and cocoa, which are the mainstay of the economy, other agricultural exports include sugar, rubber, bananas and cotton. Industry is dominated by processing agricultural produce and the import substitution of consumer goods. A growing financial services sector and tourism have also been important to the economy in recent years.

With a population growth rate of around 1.7 per cent, GDP per capita declined from US$707 in 1999 to US$573 in 2000. The slowdown in growth was mostly due to the fall in international commodity prices leading to declining revenue for the country's principle exports – coffee and cocoa – which form 60 per cent of the country's economy. As a result of the two-year fall in agro-export prices, there was negative growth of 1.7 per cent in the agricultural sector in 1999. The 54 per cent of the working population employed in agriculture were hit particularly hard, notably peasant farmers who are unable to increase their productivity to maintain their incomes. There were better times to come with the World Bank reporting positive growth of 13.3 per cent in the sector in 2000.

The insecurity that followed the military coup in 1999 had a negative effect on the economy but international funding has commenced and in July 2002, the African Development Fund approved a CFAf14 billion loan to finance the economic recovery support programme. With this boost, there is renewed confidence in the economy

External trade

The trade balance consistently registered a surplus throughout the 1990s, with the devaluation of the CFA franc in 1994 initially aiding a recovery in exports. The deterioration of commodity prices and the rapid decline in the value of cocoa exports caused the surplus to fall to an estimated US$500 million or less in 2000.

Côte d'Ivoire's current account has shown a shrinking deficit in recent years, largely due to large financial outflows in the form of debt service obligations. The current account registered a deficit of US$120.5 million in 1999, compared to US$312.6 million a year earlier.

Exports

Principal exports include cocoa (typically 36 per cent of total), oil products (18 per cent), wood (11 per cent), coffee (5 per cent).

Main destinations: France (typically 18 per cent of total), Netherlands (8 per cent), Germany (8 per cent).

Imports

Principal imports include medicinal/pharmaceutical products, transport equipment, road vehicles, fish, crustaceans, molluscs, cereals, cereal preparations, general industrial machinery, dairy products.

Main sources: France (typically 52 per cent of total), Nigeria (20 per cent), USA (6 per cent), Germany (4 per cent).

Agriculture

The agricultural sector forms the mainstay of the economy. It accounted for 29.2 per cent of GDP in 2000, up from 26.8 per cent in 1999. Agriculture earns over 60 per cent of export revenues, employing some 54 per cent of the workforce.

Growth in the sector improved in 2000 to 13.3 per cent after negative growth of 1.7 per cent in 1999 caused by a fall in international commodity prices.

Approximately 12 per cent of total area is cultivated, 25 per cent is pasture, 20 per cent forest.

Production of principal cash crops, which are grown in the southern half of the country, has been badly affected by shifts in world commodity prices. Other export crops include sugar, cotton, rubber, bananas, pineapples and palm oil.

Diversification led to an improvement in output of basic food crops (mainly rice, maize, manioc) and the country is now nearer its long-term aim of self-sufficiency.

The UK Commonwealth Development Corporation (CDC) has taken over the state rubber plantations; the total investment is about CFAf19 billion. Around 1,500 new jobs will be created by the year 2005 and about 9,000 smallholders will also benefit from the investment.

Farming

Emphasis has been on co-operative farming, overhauling the marketing system, use of selective incentives and also management training and technical advice programmes.

Forestry

Forestry is important, although exports of wood and wood products have steadily fallen – a reafforestation programme is in progress.

Industry and manufacturing

The industrial sector contributed 22.4 per cent to GDP in 2000, down from 24.4 per cent in 1999. Manufacturing alone accounted for 18.7 per cent in 2000, down from 19.9 per cent in 1999. The World Bank reported negative growth of 11.2 per cent in the sector in 2000 after positive annual growth of 2.7 per cent in 1999.

The industrial and manufacturing sectors have expanded rapidly since independence in 1960 but suffered some setbacks in the late 1980s as a result of increased foreign competition and a decline in consumer purchasing power. In addition, the industrial plant is ageing and has often not been renewed on account of the low level of private investment.

During the 1990s, privatisation reduced the state's custodial role in industry and manufacturing. Consequently, policy has focussed upon encouraging private sector involvement in the hydrocarbons sector which it is hoped will encourage the expansion of the industrial and manufacturing sectors.

Mining

The mining sector holds considerable potential and could become the second mainstay of the economy. It contributes around 3.7 per cent to GDP annually and employs 1 per cent of the workforce.

State company, Société pour le Développement Minier Ivorien (Sodemi) carries out exploration and production, in some cases in joint ventures with foreign companies.

Gold is found in three main reserves: Issia, Lobo and Ity.

Diamonds have traditionally been mined by small independent prospectors, but the incidence of diamond smuggling and consequent loss of revenue prompted the Ministry of Mines to introduce licences for prospectors and diamond purchasing offices in 2000. Diamonds are produced at Séguéla and Tortiya. Reserves at Seguela are estimated at 150,000 carats, and at Tortiya 450,000 carats.

Grand-Lehou produces 90,000 to 100,000 tonnes of manganese per year. A further deposit, estimated at 1.2 million tonnes (47 per cent manganese), has been discovered at Ziemougoula, near Odienne, and is being developed.

A large iron ore deposit at Monogaga-Victory has estimated reserves of 140 million tonnes of 42 per cent ore. Further reserves, estimated at three billion tonnes, are located on the border with Guinea at Mount Nyumba and Mount Kalayo. Officials plan to use gas piped from the port of San Pedro to fuel a processing plant providing nickel and iron ore pellets.

Hydrocarbons

In June 1994, United Meridien Corporation (UMC), a US-based company, developed two offshore oil and gas fields, Lion One and Panther One, which made Côte d'Ivoire self-sufficient in oil and natural gas.

Oil

Oil reserves are estimated at 100 million barrels, while production was estimated at 12,000 barrels per day (bpd) in 2001.

Gas

Total gas reserves are estimated at 308 billion cubic metres (1.1 trillion cubic feet) and annual production at 683 million cubic metres (24.4 billion cubic feet).

Gas-powered turbines are enabling the country to export electricity to Ghana, Togo and Benin and to make butane gas.

Energy

Electricity generation, transmission and distribution in Côte d'Ivoire is the responsibility of the Compagnie Ivorienne d'Electricité.

The country has a hydroelectric potential of around 2,000MW and installed electric generation capacity of 1.2 gigawatts. The construction of more plants is planned.

Demand for electricity in Côte d'Ivoire is expected to grow at about 10 per cent per annum between 2000–05. This will require the upgrading or replacement of inefficient and obsolete plants. The 288MW Azito power plant is to be built on a build-own-operate-transfer (BOOT) basis on the outskirts of Abidjan in order to meet growing demand.

As part of a rural electrification programme, rural communities are being connected to the distribution system, making increasingly large numbers of isolated diesel units obsolete.

Financial markets

Stock exchange

The Abidjan bourse is a regional stock exchange serving eight West African Economic and Monetary Union countries – Côte d'Ivoire, Benin, Burkina Faso, Mali, Niger, Senegal, Togo and Guinea-Bissau.

Banking

Central bank

Banque Centrale des Etats de l'Afrique de l'Ouest

Main financial centre

Abidjan

Time

GMT

Geography

Côte d'Ivoire lies on Africa's Atlantic coast, bordering Liberia and Guinea to the west, Mali and Burkina Faso to the north, and Ghana to the east. To the south is a 470 kilometre coastline on the Gulf of Guinea, the eastern part of which is inset with lagoons.

The terrain rises from the coastal plains to a plateau, 300 metres high for most of its length, rising to 1,200 metres near the country's western border.

The three main geographical areas are the equatorial zone along the coast, the tropical rain forests of the south and the drier savannah belt in the north.

There are four main rivers, the Bandama, Comoe, Sassandra and Cavally, but they are not navigable for long distances due to rapids.

Climate

In the southern coastal region the climate is tropical and humid. Dry seasons from December–April and from August–September. Rainy seasons from May–July and from October–November. Temperatures remain fairly constant throughout the year ranging from about 20 degrees Celsius (C) at night to 30–33 degrees C during the day. In the north the climate is more extreme, but less humid, with a dry season from December–June and a rainy season from July–November.

Average temperatures in the coastal plains are 21–34 degrees C. Humidity is 80–90 per cent. Annual rainfall can be as heavy as 2.5 metres spread over about 140 days.

There are four seasons in the south. The long dry season runs from December–April and the long rains from May–July. Then comes the short dry season in August and September and the short rains during October–November.

In the tropical zone, temperatures range are 14–39 degrees C. Annual rainfall varies from 1–2.5 metres.

In the northern savannah, temperatures are 21–40 degrees C. Rainfall averages 1.4 metres a year. Here, there are just two seasons, rains from July–November and the dry season from December–June.

Dress codes

Businessmen should wear suits, even though this may be uncomfortable in Abidjan's hot and humid climate. Otherwise loose-fitting, lightweight clothing is advisable.

European women generally wear sleeveless cotton dresses or lightweight skirts and blouses, and this mode of dress is adequate for business calls.

Entry requirements

Passports

Required by all except particular document holders of certain African countries.

Visa

For stays of less than three months, a visa is not required for visitors from Andorra, Belgium, Cameroon, Chad, Central African Republic, Congo Brazzaville, Gabon, Mauritius, Monaco, the Netherlands, USA and Ireland. Visas are required by British nationals. A surety bond is required by visitors who do not have a return ticket.

Currency advice/regulations

There is no limit to the amount of foreign currency which can be taken in. A limited amount of CFA francs per person may be taken out. It is advisable to check with the embassy. Unused traveller's cheques must be declared on exit.

Health (for visitors)

Mandatory precautions

Yellow fever vaccination certificate.

Advisable precautions

Hepatitis, typhoid and polio vaccinations recommended. Malaria prophylaxis should be taken as risk exists throughout the country all year. Avoid tap water and drink only bottled beverages (including water) or beverages made with boiled water. It is advisable to pack a sterilised syringe kit.

Hotels

Abidjan has several high-class hotels. Wide range in the other main centres. Tipping usually 10–15 per cent.

Public holidays

Fixed dates

1 Jan, 1 May, 2 May (Bank Holiday), 15 Aug (Assumption), 1 Nov (All Saints'), 15 Nov (Peace Day), 7 Dec (National Day), 24, 25 & 26 Dec.

Variable dates

Good Friday, Easter Monday, Ascension Day, Eid Al-Fitr, Whit Monday, Eid Al-Adha.

Working hours

Banking

Mon–Fri: 0800–1130 and 1430–1630.

Business

Mon–Fri: 0800–1200 and 1430–1700.

Government

Mon–Fri: 0730/0800–1200 and 1430–1730.

Shops

Mon–Fri: 0800–1200 and 1530–1830/1900, Sat: 0800–1200 and 1430–1730.

Telecommunications

Telephone/fax

In January 1997 there were 0.81 lines per 100 inhabitants. Privatisation should improve service.

Postal services

Côte d'Ivoire is covered by a comprehensive network of post offices, with distribution based on the use of post office boxes. Efficiency can be erratic.

Courier services

Express correspondence is handled by national and international courier services.

Electricity supply

220V AC, 50 cycles

Security

The government is concerned about the level of street crime in the cities and it is advisable not to walk around the city streets after dark.

Getting there

Air

National airline: Air Ivoire (Société Ivoirienne de Transport Aériens) (government-owned) operates internally and to Mali and Burkina Faso.

International airport/s: Abidjan–Port Bouet (Code: ABJ), 16km from city; duty-free shop, restaurant, bank, post office, shops, car hire.

Airport tax: There is no airport tax.

Surface

Road: There are links from Accra, Ghana, Burkina Faso, Guinea and Liberia.

Rail: Regular daily services from Burkina Faso, connecting Ouagadougou with Abidjan. Sleeping and restaurant facilities are available.

Getting about

National transport

Air: Air Ivoire operates regular flights from Abidjan to Bouaké, Daloa, Man, Korhogo, Sassandra, San Pedro, Berebi, Tabou, Bondoukou, Odiénné and Guiglo.

Road: Extensive network of good roads stretching from south to north with transverse roads interconnecting.

Rail: A 1,145km network from Abidjan to Ouagadougou passes through Agboville, Dimbokra, Bouaké, Katiola and Ferkessedougou including express trains (with first and second class, sleeping and dining cars).

City transport

Taxis: Red taxis with meters can be hailed or ordered by telephone in main centres. Two tariffs operate: one from 0600–2400, the other 2400–0600. The early morning tariff is double that for the day and evening. Do not hesitate to haggle over the fare, especially if the meter is not running, or if arriving at the airport.

Buses, trams & metro: Extensive service, with air-conditioned vehicles, operated in Abidjan by state-run Sotra and countrywide by private operators.

Most hotels have their own free airport buses. Check at hotel booths near the terminal exit.

Car hire

Self-drive and chauffeur-driven cars can be hired in Abidjan, Bouaké, Daloa, Gagnoa, Man and Sassandra.

An international driving licence is required (not less than 12 months old). Drivers must be at least 21 years old. Seat-belts must be worn in front seats. Traffic drives on the right.

BUSINESS DIRECTORY

Telephone area codes

The international direct dialling (IDD) code for Côte d'Ivoire is +225, followed by subscriber's number (there are no area codes).

Useful telephone numbers

Ambulance (SAMU): 185, 443-445, 445-353.

Police (emergency): 111, 170.

International telephone enquiries: 160.

National telephone enquiries: 120.

Chambers of Commerce

Chamber of Agriculture of Côte d'Ivoire, 11 Ave Lamblin, Abidjan (tel: 321-611).

Chamber of Commerce and Industry of Côte d'Ivoire, 6 Ave Joseph Anoma, 01 BP 1399, Abidjan 01 (tel: 331-600; fax 323-942).

Banking

African Development Bank, Ave Joseph Anoma, Abidjan (tel: 2020-4444; fax: 2020-4006, 2021-7753).

Bank of Africa Côte d'Ivoire, BP 4132, 11 Ave Joseph Anoma, Abidjan 01 (tel: 2033-1536; fax: 2033-2398, 2032-8993).

Banque de l'Habitat de Côte d'Ivoire, BP 2325, 22 Ave Joseph Anoma, Abidjan 01 (tel: 2022-6000; fax: 2022-5818).

Banque Internationale pour le Commerce et l'Industrie de la Côte d'Ivoire SA; Avenue Franchet d'Espérey, 01 BP 1298 Abidjan 01 (tel: 2020-1600; fax: 2020-1700) .

Banque Paribas Côte d'Ivoire; BP 09, 17 Avenue Terrasson de Fougères, Abidjan 17 (tel: 2021-8686; fax: 2021-8823).

BIAO-Côte d'Ivoire; BP 1274, 8/10 Avenue Joseph Anoma, Abidjan 01 (tel: 2020-0720; fax: 2020-0700).

Caisse Autonome d'Amortissement Société d'Etat, BP 670, Immeuble SCIAM, Ave Marchant, Abidjan 01 (tel: 2021-0611, 2032-8575; fax: 2021-3578).

Cofipa Investment Bank Cóte d'Ivoire, BP 411, Rue Botreau Roussel/ Ave Delafosse, Abidjan 04 (tel: 2021-8452; fax: 2021-8599).

Compagnie Bancaire de l'Atlantique en Côte d'Ivoire,01 BP, Immeuble Atlantique, Avenue Nogues, 522 Abidjan 01 (tel: 2021-2804, 2030-1520; fax: 2021-0798).

Compagnie Financière de la Côte d'Ivoire; BP 1566, Tour BICICI 01, Rue Gourgas 15e étage, Abidjan 01 (tel: 2021-2732; fax: 2021-2643).

Ecobank Côte d'Ivoire SA, BP 4107, Immeuble Alliance, 1 Av Terrasson de Fougères, Abidjan 01 (tel: 2031-9200, 2021-1041; fax: 2021-8816).

Société Générale de Banques en Côte d'Ivoire SA; BP 1355, 5 & 7 Avenue Joseph Anoma, Abidjan 01 (tel: 2020-1234; fax: 2020-1486).

Société Générale de Financement et de Participation en Côte d'Ivoire (SOGEFINANCE); BP 3904, 5-7 Avenue Joseph Anoma, Abidjan 01 (tel: 2022-5530; fax: 2020-1492).

Société Ivoirienne de Banque, BP 1300, Immeuble Alpha 2000, 34 Boulevard de la Republique, Abidjan 01 (tel: 2020-0000; fax: 2021-9741).

Central bank

Banque Centrale des Etats de l'Afrique de l'Ouest, PO Box 3108, Avenue Abdoulaye Fadiga, Dakar, Senegal (tel: (221)390-500; fax: (221)239-335).

Travel information

Air Ivoire, 2 Avenue du Général de Gaulle, PO Box 1027, Abidjan 01 (tel: 213-429).

Félix Houphouet-Boigny International Airport (tel: 277-322, 234-000).

Tourist Information, Office Ivoirien du Tourisme et de l'Hôtellerie (OITH), Place de la République, BP 8538, Abidjan 01 (tel: 206-528; fax: 225-624).

Wagonlits (Railway Information), Boulevard de Marseille, Abidjan (tel: 212-066, 213-910).

Ministry of tourism

Ministry of Tourism, BP V184, Abidjan (tel: 445-500; fax: 445-580).

Ministries

Ministry of Agriculture and Animal Resources, Immeuble de la Caisse de Stabilisation, BP V84, Abidjan (tel: 2021-3858; fax: 2021-4618; e-mail: minagra@cimail.net).

Ministry of Communication and Information Technology, Tour C, Tours Administratives, BP V138, Abidjan (tel: 2021-1116; fax: 2021-8495).

Ministry of Construction and Urbanism, Tour D, Tours Administratives, 20 BP 650, Abidjan (tel: 2021-8235; fax: 2021-3568).

Ministry of Defence and Civil Protection, Immeuble EECI, BP V 241, Abidjan (tel: 2021-2682; fax: 2022-4175).

Ministry of Economic Infrastructures, Immeuble Postel 2001, 18 BP 2203, Abidjan (tel: 2034-4273; fax: 2034-7322).

Ministry of Economy and Finance, Immeuble SCIAM, BP V163, Abidjan (tel: 2020-0842; fax: 2021-3208).

Ministry of Education, Tour D, Tours Administratives, BP V 120, Abidjan (tel: 2022-7406; fax: 2022-9322).

Ministry of Family, Women and Children, Tour E, Tours Administratives, BP 200, Abidjan (tel: 2021-7626; fax: 2021-4461).

Ministry of Foreign Affairs, Bloc Ministériel, Boulevard Angoulvand, BP V109, Abidjan (tel: 2022-7150; fax: 2033-2308).

Ministry of Health, Tour C, Tours Administratives, 01 BP V 04, Abidjan (tel: 2021-0871; fax: 2021-5240).

Ministry of Higher Education and Scientific Research, Tour C, Tours Administratives, BP V 151, Abidjan (tel: 2021-3316; fax: 2021-2225).

Ministry of the Interior and Decentralisation, Bloc Ministériel, Boulevard Angoulvand, BP V 121, Abidjan (tel: 2022-3816; fax: 2022-3648).

Ministry of Justice and Public Freedom, Bloc Ministériel, Boulevard Angoulvand, BP V 107, Abidjan (tel: 2021-1727; fax: 2033-1259).

Ministry of Labour, Civil Service and Administrative Reform, Immeuble Fonction Publique, Boulevard Angoulvand, BP V 93, Abidjan (tel: 2021-4290; fax: 2021-1286).

Ministry of Mines and Energy, Immeuble Postel 2001, BP V 40, Abidjan (tel: 2034-4851; fax: 2021-3730).

Ministry of Trade, Immeuble CCIA, Rue Jean-Paul II, BP V65, Abidjan (tel: 2021-6473; fax: 2021-6474).

Ministry of Transport, Immeuble Postel 2001, BP V 06, Abidjan (tel: 2034-7315; fax: 2021-3730).

Other useful addresses

Agence des Télécommunications de Côte d'Ivoire (ATCI), BP 2203, Immeuble Postel 2001, Rue le Coeur, Abidjan 18 (tel: 344-255; fax: 344-254).

Association of Exporters of Coffee-Cocoa, Imm CCIA, 01 BP 1399, Abidjan 01 (tel: 225-446/5).

Association of Fishing Industry, Port de Pêche, 01 BP 14, Abidjan 01 (tel: 257-998; fax: 252-065).

Association of Import and Export Traders, Imm Résidence du Front Lagunaire 2 étage, 01 BP 3792, Abidjan 01 (tel: 325-427; fax: 325-652).

Association of West African Home Grown Product Dealers, Imm CCIA 7 étage, O & BP 5407, Abidjan 01 (tel: 225-795).

Bourse des Valeurs Abidjan, Ave Marchand 10, BP 1878, 01 Abidjan (tel: 215-783, 215-742; fax: 221-657).

Bureau National d'Etudes Techniques et de Dévéloppement (BNETD) (National Office for Technical and Development Studies), BP 945, 04 Abidjan (tel: 442-805, 445-877; fax: 445-666; e-mail: nzoro@bnetd.sita.net).

Caisse de Stabilisation (CAISTAB), BP V132, Abidjan (tel: 202-700; fax: 218-994).

Centre de Promotion des Investissements en Côte d'Ivoire (CEPICI), CCIA-V/TR 5th Floor, BP V152, Abidjan 01 (tel: 214-070; fax: 214-071).

Committee of Insurers, Imm Les Arcades, 01 BP 3873, Abidjan 01 (tel: 225-437; fax: 211-835).

Committee of Privatisation, 6 Boulevard de l'Indénié, Abidjan-Plateau, BP 1141, Abidjan 01 (tel: 222-231; fax: 222-235).

Compagnie Ivoirienne pour le Dévelopement des Textiles, BP 622, Bouaké (tel: 633-113; fax: 634-167).

The Customs Department, Boulevard de la République, BP V 25, Abidjan (tel: 215-223).

Direction et Controle des Grands Travaux, Département Industrie et Energie, Boulevard de la Corniche, Cocody, 04 BP 945, Abidjan 04 (tel: 442-118; fax: 445-866).

Energie Electrique de la Côte d'Ivoire, BP 1345, 1 place de la RÉpublique, Abidjan (tel: 206-000; fax: 327-477).

General Surveillance Co (Responsible for Import Controls), PO Box 795, Abidjan (tel: 211-290).

Ivorian Investment Promotion in Côte d'Ivoire (CEPECI), PO Box V 152, Abidjan 01 (tel: 214-070; fax: 214-071).

Ivory Coast Embassy, 2424 Massachusetts Avenue, NW, Washington DC 20008 (tel: 797-0300).

National Enterprise Assistance and Promotion Centre (CAPEN), Immeuble La Pyramide, 9th floor, 08 BP 868, Abidjan 08 (tel: 320-145).

Organisation Centrale pour la Commercialisation de l'Ananas et la Banane (OCAB), Imm Corniche, 16 BP 1908, Abidjan 16 (tel: 325-882; fax: 321-060).

Port Autonome d'Abidjan, BP V85, Abidjan (tel: 240-866, 242-640; fax: 242-328).

Société des Mines d'Ity, BP 872, Abidjan 08 (tel: 446-363; fax: 444-100).

Société Ivoirienne de la Poste et de L'Epargne, BP 105, Abidjan 17 (tel: 347-004; fax: 347-107).

Société Ivoirienne de Raffinage (SIR), Boulevard de Petit-Bassam, BP 1269, Abidjan 01 (tel: 270-427, 270-160; fax: 271-798, 273-217).

Société Nationale d'Opérations Petroliéres de la Côte d'Ivoire, BP V194, Abidjan (tel: 214-058).

Société pour le Développement Minier de la Côte d'Ivoire, BP 2816, Abidjan (tel: 212-994).

SODEMI (State Company for Mineral Development), BP 2816, 31 Boulevard Latrille, Abidjan Cocody-Nord, Abidjan 01 (tel: 4420994; fax: 440-821).

Internet sites

Bureau National d'Etudes Techniques et de Dévélopement (BNETD): http://www.bnetd.sita.net.

Africa Business Network: http://www.ifc.org/abn

AllAfrica.com: http://allafrica.com

African Development Bank: http://www.afdb.org

Africa Online: http://www.africaonline.com

Investment promotion bureau: http://www.cepici.go.ci

Mbendi AfroPaedia (information on companies, countries, industries and stock exchanges in Africa): http://mbendi.co.za

Djibouti

Nicholas Awde & Fred J Hill

KEY FACTS

Official name: République de Djibouti/Jumhouriyya Djibouti (Republic of Djibouti)

Head of State: President Ismail Omar Guelleh (since May 1999)

Head of government: Prime Minister Dilleita Mohammed Dilleita (appointed 4 Mar 2001)

Ruling party: Coalition government consisting of Rassemblement Populaire pour le Progrès (RPP) (Popular Rally for Progress); Front pour la Restauration de l'Unité et de la Démocratie (FRUD) (Front for the Restoration of Unity and Democracy)

Area: 23,200 square km

Population: 644,000 (2001)

Capital: Djibouti-ville

Official language: French/Arabic (Somali/Afar are the national languages)

Currency: Djibouti franc (Df) = 100 centimes

Exchange rate: Df175.00 per US$ (Jan 2003)

GDP per capita: US$899 (2001)

GDP real growth: 3.00% (2001)

Inflation: 1.80% (2001)

Balance of trade: -US$206.00 million (2001)

Foreign debt: US$322.00 million (2001)

For the latest Key Facts, go to www.worldinformation.com

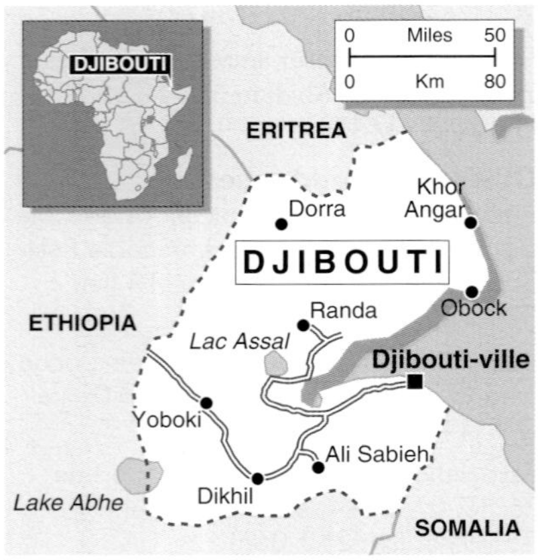

In 2001 and 2002, the small and impoverished state of Djibouti managed to put behind it the shock of a failed coup attempt staged by former chief of police General Yacin Yabeh Galab in December 2000. Despite low GDP growth, Djibouti made modest advances in implementing structural reforms and vigorously pursued ongoing economic development programmes. Djibouti's standing with its immediate neighbours and trading partners in the rest of Africa also improved.

Building stability

Precarious peace held during 2001 and 2002, despite the war between neighbouring Ethiopia and Eritrea. Djibouti took a step forward in patching up its differences with Eritrea. Diplomatic ties between the two countries, severed in 1998, were restored through bilateral co-operation in January 2002.

Improved security also boded well for the future. In May 2001, a peace deal was signed between the government and the Front pour la Restauration de l'Unité et de la Démocratie (FRUD) (Front for the Restoration of Unity and Democracy), finally bringing an end to a civil conflict that had dogged the country for 10 years. FRUD's members belong mainly to the country's Afar community, the principal rivals of Djibouti's dominant Issa ethnic group. In 1991, FRUD had launched a civil war in the north of the country and a radical wing of the group continued to pose a serious threat to national security.

The peace deal, along with the improvements in regional security, helped the government's demobilisation programme, which had been allowed to slip during 2000. Accordingly, more than 700 armed members of FRUD were demobilised with EU assistance in June 2001 and a timetable was set out to demobilise 3,700 government forces by the end of 2003. This, combined with plans to reduce significantly the number of civil servants and contractual employees, was expected to enable the government to significantly reduce the 2002 wage bill.

On 6 February, 2001, after 22 years as prime minister, Barkat Gourad Hamadou finally bowed out as a result of continuing bad health. Dilleita Mohammed Dilleita replaced him. Although Dilleita Mohammed Dilleita has no ministerial experience, he served as ambassador to Ethiopia and was a former presidential chief of staff.

Djibouti's first multi-party parliamentary election since independence in 1977 is expected in January 2003. President Ismail Omar Guelleh's position will be strengthened if the four party Union pour la Majorité Présidentielle (UMP) (Union for a Presidential Majority) alliance, which includes the ruling Rassemblement Populaire pour le Progrès (RPP) (People's Rally for Progress) and FRUD, wins the parliamentary election as expected. It is unlikely that the opposition bloc, the Union pour l'Alternance Démocratique (UAD) (Union for a Democratic Change), will be able to muster enough votes to pose any serious challenge to the UMP.

Port gains trade

With few natural resources, little agricultural activity and a small industrial sector, economic success lies in exploiting Djibouti's expanding service sector, which accounts for more than 80 per cent of GDP. The war between Ethiopia and Eritrea unexpectedly handed Djibouti a new lease of economic life after Ethiopia abandoned Eritrea's port at Assab and rechannelled its transit trade through the port of Djibouti. During the first five months of 2001, the docks recorded a 5 per cent increase in tonnage compared to the same period for the previous year.

The port has undergone extensive modernisation financed by loans from the Arab Fund and other Arab financial institutions as well as the government of Djibouti itself.

In July 2001, rules governing the operation of foreign companies in the port were tightened. Laws passed by presidential decree reserved stevedore operations exclusively for Djibouti nationals. These restrictions may be eased in exchange for reciprocal rights overseas.

IMF extends credit

In November 2001, a somewhat reticent IMF was persuaded to overlook Djibouti's shortcomings in meeting targets. It announced that it would extend a new US$5 million line of credit as part of the state's Poverty Reduction and Growth Facility (PRGF). A second disbursement of US$6 million was approved in December 2002. Since Djibouti adopted the PRGF in 1999, it has been offered credit of US$26 million, but had only drawn on US$12 million by December 2002.

In its letter of intent (December 2002) to the IMF, the government expressed its commitment to pushing ahead with structural reforms. Following slippages and delays in reforms in 2001/02, it set out clear macroeconomic objectives for 2002/03. Among its aims were to achieve GDP growth of 2.5 per cent and limit inflation to 1.5 per cent.

Djibouti recorded real GDP growth of 3 per cent in 2001, compared to 0.7 per cent in 2000. While no reliable data was available for 2002, economic growth continued to be driven by the increased port activity. Ethiopia's attempts to diversify its trade routes since the war should adversely affect Djibouti's growth in future. Meanwhile, inflation was moderate, rising by 1.8 per cent in 2001.

Tax system update

A key focus of the government is to regain control over public finances with clear fiscal objectives. In August 2001, as part of its drive to introduce a modern tax system, the government adopted a supplementary budget law. This included important revenue measures, the collection of taxes on hotels and the reintroduction of surtax on the narcotic qat. The government was also confident its introduction of a new tax penalty system would significantly improve the collection of outstanding taxes.

The telecommunications sector was also targeted, with taxes on telephone bills set to be rigorously enforced. The sector looks set for a major boost after Djibouti Telecom awarded Alcatel contracts to increase substantially the capacity and extent of its fixed and mobile network.

Free trade zone

Together with nine other member states of the Common Market for Eastern and Southern Africa (Comesa), Djibouti became part of the continent's first free-trade zone. The participating countries have formulated ambitious plans to introduce step-by-step measures that include a customs union in 2004 and a single currency by 2025.

Djibouti, along with Malawi, Mauritius and Sudan, expressed its interest in hosting the permanent seat of the Comesa Court of Justice. The court is the second of its kind in the world and has jurisdiction over cases brought by member states and companies. Should Djibouti be successful in its bid, it would prove to be an extremely prestigious role.

In an attempt to improve trade relations, Djibouti and Ethiopia agreed to establish a joint business council in October 2001. The council will be charged with reviewing business practices and recommending measures designed to facilitate bilateral trade.

There are also plans afoot to launch a joint programme to rehabilitate the railway line between the two countries. Rail traffic experienced a sharp decline of around 40 per cent in the second quarter of 2001 compared to the same period in 2000.

Anti-terrorist measures

The international fight against terrorism after the 11 September 2001 terrorist attacks in the US came to Djibouti in the form of a 17-member German military delegation. Its purpose was to set up a naval supply and training base from which to patrol the waters off the coast of Djibouti, as part of a wider nine-country operation to control terrorist activities in the region of the Sea of Oman. In late 2002, the US established a command base in Djibouti and by November 2002, it had deployed over 1,000 troops in the country to undertake operations against suspected Islamic militants in the Horn of Africa. It was also reported that the US was using Djibouti as a transit to deploy its troops in Kuwait in preparation for a possible war against Iraq.

Outlook

Despite ongoing concerns for regional stability, there were positive developments in 2001–02 with Djibouti taking an active and forward-looking role in strengthening relations with its neighbours. Similarly, events at home, including the speedy resolution of the crisis resulting from the attempted coup as well as the peace deal with the FRUD, boded well for the future, bringing hope of added political stability in which to push ahead with badly needed reforms and developmental projects.

While the service sector looked set to continue performing well in 2003, its heavy dependence on Ethiopian trade leaves it vulnerable. The regional situation remains fluid, but Ethiopia's re-evaluation

KEY INDICATORS — Djibouti

	Unit	1996	1997	1998	1999	2000
Population	m	0.61	0.62	0.62	0.63	0.64
Gross domestic product (GDP)	US$bn	0.49	0.50	0.51	0.53	0.55
GDP per capita	US$	872	862	857	859	873
GDP real growth	%	-3.8	0.5	0.8	1.5	0.7
Inflation	%	2.6	2.5	2.0	1.9	2.3
Exports (fob) (goods)	US$m	40.0	43.0	59.0	*69.0	72.0
Imports (fob) (goods)	US$m	201.0	204.0	238.0	0.0	272.0
Imports (cif)	US$m	0.0	0.0	0.0	*264.0	0.0
Balance of trade	US$m	-161.0	-161.0	-179.0	-195.0	-200.0
Current account	US$m	-77.0	-12.0	-16.0	-19.0	-43.0
Foreign debt	US$bn	0.3	0.3	0.3	0.3	0.3
Total reserves minus gold	US$m	77.0	66.6	66.5	70.6	67.8
Foreign exchange	US$m	76.8	65.8	66.1	69.0	66.0
Exchange rate	per US$	177.72	177.72	177.72	177.72	177.72

* estimated figure

of its options and desire to diversify its trade routes could see GDP growth remaining low.

Risk assessment

Economic	Improving
Political	Improving
Regional stability	Poor/improving
Stock market	Poor

COUNTRY PROFILE

Historical profile

1862 France reached agreements with local leaders which gave the French the right to settle in Djibouti. The country was called French Somaliland and later the French Territory of Afars and Issas (TFAI).
1888 Construction of Djibouti-ville began on the southern shore of Tadjoura Bay. At the end of the century, France signed an agreement with the Emperor of Ethiopia designating French Somaliland as the 'official outlet of Ethiopian commerce'. The agreement led to the construction of the vital Addis Ababa-Djibouti railway.
1967 A referendum produced a 60.6 per cent vote in favour of continued French rule. Djibouti became a French territory.
1977 The re-named Republic of Djibouti was granted independence by France after several years of growing protests and demonstrations. Hassan Gouled Aptidon of the Rassemblement Populaire pour le Progrès (RPP) (Popular Rally for Progress) was appointed president. The RPP became the only legal political party.
1991 The Front pour la Restauration de l'Unité et de la Démocratie (FRUD) (Front for the Restoration of Unity and Democracy) launched a civil war in northern Djibouti. The ethnic Afar organisation demanded multi-party elections.
1992 Following several months of fighting, President Aptidon agreed to a referendum in September, which led to the creation of a multi-party constitution. The multi-party system was limited to four parties as a first stage. Elections to the Chamber of Deputies took place in December; the RPP won 72 per cent of the vote while the newly formed Party of Democratic Renewal won the remainder.
1993 President Hassan Gouled Aptidon was re-elected for a fourth term in May.
1994 Despite the new constitution, FRUD did not end its armed struggle until 24 December, when the government and FRUD signed a peace accord confirming the constitutional and electoral reforms of 1992.
1995 FRUD joined RPP in coalition government in June.
1997 President Aptidon was re-elected for a fifth term on 19 December.
1999 In April, the 83-year-old president decided to stand down after 22 consecutive years in power. Ismail Omar Guelleh was elected president.
2000 Police officers failed in an attempted coup in December.
2001 Prime Minister Barkat Gourad Hamadou, re-appointed May 1999, prime minister since 1978, offered his resignation in February on grounds of ill health. He was replaced by Dilleita Mohammed Dilleita, a diplomat and former senior civil servant.

Political structure

Djibouti is a republic with executive power vested in the Council of Ministers, headed by a prime minister, and responsible to the directly elected president who serves a six-year term.
The government is formed from a 65-member Chamber of Deputies (elected for five years by universal suffrage).

Political parties

Ruling party
Coalition government consisting of Rassemblement Populaire pour le Progrès (RPP) (Popular Rally for Progress); Front pour la Restauration de l'Unité et de la Démocratie (FRUD) (Front for the Restoration of Unity and Democracy).
Main opposition party
Parti Renouvellement Démocratique (PRD) (Democratic Renewal Party); Parti National Démocratique (PND) (Democratic National Party). Neither of the legal opposition parties have seats in the Chamber of Deputies.

Population

643,230 (2000)
The annual population growth rate was 2.1 per cent in 1994–2000. Approximately 43 per cent of the total population is under 14 years.
Population density: 28 inhabitants per square km. Urban population: 83 per cent (1994–2000). Djibouti is overpopulated and ethnically divided.
Ethnic make-up
About 60 per cent of the national total are Issas, of Somali origin and about 35 per cent are Afars who have links with Ethiopia; there are about 5 per cent European residents.
The population also includes refugees from the Ogaden and Eritrean wars in Somalia and Ethiopia.
The nomadic population (principally Afars) totals around 100,000.
Religions
Islam (94 per cent), Christianity (6 per cent)

Education

In 2000 the adult illiteracy rate was estimated at 24.4 per cent and 45.6 per cent for men and women respectively. World Bank estimates show that the total primary school enrolment of the relevant age group typically stood at 45 per cent for boys and 33 per cent for girls (including repetition rates) between 1994 and 2000.
In 2000, the World Bank initiated the School Access and Improvement Program Project in Djibouti to enhance the quality of education, and to increase enrollment in primary schools.

Health

The life expectancy is 51 years. The infant mortality rate is 102 deaths per 1,000 live births. It is estimated that around 23 per cent of children are malnourished. The government typically spends 7 per cent of GDP on health each year but the results are limited. This is due mainly to poor management and the high costs of foreign staff and medicines.
The HIV infection rate is extremely high in Djibouti and poses a significant threat to the country's future prosperity. In 2000, it was estimated that around 35,000 adults between the ages of 15 and 49 years were infected with HIV. A further 1,500 children are infected (2000). The country has the highest known prevalence of AIDS in the sub-Saharan region. The pandemic is seriously threatening the state's ability to operate effectively, with a significant number of public sector employees dying of AIDS. In 2002, the government announced its plans to launch a national AIDS campaign and improve basic health care services in the country. The initiative is supported by the World Bank. The Ministry of Health has also been restructured to create four special directorates for health care, one of which will deal with HIV/AIDS cases.

Welfare

The average unemployment rate in the country is about 45 per cent and exceeds 60 per cent among the poor. Although poverty is more acute in the rural areas, 72 per cent of the extremely poor live in the city. As Djibouti has been reeling under the massive influx of refugees from among the Ethiopians, Somalis and Eritreans, its financial resources are hugely strained. In 2002, the World Food Programme (WFP) warned that some 25,000 refugees living in Djibouti are at risk of malnutrition. The WFP had cut the rations for the refugees by 20 per cent in an effort to save precious resources. In March 2002, it had launched an 18-month relief and recovery programme, with an estimated expenditure of US$4 million.
In 2002, the Abidjan-based African Development Bank (ADB) had signed a number of agreements with Djibouti aimed at poverty reduction and improving the situation of women. These include two loans and two grants amounting to a total of US$7.22 million.

Main cities
Djibouti-ville (capital city), Obock, Tadjoura and Dikhil.

Languages spoken
French and Arabic are the main business languages, although English is understood by the larger trading houses. Cushitic languages, also Somali and Saho-Afar are widely spoken.

Official language/s
French, Arabic (Somali/Afar are the national languages)

Media

Press
Journalists have to generally avoid sensitive press issues covering human rights, the army, FRUD, relations with Ethiopia and French financial aid. Numerous journalists have been expelled or detained for publications without government approval. There are also internal pressures on the media. Journalists are largely untrained and poorly paid.
The Djiboutian court enjoys 'an arsenal of laws', that permit it to ban any critical publication affecting the image of the regime. Although the constitution provides for a free press, circulation of information is highly restricted in practice. A law prohibits the dissemination of false information and regulates the publication of newspapers.
Dailies: The government owns the main Djiboutian newspaper, *La Nation de Djibouti*.
In 2001, the opposition paper *Le Renouveau* was temporarily suspended after it published an article criticising the destruction of the central market by the chief of police, Daher Ismael Kahin. The Editor of the newspaper, Ahmed Farah, was detained then released. *Le Renouveau* is the newspaper of the Parti Renouvellement Démocratique (PRD) (Democratic Renewal Party). Reporters Sans Frontières (RSF) (Reporters Without Borders), an international organisation fighting for press freedom, has repeatedly called on Djibouti to ratify the international covenant on civil and political rights.

Broadcasting
The government owns the radio and television stations, and the official media are generally uncritical of the government or government policy.
The Société de Telecommunications Internationales de Djibouti (STID), a commercialised company owned 75 per cent by the government and 25 per cent by France Cable & Radio (FCR), controls DJIBNET, which was set up in 1996 and is the sole provider of Internet services in the country. It operates via a link with France Telecom.
Radio: There are two AM and one FM radio stations. Radio service in French, Afar, Somali and Arabic. In May 2000 the British Broadcasting Corporation (BBC) was granted permission to broadcast its World Service in the country, in conjunction with the official government-owned station, Radio Télévision Djibouti (RTD). BBC and RTD broadcasts 24 hours a day in four languages.
In 2000, Radio France Internationale was granted license to continue broadcasting on the local FM band.
Television: There is one state-owned television station, broadcasting five hours per day.

Economy
Djibouti's economy is reliant on services – there is virtually no agriculture, apart from nomadic herdsmen, and very little manufacturing. Economic activity centres on the port, the railway and other services
The French military base, which once contributed around a quarter of Djibouti's GDP, has declined in importance since 1997 when the French government decided to scale down its military presence in Africa. As of 2002, there was still a French military base in Djibouti.
The 1991–94 civil war had a severe effect on the economy, hampering economic development and imposing a considerable burden on scarce government resources. Since 1994, the government has implemented a programme of economic reforms with assistance from multilateral and bilateral creditors and donors. The reforms were aimed at macroeconomic stabilisation, with control of public expenditure and reduction in the level of domestic and foreign debt. It has engaged in a programme of privatisation. In 2000, the Dubai Port Authority (DPA) won the contract to manage Djibouti port for 20 years. This is expected to double the port's handling capacity. The government also began the restructuring of telecommunications under the direction of Djibouti Telecom. However, problems remain with high wage levels – wages are on average up to six times the level in Somalia, Eritrea and Ethiopia – which deter foreign investors.
Djibouti is highly dependent on foreign aid to fund its economic development programme. In 2001, it was clear that Djibouti had failed to meet economic targets set by the IMF a year earlier. This was mainly due to a severe drought that had caused problems for the economy, resulting in an increase in expenditure and a fall in revenue. However, in November 2001, the IMF agreed to offer the country US$5 million as part of the state's Poverty Reduction and Growth Facility (PRGF) programme. Under pressure from the IMF to speed up economic reform, the government set out concrete macroeconomic targets for 2002, that include achieving GDP growth of 1.5 per cent and reducing unemployment. The unemployment rate of 45 per cent continues to be a major burden on the economy.
In July 2002, the African Development Fund approved a US$3.9 million loan and a US$1.3 million grant to finance the basic health services reinforcement project in Djibouti.

External trade
The large visible trade deficit is partly offset by net income from services and transport, aid flows and concessionary loans. There is a free trade zone near the port of Djibouti.

Exports
Principal exports are re-exports, manufactures, live animals, skins, leather, coffee and cereals.
Main destinations: Somalia (55.9 per cent of 2000 total), Yemen (24 per cent), France (5.8 per cent), United Arab Emirates (4.6 per cent), Ethiopia (4.4 per cent).

Imports
Principal imports are machinery and transport equipment (typically 12–14 per cent of total), fuel and energy, food, beverages and tobacco (12–14 per cent), basic manufactures (6 per cent), textiles.
Main sources: Saudi Arabia (17.6 per cent of 2000 total), France (10.1 per cent), China (9.7 per cent), Ethiopia (9.6 per cent), Italy (6.1 per cent).

Agriculture
The underdeveloped agricultural sector contributed 3.7 per cent to GDP in 2000 and employs around 75 per cent of labour.
Due to poor terrain (mostly desert), agricultural population consists mainly of nomads engaged in herding goats, sheep and camels. Drought has severley affected the livelihoods of the herd owners.
Around 95 per cent of food requirements are imported.
Projects under consideration include increasing the amount of arable land by irrigation schemes and rehabilitation of water dams and wells to aid during periods of drought.

Industry and manufacturing
The industrial sector accounted for around 22 per cent of GDP in 2000 and employed 10 per cent of the working population. Manufacturing contributed 5.4 per cent.
It is limited to construction and small-scale concerns such as mineral water bottling, tanning, dairy and animal food plants. Contracts have been awarded for the setting up of a number of new industries (cement, tiles, paints, meat processing).

Foreign investment is being encouraged and should be aided by renewed political stability in the region.

Mining
Surveys have indicated the presence of minerals such as copper, gypsum and sulphur. No minerals are mined commercially. Salt has been extracted and exported. There are plans to build a cement factory with deposits of limestone gypsum and other materials.
In 1998, US mining firms, Quest International Resources and Seven Star Minerals won exploration/exploitation permits for seven sites. The joint venture was dissolved in 1998 and Seven Star purchased Quest's share in the project. Since then Seven Star has carried out surface exploration.

Hydrocarbons
Reported discoveries of gas reserves are hoped to make the country self-sufficient in gas and provide a surplus for export, although the exact amount is unknown. Chevron is engaging in oil exploration in the country. The downstream industry serves as a supply centre for the export of petroleum products, mostly for Ethiopia.

Energy
There is a geothermal power station and supply and distribution is overseen by the state-owned Electricité du Djibouti. In April 2001, the Ethiopian Electric Power Corporation (Eepco) announced it would install a 691km line costing US$75 million, and build a number of power distribution centres that would export electricity to Djibouti by 2004.

Banking
Central bank
National Bank of Djibouti
Main financial centre
Djiboutiville

Time
GMT plus three hours

Geography
Djibouti is in the Horn of Africa, at the southern entrance to the Red Sea. It is bounded on the north, west and south-west by Ethiopia, and on the south-east by Somalia. The land is volcanic desert.

Climate
Very hot and arid from April–August; average temperature 32 degrees Celsius and can reach 45 degrees Celsius. Slightly cooler from October–March, with occasional light rain.

Dress codes
Djibouti has a large Muslim population so visitors should dress modestly, especially in the city. However, it is far less strict than other Islamic countries.

Entry requirements
Passports
Required by all. Must be valid for six months beyond date of departure.
Visa
Required by all except nationals of France on short-stay visits. Ten-day visas are available on arrival for nationals of European Union (EU) countries and US. A return ticket is not required.
Currency advice/regulations
No restrictions on import/export of local or foreign currency.

Health (for visitors)
Mandatory precautions
Yellow fever vaccination certificate if arriving from an infected area.
Advisable precautions
Yellow fever, typhoid, tetanus, hepatitis A and polio vaccinations. Malaria prophylaxis recommended as risk exists throughout the country. There is a rabies risk. Water precautions should be taken.
In March 2002, there was a threat from hundreds of tons of toxic chemical leaking from shipping containers at the Port of Djibouti.

Hotels
Available in Djibouti-ville – limited elsewhere. Service charge is normally included. Tipping is not usual.

Credit cards
Generally not accepted, except by airlines and Sheraton Hotel.

Public holidays
Fixed dates
1 Jan, 1 May, 27 June (Independence), 25 December.
Variable dates
Lailat al-Miraj, Eid al-Fitr, Eid al-Adha, First of Muharram, Ashura, Prophet's Birthday.

Working hours
Banking
Sat–Thu: 0715–1145.
Business
Sat–Thu: 0630–1300.
Government
Sat–Thu: 0630–1300.
Shops
0730–1200, 1600–1900; closed Fri.

Telecommunications
Telephone/fax
Dialling code for Djibouti: IDD access code + 253 followed by subscriber's number. There are no area codes.
A 100 per cent automatic service; outside town of Djibouti-ville there are very few telephones.

Electricity supply
220/380V AC, 50 cycles.

Getting there
Air
International airport/s: Djibouti-d'Ambouli (Code: JIB), 5 km south of city.
Airport tax: US$20
Surface
For most of 2001 the border with Somalia was closed due to political differences. In October 2001, Djibouti and Somalia agreed to normalise relations. This agreement allows the free movement of people and goods between the two countries.
Road: There is a surfaced road from Addis Ababa (Ethiopia). Local advice should be taken as to when to travel by road as it can be difficult, with problems caused by the political situation.
Rail: There is a rail link with Ethiopia. The Ethio-Djibouti Railway Company plans to rehabilitate the railway, to provide an alternative import route, by 2003.
Main port/s: Djibouti-ville has 12 berths and a container terminal. The port has been modernised and serves both as a transit hub for the region and as an international trans-shipment and refuelling centre. The consequences of hostilities between Ethiopia and Eritrea, has been an increase in port trade as a result of the transfer of Ethiopia's foreign trade from Eritrea's ports to Djibouti's.
In March 2002, the government announced that it would construct a second port by 2005, 8km west of the main port. The new port will contain a refinery plant and oil terminal.

Getting about
National transport
Air: Djibouti Airlines operates a daily domestic service to Obock and Tadjoura from Djibouti. Dikhil and Ali-Sabieh can be reached by chartered aircraft.
Road: There are surfaced roads to the Ethiopian border and to Arta, and from Djibouti-ville to Tadjoura; most roads are in need of repair. Take local advice when planning to travel by road.
Rail: Certain towns are served on the Djibouti–Addis Ababa track which was damaged in a mine explosion in August 1999.
Water: Ferry service linking Djibouti-ville with Tadjoura and Obock.
City transport
Taxis: They are available in main towns. Tipping is not usual as fares include gratuities; there is an official tariff, but it is usual for visitors to be charged 50 per cent more; there is a similar increase at night.
The journey from the airport to the city centre takes 10 minutes.
Car hire
Available in Djibouti-ville and at the airport. Valid international driving licence recommended. A temporary licence can

be obtained on presentation of national licence. Traffic drives on right.

BUSINESS DIRECTORY

Telephone area codes

The international dialling code (IDD) for Djibouti is + 253 followed by the customer number.

Useful telephone numbers

Police: 17

Fire: 18

Chambers of Commerce

Chambre Internationale de Commerce et d'Industrie de Djibouti, BP 84, place Lagarde, Djibouti-ville (tel: 351-070, 350-826, 350-673).

Banking

Banque de Développement de Djibouti; PO Box 520, Angle Ave Georges Clémenceau et rue Pierre Curie, Djibouti-ville (tel: 353-391; fax: 355-022).

Banque Indosuez Mer Rouge; PO Box 88, 10 Place Lagarde, Djibouti-ville (tel: 353-016; fax: 351-638).

Banque pour le Commerce et l'Industrie-Mer Rouge; PO Box 2122, Place Lagarde, Djibouti-ville (tel: 350-857; fax: 354-260).

Central bank

Banque Nationale de Djibouti, PO Box 2118, Ave Saint Laurent du Var, Djibouti-ville (tel: 352-751 fax: 356-288).

Travel information

Daallo Airlines (Airline of Horn of Africa), PO Box 1954, Djibouti-ville (tel: 353-401, 356-660; fax: 351-765).

Djibouti Airlines, Place Lagarde, PO Box 2240, Djibouti-ville (tel: 351-006; fax: 352-429).

Djibouti Airport, BP 204, Djibouti-ville (tel: 340-10[illegible] ext 300, 382-322; fax: 340-723).

Puntavia Airline de Djibouti, CP 2240, Djibouti-ville (tel: 351-036, 351-006; fax: 353-429, 356-660).

National tourist organisation offices

L'Office National du Tourisme et de l'Artisanat, BP 1938, place du 27 Juin, Djibouti-ville (tel: 352-800, 353-632, 353-790; fax: 356-322).

Ministries

Ministry of Agriculture and Rural Development, BP 453, Djibouti-ville (tel: 351-297).

Ministry of Commerce, Transport and Tourism, BP 121, Djibouti-ville (tel: 352-540).

Ministry of Foreign Affairs and Co-operation, BP 1863, Djibouti-ville (tel: 353-342).

Ministry of Industry and Industrial Development, BP 175, Djibouti-ville (tel: 350-340).

Other useful addresses

British Consulate, BP 81, Gellatly Hankey et Cie, Djibouti-ville (tel: 355-718, fax: 353-294); c/o Inchcape Shipping Office, Djibouti-ville (tel: 353-836/844).

Central Post Office, boulevard de la République, Djibouti-ville (tel: 350-669).

Compagnie du Chemin de Fer Djibouti-Ethiopien, BP 2116, Djibouti-ville (tel: 350-353).

Djibouti Embassy (USA), Suite 515, 1156 15th Street, NW, Washington DC 20005 (tel: 331-0270; fax: 331-0302).

Office National d'Approvisionnement et de Commercialisation (ONAC), BP 75, Djibouti-ville (tel: 350-327).

Office of the Prime Minister, BP 2086, Djibouti-ville (tel: 351-494; fax: 355-049).

Radiodiffusion Télévision de Djibouti (RTD), BP 97, Djibouti-ville (tel: 352-294).

Service de Statistique et de Documentation, BP 1846, Djibouti-ville (tel: 353-331).

US Embassy, BP 185, Villa Plateau du Serpent, boulevard Maréchal Joffré, Djibouti-ville (tel: 353-995).

Internet sites

Africa Business Network: http://www.ifc.org/abn

AllAfrica.com: http://allafrica.com

African Development Bank: http://www.afdb.org

Africa Online: http://www.africaonline.com

Harambee Afrika (UK business club for traders with east, central and southern Africa; includes annotated web resource list): http://www.harambee.co.uk

Mbendi AfroPaedia (information on companies, countries, industries and stock exchanges in Africa): http://www.mbendi.co.za

Egypt

Philip Alexander

KEY FACTS

Official name: Jumhuriyat Misr Al-Arabiya (The Arab Republic of Egypt)

Head of State: President Hosni Mubarak (re-elected for fourth term Sep 1999)

Head of government: Prime Minister Atef Obeid

Ruling party: National Democratic Party (NDP) (re-elected Nov 2000)

Area: 1,001,499 square km

Population: 65.30 million (2001)

Capital: Cairo

Official language: Arabic

Currency: Egyptian pound (LE) = 100 piastres

Exchange rate: LE4.64 per US$ (Jan 2003) (in 2001, the central bank devalued the Egyptian pound to LE4.5 per US$)

GDP per capita: US$1,299 (2001); US$1,143 (2002)*

GDP real growth: 2.50% (2001); 0.8% (2002)*

Unemployment: 12.00% (2001); 12.5% (2002)*

Inflation: 2.30% (2001); 4.7% (2002)*

Oil production: 758,000 bpd (2001)

Balance of trade: -US$9.30 billion (2001); -US$8.0 billion (12 months to Sep 2002)

Foreign debt: US$28.12 billion (2001)

* estimated figure

For the latest Key Facts, go to www.worldinformation.com

As the Israeli-Palestinian conflict continued, it always seemed probable that 2001 and 2002 would prove a difficult period for neighbour and regional power-broker Egypt. Slowing global economic growth, population growth pushing 2 per cent per annum and a massive currency devaluation in 2001 in another regional giant, Turkey, created an increasingly hostile environment in which the country attempted to seek the foreign investment crucial for development. The 11 September 2001 terrorist attacks in the US and the subsequent war on terrorism hit Egypt especially hard, as risk perceptions of a country with its own record of Islamist militancy appeared to frighten away both tourist visitors and potential investors. The threat of a US-led war against Iraq could also prove disastrous for Egypt.

Facing the consequences

In early 2001, President Hosni Mubarak gave clear indications that he was staking the future of his country on closer relations with the US and the EU. In January the government signed an EU Association Agreement, following in the footsteps of other North African states such as Tunisia and Morocco. Yet Egypt was also prepared to contemplate aiding the rehabilitation of the regional pariah state, Iraq, with a free trade agreement also signed in January.

Geopolitical calculations across the world were transformed by US President George W Bush's warning after 11 September that regional leaders would have to choose whether they were 'with us or against us'. Any lingering hopes of Iraq coming in from the cold were comprehensively dashed at the end of January 2002 as Bush maintained his bellicose rhetoric by railing against an 'axis of evil' (formed by the unlikely grouping of Iraq, Iran, North Korea and later Cuba, Libya and Syria) and threatening a war against Iraq.

Although the US's 'B-52 diplomacy' created tense times for the whole region, the reconfiguration of global allegiances did provide an opportunity for Mubarak to increase the pressure on Islamist critics of his own regime. A number of Egyptians were alleged to form the elite of Osama bin Laden's Al-Qaeda network and the Al-Gama'a Al-Islamiya (The Islamic Group), an Islamic militant group accused of the 1997 massacre of tourists at Luxor, was also believed to be linked to Al-Qaeda. In October 2001, some 250 suspected militants were detained by the Egyptian authorities and 94 were tried by special military courts, which allowed no appeal. In September 2002, an Egyptian court sentenced 51 Islamists for up to 15 years in prison for attempting to overthrow the government and assassinate political leaders. Still, careful efforts were made to appease non-violent Islamists, including a clampdown on alleged homosexuals, which hardly endeared the authorities to Egyptian and international human rights organisations.

In practice, Mubarak's grip on power appears strong, given his following in the army, and choosing his successor is likely to present more of a challenge than any rival while he still rules. The government's dependence upon US military aid will remain a source of domestic criticism as long as violence continues between Israelis and Palestinians. Islamist groups may also make more mileage out of the alleged immorality of corrupt government officials, rather than any private sexual practices.

Reformers in de-Nile

Understandably, one method of reducing the opportunities for corruption, which has consistently been recommended by multilateral organisations such as the IMF, is a comprehensive programme to take major industries out of state hands. This would also stimulate an economy where several major sectors are in need of reform or consolidation. The potential of a domestic market of 66.7 million in 2001 was tempered by an average GDP per capita of US$1,274. GDP growth slowed to around 4 per cent in 2001, having stayed steadily above 5 per cent during the previous five years. In 2002, GDP growth slowed further to 0.8 per cent.

Solid foundations were laid with the privatisation of all three major cement companies: Helwan, National and Tora. A 75 per cent stake in National Cement was sold to French-based Ciments Francais. However, the government's uneasiness at allowing foreign investors to gain direct control of major companies (even in a sector of rather limited strategic or political significance) meant the other two cement companies were sold to companies with majority Egyptian ownership. As well as diluting the potential benefits of overseas managerial expertise, this practice limits the quantity of foreign investment necessary to improve the dollar liquidity of state finances. Indeed, the problem was gravely intensified by 11 September, after which the privatisation programme appeared to grind to a halt. This inactivity by the government is thought to have caused foreign investment to fall by as much as 70 per cent year-on-year, perhaps to as little as US$390 million. Nonetheless, a further boost to the construction sector in general was provided by another key reform, the passing of a bill in June 2001 to allow formal mortgage lending, which could greatly improve the access of ordinary Egyptians to the property market.

The other vital area of fiscal reform is to address the mismatch between relatively inflexible patterns of expenditure (including high public sector wages) and the volatile budget revenues. A significant step here was the introduction of value-added taxes (VAT) on retail and wholesale trades in July 2001. These measures will need to be implemented effectively, given that the budget deficit seems to have increased from 4.8 per cent of GDP in 2000 to 5.8 per cent in 2001. This was due to slowing economic growth, and falling revenues from the decline in oil prices and Suez Canal duties as global trade contracted.

Debt servicing

The positive news for Egypt is that, unlike struggling Turkey, the levels of external debt remain manageable, especially as incomes from oil and the Canal are earned directly in US dollars, giving state finances some insulation from devaluations of the local currency. Overall, foreign debt stood at US$28.5 billion in early 2002 and much of this is owed to official creditors at concessionary rates. With only 8 per cent of the total in the form of short-term liabilities, debt servicing is readily affordable and Egypt's ratio of servicing to export earnings is on a par with such reliable sovereigns as Latvia and South Africa. As in Turkey, the international community has proved a ready source of support to a country of such obvious strategic importance in the 'War on Terror'.

In February 2002, a conference of donors at Sharm El-Sheik, on the Red Sea, provided winter warmth in the form of pledges totalling US$10.3 billion over three years, with US$2.1 billion to be

KEY INDICATORS — Egypt

	Unit	1996	1997	1998	1999	2000
Population	m	60.33	61.50	62.69	63.90	65.20
Gross domestic product (GDP)	US$bn	66.43	75.50	84.30	92.00	93.00
GDP per capita	US$	1,120	1,136	1,310	1,422	1,360
GDP real growth	%	5.0	5.5	5.6	6.0	5.1
Inflation	%	8.3	6.2	3.8	3.8	2.7
Unemployment	%	9.5	10.0	12.0	8.9	11.5
Oil output	'000 bpd	900.0	880.0	860.0	835.0	795.0
Natural gas output	bn cu m	11.5	11.6	12.2	14.7	18.0
Exports (fob) (goods)	US$m	4,780.0	5,530.0	4,400.0	5,240.0	7,061.0
Imports (fob) (goods)	US$m	13,170.0	14,160.0	14,620.0	15,170.0	15,382.0
Balance of trade	US$m	-8,400.0	-8,630.0	-10,210.0	-9,930.0	-8,321.0
Current account	US$m	-192.0	-711.0	-2,566.0	-1,635.0	-971.0
Foreign debt	US$bn	34.8	29.9	32.2	29.4	29.2
Total reserves minus gold	US$m	17,400.0	18,670.0	18,120.0	14,480.0	13,118.0
Foreign exchange	US$m	17,200.0	18,480.0	17,890.0	14,280.0	12,913.0
Exchange rate	per US$	3.39	3.39	3.39	3.41	3.69

dispensed in the near future. While some of the exact sources of funding were mildly hazy, the Arab Monetary Fund, EU and US governments all look set to deliver.

Pegged out

By far the most scrutinised area of economic policy during 2001 and 2002 was on the monetary front, where uncertainty continues to be the order of the day. The Egyptian government has always shown itself reluctant to allow market forces to come into play. A brief experiment with a float in January 2001 was abruptly halted after only a few weeks, due to a rather modest slide (of less than 2 per cent) in the value of the currency, with the government restoring a fixed peg at LE3.85 per US$. The prospects for this being maintained were poor from the start. The pound had traded as weakly as LE3.95 per US$ on the open market and economists immediately claimed that the rate was overvalued by as much as 10 per cent. To add to the problem, a high proportion of Egypt's exports, especially of goods relying on competitive pricing, such as agricultural products, glassware and construction materials, go to the euro-zone countries. With the euro's weak performance against the US dollar in 2001, the price of Egyptian exports in euros climbed and squeezed them out of low-cost markets. The rapid appreciation of the euro in 2002 should increase the value of exports in 2002/03.

Competitive devaluation

The final blow in 2001 was the collapse of the Turkish currency peg in February. This immediately created substantial commercial pressure for a competitive devaluation of the Egyptian pound. A minor devaluation in May, to LE3.90 per US$, did little to help, with the pound trading as far out as LE4.50 per US$ at unlicensed bureaux de change and inter-bank dollar interest rates rising to a high of 15 per cent. Therefore, a bolder step was taken in August, when the currency was devalued almost 6.5 per cent, to LE4.15 per US$. This appeared to be what was needed and the unofficial market in US dollars ebbed away.

Unfortunately, one month later, 11 September transformed the situation. The impact on global trade and tourism caused a massive deterioration in Egypt's current account position, with visitor receipts sliding by at least 40 per cent. Although the current account deficit is actually believed to have narrowed to under 1 per cent in 2001, this was mainly due to the decline in imports as domestic demand weakened, and foreign exchange inflows declined significantly enough to drive down the value of the pound on the parallel market.

The government's response was characteristically ambivalent. In November, the economic portfolio was removed from trade minister Youssef Boutros-Ghali, officially to allow new Central Bank of Egypt (CBE) governor Mahmoud Abu El-Ayoun (a man of impeccable private sector credentials) greater independence in monetary policy. Yet, within weeks, the state turned back to command economy measures, placing restrictions on non-essential imports. The result was disastrous, with a chorus of criticism from the commercial sector and scarce US dollars reportedly selling for as much as LE5.80 on street corners.

In a positive development, the authorities responded sympathetically to this outcry, lifting restrictions and undertaking the largest devaluation yet, by over 8 per cent, to a central parity of LE4.50 per US$, in early December 2001. To reinforce the market-friendly nature of this move, El-Ayoun also pledged to review the central peg on a weekly basis, and kept his word with a small adjustment to LE4.51 per US$ in January 2002. This, combined with the Sharm El-Sheik conference, improved sentiment enough to see the pound strengthen initially, although it had depreciated to LE4.61 per US$ by April 2002. Maintained economic pressure could force the government to place the pound in free float.

Still, El-Ayoun has made clear he would like to experiment with more ambitious solutions, such as a peg to a basket of currencies which included the euro, to reflect Egypt's export destinations more accurately, or even an outright float. Fundamental conditions are not particularly conducive to this as yet, although the strengthening of the Turkish lira in early 2002 helped to erode that country's competitive advantage. Nonetheless, if the economy shows signs of improvement during the first half of 2003, the government's willingness to contemplate permitting the CBE greater autonomy will be truly tested.

Don't bank on it

Equity valuations fell for much of 2001 and 2002, with a brief upward interlude in the weeks following the August 2001 currency devaluation, brought to an abrupt halt by 11 September. Uncertain monetary conditions and rising interest rates, heightened by risk aversion after the US terrorist attacks, went some way towards explaining this. A growing number of emerging markets are competing for funds that, during 2001, became increasingly scarce. Even the usually steady source of dedicated Egyptian portfolios among Middle Eastern institutions and high-net-worth individuals to some extent dried up after the slide in oil prices which resulted from 11 September, as fuel demand from the aviation sector plummeted.

Indeed, the 1999 inclusion of Egyptian shares in the influential Morgan Stanley index (hailed as the start of a new era for the stock market at the time) may even have aggravated the difficulties of attracting overseas funds, by encouraging direct comparisons with corporate peers across the Middle East and Africa. The banking sector in particular appears to have suffered from this syndrome. Opaque accounts and dubious management quality mean that even Egypt's leading lenders generally lose out when held up for scrutiny alongside groups such as the National Bank of Bahrain and South Africa's Stanbic, which have established stronger reputations for openness and corporate governance.

Adding jitters to this gloomy situation were the on-off negotiations for the takeover of powerful local player Egyptian American Bank (EAB) by UK-based international financial giant Standard Chartered. This move might have delivered an invigorating injection of management expertise from an institution with a respected speciality in developing countries. The talks foundered altogether, due to EAB's excessive asking price, in December 2001, and the Egyptian lender indicated that it is not inclined to look for another strategic investor.

Outlook

Egypt appears to be one of a number of countries at something of a crossroads. Continued economic liberalisation, together with closer political and commercial relations to the EU and US, could signal that Egypt is following the North African example set by pro-reform Tunisia, which is already being talked of as a 'proxy EU convergence' country. The autocratic nature of the Egyptian government could equally lead the state in the direction of Libya or Syria, where isolated leaders with limited power bases retain a vice-like grip on economic activity, causing incoherent and sometimes arbitrary policies.

President Mubarak and his team seem aware of this choice, which is in itself positive. Yet, there is an urgent need for some let-up in the Israeli-Palestinian conflict, to permit a relaxation of political paranoia gripping the region, reduce the risks of Islamist militancy and stop businessmen and tourists alike running for cover. Though Egypt may influence this problem, it cannot alone bring about its resolution. By contrast, another source of anxiety, which the government could most definitely clear up, would be the future of the exchange rate peg, and this is a key element of economic policy to watch during 2002–03.

Risk assessment

Economic	Satisfactory but deteriorating
Political	Satisfactory
Regional stability	Poor
Stock market	Poor

COUNTRY PROFILE

Historical profile

1571 Egypt became part of the Ottoman Empire. Mohammed Ali assumed the rule of Egypt. His descendants ruled until 1952.
1869 Inauguration of the Suez Canal during the reign of Khedive Ismail.
1914 Egypt became a British protectorate.
1922 Following the revolution of Saad Zaghloul in 1919, Britain granted partial independence to Egypt, but retained the right to defend the Suez Canal and Egypt itself.
1936 Signing of the Anglo-Egyptian Treaty, which restricted British military presence to the Suez Canal Zone.
1948 Egypt contributed to a pan-Arab military force that failed to occupy the newly-created state of Israel.
1952 The 23 July Revolution, led by the army, ousted King Fu'ad, who had just succeeded his father, King Faruq.
1953 General Mohammed Neguib became president.
1954 Colonel Gamal Abdel Nasser was appointed prime minister.
1956 Nasser became president and nationalised the Suez Canal. Israeli forces attacked and occupied the Sinai penisula and were later joined by Britain and France, which sought to regain control of the Canal zone. In the face of strong international opposition, paricularly from the US, all three withdrew their forces.
1967 In June, Israel launched pre-emptive airstrikes against Egypt, followed by a quick ground offensive against Egyptian, Jordanian and Syrian forces. The Six-Day War ended in Egypt's defeat and Israel took control of Sinai and the Gaza Strip, which had been Egyptian territory.
1970 Anwar Al-Sadat was elected president following the death of Nasser.
1971 The building of the Aswan High Dam was completed.
1973 The 6 October War (also known as the Yom Kippur War). Egypt and Syria invaded Israel. Despite some early successful strategic gains for Egypt and Syria, Israel counter-attacked and repelled the invasion.
1977 Visit of Sadat to Jerusalem which led to the Camp David Peace Accords, the signing of the Egyptian-Israeli Peace Treaty in 1979 and the eventual Israeli withdrawal from Sinai.
1981 Hosni Mubarak became president following the assassination of Sadat. A state of emergency was declared.
1991 Egypt contributed to the US-led military campaign against Iraq. The outcome of the Gulf War established the political and economical framework for an Arab-Israeli peace process.
1994 Egypt was a party to peace agreements between Israel and the Palestinians, which began negotiations on the status of the former Egyptian territory of Gaza.
1995 Mubarak survived an assassination attempt during a visit to an Organisation of African Unity (OAU) meeting in Ethiopia.
1997 The People's Assembly approved a presidential decree extending the state of emergency until May 2000.
1999 Mubarak was re-elected as president for a further six-year term.
2000 The ruling National Democratic Party (NDP) won the legislative elections in October/November.
2001 In March, Mubarak, President Bashar al-Assad of Syria King Abdullah of Jordan inaugurated a US$300 million electricity line linking the grids of the three countries.

Political structure

Constitution
Under the 1971 constitution, amended in 1980, Egypt is an Arab Republic with a democratic socialist system. The constitution states that there should be no discrimination on the grounds of race or religion. The country is divided into 26 governorates, with governors appointed by the president. There is universal suffrage with a voting age of 18.

Form of state
Democratic socialist republic

The executive
Executive power rests with the president, who is elected by universal suffrage for a six-year term (and may be re-elected), having been nominated by at least one-third of the People's Assembly and approved by at least two-thirds. The president may choose one or more vice presidents, and appoints, and may dismiss, the prime minister and cabinet. The president may take emergency measures, but these must be approved by a referendum within 60 days; he may also dissolve the People's Assembly (the legislative body) prematurely, but a referendum and elections must be held within 60 days. The president is supreme commander of the armed forces and head of the police.

National legislature
The legislative body is the *Majlis Al-Shaab* (People's Assembly). Most members (444 out of the total 454) are elected every five years by universal suffrage. The remaining 10 representatives are appointed by the president.
A second 264-member chamber, the *Majlis Al-Shura* (Consultative Assembly), has no legislative powers and acts only in an advisory capacity. Two-thirds of the members are elected by direct universal suffrage, with the proviso that half are blue-collar workers and peasants, and the remaining one-third are appointed by the president. The term of office is six years, with half of the members standing for re-election every three years.

Legal system
The legal system is based on the constitution of 1971. Officially, Egyptian law is based on *sharia* (Islamic law), although in practice it is based on English common law and the French Napoleonic code. Christians and Jews are subject to their own jurisprudence in personal status affairs. The Court of Cassation, consisting of five judges, is the highest court of appeal. Courts of appeal (three judges) sit in Cairo and four other cities. Assize courts (three judges) deal with serious crimes. Central tribunals (three judges) handle ordinary civil and commercial cases. Summary tribunals (one judge) deal with both civil and criminal cases and have the power to impose fines and decree three-year prison terms.

Last elections
October/November 2000 (legislative); September 1999 (presidential).

Next elections
By October 2005 (presidential); October/November 2005 (legislative).

Political parties

Ruling party
National Democratic Party (NDP) (re-elected Nov 2000)

Main opposition party
New Wafd Party (NWP)

Population

65.2 million (2000 census); 66.7 million (2001).
Annual population growth rate: 1.9 per cent (1994–2000). The projected annual average growth rate for 1997–2015 is 1.5 per cent. The birth rate is projected to

fall by 0.2 per cent per annum in the period 1997–2010, while the population aged over 15 years will grow by 2.5 per cent per annum. Approximately 37 per cent of the population is under 14 years. Population density: 63 inhabitants per square km. Urban population: 45 per cent of the total (1994–2000). An estimated 99 per cent of the total population is based on or around the river Nile.

Ethnic make-up

Eastern Hamitic (99 per cent); the remaining 1 per cent comprises minorities including Armenian, Italian and Greek.

Religions

Muslim (mostly Sunni) (92 per cent); Coptic Christian and others (8 per cent).

Labour market and unemployment

In 1997, the total labour force was 22 million. The labour force is projected to grow by 2.7 per cent per year in the period 1998–2010. The unemployment rate in 1998 stood at approximately 12 per cent before falling to 8.9 per cent in 1999.

Unemployment is a major problem, particularly in the cities. The World Bank estimates that 70 per cent of jobseekers are under 20 years of age. Independent estimates place the number of Egyptian expatriates working in Gulf and other Arab countries at up to four million. Before the 1990 Iraqi invasion of Kuwait, nearly two million Egyptians worked in Iraq.

Unofficial estimates claimed that adult literacy was only 49 per cent in 1995 (61 per cent for men, 36 per cent for women). However, official figures for 1998 put the literacy rate at 63 per cent.

Main cities

Cairo (capital, estimated population 6.7 million (2000 census), Greater Cairo 10.6 million in 2000) is the largest city in Africa.

Other cities include Alexandria (3.3 million), Port Said (500,000), Suez (458,000), Aswan, Luxor, El-Faiyum, Ismailia, Asyut, El-Minya.

Languages spoken

French and English are widely spoken, especially in business circles.

Official language

Arabic

Media

Cairo is the largest publishing centre in the Middle East. The state controls the main newspapers as well as the Egyptian Radio and Television Corporation (ERTC) and the Egyptian Television Organisation (ETO).

Press

Tensions between a free press and government are a normal part of the political process. In 2000, the government attempted to ban *Al-Sha'ab*, the newspaper run by the Socialist Labour Party. However, the decision was overturned by the courts, who deemed it unconstitutional.

Dailies: Daily newspapers are maily published in the Arabic language. These include *Al-Ahram*, *Alalam Alyoum*, *Al-Sha'ab*, *Al-Akhbar*, *Al-Gomhouriya* and *Al-Wafd*. There are also daily French papers, *Progrès Egyptien* and *Le Journal d'Egypte*. *Egyptian Gazette* provides daily local information in English.

Weeklies: The weeklies with the largest circulation are *Akhbar Al-Yom*, *Al-Mussawar*, *Alahali Newspaper*, and *Akher Sa'a*. There are a large number of weekly magazines including *Hawadeth Magazine*, *Riada Magazine* and the *Sayarat Magazine*. *The Cairo Times* is the best selling English language biweekly magazine reporting from Egypt and the region. The Egypt edition of the *Middle East Times* provides independent weekly coverage of politics, culture and religion in the Arab and Islamic worlds.

Business: Daily financial newspaper, *Al-Alam Al-Youm*. Business news is covered by *Egypt Today*, *Business Today Egypt* and the economic weekly *Al-Ahram Al-Iqtisadi*. The main English-language commercial weekly *Middle East Observer* also provides financial information.

Periodicals: Monthly publications in Arabic language include *Al-Manar Magazine* and *Al-Murabeton*. English language periodicals include the *Arab Ambassador*. IBA Media is Egypt's leading English-language publisher and publishes three monthly titles: *Egypt Today* (http://www.egypttoday.com), *Business Today Egypt* (businesstoday-eg.com) and PC World Egypt (pcworld.com.eg).

Broadcasting

Radio: The national service is broadcast by the ERTC. There are 12 stations operating. The state's radio programmes are in Arabic, but it has an FM foreign language programme with daily news bulletins in English, French, Italian, German and Greek.

Television: A number of channels are operated by ETO. Channel 1 specialises in Arab programming while Channel 2 has a larger selection of Western shows. More than 90 per cent of households have a television.

In 1998, Egyptian satellite broadcasters started transmitting programmes throughout the Middle East and Mediterranean after the launch of US$158 million Nilesat 101, which allows 84 channels across the region previously dominated by non-Arab or Saudi Arabian satellite broadcasters. Egypt broadcasts Egyptian programmes throughout the Arab World. Libya and Egypt have cable telecommunications and radio links between the two countries.

Advertising

Egypt's advertising sector is one of the fastest-growing in the region.

Economy

The Egyptian economy is one of the strongest in Africa. In recent decades, it has traditionally been driven by oil, tourism, Suez canal tolls and workers' remittances. Egypt's increasing need to import food is becoming a grave economic concern.

The Egyptian economy remains heavily centralised, and the large public sector established in the 20 years after the 1952 revolution still dominates economic life. However, since the mid-1990s the government has made strong efforts to develop the industrial and financial sectors of the economy. This is being done by rationalising, deregulating and divesting state control of the economy. The government's encouragement of privatisation is motivated by a desire to mobilise domestic capital and attract foreign investment. Both Egyptian officials and foreign observers remain concerned by the country's low levels of domestic savings, which continue to limit available funds for much-needed investment, and the stubbornly high levels of unemployment. The strict monetarist policy has also attracted criticism as low inflation has led to rising real interest rates, which restricts growth, and an over-valued exchange rate, which has undermined export competitiveness.

External trade

During the late 1990s, Egyptian trade grew impressively in both directions, although import growth consistently outstripped the growth rate for exports, leading to a widening balance of trade deficit. Egypt's current account has traditionally benefited from a unique source of invisible earnings, Suez Canal dues, which typically earn Egypt US$1.8 billion annually. However, the government has frozen tolls since 1997, mainly to counter growing competition from oil and gas pipelines.

Exports

Principal exports are petroleum products (typically 45 per cent of total), cotton yarn, textiles and fabrics. Other exports include engineering and metallurgical goods (typically 11 per cent of total), refined sugar-cane, raw cotton, potatoes, rice and oranges.

Main destinations: Italy (17.3 per cent of 2000 total), US (14.8 per cent), France (6.1 per cent), Germany (4.3 per cent), Netherlands (3.6 per cent), Australia (0.2 per cent).

Imports

Principal imports are foodstuffs, fuel and energy, transport goods and machinery, chemicals, cement, iron rods and bars.

Main sources: US (67.7 per cent of 2000 total), Germany (29.5 per cent), Italy (28.5 per cent), France (24.2 per cent), Saudi Arabia (15.7 per cent), Australia (6.2 per cent).

Agriculture

The agriculture sector typically contributes 15 per cent to GDP and employs around 30 per cent of the workforce. Its importance is declining in relation both to industry and to population growth.

Irrigation is supplied by the River Nile and the government is looking at ways to improve the efficiency of water use through the construction of lined canals and pipes. Problems surrounding the ecological effects of the Aswan High Dam persist.

In 2001, the Nile Basin Initiative (NBI) (signed by Egypt, Sudan, Tanzania, Kenya, Rwanda, Burundi, Uganda and Democratic Republic of Congo) launched seven feasibility studies backed by a US$140 million granted by the World Bank and donor governments.

Farming

Background and government policy: The construction of the Aswan High Dam in the 1970s initially improved crop yields by providing a constant source of irrigation. However, the dam has had a damaging long-term effect on agriculture. It has permanently raised the water table, causing serious drainage problems and high salinity as well as depriving the valley of annual silt, a natural fertiliser, previously brought down by the river during the flood season. The silt has had to be replaced by costly chemical fertilisers.

The government is aiming to boost output by reclaiming the desert for cultivation. Fertile land is found in the Nile Valley and Delta – the cultivable area accounts for only 2.4 per cent of the total land area. About 7.4 million feddans are cultivable (approximately 2.25 feddan per hectare). Virtually all water comes from the River Nile, from which Egypt is allowed to take 55.5 billion cubic metres a year under its agreement with other Nile basin countries. This imposes strict limitations on the expansion of agriculture.

A number of major irrigation schemes are under way. These are along the coast north-west of Alexandria, the Nile border with Sudan, East Oweinat in the desert and the largest project of them all, the Southern Valley Scheme. The cost of the Southern Valley Scheme is projected to reach US$85 billion by 2017. Saudi investment will build the largest farm in the world (six times bigger than Singapore) which will reach full production in 2010 and will employ 25,000 people permanently as well as additional seasonal labour.

Production: Agricultural production in Egypt is highly labour-intensive. Output suffers from crop infestation, price controls, fragmented land tenure, increased soil salinity and consumer preference for imported foods.

Consumption: Major subsistence crops include maize, sorghum, rice, wheat beans and vegetables. Egypt's wheat consumption far outstrips local production, with Egyptian wheat crops supplying just 40 per cent of annual domestic demand.

External trade: Rapid population growth has contributed to a dependence on imported food, especially grain. Some 65 per cent of food requirements are imported and Egypt's annual food import bill totals around US$5.5 billion.

Cotton is a major export crop. High-quality long staple cotton is exported, particularly to Europe, the US and Japan, and cheaper short staple US cotton is imported.

Egypt is the world's seventh largest sugar producer, and joined the International Sugar Organisation in 1998. It also produce an exportable surplus of fruit and vegetables.

Fishing

There are active Egyptian fishing industries in the Mediterranean and the Red Sea, as well as more limited freshwater fishing on the Nile and Lake Nasser. Egypt typically produces over 300,000 tonnes of seafood and 190,000 tonnes of freshwater fish per annum. Virtually all of this is used for domestic consumption.

Industry and manufacturing

In the first two decades after the 1952 revolution, the government carried out an extensive nationalisation programme. While the open door policy, launched in 1974, aimed to increase private-sector investment, initiatives from the private sector tended to focus on the consumer goods and service industries and avoided competition with state-controlled enterprises (SSEs). SSEs still dominate Egypt's economy. The main state-owned companies include: Egyptian General Petroleum Corporation, Egyptian Petrochemical Company, El-Nasr Pharmaceutical Chemicals Company, Egyptian Iron and Steel Company, Egyptian General Company for Tourism and Hotels and the El-Nasr Automotive Company.

The government places emphasis on industrial diversification and import substitution, the development of downstream chemicals and of heavy industry, including the Helwan Iron and Steel Company, the Nag Hammadi aluminium plant and El Dikheila integrated steel works. Four industrial cities, the Tenth of Ramadan, Sadat, Sixth of October and Borg El-Arab, have been established since the early 1990s.

Tourism

Egypt has always received substantial revenues from its tourist industry, which is Africa's largest. Developing the sector remains an urgent government priority. The government has undertaken measures to tighten internal security while the renunciation of violence by Gama'a Al-Islamiyya terrorist movement in 1999 reassured foreign visitors. In 2000, Egypt earned US$4.3 billion from tourism. However, the revenue for 2001 was badly hit by the 11 September terrorist attacks in the US and was down to an estimated US$2.6 billion.

Mining

The mineral sector in 2002 is being developed through new exploration projects, extension of leases, new tenders and foreign contracts to meet production targets. Government policy aims to encourage foreign and local companies to explore for and exploit raw materials. Agreements have been reached for exploration and production of sulphur, phosphate and gold. The government is keen to extend franchises for other minerals, especially titanium and silver. Among non-oil raw materials, only iron ore, phosphate rock and limestone is produced on a significant scale. Other minerals produced include baryte, clay, feldspar, fluorspar, gypsum, kaolin, quartz, salt, silica sand and talc. Manganese and chrome deposits have also been exploited, while commercial deposits of zinc, tin, lead and copper have been discovered in Sinai. A contract to mine sulphur in Sinai is held by Freeport Egyptian Sulphur Company, a wholly owned subsidiary of US firm Freeport McMoran. The annual production capacity is thought to be around 250,000 tonnes per year (tpy). Egypt also has deposits of uranium. The government is keen on inviting tenders for exploration of base metals and the development of ornamental stone deposits. Although Egypt has no bauxite, it has developed a significant aluminium industry based on electric power from the Aswan High Dam. Production was initially used for basic consumer goods but Egypt now exports a wide range of basic aluminium products.

The Australian mining venture, Centamin Egypt, announced in October 2001 the discovery of what could potentially be one of the largest gold mines in the world in the Sukari concession in the Eastern Desert.

Hydrocarbons

The upstream oil and gas industry generates around 10 per cent of GDP and represents one of Egypt's main sources of foreign currency, with oil accounting for about 40 per cent of total export revenues.

By the mid-1990s, despite the continued encouragement of oil exploration, it had become clear that oil production was set to decline as only small fields had been discovered. At current production rates, oil reserves of 3.5 billion barrels could be exhausted by 2020. Falling production levels coupled with industrialisation and the rise in domestic oil consumption mean that the country is likely to become a net oil importer by 2005.

Foreign oil companies continue to explore the Western Desert, an area where extraction is considerably cheaper than the offshore operations in the Red Sea. Deposits have been discovered in the Qaran area of Egypt's Western Desert by the US-based Apache Corporation.

In view of limited oil reserves, interest has switched to gas exploration and proven reserves of one trillion cubic metres (35.2 trillion cubic feet) should last well into the twenty-first century at current rates of production. Natural gas production is expected to reach over 60 million cubic metres by 2010, meeting much of Egypt's domestic energy requirement, as well as becoming a substitute for oil in certain industries, and with the possibility of exports.

Energy

Electricity is generated at thermal power stations throughout the country, and about a quarter of the total is supplied by the hydroelectric plant at the Aswan High Dam in Upper Egypt. Domestic demand is growing faster than production.

A high priority energy programme is centred on coal-fired power stations, but also includes the construction of hydroelectric and gas-powered electricity generating stations.

Banking

The banking sector is dominated by four public-sector commercial banks – Banque Misr, Bank of Alexandria, Banque du Caire and the National Bank of Egypt – which hold about 60 per cent of deposits, 70 per cent of assets and 65 per cent of loans, and are the main conduit for public-sector trade, savings and financing. Early in the 1960s, they were given specialisation in contracting (Banque du Caire), foreign trade (National Bank), agriculture (Banque Misr) and industry (Bank of Alexandria). The specialisations were abolished in 1976, but much of the banks' business remains in their former speciality areas. The four-state owned banks were ordered in 1996 to reduce their stakes in the 23 joint venture banks to a maximum of 20 per cent, although this has been a slow process. There are also four Islamic banks, including the Faisal Islamic Bank.

State-owned banks suffer from outstanding debt owed by both the government and private companies and lack of political will to reform the sector is likely to continue to limit their commercial value and growth. Moreover, the government is yet to introduce regulatory laws governing mortgages, pensions or insurance policies. The government has ruled out any privatisation programme aimed at large state-owned banks before 2003.

The Egyptian banking market has a great potential for extension but is marred by bureaucratic procedures and large debts which is off-putting to potential investors. Mortgages, consumer loans, private pensions and investment trusts are relatively unknown. Only six million Egyptians have bank accounts, with just 500,000 conducting more than two transactions a year.

After an upsurge in foreign banking activity in Egypt in 1999 – mostly from UK, US and French banks such as Crédit Commercial de France, American Express and Citibank – investment slowed as Egypt's economy slowed down over the course of 2000 and 2001. By 2001, there were over 30 foreign banks with interests in Egypt, although many of these only have a small investment in Egypt's banks.

In May 2001, however, Crédit Agricole Indosuez bought the small Egyptian bank, Crédit Internationale d'Egypte from HSBC, which has increased its activity in Egypt. Msir International plans to increase its banking presence in Egypt by opening 15 new branches over the course of 2001/02.

Central bank

Central Bank of Egypt

Main financial centre

Cairo

Time

GMT plus two hours (GMT plus three hours from May to September),

Geography

Most of Egypt is located in the north-east corner of Africa between the Mediterranean Sea, the Red Sea, Sudan and Libya. The Sinai peninsula, separated from the African continent by the Suez Canal and the Red Sea, borders Israel. The peninsula also faces Jordan and Saudi Arabia across the Gulf of Aqaba. About 95 per cent of Egypt is uninhabitable desert.

Climate

The climate is dry with very little rainfall, hot in summer and cool in winter. Temperatures in the capital Cairo in the north vary from 43 degrees Celsius (C) maximum in summer to 18 degrees C maximum in winter. Sandstorms (the *khamsin* or *simoon* winds) can disrupt air traffic between March and May.

Rainfall is largely confined to the Mediterranean coast, with around 200 millimetres a year in Alexandria. Egypt is dependent on the Nile for nearly all its water needs. The government is pressing ahead with desert reclamation schemes, but these are also dependent on limited Nile waters as reserves of water under the desert have so far proved relatively insignificant.

Dress codes

Lightweight clothing is necessary for the hot summer months (May to September). Business dress is formal – suits are worn for all occasions. Men should not wear shorts, except at the beach and women should wear modest clothing in public, covering their arms and legs.

Entry requirements

Passports

Required by all except certain Palestinians and some merchant seamen. Passports must be valid for six months beyond the intended length of stay.

Visa

Required by all except nationals of Bahrain, Djibouti, Guinea, Jordan (if holding a passport valid for five years), Libya, Malta, Oman, Qatar, Saudi Arabia, South Africa, United Arab Emirates and Yemen. Palestinians holding a residence card do not need a visa if their stay outside Egypt did not exceed six months. Transit visas may also be required for other nationalities.

All visitors except West Europeans and US nationals must register at the Office of Foreigners and Nationality within seven days of arrival. Hotels will normally attend to this on the visitor's behalf. Restrictions governing visas and transit visas should be checked before visiting Egypt.

Currency advice/regulations

Import and export of local currency is restricted to LE1,000 per person. Import of foreign currency is unrestricted, but must be declared. Export of foreign currency is restricted to this declared amount.

Customs

It is permitted to import one bottle of alcohol and 200 cigarettes. Video equipment must be declared at customs.

Health (for visitors)

Mandatory precautions

A vaccination certificate against yellow fever is required if travelling from an infected area.

Advisable precautions

Typhoid, hepatitis 'A', tetanus and polio vaccinations are recommended. Malaria exists from June–October in the El Faiyum area. There is also a rabies risk. Avoid drinking tap water. Raw vegetables are inadvisable except in top-class restaurants.

Hotels

There is a wide range available. Bills are quoted in US dollars and may be settled in Egyptian currency. A 20 per cent tax and service charge should be added to all prices.

Credit cards

Most credit cards are widely accepted. Excepting airline tickets, the free market exchange rate is used in calculating credit card transactions.

Public holidays

Fixed dates

22 Feb (Unity Day) (schools, universities), 25 Apr (Sinai Day), 1 May (Labour Day), 18 Jun (Evacuation Day), 23 Jul (Anniversary of the Revolution), 6 Oct (Armed Forces' Day), 24 Oct (Suez Day), 23 Dec (Victory Day) (schools, universities).

Variable dates

The Islamic year contains 354 or 355 days, with the result that Muslim feasts advance by 10–12 days against the Gregorian calendar each year. Dates of feasts vary according to the sighting of the new moon so cannot be forecast exactly.
Eid Al-Fitr (end of Ramadan), Eid Al-Adha, Sham El-Nessim (Coptic Easter Monday), Prophet Mohammed's Birthday, Eid Al-Fitr.

Working hours

Egypt is a Muslim country and the official day off is Friday. Embassies and the offices of some foreign companies also close on Saturday and Sunday. Some companies treat Thursday as a half day. Hours may also vary between winter and summer.

Banking

Sun–Thu: 0830–1500

Business

Sat–Thu: 0900–1400

Government

0900–1400: Fri closed

Shops

Shops are closed on Sundays. In summer they are open 0900–1230 every day and 1600–2000 every day except Thursday and Monday. In winter they open 0900–1900 except Monday and Thursday when they open until 2000.

Telecommunications

Telephone/fax

Egyptian residents/firms are indexed under the initial letters of their first names. Non-Egyptians are indexed under the initials of their surname.

Postal services

It is advisable to use airmail, which takes around five days to reach Europe. Postal censorship is in force and the internal postal service is unreliable

Mobile phones

There are two network operators, MobiNil and MisrFone.

Internet/e-mail

The country's largest Internet service provider (ISP) is InTouch, which was set up jointly with Infonet Services of California.

Electricity supply

220–440V AC in most areas; in some rural districts 110–380V AC is still found.

Weights and measures

Metric system (local units also in use).

Social customs/useful tips

Hospitality is considered a prime virtue and it would be rude for visitors not to accept a token drink or other invitation. Many hosts will not allow a guest to pay for anything during his or her stay. Guests should therefore not squabble over paying at a restaurant, for example. In address, use the first name with the appropriate title (for instance Mr, Madame, Doctor, Engineer). Business cards in Arabic are appreciated.

Security

Violent crime against foreigners is rare. However, thieves operate in busy tourist areas such as Giza and Luxor. In these areas it is best to avoid wearing flashy or expensive jewellery.
Given its strategic position in the Middle East, Egypt is particularly sensitive regarding national security. Photographing bridges, railway stations and military installations is forbidden. Carrying a video camera can cause problems with the Egyptian authorities.

Getting there

Air

International air links to Egypt are extensive and include services from all major airliners and international destinations.

National airline: Egyptair

Main airport: Cairo Heliopolis

Airport tax: There is no airport tax.

Surface

Road: There are road links from Libya and Israel.

Water: There are ferry services to Port Said and Alexandria from many destinations across the Mediterranean, run by Menatours. There are ferries between Aqaba in Jordan and Nuweiba on the Sinai peninsular. There are ferries to Suez from Jeddah in Saudi Arabia. There are steamer services across Lake Nasser from Sudan, although these are suspended during periods of instability in Sudan.

Main ports: Alexandria, Al-Ghardaqch, Aswan, Bur Safajah, Damietta, Marsa Matruh, Port Said and Suez.

Getting about

National transport

Air: Egyptair operates domestic services from Cairo to Luxor, Aswan, Hurghada, Abu Simbel and Alexandria. Air Sinai operates services to North and South Sinai. If planning to fly south, book well in advance. Travel to certain areas of the Nile Delta is restricted.

Road: There are four intercity bus companies: luxury service Superjet, West Delta Bus Company, East Delta Bus Company, and Upper Egypt Bus Company. There are fast and comfortable services between most towns and cities, although they tend to be crowded, and tickets should be booked in advance where possible.

Rail: There are train services to all main cities and towns in Egypt. Tickets must be reserved, sometimes up to two days in advance. There are three classes of carriage.

Water: Traditional sailboats (*felucca*) offer rides along the Nile river.

City transport

Taxis: Metered and unmetered taxis are readily available, but meters where fitted are often not used. Fares should be agreed in advance.
Air-conditioned limousines are available at airports and main hotels. Chauffeured taxis from Cairo airport to the city centre are recommended. Hotels have their own shuttle services. Hotel taxis or chauffeured hire cars are more efficient and can be hired by the day, subject to negotiation. Fares are usually listed in the major hotels.
City centre taxis are cheap although often uncomfortable and never have air-conditioning. If you are travelling beyond the city centre it is a good idea to carry a map to guide the taxi driver. The journey time from Cairo international airport to the city is about 40–60 minutes. Tipping is usually 10 per cent.

Buses/trams: Cairo and Alexandria have inexpensive but crowded bus systems. Alexandria has an efficient tram system, but Cairo's trams are gradually being replaced by the metro system.

Metro: The Cairo metro was built in the mid-1980s.

Car hire

An international driving licence and third-party insurance are needed. Hire charges should be negotiated in advance. The maximum speed limit on main roads is 90km per hour, and there are heavy fines for infringements. Traffic in Cairo is heavily congested.

BUSINESS DIRECTORY

Telephone area codes

The international direct dialing (IDD) code for Egypt is +20, followed by the local area codes:

Alexandria	3	Ismailiya	64
Asyut	88	Luxor	95
Aswan	97	Maeria	3
Cairo	2	Marsa Matrah	3
Damietta	57	Port Said	66
El Arish	68	Pyramids	2

Fayoum	84	Suez	62
Giza	2	Zagazig	55
Heliopolis	2		

Useful telephone numbers

Police: 122 (Cairo), 22147 (Aswan), 960-151-122 (Alexandria), 23-929 (Suez)

Fire: 125 (Cairo)

Ambulance: 123 (Cairo)

Chambers of Commerce

Alexandria Chamber of Commerce, 31 Chamber of Commerce Street, Alexandria, Egypt (tel: 809-339; fax: 808-993).

Assiut Chamber of Commerce, El Khedewi Esmail Street, Assiut (tel: 832-2082).

Aswan Chamber of Commerce, Abtal El Tahreer Street, Aswan (tel: 732-3084).

Cairo Chamber of Commerce, 4 Midan El Falaki, Cairo (tel: 355-8261; fax: 356-3603).

Damietta Chamber of Commerce, Saad Zaghloul Street, Damietta (tel: 322-799; fax: 320-632).

Egyptian Chamber of Commerce, 31 El-Ghorfa, El Tugareya Street (tel: 480-8434).

Fayoum Chamber of Commerce, El Nadi El Reyadi Street, El Fayoum (tel: 322-148).

Federation of Egyptian Chambers of Commerce, 4 Falaky Square, Cairo (tel: 355-1813; fax: 355-7940).

Federation of Egyptian Industries, Cairo (tel: 748-945).

Giza Chamber of Commerce, 6 El Ghorfa El Tegarya Street, giza (tel: 721-761; fax: 623-971).

Ismailia Chamber of Commerce, 163 Saad Zaghloul Street, Ismailia (tel: 221-663; fax: 322-515).

Port Said Chamber of Commerce, Benayet Souk El Goumla, Port Said (tel: 222-733; fax: 236-141).

Suez and South Sinai Chamber of Commerce, 47 Salah Eldin Elayoubi Street, Suez (tel: 227-783).

The Red Sea Chamber of Commerce, Old City Council Building, Hurghada (tel: 440-761).

Banking

Alexandria Commercial and Maritime Bank, PO Box 2376, 85 El Horreya Avenue, 21519 Alexandria (tel: 392-1237; fax: 391-3706).

Arab African International Bank, 5 Midan Al-Saray Al Koubra, Garden City, Cairo (tel: 794-5094/5/6; fax: 795-8493).

Arab International Bank, 35 Abdel Khalek Sarwat Street, Cairo (tel: 391-8794, 391-6391; fax: 391-6233).

Bank of Alexandria, 49 Kasr El Nil Street, Cairo (tel: 393-6262; fax: 391-0481).

Bank of Commerce & Development, 'Al-Tegaryoon', PO Box 1373, 13 26th July Street, Sphinx Square, Mohandessin, Cairo (tel: 302-8156; fax: 302-3963).

Cairo Barclays Bank, PO Box 110, Maglis El Shaab, 12 Midan El Sheikh Youssef, Garden City, Cairo (tel: 366-2600; fax: 366-2810/11).

Cairo Far East Bank, PO Box 757, 104 El Nil Street, Dokki, Cairo (tel: 336-2516; fax: 348-3818).

Crédit International d'Egypte, 46 El Batal Ahmed Abdel Aziz Street, Mohandessin, Cairo (tel: 336-1897; fax: 360-8673).

Delta International Bank, PO Box 1159, 1113 Corniche El-Nil Street, Cairo (tel: 575-3492; fax: 574-3403).

Egyptian American Bank, PO Box 1825, 4 & 6 Hassan Sabri Street, Zamalek, Cairo (tel: 738-0126; fax: 738-0609).

Misr Exterior Bank; Cairo Plaza Building, Cornish El-Nil, Boulaque, Cairo (tel: 778-701, 778-619, 766-381, 766-360; fax: 762-806, 578-0238).

Misr International Bank, PO Box 218, Embaba, 54 El Batal Ahmed Abdel Aziz Street, Mohandessin, Cairo (tel: 749-4424, 749-7091; fax: 700-928) .

National Bank for Development (NBD), PO Box 647, 5(A) El Borsa El Gedida Street, 11511 Cairo (tel: 392-3245; fax: 390-5681).

National Bank of Egypt, PO Box 11611, National Bank of Egypt Tower, 1187 Corniche El Nil, Cairo (tel: 574-9101; fax: 576-2672).

Nile Bank, PO Box 2741, 35 Ramses Street, Abdel Moneim Riyad Sq, Cairo (tel: 574-1417, 574-3502, 575-1105; fax: 575-6296, 575-3640).

Suez Canal Bank, PO Box 2620, 11 Mohamed Sabri Abu Alam St, Cairo (tel: 393-1066; fax: 391-3522).

Central bank

Central Bank of Egypt, 31 Kasr El-Nil Street, Cairo, Egypt (tel: 393-1514; fax: 392-6361, 392-5045).

Travel information

Cairo International Airport, Heliopolis, Cairo (tel: 291-4255; fax: 243-2522).

Egyptair, Cairo International Airport, Cairo (tel: 245-4400; fax: 418-3715).

Ministry of tourism

Ministry of Tourism, Misr Tourist Tower, Abbassiya Square, Abbassiya (tel: 282-8439; fax: 285-9551; e-mail: mot@idsc.gov.eg).

National tourist organisation offices

Egyptian Tourist Authority, Misr Building, Abbassia (tel: 482-0283; fax: 483-0844).

Ministries

Ministry of Agriculture, Animal and Fish Wealth and Land Reclamation, Nadi El Seid Street, Dokki, Giza (tel: 702-677; fax: 703-889; e-mail: capi@idsc.gov.eg).

Ministry of Awkaf, 5 Sabry Abou Alam Street, Bab El-Louq, Cairo (tel: 392-6163; fax: 392-6305; e-mail: mawkaf@idsc1.gov.eg).

Ministry of Cabinet Affairs and Administrative Development, 1 Magles El Shaab Street, Cairo (tel: 354-1722; fax: 355-6306; e-mail: cabinet1@idsc.gov.eg).

Ministry of Culture, 2 Shagaret El Dor St, Zamalek Cairo 03 (tel: 341-5568; fax: 340-6449; e-mail: mculture@idsc.gov.eg).

Ministry of Defence and Military Production, 5 Ismail Abaza Street, Cairo (tel: 355-3063; fax: 354-8739; e-mail: mod@idsc.gov.eg).

Ministry of Economy and International Co-operation, 8 Adly St, Cairo (tel: 390-6796; fax: 390-3029; e-mail: mineco@idscl.gov.eg; internet site: http://www.sis.gov.eg).

Ministry of Education, 4 Ibrahim Naguib St, Garden City, Cairo (tel: 355-7952; fax: 356-2952; E-mail: moe@idsc.gov.eg).

Ministry of Electricity and Energy, Ramses Street, Abbassia, Nasr City Cairo (tel: 261-6514; fax: 261-6302; e-mail: mee@idsc.gov.eg).

Ministry of Finance, Lazoughly Square, Justice and Finance Building, Cairo (tel: 354-1055; fax: 354-5433; e-mail: mofinance@idsc1.gov.eg).

Ministry of Foreign Affairs, Press and Information Department, Maspero, Corniche El Nil, Cairo 02 (tel: 354-1414; fax: 354-6285; e-mail: minexter@idsc1.gov.eg).

Ministry of Health and Population, Magles El Shaab St, Cairo (tel: 354-1076; fax: 355-3966; e-mail: moh@idsc.gov.eg).

Ministry of Higher Education, 4 Ibrahim Naguib Street, Garden City, Cairo (tel: 355-7952; fax: 356-2952; e-mail: mheducat@idsc1.gov.eg, info@sti.sci.eg).

Ministry of Housing, Reconstruction and New Urban Communities, 1 Ismail Abaza St, Cairo (tel: 355-3320; fax: 355-7836; e-mail: mhuuc@idsc1.gov eg).

Ministry of Industry and Mineral Wealth, 2 Latin America Street, Garden City (tel: 355-7034; fax: 354-8362; e-mail: moimw@idsc.gov.eg).

Ministry of Information, Mcspero, Corniche El Nil, Cairo (tel: 747-193; fax: 757-144; e-mail: rtu2@idsc.gov.eg).

Ministry of Insurance & Social Affairs, El Sheikh Rihan Street, Bab El-Louq, Cairo (tel: 337-0039; fax: 337-5390; e-mail: msi@idsc.gov.eg).

Ministry of Interior, El Sheikh Rihan St, Cairo (tel: 355-7500; fax: 355-7792; e-mail: moi1@idsc.gov.eg).

Ministry of Justice, Justice and Finance Building, Lazoughli Sq, Cairo 15 (tel: 355-1176; fax: 355-8103; e-mail: mojeb@idsc1.gov.eg).

Ministry of Land Reclamation, Nadi El Seid St, Cairo 10 (tel: 703-011).

Ministry of Local Administration, Kasr El Aini St, Cairo 04 (tel: 355-3566).

Ministry of Manpower and Immmigration, 3 Youssef Abbas St, Nasr City, Cai (tel: 260-9363; fax: 260-9891; e-mail: mwlabor@idsc1.gov.eg).

Ministry of Petroleum, 16 El Mokhayyam El Da'em Street, Nasr City (tel: 262-2268; fax: 263-6060; e-mail: mopm@idsc1.gov.eg).

Ministry of Planning, Salah Salem Road, Nasr City (tel: 602-935; fax: 263-4747).

Ministry of Public Enterprises, Magles El Shaab Street, Cairo (tel: 355-8026; fax: 355-3606).

Ministry of Public Works and Water Resources, El Nil St, Embaba, Cairo 04 (tel: 354-5884; fax: 355-8008; e-mail: mpwwr@idsc.gov.eg).

Ministry of Rural Development, 4 Shooting Club Street, Dokki, Cairo (tel: 349-7470; fax: 349-7785).

Ministry of Shipping, 7 Abdel Khalek Sarwat St, Cairo, 01 (tel: 764-343).

Ministry of Social Affairs and Insurance, El Sheikh Rihan St, Bab El Louk, Cairo 06 (tel: 354-2900; fax: 917-799).

Ministry of State for Administrative Development and Environment and Ministry of the Public Enterprise, 1 Magles El Shaab Street, Lazoughli Square, CAI 06 (tel: 355-8026; fax: 355-5882; e-mail: mops3@idsc.gov.eg).

Ministry of State for the Affairs of the People's Assembly and the Shoura Council, Magles El Shaab St, Cairo 04 (tel: 355-7750; fax: 355-7681; e-mail: parli@idsc.gov.eg).

Ministry of State for Environmental Affairs, Helwan Road, Cairo (tel: 375-7306; fax: 378-4235; e-mail: eeaa@idsc.gov.eg).

Ministry of State for Military Production, 23 Kobri Al Kubba St, Cairo 36 (tel: 257-8697/2915).

Ministry of State for Planning and International Co-operation, Salah Salem Street, Nasr City (tel: 401-4615; fax: 401-4733; e-mail: miceu@idsx.gov.eg).

Ministry of State for Scientific Research Affairs, 101 Kasr El Aini St, Cairo 04 (tel: 355-7952).

Ministry of Trade and Supply, 99 Kasr El Aini St, Cairo 04 (tel: 355-0360; fax: 354-4973; e-mail: msit@idsx.gov.eg).

Ministry of Transport, Communications and Civil Aviation, 105 Kasr El Aini Street, Cairo (tel: 354-3623; fax: 355-5564; e-mail: garb@idsc.gov.eg).

Ministry of Wakfs, 5 Sabri Abou Alam St, Cairo (tel: 392-6305).

Prime Minister's Office, 1 Magles El Shaab St, Lazoughli Square, Cairo 04 (tel: 354-7376; fax: 355-8048).

President's Office, Abdin palace, CAI 06 (tel: 391-0130).

Other useful addresses

Arab League, The Arab League Building, Corniche El Nil, Cairo (tel: 393-4499; fax: 775-626).

Arab Organisation for Industrialisation, 2D Abassiya Square, PO Box 770 (tel: 823-377; fax: 826-010).

Arab Republic of Egypt National Telecommunications Organisation (ARENTO), 26 Ramses Street (tel: 760-333; fax: 771-306).

Cabinet Office, 1 Maglis El Shaab Street, Lazoughli Square, CAI 04 (tel: 354-7376; fax: 355-8048).

Cairo Regional Center for International Commercial Arbitration, 3 Aboul Feda Street, Zamalek, Cairo (tel: 340-1330; fax: 340-1336).

Cairo Stock Exchange, 4 Sharia esh-Sherifein, Cairo (tel: 392-1402; fax: 392-8526).

Capital Market Authority, 20 Emad El Din Street, Sixth Floor, Downtown (tel: 777-774; fax: 755-339).

Central Agency for Public Mobilisation and Statistics (CAPMAS), Saleh Salem Street, Nasr City, Cairo (tel: 603-717; fax: 604-099).

Commission of the European Communities Delegation in Egypt, 6 Ibn Zenki Street, Zamalek, Cairo (tel: 340-8388; fax: 340-0385).

Customs Information Centre, 4 El Tayaran Street, Nasr City (tel: 260-5711; fax: 261-2672).

Egyptian Electricity Authority, Abassia, Cairo (tel: 261-6537; fax: 261-6512, 401-1630).

Egyptian General Petroleum Corporation (EGPCC), 4 Palestine Street, Fourth Sector, new Maadi (tel: 353-1438; fax: 353-1457).

Egyptian Radio and Television Corporation (ERTC), Radio and TV Building, Sharia Maspiro, Corniche en-Nil, PO Box 504, Cairo (tel: 749-508; fax: 746-989).

General Authority for Control of Imports and Exports, Atlas Building El Sheikh Maarouf and Ramses Streets (tel: 574-2830; fax: 766-971).

General Authority for Investment and Free Zones, 8 Sharia Adly, PO Box 1007, Cairo (tel: 390-6804).

General Organisation for Industrialisation (GOFI) 6 Khali Agha Street, Garden City (tel: 355-7005; fax: 354-4984).

General Organisation for International Exhibitions and Fairs (GOIEF), Exhibition Ground, Nasr City, Cairo (tel: 260-7811; fax: 260-7845, 260-7848).

Internatinal Monetary Fund (IMF), 31 Kasr El Nil Street, Central Bank, Cairo (tel: 392-4257; fax: 351-7137).

Local Governorates, El-Islah El-Zerai Building, 10th Floor, 4 Nadi El-Seid Street, Dokki (tel: 349-4770; fax: 349-7788).

Sales Tax Authority, 4 El Tayaran Street, nasr City (tel: 260-7500; fax: 260-7501).

Social Fund for Development (SFD), Hussein Hegazy and El Aini Streets, Cairo (tel: 354-8339; fax: 355-0628).

Taxation Authority, 5 Hussein Hegazi Street (tel: 355-7784; fax: 355-5438).

Internet sites

Africa Business Network: http://www.ifc.org/abn

AllAfrica.com: http://allafrica.com

Africa Online: http://www.africaonline.com

Arab Bank: http://www.arabbank.com

Egypt Business Directory: http://www.telefax.com.eg/default.htm

Egypt corporate information: http://www.corporateinformation.com/egcorp.html

Egypt economic indicators: http://www.economic.idsc.gov.eg/

Egypt www index: http://ce.eng.usf.edu/pharos/

KEY FACTS

Official name: República de Guinea Ecuatorial (The Republic of Equatorial Guinea)

Head of State: President Teodoro Obiang Nguema Mbasogo (PDGE) (since 1989; re-elected 1996; re-elected Dec 2002 with 97.1 per cent of the vote; opposition parties withdrew their candidates about two hours after voting started, citing irregularities)

Head of government: Prime Minister Cándido Muatetema Rivas (PDGE) (appointed by the President, 26 Feb 2001)

Ruling party: Partido Democrático da Guinea Ecuatorial (PDGE) (Democratic Party of Equatorial Guinea) (re-elected Mar 1999)

Area: 28,051 square km

Population: 522,000 (2001)

Capital: Malabo

Official language: Spanish

Currency: CFA franc (CFAf) = 100 centimes (Communauté Financière Africaine (African Financial Community) franc)

Exchange rate: CFAf629.73 per US$ (Jan 2003); CFAf655.95 per euro (pegged from Jan 1999)

GDP per capita: US$3,448 (2001)

GDP real growth: 46.50% (2001)

Inflation: 12.00% (2001)

Oil production: 181,000 bpd (2001)

Balance of trade: US$779.00 million (2001)

Foreign debt: US$259.00 million (2001)

For the latest Key Facts, go to www.worldinformation.com

Equatorial Guinea

Nils P Mork

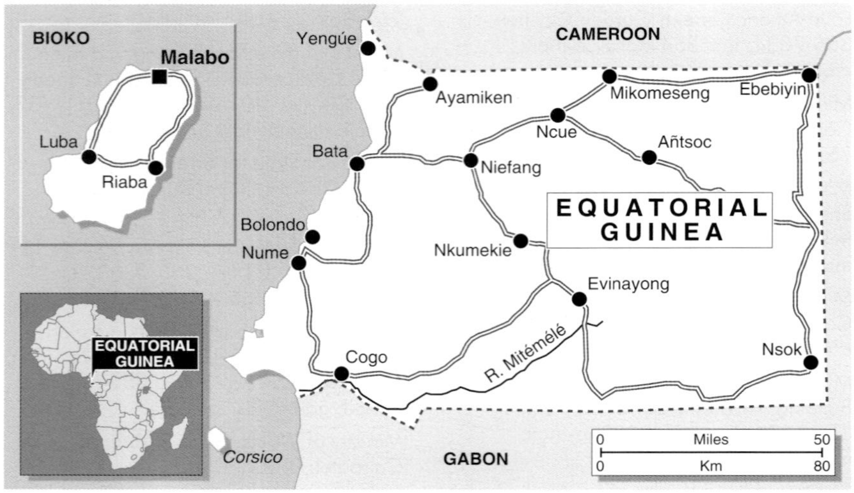

Equatorial Guinea's lasting social problems persisted, despite sky-rocketing growth rates and new oil finds, in April 2002. In October 2001, the government of President Teodoro Obiang Nguema asked oil companies and the IMF for help and expertise in diversifying the country's economy to the benefit of the people. Obiang simultaneously clamped down on opposition politicians after the UN's human rights special representative withdrew in May 2002 and censored what remained of a free press.

Authoritarian stability

Equatorial Guinea remains a democracy in name only. In reality, politics in the former Spanish colony bear more semblance to a family affair. President Obiang and his extended family hold the most important ministerial posts. Obiang's party, the Partido Democrático da Guinea Ecuatorial (PDGE) (Democratic Party of Equatorial Guinea), is dominated by the president's clan, the Mongomo. Obiang also controls the judiciary and the parliament.

The PDGE attempts to control all aspects of national life. With widespread censorship, a gagged press and much of the rest of the media under the control of the president's son, MP Teodoro Nguema Obiang Jr, it is a small wonder that much of the national opposition prefers to lobby from exile in Spain.

The December 2002 presidential election did not lead to the succession of one of Obiang's two sons as analysts had predicated. President Obiang was re-elected with 100 per cent of the vote. Obiang's high support was due to four opposition presidential candidates withdrawing at the last minute, blaming irregularities in the polling. Indeed, earlier elections, presidential in 1996 and parliamentary in 1999, were widely seen as severely flawed.

The existing domestic opposition was heavily clamped down upon in March and April 2002. In a move that outraged international human rights activists, security agents arrested leading figures in all the three main opposition groups, the Convergencia para la Democracia Social (CPDS) (Convergence for a Social Democracy), the Fuerza Democrática Republicana (FDR) (Democratic Republican Front) and the Unión Popular (UP) (Popular Union). The arrested activists were reportedly accused of plotting a <I>coup d'état<WO>, but no evidence was produced. Subsequent confessions were criticised for having been given during torture. Human rights abuses continue to be all too prevalent in Obiang's Guinea.

Petroleum and human rights

During the repression and arrests in April 2002, the UN Commission on Human Rights (UNCHR) announced an end to the mandate of the special representative for Equatorial Guinea, a mandate that has been reappointed every year since 1979. Opposition politicians, international observers and the special representative himself, Gustavo Gall, all delivered outraged criticism to what they saw as political meddling by Nigeria, whose proposal it was to end the mandate. Nigeria and Equatorial Guinea had resolved a territorial border dispute earlier in April 2002 and share plans for extensive petroleum developments in the area. Without a UNCHR mandate in the country, the regime enjoys a near impunity for further human rights abuses.

The loss of the UNCHR special representative was followed by further arrests of opposition leaders in Mongomo and Bata in May 2002 and rumours of widespread torture were apparently verified by alleged coup plotters in court, some in obviously impaired physical condition. Nonetheless, trials held in the capital of Malabo in June 2002 handed down sentences of up to 20 years to the 68 accused, among which were substantial parts of the opposition leadership. Perhaps as a result of such intimidation, reports in July 2002 stated that the numbers of opposition politicians defecting to the ruling PDGE has increased.

The Kuwait of Africa

Equatorial Guinea is often hailed as the Kuwait of Africa. Indeed, the country has seen a remarkable economic transformation since the 1980s, when it eked out a living from its traditional agricultural sector. In 2001–02, the small nation pumped out 181,000 barrels of crude oil per day (bpd), and oil-induced growth was reportedly around 50 per cent in 2001. Amarada Hess, the US petroleum company, announced substantial new finds in April 2002 and there seems to be no reason to expect the boom to subside in the near future. Petroleum output growth of 140 per cent has been predicted until 2005, the highest on the continent.

The growth has yet to produce wider, cross-sectoral development. There are still few linkages between petroleum and other sectors of the economy. There is also a concern that the wealth will not benefit others than the ruling political and economic elite. Observers warn of the fate of Nigeria, still impoverished decades after selling its first barrel.

Even at the current high rates of growth, Equatorial Guinea faces a steady balance-of-payments deficit, as the petroleum boom is being spent on imports rather than the development of domestic production capacities. The same stagnation is apparent in terms of debt service, obligations of which the country still struggles to meet.

The reality of these failures is that infant mortality remains high, that only 43 per cent have access to safe drinking water, and that the country's HIV infection rates are still growing. In addition, reports were issued in June 2002 that the increased oil production might have disastrous ecological effects, and pointed out that the government does not consult with any environmental control agencies.

Against this backdrop, in October 2001 Equatorial Guinea asked the IMF for assistance and expertise in shaping policies towards human development and poverty reduction programmes. In May 2002, the president also urged the international oil companies operating in the country to increase their contributions to the overall economy of the country, especially infrastructure.

Outlook

Equatorial Guinea is at the threshold of oil wealth that may indeed compare to that of Kuwait. Current predictions state that the boom has only just started, with production capacity yet to be maximised. There is a pressing need to foster stronger links between the petroleum sector and the overall national economy, as well as to renew past commitments to economic reform. There are already signs of a struggle for the succession after the ageing president, but it remains uncertain if a change of leadership will include a change in policies. The only realistic way to safeguard prolonged stability in Equatorial Guinea is the institutionalisation of democracy and transparent governance. Such hopes currently seem faint.

Risk assessment

Economic	Satisfactory
Political	Poor
Regional stability	Satisfactory

COUNTRY PROFILE

Historical profile

1470 The island of Anobon was first visited by the Portuguese, who subsequently settled it and the other islands in the Gulf of Guinea, including Bioko (formerly Fernando Pó).

During the eighteenth century, Portugal exchanged Bioko and its other possessions in the region with Spain.

Bioko became an important slave-trading base for several European nations during the nineteenth century; the mainland enclave remained relatively unexplored by the Spanish until the 1920s.

1968 Equatorial Guinea was granted independence from Spain in October. Macias Nguema became president. During Nguema's period in power, the country's population fell to around one-third of pre-independence levels.

1979 Teodoro Obiang Nguema Mbasogo seized power in a coup in August and established the ruling Supreme Military Council (composed of both military and civilians since December 1981).

KEY INDICATORS — Equatorial Guinea

	Unit	1996	1997	1998	1999	2000
Population	m	0.41	0.42	0.43	0.44	0.46
Gross domestic product (GDP)	US$bn	0.23	0.29	0.36	0.92	1.60
GDP per capita	US$	561	691	837	2,091	3,478
GDP real growth	%	29.1	71.2	22.0	50.1	18.1
Inflation	%	6.0	3.0	3.0	6.5	6.0
Oil output	'000 bpd	20.0	65.0	90.0	100.0	113.0
Exports (fob) (goods)	US$m	175.3	498.0	461.0	615.0	767.0
Imports (fob) (goods)	US$m	0.0	0.0	0.0	93.0	170.0
Imports (cif)	US$m	292.0	353.0	434.0	0.0	0.0
Balance of trade	US$m	-116.7	145.0	26.5	522.0	597.0
Current account	US$m	-344.0	-189.0	-374.0	-223.0	-240.0
Total reserves minus gold	US$m	0.5	4.9	0.8	3.4	23.0
Foreign exchange	US$m	0.5	4.9	0.8	3.4	22.9
Exchange rate	per US$	511.55	583.67	589.95	615.70	711.98

1984 and 1989 President Obiang was re-elected unopposed.
1992 In January the President dismissed the government as a prelude to the introduction of multi-partyism.
1993 In August the first multi-party elections were held with the President's Partido Democrático de Guinea Ecuatorial (PDGE) (Democratic Party of Equatorial Guinea) taking 68 of the 80 seats; the main opposition parties boycotted the election.
1996 In the presidential election held on 25 February, President Obiang gained 99.2 per cent of the vote. The election was described as a farce by international observers.
1999 PDGE won 75 seats in the first fully contested parliamentary elections held in March. Opposition parties alleged fraud and refused to take up their seats in parliament.
2000 Equatorial Guinea and Nigeria signed a treaty in September agreeing to the demarcation of their maritime border.
2001 In February, the President accepted the resignation of Angel Serafin Seriche Dougan and his government and appointed Cándido Muatetema Rivas prime minister. A treaty establishing the Gulf of Guinea Commisssion was signed by five of the seven member states in July (Gabon, Congo, São Tomé and Príncipe, Nigeria and Angola). Equatorial Guinea did not sign, for which no reason was given.
2002 In March and April, the government clamped down on members of the opposition, leading to accusations of mass human rights abuse.

Political structure

Constitution

Constitutional amendments, approved by referendum in August 1982, provided for the holding of presidential and legislative elections in the course of a gradual transition from military to civilian rule.
A new constitution designed to usher in multi-party politics was adopted on 16 November 1991, again by referendum. It provided for the separation of powers between the president and prime minister and gave the president protection from impeachment, prosecution and subpoena before, during and after his term of office.

Form of state

Republic

The executive

The president is elected for a seven-year term by universal suffrage. The prime minister is appointed by the president.

National legislature

There is an 80-seat Cámara de Representantes del Pueblo (legislative assembly) elected for six years.

Legal system

Although the constitution provides for judicial independence, the judicial system does not appear to operate independently, thus undermining basic rights. Judges are appointed, transferred and dismissed for political reasons.

Last elections

March 1999 (parliamentary); 25 February 1996 (presidential).

Next elections

2003 (presidential); 2004 (parliamentary).

Political parties

In January 1992 the president promulgated a bill authorising the formation of political parties.

Ruling party

Partido Democrático da Guinea Ecuatorial (PDGE) (Democratic Party of Equatorial Guinea) (re-elected Mar 1999)

Main opposition party

Unión Popular (UP) (Popular Union); Convergencia para la Democracia Social (CPDS) (Convergence for a Social Democracy); Fuerza Democratiza Republicana (FDR) (Democratic Republican Front).

Population

460,000 (2000)
Annual population growth rate: 2.6 per cent (1994–2000). Approximately 43 per cent of the total population is under 15 years.
Population density: 16 inhabitants per square km. Urban population 48 per cent (1994–2000).
Despite the arrival of oil revenue, the majority of the population remains very poor, with electricity and clean running water considered luxuries.

Ethnic make-up

The mainland region of Rio Muni has 75 per cent of the population, 90 per cent of whom belong to the Fang ethnic group. The island province of Bioko consists of Bubis, Fangs and Creoles.

Religions

Christianity (98 per cent, mostly Roman Catholic), traditional beliefs (2 per cent).

Education

In 2000, the UN estimated that adult illiteracy rates for men and women aged 15 years or over stood at 7.5 per cent and 25.6 per cent respectively. The number of pupils per primary school teacher is typically 41.
Public expenditure on education typically amounted to 2.3 per cent of annual gross national income between 1994 and 1997 according to the latest World Bank estimates.

Health

World Bank estimates during the period 1994 and 2000 showed that the average life expectancy was 51 years and the infant mortality rate stood at 104 per 1,000 live births. World Bank surveys in 2000 showed that 43 per cent of the population had access to improved water sources.
There are an estimated 1,100 people living with HIV/AIDS in Equatorial Guinea – less than 100 are under the age of 15 (2000). With infection rates at around 0.5 per cent of the adult population, Equatorial Guinea has so far escaped much of the African pandemic. However, with the government's distinct inability to formulate an AIDS strategy owing to its general disinterest in the problem, HIV/AIDS is likely to become a problem in the near future.

Welfare

Welfare conditions in the country are appalling with limited access to primary health care, education and job opportunities. The minimum monthly wage is approximately CFAf27,500 (US$43) and it does not provide a decent standard of living for a worker and family. Underage youth perform both family farm work and street vending. The government does not enforce the legal minimum age for child employment strictly.
The security forces continue to harass civilians and serious political dissidents, imprisoning, torturing and killing opponents in all parts of the country. The Amnesty International reported in 2002 that human rights conditions in the country are alarming amid heavy drug trafficking.

Main cities

Malabo (capital, on island of Bioko, estimated population 52,000), Bata (Rio Muni), Mongomo.
In June 2000, it was announced that the administrative capital is temporarily being moved from Malabo to Bata. Malabo will remain the constitutionally recognised capital.

Languages spoken

Fang, Bubi and Creole are spoken.

Official language/s

Spanish

Media

Equatorial Guinea is a multi-party state with guaranteed freedom of the press. However, the government continues to use military courts, repressive laws and arbitrary arrests and prosecutions to restrict political freedom and civil rights. The rights to freedom of opinion, expression, sharing and publication of information are severely restricted, contrary to international standards.

Press

The Convergencia para la Democracia Social (CPDS) (Convergence for a Social Democracy), an opposition political party which was officially recognised in 1993, publishes *La Verdad*, a review issued two or three times a year. The AFP - Equatorial Guinea, a French news agency (http.//www.wash.afp.com/english/home) is probably the most regular provider of news from Equatorial Guinea, with several articles a week. Other Spanish-language newspapers include *La Diaspora* and *Noticias de Guinea Ecuatorial*. The *Periódico en Español en Guinea Ecuatorial* published in Spanish, has its editorial offices in Germany, but its area of coverage is the Republic of Equatorial Guinea.

Periodicals: *La Diaspora* (Spanish) has a new edition every second month.

Broadcasting

Radio: Two radio stations (one commercial) broadcast in Spanish and local African languages.

Television: There is a limited television service.

Economy

Government officials believe the oil industry has the capacity to transform Equatorial Guinea into an African Kuwait. However, the European Union and World Bank have suspended their involvement in the country and the IMF's relations with the government remain at an impasse. Consequently, the government's growth figures of between 50–70 per cent during the late 1990s are difficult to prove. Independent analysts put GDP growth at 18.1 per cent in 2000, compared to the official figure of 48.2 per cent. Even the more objective independent figures show extraordinary growth, which is spurred on entirely by oil production. Meanwhile, consumer price inflation is relatively low at around 6 per cent, although official figures suggest rates of 3 per cent for every year since 1997.

Buoyed by oil revenue, the government feels confident enough to dismiss the role of international financial institutions, which once kept the country afloat with substantial external financing. Before oil production came on stream, external aid accounted for about 25 per cent of GDP. The reduction in foreign aid has largely been compensated by the country's considerable oil revenues.

Foreign oil companies – particularly ExxonMobil and TotalFinaElf – are turning a blind eye to Obiang's corrupt dictatorship, which has given them open access to one of the world's largest oil reserves. Meanwhile, the large numbers of poor people who live under his dictatorship endure increasing hardship.

Other than the oil sector, Equatorial Guinea's economy is underdeveloped. Equatorial Guinea is rich in timber, fishing and agricultural land and there is significant room for expansion in all these areas. However, in the past Obiang has curtailed the fishing industry in fear that fishing boats might allow people to flee his regime. The cocoa industry is troubled by falling world prices and export revenues from the commodity are gradually falling.

External trade

Exports

Principal exports are oil, timber and cocoa.

Main destinations: Spain (typically 34 per cent of total), Japan (23 per cent), Netherlands (11 per cent), US (11 per cent).

Imports

Principal imports are capital goods fuel, energy, foodstuffs, petroleum products, transport equipment.

Main sources: Cameroon (typically 36 per cent of total), Spain (22 per cent), France (13 per cent), Netherlands (6 per cent).

Agriculture

Agriculture accounted for 7 per cent of GDP in 2000, down from 12.8 per cent in 1999, and employed 70 per cent of the workforce. The sector grew by 9.4 per cent in 2000, down from 9.9 per cent the previous year.

Farming

The main cash crop on Bioko is cocoa and Rio Muni also produces timber and coffee for export.

Main food crops are cassava, sweet potatoes, bananas, palm oil/kernels.

Annual cocoa production has declined and the industry is affected by declining prices. Livestock is raised.

Fishing

Fishing is important.

Forestry

There are 1.3 million hectares of forest land. Average annual production totals 811,000 cu metres of timber.

Industry and manufacturing

The industrial sector contributed 88 per cent to GDP in 2000, up from 80 per cent in 1999, and employed 5 per cent of the workforce. In 2000, the sector grew by 20.1 per cent, down from 61 per cent in 1999. The manufacturing sector is very small, contributing only 1.9 per cent to GDP in 2000.

Industry is underdeveloped, with activity centred on very small-scale food and timber processing.

The traditional industries of cocoa and coffee suffer from a lack of investment and low world prices.

Mining

Activity is limited to exploitation of alluvial gold. There are also reserves of copper, iron ore, uranium, tantalum and manganese, but all are judged to be uneconomic for exploitation.

Hydrocarbons

The hydrocarbons sector accounts for more than 60 per cent of GDP and 90 per cent of exports.

Oil

Oil is the country's most important foreign exchange earner and Equatorial Guinea has become one of the largest oil producers in the Gulf of Guinea. Proven oil reserves are 12 million barrels.

By 2001, oil production reached 181,000bpd, up 60.1 per cent on the 2000 output, and has the potential to increase to 300,000bpd by 2005. With political stability ensured by the police state, a liberal investment framework, few regulations and a favourable Production Sharing Contract (PSC) (in which the government has a 20 per cent stake), oil companies are flocking to the small west African state.

Arguments raged between Equatorial Guinea and its neighbours – Nigeria, Cameroon and São Tomé and Principé – over the demarcation of maritime borders, which could determine the share each country has in the massive Gulf of Guinea oil reserves. Nigeria disputed Equatorial Guinea's sole ownership of the large Zafiro oil field, which it claimed extended into its territory. In September 2000, the two countries signed a pact that delineated maritime borders in which Nigeria recognised Equatorial Guinea's sovereignty over the Zafiro field.

Gas

Gas reserves are estimated at 36.6 billion cubic metres.

In October 2000, CMS Energy and its partners in the Alba gas field (Samedin, Globex International and the government) commissioned an extension to its activities in the field which increased production capacity from 2.5 million cubic metres per day (cu m/d) to 6.3 million cu m/d. Around 3.4 million cu m/d is destined for AMPCO plant once it is complete. Condensate production was also increased from 6,700bpd to 14,500bpd by the beginning of 2001 as a result of the development. Natural gas liquid production increased to 1,800bpd. The project includes a 32km pipeline from the Alba field to Bioko.

There is a possibility for a further increase in production in the Alba field with the discovery of an offshore find near Bioko. In its initial test drilling it produced over 500,000 cu m/d of natural gas and 2,100bpd of condensate.

Banking

Central bank

Banque des Etats de l'Afrique Centrale

Main financial centre

Malabo

Time

GMT plus one hour

Geography
Equatorial Guinea consists of the islands of Bioko, Corisco, Great Elobey, Small Elobey and Annobón and the mainland territory of Río Muni (Mbini) on the west coast of Africa. Cameroon lies to the north and Gabon to the east and south of Río Muni.
The mainland region of Rio Muni covers 26,000 square km while the island province of Bioko, which hosts the capital Malabo, is 2,000 square km. The island of Pagalu (17 square km), 600km south-east of Bioko, and three rocky outcrops – Elobey Grande, Elobey Chico and Corisco – close to the mainland, are all part of Rio Muni region.

Climate
Equatorial with heavy rainfall for most of the year except for slightly drier period from December–February. The mainland Rio Muni is drier and cooler than Bioko. Average temperature 26 degrees Celsius throughout the year, and generally very humid.

Entry requirements
Passports
Required by all.
Visa
Required by all except nationals of the US.
Currency advice/regulations
Visitors for business and tourism must declare any currency in excess of CFAf50,000 (approximately US$75) upon arrival. Travellers who fail to declare excess currency, risk forfeiture of any amount over the CFAf50,000 limit upon departure.
Cash in CFA francs is usually the only form of payment accepted in Equatorial Guinea.

Health (for visitors)
Mandatory precautions
A yellow fever vaccination certificate is required if arriving from an infected area.
Advisable precautions
Vaccinations against hepatitis A and B, tetanus, diphtheria, polio, typhoid and meningitis are strongly recommended. Malaria prophylaxis is advisable as risk exists throughout the country. There is a rabies risk. Water precautions should be taken. Medical facilities are limited so it is advisable to pack any special medications required.

Hotels
Accommodation is very limited but there are hotels in Malabo and Bata. It is essential to book a hotel before travelling, preferably through local business contacts. Food is rarely available at the Bata Hotel and, in Malabo, air-conditioning is available only in some rooms in the Apartotel Impala.
When there is no service charge, gratuities are around 10 to 15 per cent.

Public holidays
Fixed dates
1 Jan (New Year), 5 Mar (Independence Day), 1 May, 25 May, 10 Dec (Human Rights' Day), 25 Dec.
Variable dates
Good Friday, Easter Sunday and Monday.

Working hours
Banking
Mon–Sat: 0800–1200.
Business
Mon–Fri: 0800–1500.
Government
Mon–Fri: 0830–1500; Sat: 0830–1200, (alternate Sat) 1000–1200.
Shops
(Mon–Sat) 0800–1300 and 1600–1900.

Telecommunications
Telephone/fax
Dialling code for Equatorial Guinea: IDD access code + 240 followed by area code (8 for Bata, 9 for Malabo), followed by subscriber's number.

Electricity supply
220 V AC, 50 cycles

Social customs/useful tips
Corruption is endemic. Special permits from the Ministry of Information and Tourism are required for most photography, including the presidential palace and its environs, military installations, government buildings, airports, harbours and other areas.

Getting there
Air
There are three direct flights a week from Europe (Iberia).
International airport/s: Malabo international (SSG), 7km from the capital city on the island of Malabo.
Bata international, 7km from city, on the mainland of Equatorial Guinea, has recently been modernised.
Surface
Road: There is access by semi-surfaced road from Gabon to Mbini and Bata, although this route is not generally recommended.
Main port/s: Malabo, Bata, Luba, Mbini and Kogo.

Getting about
National transport
Air: Air Afrique Affaires, a private company based in Douala, Cameroon, operates air service between Bata and Malabo.
Road: On Bioko a surfaced road links major towns in the north. On mainland Rio Muni a surfaced road links Bata with Mbini and a partly surfaced road links Bata with Ebebiyin (near Gabon border). Other roads are unsurfaced and can be difficult.
Water: There is a weekly boat service between Malabo and Bata.

BUSINESS DIRECTORY

Telephone area codes
Dialling code for Equatorial Guinea: IDD access code +240 followed by area code (8 for Bata, 9 for Malabo), followed by subscriber's number.

Banking
Banco de Crédito y Desarrollo (credit and development bank), 1 Avenida de la Libertad, PO Box 39, Malabo (tel: 2146).

Banco Exterior de Guinea Ecuatorial, Carretera de Aeropuerto, Malabo (tel: 2001).

Banque Internationale pour l'Afrique Occidentale, Calle de Argelia No 6, PO Box 686, Malabo (tel: 2367, 2887).

Caisse Commune d'Epargne et d'Investissement en Guinée Equatoriale (CCEI-GE); PO Box 428, Malabo (tel: 2003, 2910; fax: 3311).

Société Générale de Banque GE; PO Box 686, Calle Argelia, Malabo (tel: 3337; fax: 2743).

Central bank
Banque des Etats de l'Afrique Centrale (BEAC), Services Centraux, PO Box 1917, Yaoundé, Cameroon (tel: (237)222-505); Direction Nationale, Malabo (tel: 2011).

Other useful addresses
Comite Sindical de Cacao (cocoa growers' organisation), Bioko.

Equatorial Guinea Embassy (USA), 2020 16th Street, NW, Washington DC 20009 (tel: (001-202)518-5700; fax: (001-202)518-5252).

Dirección General de Correos y Telecomunicaciones, Malabo.

Empresa Estatal de Comercio Interior y Exterior, Malabo.

Empresa General de Industria y Comercio (EGISCA), Malabo.

Empresa Guineano-Española de Petróleos (Gepsa), Malabo.

Internet sites
Africa Business Network: http://www.ifc.org/abn

AllAfrica.com: http://allafrica.com

African Development Bank: http://www.afdb.org

Africa Online: http://www.africaonline.com

Mbendi AfroPaedia (information on companies, countries, industries and stock exchanges in Africa): http://mbendi.co.za

Eritrea

Nicholas Awde & Fred J Hill

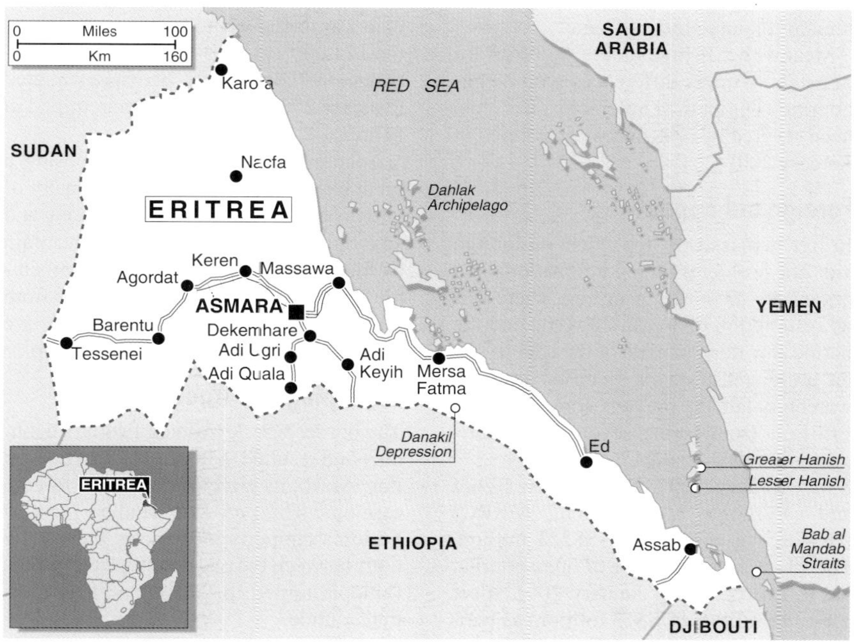

Eritrea's first years of independence, gained from Ethiopia in 1993, have been fraught with political, economic and social upheaval. A border dispute with Ethiopia ignited a two-year war between the two countries in 1998, leaving the Eritrean economy and social fabric in shreds. During 2001 and 2002, the peace process, following a ceasefire brokered in June 2000, was decidedly bumpy owing to the marked lack of goodwill and co-operation on both sides, which on several occasions hampered efforts on the part of the UN Mission in Ethiopia and Eritrea (UNMEE). Nevertheless, at the end of 2002, the peace process was still on track.

Political setback

In September 2001, optimism for political and economic stability suffered a major setback after President Issaias Afwerki ordered a wave of arrests of dissidents three months before the country's first elections since independence were due to take place.

The elections, scheduled for December 2001, were subsequently postponed indefinitely. Not that there were great hopes for the democratic process – the elections had been dismissed long before as a foregone conclusion due to the absence of any opposition parties to mount an effective challenge to Afwerki's ruling People's Front for Democracy and Justice (PFDJ). Nevertheless, their cancellation together with the crackdown, constituted a major failure by the government to present itself, at home and internationally, as a credible force for positive change.

Those detained without formal charges included scores of politicians, journalists, members of opposition groups and students. Also arrested were 11 senior PFDJ representatives – all active members of a reform group known as G-15. The group was responsible for the publication of an open letter addressed to the president, accusing him of acting illegally and unconstitutionally. Afwerki also targeted the press, closing all but the state-run paper *Hadas*.

This brought condemnation by the EU, to which the Eritrean government responded by ordering the expulsion of the Italian ambassador Antonio Bandini – also dean of the EU Mission in Eritrea –

KEY FACTS

Official name: Hagere Ertra (The State of Eritrea)

Head of State: President Issaias Afwerki (assumed power May 1991; elected President by National Assembly 8 Jun 1993)

Ruling party: People's Front for Democracy and Justice (PFDJ) (formerly the Eritrean People's Liberation Front (EPLF))

Area: 125,000 square km

Population: 4.20 million (2001)

Capital: Asmara

Official language: There is no official language but the working languages are Tigrinya/Arabic/English.

Currency: Nakfa (Nk) = 100 cents

Exchange rate: Nk8.30 per US$ (Jan 2003)

GDP per capita: US$144 (2001)

GDP real growth: 3.00% (2001)

Inflation: 15.00% (2001)

Balance of trade: -US$470.00 million (2001)

Foreign debt: US$415.00 million (2001)

Annual FDI: US$12.00 million (2001)

For the latest Key Facts, go to www.worldinformation.com

after he publicly voiced his concerns. The EU and individual European countries were quick to denounce the events and ordered their diplomats home for consultation. Although they subsequently returned in November 2001, Bandini was conspicuous by his absence.

An uneasy peace

Relations between Eritrea and Ethiopia remained rocky throughout 2001 and 2002 as the two sides engaged in repeated rounds of accusations and counter-accusations. The peace process looked perilously close to collapse.

In April 2001, after months of delay, peacekeeping troops moved into a specially created Temporary Security Zone (TSZ), marking a crucial step in the implementation of the peace agreement brokered in Algiers in June 2000 and overseen by UNMEE. The TSZ, proposed in December 2000, was intended to create a buffer zone between the two. In September 2002, as a result of the progress made, the UNMEE mandate was extended until 15 March 2003.

Despite the establishment of the TSZ tensions failed to ease. In November 2001, Ethiopia accused Eritrea of deploying as many as 30,000 troops in the off-limits zone and went as far as accusing the UN of appeasing Eritrea. Subsequent UNMEE investigations found no evidence of such a deployment. In December, Eritrea accused Ethiopia of intensifying military activity and making increased incursions into Eritrea. Ethiopia responded with its own accusations that Eritrea was gunning for another war. In the event, UNMEE observers, who concluded that the TSZ had not been breached, did not back Eritrean claims.

In December 2001, both countries put their cases to the Boundary Commission at the Permanent Court of Arbitration, sitting in The Hague in the Netherlands. Both sides agreed to accept as binding the commission's decision. In April 2002, the commission issued its ruling. A 1,000km borderline was established between the two countries, although it remained unclear as to how Eritrea was to benefit from the decision. It is likely that hostilities and suspicions between the two countries will remain for some time to come.

Meanwhile, Eritrea took a step forward in patching up its differences with neighbouring Djibouti. Diplomatic ties had been severed in 1998 and were restored in January 2002.

Foreign aid appeal

Eritrea is massively dependent on foreign aid. The problems facing international aid organisations remain daunting. There was no resumption of war in 2001–02 and the period saw rains in parts of the country after prolonged drought. Evenso, the rains were too late to prevent some 800,000 Eritreans from facing severe food shortages and related hardships.

In February 2001, the Eritrean Relief and Refugee Commission (ERRC) launched an appeal for US$223 million. The EU is a major donor of humanitarian aid to Eritrea and in January 2001, it set aside 15 million (US$13 million) as part of a food aid programme and a further 7 million (US$6 million) in June as part of a wider programme to improve drinking water supplies, provide shelters and address the problem of landmines.

Ominously, the political crackdown in September led to the possibility of international financial assistance being substantially cut back, after Sweden, Holland and Norway took Eritrea off their list of top priority countries receiving aid. In January 2002, Denmark announced that as a result of the crackdown it was to phase out development aid, (although, it appeared, not humanitarian) to the country. In November 2002, the ERRC once again warned of a famine, claiming that up to 2.3 million Eritreans needed assistance.

Refugees flow in

The refugee problem is daunting. A major plan was under way to repatriate 90,000 of the 174,000 refugees living in Sudan. Between 1991 and 2002, it was estimated that over 250,000 refugees had returned to Eritrea.

Adapting to life in Eritrea is posing a great challenge for the refugees, many of whom had set roots in Sudan, working and studying there and who are now uncertain of finding a better life or indeed any employment prospects in Eritrea. Aside from transport, refugees wishing to return are eligible for practical and financial help.

Recouping lost trade

The border war devastated Eritrea's economy and resulted in the collapse of trade at Port Assab, its principal source of foreign earnings. The port had handled most of Ethiopia's imports and exports, but as relations between the two countries worsened, Ethiopia turned to Djibouti to handle its transit trade.

While the situation remained bleak, there were glimmers of hope when, in December 2001, Port Massawa handled the first substantial consignment of goods since war broke out with Ethiopia in 1998 – 15,000 tonnes of US-donated relief food under the auspices of the UN World Food Programme (WFP).

It was hoped that apart from helping relief operations, increased port activity would bring back desperately needed local employment. Frosty relations with Ethiopia meant that there were few signs that the country would win back its lost trade. Indeed, with Ethiopia facing famine in 2002–03, Eritrea offered its Red Sea ports in November 2002 for the transport of food aid destined to Ethiopia. Ethiopia declined Eritrea's offer, claiming that more aid was needed rather than more transportation access.

Outlook

The crackdown on political dissent and the postponement of the elections constitutes a major blow for the chances of democracy in Eritrea. Government claims that the country would not be in a position to hold elections until favourable conditions had been reached, especially with

KEY INDICATORS — Eritrea

	Unit	1996	1997	1998	1999	2000
Population	m	3.60	3.70	3.80	3.90	4.00
Gross domestic product (GDP)	US$bn	0.80	0.85	0.81	0.80	0.78
GDP per capita	US$	219	225	208	200	191
GDP real growth	%	6.8	7.9	4.0	0.0	6.5
Inflation	%	3.4	1.8	16.6	12.0	19.9
Exports (fob) (goods)	US$m	95.0	53.0	30.0	20.0	35.0
Imports (fob) (goods)	US$m	514.0	490.0	494.0	495.0	471.0
Balance of trade	US$m	-419.0	-447.0	-464.0	-475.0	-436.0
Current account	US$m	-104.0	-21.0	-216.0	-205.0	-107.0
Foreign debt	US$bn	0.1	0.1	0.1	0.2	0.3
Exchange rate	per US$	6.35	6.17	7.12	7.94	8.22

regard to peace with Ethiopia, offered little hope for elections in 2002.

Furthermore, relations with the international community, upon which so many of the country's people depend, have taken a severe battering. While there is no reliable data, the recent political upheavals came at a time when there were signs of a strengthening of the Eritrean economy amid decreased defence spending and falling inflation. Yet the crackdown is bound to have a negative impact on the country's precarious economy and thus affect GDP growth.

Only a momentous effort can turn around the situation to prevent the country from closing up to the outside world and facing a future of authoritarian government and, worse still, renewed war.

Risk assessment

Economic	Poor
Political	Poor
Regional stability	Poor/improving
Stock market	Poor

COUNTRY PROFILE

Historical profile

1890–1941 Under Italian rule. Eritrea first emerged as a political entity following the Italian occupation of the Red Sea port of Massawa and other coastal enclaves in the 1880s. In 1889, Italy signed the Treaty of Ucciali with the Ethiopian Emperor, Menelik, and in 1890, named the country Eritrea.
1941 The UK defeated Italy during the second world war and Eritrea became a British protectorate.
1952 UN-sanctioned federation with Ethiopia.
1962 Annexed to Ethiopia as a province under Emperor Haile Selassie.
1991 In May, the Eritrean People's Liberation Front (EPLF) overthrew Ethiopian Colonel Mengistu's forces and liberated the territory; Issaias Afwerki assumed power.
1993 In April, vote resulted in a virtually 100 per cent acceptance of independence.
1994 Eritrea achieved nationhood on 24 May. Afwerki was elected president by National Assembly in June.
1998 Eritrea and Ethiopia resumed border warfare in June. The World Court ruled in October that Yemen should have the Red Sea island of Greater Hanish, fought over in 1995 by Eritrea and Yemen, and in November it was announced that Eritrea would return it to Yemen.
2000 In November, UN peacekeepers opened a 1,000km ceasefire land corridor between Ethiopia and Eritrea. The two countries signed a peace deal in Algiers in December, ending the two-year war.
2001 In April, the UN established a buffer zone along the border of Ethiopia and Eritrea. In September, the UN Security Council extended the mandate of the UN Mission in Ethiopia and Eritrea (UNMEE) until 15 March 2002.
2002 In April, Eritrea and Ethiopia accepted a ruling, made by the Boundary Commission at Permanent Court of Arbitration of The Hague, on the border dispute. A new 1,000km boundary was established between the two countries.

Political structure

A transition period is in effect until pluralist elections.

Constitution

A new constitution was adopted in May 1997.
A 150-member National Transitional Council was set up, with 75 seats allocated to the People's Front for Democracy and Justice (PFDJ), 60 to the Constitutional Assembly and 15 to overseas Eritreans.
The president governs with the help of his 24-member Consultative Council. The Consultative Council is composed of ministers and regional governors.
There are six administrative regions, each with regional, sub-regional (55) and village administrations (651). The regions enjoy a degree of autonomy.

Next elections

2002 (legislative) (postponed)

Political parties

The ruling People's Front for Democracy and Justice (PFDJ) (formerly the Eritrean People's Liberation Front (EPLF)) is the only legal party.
The opposition is centred around the Eritrean National Pact Alliance.

Ruling party

People's Front for Democracy and Justice (PFDJ) (formerly the Eritrean People's Liberation Front (EPLF))

Population

4.0 million (2000)
Annual population growth rate: 2.7 per cent per annum (1994–2000). Approximately 44 per cent of the total population is under 15 years; 53 per cent 15–64; 3 per cent over 65.
Population density: 32 inhabitants per square km. Urban population: 19 per cent (1994–2000).

Ethnic make-up

There are nine ethno-linguistic groups.

Religions

Tigrigna-speaking Christians (mainly Orthodox), are the traditional inhabitants of the highlands, with some Protestant and Roman Catholic communities (49 per cent); Muslim communities of the western lowlands, northern highlands and east coast are 49 per cent. A small number of the population adhere to traditional beliefs.

Health

Average life expectancy at birth is around 46 years. An estimated 60,000 children were left cripped by the war, and another 45,000 orphaned. Infant mortality rate is 62 per 1,000 live births (2000). There is one doctor per 48,000 people.
The HIV infection rate is fairly high, affecting 2.87 per cent of the adult population or 49,000 adults aged 15–49 (2000). The main incidences are in Asmara, the capital, and Assab, the sea port, where prostitution is rife. Up to 30 per cent of prostitutes are HIV positive. Although the government has set up a strategy to combat AIDS, there is as yet no budget allocated to finance it.

Main cities

Asmara (capital, estimated population 400,000), Massawa (80,000), Assab (Aseb) (25,000).

Languages spoken

The principal language group in Eritrea is Afro-Asiatic; Arabic, Afar, Bilen, Hedareb, Kunama, Nara, Saho, Tigray and Tigrinya are spoken. English is rapidly becoming the language of business and is the medium of instruction at secondary schools and at university.

Official language

There is no official language but the working language is Tigrinya/Arabic.

Media

Press

The government strictly controls the media. In 2001, the government imposed a ban on all private newspapers operating in the country. The editors of private publications were arrested, including the editors of *MeQaleh*, a private newspaper published in Tigrinya Asmara and *Keste Debena*. The move was designed to suppress criticism of the ruling People's Front for Democracy and Justice (PFDJ) before the next legislative elections, scheduled for 2002.
Weeklies: The government publishes *Hadas Eritrea* (New Eritrea) twice weekly in Tigrinya and Arabic. In 2001, this was the only newspaper in operation in December 2001.
Business: Asmara Chamber of Commerce publishes *Chamber News* in Tigrinya and English, and *Business* a quarterly publication in Tigrinya, Arabic and English.
Periodicals: *The Mirror* is an independent English-language monthly magazine published in Asmara. *The Eritrean Edition* is a quarterly publication.

Broadcasting

Radio: Voice of the Broad Masses of Eritrea (Dimtsi Hafash) broadcasts in Arabic, Tigrinya, Tigre, Afar and Kunama.

Television: The government television station is ERI-TV that broadcasts in Arabic, Tigrinya and Tigre. Transmissions are limited to Asmara and surrounding areas.

Economy

The main problems affecting the Eritrean economy are inadequate and war-ravaged infrastructure, a lack of hard currency to pay for imports, a weak tax collection system and the predominance of unproductive subsistence agriculture.

Eritrea is still reeling from the war, which cost the economy up to US$800 million. A long period of violence on the borders has not helped attract investment or maintain macroeconomic stability. Inflation exceeded 20 per cent in 2001 while the economy nose-dived, with GDP contracting by 9 per cent. War and drought have weakened Eritrea's agricultural sector. Despite better rainfall in 2001, the country still faces severe food shortages.

The government wants to diversify the economy (70 per cent of Eritreans are farmers) so that it can afford to buy abroad what it cannot grow itself. Some 70 per cent of the population depends on foreign aid for all or part of its food supply. There is a danger that the foreign aid inflow may decrease after Sweden, Denmark, Norway and Holland announced cutbacks in aid after Afwerki's 2001 political crackdown. In the long term, Eritrea may benefit from the development of offshore oil, fishing and tourism industries. The country's economic future however, depends on its ability to eradicate major social and economic problems. These include widespread illiteracy, unemployment and poor levels of foreign investment. The borderline between Ethiopia and Eritrea, implemented after the Boundary Commission ruling in 2002, should encourage stability and allow Eritrea to focus on these problems.

External trade

Exports

Principal exports include textiles, footwear and basic household goods.

Main destinations: Somalia (typically 56 per cent of the total), Yemen (24 per cent), France (6 per cent), United Arab Emirates (5 per cent) and Ethiopia (4 per cent).

Imports

Principal non-petroleum imports include machinery and transport equipment (typically 37% of total) and basic manufactures.

Main sources: Import sources include Saudi Arabia (18 per cent of the total), France (10 per cent) China (10 per cent) Ethiopia (10 per cent) and Italy (6 per cent).

Agriculture

The agriculture sector accounted for 16 per cent of GDP in 2000 and employed 70 per cent of the workforce.

Approximately 3.5 per cent of the total land is cultivated. Land has been nationalised but leases to use the land are available.

Serious environmental degradation has been caused directly and indirectly by the war. Careful water management and conservation are essential.

Main crops are millet, sesame, maize, beans, wheat, sorghum, barley, vegetables, pulses, cotton, fruit, some coffee.

The Nile Basin Initiative (NBI) (launched by Dar Es Salaam, Tanzania, Burundi, Democratic Republic of Congo, Egypt, Ethiopia, Eritrea, Kenya, Rwanda, Sudan and Uganda) developed seven feasibility studies backed by US$140 million granted by the World Bank and donor governments in June 2001. It will also develop a parallel legal framework for shared water management.

Fishing

Fishing of sardines, anchovies, tuna, shark and mackerel is practised in the Red Sea on a very small scale. There are over 1,000 different species of fish off Eritrea's shores, with the stocks virtually untouched since the 1950s. The government believes there is potential for exporting 80,000 tonnes of fish annually.

Industry and manufacturing

The industrial sector contributed 27 per cent of GDP in 2001 and employed 10 per cent of the workforce.

The industrial base is traditionally centred on the production of glass, cement, footwear and canned goods, but most industrial enterprises were badly damaged during the war. All state-owned distribution and import/export enterprises established by the former government have been dissolved.

Major problems include outdated machinery and techniques, supply of energy, and the need for imports throughout the sector. With a lack of foreign currency and investment, industry is suffering from out-dated machinery and intermediary goods which need to be imported.

Mining

Fighting along the border regions disrupted mining activities, although exploration continued elsewhere in Eritrea. The Phelps Dodge Exploration Corporation conducted exploration on the Debarwa Copper-Zinc deposits and identified up to four million tonnes of reserves, including at least two million tonnes of mineable high-grade copper and a large amount of gold.

Gold-bearing seams exist in many of the igneous rocks forming the highlands of Eritrea. There are over 15 gold mines and a large number of prospects close to Asmara. The potential for new discoveries in the area is good. Substantial gold reserves have also been identified at Adi Nefas by LaSource Development SAS.

Artisanal mining production is estimated to produce around 550kg per year, although the Eritrean government with the support of the Norwegian government is assessing its environmental impact, including the amount of mercury which ends up in the soil and water supplies. The Australian Mining Company, Subsaharan Resources began exploring Eritrea for gold deposits in 2001. Eritrean Minerals Corporation (EMC) and Canadian Adulis Minerals Corporation completed gold exploration in four areas in Eritrea. This included diamond drilling.

The government is examining the possibility of developing industrial minerals such as silica, gypsum, salt, kaolin, feldspar and talc.

Despite Eritrea's mining potential, salt and marble remain the country's main exported minerals.

Hydrocarbons

Large offshore reserves of petroleum beneath the Red Sea and substantial natural gas reserves in the Danakil depression have yet to be effectively exploited.

In 1993 the government promulgated a liberal petroleum operation code, allowing companies a 25-year licence, renewal periods of 10 years and fiscal advantages. Several oil companies, including Mobil, Amoco and Hunt, have negotiated oil exploration contracts for the shallow waters off Eritrea's Red Sea coast.

Energy

Most electricity is generated by four thermal power stations.

Banking

Central bank

Bank of Eritrea

Time

GMT plus three hours

Geography

Eritrea extends inland from the Red Sea coast of eastern Africa. To the south, the country has a long frontier with Ethiopia, and a short frontier with Djibouti. Sudan lies to the north and west.

Climate

Coastal and lowland regions very hot and dry throughout the year. On the plateau which includes Asmara, the dry season runs from October–May with temperatures ranging from as low as 6 degrees Celsius (C) in December to 26 degrees C in March (light rain from February–April). Temperatures can fall sharply at night during the dry season.

The rainy season runs from June–September with average temperature 21 degrees C. Rainfall is less than 500mm per year in lowland areas, increasing to 1,000mm in the highlands. The temperature gradient is similarly steep: average annual temperatures range from 17 degrees C in the highlands to 30 degrees C in Massawa. The Danakil depression in the south-east, which is more than 130 metres below sea-level in places, experiences some of the highest temperatures recorded, frequently exceeding 50 degrees Celsius.

Entry requirements

Passports

Passports must be valid six months beyond intended length of stay.

Visa

Required by all except holders of passports issued to nationals of Kenya and Uganda. Transit passengers continuing their onward journey to another country within six hours of entering Eritrea.

Visas can be authorised to be issued at the airport.

British nationals should register on arrival at the British Consulate in Asmara (tel: 123-415).

Currency advice/regulations

There are no restrictions on import/export of local and foreign currency.

Health (for visitors)

Mandatory precautions

Yellow fever vaccination certificate required if travelling from an infected area.

Advisable precautions

Yellow fever, hepatitis A, tetanus, typhoid and polio vaccinations. Malaria prophylaxis recommended for visits outside Asmara. Water precautions should be taken. There is a rabies risk.

Hotels

Both Asmara and Massawa suffer from a severe shortage of hotel space; booking is advisable. Standards are low but are being improved. Service charge of 10 per cent and a small tip is usual in addition to service charge. Visitors are expected to pay bills at government-run hotels in US dollars or denominated traveller's cheques.

Credit cards

Credit cards are only accepted at a few outlets in Asmara.

Public holidays

Fixed dates

1 Jan (New Year's Day), 7 Jan (Lidet), 19 Jan (Epiphany), 8 Mar (International Women's Day), 1 May (Workers' Day), 24 May (Independence Day), 20 Jun (Martyrs' Day), 16 Jul (Mewlid Al Neby), 1 Sep (Anniversary of the Armed Struggle), 11 Sep (New Year), 27 Sep (Meskel), 25 Dec (Christmas).

Variable dates

Eid Al-Fitr, Eid Al-Adha, Easter.

Working hours

Banking

(Mon–Fri) 0800–1200, 1400–1800; (Sat) 0800–1230.

Business

Mon–Thu: 0700–1200, 1400–1800; Fri: 0700–1130, 1400–1800.

Shops

Mon–Fri: 0830–1300, 1430–2030.

Telecommunications

Telephone/fax

Dialling code for Eritrea: IDD access code + 291 followed by area code (1 for Asmara, 1 for Massawa).

The telephone system is undergoing modernisation. Calling out can be laborious as calls go through an operator.

Sending or receiving faxes can be difficult and is always expensive.

Eritrea is taking part in a regional programme designed to link 19 African countries to the world and to each other through a 39,000km marine fibre optic cable network. It is due to start operation in 2002.

Electricity supply

220V AC, 50 cycles.

Weights and measures

The metric system is in force.

Getting there

Air

Main airport: Asmara International (ASM), 6km south-west of Asmara.

Airport tax: International departures: Nk60 (nationals), US$12 (all others); domestic departures Nk15.

Surface

Road: The 300km road from Kassala in Sudan, to Tessenai, is largely unsurfaced. Many bridges were destroyed during civil war. Repairs and modernisation were being carried out in 2001.

Getting about

National transport

Road: Taxis are available for trips outside the city, but the fares are higher.

City transport

Taxis: The journey time by taxi from the Asmara International Airport to the city is 15 minutes. Taxi drivers do not expect a tip.

BUSINESS DIRECTORY

Telephone area codes

Dialling code for Eritrea: IDD access code +291 followed by area code (1 for Asmara, 1 for Massawa).

Chambers of Commerce

Asmara Chamber of Commerce, PO Box 856, Asmara (tel: 121-388; fax: 120-138).

Banking

Commercial Bank of Eritrea; PO Box 291, 212 Liberty Avenue, Asmara (tel: 116005, 121844-48 fax: 1248871, 121849).

Eritrean Development & Investment Bank; PO Box 1266, 29 Atse Yohannes Street, Asmara (tel: 123787, 114520, 126777).

Housing & Commerce Bank of Eritrea; PO Box 235, Bahti Meskerem Square, Asmara (tel: 120350 fax: 120401).

Central bank

Bank of Eritrea, PO Box 849, 21 Victory Avenue, Asmara (tel: 123033, 123036 fax: 123162, 12209).

Travel information

Egypt Air, Asmara (tel: 181-461, 181-040).

Ethiopian Airlines, Asmara (tel: 127-512, 126-827, 125-436).

Lufthansa, Asmara (tel: 182-707).

Saudi Airlines, Asmara (tel: 120-166).

Yemenia, Asmara (tel: 120-199).

Ministry of tourism

Ministry of Tourism, PO Box 1010, Asmara (tel: 126-997).

Other useful addresses

African Minerals Inc (AMI), PO Box 3508, Asmara (tel: 120-280, 120-030; fax: 120-332).

British Consulate, 27 Lorenzo Tazaz Street, PO Box 997, Asmara (tel: 123-415; fax: 127-230).

Communications and Postal Authority, PO Box 234, Asmara (tel: 112-900; fax: 110-938).

Eritrean Association in London, UK (tel: (0)181-748-0547).

Eritrean Business Licence Office, PO Box 3045, Asmara (tel: 114-809, 114-752; fax: 126-694).

Eritrean Embassy (USA), 1708 New Hampshire Avenue, NW, Washington DC 20009 (tel: 319-1991; fax: 319-1304).

Eritrean Shipping Lines, PO Box 1110, Asmara (tel: 120-308/359/257; fax: 120-331).

Grain Board of Eritrea, PO Box 1234, Asmara (tel: 115-624; fax: 120-586).

Investment Promotion Centre, Asmara (tel: 118-822, 118-124; fax: 124-293).

Massawa Municipal Library, PO Box 17, Massawa.

Ministry of Agriculture, PO Box 124, Asmara (tel: 181-499; fax: 181-415).

Ministry of Defence, PO Box 629, Asmara (tel: 113-349; fax: 114-920).

Ministry of Education, PO Box 5610, Asmara (tel: 113-044; fax: 113-866).

Ministry of Energy and Mines, PO Box 5285, Asmara (tel: 116-872; fax: 127-652); Department of Energy (fax: 112-339); Department of Mines (fax: 112-994).

Ministry of Finance and Development, PO Box 896, Asmara (tel: 113-633; fax: 117-947).

Ministry of Fisheries, PO Box 923, Asmara (tel: 114-271; fax: 112-185).

Ministry of Foreign Affairs, PO Box 190, Asmara (tel: 113-811; fax: 123-788).

Ministry of Health, PO Box 212, Asmara (tel: 112-877; fax: 112-899).

Ministry of Information, PO Box 242, Asmara (tel: 115-171; fax: 119-847).

Ministry of Justice, PO Box 241, Asmara (tel: 111-822).

Ministry of Local Government, PO Box 225, Asmara (tel: 113-006).

Ministry of Public Works, PO Box 841, Asmara (tel: 119-077).

Ministry of Tourism, PO Box 1010, Asmara (tel: 126-997).

Ministry of Trade and Industry, PO Box 1844, Asmara (tel: 118-386, 113-910; fax: 120-586).

Ministry of Transport and Communications, PO Box 204, Asmara (tel: 110-444; fax: 127-048).

Prima Eritrea Oil Company, Asmara (tel: 120-050; fax: 120-099).

Red Sea Trading Corporation (import/export services operated by the PFDJ), 29/31 Ras Alula Street, PO Box 332, Asmara (tel: 127-846; fax: 124-353).

US Embassy, PO Box 211, Asmara (tel: 120-004, 120-009; fax: 127-584).

Voice of the Broad Masses of Eritrea (Dimtsi Hafash), Ministry of Information, Radio Division, PO Box 872, Asmara.

Internet sites

Eritrean news: http://www.messelna.com

Africa Business Network: http://www.ifc.org/abn

AllAfrica.com: http://www.allafrica.com

African Development Bank: http://www.afdb.org

Africa Online: http://www.africaonline.com

Harambee Afrika (UK business club for traders with east, central and southern Africa; includes annotated web resource list): http://www.harambee.co.uk

Mbendi AfroPaedia (information on companies, countries, industries and stock exchanges in Africa): http://mbendi.co.za

Ethiopia

Marybeth McKeever

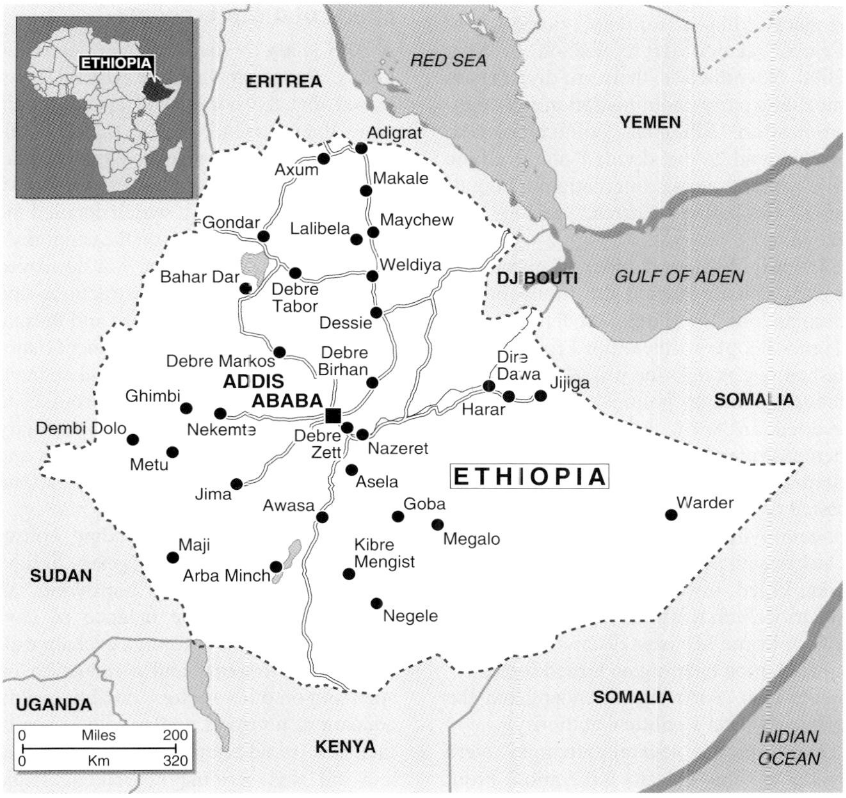

As one of the poorest countries in the world, Ethiopia faced considerable, although not entirely unpredictable, challenges in 2002. Africa's oldest independent country has become known for its periodic droughts and famines, an enduring civil war and subsequent border tensions with its neighbours. Yet an official border agreement with Eritrea ending any remaining tensions and admittance to the joint IMF-World Bank Heavily Indebted Poor Countries (HIPC) initiative, which qualifies the country for debt relief, should point Ethiopia in the right direction.

War and peace

Two-and-a-half-years of bloody conflict with neighbour (and former federated state) Eritrea ended peacefully in December 2000. The peace agreement ushered in the exchange of prisoners, a return of a displaced population of more than 350,000 civilians and a UN commission to delineate the disputed border. By February 2001, Ethiopia had completed the withdrawal of its troops in line with the UN-sponsored peace agreement, thereby restoring hope among its people and the international community that a border war would not recur. Tensions between the two nations persisted until April 2002 when the International Court in The Hague in the Netherlands decreed a final 1,000km boundary according to colonial maps and treaties. Both sides reluctantly adopted the common border, but laid claim to the town of Badme where the war had started. A request by the Ethiopian government to revise the ruling was denied in July 2002.

Relations between Ethiopia and Eritrea remained frosty during 2001 and 2002. In November 2001, Ethiopia accused Eritrea of deploying troops in the

KEY FACTS

Official name: Ityopia (Federal Democratic Republic of Ethiopia)

Head of State: President Girma Wolde Giorgise (elected by parliament, 8 Oct 2001)

Head of government: Prime Minister Meles Zenawi (leader of EPRDF) (since 1995; re-elected Oct 2000)

Ruling party: Ethiopian People's Revolutionary Democratic Front (EPRDF), an alliance led by the Tigray People's Liberation Front (TPLF)

Area: 1,251,282 square km

Population: 65.40 million (2001)

Capital: Addis Ababa

Official language: Amharic

Currency: Birr (Birr) = 100 cents

Exchange rate: Birr8.30 per US$ (Jan 2003)

GDP per capita: US$94 (2001)

GDP real growth: 7.30% (2001)

Inflation: -7.50% (2001)

Balance of trade: -US$1.12 billion (2001)

Foreign debt: US$5.70 billion (2001)

For the latest Key Facts, go to www.worldinformation.com

25km Temporary Security Zone (TSZ), which was created after the 2000 peace agreement to act as a buffer zone between the two countries and which is patrolled by peace-keeping troops of the UN Mission in Ethiopia and Eritrea (UNMEE). In November 2002, Eritrea made a move towards reconciliation by offering its Red Sea ports to transport Ethiopian aid; but Ethiopia declined the offer.

Ethiopia has yet to witness unadulterated peace, as its political and economic situations remain tenuous. Although it is relatively free from the coups that have beleaguered many other African nations, Ethiopia's political turmoil has been no less damaging in the twenty-first century. Two decades of brutal dictatorship under Colonel Mengistu Haile Mariam incurred severe droughts, famines and poorly conceived policies that brought millions to the brink of starvation.

A transitional government led by Ethiopia's current prime minister, Meles Zenawi, ousted the former Marxist dictator in 1991 and developed a constitution that called for its first democratic elections, which were held in 1995 and again in May 2000. Prime Minister Zenawi's Ethiopian People's Revolutionary Democratic Front (EPRDF) helped to stabilise Ethiopia's political and economic conditions with significant assistance from the international community. The war with Eritrea set back any modest development gains and triggered the withdrawal of international financial aid from disapproving donors. The country remains one of Africa's poorest nations, with a majority of the population malnourished and illiterate.

Internal politics

Ethiopia is a democratic federation of 11 regions, governed by a bicameral legislature with 658 combined representatives, a prime minister and a president. The EPRDF has been in power since 1991, yet six other major parties and 50 smaller ones participate in the political system. The EPRDF's re-election may have been in jeopardy, but a military victory over Eritrea secured its re-election in May 2000. Nevertheless, there are divisions in the ruling party's administration and opposition from Ethiopia's political parties, which tend to be divided along ethnic lines; many cross international boundaries, including Eritrea, Sudan and Somalia.

In early 2001, a number of events occurred that threatened the ruling party's domination. In March, rebels from the Tigray People's Liberation Front (TPLF) lashed out against the prime minister, although a major political upheaval was averted. In April, thousands of students demonstrated in support of academic freedom for universities while others protested for greater political support against unemployment in Addis Ababa. Violent clashes with police ensued and 130 people were killed. In May, the intelligence and security chief, Kinfe Gebre-Medhin, a key ally of Prime Minister Zenawi, was assassinated upon entering an armed forces officers club. Such events endangered the prime minister's political authority.

Furthermore, several attempts were made by the Oromo Liberation Front (OLF), a dissident group originally part of a rebel coalition that ousted Mengistu, to undermine political stability. The OLF seems to have fallen out of favour with the EPRDF and has since sought greater respect for human rights and greater autonomy for the south-western Oromiya region. In July 2002, much to the OLF's dismay, 150 Oromo rebels were killed and 340 were captured in two short-lasting battles with the national army near Gambela (442km west of Addis Ababa).

KEY INDICATORS — Ethiopia

	Unit	1996	1997	1998	1999	2000
Population	m	56.37	58.12	59.88	61.67	63.49
Gross domestic product (GDP)	US$bn	6.00	6.20	6.30	5.80	6.30
GDP per capita	US$	106	106	212	94	99
GDP real growth	%	10.6	5.2	-0.5	1.5	4.5
Inflation	%	-5.1	-3.7	0.9	4.8	5.0
Exports (fob) (goods)	US$m	417.5	588.3	560.3	467.4	486.0
Imports (fob) (goods)	US$m	1,002.2	1,018.7	1,309.8	1,387.2	1,131.4
Balance of trade	US$m	-584.7	-430.5	-749.4	-919.8	-645.4
Current account	US$m	-80.3	-40.2	-265.8	-465.2	16.2
Total reserves minus gold	US$m	732.2	501.1	511.1	458.5	306.3
Foreign exchange	US$m	722.0	491.4	501.0	448.7	297.1
Exchange rate	per US$	6.35	6.71	7.12	7.94	8.22

Effects of a war economy

A 2001 study by the Ethiopian Economic Policy Research Institute (EEPRI) reported that the border war cost Ethiopia more than Birr24.2 billion (US$2.9 billion), while the average daily salary in the northern Meket district is Birr10 (US$1.20). The report, which detailed the impact of the border war on the economy's performance, affirmed that war destroyed economic and social infrastructures and disrupted economic activities and normal human settlement. The government maintained that it was forced to mobilise manpower, material and financial resources to defend its nation. Accordingly, military expenditure increased by eight times and became 50 per cent of the country's total recurring expenditure.

Such an increase in spending consequently led to a higher budgetary deficit, an increase in domestic borrowing, an augmented gap in the balance of payments, a limitation in foreign exchange allocation for imports and a reduction on spending on other sectors, notably health, education, nutrition and livestock health facilities. In addition, foreign investment and aid was seriously curtailed. Trade with Eritrea, its primary partner, was halted and has yet to resume.

Figures show that military expenditure (US$176 million in 2001) is decreasing and that the government has undertaken measures to demobilise a large number of soldiers.

Pressures of an agrarian economy

Ethiopia's mixed farming economy raises most of its domestic revenue from both crops and livestock. Manufacturing plays only a minor role. Ethiopia typically has one of the lowest exports per capita in the world. Coffee is the principal export, but commands a low market price.

Due to its agrarian economy, Ethiopia is especially vulnerable to trade shocks and frequent erratic weather patterns, subsequently leading to food insecurity and famines affecting millions.

Ethiopia's centralised state-run economy has been showing signs of improvement, growing by 4.5 per cent in 2000 and

7.9 per cent in 2001. The economy is projected to improve as it changes from a command to a market-based economy. Inflation has decreased, a new taxation system is in place in order to lower tax rates, a number of restrictions that have been placed upon the private sector have been removed, and its widespread system of price controls has been disbanded. Poverty-targeted outlays have increased and public expenditure has slightly lowered.

Climactic dangers

Despite modest levels of GDP growth, Ethiopia is plagued by unco-operative weather and is susceptible to drought. Ironically, in August 2001, 6,000 people were displaced as a result of heavy floods due to torrential rains in the western region of Gambela. Many were left without food and survived on leaves and roots. In the north-east region of Afar, the rainy season (typically lasting September to December) of 2001 came and went without so much as one *kiremt* (big rain) or a *belg* (small rain).

Periodic drought since the 1990s, together with two consecutive years of no rain, has forced thousands to flee in search of food, grazing pastures and clean water. By July 2002, it was reported that over 270,000 people were in need of food, and that a famine would loom if help was not forth coming. The population in this arid Afar region is 3.5 million, mainly farmers and nomadic pastoralists; the latter group being very difficult to locate when food aid is available and being distributed. In addition, the Afari tend to travel far distances in search of good land irrespective of borders, which can further complicate matters with rival ethnic groups, like the Somali Issas, who obstruct their migration in order to protect valuable grazing pastures and water points.

Scant resources

Famines and food shortages do not happen overnight. So who is to blame? It cannot be totally blamed on mother nature. The government's Disaster Prevention and Preparedness Commission (DPPC) claims that their late response to the food shortages was mainly due to the fact that donors had not fully responded to the government's appeal for food assistance requirements; only 46 per cent of what was requested was delivered. As a result, such resource limitations prevented the government from intervening in a timely manner. However, Ethiopia is the World Bank's International Development Association's (IDA) largest beneficiary in Africa, with US$666.8 million committed in 2001. Moreover, the World Bank Institute stated that it has helped train Ethiopian nationals in subjects such as safety nets and social funds, economic growth, poverty reduction and macroeconomic management, among others. A country that has experienced several famines in less than a decade should undoubtedly be more prepared for bad weather.

Getting by with a little help

The biggest boost to Ethiopia's ego came in November 2001. The World Bank and IMF agreed to US$1.9 billion in debt service relief for Ethiopia under its Enhanced HIPC initiative. Having ranked number 158 out of 162 in the UN Development Programme's (UNDP) 2001 Human Development Index, Ethiopia took the necessary steps to become the 24th country to qualify for debt relief, joining its near neighbours Uganda and Tanzania. The initiative allows for Ethiopia's official external debt to be cut by 50 per cent, whereas the savings netted from debt relief – approximately US$763 million – are to be allocated to key anti-poverty programmes as outlined by the government in its Interim Poverty Reduction Strategy Paper. In March 2002, the IMF granted Ethiopia US$17 million to offset a loss of exports and an increase to the balance of payments deficit following the 11 September 2001 terrorist attacks in the US. A further US$14 million was approved in September 2002, bringing the total money available under the IMF's Poverty Reduction and Growth Facility (PRGF) to US$115 million. As of September 2002, Ethiopia had drawn US$77 million.

In a country where life expectancy is 43 years, illiteracy is the norm, and HIV infections are rising, debt relief is most welcomed. Continued foreign assistance to alleviate such extreme poverty is necessary, but will be largely ineffective without better financial policies and efficient management of funds.

Outlook

Having salvaged a peace agreement and adopted a border demarcation, Ethiopia's relations with its hostile neighbour Eritrea seem to be improving. Nevertheless, a thirty-year civil war in Sudan that shows no sign of ending and an ever-tumultuous Somalia plant the Horn of Africa on shaky ground. The internal politics of Addis Ababa – the host of the first ever meeting in May 1963 of the predecessor of the African Union (AU), the Organisation for African Unity (OAU) – are no less shaky. Ethiopia has endured two major coups in the last 30 years, both of which have been followed by significant changes in governance and economic performance. Contention from different ethnic groups and student protests are likely to carry on playing a role in the country's tepid political stability.

From 2000 and predominantly since the war ended, Ethiopia has achieved modest economic growth, bolstered by the government's promise of economic reform, liberalisation and poverty reduction as well as a commitment by the World Bank and IMF for debt relief. In spite of this, Ethiopia's agricultural sector continues to be haunted by unfavourable weather conditions, low market prices, a deflated currency and overall food and water shortages.

Debt relief and democracy are small steps in the right direction, although this will not be enough for the millions of Ethiopians that suffer daily from malnutrition, disease, unemployment, illiteracy, and abject poverty. The government will continue to be challenged to take giant leaps in the development of sound and transparent fiscal policies, the maintenance of peace among the competing Ethiopian ethnic groups, and the promotion of peaceful borders with all its neighbours.

The DPPC is likely to be confronted by more erratic weather in the long-term. What is needed are stronger measures to prepare against and mitigate the effects of droughts and floods, secure foodstuffs, dams to conserve scarce water, improved irrigation and better roads. Such measures will invariably promote improved agricultural activity and for the 86 per cent of Ethiopians that work in the agriculture sector, many of them women and children, their livelihoods will be improved.

The government claims that the only predictable thing about Ethiopia is its unpredictability. Unpredictable weather and markets result in poverty. Yet recurring famines, cycles of drought, and rises and falls in the market are anything but unpredictable. Unfortunately, for the majority of Ethiopians, their government fails to recognise this and has failed to make changes.

Risk assessment

Economy	Modest growth
Political	Poor
Regional stability	Poor

COUNTRY PROFILE

Historical profile

100 BC A kingdom including part of modern-day Ethiopia existed around Axum.

450 AD The kingdom was converted to Christianity and the Ethiopian church became part of the Coptic community.
1896 Italy tried to seize Ethiopia but lost the Battle of Adwa. The Italians held on to Eritrea on the Red Sea coast.
1916 Ras Tafari, later known as Emperor Haile Selassie, gained power over local lords but his appeal to the League of Nations for help against the invading Italians went unheeded.
1936 Benito Mussolini's army occupied all of Ethiopia.
1945 Emperor Haile Selassie returned to power after the Second World War.
1975 Ethiopia was a monarchy until August, when the 84-year-old emperor was strangled in his bed. He was replaced by Colonel Mengistu Haile Mariam who led a brutal regime known as the Dergue, when at least 100,000 opponents or critics were killed.
1977 Somalia tried to annex part of Ethiopia's Ogaden region, where most people are ethnic Somalis. Cuban and Soviet troops and tanks beat them off.
1984 Drought led to a famine in which as many as one million people may have died.
1987 A Soviet-style constitution was adopted and the People's Democratic Republic of Ethiopia was formed. The regime was supported by the former Soviet Union.
1991 Rebellions gathered momentum in Eritrea, led by the leftist Eritrean People's Liberation Front (EPLF) and in Tigray province by the Tigray People's Liberation Front (TPLF). The 14-year dictatorship of Mengistu ended as the EPLF took control of Eritrea and a TPLF-led coalition, the Ethiopian People's Revolutionary Democratic Front (EPRDF), marched into Addis Ababa. Mengistu fled to Zimbabwe.
1994 The transitional EPRDF government under Meles Zenawi organised the election of a constituent assembly in June.
1995 In August a general election was held and the country was officially renamed the Federal Democratic Republic of Ethiopia. Negaso Gidada became president.
1998 Border disputes resulted in Eritrea and Ethiopia resuming full-scale fighting in May and June and sporadic clashes thereafter.
1999 War broke out again in February because of Eritrea's refusal to withdraw from the disputed Badme area.
2000 Partial results of the May legislative elections showed that the EPRDF parties had done well in Addis Ababa. Meles Zenawi was re-elected prime minister on 10 October. In November, the UN peacekeepers opened a 1,000km cease-fire land corridor between Ethiopia and Eritrea. Ethiopia and Eritrea signed a peace deal in Algiers in December, ending the two-year war.
2001 In April, the UN established a buffer zone along the border of Ethiopia and Eritrea. President Negaso Gidada had a dispute with Prime Minister Meles Zenawi in June and although he quit the ruling coalition, the president stayed on to finish his term. A report in July stated that the prime minister survived an assassination attempt by his own bodyguards. In October, parliament elected Girma Wolde Giorgise to replace Negaso Gidada in the largely figurehead position of president.
2002 The mandate of the UN Mission in Ethiopia and Eritrea (UNMEE) was extended until 15 September. In April, Eritrea and Ethiopia accepted a ruling, made by the Boundary Commission at Permanent Court of Arbitration of The Hague, on the border dispute. A new 1,000km boundary was established between the two countries.

Political structure

Constitution

A constitution was adopted 8 December 1994 which established a federal system of government. The constitution formally came into force in August 1995 when the Federal Democratic Republic of Ethiopia was proclaimed.
Ethiopia comprises 11 semi-autonomous administrative regions organised loosely along major ethnic lines.

Form of state

Federal democratic republic

The executive

The role of president is largely a figurehead position. The prime minister, who is elected by parliament for a five-year term, has the most power.
The president is elected by parliament for a six-year term.

National legislature

There is a bicameral legislature: the directly elected lower house, the 656-member Council of People's Representatives, and the upper house, the Federal Council, which represents ethnic minorities and professional groups.

Last elections

October 2001 (presidential); 14 May 2000 (legislative).

Next elections

2007 (presidential)

Political parties

Ruling party

Ethiopian People's Revolutionary Democratic Front (EPRDF), an alliance led by the Tigray People's Liberation Front (TPLF)

Population

63.49 million (2000), 67.98 million (2002).
Ethiopia is the third most populous country in Africa.
Annual growth rate: 2.6 per cent (1994–2000). About 46 per cent of the population is under 14 years; 51 per cent 15–64; 3 per cent over 65.
Population density: 49.9 inhabitants per square km. Urban population: 18 per cent (2000).
With the population due to double by 2015 and rain shortages three years in every 10, famine constantly looms. An estimated 55 per cent of the population lives below the poverty line of US$1 per day. By June 2002, over 95,000 Ethiopians had returned home, having been deported from Eritrea.

Ethnic make-up

Oromo (40 per cent), Amhara and Tigrayan (32 per cent), Sidamo (9 per cent), Shankella (6 per cent), Somali (6 per cent), Afar (4 per cent), Gurage (2 per cent).

Religions

The Ethiopian Coptic Church is influential, particularly in the north. There is a large Muslim community in the south, made up mainly of Arabs, Somalis and Oromos.
Ethiopian Orthodox (40 per cent), Muslim (40 per cent), animist and other (20 per cent).

Education

Ethiopia has one of the world's lowest enrolment rates and needs to enrol 5.3 million children in primary schools by 2005. World Bank estimates show that the total primary school enrolment of the relevant age group typically stood at 55 per cent for boys and 31 per cent for girls (including repetition rates) between 1994 and 2000. There are typically 43 pupils per primary school teacher.
Enrolment in primary education increased by 20 per cent as tuition fees were abolished in the East Gojam region.
The pattern of enrolment shows large gender gaps with girls being more likely to drop out in the early stages. Oxfam estimates that fewer than one-third of boys and one-tenth of girls aged 6-11 start school, and one-quarter of these drop out during the first two grades. Female literacy rates are still below 30 per cent, and girls of primary-school age work 14–16 hours a day on a variety of tasks.
In secondary schools, English has replaced Amharic as the medium of instruction, although several local languages are being used for instruction.
Ethiopia spends 4 per cent of its GDP on education.

Health

The government aims to reorganise health services through a 20-year health development strategy, with a series of five-year investment programmes. The first Health Sector Development Programme (HSDP) covered the period 1997/98–2001/02.

The system provides access to health services for only about half of the population, mainly in the urban areas.
World Bank estimates during the period 1994 and 2000 showed that the average life expectancy was 43 years and the infant mortality rate stood at 107 per 1,000 live births. The fertility rate shows that 6.3 children are born per adult woman with 4 per cent of them using contraceptives.
World Bank estimates in 2000 showed that 24 per cent and 15 per cent of the population had access to improved water and sanitation facilities respectively. There are less than 0.05 physicians and 0.2 hospital beds typically available for 1,000 people.
Government expenditure on healthcare averaged 4.1 per cent of GDP of which 1.7 per cent is public expenditure according to latest available World Bank surveys between 1990 and 1998. Expenditure on private healthcare (such as private household expenditure and insurance) averaged 2.4 per cent of GDP over the same period.
Around three million people suffer from HIV/AIDS in Ethiopia and 10.63 per cent of the adult population is infected (2000). An estimated 1.2 million children have either lost their mother or both parents due to AIDS (2000). The loss in annual GDP growth per capita is estimated at 0.6 per cent between 2002–10 due to the impact of the disease.

Welfare

Ethiopia is one of the poorest countries in the world with the lowest income at US$99 per capita, according to the World Development Report in 2000. Based on recent data, 46 per cent of the people were classified as poor (48 per cent of the rural and 33 per cent of the urban people).
Following the end of the border conflict with Eritrea in 2000, the government of Ethiopia started to implement an ambitious adjustment and reform programme and renewed its commitment to poverty reduction. These reform efforts are supported by the IMF under a three-year Poverty Reduction and Growth Facility (PRGF) arrangement approved on March 22, 2001. Poverty-targeted expenditures are projected to increase steadily, from 14.7 per cent in 2001/02 to 15.5 per cent 2002/03. In March 2002, the IMF approved US$17 million under the PRGF arrangement to help mitigate the impact on the balance of payments following a continued deterioration of the terms of trade and the events following the 11 September 2001 terrorist attacks in the US.
In November 2001 the World Bank and the IMF agreed that Ethiopia had qualified for debt relief under the Heavily Indebted Poor Countries (HIPC) Initiative. HIPC debt relief from all of Ethiopia's creditors will amount to approximately 47 per cent of Ethiopia's total official external debt, after traditional debt relief (corresponding to US$1.9 billion in debt service relief over time).

Main cities

Addis Ababa (capital, estimated population 2.6 million in 2002), Dire Dawa (208,000), Harar (96,000), Dessie (Dese), Gondar (Gonder), Debre Mark'os and Jimma (Jima).

Languages spoken

Oromigna and Tigrigna are widely spoken. English is the second official language and is taught in schools. It is used in business circles and understood in most hotels and major towns. Arabic, French and Italian are also widely understood. Over 80 local languages are spoken.

Official language/s

Amharic

Media

Press

In November 2001 the government resumed its harassment of Ethiopian journalists who began reporting news in the free press. Fana Democracy Publishing, that used to publish the weekly newspaper *Efoyta* was closed down in November 2001. The newspaper is no longer published.
Tamrat Zuma, the publisher and editor of the defunct newspaper *Atkurot* was released from nine months imprisonment in March 2002. Zuma announced his intention to restart the newspaper as soon as he can raise the required funds.
Dailies: *Addis Zemen* is a state-owned daily. *Ethiopian News Headlines* (http://www.ethiozena.net) provides daily on-line news service.
Weeklies: Several newspapers and periodicals are published in Amharic and English languages. There are several privately owned weeklies published from Addis Ababa including *Ilete Addis*, *Seifenebelbal*, *Tobya*, *Wonchif*, *Tomar*, *Mahlet* and the English language *Addis Tribune*. *Andenat* is a semi-monthly publication.

Broadcasting

Radio: Service by Voice of Ethiopia, chiefly in Amharic, but also in English, Arabic, Somali, French and local languages.
Television: The state-controlled commercial Ethiopian Television broadcasts to most of the country via a microwave link-up.

Economy

Ethiopia's economy is largely reliant on coffee exports, which provide nearly half its foreign exchange earnings.
The government is keen to diversify, although it is hampered by poor infrastructure and desertification. As a result, the agricultural sector, which dominates the economy, endures volatile output and supply, bottlenecks creating substantial variations in economic growth.
The country's development has been undermined by external and non-economic factors, namely recurrent droughts, a deterioration in the terms of trade, and the border war with Eritrea. This has pushed up the government's fiscal deficit, with external support being cut off due to the conflict and an increase in defence expenditure.
The signing of the peace agreement with Eritrea brought with it the resumption of international support for the Ethiopian economy, which had lessened with the government's increased military expenditure and reports of human rights atrocities.
In November 2001, Ethiopia became the twenty-fourth country to qualify for debt relief under the Heavily Indebted Poor Countries (HIPC) initiative.
The African Development Bank approved US$216.47 million debt relief to Ethiopia in February 2002 under the enhanced HIP initiative to boost food security, agriculture, road development and rural energy supplies and the EU granted US$483.3 million for transport infrastructure.
The government recognises that Ethiopia's economic future lies in the transformation of the agricultural sector and rural Ethiopia.

External trade

Exports

Principal exports are coffee, gold, leather and leatherwear, oilseeds, tea, pulses, live animals, meat products, marble and other minerals.
Main destinations: Germany (18.3 per cent of 2000 total), Japan (10.8 per cent), Djibouti (10.6 per cent), Saudi Arabia (7.8 per cent), Italy (6.6 per cent).

Imports

Principal imports are machinery, transport equipment, petroleum and petroleum products, consumer goods, food, raw materials, semi-manufactured goods and fertilisers.
Main sources: Saudi Arabia (25.9 per cent of 2000 total), US (9.2 per cent), Italy (7 per cent), India (5.9 per cent), Germany (4 per cent).

Agriculture

The agricultural sector is the mainstay of the economy, accounting for around 52 per cent of GDP, 79 per cent of employment and about 85 per cent of exports. Only about two-thirds of Ethiopia's 112 million ha of land suitable for agriculture is actually cultivated, with a large part affected by soil erosion. Intensive subsistence agriculture has so depleted the soil that Ethiopia can no longer feed its population, even when the weather is good.

Only around 6 per cent of the cultivated area is irrigated.
Horticulture is seen as a future industry for Ethiopia, which has a high altitude climate offering good natural conditions for cultivating flowers. The chief cash crop is coffee which is grown on the plateau in the south-west and accounts for around half of export earnings. Other cash crops include cotton and sugar; also exports of hides and skins. The main food crops are maize, sorghum, wheat, barley, millet and teff.
The Nile Basin Initiative (NBI) (signed by Egypt, Sudan, Tanzania, Kenya, Rwanda, Burundi, Uganda and Democratic Republic of Congo) is launching seven feasibility studies backed by US$140 million granted by the World Bank and donor governments in June 2001. It will also develop a parallel legal framework for shared water management. Ethiopia refused to sign the NBI and Eritrea's membership is pending.

Farming

Ethiopia possesses the ninth-largest asset of livestock in the world. A ban imposed in 1998 by Saudi Arabia on livestock imports from Ethiopia was lifted in 2002.
External trade: Germany is the largest market for Ethiopian coffee. Saudi Arabia is the main buyer of Ethiopian cattle and camels.

Industry and manufacturing

The industrial sector contributes around 11 per cent of GDP and employs about 7 per cent of the workforce. Manufacturing of small handicrafts, and other small industry sub-sectors makes up around 7 per cent of GDP.
Industry is primarily based on the processing of agricultural raw materials. Principal among these is food processing, but textiles, handicrafts, and leather production are also significant.
Growth is constrained by a lack of raw materials, outdated machinery and techniques and the need for imports throughout the sector.

Tourism

Although there are many tourist attractions, facilities are minimal.

Mining

The mining sector accounts for around 6 per cent of GDP.
The government says there are at least 500 tonnes of proven gold reserves in the country. Activity is limited to small-scale gold mining. A non-alluvial gold treatment plant at the Legadembi mine was privatised in 1997 in a deal worth around US$172 million. It is estimated to have 1.5–2.0 million ounces of proven open pittable reserves, and the government estimates the total resource is between 60–200 tonnes.
The country has substantial reserves of iron ore and untapped reserves of platinum, tantalum (used in the electronics industry), nickel, phosphate, diatomite, copper, zinc, soda ash and potash. Tantalum reserves are estimated at 25,000 tonnes at one site alone.
The output of non-metallic minerals such as limestone and marble has increased significantly.
A number of foreign mining companies have been awarded exploration concessions.

Hydrocarbons

Foreign oil and gas companies are planning joint ventures with the Ethiopian government, although there is no hydrocarbon production as yet.

Gas

There are known reserves of natural gas with proven reserves amounting to an estimated 24 million cubic metres. Other reserves have been located in the oil- and gas-rich Ogaden region amounting to around 67.6 million cubic metres and there are substantial deposits in the Calub field.

Coal

Ethiopia has substantial reserves of coal.

Energy

Ethiopia has considerable hydroelectric capacity. Installed generating capacity is around 380MW, but it is hoped to double by 2004. Only 4 per cent of the population has access to electricity.
Wood has always been a traditional source of energy, but it is hoped increased availability of electricity will reduce this, as many forests have become severely depleted.
The Ethiopian Electric Power Corporation (EEPCO) reported that the US$63 million Tis Abay II hydroelectric power station project, near Lake Tana in the north-west of the country began supplying electricity to the Kaliti main power distribution station in April 2001. The second Tis Abay Power Project has raised electric power capacity in the country from 371.6 to 444.6MW.
The construction of Ethiopia's first independent power project is set to commence in 2002. A 150MW hydroelectric facility will be built in western Ethiopia. The project is being managed by the Saudi Arabian company Mohammed International Development Research (Midroc) and when completed, output will be sold to EEPCO.

Banking

Central bank

National Bank of Ethiopia

Main financial centre

Addis Ababa

Time

GMT plus three hours
The Ethiopian day officially begins at 0600 (midnight elsewhere).

Geography

Ethiopia extends inland from the Red Sea coast of eastern Africa. The country has a long frontier with Somalia near the Horn of Africa. Sudan lies to the west, Djibouti to the east, Eritrea to the north and Kenya to the south.

Climate

Dependent on altitude. Lowland regions are very hot and dry throughout the year. On the plateau (including Addis Ababa) dry season from October–May with temperature range from as low as 6 degrees Celsius in December to 26 degrees Celsius in March (light rain from February–April). Temperatures can fall sharply at night during the dry season. Rainy season from June–September with average temperature 21 degrees Celsius.

Entry requirements

Passports

Required by all. Must be valid for at least six months.

Visa

Required by all, except nationals of Kenya and Djibouti.
Business visas are valid for 30 days.
For longer stays visitors must register with the Immigration Office for an Alien's Registration Card and an exit visa.
British visitors are advised to register on arrival at the Consular Section of the British Embassy, Addis Ababa (tel: 612-354).
Transit visas are available at Bole Airport.
From January 2002, citizens of the US can obtain tourist visas upon arrival (only at Bole International Airport) for a fee of Birr315 (approximately US$40) payable only in Ethiopian currency. An exit visa from the main immigration office in Addis Ababa is required if the entry visa has expired by the time of departure.

Currency advice/regulations

Up to Birr100 can be imported and exported.
While there is no limit on the import of foreign currency, it must be declared on arrival. Export of foreign currency is allowed up to the amount declared.
Penalties for exchanging money on the black market range from fines to imprisonment.

Customs

Skins, hides and any antique articles require an export certificate. Laptop computers must be declared upon arrival and departure. Tape recorders require special customs permits.

Health (for visitors)

Health facilities are extremely limited in Addis Ababa and totally inadequate

outside the city. Travellers should bring their own prescription drugs and a doctor's note describing the medication. If the quantity of drugs exceeds that expected for personal use, a permit from the ministry of health is required.
The altitude may cause health problems.

Mandatory precautions
A yellow fever inoculation certificate is required if arriving from or via an infected area.

Advisable precautions
Visitors should be in date for the following vaccinations: yellow fever (within 10 years), polio vaccinations (within 10 years), typhoid, tetanus (within 10 years), hepatitis A and B, meningitis. There is a rabies risk.
Malaria prophylaxis recommended before visiting the lowlands. There is no malaria risk in Addis Ababa.
Water precautions should be taken.

Hotels
Hotels are available in Addis Ababa and other main centres. A service charge of 10 per cent and a tax of 2 per cent are added to bills but a small tip is usual in addition to the service charge. Payment is generally required in foreign currency.

Credit cards
Credit cards are accepted by airlines and the larger hotels only.

Public holidays
Ethiopia follows the Julian calendar, instead of the Gregorian calendar used in most other parts of the world. The Ethiopian calendar year is divided into 13 months: 12 months of 30 days each and one month of five days (six in a leap year). The Ethiopian new year commences on 10 or 11 September every year.

Fixed dates
7 Jan (Gena/Christmas), 19 Jan (Timket/Epiphany), 2 Mar (Victory of Adwa Day), 6 Apr (Patriots' Victory Day), 1 May (International Labour Day), 28 May (Downfall of the Dergue), 11 Sep (Enkutatash/New Year's Day; 12 Sep in year before leap year).

Variable dates
Ethiopian Good Friday, Ethiopian Easter Day, Eid Al-Fitr, Eid Al-Adha, Maulid/Birthday of the Prophet Mohammed.

Working hours
Banking
Mon–Fri: 0800–1100, 1300–1600; Sat: 0800–1200.

Business
Mon–Thu: 0830–1230, 1330–1730; Fri: 0830–1130, 1330–1730. Most private businesses also work on Saturdays.

Government
Mon–Thu: 0830–1230, 1330–1730. Fri: 0830–1130, 1330–1730.

Shops
Mon–Sat: 0800–1300, 1400–2000. Local variations.

Telecommunications
Telephone/fax
Dialling code for Ethiopia IDD access code + 251 followed by area code (1 for Addis Ababa) followed by subscriber's number.
Calls to Europe and neighbouring African countries can be made from Addis Ababa. Telephone, telex, postal and fax facilities are available in most main towns.

Electricity supply
220V, 50 cycles AC. Plugs are of the two-pin variety.

Social customs/useful tips
Handshaking is the usual mode of greeting.
The first name is the name of the Ethiopian and is followed by that of his father. There are no family names which are passed on to successive generations. The words Ato, Woizero and Woizrity are the equivalents of Mr, Mrs and Miss, respectively, and should be used when addressing people.
Smoking is not popular among traditional people, or in front of priests. Dress should be modest.
Shoes are removed on entering churches/mosques.
Private formal entertaining is common in Addis Ababa, and cocktail parties are not uncommon.
Ethiopian law strictly prohibits the photographing of military installations, police/military personnel, industrial facilities, government buildings and infrastructure.

Security
Crime is an increasing problem in Addis Ababa. Normal precautions should be taken.
Exercise caution if travelling to the northern Tigray and Afar regions (within 50km of the Ethiopian/Eritrean border) because of landmines and unsettled conditions in the border area. Travel to the Ogaden Region is considered very dangerous and should not be attempted. Limit road travel outside major towns to daylight hours only.

Getting there
Air
National airline: Ethiopian Airlines (government-owned)
International airport/s: Addis Ababa-Bole International (Code: ADD), 8km from city, bar, buffet, restaurant, bank, post office, shops, car hire.
Airport tax: International departures Birr100 and domestic departures Birr10 (nationals), US$20 (others) excluding infants under two years and transit passengers departing the same day and passengers who do not leave the airport.

Surface
Road: Entry by land into Ethiopia is possible via Dewale and Galafi (Ethiopia-Djibouti), Moyale (Ethiopia-Kenya), Humera and Metema (Ethiopia-Sudan), Jijiga (Ethiopia-Somalia). The road linking Nairobi and Addis Ababa forms part of the Trans-East African Highway. There can be difficulties gaining access at the border crossing.
Rail: The rail route from Djibouti to Addis Ababa is subject to disruption.
Water: Ethiopia has been landlocked since Eritrea gained independence.
Main port/s: Until the outbreak of hostilities with Eritrea in 1998, Ethiopia relied heavily on the Eritrean ports of Assab and Massawa. Djibouti has subsequently become Ethiopia's principal trading gateway.

Getting about
National transport
Air: Ethiopian Airlines operates domestic service to main towns.
Road: An all-weather road network connects principal towns. The road system is undergoing expansion.
There are border posts at Moyale on the Kenyan border, Adwa and Adigrat near the border with Eritrea, and Dewelle for Djibouti.
Roads are impassable to Lalibela from June to September.
Drivers bringing their own vehicles to Ethiopia will require a *carnet de passage*.
Buses: Coach services (liable to suspension) Addis Ababa-Gondar.
Rail: A line runs from Addis Ababa to Dire Dawa (and on to Djibouti). However, visitors are advised not to use this line for security reasons.

City transport
Taxis: In Addis Ababa, the National Tour Operations (NTO) provides taxis at the main hotels and the airport, although independent and communal cabs are available.
It is advisable to check the fare and the destination before you enter the cab. The most reliable taxis are available from the office of the Hilton Hotel.
The taxi journey from the airport to the city centre takes about 30 minutes.
Buses, trams & metro: Fare from airport to city centre Birr4, journey time 30 minutes.
Tipping is not usual.

Car hire
Car hire (with or without driver) is available in the main centres. A valid international driving licence is required. Traffic drives on the right.
Payment for car rental is generally required in foreign currency.

BUSINESS DIRECTORY

Telephone area codes
The international dialling code (IDD) for Ethiopia is +251 followed by area code (1 for Addis Ababa) followed by subscriber's number.

Chambers of Commerce
Addis Ababa Chamber of Commerce, PO Box 2458, Addis Ababa (tel: 513-814; fax: 511-479).

Ethiopian Chamber of Commerce, PO Box 517, Addis Ababa (tel: 518-240; fax: 517-699).

Banking
Awash International Bank SC; PO Box 12638, Bole Road, Addis Ababa (tel: 614-482/83, 612-919; fax: 614-477).

Bank of Abyssinia SC; PO Box 12947, Addis Ababa (tel: 514-130, 514-752; fax: 511-575) .

Commercial Bank of Ethiopia; PO Box 255, Unity Square, Addis Ababa (tel: 511-271, 515-004; fax: 514-522.

Construction and Business Bank, PO Box 3480, Addis Ababa (tel: 512-300; fax: 515-103).

Dashen Bank SC; PO Box 12752, Garad Building, Debre Zeit Road, Addis Ababa (tel: 661-380, 655-525; fax: 661-640, 653-037).

Development Bank of Ethiopia, PO Box 1900, Josep Broz Tito, Addis Ababa (tel: 511-188; fax: 511-606).

Wegagen Bank SC; PO Box 1018, Addis Ababa (tel: 655-015; fax: 653-330).

Central bank
National Bank of Ethiopia, PO Box 5550, Addis Ababa, Ethiopia (tel: 517-430; fax: 514-588).

Travel information
Addis Ababa-Bole Airport, PO Box 978, Addis Ababa (tel: 180-455; fax: 612-533).

Ethiopian Airlines, PO Box 1755, Bole International Airport, Addis Ababa (tel: 612-222; fax: 611-474); town office (tel: 517-000; fax: 611-474).

National tourist organisation offices
Ethiopian Tourism Commission, PO Box 2183, Addis Ababa (tel: 517-470, 150-609, 513-962; fax: 513-899).

National Tour Operations (NTO), PO Box 5709, Addis Ababa (tel: 512-955; fax: 517-688).

Other useful addresses
Antiquities Authority, National Museum of Ethiopia, PO Box 76, Addis Ababa (tel: 117-150; fax: 553-188).

British Embassy, Commercial Section, Fikre Mariam Abatechan Street, Addis Ababa (tel: 612-354; fax: 610-588).

Central Statistical Office, PO Box 1143, Addis Ababa (tel: 113-010).

Department of Immigration and Refugee Affairs, PO Box 5741, Addis Ababa (tel: 553-899).

Djibouti–Ethiopian Railway Corporation, PO Box 1051, Addis Ababa (tel: 517-250; fax: 513-533).

Ethiopian Customs Office, PO Box 3248, Addis Ababa (tel: 513-100; fax: 518-355).

Ethiopian Embassy (US), 3506 International Drive, NW, Washington DC 20008 (tel: 364-1200; fax: 686-9551; e-mail: ethiopia@ethiopianembassy.org).

Ethiopian Investment Authority, PO Box 2313, Addis Ababa (tel: 510-033; 514-396).

Ethiopian Privatisation Agency, PO Box 11835, Bole Road, Woreda 18, Kebele 18, Room No 504, Addis Ababa (tel: 150-370; fax: 513-955).

Ethiopian Private Industries' Association, PO Box 8739, Addis Ababa (tel: 512-384; fax: 552-633).

Ethiopian Television, PO Box 5554, Addis Ababa.

Ethiopian Tourist Trading Enterprise, PO Box 8640, Addis Ababa (tel: 612-277; fax: 610-500).

Maritime and Transit Services, PO Box 1186, Addis Ababa (tel: 510-666; fax: 514-097).

Ministry of Culture and Information, PO Box 1364, Addis Ababa (tel: 551-011; fax: 551-609).

Ministry of Economic Development & Co-operation, PO Box 2428, Addis Ababa (tel: 519-684; fax: 517-988).

Ministry of Foreign Affairs, PO Box 393, Addis Ababa (tel: 517-345; fax: 514-300).

Ministry of Trade and Industry, PO Box 2559, Addis Ababa (tel: 518-200; fax: 514-288).

Organisation of African Unity (OAU), PO Box 3243, Addis Ababa (tel: 557-700; fax: 511-299).

Voice of Ethiopia, PO Box 1020, Addis Ababa.

Wildlife Conservation Department, PO Box 386, Addis Ababa (tel: 510-455; fax: 510-168).

Internet sites
Africa Business Network: http://www.ifc.org/abn

AllAfrica.com: http://www.allafrica.com

African Development Bank: http://www.afdb.org

Africa Online: http://www.africaonline.com

Harambee Afrika (UK business club for traders with east, central and southern Africa; includes annotated web resource list): http://www.harambee.co.uk

Mbendi AfroPaedia (information on companies, countries, industries and stock exchanges in Africa): http://mbendi.co.za

Gabon

Nicole Goldin

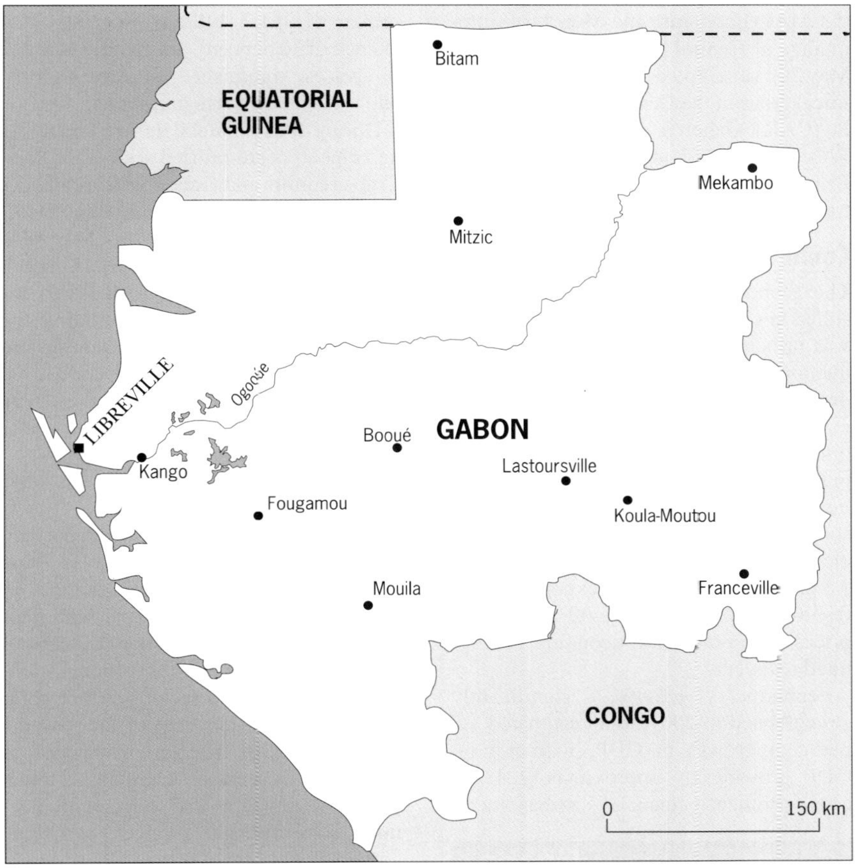

In 2002, Gabon continued to represent a relative oasis of democracy in an otherwise troubled region. Although the country's dependence on oil could ultimately be the downfall of the economy, stable world prices and solid production levels have kept the Gabonese economy steady.

Relative political stability

Gabon has experienced a relatively stable political climate since Omar Bongo began his presidential tenure on 2 December 1967. With the introduction of multi-party politics in 1990, Bongo has since had to compete on a democratic and transparent basis.

In the December 1998 general election, Bongo emphatically maintained power, garnering two-thirds of the popular vote. Following a period of tension and re-alignment among the opposition parties, legislative elections were held in December 2001. As expected, President Bongo's ruling Parti Democratique Gabonais (PDG) (Gabonese Democratic Party) and its allies retained control, winning 107 out of 120 seats in the National Assembly. Although no violence occured, eight minor opposition parties boycotted the elections on claims of a flawed electoral register, international observers reported insufficiencies in the balloting process, and opposition leader Pierre Mamboundou challenged the result.

In January 2002, a government of national unity was established comprising 39 cabinet ministers (increased from 33), including four ministers from the two

KEY FACTS

Official name: République Gabonaise (Gabonese Republic)

Head of State: President El Hadj Omar Bongo (PDG) (since 1967; last re-elected Dec 1998)

Head of government: Prime Minister Jean-François Ntoutoume-Emane (PDG) (since Jan 1999)

Ruling party: Parti Démocratique Gabonais (PDG) (Gabonese Democratic Party) (since 1960)

Area: 267,667 square km

Population: 1.30 million (2001)

Capital: Libreville

Official language: French

Currency: CFA franc (CFAf) = 100 centimes (Communauté Financière Africaine (African Financial Community) franc)

Exchange rate: CFAf629.73 per US$ (Jan 2003); CFAf655.96 per euro (pegged from Jan 1999)

GDP per capita: US$3,023 (2001)

GDP real growth: 2.50% (2001)

Unemployment: 25.00% (2001)*

Inflation: 2.00% (2001)

Oil production: 301,000 bpd (2001)

Balance of trade: US$1.70 billion (2001)

Foreign debt: US$3.80 billion (2001)

Annual FDI: US$150.00 million (2001)*

* estimated figure

For the latest Key Facts, go to www.worldinformation.com

main opposition parties. Municipal elections, originally scheduled for April 2002, were pushed back to the end of the year and are due to be followed by the immediate election of a new Senate.

Health crisis

In December 2001, the first death in the Gabonese interior caused by the existence of a new outbreak of the Zaire-strain of the Ebola virus was confirmed by the World Health Organisation (WHO). The number of cases rose to 65, with a death toll of 53, before the haemorrhagic fever outbreak that plagued the Ogooue-Ivindo region was confirmed by the Gabonese ministry of public health and the WHO in May 2002. Ebola claimed 66 lives in the same region during a 1996 outbreak.

The HIV pandemic received renewed attention in February 2002 when evidence revealing a shockingly rapid spread of the disease among the population was released. It has been said that one Gabonese citizen is infected with HIV every three hours, amounting to eight new cases per day for a population of only 1.21 million.

Gabon's health standards remain mediocre and delivery of services is not improving. HIV's dramatic effect of reducing household income and aggregate GDP, eating away the fabric of economic future, is only just being realised, as individual productivity is challenged.

Regional role

As the leader of one of the traditionally more tranquil and stable nations of West African, President Bongo maintains a high profile. The fight against child-trafficking has become a critical issue for the international community and, displaying Gabon's commitment to regional leadership, in March 2001, Libreville hosted a Unicef-organised conference discussing strategies to combat the problem.

Another mark of regional leadership was Bongo's initiation of a heads of state meeting of the Communautaire Economique et Monetaire de l'Afrique (CEMA) (Economic and Monetary Community of Central Africa) to address the May 2001 attempted coup and ensuing political crisis in the Central African Republic (CAR). Gabon is also a member of the West African Economic and Monetary Union (Waemu), which signed a new trade pact with the US in April 2002.

Continued recovery

The economic crisis in 1999, which resulted in GDP contraction of 9.6 per cent, was principally due to a drop in oil production, falling world oil prices, and weak demand for key Gabonese non-oil products timber and rubber. Political wrangling also contributed to the recession as public spending by the Bongo administration soared in efforts to secure popular support and votes in the December 1999 elections. Although GDP sank a further 1.5 per cent in 2000, rising export earnings resulting from increasing oil and timber prices invigorated the economy and ignited recovery.

Economic activity significantly strengthened in 2001, to an estimated 1.7 per cent growth in GDP, with non-oil GDP growing by approximately 4 per cent. Prudent financial management, along with favourable oil prices, yielded a fiscal surplus of approximately 17 per cent of GDP compared with a fiscal deficit of 6.3 per cent in 1998. The majority of the surplus went towards servicing the external debt, which accounted for almost 40 per cent of government revenue and 14 per cent of GDP. The trade surplus, however, dropped steeply from CFAf1,612 billion (US$2.4 billion) in 2000 to CFAf1,114 billion (US$1.7 billion) in 2001 – a change of 30 per cent, due mainly to lower oil prices, diminished forestry exports, and a 12 per cent rise in imports.

During 2001, bilateral debt rescheduling agreements were ratified with eight Paris Club creditors and Gabon was in final negotiations with the remaining three creditors. Other structural reforms have also been implemented under the 18-month Standby Arrangement with the IMF, approved in October 2000, including the new integrated budget information system (CRYSTAL), a new forestry code, civil service reform, and passage by the senate of anti-corruption legislation in December 2001.

Oil economy

Given that an average of nearly 60 per cent of total fiscal revenue between 1999 and 2001 was attributed to oil tax, and that oil exports comprised about 80 per cent of total exports over the same period, Gabon's dependence on the resource is unquestionable. Moreover, the sector accounted for an estimated 40 per cent of the national economy in 2001. The non-oil economy is dominated by services – commerce, transportation, tourism and telecommunications. Government services constitute around 20 per cent of non-oil GDP, nearly equivalent to the contribution of agriculture, fisheries and industry. Of the non-oil commodities, timber and rubber are the leading exports. World crude oil prices fell throughout 2001 from about US$24 a barrel in January to US$17 in December. Prices rebounded in the early months of 2002, fluctuating between US$23 and US$26 a barrel.

Although falling sharply from the 2000 average daily production of 330,000 barrels per day (bpd), Gabonese crude oil production remained constant during 2001 with a year-end average of 301,000bpd. Reports from the first half of 2002 indicate steady production at 2001 levels. The 2001 drops comprise an approximate 10 per cent decline at Elf Gabon oilfields, and nearly a 20 per cent fall at the Shell-operated Rabi field – two fields that together

KEY INDICATORS — Gabon

	Unit	1996	1997	1998	1999	2000
Population	m	1.11	1.14	1.19	1.39	1.21
Gross domestic product (GDP)	US$bn	5.78	5.15	5.52	4.63	4.90
GDP per capita	US$	5,207	4,518	4,639	3,331	3,451
GDP real growth	%	3.6	5.7	3.5	-9.6	-1.5
Inflation	%	4.5	4.1	2.3	-0.7	1.0
Oil output	'000 bpd	365.0	365.0	335.0	340.0	301.0
Exports (fob) (goods)	US$m	3,190.0	3,067.0	1,907.0	2,498.8	2,750.0
Imports (fob) (goods)	US$m	969.0	970.0	1,103.0	910.5	1,100.0
Balance of trade	US$m	2,221.0	2,097.0	804.0	1,588.3	1,612.0
Current account	US$m	317.0	148.0	-839.0	390.4	128.0
Foreign debt	US$bn	4.3	4.3	4.1	4.0	3.3
Total reserves minus gold	US$m	248.7	282.6	15.4	17.9	190.1
Foreign exchange	US$m	248.6	282.5	15.3	17.8	189.8
Exchange rate	per US$	511.55	583.67	589.95	615.70	711.98

account for two-thirds of Gabon's oil production.

Outlook

Bongo appears set to enjoy the rest of another seven-year term after 33 years already spent in the state house. His control over Gabonese politics remains supreme, with a disparate and poorly organised opposition unable to shake the president. However, there are signs that the government's procrastination over political reform could yet mobilise the masses. Since the mid-1990s there has been a significant increase in urban unrest as those flocking to the cities have found their expectations of jobs and a better life fall on infertile ground (an estimated 80 per cent of the population live in urban areas). While unrest has been concentrated in Libreville, there are signs of it spreading throughout the country, with protests also hitting Port Gentil, the heart of Gabon's oil wealth. The government has taken a dim view of industrial unrest and since 2001 has taken an increasingly tougher line on public demonstrations. Meanwhile, Bongo's co-option of his opponents, such as Father Abessole, will help neutralise the opposition, although opposition cabinet ministers hold relatively minor portfolios. Moreover, the appointment of a new cabinet in early 2002 saw a shift towards the old guard, indicating that Bongo was unwilling to let a new generation of modernisers into government.

Risk assessment

Political	Fair
Economics	Dependent
Regional stability	Poor

COUNTRY PROFILE

Historical profile

The region that is now Gabon was inhabited by the Omiéné by the sixteenth century. They were outnumbered by the Fang by the eighteenth century. Between the sixteenth and eighteenth centuries, Gabon was part of the Loango empire, which stretched from the Ogooué river to the Congo (Zaïre) river.

1472 Portuguese navigators arrived in the Ogooué estuary and Gabon soon became an important centre for slave trading for the Portuguese, Dutch, British and French.

1839 Having gained a dominant position in the area and despite Fang resistance, Gabon became part of the French Congo. The French began work to abolish the slave trade.

1910 Gabon became part of French Equatorial Africa.

1939–1945 Gabon was held by the Free French during the Second World War.

1946 Gabon became a province of French Equatorial Africa. In gratitude for the support the local population gave to the Free French, French President Charles de Gaulle granted French citizenship to all the territory's people.

1957 Gabon gained internal autonomy.

1958 It achieved self-government within the French community in November.

1960 Gained full independence from France in August, under President Léon M'Ba. The Parti Démocratique Gabonais (PDG) (Gabonese Democratic Party) assumed power.

1964 In February President M'Ba was deposed by a military coup, but was reinstated by French forces.

1967 President M'Ba died in November. Vice President Albert-Bernard Bongo took over the one-party state.

1973 Bongo was re-elected president and converted to Islam, adopting the forename Omar.

1981 Bongo relinquished the title of head of government, which was given to the prime minister.

1981–89 Political unrest was orchestrated by an illegal opposition group, Mouvement de Redressement National (MORENA) (Movement for National Regeneration).

1990 After demonstrations by students and strikes by workers, President Bongo said he would support democracy and opposition parties were legalised. The government was accused of electoral fraud following elections held in September and October, which secured Bongo's power with a PDG victory.

1991 A new constitution was introduced, which formalised the multi-party system.

1993 Bongo narrowly won the presidential election, although the opposition claimed massive electoral fraud.

1996 Parliamentary elections gave the PDG an overwhelming majority.

1997 France reduced its garrison of 600 troops.

1998 President Bongo won another seven years in power with more than two-thirds of the vote in December presidential election.

1999 The country plunged into a deep recession due to the fall in the world price of oil.

2000 The recession continued. There were cuts in public expenditure, strikes and social unrest.

2001 A treaty establishing the Gulf of Guinea Commisssion was signed by five of the seven member states in July (Gabon, Congo, São Tomé and Príncipe, Nigeria and Angola). Cameroon and Equatorial Guinea did not sign, for which no reason was given.

2002 In January, the PDG won 53 out of 120 seats in the December parliamentary election. The PDG formed a coalition government with the opposition Rassemblement National des Bûcherons/Rassemblement pour le Gabon (RNB/RPG) (National Rally of Lumberjacks/Rally for Gabon).

Political structure

Constitution

In 1991 a new constitution was introduced which restored multi-party elections and protected civil liberties. The constitution maintained a strong presidential role but allowed for a more influential prime minister.

Form of state

Presidential democracy

The executive

Executive power is divided between the president, elected by universal suffrage every seven years, and the prime minister and Council of Ministers (Cabinet) who are appointed by the president.

Government members must be more than 35 years of age and have at least seven years' professional experience.

The president is head of state, head of administration and chief of the armed forces.

National legislature

Legislative power is vested in the 120-member Assemblée Nationale (National Assembly), with 111 members elected for five-year terms in single seat constituencies and nine members appointed by the president. Members of the 91-seat Sénat (Senate) are elected for six year terms by local and departmental councillors.

Last elections

26 January/9 February 1997 (Senate); 6 December 1998 (presidential); 9/24 December 2001 (National Assembly).

Next elections

2003 (presidential and Senate); 2006 (National Assembly).

Political parties

Ruling party

Parti Démocratique Gabonais (PDG) (Gabonese Democratic Party) (since 1960)

Main opposition party

Rassemblement National des Bûcherons/Rassemblement pour le Gabon (RNB/RPG) (National Rally of Lumberjacks/Rally for Gabon)

Population

1.21 million (2000) 1.31 million (2002)

Annual population growth rate: 2.4 per cent (1994–2000); projected annual growth rate: 2.1 per cent per annum (1999–2015).

Population density: five inhabitants per square km. Urban population: 81 per cent of total (1994–2000). The rural population is lightly spread over a large area. Although the Gabonese enjoy one of the highest per capita incomes in sub-Saharan Africa, income distribution is unequal and it is estimated that half the population live below the poverty line.

Ethnic make-up

There are some 40 different ethnic groups, of which the Fangs are the largest (40 per cent of the total) and the Bapounous (20 per cent) are also highly significant. There are some 25,000 Europeans, mainly of French nationality.

Religions

Christianity (59 per cent), mostly Roman Catholic; indigenous animist beliefs (40 per cent). There is a small Muslim community (less than 1 per cent).

Education

School is compulsory and free for all Gabonese children up to the age of 16 years. Secondary education covers seven years, divided into a lower (premier) cycle lasting four years and an upper (deuxième) cycle lasting three years. On completion of the cycle, pupils take the examinations for the Baccalauréat. Pupils who do not qualify for the Baccalauréat are awarded the Certificat de Fin d'Etudes secondaires, a record of attendance and performance in the final year. On completion of the lower cycle pupils may opt to take a 'short' or a 'long' course of technical secondary education. The former leads to the Brevet de Technicien and the latter to the Baccalauréat technique.

Two universities – Omar Bongo University at Libreville and the University of Science and Technology of Masuku (USTM at Franceville) – as well as various independent institutions provide higher education. The universities benefit from a certain degree of autonomy. Higher education is financed exclusively by public funds.

The adult illiteracy rate is estimated at 20.2 per cent and 37.8 per cent for men and women respectively. The number of pupils available to every primary school teacher is typically 56. World Bank estimates between 1994 and 2000 showed that the total primary school enrolment of the relevant age group stood at 62 per cent.

Public expenditure on education typically amounts to 2.9 per cent of annual GDP.

Health

Gabon is plagued by poor health conditions, which are aggravated by the hot and humid climate. It is the country worst affected by malaria in sub-Saharan Africa. World Bank estimates show that only 21 per cent and 70 per cent of the population have access to sanitation and safe water facilities respectively.

Gabon has a birth and death rate of 36 births and 16 deaths per 1,000 population respectively. Life expectancy at birth was 53 years. Infant mortality rate stood at 86 per 1,000 live births. Gabon's infant mortality rate is only slightly below average for countries in sub-Saharan Africa. The fertility rate is 5.1 children born to each adult woman. Maternal mortality ratio is high and is estimated at 600 deaths per 100,000 live births. Gabon faces a growing crisis of male impotence affecting 25 per cent of all adult men mainly caused by high levels of alcohol and tobacco use.

Total health expenditure is typically 3.1 per cent of GDP, of which public expenditure is equivalent to 2.1 per cent and private expenditure amounts to 1 per cent of GDP.

AIDS in Gabon is also a rapidly growing crisis and disease has reached catastrophic proportions. The World Health Organisation (WHO) estimates that 30,000 people in Gabon are being infected with HIV each year and 7.6 per cent of sexually active people between ages 18–45 years were infected by 2000. With infection rates at around 4.16 per cent of the adult population, Gabon is beginning to experience the serious effects of the African pandemic. Around 8,600 children have been orphaned by the disease. The main concentration of HIV/AIDS cases is in Libreville, the country's capital. The government has launched a campaign to prevent the disease spreading further. In 2000, a presidential decree led to the creation of an inter-ministerial committee on AIDS, chaired by the prime minister. In 2001, the government launched a new strategic plan which identified a number of priorities, including education initiatives among Gabonese youth.

Welfare

Gabon's social welfare system, while deeply flawed, is one of the best in sub-Saharan Africa. It operates a social insurance system and a separate system for self-employed and state workers under contract.

The social insurance system covers benefits including old age, disability, sickness, maternity and work injuries with provision for certain categories of self-employed workers. Old age pensions are available to men aged 55 with 20 years of insurance and 120 months of contribution during the last 10 years. It is set at a minimum of 40 per cent of average earnings during the last three or five years of pay. There is also provision for old-age settlement with a lump sum equal to 50 per cent of average monthly earnings for every six months of contribution, if the person is ineligible for pension.

Medical services are provided by hospitals and dispensaries operated by the National Social Security Fund, and by other establishments. Free maternity care is payable up to six weeks before and eight weeks after confinement. A family allowance law also offers benefits to employees with one or more children under the age of 16 years. Family Allowance Benefits are set at a maximum of CFAf3,000 (US$4) a month for each child and school allowances of CFAf10,000 (US$13.5) per year to primary, secondary and technical school students.

Main cities

Libreville (capital, estimated population 541,000 in 2002), Port-Gentil (102,000), Franceville (42,000).

Languages spoken

French is the medium for all documentation. The main native language is Fang, with a number of other Bantu dialects spoken.

It is essential that business visitors should be able to conduct business in French. Interpreters can be hired locally.

Official language/s

French

Media

Press

The official news agency is Agence Gabonaise de Presse (AGP).

Dailies: Gabon has two daily newspapers. *L'Union* is published by Sonapresse, owned jointly by the state, Sonadig, Multipresse Gabon and France Edition. *Gabon-Matin* is the second daily paper.

Periodicals: *L'Union* also publishes a monthly magazine, with a similar circulation. *M'Bolo* has three issues on holiday and travel.

Broadcasting

Gabon is developing as the centre of Francophone broadcasting for central and west Africa, being the base of the radio service Africa No 1 and for the African operations of France's Canal Plus. The state has taken a financial interest in these broadcasting media, as well as in the main newspaper, directly and through parastatal groups. It therefore retains a degree of control.

Radio: Gabon is host to the radio service Africa No 1, broadcasting mostly programmes from Radio France Internationale (RFI). Africa No 1, which is 35 per cent state-owned, began transmissions in 1981. Africa No 1 broadcasts news from RFI, Radio Japan and Swiss Radio International to South America, the Middle East, southern Africa, west Africa, as well as the whole of central Africa.

Television: Gabon's state broadcaster is Radiodiffusion-Télévision Gabonaise (RTG), known as La Voix de la Rénovation. RTG has two television

channels: RTG 1 is a national service, broadcast in Libreville and Franceville; while RTG 2 can be received only in the Libreville and the coastal area.
Téléafrica, a private commercial channel, began transmissions in 1988. Broadcasting 24 hours a day, it prepared the way for the establishment of Canal Plus Gabon, a subscription channel which will eventually serve the whole of Francophone central Africa.

Advertising
Extremely limited facilities. The only active agency is Havas-Gabon.

Economy
Gabon is sub-Saharan Africa's third-largest oil exporter and oil revenues account for 80 per cent of export revenues and almost 60 per cent of government revenues. At US$3,451 in 2000, Gabon's per capita GDP is significantly above the US$500 average of sub-Saharan Africa, although income is distributed extremely unevenly and the standard of living is well below that in countries with a similar per capita income.
Gabon's reliance on oil – which contributes around 40 per cent to GDP – has subjected the economy to the vagaries of the international price of oil. Falling production levels are also a threat to the medium-term health of the economy: without significant new finds, at 2001 production levels of 301,000 barrels per day (bpd), Gabon's oil reserves are expected to last only another 10 years.
Efforts to diversify the economy have been slow. Privatisation in the telecommunications industry and the national airline have been slow, made more difficult by government mismanagement and corruption.
The government failed to meet its privatisation targets in 2001 and several sales did not go through. However, there are a number of companies slated for privatisation in 2002/03. These include shipping, housing and oil products companies.

External trade
Gabon is spearheading moves towards greater regional integration. In 1999, Gabon and five other African states that form the Central African Economic and Monetary Community (CAEMC) agreed to converge their macroeconomic policies, stabilise their common currency, create a common market and harmonise their sectoral policies. This culminated in the creation of the Gulf of Guinea Commission by the beginning of 2000, giving the countries a forum for dialogue on conflicts over the exploitation of natural resources.

Exports
Principal exports are crude oil (typically 80 per cent of total), timber (10 per cent), manganese and uranium (10 per cent).
Main destinations: The US buys over US$1.6 billion of crude oil annually (and absorbs typically 47 per cent of total exports), France (19 per cent), China (8 per cent), Japan (1.3 per cent).

Imports
Principal imports are equipment and tools (typically 37 per cent of total), chemicals, petroleum products, construction materials, food.
Main sources: France (typically 64 per cent of the total), US (4 per cent), UK (2 per cent), Netherlands (2 per cent).

Agriculture
The agricultural sector in Gabon has been neglected, forcing the importation of a large percentage of the country's food needs. Only about 1 per cent of total land area is under cultivation and agriculture is further limited by the small size of the population. A shortage of cultivated lands has been the major problem facing the agricultural sector which, mostly through subsistence farming, supports a large portion of the population.
Principal cash crops are palm oil, coffee, cocoa and refined sugar, while subsistence crops are cassava, maize and plantains. Cocoa is grown mainly in Woleu Ntem province and coffee mainly in Ogooué-Ivindo, Ogooué-Lolo and Haut Ogooué provinces. Sugar-cane is grown and refined by the Société Sucrérie du Haut-Ogooué (Sosuho). Annual sugar output is around 30,000 tonnes.
Agrogabon set up three cattle ranches in the 1980s, importing tsetse-resistant cattle. They are located at Lekabi, Nyanga and N'Gounie. The only industrial-scale poultry farm is run by the Société Industrielle d'Agriculture et d'Elevage de Boumango (SIAEB).
The agricultural sector typically contributes around 7 per cent to GDP and employs up to half the workforce. The sector suffers from urban drift, under-investment and weak rural infrastructure.

Fishing
Gabon has well-stocked fishing grounds, which are only partially exploited. Reserves are estimated at around 180,000 tonnes of fish and 2,000 tonnes of shellfish, with an additional 40,000 tonnes of tuna fish in the Gulf of Guinea region. Domestic demand is estimated at around 36,000 tonnes per annum. Traditional fishing accounts for two-thirds of national output. There are about a dozen fleets, most of which are foreign, engaged in industrial fishing in Gabonese waters.

Forestry
Forests cover 75 per cent of the land area in Gabon and the forestry industry is the second major industry in the country. Gabon commercially exploits and exports both soft and hard woods, but cultivation and processing of timber comprises the main portion of forestry activities. Despite concerns of deforestation, the timber industry picked up in 2000.
Exploitable forest potential is more than 300 million cubic metres. One-third of this is okoume, which is particularly suited to the production of plywood. The forest is divided into three administrative zones. The coastal area is already fairly well exploited. The zone around Ngounie, Nyanga and Haut-Ogooué has the bulk of current activity. The Booue-Lastourville axis of the Transgabon railway is largely undeveloped. Seven large companies dominate okoume production. The largest is the majority state-owned Compagnie Forestière du Gabon (CFG).

Industry and manufacturing
A fair proportion of the very modest industrial sector has been based on a policy of import substitution. This is now being abandoned as part of structural adjustment measures. The outlook for industry is therefore bleak but there are plans to develop a regional export market within the Union Douanière des Etats de l'Afrique Centrale (UDEAC) (Central African Customs and Economic Union) countries. In theory, this larger potential market would allow industry to develop economies of scale that the small domestic market does not justify. In practice, however, high labour costs are likely to frustrate efforts to promote the regional market. Gabon's labour costs are high on account of the well-established social security system, most of the cost of which is borne by employers, offering benefits that are not found in many other West and Central African countries.
The main industrial activities are oil refining and timber processing, although these activities are treated separately from other industry in the national accounts. The main manufacturing sectors, apart from these, are food processing, drinks and tobacco, metal transformation (mainly connected with shipyard activities and supplying the oil and wood industries) and building materials. Small sub sectors include textiles and chemicals (lubricants, paints, varnishes and detergents).

Tourism
Gabon receives around 120,000 foreign visitors annually, however, only around 1 per cent are tourists. The ministry of tourism is beginning to market Gabon as an eco-tourism destination. La Lopée Reserve in south-east Gabon, covering 4,940 square km, was the country's first national park. Tourism is not yet well developed and the high local cost of living makes it difficult to compete internationally. However, Gabon has a good hotel infrastructure, marvellous sandy beaches, generally

safe bathing and many wildlife attractions. There are about 6,000 hotel beds in the country. Gabon has five game reserves: La Lopée, Mouklaba, Wonga-Wonge, Sette-Cama and Iguela.

Mining

Mining and hydrocarbons together contribute around 50 cent to GDP and employ 10 per cent of the workforce.
Gabon is one of the world's leading producers of manganese and uranium. Other areas of interest are gold and iron ore. Activity is concentrated on extraction and export of manganese ore (reserves of 200 million tonnes) and uranium (reserves of 35,000 tonnes). Both are crudely refined before export, the manganese as a 51 per cent concentrate and the uranium as 74 per cent pure yellow cake. Manganese goes mainly to Europe, but also to the US and the Far East. Uranium goes mainly to France (about 10 per cent of France's requirements), the rest to Belgium and Japan. Manganese and uranium account for 10 per cent of merchandise exports.
Large deposits of iron ore, barytes (used in paint-making) and niobium, discovered during construction of the Transgabon railway, have yet to be exploited.
There are 50 million tonnes of phosphate reserves.
Manganese production is declining.

Hydrocarbons

Oil

Gabon is sub-Saharan Africa's third-largest oil producer, after Nigeria and Angola. In 2001, the proven reserves were 2.5 billion barrels, almost double the 1996 figure of 1.3 billion barrels. Oil production in 2001 averaged 301,000 barrels per day (bpd), but oil production has been declining. The World Bank estimates that oil production is likely to decline by 50 per cent by 2007, which will strain government revenues.
Exploration and production occur both onshore and offshore. The country's downstream industry consists of the Sogara refinery, which has a capacity of 21,000bpd.
The government has consistently maintained a market-oriented policy towards its sizeable oil reserves and has one of the most attractive hydrocarbons codes in Africa. Under this law, the state has a minimum 25 per cent holding in all oil-producing companies operating in Gabon. Current practice is to award oil exploration permits under production sharing agreements, which are individually negotiated.
Companies holding exploration permits include: Elf Gabon, Occidental Gabon, Amoco, Shell Gabon, Marathon Gabon, Total Gabon, Ocelot, Vaalco, Santa Fe, Chauvco, Phillips, Petrofields, Broken Hill Petroleum, Energy Africa, Mitsubishi, Forcenergy and Elf Aquitaine. The most important discoveries have been onshore fields at Gamba, Rabi, Echira, Coucal and Avocette.
Production at Gabon's largest oil field, Rabi-Kounga, fell to 100,000bpd in 2000 – less than half the output of 1997. In an effort to increase new investment and boost production, the government offered licences for 27 blocks in April 2000. After the licensing round had ended in January 2001, the government admitted that international interest had been 'disappointing' but has continued to promote the blocks.
In February 2001, PanAfrican Energy signed a concession agreement to reactivate the Remboue field. Production began in July 2001. Initial crude oil production was 1,299bpd in 2001. By May 2002, this had risen to 3,300bpd.

Gas

Natural gas reserves total approximately 33.8 billion cubic metres with production at around 1 billion cubic metres per annum. All gas produced in Gabon is used for electricity or refinery fuel.

Energy

Gabon has a total electricity generating capacity of 300MW. Société d'Energie et d'Eau du Gabon (SEEG) is responsible for the production and distribution of electricity and water throughout the country – 51 per cent was sold to a French consortium in 1997, representing sub-Saharan Africa's first privatisation of a water and electricity utility. Consumption is principally concentrated in the regions of Libreville, Port-Gentil and Franceville. Hydroelectricity accounts for two-thirds of output and there is hydroelectric potential of around 6,000MW.

Banking

Central bank

Banque des Etats de l'Afrique Centrale.

Main financial centre

Libreville.

Time

GMT plus one hour

Geography

Gabon is an equatorial country on the west coast of Africa, with Equatorial Guinea and Cameroon to the north, and the Republic of Congo to the south and east.
The eastern boundary lies along the watershed of the Democratic Republic of Congo (DRC), so that all rivers flow broadly west through Gabon into the sea. The sandy coastal strip consists of palm-fringed bays, lagoons and estuaries. The uplands are heavily eroded by river action, and there is a wide coastal plain, which is largely alluvial in nature. The natural vegetation is dense rain forest.

Climate

The climate is equatorial with an annual mean temperature of 28 degrees Celsius and high levels of humidity. The rainy seasons are between October and mid-December, and between mid-January and May. The dry season from June to September.

Dress codes

Lightweight or tropical clothing is suitable, with rainwear for the monsoon season. Businessmen should wear a lightweight or tropical suit and women a lightweight suit or equivalent.

Entry requirements

Passports

Required by all. Passports must be valid for more than six months.

Visa

Required by all. To encourage tourism, Gabon introduced a tourist visa, issued free.

Currency advice/regulations

There are no limits on the import of foreign or domestic currency, although any currency brought into the country should be declared on arrival. Exports of local currency are controlled, however, and there is a limit of CFAf200,000 (around US$250) for export to countries outside the franc zone. Visitors are advised to carry traveller's cheques in French francs. Credit cards are not widely accepted.

Health (for visitors)

Mandatory precautions

A yellow fever vaccination certificate is required if coming from an infected area.

Advisable precautions

Immunisations are advisable for yellow fever, hepatitis 'A', tetanus, typhoid and polio. There is a rabies risk.
Malaria and AIDS are prevalent and standard measures should be taken to avoid these diseases.
Dysentery can be caught from raw fruit and vegetables and unboiled water. Water which is used for drinking, brushing teeth or making ice should first be boiled. Dairy products made from local milk should be avoided. Meat and fish should be well cooked.
There was an outbreak of ebola in December 2001.

Hotels

Available in Libreville, Port Gentil, Lambaréné and other main centres. Service charge is usually included in bill, if not a tip of 10–15 per cent is usual.

Credit cards

Credit cards can be used in some hotels and restaurants in Libreville; there is limited acceptance further afield – use is becoming more widely spread.

Public holidays
Additional holidays may be announced at short notice.

Fixed dates

1 Jan (New Year's Day), 12 Mar (Anniversaire de la Rénovation), 1 May (Labour Day), 17 Aug (Independence Day), 1 Nov (All Saints' Day), 25 Dec (Christmas Day).

Variable dates

Easter Monday, Eid Al-Fitr, Whit Monday, Eid Al-Adha, Prophet's Birthday.

Working hours
Banking

Mon–Fri: 0730–1130, 1430–1630.

Business

Mon–Fri: 0730–1200, 1430–1800.

Government

Mon–Fri: 0800–1200, 1500–1800; Sat: 0800–1300.

Shops

Mon–Sat: 0800–1200, 1500–1900.

Telecommunications
Telephone/fax

Network comprises an international automatic exchange and 14 domestic automatic exchanges.

Gabon has direct telephone links with Europe, North America and other African countries. The high quality of international communications contrasts with the sparse domestic network outside Libreville and Port Gentil.

There are around 50,000 telephone lines in Gabon, of which 10,000 are mobile and 40,000 are fixed with microwave and satellite connections.

Postal services

The Office des Postes et Télécommunications (OPT) has responsibility for postal services and domestic telephone, telex and fax services.

Internet/e-mail

Internet service is available although limited.

Electricity supply
220–230V AC, 50 cycles. Round two-pin plugs are standard.

Social customs/useful tips
Business is conducted in French. Appointments should be made in advance. It is customary to shake hands on meeting and taking leave. Business cards are exchanged after introduction.

Gratuities around 10 per cent to 15 per cent are proffered if there is no service charged.

The lifestyles of the middle classes in Libreville, Port-Gentil and Franceville have been heavily influenced by the French, and French etiquette has been largely adopted. As elsewhere in Africa, it is extremely unwise to attempt to photograph any military installations or troop movements, security checkpoints, etc.

Security
Political and social unrest, as a result of the economic recession during the 1990s, have led to a deterioration in the security situation. Previously, in the large towns and along the beaches in Libreville, security was excellent, with little incidence of theft and mugging. Unfortunately, visitors are now advised to exercise considerable caution. It is unwise to walk on the streets after dark and there have been muggings and thefts in the car parks of the main hotels.

Getting there
Air

National airline: Air Gabon (Compagnie Nationale Air Gabon).

International airport/s: Libreville-Léon M'Ba (Code: LBV), 12km from city; restaurant, currency exchange; Port Gentil (POG), 4km from city; Franceville.

Other airport/s: There are 65 other public and 50 private airfields linked mostly with the forestry and petroleum industries.

Airport tax: None.

Surface

Road: The major routes are from the Republic of Congo, Cameroon or Equatorial Guinea. These are semi-surfaced but generally are in good condition and well maintained.

Water: There is a boat to and from São Tomé every five days.

Main port/s: The principal deep-water ports are Port Gentil, Owendo (Libreville). Mayumba and Nyanga are used for shipping timber. There is a fishing port in Libreville.

Getting about
National transport

Air: Air Gabon operates scheduled and charter flights to all main centres.

Road: There are an estimated 8,590km of roads, including 3,290km of main roads and 1,950km of secondary roads. Except for the routes Libreville to Ndende, Booué and Bitam, roads can be difficult in the rainy season. Travel by bush taxis and truck can be dangerous in the rainy season, especially.

Buses: Regular coach and minibus services link Libreville with Lambaréné, Oyem, Mouila and Bitam. Some services are subject to rainy season conditions.

Rail: Regular services operate on the Transgabon railway linking Libreville with Booué, Ndjolé and Franceville. There are two classes. The railcars are air-conditioned for some services but no refreshment or sleeping accommodation is scheduled. The rolling stock is generally new.

Water: The principal river is the Ogooué, navigable from Port-Gentil to Ndjole (310km), and serving the towns of Lambaréné, Ndjolé and Sindara.

A ferry service (taking two hours) operates between Libreville and Port-Gentil.

City transport

Taxis: Unmetered 'collective' and private taxis are available in main towns; tipping is not usual; rates vary according to the time of day. The journey from the airport to the Libreville city centre takes 10 minutes

Car hire

Available in main towns, at airports and through hotels. International driving licence required. Charges are high.

BUSINESS DIRECTORY

Telephone area codes
The international dialling code (IDD) for Gabon is + 241 followed by the customer number.

Useful telephone numbers
Police: 732-036, 761-044, 760-950, 720-951

Fire: 18, 761-520

Ambulance: 732-771, 762-344

Chambers of Commerce
Chambre de Commerce d'Agriculture, d'Industrie et des Mines du Gabon, BP 2234, Libreville (tel: 720-753, 722-064).

Centre Gabonais du Commerce Extérieur, 3ème étage, Immeuble Rénovation, BP 3906, Libreville (tel: 746-974/80; fax: 747-153).

Banking
Banque Gabonaise de Développement; PO Box 5, Rue Alfred Marche, Libreville (tel: 762-429, 762-489; fax: 742-699).

Banque Gabonaise et Francaise Internationale (BGFI) (BGFI), PO Box 2253, Blvd de l'Indépendance, Libreville (tel: 732-326, 764-035; fax: 740-894, 744-456).

Banque Internationale pour le Commerce et l'Industrie du Gabon SA, PO Box 2241, Avenue du Colonel Parant, Libreville (tel: 762-613, 763-811; fax: 746-410).

Banque Nationale du Crédit Rural, PO Box 1120, Avenue Bouët, Libreville (tel: 724-742, 766-144, 763-045; fax: 740-507).

Banque Populaire du Gabon, PO Box 6663, Blvd de l'Indépendance, Libreville (tel: 724-719; fax: 728-691).

Caisse Nationale d'Epargne, Siège Social, Libreville (tel: 766-509).

Centre de Chéques Postaux, Siége Social, Libreville (tel: 766-509).

Union Gabonaise de Banque SA, PO Box 315 & 2238, Avenue du Colonel Parant, Libreville (tel: 777-000; fax: 764-616).

Central bank

Banque des Etats de l'Afrique Centrale (BEAC) Direction Nationale; PO Box 112, Libreville (tel: 761-352, 760-209, 760-206).

Travel information

ADL (Aeroport de Libreville), BP 363, Libreville (tel: 736-128).

Air Gabon (Compagnie Nationale Air Gabon), BP 2206, Aeroport International Léon M'ba, Libreville (tel: 730-027; fax: 731-156).

Eurafrique Voyages, BP 4026, Libreville (tel: 762-787; fax: 761-897).

Libreville Léon M'Ba International Airport, BP 363, Libreville (tel: 736-244/246/247; fax: 736-128).

Other useful addresses

There is no British Embassy in Libreville; Gabon is covered from: British High Commission, Commercial Section, Avenue Winston Churchill, BP 547, Yaoundé, Cameroon (tel: (00 237) 220-545; fax: (00 237) 220-148).

Compagnie Minière de l'Ogoué (COMILOG), BP 578, Libreville (tel: 722-474).

Conseil Economique et Sociale de la République Gabonais, BP 1075, Libreville (tel: 762-668).

European Development Fund, BP 321, Libreville (tel: 732-250).

Gabon Embassy (US), 2233 Wisconsin Avenue, NW, Washington DC 20007 (tel: 797-1000; fax: 332-0668).

Ministry of Agriculture and Rural Development, BP 551, Libreville (tel: 721-579).

Ministry of the Arts, Culture and People Education, BP 1007, Libreville (tel: 724-028).

Ministry of Defence, Security and Immigration, BP 13493, Libreville (tel: 760-835).

Ministry of Economy, Planning and of the Reform of the Parapublic Sector and Privatisation, BP 747, Libreville (tel: 721-421).

Ministry of Finance, Budget and Participations, BP 165, Libreville (tel: 761-210); Privatisation Committee, 4th Floor, Room 410, BP 9672, Libreville (tel: 760-677, 775-723; fax: 721-818; e-mail: meye.bekourou @internetgabon.com).

Ministry of Foreign Affairs and Co-operation, BP 2245, Libreville (tel: 762-251).

Ministry of Forestry and Environment, BP 199, Libreville (tel: 733-191).

Ministry of Higher Education, BP 3919, Libreville (tel: 763-252).

Ministry of Home (in charge of Local Collectivities and Mobile Security), BP 2110, Libreville (tel: 762-181).

Ministry of Housing, Land Registry and Town Planning, BP 512, Libreville (tel: 740-461).

Ministry of Justice, BP 547, Libreville (tel: 720-160).

Ministry of Labour and Human Resources, BP 2256, Libreville (tel: 732-739).

Ministry of Mining, Energy and Hydraulic Resources, BP 4041, Libreville (tel: 762-863).

Ministry of National Education and Professional Training, BP 6, Libreville (tel: 721-741).

Ministry of Public Health, BP 50, Libreville (tel: 762-522).

Ministry of Public Service and Administrative Reform, BP 496, Libreville (tel: 762-150).

Ministry of Shipping, BP 803, Libreville (tel: 733-210).

Ministry of Small and Medium Businesses, BP 4120, Libreville (tel: 720-636).

Ministry of Social Affairs, Family and Solidarity, BP 5684, Libreville (tel: 761-700).

Ministry of State Control, Decentralisation, Administration of Territory and Regional Integration, BP 178, Libreville (tel: 763-550).

Ministry of Trade Industry, BP 3906, Libreville (tel: 722-887).

Ministry of Transport, Tourism and National Parks, BP 3974, Libreville (tel: 763-240).

Ministry of Youth and Sport, BP 3904, Libreville (tel: 763-576).

Société de Développement de l'Agriculture au Gabon (AGROGABON), BP 2248, Libreville (tel: 764-082).

Société Equatoriale de Travaux Pétroliers Maritimes, BP 493, Libreville (tel: 753-509).

Société Gabonaise de Financement et d'Expansion, BP 2151, Libreville.

Société Gabonaise de Participation et de Développement, BP 1624, Libreville.

Société Gabonaise de Raffinage, BP 530, Libreville (tel: 752-365).

Société Nationale de Transports Maritimes (SONATRAM), BP 3841, Libreville (tel: 740-632; fax: 745-967).

US Embassy, Boulevard de la Mer, BP 4000, Libreville (tel: 762-002).

Internet sites

Africa Business Network: http://www.ifc.org/abn

AllAfrica.com: http://allafrica.com

African Development Bank: http://www.afdb.org

Africa Online: http://www.africaonline.com

Harambee Afrika (UK business club for traders with east, central and southern Africa; includes annotated web resource list): http://www.harambee.co.uk

Mbendi AfroPaedia (information on companies, countries, industries and stock exchanges in Africa): http://www.mbendi.co.za

The Gambia

Anver Versi

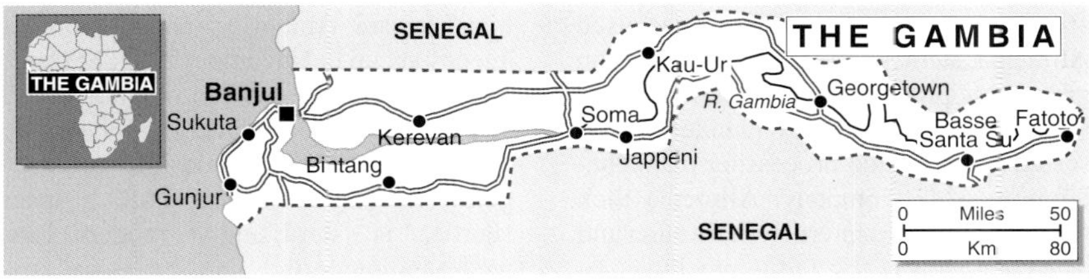

President Yahya Jammeh, probably still holding on to his title as the world's youngest head of state at the age of 37, spent most of 2001 and 2002 consolidating his credentials as a democratically-elected civilian president. With his party, the Alliance for Patriotic Reorientation and Construction (APRC), holding 45 of the 50 seats in parliament, he felt confident enough to push through the National Media Commission bill in April 2002 – considered by most as the last nail in the coffin of the country's free press.

Good groundnut harvests two years running and an IMF/World Bank debt reduction package worth US$67 million was expected to see GDP growth hit the 5 per cent mark in 2002. With tourism beginning to pick up after the disastrous slump following the 1994 coup, which brought Jammeh to power, and debt servicing reduced by 43 per cent, the government will be in a position to start implementing some of its social policies. However, it is unlikely that the status of The Gambia as one of the poorest countries in Africa will be much changed.

Taking off the uniform

Yahya Jammeh began his transformation from military to civilian ruler in earnest in July 2001 when he lifted a ban on political parties which had been active before the 1994 coup. In 1996, he had cast off his uniform, but not his military mind-set, when he and his party, the APRC, stormed through to win the presidential and general elections amid accusations of electoral fraud from international observers.

After lifting the ban on political parties, Jammeh announced presidential elections for October 2001 and general elections for November. Although there was a spirited regrouping of The Gambia's old guard, led by human rights lawyer Ousainou Darboe of the United Democratic Party (UDP) and the country's first ever vice president, Sherriff Diba of the National Convention Party (NCP), Jammeh kept a tight leash on the media and mounted a vigorous campaign of his own.

The government's relations with the UK have not been good under Jammeh. The UK made no secret of its desire to see the ousted ex-president Sir Dawda Jawara back in power. Relations deteriorated further when Jammeh expelled the British deputy high commissioner, Bharat Joshi, for consorting with the opposition.

While relations with the UK remained poor during 2001–02, the government did allow Jawara to return to The Gambia in June 2002 from exile in the UK. The decision to allow Jawara to return was made as part of a reconciliation process enacted by Jammeh. Upon his return on 24 June, Jawara announced that he was retiring from politics.

Ousainou Darboe, who had given Jammeh several uneasy moments during the farcical 1996 elections, was again the main contender for the presidency. A Muslim like Jammeh, he had the strong backing of the country's trading classes and was popular in the rural areas. His arrest, on charges of murdering an APRC activist in June 2000, had made him something of a martyr and enhanced his reputation as a man of impeccable honesty.

The presidential election in October 2001 was generally deemed free and fair although there were several flash points and one man was killed. With Jammeh leaning heavily on the press and using the state publicity apparatus to the full, the result was a foregone conclusion.

KEY FACTS

Official name: Republic of The Gambia

Head of State: President Yahya Alphonse Jamus Jebulai Jammeh (Chairman of APRC) (re-elected 18 Oct 2001)

Head of government: President Yahya Alphonse Jamus Jebulai Jammeh

Ruling party: Alliance for Patriotic Reorientation and Construction (APRC) (re-elected Jan 2002)

Area: 11,295 square km

Population: 1.40 million (2001)

Capital: Banjul

Official language: English

Currency: Dalasi (D) = 100 butut

Exchange rate: D22.38 per US$ (Jan 2003)

GDP per capita: US$253 (2001)

GDP real growth: 4.60% (2001)

Inflation: 4.30% (2001)

Balance of trade: -US$70.00 million (2001)

Foreign debt: US$441.00 million (2001)

Annual FDI: US$6.00 million (2001)

For the latest Key Facts, go to www.worldinformation.com

Nevertheless, voter turnout was surprisingly high, with an estimated 80 per cent of the country's half million electorate turning out to cast their marbles into a 'ballot' drum. This was The Gambia's unique system of casting ballots, the aim being to prevent multiple voting.

Jammeh won as expected and obtained 52.9 per cent of the vote, making a second round unnecessary. Darboe came in second with 32.67 per cent and all other presidential candidates combined obtained 14.3 per cent.

Having secured public endorsement for his tenure as a civilian president, Jammeh set about sealing his authority by mounting a well orchestrated campaign for the parliamentary elections, which had been postponed from November 2001 to January 2002.

With a week to go to the elections, Darboe pulled the UDP out of the race, saying the field had been severely tilted when voter lists had been switched between constituencies. This left the field clear for the APRC – it was unopposed in 33 constituencies and took 12 out of the 15 seats contested by other parties.

In April 2002, despite strong opposition from journalist trade unions and international organisations, The Gambia passed the National Media Commission Bill. The new Media Commission will have sweeping powers to call journalists to task, fine and even imprison them. Media companies which fall foul of the commission could lose not only their licences but also their properties.

Nuts about the economy

Groundnuts form the basis of this small country's economy. The Gambia is the world's second largest producer of groundnuts. Yields have varied from the very poor 45,000 tonnes in the 1996/97 season to the bumper crops of around 130,000 tonnes in 2001 and 2002.

Severe groundnut processing and marketing problems involving the Swiss based company, Alimenta, which adversely affected harvests from 1998 to 2000, were still unresolved in 2002. In 1999, the had government accused Alimenta, which enjoyed a monopoly on groundnut processing and marketing, of being involved in money laundering and seized property and processing plants belonging to the company. Alimenta took the government to international courts and The Gambia was ordered to pay the company US$11.4 million.

The IMF and World Bank have expressed satisfaction at the way the government has so far managed its economy, with inflation down to around 4 per cent and GDP growth of around 6 per cent. The US$67 million debt relief (which will translate into US$91 million over 20 years) will free up sufficient resources to test Jammeh's social reform pledges.

The IMF was prepared to overlook the budget deficit in 2001 because of the payment made to Alimenta, but insisted that the budget deficit of 20 per cent of GDP in 2001 had to be reduced to at least 15 per cent of GDP in 2002.

In an effort to step up the pace of the economy, Jammeh announced in 2001 an across the board wage increase of 6 per cent and authorised commercial banks to introduce foreign currency deposits. Several state-owned entities, such as the National Printing Services Corporation, Management Services Agency, Gambia International Airlines and Banjul Shipyards, were being prepared for privatisation.

Tourism, which generates around 12 per cent of GDP, is slowly picking up after the disastrous decline following the 1994 coup and tensions with the UK. Average tourist arrivals before the coup were around the 100,000 mark with about 60 per cent coming from the UK. The Gambia Tourism Authority, an autonomous agency set up in November 2001, has been looking for investment in order to diversify the tourism product. Banjul airport, which is one of the US-designated emergency landing strips for NASA's space shuttle, is surprisingly modern and well-appointed and can be easily expanded to accommodate greater passenger traffic.

Domestic organisations, such as Gambia Tourism Concern, complain that very little of the revenue from tourism, which is made up almost exclusively of package holidays, actually finds its way back to the country. Most of the support services, such as transport, retail and catering, are operated by overseas subsidiaries of holiday package companies. This, coupled with the visible disparity between the affluent tourist areas and the poverty stricken local conditions, is causing a degree of resentment against tourism. When Jammeh took power, he promised that The Gambia would once again belong to Gambians; now he has the public mandate and a reasonable purse to make good his word.

Risk assessment

Economic	Fair
Political	Stable
Regional stability	Poor

KEY INDICATORS — The Gambia

	Unit	1996	1997	1998	1999	2000
Population	m	1.15	1.19	1.23	1.38	1.39
Gross domestic product (GDP)	US$bn	0.39	0.42	0.43	0.45	0.42
GDP per capita	US$	354	366	360	368	312
GDP real growth	%	5.3	4.9	4.9	5.6	5.6
Inflation	%	1.1	2.8	1.1	3.8	0.9
Exports (fob) (goods)	US$m	118.8	119.6	130.0	120.0	133.0
Imports (fob) (goods)	US$m	217.1	207.1	207.0	194.0	202.0
Balance of trade	US$m	-98.3	-87.5	-77.0	-74.0	-69.0
Current account	US$m	-47.7	-23.6	-46.0	-19.0	-21.0
Total reserves minus gold	US$m	102.1	96.0	106.4	111.3	109.4
Foreign exchange	US$m	99.7	93.9	103.8	108.5	107.3
Exchange rate	per US$	9.79	10.20	10.64	11.40	12.79

COUNTRY PROFILE

Historical profile

1455 The Portuguese established trading stations along the Gambia river.

1889 The boundaries of The Gambia were agreed by the British and French.

1894 The Gambia became a British protectorate.

1965 The Gambia became independent. Dawda Jawara, at the head of the People's Progressive Party (PPP), became prime minister with the British monarch as head of state.

1970 The Gambia became a republic following a referendum. Dawda Jawara was elected president.

1981 Around 500 people were killed after Senegalese troops intervened to suppress a coup.

1982 Senegal and The Gambia formed a confederation called Senegambia.

1989 Senegambia collapsed as a confederation.
1991 The Gambia and Senegal signed a friendship treaty.
1994 In July, President Jawara was deposed by a military coup. Lieutenant Yahya Jammeh of the Alliance for Patriotic Reorientation and Construction (APRC) was installed as president.
1996 Jammeh was elected president by the APRC and the majority of the popular vote. However, the three main opposition parties abstained from participating in the elections.
1997 There was a return to civilian rule in January. In the National Assembly elections, the ruling APRC won an absolute majority with 33 seats.
2000 In April, police fired on young demonstrators killing at least 12 people and injuring many others. Political tensions remained high throughout the year with clashes between members of the APRC and the United Democratic Party (UDP).
2001 In July, President Jammeh lifted the ban on the political parties he overthrew in 1994. He was re-elected in October. The British Deputy High Commissioner was expelled in August for meeting opposition leaders.
2002 On 17 January, President Jammeh's ruling APRC won a victory in the parliamentary elections, in which most APRC candidates were unopposed and the main opposition party, the centrist UDP, boycotted the elections.

Political structure

Constitution
The constitution was promulgated in 1970 and amended in 1982.

Form of state
Republic.

The executive
Executive power rests with the president, who is elected by universal suffrage every five years.

National legislature
Legislative power is vested in the unicameral 53-member House of Representatives, comprising 48 members directly elected for a five-year term and five members appointed by the president.

Last elections
18 October 2001 (presidential); 17 January 2002 (parliamentary).

Next elections
2006 (presidential); 2007 (parliamentary).

Political parties

Ruling party
Alliance for Patriotic Reorientation and Construction (APRC) (re-elected Jan 2002)

Main opposition party
United Democratic Party (UDP) is regarded as the main opposition party, although it has boycotted elections. The People's Democratic Organization for Independence and Socialism (PDOIS) is the only opposition party represented in parliament with three of the 53 seats.

Population
1.39 million (2000)
Annual population growth rate: 3 per cent (1994–2000). Approximately 41 per cent of the total population is under 14 years. Population density: 105 habitants per square km. Urban population: 33 per cent (1994–2000).

Ethnic make-up
Three major ethnic groups: Mandinka (42 per cent), Fula (18 per cent), Wolof (16 per cent). Other substantial ethnic groups: Jola, Serahule, Serere, Manjago, Bambara, Creole/Aku.
The census of 1993 showed that just over 13.7 per cent of the population came from other African countries, with non-Africans (mostly European expatriates and Lebanese businessmen) accounting for less than 1 per cent.

Religions
Muslim (90 per cent), Christian (9 per cent), animist beliefs (1 per cent).

Education
In 2000 the adult illiteracy rate was estimated at 56 per cent and 70.6 per cent for men and women respectively. Primary schooling lasts for six years between ages seven and 13. World Bank estimates show that the total primary school enrolment of the relevant age group typically stood at 87 per cent for boys and 57 per cent for girls (including repetition rates) between 1994 and 2000. It has been estimated by Oxfam that 74 per cent of children age 6–11 will enrol for school in 2015. The number of pupils per primary school teacher is typically 30.
Secondary education is divided into junior secondary schools, which offer a three-year course leading to the Junior School Leaving Certificate, and Senior Secondary schools, which offer another three-year course. This is followed by two years of schooling in the sixth Form.
Higher education in The Gambia is provided by the University of The Gambia, created in 1999, and Gambia College which offers courses in agriculture, education, nursing, midwifery, and public health.
Public expenditure on education typically amounted to 5.3 per cent of annual gross national income between 1994 and 1997.

Health
World Bank estimates during the period 1994 and 2000 showed that the average life expectancy was 53 years with a high infant mortality rate of 75 deaths per 1,000 live births. There were 26 per cent of malnourished children under the age of five in the same period. The fertility rate shows that 5.5 children are born per adult women. World Bank estimates in 2000, showed that 62 per cent and 37 per cent of the population had access to safe water and improved sanitation facilities respectively. There are less than 0.5 physicians and 0.6 hospital beds typically available for 1,000 people. There are an estimated 13,000 people living with HIV/AIDS in The Gambia – 520 are under the age of 15 (2000). With infection rates at around 1 per cent of the total population, The Gambia has so far escaped much of the African pandemic. However, with 14 per cent of sex workers testing positive, there is a chance that the infection could spread.
The total health expenditure typically amounts to 3.8 per cent of GDP, of which public and private expenditure each amount to 1.9 per cent of GDP.

Welfare
The Gambia has two important funds including the social security fund and the housing finance fund that receive contributions of the employers and employees either directly or indirectly. The Department of Social Welfare in Banjul has been restructured with four major units covering child care, adult, elderly and disabled services. There is provision for maternity leave up to 12 weeks on full payment of wage. The Gambia government and the Social Security and Housing Finance Corporation (SSHFC) have initiated mass housing projects including a rural electrification programme covering all major towns and villages.

Main cities
Banjul (capital) (population 240,000 in 1998), Brikama, Gunjur, Soma, Farafenni, Bansang, Georgetown, Basse.

Languages spoken
Mandinka, Wolof and Fula spoken. French is taught in some secondary and high schools. German, Italian, Dutch and the Scandinavian languages are also spoken by tourism staff.

Official language
English

Media

Press
Dailies: Daily newspapers include the *Daily Observer* and *The Gambia Daily*.
Weeklies: Main weekly newspapers are *Weekend Observer*, *New Citizen* (formerly *Newsmonth*) and a bi-weekly publication *The Point*.
Business: Business information is covered by *Business Weekly*, a weekly publication by The Gambia Communication Agency and Baroueli Enterprises.

Periodicals: Periodicals include the *Gamco-op News* (quarterly), *Gambia Times* (monthly) and *The Nation* (irregular).

Broadcasting

Radio: Radio Gambia, a government non-commercial station, operates 19 hours daily in English and Gambian languages. The commercial station, Radio Syd, also broadcasts in English, French and African languages, and provides tourist information in German and Swedish.

Television: Senegalese transmissions are received.

Economy

The Gambia is classified by the World Bank as a low-income country. Agriculture, forestry and fisheries remain the dominant sectors of the economy and have actually grown as a proportion of GDP, reflecting the country's industrial stagnation. The economy depends almost entirely on the cultivation and export of groundnuts in the form of nuts, oil and cattle cake.

The general policy is to diversify and broaden the productive base of the economy and foster economic growth and development. The Economic Recovery Programme (ERP) includes institutional reform, price liberalisation and the adoption of a flexible exchange rate regime. There is potential for tourism and re-exports, but political instability and poor infrastructure have hampered the development of these sectors.

Since the mid-1990s, inflation has remained below 5.0 per cent, averaging 2.3 per cent in 1996–2001. Meanwhile, GDP growth has been strong, averaging 5.4 per cent in the same period and reaching a record 5.8 per cent in 2001 on the back of good groundnut harvests and rising tourism.

In December 2000, the IMF and World Bank agreed to support a US$67 million debt-reduction package under the enhanced Heavily Indebted Poor Countries (HIPC) Initiative. This will be worth a total of US$91 million over 20 years. It is envisaged that external debt service as a percentage of goods and travel income will fall from more than 11 per cent in 2000 to around 6 per cent by 2010 as a result of HIPC. The ratio of the total net present value of debt to exports is scheduled to fall from about 206 per cent in 2000 to under 130 per cent in 2010 and about 120 per cent in 2010–20.

The bulk of assistance is contingent on The Gambia fulfilling a number of criteria, including a poverty reduction strategy in line with the IMF's structural adjustment strategies. The Poverty Reduction Strategy Paper (PRSP) was expected to be finalised by the end of 2001 but was delayed until 2002.

External trade

Banjul is an important transit trade centre.

Exports

Principal exports are groundnuts (typically 85 per cent of total) and fish. Minor exports include horticultural products, cattle, hides and skins.

Main destinations: Belgium (typically 55 per cent of total), Japan (9 per cent), UK (8 per cent), Brazil (4 per cent), Netherlands (3 per cent).

Imports

Principal imports are food, live animals, beverages, basic manufactures, machinery and transport equipment, mineral fuels, energy. Imports which support transit trade are estimated at 34 per cent of total imports.

Main sources: China (typically 23 per cent of total), Hong Kong (10 per cent), UK (9 per cent), Netherlands (8 per cent), Brazil (5 per cent).

Agriculture

Agriculture remains the main sector of the economy, typically contributing 30 per cent to GDP and employing over 70 per cent of the workforce.

Approximately 17 per cent of the total land area is cultivated. Groundnuts are cultivated on about 60 per cent of the planted area, and provide 85 per cent of official export earnings. The Gambia is the second largest producer of groundnuts in the world, after Senegal. Production of food crops (rice, maize, millet, sorghum, cassava) is insufficient to meet local needs, but receives a great deal of official encouragement. Small-scale fruit and cotton farming are also important while some livestock is exported to neighbouring countries for breeding.

The government, backed by international development agencies and donors, is attempting to increase agricultural production. The on-going US$2.5 million Lowlands Agricultural Development Project (LADEP) is aimed at developing 6,000 hectares for cultivation and the rehabilitation of 1,500 hectares in various lowland ecologies. US$2 million has been allocated to assist women's groups engaged in sheep, goat and poultry production while US$1.5 million is dedicated to an integrated rural development scheme.

Fishing

Fishing has also increased in importance with the annual catch rising to over 22,000 tonnes. The government, with assistance from the United Nations Development Programme (UNDP), is encouraging improved methods and modernisation of boats. Illegal fishing by foreign trawler fleets remains a problem.

Industry and manufacturing

The industrial sector contributes around 6 per cent to GDP and employs 4 per cent of the workforce.

The manufacturing sector is small-scale and underdeveloped.

The main activities (most of which are centred around Banjul, particularly in the Kanifing Industrial Estate) include groundnut and fish processing, brewing, footwear, perfume, cement and brick production.

Tourism

The tourism sector is strong. It attracts an increasing number of Europeans, of whom between 50–60 per cent are British.

There are over 24 hotels with 6,000 beds in Banjul and along the coast.

Environment

Concerns are mounting over the ecological effects of tourism on the local environment, particularly shore erosion and the depletion of water resources.

Mining

Most mining activity is centred on the production of industrial minerals for local consumption. The Australian Carnegie Corporation is investigating the Brufut deposits located along the coast and around 11,000 tonnes of zircon has been found. There are known deposits of kaolin, tin, ilmenite and rutile as yet unexploited.

Hydrocarbons

There are no known deposits of oil or gas in Gambia, although offshore oil exploration is continuing. Oil prospectors believe that Gambia has potential offshore reserves. The downstream market has a total consumption of around 75,000 tonnes per annum.

Energy

There is total dependence on imported petroleum. Fuelwood is the main source of domestic energy. Hydroelectric resources are being developed on the River Gambia.

Banking

The banking sector is under-developed, but is growing as a result of increased economic activity and macroeconomic stability. The sector has seen consolidation, with two large mergers and privatisations.

Central bank

Central Bank of The Gambia

Main financial centre

Banjul

Time

GMT

Geography

The Gambia is a narrow territory around the River Gambia on the west coast of Africa. The country has a short coastline on the Atlantic Ocean but is otherwise surrounded by Senegal.

Climate
Sub-tropical with distinct dry and rainy seasons. Dry season from November–May with average temperatures around 21–27 degrees Celsius (C). The dry Harmattan wind keeps the humidity low. Rainy season from June–October with high humidity and average temperatures around 26–32 degrees C.

Entry requirements
Passports
Required by all. Passports must be valid for three months from date of return.
Visa
Required by all except nationals of UK, Commonwealth countries, Economic Community of West African States (ECOWAS) member countries, Germany, Scandinavian countries, Greece, Italy, Netherlands and some other European countries, for a period not exceeding 90 days. All visitors must hold tickets and documents for onward or return travel.
For those who require a visa and who are travelling to The Gambia on last minute bookings, arrangements can be made to get visas issued at The Immigration Office in Banjul after arrival.
Currency advice/regulations
No restrictions on import or export of local and most foreign currency, although a declaration form must be completed on arrival. Exceptions: currency from Algeria, Ghana, Guinea, Mali, Morocco, Nigeria, Sierra Leone and Tunisia will not be accepted and cannot be exchanged.

Health (for visitors)
Mandatory precautions
Yellow fever vaccination certificate required only if travelling from an infected area.
Advisable precautions
Yellow fever, typhoid, hepatitis A and polio vaccinations are recommended. Malaria prophylaxis should be taken as risk exists throughout the country. There is a rabies risk.
In the Banjul and Fajara area, the water supply is fed from deep bore holes and is considered safe to drink. Bottled water is available from all hotels and most supermarkets. Water precautions are necessary outside these areas.

Hotels
Book well in advance, especially if arriving during tourist season (Nov–May). Many Gambian hotels are geared to package holidays. Ten per cent tip is usual.

Credit cards
Limited acceptance of credit cards. American Express is normally accepted in most hotels but this must be arranged at the beginning of your stay with the hotel management.

Public holidays
Fixed dates
1 Jan (New Year's Day), 18 Feb (Independence Day), 15 Sep (St Mary's Day), 25 Dec (Christmas Day).
Variable dates
Good Friday, Easter Monday, Eid Al-Fitr, Eid Al-Kabir (Eid Al-Adha), Ashura, Maulid Al-Nabi.

Working hours
Banking
Mon–Thu: 0800–1330; Fri: 0800–1100.
Business
Mon–Thu: 0800–1600; Fri: 0800–1230.
Government
Mon–Thu: 0800–1600; Fri: 0800–1230.
Shops
Mon–Thu: 0900–1200, 1400–1700; (Fri–Sat) 0900–1300.

Telecommunications
Telephone/fax
Dialling code for The Gambia: IDD access code + 220 followed by subscriber's number. There are no area codes.

Electricity supply
220V AC, 50 cycles.

Social customs/useful tips
Handshaking is widely used as a form of greeting, whereas 'Salam alaikum' is the traditional greeting.
Many Gambians are Muslim and their religious customs and beliefs should be respected.

Getting there
Air
National airline: Gambia Airways.
Airport tax: International departures D150; not applicable to transit passengers.
Surface
Road: Road access to Banjul is possible from Dakar (Senegal), by the Trans-Gambia Highway which crosses the River Gambia by ferry between Farafenni and Mansa Konko. There is an alternative car ferry crossing between Barra and Banjul. Government buses run between The Gambia and Senegal, via Barra, to Koalack and Dakar; there is also a high-class Gambian coach service.

Getting about
National transport
Road: Approximately 3,000km of roads of which 450km are paved. Roads in and around Banjul are mostly bituminised, but unsealed roads often become impassable in the summer season.
Highways run along each bank of the river Gambia; the Trans-Gambia highway runs north to south, crossing the river at Farafenni-Mansa Konko (car ferry); other inland roads may become impassable in the rainy season.
Take care because of the lack of adequate traffic signs.
Buses: The Gambia Public Transport Corporation (GPTC) operates cheap and reliable services linking Banjul with the coastal hotel area and other main centres.

There are several commercial bus services, such as Amdalaye and Transgambia services.
Water: An hourly car ferry service operates between Banjul and Barra (journey time 20–30 minutes).
There is a boat that travels from Banjul to Basse once a week. The journey takes about three days. It is possible to return overland by coach.
City transport
Taxis: Tourist taxis are registered and licensed drivers and vehicles are authorised by the Tourist Office to transport customers on a fixed tariff. They tend to be expensive. Rates are displayed on notice boards. Check and confirm with driver before departure. Take down the vehicle and driver registration number in case of queries, and report to the Tourist Office immediately.
It is advisable to agree the fare in advance when hiring collective taxis.
A 10 per cent tip is usual.
The journey from the international airport to the city centre takes 30–40 minutes.
Car hire
International driving licence accepted for a period of three months. National licence can be used for a short visit. Traffic drives on the right.
Car hire facilities are somewhat limited and local enquiries (eg to Tourist Office (tel: 229-563, 227-881/3) are advised.

BUSINESS DIRECTORY

Telephone area codes
Dialling code for The Gambia: IDD access code +220 followed by subscriber's number. There are no area codes.

Useful telephone numbers
Police: 17
Fire: 18
Ambulance: 16 or 18 (Banjul)

Chambers of Commerce
Gambia Chamber of Commerce & Industry, PO Box 333, Banjul (tel: 27-765).

Banking
Arab Gambian Islamic Bank Ltd, 7 Ecowas Avenue, Banjul (tel: 223-773; fax: 223-770).

Continent Bank Ltd, 61 Ecowas Avenue, Banjul (tel: 226-986, 229961; fax: 229-711, 229-706) .

First International Bank Ltd, PO Box 1997, 6 OAU Boulevard, Banjul (tel: 202-000/5; fax: 202-001, 202-000).

International Bank for Commerce (Gambia) Ltd, PO Box 211, 11a Liberation Avenue, Banjul (tel: 228-144, 228-145; fax: 229-312).

Standard Chartered Bank Gambia Ltd, PO Box 259, 8 Ecowas Avenue, Banjul (tel: 228-681/4; fax: 227-714).

Trust Bank Limited (TBL), PO Box 1018, 3-4 Ecowas Avenue, Banjul (tel: 225-777, 225-778/9; fax: 225-781).

Central bank

Central Bank of The Gambia, 1/2 Ecowas Avenue, Banjul, Gambia (tel: 228-103, 227-633, 226-614, 227-786; fax: 226-969).

Travel information

Banjul (Yundum) International Airport, PO Box 285, Banjul (tel: 473-000; fax: 472-190).

Gambia Airways, PO Box 268, 68-69 Wellington Street, Banjul (tel: 226-733, 227-778/9, 226-347; fax: 229-339).

Ministry of tourism

Department of State for Tourism and Culture, The Quadrangle, Banjul (tel: 229-563, 223-210; fax: 227-753; internet site: http://www.gambiatourism.info).

Ministries

Ministry of Agriculture and Natural Resources (MANR), The Quadrangle, Banjul (tel: 472-888; fax: 237-034).

Ministry of Finance and Economic Affairs, The Quadrangle, Banjul (tel: 227-221; fax: 227-954).

Ministry of Tourism and Culture, The Quadrangle, Banjul (tel: 227-881; fax: 227-753).

Other useful addresses

Central Statistics Office, Central Bank Building, Buckle Street, Banjul (tel: 228-105).

Gambia Embassy (USA), Suite 1000, 1155 15th Street, NW, Washington DC 20005 (tel: 785-1399; fax: 785-1430).

Gambia Hotel Association, c/o The Bungalow Beach Hotel, PO Box 2637, Serrekunda (tel: 465-288; fax: 466-180).

Gambia Investment Promotion and Free Zones Agency (GIPFZA), 5 Nelson Mandela Street, PO Box 757, Banjul (tel: 222-412, 222-836; fax: 222-829; e-mail: dipm.gipfza@qanet.gm; ceo.gipfza@qanet.gm).

National Investment Promotion Authority (NIPA), Independence Drive, Banjul (tel: 228-332; fax: 229-220).

Internet sites

Africa Business Network: http://www.ifc.org/abn

AllAfrica.com: http://allafrica.com

African Development Bank: http://www.afdb.org

Africa Online: http://www.africaonline.com

Mbendi AfroPaedia (information on companies, countries, industries and stock exchanges in Africa): http://mbendi.co.za

The Gambia: http://www.gambia.com

Ghana

Desmond Davies

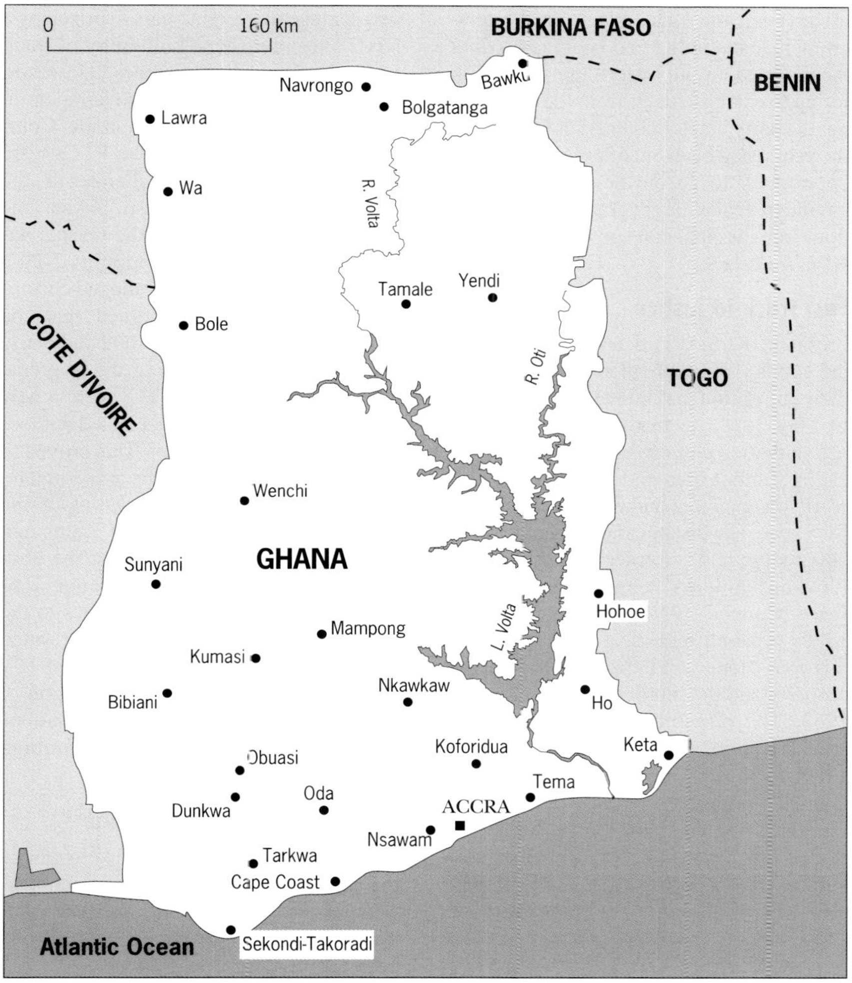

The year 2002 began successfully for the ruling New Patriotic Party (NPP). The result of the by-election in the northern constituency of Bimbilla resulted in an NPP victory. The win gave the NPP a total of 101 seats out of 200 in parliament, securing a majority. The result was a real blow to the opposition National Democratic Congress (NDC), which had previously viewed Bimbilla as one of the NDC's most loyal constituencies.

Clans clash

Despite this confident victory, things soured in March 2002, when the NPP had to face its first political crisis. This was caused by inter-clan clashes in Yendi in the northern region, which were a result of simmering tension between rival claimants to the skin (throne). The government declared a state of emergency in the region following the assassination of the Dagbon king, Ya Naa Yakubu Andani II, and 30 of his supporters at the Dagbon palace in March 2002. The killings followed clashes between the Andani and Abudu clans. The clan rivalry was stirred up after the Abudu claimed the kingship as a reward for its support for the NPP during the 2000 elections. In September 2002,

KEY FACTS

Official name: Republic of Ghana

Head of State: President John Kufuor (leader of NPP) (sworn in 7 Jan 2001)

Head of government: President John Kufuor

Ruling party: New Patriotic Party (NPP) (won the greatest number of seats in the Dec 2000 elections but failed to secure a majority)

Area: 239,460 square km

Population: 19.70 million (2001)

Capital: Accra

Official language: English

Currency: Cedi (C) = 100 pesewas

Exchange rate: C8,400.00 per US$ (Jan 2003)

GDP per capita: US$270 (2001); US$286 (2002)*

GDP real growth: 4.30% (2001); 4.3% (2002)*

Labour force: 9.30 million (2001); 9.5 million (2002)*

Inflation: 32.90% (2001); 13.8% (2002)*

Balance of trade: -US$1.40 billion (2001)

Foreign debt: US$6.69 billion (2001)

* estimated figure

For the latest Key Facts, go to www.worldinformation.com

President Kufuor appointed 11-member committees to run the affairs of six Dagbon districts. The committees were designed to fill the power vacuum created after the local assemblies were dissolved in preparation for local elections in August 2002. The elections were postponed until the state of emergency is lifted.

Molesting the media

The government was taken unawares by the ethnic tension and the murder of the Dagbon king. In an apparent knee-jerk reaction to media coverage of the conflict, the government ordered that reports on the crisis should be first submitted to the information ministry for vetting before publication or broadcast. The government's decision came after a state of emergency was declared in the Yendi area.

But the opposition NDC quickly seized upon the government's media edict to score political points. The party had been under considerable pressure from the NPP as the new government delved into the activities of the previous NDC government. No sooner had the government given its directive to the media than the NDC was urging the Ghana Journalists Association (GJA) and the National Media Commission (NMC) to challenge the edict, arguing that it was unconstitutional. The government's defence was that the media were publishing and broadcasting 'inflammatory' reports and that some were 'totally untrue' while 'many more' were 'ill-founded and/or motivated by speculation'. The government statement added that in the cases where the reports were correct, they had been 'calculated to inflame the situation'.

But the opposition saw this as a move by the government to clamp down on press freedom, arguing that journalists covering the Yendi conflict had 'exercised maturity and a sense of responsibility'. The NDC said that although it did not have anything against the declaration of a state of emergency at Yendi, it would not 'support any attempt to circumvent or violate constitutional procedures and the rule of law'.

However, the NDC attack on the government had nothing to do with upholding media freedom but everything to do with trying to extricate itself from the tight corner the party had found itself in for most of the year it had been out of power. It was an opportunity to go on the offensive after having to deal with government investigations into the financial activities of former NDC ministers.

Fast track to justice

President Kufuor is determined to bring the country's former rulers to account for their corruption and human rights abuses. In May 2002, he inaugurated a national reconciliation commission, similar to panels in South Africa and Nigeria. It began work in September and was expected to sit for a year. The disappearance of more than 200 people under former president, Jerry Rawlings' military People's National Defence Council (PNDC) regime of the 1980s is being investigated by the commission, along with the confiscation of property and the murder of four judges in 1982. The nine-member commission is seen as a political witch-hunt by the NDC, although those who testify before it are granted immunity from prosecution. Rawlings reacted angrily to the formation of the commission and called on Ghanaians to practise what he called 'positive defiance', which many saw as incitement to revolution.

The commission comes alongside the formation of Fast Track Courts (FTC), which were set up to convict those accused of corruption under the NDC government. In December 2001, former deputy finance minister Victor Serlomery was sentenced to eight years in prison by a FTC. The court found him guilty of fraud and other financial offences. However, there was a setback for the government in March 2002, when the Supreme Court ruled by five to four that the FTCs were unconstitutional. The challenge to the court had come from Tsatsu Tsikata, the former chief executive of the Ghana National Petroleum Corporation (GNPC), who was facing charges of alleged corruption. The government argued that the FTCs were part of the normal judiciary, but in their majority ruling the Supreme Court claimed that the FTCs were a new type of court that had been created without the approval of parliament. This proved to be a major setback for the government, which had been accused of setting up the FTCs as part of a political campaign against the NDC. Nevertheless, the government was able to circumvent the problem by appointing two new judges to the Supreme Court which, in June 2002, ruled by a majority of six to five that the FTCs were legal. The political manipulation of the judiciary led to opposition accusations that President Kufuor was transforming Ghana into a 'fascist dictatorship'.

Tightening the purse strings

In 2001, the government battled to ensure that there was stability in the economy. This meant keeping a tight rein on inflation and the value of the cedi, which had been in free-fall for many years.

In the case of inflation, from a high of 41.9 per cent in March 2001, the rate fell to 21.3 per cent by the end of 2001. This was a marked improvement on the 25 per cent that had been targeted by the government. As far as the cedi was concerned, after a sharp depreciation in 2000, the currency hovered around C7,300 to the US$ throughout 2001.

Ghana's gross international reserves rose from US$232 million at the end of 2000 to a provisional estimate of some US$336 million – equivalent to 1.5 months of imports – by December 2001.

Finance Minister Yaw Osafo-Maafo put this down to firm financial discipline on the part of the government. He said in his

KEY INDICATORS — Ghana

	Unit	1996	1997	1998	1999	2000
Population	m	18.15	18.66	19.16	19.68	20.15
Gross domestic product (GDP)	US$bn	7.00	6.90	7.50	7.80	5.00
GDP per capita	US$	399	387	407	413	258
GDP real growth	%	4.6	4.2	4.7	4.4	3.7
Inflation	%	46.6	27.9	14.6	12.4	25.2
Exports (fob) (goods)	US$m	1,570.0	1,490.0	2,090.0	2,120.0	1,898.4
Imports (fob) (goods)	US$m	1,940.0	2,130.0	2,900.0	3,230.0	2,741.3
Balance of trade	US$m	-366.9	-638.3	-805.7	-1,111.5	-842.9
Current account	US$m	-324.7	-549.7	-380.0	-766.0	-412.6
Foreign debt	US$bn	6.0	6.1	6.2	7.2	6.7
Total reserves minus gold	US$m	828.7	0.0	377.0	453.8	232.1
Foreign exchange	US$m	801.5	0.0	292.8	379.1	231.5
Exchange rate	per US$	1,200.43	1,637.23	2,050.17	2,314.15	5,455.06

March 2002 budget that aided by strict control of cash expenditures by the government, the Bank of Ghana had succeeded in reducing the rate of expansion of reserve money, thus reducing the excessive monetary expansion that occurred in 2000. 'The 2001 targets for the government's domestic primary balance, the overall budget balance and the net international reserves of the Bank of Ghana were all achieved', he reported.

There was good news also on the collection of tax, which saw the government achieve a 5 per cent increase over the projected target, mainly because the VAT service and the customs department tightened revenue collection.

Although the NPP government had presented a budget in March 2001, the budget of March 2002, according to Osafo-Maafo, encompassed the first full year of the implementation of President Kufuor's agenda for economic and social development for Ghana. 'This budget is founded on his conviction that by improving the management of the nation's economic affairs and mobilising its potential resources more intensively, it is possible to propel Ghana into a new trajectory of rapid national development', the finance minister said. 'It is only by growing our economy at rates eventually running close to double digits that our people can expect, within the period of a decade, to enjoy the standards of living and the social benefits of a substantially transformed and modernised economy', Osafo-Maafo said.

An impoverished populace

The 2002 budget also represented the first year of the implementation of the Ghana Poverty Reduction Strategy (GPRS), which is basically aimed at creating a wider wealth base that would develop the farming communities. The government believes that by 2004 it would be possible to substantially reduce mass poverty and provide better protection for the most vulnerable in Ghanaian society.

But in all this, the government was ever conscious of stabilising the economy and improving the business climate. Finance Minister Osafo-Maafo spoke of killing 'the inflation psychology', reducing fears of exchange risks and bringing back confidence to local and foreign investors.

In this regard, the 2002 budget was aimed at strengthening the base that would sustain economic growth. At the same time, the government was exercising caution on fiscal and monetary policy and that was why it set a relatively modest growth rate of 4.5 per cent for 2002. This projection was based on the level of investment envisaged and development funding committed by donor countries.

But Finance Minister Osafo-Maafo insisted that the government would be looking for other avenues of raising revenue to fund development projects, stressing that the NPP would stick to its election manifesto of empowering 'the most deprived sections of our society to lift themselves up towards higher levels of productivity'. Consequently, the national development agenda would be closely linked to the government's annual budget so that there would be regular financing for projects.

This arrangement was grounded in the fact that so many development initiatives that had been launched in the past had failed because of poor management and support from those involved in these initiatives. The government expected this to change, promising to pay more attention to the implementation of the projects.

The government's macroeconomic policy for 2002 was aimed at pushing for economic growth, using the private sector as the backbone for such growth. As an incentive to the private sector, the government planned to create the framework for increased access to bank finance for businesses.

The government also hoped that the advantages presented by the Enhanced Highly Indebted Poor Country (EHIPC) initiative would relieve pressure on the economy. Indeed in 2001, after Ghana became eligible for HIPC, the government was able to suspend debt repayments to bilateral donors; this brought about budgetary savings of some US$190 million.

Outlook

Ghana's government is slowly getting the economy right. The ultimate aim is to create a suitable economic climate to entice foreign investment. However, the continued probe into the affairs of the former NDC government is leading to rancour among Ghanaians, many of whom believe that the government should concentrate on looking after the interests of the people rather than pursuing what is viewed as a political agenda. Given the determination of the government to pursue former NDC functionaries, it is leaving itself open to accusations of a witch-hunt – thus providing a boost for an embattled NDC opposition.

Political infighting within the NPP could also present problems for the government. It is no secret that Attorney-General Akufo-Addo does not get along with President Kufuor. Both men have been at loggerheads since Kufuor beat Akufo-Addo in highly contentious circumstances to become the NPP's presidential candidate. The party will have to ensure that the low-level civil war within its ranks does not escalate and throw Ghana's democratic credentials overboard or hamper its economic advance.

Risk assessment

Economy	Improving
Political	Good
Regional stability	Satisfactory
Stock market	Improving

COUNTRY PROFILE

Historical profile

1957 Ghana (formerly the Gold Coast) was granted independence from British rule.

1960 Dr Kwame Nkrumah of the People's Convention Party became President.

1966 Lt-Gen J A Ankrah of the National Liberation Council seized power.

1969 Dr Kofi Busia of the Progress Party secured victory in the parliamentary elections and became prime minister.

1972 Another military coup saw Col Ignatius Acheampong of the National Redemption Council take control.

1978 Lt-Gen F Akuffo, previously chief of the defence staff, replaced Acheampong as Head of State.

1979 A successful coup was launched by Flt-Lt Jerry J Rawlings of the Armed Forces Revolutionary Council. Democratic elections in June established Dr Hilla Limann of the People's National Party as President.

Flt-Lt Jerry J Rawlings and the Provisional National Defence Council returned to power through a second military coup.

1983–89 There was discontent with the regime and the ineffectiveness of its economic policies was reflected in a series of attempted coups, student unrest and alleged anti-government conspiracies.

1990 A national referendum on the restoration of multi-party politics was demanded.

1992 A new constitution was endorsed in a referendum to allow for a multi-party system. Jerry Rawlings was elected President and his National Democratic Congress (NDC) secured an overall majority in legislative elections.

1993 The Fourth Republic was inaugurated on 7 January.

1996 Jerry Rawlings won the presidential election held on 7 December with 57.2 per cent of the vote. His NDC won the legislative elections.

2000 John Kufuor of the New Patriotic Party (NPP) won run-off presidential elections in December with 56.73 per cent of the vote. The NPP also became the largest party in parliament.

2001 After 19 continuous years as president, Jerry Rawlings stepped down in January. A 25-member Council of State was sworn in on 20 June. President John Kufuor appointed the Council to fulfil an advisory role.

2002 The ruling NPP won the March by-elections in the northern constituency of Bimbilla, giving them a majority in parliament.

In the same month, ethnic battles in the north led to the murder of Ghana's second most important king, Ya Na Yakubu Andani of the Dagbon people. The death of the tribal king led to the resignation of two senior government ministers.

Political structure

Constitution

The 1992 constitution is based on the US model. It allows for a multi-party system. The president is elected by universal suffrage for a maximum of two four-year terms.

Ghana has 10 administrative regions which are subdivided into districts.

Form of state

Unitary republic

The executive

Executive power is vested in the president, vice president and Council of Ministers; both the vice president and the Council of Ministers are appointed by the president. If no candidate receives more than 50 per cent of votes in the presidential election, a new election between the two candidates with the highest number of votes is to take place within 21 days.

National legislature

Legislative power is held by a 200 member unicameral parliament, which is elected every four years by direct adult suffrage.

Last elections

7 December 2000 (parliamentary); 7/28 December 2000 (presidential).

Next elections

2004 (presidential and parliamentary)

Political parties

Ruling party

New Patriotic Party (NPP) (elected Dec 2000)

Main opposition party

National Democratic Congress (NDC)

Population

20.15 million (2000).

The population grew by 2.9 per cent in 2001 and is projected to grow by 2.3 per cent per annum between 2001 and 2015. About 44 per cent of the population is under 15 years.

Population density: 79 inhabitants per square km. Urban population: 38 per cent. The highest population densities are in the urban areas. Cocoa processing and mining areas in the south have relatively large populations.

Ethnic make-up

Akan (including Ashanti) (44 per cent), Mole-Dagbani (15 per cent), Ewe (13 per cent), Ga-Adangbe (8.3 per cent), Guan (3.7 per cent), Gurma (3.5 per cent).

Religions

Christian (43 per cent), traditional religions (38 per cent), Muslim (12 per cent). There is complete freedom of worship in Ghana.

Education

The government's official medium-term strategy is to provide compulsory, free basic education for all. Government expenditure on education is about.a quarter of total government spending. The Provisional National Defence Council (PNDC), the previous military government, introduced school fees and a loan scheme for tertiary education.

Some 50,000 literacy groups have been working to eliminate illiteracy in the country.

Ghana boasts the oldest university in sub-Saharan Africa – at Legon in Accra.

Health

Health spending averages 4.7 per cent of GDP, of which public expenditure is equivalent to 1.8 per cent of GDP and private expenditure 2.9 per cent.

There are approximately 1.5 hospital beds per 1,000 people. Life expectancy at birth was 60 years. The infant mortality rate is 65 per 1,000 live births and 26 per cent of children under five years are malnourished. In 2000, around 210,000 people were classified as HIV positive, representing 2.38 per cent of the population.

Main cities

Accra, capital, estimated population 1.6 million (2002). Other main cities include Kumasi (627,600), Tamale (269,200) Tema (237,700), Obuasi (122,600), Teshi (117,200), Bolgatanga (88,200) and Takoradi (86,400).

Languages spoken

There are over 25 major languages with numerous dialects. The principal African languages spoken are Twi and Fante (spoken by the Akans), Ga, Hausa, Dagbani, Ewe and Nzema.

French is taught in most schools. There is an official policy to encourage Ghanaians to be multilingual.

Official language

English

Media

Press

The Newspaper Licensing Law of 1989 (Provisional National Defence Council Law 211) regulates all newspapers and periodicals. It was passed largely to combat a spate of sensational fly sheets which had sprung up and which were said to have a combined circulation of 60,000. The government's stated policy is to introduce 'order and decency' into journalism. Licences are obtainable on application to the PNDC Information Secretary. A fee of C25,000 is payable and renewable annually. In-house publications and religious, educational, cultural, military and scientific newspapers or magazines may be exempted from the payment of the fee.

There is one official agency, the Ghana News Agency.

Dailies: English language dailies include *The Mirror*, *The Independent*, *The Ghanaian Times*, and *The Daily Graphic*.

Weeklies: Weeklies include *The Ghanaian Democrat*, *The Accra Mail*, *The Independent*, *The Statesman*, *Public Agenda*, *Ghanaian Chronicle*, *Crusading Guide*, *Christian Messenger*, *The Guide*, *Mirror*, *P&P*, *Pioneer*and *Weekly Spectator*.

Business: There are a number of weekly business newspapers including the *Business and Financial Times*, *Business Chronicle*, *High Street Journal* and *The Financial Guardian*.

Periodicals: *Ghanaian Voice* is published irregularly.

Broadcasting

Radio: Ghana Broadcasting Corporation runs three radio stations. They include a radio service in English, Hausa and other African languages and an external radio service in English, French and Hausa. There are also private radio stations. These include Atlantis Radio, Vibe FM, Joy FM, Choice FM, Radio Universe and Groove FM.

Television: Ghana TV (GTV) is a state-owned company operated by the Ghana Broadcasting Corporation. Metro TV is owned by both the government and a private company.

Economy

The Vision 2020 programme launched by the government in 1994, aimed at developing Ghana into a middle income country by 2020, was replaced by the Ghana Poverty Reduction Strategy (GPRS) in 2002. The focus of the GPRS is to expand the wealth base of the country and raise the incomes of Ghana's poorest farming communities.

To make Ghana's development objectives realisable, it has been necessary to obtain funds from the donor organisations such as the World Bank and IMF. In the past, economic policy has strayed from the World Bank's aims of tight monetary and fiscal control, particularly around the time of the 2000 elections when austerity measures could have led to electoral defeat. However, Ghana achieved reasonable levels of economic growth while maintaining political stability and democratic government. Investment in the country's significant industrial sector, which contributes 25 per cent of national output, and the government's commitment to human development depended in large part on foreign exchange earnings from cocoa and gold, which form over 70 per cent of total exports.

Very few of the economic performance targets set by the World Bank were met in 2000, including the objective of 4 per cent growth and a current account deficit of 10 per cent of GDP. Critics argue that the country's capacity to absorb external shocks was compromised by the government's policy, backed by international donors, of depleting foreign reserves and maintaining high interest rates to curb exchange rate volatility. They maintain this resulted in a sharp devaluation and subsequent difficulties for the private sector which had relied on foreign credit.

In 2001, the government restored financial discipline. The economy recorded growth of 4.0 per cent. The government has set a growth target of 4.5 per cent for 2002. As a result of this promising economic performance, the IMF and World Bank have agreed a US$3.7 billion debt relief package for Ghana. This will help cover some of Ghana's debt-servicing obligations and help finance education, health and social development projects as part of the GPRS.

To further regional economic integration, the Economic Community of West African States (Ecowas) decided to create a second monetary zone in the region by 2003. There are also plans for a single currency in 2004.

External trade

Ghana has a steadily growing trade deficit, with cocoa, gold and timber the principal export products. In 2002, the government was trying to encourage the export of textiles, garments and processed goods with the aim of earning the country US$3.6 billion by 2006.

Exports

Principal exports are gold (typically 40 per cent of total), cocoa and cocoa products (30 per cent), timber and timber products (13 per cent), manganese, diamonds, electricity, bauxite, pineapples, tuna, prepared fish and petroleum oil

In 2002, cocoa prices were rising. Between September 2001 and March 2002, cocoa prices increased by 70 per cent. Ghana saw its production of cocoa fall in 2001 and it was feared that it may not be able to meet demand. Ghanaian farmers will not be able to benefit from the price rise since prices are agreed by a Ghanaian government board at the start of the season.

Main destinations: Togo (15.5 per cent of 2000 total), Netherlands (13.7 per cent), US (11.3 per cent), UK (7.5 per cent), Germany (6.2 per cent).

Imports

Principal imports are machinery and transport equipment, basic manufactures, petroleum and products, chemicals, food, beverages and tobacco, miscellaneous manufactures.

Main sources: Nigeria (19.3 per cent of 2000 total), Italy (11.6 per cent), UK (9 per cent), US (6.6 per cent), Côte d'Ivoire (4.7 per cent).

Agriculture

Agriculture is the main sector of the economy, accounting for 36 per cent of GDP in 2000 and employing over 60 per cent of the working population.

An estimated 43 per cent of total area is potential arable land – only 12 per cent is under cultivation; around 60 per cent is woodland/forest (estimated 25 per cent rain forest).

Cocoa is traditionally the most important crop and provides approximately 25 per cent of export earnings. Ghana is the world's third-largest cocoa producer. Although world prices of cocoa were rising in 2002, Ghanaian farmers were unable to benefit from it because prices of the commodity are set by the Ghanaian government.

The monopoly of the Ghana Cocoa Board (GCB) was lifted in 1993, allowing private trading companies to purchase directly from farms.

Other cash crops for export include bananas, kola nuts, limes, coffee, copra and palm kernels.

Crops grown for the local agro-industry include rubber, sugar, cotton, and oil palms.

Subsistence farming of food crops (cassava, plantains, rice, maize, sorghum, millet, yams) has been affected by prolonged drought and shortages of fertilisers, but there has been a recovery, particularly in maize and rice production.

Fishing

The annual domestic fish catch averages 300,000 tonnes, satisfying over 75 per cent of domestic demand. Fish farms have been set up in the northern regions in an effort to achieve total fish self-sufficiency. Tuna is one of Ghana's non-traditional exports, but the maximum sustainable yield from the 28,000 square km territorial waters is far from being realised.

Forestry

Most commercial forestry is concentrated in the southern part of the country. Deforestation occurred at an alarming rate in the 1980s, and the government imposed restrictions on the export of various types of timber and wood products. The government's long-term plan is to produce high-quality finished wood products.

Ghana has over 200 species of tropical hardwood. The annual capacity for sawn timber is approximately 2.5 million cubic metres and 450,000 cubic metres for processed timber. The extent of productive forest reserves is put at 1.2 million hectares, containing 190 million cubic metres of potential wood volume in trees over 30 cm in diameter. Timber is Ghana's third-largest export commodity. The current export level of some 600,000 cubic metres a year of commercially viable species and sizes (trees with diameters of 70 cm or more) can only be maintained if reliance on redwoods is lessened and exploitation of other species is increased.

The forestry sector in Ghana is facing competition from emerging south-east Asian producers.

The National Forests Protection Strategy resulted in decreasing deforestation during the 1990s. The strategy plans to make the private sector responsible for the costs of forest depletion. The Environmental Protection Agency (EPA) monitors developments and policy affecting wildlife, forests and mining activities.

Industry and manufacturing

The industrial sector accounts for approximately 25 per cent of annual GDP. Of this, the manufacturing sector contributes 9 per cent to GDP, electricity, gas and water 2.6 per cent and construction 8.5 per cent.

Tourism

Ghana has clean beaches, game reserves and many traditional festivals. Adventure tourism, convention and business tourism are being highlighted, but as yet, the potential for a significant level of tourism has not been exploited.

Most arrivals are from the US, UK, Germany and the Netherlands.

There were an estimated 400,000 tourist arrivals in 2000; receipts were around US$386 million.

Mining

Mining typically accounts for 18 per cent of GDP and employs 3 per cent of the workforce. It is the largest single foreign exchange earner in Ghana, and is expanding. Minerals include gold, manganese, diamonds, bauxite, iron ore, limestone, silica, columbite, tantalite and several rich clays.

Gold is the principal mineral export and Ghana is Africa's second-largest gold producer, after South Africa. Ashanti Goldfields Corporation (AGC) accounts for 85 per cent of total output. The other major producer is the State Gold Mines

Corporation. Recoverable gold reserves are estimated at 57 million kg. AGC recorded profits of US$62.7 million in 2001, more than double its 2000 earnings. The year 2002 was one of consolidation in Ghana's gold mining industry with expectations that Gold Fields of South Africa would merge with AGC before the year's end.
Diamonds and manganese each account for 1–2 per cent of export earnings. Diamonds (mostly industrial) are mined by Ghana Consolidated Diamonds Ltd in the Birim Basin. Ghana is the eighth-largest diamond producer in the world. Manganese ore is mined at Nsuta by the National Manganese Corporation.
Manganese production averages 280,000 tonnes per annum.
Ghana has vast bauxite reserves near Kibi, but heavy transport/extraction costs have limited commercial development of local bauxite for use by the Valco aluminium smelter.
Periodic droughts have disrupted power supplies, resulting in a drop in production in many mining operations. This was partly solved in 2000 when a 220MW power plant was commissioned to supply electricity to Ashanti Goldfields.

Hydrocarbons

Oil

Ghana's oil reserves are estimated at 16.5 million barrels. However, although local reserves could supply a substantial proportion of the one million tonnes per year domestic oil requirement, the bulk of these needs are imported from Nigeria.
Petroleum products account for about a quarter of the country's energy requirements. Arco and Petro Ghana, among other companies, are drilling offshore in the South Tano area in the west of the country.
Oil reserves are located in the Accra/Keta Basin, the Cape Three Points Basin, Saltpond Basin, Tano Basin and the Voltaian Basin. GNPC produces approximately 300,000 tonnes of oil from the Saltpond Basin annually.

Gas

Estimated natural gas reserves of 23.52 billion cubic metres (840 billion cubic feet) are located primarily in the Tano fields. GNPC and the Volta River Authority are considering plans to develop natural gas for power generation as a back-up to the hydroelectric based power generation at Akosombo. There is official backing for a project to develop liquefied petroleum gas as a source of local energy to reduce the depletion of forests through the use of wood-based fuels. In recent years, the ministry of energy has provided assistance to allow enterprises to convert from firewood to LPG; this is expected to save 7,000 tonnes of firewood a year.

Energy

The Volta River Authority (VRA) has responsibility for the development, generation and distribution of electricity in Ghana.
Ghana is heavily dependent on imported oil, primarily from Nigeria.
The 912MW Akosombo hydropower plant and the 160MW Kpong plant are overstretched. The World Bank financed a 300MW thermal power station near Takoradi.
Electricity is exported to Togo and Benin. Western Power Company, a subsidiary of the Ghana National Petroleum Corporation (GNPC) has secured funding for two barge-mounted gas turbines in the Western Region.
The private sector is encouraged to invest in the energy sector.
The West African Gas Pipeline project to bring gas from Nigeria would bring huge benefits to Ghana by securing cheap long-term energy supplies.
Several reforms have transformed Ghana's energy sector. In March 2001, the government removed subsidies on petroleum products that resulted in a 64.3 per cent increase in fuel prices.

Financial markets

Stock exchange

The Ghana Stock Exchange (GSE) has two main indices, the GSE All-Share Index and the Databank Stock Index (DSI). In April 2002, stock market capitalisation was US$500 million. However, there were only 22 companies listed on the exchange which is dominated by the Ashanti Goldfields Corporation.

Banking

Central bank

Bank of Ghana.

Main financial centre

Accra.

Time

GMT

Geography

Ghana's southern border is the Gulf of Guinea. To the north, east and west lie the states of Burkina Faso, Togo and Côte d'Ivoire. From north to south the country extends a distance of about 680 km.
The River Volta, which flows from the north to the south-east, is the most conspicuous landmark. There is a coastal area of thicket and mangrove which gives way in the east and north-east to more open plains and semi-deciduous forest.
To the west and north-west of the coastal strip is high forest, which still covers the greater part of Ashanti and part of the Northern Region. The forest gives way in the north to Guinea savannah woodland; the extreme north-eastern corner of Ghana forms part of the drier Sudan savannah woodland.

Climate

Ghana lies entirely within the tropics. In the northern savannah the climate is hot and dry, with intermittent rainfall during March–September. In the hot and humid forest regions there are two rainy seasons, during March–June and September–November. At the coast, which is only 4.5 degrees from the Equator, the heat is intense.
The capital city, Accra, is only 65 metres above sea level. The capital's hottest month is March, with temperatures of 24–32 degrees Celsius (C); August is the coldest month, with temperatures of 21–27C. The annual rainfall in the capital averages 865mm. The driest month is December when rainfall averages 18mm, and the wettest month is June when rainfall averages 235mm.

Dress codes

Western-style clothes are usually worn for business purposes, including shorts for outdoor occupations. On social or ceremonial occasions traditional costume or Western-style clothes are equally acceptable.
Local dress includes the expensive, hand-woven Kente cloth for which Ghana is famous: this is worn by men like a toga. Cheaper local-style prints (which are frequently imported) feature traditional patterns or the portraits of popular politicians.

Entry requirements

Entry permits are required by all Commonwealth citizens and must be obtained prior to arrival.

Passports

Required by all, except by members of the Economic Community of West African States (ECOWAS) who can obtain a Travel Certificate instead. Passports must be valid three months.

Visa

Required by all except nationals of Benin, Botswana, Burkina Faso, Cape Verde, Côte d'Ivoire, Egypt, Gambia, Guinea, Guinea-Bissau, Hong Kong (SAR), Lesotho, Liberia, Malawi, Mali, Mauritania, Mauritius, Niger, Nigeria, Senegal, Sierra Leone, Swaziland, Tanzania, Togo, Uganda, Zambia and Zimbabwe.
Multiple entry visas can only be obtained after arrival. Foreign visitors must hold a return ticket or letter from an employer guaranteeing repatriation. To encourage tourism, visas can be arranged for collection on arrival at the Kotoka International Airport.

Currency advice/regulations
It is advisable to check the latest currency regulations prior to visit.
It is easy to exchange US dollar bills for cedis. Visa cards can be used to withdraw cedis from Barclays Bank automatic telling machines (limit C200,000 per transaction; daily maximum C2 million).
Unlimited import of foreign currency but it must be declared. Foreign unused currency, traveller's cheques, etc, declared on arrival, can be exported. Foreign currency must be exchanged with authorised dealers only. Keep the foreign exchange form. Import of local currency is prohibited and export is limited to C5,000, which must be recorded in passport.
Unused cedis can be re-exchanged into foreign currency by local banks or the Bank of Ghana, but the declaration form T.5 must show that the monies were obtained while in Ghana from an authorised dealer in foreign exchange.

Health (for visitors)
Mandatory precautions
A yellow fever vaccination certificate is required by all.
Advisable precautions
Typhoid, polio, tetanus, hepatitis 'A' and meningitis vaccinations are recommended. A hepatitis 'B' vaccination is recommended if staying in Ghana over six months. A vaccination for rabies is recommended if travelling to rural areas. Malaria prophylaxis should be taken as risk exists throughout the country.
Water precautions are essential. There is a growing bilharzia risk and swimming or paddling in rivers is not advisable. AIDS is present in Ghana. Guinea worm is rife and increasing in northern regions.

Hotels
Available in Accra, Kumasi, Takoradi and other regional capitals. Several hotels are being built or renovated. Prices are high. A 10 per cent government tax is added.
Tipping is permitted in hotels, restaurants, etc. It is rarely added to the bill.

Credit cards
The most widely accepted credit cards are American Express, Diners' and Visa. They may be used for payment at nearly all airlines, leading hotels and major supermarkets.
Many restaurants and airlines prefer to be paid in cash.

Public holidays
Fixed dates
1 Jan (New Year's Day), 6 Mar (Independence Day), 1 May (Labour Day), 1 Jul (Republic Day), 25 Dec (Christmas Day), 26 Dec (Boxing Day).
Variable dates
Eid Al-Fitr, Good Friday, Holy Saturday, Easter Monday.

Working hours
Banking
Mon–Thu: 0830–1400; Fri: 0830–1500.
Business
Mon–Fri: 0800–1200, 1400–1700. Sat: 0830–1200.
Government
Mon–Fri: 0800–1230, 1330–1700.
Shops
Mon–Tue and Thu–Fri: 0800–1200, 1400–1730. Wed and Sat: 0800–1300. Closed on Sundays.

Telecommunications
Telephone/fax
There is a shortage of landlines. Ghana Telcom plans to provide 225,000 new lines and about 1,500 payphones by 2002. In 2002, the government announced that it would not renew its agreement with Ghana Telecom and Westel Telesystems Limited (WESTEL), in an effort to break their duopoly and attract other investors to the sector.
Postal services
Internal services are not always reliable. Air mail is slow.
Courier services
Air courier services are available.
Internet/e-mail
Internet usage in Ghana is growing. Dial-up access is provided by Ghana Telecom. Internet bars can be found in every part of the country, mostly in Accra, the capital. There are nine Internet providers in the country and an estimated 20,000 users with direct connection. The connection speed is very slow. A dial-up subscriber must dial, on average, 40 times, before a connection is established.

Electricity supply
220V AC, 50 cycles.

Social customs/useful tips
It is traditional to arrive with a gift when accepting private hospitality, particularly in rural areas. It is customary to use the right hand when presenting an object to another person, particularly in the case of food or a gift.
In northern Ghana, where the population tends to be Muslim, Islamic customs should be respected: it is considered unclean to eat or drink with the left hand; it is insulting to point the sole of your shoe at a Muslim. Older people are treated with special respect in Ghana.
It is inadvisable for foreigners to refer to tribalism or ethnic affiliations when discussing current affairs.
Body language differences include the custom of a greater degree of physical contact – touching and holding hands – between men and between women.
Business people need patience when dealing with bureaucracy. There are regular power cuts in Accra and although the telephone system has improved, it may take several attempts to make an international call.
There are no unusual or particularly strict laws, but foreign visitors should observe all rules and regulations as Ghana does not take ignorance of the law as an excuse for non-observance. It is prudent to carry proof of identity.

Security
Due to growing unemployment and falling wage levels, there has been a rise in crimes such as theft, including the pilfering of luggage, bag snatching and breaking into cars. There has also been an increase in the demand for bribes.

Getting there
Air
National airline: Ghana Airways
Main airport: Accra Kotoka International Airport (ACC), 10 km north of Accra.
Airport tax: US$15

Getting about
National transport
Transport in northern Ghana can be more difficult than in southern Ghana.
Air: Ghana Airways operates flights to Accra, Kumasi and Tamale.
Road: Roads are often potholed and badly marked.
City transport
Taxis: There are cheap and reliable taxis in Accra.
Tipping is not usual; taxis are unmetered – fare is by negotiation; current rates are often posted in hotels.
Car hire
Car hire is expensive. An international driving licence is recommended; this must be endorsed by Police Licensing Officer if stay exceeds 90 days. Traffic drives on the right.
The driving standards are poor. Driving at night is not advised.

BUSINESS DIRECTORY

Telephone area codes
Dialling code for Ghana: IDD access code +233 followed by area code (21 for Accra), followed by subscriber's number.

Useful telephone numbers
Police, fire and ambulance: 999.

Chambers of Commerce
Ghana National Chamber of Commerce, PO Box 2325, Accra (tel: 662-427/210; fax: 662-210).

Banking
Agricultural Development Bank; PO Box 4191, Cedi House, Liberia Road, Accra (tel: 662-758, 662-762; fax: 662-912, 662-846).

Amalgamated Bank Limited; PO Box C1541, C131/3 Farrar Avenue, Accra (tel: 249-690; fax: 249-697), e-mail: amalbank@ighmail.com.

Barclays Bank of Ghana Ltd; PO Box 2949, Barclays House, High Street, Accra (tel: 664-901/4, 665-382; fax: 667-420).

CAL Merchant Bank Ltd; PO Box 14596, 45 Independence Avenue, Accra (tel: 221-056, 231-098, 222-345, 221-091, 231-912-7; fax: 231-104, 231-913).

Ecobank Ghana Ltd; 19 Seventh Avenue, Ridge West, Private Mail Bag, General Post Office, Accra (tel: 229-532, 228-812, 221-103, 667-109; fax: 667-127, 232-086).

First Atlantic Merchant Bank Ltd; PO Box C1620, Atlantic Place, No. 1 Seventh Avenue, Ridge West, Cantonments, Accra (tel: 231-433-5; fax: 231399).

Ghana Commercial Bank Ltd, PO Box 134, Accra (tel: 664-914 (5 lines), 664-911, 664-918; fax: 662-168).

International Commercial Bank Ltd; PO Box 20057, Accra (tel: 666-190, 665-779; fax: 668-221).

Merchant Bank (Ghana) Ltd; PO Box 401, Merban House, 44 Kwame Nkrumah Ave, Accra (tel: 666-331/2, 666-336; fax: 663-398).

Metropolitan and Allied Bank (GH) Ltd; PO Box C 1778, Valco Trust House, Castle Road Branch, Cantonments, Accra (tel: 232-770, 232-776; fax: 232-728).

National Investment Bank Ltd; PO Box 3726, 37 Kwame Nkrumah Avenue, Accra (tel: 240-001, 240-024; fax: 240-030/34).

Prudential Bank Ltd; PO Box 9820, Airport, Accra (tel: 226-322, 226-803; fax: 226-803).

SSB Bank Ltd; 1 Cola Avenue, Kokomlemle, Accra (tel: 222-564; fax: 222-136).

Stanbic Bank Ghana Limited; PO Box CT 2344, Valco Trust House, Castle Road, Ridge, Accra (tel: 234-683-4; fax: 234-685).

Standard Chartered Bank Ghana Ltd; PO Box 768, 3rd Floor, Accra High Street Building, Accra (tel: 664-591-8; fax: 667-751).

The Trust Banl Ltd; PO Box 1862, Re-insurance House, 68 Kwame Nkrumah Avenue, Accra (tel: 240-049fax: 240-056).

Central bank

Bank of Ghana, PO Box 2674, Thorpe Road, Accra (tel: 666-174/6, 666-902/8; fax: 662-996).

Travel information

Accra Kotoka International Airport, PO Box 87, Accra (tel: 776-171).

Ghana Airways, Ghana House, PO Box 1636, White Avenue, Accra (tel: 777-673; fax: 777-675).

National tourist organisation offices

Ghana Tourist Board, PO Box 3106, Accra (tel: 238-330; fax: 231-779; e-mail: gtb@africa-on-line.com.gh).

Ghana Tourist Development Co Ltd, PO Box 8710, Accra (tel: 772-084; fax: 772-093).

Ministries

Ministry of Communications: PO Box M.41, Accra (tel: 229-870; fax: 229-786).

Ministry of Defence, Burma Camp, Accra (tel: 774-727; fax: 773-951).

Ministry of Education, PO Box M45, Accra (tel: 662-772; fax: 664-067).

Ministry of Employment and Social Welfare, PO Box M84, Accra (tel: 665-421; fax: 667-251).

Ministry of Environment, Science and Technology, PO Box M39, Accra (tel: 662-626; fax: 666-828).

Ministry of Finance and Economic Planning, PO Box M40, Accra (tel: 665-441, 665-587, 666-512; fax: 667-069).

Ministry of Food and Agriculture, PO Box M37, Accra (tel: 663-036, 665-421; fax: 663-250).

Ministry of Foreign Affairs, PO Box M53, Accra (tel: 664-008; fax: 665-363).

Ministry of Health, PO Box M44, Accra (tel: 665-323; fax: 663-810).

Ministry of Information, PO Box M41, Accra (tel: 228-0211).

Ministry of Interior, PO Box M42, Accra (tel: 665-421; fax: 662-688).

Ministry of Justice & Attorney General, PO Box M60, Accra (tel: 665-051).

Ministry of Land and Forestry, PO Box M212, Accra (tel: 665-949; fax: 666-801).

Ministry of Local Government, Rural Development and Co-op, PO Box M50, Accra (tel: 664-763; fax: 667-911).

Ministry of Mines and Energy, PO Box 40, Stadium Post Office, Accra (tel: 667-090; fax: 668-262).

Ministry of Mobilisation (tel: 665-349; fax: 667-251).

Ministry of Roads and Transport, PO Box M43, Accra (tel: 666-465; fax: 667-911).

Ministry of Tourism, PO Box 4386, Accra (tel: 666-314; fax: 666-182; e-mail: MOT@ghana.com; internet site: http://www.estghana.gov.gh; www.africaonline.com.gh/Tourism).

Ministry of Trade and Industry, PO Box M47, Accra (tel: 663-327; fax: 665-114).

Ministry of Works and Housing, PO Box M43, Accra (tel: 662-242; fax: 663-268).

Ministry of Youth and Sports, PO Box M 252, Accra (tel: 664-71; fax: 663-927).

Other useful addresses

Accra International Conference Centre, PO Box C1054, Accra (tel: 669-600; fax: 669-825).

Ashanti Goldfields Co Ltd, Gold House, Patrice Lumumba Road, Roman Ridge, PO Box 2665, Accra (tel: 772-190, 776-224, 778-155; fax: 775-947).

Association of Ghanaian Industry, PO Box 8624, Accra (tel: 777-283; fax: 773-143).

Black Star Line, PO Box 2760, Accra (tel: 776-161; fax: 775-140).

British Diplomatic Mission, Accra (tel: 221-665).

Civil Aviation Authority, Kotoka International Airport, PO Box 87, Accra (tel: 773-283).

Coffee, Sheanuts Exporters' Association, c/o Mr J W Biney, Agrotrade Ltd., PO Box 226, Accra (tel: 224-820; fax: 224-564).

Customs, Excise and Preventive Service, PO Box 68, Accra (tel: 666-841; fax: 660-019).

Department of Co-operatives, PO Box M150, Accra (tel: 666-212).

The Department of Urban Roads, Ministry of Roads and Transport, PO Box 38, Accra (tel: 230-381, 223-908; fax: 234-522).

Divestitute Implementation Committee, F35/5 Ring Road East, North Labone, PO Box C102, Cantonments, Accra (tel: 772-049, 773-119, 760-281; fax: 773-126; e-mail: dicgh@ncs.com.gh).

Export Finance Company, Bank of Ghana, PO Box 2674, Accra (tel: 666-902; fax: 662-996).

Federation of Association of Ghanaian Exporters (FAGE), c/o Kiku Ltd., PO Box M378, Accra (tel: 223-215; fax: 776-755).

Ghana Assorted Foodstuffs Exporters Assocation, PO Box 16073, Airport - Accra (tel: 220-746; fax: 223-663).

Ghana Chamber of Mines, PO Box 991, Accra (tel: 665-355; fax: 662-926).

Ghana Civil Aviation Authority, Private Mail Bag, Kotoka International Airport, Accra (tel: 776-171; fax: 773-293; e-mail: centre-GCAA@ighmail.com; internet site: http://www.gcaa.com.gh).

Ghana Cocoa Board, PO Box 933, Accra (tel: 221-212; fax: 667-104, 665-076; e-mail: cocobod@africaonline.com.gh).

Ghana Export Promotion Council, Republic House, Tudu, PO Box M 146, Accra (tel: 228-813/830/623; fax: 668-263, 233-715; e-mail: gepc@ighmail.com).

Ghana Free-Zones Board, PO Box M626, Accra (tel: 670-532/5; fax 670-536; e-mail: freezone@africaonline.com.gh; internet site: http://www.ghanaclassifiec.com.ghzb).

Ghana Furniture Producers/Exporters Association, PO Box 32, Trade Fair Centre, Accra (tel: 775-311).

Ghana Highway Authority, PO Box 1641, Accra (tel: 666-591; fax: 665-571).

Ghana Investment Promotion Centre (GIPC), PO Box M193, Accra (tel: 665-125/9; fax: 663-801; e-mail: gipc@ghana.com; internet site: http://www.gipc.org.gh).

Ghana Liaison Office, Cotecna Inspection S A, 10 Drake Avenue, Airport Residential Area, PO Box C2212, Cantonments, Accra (tel: 775-698; fax: 553-522).

Ghana National Petroleum Corporation (GNPC), Private Mail Bag, Tema (tel: 232-056; fax: 774-143).

Ghana National Procurement Agency, Ministries Post Office, Private Mail Bag, Accra (tel: 220-851; fax: 221-049).

Ghana Shippers Council, Private Mail Bag, Ministries Post Office, Accra (tel: 666-915; fax: 668-768).

Ghana Stock Exchange, Marketing Department, 5th Floor, Cedi House, Liberia Road, Accra (tel: 669-914; fax: 669-913; e-mail: stockex@ncs.com.gh; internet site; http://www.gse.com.gh).

Ghana Trade and Investment Gateway Project (GHATIG), PO Box M47, Accra (tel: 663-439, 664-074; fax: 665-423; e-mail: gateway1@ghana.com).

Ghana Yam Producers and Exporters' Association, PO Box 5233, Accra (tel: 775-311; fax: 668-263).

Ghanaian Embassy (USA), 3512 International Drive, NW, Washington DC 20008 (tel: 686-4520; fax: 686-4527; e-mail: hagan@cais.com).

Horticulturists' Association of Ghana, PO Box 9303, Accra (tel: 772-139; fax: 772-350).

Institute of Economic Affairs (tel: 776-641; fax: 776-724).

Internal Revenue Services, PO Box 2202, Accra (tel: 664-961; fax: 664-938).

Organisation for Export Development for Seafood, c/o Signotrade Ltd., PO Box 16851, Accra (tel: 712-762; fax: 668-263).

Precious Metals Marketing Corporation, PO Box M108, Accra (tel: 664-931; fax: 772-350).

Private Enterprises Foundation (PEF), PO Box C1671, Cantoments, Accra (tel: 222-313; fax: 231-487).

Registar-General's Department, PO Box 118, Accra (tel: 666-469).

US Diplomatic Mission, Accra (tel: 228-440).

Vegetables Exporters' Association, c/o Ghana Export Promotion Council, PO Box M146, Accra (tel: 221-212; fax: 668-263).

Volta River Authority, PO Box MB77, Accra (tel: 664-941, 221-124; fax: 662-610; e-mail: orgsrv@accra.vra.com).

Internet sites

Ghana Drum Magazine: http://www.erols.com/ghanadrm/Africa Business Network: http://www.ifc.org/abn

AllAfrica.com: http://allafrica.com

African Development Bank: http://www.afdb.org

Mbendi AfroPaedia (information on companies, countries, industries and stock exchanges in Africa): http://mbendi.co.za

Yellow Pages: http://www.ghanaforum.com/directory.htm

Guinea

Alvise Forcellini

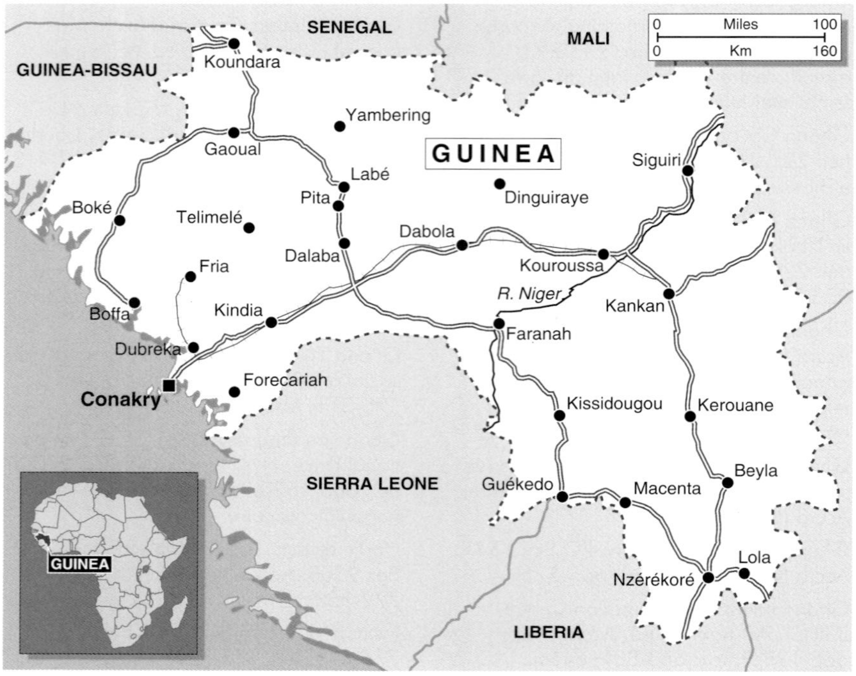

KEY FACTS

Official name: République de Guinée (Republic of Guinea)

Head of State: President General Lansana Conté (PUP) (since 1984; the Nov 2001 constitutional referendum permitted President Conté to retain the presidency and run for a third, extended term in 2003)

Head of government: Prime Minister Lamine Sidime (PUP) (since 1999)

Ruling party: Parti de l'Unité et du Progrès (PUP) (Party of Unity and Progress) (since 1995; re-elected 30 Jun 2002, elections)

Area: 245,857 square km

Population: 8.15 million (2001)

Capital: Conakry

Official language: French

Currency: Guinean franc (Gf)

Exchange rate: Gf1,985.00 per US$ (Jan 2003)

GDP per capita: US$368 (2001)

GDP real growth: 3.60% (2001)

Inflation: 5.40% (2001)

Balance of trade: US$169.00 million (2001)

Foreign debt: US$2.94 billion (2001)

For the latest Key Facts, go to www.worldinformation.com

The parliamentary elections of June 2002 were largely ignored by the media. The opposition parties boycotted the elections, believing them to be rigged, and as expected, the ruling Parti de l'Unité et du Progrès (PUP) (Party of Unity and Progress) secured a majority. While President Lasana Conté's aim was to show the international community his commitment to democratic reforms, his determination to keep hold of power for the rest of his days became more obvious prior to the elections.

Keeping hold of power

President Conté has been momentarily successful in reducing political opposition. His grip on the country's political system is not likely to be questioned until the next presidential elections due at the end of 2003. To secure a life-long presidential mandate, he introduced all the necessary constitutional amendments in 2001. In particular, his revision extended the presidential mandate from five to seven years. The legal limit to how many times a president can be re-elected was removed (Conté had already stood for two elections), and the age limit at which a candidate can stand for president, previously 70 years, was abolished. Despite concerns from the West about the logical outcome of this tailor-made constitutional reform, the president's entourage described it as a reward for President Conté's 'successful fight against the primal hordes of rebellion'. According to officials, the constitutional revision was approved by a large majority of the population through a referendum held in November 2001.

An outright boycott

The immediate consequence of the revision was the decision by a large part of the political opposition to boycott the June 2002 parliamentary elections. A small fraction of the opposition disagreed and put forward a list of candidates. Alpha Condé, a long serving opposition leader who challenged Lasana Conté twice and was sent to prison in 1998 was set free by the president in May 2001. This appeared to be a pragmatic response to international pressures in favour of Condé's liberation rather than a serious commitment to the legal rights of political opponents.

With the opposition's boycott and the fear of possible violence, it was not surprising that the election turnout was extremely low. The EU seemed to concur with the opposition's views and decided neither to send observers nor to fund the elections.

Relief for refugees

During most of 2001 and 2002, Guinea was involved and seriously affected with what was described by UN High Commissioner for Refugees, Rudd Lubbers, as the worst refugee crisis in the world. Hundreds of thousands of refugees from Liberia and Sierra Leone were camped in southern Guinea. Refugees constituted around 7 per cent of the country's population and public opinion grew increasingly hostile in 2001. The authorities fostered and manipulated antagonism by blurring the significant differences between rebel armed movements and refugees. In early 2002 tension started decreasing, as thousands of refugees left Guinea and returned to their villages in Sierra Leone. These repatriations were made possible through the robust presence and active role of the UN.

Positive moves in Sierra Leone were overshadowed by worsening conditions in Liberia, where rebels made rapid advances towards the capital, Monrovia. There is arguably some truth in President Conté's and Liberian President Charles Taylor's reciprocal accusations of each fostering rebel movements in their two countries as a way to prevent any co-operation between them. Nevertheless, talks that seemed unlikely in early 2001 finally took place in February 2002: a summit was held in Rabat between the presidents of the three neighbouring countries, Guinea, Sierra Leone and Liberia, to discuss the regional conflict.

As a consequence of Guinea's border conflicts, the number of war weapons in civilian hands and of organised armed attacks rose in 2001 and into 2002. Criminal activity in the country led to frequent human right's abuses and to the end of the 17-year moratorium on the death penalty in February 2002.

Conditional aid

The G8 summit held in Canada in June 2002 agreed to strengthen both financial aid and debt relief. In 2000, Guinea benefited from a comprehensive debt reduction package under the Heavily Indebted Poor Countries (HIPC) initiative aiming to reduce the country's debt service obligations by a third by 2020. While the HIPC initiative could be as much as US$1,000 million, the G8 emphasised that only legally constituted states fostering good governance and democracy will be considered. The majority of observers of African politics are convinced that Guinea will not respect these conditions and will therefore not be part of what has been called a 'Marshall plan for Africa'.

Economic reforms and the IMF

Guinea embarked on economic liberalisation when Conté took over as president in 1984. As agreed with the IMF, price controls were abolished, foreign trade was liberalised and monetary and banking reforms were implemented. Reform efforts have not produced the expected results, regional instability playing a major role in the worsening economic situation.

A Poverty Reduction and Growth Facility (PRGF), a concessional facility ideally based on poverty reduction strategies, was delayed in 2000 as a consequence of the growing border conflict, the shortfall in expected external assistance and of a marked decline in the terms of trade. As a result, Guinean authorities revived the trend towards structural reforms and established a National Anti-Corruption Committee (NACC) as required by the IMF. Consequently, in May 2001, a three-year PRGF arrangement of US$81.3 million was approved by the IMF, aiming at, according to Stanley Fischer, first deputy managing director of the IMF, 'maintaining macroeconomic stability and accelerating growth as the foundation of the government's poverty reduction strategy'. The IMF also expects the privatisation agenda to give a positive outcome, despite the fact that these reforms have proved extremely laborious in the past.

In June 2002, the IMF approved a US$17 million tranche under the PRGF programme and an additional US$3.6 million under the Highly Indebted Poor Countries (HIPC) initiative.

The IMF's emphasis on increasing revenue was echoed in the 2001/02 budget: overall revenue was raised from 11.1 to 13.4 per cent of GDP and expenditure was cut by 4 per cent. According to Sheik Amadou Camara, the economy and finance minister, a 'budget of austerity and caution' was necessary due to the 'difficult economic situation' of the last few years. The financial plan also predicted 3 per cent GDP growth in 2003 with inflation at 4 per cent.

Even though IMF projections see GDP growth rate rising to 6.5 per cent in 2004, this will depend on the government's ability to cope with regional instability and the resultant humanitarian costs and social unrest.

Mining

State revenue will be, as always, dependent on the extraction of bauxite, of which Guinea possesses the world's largest deposits and is the world's second largest exporter after Australia. Production has intensified and income from bauxite represents approximately 80 per cent of total export and 65 per cent of tax revenues. The production of alumina is also progressing.

Diamonds are Guinea's second largest export commodity, but deposits in the

KEY INDICATORS — Guinea

	Unit	1996	1997	1998	1999	2000
Population	m	7.53	7.71	7.81	8.02	8.15
Gross domestic product (GDP)	US$bn	3.96	3.92	3.62	3.50	3.10
GDP per capita	US$	526	508	463	436	380
GDP real growth	%	5.1	4.8	4.6	3.6	2.0
Inflation	%	3.0	1.9	5.1	4.6	6.8
Exports (fob) (goods)	US$m	636.5	630.1	693.0	677.9	695.0
Imports (fob) (goods)	US$m	525.3	512.5	572.0	583.4	555.0
Balance of trade	US$m	111.2	117.6	121.0	94.5	140.0
Current account	US$m	-177.3	-91.1	-183.6	-151.6	-201.0
Total reserves minus gold	US$m	87.3	121.6	236.7	199.7	147.9
Foreign exchange	US$m	86.5	118.9	235.2	198.3	147.6
Exchange rate	per US$	1,004.00	1,095.30	1,236.80	1,327.10	1,746.90

forested triangle of Kerouané-Beyla-Macenta, in the south, fuel illegal trafficking with Sierra Leone. In 2001, violent clashes with rebel groups occurred in the region, while diamond deposits in that area have not yet stimulated much industrial investment. Gold is gaining importance as international exploration funding increases: besides the two main gold producers, Société Minière de Dinguiraye (SMD) and Société Aurifère de Guinée (SAG), a third one, Semafo Incorporated, officially opened its gold mine in 2002.

Outlook

Relative stabilisation in the region has been beneficial to Guinea and economic prospects would be promising if the conflict in Liberia was not a constant threat to its neighbours. The authorities are increasingly committed to sound economic policies, aiming to keep inflation low and ensure macroeconomic stability, in the expectation that economic growth will help to reduce widespread discontent against the government.

With Lansana Conté's regime drawing to an end, the democratisation process that was half-heartedly begun in 1990 has been consciously jeopardised during the last 12 months, lessening prospects for a peaceful shift of power.

Risk assessment

Economic	Poor
Political	Deteriorating
Regional stability	Improving

COUNTRY PROFILE

Historical profile

From the thirteenth–fifteenth centuries Guinea was part of the Mali empire which covered a large part of west Africa.
1450s The coastal region began to be settled by European traders.
1891 The country became a French colony.
1958 Formerly French Guinea, Guinea became independent under the leadership of Sekou Touré.
1960s Touré modelled Guinea on the Chinese system; French financial and technical aid was cut off.
1977 The Market Women's Revolt (against state plans to discourage private trading) led to a change in government policy.
1984 Touré died in March. One month later a group of army colonels launched a military coup. Lansana Conté became president and introduced IMF-backed austerity measures as well as a new currency, the Guinean franc, which replaced the syli.
1993 Conté won the December presidential election with 51 per cent of the vote.
1995 In multi-party legislative elections held on 11 June, the Parti de l'Unité et de Progrès (PUP) (Party of Unity and Progress), led by President Conté, won 71 of the 114 seats in the National Assembly.
1996 An army mutiny in February almost led to the end of President Lasana Conté's rule, but order was restored within a few days. In July, the post of prime minister was created by the president who appointed Sidya Touré (a leading Guinean businessman) as Guinea's first prime minister. The 22-strong cabinet was essentially made up of technocrats. Touré's appointment led to increased co-operation with the IMF and the World Bank.
1998 President Lansana Conté was re-elected in December.
1999 Lamine Sidime (PUP) was appointed prime minister, replacing Sidya Touré.
2001 In January, Sierra Leone's war spread deeper into Guinea, displacing a number of refugees. There were also rebel attacks on the border between Guinea and Liberia. A constitutional referendum held in November permitted President Lasana Conté to retain the presidency and run for a third, extended term in 2003.
2002 Turnout was low in the parliamentary elections held in June. The elections had been delayed by two years, allegedly due to the fighting that had been going on between Sierra Leone and Liberia. The oppostion boycotted the election which was won by the ruling PUP.

Political structure

Constitution
The constitution was promulgated in 1990.

Form of state
Republic

The executive
Prior to the constitutional amendments, made in 2001, the president was elected for a five-year term, renewable only once. Following the changes, the mandate increased to a seven-year term with no legal limit as to the number of times that it could be renewed.
The prime minister and the Council of Ministers are appointed by the president.

National legislature
The unicameral Assemblée Nationale Populaire (People's National Assembly) has 114 deputies serving five-year terms.

Legal system
The legal system is based on French civil law, customary law and decree.

Last elections
30 June 2002 (legislative) (originally scheduled for November 2000)

Next elections
2003 (presidential)

Political parties

Political parties were legalised from April 1992.

Ruling party
Parti de l'Unité et du Progrès (PUP) (Party of Unity and Progress) (since 1995; re-elected 30 Jun 2002, elections).

Main opposition party
Rassemblement du Peuple Guinéen (RPG) (Rally of the Guinean People).

Population

8.15 million (2000)
Annual population growth rate: 2.4 per cent (1994–2000). About 47 per cent of the total population is under 15 years.
Population density: 28 per square km. Urban population: 30 per cent (1994–2000).
Guinea has about 700,000 refugees from Liberia, Sierra Leone and Guinea-Bissau.

Ethnic make-up
Fulani (35 per cent), Malinke (30 per cent), Soussou (20 per cent).

Religions
Islam (85 per cent), a small number of Roman Catholics (8 per cent) and traditional beliefs (7 per cent).

Education

Guinea shows an upward trend in gross enrolment rate with increasing demand for teachers, school facilities, and other resources. The gross illiteracy rate is estimated at 69 per cent. The government has initiated the third phase of the project Basic Education for All (2001–2012) focusing on increased access, improved quality and efficiency through decentralisation processes.
Despite significant urban/rural and gender disparities in enrolment ratios, there is overall improvement. Enrolment for girls is estimated at 44 per cent compared to the boys at 70 per cent for the year 2000. In rural areas the enrolment rate for girls remains at only 26 per cent. The crisis in teacher supply persists despite the World Bank and the government's intensive teacher-training program (FIMG), which had planned recruitment of approximately 6,000 teachers for the entire 1998-2001 period.
Government expenditure in education increased to 25 per cent of the total national budget in 2000.

Health

World Bank estimates for the period 1994 and 2000 show that the average life expectancy was 44 years and the infant mortality rate stood at 98 per 1,000 live births. It is estimated that around 24 per cent of children under the age of five are malnourished. The total fertility rate is around 5.3 children born per woman while the rate of contraception practices is estimated at 6 per cent among women aged 15–49. The maternal mortality rate is typically 670 deaths per 100,000 live births. World Bank estimates in 2000 showed that 49 per cent and 58 per cent of the population had

access to improved water and sanitation facilities respectively. There are 0.2 physicians and 0.6 hospital beds typically available for 1,000 people. The HIV rate is 1.54 per cent among adults.
Between 1990 and 1998, government expenditure on healthcare averaged around 4 per cent of GDP of which 2.2 per cent was public expenditure, according to World Bank estimates. Expenditure on private healthcare (such as private household expenditure and insurance) averaged around 1.4 per cent of GDP.

Welfare
Guinea's social insurance system provides coverage for employed people, pensions, old-age benefits and survivor benefits (payable to widows, orphans and dependant relatives). Old age pensions are applicable to all those aged 55 and over. The system also provides sickness and maternity benefits as well as allowance for those families with children under the age of 17.

Main cities
Conakry (population 1.2 million in 1998), Kankan (60,000), Labé, Siguiri, Kindia, Boké.

Languages spoken
African languages are in daily use. English is seldom used.

Official language/s
French

Media
Press
Most newspapers in circulation are weeklies including *3P-Plus*, *La Lance*, *Le Lynx*, Oroya and *L'Indépendent*.

Broadcasting
Television and radio programmes in French, English, Arabic, Portuguese and local languages. Services operated by Radiodiffusion-Télévision Guinéenne (RTG) from Conakry and carry advertising.

Economy
Guinea is rich in minerals and fertile land, but remains one of Africa's more underdeveloped economies. However, the government has managed to create moderate economic conditions, with typical GDP growth of around 4 per cent (GDP grew only 2.9 per cent in 2001 as a result of the unstable world economy) with inflation in single figures. Government revenues are healthy following the implementation of a tight fiscal regime.
Despite liberalising the investment environment, Guinea is still dependent on primary commodities and lacks the capital and infrastructure to diversify the country's export markets as well as providing for the domestic market. Moreover, the country's dependence on the export of bauxite and other minerals means the economy is highly vulnerable to fluctuations in global commodity prices, creating potential problems for sustainable economic development in the future.

External trade
Bauxite and alumina are Guinea's main export earners. Although diamond exports are rising, the balance of payments situation is precarious, despite large volumes of concessionary assistance from the World Bank, IMF and foreign aid donors. Guinea does not belong to the West African Monetary Union (franc zone).

Exports
Exports are dominated by bauxite and alumina (up to 90 per cent of total), gold, diamonds, coffee, fish, fresh fruit and vegetables.
Main destinations: US (typically 25 per cent of total), France (10 per cent), Spain (9 per cent), Germany.

Imports
Principal imports are foodstuffs, capital and manufactured goods and primary commodities.
Main sources: France (typically 29 per cent of total), Côte d'Ivoire (12 per cent), US (9 per cent), Hong Kong (8 per cent).

Agriculture
Traditional farming generates around 23 per cent of GDP and around 67 per cent of the population is engaged in subsistence farming.
Only 7 per cent of land is cultivated, although there is considerable potential for development due to fertile land.
Main cash crops are bananas, groundnuts, oil palm, cotton, pineapples, citrus fruits and coffee. Main subsistence crops are rice (60 per cent of cultivated land), cassava, maize and vegetables.
Output has stagnated due to transport problems, low levels of mechanisation, poor marketing and a lack of vital inputs. Although infrastructural projects have rectified some problems, the country is in need of further investment to improve roads linking agricultural areas to domestic and foreign markets.
The fishing, forestry and livestock sectors are small. There is potential for lucrative fishing but the fishing fleet suffers from lack of funds.

Industry and manufacturing
The industrial sector contributes around 4 per cent to GDP and employs 5 per cent of the workforce.
Except for aluminium smelting it is small-scale and designed to meet local requirements. Aluminium smelting from locally mined bauxite is being modernised with French aid.
The other main industries, textiles, food processing and plywood, are handicapped by supply bottlenecks and shortages of skilled labour.
The investment code and economic liberalisation are expected to attract more foreign capital.

Mining
Mining is the most dynamic sector of the economy, accounting for around 30 per cent of GDP and almost all export earnings. Eight per cent of the workforce is employed in the sector. A mining code introduced in 1995 renewed foreign interest in the mining sector, offering a range of guarantees and tax incentives to foreign investors, who may own up to 85 per cent of any venture.
Reserves of bauxite account for around one-third of the world reserves. Bauxite accounts for around 20 per cent of Guinea's GDP and around 90 per cent of exports. Around 650,000 tonnes of alumina are produced from the country's single refinery at Fria. The largest bauxite producer is the Sangarédi mine, operated by Compagnie des Bauxites de Guinée (CBG), a joint venture between the government and Halco. CBG has an annual production capacity of 14 million tonnes.
Guinea is rich in uranium, titanium, copper, manganese, iron ore, gold and diamonds. Diamond reserves are estimated at 40 million carats (93 per cent gem quality). The Aredor diamond mine, near Banankore, is 50 per cent owned by the government and 50 per cent by a consortium led by Bridge Oil of Australia and produces around 25,000 carats per year. Diamond mining capacity in Guinea is far lower than recorded exports. It is thought that many gems purchased originate in Sierra Leone. Key sites of precious stones include Siguiri, Mandiana, Dinguiraye, Kissidougou and Kérouané, and along the rivers of Baoulé, Milo and Diani.

Hydrocarbons
Exploration for offshore petroleum is under way.

Energy
There is considerable potential for hydropower from several large rivers, as yet untapped.
The country imports oil to run power stations.
The Garafiri Dam, with power production capacity of 75MW, was built by France at a cost of US$211 million. It was opened in 1999.

Banking
Central bank
Banque Centrale de la République de Guinée.

Main financial centre
Conakry.

Time
GMT.

Geography
Guinea lies on the west coast of Africa, with Sierra Leone and Liberia to the south, Senegal to the north, and Mali and Côte d'Ivoire inland to the east.

Climate
The climate is tropical and humid. South: rainy season falls in June–October, rainfall is particularly heavy in Conakry, average temperature range from 22–30 degrees Celsius. The dry season is from November– April, likely temperature range 24–35 degrees Celsius. The north is generally cooler and drier.

Entry requirements
Passports
Required by all.
Visa
Required by all except nationals of some African countries.
Currency advice/regulations
No restrictions on foreign currency and traveller's cheques. The import and export of local currency is strictly forbidden.

Health (for visitors)
Mandatory precautions
Yellow fever vaccination certificate.
Advisable precautions
Typhoid and polio vaccinations. Malaria prophylaxis essential as risk exists throughout the country. Water precautions should be taken.

Hotels
Limited first-class accommodation available in Conakry and Kankan; good hotels are expensive. Hotel bills may be paid in foreign currency or by credit card. A service charge is usually included in the bill. Tipping is optional.

Public holidays
Fixed dates
New Year's Day, 3 Apr, 1 May (Labour Day), 25 May, 15 Aug, 2 Oct, 25 Dec.
Variable dates
Ramadam, Tabaski, Le Maouloud, Le lundi de Paques.

Working hours
Banking
Mon–Sat: 0800–1300.
Business
Mon–Thu: 0800–1500; Fri: 0800–1300; Sat: 0800–1500.
Government
Mon–Thu: 0800–1500; Fri: 0800–1300; Sat: 0800–1500.

Telecommunications
Telephone/fax
The number of telephone lines have been doubled to 50,000 since Telekom Malaysia took over the previously state-controlled telecommunication services.

Electricity supply
220V AC, 50 cycles.

Getting there
Air
National airline: Air Guinée.
International airport/s: Conakry (Code: CKY), 13km from city, restaurant, bank, post office. Taxis are available to and from the city.
Airport tax: Domestic departures Gf3,000; international departures (destinations in Africa) US$20; international departures (non-African destinations) US$25; not applicable to transit passengers.
Surface
Road: Best route is the coastal road from Sierra Leone (Freetown) to Conakry. Roads from Ganta (Liberia) to N'zérékoré and from Mali (to Kankan and Siguiri) can be difficult.

Getting about
National transport
Air: Air Guinée operates regular domestic service between Conakry, Boké, Kankan, Kissidougou, Labé, Macenta, N'zérékoré, Siguiri.
Road: A few main roads are surfaced, eg from Conakry north to Kindia and Kissidougou, and parts of the road east to Freetown in Sierra Leone. Most roads are laterite and become impassable during the rainy season (May–Oct).
Buses: Coach services Conakry-Kindia-Gaoual and Dabola-N'zérékoré.
Rail: Narrow-gauge railway from Conakry to Kindia and Kankan, which is in poor condition.
City transport
Taxis: Available in Conakry, limited availability elsewhere; can be hired from hotels by the hour or day. Standard fares apply within towns but for longer journeys, fares should be agreed in advance. Tipping is optional.
Car hire
International and national driving licence required. Driving outside city limits with chauffeur and special authorisation only.

BUSINESS DIRECTORY

Telephone area codes
The international dialling code (IDD) for Guinea is + 224; no area code.

Banking
Banque Internationale pour le Commerce et l'Industrie de la Guinée SA; PO Box 1484, Avenue de la République, Conakry (tel: 414-515; fax: 413-962).

Banque Islamique de Guinee; PO Box 1247, 6è Avenue de la Republique, Conakry (tel: 415-086, 412-108; fax: 415-071).

Banque Populaire Maroco-Guineenne; PO Box 4400, Avenue de la Republique, Conakry (tel: 411-599, 419-0206, 412-360; fax: 413-261).

Ecobank - Guinee; PO Box 5687, Avenue de la Republique, Conakry (tel: 453-423; fax:454-241).

International Commercial Bank; PO Box 3574, 4è Avenue Boulbinet, Conakry (tel: 412-590, 412-591, 412-592; fax:415-450).

Société Générale de Banques en Guinée; PO Box 1514, Avenue de la République, Conakry (tel: 411-741, 411-746, 412-558 fax: 412-565).

Union Internationale de Banque en Guinée UIBG; PO Box 324, Angle 5è Boulevard, 6è Avenue de la République, Conakry (tel: 412-096, 414-309).

Central bank
Banque Centrale de la République de Guinée; PO Box 692, 3 Boulevard du Commerce, Conakry (tel 412-651, 415-072; fax: 414-898).

Travel information
Air Guinée (Compagnie Nationale Air Guinée), Route du Niger, BP 12, 12 Côte Commissariat Central, Conakry (tel: 444-602, 442-981 for reservations, 461-537 for airport, 444-614 for office).

Other useful addresses
Agence Guinéenne de Presse, BP 191, Conakry.

Bureau Veritas, BP 1451, Conakry (tel: 441-841, 442-202; fax: 412-112).

Chambre Economique de Guinée, BP 609, Conakry.

Comité d'Etat pour la Co-opération avec l'Europe Occidentale, Conakry.

Direction Nationale des Marchés Publics et du Portefeuille de l'Etat (privatisation office), La Division du Portefeuille du Ministère des Finances, avenue de la République, face á l'hôpital Ignace DEEN, BP 2006, Conakry (tel: 413-957; fax: 414-220).

ENTRAT (state forwarding firm), BP 315, Conakry.

Entreprise Nationale Import–Export (Importex), BP 152, Conakry (tel: 442-813, 442-809).

Guinea Embassy (US), 2112 Leroy Place, NW, Washington DC 20008 (tel: 483-9420; fax: 483-8688; e-mail: emgui@sysnet.net).

L'Office de Promotion des Investissement Privés – Guichet Unique (OPIP) (assistance for foreign investors), BP 2024, Conakry (tel: 451-830, 414-985; fax: 413-990; e-mail: dg@opip.org.gn).

Port Autonome, BP 805, Conakry (tel: 442-728, 442-737; fax: 414-564).

Radio-Télévision Guinéenne (RTG), BP 391, Conakry.

Statistical Office, Bureau du Premier Ministre, Conakry (tel: 442-148).

Internet sites
Guinea: http://www.Boubah.com/

Guinea-Bissau

Nils P Mork

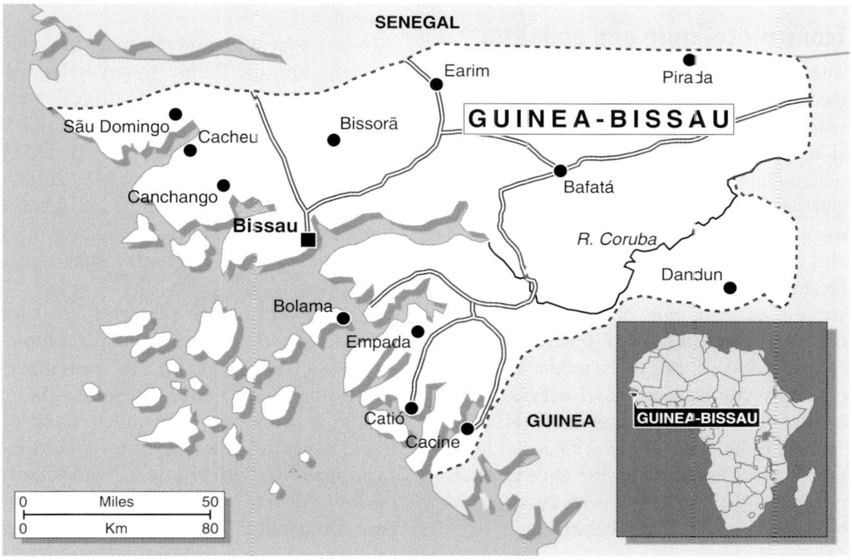

Following the election in January 2000 of President Kumba Ialá and his Partido para a Renovaçáo Social (PRS) (Social Renewal Party), troubled Guinea-Bissau has seen a prolonged power struggle between a Machiavellian president, an authoritarian military and a parliament in defiant opposition. Against a familiar backdrop of corruption scandals, human rights abuses, regional tension and a string of attempted or invented *coups d'état*, one of the poorest countries in Africa saw another period of failed development in 2001 and 2002.

Count the coups

The election that brought President Ialá to power was seen as a victory for democracy and the rule of law in Guinea-Bissau. After the destructive civil war of 1998 that led to a GDP decrease of 28.1 per cent, the mainly agricultural country badly needed a stable political environment to ensure domestic growth and the return of international investment and development assistance.

In May 2001, the World Bank and the IMF placed the country under quarantine after a corruption scandal that saw the embezzlement of US$15 million of development assistance. For a country that relies on international aid for up to 80 per cent of its budget, such ostracism is very serious indeed. The budget, adopted in June 2001, lacked any notable commitment to poverty reduction or productive sector developments, with more than 50 per cent earmarked for military expenditure and presidential costs.

The corruption scandal and the subsequent unconstitutional dismissal of Supreme Court Judges led to a parliamentary withdrawal of confidence in President Ialá in October 2001. He replied in November 2001 by threatening to suspend parliament for no less than 10 years in 'the time it would take for them to learn about democracy'.

This constitutional crisis was interrupted by an attempted *coup d'état* in December 2001. The coup attempt, allegedly instigated by the deputy head of the army, Lieutenant Colonel Almame Camara, was officially seen as related to the military revolt of November 2000 as well as another alleged attempt on the president's life in February 2001. All three instances are shrouded in secrecy, but have in common the fact that they have led to arbitrary arrests and widespread repression of dissent.

KEY FACTS

Official name: República da Guiné-Bissau (Republic of Guinea-Bissau)

Head of State: President Kumba Ialá (leader of PRS) (sworn in 17 Feb 2000)

Head of government: Prime Minister Mário Pires (sworn in 17 Nov 2002)

Ruling party: Partido para a Renovação Social (PRS) (Social Renewal Party) in coalition with the Resistência da Guiné-Bissau-Movimento Bafatá (RGB-Bafata) (Guinea-Bissau Resistance-Bafata Movement) (government sworn in Dec 2001) (parliamentary election 25 Feb 2003)

Area: 36,125 square km

Population: 1.20 million (2001)

Capital: Bissau

Official language: Portuguese

Currency: CFA franc (CFAf) = 100 centimes (Communauté Financière Africaine (African Financial Community) franc) (replaced peso Aug 1997)

Exchange rate: CFAf629.73 per US$ (Jan 2003); CFAf655.95 per euro (pegged from Jan 1999)

GDP per capita: US$167 (2001)

GDP real growth: 0.20% (2001)

Inflation: 3.30% (2001)

Balance of trade: -US$34.00 million (2001)

Foreign debt: US$674.00 million (2001)

For the latest Key Facts, go to www.worldinformation.com

Opposition politicians and international observers doubted the veracity of the rather conveniently timed coup attempt. Amnesty International issued concerned statements in December 2001 regarding the many detainees that were held without evidence or plans of forthcoming trials. The opposition called for evidence of the putsch and claimed that the president was using it as an excuse to clamp down on democratic rights as well as to silence independent newspapers and radio stations. The crisis also led to another occasion for a long line of ministerial reshuffles with the appointment of Alamara Nhassé as prime minister in December 2001.

The sacking of Prime Minister Faustino Imbali, who lasted a relatively respectable year in office was reportedly due to corruption. Guinea-Bissau's worsening economic situation led to Ialá also replacing Nhasse as prime minister in November 2002. Mário Pires was named as Nhassé's replacement – the sixth executive in less than two years. A parliamentary election is expected in early 2003.

It was reported in January 2002 that the attorney general requested the rather arbitrary lifting of parliamentary immunity for three leading opposition deputies, all members of an inquiry into the corruption scandal of May 2001. Although reasons were not officially given, opposition politicians feared they were being framed for the coup in an attempt to sabotage their investigation.

Relations with The Gambia became tense as President Ialá announced in May 2002 the foiling of yet another coup, this time allegedly supported by Gambian President Jahya Jammeh. In June 2002, Ialá threatened to 'squash' his west African neighbour, a statement that increased regional tension considerably. The Gambia denied any involvement and mediation efforts by the UN secretary general special representative, James Victor Gbehu, commenced in July 2002. Yet again, observers claimed that the coup was an invention to divert attention away from domestic discontent.

Economic collapse and populism

The economy has suffered profoundly from the lack of political stability. The corruption scandal in May 2001 led to increased tension with the World Bank and the IMF, on which Guinea-Bissau is heavily dependent, and threatened a prolonged stop in disbursements. The three-year Poverty Reduction and Growth Facility (PRGF), approved in December 2000 and heralded as a major success of economic policy, was also in danger. In May 2002, the World Bank called for expanded reforms and a reduction of the country's cumbersome civil service from 40,000 to a more economically efficient 14,000. Relations with these financial institutions serve as a door-opener to other international aid programmes, the cessation of which would be catastrophic for Guinea-Bissau.

The political unrest lead to the failure to achieve the stated goal of 8 per cent growth in 2002. Instead, GDP fell considerably to -4.3 per cent of the GDP. The Ialá presidency may well herald the end of the optimism of 1999/2000, where economic productivity and growth steadily improved.

Plans for diversification of the economy towards the oil and phosphate sector hold the potential for increased future revenues. The oil-rich joint zone between Guinea-Bissau and Senegal is especially promising, but commitment from international oil companies for investments in the region depend crucially on political stability. Nonetheless, US oil company Amerada Hess continued to consolidate its holdings in the region in May 2002. Concrete development plans are yet to be announced.

In response to the government mismanagement and the failure to pay salary arrears, several prolonged strikes were organised from April to June 2002. Eastern parts of the country were threatened by widespread food shortages in May 2002, a result of combined drought and general economic collapse, as people increasingly saw the basis of their subsistence disappear.

The government's response to such events, and the widespread discontentment that followed them, has been inadequate and inefficient – despite talk of bringing economic adjustment back on track. Only on the question of land reform has the government consistently performed, but observers worry that the parcelling out of up to 10,000 hectares (ha) of good land in January 2002 was a result of political populism, not of competent economic management. The distribution of land that formerly belonged to the deposed President Vieira to 'veterans of the liberation struggle' is reminiscent of similar 'land reforms' in Zimbabwe. Such policies may be politically rewarding, but not necessarily economically efficient.

Outlook

Most observers agree that the future of Guinea-Bissau depends heavily on its ability to re-impose a constitutional and law-abiding political regime. President Ialá , for all his shortcomings, was nonetheless democratically elected and will no doubt complete his term in office. Much responsibility lies on the opposition-dominated parliament to curb executive power, a struggle that will be closely watched in the region in the following years. Guinea-Bissau, although miserably poor, demonstrated its potential for growth in 1999 and 2000, which could be stronger still if coupled with development of the mining and petroleum industry. Guinea-Bissau desperately needs a modicum of political peace and competent governance to produce the growth required to pull it out of its quagmire of economic stagnation.

KEY INDICATORS — **Guinea-Bissau**

	Unit	1996	1997	1998	1999	2000
Population	m	1.10	1.13	1.15	1.17	1.12
Gross domestic product (GDP)	US$bn	0.25	0.25	0.30	0.22	0.22
GDP per capita	US$	227	221	261	188	196
GDP real growth	%	4.6	5.5	-28.1	7.8	7.5
Inflation	%	50.7	49.1	8.0	-2.1	8.6
Consumer prices	1995=100	150.7	224.7	239.4	237.7	258.2
Exports (fob) (goods)	US$m	21.6	48.9	27.0	56.0	68.0
Imports (fob) (goods)	US$m	56.8	62.5	52.0	66.0	86.0
Balance of trade	US$m	-35.2	-13.6	-25.0	-10.0	-18.0
Current account	US$m	-60.4	-30.3	-30.0	-28.0	-38.0
Total reserves minus gold	US$m	11.5	33.7	35.8	35.3	66.7
Foreign exchange	US$m	11.5	33.6	35.7	35.2	66.7
Exchange rate	per US$	26,373.00	583.67	589.95	615.70	711.98

Risk assessment

Economic	Poor
Political	Poor/deteriorating
Regional Stability	Poor/deteriorating

COUNTRY PROFILE

Historical profile

1400s Until Portuguese traders first came to Guinea-Bissau, the country was part of the Mali empire.

1915 The Portuguese finally gained control of the interior, although unlike its other colonies, Portugal made little attempt to develop the then Portuguese Guinea.

1960–1974 Portugal refused to relinquish power, which resulted in Africa's longest war of independence. The Partido Africano da Independéncia da Guiné e Cabo Verde (PAIGC) (African Party for the Independence of Guinea and Cape Verde) fought throughout the late 1960s and into the 1970s.

1973 Independence was unilaterally declared, by which point nearly all the necessary preparations for government had been made by the rebels.

1974 Portugal finally withdrew following the fall of the dictatorship in Lisbon. Luis Cabral, leader of the PAIGC, became president.

1980 The PAIGC was committed to the unification of Guinea-Bissau and Cape Verde, but this aim was dropped when President Cabral was removed by his prime minister, João Bernardo Vieira.

1994 Multi-party legislative and presidential elections were held in July/August. Vieira was re-elected president with 52 per cent of the vote. The PAIGC won 62 out of the 100 seats available at the general election. Turnout was an impressive 80 per cent.

1997 The CFA franc replaced the peso as national currency.

1998 Civil war started in June. A cease-fire agreement was signed on 24 August, but fighting broke out again in October. An agreement was signed at Abuja, Nigeria, on 1 November, under which President Vieira would remain in office. On 3 December, Francisco Fadul was appointed prime minister.

1999 Ecowas forces arrived to keep the peace. On 8 May fighting broke out again and President Vieira was ousted. Malam Bacai Sanha became interim president. In the first round of the presidential election held in December, Kumba Yala, leader of the Partido para a Renovação Social (PRS) (Social Renewal Party), won 38.8 per cent of the vote, and Malam Bacai Sanha, leader of the former ruling PAIGC, polled 23.4 per cent.

2000 A second round of voting was held on 16 January, and Kumba Yala was elected president with 70 per cent of the vote.

2001 Faustino Imbali was appointed prime minister in March 2001 but only served 10 months in the post. He was dismissed by the president in December and the interior minister, Alamara Ntchia Nhasse, was chosen to take over.

Political structure

Constitution

In 1999 the National Assembly passed a law reserving the highest posts in the country for 'native Bissau-Guineans'.

The executive

Executive power rests with the president who is the head of state and serves a five-year term.

National legislature

The National Assembly has 102 seats and is elected for a five-year term.

Last elections

November 1999 (legislative and presidential); January 2000 (presidential).

Next elections

2004 (presidential and legislative).

Political parties

Ruling party

Partido para a Renovação Social (PRS) (Social Renewal Party) in coalition with the Resistência da Guiné-Bissau-Movimento Bafatá (RGB-Bafata) (Guinea-Bissau Resistance-Bafata Movement) (government sworn in Dec 2001)

Main opposition party

The former ruling party, Partido Africano da Independéncia da Guiné e Cabo Verde (PAIGC) (African Party for the Independence of Guinea and Cape Verde), came third with 24 seats, bringing to an end 26 years of PAIGC rule.

The PAIGC was excluded from the cabinet appointed by President Kumba Yala in February 2000.

Population

1.12 million (2000)

Guinea-Bissau's population is among the poorest in Africa.

Annual average population growth rate: 2.2 per cent per annum (1994–2000). Many people fled from the fighting to Guinea and there was a decline in population from 1.17 million in 1999 to 1.12 million in 2000. Approximately 44 per cent of the total population is under 15 years.

Population density: 31 per square km. Urban population: 23 per cent (1994–2000).

Ethnic make-up

Balanta (30 per cent), Fula (20 per cent), Manjaca (14 per cent).

Religions

Some 65 per cent of the population are animist, 30 per cent Muslim and 5 per cent Christian.

Education

Adult literacy is low, with illiteracy typically at around 40 per cent of men and 80 per cent of women. It has been estimated by Oxfam that 58 per cent of children age 6–11 will enrol for school by 2015.

Health

World Bank estimates during the period 1994 and 2000 showed that the average life expectancy was 44 years and the infant mortality rate stood at 128 per 1,000 live births. It is estimated that 23 per cent of children under the age of five were malnourished in the same period. The total fertility rate is around 5.5 children born per woman. The maternal mortality rate is typically 910 deaths per 100,000 live births. World Bank estimates in 2000 showed that 53 per cent of the population had access to improved water sources. There are 0.2 physicians and 1.5 hospital beds typically available for 1,000 people. There are an estimated 14,000 people living with HIV/AIDS in Guinea-Bissau – 560 are under the age of 15 (2000). With infection rates at less than 1 per cent of the total population, Guinea-Bissau has so far escaped much of the African pandemic.

Public health expenditure according to World Bank estimates averaged 1.1 per cent of GDP between 1990 and 1998.

Main cities

Bissau (estimated population 220,000), Bafata, Buba, Bolama.

Languages spoken

Creole, Balanta, Bijago and Fulani are widely used. Very little English is used and all correspondence and documentation should be in Portuguese and French.

Official language/s

Portuguese

Media

The media has come under severe threat from the military operations in recent years. In April 2001, the opposition PAIGC had accused a number of senior military officers of attempting to 'gag' the press. The Reporters sans Frontieres (RSF) had also condemned the attacks against journalists by soldiers to the chief of staff of Guinea-Bissau's armed forces, Verissimo Correia Seabra. The RSF complained of other abuses against journalists, including the detention for one night of a journalist representing a private newspaper, *Diario de Bissau*.

Press

all Africa.com provides on-line news service on Guinea-Bissau's latest political and economic developments (http://allafrica.com/guineabissau/). The local weekly publication is *Correio-Bissau*.

Broadcasting

Radio: Radiodifusão Nacional da República da Guiné-Bissau broadcasts services in Portuguese.

Television: TV broadcasts are on Friday, Saturday and Sunday evenings.

Economy

Guinea-Bissau is one of the most deprived economies in West Africa and one of the most aid-dependent in the world. Around 88 per cent of the population lives on less than US$1 per day and welfare services are insignificant.

Guinea-Bissau entered the Franc Zone in 1997. In 1998 its economy was disrupted by civil war, with total GDP contracting by 28.1 per cent. However, with the advent of peace and democracy, the economy grew by 7.5 per cent in 2000 and 7.8 per cent in 2001.

Consumer price inflation has fallen to manageable levels since the mid-1990s when it reached between 45–50 per cent. In the first quarter of 2000, a seasonal increase in bank credit related to cashew production coupled with power shortages led to a rise in inflation of over 20 per cent. However, the government's efforts to reduce the fiscal deficit paid off and monthly inflation fell to 1 per cent per month. The average inflation for 2000 was 8.6 per cent, compared with -2.1 per cent in 1999, declining to 6.4 per cent in 2001.

By the end of the 1990s, the primary fiscal balance was in the black, indicating the government's success in raising revenues. However, the overall fiscal deficit was the equivalent of 9.9 per cent of GDP in 1999 due to capital expenditure growth beyond government projections.

The government's three-year Poverty Reduction and Growth Facility (PRGF) for 2000–03, agreed in December 2000, aims at achieving growth of 8–9 per cent per annum, reducing annual inflation to 3 per cent by 2003 and contributing to the build-up of international reserves by the Banque Centrale des Etats de l'Afrique de l'Ouest (Central Bank of West African States).

The PRGF was given a boost in December 2000 when the IMF and the World Bank agreed US$790 million in debt service relief, equivalent to US$417 million in net present value, under the enhanced Heavily Indebted Poor Countries (HIPC) initiative.

The IMF promised to cover 100 per cent of debt repayment in 2001/02 in order to help with the post-conflict transition. However, in May 2001, the IMF and the World Bank suspended their aid schemes after around US$15 million mysteriously disappeared from an amount placed at the disposal of the government for the country's development.

The government's economic strategy includes encouraging greater domestic and foreign private participation in economic activities and infrastructure rehabilitation and reform, and enhancing the investment climate through legal and business environment reform. However, the country's political unrest is threatening progress in these directions and economic growth in 2002.

External trade

Guinea-Bissau has a large trade deficit and heavy dependence on foreign aid and credits.

Exports

Principal exports are cashew nuts, frozen shrimp, frozen fish, groundnuts, palm nuts, sawn timber, cotton.

Main destinations: Portugal (typically 34 per cent of total), Spain (19 per cent), France (18 per cent), India, Senegal.

Imports

Principal imports are foodstuffs, transport equipment, fuels and lubricants, machinery and equipment.

Main sources: France (typically 27 per cent of total), Portugal (20 per cent), Senegal (4 per cent), CIS, the Netherlands.

Agriculture

The agricultural sector (including fishing) is the principal economic activity, accounted for 58.8 per cent of GDP in 2000 (down from 60.6 per cent in 1999), over 70 per cent of total export earnings and employed 70 per cent of the workforce. Average annual growth declined to 4 per cent in 2000, from 7.5 per cent in 1999.

Only 9 per cent of total area is cultivated; inland areas are largely savannah, coastal areas are forest and mangrove swamps. Construction of a bridge on the Mansoa river between Dakar and Bissau – completed in 1999 – has improved links between Cacheu and Oio regions (which produce half of the country's agricultural output) and markets.

There are chronic food shortages, despite the emphasis on food self-sufficiency and co-operative farming.

The main food crop is paddy rice (19 per cent of cultivated land); other food crops include millet (9 per cent), sorghum, plantains, root crops, some maize and groundnuts. Guinea-Bissau is the sixth-largest world producer of cashew nuts. Other cash crops include palm kernels, coconuts, tobacco, sugar.

Farming

The sector is dominated by subsistence farming and animal husbandry.

Fishing

The fishing sector is important. Exports of fish and shellfish are expected to increase as the country's enormous fish resources are exploited. In May 2001, the country was included in a five-year fishing development programme, under the auspices of the European Development Fund. As a result, the country will receive US$35 million in aid to develop the fishing industry, including an ice-making plant.

Industry and manufacturing

The industrial sector contributed 12.3 per cent to GDP in 2000, equal to 1999, and employed 10 per cent of the workforce. Manufacturing's contribution declined from 10.2 per cent in 1999 to 9.9 per cent in 2000. Average annual growth in the industrial sector rose in 2000 to 4 per cent from 1.5 per cent in 1999.

Production is mostly agro-related: processing groundnuts, fish processing, rice dehusking, sugar refining. There is also a large brewery plant, a small Citroën assembly plant, brick making and textiles industries. Since the end of the civil war, there has been a drive to modernise transport facilities.

Tourism

The sector is undeveloped.

Mining

There are some 200 million tonnes of bauxite reserves in the region of Boé, but exploration costs are too high to justify extraction. There are also known deposits of phosphate near Farim, gold and possibly diamonds. The main barrier to investment in the mining sector is the country's poor infrastructure.

In November 1999, the government of Guinea-Bissau passed a new mining law to reform mineral exploration and mine development and production.

In 2000, test drilling by Champion Resources Inc at the Farim phosphate deposit was completed. Champion indicated that commercially viable production could be achieved due to high phosphate recovery rates (84.1 per cent) and potentially low production costs. When developed, the company, which holds a 100 per cent interest in the deposit, expects to produce up to 2.1 million tonnes of phosphate rock per annum.

Hydrocarbons

The 1993 maritime border agreement with Senegal was ratified in December 1995 and joint oil exploration can be carried out in this area, which could contain substantial reserves.

Estimated offshore oil production is 7 million tonnes per year, although this is still in the exploration phase.

Energy

Guinea-Bissau is dependent on imported oil, although offshore exploration is under way.

Hydroelectric potential remains largely untapped.
A government commission co-ordinates the energy sector.

Banking
Central bank
Banque Centrale des Etats de l'Afrique de l'Ouest
Main financial centre
Bissau

Time
GMT

Geography
Guinea-Bissau lies on the west coast of Africa, with Senegal to the north and Guinea to the east and south.

Climate
Tropical with rainy season from mid-May to November and dry season from December–April. Average temperatures range from 20–38 degrees Celsius (C) in April–May, and from 15–33 degrees C in December–January. High humidity from July–September.

Entry requirements
Passports
Required by all.
Visa
Required by all except nationals of all ECOWAS countries. An exit visa, obtainable from the central police station in Bissau, is necessary before leaving. Visa extensions are also available from the central police station.
Currency advice/regulations
Import/export of local currency is prohibited. Foreign currency import is unlimited, but amounts should be declared; export allowed up to declared amount.

Health (for visitors)
Mandatory precautions
Yellow fever vaccination certificate
Advisable precautions
Typhoid and polio vaccinations. Malaria prophylaxis should be taken as risk exists throughout country. Water precautions are necessary.

Hotels
Accommodation is very limited and difficult to obtain at short notice. Reservations should be made well in advance, preferably through business contacts. Hotel tariffs are liable to change at short notice, therefore confirmation of booking is recommended.

Public holidays
Fixed dates
1 Jan, 20 Jan (Death of Amilcar Cabral), 8 Mar (International Women's Day), 1 May, 3 Aug (Assassination of Pidjiguiti), 24 Sep (National Day), 14 Nov (Movement of Readjustment), 25 Dec.
Variable dates
Eid Al-Fitr, Eid Al-Adha, Islamic New Year, Ashura.

Working hours
Banking
Mon–Fri: 0730–1430.
Business
Mon–Fri: 0730–1400.
Shops
Mon–Fri: 0730–1230, 1430–1830.

Telecommunications
Telephone/fax
Dialling code for Guinea-Bissau: IDD access code + 245 followed by subscriber's number. There are no area codes. Communications are poor.

Getting there
Air
International airport/s: Bissau (Code: BXO), 8km from city. Taxis and minibuses are available to take visitors to the city.
Airport tax: International departures US$20
Surface
Road: The road form Guinea is mostly paved, however that which is not, from the border to Labé, gets boggy in the rainy season. Petrol is readily available only in the cities.
The road from Senegal is not generally recommended.
Water: There are weekly sea links between Cape Verde and Guinea-Bissau.
Main port/s: Bissau

Getting about
National transport
Air: There are no mainland internal flights. Flights go between Bissau and Bubaque Island and a small plane flies to Orango Island from Bissau.
Road: Total network over 3,250km, of which about a third is all-weather. A 720-metre bridge over the Mansoa river has improved the traffic flow on the trans-African coastal road between Dakar and Bissau.
US$1.4 million was allocated in January 2000 by the EU and the World Bank for refurbishment of the road network in Bissau.
Buses: There are minibuses and bush taxis operating on the main roads.
Water: Boats serve most towns on the coast and up-river. Tickets available from the Guinémar Office.
City transport
Taxis: Available in Bissau and serve all main towns. Long-distance taxis leave from the market square in Bissau.

BUSINESS DIRECTORY

Telephone area codes
The international dialling code (IDD) for Guinea-Bissau is + 245 followed by the customer number.

Chambers of Commerce
Associação Commercial e Industrial e Agricola da Guiné-Bissau, Bissau.

Banking
Banque Centrale des Etats de l'Afrique de l'Ouest; PO Box 38, Bissau (tel: (221)215-548, 214-173, 211-482; fax: (221)201-305, 201-321).
Central bank
Banque Centrale des Etats de l'Afrique de l'Ouest, PO Box 3108, Avenue Abdoulaye Fadiga, Dakar, Senegal (tel: 390-500; fax: 239-335).

Ministries
Ministry of Economy and Finance, Rua Justino Lopes 74A, Bissau (tel: 203-495; fax: 203-496).

Ministry of Finance, Avenue Domingos Ramos, Caixa Postal 67, Bissau (tel/fax: 201-037).

Ministry of Mines and Energy, Caixa Postal 387, Bissau.

Other useful addresses
Empresa Nacional de Comércio Geral, CP 5, Bissau (tel: 212-925).

Empresa Nacional de Pesquisas e Exploração Petroliferas e Mineiras (Petrominas), 58 Rua Eduardo Mondlane, Bissau (tel: 212-279).

Guinea-Bissau Embassy (USA), 15929 Yukon Lane, Rockville MD 20855 (tel: 947-3958).

Guinémar Office, 21A Rua Guerra Mendes, Bissau.

Petroguin, Caixa Postal 387 Bissau (tel: 221-155, 222-625; fax: 221-155, 222-625).

Radiodifusão Nacional da República da Guiné-Bissau, CP 191, Bissau.

Internet sites
Africa Business Network: http://www.ifc.org/abn

AllAfrica.com: http://allafrica.com

African Development Bank: http://www.afdb.org

Africa Online: http://www.africaonline.com

Mbendi AfroPaedia (information on companies, countries, industries and stock exchanges in Africa): http://mbendi.co.za

Kenya

Falguni Patel

Falguni Patel

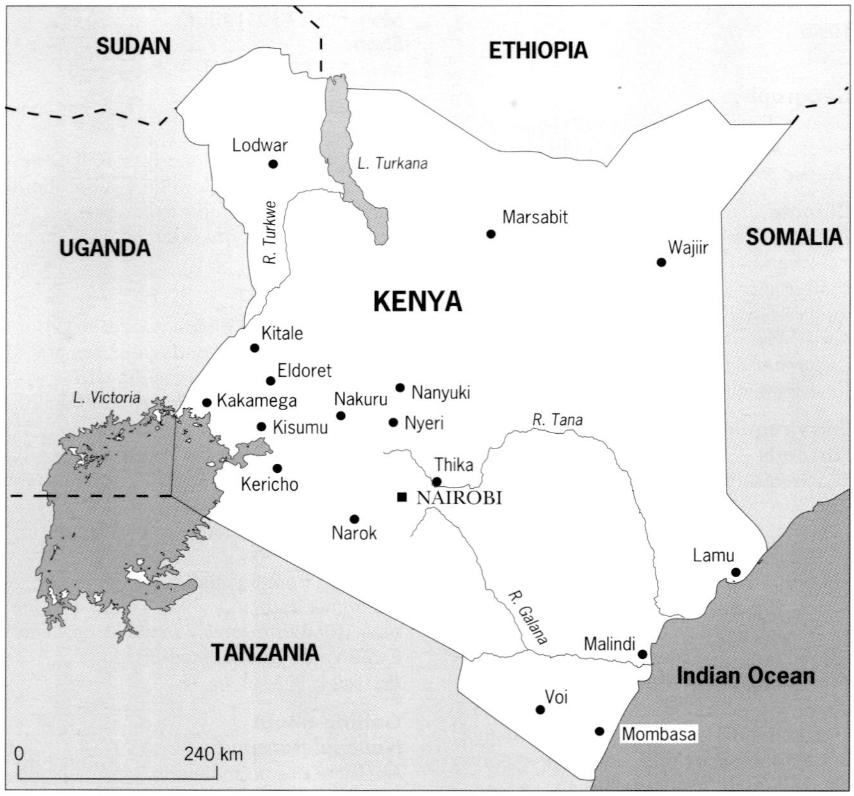

KEY FACTS

Official name: Jamhuri ya Kenya (Republic of Kenya)

Head of State: President Mwai Kibaki (NARC) (sworn in 30 Dec 2002) (results of 27 Dec 2002 presidential elections: Mwai Kibaki won 62.3 per cent of the vote against 31.2 per cent for Uhuru Kenyatta, candidate of the ruling Kanu)

Head of government: President Mwai Kibaki

Ruling party: National Rainbow Coalition (NARC) (results of 27 Dec 2002 parliamentary elections: NARC won 124 seats out of 210, former ruling party Kenya African National Union (Kanu) 64 and Ford-People 14)

Area: 582,646 square km

Population: 30.80 million (2001)

Capital: Nairobi

Official language: KiSwahili and English

Currency: Kenyan shilling (Ksh) = 100 cents (convertible with currencies of Tanzania and Uganda)

Exchange rate: Ksh77.45 per US$ (Jan 2003)

GDP per capita: US$337 (2001); US$331 (2002)*

GDP real growth: 1.20% (2001); 1.4% (2002)*

Labour force: 11.70 million (2001); 11.6 million (2002)*

Inflation: 0.80% (2001); 1.6% (2002)*

Balance of trade: -US$1.51 billion (2001)

Foreign debt: US$6.03 billion (2001)

* estimated figure

For the latest Key Facts, go to www.worldinformation.com

The December 2002 elections were a landmark in Kenyan history. The Kenya African National Union (Kanu), which had dominated Kenyan politics since independence, was forced out of power by an umbrella organisation, the National Rainbow Coalition (Narc), consisting of a number of opposition parties and Kanu dissidents. The elections were preceded by the retirement of President Daniel arap Moi, who had ruled the country since 1978 and had overseen the transition to multi-party politics in 1991. The distinct lack of political violence surrounding the polls and the generally free and fair nature of the election led many to praise the strength of Kenya's relatively new democratic institutions. While only a minority of Kenyans will miss Moi, the former president enabled a dignified hand-over of power to Mwai Kibaki which won him praise from other African leaders and helped minimise the risk of civil unrest.

Kenya and foreign aid

Kenya's deteriorating economy is set for a rebound under President Kibaki, who has promised to introduce anti-graft legislation to appease donors. In 2000, the IMF froze financial aid to the country after the government failed to introduce anti-corruption measures. It was followed by the World Bank and major bilateral donors who stopped or reduced aid to Kenya. Concerned about high levels of corruption and the lack of transparency in the management of donor funds under President Moi's leadership, the IMF's conditions for resuming its loans to Kenya are that the government should complete reforms on privatisation and good governance. However, little progress was made on combating corruption in Moi's last two years in office.

In August 2001, the Kenyan parliament voted against an anti-corruption bill, which, if passed, would have revived the Kenya Anti-Corruption Authority (KACA) and fulfilled one of the IMF's main conditions for resuming the flow of aid. Critics, however, insisted that the poorly drafted bill would have led to a KACA that, rather than reduce corruption, would simply 'paper over' it. In its previous incarnation, KACA ran into constitutional and legal problems before eventually being dissolved in December 2000 after the Kenyan constitutional court declared its powers of prosecution to be illegal. The government planned to rectify this situation by passing two bills – the anti-corruption economic crimes bill and the code of ethics bill – so that a resurrected KACA would not face the same constraints again. However, the government did not bring these two bills before parliament, making the revival of KACA almost impossible in the eyes of many MPs and observers. Opposition politicians would have welcomed an effective anti-corruption law, but the government's proposed bill did not measure up to their expectations.

Many Kenyans, while understanding the shortcomings of the anti-corruption bill, were nonetheless dismayed at the vote against it because of its economic implication – it prevented the desperately needed injection of foreign aid from the IMF and other donors into the economy. Indeed, a wave of negative economic predictions followed the parliamentary vote, with many analysts and businessmen predicting a collapse of the Kenyan economy because of the lack of foreign aid. For a start, the US$300 million inflow of foreign aid assumed in Kenya's 2001 budget did not materialise. In addition, until Kenya wins back the favour of its foreign donors, it is widely expected that the economy will be characterised by high interest and tax rates, high unemployment and low investor confidence.

Aside from the implementation of agreed anti-corruption measures, the IMF also stipulated progress in the country's privatisation programme. A key element of this was the sale of the state-run telecommunications provider, Telkom Kenya. Originally planned for April 2000, the sale has suffered several setbacks, the latest of which occurred in November 2001 when talks with a prospective buyer consortium collapsed. Although the government insisted that it was still committed to privatising Telkom in 2002, the IMF remained aloof and unconvinced of the government's commitment to the privatisation programme. The privatisation was put off until after the election.

One positive development was the announcement by the US that it planned to increase foreign aid to East Africa, with Kenya's US$40 million allotment for 2002 rising to US$47 million in 2003. In addition, the federal budget proposal submitted to Congress in February 2002 also indicated that Kenya would benefit from extra funds to combat the country's HIV/AIDS epidemic.

Peaceful hand-over

The elections of December 2002 brought an end to the rule of the Kenya African National Union (Kanu), which had ruled Kenya since independence in 1963. Mwai Kibaki was elected president with 62 per cent of the vote, roundly beating Kanu's Uhuru Kenyatta, who had been Daniel arap Moi's favourite to succeed him. Regardless of who won the election, change was inevitable after Moi, Kenya's longest-serving president, agreed to retire. What was not expected was the scale of Kanu's defeat, brought about by an alliance of opposition groups in the umbrella National Rainbow Coalition (Narc), led by Kibaki. Narc secured an absolute majority in parliament, winning 132 of the 224 seats, while Kanu took just 68 seats and the Forum for the Restoration of Democracy-People (Ford-P) won 15. The remaining seats were won by minor parties.

Narc's success was partly due to disillusionment with Moi's rule, which had been widely regarded as corrupt and dictatorial. The failure to instigate constitutional reform, combat corruption and the method of Kenyatta's selection had alienated Kanu from its grassroots supporters. The battle for the Kanu candidacy was also divisive and highly damaging for the party, with senior figures such as former vice president, George Saitoti, who had competed with Kenyatta for the Kanu nomination, quitting Kanu to back Kibaki. Although they claimed the undemocratic nature of the contest had forced them to desert Kanu, many suspected they were using the controversy surrounding Kenyatta's selection to jump on the Narc bandwagon, thereby retaining a foothold in the future government.

One notable defection ahead of the election was that of Raila Odinga, the former leader of the National Development Party (NDP), which merged with Kanu in March 2002. Odinga had come third in the 1997 presidential elections with 10.9 per cent of the vote on the back of support from the economically marginalised Luo people. The NDP had been the third-largest party in parliament with 22 seats. It was widely believed that the merger was a ploy by Odinga to secure the Kanu candidacy for himself. Odinga served as energy minister from March to October, but helped lead the Rainbow Alliance faction within Kanu which objected to Moi's interference in the race for the presidential candidacy. He quit Kanu and resigned his cabinet post following Kenyatta's appointment as the ruling party's presidential candidate and created the Liberal Democratic Party (LDP), helping to form Narc with other political parties, including Kibaki's Democratic Party of Kenya (DPK).

Although disillusionment with nearly 40 years of Kanu rule had led to an increase in the opposition vote, the main

KEY INDICATORS **Kenya**

	Unit	1996	1997	1998	1999	2000
Population	m	26.70	27.30	27.50	27.70	29.30
Gross domestic product (GDP)	US$bn	8.49	9.66	11.11	8.23	8.82
GDP per capita	US$	318	354	404	297	301
GDP real growth	%	4.6	2.4	1.8	1.4	-0.3
Inflation	%	8.8	11.2	6.6	3.5	7.8
Exports (fob) (goods)	US$m	2,083.0	2,062.6	2,017.0	1,748.6	1,733.4
Imports (fob) (goods)	US$m	2,598.0	2,948.4	3,028.7	2,731.8	3,044.0
Balance of trade	US$m	-514.8	-885.9	-1,011.7	-983.2	-1,270.6
Current account	US$m	-73.5	-456.8	-475.3	-97.7	-23.8
Foreign debt	US$bn	6.1	6.5	7.0	6.4	6.3
Total reserves minus gold	US$m	746.5	787.9	7,831.0	791.6	897.7
Foreign exchange	US$m	728.0	770.6	765.0	772.2	881.2
Exchange rate	per US$	57.12	58.73	60.37	70.33	76.18

reason for Kanu's defeat was the efforts made by its opponents to unify behind a single candidate. In the past, the opposition vote has been split along tribal lines. In 1997, Moi managed to get elected on little over 40 per cent of the vote. The 2002 elections saw Kenyatta receive 31 per cent, while Kibaki's vote was almost double the 32 per cent he received five years before. Narc achieved a landslide majority on a swing of just 10 per cent to the opposition, indicating that opposition unity had paid off.

Nevertheless, Kibaki's selection as Narc's candidate was not without controversy.His leading critic, Simeon Nyachae of Ford-P, claimed that Narc is little more than a clique of self-interested individuals keen to distribute positions among themselves and that Kibaki's candidacy was not decided by democratic means. Nyachae decided against joining NARC and put himself forward as an alternative opposition presidential candidate, receiving just 6 per cent of the vote.

Economic performance

Kenya's modest economic recovery in 2001 was due largely to an increase in agricultural production. In January 2002, the Central Bank of Kenya (CBK) reported that the production of tea, horticultural produce, pyrethrum and sisal increased in the first ten months of 2001 by 32.2 per cent, 16.1 per cent, 39.9 per cent and 6.5 per cent respectively compared with declines of 7.7 per cent, 6.4 per cent, 18.8 per cent and 4.6 per cent respectively, for the same period of 2000. Kenya's flower farms, in particular, flourished. Reports in February 2002 indicated that the country had overtaken Israel as the EU's biggest source of flower imports and now enjoyed a 25 per cent share of the EU market. However, there are concerns that the success of the flower farms is not benefiting farmers as it should and in early 2001 hundreds of pyrethrum farmers demonstrated against poor payment by the Pyrethrum Board of Kenya.

The CBK reports that the manufacturing sector also strengthened in 2001, boosted by the growth in agricultural production, tax incentives introduced in the financial year and increased access to the wider market within the US African Growth and Opportunities Act (AGOA), the Common Market for Eastern and Southern Africa (Comesa) and the East African Community (EAC). The Ministry of Trade and Industry announced in February 2002 that Kenya had earned Ksh5.4 billion (US$69.2 million) from textile exports to the US since the AGOA trade initiative began.

Tourism, a mainstay of the Kenyan economy, saw a marked increase from 2000 in both arrivals and earnings in 2001. The CBK reported that tourism earnings in US dollars increased in the first 10 months of 2001 by 19.3 per cent compared with a decline of 21.9 per cent in the same period of 2000.

Outlook

President Kibaki is faced with numerous challenges, largely due to the threats posed by a number of opportunists within the disparate Narc alliance. Unlike Kanu, Narc has no identity of its own or any coherent organisation. Rather, it was patched together in the last weeks of the Moi presidency. Moreover, it includes former Kanu politicians who are associated in the public mind with the endemic corruption of the Moi era. Kibaki's main task will be to keep the organisation together and transform it from a coalition to a fully functioning party, something which some within Narc's constituent parties are uneasy about. Narc's founding document, a memorandum of understanding between anti-Kanu parties, is vague on the subject of policy or organisation, an indication that party leaders would set aside their differences until after the election. Narc's manifesto mainly listed the problems of the Kanu administration, but was short on detailed policy.

The transition from an opposition front to a party of government is not likely to be easy. The question of Kibaki's successor is likely to grow in importance as Kenya approaches the next presidential elections in 2006. Kibaki will be 75 years old when he finishes his current term in office; Moi was 78 when he retired. He could stand for a second term, but by then he may not have the same level of support he achieved in 2002. Although the elections appear a long way off, ambitious figures within the government are likely to start manoeuvring themselves into position. This could lead to Narc's fragmentation.

The economic situation could improve in 2003, with growth forecast at 2.3 per cent. The progress of anti-corruption legislation, the new government's first full budget due in June 2003 and the level of food output, which depends on rainfall, will be key determinants of growth in 2003 and 2004.

Risk assessment

Economic	Satisfactory
Political	Satisfactory
Regional stability	Satisfactory
Stock market	Poor

COUNTRY PROFILE

Historical profile

From the mid-nineteenth century, British interest in the region grew and in 1895 Kenya was declared a British protectorate.
1944 The Kenyan African Union (KAU) was created to voice local demands for good land. From 1947, it was led by Jomo Kenyatta, a prominent member of the Kikuyu tribe, who later became the first President of the Republic of Kenya.
1952 The Kikuyu-led secret society, the Mau Mau, launched a guerrilla campaign against white farmers. More than 13,500 Africans were killed during the uprising, compared to around 100 Europeans.
1953 The KAU was suspended and Kenyatta detained, suspected of having links with the Mau Mau.
1957 Africans were elected to the Legislative Council and offered ministerial posts.
1960 A new constitution gave Africans a majority in the Legislative Council. The KAU split: the Kenya African National Union (Kanu) (which had a strong Kikuyu and Luo membership) and the Kenya African Democratic Union (Kadu) were established.
1961 Kenyatta was freed and became president of Kanu and leader of an all-party African government.
1963 The Republic of Kenya was proclaimed on 12 December and Kenyatta became president.
1964 Kadu was dissolved.
1978 President Kenyatta died and was succeeded by Daniel arap Moi.
1979, 1983 and 1988 Only Daniel arap Moi stood in the presidential elections and there was no vote.
1992 After a lengthy period as effectively a one-party state, multi-party elections were held and President Moi was re-elected.
1997 Presidential and parliamentary elections were held. President Moi secured victory over a divided opposition, gaining 40.1 per cent of the vote; Kanu won 102 seats in the National Assembly.
1999 In July George Saitoti was appointed vice president. President Moi stated that he would step down in 2002.
2001 On 11 June, President Daniel arap Moi appointed the opposition National Development Party (NDP) leader, Raila Odinga, to his 26-member cabinet, forming Kenya's first coalition government.
2002 In February, the NDP and Kanu announce a merger of the two parties in the run-up to the general election.

Political structure

Constitution

The constitution was promulgated in 1963. In 1997, a number of constitutional changes took place; these allowed the formation of a coalition government, the review of the constitution by an independent commission and increased the number of directly elected seats in the Kenyan National Assembly from 188 to 210. A further 12 seats are nominated by the government.

A constitutional amendment affirming the National Assembly's supremacy and curbing the powers of the presidency was approved in November 1999. This removed the president's right to appoint the clerk of the house, enabling the legislature to appoint and dismiss the clerk, who is no longer answerable to the president's office. The clerk manages everything from the National Assembly's agenda to its budget.

The country is divided into seven provinces run by provincial commissioners appointed by the president. The provinces are divided into districts run by district commissioners. Towns and districts have municipal and country councils, which are partly elected and partly nominated, but the commissioner has wider powers than the councils. The Nairobi area has a separate government-appointed city commission.

Form of state

Republic

The executive

Executive power in Kenya is in the hands of the president, assisted by the vice president and cabinet, both named by the president. In theory, the president is elected for a five-year term by direct popular vote. In 1979, 1983 and 1988, only one candidate stood, Daniel arap Moi, and there was no vote. However, multi-party elections took place in 1992 and 1997.

The office of the president is responsible for defence, the police, immigration and the provincial administration.

National legislature

The unicameral *Bunge* (National Assembly) has 222 members: 210 elected in single-seat constituencies for a five-year term and 12 members appointed by the president.

Legal system

Kenya's legal system is based on English common law, Islamic law and tribal law, with a High Court and Court of Appeal. The Chief Justice of the Court of Appeal is appointed by the president.

Last elections

29/30 December 1997 (presidential and parliamentary)

Next elections

December 2002 (presidential and parliamentary)

Political parties

Ruling party

Kenya African National Union (Kanu) (re-elected Dec 1997); from Jun 2001, Kanu leads a coalition government, which includes two ministers from the second-largest opposition party, National Development Party (NDP).

Main opposition party

Democratic Party (DP)

Population

29.30 million (2000)

Annual population growth rate: 2.4 per cent (1994–2000). Between 1999 and 2015 the population growth rate is projected to average 1.5 per cent per annum.

Population density: 52 inhabitants per square km. Urban population: 31 per cent (1994–2000). The high population density exerts pressure on and resources. It is estimated that 75 per cent of the population is confined to 10 per cent of the land area as most of the country is classified semi-arid or arid. Northern Kenya is arid and sparsely populated and most of its people lead a nomadic life.

Ethnic make-up

Kenya is a multi-cultural society. Most of Kenya's people belong to 13 ethnic groups although there are a further 27 smaller groups. Most Kenyans belong to Bantu tribes such as the Kikuyu (22 per cent), Luhya (14 per cent) and Kamba (11 per cent). The Luo (13 per cent) are of Nilotic origin, as are the smaller Kalenjin (12 per cent), Maasai, Turkana and others.

The Kikuyu live in the central highlands and have traditionally been dominant in commerce and politics, although this is changing. A small European settler population remains in the highlands, involved in farming and commerce. In the north live the Somalis and the nomadic Hamitic peoples (Turkana, Rendille and Samburu); Kamba and Maasai peoples are concentrated in the south and eastern lowlands, and the Luo live around Lake Victoria.

Religions

Protestant, including Anglican (38 per cent), Roman Catholic (28 per cent), animist (26 per cent), Muslim (6 per cent), others (including small Hindu, Sikh and Jain minorities) (2 per cent).

Education

Education has expanded rapidly since independence in 1963. The number of primary schools has more than doubled, while that of secondary schools has increased eighteen-fold. Enrolment at primary schools is virtually universal. Primary education begins at the age of six and is provided free of charge at state schools. Secondary school enrolment has grown rapidly, but still covers only a small proportion of the relevant age group.

Declining living standards have resulted in a drop in higher education enrolment as fewer Kenyan families can afford the rising fees. This, as well as the continuing unrest in the teaching profession, is bound to have a negative impact on the quality of the labour force in the future. Approximately 85 per cent of the relevant age group has access to primary school education, 24 per cent to secondary education and 2 per cent to tertiary education. It has been estimated by Oxfam that 75 per cent of children age 6–11 will enrol for school by 2015.

Health

Life expectancy is around 50 years and infant mortality rate is 74 per 1,000 live births. Kenya's child mortality rate has been increasing since the early 1990s, mainly due to the spread of HIV/AIDS infection. Annual expenditure on the government's AIDS strategy is US$33 million, although this was expected to rise to US$37.4 million annually over the 1999–2004 period.

Prevalence of HIV rose from 8.3 per cent of adults in 1990 to 14 per cent by 2000. For the first time in a generation, life expectancy is predicted to drop. There are an estimated two million adults and a further 100,000 children under the age of 15 with HIV/AIDS in Kenya. In 1999 alone, there were an estimated 180,000 AIDS deaths, leaving around 730,000 AIDS orphans. More than 95,000 children lost a teacher to AIDS in 1999. Around 30 per cent of hospital beds are occupied by AIDS sufferers. The annual loss in terms of GDP per capita growth is estimated to be 1.3 per cent per annum between 2000–10. Households in which one family member dies of AIDS are estimated to lose between 49–78 per cent of their income.

The United Nations food agency, the World Food Programme (WFP), has warned of disturbingly high levels of malnutrition in north-eastern Kenya. Caused by a lack of rainfall and compounded by a crop infestation, the number of malnourished children was recorded as doubling to nearly 40 per cent by 2001.

Welfare

Approximately 47 per cent of the total population is under 15 years. Around 50 per cent of the population is thought to live on less than US$1 a day. Around 80 per cent of the population is at risk from drought, famine and AIDS.

The social security system, administered separately from the government budget, covers only government employees and workers in the small modern sector of the economy. The welfare system is financed by the National Social Security Fund (NSSF), set up in 1965.

The NSSF has approximately 2.7 million members. In theory, social security contributions are compulsory and are deducted from wages at source. Deductions range from one-thirtieth to one-tenth of earnings. The employer pays half of each employee's contribution. In practice, few families or small businesses enrol their servants or workers. In November 2001, President Moi announced the establishment of a mandatory National Social Health Insurance (NSHI) scheme that would cover all Kenyans.

Social security benefits are limited to survivor's benefit (paid on the death of contributor), invalidity benefit, withdrawal benefit (a fixed sum paid on retirement) and an emigration grant. There is no unemployment benefit. Every Kenyan is entitled to supplementary health benefit under the National Hospital Insurance scheme, founded in 1966.

Main cities

Nairobi (capital, estimated population 1.84 million in 1999, some 1,650 metres above sea-level), Mombasa (main port, 800,000), Nakuru, Kericho, Thika, Kisumu, Eldoret, Machakos, Nyeri, Kitale.

Languages spoken

KiSwahili is the lingua franca. In addition, most tribes have their own language. English is universally used in business and spoken by most people in the tourist industry. Other languages are Gikuyu, Kiluhya, Dholuo, Kikamba, Maasai and Somali.

Official language

KiSwahili and English

Media

Press

Newspaper distribution is limited to large towns and a low level of literacy means that readership is small.

Dailies: The principal daily newspapers are *Daily Nation* (owned by the Aga Khan), *East African Standard*, *Taifa Leo*, *Kenya Times* and *Mombasa Times*.

Weeklies: Weeklies and Sunday newspapers include *Sunday Nation*, *Sunday Standard*, *Sunday Times*, *Post on Sunday*, *Star*, *Herald*, *Dispatch*, *The East African* and *Kenya Leo*.

Business: Business publications are *Business Africa* and the *Business Chronicle*.

Periodicals: There are a number of general and specialised periodicals.

Broadcasting

Radio: State-run Kenya Broadcasting Corporation (KBC) operates extensive national services in KiSwahili, English, Hindi and numerous African languages. Radio is listened to by over 66 per cent of adults.

Television: KBC operates one channel for 126 hours per week. The commercial service is in KiSwahili and English.

A satellite channel, Kenya Television Network (KTN) was launched by Kenya Times Media Trust in 1990. KTN operates 24 hours per day and can only be viewed in the Nairobi area.

Television is watched by only around a sixth of households.

Economy

Kenya is predominantly rural, severely indebted and a low income economy. Seventy-five per cent of its land area is arid or semi-arid, leading to high concentrations of population, notably in the large shanty towns that skirt the major cities such as Nairobi. Agriculture dominates employment and is comprised of 50 per cent subsistence farming. Available arable land is scarce and output depends on a climate which frequently brings drought.

Despite this, Kenya probably has the most developed economy in East Africa and is well placed to take advantage of the successful Structural Adjustment Programmes (SAPs) taking place in Tanzania and Uganda. Industrial activity is more diversified and includes more private sector involvement than in its neighbouring countries. Kenya's important industries include food processing, tobacco, beverages and transport. It also has a strong service sector, mainly tourism and financial services, which contributes the bulk of GDP and is a major source of employment and foreign exchange.

The economy has made moderate progress, aided by a domestic austerity programme, but population growth threatens to overtake economic advances. Large current account deficits have been partly funded by foreign borrowing.

The drought in 2000 was declared a national disaster and President Daniel arap Moi appealed for food aid. In 2001, NGOs warned of an imminent famine with the number of families dependent on food assistance increasing. They urged the international community to support long-term development initiatives as a method of averting emergencies.

In August 2000, the IMF approved a three-year SDR150 million Poverty Reduction and Growth Facility (PRGF) – the first loan since 1997. This news encouraged donor flows to the country. The Paris Club approved a debt rescheduling in November 2000. However, IMF lending was halted again in January 2001 in response to the Kenyan government's alleged foot-dragging on implementing anti-corruption measures, with many of the measures proposed by multilateral agencies being rejected by parliament and the High Court as unconstitutional. The failure to implement anti-corruption laws has led to a sharp decline in donor aid, putting the country's precarious economic recovery in jeopardy.

In March 2002, the government released the Ninth National Development Plan (2002–08), forecasting average economic growth of 4 per cent per annum across the period. Agricultural growth is expected to rise from its 1996–2001 average of 1.1 per cent to 3.3 per cent with similar growth expected in the manufacturing sector. However, these economic growth projections are below the 6.6 per cent GDP growth required to achieve the poverty eradication targets set out in the National Poverty Eradication Plan (NPEP).

External trade

Exports

Principal merchandise exports are tea (typically 28 per cent of total), horticultural products and coffee. Other exports include petroleum products, fruit and vegetables, cement and sisal.

Main destinations: Uganda (typically 14 per cent of total), UK (14 per cent), Tanzania (11 per cent), Pakistan (7 per cent), France (6 per cent), Netherlands (5 per cent), Germany (5 per cent), US (5 per cent), Egypt (3 per cent), Rwanda (2 per cent).

Imports

Principal imports are crude petroleum, industrial supplies, machinery and capital equipment, food and live animals, transport equipment.

Main sources: UK (typically 11 per cent of total), United Arab Emirates (10 per cent), South Africa (7 per cent), Saudi Arabia (7 per cent), US (7 per cent), France (6 per cent), Japan (6 per cent), India (5 per cent), Germany (4 per cent), China (4 per cent).

Agriculture

The agricultural sector contributes around 30 per cent to GDP and provides a livelihood for around 50 per cent of the workforce. Primary and processed agricultural products account for over 55 per cent of export earnings. Subsistence farming comprises more than half of output and less than 20 per cent of Kenya's land surface is arable.

Maize is the most important food crop. Sorghum, cassava, beans and fruit are also grown. The principal cash crops are tea, coffee (mainly arabica grown by smallholders), sugar, cotton, pyrethrum, sisal, tobacco, pineapples and wattle.

Horticultural produce is increasingly important and by 2000 it became the second-largest export earner after tea with flowers making up the largest share (close to 40,000 tonnes).

The sugar industry was hit by a massive illegal dumping of sugar imports. Launched as a cash crop in the early 1970s, sugar-cane thrived in the perfect climate conditions in the 1980s, but now fails to meet local demand of 550,000 tonnes due to poor management.

Since 1989, a gradual reduction of state control of grain marketing, giving co-operatives and private entrepreneurs an initial 20 per cent of the market, has stimulated production. Early in 1991 the government relaxed its controls on the distribution of maize and several other commodities. By the end of 1993 the government's maize import and marketing monopoly had been abolished. However, the deregulation of price controls was not included in this liberalisation move. The government's goal during the 1990s was to maintain at least 5 per cent annual growth in agricultural output to the end of the century. However, production consistently fell behind these targets. Inadequate storage facilities, little irrigation, recurrent drought and a severe shortage of arable land have restricted growth in the sector. There is an acute shortage of arable land and uneven distribution has resulted in most farmers working plots of two hectares or less. Landlessness, an annual population growth of 2.4 per cent and rapid urbanisation place increasing pressure on the ability of current food production and distribution to meet demand at affordable prices. In addition, there is an ecological risk to some of the most fertile areas of western and central Kenya, which are already severely overpopulated. Given the pressure on the land, increased food production depends on the development of new high-yielding crops.

The Nile Basin Initiative (NBI) (signed by Egypt, Ethiopia, Sudan, Tanzania, Kenya, Rwanda, Burundi, Uganda and Democratic Republic of Congo) launched seven feasibility studies backed by US$140 million granted by the World Bank and donor governments in June 2001. It will also develop a parallel legal framework for shared water management.

Fishing

Fishing resources remain under-exploited. Kenya has a coastline of 680km and the annual catch is between 5,000 and 7,000 tonnes per year (tpy). Analysts believe that the sustainable level of tuna fishing alone is 200,000tpy.

Forestry

The government is attempting to protect timber resources which are being depleted because of wood fuel demands. However the need for land is placing increased pressure on Kenya's forestry reserves. Deforestation is a major problem. A Permanent Presidential Commission on Soil Conservation and Afforestation was created to correct the situation. In April 2001, Kenyan opposition MPs and some members of the ruling party accused the government of systematically destroying forests. The attacks came in a debate on deforestation in response to the government's plans to convert 167,000ha of forest into settlement and farming.

The government estimates that only 70 per cent of Kenya's wood fuel demands are met by regenerative growth. Some 38 million cubic metres of wood, or one million tonnes of oil equivalent (toe), are believed to be consumed annually.

Industry and manufacturing

Foreign investment, particularly from the UK, Japan and US, plays a significant role. Emphasis is on developing joint venture, export-oriented industries and encouraging greater utilisation of local raw materials and other inputs. Large sections of industry continue to operate well below full capacity as a result of import controls, rising costs and marketing difficulties.

The manufacturing sector accounted for 13.1 per cent of GDP in 2001, but has been on the wane due to power shortages, a fall in the growth of foreign direct investment (FDI) and rising costs of fuel imports. The sector was in recession in 2000 and 2001. However, it remains the most developed manufacturing sector in east Africa. Principal industries include food and tobacco processing, beverages, chemicals, machinery and transport equipment, textiles, glass, vehicle assembly and construction materials. Despite the sector's overall decline, the government claimed that certain select industries were growing in 2001, particularly leather shoes, soda ash, tyres and mineral water. This reflected a pick-up in electricity output and fuel consumption. Increased rainfall is improving the supply of energy as well as primary agricultural produce which will have a knock-on effect in the manufacturing sector.

The building and construction sector contributes 2.4 per cent of GDP, but was in recession in 2001 due to the high cost of inputs, particularly fuel and power, and the decline in public sector construction works owing to expenditure cut-backs.

Tourism

Tourism is the country's largest foreign exchange earner, and employs 150,000 people. Kenya's tourist assets are its wildlife, mostly accessible through a system of parks and reserves, extensive white sand beaches protected by coral reefs, and dramatic scenery from deserts to tropical rain forest. About 100,000 Germans visit Kenya each year. Other visitors originate from the UK, Switzerland, France, Italy and the US.

The sector took a knock after the 11 September 2001 attacks in the US. It had already suffered a sharp decline in the late 1990s due to political violence, deteriorating infrastructure and poor marketing. The sector recovered by 2000 when visitor numbers reached 1.04 million compared to 690,000 in 1998. In the immediate aftermath of the terrorist attacks, up to 80 per cent of US tourists cancelled their bookings, causing concern that the sector might go into recession in the fourth quarter of the year. However, the Central Bank of Kenya (CBK) reported that in the first 10 months of 2001, tourist arrivals and earnings were up by 16 per cent and 19 per cent respectively compared to the same period in 2000. Nevertheless, advance hotel bookings saw a decline in the fourth quarter, sparking concerns that the sector might experience further difficulties throughout 2002. Tour operators are hoping that the threat of terrorism and US military action in Asia and the Middle East will see tourists switching to African destinations, such as Kenya.

Mining

The Kenyan government's policy is to encourage private sector participation in further exploration, prospecting and development of the mineral resources sector. It had started pressing for greater security of tenure and environmental protection in 1993, with a review of the laws governing mineral exploration. Geophysical work is under way to assess the potential of precious minerals such as rubies, gold, silver and metal-based sulphides. French, Norwegian and Swiss companies are involved in gold exploration. AAPS (Kenya), part of the Anglo American Group, in a joint venture agreement with Sebimu, has conducted exploration activities for gold. AAPS is also exploring base metals primarily including zinc, nickel and copper. A geochemical survey has also been carried out in the Coast province for base metal assessment. Diamond occurrences in various parts of the country have yet to be verified. Kenya, with three other countries outside South Africa, is listed in a UN Fund for Natural Resources preliminary evaluation of Africa's mineral prospects, as having known or probable reserves of platinum and platinoids. It is also believed to have potential for extraction of the strategic mineral rutile.

Major evaluation programmes already undertaken have included the assessment of some industrial minerals, such as limestone in western Kenya, kaolin in central Kenya, wollastonite in Kajiado (southern Kenya), phosphates at Ikutha in south-east Kenya and Homa Bay on Lake Victoria. The Athi River Mining Company produces a wide variety of industrial minerals. Several local prospectors are engaged in prospecting and mining a wide range of gemstones.

In value terms, the most important raw materials are soda ash, fluorspar and salt. Soda ash is produced from the mineral trona that occurs at Lake Magadi, which is situated within the Great Rift Valley, by the Magadi Soda Company. This is the biggest known natural source of trona in the world. Lake Magadi is also the major source of crude salt and output has risen to 103,000 tonnes per year. Fluorspar, mined in the Kerio Valley since 1975, is exported to the US, Germany and Japan. The most promising mining prospects in Kenya are within the licences held by the Canadian mining company Tiomin Resources for deposits covering four areas – Mambrui, Sokoke, Vipingo and Kwale – which hold 12 per cent of the world's rutile and ilmenite resources. Tiomin came under fire from conservationists and farmers in 2000 and 2001. It holds a license to mine titanium along the Kenyan coast, but its activities have allegedly threatened a marine reserve and its compensation to farmers living on land due for exploitation is paltry. In September 2001, the High Court blocked the project. Tiomin's appeal against the ruling was heard in February 2002 and a judgement was expected by mid-2002.

Hydrocarbons

Exploratory oil wells in the Rift Valley and north-eastern provinces have been carried out. However, no commercial oil discoveries have been found. Kenya has a 4.2 million tonne capacity oil refinery at Mombasa, which is a major foreign exchange earner.

Energy

Around 70 per cent of domestic energy requirements are imported. The United Arab Emirates is chief supplier of crude oil. Government efforts to reduce oil imports are succeeding. New energy sources being developed include ethanol from molasses and geothermal power.

Hydroelectric and geothermal power supplies around 25 per cent of energy needs. Electricity is supplied inland by hydroelectric plants in the Tana river basin, by the geothermal station at Olkaria, and at Kipevu, on the coast, by an oil-fired plant. This is irregularly supplemented by a bulk supply of 30MW from Owen Falls in Uganda, under a 50-year agreement signed in 1958.

Kenya has a total generating capacity of 805MW.

Development of the electricity sector is a priority in economic planning. Two independent producer projects are being constructed – one in Nairobi to provide 44.5 MW and a barge-mounted diesel plant at Kipevu in Mombasa, to provide 44.5MW. A major development project is the US$417 million construction of the 100MW Turkwell hydroelectric plant.

The Olkaria II Geothermal Power Station will be constructed near Naivasha, 100km from Nairobi and 5km from the existing 45MW Olkaria I Power Plant, and will have two steam turbine generators with a total capacity of 54MW.

Financial markets

Stock exchange

The Nairobi Stock Exchange (NSE) in Kenya is small and speculative. The NSE was established in 1954 and is sub-Saharan Africa's fourth-largest bourse. It originally operated as an association of stockbrokers with no trading floor until October 1991. The introduction of the trading floor has led to a substantial increase in trading volumes and dramatic upward movement in the various indexes. On 2 January 1995, foreign investors were allowed back into the NSE for the first time in 30 years, but were limited on the amount of shares they could own. The NSE has been instrumental in enabling the public and private sectors in Kenya to raise large amounts of capital for expansion projects and for the financing of new businesses.

The continued delay and setbacks in the sale of Telkom depressed general confidence in the stock market throughout 2001.

Banking

Kenya contains a thriving community of foreign banks, which were attracted during the 1970s and 1980s by its reputation for political and commercial stability, good telecommunications infrastructure and the large number of multinationals based in the country. However, the sector is plagued by high levels of non-performing loans which threaten to undermine banking liquidity, affecting the wider economy.

In 2001, the banking system comprised 49 commercial banks, five non-bank financial institutions, two mortgage finance companies, four building societies and 47 foreign exchange bureaux.

Central bank

Central Bank of Kenya

Main financial centre

Nairobi

Time

GMT plus three hours

Geography

Kenya lies almost exactly astride the equator on the east coast of Africa. It is bounded by Ethiopia and Sudan to the north, Uganda and Lake Victoria to the west, Tanzania to the south and Somalia and the Indian Ocean to the east.

From the Indian Ocean, the land rises gradually through dry bush to the arable land of the highlands. The highest peak is Mount Kenya at 5,200 metres. The west of the country is dissected by the Great Rift Valley, partly filled by a chain of lakes.

Climate

The climate is tropical in low-lying districts, especially along the coast, but is more temperate on the plateau and in the highlands. Kenya has two rainy seasons when temperatures can fall sharply: the long rains from April to June and the short rains in October and November. The hottest month is February, with temperatures of 20–30 degrees Celsius (C), while the coolest month is July, with temperatures of 11–22 degrees C. Nairobi, at an altitude of 1,661 metres, has a mean annual temperature of 17 degrees C and annual rainfall averaging 864mm.

Dress codes

A lightweight suit, collar and tie or other formal clothing should be worn for business meetings. Despite a hot tropical climate, nights can be cool and it is advisable to have a sweater to cover day wear, which should be light cotton casual at the coast. Warmer clothing is needed especially in June and July. Evening dress should normally be smart casual. Nairobi is considerably cooler than Mombasa.

Entry requirements

Passports

Required by all, except holders of *Kinderausweis* Identity Card with photograph, issued by Germany. Passports must be valid for six months from date of entry.

Visa

In March 2001 the Kenyan government reinstated the visa requirement for tourists visiting the country for up to 30 days. Check current regulations as they are liable to change at short notice.

Possession of a visa is not the final authority to enter Kenya.

Currency advice/regulations

Import of local currency up to Ksh200 is allowed. No restrictions on foreign currency imports.

Export of local currency is prohibited. Unlimited foreign currency can be exported. Tanzanian and Ugandan currency is only negotiable in the form of traveller's cheques.

Health (for visitors)

Mandatory precautions

Yellow fever vaccination certificate if arriving from an infected area.

Advisable precautions

Yellow fever, typhoid, tetanus, hepatitis A, meningitis and polio vaccinations. Malaria prophylaxis necessary for coastal and other lower altitude regions. Water precautions should be taken – bilharzia is present. Vaccinations for rabies are recommended if travelling to rural areas.

Hotels

There is a wide range available in main centres. It is advisable to book well in advance during peak season (November–April).

Credit cards
Major cards widely accepted.

Public holidays
Fixed dates
1 Jan (New Year's Day), 1 May, 1 Jun (Madaraka Day), 11 June (KANU Day), 10 Oct (Moi Day), 20 Oct (Kenyatta Day), 12 Dec (Independence/Jamhuri Day), 25 Dec, 26 Dec.
Variable dates
Good Friday, Easter Monday, Eid Al-Fitr, Eid Al-Adha.

Working hours
Banking
Mon–Fri: 0900–1400. Open first and last Sat in each month 0900–1100.
Barclays Bank, Kenyatta Avenue, Nairobi, open daily for foreign exchange until 1600.
Airport banks are open until midnight every day.
Business
Mon–Fri: 0800–1300, 1400–1700; Sat: 0830–1200/1230. Mombasa offices normally open and close half-an-hour earlier.
Government
Mon–Fri: 0800–1300, 1400–1700; Sat: 0830–1200/1230. Mombasa offices normally open and close half-an-hour earlier.
Shops
Sat: 0830–1300. Many shops open outside these hours.

Telecommunications
Telephone/fax
Links between Mombasa and Nairobi and along the coast from Kwale on the Tanzanian border to Mukowe near the Somali frontier via Garsen, Lamu and Garissa offer digital dialling in the country's main tourist areas. The Mombasa-Nairobi link also carries a high quality television channel.
Officials state that telephone penetration in rural areas is 0.16 lines per 100 people and in urban areas is four lines per 100 people. By 2015 the government plans to increase respective figures to one line per 100 people and 20 lines per 100 people.
Postal services
All the usual postal facilities are available, plus air courier services.

Electricity supply
230/240V AC, 50 cycles. Subject to power surges outside main centres.
Sockets are usually three-pin square (British type).

Social customs/useful tips
Personal contact is an important way of doing business in Kenya.
Bureaucracy can be frustratingly slow, although persistence pays. Going in person to the relevant office is often the best way of getting things done.
There is a large Arab influence on the coast and most hotels display government signs saying nudity is banned. Topless bathing for women is, however, tolerated in areas where there are large concentrations of hotels.
Kenyans are friendly and open, and the greeting, *jambo*, will be returned with a smile.
The purchase or export of ivory is banned.

Security
Security is not a problem in the major towns during the day but flashy displays of jewellery are not recommended. Do not carry large amounts of cash. US dollar or other hard currency traveller's cheques recommended.
Nairobi is practically deserted after 2200. Walking around the African quarters of town without a guide or in the shanty towns around the capital is not advised.
Visitors are advised to avoid political meetings and demonstrations.
Incidents of armed car-hijacking are prevalent in Nairobi and Mombasa.
Do not attempt to escape from hijackers or resist their demands.

Getting there
Air
National airline: Kenya Airways (privatised).
Main airport: Mombasa Moi International (MBA), 13km west of Mombasa; Jomo Kenyatta International (NBO), 13km south-east of Nairobi.
Airport tax: There is no airport tax.
Surface
Road: An all-weather road links Nairobi to Addis Ababa, Ethiopia, and there is a 590 km road link between Kitale and Juba (Sudan).
The growth in road transportation has led to overloading of some highways, and both the maintenance and improvement of these routes have been neglected. This also applies to roads which come under the jurisdiction of town authorities.
In rural areas some of the unsurfaced roads can be difficult in wet weather.
You can travel by road to Uganda, Ethiopia, Sudan (under improvement), and Tanzania. Entry by these routes can be difficult. Regulations and conditions should be checked with Kenyan authorities before travelling.
Rail: The Kenya Railways system comprises approximately 1,920km of one metre gauge single track. A 1 085km main line runs from the port of Mombasa through Nairobi, Nakuru and Eldoret to the Ugandan border. There are departures daily, offering modern, first- and second-class service from Nairobi-Mombasa; the overnight service is popular. The journey time is approximately 14 hours.
Trains often run late, but are fairly comfortable. It is advisable to book sleeping compartments in advance.

Getting about
National transport
Air: Kenya Airways operates an extensive and regular service linking Mombasa, Malindi, Kisumu, and other major centres, from Nairobi.
Local light aircraft companies, such as Airkenya Aviation and Eagle Aviation, fly regular services to smaller airfields, such as Lamu, a tourist attraction on the coast. Charter flights are also available to game reserves, such as Maasai Mara, and main centres. The major charter companies include Africair, Caspair, Pioneer, Sunbird, Air Kenya, operating from Nairobi's Wilson Airport.
City transport
Taxis: Available in most major towns. Some licensed taxis are metered and often shared, with fares according to time and distance. However, fares for long trips should be agreed in advance. Taxis cannot be hailed in the street. A 10 per cent tip is usual. The taxis of companies that run fleets, such as Kenatco, are the most reliable. Most of the older yellow band taxis are unmetered and fares must be negotiated.
Buses/trams: Fairly cheap services operate in Nairobi and Mombasa. There are also the Matatu-minibuses and vans; these are unregulated and can be overcrowded. They are not recommended for visitors.
Car hire
Can be hired from travel operators and hotels in Nairobi, Mombasa and Malindi. International driving licence accepted, or national driving licence endorsed at a Kenyan police station or at the Registrar of Motor Vehicles in Nairobi (valid for 90 days).

BUSINESS DIRECTORY

Telephone area codes
The international direct dialling (IDD) code for Kenya is +254, followed by the area code:

Athi River	150	Nairobi	2
Diani Beach	127	Nakuru	37
Eldoret	321	Nanyuki	176
Kisumu	35	Nyeri	171
Malindi	123	Thika	151
Mombasa	11		

Chambers of Commerce
National Chamber of Commerce & Industry, Ufanisi House, Harambee House, PO Box 47024, Nairobi (tel: 228-016).

Banking
African Banking Corporation Ltd; PO Box 46452, Mezzanine Floor, ABC-Bank, Koingange Street, Nairobi (tel: 223922; fax: 222437)

Barclays Bank of Kenya Ltd; PO Box 30120, Barclays Plaza, Loita St, Nairobi (tel: 214270; fax: 213915)

The Co-operative Bank of Kenya Ltd, PO Box 48231, Union Towers, Kenya-Re Plaza - Taifa Rd, Moi Ave, Nairobi Tel: 225579; fax:246635)

Commercial Bank of Africa Ltd; Commercial Bank Building, Standard/Wabera Streets, Nairobi (tel: 228881 Fax: 335827, 340157)

Development Bank of Kenya Ltd; PO Box 30483, Finance House, Loita Street, Nairobi (tel: 340401; fax:338426)

Imperial Bank Ltd, PO Box 44905, 8th Floor, IPS Bldg, Kimathi St, Nairobi (tel: 252175; fax: 230994)

Investments & Mortgages Bank Ltd, PO Box 30238, I & M Bank House, 2nd Ngong Avenue, Nairobi (tel: 711994-8; fax: 713757, 716372)

Kenya Commercial Bank Ltd, PO Box 48400, Moi Avenue, Nairobi (tel: 339441 fax: 215565)

National Bank of Kenya Ltd, PO Box 72866, National Bank Building, Harambee Avenue, Nairobi

Standard Chartered Bank Kenya Ltd, PO Box 30003, Stanbank House, Moi Avenue, Nairobi (tel: 330200, 331210 fax: 214086)

Central bank

Central Bank of Kenya, PO Box 60000, Haile Selassie Avenue, Nairobi, Kenya (tel: 226431, 246000 fax: 340192)

Travel information

AA of Kenya, PO Box 40087, Nairobi.

Kenya Aviation, PO Box 30357, Wilson Airport, Nairobi (tel: 502-421, 501-601; fax: 500-845).

Kenya Airways, Kenyatta International Airport, PO Box 19002, Nairobi (tel: 822-171; fax: 822-707).

Kenya Railways, PO Box 30121, Nairobi (tel: 221-211).

National tourist organisation offices

Ministry of Tourism, PO Box 54666, Nairobi.

Ministries

Ministry of Agriculture, Livestock Development and Marketing, Kilimo House, Cathedral Road, PO Box 30028, Nairobi (tel: 718-870; fax: 725-774).

Ministry of Commerce and Industry, Co-operative House, Haile Selassie Avenue, PO Box 30430, Nairobi (tel: 340-010, 340-224; fax: 218-845).

Ministry of Energy, Nyayo House, Kenyatta Avenue, PO Box 30582, Nairobi (tel: 333-551).

Ministry of the Environment and Natural Resources, Kencom House, Moi Avenue, PO Box 30126, Nairobi (tel: 229-261).

Ministry of Finance, Treasury House, Harambee Avenue, PO Box 30007, Nairobi (tel: 338-111; fax: 330-426).

Ministry of Information and Broadcasting, Jogoo House 'A', Taifa Road, PO Box 30025, Nairobi (tel: 334-688; fax: 340-659).

Ministry of Planning and National Development, PO Box 3007, Nairobi (tel: 338-111; fax: 330-426).

Ministry of Tourism and Wildlife, Utali House, Uhuru Highway, PO Box 30027, Nairobi (tel: 331-030; fax: 217-604).

Ministry of Transport and Communications, Transcom House, Ngong Road, PO Box 52692, Nairobi (tel: 729-200; fax: 726-362).

Office of the President, Harambee House, Harambee Avenue, PO Box 30510, Nairobi (tel: 227-411; fax: 723-666).

Other useful addresses

Africa Growth Fund, PO Box 34045, Nairobi (tel: 721-566; fax: 722-240).

Agricultural Development Corporation, PO Box 30367, Nairobi (tel: 338-530).

Attorney-General's Office, State Law Office, Harambee Avenue, PO Box 40112, Nairobi (tel: 227-461; fax: 211-082).

Capital Markets Authority (CMA), Re-Insurance Plaza, Taifa Rd, PO Box 74800, Nairobi (tel: 221-910/869; fax: 216-681).

Central Police Station, University Way, Nairobi (tel: 222-222).

Customs and Excise, PO Box 40160, Nairobi.

Development Finance Company of Kenya, Finance House, Loita Street, PO Box 30483, Nairobi (tel: 340-401; fax: 338-246).

Economic Development for Equatorial and Southern Africa, PO Box 56038, Nairobi (tel: 822-920/4; fax: 822-925/907).

Executive Secretariat and Technical Unit (ESTU), Anniversary Towers, University Way, 7th Floor, PO Box 34542, Nairobi (tel: 222-127/57/68; fax: 216-945).

Export Processing Zones Authority, British American Centre, Mara Rd, PO Box 50563, Nairobi (tel: 712-800; fax: 713-704).

Export Promotion Council (EPC), Anniversary Towers, 1st Floor, University Way, PO Box 40247, Nairobi (tel: 228-534/5; fax: 218-013).

Federation of Kenya Employers (FKE), Argwings Kodhek Road, PO Box 48311, Nairobi (tel: 721-929; fax: 721-948).

General Post Office, Kenyatta Avenue, Nairobi.

Horticultural Crops Development Authority (HCDA), Uniafric House, Koinange St, PO Box 42601, Nairobi (tel: 337-381/3).

Industrial and Commercial Development Corporation, Uchumi House, Nkrumah Avenue, PO Box 45519, Nairobi (tel: 229-213; fax: 333-880).

Industrial Promotion Services Ltd, IPS Building, PO Box 30500, Nairobi (tel: 228-026, 728-207; fax: 214-563).

International Finance Corporation, View Park Towers, PO Box 30577, Nairobi (tel: 224-726; fax: 219-980).

Investment Promotion Centre, National Building, 8th Floor, Harambee Avenue, PO Box 55704, Nairobi (tel: 221-401/4; fax: 336-663).

Kenya Association of Manufacturers (KAM), Mpaka Rd, Westland, PO Box 30225, Nairobi (tel: 746-005/7; fax: 746-028).

Kenya Association of Tour Operators (for information on conference facilities throughout Kenya), PO Box 48461, Nairobi (tel: 227-005).

Kenya External Trade Authority, PO Box 43137, Nairobi (tel: 226-016).

Kenya Power Company Limited, Stima Plaza, Kolobot Road, PO Box 47936, Nairobi (tel: 741-181/9; fax: 337-351).

Kenya Revenue Authority, Tax Programmes and New Business Initiatives, Nairobi (tel: 715-428; fax: 715-432).

Kenya Tea Development Authority, Commonwealth House, Moi Avenue, Nairobi (tel: 221-441).

Nairobi Stock Exchange, Kimathi Street, IPS Building, 2nd Floor, PO Box 43833, Nairobi (tel: 230-692; fax: 224-200).

Internet sites

Africa Business Network: http://www.ifc.org/abn

AllAfrica.com: http://allafrica.com

African Development Bank: http://www.afdb.org

Africa Online: http://www.africaonline.com

Harambee Afrika (UK business club for traders with east, central and southern Africa; includes annotated web resource list): http://www.harambee.co.uk

KenyaWeb: http://www.kenyaweb.com/

Mbendi AfroPaedia (information on companies, countries, industries and stock exchanges in Africa): http://mbendi.co.za

Lesotho

Daniel Brett

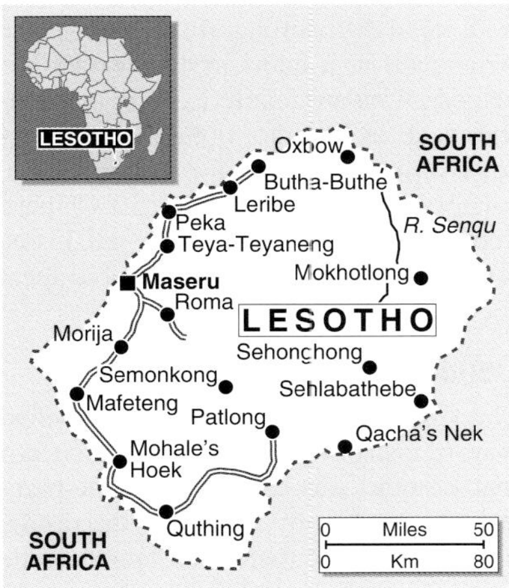

The tiny mountain kingdom was faced with one of its greatest challenges when it went to the polls in May 2002. Previous elections held in 1998 led to a civil uprising and an army mutiny after opposition parties accused the ruling Lesotho Congress for Democracy (LCD) of electoral fraud. The Interim Political Authority (IPA), set up after South African troops intervened on behalf of the government, has overseen a radical overhaul in the electoral system. The introduction of proportional representation did not significantly alter Lesotho's political landscape, with the LCD winning an outright majority both in terms of the proportion of the vote and the number of seats in the national assembly. Prime Minister Pakalitha Mosisili was subsequently sworn in for a second term and promised to prioritise the fight against HIV/AIDS, food shortages and high levels of unemployment. Although foreign observers declared the election to be free and fair, the opposition was unhappy and led a series of protests claiming electoral irregularities.

Electoral reform

The previous first-past-the-post (FPTP), constituency-based system was widely seen as one of the chief culprits of the political crisis of 1998. The LCD received 60 per cent of the vote, but won 79 of the 80 parliamentary seats, leaving the opposition Basotho National Party (BNP) with just one seat. The introduction of a mixed-member system is intended to give smaller parties a greater voice in parliament. The new system involved 80 seats elected by FPTP, with a further 40 seats allocated to parties according to the proportion of votes they received. This involved voters casting two votes, one for their constituency and one for the party of their choice.

Non-governmental organisations had warned that the electoral system was too confusing and could destabilise the country. Opponents of the new electoral system claimed that similar systems in other countries, such as Italy, had produced rapid changes in government. They argued that a similar situation in Lesotho could result in another political crisis.

Nevertheless, turn-out was average for the region at 68 per cent and only two constituencies – Mount Moorosi and Hlotse – were unable to elect representatives due to the death of a candidate. The elections gave the LDC 77 of the 78 constituencies up for election by FPTP. The only constituency election won by an opposition party was Seqonoka, which was won by Kelebone Maope, the leader of the Lesotho People's Congress (LPC), a party formed in 2001 after a number of MPs broke away from the LCD. Votes by proportional representation gave the main opposition party, the Basotho National Party (BNP), 21 seats, the National Independence Party five seats and LPC a further four seats. Ten other seats were shared out to six smaller parties.

Highland fling

The construction of the Lesotho Highlands Water Project (LHWP), one of Africa's largest engineering schemes, has become the focal point of economic development. Financed with the help of the World Bank, it will eventually consist of six dams and hundreds of kilometres of tunnels to generate electricity for Lesotho and supply South Africa with water. The project, begun in 1986 and due for completion in 2020, has provided new housing, infrastructure and welfare services, such as health clinics and community centres. The LHWP has even boosted

KEY FACTS

Official name: Kingdom of Lesotho

Head of State: King Letsie III (sworn in Feb 1996; crowned Oct 1997)

Head of government: Prime Minister Bethuel Pakalitha Mosisili (LCD) (since 1998)

Ruling party: Lesotho Congress for Democracy (LCD) (re-elected May 2002)

Area: 30,355 square km

Population: 2.20 million (2001)

Capital: Maseru

Official language: Sesotho and English

Currency: Loti (maloti, plural) (L) = 100 lisente; has parity with the South African rand, which is legal tender.

Exchange rate: L8.51 per US$ (Jan 2003)

GDP per capita: US$367 (2001)

GDP real growth: 3.20% (2001)

Unemployment: 40.00% (2002)

Inflation: -9.60% (2001)

Balance of trade: -US$389.00 million (2001)

Foreign debt: US$734.00 million (2001)

For the latest Key Facts, go to www.worldinformation.com

tourism, with 30,000 tourists a year visiting the Katse Dam, the project's biggest dam.

However, since 1995, the LHWP has been immersed in a corruption scandal. Fourteen foreign construction companies are accused of paying around US$3 million in bribes to the project's former chief executive, Masupa Sole, and other officials. In May 2002, Sole was convicted on 13 counts of bribery linked to LHWP.

Acres International, a Canadian multi-national construction company at the heart of the bribery scandal, was fined US$2.2 million in October 2002. Acres claimed that its representative, Zalisiwonga Bam, had acted without its knowledge when he paid Sole 60 per cent of more than C$680,000 (US$436,000) given to him by the company. It also accused the presiding judge in the case, Mahapela Lehohla, of incompetence and 'hell-bent on getting a conviction', whatever the evidence. In December 2002, the fine against Acres was suspended while the case went through the appeals court. If Acres fails to win its appeal in 2003, it could be put on the World Bank's List of Ineligible Firms, which would prevent it from entering into any other contracts supported by the development institution.

Textiles lead the way

Economic growth has been modest since the 1998 political crisis, with annual GDP growth averaging around 2.5 per cent. However, GDP rose to 3.2 per cent in 2000, indicating the economy was still making modest progress, although it declined again to 2.9 per cent in 2001. As a result of this mediocre performance, per capita incomes have stagnated with certain areas of the economy recording slower growth. With activity related to the LHWP winding down as the project enters its final phase, growth in the construction sector has slowed from 7.7 per cent in 1999 to around 1 per cent in 2001. This has been partly offset by a boom in manufacturing growth, which rose from -1.5 per cent in 1999 to 9 per cent in 2000 and 10 per cent in 2001.

The manufacturing sector is led by the production of garments and textiles for export, which have maintained a competitive edge due to the depreciation of the South African rand-linked loti throughout 2001. The inclusion of Lesotho in the US Africa Growth and Opportunities Act (AGOA), designed to allow textile and garment producers access to US markets, in April 2001 helped boost the country's exports to the US by over 50 per cent. The government has also attempted to attract foreign investors with various incentives, such as a six-year tax holiday. As a result, the textile industry is now the country's largest employer with more than 40,000 workers.

The manufacturing boom has led to increased union mobilisation around the issue of foreign exploitation of Lesotho's working class. The Lesotho Clothing and Allied Workers Union (LECAWU) claims that workers in the sector are being exploited, with low wages, long working hours, repression of trade union rights and illegal dismissals. In 2001, LECAWU demanded a minimum wage in line with the guidelines of the International Labour Organisation (ILO) and the implementation of labour codes to protect workers. However, one union official claimed that 'Taiwanese companies together with ministers in our government who are shareholders are running the companies so it is very difficult to enforce the law'. Meanwhile, some fear that Lesotho's factories may be forced out of business following the accession of China to the World Trade Organisation (WTO) in 2001. In November 2001, the International Textile, Garment and Leather Workers' Federation (ITGLWF) warned that China is pushing for a rapid dismantling of the Multi-Fibre Arrangement, a quota system which has helped stimulate textile exports in countries such as Lesotho. It claimed that Lesotho is not prepared for the transition, cannot compete with lower-cost Chinese goods and 'will face serious job losses with the potential for considerable local social unrest'.

Outlook

The size of the LCD's majority dispelled fears of instability, but also raised concern that Lesotho was effectively a one-party state. Consequently, whatever the results of the elections, there was bound to be controversy. It is unlikely that the events of 1998 will be repeated, particularly given South Africa's willingness to intervene on behalf of Lesotho's authorities. The split within the LCD seen in 1998 has managed to strengthen Mosisili, with the LPC seeing its representation in parliament drop from 27 to just five seats. Now that the dominant LCD comprises government loyalists, the executive's power over the legislature has strengthened, while the parliamentary opposition, comprising 15 parties, remains fragmented.

Meanwhile, Lesotho still faces an uphill struggle to diversify the economy and find jobs for the 40 per cent of its workforce who are unemployed. The surge in clothing and textile exports coupled with a commitment to structural reform under the Poverty Reduction and Growth Facility (PRGF) arrangement with the IMF are likely to keep the economy stable in the medium-term. However, in the long-term, Lesotho is faced with a burgeoning AIDS epidemic, food shortages and the rationalisation of the South African mining sector, which is a major employer for Lesotho's migrant labour force. Therefore, it is unlikely that Lesotho will be able to move from aid-dependency to a dynamic export-oriented economy in the foreseeable future.

KEY INDICATORS — Lesotho

	Unit	1996	1997	1998	1999	2000
Population	m	1.97	2.02	2.06	2.11	2.16
Gross domestic product (GDP)	US$bn	0.94	1.02	0.89	0.92	0.99
GDP per capita	US$	479	507	432	437	458
GDP real growth	%	8.0	7.2	-3.6	2.1	2.4
Inflation	%	9.1	8.5	7.8	7.3	6.2
Exports (fob) (goods)	US$m	186.9	196.1	193.4	172.5	211.1
Imports (fob) (goods)	US$m	998.6	1,024.4	866.0	779.2	727.6
Balance of trade	US$m	-811.8	-828.3	-672.5	-606.7	-516.5
Current account	US$m	-302.5	-269.2	-280.2	-220.8	-151.4
Total reserves minus gold	US$m	460.5	571.7	575.1	499.6	417.9
Foreign exchange	US$m	454.1	565.8	568.9	493.5	412.6
Exchange rate	per US$	4.30	4.61	5.35	6.11	6.94

Risk assessment

Economic	Fair
Political	Stable
Regional stability	Poor

COUNTRY PROFILE

Historical profile

1600s Modern-day Lesotho was settled by the Sotho people; the area was already home to the San people.
1800s European traders and missionaries arrived in the area, and were soon followed by the Boers on their Great Trek. The Boer trek coincided with the expansion of the Zulu state. King Moshoeshoe the Great ensured the survival of his people by taking them to a mountain stronghold in about 1820. The policy of assisting refugees on condition that they help in defence proved successful – by 1842 the King's people numbered around 40,000 and were protected by outlying refugee settlements.
1870 By the time King Moshoeshoe died, a Basuto nation of 150,000 had been established.
1910 After annexing Basutoland, the British established the Basutoland National Council comprising members nominated by chiefs.
1960 After a new constitution was introduced, elections were held. The Basutoland Congress Party (BCP) won the election ahead of the Basutoland National Party (BNP) headed by Chief Leabua Jonathan.
1965 The BCP lost the election to the BNP; Chief Jonathan became the first Prime Minister of the Kingdom of Lesotho. King Moshoeshoe II was stripped of most of his powers.
1966 Independence was granted on 4 October.
1970 The constitution was suspended and opposition political parties banned.
1986 In January, the government of Chief Leabua Jonathan was overthrown in a military coup by Major General JM Lekhanya. The new regime was more amenable to South Africa's wishes.
1990 A constituent assembly was set up in April to frame a new constitution; a timetable was announced for a return to civilian rule. King Moshoeshoe II abdicated in favour of his eldest son, Crown Prince David Mohato who became King Letsie III.
1991 Lekhanya was overthrown by a group of military officers led by Major-General Elias Ramaema and King Moshoeshoe II went into exile.
1992 King Moshoeshoe returned from exile under a deal with the military regime, but did not take up his throne.
1993 Elections in March signalled a return to democracy; the BCP won a convincing victory. King Letsie III became a purely constitutional monarch.
1994 After growing unrest, King Letsie III suspended the constitution in August. The settlement eventually negotiated allowed for both the re-establishment of parliamentary rule and the return of King Moshoeshoe II.
1996 In January, King Moshoeshoe II was killed in a road accident and was again succeeded by his son, who was sworn in as King Letsie III on 7 February.
1997 King Letsie III was formally crowned in October.
1998 In the May elections, the Lesotho Congress for Democracy (LCD) won 79 of the 80 seats in parliament with 60 per cent of the total vote. The result was rejected by opposition groups. After riots broke out in Maseru and in September reports circulated of an imminent military coup, 800 South African and Botswanan soldiers entered Lesotho with the aim of restoring order. Only after the capital was ransacked by rioters did the troops succeed in restoring order. A deal was reached in October and the Interim Political Authority (IPA) was created to work alongside the government to prepare for elections.
2000 King Letsie III married Karabo Motsoeneng. Elections were postponed until 2002.
2001 President Thabo Mbeki of South Africa visited Lesotho to mend diplomatic relations and develop economic links. In October, 27 LCD members of parliament quit the party to form the Lesotho People's Congress (LPC).
2002 In 25 May parliamentary elections, the ruling LCD won 54 per cent of the vote (76 seats), the Basotho National Party 21 per cent and the Lesotho People's Congress 7 per cent (one seat). These 77 seats go to the top vote-getter in each district and the remaining 40 seats go to the parties, based on their proportion of the national vote. It is unlikely that the LCD will get any of those seats; they will most likely bolster the opposition's representation. Turnout was more than 70 per cent.

Political structure

The National Assembly is to be enlarged from 80 seats to 120 for the elections scheduled for 2002. The voting system will be a combination of proportional representation (40 seats) and first past the post (80 seats).

Form of state
Constitutional monarchy

The executive
Executive power is vested in the prime minister, leader of the majority parliamentary party, and the cabinet appointed by the prime minister.

National legislature
Legislative power is held by a bi-cameral National Assembly. The lower house is directly elected and the upper house (Senate) has 22 principal chiefs and 11 members appointed by the King.

Last elections
May 1998 (legislative)

Next elections
25 May 2002 (general)

Political parties

Ruling party
Lesotho Congress for Democracy (LCD) (results of 25 May 2002 parliamentary elections: LCD won 54 per cent of the vote (76 seats), the Basotho National Party 21 per cent and the Lesotho People's Congress 7 per cent (one seat); turnout more than 70 per cent)

Main opposition party
Basotho National Party (BNP)

Population

2.16 million (2000)
Annual population growth rate: 2.2 per cent (1994–2000). Approximately 41 per cent of the population is below the age of 15 years.
Population density: 66 inhabitants per square km. Urban population: 27 per cent of the total population (1994–2000). Seventy per cent of the population live in the lowlands along the western strip.
Collectively the nationals are called Basotho, the singular of which is Mosotho.

Ethnic make-up
The Basotho nation is an amalgam of mainly Sesotho-speaking people. Some 45 per cent of the population is of Nguni origin. A number of smaller groups, including San Griqua, Indian and European, have also become naturalised Basotho.

Religions
Christianity (approximately 80 per cent, mainly Roman Catholic), various traditional beliefs and others (20 per cent).

Labour market and unemployment

Approximately 37 per cent of the labour force is female.
The labour force is estimated to be growing at the rate of 20,000 annually.
Unemployment is a major problem due to the low rate of domestic employment, retrenchment of Basotho migrant workers and the expansion of the workforce. The government is implementing a works programme under the Lesotho Highlands Revenue Fund.
The highly literate (adult literacy 62 per cent), dependable and productive labour force is attracting increased investor interest.

Education

It has been estimated by Oxfam that 65 per cent of children age 6–11 will enrol for school in 2015. Lesotho has one university, located in the capital, Maseru. Public expenditure on education typically amounts to around 8.5 per cent of gross national income (GNI). Adult literacy showed improvement in the 1990s and by

2000 only 7 per cent of women and 28 per cent of men were illiterate, compared to 11 per cent and 35 per cent respectively in 1990.

Health

Life expectancy is 45 years. The infant mortality rate is 92 per 1,000 live births (1994–2000). About 16 per cent of children were malnourished in the same period. Public expenditure on health typically amounts to 3.5 per cent of GDP. On average, there was just one doctor per 10,000 people in the 1990s.
In 2000, 91 per cent of the population had access to an improved water source while 92 per cent had access to improved sanitation facilities. HIV prevalence is among the highest in the world, at 23.57 per cent of adults in 1999.

Main cities

Maseru (capital, estimated population 150,000 1998), Leribe, Mafeteng, Mohale's Hoek, Butha Buthe, Quthing, Qacha's Nek, Mokhotlong.

Languages spoken

English and Sesotho are the official languages. English becomes the medium of instruction from the fifth year of primary education.

Official language

Sesotho and English

Media

Press

Dailies: *Public Eye Daily* (www.publiceye.co.ls) is an important newspaper with on-line edition.
Weeklies: There are several weeklies including *Lentsoe la Basotho*, *Leselinyana la Lesotho* (bi-weekly), *Lesotho Today*, *Makatolle*, *Mirror*, *Mphatlalatsane* and *Setsomi Sa Litaba*. *Mopheme* is the most popular semi-weekly newspaper in Lesotho.
Periodicals: Monthly periodicals include the *Southern Star* and *Thebe*. *Leseli ka sepolesa* is published irregularly from Maseru.

Broadcasting

Radio: Radio Lesotho broadcasts in English and Sesotho.

Economy

Lesotho's economy is highly integrated with that of South Africa. The government is pursuing economic growth and employment through export diversification, development of water resources and greater vocational and technical training.
The major priorities are food security and industrial development. Around half of Lesotho's GDP comes from remittances sent back by migrant workers in South African gold mines. Another sector growing in importance is manufacturing (particularly textiles), which is increasingly geared towards markets outside Southern Africa.
The US$4 billion Lesotho Highlands Water Programme (LHWP) is one of the largest and most ambitious multi-purpose water schemes anywhere in the world, in addition to being one of Africa's biggest civil engineering project. Once complete, the LHWP will provide South Africa with 79 cubic metres of water a second by diverting the flow of the Senqu and its tributaries northwards to South Africa. By 2044, revenues are predicted to contribute some 5 per cent to Lesotho's annual GDP. The LHWP is due to be fully completed in 2020. However, construction is slowing thereby reducing economic activity.

External trade

Lesotho is a member of the Southern African Customs Union (Sacu) (together with South Africa, Namibia, Swaziland and Botswana), administered by South Africa, which provides for free trade within the Union and, as member countries all apply to South Africa's external customs tariff, a common pool of customs duties. It is also a member of the Southern African Development Community (SADC), which is reducing trade barriers within the region allowing for greater movement of goods and services.

Exports

Principal exports are ceramics, clothing, cut diamonds, footwear, furniture and wool.
Main destinations: Southern African Customs Union (Sacu) (typically 54 per cent of total), North America (46 per cent).

Imports

Principal imports include cereals, electricity, machinery, medicines and oil and petroleum products.
Main sources: Southern African Customs Union (Sacu) (typically 90 per cent of total), Asia (7 per cent).

Agriculture

Lesotho's agricultural sector has traditionally been a major contributor to the economy. Between 1980 and the mid-1990s, the government's agricultural policy was centred on the Food Self-Sufficiency Project (FSSP), which aimed to reduce the country's dependency on South Africa for the supply of staple foods. However, the objectives were never achieved and the sector's performance declined dramatically throughout the 1990s, with its contribution to GDP falling from 24 per cent in 1990 to about 17 per cent in 2000. The sector's share of total exports has fallen from 16.0 per cent in 1998 to just 9.7 per cent in 2000. A series of programmes were implemented from 1996 to boost agricultural development through commercialisation and privatisation. Progress has been slow and the programmes have concentrated on the medium-term without any long-term programme.
There are a number of factors constraining the development of agriculture in Lesotho. Firstly, the government has been heavily involved in the production, marketing and processing in the sector. This involved controlled commodity prices and strict control of imports and exports. These policies deterred private sector involvement and hampered growth. Also, the country faces a severe lack of land suitable to arable farming as well as poor soil fertility, unreliable rainfall and a lack of adequate capital inputs. Poverty is widespread in rural areas, which rely on miners' remittances to remain in operation. With the fall in demand for labour in South Africa's mines, the agricultural sector is finding it hard to maintain production levels.
Moreover, the construction of the Mohale dam as part of the Lesotho Highlands Water Project (LHWP) will mean flooding the most fertile land area, the only region producing a food surplus. The World Bank insists US$55 million earnings from water sales to South Africa will far exceed the US$2 million value of Mohale valley crops. Farmers from the Katse Dam area have been given food aid and skills training and communities have been resettled. Environmental organisations expressed concern over increased unemployment, food security and water shortages downstream due to dams.

Industry and manufacturing

The industrial sector as a whole typically contributes around 38 per cent of GDP and employs around 26 per cent of the labour force.
Most firms are small and are in joint ventures with the Lesotho National Development Corporation (LNDC). Production is largely for export (clothing, footwear, textiles) or import substitution (food processing, bricks). Other enterprises include handicrafts, ceramics and furniture making.
Pharmaceuticals and leather/hide processing are under development.
There has been a surge in manufacturing made possible by increased investor interest in Lesotho, however growth in this sub-sector has been hampered by a lack of factory space. Throughout 2001, the LNDC funded the construction and expansion of a number of factories in Lesotho. The largest investment in 2001 was by a Taiwan-based textiles manufacturer, Nien Hsing, which pledged US$800 million for a new plant at Thetsane industrial estate, representing the second-largest investment in Lesotho after the LHWP. When completed, it will directly employ more than

5,000 people. Construction alone will involve creating at least 5,000 new jobs.

Tourism

Tourism is being energetically developed and will benefit from the Lesotho Highlands Water Project. The tourism authorities are packaging the development, particularly the Katse Dam, as a major tourist attraction.

Mining

Lesotho produces a negligible amount of diamonds and annual exports are estimated at around 1,000 carats. There are plans to revive the diamond industry with the re-opening of the Letseng la Terae mine by the locally-owned Letseng Diamonds company. Letseng Diamonds and the New Mining Corporation each have a 38 per cent share in the project while government retains a 24 per cent share. The mine was previously run by De Beers between 1976–92, producing a total of 280,000 carats. Letseng estimates that the mine could produce around 50,000 carats per annum.

In 2000, a feasibility study conducted by Liqhobong Mining Development Ltd, a subsidiary of Canada-based MineGem, found reserves that could produce an average of 300,000 carats per annum over a five-year period. It was awarded a mining licence in mid-2001.

Energy

The electricity supply is the responsibility of the Lesotho Electricity Corporation (LEC), although Lesotho, at present, relies on South Africa for most of its power requirements.

However, the first phase of the ambitious US$4 billion Lesotho Highlands Water Project (LHWP) should produce enough hydroelectricity to meet almost all Lesotho's needs. South Africa is funding a large part of the Project while Lesotho is paying for the 110MW hydropower station, which should be completed in 2003.

Banking

Throughout the 1990s, the banking sector was plagued by a high level of non-performing loans and low liquidity, largely due to poor management and political interference. Two state-owned banks – LADB and Lesotho Bank – were technically insolvent by 1999, with the Central Bank injecting L2 million (US$330,000) and L20 million (US$3.3 million) respectively per month to keep them in operation and to safeguard depositors' funds. The situation affected the investment activity across the economy as a whole. In 1999, the Central Bank was given the power and autonomy to intervene in the activities of commercial banks. The LADB was closed in 1999 and depositors' funds were reimbursed by the government. Lesotho Bank was saved from closure, as it represented a far larger part of the market – 70 per cent. Instead, the central bank brought in the Standard Bank of South Africa (SBSA) as a strategic partner, which created a new bank – Lesotho Bank Limited (LBL) (70 per cent SBSA; 30 per cent Lesotho government). LBL assumed the deposits of the old Lesotho Bank, which was kept in operation by liquidators to recover bad debts.

The restructuring of the banking sector led to widespread job losses, but has strengthened the position of Lesotho's banking sector by improving asset management and the capital base of domestic banks. Along with the liberalisation of interest rates, restructuring has enabled domestic banks to respond to interest rate movements in South Africa and strengthened the Central Bank's ability to influence the money supply. By January 2002, the commercial bank liquidity ratio was 43.3 per cent, well above the Statutory Liquidity Ratio which is set at 25 per cent of commercial banks' short-term liabilities.

Central bank

Central Bank of Lesotho

Time

GMT plus two hours

Geography

Lesotho is a landlocked country, entirely surrounded by South African territory.

Climate

Temperate climate with well-marked seasons.

More than 85 per cent of the country's rainfall – averaging 700mm mountain areas – falls from October to April Spring comes in August. Summer from November–January with average temperature 27 degrees C, rising to 32 degrees C in lowland areas.

Autumn days are warm. Winter from May–July with temperatures as low as -7 degrees C in lowlands and -18 degrees C in highlands.

Snowfalls can occur on the highlands at any time of the year.

Clothing: In summer light, loose clothing is most comfortable, but include a raincoat. Spring and autumn clothing should include a jersey for the cool evenings. Heavy woollens, vests, windcheaters, socks and jackets are a must in winter. Warm clothing is also essential for a journey into the Maloti where severe weather conditions can be encountered any time of the year.

Entry requirements

Passports

Required by all. Passports must be valid for six to 12 months beyond length of stay.

Visa

Visas are required by most countries although they are not required by tourists staying less than 30 days. Entry and exit cards must be completed.

Visitors intending to remain in Lesotho for longer than 30 days should make application in advance to the Director of Immigration and Passport Services.

Currency advice/regulations

There is no restriction on foreign currency, but all transactions must be conducted in Maseru.

The Lesotho maloti is at parity with the South African rand, which is also accepted as legal currency.

Traveller's cheques are acceptable.

Health (for visitors)

Mandatory precautions

Yellow fever vaccination for visitors from infected areas.

Advisable precautions

Immunisations for hepatitis 'A', polio, tetanus and typhoid. There is a rabies risk.

Hotels

Lesotho has a number of comfortable, international-class hotels in Maseru.

Throughout the rest of the country accommodation consists of medium-sized hotels ranging to smaller tourist lodges.

Bills are subject to tax of 12 per cent. Tip of 10 per cent is usual.

Credit cards

Major credit cards are accepted.

Public holidays

Fixed dates

1 Jan (New Year's Day), 11 Mar (Moshoeshoe's Day), 4 Apr (Hero's Day), 1 May (Workers' Day), 17 Jul (King's Birthday), 4 Oct (Independence Day), 25 Dec (Christmas Day), 26 Dec (Boxing Day).

Variable dates

Good Friday, Easter Monday, Ascension Day.

Working hours

Banking

(Mon, Tue, Thu, Fri) 0830–1530; (Wed) 0830–1300; Sat: 0830–1100.

Business

Mon–Fri: 0800–1245, 1400–1630; Sat: 0800–1300.

Government

Mon–Fri: 0800–1245, 1400–1630.

Shops

Mon–Fri: 0800–1700; Sat: 0800–1500.

Telecommunications

Lesotho Telecommunications Corporation was set up in 1980. There is a satellite earth station at Maseru.

Telephone/fax

Automatic trunk services operate between Lesotho and South Africa. Satellite connections facilitate communication between

Lesotho and most European countries, the USA and some countries of South America and the Far East. Dial 109 to book.

Getting there

Air

National airline: Lesotho's national airline, Air Lesotho, closed down on 6 February 1999 due to heavy losses incurred from August 1997 until December 1998. International air traffic between Lesotho and Johannesburg continues to be conducted by South African Airlink.

Airport tax: International departure tax of L20; children under five years and transit passengers are exempt.

Surface

Road: Good tarred roads from South Africa into the south and west of the country. With the implementation of the Highlands Water Project, the road network is being expanded.

There are 12 border control posts from South Africa.

Rail: Lesotho does not have its own rail system, although Maseru is linked to the South African system for freight traffic only.

Getting about

National transport

Air: Air Lesotho's domestic air services were terminated on 31 January 1999. Charter companies in Lesotho are Highlands Air and Senqu Air.

Car hire

Driving licences issued in most countries are valid in Lesotho for a period of up to six months, provided they are printed in English or are accompanied by a certified translation. International driving permits are also recognised.

BUSINESS DIRECTORY

Telephone area codes

Dialling code for Lesotho: IDD access code +266, followed by subscriber's number (no area codes).

Useful telephone numbers

Queen Elizabeth II Hospital: 312-501.
Police: 123.
Fire brigade: 122.
Ambulance: 121.

Chambers of Commerce

Lesotho Chamber of Commerce & Industry, PO Box 79, Maseru 100 (tel: 323-482; fax: 310-414).

Banking

Lesotho Bank Ltd; PO Box 1053, Kingsway, Maseru 100 (tel: 314333 fax: 310348).

Barclays Bank plc, PO Box 115, Kingsway, Maseru (tel: 312-423; fax: 310-068).

Lesotho National Development Bank, PMB A96, Maseru (tel: 312-012; fax: 310-038).

NedBank, 1st Floor, Standard Bank Bldg, Kingsway, PO Box 1001, Maseru 100 (tel: 322-696; fax: 310-025).

Central bank

Central Bank of Lesotho, PO Box 1184, Maseru 100 (tel: 314-281; fax: 310-051; cbl@pixie.co.za).

Travel information

Air Lesotho (reservations), PO Box 861, Mejametalana Airport, Maseru (tel: 317-317; fax: 310-126).

National tourist organisation offices

Lesotho Tourist Board, PO Box 1378, Maseru 100 (tel: 312-896, 313-760; fax: 310-108).

Ministries

Minister to the Prime Minister, PO Box 527, Maseru 100 (tel: 311-000; fax: 310-102).

Ministry of Agriculture, Co-ops, Marketing and Youth Affairs, PO Box 24, Maseru 100 (tel: 323-561; fax: 310-349).

Ministry of Defence and Public Service, PO Box 527, Maseru 100 (tel: 311-000; fax: 310-102).

Ministry of Education and Manpower Development, PO Box 47, Maseru 100 (tel: 313-045; fax: 310-206).

Ministry of Finance and Economic Planning, PO Box 395, Maseru 100 (tel: 311-101; fax: 310-157).

Ministry of Foreign Affairs, PO Box 1378, Maseru 100 (tel: 311-150; fax: 311-150).

Ministry of Health and Social Welfare, PO Box 514, Maseru 100 (tel: 324-404; fax: 310-467).

Ministry of Home Affairs and Local Government, Rural and Urban Development, PO Box 174, Maseru 100 (tel: 323-771; fax: 310-319).

Ministry of Information and Broadcasting, PO Box 36, Maseru 100 (tel: 323-561; fax: 310-003).

Ministry of Justice, Human Rights, Law and Constitutional Affairs, PO Box 402, Maseru 100 (tel: 322-683).

Ministry of Labour and Employment, Private Bag A116, Maseru 100 (tel: 322-565).

Ministry of Natural Resources, PO Box 426, Maseru 100 (tel: 313-632).

Ministry of Tourism, Sports and Culture, PO Box 52, Maseru 100 (tel: 313-034).

Ministry of Trade and Industry, PO Box 747, Maseru 100 (tel: 322-138; fax: 310-326).

Ministry of Transport and Telecommunications, PO Box 413, Maseru 100 (tel: 323-691).

Ministry of Works, PO Box 20, Maseru 100 (tel: 311-362; fax: 310-125).

Other useful addresses

Lesotho National Development Corporation, Private Bag A96, Maseru 100 (tel: 312-012; fax: 310-038).

Lesotho National Insurance Corporation, Private Bag A96, Maseru 100 (tel: 313-031; fax: 310-007).

Livestock Marketing Corp, PO Box 800, Maseru (tel: 322-444) (sole marketing concern for all livestock and products, including mohair).

Multilateral Investment Guarantee Agency (MIGA), 1818 H Street NW, Washington DC 20433, USA (tel: (1 202)473-1079; fax: (1 202)334-0265).

Radio Lesotho, PO Box 552, Maseru (tel: 323-561).

Statistics Bureau, PO Box 455, Maseru (tel: 323-852).

Trade Promotion Unit, Ministry of Trade and Industry, PO Box 747, Maseru (tel: 323-414; fax: 310-121).

Internet sites

Africa Business Network: http://www.ifc.org/abn

AllAfrica.com: http://allafrica.com

African Development Bank: http://www.afdb.org

Africa Online: http://www.africaonline.com

Harambee Afrika (UK business club for traders with east, central and southern Africa; includes annotated web resource list): http://www.harambee.co.uk

Public Eye (on-line edition of daily newspaper): http://www.publiceye.co.ls

Central Bank of Lesotho: http://www.centralbank.org.ls/

Lesotho news agency: http://www.lena.gov.ls/news.htm

Lesotho National Development Corporation (LNDC): http://www.lndc.org.ls/

Mopheme newspaper: http://www.lesoff.co.za/news/

Lesotho Council of Non-Governmental Organisations (LCN): http://www.lecongo.org.ls/

Liberia

Desmond Davies

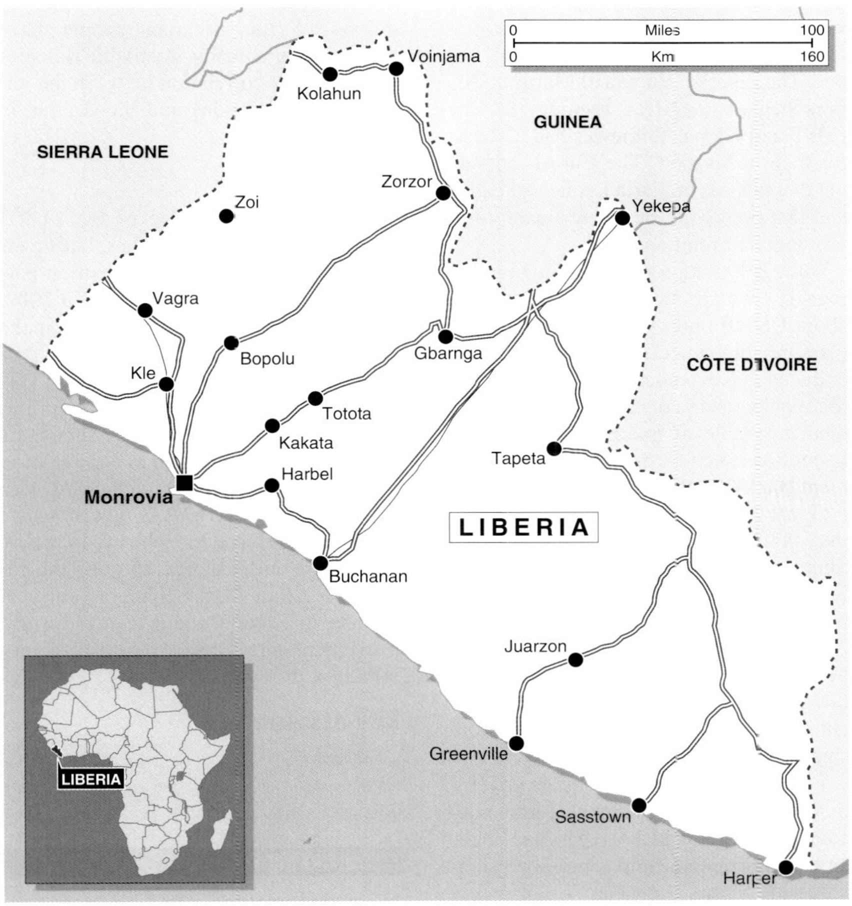

Less than two months into 2002 and Monrovia, the seat of political power, was under threat from the rebel group, Liberians United for Reconciliation and Democracy (LURD). The speed with which the city was threatened by the LURD, which had been carrying out sporadic attacks in the countryside against the government of President Charles Taylor since the late 1990s, came as a surprise to many. One minute the city was running normally, the next it was a scene of chaos as its residents fled in droves to neighbouring Côte d'Ivoire.

The rebel commanders announced that they were going to overrun Monrovia and drive Taylor out of the city. After weeks of tension the matter took another turn. The expected invasion of Monrovia did not materialise. Instead, the protagonists retired to Abuja in March 2002 where, under the aegis of the Economic Community of West African States (Ecowas), they began peace talks.

Ecowas had to act after its leaders were accused of failing to deal decisively with the conflict in Liberia, which had the potential of engulfing neighbouring Sierra Leone again. The upshot of the March 2002 Abuja meeting was that the opposition forces ranged against Taylor finally managed to gain a considerable amount of political leverage.

Taylor, who in December 2001 was talking tough – promising to meet head on the LURD advance – had changed his tune by

KEY FACTS

Official name: Republic of Liberia

Head of State: President Charles Taylor (since 1997)

Area: 111,370 square km

Population: 3.20 million (2001) (no census has been taken since the end of the civil war)

Capital: Monrovia

Official language: English

Currency: Liberian dollar (L$) = 100 cents (new Liberian $ banknotes introduced Mar 2000)

Exchange rate: L$1.00 per US$ (official) (fixed peg)

GDP per capita: US$176 (2001)

GDP real growth: 15.00% (2001)

Unemployment: 70.00% (2001)

Inflation: 9.90% (2001)

Foreign debt: US$1.99 billion (2001)

For the latest Key Facts, go to www.worldinformation.com

February 2002 when he organised three days of national prayer in the hope of getting divine intervention in the conflict. Taylor was under pressure after his closest ally in West Africa, Blaise Compaoré, the president of Burkina Faso, dropped his support for the Liberian leader at the end of 2001. The about face came after opposition leaders, including Ellen Johnson-Sirleaf and Amos Sawyer, had a meeting with Compaoré in Ouagadougou to urge him to remove his backing for Taylor.

The Liberian leader's choices – after the desertion of Compaoré – were rather limited. UN sanctions and the arms embargo on Liberia were biting deep and as such Taylor was prepared to talk to the opposition parties, which had their eyes on the 2003 presidential and assembly elections. A meeting planned for July 2002 in Monrovia was meant to end hostilities and prepare the ground for the return of exiled opposition politicians. In the same month, UN Secretary General Kofi Annan warned the international community that the conflict in Liberia was threatening to destabilise the whole of Western Africa.

Ship shape

Although Taylor tried to weather the political storm in late 2001 and 2002, the economic climate was far less salubrious. At the height of the threat from the LURD, there was a run on foreign currency holdings in local banks as residents of Monrovia withdrew their savings in preparation for their flight from the rebel advance. The pressure on the US dollar, which is legal tender in Liberia, in conjunction with the Liberian dollar, was so great that the banks began paying out Liberian instead of US dollars. This served no purpose, because the one airline serving Monrovia and Abidjan (Côte d'Ivoire) accepted only US dollars.

International pressure on Liberia ensured that the avenues through which the government could raise funds were seriously restricted. The country's ship registry, which has been the mainstay of the economy for many years, came under the spotlight in September 2001 when the International Transport Workers' Federation (ITWF) and the London-based human rights group, Global Witness, called on shipowners to withdraw from the 50-year registry. Their argument was that Liberia was a 'rogue state', which was 'sponsoring terror' – that is, the conflict in Sierra Leone. The Liberian Bureau of Maritime Affairs begged to differ, arguing that the ITWF and Global Witnesses had no basis for their accusation. The Bureau pointed out that the war in Sierra Leone had ended and that both countries were steadily improving their relations.

Some 2,000 ships are under the Liberian registry, which received an income of about US$20 million in 2000. In a bid to reassure shipowners, the government announced in November 2001 that the registry would open up its books and make them available to international financial institutions such as the African Development Bank (AfDB) and the World Bank.

Finance Minister Nathaniel Barnes said that the US-based Liberia International Ship and Corporate Registries (LISCR), which has been running the Liberian registry since 2000, would 'ring fence' its revenue. He said that 'we have taken this step because we want the whole world to know that the Liberian registry runs a transparent operation, which benefits both shipowners and the people of Liberia'.

The pressure on the Liberian government from the international community continued to grow in 2001. The ban on diamonds emanating from Liberia (presumably of Sierra Leonean origin) was maintained. An attempt to include Liberian timber on the sanctions list was turned down by Kofi Annan who argued that the Liberian government needed funds to tackle the serious humanitarian situation that prevailed in the country in 2001.

Addressing the UN General Assembly in November 2001, Foreign Minister Monie Captan noted: 'Since the imposition of sanctions by the Security Council, and despite the claim by the Council that the sanctions would not have any adverse effect on the ordinary people, socio-economic indicators show that the living conditions of the Liberian people have declined dramatically. Available statistics show a direct correlation between the imposition of sanctions and the decline in living standards.'

Outlook

The audacious offensive of the LURD appeared to have had quite a sobering effect on Taylor. With the opposition parties also gaining the upper hand in 2002, the Liberian leader would have to make concessions that would lead to them participating in the elections in 2003. This was what Taylor did not want. The intimidation and the attacks on his opponents had always been intended to weaken their political resolve. All this changed with the LURD offensive. It is now down to the opposition leaders, who are in reality not quite a unified force, to press the advantage. All in all, the changing political climate in Liberia could lead to an improvement in peace and stability in a very volatile sub-region.

Risk assessment

Economic	Poor
Political	Poor
Regional stability	Poor

KEY INDICATORS — Liberia

	Unit	1996	1997	1998	1999	2000
Population	m	2.81	2.88	2.50	2.71	2.92
Gross domestic product (GDP)	US$bn	0.62	0.67	0.71	0.51	*0.52
GDP per capita	US$	210	230	240	188	*176
Foreign debt	US$bn	1.5	1.1	2.1	2.1	2.0
Total reserves minus gold	US$m	0.4	0.4	0.6	0.4	0.3
Foreign exchange	US$m	0.3	0.4	0.6	0.4	0.2
Exchange rate	per US$	1.00	1.00	1.00	1.00	1.00

* estimated figure

COUNTRY PROFILE

Historical profile

1822 Liberia was created by a number of US philanthropists with the idea that freed slaves would be resettled in Africa. Many refused to go and those who did were met with hostility from the indigenous population.

1847 Liberia was established as an independent state. The US did not formally recognise this status until 1862.

1944–71 Under President William Tubman of the True Whig party (which monopolised power from early in Liberia's existence) the country received massive foreign investment, but this only exacerbated tension between the descendants of the settlers and the indigenous people.

1963 The local people were enfranchised – around 97 per cent of the total population.

1971 Tubman was succeeded by William Tolbert.

1980 Following protests against the government the previous year, Tolbert's government was overthrown in a coup led by Master Sergeant Samuel Doe. Doe survived several coup attempts and won an 'election' held in 1985, but his government proved widely unpopular.
1990 Opposition groups led by Prince Johnson and Charles Taylor overran most of Liberia and captured Monrovia. With Johnson and Taylor both claiming the presidency, the west African peacekeeping force, the Economic Community of West African States Monitoring Group (Ecomog), installed Amos Sawyer as head of an Interim Government of National Unity (IGNU). Taylor's National Patriotic Front of Liberia (NPFL) controlled around 90 per cent of Liberia; the remnants of Doe's supporters and Johnson's forces were both encamped within the capital.
1993 After a period of heavy fighting, a UN-sponsored peace accord was signed in August, calling for the creation of a six-month transitional government representing the IGNU, the NPFL and Doe's supporters and the United Liberation Movement for Democracy (Ulimo).
1994–95 A series of agreements were reached, none of which brought a final peace.
1996 An attempt to arrest one faction leader for breaking the truce led to two weeks of serious street fighting in Monrovia until Ecomog regained control. Following the renewed conflict, both the faction leaders and Ecowas agreed to hold elections in 1997.
1997 Presidential and Congressional elections were held in August in which Charles Taylor and his NPFL won a landslide victory.
1999 The Ghanaian and Nigerian troops, who were part of Ecomog, withdrew from Liberia in October.
2000 In January, President Charles Taylor announced that his government was forming a new army.
2001 There were rebel attacks on the border between Guinea and Liberia in January. Liberia closed its border with Sierra Leone in March.
2002 A state of emergency was declared in February after rebels attacked a town near the capital, Monrovia.

Political structure

Constitution
A multi-party constitution was approved by referendum in July 1984.

The executive
Executive power rests with the president.

National legislature
Legislative power rests with the 26-member Senate and the 64-member House of Representatives.

Political parties

Ruling party
National Patriotic Front of Liberia (NPFL)

Main opposition party
United Liberation Movement for Democracy in Liberia (Ulimo)

Population

2.92 million (2000)
Annual population growth rate: 2.7 per cent (1994–2000). Approximately 46 per cent of the total population is under 15 years.
Population density: 32 inhabitants per square km. Urban population: 45 per cent (1994–2000).

Ethnic make-up
Indigenous tribes (95 per cent), Americo-Liberians (5 per cent).

Religions
Christianity (68 per cent), traditional beliefs (18 per cent), Muslim (14 per cent).

Main cities

Monrovia (population 820,000 in 1998), Robertsport (7,149), Totota (2,057), Buchanan, Greenville.

Languages spoken

English is both the official and business language. There are three main Liberian dialects – Golla, Bassa, Kpelle, Kru and Vai.

Official language
English

Media

Press
Dailies: The Liberia Communications Network (LCN), owned by President Charles Taylor, publishes two dailies *The Patriot* and *Newsbeat*. Other dailies published mainly from Monrovia include *News*, *Daily Times*, *Inquirer* and the *National Chronicle*.
Weeklies: Weeklies published from Monrovia are *By Monrovia Weekend* (bi-weekly), *Eye* and the *New Democrat Weekly*.

Broadcasting
State-owned TV and radio suffered particularly from looting in the civil war and lost its TV and FM radio transmitters in 1991. The Liberia Broadcasting System (LBS) has one FM small transmitter than can reach only Monrovia, and no television
The LCN, owned by the President, controls a TV and radio network which uses the frequency 89FM, previously used by LBS, and which, by law, belongs to the state.
Radio: There are two aid-funded radio stations – Star and Veritas.

Economy

The economy has been severely damaged by the civil strife of the 1990s. Large proportions of Liberia's income comes from the Liberian Maritime Programme (which registers ships under the Liberian flag). Maritime revenue increased by US$60 million per annum following the announcement in 2000 that the Liberia International Ship and Corporate Registry (LISCR) would take over Liberia's maritime affairs from the US-based International Registries Inc. There are 2,000 ships under the Liberian registry.
However, the government's political isolation has been accompanied by a breakdown in relations with multilateral and bilateral donors and creditors, particularly the World Bank. This has resulted in the freezing of a post-conflict assistance programme worth up to US$50 million. The government will need to mend relations with donors and external creditors if it stands a chance of financing its development programme.
The government has faced criticism from the IMF for its handling of the economy, which has condemned the government's weak fiscal policy which has been undermined by rising extra-budgetary expenditure and a failure to liberalise rice and petroleum imports. Up to a third of the government's annual revenues is used to bolster President Taylor's personal wealth. Other large areas of expenditure included security and defence, which increased as Taylor began fighting rebels in the border areas – as well as supporting rebels in other west African states. The control of fiscal policy, a reduction in budget deficits and a programme of liberalisation will be required if the government wishes to gain further external help.
Despite the gloom that hangs over Liberia, the country is enjoying high growth levels of between 15–20 per cent and inflation rates of under 10 per cent, although per capita incomes are only a half of what they were before the conflict and unemployment is rampant.
The political stabilisation of Liberia is essential if it is to reap the economic benefits of finding peace with its regional neighbours. A lifting of economic sanctions would lead to an economic boom with a resumption of diamond exports.

External trade

Increased outflow of foreign company remittances, debt repayments and falling exports have kept the current account in deficit.

Exports
Principal exports include iron ore (pre-civil war typically 62 per cent of total; stopped completely in civil war), rubber (20 per cent), timber (5 per cent), coffee (4 per cent), diamonds (3 per cent). Informal exports continued in rubber and forestry areas.
Main destinations: Germany (pre-civil war typically 30 per cent of total), US (18 per cent), Italy (18 per cent).

Imports
Principal imports include machinery and transport equipment (pre-civil war typically 27 per cent of total), other manufactures (23 per cent), foodstuffs (23 per cent) and fuels and lubricants (18 per cent). During the civil war food imports increased significantly due to large cereal deficits.
Main sources: US (pre-civil war typically 25 per cent of total), Germany (13 per cent), Netherlands (10 per cent), Japan (8 per cent).

Agriculture
Hit by hostilities and migration from rural areas, production has been reduced from pre-war levels. Agriculture is still the most important sector of the economy, contributing approximately 35 per cent to GDP and employing 55 per cent of the workforce.
The principal cash crop is rubber, which provides 20 per cent of exports. Although mostly grown in foreign-owned plantations, smallholders are responsible for over half the total acreage planted. Coffee, cocoa and timber are also grown for export, but, as with rubber, earnings have been reduced due to falling world prices. Palm oil is produced mostly for the domestic market. The main food crops are rice, cassava and sweet potatoes, followed by eddoes and yams. The government is attempting to improve production to reduce the need for imports of rice which have become necessary to meet domestic demand.
Timber is an important export earner with total fellings around 800,000 cubic metres a year. Commercial ocean fishing is a growing activity, particularly shrimps.

Industry and manufacturing
The industrial sector contributes 10 per cent to GDP and employs 10 per cent of the workforce. The manufacturing sector is relatively underdeveloped, contributing less than 5 per cent to GDP, with very few firms employing more than 50 people. Activity is mainly confined to textiles, food processing, wood products, cement and chemicals.
Growth in the sector has been constrained by the small size of the domestic market, the need to import practically all raw materials and financial problems. However, the government has managed to attract some foreign investment for the setting-up of new companies aimed at exploiting local resources.
There is an industrial free zone near Monrovia for the duty-free assembly and manufacture of goods destined for re-export.
Liberia is famous for its 'flag of convenience' in the merchant shipping world.

Mining
Mining is the most important sector of the external economy. Before sanctions, it accounted for two-thirds of visible exports, employing 15 per cent of the workforce and contributing 20 per cent to GDP.
Prior to the civil war, Liberia was one of the world's major producers of iron ore (mainly extracted from mines at Mount Nimba, Mano River and Bong). Production was estimated at 23 million tonnes a year but stopped during the war. Major producers were Lamco, NIOC and the Bong Mining Company.
Diamonds are mined, previously earning Liberia an estimated US$300 million annually. During the war, factions exploited production. Current production figures are hard to gauge due to the allegations of diamond smuggling with Sierra Leone, Guinea and Côte d'Ivoire. The government's official figures are around 8,500 carats along with around 50kg of gold. However, it is estimated that up to six million carats of diamonds marked as of Liberian origin are produced and exported every year, although this may be far less. There are up to 30,000 artisinal miners in Liberia.
The rehabilitation of the infrastructure, especially destroyed railways, is needed to aid the recovery of the mining industry.
In March 2001, the UN Security Council imposed an embargo on all diamonds sold by Liberia after 7 May 2001.

Hydrocarbons
Liberia's upstream oil industry is tiny and there have been no commercially viable oil or gas finds in recent years. However, there may be some potential in the country's offshore, which has only recently attracted the interests of oil prospectors.

Energy
Total installed generating capacity is over 300MW, most of which is diesel-generated. Liberia has a hydroelectric potential of around 1,000MW. The Liberian Electricity Corporation (LEC) is state-owned and operates two power networks: the Monrovia Grid and the Rural Electrification Network. The Monrovia Grid serves five counties and has over 40,000 customers while the Rural Electification Network operates in eight counties with isolated diesel generators. LEC estimates that it will need US$100 million to increase capacity and extend distribution.

Banking
One of the banking sector's most attractive elements to foreign depositors is its reputation as one of the world's oldest tax havens. A lack of local lawyers and accountants means foreign corporations can register in Liberia with minimal restrictions. It is a popular tax haven for registering ships and Liberia has a merchant shipping fleet more than three times that of the US fleet. The lack of restrictions also make it popular for laundering money.
However, the civil war has led to a virtual collapse of the banking system and lending services have declined dramatically. The country's five commercial banks have found it hard to attract capital savings, as the public and businesses have tended to hoard money rather than put it in banks due to a general crisis of confidence in the banking system. The subsequent lack of liquidity in the banking sector has led to a wide spread between the average deposit and lending rates. Lack of affordable bank credit has hampered growth across the economy, particularly the agricultural sector. Unless the government can ensure political stability and security and a policy is instituted to increase bank savings, Liberia's banking sector will remain in the doldrums.

Central bank
In October 1999 the National Legislature enacted a law creating the Central Bank of Liberia, which replaced the National Bank of Liberia. Monetary authority functions are undertaken by the central government.

Main financial centre
Monrovia

Time
GMT

Geography
Liberia lies on the west coast of Africa, with Sierra Leone and Guinea to the north and Côte d'Ivoire to the east.

Climate
Hot and tropical with high levels of humidity (85–90 per cent) and there is little temperature variation throughout the year. Average temperatures range between 20–22 degrees C at night and 28–32 degrees C during the day. Wet season lasts from May–October with especially heavy rain June–July.

Entry requirements
Passports
Required by all. Passports must be valid for six months from date of entry.

Visa
Required by all except nationals of most West African countries. A return or onward ticket is required when applying for a visa. Visitors wishing to stay for more than 15 days must report to the Immigration Office, Broad Street, Monrovia, within 48 hours of arrival. Two passport-size photographs are required.

Currency advice/regulations
There are no restrictions on import and export of local or foreign currency. US dollars are legal tender.

Health (for visitors)

Mandatory precautions

Yellow fever vaccination certificate is required.

Advisable precautions

Typhoid, hepatitis 'A', tetanus and polio vaccinations are recommended. Malaria prophylaxis should be taken as risk exists throughout the country. There is a rabies risk. Drinking water should be boiled and filtered.

Hotels

The airport hotel and other major hotels in Monrovia should be booked in advance. Rates are expensive and tipping is optional.

Credit cards

There is limited acceptance of credit cards.

Public holidays

Fixed dates

1 Jan (New Year's Day), 11 Feb, 15 Mar, 12 Apr, 14 May, 25 May, 26 Jul, 24 Aug, 24 Oct, 29 Nov, 25 Dec (Christmas).

Variable dates

Decoration Day (second Wed in Mar), Good Friday, Fast and Prayer Day (second Fri in Apr), Thanksgiving (first Thu in Nov).

Working hours

Banking

Mon–Thu: 0900–1200; Fri: 0800–1400.

Business

Mon–Fri: 0800–1200, 1400–1600.

Government

Mon–Fri: 0800–1200, 1300–1600.

Shops

Mon–Sat: 0800–1300, 1500–1800.

Telecommunications

Telephone/fax

Dialling code for Liberia: IDD access code + 231, followed by subscriber's number (there are no area codes)

Getting there

Air

Main airport: Monrovia (MLW) Roberts International (ROB), 60km south-east of Monrovia.

Airport tax: International departures US$20; not applicable to children under 12 years and transit passengers.

Surface

Road: Monrovia–Sierra Leone road is paved. Routes from Côte d'Ivoire and Guinea are not generally recommended during rainy season.

Getting about

National transport

Air: Air Liberia operates a domestic service between Monrovia and main towns (services suspended due to unrest).

Air taxi companies charter planes between Monrovia and airfields throughout the country.

City transport

There are buses and taxis available from the airport to the city centre.

Taxis: Zoning system in operation. Negotiate fares in advance for long-distance journeys. Tipping is not usual.

Car hire

Chauffeur-driven or self-drive cars are available in Monrovia. International driving licence or national driving licence with permit (valid for up to 30 days) accepted. Traffic drives on the right. Self-drive cars are not generally recommended.

BUSINESS DIRECTORY

Telephone area codes

Dialling code for Liberia: IDD access code +231, followed by subscriber's number (there are no area codes).

Banking

Liberian Bank for Development and Investment (LBDI), Corner of Randall and Ashmun Streets, PO Box 547, Monrovia (tel: 227-140; fax: 226-939).

International Bank (Liberia) Limited; 64 Broad Street, Monrovia (tel: 227438 fax: 226092/3)

Liberian Trading And Development Bank Ltd, PO Box 293, Tradevco Building, Ashmun Street, 1000 Monrovia 10 (tel: 226072, 226074 fax: 226471)

Central bank

Central Bank of Liberia; PO Box 2048, Warren and Carey Streets, Monrovia (tel: 222497, 222580, 222767 fax: 226144, 227685)

Travel information

Air Liberia, PO Box 2076, Monrovia (tel: 222-144, 226-404).

Ministry of tourism

Ministry of Information, Cultural Affairs and Tourism, PO Box 10-9021, UN Drive, 1000 Monrovia 10 (tel/fax: 226-078).

Ministries

Ministry of Commerce, Industry, PO Box 10-9041, 1000 Monrovia 10 (tel: 226-283).

Ministry of Finance, Bureau of Customs and Excise, PO Box 10-9013, 1000 Monrovia 10.

Ministry of Foreign Affairs, PO Box 10-9002, 1000 Monrovia 10 (tel: 226-763, 221-029, 221-751).

Ministry of Information, Cultural Affairs and Tourism, PO Box 10-9021, UN Drive, 1000 Monrovia 10 (tel/fax: 226-078).

Ministry of Justice, Bureau of Immigration, PO Box 10-9006, Broad Street, 1000 Monrovia 10.

Ministry of Lands, Mines and Energy, PO Box 10-9024, 1000 Monrovia 10 (tel: 226-281, 221-580, 221-488, 221-460).

Ministry of Planning and Economic Affairs, PO Box 10-9016, 1000 Monrovia 10 (tel: 226-962, 227-987, 222-121, 222-331, 223-208, 221-971).

Ministry of Youth and Sports, PO Box 10-9040, 1000 Monrovia 10 (tel: 226-284).

Other useful addresses

Commonwealth Development Corporation, PO Box 2015, Monrovia.

ELTV (Liberian television system), PO Box 594, Monrovia.

Liberian Development Corporation, PO Box 9043, Monrovia.

Liberian Embassy (USA), 5201 16th Street, NW, Washington DC 20011 (tel: 723-0437; fax: 723-0436; e-mail: info@liberiaemb.org).

Liberian News Agency (LINA), Ministry of Information, PO Box 9021, Capitol Hill, Monrovia (tel: 222-229).

National Investment Commission, PO Box 10-9043, 1000 Monrovia 10 (tel: 226-685, 226-575).

National Ports Authority, PO Box 14, Monrovia.

Statistics Bureau, PO Box 9016, Monrovia (tel: 222-622).

Internet sites

Africa Business Network: http://www.ifc.org/abn

African Development Bank: http://www.afdb.org

Africa Online: http://www.africaonline.com

AllAfrica.com: http://allafrica.com

Harambee Afrika (UK business club for traders with east, central and southern Africa; includes annotated web resource list): http://www.harambee.co.uk

Mbendi AfroPaedia (information on companies, countries, industries and stock exchanges in Africa): http://mbendi.co.za

Libya

Daniel Brett

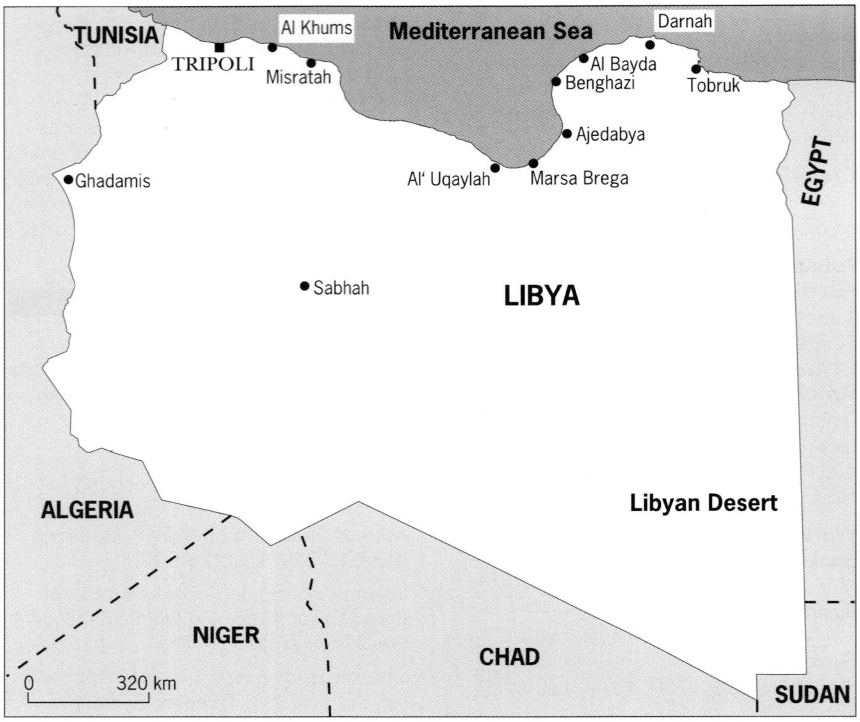

Western attitudes towards Libya are slowly shifting as Muammar Al-Qadafi, the Leader of the Revolution, has turned away from conflicts in the Middle East to concentrate on strengthening his hold on Africa. His disdain towards other Arab leaders on issues such as Iraq and the Palestinians resulted in a threat to leave the Arab League in October 2002, although his enthusiasm for funding Palestinian militants has waned. Meanwhile, Libyan influence has grown in Africa's trouble spots, notably Zimbabwe and the Central African Republic (CAR).

Cult of personality

Muammar Al-Qadafi, the Leader of the Revolution, has sought to rebrand Libya as an economic eldorado while portraying himself as a crusader for African unity and peace. The collapse of the Soviet Union and the communist bloc left Libya politically and economically isolated from the late 1980s. The country's desperate need for international capital and trade with the West has seen the government opening the country up to foreign investment. Meanwhile, it has ditched its involvement in international terrorism, which proved to be more trouble than it was worth.

Nevertheless, Qadafi is still perceived as dangerous because nobody knows when his anti-Western antagonism is simply grandstanding or evidence of a lingering terrorist mindset. He has moved from Arab nationalism to pan-Africanism without any apparent shift in his familiar aggressive dogmatism or underhand tactics. Yet, while Qadafi's erratic and vain behaviour makes him seem dangerous, he is more rooted in secular politics than ever and shares with Western states a common enemy in Al-Qaeda. The group, believed to be behind the 11 September 2001 attacks in the US, has links with Libyan rebels seeking to replace Qadafi's regime with an Islamic state. The co-operation between Libyan and Western intelligence services in 2002 helped strengthen

KEY FACTS

Official name: Al-Jamahiriya Al-Arabiya Al-Libiya Ash-Shabiya Al-Ishtirakiya Al-Uzma (The Great Socialist People's Libyan Arab Jamahiriya)

Head of State: Leader of First of September Revolution, Colonel Muammar Al-Qadafi

Head of government: Secretary General of the General People's Committee, Mubarak Abdullah Al-Shamikh (from Mar 2000)

Area: 1,775,500 square km

Population: 5.50 million (2001)

Capital: Tripoli

Official language: Arabic

Currency: Libyan dinar (LD) = 1,000 dirhams

Exchange rate: LD1.23 per US$ (Jan 2003) (on 1 Jan 2002, the Libyan dinar was devalued by 51 per cent against the US dollar)

GDP per capita: US$5,082 (2001); US$3,216 (2002)*

GDP real growth: 3.10% (2001); 0.8% (2002)*

Labour force: 1.40 million (2001); 1.5 million (2002)*

Unemployment: 30.00% (2001)*

Inflation: -8.50% (2001); 6.0% (2002)*

Oil production: 1.43 million bpd (2001)

Balance of trade: US$4.40 billion (2001)

Foreign debt: US$4.70 billion (2001)

* estimated figure

For the latest Key Facts, go to www.worldinformation.com

Qadafi's hand over armed rebels within his own country. This has encouraged many Libyan businessmen, who have yearned to break out of the sanctions straightjacket which curtailed economic growth throughout the 1990s.

Lockerbie lingers on

The conclusion of the trial in 2001 of two suspected Libyan agents accused of blowing up a Pam Am jet over Scotland in 1988 saw many countries bury the hatchet to enable their business interests to gain a foothold in Libya. The country's image was further enhanced by the sharing of intelligence between Libya and Western governments in the wake of the 11 September 2001 terrorist attacks on the US. This has come on top of a gradual dissociation of the Libyan regime from Palestinian militant groups and the expulsion of Islamic militants.

The Libyan reaction to the trial has not clarified the question of whether the West can trust the Qadafi regime. In 1999, the government reached a deal in which it handed over the suspects to an international court in the Netherlands to be tried by a Scottish judge and pledged to accept the judge's verdict. This led to the suspension of UN and EU sanctions, although the US maintained its sanctions regime under the Iran-Libya Sanctions Act (ILSA), which was extended for a further five years in August 2001. The UN maintained that the sanctions would not be completely lifted until Libya paid compensation to the victims of the Lockerbie disaster, admitted responsibility for the bombing, renounced all forms of terrorism and disclosed all information it has about the bombing.

In January 2001, Abdelbaset Ali Mohmed Al-Megrahi was found guilty while his co-accused, Al-Amin Khalifa Fhimah, was acquitted. In March 2002, Al-Megrahi's appeal was thrown out and he began his life sentence in an isolated wing of a Scottish jail. Libya rejected the decision, calling it 'an insult to Scottish justice' and claimed that 'the appeal court handed down a political verdict imposed by certain parties and ignored the new evidence submitted by the defence'. Consequently, the government refused to pay US$6 billion in compensation to the Lockerbie victims, opening the door to a renewal of sanctions.

There was brief optimism about a settlement in May 2002 when Libya reportedly reached a deal with the Lockerbie victims' relatives and offered US$2.73 billion in compensation, which was contingent on a progressive lifting of sanctions. However, it was later revealed that the deal had not been officially sanctioned by the government and was brokered by a Libyan entrepreneur representing businesses which are severely restricted by the sanctions regime. The move therefore failed to meet all the UN's demands and sanctions were maintained.

The Lockerbie case eclipsed another important trial, which also opened up old wounds. On 13 November 2001, a German court blamed Libya's intelligence service for the bombing of a Berlin disco in 1986, an attack that killed two US servicemen. Four people, including a former Libyan diplomat, were sentenced to prison terms of between 12–14 years while a fifth defendant was acquitted. The trial came while US nerves were still raw after the 11 September terrorist attacks and the judge's verdict resonated with US President George W Bush's 'war on terror' rhetoric. Therefore, although the Berlin terrorist attack was carried out in a very different era, the case appeared to many in the US as justifying the continuation of a war of words and sanctions against Libya.

Americans in two minds

The handing-over of the Lockerbie suspects was an important leap towards reconciliation with Western states. The UK, France and Germany, which had suffered alleged Libyan-backed terrorist attacks during the 1980s and 1990s, joined other EU states in the rush to break with the past in order to exploit investment opportunities in Libya. The US's position is more confusing, largely due to a split within the upper echelons of government.

US attitudes towards Libya appeared to soften when Qadafi threw his weight behind the US 'war on terrorism'. In an unusual move, Qadafi sent his condolences to the US following the 11 September attacks and stated that the US 'is right to seek retaliation' and confirmed that 'anyone who suffers such a disastrous blow has the right to be angry and retaliate'. Libyan security chiefs are said to have met their US counterparts to exchange intelligence on Islamic militant groups and in January 2002 the two countries began top-level talks aimed at rebuilding bridges.

Libya's stance on Islamic militancy and its acquiescence in the 'war on terrorism' has left many policy-makers in the US scratching their heads, opening up a rift within the US government on policy towards Libya. The traditional thinking is that Libya is acquiring and developing nuclear, chemical and biological weapons to threaten US interests as well as co-operating with pariah states such as Iran and Iraq. However, Libya's willingness to co-operate with the US and move towards reconciliation has led some within the US government to believe that once it begins compensating the Lockerbie victims, sanctions should be lifted.

The rapprochement following 11 September was welcomed by US oil companies, which had been operating in Libya before the imposition of US sanctions in 1986. In September 2001, they were told by the Libyan authorities that they would lose their operating licences unless they returned to Libya within a year. With the Bush administration closely tied to oil

KEY INDICATORS

	Unit	1996	1997	1998	1999	2000
Population	m	4.85	4.96	5.06	5.18	5.29
Gross domestic product (GDP)	US$bn	33.20	34.20	31.80	32.30	39.20
GDP per capita	US$	5,937	5,925	5,947	5,896	6,939
GDP real growth	%	1.1	0.5	-2.0	5.4	6.5
Inflation	%	38.9	25.0	24.2	18.0	12.0
Oil output	'000 bpd	1,450.0	1,490.0	1,480.0	1,425.0	1,475.0
Natural gas output	bn cu m	6.2	6.4	6.2	5.9	5.5
Exports (fob) (goods)	US$m	9,578.0	9,876.0	6,328.0	6,758.0	13,900.0
Imports (fob) (goods)	US$m	7,059.0	7,160.0	5,857.0	3,996.0	7,600.0
Balance of trade	US$m	2,519.0	2,716.0	471.0	2,762.0	6,300.0
Current account	US$m	1,477.0	1,875.0	-391.0	1,984.0	4,470.0
Foreign debt	US$bn	3.3	3.7	3.9	3.8	4.1
Total reserves minus gold	US$m	0.0	0.0	7,270.0	6,995.0	12,461.0
Foreign exchange	US$m	0.0	0.0	6,221.0	5,940.0	11,408.0
Exchange rate	per US$	0.36	0.37	0.38	0.45	1.85

interests, the threat probably led to increased pressure for the scrapping of ILSA, which prohibits investment in Libya.

President George W Bush's State of the Union address to Congress in January 2002 represented a tentative step towards reconciliation with Libya when he failed to include Libya in the 'axis of evil', which included Iran, Iraq and North Korea. However, when the Libyan government refused to pay compensation for the Lockerbie victims following the results of Al-Megrahi's appeal trial, US feelings hardened again. By mid-2002, the US stated that it still regarded Libya as a 'rogue state' and accused it of hoarding 'weapons of mass destruction'. In May, US Under Secretary of State John Bolton claimed that Libya was trying to re-establish its 'offensive chemical weapons capability' and that it 'may be capable of producing small quantities of biological agent'. Bolton also reiterated past US accusations that Libya was seeking to acquire nuclear weapons. The distinct lack of proof to back up these allegations suggested that the US was simply posturing to appeal to the powerful Zionist lobby in the US. It is extremely unlikely that Libya will become a target in the 'war on terrorism', particularly given its warmer relations with the EU.

Libya's dream

Qadafi's vision of a united Africa came a step closer with the creation of the African Union (AU) to replace the Organisation of African Unity (OAU), a process that was completed with the AU's launch in July 2002. The AU is supposed to overcome the shortcomings of its predecessor and its founding constitution enables it to intervene in member states where there is evidence of serious human rights violations. It also sets out plans for a Pan-African Parliament (PAP), a court of justice and a central bank with a single currency. Libya is keen to host all these proposed institutions, which Qadafi is keen to dominate.

Qadafi has portrayed himself as the AU's father figure, but many African governments remain wary of him due to past experience and his anti-Western sentiments. South Africa's Thabo Mbeki is likely to be Qadafi's main opponent in the AU. Qadafi clashed with Mbeki over the South African-led New Partnership for Africa's Development (Nepad), which pledges democratic and economic reform in return for investment and aid. He claimed the programme constituted a new form of colonialism. The rivalries between the two styles of African leadership — Mbeki's neo-liberal capitalism versus Qadafi's pan-African nationalism — are likely to intensify as Qadafi continues to impress his personality on the rest of Africa. While donors and Western governments favour Mbeki, Qadafi is picking up the support of those governments isolated by the West as well as many African citizens who feel increasingly marginalised by economic liberalisation. Indeed, Qadafi has played on this resentment of alleged Western interference to increase his sphere of influence, backed by large amounts of financial and military aid. Yet, South Africa and its chief African ally, Nigeria, remain highly influential and can head off Qadafi's ideological encroachment.

Qadafi is also a champion of hopeless causes in Africa. This tends to undermine any credibility he might have built up through liberally throwing his cash around. His support for the violent Revolutionary United Front (RUF) in Sierra Leone left him with egg on his face after the rebels' defeat. Similarly, his campaign to bolster Robert Mugabe's dictatorship in crisis-ridden Zimbabwe has upset many southern African governments who want the issue solved within the context of the Southern African Development Community (SADC). Nevertheless, in November 2002 Libya ended an oil deal with Zimbabwe, which relies on Libyan oil imports for 70 per cent of its needs. The decision was supposedly made for 'commercial' reasons, since Zimbabwe failed to keep up with its payments and was in arrears by an estimated US$90 million. Commercial reasons were also allegedly behind Libya's military adventure into the CAR in 2001, ostensibly to prevent a mutiny and to ensure President Ange-Felix Patasse's security. Reports in late-2002 suggested that Patasse was preparing to sign a 99-year treaty with Libya, giving it the right to exploit its oil, uranium and other mineral resources. Libya's unilateral interference in the affairs of other states will continue to annoy other regional powers and is likely to increase distrust of the Qadafi regime among African governments.

Oil boom bonanza

GDP growth was estimated at around 5.6 per cent in 2001, a slight fall from 6.5 per cent in the previous year. Growth has been fuelled by rising oil export revenues, which form about 95 per cent of the country's foreign exchange earnings and three-quarters of government revenue.

In January 2002, the government unified the country's official and unofficial exchange rates and devalued the dinar by 51 per cent. This will substantially enhance the competitiveness of Libya's non-oil exporters and boost inward investment. However, since the non-oil sector only contributes a marginal amount to total exports, the effects of devaluation on overall external performance are likely to be negligible since Libyan oil exports are traded in US dollars. The inflationary effects of devaluation will be partly offset by a 50 per cent cut in the customs duty rate on most imports. However, inflation could rise to up to 20 per cent in 2002 as a result of devaluation and its effects on import prices.

Central to the Libyan economy is its hydrocarbons sector. Libya has 12 large oil fields with reserves of at least one billion barrels each and two others with reserves of between 500 million and one billion barrels. In early 2002, oil production was estimated at around 1.4 million barrels per day (bpd), over 90 per cent of which is exported. Libya plans to increase production to two million bpd by 2006, backed by around US$10 billion of foreign investment expected in the period 2000–10.

Oil export revenues totalled an estimated US$12.5 billion in 2001, down from US$12.9 billion in the previous year. The dramatic rise in oil receipts since 1999 has boosted government revenue. Although the global slowdown is likely to diminish these revenues, lost income from oil will be made up by remittances from Libya's large foreign investment portfolio. Consequently, both the external current account and the government's fiscal position are likely to remain relatively stable in 2002, maintaining their surpluses for the foreseeable future. Healthy government revenue caused by oil windfalls ensures rising expenditure on capital projects as well as public sector wages.

Outlook

Libya's oil sector is likely to have a great impact on the country's economy and its international position. European and Asian oil companies will continue to flock to Libya, leading to a softening of international attitudes towards the government. Unless Qadafi does something drastically stupid, international sanctions, with the exception of the US, are likely to remain suspended, even without a resolution of the Lockerbie compensation issue. The booming oil sector will help Qadafi to buy influence in Africa, enabling him to influence the AU's direction. His predilection for supporting African governments that are resistant to Western demands for democracy and reform is likely to affirm suspicions that Al- Qadafi is still up to his old tricks. Meanwhile, the large number of unemployed young Libyans will be questioning why so much money is being channelled into Qadafi's political ventures abroad rather than job-building measures at home.

Risk assessment

Economic	Good
Political	Stable
Regional stability	Good

COUNTRY PROFILE

Historical profile

According to archaeological surveys, Libya's coastal plain has hosted permanent settlements since at least 8000BC. Berber tribes began to migrate to the area in 3000BC. The people of what is now Libya came under the influence of several empires, including the Egyptian pharaohs, the Phoenicians, the Greeks, the Romans and the Byzantines.

The rise of Islam in the seventh century saw the conquering of the region by Arabs under the rule of Caliph Umar I. After the Arab conquest, Libya came under the jurisdiction of a succession of *amirs* (commanders) who were subordinate to the caliph, the leader of the Islamic world.

1510 During the struggle between Hapsburg Spain and the Ottoman Turks for supremacy in the Mediterranean, Spanish forces captured and destroyed Tripoli.

1524 Tripoli was entrusted to the Knights of St John of Malta.

1551 The Knights were driven out of Tripolitania by the Turks who began consolidating their control over the Maghreb region. The Ottoman Empire joined the three provinces of Tripolitania, Cyrenaica and Fezzan into one regency in Tripoli.

1711–1835 Although nominally part of the Ottoman empire, the Turks in effect gave way to the local Karamanli dynasty until 1835 when the Turks strengthened their control again. The local rulers levied a toll on every Christian fleet using the Mediterranean.

1870–1911 The area was dominated by the Sanusi religious order, although the Turks and the Italians continued to invade periodically.

1911–42 By the time of the First World War an Italian force had taken control of the coastal towns. After the war, Italy captured the Libyan nationalist hero, Omar Mukhtar, hanging him in 1931. Italy introduced an Italianisation programme; by the end of the Second World War in 1945 an estimated half the indigenous population of one million had been exiled or killed.

1942 Italy's colonisation of Libya ended, when the Italians and Germans lost the war in the Western Desert. The British took over Tripolitania and Cyrenaica and the French took over the Fezzan.

1951 Libya was granted independence under King Idris (originally Mohammed Idris Al-Sanusi, a member of the Sanusi religious order).

1956 Libya became an oil producing nation after the government granted two US companies a concession of 35 million hectares.

1961 King Idris opened a 167km pipeline, which linked important oil fields in the interior to the Mediterranean Sea, making it possible for Libya to export oil.

1969 As pan-Arabism swept the Arab world, Colonel Muammar Al-Qadafi seized power as Leader of the Revolution in September. Most economic activities were nationalised, including the oil industry.

1970 The government closed the British airbase in Tobruk and the US Air Force base in Tripoli. Property belonging to Italian settlers was nationalised.

1971 The Federation of Arab Republics (FAR), comprising Libya, Egypt and Syria, was approved by national referendum, but was never realised.

1972 Libya and Egypt agreed to merge into a single state, but the plans were abandoned.

1973 Qadafi announced a cultural revolution in which people's committees were established throughout the country. Libyan forces invaded the Aozou Strip in northern Chad.

1974 A plan to unify Libya and Tunisia was agreed but never implemented.

1977 Qadafi set up the General People's Congress and the country was renamed the Great Socialist People's Libyan Arab Jamahiriya.

1980 An agreement to merge Libya and Syria was made but failed to materialise.

1981 The US shot down two Libyan aircraft which challenged its warplanes over the Gulf of Sirte, claimed by Libya as its territorial waters.

1984 Police Constable Yvonne Fletcher was killed during an armed siege in the Libyan embassy in London. The UK suspended diplomatic relations with Libya.

1986 In an unsuccessful attempt to bring down the Qadafi regime, the US launched a major airstrike on Tripoli, causing substantial damage. The US claimed its raids were in response to an alleged Libyan involvement in the bombing of a nightclub in Berlin which was used by US military personnel. The US imposed economic sanctions against Libya.

1988 Libyan terrorists were blamed for the bomb which destroyed a Pan Am passenger aircraft over Lockerbie in Scotland.

1989 Algeria, Libya, Mauritania, Morocco and Tunisia formed the Arab Maghreb Union.

1992 UN sanctions were imposed upon Libya for refusing to hand over two men suspected of the Lockerbie bombing.

1994 Libya returned the Aozou Strip to Chad.

1995 Qadafi ordered the expulsion of 30,000 Palestinians in protest at the Oslo accords signed by the Israeli government and the Palestine Liberation Organisation (PLO).

1999 UN and EU sanctions were suspended after Libya agreed to arrest and extradite Lockerbie bombing suspects. In July, the UK re-established diplomatic links with Libya.

2000 Qadafi visited Arab states in North Africa and the Middle East, seeking to promote Arab co-operation. Libya was one of the key signatories to the creation of the African Union (AU) made at an Organization of African Unity (OAU) conference in Lomé, Togo.

2001 Abdelbaset Ali Mohmed Al-Megrahi, a Libyan intelligence agent, was found guilty of the Lockerbie bombing in a Scottish court based in the Netherlands, while his co-accused, Al-Amin Khalifa Fhimah, was acquitted. The parliament building for the AU, launched at a summit of the OAU in Lusaka, was built in Tripoli. In August, the US imposed a five-year extension to sanctions against Libya. In November, a German court convicted four Libyans of the 1986 Berlin nightclub bombing.

2002 From 1 January, the Libyan dinar was devalued by 51 per cent against the US dollar – the first step in setting a unified, market-driven exchange rate. In March, Al-Megrahi's appeal failed and he was sentenced to life imprisonment at a Scottish jail. The Libyan government refused to recognise the verdict. In May, a Libyan businessmen offered to pay US$2.73 billion in compensation to the relatives of the Lockerbie victims, but the offer fell short of meeting the terms of UN resolutions. The AU was launched in July.

Political structure

Constitution

Libya has no constitution. In 2000, 14 ministries were abolished and their powers devolved to provincial committees or other bodies.

Form of state

Libya is officially a Jamahiriya, or state of the masses.

The executive

Libya has no official head of state, but Colonel Qadafi exercises absolute authority in his role as Leader of the First of September Revolution. Federal executive power is exercised by the General

People's Committee (council of ministers). The Secretary General of the General People's Committee is a post broadly equivalent to that of prime minister.

National legislature

Political power is vested in the General People's Congress (GPC).

Libya is officially run by popular committees and congresses. Each sends delegates to the GPC, which approves laws and sets policy guidelines. There are 300 congresses, each having an executive popular committee, which can effectively take some decisions at a local level.

Legal system

The Libyan legal system is based on *sharia* (Islamic law) and the Italian civil law system. There are separate religious courts and no constitutional provision for judicial review of legislative acts. The judicial system consists of the Supreme Court, courts of appeal, courts of first instance and summary courts. Libya has not accepted compulsory International Court of Justice (ICJ) jurisdiction.

Political parties

There are no official political parties in the country.

Main opposition party

The two most active internal opposition movements are the Islamic Liberation Party and the Muslim Brotherhood. The main exiled opposition is the US-based National Front for the Salvation of Libya (NFSL).

Population

5.29 million (2000)

Annual population growth rate: 2.2 per cent (1994–2000). Approximately 40 per cent of the population is under 14 years of age; 57 per cent 15–64 years; 3 per cent over 65.

Population density: three inhabitants per square kilometre. Urban population: 88 per cent (1994–2000). Around 90 per cent of the population live in coastal regions, with half residing in Tripoli itself.

Ethnic make-up

Berber-Arab (97 per cent). There are small communities of Greeks, Maltese, Italians, Egyptians, Pakistanis, Turks, Indians and Tunisians.

Religions

Sunni Muslim (97 per cent). A third of Libya's Muslims are affilitated to the Sanusi religious sect, which had fought against European colonialism in the first half of the twentieth century.

Education

Libya has paid particular attention to its education system, with the aim of reducing illiteracy and improving the education available to women. In 2000, the UN estimated that adult illiteracy rates for men and women aged 15 years or over stood at 9.2 per cent and 31.7 per cent, respectively.

Education is mandatory and free for all children from six to 15 years of age. Primary school starts from the age of six and lasts until 12 years of age. Secondary school begins at the age of 12 and the curriculum is divided into two- to three-year courses.

Intermediate level education extends from three to four years and comprises a number of secondary school types including both general and specialised secondary schools and intermediate vocational centres.

Higher education is offered in 14 universities and 54 higher vocational institutes. English and Arabic are the main languages for instruction.

Health

World Bank estimates during the period 1994–2000 showed that the average life expectancy was 71 years and the infant mortality rate stood at 22 per 1,000 live births. The fertility rate showed that 3.6 children were born per adult woman. Contraceptives are used by 45 per cent of adult women aged 15–49. The maternal mortality ratio is estimated at 75 per 100,000 live births. Approximately 5 per cent of children under the age of five are malnourished and 72 per cent of the population have access to improved water facilities. There are 1.3 physicians and 4.3 hospital beds typically available per 1,000 people.

The government provides free health services. There are two large hospitals in Tripoli and Benghazi. Despite claims that Libya provides 100 per cent of the population with access to healthcare, there has been a perceptible decline in health standards since the 1980s. Since 1992, UN sanctions have had a detrimental impact on the quality of healthcare provision and many medical services and pharmaceutical products have become unavailable. Consequently, many Libyans seek medical treatment in neighbouring Tunisia, Egypt or in Western Europe.

Welfare

The government is theoretically committed to full provision of welfare services to all Libyan nationals. However, in reality parts of the population are often not covered by welfare provisions. The most common welfare benefit is housing to those in need.

The government provides a national social security system covering pensions and other social insurance, but the availability of such services regularly depends on annual oil receipts, which make up a large proportion of total government revenues.

Main cities

Tripoli (estimated population 1.5 million), Benghazi (750,000), Misratah (Misurata) (360,000), Az Zawiya (300,000), Al Khums (Homs) (200,000).

Languages spoken

Italian and English are spoken and there are also pockets of native Berber speakers.

Official language/s

Arabic

Media

Press

Newspapers and periodicals are published by the official Jamahiriya News Agency (Jana) and Trades Unions. The main newspapers are the *Al-Fajr Al-Jahid* and *Shu'un Libiyah*. A number of weekly, fortnightly, monthly and occasional periodicals are also produced. These include the *Al Sidra Magazine*, *Ath-Thaqafa Al-Arabiya* (*Arab Culture*), *Ad-Daawa Al-Islamia* (*Islamic Call*) and the monthly *Risala Al-Jihad* (*Holy War Letter*) in Arabic, English and French.

Broadcasting

The broadcast media is controlled by the state-owned Great Socialist People's Libyan Arab Jamahiriya Broadcasting Corporation.

Radio: Programmes are broadcast in Arabic and English from Tripoli and Benghazi.

Television: The television service broadcasts in Arabic, but there are also channels which broadcast in Italian, English and French.

Economy

Libya's economy, which depends primarily upon revenues from the oil sector, is traditionally run on an *ad hoc* basis, subject both to the whims of Qadafi and the vagaries of the international oil market. With the introduction of sanctions, the country's economy stagnated. UN sanctions, a response to Libya's refusal to hand over two security agents suspected of the Lockerbie bombing in 1988, banned flights to and from Libya, forbade the sale of spare parts for oil refineries and froze all Libyan funds abroad (excluding earnings derived from sales of oil, gas and petrol products, and agricultural products). The government's policy of economic liberalisation, proclaimed in 1988, proved extremely difficult to implement in the restricted trading environment sanctions imposed.

In Libya's state-dominated economy, import restrictions and inefficient resource allocations have led to periodic shortages of basic goods and foodstuffs. The non-oil manufacturing and construction sectors, which account for about 20 per cent of GDP, have expanded from processing mostly agricultural products to include the production of petrochemicals, iron, steel, and aluminum. Climatic conditions and poor soils severely limit agricultural output, and Libya imports about 75 per cent of its food requirements.

Higher oil prices since 1999 have seen an increase in export revenues, which improved macroeconomic balances and helped to stimulate the economy.

Following the handing over of the Lockerbie suspects and the subsequent suspension of UN sanctions in 1999, Libya has been trying to increase its attractiveness to foreign investors and several foreign companies have visited in search of contracts. The speed with which European businesses returned to the country once the Lockerbie suspects had arrived in the Netherlands suggested that a turf war would soon emerge as they fought to obtain new contracts. Libya's re-emergence into the international community should lead to a rapid improvement in trade and development. While the suspension of UN sanctions may go a long way to assisting the development of Libya's economy, US sanctions, in the form of the 1996 Iran-Libya Sanctions Act (ILSA), extended for five years in July 2001, are still an impediment to foreign investment in Libya's energy industries.

External trade

Exports

Oil accounts for 95 per cent of exports.

Main destinations: Italy (42 per cent of the 2000 total), Germany (19.2 per cent), Spain (12.9 per cent), Turkey (5.6 per cent), France (4.5 per cent).

Imports

Goods imported range from food to scientific instruments.

Main sources: Italy (25.4 per cent of the 2000 total), Germany (9.8 per cent), UK (7.6 per cent), Tunisia (7.1 per cent), France (7 per cent), Australia (0.5 per cent).

Agriculture

Agriculture is estimated to account for 8 per cent of GDP and to employ 20 per cent of the labour force.

The cultivated land is only 1.2 per cent of the total land area and over 80 per cent of all agricultural production is concentrated around oases and northern coastal regions, especially near Benghazi and Tripoli. Less than 1 per cent is irrigated. Climatic conditions and irrigation problems limit output. About 30 per cent of food is imported.

The main crops are barley (the staple diet for most of the population), dates, castor beans, tomatoes, almonds, potatoes, wheat, oats, olives, citrus fruits and groundnuts.

Farming

Libya is self-sufficient in fruit and vegetables, dairy products and poultry.

The large-scale Great Man-Made River (GMR) project, which delivers water from underground reservoirs in the Sahara to Libya's main cities and farms in the more cultivable coastal areas, provides irrigation for 500,000ha. Phase 3 of the GMR project was in the planning stages in 2002.

Fishing

The fishing industry has considerable potential. The total fisheries catch is estimated at around eight million tonnes per year, with small quantities being exported to Greece, Malta and Tunisia. There is a tuna cannery at Zanzur, and sardine canneries at Zuara and Khoms.

Industry and manufacturing

The industrial sector is estimated to contribute 18 per cent to GDP and to employ 15 per cent of the workforce. Virtually all industry is state-owned.

Traditionally the industrial sector was limited to small-scale processing operations, mostly in food, wood and paper, textiles and soap. However, traditional small-scale agro-allied industries have given way to the growth of import substitution industries (such as building materials manufacture) and heavy industries (such as petrochemicals, iron and steel, concrete pipes and vehicle assembly). The National Petrochemicals Company (Napectco) has built up a substantial petrochemicals capacity since the late 1970s using local feedstock. The large Marsa Brega complex is owned by Napectco which hosts a number of plants producing petrochemicals, ethanol, ammonia and urea. Much industrial investment has gone into expanding capital intensive chemicals capacity as a means of increasing the value added content of exports. Major metal smelting projects have been impeded by low incomes and depressed world prices in recent years. Other constraints to development are insufficiently trained Libyan manpower and the small domestic market.

Tourism

The main obstacle to the development of the tourist sector has been Libya's political isolation and its international image. Libya's Mediterranean beaches and historical sites, including the Roman ruins at Leptis Magna, together with its proximity to Europe provide the country with good potential for attracting foreign visitors. However, as with many other issues in Libya, the government has failed to produce a coherent and realistic agenda for the sector and the prospects of tourism as a major contributor to the economy remain slim over the short- to medium-term. A significant proportion of the government's US$35 billion investment programme, which finishes in 2005, is being directed towards tourism projects with the emphasis on starting and upgrading beachside tourist facilities.

Mining

The mining and hydrocarbons sectors are estimated to contribute 35 per cent to GDP and to employ 10 per cent of the working population.

Major mineral deposits include iron ore (which supplies the steel complex at Misurata), potassium, magnesium, sulphur, gypsum and phosphate. There are also potential uranium deposits. Commercial exploitation of minerals is restricted by high development costs.

Salt and construction materials are produced, but large reserves of iron ore at Wadi Shatti remain undeveloped, although this is being reconsidered.

Hydrocarbons

Oil

Crude oil production is the mainstay of the economy. Libya is the second-largest oil producer in Africa, after Nigeria, and holds 42 per cent of all Africa's proven reserves. Proven oil reserves totalled 29.5 billion barrels (end-2001) (mostly high-quality light crudes). Most of the principal oil fields are in the Sirte Basin in north-central Libya. There are 14 large oil fields, 12 of which contain reserves of over one billion barrels and two contain 500 million to one billion barrels. Total refining capacity, located chiefly in Zawia, Brega, Misurata and Ras Lanuf, stands at approximately 360,000bpd.

The suspension of UN sanctions has led to fierce competition among European oil companies for concessions in Libya. The continuation of US sanctions have helped increase interest among small oil firms, which are free from competition with US corporations. Libya is also attractive to investors due to the low cost of oil recovery, its close proximity to European markets (particularly Italy) and its relatively high standard of infrastructure. The only frustration investors have faced is the state-owned National Oil Company's (NOC) slow pace in awarding exploration licenses.

Oil production and export (domestic demand absorbs less than 10 per cent of total production) have fluctuated in line with world demand/price shifts and allocation of OPEC quotas. Oil production in 2001 amounted to 1.4 million barrels per day (bpd), a fall of around 4 per cent over 2000 output. Libya plans to increase production to two million bpd by 2006.

In 1986, US unilateral sanctions were imposed, forcing five major US oil companies to abandon up to US$2 billion in fixed assets, and forfeit business worth up to US$2.1 billion annually. Libya said that their assets will be returned to the companies when they resume operations in the country. UN sanctions were suspended in 1999, but the US maintains its own sanctions on investing into Libya's energy industries. In September 2001, the Libyan government told the four US companies holding operating licences in Libya that unless they returned within one year they would put the licences up for tender.

Gas

There are extensive natural gas reserves of 1.31 trillion cubic metres (end-2001) (46.4 trillion cubic feet), with up to 300 billion cubic metres in the Bouri offshore field.

Natural gas is liquefied in Marsa Brega. There are plans for a major extension of the gas pipeline network as part of the Organisation of Arab Petroleum Exporting Countries (OAPEC) scheme for a regional gas network.

Natural gas production totalled 5.4 billion cubic metres in 2001 (4.9 million toe), slightly less than the 2000 output.

ENI, Italy's partly privatised energy and chemicals conglomerate, and Libya's National Oil Corporation, reached an agreement in July 1999 on the development of offshore block NC41 and onshore block NC169. The project is expected to start production at the end of 2003 and will require investment of US$5.5 billion. Infrastructure will be built, enabling other Libyan onshore and offshore reserves to be developed.

Energy

Libya has been self-sufficient in energy since the 1960s. Its electricity generating capacity was 4.6GW in 2000 and power demand is growing rapidly at 6 per cent per annum. During the 1990s, there was a rapid expansion of electricity capacity, with two new 720MW plants being constructed at Zuwara and Zuweitina. The vast majority of electricity is from oil-fired power plants. The government hopes to double generating capacity by 2010 at a cost of US$3.5 billion. In February 2002, Russia's Tekhnopromexport signed a US$600 million deal to build a 650MW power plant. Libya's national transmission grid is linked to Egypt and Tunisia.

Banking

The banking sector is highly centralised and dominated by state-owned banks, many of which were nationalised after Muammar Al-Qadafi seized power in 1969. A banking law passed in 1993 allowed private banks to operate in Libya, but by 2002 there was only one private banking institution operating in Libya.

Central bank

Central Bank of Libya

Main financial centre

Tripoli

Time

GMT plus one hour (GMT plus two hours April–September)

Geography

Libya is the fourth-largest country in Africa. It extends along the Mediterranean coast of North Africa with Tunisia and Algeria to the west, Niger and Chad to the south, Egypt to the east, and Sudan to the south-east. Most of the country is part of the Sahara Desert. Only the narrow coastal strip receives sufficient rainfall to be suitable for agriculture and it is here that 90 per cent of the population live.

Climate

The coastal areas enjoy a temperate Mediterranean climate. Summer (May–September) temperatures are up to 40 degrees Celsius (C), while winter (November–April) temperatures reach 25–32 degrees C during daytime but can fall to 4–5 degrees C at night. Otherwise, with 90 per cent of the country desert, very hot days (to 50 degrees C), cold nights and sandstorms are likely in May–June. There is low rainfall, mainly between October and March in the highlands and semi-desert.

Dress codes

A lightweight suit or jacket and trousers are advised. A tie and a long-sleeved shirt should be worn at business meetings, but a jacket is not essential. Women should dress modestly, covering their arms and knees.

Entry requirements

Passports

Required by all. From 11 December 1981, US passports require a special validation for travel to Libya.

Visa

Visas are required by all except nationals of Algeria, Malta and Mauritania, who require No Objection Certificates. An Arabic translation of the passport holder's particulars is necessary. All visitors must register with authorities on arrival – this is usually taken care of by the hotelier.

Prohibited entry

Nationals of Israel and passport holders with Israeli visas.

Currency advice/regulations

Passengers arriving in Tripoli are required to bring into Libya a minimum of US$500 (this amount can change, so it is advisable to check). This requirement is subject to a border check and the passenger faces possible deportation if the requirement is not met. Import of foreign currency is subject to declaration while export of foreign currency is limited. All currency must be declared.

Traveller's cheques are often hard to cash. Carrying cash is the only realistic option, and the favoured currency is the US dollar. Penalties for the use of unauthorised currency dealers are severe.

Customs

There are strict customs regulations about the import or export of firearms, religious materials, antiquities and medications.

Prohibited imports

Imports of alcohol, pork and certain other items are prohibited.

Health (for visitors)

The hospital with the best reputation is the Oil Clinique-NOC.

Mandatory precautions

Yellow fever and cholera vaccination certificates are required if travelling from infected areas.

Advisable precautions

Visitors should have typhoid and polio vaccinations. Malaria prophylaxis is recommended for visits to certain areas.

Avoid drinking tap water.

It is advisable to pack necessary medication as some medicines may not be available in Libya.

Hotels

Limited availability and usually expensive.

Credit cards

Credit cards are not accepted.

Public holidays

Fixed dates

28 Mar, 11 Jun, 1 Sep, 7 Oct.

Variable dates

Birth of the Prophet, Eid Al-Fitr and Eid Al-Adha, Ascension of Muhammad, Islamic New Year, Ashoura.

Working hours

Friday is the Muslim holy day and all offices, businesses and banks are closed. The oil industry is also closed on Saturday.

Banking

Monday, Wednesday and Saturday: 0730–0800, 1230–1300 and about 1500–1700; Friday: closed. Hours may vary between winter and summer and be reduced during Ramadan.

Business

Saturday–Thursday: 0700–1400 summer, 0730–1430 winter.

Government

Saturday–Thursday: 0700–1400 summer, 0730–1430 winter.

Shops

Shops are mainly open 0800–1800, often closing for a few hours during the middle of the day.

Telecommunications

Telephone/fax

Public telephones are available in post offices. There are 84 landlines per 1,000 people, 94 per 1,000 people in Tripoli.

Postal services

Libya's postal service is often infrequent and there is a relatively high incidence of delivery failure. The suspension of UN sanctions in 1999 resulted in the resumption of airmail services to Libya.

Mobile phones

There is a low userbase of approximately three mobile phones per 1,000 people.

Internet/e-mail

Access to the Internet is extremely limited, often only available to government officials and agencies. As a result of lack of accessibility there are very few service providers (ISPs) in Libya.

Electricity supply

110 or 220V AC

Social customs/useful tips

Alcohol is banned throughout Libya and visitors arriving with alcohol will have it confiscated. Women often do not attend Arab social or business meetings, despite gender equality enshrined in the constitution.

Photography of public buildings and anything of military or security interest is not permitted. It is best to avoid criticism of the country, its leadership or Islam while in Libya since this could potentially result in a heavy-handed response from the authorities.

During Ramadan, eating, drinking and smoking in public is banned throughout the hours of daylight. Islamic and Arab customs prevail and must be respected by visitors. Pork is forbidden by Muslim law. Food is traditionally eaten with the right hand only.

Security

Crime is growing in Libya. The most common crimes are car theft and theft of items left in vehicles. Muggings have occurred on the beaches. Travel to remote areas is best undertaken in groups.

Getting there

Air

National airline: Jamahiriya Libyan Arab Airlines.

International airport/s: Benina International (Code: BEN), 29km from Benghazi; Sebha (Code: SEB), 11km from town; Tripoli International (Code: TIP), 34km from city.

Airport tax: The Tripoli International levies an embarkation tax of LD3 for international departures.

Surface

Road: There are entry points via Tunisia and Egypt by the main coast road, Algeria (via Sabha and Ghat) and Niger and Chad (via Sabha).

Water: There are weekly ferry services from Malta to Tripoli. There also occasional services from Casablanca (Morocco) and Alexandria (Egypt).

Main port/s: Benghazi, Misratah, Marsa Brega and Tripoli (established as a free port in 1999). Libya aims to resuscitate its trading role using the free port as the nucleus for trade between Africa and Europe.

The air embargo led to an expansion of Libya's port facilities.

Getting about

National transport

Air: Travel between western and eastern provinces is generally by air. Libyan Arab Airlines operates a domestic service between main centres.

Road: The road system in Libya is excellent. There is a surfaced road system comprising an estimated 32,000km linking all main centres. The main roads include the 1,820km national coast road from the Tunisian to the Egyptian border, Sabha-Ghat, Tripoli-Sabha, Agedabia-Kufra, Sabha-Chad and Niger borders. The maintenance of rural roads is generally poor and many are unpaved.

Buses: There are services between main centres.

Rail: No commercial railway operates.

City transport

Taxis: Yellow government taxis are generally cheaper than private taxis. It is advisable to negotiate the fare in advance. Taxis are often on a shared basis.

Buses, trams & metro: State-run services operate in Benghazi and Tripoli. They can be unreliable and overcrowded.

Car hire

There are car hire agencies in Tripoli and Benghazi, although rates can be quite high.

BUSINESS DIRECTORY

Telephone area codes

Dialling code for Libya: IDD access code +218, followed by area code (21 for Tripoli, 22 for Tripoli International Airport, 61 for Benghazi) followed by subscriber's number.

Chambers of Commerce

Chamber of Commerce, Trade, Industry and Agriculture for the Eastern Province, PO Box 208, 1286 Benghazi (tel: 94-526).

Chamber of Commerce, Trade, Industry and Agriculture for the Western Province, PO Box 2321, Sharia el-Fatah September, Tripoli (tel: 33-755).

Banking

Libyan Arab Foreign Bank, PO Box 2542, That al-Imad Administrative Complex, Tripoli (tel: 335-0155, 335-0160, 335-0086/7; fax: 335-0164/8).

Sahara Bank, PO Box 270, 10 First of September Street, Tripoli (tel: 333-9804; fax: 333-7922).

Wahda Bank, PO Box 452, Sharia Gamal Abd an-Naser, Benghazi (tel: 222-4122; fax: 222-4122, 222-4709).

Umma Bank Sal, PO Box 685, 1 Giaddat Omar El-Mokhtar Street, Tripoli (tel: 333-4031/35, 444-2541, 444-25 44; fax: 333-2505, 444-2476).

Central bank

Central Bank of Libya, PO Box 1103, Tripoli, Libya (tel: 444-1481/2/3, 333-3591/9; fax: 444-1488).

Other useful addresses

General National Organisation for Industrialisation, PO Box 4388, Tripoli (tel: 44-680, 34-995).

Kufrah & Serir Authority, Council of Agricultural Development, Benghazi.

National Oil Corporation, PO Box 2655, Tripoli (tel: 46-180).

National Trade Union Federation, PO Box 734, Tripoli.

Internet sites

Africa Business Network: http://www.ifc.org/abn

African Development Bank: http://www.afdb.org

Africa Online: http://www.africaonline.com

AllAfrica.com: http://allafrica.com

Libya on the Web: http://www.libyaweb.com/news.htm

Libyans Online: http://www.libyaonline.com

Libyan Mission at United Nations: http://www.un.int/libya/

Azar Libya Travel and Tour Company: http://www.angelfire.com/az/azartours/index.html

Juddaim Tourism Service: http://www.libya-juddaim.com/eng/index.html

Bright Focus: http://www.brightfocus.com/ly

Caravanserai Tours: http://www.caravanserai-tours.com

Madagascar

Dominique Rakotomalala

KEY FACTS

Official name: Repoblikan'i Madagasikara (The Republic of Madagascar)

Head of State: President Marc Ravalomanana (sworn in, 6 May 2002) (recognised as Madagascar's leader by France and the US in Jul 2002; his rival, Didier Ratsiraka, fled with his family to the Seychelles)

Head of government: Prime Minister Jacques Sylla (appointed 16 Jun 2002)

Ruling party: Coalition government, including technocrats (results of Dec 2002 parliamentary elections: President Marc Ravalomanana's Tiako i Madagsikara (TIM) (I Love Madagascar) alliance won 102 seats out of 160 and his allies within the Firaisankinam-Pirenena (FP) (National Union) coalition 23; turnout was 67.6 per cent)

Area: 592,000 square km (the fourth-largest island in the world)

Population: 16.40 million (2001)

Capital: Antananarivo

Official language: Malagasy, French

Currency: Franc Malgache (Mf) = 100 centimes

Exchange rate: Mf5,900.00 per US$ (Feb 2003)

GDP per capita: US$286 (2001)

GDP real growth: 6.70% (2001)

Inflation: 7.00% (2001)

Balance of trade: -US$148.00 million (2001)

Foreign debt: US$4.15 billion (2001)

For the latest Key Facts, go to www.worldinformation.com

At the beginning of 2001, the incumbent President Didier Ratsiraka had reasons to be optimistic about his re-election as president of the Republic of Madagascar. Despite declared candidatures from some members of the opposition, it was widely assumed that he would win the election at the first ballot. In June 2001, the mayor of Antananarivo, Marc Ravalomanana, announced that he would also stand in the presidential election due in December. Ravalomanana, whose background is in the private sector as the owner of the Tiko group of companies, had emerged on the political scene some years before, becoming the mayor of Antananarivo, the capital of Madagascar. From the moment he declared his candidacy for the president's post, it became apparent that there would be no victory in the first round for Ratsiraka. It was the beginning of the political turmoil that would paralyse the island and threaten to ruin the economic progress that had been achieved.

Ratsiraka vs Ravalomanana

Ratsiraka strengthened his position in power after the 18 March 2001 election of the 90-member Senate, the second chamber of the Antenimieram-Pirenena/ Assemblée Nationale (National Assembly). In addition to the 60 senators elected representing Madagascar's six provinces, Ratsiraka appointed 30 additional senators, as provided for by the constitution. The result was that 90 per cent of the senators were members of Ratsiraka's Andry sy Riana Enti-Manavotra an'i Madagasikara (Arema) (Association for the Rebirth of Madagascar), or political friends of the president.

The governors of the provinces were then elected on 12 June. The six elected governors were expectedly close allies of Ratsiraka. Arema also dominated the National Assembly and it was becoming obvious that Ratsiraka was making efforts to ensure his victory by the thorough domination of the political institutions and the administrative apparatus. Ratsiraka himself declared his candidacy for the presidency during the ceremony celebrating independence on 26 June 2001, and although other candidates earlier on declared their intention to stand, there was no doubt then that Ratsiraka would win the first round (the system for the election of the president in Madagascar is similar to that in France, where the elected candidate has to win an absolute majority of the votes by universal franchise).

On 5 August 2001, Marc Ravalomanana announced his candidature. With the help of seven helicopters and freight planes full of T-shirts and baseball caps, Ravalomanana campaigned around the island and mobilised the population; about 80,000 people came to his inaugural campaign at the Mahamasina stadium in Antananarivo. Everybody understood that he was the only candidate who would be able to prevent a victory by Ratsiraka at the first ballot on 16 December 2001, and even possibly beat him.

The official result of the first ballot gave Ravalomanana 46 per cent. But as this was not enough to win, a second ballot was announced for 24 February 2002. However,

Ravalomanana refused to take part and proclaimed himself president on 22 February. Ratsiraka declared a state of emergency and banned further demonstrations. In April, the High Constitutional Court declared that the recount of the December presidential election showed Marc Ravalomanana was the winner with 51.5 per cent of the vote, while Didier Ratsiraka won 35.9 per cent (Ratsiraka did not recognise the result). In Antananarivo, Ravalomanana was sworn in as the president on 6 May and his new government was named on 14 May. Ravalomanana held power in Antananarivo, but the governors of the other provinces remained loyal to Ratsiraka and independent states were declared in Toamasina, Toliara and Mahajanga. Ratsiraka then attempted to form his own government and introduced a fuel blockade against Antananarivo. In June 2002, troops loyal to Ravalomanana ended the blockade and captured the Ratsiraka strongholds. Ravalomanana appointed a new cabinet composed of his supporters and technocrats. Jacques Sylla, the former foreign minister in the Albert Zafy administration in the early 1990s, was installed as prime minister. In July, after the US and France recognised Ravalomanana as Madagascar's president, Ratsiraka and his family fled to the Seychelles. Ravalomanana then authorised the arrest of former government officials and military commanders involved in the blockade and attempt to establish rival governments.

With Ratsiraka's supporters out of the way, Ravolomanana tried to cement his position during the 15 December 2002 parliamentary election. Ravolomanana's Tiako i Madagasikara (TIM) (I Love and Care for Madagascar) alliance emerged as the largest party in the 160-member National Assembly by winning 102 seats. TIM's ally, the Firaisankinam-Pirenena (FP) (National Union), won 23 seats. Other parties, including Arema, won 13 seats between them. There are 22 independents.

General economic performance

Despite distribution imbalances and the lack of good governance, which eventually led to the rejection of Ratsiraka by the voters, overall economic performance in 2001 and 2002 was satisfactory and even won praise from the IMF, which approved in March 2001 US$101 million as part of the Poverty Reduction and Growth Facility (PRGF) initiative. A further US$15 million was approved in December 2002. The IMF commended the new government for the 'decisive actions taken since the middle of 2002 to spur economic activity through a careful prioritisation of public expenditures, faster implementation of externally funded projects, and adoption of measures to boost confidence and encourage the return of private investors'.

The GDP growth rate for 2001 was 6.7 per cent due a rise in agricultural production and a boom in the construction and trade sectors, and export processing companies. Exports were expected to grow by 14 per cent; exports of the textile sector in particular grew by 25 per cent due to the US government's Africa Growth and Opportunity Act (AGOA): during the AGOA forum which took place in the US in October 2001, it emerged that Madagascar's exports to the US grew by 126 per cent.

The results were mixed as far as public finances were concerned: during the first half of 2001, the overall fiscal deficit was less than forecast due to diminishing income from customs duties. This was explained by low consumption of oil products caused by the appreciation of the Franc Malgache (Mf) against the US$ during the first half of 2001. By May 2002, the currency was worth Mf6,510.00 per US$.

The only privatisation that was fully completed in 2001 was the oil company Solitany Madagascar (SOLIMA), which was sold on 8 May 2001 to South Africa's Engen offshore holdings, France's Mascareignes Investissements and Total Outre-Mer as well as Shell Indian Ocean Holding.

The tender for the privatisation of Telecom Malagasy (TELMA) was launched in May 2001 and the offers were opened on 17 December: two offers – France Télécom and Distacom (a company from Mauritius and which already owns the cellular phone company Madacom) – were received. Distacom eventually won the bid, but the process was still incomplete by late 2002 due to the political impasse.

Outlook

The political instability that has prevailed in the wake of the presidential elections has taken its toll on the economy and social conditions in Madagascar. During a conference on the impact of the crisis, the resident mission of UN Development Program (UNDP) announced that the growth rate expected for 2002 would be less than 10 per cent. The World Bank declared in May 2002, that the cost of the crisis amounted to US$600 million.

On the political front, President Ravalomanana has received recognition by the international community, which has relied on the African Union (AU) (formerly the Organisation of African Unity (OAU)) to find a solution for the problems in Madagascar. Even if Ravalomanana brings some stability to Madagascar, economic progress will still be difficult to achieve in the short-term.

Risk assessment

Economic	Poor
Political	Poor
Regional stability	Satisfactory

KEY INDICATORS — Madagascar

	Unit	1996	1997	1998	1999	2000
Population	m	14.20	14.62	15.06	15.51	15.97
Gross domestic product (GDP)	US$bn	4.00	3.50	3.70	3.70	3.90
GDP per capita	US$	281	243	248	240	243
GDP real growth	%	2.1	3.7	4.0	4.6	4.8
Inflation	%	20.8	4.5	6.2	9.9	11.9
Consumer prices	1995=100	119.8	125.1	132.9	146.1	163.7
Exports (fob) (goods)	US$m	509.0	516.0	538.0	584.0	824.0
Imports (fob) (goods)	US$m	629.0	694.0	693.0	742.0	997.0
Balance of trade	US$m	-120.0	-178.0	-154.0	-158.0	-174.0
Current account	US$m	-291.0	-266.0	-301.0	-252.0	-283.0
Foreign debt	US$bn	3.8	3.7	3.3	4.4	4.4
Total reserves minus gold	US$m	240.9	281.6	171.4	227.2	285.2
Foreign exchange	US$m	240.8	281.5	171.3	227.0	285.1
Exchange rate	per US$	4,061.30	5,090.90	5,441.40	6,283.80	6,767.50

COUNTRY PROFILE

Historical profile
1500 The first Europeans landed in Madagascar.
1790s King Andrianampoinimerina unified the Merina tribe which soon became the island's dominant tribe, controlling nearly half of Madagascar.
1820 Britain signed a treaty recognising Madagascar as an independent state under Merina rule.
1890 An Anglo-French treaty gave control of the island to France.
1894 Queen Ranavalona III was forced to abdicate and Madagascar was declared a French colony.
1947 After several decades of growing resentment and resistance to French rule, an insurrection was crushed by France with the loss of several thousand lives.
1960 The Republic of Madagascar (known between 1960–72 as the Malagasy Republic) gained full independence in June. Philibert Tsiranana became president.
1972 Tsiranana was forced from office; he was replaced by General Gabriel Ramantsoa, the army commander.
1975 Ramantsoa was replaced by Colonel Richard Ratsimandrava; within one week he had been killed and a rebel army group announced a military takeover. They, in turn, were quickly defeated by army elements loyal to the ex-president. A new government was installed under Didier Ratsiraka.
1992 Following three years of protests and civil disturbances after Ratsiraka's third presidential election victory, a referendum endorsed a multi-party constitution which enshrined a unitary state and reduced the powers of the president. In the 1992/93 presidential election Ratsiraka was defeated by Albert Zafy.
1997 Didier Ratsiraka beat Albert Zafy in the presidential election, gaining 50.7 per cent of the vote, and was sworn in as president on 9 February.
2000 Elections continued to give Didier Ratsiraka and his party considerable political power.
2001 There was no clear winner in the presidential elections in December.
2002 The constitutional court ordered a recount in January. Supporters of the opposition candidate, Marc Ravalomanana, insisted that he won the first round and they staged a huge protest in Antananarivo. The second round was scheduled for 24 February but Ravalomanana refused to take part and proclaimed himself president on 22 February. Ratsiraka declared a state of emergency including a ban on further demonstrations. Nevertheless, thousands of people jammed the capital. Government officials stated results showed neither Ravalomanana nor Didier Ratsiraka won an outright majority. On 17 April, the disputed presidential election was annulled by the Supreme Court. At the end of April, the High Constitutional Court declared a recount of the December presidential election showed Marc Ravalomanana was the winner with 51.5 per cent of the vote, while Didier Ratsiraka won 35.9 per cent (Ratsiraka did not recognise the result). Ravalomanana held power in the capital, Antananarivo, but the governors of the other provinces remained loyal to Ratsiraka and on 30 April 2002, Governor Jean Robert Gara proclaimed his state, Antsiranana, a 'sovereign state, independent in the confederation of Madagascar'. The governor of Toamasina, Samuel Lahady, proclaimed himself 'head of state of the independent state of Toamasina' on 2 May and on 3 May, the provinces of Toliara and Mahajanga proclaimed independence. In the capital, Marc Ravalomanana was sworn in as president on 6 May; his government was named on 14 May. Meanwhile, Didier Ratsiraka proceeded to form his government, retaining support in rural and coastal areas. However, in June Ratsiraka fled to France. After the resignation on 13 June of the governor of Mahajanga, Étienne Hilaire Razafindehibe, President Marc Ravalomanana's forces took control of Mahajanga and also of Toliara. On 16 June, Ravalomanana dissolved the government and appointed a new prime minister, Jacques Sylla. President Ravalomanana's army took the city of Antsiranana on 2 July.

Political structure
Constitution
A constitutional referendum in September 1995 gave the president the power to appoint or dismiss the prime minister.
Form of state
Republic
The executive
Under the constitution the prime minister is head of government and exercises virtually all executive power. The president is directly elected for five years.
National legislature
Legislative power is vested in a 138-member Antenumierampirenena/Assemblée Nationale (National Assembly), elected for four years by proportional representation. The constitution also provides for a Senate, of which two-thirds of the members are appointed by an electoral college, and the remainder nominated by the president. The mandate of the senators is four years; half of them are elected or appointed every two years.
Last elections
24 February 2002 (second round presidential) – Marc Ravalomanana refused to take part and proclaimed himself president on 22 February; 16 December 2001 (first round presidential).
Next elections
2007 (presidential)

Political parties
Ruling party
Présidentielle (coalition government) dominated by the Andry sy Rihana Enti-Manavotra an'i Madagasikara/Association pour la Renaissance de Madagascar (Arema) (Association for the Rebirth of Madagascar) (government dissolved by President Ravalomanana, 16 Jun 2002).
Main opposition party
In May 1999, former president Albert Zafy announced the Herim Panavotam Pirenena (HPP), an alliance of opposition parties. In 2000, opposition parties not represented in the legislature formed the Cellule de Crise (Crisis Cell) to unite against the ruling coalition.

Population
15.97 million (2000)
Annual population growth rate: 3.1 per cent (2000). Approximately 45 per cent of the total population are under 15 years. Population density: 24 inhabitants per square km. Urban population: 29 per cent (2000).
Ethnic make-up
Madagascar's population is a broad composite of Malayo-Polynesian, Arab and African ethnic groups. The Merinas represent about 26 per cent of the total, while the Betsimisaraka on the east coast account for 15 per cent and the Betsileo 12 per cent. There are some 35,000 Europeans, mainly French nationals, also 35,000 Indians and Pakistanis, and 20,000 Chinese.
Religions
Traditional beliefs (50 per cent), Christianity (about 43 per cent), Islam (7 per cent).

Education
In 1999, illiteracy affected nearly half of the population, of which 61 per cent affected rural areas against one-third from urban areas. It is estimated that 56.5 per cent of women are illiterate with a higher rate among the youngest. Although some improvement has been observed compared to the 1997 situation, nearly half of the school age children are not enrolled in schools, net primary school attendance rate being only 70.1 per cent for the whole country. The majority of those who do not attend school or who are early school leavers come from the poorest sections of the population and those living in rural areas. It has been estimated by

Oxfam that 58 per cent of children age 6–11 will enrol for school in 2015. Between 1995 and 1999, public expenses in education were increased from 8.7 per cent to 18.3 per cent of total budgetary expenses and from 1.5 per cent to 3 per cent of GDP. Higher education expenses amount to only 0.5 per cent of GDP.

Health

Life expectancy at birth is estimated at 57.5 years, although nearly one-third of the population's life expectancy is below the age of 40. The maternal mortality rate is typically 488 per 100,000 live births. The infant mortality rate is typically 94 per 1,000 live births. The child-juvenile mortality rate is 164 per 1,000 live births. In some areas, malnutrition levels among children under five have risen by up to 45 per cent as a result of the crisis that has gripped the country following the presidential elections held in December 2001. Vaccination facilities remain poor with 32.4 per cent of children completing vaccination before their first year of age. More than three-quarters of the people have no access to drinking water. The government has a national AIDS policy that covers all economic sectors. Households allocate only 2.4 per cent of their expenses in health care. Besides, about 60 per cent of the population live within 5km of or about one hour's walk from a public health centre. On average one doctor is in charge of approximately 10,000 people and most health officers work in urban areas.

Although health care expenses have increased from 3.4 per cent to 7.6 per cent of the total public expenses on average between 1995 and 1999. the percentage in relation to GDP has risen from 0.6 per cent to 1.2 per cent.

Welfare

As the political deadlock in Madagascar continues to isolate the newly declared president in Antananarivo, the economic conditions have worsened, with thousands of people losing their jobs. Aid agencies have warned of an impending humanitarian crisis as the price of essential commodities in the capital increases. The United Nations World Food Programme (WFP) in June 2002 had stepped in to assist the urban poor. WFP had started emergency food distribution to help feed 35,000 malnourished children in the capital.

Main cities

Antananarivo, capital, and principal business centre (population 1.5 million in 2002); Toamasina (Tamatave), on the east coast, the island's main port and the centre of the main area for producing cloves (169,000); Antsirabe (150,000); Mahajanga (Majunga), the west coast's main port (130,000); Fianarantsoa, a rich agricultural region (130,000); Antsiranana (formerly Diégo-Suarez), port in the extreme north of the island (43,000); Toliara (formerly Tuléar), port on the south-west coast (36,000).

Languages spoken

French is the usual business language and the medium for all documentation.
Very little English is spoken.

Official language/s

Malagasy, French

Media

Press

Dailies: The 1990 law on press freedom was followed by a boom in privately-owned newspapers and encouraged more critical political reporting by the print media. Daily newspapers in French include the privately owned *Midi Madagasikara* and *Madgascar Tribune* and the Antananarivo daily *L'Express de Madagascar*. Other popular dailies are *Gazetiko* and *Maresaka*.

Weeklies: Weeklies include a Roman Catholic publication *Lakroa* (Cross) covering rural and remote areas and a bi-weekly *Telo Nohorefy*. *Dans les media demain* (In The Media Tomorrow) is a privately-owned Antananarivo weekly news digest with a large circulation in the Madagascan diaspora. *Feon'ny Merina* (Voice of the Merina) promotes the interests of Merina people of Malay origin.

Periodicals: Monthly magazines are *Jureco* and the news magazine *Revue de l'Ocean indien* covering other Indian Ocean islands.

Broadcasting

State monopoly of radio and television has been abolished. Radio-Télévision-Antenne 2 Malagasy (RTM) and Radio Madagasikara broadcast in Malagasy and French. There are several private stations as well as state radio and television.

Radio: *Echo du Capricorne* is a weekly radio broadcast dealing with Madagascar in general, presented in both Malagasy and French.

Economy

Madagascar is the fourth-largest island in the world and covers a land area larger than France, Netherlands, Belgium and Luxembourg put together. Agriculture is the predominant sector in the economy, although the government has led moves to diversify into export processing, particularly in the textile sector.

The environment for foreign investors is improving. Foreign exchange has been liberalised, import licences removed and some state monopolies ended. The planned privatisation of state industries should provide opportunities for investment, including telecommunications, petroleum distribution and Air Madagascar. However, much of the population is resistant to IMF calls for the privatisation of utilities such as water, which they fear could see prices spiral thereby entailing further impoverishment. The opening up of the Malagasy economy should also generate niche opportunities in aid-funded areas such as infrastructure, education, health, mining/energy, tourism, agriculture (including cotton and non-traditional exports) and consumer goods.

To tackle poverty, the government plans to foster high economic growth by moving towards exports and labour intensive industries, boosting manufacturing and services and greatly increasing agricultural output.

Over 70 per cent of the population live in poverty. Floods and cyclones in 2000 left some 500,000 people homeless.

The IMF and the International Development Association (IDA) agreed to support a debt-reduction package under the enhanced Heavily Indebted Poor Countries (HIPC) Initiative in December 2000 worth around US$1.5 billion. This was accompanied by a 90 per cent reduction in debt owed to the Paris Club of creditors, agreed in March 2001. Also in March, the IMF approved a US$103 million loan under the country's three-year Poverty Reduction and Growth Facility (PRGF), due to run until 2003. The objectives of the PRGF are GDP growth of 6 per cent, inflation of 5 per cent, an increase in international reserves to cover three months of imports and a reduction in the current account deficit to an average of 7.5 per cent GDP. To do this, the IMF has ordered a reduction in the fiscal deficit, exchange rate flexibility and continued privatisation of state assets.

The political situation has led to a multitude of job losses estimated at around 150,000. Foreign investment has declined considerably and many manufacturing companies have closed. In 2002, a two-month blockade organised by supporters of Ratsiraka and soldiers starved the capital, Antananarivo of essential goods.

External trade

Regular trade and current account deficits are largely financed by aid flows and external borrowing.

Exports

Principal exports are prawns, coffee, vanilla, cotton, sugar and cloves.

Main destinations: France (35.4 per cent of 2000 total), US (18.3 per cent), Germany (6.7 per cent), Indonesia (5 per cent), Singapore (5 per cent).

Imports
Prior authorisation and an import permit are no longer required. However, control and inspection of goods with FOB value above US$5,000 are obligatory.
Principal imports are capital goods, food, raw materials, consumer goods and fuel products.
Main sources: France (29.2 per cent of 2000 total), Mauritius (9.3 per cent), China (8.7 per cent), Hong Kong (8.5 per cent), South Africa (5.4 per cent).

Agriculture
The agricultural sector dominates the economy. It contributes around 32 per cent to GDP and employs 75 per cent of the working population. Madagascar has a wide range of soil types.
Main cash/export crops are prawns, coffee, cotton, cloves and vanilla, production of which has fluctuated due to recurrent droughts and cyclones. Vanilla used to be the country's main export crop but high local taxes and increased competition from Indonesia and Mexico has inhibited the vanilla sector. In 2000, coffee production was 64,200 tonnes, higher than in recent years. However, depressed world commodity prices continue to plague the sector.
Main food crops are rice, maize, bananas and sweet potatoes. Groundnuts, pineapples, coconuts and sugar are also grown, mostly for internal use. The decline in coffee prices led to many growers switching production to rice, increasing production by 5 per cent, and making Madagascar self-sufficient in rice (the staple diet of the country) for the first time since the mid-1970s, with annual production at around 2.5 million tonnes per year.
Divestiture of vanilla, cotton and sugar parastatals is expected to encourage greater foreign investment.
The potential future development of the cotton industry is of particular interest, as it may supply the growth in the textile trade being promoted by companies from Mauritius and elsewhere.
The livestock sector is dominant in the west and south of the country.

Fishing
Since 1996, prawns have been the number one export earner, with 7,000 tonnes of prawn exports earning revenues of US$63 million per annum.

Forestry
Only 15 per cent of Madagascar's ancient forest remains. Deforestation has left the hills exposed to the wind and rain which strips away the soil. Forest preservation and the creation of national parks are receiving large-scale international support.

Industry and manufacturing
The industrial sector contributes around 12 per cent of GDP and employs around 9 per cent of the workforce.
Industry is dominated by food processing and the manufacture of textiles for the domestic market. Other major sectors include rice milling, sugar refining, distilling, oil-seed crushing, meat, fruit and vegetable canning, processing of cashew nuts, fruit juices, milk products and jams, cigarettes, soap and rope manufacturing, cotton spinning and brewing. Major capital-intensive industries are oil refining, fertiliser and cement production.
There are 150 firms based in industrial free zones, representing mainly textiles, food processing and information technology, and creating 6,000 jobs in the Antananarivo area alone. Many textile companies in Mauritius are relocating to Madagascar due to the cheaper labour rates.
Under the US government's Africa Growth and Opportunity Act (AGOA), Madagascar expects the textile sector to expand, creating 70,000 new jobs between 2001–06.

Tourism
Construction of new hotels is planned as well as modernisation and refurbishment of existing ones. In 2002, the government was in the process of creating special investment zones to facilitate investment in the ecotourism sector.

Environment
Madagascar has plants and wildlife found nowhere else on earth, and growth of both tourism and mining needs to be controlled to protect the fragile environment.

Mining
Excluding gold and gem production by artisinal miners, mining contributes around less than 1 per cent of GDP and employs 1 per cent of the workforce. If the informal sector is included, the contribution to GDP is around 3 per cent.
Madagascar is rich in mineral resources, although it is still only a minor mineral producer by regional standards. There are sizeable deposits of a number of minerals, industrial ores and precious and semi-precious gemstones including chrome ore, mica, graphite, gold, bauxite, uranium, iron ore, ilmenite/titanium, quartz, nickel, copper, lead, platinum, labradorite, rock-crystal, rhodolite, marble, garnets, emeralds, rubies and sapphires. There are known deposits containing 100 million tonnes of bauxite and 400 million tonnes of iron ore, although these have not been developed due to the country's poor infrastructure.
Only chrome, mica and graphite have been exploited to any great extent, and export earnings from these are limited due to lack of demand. The world's largest known emerald cluster was discovered in Madagascar in 1996.
Small quantities of semi-precious stones (garnets and amethysts) are mined for export.
Madagascar is the world's tenth largest chromite producer. The state-owned Société Kraomita Malagasy (Kraoma) is Madagascar's main chromite producer. It extracts around 40 000 tonnes of concentrates and 80,000 tonnes of lumpy ore per year from the Andriamana complex and a further 20,000 tonnes from the Behandrinana mine.
Madagascar produces between 3–4 tonnes per year (tpy) of gold, mainly from the artisinal sector which includes 100,000 individual miners and small synidates. Although the government tolerates this form of mining, it is worried about its ecological effects which include a high level of mercury being leaked into streams and rivers.
The country also produces graphite, 66 per cent of which comes from the Gallois mine. It exports up to 15,000tpy, mostly to UK, US and Germany.

Hydrocarbons
There is confirmation that oil and gas reserves exist in Madagascar, but the island has been overlooked by prospectors and developers.
Madagascar relies on imported oil, some of which is refined for re-export. Typically, Madagascar imports around 4,600 barrels per day (bpd) of refined oil and 4,200bpd of crude oil, of which 370bpd is then re-exported after refinement.
There is one oil refinery at Tamatave, with an initial capacity of 14,400bpd, although capacity has fallen since it was struck by a hurricane in 1994. The oil distribution infrastructure is in desperate need of repair.
There are identified reserves of around 100 million tonnes of good quality coal. However, exploitation and investment is deterred by poor infrastructure around the location of the deposits.

Energy
The majority of the country's energy needs are supplied by imported fuel.
Besides fuelwood, hydropower is the main domestic energy source. Some mines and factories have their own small diesel or stream-powered generators. Construction of the country's second dam, at Ankorahotra, has been suspended pending evaluation of the oil fields.

Banking
Central bank
Banque Centrale de la République Malgache

Time
GMT plus three hours

Geography
The Democratic Republic of Madagascar comprises the island of Madagascar, the fourth-largest in the world, and several much smaller offshore islands, in the western Indian Ocean, about 500km (300 miles) east of Mozambique, in southern Africa.

Climate
Tropical, cooler in highlands. The summer period spans the months of November to April. Numerous areas have their own micro-climates – the highlands are subject to mild freshness in the winter, while the eastern parts of the island experience high temperatures and humidity, with barren and arid conditions dominating the western sector.
In Antananarivo hottest month December (15–28 degrees Celsius), coldest July (9–19 degrees Celsius). Wettest month (January). Winter in the capital lasts from April to October, when it is both cold and dry.
Madagascar falls within the cyclone belt and cyclones tend to occur during the rainy season December–March, which is hot. It is rainy until June or July on the east coast and is hotter throughout the year. It is drier but hotter on the west coast.

Dress codes
In Antananarivo, in the winter months, normal weight clothing is suitable, with a woollen sweater/cardigan recommended. In the summer men should wear tropical suits and women, cotton dresses. On the coast, tropical clothing is recommended all year round.

Entry requirements
Passports
Required by all. Passports must be valid for six months of visa issue date.
Visa
Required by all. Visas can be obtained from foreign consulates upon request and on presentation of flight tickets.
Currency advice/regulations
Local currency: up to Mf5,000 may be imported and exported.
No limit on import of foreign currency, but amounts over Mf50,000 in value must be declared on arrival, and export is allowed up to the declared amount.

Health (for visitors)
Mandatory precautions
Yellow fever vaccination certificate required if arriving from an infected area.
Advisable precautions
Typhoid, polio, tetanus and hepatitis A vaccinations recommended. Malaria risk exists throughout the country and prophylaxis is necessary. There is a rabies risk. Water precautions should be taken.

Hotels
Good hotels are available in Antananarivo, Toamasina, Nosy Be, Ste Marie and Taolanaro. A service charge is added to bills at some hotels. Discretionary tipping is usual.

Credit cards
Credit cards are of limited use in Madagascar and few establishments accept them.

Public holidays
Fixed dates
1 Jan (New Year's Day), 8 Mar (International Women's Day), 29 Mar (Commemoration Day – 1947), 1 May (Labour Day), 25 May (OAU Day), 26 Jun (National Day), 15 Aug (Assumption Day), 1 Nov (All Saints' Day), 25 Dec (Christmas Day).
Variable dates
Easter Monday, Ascension Day, Whit Monday.

Working hours
Banking
Mon–Fri: 0800–1500.
Business
Mon–Fri: 0800–1630.
Government
Mon–Fri: 0800–1200, 1400–1800.
Shops
Mon–Fri: 0800–1200, 1400–1800.

Telecommunications
Telephone/fax
Dialling code for Madagascar: IDD access code + 261 followed by area code (2 for Antananarivo, 8 for Antseranana (formerly Diégo-Suarez), 7 for Fianarantsoa, 5 for Toamasina (Tamatave), followed by subscriber's number.
Postal services
Air mail is advised. Surface mail can take between three and four months.

Electricity supply
110 or 220V AC, 50 cycles; also 380V AC, 50 cycles.

Getting there
Air
National airline: Air Madagascar (Société Nationale Malgache de Transports Aériens); 3.48 per cent owned by Air France.
International airport/s: Antananarivo (Code: TNR), 14km southeast of city; restaurant, currency exchange.
Airport tax: None. Any departure tax is usually included in the price of the ticket.
Surface
Water: There are few scheduled sea passages.
Main port/s: Toamasina (Tamatave), on the east coast, is the island's main port. It is used by numerous foreign shipping lines. Mahajanga (Majunga) is the west coast's main port. Antseranana (formerly Diégo-Suarez) is in the extreme north of the island, and Toliara (formerly Tuléar) is on the south-west coast.

Getting about
National transport
Air: Ivato airport caters for more than 60 domestic air routes on Air Madagascar and TAM airlines. There are connections between all major towns, apart from Antsirabe, operated by Air Madagascar. Air travel is the most used and generally recommended form of transport. There are over 100 airfields on the island, although many are just airstrips.
Road: Generally poor and in need of repair, and only passable in good weather (the dry season).
Three main roads leave Antananarivo – (RN4) to Mahajanga (Majunga), (RN2) to Toamasina (Tamatave), and the plateau route south to Fianarantsoa (RN7).
Rail: Two classes; light refreshments may be available; air-conditioning available on first-class trains.
Routes are: between Toamasina and Antsirabe, via Antananarivo, incorporating a connection between Moramanga and Lake Alaotra; and between Fianarantsoa and Manakara on the east coast. Daily services operate on most routes.
City transport
Taxis: Flat fare system for short journeys in most towns, otherwise by negotiation; tipping is not usual.
Car hire
Available in main centres. International driving licence required.

BUSINESS DIRECTORY

Telephone area codes
The international dialling code (IDD) for Madagascar is +261 followed by area code (20 for Antananarivo).

Useful telephone numbers
Police: 17

Fire: 18

Ambulance: 2235-753

Chambers of Commerce
Fédération des Chambres de Commerce, d'Industrie et d'Agriculture de Madagascar, BP 166, Antananarivo (tel: 2221-567).

Banking
BNOI (linked with Banque Nationale de Paris), PO Box 25 bis, 101 Antananarivo (tel: 2234-609; fax: 2234-610).

Bank of Africa-Madagascar, PO Box 183, 2 Place de L'Independance, Antananarivo

101 (tel: 2239-100/ 2239-250, 2223-641; fax: 2229-408).

Banque SBM Madagascar, 1 Rue Andrianary Ratianarivo Antsahavola, Antananarivo 101 (tel: 2266-607/ 2266-646-47; fax: 2266-608).

BFV-Société Générale, PO Box 196, 14 Lalana Jeneraly Rabehevitra, Antananarivo 101 (tel: 2220-691; fax: 2234-554).

BNI-Crédit Lyonnais Madagascar, PO Box 174, 74 Rue du 26 Juin 1960, Antananarivo 101 (tel: 228-00/239-51; fax: 337-49).

Investco Southern Investment Bancorp, PO Box 8510, Immeuble NIAG, 8 Lalana Rainizanabololona, Antanimena, Antananarivo 101 (tel: 2264-820/ 2229-114; fax: 2261-329).

Union Commercial Bank SA, PO Box 197, 77 Rue Solombavambahoaka Frantsay, Antsahavola, Antananarivo 101 (tel: 2227-262; fax: 2228-740/ 2232-282).

Central bank

Banque Centrale de la République Malgache, avenue de la Révolution Socialiste Malgache, BP 550, Antananarivo (tel: 2221-751; fax: 2234-532).

Travel information

Air Madagascar (Société Nationale Malgache de Transports Aériens), BP 437, 31 Avenue de l'Indépendance, Analakely, Antananarivo 101 (tel: 2222-222, 2222-200; fax: 2233-760, 2225-728); Ivato Airport, Antananarivo (tel: 2244-222, ext 5200).

Air Mauritius, 77 lalana Solombavabahoaka, Frantsay, Antsahavola, Antananarivo (tel: 2235-900; fax: 2235-773).

Ministry of tourism

Direction du Tourisme de Madagascar, Tsimbazaza, BP 610, Antananarivo (tel: 2226-298).

National tourist organisation offices

Maison du Tourisme de Madagascar (Madagascar Tourist Office), Place de l'Indépendance, Antaninarenina, PO Box 3224, Antananarivo (tel: 2232-529; fax: 2232-537).

Ministries

Ministry of Private Sector Development and Privatisation, Comité de Privatisation, Zone III 1er étage, Ampefiloha, Antananarivo (fax: 2260-138).

Ministry of Tourism, PO Box 610, Tsimbazaza, Antananarivo (tel: 2226-298).

Ministry of Transport and Meteorology, Anosy, Antananarivo (tel: 2224-604, 2222-719).

Other useful addresses

Agence Nationale d'Information 'Taratra' (ANTA), 3 rue du R P Callet, BP 386, Antananarivo (tel: 2221-171).

Association des Agences de Voyages de Madagascar, BP 541, Antananarivo (tel: 2222-364).

Association of the Hotel Industry of Madagascar (SIHM), c/o Sofitrans – Soarano, Antananarivo (tel: 2222-330).

British Embassy, Commercial Section, First Floor, Immeuble 'Ny Havana', Cité des 67 Ha, BP 167, 101 Antananarivo (tel: 2227-749, 2227-370; fax: 2226-690).

Civil Aviation Management, Antananarivo (tel: 2227-715).

Comité de Privatisation, Secrétariat Technique á la Privatisation Immeuble FIARO, Zone III 1er étage, Ampefiloha, 101 Antananarivo (fax: 2260-138).

Customs Services, Ivato Airport, Antananarivo (tel: 2244-032).

Institut National de Géodésie et Cartographie/FTM, BP 323, Antananarivo (tel: 2222-935).

Institut National de la Statistique et de la Recherche Economique (DGBDE), Direction Générale, BP 485, Antananarivo (tel: 2221-652).

Madagascan Embassy (US), 2374 Massachusetts Avenue, NW, Wasghington DC 20008 (tel: 265-5525; fax: 265-3034; e-mail: malagasy@embassy.org).

Office Militaire National pour les Industries Stratégiques (monitors major industrial projects), 21 Lalana Razanakombana, Antananarivo.

Réseau National des Chemins de Fer, BP 259, Soarano, Antananarivo (tel: 2220-521).

Société d'Etude et de Réalisation pour le Développement Industriel, BP 3180, Antananarivo (tel: 2221-335).

Syndicat de l'Industrie Hôteliére de Madagascar, BP 341, Antananarivo (tel: 2220-202).

Internet sites

Africa Business Network: http://www.ifc.org/abn

African Development Bank: http://www.afdb.org

Africa News Online: http://www.allafrica.com

Africa Online: http://www.africaonline.com

Harambee Afrika (UK business club for traders with east, central and southern Africa; includes annotated web resource list): http://www.harambee.co.uk

Mbendi AfroPaedia (information on companies, countries, industries and stock exchanges in Africa): http://mbendi.co.za

Malawi

Anver Versi

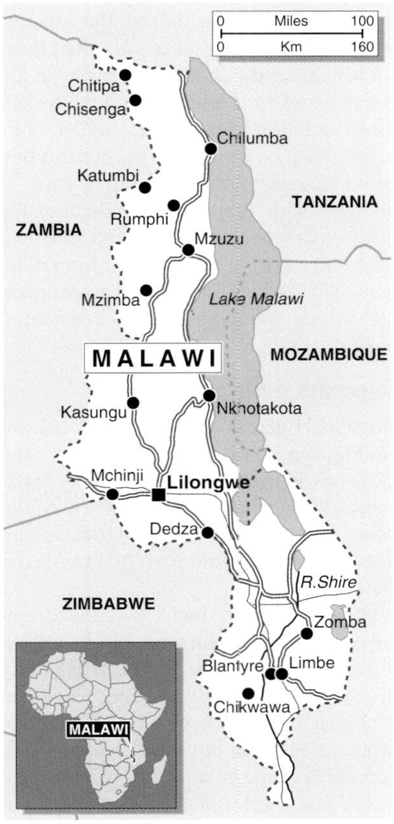

It has never rained in Malawi since the late 1990s, but it has poured – literally and figuratively. Floods in 2001, destructive dry spells and unseasonably heavy downpours in 2002 all conspired to knock the country's agricultural output totally off-balance so that by mid-2002 most of Malawi was dependent on food aid for survival. In February, the government declared a 'state of disaster' and appealed for help. International donors chose this period to put the squeeze on the government of President Bakili Muluzi and withheld millions of dollars of budgetary support aid. The Danish aid agency abruptly upped and left the country, throwing several key education and health projects into complete chaos.

Inflation was 27.2 per cent in 2001 and the Malawi kwacha continued to lose ground against the US$ – in February 2002 alone, it fell from an already low K68 per US$ to K77, making food imports prohibitively expensive and undermining industrial expansion programmes. With the World Bank, the IMF and international donors poring over the national accounts with a magnifying glass, the Malawi government found itself in the awkward position of having to admit that it had overspent its 2001/02 budget of K42 billion (US$600 million) by at least a couple of billion kwacha.

Fiscal discipline falters

Promises by the finance minister, Friday Jumbe, that the government was about to launch a new regime of fiscal discipline by limiting trips of government officials and not repeating such *faux pas* as purchasing fleets of Mercedes saloons for all 39 ministers seemed to convince nobody.

In April 2002, with the government already having had to borrow heavily to pay salaries and settle domestic debts, President Muluzi launched yet another ambitious and costly programme: he unveiled the comprehensive Malawi Poverty Reduction Strategy Paper (MPRSP). He had little choice. This was the first of many slippery steps if the country is to gain unqualified relief on US$2.5 billion foreign debt under the enhanced Heavily Indebted Poor Countries (HIPC) initiative. In May 2002, the president claimed that the IMF was responsible for his government's decision to sell off maize reserves, exacerbating the country's famine. The IMF strongly denied this and claimed the government's judgement on the level of agricultural output had been to blame. Nevertheless, the IMF approved US$23 million in emergency credit in September 2002 to increase imports as a food shortage loomed.

After almost 30 years of iron rule under Kamuzu Banda's dictatorship, Malawi is still struggling to come to terms with multi-party democracy. The ruling United Democratic Front (UDF) party, which won the 1999 elections with an uncomfortably narrow margin (52 per cent), has consolidated its position mainly as a result of damaging and often violent splits among the opposition parties. The UDF stepped up its campaign to amend the

KEY FACTS

Official name: Dziko la Malawi (The Republic of Malawi)

Head of State: President Bakili Muluzi (UDF) (since 1994; re-elected in 1999)

Head of government: President Bakili Muluzi

Ruling party: United Democratic Front (UDF) (since 1994; re-elected Jun 1999)

Area: 118,484 square km

Population: 11.40 million (2001)

Capital: Lilongwe

Official language: English, Chichewa

Currency: Kwacha (K) = 100 tambala

Exchange rate: K86.91 per US$ (Jan 2003)

GDP per capita: US$165 (2001); US$186 (2002)*

GDP real growth: -1.50% (2001); 1.0% (2002)*

Inflation: 27.20% (2001); 18.5% (2002)*

Balance of trade: -US$125.00 million (2001)

Foreign debt: US$2.73 billion (2001)

Annual FDI: US$28.00 million (2001)

* estimated figure

For the latest Key Facts, go to www.worldinformation.com

constitution and allow Muluzi to stand for a third term in 2004, leading to fears that the country might be slipping back to the detested one-party system.

The only silver lining was that when tobacco auctions opened in Lilongwe and Limbe early in April 2002. Burley – which is the most important of six types of tobacco grown in Malawi – fetched the highest price of the past three years. However, large scale smuggling of the tobacco crop to Mozambique and Zambia cost the exchequer billions of kwacha.

Personality politics

The first half of 2002 was dominated by deteriorating relations with international donors, including the ugly row with Denmark. Malawi was accused of financial indiscipline, misuse of funds, a lack of transparency and inability to check corruption. Denmark added 'political intolerance, weak governance and interference with the judiciary' in its list of grievances.

On the domestic front, old habits die hard and Malawi's main political parties still seem bent on a winner-takes-all attitude. Since the advent of pluralism in 1992, there have been a bewildering series of alliances made and broken and major leadership splits within the main opposition parties – the Malawi Congress Party (MCP) and the Alliance for Democracy (Aford).

With little or no ideological or policy differences between the parties, the power struggle is largely regionally and ethnically based. The cult of personality, taken to extreme limits under Banda's dictatorship, still underlines political tactics.

Aford president, Chakufwa Chihana, having once again dissolved an opposition alliance with the MCP, sought to mend fences with the ruling UDF by calling for a 'government of national unity' and hinted that he would not oppose moves to amend the constitution and allow Muluzi to stand for a third term of office. This split his party and in March 2002 there were pitched battles between his supporters and a faction led by party vice president Du Mhango at the party's heartland in Karonga in Malawi's northern region.

Taking advantage of the in-fighting among the opposition, the UDF stepped up its campaign to amend the constitution and allow Muluzi to stand for yet another term as both party and national president in 2004. Although publicly both the government and party said there were no moves to amend the constitution, they nevertheless insisted that it was a matter of debate and that if both party and country felt Muluzi should stand in 2004, they would be powerless to oppose such strong sentiments. Observers took this as an early signal that at some point in 2003, parliament would be asked to vote on the amendment. Given the opposition's fickleness, the chances of Bakili Muluzi taking office again after the 2004 elections appear high.

In early 2001, the Catholic church challenged Muluzi's rule. In a letter, signed by all seven Catholic bishops in Malawi, the church warned that Malawi was slipping back into a one-party state and took the government to task over several issues. It was a similar letter in 1992 that finally tilted the political balance against Banda and brought his dictatorial era to an end.

The bishops said that there was a declining respect for life, disregard for the rule of law, an unfair judiciary, police brutality and a blurring of the separation of power between the legislative, the executive and the judiciary. They blamed the government for not having taken sufficient measures to avert the shortage of maize in the country and for not doing enough to halt the devastating march of HIV/AIDS. They insisted that no changes to the constitution could be made without a referendum.

Faced with this direct challenge, the government backed down and Clement Stambuli, the minister of information, who had earlier started the amendment ball rolling, quickly withdrew to a neutral position.

Denmark pulls out

Denmark's decision to curtail all aid, including on-going project support, and close down its embassy by end-May 2002, came as a severe shock, not only to Malawians, but to some 36 other African countries that have come to rely heavily on Danish aid.

Malawi officials insist that the disengagement came following the expulsion of Danish ambassador, Orla Bakdal, early in 2002 for allegedly calling President Muluzi a 'fat pig'. There is little doubt that Bakdal had made himself thoroughly unpopular with the government when he had insisted on a series of audits into the use of aid money. There were allegations that some K10 million (US$140,000) allocated to resolving inter-party conflicts had been misappropriated and that the trail was leading dangerously close to people in very high positions.

Although Denmark, which contributes 1 per cent of its GDP to development aid, is still the most generous donor per capita in the world, in November 2001, a new centre-right Danish government slashed 10 per cent of development aid worldwide in an attempt to bolster the domestic health service. At the beginning of 2002, it was clear that countries would have to be on their best behaviour if they were to avoid cuts.

A number of Danish embassies around the world (including in Eritrea and Zimbabwe) were closed down, but programmes entered into with the respective governments will continue to be honoured up to and including 2005.

KEY INDICATORS — Malawi

	Unit	1996	1997	1998	1999	2000
Population	m	10.14	10.44	10.74	11.03	11.31
Gross domestic product (GDP)	US$bn	2.40	2.60	1.80	1.80	1.50
GDP per capita	US$	248	263	186	176	150
GDP real growth	%	7.3	3.8	2.0	4.0	1.7
Inflation	%	37.6	9.2	29.8	44.8	29.6
Consumer prices	1995=100	137.6	150.2	194.9	282.4	365.6
Industrial production	1995=100	103.6	102.7	106.3	90.3	89.6
Exports (fob) (goods)	US$m	436.0	567.0	509.0	447.0	431.0
Imports (fob) (goods)	US$m	352.0	783.0	677.0	673.0	600.0
Balance of trade	US$m	84.0	-216.0	-168.0	-226.0	-169.0
Current account	US$m	-271.0	-318.0	-289.0	-308.0	-260.0
Foreign debt	US$bn	2.4	2.3	2.3	2.6	2.5
Total reserves minus gold	US$m	225.7	162.2	269.7	250.6	246.9
Foreign exchange	US$m	221.2	159.2	259.8	247.2	243.5
Exchange rate	per US$	15.31	16.44	31.07	44.09	59.54

Malawi, which received considerable extra resources from the Danish Mifrifesta (loosely translated as 'environment and peace') project, in addition to the normal development aid, seemed to have been singled out for special treatment because the Danes claimed the government had made no attempt to control the corruption that had been eating into development funds. As a result, Malawi stood to lose a large proportion of the US$87 million in aid granted for the period 2001–04.

Economy

Malawi's GDP growth rose from 1.7 per cent in 2000 to 2.8 per cent in 2001. Projections of a 3.8 per cent growth in 2002 looked highly optimistic given a very poor agricultural season and the suspension of foreign aid. By the end of 2002, analysts were predicting that GDP growth would only be around 1 per cent. Inflation had been beaten down to 27.2 per cent in 2001 from highs of almost 50 per cent in 1999, but was still way over the 10 per cent target set by former finance minister Mathews Chikaonda. The prime lending rate in April 2002 was around 46 per cent with few prospects of a reduction given the government's heavy borrowing to offset a massive budget deficit.

Malawi is the second largest producer of tobacco in Africa after Zimbabwe and early tobacco auction prices (beginning April 2002) were encouraging. The new finance minister, Friday Jumbe – who replaced Chikaonda in March much to the chagrin of the international community – warned against reading too much into the early rally in prices. Tobacco traditionally accounts for around 70 per cent of export earnings. It sustains some 6,400 estates and around 70,000 smallholders. Poor tobacco prices since 1999 have forced many smallholders to switch to other cash crops.

Malawi is also Africa's second largest producer of tea, most of it grown on large commercial estates, but world demand for the dominant Indochinese variety has been falling. Adverse weather conditions indicated that the 2002 crop would be both smaller and poorer in quality.

Outlook

Despite the country's considerable potential in agriculture and agro-processing, Malawi remains one of the poorest countries in the world. At the heart of Malawi's economic recovery is the MPRSP, which was launched in April 2002. Implementation of the strategy will be monitored for one year before the country can expect relief on US$2.5 billion foreign debt under the HIPC initiative. Jubilee 2000, the anti-debt campaign, estimates that for every US dollar given to Malawi in aid grants, it has paid US$0.39 in debt servicing. As a percentage of output, spending on debt has been twice the level of health expenditure.

Even in the best of circumstances, implementation of the MPRSP would be difficult; only 24 countries worldwide have reached 'decision point' under the HIPC initiative but only four – Bolivia, Mozambique, Tanzania and Uganda – have actually qualified for debt forgiveness. In 2000, after an 'interim' MPRSP, Malawi qualified for debt relief of US$40 million. If Malawi can qualify for relief for its US$2.5 billion, it might have a realistic chance of breaking out of the poverty cycle.

In the meantime, Malawi faces the daunting task of persuading international donors such as Britain (which withheld a £122 million (US$170 million) aid package), the IMF (which was refusing to part with US$47 million from a US$55 million three-year poverty reduction and growth facility) and the EU to resume the flow of aid.

Risk assessment

Economic	Poor
Political	Poor
Regional stability	Poor

COUNTRY PROFILE

Historical profile

In the eighth century the Bantu people of Nyasaland began trading with Portuguese merchants on the east African coast.

1891 The British declared the area a protectorate and in the wake of David Livingstone's explorations, an increasing number of Europeans went to Nyasaland, particularly missionaries. The settlers expropriated land and imposed taxes which led to ever growing numbers of Africans working in settler plantations or emigrating to the then Rhodesia or South Africa.

1950s Opposition to colonial rule, which had begun in the southern highlands, became more widespread. The Nyasaland African Congress was established to oppose the planned Central African Federation (CAF) with Northern and Southern Rhodesia, and the heavy-handed interference by white settlers in traditional agricultural methods.

1954 The Nyasaland African Congress grew rapidly upon the return from Britain of Dr Hastings Kamuzu Banda; within a year the colonial authorities had jailed him and other leaders.

1961 The authorities released Dr Banda and invited him to London for a constitutional conference, at which Nyasaland was promised eventual independence regardless of constitutional developments in the rest of the CAF. Elections followed, which Dr Banda's Malawi Congress Party (MCP) won.

1963 The CAF was officially dissolved, paving the way for independence in Nyasaland a year later, with Dr Banda as Prime Minister.

1966 Nyasaland became a republic and was renamed Malawi; Dr Banda became president.

1971 Banda declared himself president-for-life.

1978 Dr Banda and the MCP won the first election since independence.

1992 A letter by Catholic bishops condemning the government sparked mass demonstrations against the Banda regime and all non-humanitarian aid to the country was cut off.

1993 A referendum was held to choose between a multi-party system or the existing one-party system; the multi-party option won comfortably and political parties began to develop.

1994 At the multi-party legislative and presidential elections held in May, the United Democratic Front (UDF) beat the MCP and the newly established Alliance for Democracy (Aford). Bakili Muluzi, leader of the UDF, became president, replacing Dr Banda.

1995 Banda was put on trial for ordering the murder of three government ministers but was acquitted, later apologising for any suffering he may have 'unknowingly caused.'

1999 President Muluzi retained power after the elections on 15 June.

2000 Corruption scandals which began to threaten aid flow forced Muluzi to dismiss his government in October. A new government was appointed in November.

2002 Malawi's bishops condemned Muluzi's rule, warning it was becoming a dictatorship. International aid was cut to Malawi due to a lack of reform and transparency, despite the onset of a famine.

Political structure

Constitution

The constitution dates from 1966. Malawi voted to change from a one-party to a multi-party system in 1994.

Malawi is divided into 24 administrative divisions.

Form of state

Republic

The executive

The president is both the head of state and the head of government. The president names the 36-member Cabinet and is elected by popular vote for a five-year term.

National legislature
The unicameral 193-member National Assembly is elected by popular vote to serve a five-year term.
Last elections
15 June 1999 (presidential and legislative)
Next elections
2004 (presidential and legislative)

Political parties
Ruling party
United Democratic Front (UDF) (since 1994; re-elected Jun 1999).
Main opposition party
Malawi Congress Party (MCP)

Population
11.31 million (2000)
Annual population growth rate: 2.5 per cent (1994–2000).
Population density: 87 inhabitants per square km. Urban population: 25 per cent (1994–2000).
Ethnic make-up
Maravi (60 per cent), Lomwe (18 per cent), Yao (13 per cent), Ngoni (7 per cent).
Religions
Christianity (75 per cent), Muslim (10 per cent), traditional beliefs (10 per cent).

Education
Literacy rate is 58 per cent while educational attainment, defined as completion of standard eight, is only 11.2 per cent. While education is free, it is not compulsory, and provision has not kept up with demand. In some rural areas children have to walk up to 13km to the nearest school. The government's decision to provide free primary education has brought a crisis in the system, placing severe restrictions on its education budget. An official report in 2001 stated that increased enrolment has overwhelmed the existing institutions, which are severely understaffed. Secondary schools have less than half the teachers they need and about two-thirds of these are not trained to teach at secondary level. The government proposes to convert Malawi Distance Education Centres (DECs) into Community Day Secondary Schools (CDSS) in order to alleviate the shortage of secondary school teachers.
The University of Malawi typically has approximately 3,000 students, with roughly 1,000 new enrolments every year. However, it has been closed for extended periods since 2000 as students protested against rising fees and shortage of facilities.
The health and education budget by 1999/2000 was cut back to under US$100 million as pressures from the IMF and the World Bank mounted.

Health
With the most productive section of the population at the highest risk from HIV infection, there is a concern at the long-term effect on the country's economic growth. Studies indicate that current trends of HIV infection will result in a drop in GDP by at least 10 per cent by 2010. Women, who engage in most of Malawi's subsistence farming, are most vulnerable to the disease. With between a quarter and a half of civil servants possibly dying from AIDS by 2010, the government's ability to implement policy will be severely hampered in coming years.
Up to 70 per cent of hospital beds are occupied by patients who are HIV positive. It is estimated that to treat just one person with AIDS, it costs the equivalent to the average income for a Malawian for four years. The growing impact of AIDS related deaths has driven up the state's health spending in the army and civil service by an estimated 50 per cent, diminishing the amount available to other sectors.
Life expectancy at birth dropped from 43 years in 1996 to 39 years in 2000. Infant and under-five mortality rates are estimated at 104 and 189 deaths per 1,000 live births respectively – one of the worst figures in the world. Estimates between 1994 and 2000 showed that 30 per cent of children were malnourished and 45 per cent of the population had access to an improved water source.
In addition to severe HIV and AIDS infections, which have had a catastrophic impact on agricultural output, the worst outbreak of cholera in 10 years claimed the lives of at least 1,000 people in the central province in 2001. In mid-2002, the World Health Organisation (WHO) reported an outbreak of the bubonic plague in the south of the country.

Welfare
According to a 1998 Integrated Household Survey Consumption survey, 65.3 per cent of the country's population are officially poor – their consumption of basic needs (food and non-food) is below the minimum level estimated at US$0.13 per day. Meanwhile, 2.8 million are in dire poverty. Some 52 per cent of the poor are female and females make up 25 per cent of household heads.
In April 2002, the government launched a Poverty Reduction Strategy Paper (PRSP) to gain unqualified relief on its US$2.5 billion foreign debt under the controversial Highly Indebted Poor Countries (HIPC) initiative. Malawi launches its war on poverty at a time when the country is facing a severe food shortage. The government declared a state of disaster in February 2002, when over 500 people had reportedly died from hunger-related diseases and seven million had run out of food.

Main cities
Lilongwe (capital, estimated population 400,000 in 1998), Blantyre (430,000), Zomba (43,000), Mzuzu (44,000).

Languages spoken
English is the usual medium for business. Chichewa is the major national language, although Chitumbuka is spoken in much of the north. Tumbuka, Lomwe and Yao are also spoken.
Official language
English, Chichewa

Media
Press
Dailies: *The Nation* is the most important daily in Malawi.
Broadcasting
Radio: Domestic radio service broadcasts in English and Chichewa by Malawi Broadcasting Corporation.
Television: A pay-TV service was lauched in 1998.

Economy
The country's economy has weakened, largely due to a decline in the agricultural sector which is linked to poor rainfall. Malawi needed large amounts of food aid in 2002 following poor harvests. Around three-quarters of the population faced food shortages and possible starvation. The IMF withheld US$47 million in funds under the country's poverty reduction and growth facility (PRGF), approved in December 2000, claiming 'lack of good governance has resulted in a misallocation of resources, increased the cost of doing business, created a general distrust in public sector activities and weakened civil service morale'. This undermined Malawi's hopes of receiving debt relief. The IMF and the World Bank had agreed to support a US$1.1 billion debt-reduction package under the enhanced heavily indebted poor countries (HIPC) initiative. According to the IMF, this plan would save an average of US$50 million per year in debt service payments by 2020, an amount equivalent to around 2.5 per cent of annual GDP for the 2001–09 period and 1.2 per cent of annual GDP for the 2010–20 period. However, with slowly deteriorating terms of trade, few possibilities for diversification, poor relations between donors and the government and the growing problems associated with HIV/AIDS, debt relief, if it is ever granted, is not likely to have a significant impact on the country's economic woes.
Another problem is the sharp depreciation of the kwacha, which has pushed up the price of imports. Between 2000 and mid-2002, the currency declined by nearly 30 per cent in nominal terms.
Further development is hampered by poor road infrastructure and a low-skilled labour force which have deterred foreign investment. With public funds increasingly diverted towards fighting the country's AIDS crisis, capital expenditure is threatened. Large budget deficits have diverted private savings from investment and Malawi's

savings rate is among the lowest in the region. Most domestic investment is financed through foreign savings, thereby threatening the country's current account and worsening its foreign debt situation. Structural adjustment has not led to an increase in private domestic savings which have diminished partly due to the AIDS pandemic.

External trade

Malawi is a member of the Southern African Development Community (SADC) and the Common Market for Eastern and Southern Africa (Comesa).

Exports

Principal exports are tobacco (typically 70 per cent of total), tea (14 per cent), sugar (11 per cent) and coffee (5 per cent). Newly industrialising countries are increasingly important destinations for tobacco exports.

In 2001, the Malawian government accepted the textile and garments export quotas of the SADC Trade Protocol. This will give Malawi's textile industry preferential market access, including the lucrative South African market.

Main destinations: South Africa (20.3 per cent of 2000 total), US (12.8 per cent), Japan (11 per cent), Germany (7 per cent), Netherlands (6.8 per cent).

Imports

Principal imports are industrial material, basic and auxiliary (typically 43 per cent of total), plant machinery and equipment (13 per cent), transport equipment (12 per cent), consumer goods (9 per cent).

Main sources: South Africa (typically 43 per cent of total), Zimbabwe (15 per cent), Zambia (10 per cent), India (3 per cent), UK (3 per cent).

Agriculture

The agricultural sector is the most important single sector of the economy, accounting for around 37 per cent of GDP and employing over 85 per cent of the workforce. The sector consists of two modes of production: smallholders, growing mainly food crops such as maize and groundnuts but also tobacco, and estate farmers, growing export crops. Other food crops include cassava, millet, sorghum and rice. Tobacco production generates about 70 per cent of the country's exports. Formerly a food exporter, Malawi has become a net importer due to the increasing population, adverse weather conditions (especially drought), a decline in farming subsidies and smallholders switching to tobacco.

The Malawian government clashed with the IMF in May 2002 when it accused the IMF of forcing it to sell its maize reserves. The IMF denied the claim, maintaining that the government had depleted food reserves to dangerous levels due to its own poor estimates for food production in the 2002 harvest. Whoever is to blame for the problem, Malawi will need substantial food aid in 2002 to avoid famine.

In the long-run, the country needs more investment in food production. Much of the investment in agriculture in the past has been directed at improving export-oriented production, while food production has been neglected. Donors and the government will need to work together to ensure a more even pattern of investment in farming.

Fishing

Malawi has the western and southern shores of Lake Malawi, one of the world's largest lakes. Consequently, the fishing industry is an important sector, augmenting the country's diet. Production can vary between 50–65,000 tonnes per year.

Forestry

Around 35 per cent of Malawi's land area is forested and there are significant areas of plantation forests. There are nine national parks and game reserves and a large number of forest reserves which provide varying levels of protection against deforestation. However, during 1990–2000, Malawi's forests disappeared at a rate of 2.41 per cent per year, one of the highest rates of deforestation in the world. This is largely due to the use of wood for fuel for domestic and industrial uses as well as the production of sawn timber and wood-based panels. Total forest exports amounted to US$689,000 in 2000.

Industry and manufacturing

The industrial sector contributed around 15 per cent to GDP in 2001, and employed 15 per cent of the workforce. The industrial sector is centred on agro-processing.

The major constraints on growth are the country's relatively limited resource base, small domestic market and difficulties in importing raw materials and intermediate goods.

Tourism

Tourism is being developed with foreign involvement.

Mining

Industrial mineral production dominates the mining sector and services domestic markets. The sector is underdeveloped, but has potential in the extraction of heavy mineral sand, bauxite, phosphate, uranium and rare earth elements.

There are three heavy mineral sand deposits with considerable titanium resources: Tengani with over 100 million tonnes of heavy minerals, Mpyukyu/Kachulu with over four million tonnes of ilmenite, 300,000 tonnes of zircon and 10,000 tonnes of rutile and beach deposits along the shores of Lake Malawi.

The Kayelekera uranium deposit has reserves of 11,000 tonnes of uranium ore at 0.16 per cent grade. Paladin Resources of Australia has a 90 per cent interest in the deposit, while Balmain Resources of Australia has the remaining 10 per cent share. The mine's total capital costs are estimated at up to US$65 million, while the revenue from the mine's 10-year life-span is estimated to average between US$30–US$34 million per year. It is due to begin production in 2003 with output of 1,000 tonnes of ore per year.

Hydrocarbons

Around 80 per cent of the country's commercial energy consumption is dependent on imported refined oil products. There is no upstream oil production and there are no refineries. The coal industry produced around 34,500 tonnes of coal in 2000, nearly half the output achieved in the mid-1990s. The decline is attributed to ageing machinery and a decline in capital investment.

Energy

Malawi has around 285MW of electricity generating power, although distribution is hampered by serious disruptions caused by crumbling infrastructure and poor investment. Only 4 per cent of the population has access to electricity and only 1 per cent of these live in rural areas, compared to an average accessibility rate of 20 per cent for the whole of the Southern African Development Community (SADC). All liquid fuels are imported, except for a small amount of ethanol produced from sugar cane. Imported liquid fuels are blended 4:1 with ethanol. Approximately 90 per cent of energy requirements are met by wood-burning. A planting programme has had to be implemented to replace dwindling resources with shortages becoming acute in the southern region. Fuel price rises have increased pressure on wood resources.

Financial markets

Stock exchange

A stock exchange was established in 1996. With just eight listed stocks active on the market in 2001, the Malawi Stock Exchange (MSE) is one of the smallest in the world. In 2001, the average daily turnover of shares amounted to K5.59 million (US$82,000), a 163 per cent increase over the previous year. The daily average share volume increased by 67 per cent in 2001 compared to 2000. The MSE's better performance in 2001 is attributed to the sale of 120 million shares in the Commercial Bank of Malawi to Stanbic of South Africa.

The Malawi All Share Index (MASI) opened in 2001 at 518.40 points, rising to a record high of 578.47 points in May 2001 and falling to a low of 458.74 points. Overall, the MASI fell 11.5 per cent by the end of 2001. The stock market's liquidity ratio was estimated at 13.82 per cent in 2001, up from 4.92 per cent in 2000.

An initial public offering by Blantyre Hotels was expected by mid-2002. The MSE expected at least one new listing by mid-2002, namely Sunbird Tourism and Hotels Ltd.

Banking

The banking system is underdeveloped and the vast majority of lending is to the government and parastatals. There is little lending to private individuals. There are five commercial banks in operation in Malawi. Although the sector is open to foreign participation, few foreign banks have shown an interest in establishing operations in Malawi, although a subsidiary of a Mauritian bank opened its doors in 1999. In 2001, Stanbic of South Africa bought a controlling share in the Commercial Bank of Malawi (CBM) to increase it's shareholding to 60.18 per cent of the company. This should help boost CBM's commercial operations in the future.

Central bank

Reserve Bank of Malawi

Main financial centre

Blantyre and Lilongwe

Time

GMT plus two hours

Geography

Malawi is a landlocked country in southern central Africa, with Zambia to the west, Mozambique to the south and east, and Tanzania to the north. Lake Malawi forms most of the eastern boundary.

Climate

Tropical, cooler in highlands. Hottest months October–November, rainy season November–April. 'Chiperoni' wind can be chilly during July–August.

On the shores of Lake Malawi and upper Shire River, the weather is pleasantly warm most of the year, hotter in the rainy season between November and March.

It is more temperate in the highlands and on the plateaux, with cool nights all year. Around the lower Shire River and the south it is more tropical and very hot during the rains.

Entry requirements

Strict rules apply concerning clothing and appearance. Male visitors with long hair or shabbily dressed may be refused entry.

Passports

Required by all.

Visa

Required by all except citizens of the EU and Commonwealth countries, and the US for stays of up to three months.

Currency advice/regulations

Import/export of local currency is allowed up to K3,000.

Foreign currency import unlimited but amounts should be declared.

Currency declaration forms issued on arrival should be kept throughout stay.

Traveller's cheques and foreign currency of all major currencies are accepted by banks, authorised hotels and other institutions. Recommended traveller's cheques are South African rand, British sterling, euros and US dollars.

Customs

Travellers to Malawi should be aware that criminals have been planting drugs in luggage and then posing as policemen, demanding bribes from passengers.

Health (for visitors)

Mandatory precautions

Yellow fever vaccination certificate required if arriving from an infected area.

Advisable precautions

Typhoid, polio, tetanus and hepatitis A vaccinations.

Take malaria prophylactics (choice of prophylactic should be checked); use mosquito nets at night when provided, as well as insect repellent spray or cream, especially in lower-lying areas.

Bilharzia is an increasing problem in still or slowly moving water. Swim only in designated areas or in swimming pools.

HIV is endemic.

Although tap water is safe to drink in Lilongwe, Blantyre, Limbe and Zomba, you should boil water or use purifying tablets in remote areas.

There is a rabies risk.

Hotels

Good hotels available in all main commercial centres. However, space can be limited so reservations should be made well in advance and a booking confirmation obtained. Service charge of 10 per cent and a 10 per cent tax are added to bills, and a small tip is occasionally expected.

Credit cards

Only accepted in major hotels, not in shops.

Public holidays

Fixed dates

1 Jan, 3 Mar (Martyr's Day), 14 May (Kamuzu Day), 6 Jul (Republic Day), 17 Oct (Mother's Day), 21 Dec (Tree Planting Day), 25 Dec, 26 Dec.

Variable dates

Good Friday, Easter Monday.

Working hours

Banking

Mon–Fri: 0800–1300.

Business

Mon–Fri: 0730–1700, with one-hour lunch break 1200–1300.

Government

Mon–Fri: 0730–1700, with one-hour lunch break 1200–1300.

Shops

Mon–Fri: 0730 or 0800–1600 or 1700; Sat: 0730 or 0800–1200.

Telecommunications

Telephone/fax

The telecommunications network is operated by Malawi Post and Telecommunications Corporation (MPTC).

Mobile phones

MPTC and Telekom Malaysia formed Telekom Networks Malawi, which commissioned a national cellular network.

Internet/e-mail

MalawiNet is the only Internet service provider.

Electricity supply

230–240V AC. Three-pin UK plugs the norm in modern buildings.

Getting there

Air

National airline: Air Malawi.

Main airport: Lilongwe-Kamuzu International (Code: LLW), 12km from city; bar, restaurant, buffet, bank, post office, shops, car hire.

Airport tax: International departures (nationals and permanent residents) K950; international departures (others) US$20; domestic departures K100, excluding 24 hour transit passengers and infants under two years.

Surface

The lake–ship–road–rail 'Northern Corridor' route to Dar es Salaam carries half of Malawi's fuel imports. It has the potential capacity to carry up to two-thirds of foreign freight.

Road: There are two main routes from Zambia: via Chipata on the Lilongwe to Lusaka road, and via Chitipa on the Karonga to Nakonde road in the extreme north. Roads also link Zimbabwe, via Tete, Mozambique.

Rail: Link with Nacala (Mozambique) but capacity is severely limited by poor track condition.

Getting about

National transport

Air: Air Malawi flies regular services linking Lilongwe, Blantyre, Mzuzu and Karonga. There are also charter services to several locations. Twice-daily services between Blantyre and Lilongwe.

Road: Over 11,500km of roads linking main centres. A quarter are main roads and a further quarter secondary roads, most of which are all-weather routes. Other roads become impassable during rainy season.

Buses: Useful bus network covers most of the country. Luxury coaches operate on the Blantyre-Zomba-Lilongwe route.

Rail: Regular services from Blantyre to Lilongwe but very much slower than buses; connection with ferries at Chipoka on Lake Malawi for services to other lake towns; three classes; first class limited availability; restaurant, sleeping cars.

Water: There is a weekly steamer service on Lake Malawi.

City transport

Taxis: In short supply and cannot be hailed. Available by telephone in Blantyre (tel: 636-402).

Buses/trams: There are regular services in all the major urban areas, with double-decker buses in Blantyre and Lilongwe.

Car hire

Available in main cities. Demand is high so cars should be booked in advance. Self-drive cars are hired at a daily rate, which includes first 40km.

Chauffeurs also charged at a daily rate plus overtime after 1600 and at lunch-time.

Traffic drives on the left. General speed limit of 80kph, and 40kph in urban areas.

BUSINESS DIRECTORY

Telephone area codes

The international direct dialling (IDD) code for Malawi is +265 subscriber's number. There are no area codes.

Chambers of Commerce

Associated Chamber of Commerce and Industry of Malawi, Chichiri Trade Fair Grounds, PO Box 258, Blantyre (tel: 671-988; fax: 671-147).

Banking

CBM Financial Services Limited; PO Box 2619, Victoria Ave, Blantyre (tel: 621280, 623287 fax: 624525).

Commercial Bank of Malawi Ltd; PO Box 1111, Capital City, Blantyre (tel: 620144 fax: 620117, 620360).

Finance Bank of Malawi; PO Box 421, Finance Hse, Victoria Ave, Blantyre (tel:624799, 623209 fax: 622957, email: makhan@malawi.net).

First Merchant Bank Limited; PO Box 122, First Hse, Glyn Jones Rd, Blantyre (tel: 622787, 621955, 621942, 621943, 624840 fax: 621978).

Investment & Development Bank of Malawi; PO Box 358, Indebank House, Kaushong Rd, Top Mandala, Blantyre (tel: 620055 fax: 623353).

Loita Investment Bank Ltd; Loita House, Victoria Avenue - Private Bag 389, Chichiri, Blantyre 3 (fax: 622683).

Malawi Savings Bank, PO Box 521, Umoyo Hse, Blantyre (tel: 625111 fax: 621929).

National Bank of Malawi, PO Box 945, Victoria Avenue, Blantyre (tel: 620622 fax: 620464).

Central bank

Reserve Bank of Malawi, PO Box 30063, Convention Drive, Lilongwe 3, Malawi (tel: 770600 fax: 772752, 774289).

Travel information

Air Malawi, PO Box 84, Chibisa House, Glyn Jones Road, Blantyre (tel: 620-811; fax: 620-042, 623-070; e-mail: it@airmalawi.malawi.net).

Department of Parks and Wildlife, PO Box 30131, Lilongwe 3 (tel: 723-566).

Malawi Railways, PO Box 5492, Limbe (tel: 640-844; fax: 640-683).

Malawi Tourism Association, Aquarius House, PO Box 1044, Lilongwe (tel: 770-010, 774-713; tel/fax: 770-131; e-mail: mata@malawi.net).

Ministry of tourism

Ministry of Tourism, Delamere House, PO Box 402, Blantyre (tel: 620-300; fax: 620-947).

Ministries

Ministry of Economic Planning and Development, PO Box 30136, Capital City, Lilongwe 3 (tel: 782-300; fax: 782-224).

Ministry of Energy and Mining, Private Bag 309, Lilongwe 3 (tel: 784-178; fax: 784-236).

Ministry of Lands and Valuation, Tikwere House, Private Bag 311, Lilongwe 3 (tel: 780-755; fax: 780-727).

Ministry of Physical Planning and Surveys, PO Box 30385, Capital City, Lilongwe 3 (tel: 784-655).

Ministry of Trade and Industry, PO Box 30366, Lilongwe 3 (tel: 732-71?; fax: 732-551).

Other useful addresses

Agricultural Development & Marketing Corporation (ADMARC), PO Box 50512, Limbe (tel: 640-500; fax: 640-436).

Civil Service Commission, PO Box 30133, Capital City, Lilongwe 3 (tel: 783-311).

Department of Customs and Excise, Private Bag 20, Blantyre (tel: 620-288).

Department of Forest, PO Box 30048, Lilongwe 3 (tel: 781-000).

Department of Income Tax, PO Box 162/250, Blantyre (tel: 620-844).

Department of Parks, Wildlife and Tourism, PO Box 402, Blantyre (tel: 620-300; fax: 620-947).

Department of Posts and Telecommunications, PO Box 537, Blantyre (tel: 620-977).

Department of Statutory Bodies, PO Box 30061, Capital City, Lilongwe 3 (tel: 784-266; fax: 784-110).

Electricity Supply Commission of Malawi, PO Box 2047, Blantyre (tel: 622-000; fax: 622-008).

European Development Fund, Lingadzi House, PO Box 30102, Lilongwe 3 (tel: 730-255).

Geological Survey Department, PO Box 27, Zomba (tel: 522-166; fax: 522-716).

Immigration Office, PO Box 331, Blantyre (tel: 623-777; fax: 623-065).

Import & Export (Malawi) (1984) Ltd., PO Box 1106, Blantyre (tel: 670-999; fax: 671-160).

Judicial Department, PO Box 30244, Chichiri, Blantyre 3 (tel: 670-255; fax: 670-213).

Malawi Broadcasting Corporation, PO Box 30133, Chichiri, Blantyre 3 (tel: 671-222; fax: 671-257).

Malawi Bureau of Standards, PO Box 946, Blantyre (tel: 670-488; fax: 670-756).

Malawi Development Corporation, Development House, PO Box 566, Blantyre (tel: 620-100; fax: 620-584

Malawi Export Promotion Council, Delamere House, Victoria Avenue, PO Box 1299, Blantyre (tel: 620-499).

Malawi Investment Promotion Agency, Private Bag 302, Lilongwe 3 (tel: 780-800; fax: 781-781).

Malawi Iron and Steel Corporation, PO Box 2165, Blantyre (tel: 671-455).

National Statistical Office, PO Box 333, Zomba (tel: 522-377; fax: 523-130).

Registrar General's Department (Companies etc), Private Bag 100, Blantyre (tel: 635-077; fax: 640-877).

Road Transport Operators' Association, PO Box 950, Blantyre (tel: 670-442).

United Nations Development Programme, Resident Representative, PO Box 30135, Capital City, Lilongwe 3 (tel: 783-500; fax: 783-637).

Internet sites

Africa Business Network: http://www.ifc.org/abn

AllAfrica.com: http://allafrica.com

African Development Bank: http://www.afdb.org

Africa Online: http://www.africaonline.com

Harambee Afrika (UK business club for traders with east, central and southern Africa; includes annotated web resource list): http://www.harambee.co.uk

MalawiBiz.com: http://www.malawibiz.com/complist.html

Mbendi AfroPaedia (information on companies, countries, industries and stock exchanges in Africa): http://mbendi.co.za

Mali

Falguni Patel

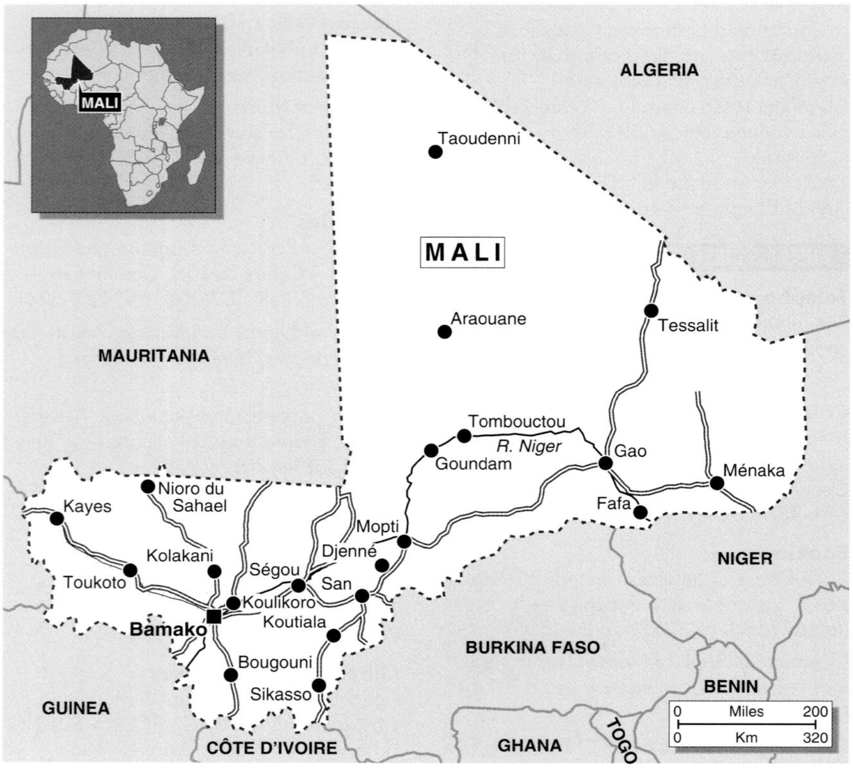

KEY FACTS

Official name: République du Mali (Republic of Mali)

Head of State: President Amadou Toumani Touré (sworn in 8 Jun 2002)

Head of government: Prime Minister Ahmed Mohammed Ag Hamani (appointed by the president, 9 Jun 2002)

Ruling party: Alliance pour la Démocratie au Mali-Parti pan-Africain pour la Liberté, la Solidarité et la Justice (ADEMA-PPLSJ) (Alliance for Democracy in Mali-Pan African Party for Liberty, Solidarity and Justice) (on 8 Aug 2002, the Constitutional Court reversed the outcome of the Jul 2002 parliamentary elections, giving the Hope 2002 coalition 66 of the 147 seats, compared to 51 for the Alliance for Democracy in Mali, which had the lead in the previously announced results.)

Area: 1,241,238 square km

Population: 11.30 million (2001)

Capital: Bamako

Official language: French

Currency: CFA franc (CFAf) = 100 centimes (Communauté Financière Africaine (African Financial Community) franc)

Exchange rate: CFAf629.73 per US$ (Jan 2003); CFAf655.95 per euro (pegged from Jan 1999)

GDP per capita: US$230 (2001)

GDP real growth: 1.40% (2001)

Inflation: 5.20% (2001); 0.6% (year-on-year, Feb 2002)

Balance of trade: -US$213.00 million (2001)

Foreign debt: US$2.89 billion (2001)

Annual FDI: US$55.00 million (2001)

For the latest Key Facts, go to www.worldinformation.com

The glamour of playing host to the 2002 African Nations Cup and the excitement accompanying the build-up to Africa's premier football championship could not disguise the deep-rooted poverty suffered by the average Malian.

Outgoing president, Alpha Oumar Konaré, managed to incur widespread criticism with proposed constitutional reforms, while the launch of a new political party promised to intensify competition at the 2002 presidential elections.

Change afoot

In November 1999, President Konaré announced that he had no intention of contesting an unconstitutional third-term in the 2002 presidential elections, triggering much speculation about the country's future leadership.

A split within the ruling party, the snappily named Alliance pour la Démocratie au Mali-Parti pan-Africain pour la Liberté, la Solidarité et la Justice (ADEMA-PPLSJ) (Alliance for Democracy in Mali-Pan-African Party for Liberty, Solidarity and Justice), led to the launch of a new party in July 2001.

Boubacar Keita, a former prime minister and ex-member of the ruling ADEMA-PPLSJ, became head of the new political party, Rassemblement Pour le Mali (RPM) (Rally for Mali), and was expected to be one of the more formidable candidates in the April/May 2002 presidential elections. RPM's support comes primarily from former ADEMA-PPLSJ members – 30 disaffected parliamentary deputies from the RPM defected to the party, making it the second most powerful party in the National Assembly, and a key new player on the country's political stage.

The presidential election was tainted by alleged irregularities and corruption and turnout was poor. During the first ballot on 28 April 2002, only 36.8 per cent of the electorate turned out to vote. On 12 May, this figure dropped to 30.2 per cent. Amadou Toumani Touré emerged as the new president, winning 64 per cent of the vote in the second round. Keita also made it to the second round, but won only 35.7 per cent of the vote.

On 14 July 2002, Mali also held a parliamentary election. The Espoir 2002 (Spirit 2002) alliance, led by the RPM, won 66 seats in the National Assembly and the Alliance pour la République et la Démocratie (ARD) (Alliance for the Democratic Republic) won 31 seats. The Alternance et Changement (ACC) (Alternance and Change) and African Solidarity for Democracy and Independence (SADI) won 10 and 6 seats respectively. Touré appointed Ahmed Mohamed Ag Hamani as prime minister in June 2002, replacing Modibo Keita who had only been in the job for three months.

Poverty and frustration

Mali is one of the world's poorest countries and its people are increasingly frustrated by the lack of basic services and amenities, such as access to safe, clean water. The repayment of a US$3.2 billion external debt makes the provision of basic needs even more difficult. In September 2002, the French government hinted that it would cancel up to 40 per cent of the US$200 million debt owed to it by Mali.

Many Malians are disillusioned with a leadership that finds money for grand gestures, but not for essentials, like a solution to the country's 10-year education crisis. In 2001, various sections of civil society expressed concerns over government expenditure – such as spending an estimated US$150 million hosting the 2002 African Nations Cup and US$20 million on two new monuments for the streets of the capital city Bamako.

Among the country's majority (90 per cent) Muslim population, disenchantment with the political leadership is increasingly discernible. In September 2001, at the third Muslim rally to be held in Bamako that year, imams issued grave warnings to the 40,000 assembled Muslims that the secular Malian state had become 'anti-religious' and that too much foreign influence had been allowed in under President Konaré's leadership. In a country known for moderate and tolerant Islam, politicians have been surprised by the sudden wave of religious fervour.

Economic conditions

In December 2001, upon completion of the third review of Mali's economic performance under the three-year Poverty Reduction and Growth Facility (PRGF) arrangement, the IMF approved a US$9 million disbursement to the country. In July 2002, the IMF undertook its fourth review, enabling the country to draw on another US$9 million.

Mali's citizens are increasingly sceptical about the poverty reduction effect that the country's structural adjustment deal with the IMF and the World Bank is supposedly producing. Although meetings with civil society representatives were included during a high-level visit by leaders from the Bretton Woods institutions to Mali in February 2001, most Malians were disengaged from these talks. It was felt that the summit was more to do with public relations than tackling real life poverty.

The IMF predicted that Mali's 'external current account balance is expected to deteriorate relative to earlier projections, owing to a sharp decline in private transfers from abroad and an increase in the net remittances of mining companies'. The country's other main export, cotton, is also suffering as a result of falling world commodity prices. Mali's cotton producers, having taken strike action in 2000, returned to cotton production in 2001 as cotton prices temporarily rose. The 2001/02 cotton harvest totalled 575,000 tonnes, but the deterioration in the world cotton price outlook will mean lower profitability in the cotton sector, which in turn will slow the pace of fiscal consolidation in 2002/03.

The Communauté Financière Africaine franc (CFAf) appreciated in real terms as the euro, to which it is pegged in value, strengthened against the US dollar in 2001 and 2002. This affected the competitiveness of Malian exports and squeezed producers' profits. This is one of the chief problems faced by the Economic Community of West African States (Ecowas) in introducing a single currency for the entire sub-region by 2004, as originally envisaged. Mali was a key player in Ecowas plans for monetary union with the CFAf franc, but by the beginning of 2002, it seemed unlikely that the economic convergence of member countries – vital to the success of the plan – would happen within the original timeframe.

Tourism promised much-needed income-generating opportunities in a weak economy that rests primarily on subsistence farming and animal husbandry. Most of the profits from tourism go to big tour operators rather than ordinary Malians. If the sector is going to open up economic opportunities for a wider cross-section of the population, the question of equitable profit distribution needs to be addressed by engaging the participation of local communities in tourism ventures.

Outlook

Political stability for 2003 is difficult to predict, but is not expected to deteriorate. The process of reducing poverty at both micro and macro levels will be slow, particularly so in the light of the declining terms of trade for cotton on the world market and a failure to retain within the

KEY INDICATORS — Mali

	Unit	1996	1997	1998	1999	2000
Population	m	10.19	10.44	10.69	10.96	11.22
Gross domestic product (GDP)	US$bn	0.00	2.47	2.62	2.60	2.50
GDP per capita	US$	0	260	245	240	223
GDP real growth	%	4.0	6.7	4.7	5.5	4.6
Gross national product (GNP)	US$bn	2.60	0.00	0.00	0.00	0.00
GNP per capita	US$	240	0	0	0	0
Inflation	%	6.8	-0.4	4.0	-1.2	-0.7
Consumer prices	1995=100	106.8	106.4	110.7	109.4	108.6
Exports (fob) (goods)	US$m	433.5	561.6	532.9	568.9	518.0
Imports (fob) (goods)	US$m	551.5	551.9	730.6	751.3	909.0
Balance of trade	US$m	-118.0	9.7	-197.7	-568.1	-391.0
Foreign debt	US$bn	2.9	3.3	3.1	3.0	3.0
Total reserves minus gold	US$m	426.3	409.8	398.0	349.7	381.2
Foreign exchange	US$m	418.6	403.0	390.4	337.0	337.0
Exchange rate	per US$	511.55	583.67	589.95	615.70	711.98

country more of the profits from the mining industry.

Risk assessment

Economic	Poor
Political	Satisfactory
Regional stability	Improving

COUNTRY PROFILE

Historical profile

900 Modern-day Mali was part of the empire of Ghana.
1250s Sundiata Keita, leader of the Mandinka people, established the Empire of Mali, which stretched from the Atlantic to the present day borders of Nigeria and controlled most trans-Sahara trading routes by the fourteenth century.
1464 The Songhai Empire, centred around Gao, surpassed the Mali Empire and began to conquer the Sahel.
1591 After a Moroccan invasion the Songhai Empire collapsed.
1890s Towards the end of the nineteenth century Mali became a French colony.
1960 Mali gained independence from France as part of the Federation of Mali. This was dissolved a few weeks later when Senegal broke away. The Republic of Mali was established in September 1960. Modibo Keita became the country's first president.
1968 Keita was overthrown by a military coup, led by Moussa Traoré, who became president.
1977 Protests erupted following Keita's death in prison.
1979 A new constitution provided for elections and Traoré was re-elected president.
1985 A border war erupted between Mali and Burkina Faso, but was ended after intervention by other African states.
1991 In March, following pro-democracy demonstrations, Traoré was deposed by a military coup. In April, a 25-member military/civilian Transitional People's Salvation Committee came to power, led by Lt Col Amadou Toumani Touré.
1992 Touré organised elections, in which he did not take part, before stepping down. Alpha Oumar Konaré was democratically elected president.
1995 A peace agreement with Tuareg rebels led to the return of thousands of refugees from neighbouring African states.
1997 President Konaré was re-elected in presidential elections held on 11 May.
1999 Traoré was sentenced to death for corruption, but his sentence was commuted to life imprisonment by President Konaré. President Konaré announced in November that he would not contest the next presidential election, due in 2002.
2000 Mande Sidibe, a former IMF official, was appointed prime minister in February.
2001 The President announced the indefinite postponement of a constitutional referendum scheduled for 23 December. The referendum was proposing to grant Konaré immunity from prosecution.
2002 Prime Minister Mande Sidibe resigned and Modibo Keita was appointed to the post on 18 March. General Amadou Toumani Touré received 28 per cent of the votes in the 28 April presidential election, followed by Soumaila Cisse with 26 per cent. The results of the run-off in May gave Touré 64.35 per cent of votes against 35.65 per cent for Soumaila Cisse. Turnout was low at just over 30 per cent.

Political structure

Constitution

A referendum held in January 1992 approved a constitution establishing multi-party rule.
A two-round voting system for electing parliamentarians was established.
In 1997, a new electoral code introduced an Independent National Electoral Commission (CENI) comprising 34 members: 10 representatives of government services, 10 from civil society and 14 from the political parties (seven from the opposition and seven from the parliamentary majority).
Other changes included the authorisation of independent candidacies, the reduction in the number of voters per polling station to 700 and an increase in the number of deputies in the National Assembly from 116 to 147. The principle of sponsoring presidential candidates was ended, and correspondence or proxy voting and eligibility for other African nationals were annulled.

Form of state

Republic.

The executive

The directly elected president serves a five-year term.

National legislature

Mali has a 147-member National Assembly with a five-year term.

Last elections

28 April 2002 (presidential); second round 12 May 2002; July 1997 (legislative).

Next elections

July 2002 (legislative); 2007 (presidential).

Political parties

Ruling party

Alliance pour la Démocratie au Mali-Parti pan-Africain pour la Liberté, la Solidarité et la Justice (ADEMA-PPLSJ) (Alliance for Democracy in Mali-Pan African Party for Liberty, Solidarity and Justice) (parliamentary elections Jul 2002).

Main opposition party

Rassemblement Pour le Mali (RPM) (Rally for Mali)

Population

11.22 million (2000)
Annual population growth rate: 2.4 per cent (1994–2000). Approximately 47 per cent of the total population is under 15 years.
Population density: eight inhabitants per square km. Urban population 28 per cent (1994–2000). There is a continuing population drift toward the Senegal and Niger Rivers.
The government's medium-term social objective is to achieve a broadly based improvement in living standards.

Ethnic make-up

Mande (50 per cent), Peul (17 per cent), Voltaic (12 per cent).

Religions

Muslim (90 per cent), indigenous beliefs (9 per cent), Christian (1 per cent).

Education

It has been estimated by Oxfam that 53 per cent of children age 6–11 will enrol for school by 2015. The illiteracy rate is 61.8 per cent (2000). Public expenditure on education in 1997 was 2.2 per cent of GNP. Mali has the highest pupil-teacher ratio in the world with an average of around 80 pupils per teacher (1997).

Health

Public expenditure on health typically stands at an average of 2.0 per cent of GDP while private expenditure averages 1.8 per cent of GDP. In the same period, there was on average one doctor and two hospital beds per 10,000 people. Only around 40 per cent of the population has access to safe water while 30 per cent has access to sanitation.
There are an estimated 100,000 people living with HIV/AIDS in Mali – 5,000 are under the age of 15 (2000). With infection rates at less than 1 per cent of the total population, Mali has so far escaped much of the African pandemic.

Welfare

In the mid-1990s, it was estimated that 72.8 per cent of the population lived on less than US$1 per day and over 90 per cent live on less than US$2 per day. The minimum wage for Malian workers was US$459 per annum in 1995–99. However, since the workforce is largely informal or engaged in subsistence agriculture, minimum wages are of little relevance. The distribution of wealth in Mali is highly unequal and the highest 10 per cent of the population owns 56.2 per cent of the wealth.

Main cities

Bamako (population 850,000 in 1998) is the capital and main business centre, Gao, Mopti, Tombouctou, Kayes, Sikasso.

Languages spoken

Very little English is spoken. Arabic, Bambara, Fulani, Senoufo and Dogon are commonly spoken.

Official language

French

Media

Press

Dailies: Dailies include *L'Essor*, *Info-Matin*, *Le Soir de Bamako* and *Sud-info*.

Weeklies: Eighteen opposition parties launched a weekly paper, *La Voix de l'Opposition* in 1998. Other weeklies published from Bamako include *Aurore*, *Carcan*, *Carrefour*, *Les Echos*, *Independent*, *Scorpion*, *Le Malien Magazine*, *Soudanais*, *Tambour*, *Temps* and *Le Zenith*.

Periodicals: Periodicals include the bi-monthly *Cauris* and *Courrier* (irregular).

Economy

With a GDP per capita of US$223 (2000), Mali is one of the world's poorest countries and is heavily dependent on foreign aid. Before 1991, the Soviet Union was the country's main source of aid. Since then, the country has looked increasingly toward international financial institutions (IFIs). Meanwhile the Chinese government has taken an increasingly important role in infrastructural projects and provided considerable support for the construction of the new national football stadium in Bamako for the 2002 Africa Cup.

The economy is vulnerable to price fluctuations in the world price of cotton, its main export. Although the government has implemented various structural adjustment programmes to diversify the economy and the country's export markets, it is gold mining that has attracted an increasing number of foreign investors. However, under the auspices of the increasingly powerful IFIs, the Malian authorities continue to reduce budget deficits, cut the operating losses of state enterprises and liberalise the economy.

Economic growth has been moderate and sustained since the 50 per cent devaluation of the CFA franc in 1994 helped boost export growth. Although growth in recent years has been spurred on by gold production, around 70 per cent of the labour force is engaged in agriculture and cotton makes up around three quarters of total exports.

A series of shocks, including a severe drought, rising oil prices and increased transport costs, helped undermine growth in 2001. Estimates indicate that the economy grew by only 0.1 per cent compared to 4.6 per cent in 2000. Inflation also rose due to food shortages, from -0.7 in 2000 to 4.6 per cent in 2001. The current account widened as a result of declining terms of trade of cotton and the rise in profit transfers from mining companies.

External trade

A significant amount of foreign trade goes unrecorded. The large current account deficit is partly funded by workers' remittances and official transfers.

Exports

Cotton and cotton products are the main exports, followed by gold and live animals. Other exports include groundnuts and fish.

Main destinations: Algeria, Belgium, Canada, France.

Imports

Principal imports are petroleum products, chemicals and pharmaceuticals, machinery and transport equipment, foodstuffs, construction materials.

Main sources: Côte d'Ivoire, France, Senegal, Germany, Italy.

Agriculture

The agricultural sector is the mainstay of the economy, contributing around 50 per cent of GDP, employing 73 per cent of the workforce (largely at subsistence levels) and accounting for about 70 per cent of exports. Only about 2 per cent of the total land area is cultivated, but approximately 20 per cent of the total land area along the Niger River is suitable for cultivation, with the most productive areas lying between Bamako and Mopti.

Principal food crops are millet, sorghum, paddy rice, maize and groundnuts. Supported by foreign aid, the government has co-ordinated a programme to expand production of rice, a staple food.

The main export crops are cotton, groundnuts, cereals, fresh fruit and vegetables. Mali is Africa's second-largest cotton producer. Livestock exports have experienced growth in recent years following the abolition of export taxes on livestock. The livestock sector is a mainstay of the economy in the northern half of the country, much of which is desert, and contributes 20 per cent to GDP. However, recent desertification caused by deforestation and global warming has shifted herding activity southwards. Fishing is also an important livelihood along the Niger River. The annual fish catch is around 100,000 tonnes.

There is a regular food deficit due to recurrent drought, crop smuggling and an inefficient marketing and distribution system.

Industry and manufacturing

The industrial sector is small-scale, contributing around 7 per cent to GDP and employing 6 per cent of the workforce. Manufacturing is concerned mainly with agricultural processing for domestic consumption and export.

Other industries include soft drinks, textiles, soaps, plastics, cigarettes, cement, bricks and agricultural tools and equipment. Activity is concentrated in Bamako. Around 90 per cent of production is accounted for by state enterprises, although rationalisation and privatisation plans are likely to continue.

Mining

The mining sector typically contributes around 10 per cent to GDP and employs 0.5 per cent of the workforce. Gold is Mali's principal mineral resource, and since the late 1990s it has become the country's second largest export earner after cotton. Gold production is estimated to rise from 32.2 tonnes in 2001 to 36.2 tonnes in 2002.

Following the introduction of new mining laws in 1991, which helped expand gold production, Mali has become Africa's third largest gold producer after Ghana and South Africa. Total gold reserves are estimated at up to 700 tonnes and geologists claim there is potential for further discoveries. However, commercial exploitation is hampered by the lack of adequate physical infrastructure. Gold represents 95 per cent of the country's total mineral production. Mali also contains reserves of bauxite, iron ore, base metals and phosphates, although a lack of adequate infrastructure has deterred commercial exploitation.

The first privately owned gold mine was opened by BHP-Utah at Syama in 1990, but following operational difficulties it was sold to Randgold of South Africa in 1996. The mine underwent an investment programme and production peaked at 6.1 tonnes in 1999. However, in January 2001, Randgold decided to mothball Syama after extensive flooding led to financial losses.

Opened in 1997, the Sadiola Hill open-cast mine, owned by AngloGold, IAMGold and the Mali government, has estimated reserves of around 130 tonnes. With average annual production estimated at around 10 tonnes per annum until 2010, it is the second largest gold mine in Africa and one of the biggest and lowest cost gold mines in the world.

The Yatela gold mine – owned jointly by AngloGold (40 per cent), IAMGold (40 per cent) and the Mali government (20 per cent) – lies 35km to the north of Sadiola, and was officially opened in September 2002. It has reserves of over 72 tonnes with estimated average annual

production of 6 tonnes over a period of 12 years.
The Morila gold mine, opened in early 2001, is to produce an average of 10 tonnes per year over a period of 14 years and is jointly owned by Rangold (40 per cent), AngloGold (40 per cent) and the Mali government (20 per cent). Feasibility studies are being conducted on the re-opening of the Kalana gold mine which could produce an estimated 430kg per annum. There are also large unexploited deposits at Kodieran (43 tonnes), Loulo (30.1 tonnes), Segala (15.4 tonnes) and Tabakto (1 tonne).
Artisanal gold mining has been practiced in Mali for around 1,000 years and represents 0.6 per cent of GDP and employs around 150,000 seasonal workers. Much of this kind of mining is performed without permits and is generally dangerous.
Phosphate production is around 10,000 tonnes per annum. Small quantities of salt, limestone and uranium are also mined. There are known deposits of bauxite, manganese, iron and tin, and prospecting for lithium, diamonds and copper is under way.

Hydrocarbons
There are no known reserves of oil or gas in Mali. Refined oil represents around 17 per cent of imports and is imported from Côte d'Ivoire and Senegal.

Energy
Mali is reliant on imported petroleum, although sufficent electricity is produced to meet local demand.
Bamako is supplied with hydropower from the dam at Selingué. Most other towns rely on diesel generators.

Financial markets
Stock exchange
Malian shares are listed on the regional stock exchange (bourse) which opened in Abidjan, Côte d'Ivoire, in 1998. The exchange also lists shares from companies registered in Benin, Burkina Faso, Côte d'Ivoire, Niger, Senegal and Togo. The seven members of the new bourse are also members of the Economic and Monetary Union of West Africa (UEMOA) as well as being members of the Economic Community of West African States (Ecowas). Of the 14 brokerage firms that have been established to operate on the Abidjan bourse, one is based in Mali.

Banking
Mali has an undeveloped banking sector with just nine banks and two financial institutions. Three of the banks are majority owned by the state while the state owns a minority share in three others. There are three privately owned banks. In recent years, the sector has undergone liberalisation.

Central bank
Banque Centrale du Mali
Main financial centre
Bamako

Time
GMT

Geography
Mali is a landlocked country in West Africa, with Algeria to the north, Mauritania and Senegal to the west, Guinea and Côte d'Ivoire to the south, and Burkina Faso and Niger to the east.

Climate
There is considerable variation between southern, central and northern areas, rain being rare and sporadic in the far north, Sahara region. Bamako's rainy season runs from June to October with humidity reaching 80 per cent and temperatures ranging from 20 degrees C to 36 degress C. The warm, dry season runs from November to February followed by a hot, dry season between February and May with average temperatures of 35 degrees C.

Entry requirements
Passports
Required by all. Passport must be valid six months from date of entry.
Visa
Required by all except nationals of France and certain African countries. Exit visas and proof of intended departure required.
Currency advice/regulations
No restrictions on import/export of local currency. Unlimited import of foreign currency but it must be declared. Foreign currency up to equivalent of CFAf250,000 in bank notes can be exported.

Health (for visitors)
Mandatory precautions
Yellow fever vaccination certificate is required by all.
Advisable precautions
Typhoid, tetanus, hepatitis A and polio vaccinations are recommended. Malaria prophylaxis should be taken as risk exists throughout country. There is a rabies risk. Water precautions must be taken.

Hotels
There are only a few good hotels available and these can be expensive.

Credit cards
Only accepted in main hotels.

Public holidays
Fixed dates
1 Jan (New Year), 20 Jan (Army Day), 1 May (Labour Day), 25 May (Africa Day), 19 Nov (Bank Holiday), 25 Dec (Christmas).
Variable dates
Easter, Maouloud (birth of the Prophet) (two days), Ramadan, Tabaski or Eid al Kebir.

Working hours
Banking
Mon–Thu: 0730–1200, 1315–1500. Fri: 0730–1230.
Business
Mon–Thu: 0730–1230, 1300–1600. Fri: 0730–1230, 1430–1730.
Government
(Mon–Thu, Sat) 0730–1430, Fri: 0730–1230.

Telecommunications
Telephone/fax
There are direct telephone links with Paris, Moscow and Cairo. The internal service is unreliable.

Electricity supply
220V AC, 50 cycles.

Getting there
Air
National airline: Air Mali (formed 1994).
Main airport: Bamako (Code: BKO), 15km from city.
Airport tax: CFAf2,500 is payable on domestic flights; CFAf8,000 on international flights within Africa; and CFAf10,000 is payable for flights outside Africa. The airport tax may be collected at time of ticket sale and does not apply to transit passengers on the same flight and for children under two years.
Surface
Road: Good road from Niger (Niamey); condition of routes from Côte d'Ivoire and Burkina Faso varies; those from Senegal and Algeria are not generally recommended.
Rail: A regular twice weekly rail service from Senegal (Dakar) to Bamako (with sleeping and restaurant cars and facility for conveying vehicles). Journey takes up to 29 hours.
Main ports: River ports of Bamako, Mopti, Tombouctou and Gao on the Niger.

Getting about
National transport
Air: There are no scheduled services between Bamako and other towns. Charter of light aircraft available from Société des Transports Aériens (STA). Tombouctou Air Service provide domestic flights.
Road: Main roads run from Sikasso and Bougouni in the south to Bamako, and from Bamako to Mopti and on to Gao via a new tarred road. Condition of roads are variable and secondary roads can be difficult.
Buses: Cheap but generally uncomfortable. Services run from Bamako to all main towns.

Rail: Main routes: Bamako–Koulikoro (59 km) leaves Bamako daily at 1100 and 1700; Bamako–Kayes (494km) leaves Bamako daily at 0945. There are two classes; sleeping and restaurant facilities and some air-conditioned cars are available.
Water: Three river steamers operate up and down the River Niger betwen August and late December, linking Koulikoro, Mopti, Tombouctou and Gao. Four classes are available, but first-class cabins must be booked in advance through SMERT, the tourist organisation.

City transport

Taxis: Cheap and widely available but not metered. Official standard fare system in Bamako. Tipping is not usual.

Car hire

International driving licence recommended. Hired cars are usually Renaults or Peugeots.

BUSINESS DIRECTORY

Telephone area codes

Dialling code for Mali: IDD access code +223 followed by subscriber's number (no area code required).

Useful telephone numbers

Police: 17
Fire: 18
Ambulance: 225-002

Chambers of Commerce

Chambre de Commerce et d'Industrie du Mali, BP 46, Bamako (tel: 225-036; fax: 222-120).

Chambre de Commerce de Kayes, BP 81, Kayes.

Banking

Bank of Africa Mali, BP 2249, 418 Avenue de la Marne, Bamrako (tel: 224672; fax: 224653).

Banque Commerciale du Sahel; BP 2372, 127 Rue, Bozola, Bamako (tel: 210195/97, 225536 fax: 225543, 220135)

Banque de Développement du Mali, BP 94, Ave Modibo Keita, Quartier du Fleuve, Bamako (tel: 222050, 224088 fax: 225085, 224250).

Banque de l'Habitat du Mali, BP 2614, Rue de Métal Soudan, Quartier du Fleuve, Bamako (tel: 229190, 229342 fax: 229350).

Banque Internationale du Mali; BP 15, Blvd de l'Indépendance, Bamako (tel: 225111, 225066 fax: 224566).

Banque Internationale pour le Commerce et l'Industrie du Mali; BP B72, Bd du Peuple, Immeuble Nimagala, Bamako (tel: 233370 fax: 233373).

Banque Malienne de Credit et de Dépôts, BP 45, Avenue Modibo Keïta, Bamako (tel: 225336 fax: 227950).

Banque Nationale de Développement Agricole - Mali; BP 2424, Immeuble Dette Publique, Bamako (tel: 226464, 226611 fax: 222961).

ECOBANK-Mali; BP 1272, Quartier du Fleuve, Place de la Nation, Bamako (tel: 233300 fax: 233305).

Central bank

Banque Centrale des Etats de l'Afrique de l'Ouest, PO Box 3108, Avenue Abdoulaye Fadiga, Dakar, Senegal (tel: 390500 fax:239335).

Travel information

Air Mali, Immeuble Scif, Square Lumumba, BP 27, Bamako (tel: 225-741/42; fax: 222-349).

Commissariat au Tourisme, BP 191, Bamako (tel: 225-673).

Delta Voyages SA, Immeuble Gamby (ex BNDA), BP 5005, Bamako (fax: 231-272).

Timbuctours, BP 222, Bamako (tel: 225-315).

Ministries

Ministry of Foreign Affairs, Bamako (fax: 230-327, 225-226).

Ministry of Public Works and Transport, BP 17759, Rue 214 Hippodrome, Bamako (tel: 222-901; fax: 220-874; e-mail: ssimpara@cefib.com).

Ministry of Rural Development and Water, Bamako.

Other useful addresses

Direction Nationale du Plan et de la Statistique, Koulouba, Bamako (tel: 222-753).

Direction Nationale de la Sécurité des Services de l'Immigration, Avenue de la Nation, Bamako.

Radiodiffusion-Télévision Malienne, BP 171, Bamako (tel: 222-474).

Mali Embassy (USA), 2130 R Street, NW, Washington DC 20009 (tel: 332-2249; fax: 332-6603; e-mail: info@maliembassy-usa.org).

Internet sites

Africa Business Network: http://www.ifc.org/abn

African Development Bank: http://www.afdb.org

AllAfrica.com: http://www.allafrica.com

Africa Online: http://www.africaonline.com

Mbendi AfroPaedia (information on companies, countries, industries and stock exchanges in Africa): http://mbendi.co.za

Mauritania

Daniel Brett

KEY FACTS

Official name: République Islamique Arabe et Africaine de Mauritanie (The Islamic Republic of Mauritania)

Head of State: President Colonel Maaouya Ould Sid'Ahmed Taya (PRDS) (since 1984; re-elected Dec 1997)

Head of government: Prime Minister Cheikh El-Avia Ould Mohammed Khouna

Ruling party: Parti Républicain Démocratique et Social (PRDS) (Social and Democratic Republican Party) (re-elected Oct 2001)

Area: 1,030,700 square km

Population: 2.79 million (2001)

Capital: Nouakchott

Official language: Arabic

Currency: Ouguiya (UM) = 5 khoums

Exchange rate: UM268.23 per US$ (Jan 2003)

GDP per capita: US$313 (2001)

GDP real growth: 4.60% (2001)

Inflation: 4.70% (2001)

Balance of trade: -US$12.00 million (2001)

Foreign debt: US$1.84 billion (2001)

Annual FDI: US$14.00 million (2001)

For the latest Key Facts, go to www.worldinformation.com

Mauritania's democratic facade hides a reality in which opposition parties are routinely banned and the legacy of black enslavement and oppression lingers on. In 2002, Mauritania entered the eleventh year of its democratisation process, which has supposedly transformed it from a repressive military regime into a politically tolerant society. The government was able to hide behind a wall of international indifference and maintain the repressive state structures that were in place before President Maaouya Ould Sid'Ahmed Taya discarded his military fatigues and took on the persona of a civilian leader. Nevertheless, the government's austere process of economic liberalisation continues to win praise from international financial institutions, who have turned a blind eye to widespread human rights abuses.

Paper democracy

A wave of repression helped secure a victory for the ruling Parti Républicain Démocratique et Social (PRDS) (Social and Democratic Republican Party) following the October 2001 elections to the Al-Jamiya Al-Wataniyah (national assembly). The PRDS won 64 of the 81 seats with little over half the vote.

This triumph was achieved after the main opposition party, the Union des Forces Démocratiques–Ère Nouvelle (UFD–EN) (Union of Democratic Forces–New Era), was banned and its leaders were arrested, drugged, tortured and imprisoned. A number of independent newspapers were shut down and intellectuals and activists were arrested. In June 2001, three leading members of the Front Populaire Mauritanien (FPM) (Mauritanian Popular Front), including its leader Mohamed Lemine Chbih Ould Chiekh Melaïnine, were sentenced to five years in prison for 'conspiracy to form an armed group with the intent of carrying out acts of terrorism'. The trial was denounced as a sham by human rights and lawyers groups. Amnesty International took up their cases as prisoners of conscience, claiming that 'the charges against the men are without foundation and their conviction is intended solely to stifle political opposition'. Despite a low turnout of 55 per cent compared to 75 per cent in the 1997 presidential election, the 2001 elections were hailed by EU observers as fair and open, reflecting 'the political pluralism shown by the Mauritanian electorate'.

Black power

In January 2002, the government banned the Action pour Changement (AC) (Action for Change) party, which won four seats in the national assembly making it the largest opposition group in parliament. The government accused the party of being 'violent and racist'. AC leader Messaoud Ould Belkheir dismissed the ban as 'a typical example of the absence of democracy under a dictatorial regime that does not tolerate opinions opposed to its own'.

The AC's main crime seemed to be to challenge the hegemony of the Moorish Arab elite and campaign for the rights of Haratines, the descendants of blacks enslaved by the Arabs. Belkheir drew international attention to the continuing problem of slavery and the large number of black Mauritanian refugees, most of whom live in Senegal. Thousands of blacks were exiled to the Senegalese border area following an ethnic pogrom instigated by Taya in 1989 which saw hundreds massacred. Those that have returned to Mauritania have found their lands and homes confiscated by Arabs and have not received compensation. This has heightened resentment among blacks towards the Arab elite.

Racial tensions continue to simmer as the country's black community has increasingly sought to assert itself and seek public office. The feelings over the events of 1989 are still raw, especially since Taya has officially pardoned the army officers responsible for the massacre. As they have become radicalised, the Haratines have rejected subservient attitudes to their former slave masters. This is a major challenge to Moorish Arabs, many of whom have been indoctrinated by Taya's notion of a 'black peril'. The elite has become disturbed by the wave of confrontational politics which was fuelled by the new democratic discourse and are angry that groups like AC are trying to embarrass their government in front of the international community. The government's decision to ban AC has only hardened black defiance and inflamed militant feelings which have threatened to spill over into violence.

However, black groups have only had limited success in trying to attract foreign attention. The US in particular is keen not to isolate Mauritania, which is the only member of the Arab League to maintain diplomatic ties with Israel. Taya's pro-Israel stance has enabled him to escape world attention, although it has been at the expense of some domestic legitimacy.

Debt and development

The IMF has consistently praised the government for its implementation of structural adjustment policies, including extensive privatisation and a balanced budget. In November 2001, the IMF's executive board commended the Mauritanian authorities for meeting all the performance criteria and structural benchmarks under the US$54 million three-year Poverty Reduction and Growth Facility (PRGF), which was approved in July 1999. The programme has succeeded in stabilising the economy, reducing inflation and maintaining a reasonable level of growth, which averaged around 4 per cent in 1996–2001. However, much of the population receives very few of the benefits of growth. Development has focussed on a small sector of the economy while 64 per cent of the population is engaged in subsistence farming.

Debt relief promises to free up government finances in the future, after Mauritania reached completion-point under the IMF's Heavily Indebted Poor Countries Initiative (HIPC) in June 2002. The Paris Club creditor countries quickly followed with a recommended reduction of Mauritania's stock of debt owed to bilateral creditors from US$320 million to US$16 million. In July, the African Development Bank (ADB) approved US$72 million of debt relief, reducing its debt to the bank by around 80 per cent.

Something fishy

The main task facing Mauritania is to diversify its export base, which has traditionally relied on fishing and iron production. The discovery of oil in a number of exploration blocks in 2000 and 2001 has led to hopes that the country may become an oil exporter, although development of the sector is a long way off. Despite structural reform, Mauritania retains a narrow range of exports which are vulnerable to price fluctuations. The country's capacity to broaden its export base is severely limited by a lack of resources, investment and infrastructure. Moreover, its developing manufacturing base is primarily centred on the processing of primary goods, such as iron and fish, which has simply increased the added value of traditional exports rather than increased the range of exports.

Fishing is a particularly vulnerable sector, with fish stocks depleting as foreign trawlers exploit Mauritania's seas. In August 2001, the EU and Mauritania renewed a fishery agreement for a further five years. This heightened anxieties among environmentalists who claim increased levels of fishing are unsustainable and could lead to famine. The EU is paying US$430 million for fishing rights over the period, over 60 per cent more than

KEY INDICATORS **Mauritania**

	Unit	1996	1997	1998	1999	2000
Population	m	2.35	2.46	2.53	2.60	2.67
Gross domestic product (GDP)	US$bn	1.10	1.10	1.00	1.00	0.90
GDP per capita	US$	465	454	399	376	322
GDP real growth	%	5.5	3.2	3.2	4.3	5.2
Inflation	%	4.7	4.5	8.0	4.1	3.3
Exports (fob) (goods)	US$m	480.0	424.5	358.6	333.0	345.0
Imports (fob) (goods)	US$m	346.1	316.5	318.7	329.0	329.0
Balance of trade	US$m	133.9	107.2	40.0	4.0	16.0
Current account	US$m	91.3	47.8	77.2	29.0	-22.0
Foreign debt	US$bn	2.0	2.4	2.5	2.5	2.5
Exchange rate	per US$	137.22	151.85	188.48	209.51	238.92

under the previous agreement. The new agreement has resulted in vessels being pushed further from the coast to protect local small-scale vessels. However, authorities are largely powerless to stop rampant illegal trawling or impose size limitations on EU vessels. Moreover, Mauritania's fisheries are also in jeopardy due to over-fishing in neighbouring countries' waters, notably Morocco and Senegal, where the EU has won extensive fishing rights. This is having an adverse effect on the region's fish stocks and spawning grounds, which Mauritania is powerless to do anything about.

The long-term future of Mauritanian fishing looks bleak. If the country cannot find an industry that can support those who will suffer from the sector's decline, then there is a danger that many Mauritanians will endure hunger and further destitution.

Outlook

Mauritania's paper democracy camouflages a militaristic authoritarianism legitimised by the international community's complacency and indifference. Taya's efforts to depict himself as a democratic and benevolent leader are being undermined by his own use of open repression. However, with a democratic renewal in the neighbouring states of Mali and Senegal, Mauritania stands out as a country in political and economic decay. The growing confidence of the country's black community could lead to racial conflict. Mauritania will be faced with difficult times ahead unless Taya institutes a meaningful democracy which all communities can respect.

Risk assessment

Economic	Stable
Political	Deteriorating
Regional stability	Improving

COUNTRY PROFILE

Historical profile

1800s France gained control of Mauritania, ruling it from Senegal.
1957 Limited self-government was granted under the Loi cadre.
1960 Mauritania gained full independence from France under the regime of the Mauritanian People's Party. Mokhtar Ould Daddah became president.
1974 Mauritania withdrew from the CFAf currency zone and introduced the ouguiya.
1975 An agreement between Mauritania, Morocco and Spain led to the division of the Spanish Sahara (a Spanish colony and the present day Sahrawi Arab Republic (Western Sahara)) between Mauritania and Morocco.
1978 After fighting a largely unsuccessful war against rebels of the Western Sahara, President Daddah was overthrown.
1979 The new government of President Haidallah agreed to renounce all territorial claims to Western Sahara.
1981 Slavery was banned in Mauritania.
1984 Haidallah was removed from office by Colonel Maaouya Ould Sid'Ahmed Taya.
1992 Multi-party elections were held in which President Taya was returned to office with 63 per cent of the vote.
1996 The governing Parti Républicain Démocratique et Social (PRDS) (Social and Democratic Republican Party) won elections held in October.
1997 President Taya was re-elected in the December presidential election with 90 per cent of the vote.
1999 Full diplomatic relations were established with Israel on 28 October. After criticism by Iraq, on 4 November the foreign ministry announced that Mauritania had severed its relations with Iraq.
2001 The PRDS was re-elected with 51 per cent of the vote in the parliamentary elections held on 19 and 26 October 2001.

Political structure

Constitution
In July 1991, a constitution was approved which provided for a president to be elected by universal suffrage for a six-year term and a prime minister to be appointed.
Form of state
Islamic republic
The executive
The president is elected by universal suffrage for a renewable six-year term.
National legislature
Legislative power is vested in a bicameral legislature, with the 81-member Al-Jamiya Al-Wataniyah (national assembly, the lower house) being directly elected every five years, and a 56-member Majlis Al-Shuyukh (senate, the upper house), indirectly elected every six years.
Legal system
The legal system is based on the 1991 constitution and is strongly influenced by Sharia (Islamic law).
Last elections
19 October 2001 (National Assembly); December 1997 (presidential).
Next elections
April/May 2002 (Senate); December 2003 (presidential); 2006 (National Assembly).

Political parties

Political parties were legalised in July 1991 but were forbidden to be organised on racial or regional lines, or to be opposed to Islam. The government has also banned a number of political parties due to their involvement in alleged 'terrorist activities'.
Ruling party
Parti Républicain Démocratique et Social (PRDS) (Social and Democratic Republican Party) (re-elected Oct 2001)
Main opposition party
Union des Forces Démocratiques-Ère Nouvelle (UFD-EN) (Union of Democratic Forces-New Era) (banned); Action pour Changement (AC) (Action for Change) was the largest opposition party in parliament following the 2001 elections, but was banned in January 2002.

Population

2.67 million (2000)
Annual population growth rate: 2.7 per cent (1994–2000). Approximately 45 per cent of the total population is under 15 years.
Population density: two inhabitants per square km. Urban population: 58 per cent (1994–2000).
The standard of living was below the national poverty line for around 47 per cent of the population (1994–2000).
Ethnic make-up
The population comprises a majority of Arabised Moors. The rest are ethnically linked with the peoples of Senegal and Mali. Moor-black (40 per cent), Moor (30 per cent), black (30 per cent).
Religions
Islam (99 per cent)

Education

Public expenditure on education typically amounts to around 5 per cent of gross national income (GNI). On average, there are around 50 teachers per pupil. Literacy levels rose in the 1990s, from 47 per cent for men and 26 per cent for women in 1990 to 52 per cent and 31 per cent respectively.

Health

Life expectancy: 53 years (1994–2000).
Infant mortality rate: 106 per 1,000 live births (1994–2000); approximately 48 per cent of children were malnourished in the same period. Public expenditure on health typically amounts to around 1.5 per cent of GDP. On average, there were just seven doctors per 10,000 people in the 1990s.
In 2000, 37 per cent of the population had access to an improved water source and 33 per cent had access to improved sanitation facilities. HIV prevalence is relatively low among adults, at around 0.52 per cent in 1999.

Main cities

Nouakchott, administrative capital (estimated population 750,000 in 1998);

Nouadhibou (formerly Port-Etienne, 45,000); Zouerate (35,000).

Languages spoken

French is the usual language spoken in business circles.
Hassaniya, Pulaar and Wolof are the major languages in everyday use.
English is rarely spoken.

Official language

Arabic

Media

Press

The only daily newspaper is *Ach-Chaab* printed in both Arabic and French. There are a large number of weekly papers. Issues of weekly newspapers are routinely seized under Article 11 of the 1991 Press Law, which allows government to censor arbitrarily publications that attempt any open criticism of state action. Pre-publication censorship, the arrest of journalists and bans of newspapers are very common government actions in Mauritania. The weekly *Rajoul al-Chari* has been under attack and the independent weekly *Le Calame* has faced suspension. Other newspapers targeted by the government include *La Tribune* and the weekly *Al Alam*.
Agence Mauritanienne d'Information (http://www.mauritania.mr/ami) in Nouakchott is the official government press agency that publishes the daily editions of the *Chaab* newspapers (circulated in Arabic), *Horizons* (French) and the official *Bulletin* of the Agency.

Broadcasting

Office Mauritanien de Radiodiffusion et de Télévision (OMRT) broadcasts in Arabic and French.

Advertising

Radio Mauritanie accepts advertisements. TV advertising rates are reasonable.

Economy

Mauritania has a strong reliance on aid flows and earnings from fish and iron ore. Since 1992, Mauritania has been implementing a comprehensive programme of economic adjustment and structural reform which has won the support and praise of international financial institutions (IFIs) such as the IMF.
In July 1999, Mauritania began a three-year programme supported by a US$54 million Enhanced Structural Adjustment Facility (ESAF) – later renamed the Poverty Reduction and Growth Facility (PRGF) – agreed with the IMF. By end-2001, Mauritania had drawn on a total of around US$39 million.
In the light of sustained macroeconomic stability, the government eased fiscal policy and allowed for a decline in budgetary revenue by 1 per cent of GDP in 2001, raising the budget deficit to 1.5 per cent of GDP. Much of the increase in government expenditure was targetted at priority areas, such as health and education, as well as infrastructural investment. The wage bill was also due to rise by around 0.1 per cent of GDP to allow for additional recruitment in the priority sectors.
Strong macroeconomic performance has made little difference to the lives of most Mauritanians. Around 47 per cent of the population live below the poverty line and GNP per capita is US$390. Most of the country's growth has come in a narrow range of industrial activities, namely fish processing and iron production. Growth is also offset by currency depreciation and real GDP in dollar terms was almost the same in 2001 as in 1989 before the country embarked on its structural adjustment programme, thereby leading to a steady decline in GDP per capita. The main task facing the government is how to expand and diversify its economy in such a way that will benefit the poor while retaining economic stability.

External trade

Mauritania belongs to the Arab Maghreb Union (UMA), together with Algeria, Libya, Morocco and Tunisia. The UMA was set up in 1989, but has been frozen in deadlock in recent years due to a breakdown in relations between Algeria and Morocco over the sovereignty of Western Sahara. However, it was revived in 2001 to resolve food security issues and strengthen trade ties throughout the region.

Exports

Principal exports are fish and fish products (typically 45 per cent of total value) and iron ore (40–50 per cent).
Main destinations: France (18.4 per cent of 2000 total), Japan (15.3 per cent), Italy (13.7 per cent), Spain (11 per cent), Belgium (8.9 per cent).

Imports

Principal imports are foodstuffs (typically 30–40 per cent of total), petroleum products (24–30 per cent), transport equipment (8–12 per cent), consumer goods (8–12 per cent).
Main sources: France (26.7 per cent of 2000 total), Belgium (9.3 per cent), Italy (6.2 per cent), Spain (6.2 per cent), Germany (4.9 per cent).

Agriculture

The agricultural and fishing sector accounts for around a quarter of GDP and employs two-thirds of the working population. Less than 3 per cent of the total area is cultivated arable and 10 per cent is pasture. Production of foodstuffs is restricted to irrigated land in the south along the north bank of the Senegal River. Most of Mauritania consists of arid and semi-arid land and although it is unsuitable for crops, livestock rearing is an important sector. Nomadic herders comprise around 10 per cent of the population, although their numbers are dwindling.
Fishing contributes up to 10 per cent of GDP and provides around 45 per cent of export earnings as well as an important source of food for Mauritanians.
International aid agencies and imported cereals are vital in supplementing the main food crops – millet, sorghum, rice, maize, potatoes and dates.

Fishing

Mauritanian coastal waters are among the richest in the world and joint venture fishing is one of the most important foreign exchange earners. The main catch is deep sea species and shellfish – particularly shrimps for the Japanese market.
In August 2001, the EU and Mauritania renewed a fishing agreement to enable EU trawlers to fish in Mauritanian waters.

Industry and manufacturing

The industrial sector contributes around 10 per cent to GDP and employs 5 per cent of the workforce.
The most important activities are fish freezing and processing and the treatment of locally mined iron ore. There are also various small import substitution industries (brewing, footwear, dairy processing etc), oil refining and a sugar refinery in Nouakchott.

Mining

The mining sector contributes around 13 per cent to GDP, employs 5 per cent of the working population and generates 42 per cent of export earnings.
The annual output of iron ore is around 12 million tonnes, of which about 11 million tonnes is exported – 36 per cent to France, 26 per cent to Italy, 16 per cent to Belgium, 8 per cent to Germany, 4 per cent to Spain and 4 per cent to the UK.
The iron mines are located in the Tiris region in the north and are owned and operated by Société Nationale Industrielle et Minière (SNIM). Other mineral resources include copper (at Akjoujt); gold (also near Akjoujt); phosphates (deposits at Bofal), diamonds and uranium.
The government has attempted to encourage foreign investment in the mining sector and in June 1999 a mining law was passed which gave the private sector and foreign investors a number of incentives, including tax incentives and exemptions. By 2001, the government had granted more than 80 exploration licences and five mining concessions to domestic and foreign mining operators.

Hydrocarbons

Offshore oil reserves have been identified, but the precise amount is not known. In June 2000, Dana Petroleum stated it had identified potential reserves in shallow and deepwater prospects in offshore blocks 1, 7 and 8. Fusion Oil and Gas Plc, which has a stake in Production Sharing Contracts (PSCs) A and B of 3 per cent and 6 per cent respectively, began drilling oil exploration wells in April 2001. PSCs A and B cover a total of 28,000 square kilometres. In May 2001, Woodside, another participant in the prospects, estimated proven reserves of 370 million barrels. Mauritania's downstream industry consists of one refinery located at Nouadhibou which is operated by an Algerian company.

Energy

Primary energy resources consist of fuelwood and small-scale thermal electricity (generating capacity 110MW). A majority of thermal generation is provided by isolated diesel generators.

The Société Mauritanienne d'Electricité (Maurelec) is responsible for electricity generation, transmission and supply. The electricity network serves only a few people in urban areas. Over half of the installed generating capacity is provided by hydroelectric dams.

Completion of work on Manantali dam on the Senegal river will lead to an increase in hydroelectric power supply to Mauritania, Senegal and Mali. Work on the Manantali dam was completed in 2001 and is funded by loans from the Arab Fund, World Bank, African Development Fund, French Co-operation Fund, Islamic Development Bank, European Investment Bank and the Mauritanian government at a cost of US$340.65 million. Five generators will supply around 40MW each.

Banking

Throughout the 1980s and 1990s, Mauritania's banking sector underwent a series of crises, mainly due to poor management and the near-collapse of the fishing industry which led to heavy losses and a large ratio of bad loans. In recent years, Mauritania's banking sector has undergone liberalisation with the government selling its equity stake in commercial banks, which has made it more competitive. Reform of the banking sector has led to limits on bank lending and to new laws on debt recovery. In 2001, there were seven banks operating in the country.

Domestic confidence in the banking sector remains low and 60 per cent of cash is still not placed in banks. However, this represents an enormous opportunity for the banking sector to increase savings and improve liquidity. The government has succeeded in meeting the IMF's debt reduction requirements by producing year-on-year budget surpluses, which has reduced inflation and limited the crowding out of private sector credit. An increase in the number of bank branches and the introduction of micro-banking schemes is likely to transform the sector in coming years.

Central bank

Banque Centrale de Mauritanie

Main financial centre

Nouakchott

Time

GMT

Geography

Mauritania lies in north-west Africa, with the Atlantic Ocean to the west, Algeria and Western Sahara to the north, Mali to the east and south, and Senegal to the south. The north is mainly desert.

Climate

The climate is hot and dry. The hottest month in Noukachott is September (24–34 degrees Celsius (C); the coldest is December (12–29 degrees C); the wettest month is August.

Entry requirements

Passports

Required by all.

Visa

Required by all except nationals of Arab League countries and certain African countries. UK citizens must get their visas from the Consul Générale office in Paris (89 rue du Cherche Midi XVI).

Currency advice/regulations

Unlimited foreign currency may be imported, but the amount must be declared on arrival. Unexchanged foreign currency may be exported. Declaration forms must be produced on departure. Import and export of local currency is strictly forbidden. Controls are constantly subject to modification.

Health (for visitors)

Mandatory precautions

Yellow fever vaccination certificate required by all, unless arriving from a non-infected area and staying for less than 14 days.

Advisable precautions

Yellow fever, hepatitis A, tetanus, typhoid and polio vaccinations. Malaria prophylaxis should be taken.

Water precautions are advisable. There is a rabies risk.

Hotels

Accommodation is limited and visitors should book well in advance. A service charge is normally included in the bill, otherwise a 15 per cent tip is usual.

Credit cards

Only accepted in main hotels.

Public holidays

Fixed dates

1 Jan (New Year's Day), 1 May (Labour Day), 8 May (Women's Feast) (only for women), 25 May (Organisation for Arab Unity Day), 28 Nov (Independence Day).

Variable dates

Korité (Eid Al-Fitr – end of Ramadan), Tabaski (Eid Al-Adha), Maouloud (Prophet's Birthday), Ascension of the Prophet, Islamic New Year.

Working hours

Banking

(Sun–Wed) 0800–1115; 1430–1630; Thu: 0800–1500.

Business

Sat–Wed: 0800–1500; Thu: 0800–1300. Some stop for a lunch-time break (usually 1200–1300 or 1500).

Government

Sat–Wed: 0800–1500; Thu: 0800–1300.

Shops

Sat–Thu: 0800–1200; 1430–1800.

Telecommunications

Telephone/fax

International telephone facilities are available in Nouakchott and Nouadhibou. Dialling code for Mauritania: IDD access code + 222 followed by subscriber's number. There are no area codes.

Electricity supply

127/220V AC, 50 cycles. Plugs and sockets mostly two-pin (round).

Getting there

Air

National airline: Air Mauritanie

Main airport: Nouadhibou (Code: NDB), 4km from city; Nouakchott (Code: NKC), 4km from city.

Airport tax: International departures to Africa (including Madagascar) UM560; international departures to rest of world UM860; domestic departures UM270; excluding transit passengers not leaving the airport and continuing their journeys by same or first available connecting flight within 24 hours.

Surface

Road: Surfaced road from Dakar (Senegal) to Nouakchott; via ferry over the River Sénégal at Rosso. Also paved from Mali to Nouakchott.

Main ports: Nouadhibou and Nouakchott. The deep-water port near Nouakchott, built with Chinese assistance, has a capacity of one million tonnes per annum.

Getting about

National transport

Air: Air Mauritanie provides a daily service between Nouakchott, Nouadhibou and Zouerate, while flying bi-weekly to other towns in Mauritania such as Kaédi.

Road: There is a paved road between Rosso (on the Senegal River, where a ferry connects with the road to Dakar) and Akjoujt, via Nouakchott.

Nouakchott-Rosso 204km;
Nouakchott-Akjoujt 244km.

Rail: A track runs inland from the coast (Nouakchott-Zouerate), mainly for freight but there are some passenger services (single-class) scheduled; motor vehicles are sometimes carried.

City transport

Taxis: Taxis are numerous in the main towns. Fares are standardised but not metered. A small tip is usual. Taxis can also be rented by the hour.

Car hire

An international or national driving licence is required. It is advisable to have a driver as finding one's way around is difficult. Out of town, a four-wheel drive with chauffeur, although expensive, is recommended.

BUSINESS DIRECTORY

Telephone area codes

Dialling code for Mauritania: IDD access code +222 followed by subscriber's number. There are no area codes.

Chambers of Commerce

Chambre de Commerce, d'Agriculture et d'Industrie de la République Islamique de Mauritanie, BP 215, Nouakchott (tel: 52-214; fax: 53-895).

Banking

Banque Mauritanienne pour le Commerce International, PO Box 622, Immeuble Afarco, Avenue Gamal Abdel Nasser, Nouakchott (tel: 254353; fax: 252045).

Banque Nationale de Mauritanie; PO Box 614 & 291, Avenue Gamal Abdel Nasser, Nouakchott (tel: 251262, 252707, 252602, 252934 fax: 253397).

Central bank

Banque Centrale de Mauritania, PO Box 623, Avenue de l'Indépendance, Nouakchott, Mauritania (tel:252206, 252888 fax:252759).

Travel information

Air Mauritanie, BP 41, Nouakchott 174, (fax: 53-815).

Société Mauritanienne de Tourisme et d'Hôtellerie, BP 552, Nouakchott.

National tourist organisation offices

Direction du Tourisme, BP 246, Nouakchott (tel: 53-337).

Ministries

Ministry of Commerce, Artisans and Tourism, BP 182, Nouakchott (tel: 51-057).

Ministry of Economy and Finance, BP 197, Nouakchott (tel: 54-395; fax: 53-114).

Ministry of Fishing and Maritime Economy, BP 137, Nouakchott (tel: 52-476).

Ministry of Foreign Affairs and Co-operation, BP 230, Nouakchott (tel: 52-682).

Ministry of Health and Social Security, BP 169, Nouakchott (tel: 52-052).

Ministry of Industry and Mines, BP 183, Nouakchott (tel: 51-318).

Ministry of the Interior, Post and Telecommunications, BP 195, Nouakchott (tel: 52-020).

Ministry of Planning, BP 238, Nouakchott (tel: 51-612).

Ministry of Transport, BP 237, Nouakchott (tel: 53-337).

Ministry of Rural Development, BP 180, Nouakchott (tel: 51-500; fax: 57-574).

To contact other ministries (tel: 53-337).

Other enquiries:

Budget (tel: 52-666), Customs (tel: 51-404), Finance (tel: 53-337), Hydraulics (tel: 51-611), Imports (tel: 52-093), Industry (tel: 53-337), Information (tel: 51-931), Marine market (tel: 57-893), Post and Telecommunications (tel: 51-649), Statistics (tel: 53-070), Treasury (tel: 51-462).

National Statistics Office, BP 240, Nouakchott (tel: 51-477).

Prime Minister's Office, BP 184, Nouakchott (tel: 53-337).

Other useful addresses

Bureau d'Achats pour la République Islamique de Mauritanie (BARIM), BP 272, Nouakchott (deals with imports of food, textiles etc).

Exploitation des Mines d'Or de l'Inchin (MORAK), Akjoujt (tel: 61-263; fax: 61-079); Nouakchott (tel: 56-423, 57-499; fax: 56-320).

Fédération des Banques et Services, Nouakchott (tel: 58-343; fax: 53-301).

Fédération des Industries et Armement de Pêche (FIAP), Nouadhibou (tel: 45-089; fax: 45-430).

Fédération des Industries et des Mines (FIM), Nouakchott (tel: 52-160, 51-990; fax: 53-301).

Fédération du Commerce (FC), Nouakchott (tel: 52-160, 51-990; fax: 53-301).

Fédération Nationale des Transports (FNT), Nouakchott (tel: 57-936, 54-738; fax: 57-935).

La Confédération Générale des Employeurs de Mauritanie (CGEM), Nouakchott (tel: 52-160, 51-990; fax: 53-301).

Mauritanian Embassy (USA), 2129 Leroy Place, NW, Washington DC 20008 (tel: 232-5700; fax: 319-2623).

Mauritanienne d'Entreposage des Produits Pétroliers (MEPP), Nouakchott (tel: 52-646; fax: 54-608).

Société Arabe des Mines d l'Inchin (Samin), Akjoujt (tel: 61-104; fax: 61-279).

Société Mauritanienne de Commercialisation de Produits Pétroliers (SMCPP), Nouakchott (tel: 52-651; fax: 52-542).

Société Nationale d'Importation et d'Exportation (SONIMEX), BP 290, Nouakchott (tel: 51-472, 52-224; fax: 53-014).

Société Nationale d'Eau et d'Electricité (SONELEC), Nouakchott (tel: 52-308; fax: 53-995).

Société Nationale Industrielle et Miniére (SNIM), Nouadhibou (tel: 45-174; fax: 45-396); Nouakchott (tel: 53-689; fax: 53-689).

Société Nationale pour le Dévéloppement Rural (SONADER), Nouakchott (tel: 51-800; fax: 53-286).

Internet sites

Africa Business Network: http://www.ifc.org/abn

AllAfrica.com: http://allafrica.com

African Development Bank: http://www.afdb.org

Africa Online: http://www.africaonline.com

Harambee Afrika (UK business club for traders with east, central and southern Africa; includes annotated web resource list): http://www.harambee.co.uk

Mbendi AfroPaedia (information on companies, countries, industries and stock exchanges in Africa): http://mbendi.co.za

Mauritius

Guy Arnold

KEY FACTS

Official name: Republic of Mauritius

Head of State: President Karl Offman (elected by the National Assembly, Feb 2002)

Head of government: Prime Minister Sir Anerood Jugnauth (from Sep 2000)

Ruling party: Coalition of Mouvement Socialiste Mauricien (MSM) (Mauritian Socialist Movement) and Mouvement Militante Mauricien (MMM) (Mauritian Militant Movement) (elected Sep 2000)

Area: 1,865 square km

Population: 1.20 million (2001)

Capital: Port Louis

Official language: English, French

Currency: Mauritian rupee (MR) = 100 cents

Exchange rate: MR28.95 per US$ (Jan 2003)

GDP per capita: US$3,812 (2001); US$4,010 (2002)*

GDP real growth: 5.60% (2001); 5.0% (2002)*

Unemployment: 8.60% (2001); 8.8% (2002)*

Inflation: 5.40% (2001); 6.3% (2002)*

Balance of trade: -US$423.00 million (2001)

Foreign debt: US$1.74 billion (2001)

Annual FDI: US$223.00 million (2001)

* estimated figure

For the latest Key Facts, go to www.worldinformation.com

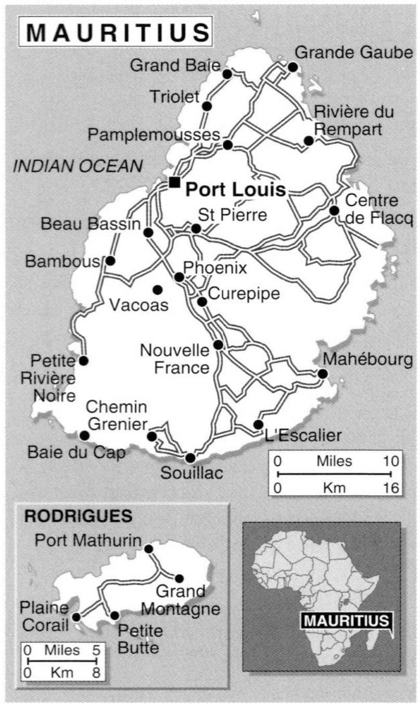

Politically, the beginning of 2002 was a difficult period for Mauritius as a result of the much-debated Prevention of Terrorism Act. The domestic climate was unstable with public violence erupting on the island. In contrast, economic conditions were good and the island seemed to be reaping the benefits of its ongoing diversification policy.

Constitutional crisis

The controversial Prevention of Terrorism Act that increased the period police can hold suspects without charging them and which denies alleged terrorists legal representation became law in February 2002. The bill caused the resignation of two presidents in the same month. The former president, Caseem Uteem, and his successor, Angidi Chettiar, both stepped down in protest against the bill, believing it constituted an erosion of citizens' rights. The law was criticised by Amnesty International as being ambiguous in its terms and giving too much power to the Mauritian police. The inauguration of the new president, Karl Offman, was met with widespread public protest as many Mauritians believed that he should have had the moral responsibility to refuse the position. The prime minister, Sir Anergood Jugnauth, maintained that the people had nothing to fear from the law. Given reports of violence in police custody and mounting public hostility towards the law, it is likely that security conditions on the island will deteriorate.

The British Indian Ocean Territory

The Mauritian claim to the Chagos Islands surfaced again in 2001 as a result of the British High Court ruling in November 2000 that the eviction of 2,000 inhabitants of the Chagos Islands, now uninhabited and called the British Indian Ocean Territory (BIOT), had been unlawful, a judgement that raised an old bone of contention between Mauritius and Britain. Díego Garcia, one of the islands, was leased by Britain to the US for use as a military base during the Cold War and was used again by the US to launch airstrikes against the Taliban and Al-Qaeda in Afghanistan from October 2001. After the military base was created in the 1970s, the islanders were sent to Mauritius, which claimed sovereignty over the Chagos Archipelago and intended to secure compensation from Britain and the US for the 'discrimination and human rights violations' that had been suffered by the islanders who want to return to their former homeland. In October 2002, the exiled islanders began steps to launch legal action against the British government to return to Díego Garcia and gain compensation for being deported in the first place.

Better than good

The economy is in reasonably healthy condition, although its high GDP growth rate of 25 per cent during 1999 had dropped to a more modest 5.6 per cent in 2001 and 5 per cent in 2002. The fall has been partly due to poor sugar harvests resulting from drought conditions. Mauritius has been better able to withstand such setbacks than in former times because of its success in diversifying the economy, reducing its dependency on sugar, the traditional staple of the economy. Mauritius has developed strong macroeconomic policies and manages a wide degree of diversification to demonstrate some of the best economic growth in Africa. Since 1980, Mauritius has registered an average annual growth rate of nearly 6 per cent, principally as a direct result of this diversification. As a result, agriculture, which contributed 12 per cent to GDP in 1990, now only contributes 10 per cent to GDP. The services sector is dominated by tourism and financial services that together account for 74 per cent of GDP. Foreign exchange earnings from services contribute over a third of all foreign exchange income. Mauritius has a more open trading policy than most African countries.

Southern Africa has taken a leaf out of Caribbean success in tackling tourism by establishing a multinational tourism body, the Regional Tourism Organisation of Southern Africa (RETOSA). Mauritius had hoped to become the headquarters of the RETOSA particularly as it has an excellent infrastructure, but in the end the headquarters were sited in Johannesburg, which is the commercial airline hub of the region. Nonetheless, RETOSA should benefit the whole Southern African Development Community (SADC) region, although tourism was adversely affected by the fallout from the 11 September 2001 terrorist attacks in the US and the 2002 Bali bombing.

The future of the EEZ

Much of the government's attention during 2001 and 2002 was directed towards the changes that globalisation is likely to bring to the island's economy. These will affect the operation of the Exclusive Economic Zone (EEZ) and require adjustments in line with the directives of the World Trade Organisation (WTO).

Mauritius' successful EEZ has given rise to adverse comments and accusations that it was 'unfair'. An OECD report of 2000 examined offshore investment centres and argued that its tax practices were not fair since they did not comply with principles that are seen to be fair in relation to taxation. In reaction to this OECD document, Minister of Finance V K Bunware stressed that 'the government of Mauritius hereby commits to the elimination of tax practices that have been determined by the Forum on Harmful Tax Competition to be harmful in accordance with the OECD Report. Mauritius undertakes to implement such measures (including through any legislative changes) as are necessary to fulfil this commitment.' The timetable for a phased elimination of the 'harmful tax practices' was set for the end of 2005. The OECD had raised controversy by this approach, which many in developing countries see as an attempt to marginalise offshore investment centres. The OECD needs to convince its critics that this is not the case.

Maritime boundaries

Graham Holden, a Commonwealth Fund for Technical Co-operation (CFTC) expert, was appointed early in 2001 for a one-year assignment to assist the government of Mauritius meet an international maritime deadline. Mauritius, which is a signatory of the UN Convention on the Law of the Sea (UNCLOS), has to redefine its territorial boundaries in order to comply with international guidelines by 2004. The government signed the Convention in 1994, thus committing Mauritius to redefine its EEZ and the continental shelf over which it has sovereignty. The CFTC, in response to a Mauritian request, appointed Graham Holden to co-ordinate the work of redefining Mauritius' maritime boundaries. The work to be done included redrafting the maritime boundaries, preparing and implementing a training programme for all local staff on every aspect of the project and negotiations with neighbouring states.

Diversification and the WTO

Diversification has paid dividends for Mauritius, which has become a net exporter of services. According to the WTO, 'Mauritius' participation in the multilateral trading system and in various regional agreements reflects its interests as a small, export-oriented economy with advantages in a few products, sugar, textiles and clothing in particular.' In addition, Mauritius has benefited because of the preferential market access granted to it by major trading partners.

Forthcoming changes that result from WTO agreements mean that Mauritius must adjust. The WTO stated that 'the end adjustment needs to emphasise the streamlining and rationalisation of existing incentives so as to lessen the aspects of duality and improve resource allocation'. As a small island economy, Mauritius constantly has to take account of external factors and pressures, and adjust to a changing economic environment and technological advances. This means further diversification. According to the WTO, there is duality in the Mauritian economy between companies producing for the domestic market, which are fairly highly protected and export enterprises, which receive various incentives, for example under the EEZ. The WTO has said 'This has led to tensions in resource allocation between the export and domestic sections and highlights the task of transforming the economy.'

Regional organisations

Mauritius is a member of four regional trading organisations: the Common Market for Eastern and Southern Africa

KEY INDICATORS — Mauritius

	Unit	1996	1997	1998	1999	2000
Population	m	1.13	1.15	1.16	1.17	1.18
Gross domestic product (GDP)	US$bn	4.29	4.17	4.20	4.22	4.60
GDP per capita	US$	3,799	3,629	3,622	3,610	3,914
GDP real growth	%	5.4	5.0	5.2	5.6	7.8
Inflation	%	6.6	6.8	6.8	6.9	4.5
Wholesale prices	1995=100	0.0	0.0	0.0	0.0	135.4
Consumer prices	1995=100	106.6	113.8	121.6	130.0	0.0
Unemployment	%	5.5	5.9	5.9	6.4	8.0
Exports (fob) (goods)	US$m	1,811.0	1,600.0	1,669.0	1,589.0	1,559.4
Imports (fob) (goods)	US$m	2,136.0	2,036.0	1,933.0	2,137.0	1,953.3
Balance of trade	US$m	-325.7	-436.0	-264.0	-547.2	-393.9
Current account	US$m	34.0	-88.9	3.3	-52.3	-33.3
Foreign debt	US$bn	1.8	1.9	2.0	2.5	2.4
Total reserves minus gold	US$m	896.1	693.3	559.0	731.0	897.4
Foreign exchange	US$m	853.7	653.0	516.5	689.1	857.1
Exchange rate	per US$	17.95	21.06	23.99	25.19	26.25

(Comesa), the Southern African Development Community (SADC), the Indian Ocean Commission (IOC) and the Regional Facilitation Forum (RIFF). Its participation in these regional groupings moves Mauritius closer to full integration in the world economy.

Outlook

Political conditions on the island seem likely to deteriorate unless the Prevention of Terrorism Act is repealed. Given the prime minister's defence of the law, this is unlikely to happen, leading to further public hostility.

The Mauritian economy is soundly based and the government is making determined efforts to endorse and adopt measures that will help the island to integrate more closely with the world economy. Its level of growth remains one of the highest in Africa.

Risk Assessment

Economic	Good
Political	Poor
Regional stability	Good
Stock market	Satisfactory

COUNTRY PROFILE

Historical profile

1598 A Dutch squadron landed at Grand Port and named the island Mauritius.
1638 Mauritius settled by the Dutch. The island became an important port of call for Dutch, English and French trading ships. The Dutch introduced sugar-cane and imported slaves to harvest it.
1710 The Dutch abandoned their settlement.
1721 France claimed the island; it also imported large numbers of slaves to harvest sugar-cane, cotton and other crops.
1810 Britain defeated a French naval squadron and the island was ceded to Britain at the end of the Napoleonic Wars.
1835 Slavery was abolished. Most freed slaves left the plantations and settled in coastal towns; workers had to be imported from the Indian sub-continent to take their place, most of whom opted to remain on the island at the end of their contracts.
1936 The Labour Party (LP) was formed and organised strikes and protests between 1937–45.
1953 A group of Mauritians under Seewoosagur Ramgoolam rose to the leadership of the LP, which won the 1953 elections to the Legislative Council. Most Creoles joined the Parti Mauricien Social-Démocrate (PMSD) (Social Democratic Party of Mauritius).
1959 New political parties emerged including the Muslim Committee of Action (CAM). CAM formed an alliance with the LP.
1968 Mauritius gained independence from Britain in March.
1969 Ramgoolam's LP-CAM (Muslim) ruling alliance was strengthened when a coalition with the PMSD was formed. In response, the Mouvement Militante Mauricien (MMM) (Mauritian Militant Movement) was established.
1982 The LP lost power as the MMM, in alliance with the Parti Socialiste Mauricien (PSM), gained power under the premiership of Anerood Jugnauth.
1983 The MMM split and Jugnauth formed the Mouvement Socialiste Mauricien (MSM) (Mauritian Socialist Movement) which formed a government with the LP.
1990 The MMM and the MSM formed a political alliance and aimed to transform Mauritius into a republic.
1995 An alliance of the LP and the MMM, led by Navinchandra Ramgoolam and Paul Berenger, won 60 seats in the December parliamentary elections. Ramgoolam became prime minister.
1997 In June the LP-MMM coalition broke up when the MMM left government and became the official opposition. Even so, the LP continued to hold an outright majority in the legislature with 35 out of the 62 seats, and for the first time since independence Mauritius was governed by a single party.
2000 The ruling LP suffered a crushing defeat when the opposition MSM/MMM won the September election. Anerood Jugnauth, leader of the MMM, became prime minister for the second time. In December, Mauritius revived a claim to sovereignty over Diego Garcia, British Indian Ocean Territory.
2001 The WTO trade policy review in November encouraged Mauritius to further liberalise and diversify its economy.
2002 President Cassam Uteem resigned on 15 February and Vice President Angidi Chettiar became interim president. However, on 18 February, he also resigned. Both Cassam Uteem and Angidi Chettiar resigned having refused to sign into law controversial anti-terrorism legislation. The National Assembly elected Karl Offman as president.

Political structure

Constitution
Mauritius is a republic with a president as head of state.
The president is elected by a simple majority of all the members of the National Assembly for a five-year term. The National Assembly is the supreme body that votes laws. The president's agreement and signature is required to sign legislation into law.

Form of state
Republic

The executive
Executive power is vested in the prime minister, leader of the majority parliamentary party.
There is a Council of Ministers consisting of the prime minister and not more than 24 other ministers.

National legislature
The unicameral National Assembly has 62 seats elected by universal adult suffrage for five years.
For the purpose of electing members of the National Assembly, the island of Mauritius is divided into 20 three-member constituencies.
The island of Rodrigues returns two members.
The official language of the National Assembly is English but any member may address the Chair in French.

Last elections
September 2000 (parliamentary) February 2002 (presidential)

Next elections
2005 (parliamentary)

Political parties

Ruling party
Coalition of Mouvement Socialiste Mauricien (MSM) (Mauritian Socialist Movement) and Mouvement Militante Mauricien (MMM) (Mauritian Militant Movement) (elected Sep 2000)

Main opposition party
Labour Party/Mauritian Party of Xavier Duval (LP/PMXD), (six seats); (Rodrigues People's Organisation) (OPR) (two seats).

Population

1.18 million (2000). The population is expected to reach 1.4 million by 2025.
Annual population growth rate: 1.2 per cent (2001). Approximately 26 per cent of the total population is under 15 years.
Population density: 588 per square km. The population densities of the island of Mauritius and the island of Rodrigues are 624 and 345 respectively.

Ethnic make-up
Indentured workers were brought from India to work on sugar estates and their descendants form a majority of the population, followed by Creoles (of mixed, predominantly African, origin), Muslim Indians, Chinese and Europeans. Hindu Indo-Mauritian (51 per cent), Creole (27 per cent), Muslim Indo-Mauritians (17 per cent), Chinese (2 per cent).

Religions
Hinduism (51 per cent), Christianity (Roman Catholic) (31.3 per cent), Muslim (16.6 per cent).

Main cities

Port Louis (capital city), Beau Bassin/Rose Hill, Quatre Bornes and Curepipe.

Languages spoken

English and French are the official languages, and are widely understood in business circles; Creole and Bhojpuri are the predominant languages in everyday life.

Official language

English, French (Creole and Bhojpuri widely spoken)

Media

Press

Several daily newspapers including *Le Mauricien*, *l'Express*, *The Sun* and some weekly newspapers and periodicals are in circulation.

Broadcasting

Mauritius Broadcasting Corporation (MBC) operates two TV and three radio channels. Broadcasts in English, French, Creole, Hindi, Tamil, Telegu, Marathi, Urdu, Chinese, Gujarati and Bhojpuri. French pay-TV station Canal Plus and Sky News from the UK British Sky Broadcasting Corporation have been transmitting programmes since 1995.

Radio: Radio Sugar FM is the main station, operated by MBC.

Economy

Mauritius has a stable, prosperous economy but changes are taking place due to WTO requirements to liberalise trade and diverisfy the economy. The government hopes to model the island on Singapore based on the free port, expansion of offshore banking, manufacturing base and modernisation of traditional industries as well as its well-placed geographical situation between Asia and Africa.

The economy experienced strong growth throughout 2000/01, when GDP growth was 7.8 per cent. This performance has mainly been driven by growth in the economy's major sectors, paricularly sugar. Careful policy-making has resulted in this economic success.

External trade

The Cotonou Agreement, which replaced the Lomé Convention in 2000, gives preferential treatment to Mauritius on European markets and supports its sugar industry.

Unexploited textile import quotas with the US have made Mauritius an attractive production location for Indian and Chinese companies, whose own national quotas have been filled.

Exports

Principal exports are textiles, sugar, canned tuna, tea, watches and flowers.

Main destinations: UK (29 per cent of 2000 total), France (22 per cent), US (20.2 per cent), Madagascar (5.1 per cent), Italy (3.9 per cent).

Imports

Principal imports are meat, fish, wheat, textile yarn, cotton fabrics, road vehicles and specialised machinery.

Main sources: South Africa (20.9 per cent of 2000 total), France (13.6 per cent), India (12.3 per cent), China (10.6 per cent), UK (6.1 per cent), Australia (4.9 per cent).

Agriculture

The agricultural sector contributed 10 per cent to GDP in 2000 and employed 13 per cent of the workforce.

Sugar-cane cultivation dominates the sector. Approximately 70 per cent of all cultivated land is devoted to the crop, and the sugar industry as a whole employs the majority of the workforce and accounts for 6 per cent of GDP. Cultivation is undertaken both on large plantations and by smallholders.

The other major export crop is tea, grown by tenant farmers. Mauritius is the fourth-largest producer of tea per capita in the world. Around 75 per cent of tea production (green leaf) is controlled by the Tea Development Authority, whose commercial activities are privately run.

Tobacco is grown for the home market.

Main food crops include potatoes and other vegetables, output of which is sufficient to meet domestic demand.

Much of the island's meat requirement is imported. Around 75 per cent of food requirements are also imported.

It is estimated that for the 2000/01 harvest year, sugar production reached 650,000 tonnes, an increase of 5 per cent from 1997/98 Another 1,800 hectares has been added to the cultivation area, making a total of 74,550ha.

Industry and manufacturing

The industrial sector contributed 29 per cent to GDP in 2000 and employed 28 per cent of the workforce.

With no natural resources, Mauritius capitalises on a selection of well-spotted market niches.

The industrial sector is based on the Export Processing Zones (EPZ) which were opened in the 1970s to take advantage of the preferential treatment which Mauritius receives under the Cotonou Agreement.

Production of textiles, and in particular knitwear, has become the most significant EPZ industry, and Mauritius is the world's third-largest exporter of pure new wool products. The EPZ textiles industry employs 91 per cent of the industrial workforce, accounts for 68 per cent of EPZ enterprises and 80 per cent of EPZ exports. The EPZs generate 23 per cent of GDP. In 2001 the knitwear industry was moving towards high-fashion apparel as part of the effort to modernise. The country's exports of textiles in 2001 increased by US$21.3 million, the result of the US Africa Growth and Opportunity Act (AGOA).

Diversification is being encouraged; other industries include the manufacture of watches and clocks, jewellery, spectacle frames and leather goods.

Informatics Park for foreign companies specialising in information technology was opened in 1994. Mauritius has plans to develop into a 'cyber island' and will receive assistance from the IMF as part of its upgrade.

Tourism

Tourism is the third most important source of foreign exchange and accounts for 12 per cent of GDP.

Approximately 28 per cent of tourists come from France, 19 per cent from Réunion, 10 per cent from South Africa, 10 per cent from Germany and 8 per cent from the UK.

There are some 95 registered hotels, total room capacity is around 6,450. Twenty new hotels are planned by 2016 at the total cost of US$450 million. Saturation point is near and there is a risk of environmental damage if development is not managed and contained accordingly.

Energy

Approximately 50 per cent of primary energy requirements are imported.

Local electricity supply is largely from diesel-powered thermal stations.

There has been rapid development of electricity generation from bagasse (refuse produced in sugar-making). Hydroelectricity produces 25 per cent and bagasse 15 per cent of electricity.

Financial markets

Stock exchange

The Stock Exchange of Mauritius was established by the government in July 1989 with five companies listed.

From June 1994 the stock market was opened to international investors.

There are ambitions to become a regional exchange, supplemented by offshore funds and listings from mainland Africa. In 1996 a central depository and settlement system was introduced. A new Securities Act also brought the framework up to world standards.

A weighted index, the SemDex, was introduced in 1998. In March 2002, market capitalisation was US$1.1 billion, with 40 listed companies. Foreign investors do not need approval to trade shares unless investment is for the purpose of management of a Mauritian company or for a holding over 15 per cent of a sugar company.

Banking

In 1989 tax and duty incentives were introduced for foreign banks licensed to engage in offshore banking. Mauritius launched Africa's first offshore banking centre at the end of 1989 which continues to expand.

Central bank
Bank of Mauritius.

Main financial centre
Port Louis.

Time
GMT plus four hours

Geography
Mauritius lies in the Indian Ocean. The principal island from which the country takes its name, lies about 800km (500 miles) east of Madagascar. The other main islands are Rodrigues, the Agalega Islands and the Cargados Carajos Shoals (St Brandon Islands).

Climate
Maritime – tropical in summer (November–April), and sub-tropical for rest of year. High humidity especially in inland areas. Summer temperatures average 25–30 degrees Celsius (C) with maximum 35 degrees C in February. Highest rainfall occurs in summer (and cyclones are likely). From May–November, drier and warm with temperatures 19–27 degrees C. Lowest rainfall from September–November. Inland areas generally 5 degrees celsius lower than coast with higher rainfall.

Entry requirements
Passports
Passports must be valid for six months from date of entry.

Visa
Required by all except nationals of Commonwealth (except Bangladesh, Cameroon, Fiji, India, Nigeria, Pakistan, Sri Lanka and Swaziland who do need a visa), EU and GCC countries, US, Scandinavian countries, Japan and certain others.
All visitors must hold valid tickets and documents for their onward or return journey and adequate funds for their intended length of stay.

Currency advice/regulations
No limits on import and export of local currency. Any amount of foreign currency may be imported, subject to declaration, and any unused balance may be exported.

Health (for visitors)
Mandatory precautions
Yellow fever and cholera vaccination certificate may be required if arriving from infected areas.

Advisable precautions
Typhoid, tetanus, hepatitis A and polio vaccinations. Seek advice about malaria precautions. Water precautions should be taken.

Hotels
Wide choice available but relatively expensive. Ten per cent tax surcharge added to bills (10 per cent tip is usual except where service charge is included). Business visitors staying longer than a day or two generally prefer beach hotels.

Public holidays
Fixed dates
1 & 2 Jan (New Year), 12 Mar (National Day), 1 May (Labour Day), 1 Nov (All Saints' Day), 25 Dec (Christmas).

Variable dates
Chinese Spring Festival (Jan), Thaipoosam Cavadee (Feb), Maha Shivratee (Feb), Ougadi (Mar), Eid al Fitr (Mar), Ganesh Chaturthi (Sep), Divali (Nov).
Exact dates are subject to visibility of the moon.

Working hours
Banking
Mon–Fri: 0930–1430; Sat: 0930–1130.

Business
Mon–Fri: 0830–1630, Sat: 0900–1200.

Government
Mon–Fri: 0845–1600.

Telecommunications
Telephone/fax
Dialling code for Mauritius: IDD access code + 230, followed by subscriber's number. There are no area codes.

Postal services
Air mail is advised. Air courier services are available.

Electricity supply
220V AC, 50 cycles.

Weights and measures
The metric system is in general use, but certain obsolete French measures are still used in connection with the measurement of land.

Getting there
Air
National airline: Air Mauritius.
Main airport: Sir Seewoosagur Ramgoolam International (MRU), 48km south-east of Port Louis.
Airport tax: International departures MR500.

Surface
Main ports: Port Louis is the island's only commercial port. It has five deep water quays, an eight hectare container park, with an annual throughput of 85,000 TEUs and provision for refrigerated containers. Its free port status underpins the island's offshore banking system.

Getting about
National transport
Air: Air Mauritius operates inter-island service between Mauritius and Rodrigues and Réunion. Two Air Mauritius Bell Jet helicopters are available for transfer from airport to hotel and tours.
Road: There are 1,831km of classified roads, of which 886km are main roads and 577km secondary roads. About 93 per cent of the road network is paved. Extensive network throughout the island. Occasional congestion. A dual highway links Port Louis and Phoenix, Port Louis and Mapou/Pamplemousses.
Buses: Good bus services cover the main island.

City transport
Taxis: Operate in all towns, villages and resorts. Generally unmetered so it is advisable to agree a fare before starting the journey. Tipping is not usual.
Buses/trams: Bus fare MR20 from airport to city centre, journey time 135 minutes. UBS bus service 198 runs every 60 minutes, fare MR16, journey time 90 minutes (March 1999).

Car hire
Widely available. International or foreign licence accepted; traffic drives on the left.

BUSINESS DIRECTORY

Telephone area codes
Dialling code for Mauritius: IDD access code +230, followed by subscriber's number. There are no area codes.

Chambers of Commerce
Mauritius Chamber of Commerce & Industry, 3 Royal St, Port Louis (tel: 208-3301; fax: 208-0076).

Banking
African Asian Bank Limited, Office 5, 8th Floor, Max City Building, Corner Louis Pasteur & Remy Ollier Streets, Port Louis (tel: 2407002, 2407350 Fax: 2407009)

Bank of Baroda, African Asian Bank Limited, PO Box 553, Sir William Newton Street, Port Louis (tel: 208-1504; fax: 208-3892).

Bank of Mauritius, PO Box 29, Sir William Newton Street, Port Louis (tel: 2023800 fax: 2089204)

Banque Nationale de Paris Intercontinentale, 1 Sir William Newton Street, Port Louis (tel: 208-4147/8/9, 208-4151/2; fax: 208-8143).

The Delphis Bank Limited, 16 Sir William Newton Street, Port Louis (tel: 2085061 fax: 2085388)

Development Bank of Mauritius Ltd, PO Box 157, Chaussée, Port Louis (tel: 208-0241; fax: 208-8498).

Indian Ocean International Bank Ltd, 34 Sir William Newton Street, Port Louis (tel: 208-0121; fax: 208-0127).

Mauritius Commercial Bank Ltd, 9-15 Sir William Newton St, Port Louis (tel: 2025000 fax: 2087054)

South East Asian Bank Ltd, 26 Bourbon Street, PO Box 13, Port Louis (tel:

208-8826/7/8, 212-2884/6/7; fax: 208-8825).

State Bank of Mauritius Ltd, PO Box 152, State Bank Tower, 1 Queen Elizabeth II Ave, Port Louis (tel: 2021111 fax: 2021234)

Central bank

Bank of Mauritius, Head Office: PO Box 29, Sir William Newton Street, Port Louis, Mauritius (tel: 2023800 fax: 2089204)

Travel information

Air Mauritius, Rogers House, 5 President John F. Kennedy Street, PO Box 441, Port Louis (tel: 208-7700; fax: 208-8331).

Ministry of tourism

Mauritius Tourist Development Authority, Emmanuel Anquetil Building, Sir Seewoosagur Ramgoolam Street, Port-Louis (tel: 201-1703; fax: 212-5142).

National tourist organisation offices

Mauritius Tourism Promotion Authority, 11th Floor, Air Mauritius Centre, President John Kennedy Street, Port-Louis (tel: 210-1545, 208-6397; fax: 212-5142; e-mail: mtpa@intnet.mu; internet site: http://www.mauritius.net).

Ministries

Ministry of Agriculture and Natural Resources, NPF Bldg, 9th Floor, Port Louis (tel: 212-7946; fax: 212-4427).

Ministry of Arts, Culture, Leisure and Reform Institutions, Government Centre, Port Louis (tel: 201-2032).

Ministry of Civil Service Affairs and Employment, Government Centre, Port Louis (tel: 201-1035; fax: 212-9528).

Ministry of Co-operatives and Handicraft, Life Insurance Corporation of India Bldg, 3rd Floor, John Kennedy St, Port Louis (tel: 208-4812; fax: 208-9265).

Ministry of Economic Planning and Development, Emmanuel Anquetil Bldg, Sir Seewoosagur Ramgoolam St, Port Louis (tel: 201-1576; fax: 212-4124).

Ministry of Education and Science, Sun Trust Bldg, Edith Cavell St, Port Louis (tel: 212-8411; fax: 212-3783).

Ministry of Energy, Water Resources and Postal Services, Government Centre, Port Louis (tel: 201-1087; fax: 208-6497).

Ministry of the Environment and Quality of Life, Barracks St, Port Louis (tel: 212-8332; fax: 212-9407).

Ministry of External Affairs, Government Centre, Port Louis (tel: 201-1416; fax: 208-8087).

Ministry of Finance, Government Centre, Port Louis (tel: 201-1145; fax: 208-8622).

Ministry of Fisheries and Marine Resources, Port Louis.

Ministry of Health, Emmanuel Anquetil Bldg, Sir Seewoosagur Ramgoolam St, Port Louis (tel: 201-1910; fax: 208-0376).

Ministry of Housing, Lands and Town and Country Planning, Moorgate House, Port Louis (tel: 212-6022; fax: 212-7482).

Ministry of Industry and Industrial Technology, Government Centre, Port Louis (tel: 201-1221; fax: 212-8201).

Ministry of Information, Government Centre, Port Louis (tel: 201-1278; fax: 208-8243).

Ministry of Internal and External Communications, Emmanuel Anquetil Bldg, 10th Floor, Sir Seewoosagur Ramgoolam St, Port Louis (tel: 201-1089; fax: 212-1673).

Ministry of Justice, Jules Koenig St, Port Louis (tel: 208-5321).

Ministry of Labour and Industrial Relations, Ming Court, cnr Eugène Laurent and GMD Atchia Sts, Port Louis (tel: 212-3049; fax: 212-3070).

Ministry of Local Government, Government Centre, Port Louis (tel: 201-1215).

Ministry of Manpower Resources and Vocational and Technical Training, Jade House, Remy Ollier St, Port Louis (tel: 242-1462).

Ministry for Rodrigues Island, Fon Sing Bldg, Edith Cavell St, Port Louis (tel: 208-8472; fax: 212-6329).

Ministry of Social Security and National Solidarity, cnr Maillard and Jules Koenig Sts, Port Louis (tel: 212-3006).

Ministry of Tourism, Emmanuel Anquetil Bldg, Sir Seewoosagur Ramgoolam St, Port Louis (tel: 201-2286).

Ministry of Trade and Shipping, Government Centre, Port Louis (tel: 201-1067; fax: 212-6386).

Ministry of Women's Rights, Child Development and Family Welfare, Rainbow House, cnr Edith Cavell and Brown Sequard Sts, Port Louis (tel: 208-2061; fax: 208-8250).

Ministry of Works, Treasury Bldg, Port Louis (tel: 208-0281; fax: 212-8373).

Ministry of Youth and Sports, Emmanuel Anquetil Bldg, Sir Seewoosagur Ramgoolam St, Port Louis (tel: 201-1242; fax: 212-6506).

Prime Minister's Office, Government Centre, Port Louis (tel: 201-1001; fax: 208-8619).

Other useful addresses

British High Commission, Commercial Section, 7th Floor, Les Cascades Building, Edith Cavell Street, Port Louis (tel: 208-9850/1; fax: 212-8470).

Export Processing Zone Development Authority, 5th Floor, Les Cascades, Edith Cavell St, Port Louis (tel: 212-9760; fax: 212-9767).

Mauritius Embassy (USA), Suite 441, 4301 Connecticut Avenue, NW, Washington DC 20008 (tel: 244-1491; fax: 966-0983; e-mail: mauritius.embassy@prodigy.net).

Mauritius Employers' Federation, Cerné House, Chausse, Port Louis (tel: 212-1599; fax: 212-6725).

Mauritius Export Processing Zone Association, 42 Sir William Newton St, Port Louis (tel: 208-5216; fax: 212-1853).

Mauritius Free Port Authority, 2nd Floor, Deramann Tower, Sir William Newton St, Port Louis (tel: 212-9627; fax: 212-9629).

Mauritius Industrial Development Authority, Level 2, BAI Bldg, 25 Pope Hennessy St, Port Louis (tel: 208-7750; fax: 208-5965; e-mail: mida@media.intnet.mu).

Mauritius Offshore Business Activities Authority, 1st Floor, Deramann Tower, 30 Sir William Newton St, Port Louis (tel: 212-9650; fax: 212-9459).

Mauritius Standards Bureau, Ministry of Industry and Industrial Technology, Réduit (tel: 454-1933; fax: 464-7675).

Internet sites

Africa Business Network: http://www.ifc.org/abn

AllAfrica.com: http://allafrica.com

African Development Bank: http://www.afdb.org

Business Directory: http://www.mauritius.co.uk/

Harambee Afrika (UK business club for traders with east, central and southern Africa; includes annotated web resource list): http://www.harambee.co.uk

Mbendi AfroPaedia (information on companies, countries, industries and stock exchanges in Africa): http://mbendi.co.za

Morocco

Jonathan Derrick

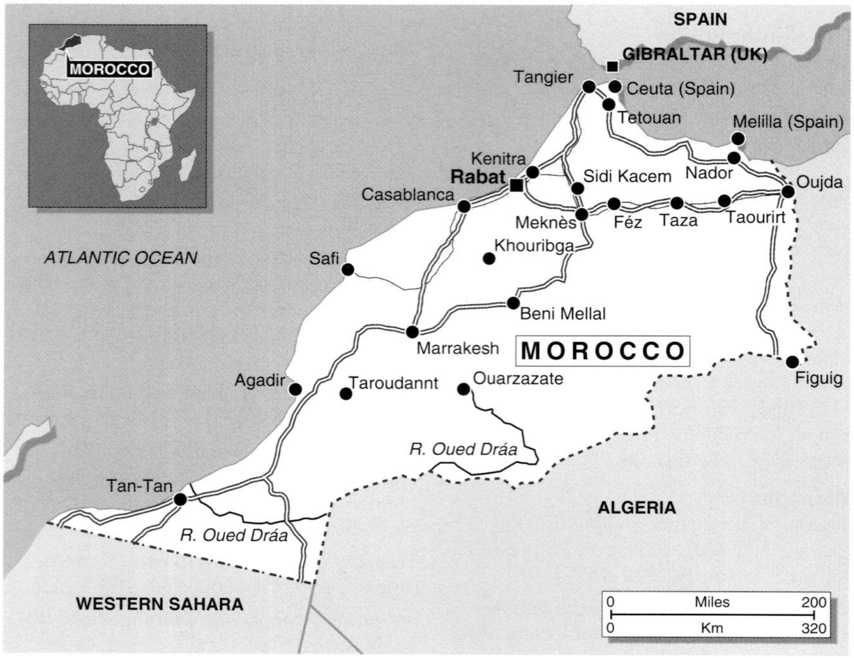

KEY FACTS

Official name: Al-Mamlaka Al-Maghrebia (Kingdom of Morocco)

Head of State: King Mohammed VI (since Jul 1999)

Head of government: Prime Minister Driss Jettou (appointed by the King, 9 Oct 2002)

Ruling party: Coalition government from Nov 2002: Union Socialiste des Forces Populaires (USFP) (Socialist Union of Popular Forces); Istiqlal (I) (Parti d'Indépendence) (Independence party) (results of the general elections on 27 Sep 2002: USFP 50 seats; Istiqlal 48 seats; Parti de la Justice et du Développement (PJD) (Justice and Development Party) 42 seats; turnout just over 50 per cent)

Area: 711,000 square km

Population: 29.20 million (2001)

Capital: Rabat

Official language: Arabic

Currency: Dirham (Dh) = 100 centimes

Exchange rate: Dh10.13 per US$ (Jan 2003)

GDP per capita: US$1,123 (2001); US$1,217 (2002)**

GDP real growth: 5.70% (2001); 3.5% (2002)**

Labour force: 10.80 million (2001)

Unemployment: 10.60% (2001); 10.8% (2002)**

Inflation: 0.60% (2001); 4.1% (2002)**

Balance of trade: -US$4.14 billion (2001)

Foreign debt: US$17.83 billion (2001)

Visitor numbers: 2.25 billion (2001); 1.28 million (Jul 2002)

* estimated figure

For the latest Key Facts, go to www.worldinformation.com

Morocco began 2001 with abundant rainfall and better crops after several years of drought. The kingdom's rural areas however, remained deprived. Overall, the number of Moroccans living in poverty was high, at 46 per cent, but the rate in rural areas was even higher, at 66 per cent. The popular new King, Mohammed VI, showed concern for the deprivation of his people and was called the 'King of the Poor'. In this spirit, he celebrated the anniversary of his accession in June 2001.

Election time

In October 2001, the King announced that legislative elections in September 2002 and called on all political partiesto ensure a free and fair election.

The voters elected 325 members to the lower house, the *Majlis Al-Nuwab* (Assembly of Representatives). Of the major parties, the Union Socialiste des Forces Populaires (USFP) (Socialist Union of Popular Forces) won 50 seats, Istiqlal/Parti d'Indépendence (Independence party) 48, Parti de la Justice et du Développement (PJD) (Justice and Development Party) 42, Rassemblement National des Indépendents (RNI) (National Rally of Independents) 41 and Mouvement Populaire (MP) (Popular Movement) 27. Analysts were surprised by the King's decision to appoint the former interior minister and technocrat, Driss Jettou, as prime minister. Many had expected that the UFSP leader, Abderrahman El Youssoufi, would remain prime minister. The King's call for a fair election also seemed a pointless exercise when he appointed the new government in November 2002. The USFP and Istiqlal/Parti d'Indépendence were selected to form the 31-member cabinet. There was no place in the government for the PJD, despite its strong performance in the election.

After more than two years of gradual reform, Morocco has still not adopted the more conventional forms of democracy and elements of repression still exist with progress on women's rights being particularly slow. International attention has centred on the trial of 36 human rights defenders, including the president and vice-president of the Association Marocaine des Droits Humains (AMDH) (Moroccan Association of Human Rights), who were accused of organising an unauthorised demonstration outside parliament in December 2000. In May 2001, they were sentenced to three months in prison and fined Dh3,000 (US$283) each. International human rights groups condemned the decision and warned that it signalled a return to Hassan II's style of repression.

The migrant problem

Poverty is particularly bad in Tangier in northern Morocco. This has forced Moroccans to either emigrate to Europe or to cultivate cannabis. In 2001 and 2002, several projects were under way to help the north, but emigration from Morocco continues because of high unemployment, estimated at 10.6 per cent in 2001. Between January and June 2001, the Moroccan authorities arrested over 20,000 people trying to cross the Straits of Gibraltar illegally, costing the government an estimated US$3 million per day. The Spanish authorities made 24-hour-a-day efforts to stop the illegal transport of Moroccans and others by boat across the Straits to Spain, but it still continues.

Rocky relations

Relations with Spain continue to be strained over the issue of Moroccan illegal immigrants. Spain accused Morocco of not doing enough to stem the flow of migrants. The King has criticised Spanish gangsters for trafficking in humans, although the Spanish government claimed that Moroccan police have colluded in the smuggling of people and drugs. Morocco has also become alarmed at the rise of racist and xenophobic anti-Moroccan rhetoric in the Spanish media. In July 2002, relations deteriorated further when 12 Moroccan soldiers invaded Isla del Perejil (Parsley Island), a small Spanish-owned and uninhabited island in the Straits of Gibraltar in July 2002. Spanish special forces peacefully recaptured the island (which the Moroccans call Leila) and later withdrew. Spain fears that Morocco could try and capture its enclaves of Ceuta and Melilla, the free ports over which Morocco has territorial claims, along with the Spanish islands of Penon de Alhucemas, Penon de Velez de la Gomera and Islas Chafarinas. Both countries tried to resolve their differences in December 2002, but talks failed to achieve any major results. Neither side restored full diplomatic relations, which were cancelled following the Perejil crisis.

Another serious problem between the two countries was the continuing impasse over the Moroccan fisheries agreement with the EU. The EU fishing vessels under the previous agreement had been mostly Spanish. Attempts to negotiate a new agreement with Brussels were still nowhere near success by the beginning of 2002, more than two years after the expiry of the previous agreement because Morocco demanded a number of changes in its favour. The EU (essentially Spain) rejected these proposals. Morocco called for 'global co-operation' to develop its fishing ports and assurances of scientific monitoring of its fish stocks. El Youssoufi and Spain's prime minister, José María Aznar, arranged to meet in December 2001, but the meeting was postponed. In December, Spain granted an offshore oil concession in waters off the Canary Islands, although Morocco disputed the maritime border in the area concerned.

Tensions in the Sahara

Another preoccupation for Moroccan foreign policy is still the Western Sahara (Sahrawi). In June 2001, the UN called on Morocco and the leaders of the Polisario Front (who lead the independence movement for Sahrawi) to set out a programme leading to a referendum within five years. He warned that the UN could consider ending its mediation role. A meeting in August at the US ranch of James Baker, the UN secretary general's special representative for the Western Sahara question, led to no significant progress. The situation worsened in 2002, when the Polisario made an outright concemnation of Morocco's territorial claims.

Much of the world now accepts Morocco's *de facto* control of the Western Sahara. Agreements on oil exploration in the Sahara's offshore waters were signed with Morocco, assumed to be the sovereign authority over those waters. An agreement with Kerr-McGee (US-based) was announced on 4 October 2001 for the Boujdour offshore area and an agreement with TotalFinaElf, the giant French conglomerate, was signed in October for the Dakhla offshore area. UN experts looked into the legality of the agreements, which were denounced by Polisario. Many African states took a different view from the West on the Sahara: even though some countries were withdrawing their recognition of the Sahrawi Republic, it remained a member of the Organisation for African Unity (OAU) and then joined the new

KEY FACTS

Official name: Western Sahara (The legal status of the territory and the issue of sovereignty are unresolved; they are contested by Morocco and Polisario, which in Feb 1976, formally proclaimed a government-in-exile of the Sahrawi Arab Democratic Republic (SADR).)

Head of State: President Mohammed Abdelazziz (Polisario) (since 1982)

Head of government: Prime Minister Bouchraya Hamoudi Bayoune (Polisario) (from Feb 1999)

Ruling party: Independence movement – Frente para la Liberación de Saguia Al-Hamra y Río de Oro (Polisario) (Popular Front for the Liberation of Saguia Al-Hamra and Río de Oro)

Area: 266,000 square km

Population: 250,559 (2001)

Capital: Laayoune (El Aaiún)

Official language: Arabic and Spanish

Currency: Moroccan dirham (Dh) = 100 centimes; the currency used in the Occupied Zone

Exchange rate: Dh10.13 per US$ (Jan 2003)

Aid flow: US$10.00 million annually

For the latest Key Facts, go to www.worldinformation.com

African Union (AU) under the Lomé treaty which came into effect (with a one-year transition period to follow) in May 2001. Morocco did however continue to develop relations with several African states: the King led a delegation of 300 to the France-Africa summit in Yaoundé in January 2001; in March 2002 talks on peace between Sierra Leone, Liberia and Guinea were held in Rabat. The Western Sahara was one obstacle to restoration of normal relations with Algeria, bilateral trade being another. The border between Algeria and Morocco had closed in 1994.

The economy

GDP growth in 2001 was 6.3 per cent and inflation was 0.6 per cent. At the end of 2001, the year's cereal harvests were estimated at 4.7 million tonnes due to better rainfall. The forecast for 2002 was 5.5 million tonnes.

Although the government has made reduction of the budget deficit a priority, expenditure on health, education and social infrastructure has increased since the late 1990s. The 2002 budget, as revised in October 2001, planned expenditure of Dh142 billion (US$13.4 billion) and revenue of Dh136 billion (US$12.8 billion). It provided for a deficit of Dh12 billion (US$1.1 billion) or 2.9 per cent of GDP. Projected public investment was down by 8.5 per cent at Dh20 billion (US$1.8 billion), but with spending by state agencies, local authorities and the Hassan II Development Fund added, the total was estimated at Dh64 billion (US$6 billion). Driss Jettou's first budget as prime minister, which was announced in late 2002, aims to increase investment and fight poverty. The 2003 budget proposes expenditure of Dh139.51 billion (US$13.1 billion) while revenue is expected to rise by 0.49 per cent to Dh136.7 billion (US$12.9 billion).

The exchange rate of the dirham was modified in April 2001 through alteration of the basket of currencies used for its calculation. The result was an average 5 per cent depreciation. This was to correct an appreciation against the euro, two-thirds of Morocco's exports being to the EU. The textile and clothing industry, one of the most important in Morocco, had wanted a 10 per cent depreciation to make its exports competitive in Europe again.

Morocco bound

Before the temporary setback of the 11 September terrorist attacks in the US, the October 2002 Bali bombing and the US's threat of a war against Iraq, the government was planning an expansion of the tourism sector. There were plans to raise the number of visitors from 3 million in 2000 to 10 million per year by 2010. Tourism revenue (US$2 billion in 2000) and private transfers (US$2.3 billion) are vital sources of foreign exchange for a country whose visible trade is in deficit. Plans to develop tourism are likely to continue and several new hotel projects were begun in 2001. In February, for example, Liwa of the United Arab Emirates (UAE) announced that it would extend its three Sheraton hotels in Morocco and there is a plan by the Saudi Arabian group, Dalla al Barraka, to invest nearly Dh1 billion (US$94 million) in four luxury hotels in Agadir.

KEY INDICATORS						Morocco
	Unit	1996	1997	1998	1999	2000
Population	m	26.85	27.31	27.78	28.24	29.00
Gross domestic product (GDP)	US$bn	36.60	33.40	35.70	35.00	33.50
GDP per capita	US$	1,365	1,224	1,284	1,248	1,155
GDP real growth	%	12.1	-2.0	6.0	-0.7	0.2
Inflation	%	3.0	0.9	2.9	0.7	1.9
Consumer prices	1995=100	103.0	103.9	106.9	107.7	109.7
Manufacturing output	1995=100	104.1	107.5	110.2	112.7	117.5
Exports (fob) (goods)	US$m	6,886.0	7,039.0	7,144.0	7,500.0	7,419.0
Imports (fob) (goods)	US$m	9,080.0	8,903.0	9,463.0	-9,957.0	10,665.0
Balance of trade	US$m	-2,193.0	-1,864.0	-2,935.0	-2,500.0	-3,235.0
Current account	US$m	35.0	-87.0	-32.0	-200.0	-501.0
Foreign debt	US$bn	21.6	20.8	22.1	19.3	19.9
Total reserves minus gold	US$m	3,794.0	3,993.0	4,435.0	5,689.0	4,823.0
Foreign exchange	US$m	3,743.0	3,951.0	4,389.0	5,507.0	4,612.0
Exchange rate	per US$	8.72	9.53	9.60	9.80	10.63

Privatisation profits

In 2001, Maroc Télécom, in which Vivendi Universal of France has a 35 per cent stake, recorded turnover of Dh1.4 billion (US$132 million), a 17 per cent rise compared with 2000. It announced a five-year investment plan, costing Dh11.5 billion (US$1 billion). Having acquired 51 per cent of Mauritania's telecommunications corporation, Mauritel, in February 2001, it expressed interest towards the end of 2001 in the corresponding parastatal in Mali. The Maroc Télécom part- privatisation proceeds of US$2 billion were the entire privatisation revenue forecast in the 2001 budget. More privatisation was scheduled, but during 2001 the privatisation of Royal Air Maroc (RAM) was postponed to 2004. In March 2001, RAM contracted to buy 20 Boeing 737s and two 767s to add to its fleet. Later in the year, a reconstruction plan for the airline was announced, involving raising new capital – up to Dh1 billion (US$94 million) – and payment of the state's Dh1.2 billion (US$113 billion) debt.

Hopes to hit oil

The search for oil continued in 2001/02. Prospects of substantial production were distant despite the excitement aroused in the kingdom after the discovery in the Talsint area in 2000. Besides the agreements for exploration off the coast of the Western Sahara, an agreement was signed earlier in 2001 with Energy Africa Morocco, a subsidiary of a South African company, for exploration on three offshore blocks south of Agadir (in Morocco's undisputed area). Meanwhile petroleum was the biggest single import item, costing Dh8.4 billion (US$793 million). The kingdom's existing mineral wealth, the phosphates of Morocco proper and the Western Sahara, continued to flow well. Morocco's share of world phosphate exports rose from 25.3 per cent to 26.2 per cent in 2000 through product diversification and partnership agreements. The Office Chérifien des Phosphates (OCP) (National Office of Phosphates) plans to invest Dh7.8 billion (US$736 million) in its production facilities and maritime transport from 2001–05.

Outlook

Under the rule of Mohammed VI, Morocco is being slowly transformed into a democratic state. The King's rule appears to have been consolidated with the royal wedding in March 2002, when he married Salma Bennani, an engineer with Guemassa, the mining arm of the giant Ominium Nord Africain (ONA) company. It marks the first time in the country's history that a member of the royal family has married a 'commoner'. Although she will not bear the title of Queen, she will be known as royal highness.

The issue of Western Sahara remains a stumbling block in foreign relations. Unless the Moroccan government can stage a plebiscite acceptable to Polisario and the UN, the lingering conflict is likely to continue.

Despite the government's enthusiasm for improving the social welfare of its people, large numbers of highly qualified young Moroccans are flooding out of Morocco and into Europe in search of better career prospects. Although it generates substantial amounts of private transfers into the economy, creating more wealth than the tourism sector, the brain drain is becoming a major impediment to further development.

Risk assessment

Economic	Improving
Political	Good
Regional stability	Good
Stock market	Good

COUNTRY PROFILE

Historical profile

In Morocco's early history, the country was ruled by Idris (788–985), a descendant of the Prophet Mohammed, and by two religious movements, the Almoravids and the Almohads.

The Almohads were succeeded by the Merinids, and an era in which there were alternating periods of anarchy and prosperity, as Berber tribes clashed with intruding Arab tribes and also with Spanish and Portuguese colonists on the Mediterranean and Atlantic coasts.

1664 Sultan Rashid II of the House of Alawi (Morocco's royal family) brought a period of peace and prosperity.

European governments were attracted to North Africa, and in 1904 Morocco was split into two zones of influence – the French in the north and the Spanish in the south.

1912 Morocco became a French protectorate.

1923 France, Spain and Britain set up the international zone of Tangier. A rebellion led by Abdel Krim began in 1921 and was quelled finally in 1926.

1956 Independence was granted by France and Spain. Sultan Sidi Mohammed ben Youssef adopted the title of King Mohammed V. Tangier became Moroccan once more.

1961 King Hassan II succeeded his father, King Mohammed V, to the throne.

1997 Local elections were held in June electing 24,000 councillors; regional elections were held in October – 16 regional councils with local financial and policy-making powers were stipulated according to the decree in March. Legislative elections were held on 14 November when no political bloc won a clear majority in the lower house. The governing parties lost control to a coalition of opposition parties, which formed the new government.

1999 King Hassan II died suddenly on 23 July. His son, Mohammed VI, acceded to the throne.

2000 King Mohammed VI begins a process of modest political liberalisation.

2001 In April, at the sixth congress of the Union Socialiste des Forces Populaires (USFP) (Socialist Union of Popular Forces) a resolution was passed that changed the Moroccan voting system from one round system to two rounds to make parliamentary elections more open and fair.

2002 In March, King Mohammed VI married Salma Bennani, a 24-year-old computer engineer from Tangier. The marriage, to a commoner, was a break with Royal Moroccan tradition.

Political structure

Constitution

Morocco is a constitutional and democratic monarchy. Islam is the state religion and Arabic the official language. The Moroccan constitution prohibits a one-party political system.

The King is Commander of the Faithful (Amir Al-Moumineen), hereditary head of state and supreme commander of the armed forces. He also appoints the cabinet. As part of the move to decentralise power and give rural areas more control over spending and policy implementation, regional elections were held in 1997 for 16 newly created regional councils.

The King is empowered to declare a state of emergency if the country's territorial integrity or constitutional institutions are threatened, and he can dissolve parliament.

Form of state

Constitutional monarchy

The executive

Executive power rests with the prime minister and cabinet, appointed by the King.

National legislature

Legislative powers are exercised by the bicameral Moroccan parliament. The 325-member *Majlis Al-Nuwab* (Assembly of Representatives, lower house) is directly elected for a five-year term in multi-seat constituencies. It debates legislation presented to it by the government. Approved legislation is automatically promulgated a month later.

Local councils elect 60 per cent of the 270 representatives to the *Majlis Al-Mustasharin* (Assembly of Councillors, upper house); the remainder are elected indirectly from unions and chambers of commerce. The upper house has the power to overrule the government with a no-confidence vote.

Legal system

The legal system is based on Islamic law and a combination of French and Spanish civil law codes. The Supreme Court is responsible for reviewing government legislation.

Last elections

November 1997 (parliamentary)

Next elections

September 2002 (parliamentary)
November 2002 (legislative)

Political parties

Ruling party

Coalition including Union Socialiste des Forces Populaires (USFP) (Socialist Union of Popular Forces), Istiqlal (Independence), Rassemblement National des Indépendents (RNI) (National Rally of Independents), Mouvement Nationale Populaire (MNP) (National Popular Movement), Parti du Renouveau et du Progrés (PRP) (Party of Renovation and Progress), Front des Forces Démocratiques (FFD) (Front of Democratic Forces) and Parti Social et Démocratique (PSD) (Social and Democratic Party).

Main opposition party

Union Constitionelle (UC) (Constitutional Union)

Population

29.0 million (2000)

Annual population growth rate: 1.7 per cent (2001); 1.4 per cent (2000–2015 projection). Around 70 per cent of the population is under 25 years of age. Population density: 68 inhabitants per square km (2001). Urban population: 55 per cent of the total (2000).

Ethnic make-up

Mostly Berbers and Arabs. There is a small Jewish minority and an estimated 60,000 foreign residents, mainly of French, Spanish and Italian origin.

Religions

Sunni Muslim (98 per cent). There are small minority Jewish and Roman Catholic communities.

Education

In 2001, the African Development Bank signed a US$32 million agreement for the strenthening of technical education in Morocco.

The adult illiteracy rate is 52 per cent (2001). The illiteracy rate is as high as 90 per cent among young girls in rural areas, who do not attend school. The government aims to reduce the illiteracy rate to 35 per cent by 2004 and 24 per cent by 2010.

Health

It is estimated that less than 20 per cent of Moroccans have access to health care. Approximately 5 per cent of the government budget is allocated to the health sector each year, less than 1 per cent of GDP. Access to public hospitals is not free and few Moroccans can afford private doctors.

Main cities

Casablanca (commercial centre, estimated population five million in 2001), Rabat (capital, 1.4 million), Marrakesh (1.39 million), Meknès (686,000), Salé (483,000), Tangier (492,000), Oujda (869,000), Fez (906,000), Agadir (672,000).

Languages spoken

French is the dominant business language in the centre and south, while Spanish is often spoken in the north. Berber is used in the countryside. English is not widely spoken, but is increasingly taught as a second foreign language.
Business literature and correspondence should be in French or Arabic.

Official language

Arabic

Media

The government uses the media to strengthen national unity and aid cultural, economic and social development. This has meant extending the state media network to remote areas, improving training and modernising technical equipment.
The government owns the official news-agency, Maghreb Arab Presse. While print media is predominantly independent, electronic media remains largely under government control.

Press

Dailies: Principal newspapers in Arabic, French and English include the government owned *Al Anbaa*, *Le Matin du Sahara et du Maghreb*, *Maroc Hebdo*, *La Nouvelle Tribune*, *La Gazette du Maroc*, *Al Annbaa*, *Al Jarida Al Maghribia*, *Al Bayane*, *Morocco Today* and *News Express*. On-line news services include the daily French *Marocnews.com* (http://www.marocnews.com).
Business: Numerous periodicals are available in French and Arabic, including the business weekly *La Vie Economique*. *l'Economiste* carries financial news.

Broadcasting

Radio: Extensive national and external services are available in Arabic, French, English, Spanish and Berber. The government controls Radio-Television Marocaine (RTM). The French language Medi-1 is a private radio station. In 2001, the government said that it would encourage more private radio stations to operate in Morocco.
Television: Local television stations broadcast for over 60 hours per week, with advertising, in Arabic and French. The nationwide network is basically state-controlled, but a private cable channel is also in operation.

Advertising

There are several local advertising agencies operating on a relatively small scale in Morocco. Television advertising has a 70 per cent share of the total market, followed by print media and billboard advertising. Advertising on the Internet is increasingly popular with companies that seek to target selected consumer groups.

Economy

Rainfall is key to the performance of Morocco's agriculture-dominated economy. A vulnerability to drought, together with high levels of public sector and external debt, remain major obstacles to investor confidence. Although the Youssoufi-led government has expressed its commitment to greater fiscal discipline and increased economic growth, much will depend on the pace of economic reform.
Even though the dominance of the agricultural sector should remain over the medium term, the manufacturing and service sectors are slowly but gradually gaining a higher share of annual GDP. In 2001, it was estimated that 30–35 per cent of GDP was contributed by industrial production (which relies heavily on inputs from the agricultural sector) and construction. This is in comparison to an estimated 13 per cent contribution to GDP from the agricultural sector.
The tourism industry is increasingly providing opportunities to the wider services sector, as well as for construction and other infrastructure development. Within the service sector the telecommunication industry is among the most deregulated and dynamic in the region and is set to become fully privatised over the short term. In 2001, a major development occurred with the sale of 35 per cent of the state-owned operator Maroc Télécom.
Meanwhile, thousands of Moroccans continue to try to get to Europe every year to seek work, often travelling illegally in small boats crossing to Spain. France, the main destination for Moroccan migrants, has called for the flow of illegal immigrants to be curbed – Morocco is committed under its 1995 EU Partnership Agreement to take measures towards this. However, remittances from Moroccans abroad (who total an estimated 1.9 million) continue to be a major source of foreign exchange for the country. At the end of 2001, foreign exchange receipts totalled US$7 billion.

External trade

Although exports steadily increased during the 1990s, the trade deficit remains large even though it is partially offset by invisible earnings from tourism and workers' remittances from abroad.
Morocco belongs to the Arab Maghreb Union (AMU) with Algeria, Libya, Mauritania and Tunisia. The EU and the European Free Trade Association (EFTA) both agreed free trade agreements with Morocco in 2000, the first such agreements with a North African country. In 2000, Morocco began implementing an EU accord that will eventually remove all tariffs between the two by 2012. Morocco wishes to become a full member of the European Union.

Exports

Principal exports are food and beverages (typically 21 per cent of the total), semi-processed goods (22 per cent) and consumer goods, including clothing and footwear (40 per cent).
Main destinations: France (25.9 per cent of 2000 total), Spain (9.6 per cent), UK (7.9 per cent), Italy (5.6 per cent), Germany (5.4 per cent).

Imports

Principal imports are machinery and transport equipment (typically 22 per cent of total value), crude oil (14 per cent), cereals (typically 7 per cent), other foodstuffs (5 per cent), chemicals (7 per cent), iron and steel (4 per cent).
Main sources: France (25.3 per cent of 2000 total), Spain (10.8 per cent), Italy (5.9 per cent), Germany (5.8 per cent), UK (5.5 per cent).

Agriculture

The agricultural sector contributed 13 per cent to GDP in 2000 and employed 40 per cent of the workforce. It accounts for some 29 per cent of exports.
Around 70 per cent of the 7.9 million hectares of arable land is cultivated, mainly by peasant smallholders.
Principal crops are wheat, barley, maize (grown in the rain-fed areas), citrus fruits, beans, chick peas and other pulses, tomatoes (mainly for export), potatoes, olives and oilseeds.
Important agro-allied crops are sugar-cane, sugar beet (the production of which is being developed to cut down on sugar imports), and cotton.
Livestock productivity and crop yields have remained low and regular food imports of grain are necessary to meet domestic cereal requirements. Agricultural development has also been hampered by the small size of the majority of holdings and restricted access to EU markets. However,

many long-term government projects are under way, including irrigation schemes, development of new techniques and financial incentives to farmers.

Morocco's agriculture is always vulnerable to drought and suffered adverse climatic conditions in 2000, resulting in a drastic fall in agricultural output. As a result growth in the sector was weak in 2001, at 1.3 per cent. As the increasing population puts pressure on available resources, access to water will become more difficult. The World Bank has estimated that Morocco will become a water deficit country by 2020.

Some 32,500 tonnes of cannabis annually has been grown in the deprived north of Morocco, for the European market. King Mohammed VI has made opening up and developing the north a priority in government policy.

Fishing

The fishing sector offers considerable potential, although export markets for the main catch, sardines, are restricted by strong competition from Spain, Portugal and France. Catch is estimated at around 750,000 tonnes a year.

After pursuing a policy of leasing fishing rights to foreign countries such as South Korea, Japan, the former Soviet Union, Spain and Portugal, the government is now encouraging national private enterprises in the sector.

The government is modernising the fleet and fishing ports to exploit the rich potential of local fishing grounds. A US$13 million expansion programme at Sidi Ifni fishing port, completed in August 2000, enables catches in excess of 50,000 tonnes per annum.

The Moroccan fishing fleet consists of around 2,500 vessels, of which 85 per cent are coastal boats. There is a deep-sea fleet of 517 craft, of which 320 are refrigerated. Around 700 boats are being modernised or replaced. Morocco's fleet fishes in both Atlantic and Mediterranean waters, and has an agreement to fish in the Gulf of Guinea. As well as its own ports, some of Morocco's catch is landed in Portugal. Fish frozen at sea is landed at Agadir and Tan-Tan.

Industry and manufacturing

The sector accounts for around 33 per cent of GDP and employs 37 per cent of the workforce. Most activity is concentrated in the Casablanca area.

The main industry is the processing of phosphates into phosphoric acid and fertilisers. Food processing is another major industry, with the agricultural sector accounting for around a third of annual exports. Other significant industries include oil refining (there are two refineries - at Sidi Kacem and Mohammedia with a combined capacity of 74,000 barrels per day (bpd)), steel, cement, chemicals, pharmaceuticals, toiletries, metallurgy, textiles, leather, paper and timber, metals, rubber, plastics and vehicle assembly. The textile and leather industries employ one quarter of the industrial workforce, and export successfully.

Industrial development has switched in recent years away from import substitution and towards encouraging the manufacture of goods for export, support for small- and medium-sized producers, devolution of spending powers to local authorities, and investment in other areas of the country away from Casablanca. Many small- to medium-sized state-owned companies are due for privatisation.

Tourism

The tourism sector accounts for 7 per cent of GDP and 6 per cent of employment and is the second largest foreign exchange earner after workers' remittances. Morocco is a competitive destination for European tourists. To further encourage tourism, the prices of accommodation, restaurants and service charges have been reduced. Police checks on tourists have also been relaxed.

The private sector pooled resources to set up a National Tourism Federation to plan renovation of hotels, development of infrastructure and seaside resorts. The continuing privatisation of state-run hotels should contribute to the growth of the sector.

By the end of 2000, 2.5 million people visited Morocco, mainly from Europe.

Mining

The mining sector contributed 6 per cent to GDP in 2000 and employed 4 per cent of the workforce.

Morocco is the world's leading exporter of phosphate rock with estimated reserves of 110 billion tonnes (third largest world producer with an estimated three-quarters of known world reserves).

Responsibility for their extraction, marketing and export is vested in the parastatal Office Chérifien des Phosphates (OCP). Although phosphates account for 92 per cent of mineral production, smaller quantities of other minerals are produced, including 500,000 tonnes of anthracite.

Iron ore deposits in northern Rif region, 25km from Beni Eznar port, consist of 18.2 million tonnes of magnetite ore, which could bring in 700,000–800,000 tonnes of ore per year.

Silver, copper, zinc and lead are mined.

Hydrocarbons

Oil

Morocco is heavily reliant on imported oil, which accounts for over 30 per cent of total energy requirements, mainly imported from Saudi Arabia. Exploration projects are under way mainly in the south-west and north-east of the country, and offshore. Big shale oil deposits at Timadhit and Tarfaya (estimated at 200 billion tonnes) are currently uneconomic. In October 2001, Morocco signed two controversial oil deals with TotalFinaElf of France and Kerr-McGee (US-based) in the disputed Western Sahara. The Polisario Front, Western Sahara's independence movement protested against the deals.

The state-owned Samir oil refinery has been partially privatised.

In August 2000 a major oil and gas deposit (possible yielding up to two billion barrels of oil equivalent) was discovered in the Talsint region, close to the Algerian border. It was anticipated that the discovery would significantly narrow the large trade deficit.

Gas

Proven recoverable reserves of natural gas are estimated at four billion cubic metres. The main producing field is at Essaouira with an annual output of around 60 million cubic metres.

Coal

There is only one coal mine, at Jerada. Morocco imports coal from the US, Colombia and South Africa.

Energy

Electricity production depends heavily on imported oil, with hydroelectric potential not yet fully realised. Hydropower accounts for approximately 75 per cent of Morocco's 11.9 billion kWh electricity consumption. Thermal energy accounts for two billion kWh, and one billion kWh is imported from Algeria. Morocco is planning to liberalise its power sector by 2003 when it hopes to open 20 per cent of the sector to competition. Morocco's National Office of Electricity (ONE) also plans to provide the countryside with electricity by 2010. In 2001, only 15 per cent of people living in rural areas had access to electricity.

Financial markets

Stock exchange

In 1993, the government approved a decree to turn the Casablanca Stock Exchange, the Bourse des Valeurs, into a private company with stock held by brokers. This created new bodies for trading in securities, and channelled small savers' funds into share issues and unit trusts.

The government's privatisation programme for state-owned enterprises has increased the volume of trading on the Bourse. The programme has dramatically altered foreign perceptions of the Moroccan economy. Once a sleepy backwater of the financial community, it is now regarded as the strongest market in Africa outside Johannesburg.

Banking
Morocco has a well-developed and liberalised banking sector. In 2000, there were 15 commercial banks in Morocco. Major reforms in 2000 include the abolition of state control, the liberalisation of interest rates and the privatisation of some public banks.
A law passed in 2000 gives Morocco's largest bank, Banque Centrale Populaire, the right to float 20 per cent of its shares on the stock exchange. The government plans to make the initial public offering by the end of 2002.
Central bank
Bank al Maghrib.
Main financial centre
Casablanca.

Time
GMT

Geography
Morocco is situated in the extreme north-west of Africa. It has a long coastline on the shores of the Atlantic Ocean and, east of the Strait of Gibraltar, on the Mediterranean Sea, facing southern Spain. Morocco's eastern frontier is with Algeria, while to the south lies the disputed territory of Western Sahara.

Climate
Varies widely with area; while Mediterranean on the coast, it is hotter and drier inland and Alpine in the High Atlas, yet Saharan in the south. Summer is from May–October. It is dry and hot, with temperatures between 23–28 degrees Celsius on the coast, 30–45 degrees C inland. Winter runs from November–April; with light rain on the coast, average temperature 15–21 degrees C, and a dry inland with temperatures between 20–30 degrees C.

Dress codes
Lightweight suits are best for formal wear. Women should dress modestly. Some visitors adopt the traditional *jellaba*, which is more comfortable in both hot and cool weather and is usually worn by men. It can get cool quickly after dark, so a light overcoat or wrap is advised.

Entry requirements
Passports
Required by all. Passports must be valid for at least six months from the date of entry.
Visa
Not required for periods of up to 90 days by nationals of Australia, Canada, UK, US, Japan, EU members and several other countries.
For a stay of over three months, application must be made to the police authorities within 15 days of arrival.
Currency advice/regulations
The import and export of local currency is prohibited, except for repatriation of salaries.
Unlimited import of foreign currency, although amounts over the equivalent of Dh15,000 should be declared. Export is allowed of foreign currency up to amount declared on arrival. Up to half of the Moroccan currency purchased by a visitor during his stay may generally be re-exchanged for foreign currency on the production of relevant receipts.
Prohibited imports
Import restrictions apply to firearms, explosives, used clothes and used tyres.

Health (for visitors)
Mandatory precautions
Vaccinations against yellow fever are required if arriving from an infected area. Water may be contaminated. Milk is unpasteurised and should be boiled.
Advisable precautions
Typhoid, tetanus and polio vaccinations are recommended. Anti-malaria precautions should be taken.

Hotels
Inexpensive and widely available. Two main types: graded hotels (which are given a one- to five-star rating by the Tourist Board) and small (and usually old) unlisted hotels. A service charge and local tax is normally added to bill.

Credit cards
Major credit cards widely accepted.

Public holidays
Fixed dates
6 Mar Fatih Mouharran (Muslim New Year), 1 May (Labour Day), 23 May (Majority Day), 9 July (Youth Day), 14 Aug (National Day), 30 Jul (Feast of the Throne), 14 August Fête Oued Eddahab (Oued Eddahab Allegiance Day), 6 Nov (Anniversary of the Green March), 18 Nov (Independence).
Variable dates
Eid Al-Fitr, Easter, Aid Al-Adha, Aid Al Mawlid.

Working hours
Banking
Winter: Mon–Fri: 0800–1130 and 1400–1830. Summer: Mon–Fri: 0800–1600. Ramadan: Mon–Fri: 0900–1530.
Business
Winter: Mon–Fri: 0800–1200 and 1400–1800/2000. Summer hours vary, some work Mon–Fri: 0800–1500/1600, others revert to winter hours. Ramadan: Mon–Fri: 0900–1500/1600.
Government
Winter: Mon–Fri: 0800–1200 and 1430–1800. Summer: Mon–Sat: 0800–1600. Ramadan: Mon–Sat: 0900–1500.
Shops
Shops are usually open between 0800 and 1800, often closing for a few hours in the middle of the day.

Telecommunications
Telephone/fax
Morocco has the most modern service among Maghreb countries. International calls in most cities can be made direct. Elsewhere calls can be made at the Central Post Office (PTT). In 2000, there were an average 54 telephone mainlines per 1,000 people, with 115 per 1,000 in Casablanca.
Postal services
The postal system is often unreliable and postal services are slow.
Mobile phones
Mobile phone has increased dramatically with 83 mobile phones per 1,000 people in 2000 compared to 1 per 1,000 in 1995.
Internet/e-mail
In 2000 there were an estimated 200,000 internet users in the country.

Electricity supply
110–127V or 220V AC, 50 cycles.

Social customs/useful tips
Business visits during the Muslim month of Ramadan are best avoided, as many businesses close during part or all of this period. During Ramadan, visitors should respect Muslim traditions and avoid drinking, eating and smoking in public during daylight hours.
Pork and alcohol are forbidden to Muslims at all times, so these should not be offered, although in practice alcohol is widely available and its consumption not considered an insult to Islam.
Business practices in most respects are similar to those in France and Spain.
Tipping is common for most services, including hotel porters, cinema usherettes, cloakroom attendants, railway porters, and so on. In hotels and restaurants a service charge is normally added to the bill.
Taxi drivers (in *grand* taxis only) will expect a 10 per cent tip.

Security
Street crime is a problem, especially in the larger cities where petty theft is rife. Women may also encounter sexual harassment on the streets at any time, especially when walking alone.

Getting there
Air
National airline: Royal Air Maroc
Main airport: Agadir-Inezgane (Code: AGA), 6.5km south of city, bar, buffet, bank car hire; Casablanca-Mohammed V (Code: CMN), 30km south of city, bar, buffet,

restaurant, bank, post office, car hire; Fez-Sais (Code: FEZ), 10 km from city; Rabat-Salé (Code: RBA), 10km from city, buffet, restaurant, bank, post office, shops, car hire; Tangier-Boukhalef Souahel (Code: TNG), 15km from city, restaurant, bank, car hire; Marrakesh (Code: RAK), 6km from city.

Airport tax: None

Surface

Road: There are good bus connections between many European centres and major destinations in Morocco. Road access is possible from Algeria via Oujda.

Several major road projects were under way in Morocco in 2001, including a four-way motorway from Casablanca to the industrial area of El Jadida/Jorf Lasfar and the 550 km northern coastal road, for which Japan agreed to loan 12,764 million yen for civil works and consulting services for the Tetuan-Jebha section (among several Moroccan projects for which Japan committed aid during 2001). The latter project was one of several intended to benefit disadvantaged northern areas. Another was a major project for waterworks and sanitation in Tangier and Tetuan, for which a 25-year concession was awarded at the end of 2001.

Rail: There are good rail connections to France, Spain and Tunisia. The international rail link is via Oujda. In 2002, rail links to Algeria had been suspended.

Water: There are daily ferry services between Tangier and Nador in Morocco and ports in France, Spain and Gibraltar.

Main ports: Agadir, Casablanca (major freight port), Jorf Lasfar, Kenitra, Mohammedia, Nador, Safi, Tangier (main passenger port). Regular car ferry and hydrofoil services connect Spain, France and Gibraltar with Tangier and the Spanish administered ports of Ceuta and Melilla. New harbour facilities are planned at Dakhla, Sidi Ifni, Tan-Tan, Agadir and Layoun.

Getting about

National transport

Air: Royal Air Maroc operates domestic services to main centres. Regional Airlines is another domestic carrrier.

Road: Morocco has approximately 30,000km of surfaced roads – the links between main centres are generally good; some of the 30,000km country roads need care and/or local knowledge.

The Atlas Mountains may be impassable in winter.

Buses: There are frequent, cheap services between towns; long-distance services include: Tangier-Oujda, Fez-Marrakesh; Agadir-Casablanca and Tangier-Casablanca. It is advisable to book in advance.

Rail: A limited (1,893km) but efficient network is operated by Office National des Chemins de Fer (ONCF). Fares are cheap. Three classes are available. Air-conditioning, air-conditioned sleeping cars – couchettes and restaurant cars are available; supplements may be payable. Routes include: Oujda-Fez-Rabat-Casablanca, Marrakesh-Casablanca-Rabat and Casablanca-Rabat-Tangier.

City transport

Taxis: The *grand* taxis (Moroccan bus-taxis), seating up to six persons, operate along specific routes and can be arranged at hotel receptions, or can be found outside bus and train stations and the airport. They are cheaper than a conventional taxi for long journeys and more comfortable and convenient than a bus. The *Petit* taxis are metered and operate within cities. Fares vary considerably; drivers prefer to set fares in advance rather than use the meter, so each journey is preceded by a negotiation. A 10 per cent tip is usual.

Buses/trams: Agadir, Casablanca, Tangier and other main towns have good bus services. Tickets can be bought in advance of journeys. There is a shuttle bus service from Casablanca rail stations to the CTM Gare Routière (bus station) which takes at least 45 minutes, depending on traffic.

Metro: A train service every 30 minutes connects Casablanca's Mohammed V Airport with the city's main railway stations, Voyageurs and Port.

Car hire

Car hire is widely available but expensive. Major hire companies operate from Agadir, Casablanca and Tangier. National or international driving licences are accepted. Driving is on the right.

BUSINESS DIRECTORY

Telephone area codes

Dialling code for Morocco: IDD access code +212 followed by area code (8 for Agadir, 2 for Casablanca, 5 for Fez, 68 for Oujda, 7 for Rabat, 4 for Marrakesh, 9 for Tangier), followed by subscriber's number.

Chambers of Commerce

American Chamber of Commerce in Morocco, Hyatt Regency Hotel, Place des Nations Unies, Casablanca (tel: 293-028; fax: 481-597).

British Chamber of Commerce for Morocco, 65 Avenue Hassan Sghir, Casablanca (tel: 448-860; fax: 448-868).

Chambre de Commerce et d'Industrie de Casablanca, 98 Boulevard Mohamed V, Casablanca (tel: 293-181; fax: 268-436).

Chambre de Commerce et d'Industrie de Marrakech, Dinan Harti, Marrakech (tel: 431-951; fax: 430-950).

Chambre de Commerce et d'Industrie de Rabat, 6 Rue Ghandi, Rabat (tel: 706-466; fax: 706-768).

Chambre de Commerce et d'Industrie de Tanger, 41 Boulevard Pasteur, Tanger (tel: 932-535; fax: 934-716).

Chambre de Commerce Internationale, Boulevard de Bordeaux, Casablanca (tel: 225-111; fax: 225-119; e-mail: icc@casanet.net.ma).

Fédération des Chambres de Commerce et d'Industrie du Maroc, 6 Rue Erfoud, Rabat (tel: 766-108; fax: 767-076; e-mail: fccjsm@maghrebnet.net.ma).

Banking

ABN Amro Bank (Maroc) SA, PO Box 13478, 47 Rue Allal Ben Abellah, Casablanca 20000 (tel: 266027 fax: 222514).

Banque Centrale Populaire, 101 Boulevard Mohamed Zerktouni, Casablanca (tel: 222-589; fax: 222-699; e-mail: aslamti@cpm.co.ma).

Banque Commerciale du Maroc, 2 Boulevard Moulay Youssef, Casablanca (tel: 224-169; fax: 469-916).

Banque Marocaine du Commerce Extérieur SA, PO Box 13.425, 140 Avenue Hassan II, Casablanca 01 (tel: 2200325; fax: 2200005).

Crédit du Maroc SA, PO Box 13579, 48-58 Boulevard Mohammed V, Casablanca 20000 (tel:477000 fax: 277127, 206076/77).

Crédit Immobilier et Hôtelier, 187 Avenue Hassan II, Casablanca 20000 (tel: 2227863; fax: 2487537).

Groupement Professionel des Banques du Maroc (Moroccan Banking Association), 71 Avenue des Forces Armées Royales, Casablanca (tel: 311-624; fax: 311-911).

Société Marocaine de Dépôt et de Crédit, 79 Avenue Hassan II, Casablanca (tel: 224-114; fax: 271-590).

Wafabank, 163 Avenue Hassan II, Casablanca (tel: 2200200; fax: 2263621).

Central bank
Bank Al-Maghrib, PO Box 445, 277 Avenue Mohammed V, Rabat, Morocco (tel: 7702626 fax: 7700097)

Travel information
Office National des Chemins de Fer (ONCF) Tourist Office, 98 Boulevard Mohammed V, Casablanca (tel: 221-524).

Royal Air Maroc, 44 Avenue des Forces Armées Royales, Casablanca (tel: 311-122; fax: 442-409).

National tourist information offices
Morocco National Tourist Board (ONMT), Rue Oued Fes, Angle Avenue Al Abtal, Agdal, Rabat (tel: 681-531; fax: 777-437; e-mail: visitemorocco@mbox.azure.net).

Ministries
Prime Minister's Office, Palais Royal, Le Méchouar, Rabat (tel: 762-709; fax: 769-995).

Ministry of Agriculture and Rural Development, Place Abdallah Chefchaouni, Quartier Administratif, Rabat (tel: 760-933; fax: 763-378).

Ministry of Culture and Communication, Rue Ghandi, Rabat (tel: 708-037; fax: 673-267).

Ministry of Economic Forecasts and Planning, Avenue Al Haj Cherkaoui, Agdal, Rabat (tel: 761-415; fax: 760-771).

Ministry of the Economy, Finance and Tourism, Boulevard Mohammed V, Quartier Administratif, Rabat (tel: 765-504; fax: 761-575; e-mail: ministre@mfie.gov.ma).

Ministry of Education, Bab Rouah, Rabat (tel: 771-822; fax: 772-042)

Minister of Employment, Vocational Training, Social Development and Solidarity (tel: 760-695; fax: 766-633).

Ministry of Equipment, Quartier Adminisatratif, Chellah, Rabat (tel: 762-811; fax: 765-505).

Ministry of Foreign Affairs and Co-operation, Avenue Roosevelt, Rabat (tel: 762-841; fax: 764-679; e-mail: mail@maec.gov.ma).

Minister of Habous and Islamic Affairs, Le Méchouar, Rabat (tel: 766-801; fax: 765-257; e-mail: webmaster@habous.gov.ma).

Ministry of Health, 335 Boulevard Mohammed V, Rabat (tel: 761-121; fax: 768-401; e-mail: webmaster@sante.gov.ma).

Ministry of Higher Education and Scientific Research, Charia Bouregreg, Rabat (tel: 707-496; fax: 737-236).

Ministry of Human Rights (tel: 673-131; fax: 671-967).

Ministry of Industry, Commerce, Energy, and Mines, Quartier Administratif, Chellah, Rabat (tel: 761-868; fax: 766-265; e-mail: ministre@mcinet).

Ministry of Interior, Quartier Administratif, Rabat (tel: 761-861; fax: 762-056).

Ministry of Justice, Place Mamounia, Rabat (tel: 732-941; fax: 730-772).

Minister of Land Management, Urban Affairs, Housing and the Environment (tel: 763-539; fax: 763-510).

Ministry of Parliamentary Relations, Quartier Admistratif, Agdal, Rabat (tel: 775-170; fax: 775-468).

Ministry of Public Service and Administrative Reform (770-894; fax: 775-690)

Ministry of Sea Fisheries, Quartier Administratif, Rabat (tel: 770-154; fax: 778-540).

Ministry of Transport and Merchant Marine (tel: 774-266; fax: 779-525).

Ministry of Youth and Sport, Boulevard Ibn Sina, Agdal, Rabat, (tel: 680-045; fax: 680-916).

Other useful addresses
Bourse de Casablanca (Stock Exchange), Avenue de l'Armée Royale, Casablanca (tel: 452-626; fax: 452-625; e-mail: contact@casablanca-bourse.com).

British Consulate-General, 43 Boulevard d'Anfa, Casablanca (tel: 221-653; fax: 265-779; e-mail: british. consulate@casanet.net.ma).

British Embassy, 17 Boulevard de la Tour Hassan, Rabat (tel: 729-696; fax: 704-531; e-mail: britemb@mtds.com).

Confédération Générale des Enterprises du Maroc (CGEM), Angle Avenue des Forces Armées Royales et Rue Mohamed Errachid, Casablanca (tel: 252-696; fax: 253-839).

Fédération des Industries Chimiques et Parachimiques (FICP), 36 Rue Chaouia, Casablanca (tel: 229-215; fax:225-613).

Fédération des Industries de la Conserve des Produits Agricoles du Maroc (FICOPAM), 77 Rue Mohamed Smiha, Casablanca (tel: 303-953; fax: 303-534).

Fédération des Industries Métallurgiques, Mécaniques, Electriques et Electroniques (FIMME), 147 Rue Mohamed Smiha, Casablanca (tel: 301-683; fax: 940-587).

Moroccan Centre for Export Promotion, 23 Rue Bnou Majed El Bahar, Casablanca (tel: 302-210; fax: 301-793).

Moroccan Embassy (USA), 1601 21st Street, NW, Washington DC 20009 (tel: 462-7979; fax: 265-0161; e-mail: sifarausa@erols.com).

National Telecommunications Regulatory Agency (ANRT), Boulevard Ennakhil, Rabat (tel: 717-312; e-mail: webmaster@anrt.net.ma).

Office pour le Développement Industriel (ODI), 10 Rue Ghandi, Rabat (tel: 708-460; fax: 707-695).

ONAREP (national oil company), 34 Avenue Al Fadila, Rabat (tel: 281-616; fax: 281-634; e-mail: benkhadr@onarep.com)

United States Embassy, 2 Avenue de Mohamed El Fassi, Rabat (tel: 762-265; fax: 765-661).

Internet sites
Information on Morocco – historical events, cities, economy, culture and media: http://www.dsg.ki.se/maroc/

Ministry of Public Sector and Privatisation: http://www.minpriv.gov.ma

Africa Business Network: http://www.ifc.org/abn

AllAfrica.com: http://allafrica.com

African Development Bank: http://www.afdb.org

Mbendi AfroPaedia (information on companies, countries, industries and stock exchanges in Africa): http://mbendi.co.za

Menara Yellow Pages (in French): http://www.menara.co.ma/pagejauneHome.asp

Mozambique

Daniel Brett

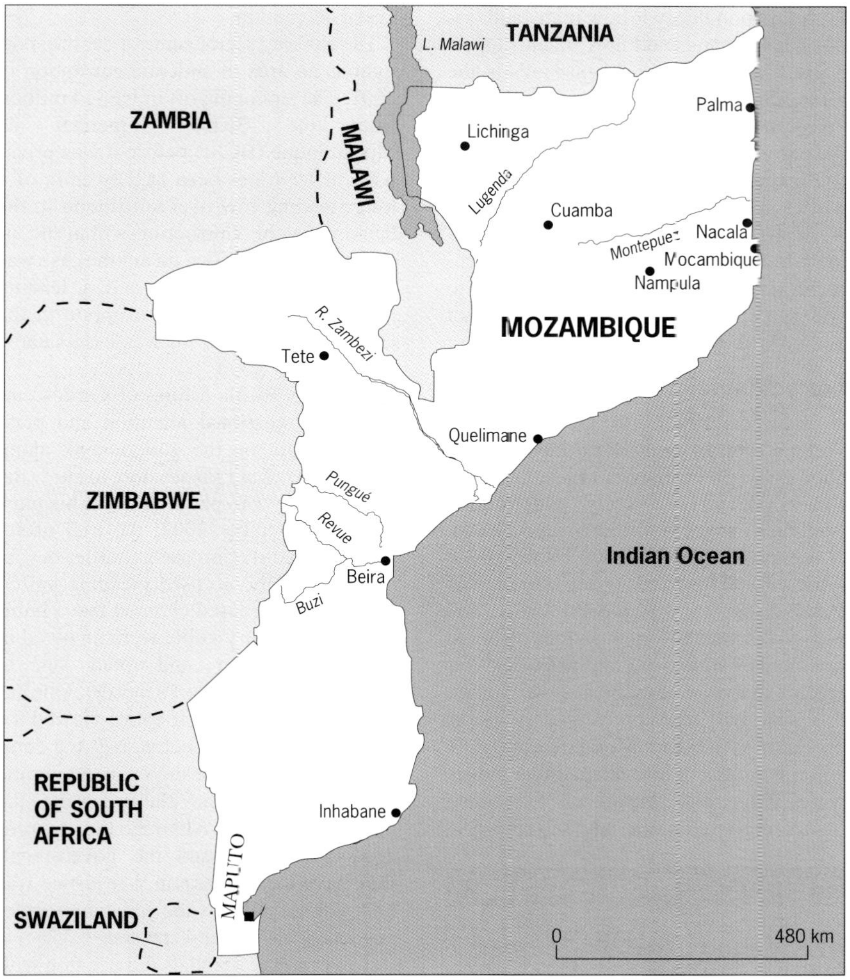

President Joaquim Chissano's decision not to seek re-election in 2004 led to a lengthy campaign for the leadership of the ruling Frente de Libertação de Moçambique (Frelimo) (Front for the Liberation of Mozambique) and therefore the party's candidacy. By standing down, Chissano has avoided a potentially destabilising political conflict with the opposition Resistencia Nacional de Moçambique (Renamo) (Mozambique National Resistance) as well as elements within Frelimo.

Political stability has been matched by economic growth, with Mozambique increasingly seen as an African success story. The country's performance has led to substantial debt reduction under the enhanced Heavily Indebted Poor Countries (HIPC) initiative, administered by the World Bank and IMF, which has led to the cancellation of much of Mozambique's debt. However, underneath the strong macroeconomic fundamentals are problems of corruption, a major food crisis and grinding poverty. While Mozambicans have benefited from an end to war, many have yet to receive the benefits of peacetime economic expansion.

KEY FACTS

Official name: República de Moçambique (The Republic of Mozambique)

Head of State: President Joaquim Alberto Chissano

Head of government: Prime Minister Pascoal M Mocumbi

Ruling party: Frente de Libertação de Moçambique (Frelimo) (Front for the Liberation of Mozambique)

Area: 799,380 square km

Population: 17.99 million (2001)

Capital: Maputo

Official language: Portuguese

Currency: Metical (MT) = 100 centavos

Exchange rate: MT23,336.50 per US$ (Jan 2003)

GDP per capita: US$204 (2001); US$106 (2002)*

GDP real growth: 13.90% (2001); 12.2% (2002)*

Inflation: 21.90% (2001); 9.0% (2002)*

Balance of trade: -US$413.00 million (2001)

Foreign debt: US$4.98 billion (2001)

Annual FDI: US$183.00 million (2001)

* estimated figure

For the latest Key Facts, go to www.worldinformation.com

New leader, new era

In June 2002, Frelimo's 156-strong central committee voted overwhelmingly for Armando Guebaza, head of Frelimo's parliamentary group, to become the party's secretary general and consequently its candidate in the 2004 presidential election. Guebaza is a natural 'unity' candidate, having been associated with the party's independence struggle during the 1960s and 1970s as well as the post-independence governments of Samora Machel and Chissano. He was first elected to the party's politburo in 1968, rising through the ranks from guerrilla commander to general during the country's struggle for independence. He has served in every government since independence in 1975 and is known as a shrewd and intelligent politician who is able to rally masses.

Guebaza has undergone something of an ideological conversion since the collapse of the Soviet Union and the end of the civil war, discarding the military fatigues of his communist past to become a pro-Western, free-market liberal under the Chissano administration. He is therefore seen as a link between the party's socialist roots and the modernising elements of the young technocratic wing, and therefore the person most able to heal the rift between traditionalists and modernists.

Election issues

Guebaza will have to reverse the party's fortunes in the run-up to the 2004 election. The results of the 1999 presidential election were a big shock to Frelimo, with Chissano receiving a slim majority over his Renamo rival, Afonso Dhlakama. Frelimo's popularity will be tested in the 2003 municipal elections. These are likely to be contested by Renamo and its political allies, which have in the past boycotted local elections. The 1998 elections saw Frelimo take control of all the local authorities, with very little opposition. With opposition parties poised to contest the elections, Frelimo is likely to lose control of many local authorities. The acid test of Frelimo's popularity is how many authorities change hands and how much support it loses in its traditional heartlands in the far north and the south.

Frelimo is aware of the dangers facing the party. Rather than opt for the destructive authoritarian route taken by the ruling parties in Malawi and Zimbabwe, Frelimo is undergoing some healthy soul-searching which is having an impact on government policy. It has begun to respond to widespread complaints that it is corrupt and inflexible.

Corruption reigns

A main contributor to the erosion of Frelimo support has been the close association between business and leading party figures. This is severely undermining Frelimo's image both at home and abroad. A report published in 2002 by the South Africa-based Institute for Security Studies (funded by foreign governments and non-governmental organisations) warned that 'unless there are dramatic and far reaching interventions by the government, this slide will lead to criminal networks operating in the shadow of the formal state administration'. It also alleged that judges were frequently bribed while 'money laundering is common and Mozambique has become an important drug warehousing and transit centre, with senior figures involved'. Some donors have disagreed with the criticism lodged against the Mozambican authorities. Bilateral donors such as the US, the UK and Belgium as well as multilaterals such as the UN Development Programme (UNDP) and the World Bank have all praised Mozambique for its transparency and lack of institutionalised corruption.

The banking sector came under the spotlight as an area of endemic corruption in 2001. The siphoning off of US$14 million from the Banco Comercial de Moçambique (BCM) before it was privatised in 1996 has been at the centre of a long-standing row over corruption in the banking sector. Corruption within the attorney general's office meant the case was never fully investigated and a leading journalist investigating corruption in the BCM, Carlos Cardoso, was assassinated in November 2000.

The high-profile killing of Cardoso attracted international attention and pressure was put on the government, along with threats of aid suspension, to allow the trial of those who participated in his murder. In November 2002, the trial of six men accused of Cardoso's murder began, with two of the accused pleading guilty. Three of the accused claimed that a number of the country's elite were involved in the assassination and paid up to US$40,000 for Cardoso's murder. One defendant, Momade Assif Satar, showed the court seven cheques belonging to a company owned by Chissano's son, Nyimpine Chissano, which he claimed were the hit-men's payment. Although the trial proceedings embarrassed the government, they gave the impression that justice was being done and that the judiciary's independence was being respected.

However, the scandals did not stop with the BCM affair. In 2001, senior political figures who refused to pay off their debts helped saddle the state-owned Banco Austral with US$150 million worth of bad debts. The bank was forced into insolvency and its assets were put up for sale. In August 2001, Banco Austral's interim president, António Siba-Siba Macuácua, was assassinated after he drew up a report on massive corruption linked to leading Frelimo figures which he intended to pass on to the South African bank, Absa, which was looking to buy the bank. Absa's own investigations confirmed large-scale fraud in Banco Austral, which involved Malaysian bankers as well as the ruling elite. However, the scandals surrounding the

KEY INDICATORS — Mozambique

	Unit	1996	1997	1998	1999	2000
Population	m	16.18	16.54	16.92	17.30	17.69
Gross domestic product (GDP)	US$bn	2.90	3.40	3.90	4.20	4.80
GDP per capita	US$	182	214	237	248	282
GDP real growth	%	7.1	11.1	9.9	10.0	1.6
Inflation	%	16.6	5.8	-1.3	3.1	12.7
Exports (fob) (goods)	US$m	226.0	230.0	244.6	283.8	364.0
Imports (fob) (goods)	US$m	704.0	684.0	735.6	1,090.0	0.0
Imports (cif)	US$m	0.0	0.0	0.0	0.0	1,046.0
Balance of trade	US$m	-478.3	-454.0	-491.0	-806.2	-682.0
Current account	US$m	-420.5	-295.6	-429.3	-912.0	-763.6
Total reserves minus gold	US$m	344.1	517.4	608.5	651.6	725.1
Foreign exchange	US$m	344.0	517.3	608.4	651.5	725.0
Exchange rate	per US$	11,293.80	11,543.60	11,874.60	12,775.10	15,447.10

bank did not stop the takeover and the bank was privatised in January 2002.

In December 2001, Attorney General Joaquim Madeira announced the formation of a special unit to fight corruption. The body is composed of magistrates investigating corruption in the judiciary. Its creation is intended to meet demands made by international donors, who have urged Chissano to prioritise the fight against corruption. However, given that investigations into the BCM affair were thwarted by corruption in the attorney general's office, there are serious doubts over Madeira's commitment to fighting graft.

Economic performance

Mozambique's economy has boomed since the mid-1990s, with the industrial sector leading growth. The government has pursued an aggressive free-market approach to development, attracting plaudits from donors, investors and financial institutions. Private sector investment has risen from 10.6 per cent of GDP in 1996 to 27.7 per cent in 2001. In 2001, GDP growth reached 12.9 per cent compared to the 1.6 per cent achieved in the previous, disaster-ridden year. Growth was boosted by the Mozal aluminium smelter, which had its first full year of operation in 2001, and a strong recovery in the agricultural sector. Mozal's exports helped reduce the trade deficit, thereby narrowing the current account deficit from 11.8 per cent of GDP in 2000 to 10.5 per cent in 2001.

Inflation rose from 1 per cent at the beginning of 2001 to 22 per cent by the end of the year, with an average of 9 per cent across the year as a whole. Inflationary pressures were caused by the depreciation of the metical, which lost a third of its value in 2001, and an expansionary monetary policy. By the fourth quarter of 2001, the authorities had moved to restrict monetary policy by raising banks' reserve requirements and interest rates. This saw broad money growth decline from 45 per cent in September 2001 to 30 per cent by March 2002. According to the IMF, this move to tighten liquidity saw cumulative inflation of less than 1 per cent in the first five months of 2002. The metical also stabilised in the first half of 2002, maintaining a value of around MT23,000 per US$. This helped prevent an increase in the value of external debt and the cost of imports and improved the country's balance of payments.

Mega-projects dominate

Industrial development is led by 'mega-projects', which have had a high impact on macroeconomic fundamentals. The largest mega-project is the Mozal aluminium smelter, which began construction in 1999. The first phase of Mozal, which was completed in 2001, doubled Mozambique's exports, generating over US$400 million per annum in foreign exchange earnings. The US$1.2 billion plant, one of the largest industrial projects in sub-Saharan Africa, is owned by BHP-Billiton (the leading shareholder), Mitsubishi, South Africa's Industrial Development Corporation (IDC) and the Mozambican government. The US$806 million second phase will see capacity rise to 506,000 tonnes of aluminium per year by 2004. By then, Mozal will have helped increase exports by over 300 per cent of 2000 levels, adding up to 20 per cent to GDP. Already, Mozal is the world's cheapest producer of aluminium and costs will fall further as capacity is increased.

The 865km Sasol pipeline, which began construction in July 2002, will also add an estimated 20 per cent to the country's GDP, creating up to 1,000 new jobs. When completed in 2004, the pipeline will transport gas from Mozambique to South Africa. The pipeline is a joint venture between South Africa's Sasol (which is investing a total of US$385 million) and the governments of Mozambique and South Africa. Other mega-projects include the Maputo Corridor (a major infrastructural development linking Mozambique with South Africa), the Chibuto heavy sand project and the Lubombo project (a joint tourism programme with Swaziland and South Africa).

Big is not beautiful

Economic growth may be impressive on paper, but given the country's low starting point, the 8 per cent annual growth target for 2001–2010 is unlikely to alter Mozambique's position as one of the world's poorest countries. With average growth of around 8 per cent in 1996–2000, GDP per capita rose by 50 per cent to just US$282. Meanwhile, income inequality increased dramatically, with the rich becoming richer and economic activity remaining focussed on capital-intensive mega-projects which have few direct benefits for most ordinary Mozambicans.

Most Mozambicans are dependent on labour-intensive agriculture, which has failed to keep up with manufacturing growth levels. Farming endures poor productivity, a lack of capital and is highly susceptible to climatic problems, such as the floods of 2000 and the drought of 2001/02. The recurrent problem of food crop failure is a major issue in Mozambique. In June 2002, the World Food Programme (WFP) estimated that 'approximately 515,000 people in poor households in 43 districts of the Southern and Central regions are facing severe food insecurity'.

Investment in physical and social infrastructure will require additional support to mitigate these periodic crises, particularly with the advent of the HIV/AIDS pandemic. The lack of resources in rural areas has led to a continuation of a high incidence of poverty, which is estimated at around 60 per cent of the rural population. However, even after the debt reductions under the HIPC, Mozambique is spending US$50 million on debt servicing, compared to just US$20 million on primary healthcare and US$32 million on primary education.

Dilemmas of development

Industrialisation through economic liberalisation and the building of large industrial projects is a mixed blessing for Mozambique. High profile mega-projects may help to boost economic growth in the medium-term, but their benefits may be short-lived and highly localised. Most of the profits from the Mozal smelter are repatriated by foreign investors and construction activity related to the smelter will tail off by 2004. The jobs created by mega-projects, either directly or indirectly, will not have a significant impact on the country's poverty levels or long-term job prospects. Moreover, Mozambique's reliance on a small number of large projects makes it highly vulnerable to external influences. Any serious under-performance at Mozal could derail the entire economic programme, frustrating the government's chances of meeting its targets under the IMF's Poverty Reduction and Growth Facility (PRGF) and undermining donor and investor confidence. This could have serious implications for the development of the wider economy.

Another common complaint against current industrial and infrastructural projects is their concentration in and around Maputo and the southern and, to a lesser extent, central provinces. The northern provinces are virtually excluded in the country's move towards industrialisation, with investment skewed towards the south. This makes the country's development highly uneven.

Meanwhile, traditional manufacturing industries are suffering under the economic liberalisation programme. Once the country's main industry, the cashew nut processing sector collapsed after Mozambique bowed to World Bank demands to end state tariffs. which had encouraged local processors to buy cheaper imported nuts rather than home-grown nuts. This devastated the sector leading to over 40,000 job losses and reducing the added value Mozambican cashew nuts once had on world markets.

So far, the gains made in job creation through foreign involvement in mega-projects are far outweighed by the losses incurred through the collapse of traditional industries.

Debt reduction

An important recent development in the Mozambican economy is foreign debt reduction. In 2000, Mozambique became the third country to be admitted to the HIPC initiative, with total debt relief under the scheme amounting to a total of US$1.7 billion. The HIPC is based on the premise that foreign debt should be reduced to a 'sustainable level'. The initiative links debt reduction to a number of performance criteria set out in the country's PRGF and its Poverty Reduction Strategy Paper (PRSP or PARPA, under its Portuguese acronym), approved by the IMF and World Bank in April 2001. These criteria involve commitments to economic liberalisation and fiscal reform as well as reducing poverty from 70 per cent of the population in 1997 to 50 per cent by 2010 and maintaining an average growth rate of 8 per cent between 2001–2010. The Mozambique government's commitment to fiscal prudence helped it meet revenue and expenditure targets in 2001 and 2002. This enabled it to receive a large reduction in its debt stock, with Russia, China, the UK and the US wiping out most of the country's bilateral debt.

Debt relief is not the panacea for Mozambique's problems, as claimed by bilateral and multi-lateral creditors. The rigid structural adjustment programme, reinforced by the HIPC, in some ways helped worsen the living standards of Mozambique's poor. For example, the IMF demanded an increase in healthcare user charges as a prerequisite for debt reduction, thereby denying the poorest people access to medical facilities. The reduction of the debt stock is also not having a significant effect on the level of annual debt servicing, as Mozambique was only paying a quarter of the debt it owed before implementation of the HIPC. According to IMF figures, during the three years prior to Mozambique's qualification for assistance under the HIPC (1995–97), Mozambique was paying an average of US$113 million per annum. In the first three years of the HIPC, this fell to US$110 million. This is a reduction of just US$0.73 per person per annum, according to the UN Office for the Co-ordination of Humanitarian Affairs. Many NGOs are also warning that the reduction of debt service obligations to the target of 10 per cent of government revenue by 2010 may still be unsustainable.

Outlook

Guebaza's ascent to the presidency is not guaranteed. A candid report by Frelimo's central committee published in June 2002 implied that Frelimo is its own worst enemy and recommended that local parties need to adopt more participatory practices and decentralise power to small, community-based units. Unless the party reforms its own internal structures, the report warned, it was at serious risk of being 'penalised by the electorate'. The public also need to be assured that Frelimo is genuinely tackling corruption within its own ranks as well as being able to deliver on a more equitable distribution of resources and wealth. Unless the government is seen to act on these issues, there is a significant danger that Frelimo will lose support in its strongholds during the 2003 municipal elections. Any widespread loss of support could open up splits within the ruling party in the run-up to the presidential election, undermining Guebaza's chances of securing the presidency in 2004.

Another issue that is likely to dominate headlines in 2003 is electoral reform. Frelimo and Renamo have been at loggerheads over the issue, with the opposition demanding radical changes. The issue has disrupted the functioning of the national assembly and threatens to upset the municipal elections, as failure to agree on government proposals for minor revisions has held back the updating of the electoral register. This raises the possibility of the kind of confusion and boycotts that surrounded the 1998 municipal elections.

Risk assessment

Economic	Good
Political	Stable
Regional stability	Poor
Stock market	Small

COUNTRY PROFILE

Historical profile

In the third century, Bantu tribes settled the area. The Shona empire was established by the eleventh century between the Limpopo and Zambezi river.

1498 Portuguese explorer Vasco da Gama landed on the shores of what is now Mozambique.

Portuguese traders and settlers arrived in the late fifteenth century. Full scale colonisation did not begin until the seventeenth century. In the eighteenth and nineteenth centuries, Mozambique served as a major slave-trading centre.

1842 Portugal abolished the slave trade, although the practice continued.

1891 Mozambique's southern and western borders were defined by the British and Portuguese.

1932 Portugal broke up the companies which owned the land and controlled trade and imposed direct rule over Mozambique.

1962 The Frente de Libertação de Moçambique (Frelimo) (Front for the Liberation of Mozambique) was established and launched a military campaign to drive out the Portuguese.

1975 Mozambique gained independence on 25 June. Following independence, a one-party system was implemented with Frelimo as the sole legal party. Mozambican support for the independence war in Rhodesia (Zimbabwe) and the African National Congress in South Africa led to frequent reprisals from the governments of those countries. Independence was followed by 16 years of civil war against the rebels of the Resistencia Nacional de Moçambique (Renamo) (Mozambique National Resistance), a guerrilla army supported first by Rhodesia and later by South Africa and the US.

1977 Frelimo adopted Marxism-Leninism as its official doctrine.

1984 Frelimo reached a deal with apartheid South Africa in which it would halt its support for the African National Congress (ANC) in return for an end to South Africa's aid to Renamo.

1986 President Machel was killed in an airplane crash; Joaquim Chissano became president.

1989 Frelimo formally abandoned Marxism-Leninism in favour of democratic socialism and a market economy. This decision reduced Renamo's support further – the civil war was already going in the government's favour.

1990 A new consititution was promulgated to allow for a multi-party electoral system.

1992 A cease-fire was agreed, followed by a full peace agreement in October.

1994 In the first multi-party elections, held in October, Frelimo won an absolute parliamentary majority. Joaquim Chissano was re-elected president.

1995 Mozambique joined the Commonwealth, the only member not to have been a British colony.

1998 Local elections were held on 30 June. Frelimo won a majority in the municipal and local councils it contested. Renamo boycotted the poll in which turnout was about 20 per cent.
1999 In the second multi-party presidential and legislative elections held on 3–5 December, President Joaquim Chissano received 52.3 per cent of the vote in the presidential elections and Frelimo increased its parliamentary majority.
2000 Mozambique was devastated by a tropical cyclone and severe flooding. In November, more than 40 people were killed in rioting over Renamo allegations that the 1999 election were rigged. International observers claimed the elections were free and fair. A further 82 Renamo activists died in police custody after they were arrested during protests.
2001 More flooding in January affected 253,000 people.
2002 A train crash in May killed 200 passengers and injured 400. In June, Armando Guebuza become Frelimo's general secretary and the party's candidate for the 2004 presidential elections.

Political structure

Constitution
The 1975 independence constitution was replaced by the 1990 constitution, which provides for a multi-party system, direct elections and a free market economy.

Form of state
Unitary republic

The executive
The head of state is the president, directly elected for a five-year term, who can be re-elected on only two consecutive occasions, and who governs with his appointed prime minister and Council of Ministers.

National legislature
Legislative power is vested in the 250-seat unicameral *Assembleia de la República* (Assembly of the Republic) elected by direct universal adult suffrage every five years.

Legal system
Based on Portuguese/Roman law and the 1990 constitution. Since 1996, there has been a Law Reform Commission which has the responsibility for revising legislation.

Last elections
December 1999 (presidential and parliamentary)

Next elections
2004 (presidential and parliamentary)

Political parties

Ruling party
Frente de Libertação de Moçambique (Frelimo) (Front for the Liberation of Mozambique)

Main opposition party
Resistencia Nacional de Moçambique (Renamo) (Mozambique National Resistance)

Population

17.69 million (2000)
Annual population growth rate: 2.2 per cent (1994–2000). The projected growth rate for the period 1999–2015 is 1.7 per cent per annum. Approximately 46 per cent of the population are under 14 years of age.
Population density: 22 inhabitants per square km. Urban population: 38 per cent (1994–2000).
About 38 per cent of the urban population and 9 per cent of the rural population have access to clean water.

Ethnic make-up
Indigenous tribal groups, including Ronga, Shangaan, Chokwe, Manyika, Sena and Makua (99 per cent); European (1 per cent).

Religions
Some 300 registered religions, including traditional beliefs (50 per cent), Christianity (majority Roman Catholic) (30 per cent), Muslim (20 per cent).

Education

The war devastated the education sector. However, by the end of the 1990s, the primary school network had recovered to levels seen in 1983. In 1999, there were 6,600 first-level primary schools (first to fifth years) attended by 2.1 million children. However, a third of primary school children attend schools that are so crowded that classes are oversubscribed by over 300 per cent. Educational provision is far worse in the second-level primary schools (sixth and seventh years), with only 440 operating in the entire country. The secondary school sector consists of just 81 schools, with fewer than 64,000 students receiving basic secondary education. There are around 7,000 students enrolled in Mozambique's six university-level institutions and 15,000 in vocational colleges.

Health

Mozambique has been one of the countries worst affected by the AIDS pandemic which is sweeping Africa. In 1999, the estimated HIV prevalence was around 10.2 per cent. Central provinces are more affected than southern and northern provinces with infection trends following the major transport routes and areas bordering Zimbabwe, Malawi and Zambia. In the cities of Chimoio and Tete, HIV seroprevalence in pregnant women is over 20 per cent.
With resources targetted at this growing problem, other healthcare needs are increasingly neglected. Moreover, the IMF forced the government to abandon its commitment to free healthcare provision and it is estimated that a rural Mozambican must walk an average of 46km to reach the nearest doctor. Modern health services reach around 40 per cent of the population and cholera has been rampant due to poor sanitation. However, mobile medical brigades have formed the backbone of the government's innoculation campaign, with polio virtually eradicated.
Mozambique has a birth and death rate of 40 births and 20 deaths per 1,000 people. World Bank estimates during the period 1994 and 2000 showed that the average life expectancy was 45 years and the infant mortality rate stood at 134 per 1,000 live births. It is estimated that 26 per cent of children under the age of five were malnourished in the same period. The fertility rate shows that 5.2 children are born per adult woman while the rate of contraception practices is estimated at 6 per cent among women aged 15–49. Maternal mortality ratio is high and estimated at 1,100 deaths per 100,000 live births. World Bank estimates in 2000, showed that 43 per cent and 60 per cent of the population had access to improved sanitation and safe water facilities respectively. Approximately 0.9 hospital beds per 1,000 people are typically available. Between 1990 and 1998, government expenditure on healthcare averaged 3.5 per cent of GDP of which 2.8 per cent was public expenditure, according to latest available World Bank estimates. Expenditure on private healthcare (such as private household expenditure and insurance) averaged 0.7 per cent of GDP over the same period.

Welfare

The World Bank figures state that 69 per cent of the population live in poverty. Floods in 2000 resulted in 700 deaths and around 500,000 internally displaced people
Economic liberalisation, hailed as the driving force behind Mozambique's high growth levels, has also removed the safety nets that existed under the command economy. The minimum wage of US$30 per month is paltry and in many companies even the minimum is not paid and workers often receive their wages weeks or months late. There is no longer a basic ration of subsidised food, leaving many in the growing informal economy with little to eat.

Main cities

Maputo/Matola conurbation (capital, estimated population 2.2 million in 1998), Beira (350,000), Quelimane, Nampula, Nacala, Tete, Lichinga, Pemba,

Inhambane, Xai-Xai, Chimoio, Chokwe, Mocuba, Cuamba.

Languages spoken

Although Portuguese is the official language, it is spoken by less than 30 per cent of the population. English is widely spoken in business circles.

There are three main African language groups: Tsonga, Sena-Nyanja, Makua-Lomwe.

In July 1996, Portugal and six of its former colonies (Angola, Brazil, Cape Verde, Guinea-Bissau, Mozambique and São Tomé) launched the Comunidade dos Países de Língua Portuguesa (CPLP) (Community of Portuguese Speaking Countries) to protect their common language.

Official language/s

Portuguese

Media

Press

There are more than 40 newspapers and magazines, including nine daily newspapers, 11 weekly publications, eight fortnightly publications, 14 monthly publications and 12 quarterly or half-yearly publications.

The 1990 constitution provides for press freedom. With the opening up of independent newspapers, the share of the civil war-era government newspapers has fallen. The most important media company to arise is the co-operative Mediacoop, which owns the successful *Media Fax*, faxed to hundreds of direct subscribers but read very widely, the periodical *Mozambique Inview*, and the weekly *Savana*.

Dailies: *Media Fax* (independent), *Imparcial* (independent), *Demos* (independent) and *Noticias de Moçambique* (government).

Weeklies: *Tempo* (government), *Savana*(independent) and *Domingo* (government) are the main weeklies in circulation.

Business: Other fax newsletters targeted at businesses include *Metical* and *Correio de Manha*.

Periodicals: Agencia de Informação de Moçambique (AIM) provides a daily bulletin in Portuguese and English and a monthly bulletin in French and English. *Mozambique Inview* is an independent bi-monthly publication.

Broadcasting

Radio: There are 10 radio stations. Each province has its own broadcasting station which transmits programmes in Portuguese and local languages.

Radio Moçambique provides programmes in Portuguese, English and local languages. The programmes consist mainly of light entertainment, interspersed with news and political broadcasts. The only radio broadcaster with national coverage, it is no longer controlled directly by the information ministry.

Television: Maputo enjoys several local TV stations, one of which also serves major cities in the rest of the country. These are Radiotelevisão Klint, Radio Televisão de Portugal and the São Paulo, Brazil-based Miramar. The national television broadcaster, Televisão de Moçambique (TVM), is hoping to broadcast nationwide using satellite, through an agreement with Radio Televisão de Portugal.

Advertising

Television is probably the most effective way of reaching Mozambique's middle classes. Prime time slots are inexpensive and may sell for a few hundred US dollars. Other target groups are avid radio listeners.

Economy

Portuguese colonisation of Mozambique brought large revenues from gold, ivory and slaves, much of which was repatriated by the colonial elite. During the nineteenth century, British, South African and Rhodesian investors set up businesses, hoping to take advantage of cheap labour, natural resources and a favourable climate for agriculture. Following independence in 1975, Mozambique inherited an economy primarily focused on providing services for South Africa. Revenues from rail freight and remittances from Mozambican miners in South Africa supported the economy. The flight of Portuguese skills and investment, however, was a severe setback to the economy, while subsequent state-led industrialisation had a social cost.

Mozambique's economy is now primarily agricultural, with farming employing 80 per cent of the working population. The sector also continues to provide a large part of export revenues and main cash crops include cashew nuts, sugar and cotton, although these products face problems competing on the international market.

The service sector employs around 10 per cent of the population and consists mainly of the tourist industry, transport, communications and clerical work. Industry employs up to 10 per cent of the population, mainly in food processing (maize and wheat flour, cashew nuts, sugar and salt), beverages, aluminium smelting and light industry, such as textiles, soap, batteries, radios and bicycles. However, the economy is diversifying rapidly and transport, metallurgy, manufacturing, energy, tourism, timber and fishing are all growth areas. There is renewed emphasis on poverty reduction and extension of infrastructure and basic social services to rural areas.

Despite damage of almost US$1 billion caused by tropical cyclones in 2000, Mozambique is recovering strongly from the low base perpetuated by the civil war. Mozambique was one of the fastest growing economies in the world before the floods. Although growth fell to 1.6 per cent in 2000, compared to double digit figures in the late 1990s, 2001 saw growth of 12.9 per cent, indicating that the country was making a strong recovery. The medium-term framework detailed in Mozambique's Poverty Reduction Strategy Paper (PRSP), agreed with the IMF and published in October 2001, envisages average growth of 8 per cent per annum between 2002–04. The government has pledged to move the country towards greater macroeconomic stability and less aid dependency by reducing expenditure. Stricter fiscal and monetary measures are being imposed in 2002 as the country returns to its normal pattern of development and growth following the completion of many post-disaster reconstruction projects. In the medium-term, the country's development will be dominated by mega-projects, such as the Mozal aluminium smelter, the 900km Sasol pipeline from Beira, the Maputo Corridor (project to develop infrastructure between southern Mozambique and South Africa), the Chibuto heavy sand project and others.

External trade

The large visible trade deficit began to fall in 2001 as the Mozal aluminium smelter picked up production and exports increased.

Exports

Principal exports are aluminium, prawns and other fish, cotton, cashew nuts, timber, sugar and copra.

Main destinations: Zimbabwe (17.7 per cent of 2000 total), South Africa (14.7 per cent), Portugal (11.6 per cent), Spain (10.7 per cent), India (4.9 per cent).

Imports

Principal imports are food and consumer goods (typically 37 per cent of the total), raw materials (17 per cent), machinery and equipment (38 per cent), crude oil (10 per cent), spare parts (7 per cent).

Main sources: South Africa (36.7 per cent of 2000 total), Portugal (8 per cent), Japan (4.4 per cent), US (3.1 per cent), France (2.1 per cent).

Agriculture

The agricultural sector is the mainstay of the economy, employing 80 per cent of the workforce, mainly engaged in subsistence farming, and accounting for around a quarter of GDP. The main cash crops are cashew nuts, tea, sugar, sisal, cotton, copra, tobacco, oil seeds and some citrus fruits. Maize is the main subsistence crop, but cassava, millet, sorghum, groundnuts, beans and rice are also grown. There is an important forestry sector, with exploitation of hardwoods from Zambezia, Sofala, Nampula, Manica and Niassa provinces.

Some 45 per cent of the land area is considered suitable for agriculture, but only 4 per cent of that is under cultivation. Most production is carried out through rain-fed farming and continues to be done by hand with only 7 per cent of farmers using traction (animal or mechanical) and only 2 per cent using fertilisers and pesticides. The agricultural sector is dominated by peasant family smallholdings, which occupy 90 per cent of the total cultivated area. Only 5 per cent of cultivated land is used by commercial operations, which grow cash or export crops. There is significant large potential for foreign investment in the agriculture sector due to the fertility and availability of unused cultivatable land.

Peace, good rains and an increase in the area under cultivation have resolved the chronic food deficit seen in the 1980s. However, food stocks are low and most families do not produce enough to build up a reserve of food and money that would see them through a bad harvest. Floods and drought in 2000–2002 have revealed the level of the country's dependence on international food aid in times of crisis. In mid-2002, the UN's World Food Programme (WFP) estimated that over 500,000 people in the south and central districts were facing severe food insecurity which requires urgent international aid.

The ongoing structural adjustment programme has exacerbated problems associated with fragile marketing systems and poor infrastructure. The state marketing body intervenes in the market in order to pay farmers for crops they have been unable to sell, either due to low prices on the open market or because the transport infrastructure is too poor. However, with bank credit in short supply and with a reluctance on behalf of international financial institutions to support marketing boards, the state has been unable to completely fulfil its role. This has encouraged the growth of unscrupulous middle-men who demand lower farm-gate prices.

Fishing

Fishing is of increasing importance and prawns have become a major export. The UK is helping to modernise the industry through the refitting of trawlers and building of a new jetty at Angoche (Indian Ocean coast).

Industry and manufacturing

During the 1980s and 1990s, government policy emphasised the production of consumer goods, especially food, beverages and textiles, where supplies can be locally sourced, in an attempt to reduce import dependency and strengthen the market for peasant farmers producing cash crops. However, industry suffered from capital shortages, poor infrastructure and the high cost of credit. Manufacturers rely largely on internal funding from operating profits or owner savings. Recent metallurgical investments promise a dramatic departure from import substituting industrialisation strategy.

The greatest problems have occurred in the food processing industry, with cashew nut and sugar production particularly hit. Cashew nuts prices have plummeted due to increased output in India, where production is more cost-effective and tree-planting has increased. India intends to become self-sufficient in cashew nuts, which is dealing a big blow to this important sector in Mozambique. The situation has been exacerbated by the damaging policy of trade liberalisation demanded by the World Bank, which had originally advised Mozambique to stop processing cashew nuts domestically, close down the processing factories and export unshelled nuts to India.

Sugar refining is another industry which was in the doldrums. Mozambican sugar mills were severely affected by the civil war, which virtually wiped out the industry. Foreign investment, mostly from South African companies such as Illovo, has been the driving force behind the rehabilitation of the sector. In September 2001, the Development Bank of Southern Africa announced that it was issuing a US$12 million loan to the Marromeu mill, the largest in the country. It is envisaged that the money will help increase capacity from 30,000 tonnes in 2001 to 100,000 tonnes by 2003, by which time the complex should be fully restored. Some of the money will also go towards replanting an area of 10,728 hectares of sugar cane.

By far the most important industrial project in Mozambique is the Mozal aluminium smelter. The plant is owned by BHP-Billiton (the leading shareholder), Mitsubishi, South Africa's Industrial Development Corporation (IDC) and the Mozambican government. The US$1.2 billion smelter is one of the largest industrial projects in sub-Saharan Africa and began production in June 2000, six months ahead of schedule. The US$1 billion second phase of the project will see capacity rise to 506,000 tonnes of aluminium per annum by 2004. Already, Mozal is the world's cheapest producer of aluminium, and costs will fall as capacity is increased. The completion of the project will lead to around US$800 million in aluminium exports per year, increasing total exports by over 300 per cent of 2000 levels and adding up to 20 per cent to GDP. However, most of the profits from the smelter will be repatriated by foreign investors and since it is highly capital intensive, it will not have a significant impact on employment. Although Mozal appears as a success story for Mozambique's development, it will have a limited long-term role in alleviating poverty and generating growth in other sectors.

Tourism

With its beautiful beaches, tropical climate and abundance of wildlife, Mozambique has considerable tourism potential. There are ongoing improvements to the country's tourism infrastructure, with the rehabilitation of the Gorongosa National Park and the improvement of airports and hotels.

The Lubombo project, an ambitious joint programme with Swaziland and South Africa, is expected to attract tourists to the three countries.

Mining

Mining is limited to gold in Manica province, pegmatites, ilmenite, zircon, rutile, monazite, tantalum, copper, marble and semi-precious stones. The sector is small and only contributes around 2 per cent of GDP. There are around 50,000 artisinal miners who concentrate their operations on gold and gemstone extraction.

The Irish company Kenmore Resources has two gold licences at Niassa, where test drills in the first half of 1996 inferred reserves of 200,000 ounces. Kenmore also has a licence for the titanium reserves at Congolone which is thought to be one of the most valuable undeveloped titanium mines in the world.

There are considerable mineral resources including iron, graphite, fluorites, mica, lime clays, tin, nickel and bauxite. However, there has been little foreign interest.

Hydrocarbons

Since the civil war ended in 1992, Mozambique has attracted foreign interest in its gas potential. Substantial gas reserves have been identified and the country is likely to become a major gas producer in the region by 2005. There are three onshore gas fields: Pande, Temane and Buzi-Divinhe. Pande has reserves of around 59 billion cubic metres, Temane has 28 billion cubic metres and Buzi-Divinhe has 281 million cubic metres.

By 2002, gas production was insignificant and limited to a small amount tapped from the Pande field to supply the needs of local villagers. The construction of a 865km pipeline began in July 2002 and when completed in 2004 it will add around 20 per cent to the country's GDP. The pipeline is a joint venture between South Africa's Sasol (which is investing a total of US$385 million) and the governments of South Africa and Mozambique. Coal is mined at Moatize in Tete province. Proven coal reserves are approximately 6 billion tonnes. Oil is imported. However, there is prospecting for oil in the Rovuma basin, in the north, close to the Tanzanian border, and BP is prospecting offshore.

Energy
Mozambique is one of the largest energy producers in the Southern African Development Community (SADC). A large proportion of the country's electricity supply is produced by a coal-fired power station. With a potential in hydroelectric power and gas-fired power stations, there is a distinct possibility that it will become an electricity exporter in years to come. However, with only 5 per cent of households connected to the electricity supply, there is room for improving domestic supply. Further generating plants are scheduled to begin operations by 2006. These include the Moatize thermal power station (1,000MW), the expansion of the Cahora Bassa hydroelectric plant (550MW) and the Mepanda Uncuna hydroelectric station (2,500MW). However, the construction of new dams is facing mounting domestic and international opposition. With flooding becoming a regular occurrence, many ecologists believe dams pose a significant threat to farming communities, particularly when dams release flood waters.

Financial markets
Stock exchange
The Bolsa de Valores de Moçambique (BVM) (Mozambique Stock Exchange) opened in October 1999.

Banking
All banks in Mozambique are privately owned, with more foreign competition entering the sector with the completion of the bank privatisation process in January 2002 when Banco Austral was sold to Absa.
Central bank
Banco de Moçambique, with branches throughout the country.
Main financial centre
Maputo

Time
GMT plus two hours

Geography
Mozambique lies on the east coast of Africa, south of the equator. It is bordered by Tanzania to the north; Malawi, Zambia and Zimbabwe to the west; South Africa and Swaziland to the south and south-west; and by the Indian Ocean to the east (2,470km of coastline).
The country is divided into the coastal lowlands and plateaux (200–600 metres over most of the central region and north, reaching 1,000 metres in the north-west). The country is crossed by a large number of rivers, including the Zambezi (navigable for 460km), the Limpopo and the Save.

Climate
Mozambique has two main seasons: a hot, normally wet season from October to March and a cooler, mostly dry season from April to September.
In the extreme south the mean annual temperature is around 23 degrees Celsius (C), with a difference of about 8 degrees C between the hottest and coldest months. In the north the mean annual temperature is about 25 degrees C. The temperature in Maputo is influenced by the direction of the wind and wide variations are experienced, especially during the cool season. Temperatures in Maputo can reach as high as 45 degrees C.
Most rain falls in the second half of the hot season. Northern regions receive 640–1,280mm and southern regions may receive 260–1,540mm. The average is 770mm.

Dress codes
During the hot wet season (October–March) light cotton clothes are advisable. During the temperate dry season (April–September) light or medium weight clothing should suffice. Warmer clothing is required for frequent cold spells.

Entry requirements
Passports
Required by all. Passports must be valid for a minimum of six months beyond the intended date of departure.
Visa
Required by all. Visas are automatically issued for official visitors. Tourist and business visas issued but not necessarily automatic. Applications should be made well in advance. Can be obtained at Mozambican diplomatic missions but usually must be obtained by someone in Maputo (three weeks in advance). Express service is available at extra cost.
Journalists should seek visas through the Ministry of Information's Foreign Press Service. These are normally granted quickly.
For tourist visas, it helps to be visiting friends or relatives in Mozambique.
Visa exemption agreements have been signed with Malawi and Zimbabwe.
Prohibited entry
Foreign nationals who had the status of 'National of Mozambique' before 25 Jun 1975, except those with documentation proving renunciation of this status within 90 days of that date.
Currency advice/regulations
Import/export of local currency prohibited. Unlimited import of foreign currency is allowed but amounts must be declared on arrival. Export of foreign currency is limited to the amount declared on arrival.
It is advisable to take travellers cheques or currency in US dollars or South African Rand. Travellers entering Mozambique have to fill out a statement detailing the amount of currency in bank notes, cheques and travellers cheques being brought into the country. The declaration is passed over to the Exchange Control Office at the point of entry.
Prohibited imports
Narcotics. A permit is required for firearms.

Health (for visitors)
Mandatory precautions
Yellow fever certificate if arriving from an infected area.
Advisable precautions
Cholera is a serious risk in the country and vaccination is advisable, particularly after the cholera outbreak of August 2001 when 2,5000 cases were reported. Typhoid, polio, tetanus and hepatitis 'A' vaccinations are also advised. Hepatitis 'B' and 'E' are present in Mozambique. Malaria prophylaxis is essential as risk exists throughout the country, and cerebral malaria occurs in some places. There is a risk of rabies.
Water precautions are advisable, especially in the rural areas where bilharzia is present. Some milk is unpasteurised and should be boiled. Avoid dairy products which could have been made from unboiled milk and only eat well-cooked, hot meat and fish. Vegetables must be cooked and fruit peeled.
Medical facilities are minimal and many medicines are not available. Carry basic medical supplies, medicines and sterile syringes. Full medical insurance is essential. Insurance cover which provides for medical evacuation by air to South Africa is extremely advisable.

Hotels
Reasonable accommodation is available in Maputo. Bills must be paid in hard currency or by American Express credit card. Tipping is permitted.

Public holidays
Fixed dates
1 Jan (New Year's Day), 3 Feb (Heroes' Day), 7 Apr (Women's Day), 1 May (Workers' Day), 25 Jun (Independence), 7 Sep (Victory Day), 25 Sep (Armed Forces' Day), 25 Dec (Family Day).

Working hours
Banking
Mon–Fri: 0745–1130.
Business
Mon–Thu: 0730–1230, 1400–1730; Fri: 0730–1230, 1400–1700.

Government
Mon–Thu: 0730–1230, 1400–1730; Fri: 0730–1230, 1400–1700.
Shops
Mon–Fri: 0800–1230; 1400–1800; Sat: 0800–1330.

Telecommunications
Telephone/fax
Dialling code for Mozambique: IDD access code + 258 followed by area code (3 for Beira, 1 for Maputo) followed by subscriber's number.
Good service internally and to other countries by Telecomunicacoes de Moçambique (TDM).

Electricity supply
220 V AC, 50 cycles.

Social customs/useful tips
The courtesies and modes of address customary in Portugal and other Latin countries are still observed. Visitors are normally addressed as *O Senhor*. Occasionally *camarada* (comrade) is used, but this is not correct outside the circles of the ruling party, Frente de Libertaçao de Moçambique (Frelimo), and is discouraged.

Security
Street crime is an increasingly serious problem, with armed robbery prevalent in Maputo. Visitors should not carry or display cash or jewellery, and are advised not to venture outside well-lit, busy streets. Unfamiliar areas and downtown Maputo at night are certainly to be avoided. Female visitors should not walk unaccompanied along any beaches in Mozambique. After heavy rains in early 2000, conditions are beginning to return to normal and it is possible to travel safely by road in southern Mozambique. Visitors should however check conditions with the local authorities before travel.
Visitors travelling outside major urban areas should also be aware that Mozambique has a severe problem with landmines left over from the bitter conflict between Frelimo and Renamo. The problem was exacerbated in early 2000 when flooding swept thousands of anti-personnel mines to new, unknown locations. Travel by convoy is advisable, as in addition to mines, there is the risk of theft of vehicles at gunpoint.
Identity documents should be carried at all times.

Getting there
Air
National airline: Linhas Aéreas de Moçambique (LAM) (Mozambique Airlines).
International airport/s: Maputo International (MPM), 3km north of Maputo. Airport facilities include bank, restaurant, bar, snack bar, car hire and post. Beira (BEW), 13km from the city, receives flights from Europe, other African countries and the US. Airport facilities include restaurant, shops and a post office.
Other airport/s: Beira (BEW), 2km from city, restaurant, post office, shops. Visitors should arrange to be met at the airport on arrival.
Airport tax: Domestic flights include an embarkation tax of MT55,000 (nationals, resident aliens & tickets paid in local currency), US$5 (non-residents & tickets paid in foreign currency). International departures include an embarkation tax of MT115,000 (nationals, resident aliens & tickets paid in local currency), US$20 (non-residents for intercontinental travel tickets paid in foreign currency), MT230,000 (non-residents for regional travel tickets paid in foreign currency); not applicable to infants under two years and transit passengers on international flights.
Surface
Road: Road access is possible from all neighbouring countries except Tanzania; good paved roads from South Africa and Zimbabwe. The condition of roads in Mozambique is poor and and banditry along major highways threatens the safety of road travellers. Travel outside Maputo often requires four-wheel drive vehicles. There is a daily bus service from Maputo to Johannesburg and good bus links to other South African cities. A minibus service runs between Maputo and towns in Swaziland, crossing the border at Namaacha. It is advisable to carry water and food on long journeys. Bus travel is the cheapest form of transport in the country.
Rail: Please note that rail services can be sporadic and unreliable. Six times a week there is a train from Johannesburg to the Mozambique border at Komatipoort where there is a connection to Maputo (journey time 15 hours). There is an overnight train from Durban to Maputo. A service runs from Harare to Beira. There are connections from Malawi to Beira but the border has to be crossed on foot. There is a goods service from Swaziland to Maputo. Rail tracks run from Malawi to Nacala (no passenger service) and Swaziland to Maputo.
Water: There are no regular passenger services.
Main port/s: Beira, Maputo, Nacala and Quelimane.

Getting about
National transport
Be aware of the situation in the area you are visiting, and remember that landmines are still present.
Air: Travel between major cities within Mozambique is best by air, although flights are heavily booked. LAM operates domestic service to main towns. Local and charter flights can also be obtained from TTA and other companies with offices at Maputo Airport. Metavia has light planes operating a shuttle service between Maputo and Nelspruit. There is little night-time flying.
Road: There are an estimated 29,810km of roads in Mozambique. Good roads connect Maputo to Xai-Xai, Maputo to Juchoke, Maputo to Beira, Maxixe to Vilanchulo, Nampula to Nacala, Beira to Chimoio and Beira to Tete. The surface of other roads varies. Bus services cover most parts of the country, but are restricted by the state of the roads.
Buses: There are services covering most parts of the country but are restricted by the state of the roads.
Rail: There is no single rail network. Instead there are three networks: one in the south (Maputo to Swaziland, South Africa and Zimbabwe), one in the centre (Beira to Zimbabwe and Malawi) and one in the north (Nacala to Malawi and to Lichinga). These systems are not connected since the Portuguese did not build any trunk lines north-south. There are also some isolated branch lines (Xai-Xai to Manjacase; Inhambane to Inharrime; and Quelimane to Mocuba)
City transport
Taxis: Available in almost every city, taxis are metered but for long journeys fares should be negotiated. A 10 per cent tip is usual. Taxis are rarely available at the airport.
Car hire
Car rental is available from airports or hotels. A car and driver can be hired by the hour or day. Only hard currency will be accepted. International licence required. Traffic drives on the left. Driving after dark can be hazardous due to other vehicles travelling without headlights.

BUSINESS DIRECTORY

Telephone area codes
The international dialling code (IDD) for Mozambique is +258 followed by the area code:

Beira	3
Chokwe	21
Maputo	1
Nampula	6

Chambers of Commerce
Camara de Comercio de Moçambique (Mozambique Chamber of Commerce), Rua Mateus Sansão Muthemba 452, PO Box 1836, Maputo (tel: 492-210, 491-970; fax: 492-211).

Mozambique–US Chamber of Commerce, Maputo (tel: 492-904).

Banking

Banco Comercial do Moçambique, PO Box 865, Av 25 de Setembro 1800, Maputo (tel: 307533, 307471, 307532, fax: 307564, 307557, 307543)

Banco Internacional de Moçambique SARL, Av Zedequias Manganhela 478, Maputo (tel: 429390/3 fax: 429389)

Banco Standard Totta de Mozambique SARL, PO Box 2086, Praça 25 de Junho Nr 1, Maputo (tel: 423041/5, 424405, 301616 fax: 426967, 423029)

Banco de Fomento SARL; Av. Julius Nyerere 1016, Maputo (tel. 494010/1 fax: 494401)

Banco de Moçambique, PO Box 423, Av. 25 de Setembro 1679, Maputo (tel: 428150/9 fax: 429721)

BIM Investimento SARL, Av Kim Il Sung 961, Maputo (tel: 490085/7 fax: 490212), bimi@vircom.com

BNP Nedbank (Mocambique) SARL, PO Box 1445, Prédio 33 Andares; Av.25 de Setembro 1230, Maputo (tel: 306700 Fax: 306305), bnpnebank@bnpnedbank.co.mz

Novo Banco SARL, Av.do Trabalho, 750-Sede, Maputo (tel:407755/6, 408209 fax: 407755/6, 408210), novobanco@teledata.mz

Uniao Comercial de Bancos (Moçambique) SARL, Av. Fredrich Engels 400, Maputo (tel: 499900, 495221-5 fax: 498675), banque_fc@teledata.mz

Central bank

Banco de Moçambique, PO Box 423, Av. 25 de Setembro 1679, Maputo, Mozambique (tel: 428150/9 fax: 429721)

Travel information

Aeroporto de Maputo (Linhas Aéreas de Moçambique), CP 2060, Maputo (tel: 465-026, 465-137, fax: 735-601, 465-564).

Empresa Nacional de Turismo (ENT) (Mozambique National Tourism Company), CP 417, Praca dos Trabalhadores 9, Maputo (tel: 421-305, 427-191; fax: 430-181).

Linhas Aereas de Moçambique, Aeroporto de Mavalane, CP 965, Maputo (tel: 465-561/9).

Transportes e Trabalhos Aéreos (TTA) (air taxi services, etc), PO Box 2054, Aeroporto de Mavalane, Maputo (tel: 465-292, 465-028).

Ministries

Ministry of Commerce, Industry and Tourism, Praça do 25 Junho 37, Maputo (tel: 426-091/7).

Ministry of Finance and Planning, Praça da Marinha Popular, CP 272, Maputo (tel: 420-648; fax: 425-240).

Ministry of Industry and Energy, Avenida 25 de Setembro, PO Box 2904, 1502 Maputo (tel: 420-963, 492-011).

Ministry of Trade, PO Box 1831, Maputo (tel: 426-091/7; fax: 421-305).

Other useful addresses

Agência de Informação de Moçambique (AIM), CP 896, Maputo (tel: 430-795).

Agência Nacional de Frete e Navegação (ANFRENA) (main national shipping agency), Rua Consiglieri Pedroson 366, CP 1430, Maputo (tel: 427-064, 428-111).

BP Mozambique, PO Box 854, Maputo (tel: 425-021/5; fax: 426-042).

British Council, Travessa da Catembe 21 (corner of Av Martires de Inhaminga 1421), CP 4178, Maputo (tel: 421-571; fax: 421-577).

British Embassy, Av Vladimir I Lenine 310, CP 55, Maputo (tel: 420-111/2/5/6/7; fax: 421-666).

Commonwealth Development Corporation, Maputo (tel: 421-325; fax: 422-150).

Direcção Nacional Portos e Caminhos de Ferro (railways), PO Box 276, Maputo (tel: 420-748, 424-133, 430-151).

Empresa Nacional de Minas, PO Box 1152, Maputo (tel: 423-933).

Empresa Nacional de Portos e Caminhos de Ferro de Moçambique, Maputo (tel: 427-173).

Empresa Nacional Petroleos de Moçambique (Petromoc), PO Box 417, Maputo (tel: 427-191/7).

FACIM, PO Box 1761, Maputo (tel: 423-713, 427-151/2; fax: 427-129) (annual international trade fair).

Hidroelectrica de Cabora Bassa (HCB) (operators of Cabora Bassa power complex), Head Office, CP 263, Songo, Tete (tel: 82-221/4; fax: 82-364); PO Box 4120, Maputo (tel: 400-551, 400-647, 491-346, 492-976).

Hotel and Tourism Business Association, Maputo (tel: 425-562).

Imprensa Nacional de Moçambique (publishes statistical bulletins, census information etc), PO Box 275, Maputo.

Maputo Development Corridor, Maputo (tel: 426-359; fax: 430-159).

Mozambique Embassy (USA), Suite 570, 1990 M Street, NW, Washington DC 20036 (tel: 293-7146; fax: 835-0245; e-mail: embamoc@aol.com).

Mozambique Institute of Export Promotion (IPEX) (Government agency for export promotion), Av 25 de Setembro 1008, PO Box 4487, Maputo (tel: 423-343).

Office for Foreign Investment Promotion (GPIE), Av 25 de Setembro 2049, 2 andar, PO Box 2049, Maputo (tel: 422-456/7; fax: 422-459).

Radio Moçambique, PO Box 2000, Maputo (tel: 434-041/5, 432-591; fax: 421-816).

Technical Unit for Enterprise Restructuring (UTRE) (information on company tenders for privatisation and investment opportunities), Ministry of Planning and Finance, Rua da Imprensa No 256, 7th Floor, Suites 704-708, PO Box 4350, Maputo (tel: 426-514/6; fax: 421-541).

Televisão de Moçambique, Av Julius Nyerere 942, PO Box 2675, Maputo (tel: 491-198).

World Bank, Maputo (tel: 492-841; fax: 492-893).

Internet sites

Africa Business Network: http://www.ifc.org/abn

AllAfrica.com: http://allafrica.com

African Development Bank: http://www.afdb.org

Africa Online: http://www.africaonline.com

Harambee Afrika (UK business club for traders with east, central and southern Africa; includes annotated web resource list): http://www.harambee.co.uk

Mbendi AfroPaedia (information on companies, countries, industries and stock exchanges in Africa): http://mbendi.co.za

Namibia

Daniel Brett

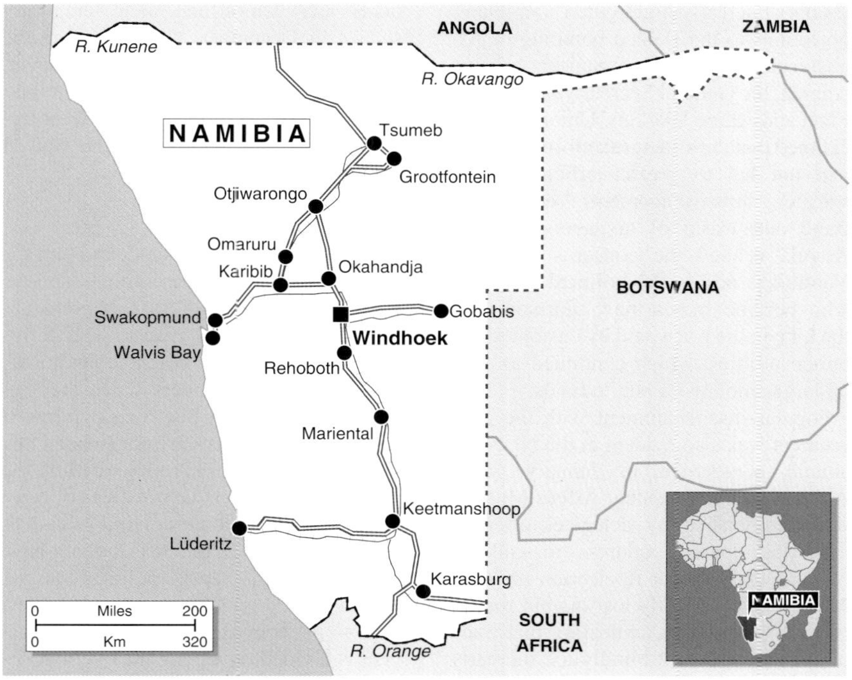

Namibia prides itself as a model of peace and democracy. However, since independence from apartheid South Africa in 1990, it has been plagued by social problems, corruption, the AIDS pandemic and low-level armed conflict. The war of independence may have given Namibians sovereignty, but the battle for development is proving to be just as tough.

The ruling South West African People's Organisation (Swapo), which led the country to freedom, has become a bureaucratic monolith, incapable of compromise and lacking any strong opposition to ensure accountability. Meanwhile, President Sam Nujoma has taken Zimbabwe's President Robert Mugabe as his ideological mentor and has launched a series of vitriolic verbal attacks on 'enemies' of Namibia, including homosexuals, human rights activists, the independent media and white farmers. The appointment of Theo-Ben Gurirab, a proponent of radical land reform measures, as prime minister in August 2002 was an indication of what is in store for Namibia's white commercial farmers. Many suspected that Nujoma was grooming Guirab as his successor, although the impetuous President may well decide to stand for re-election in 2004.

End of an ego?

In November 2001, Nujoma pledged to respect the constitution and stand down at the end of his third term in 2004. However, he has made no secret of his willingness to change the law and make a fourth election bid 'if the people demand it'. Many civic leaders are hoping Nujoma will not seek another term of office.

Namibia's National Society for Human Rights (NSHR) claimed that Nujoma's departure would be a healthy move for Namibia. It believes a new leader could enable Swapo to make the final transformation to a political party 'more concerned with bread and butter issues rather than a 'we liberated this country' attitude'. The NSHR added that an end to Nujoma's rule 'would effectively end the politics of fear and intolerance...for which he has

KEY FACTS

Official name: Republic of Namibia

Head of State: President Sam Shafiishuna Nujoma (since 1990)

Head of government: Prime Minister Theo-Ben Gurirab (appointed by the President, 28 Aug 2002)

Ruling party: South West African People's Organisation (Swapo)

Area: 824,269 square km

Population: 1.78 million (2001)

Capital: Windhoek

Official language: English

Currency: Namibian dollar (N$) = 100 cents; at par with the South African commercial Rand

Exchange rate: N$8.51 per US$ (Jan 2003)

GDP per capita: US$1,647 (2001); US$1,379 (2002)*

GDP real growth: 2.00% (2001); 3.2% (2002)*

Labour force: 700,000 (2001); 700,000 (2002)*

Inflation: 9.50% (2001); 9.5% (2002)*

Balance of trade: -US$243.00 million (2001)

Foreign debt: US$264.00 million (2001)

* estimated figure

For the latest Key Facts, go to www.worldinformation.com

been partially responsible'. However, it warned that his resignation as party leader after four decades of leadership could result in party infighting that could affect the country's peace and stability. The opposition Congress of Democrats also called for decorum among those vying to become Swapo's candidate in the presidential elections, fearing a possible dangerous outburst of tribalism.

Rumblings of dissent

The President's decision came at a time of increasing public discontent over his handling of the economy. After more than a decade of independence, the vast majority of Namibians are living in poverty and more than a third of the working population is unemployed. This was confirmed by figures published in October 2001 by Namibia's Employment Equity Commission (EEC), which highlighted the vast gap between rich and poor with senior managers awarding themselves huge increases in perks and bonuses above their normal take-home pay. The World Bank statistics also show that Namibians have the highest level of income inequality in the world. Herbert Jaunch, director of the Labour Resource and Research Institute (LaRRI), claimed the problem is a legacy of the colonial economy, 'which was built around the extraction of resources for world market production at the lowest possible price. To do this workers were used very crudely and the colonial masters promoted a system of migrant labour, which was further facilitated by institutionalised racism — apartheid.'

The failure of the government to redistribute wealth, land and resources or significantly alleviate poverty since independence led to increasing frustration among workers with the government's economic policy in 2001. In November 2001, the Swapo-affiliated National Union of Namibian Workers (NUNW), a federation of the country's main trade unions, staged a one-day national 'stay-away'. Its main target was the privatisation and mismanagement of state-owned enterprises (SOEs), but it also highlighted Namibians' objections to the US-led bombing of Afghanistan. Protest organiser Cuana Angula, the General Secretary of Namibia Food and Allied Workers' Union (Nafau), claimed that the structural reform of SOEs had not led to greater efficiency, but 'greater mismanagement, corruption, fraud and waste of taxpayers' money'. Angula echoed the concerns of many Namibians across the political spectrum who became increasingly alarmed over the hike in the price paid by customers for public utilities, which continued to soak up large amounts of public funds.

Popular disenchantment with the government was also evident at the NUNW's annual conference in January 2002. Acting NUNW President Alfeus Muheua was admonished by delegates after he used his opening address to call on Nujoma to stand for re-election in 2004. Muheua subsequently lost his bid for the NUNW presidency, indicating that trade unionists would not blindly toe the party line. Even Muheua, regarded as a Nujoma crony, attacked the government's privatisation programme, particularly the restructuring of NamWater, which has increased water prices in preparation for privatisation.

KEY INDICATORS — Namibia

	Unit	1996	1997	1998	1999	2000
Population	m	1.58	1.61	1.66	1.70	1.74
Gross domestic product (GDP)	US$bn	3.50	3.60	3.40	3.50	3.50
GDP per capita	US$	2,210	2,264	2,055	2,044	2,011
GDP real growth	%	3.2	4.5	3.3	4.3	3.9
Inflation	%	8.0	8.8	6.2	8.6	9.2
Exports (fob) (goods)	US$m	1,404.0	1,343.0	1,278.0	1,373.0	1,480.0
Imports (fob) (goods)	US$m	1,531.0	1,615.0	1,451.0	1,503.0	1,621.0
Balance of trade	US$m	-127.1	-271.7	-172.6	-130.0	-141.0
Current account	US$m	115.8	90.4	161.8	139.0	196.0
Foreign debt	US$bn	0.1	0.1	0.1	0.2	0.2
Total reserves minus gold	US$m	193.9	250.5	260.3	305.5	260.0
Foreign exchange	US$m	193.8	250.5	260.2	305.4	259.9
Exchange rate	per US$	4.30	4.61	5.53	6.11	6.94

Many other grass-roots Swapo supporters have also vented their frustrations over the lack of economic progress. In late 2001, more than 200 young unemployed Swapo supporters, calling themselves 'party loyalists', established an illegal squat near the party's headquarters demanding jobs and housing from the government. The Windhoek municipal authority and the police evicted the dissidents and demolished their temporary shacks in December 2001, accusing the youths of harbouring criminals. However, the group remained defiant and rebuilt their shelters, claiming that they were trying to uphold the ideals of the war of independence.

Land and freedom

Like Mugabe, Nujoma is quick to turn the public's attention to the emotive land reform issue. In August 2002, Nujoma announced plans to confiscate 192 farms 'belonging to foreign absentee landlords', while some tribal leaders stated their intention of seizing white-owned farms if land reform measures are not stepped up.

White land-owners are regarded by the country's poor as the last vestiges of colonialism and bad labour conditions and allegations of racism and tax-dodging have made them an easy political target. Around 4,000 white commercial farmers own 44 per cent of farmland, while 41 per cent is divided up among the overwhelming black majority. Since independence, only 35,000 black Namibians have been resettled on redistributed land, while nearly 250,000 are still on the waiting list. Although the Swapo government is committed to only buying land that is up for sale, there are growing fears that the Namibian government, faced with increasing discontent over poverty and economic inequality, might instigate forced land resettlements as seen in Zimbabwe.

The redistribution of land has largely stalled due to the failure of the government to devise and implement an effective land redistribution mechanism as well as a high degree of bureaucratic foot-dragging. Land reform is based on a 'willing-seller, willing-buyer' basis, but the government has bought up only a handful of the hundreds of farms put up for sale and has spent less than half the money set aside to buy commercial farms. In the 2000/01 financial year, the government bought only 18 out of 173 farms offered for sale. The government also lacks the skills to implement an effective land reform programme. In 2001, the ministry of land admitted there was a 'shortage of qualified land use planners, land valuers, resettlement officers and land economists' which 'has made land reform difficult'. Land-owners are also guilty of last-minute withdrawals from farm offers and of taking advantage of the reform process by hiking up the price of land and selling off agriculturally unproductive land. In the middle are impoverished landless blacks, who feel frustrated that independence has not brought with it a change in the colonial structure of the economy.

In an effort to mollify its critics, the government introduced a special land tax on commercial farmers in April 2001. This was ostensibly to prevent farmers from owning excessive amounts of land and to free under-utilised land for redistribution. Revenue from the tax was meant to be ear-marked to aid land redistribution, but many suspect it is being diverted to SOEs, which are a constant drain on public finances.

Following the imposition of the new tax, landowners who refused to co-operate with the land reform programme sought to exploit loop-holes in the taxation system by turning their farms into trusts or companies. This increased tensions between the government and white farmers, although the authorities were careful to avoid the kind of violence seen in Zimbabwe. This has not stopped many Namibians from calling for forced land redistribution and the Namibian National Farmers' Union (NNFU), representing black farmers, has called on the government to speed up land reform or face Zimbabwe-style farm invasions. In November 2001, Swapo veteran Ponhele ya France, a member of parliament and former trade union leader, warned that the land issue was a 'time bomb'. He claimed that unless white-owned land was confiscated and given to the landless, there was a distinct possibility of civil war.

This route would not only open up rifts between Namibia and the international community, it could also threaten the economy's agricultural base. Even if the NNFU gets its way and land is forcibly redistributed to the landless, there is no guarantee that this will alleviate poverty. The government's National Poverty Reduction Action Programme for 2001–05 recognises that land redestribution is not a long-term basis for poverty reduction, claiming that 'the agricultural base is too weak to offer a sustainable basis for prosperity'. The reform programme is also criticised for allocating land to rehouse squatters evicted from commercial farms, who do not have the skills, capital or motivation to become self-reliant and economically viable farmers.

By taking land out of the commercial sector, the government could be creating long-term problems by reducing private sector investment in the agricultural sector. This would undermine the long-term objective of diversifying and developing the economy by opening it up to private capital. In order to have a positive impact on the lives of the Namibian poor and avoid a Zimbabwe-style disaster, the government will have to put in place comprehensive and durable mechanisms for land redistribution that satisfy the country's development objectives as well as the demands of the poor.

Outlook

Namibia continues to show unremarkable economic growth, which has averaged 3.5 per cent since the mid-1990s. The pegging of the Namibian dollar to the South African rand has enabled the economy to retain its high level of competitiveness, but has limited the scope of monetary policy. While this did not appear to have a negative impact on inflation, which stabilised at around 9 per cent in 2001, the government's poor fiscal performance, with persistently high budget deficits, could undermine macroeconomic stability in the medium-term. Massive extra-budgetary transfers to parastatals such as Air Namibia are not only inflationary, they are highly unpopular and are fueling the public's discontent with the economic programme. Rather than plunge public money into the pockets of over-paid and corrupt parastatal bosses, Namibians are crying out for investment in jobs and social programmes that genuinely alleviate poverty. Unless the government puts its house in order, Swapo may choose a more hard-line candidate like Guirab to succeed Nujoma in 2004. This could lead to the very real scenario of economically disastrous land seizures and the kind of ad hoc policy-making seen in neighbouring Zimbabwe.

Risk assessment

Economic	Satisfactory
Political	Good
Regional stability	Poor

COUNTRY PROFILE

Historical profile

1884 Declared a German territory (except Walvis Bay which was occupied in 1878 by the British).

1920 Mandated to South Africa by the League of Nations.

1958 The South West African People's Organisation (Swapo) formed from the anti-contract labour movement.

1966 South Africa introduced apartheid laws, the UN terminated its mandate and Swapo launched an armed struggle for independence.

1973 The UN withdrew its mandate and recognised Swapo as the 'sole authentic representative of Namibian people'.

1985 South Africa established the Transitional Government (TG), an un-elected black majority government consisting of members of six different tribal parties, instructing it to draw up a constitution.

1988 South Africa turned down the TG's constitutional draft; independence was agreed by South Africa, Angola, Cuba, (the then) USSR and USA.

1989 Free and fair elections were held under the auspices of the UN. South Africa withdrew its forces. The Swapo leader, Sam Nujoma, formed a transitional ministerial team.

1990 Independence was granted in March and Nujoma became Namibia's first President.

1994 Walvis Bay and 12 offshore Penguin Islands were formally transferred from South African to Namibian sovereignty. In Namibia's first post independence presidential and National Assembly elections in December, Swapo and Nujoma defeated the Democratic Turnhalle Alliance party of Mishake Muyongo.

1999 President Sam Nujoma and the ruling Swapo won the presidential and legislative elections held on 30 November and 1 December.

Political structure

Constitution

In 1999 the constitution was altered to allow President Nujoma to serve a third term.

Form of state

Namibia is a multi-party republic.

The executive

Executive power rests with the president, who is head of state, elected by universal suffrage for a five-year term, with the assistance of a cabinet headed by a prime minister.

National legislature

Legislative power is vested in a bicameral parliament comprising a directly elected, 72-member National Assembly with a five-year term, and an indirectly elected National Council (26 members, two members from each of Namibia's 13 regions), with a six-year term.

Last elections

1999 (presidential and parliamentary).

Next elections

2004 (presidential and parliamentary).

Political parties
Ruling party
South West African People's Organisation (Swapo)
Main opposition party
Congress of Democrats (CoD)

Population
1.74 million (2000)
The annual population growth rate was 2.4 per cent (1994–2000). Over 70 per cent of the population is under 29 years. Population density: two inhabitants per square km. Urban population: 31 per cent (1994–2000). Two-thirds of the predominantly rural population live in the north: Ovamboland (now four non-tribal regions), Okavango and Caprivi.
Ethnic make-up
86 per cent black, 5 per cent mixed race (coloured) and 2 per cent other.
Religions
Christianity (approximately 80 per cent), traditional beliefs (20 per cent).

Education
It has been estimated by Oxfam that 100 per cent of children age 6–11 will enrol for school in 2015. Public expenditure on education amounts to approximately 4 per cent of annual GDP. Adult illiteracy among men is around 18 per cent and among women it is around 20 per cent.

Health
Life expectancy at birth was 50 years in 2000 compared to 53 years in 1980. The infant mortality rate was on average 67 per 1,000 live births between 1994–2000. Approximately 26 per cent of children were malnourished in the same period. There is one physician for every 5,000 people.
Around 160,000 people suffer from HIV/AIDS in Namibia and the adult infection rate is 19.54 per cent (2000). An estimated 67,000 children have lost their mother or both parents to AIDS (1999). UNAIDS estimates that the annual loss to GDP per capita growth will be 1.5 per cent by 2010. As a result of HIV/AIDS, annual cost of public healthcare has risen from 2.9 per cent of GDP in 1996 to up to 17 per cent by 2001.

Main cities
Windhoek (population 160,000 in 1998), Walvis Bay (45,000), Keetmanshoop (25,000), Swekopmund, Luderitz, Oshakati, Rundu, Ondangua, Okahandja, Otjiwarongo, Grootfontein, Tsumeb, Gobabis, Rehoboth.

Languages spoken
English is the first language of only 7 per cent of the population, although it is the country's official language. All documents, notices and directional signs are in English. German and Afrikaans are widely used throughout the country.
There are six main African languages: Oshiwambo, Herero, Nama-Damara, Kwangali (Okavango region), Lozi (Caprivi region) and Tswana.
Official language
English

Media
Press
Dailies: Dailies include the *Allgemeine Zeitung*, *Die Republikein*, *Namibian*, *Namibia News*, *National Mirror* and *Windhoek Advertiser*.
Weeklies: Weeklies include the *New Era* (published by the government since 1991), *Tempo* and *Sunday Republikein*. *Namib Times* (Walvis Bay) is a bi-weekly newspaper.
Business: *Namibia Economist* is a weekly publication covering financial and economic news.
Periodicals: *Monitor* is a monthly published from Windhoek.
Broadcasting
Radio: Local services in English, the principal African languages, Afrikaans, broadcast by state owned Namibian Broadcasting Corporation (NBC).
Television: The NBC broadcasts on one channel in English only; South Africa's M-net pay TV company also broadcasts.

Economy
South Africa remains Namibia's most important trading partner and occupies a position of major importance in Namibia's economic future. The Namibian economy is dependent on the production and export of primary products, the most important of which are diamonds, uranium, fish and beef.
The government is attempting to diversify economic activities. Namibia offers relatively low labour costs, and at Walvis Bay, a strategic location for exports to the southern African region. The government is targeting manufacturing, tourism, transshipment and energy as the prime sectors for new business.
In 2001, the country suffered from lower agricultural growth and declining fishing ouput. The 2001/02 budget aimed to strengthen fiscal management with a target ratio of government debt to GDP of no more than 25 per cent. A fiscal deficit of 3.75 per cent of GDP was forecast with deficits of 3.0 per cent of GDP in the next two financial years. This reflects a stronger commitment to fiscal consolidation as the government continues to tackle inflation. However, the IMF warned that the budget deficit was likely to rise to around 5.25 per cent of GDP in 2001/02 due to higher wage expenditure and large transfers to Air Namibia and expressed concern that this could undo the government's three-year fiscal framework.
An expansion of mining activity in 2002 is likely to see GDP growth exceed 3 per cent and increased inflows of foreign direct investment due to the US African Growth and Opportunities Act (AGOA). However, an expected fall in income from southern Africa is likely to diminish the current account surplus.

External trade
Namibia, at independence, opted for full membership of the Common (Rand) Monetary Area and Southern African Customs Union (SACU) with all tariffs, trade and exchange controls conforming to those applied in South Africa.
Exports
Principal exports are diamonds (typically 35 per cent), fish (30 per cent), uranium and beef.
Main destinations: UK (typically 50 per cent of total, including diamonds), South Africa (30 per cent), Germany (10 per cent), Spain (5 per cent), Japan, Italy.
Imports
Principal imports are food and beverages, transport equipment, machinery and electrical goods, chemicals and plastics, fuel and lubricants.
Main sources: South Africa (typically over 87 per cent of total) (mostly consumer items, intermediates, food and fuel), Germany, Japan and UK (capital goods).

Agriculture
The agricultural sector contributes 11 per cent to GDP and employs 39 per cent of the workforce. Only half the country is suitable for farming and due to overgrazing, yields in the north remain low on average.
Farming is highly susceptible to drought; it supports either directly or indirectly some 70 per cent of the population with disparity in land access between the mainly white 4,000 commercial farmers and subsistence farmers, who number some 60 per cent of the population.
Commercial farming is dominated by livestock ranching – cattle in the north-central districts, sheep (karakul and mutton) and ostriches in the south, which account for 80 per cent of total agricultural output.
Namibia normally produces some 40 per cent of its maize requirements from commercial farms and is generally self-sufficient in millet, the main food crop grown in the north by communal farmers.
Beef is the most high-value product and exports to the EU under the Cotonou Convention (which replaced the four previous Lomé Conventions in June 2000) under an annual quota of 60,000 tonnes.
Fishing
The south-east Atlantic is one of the world's richest fishing grounds, with

pilchard, hake and mackerel being the main species.

The government declared a 370km exclusive economic zone and banned unlicenced foreign trawlers after independence. However, foreign trawlers can operate in Namibian waters under charter.

Industry and manufacturing

The industrial sector contributes around 14 per cent of GDP and employs 8 per cent of the workforce. One of Namibia's most attractive elements for investors is its relatively developed infrastructure with good links with neighbouring countries through well-maintained motorways and railways.

There is a small and highly specialised manufacturing sector, concentrated in Windhoek and Walvis Bay, with food processing (meat, agronomic products, fish), and beverages (beer and soft drinks) predominant. Other activities include structural metal products, non-metal mineral products, wood furniture, leather goods. Export processing zone (EPZ) regime was established in 1995; it provides incentives to investors in manufacturing plants producing goods mainly for export, including a zero income tax liability for an unlimited period.

Tourism

The tourism industry is the third biggest industry in Namibia, growing at between 12 and 15 per cent a year, generating about 7 per cent of GDP. Namibia receives around 500,000 tourists per annum. South Africa accounts for about 60 per cent of the total number of visitors; around 30 per cent of the total originate in Germany, the UK and other European countries, 10 per cent from the US and Canada.

In 1995 the government implemented a five-year tourism development policy with financial and technical assistance from the EU. As a result hotel accommodation has expanded, especially in Windhoek and the coastal resort of Swakopmund.

Mining

The mining sector is the traditional backbone of the economy, contributing around 20 per cent to GDP.

Around 7 per cent of government revenues and a third of the country's foreign exchange earnings come from diamonds. Namdeb Diamond Corporation (50 per cent owned by De Beers and 50 per cent owned by the Namibian government) mines the world's richest source of high quality gem diamonds onshore north of Oranjemund, while offshore diamond recoveries by De Beers Marine have expanded significantly since commercial mining began in 1991. Namibia is also a major uranium producer.

Namibia Minerals Corporation (Namco) is listed on the Namibian and Toronto stock exchanges and holds the country's largest marine diamond mining concession. However, its financial results for 2001 recorded losses of US$56 million and some subsidiaries went into provisional liquidation between February and August 2001. The setback was caused by an accident to its NamSSol mining system in January 2001 which led to a withdrawal of support from its financial backers. A recovery programme was initiated in July 2001, which involved rescheduling debt, raising additional financing, increasing production and settling its insurance claims.

Although the Rosh Pina is Namibia's solid zinc producing mine, the Skorpion zinc mining complex is destined to be the biggest zinc producer in Africa and one of the top 10 by output in the world when it comes on line in 2003, with an annual output of 150,000 tonnes of refined zinc. Primary gold production started in 1989 and significant quantities of copper, lead, pyrite, salt and zinc are also produced while there are large unexploited deposits of base, precious and industrial minerals. Marble, granite and semi-precious stones such as rose quartz, tourmaline, amethyst and blue-lace agate are also mined; the government is seeking to promote local value by adding processing. Larger mines are mainly owned by foreign multinationals from South Africa and the UK.

Hydrocarbons

Dependency on South Africa for oil products has been reduced with supplies procured from Angola and overseas refineries.

The Kudu offshore gas field in the south contains 7–14 trillion cubic feet of gas and could make Namibia a major energy producer.

Financial markets

Stock exchange

The Namibian Stock Exchange (NSE) was launched in October 1992.

Banking

The banking sector is small, with four private commercial banks. The ratio of non-performing loans is relatively low, making the sector stable and financially sound.

Central bank

Bank of Namibia

Main financial centre

Windhoek

Time

GMT plus two hours

Geography

Namibia lies in south-western Africa, with South Africa to the south and south-east, Botswana to the east and Angola to the north. The country has a long coastline on the Atlantic Ocean. The narrow Caprivi Strip, between Angola and Botswana in the north-east, extends Namibia to the Zambezi river, giving it a border with Zambia. The arid Namib Desert stretches along the west coast, while the easternmost area is part of the Kalahari Desert.

Climate

Namibia has one of the driest climates in the world. Sub-tropical; hottest months January–February (20–29 degrees C); coldest June–July (6–18 degrees C).

Entry requirements

Passports

Required by all; must be valid for six months after intended departure date.

Visa

Not required by nationals of over 20 countries, including UK and all EU countries except Greece, USA, Canada, Switzerland and non EU Scandinavian countries. Other nationals applying for business visas may need covering letter and journalists/reporters a temporary work permit from Ministry of Home Affairs; 90 days is maximum period granted.

Currency advice/regulations

Import and export of local currency is limited to N$500. Foreign currency is unrestricted but must be declared on arrival, and export is allowed up to declared amount.

Traveller's cheques are accepted.

Health (for visitors)

Mandatory precautions

Yellow fever vaccination certificate required if arriving from an infected area.

Advisable precautions

Hepatitis A, tetanus, typhoid and polio vaccinations. Malaria risk exists in most areas in the north. Water in all main towns is purified and safe to drink. There is a risk of rabies.

Hotels

Classified from one to four stars. Accommodation in towns outside Windhoek is limited apart from Swakopmund so should always be booked well in advance. Luxury lodges or bungalow accommodation is available at Etosha and other national parks; there is also an expanding range of desert lodges and guest farms.

Credit cards

International cards are widely accepted throughout the country.

Public holidays

Fixed dates

1 and 2 Jan (New Year's Day), 21 Mar (Independence Day), 1 May (Workers'

Day), 4 May (Cassinga Day), 25 May (Africa Day), 26 Aug (Heroes' Day), 10 Dec (Human Rights Day), 25 and 26 Dec (Christmas).

Variable dates

Good Friday, Easter Monday, Ascension Day.

Working hours

Banking

Mon–Fri: 0900–1530; Sat: 0830–1100.

Business

Mon–Fri: 0800–1700.

Government

Mon–Fri: 0800–1700.

Electricity supply

220V AC

Getting there

Air

National airline: Air Namibia

Main airport: Windhoek International (WDH), 40km east of Windhoek.

Airport tax: None

Surface

Road: Tarred highways from South African border via Keetmanshoop and Windhoek to Oshakati and northern border with Angola, and between Windhoek and Swakopmund/Walvis Bay.

The unsurfaced road from Botswana via Ghanzi has been upgraded as the new Trans-Kalahari highway, and along with the Trans-Caprivi tarred highway, was completed in 1998; these provide direct road links between Walvis Bay and central Africa.

Rail: Main line runs from South African border via Keetmanshoop and Windhoek to Swakopmund, Walvis Bay, and via Otavi to Tsumeb and Grootfontein, the northern railheads.

Getting about

National transport

Air: Domestic flights operate from Eros Airport, near Windhoek city centre.

Air Namibia operates scheduled services between Windhoek, Walvis Bay, Swakopmund, Tsumeb (for Etosha national park), Keetmanshoop, Grootfontein, Luderitz, Oshakati, Rundu, Katima Mulilo. South African Express flies to Walvis Bay.

City transport

Taxis: Available in main towns; 10 per cent tip is usual.

Car hire

Available in Windhoek city centre, international airport, Walvis Bay.

Although all roads between major towns are generally of a high standard, the distances involved can be prohibitive; four-wheel drive is advisable if going off the main routes.

International driving licence is required. Traffic drives on the left. The general speed limit is 60kph in built-up areas and 120kph on open roads. Safety belts must be used at all times.

BUSINESS DIRECTORY

Telephone area codes

The international dialling code (IDD) for Namibia is +264 followed by the area code:

Keetmanshoop	63
Luderitz	63
Swakopmund	64
Tsumeb	671

Chambers of Commerce

Chamber of Commerce and Industry, SWA Building Society Building, Independence Avenue, PO Box 191, Windhoek (tel: 222-000; fax: 233-690).

Chamber of Mines of Namibia, First Floor, Continental Building, Independence Avenue, PO Box 2895, Windhoek (tel: 263-101; fax: 222-638).

Namibia National Chamber of Commerce and Industry, Kenya House, Corner Leutwein/Körner Streets, PO Box 9355, Windhoek (tel: 228-809; fax: 228-009).

Banking

Bank of Windhoek, 262 Independence Avenue, PO Box 15, Windhoek (tel: 299-1229; fax: 299-1285).

City Savings and Investment Bank, PO Box 63, FGI Building, Post St Mall, Windhoek (tel: 221262 fax: 221555) .

Commercial Bank of Namibia, 12-20 Bulow Street, PO Box 1, Windhoek (tel: 295-9111, 295-2014; fax: 295-2046; e-mail: cbon@iwwn.com.na).

First National Bank Namibia, 209 Independence Avenue, PO Box 195, Windhoek (tel: 229-610; fax: 225-994).

Standard Bank Namibia, Mutual Platz Building, Post Street Mall, PO Box 3327, Windhoek (tel: 294-2283; fax: 294-2583).

Central bank

Bank of Namibia, PO Box 2882, 71 Robert Mugabe Avenue, Windhoek, Namibia (tel: 2835111 fax: 2835228).

Travel information

Air Namibia, PO Box 731, Transnamib Building, Eros Airport, Windhoek 9000; (tel: 38-220; fax: 36-460); Town Office (tel: 229-630; fax: 236-460); Central Reservations (tel: 298-2552; fax: 221-382).

Automobile Association, PO Box 61, Windhoek (tel: 224-201).

Etosha Northern Tourism and Publicity Association, PO Box 779, Tsumeb (tel: 220-728; fax: 220-916).

Lodge & Guest Farm Reservations, PO Box 21783, Windhoek (tel: 226-979; fax: 226-999).

Namibia Resorts International, PO Box 2862, Windhoek (tel: 233-145; fax: 234-512).

Southern Tourism Forum, Private Bag 2125, Keetmanshoop (tel: 2095; fax: 3818).

Tour and Safari Association of Namibia, PO Box 5144, Windhoek (tel: 232-748; fax: 228-461).

National tourist organisation offices

Namibia Tourism Board, Independence Avenue, Private Bag 13346, Windhoek (tel/fax: 284-2360, 284-2364; e-mail: tourism@mweb.com.na; internet site: http://www.tourism.com.na).

Ministries

Ministry of Agriculture, Water and Rural Development, Private Bag 13184, Windhoek (tel: 202-9111; fax: 229-961).

Ministry of Basic Education and Culture, Private Bag 13186, Windhoek (tel: 293-9411; fax: 224-277).

Ministry of the Environment and Tourism, Private Bag 13346, Swabour Building, Independence Avenue, Windhoek (tel: 284-2111; fax: 229-936).

Ministry of Finance, Private Bag 13295, Windhoek (tel: 209-9111; fax: 236-454).

Ministry of Fisheries and Marine Resources, Private Bag 13355, Windhoek (tel: 205-3911; fax: 233-286).

Ministry of Foreign Affairs, Private Bag 13347, Windhoek (tel: 282-9111; fax: 223-937).

Ministry of Higher Education, Vocational Training, Science & Technology, Private Bag 13391, Windhoek (tel: 253-670; fax: 253-671).

Ministry of Information and Broadcasting, Private Bag 13344, Windhoek (tel: 283-911; fax: 222-343).

Ministry of Mines and Energy, Private Bag 13297, Windhoek (tel: 284-8111; fax: 283-643).

Ministry of Trade and Industry, Private Bag 13340, Windhoek (tel: 283-7111; fax: 220-148).

Ministry of Works Transport and Communication, Private Bag 13341, Windhoek (tel: 208-9111; fax: 228-560).

President's Office, State House, Private Bag 13339, Windhoek (tel: 220-010; fax: 221-770).

Prime Minister's Office, Private Bag 13338, Windhoek (tel: 287-9111; fax: 226-189).

Other useful addresses

British High Commission, PO Box 22202, 116 Robert Mugabe Avenue, Windhoek (tel: 223-022; fax: 228-895; e-mail: bhc@iwwn.com.na).

Investment Centre, Private Bag 13340, Windhoek (tel: 283-7335; fax: 22-0278).

Meat Board of Namibia, PO Box 38, Windhoek (tel: 233-280; fax: 228-310).

Namibia Crafts Centre, 40 Talstreet, Windhoek (tel: 222-236).

Namibia Development Corporation, Private Bag 13252, Windhoek (tel: 206-9111; fax: 23-3943).

Namibia Power Corporation, PO Box 2864, Windhoek (tel: 205-4111; fax: 23-2805).

Namibian Embassy (USA), 1605 New Hampshire Avenue, NW, Washington DC 2009 (tel: 986-0540; fax: 986-0443; e-mail: embnamibia@aol.com).

Namibian Ports Authority, PO Box 361, Walvis Bay (tel: 20-8201: fax: 20-8242).

National Planning Commission (NPC), Office of the President, Private Bag 13356, Windhoek (tel: 222-549; fax: 226-501).

Offshore Development Company, Private Bag 13397, Windhoek (tel: 239-032; fax: 231-001).

Ombudsman's Office, Private Bag 1321, Windhoek (tel: 225-998; fax: 226-838).

Telecom Namibia, PO Box 297, Windhoek (tel: 201-2221; fax: 223-323).

TransNamib Ltd, Private Bag 13204, Windhoek (tel: 298-1111; fax: 298-2053).

UK High Commission, 116A Leutwein Street, PO Box 22202, Windhoek (tel: 223-022; fax: 228-895).

US Embassy, Private Bag 12029, 14 Lossen Street, Ausspannplatz, Windhoek (tel: 221-601; fax: 229-792).

Windhoek Show Society, PO Box 1733, Windhoek (tel: 224-748; fax: 227-707).

Internet sites

Africa Business Network: http://www.ifc.org/abn

AllAfrica.com: http://allafrica.com

African Development Bank: http://www.afdb.org

Africa Online: http://www.africaonline.com

Harambee Afrika (UK business club for traders with east, central and southern Africa; includes annotated web resource list): http://www.harambee.co.uk

Mbendi AfroPaedia (information on companies, countries, industries and stock exchanges in Africa): http://mbendi.co.za

Niger

Anita Parameswaran

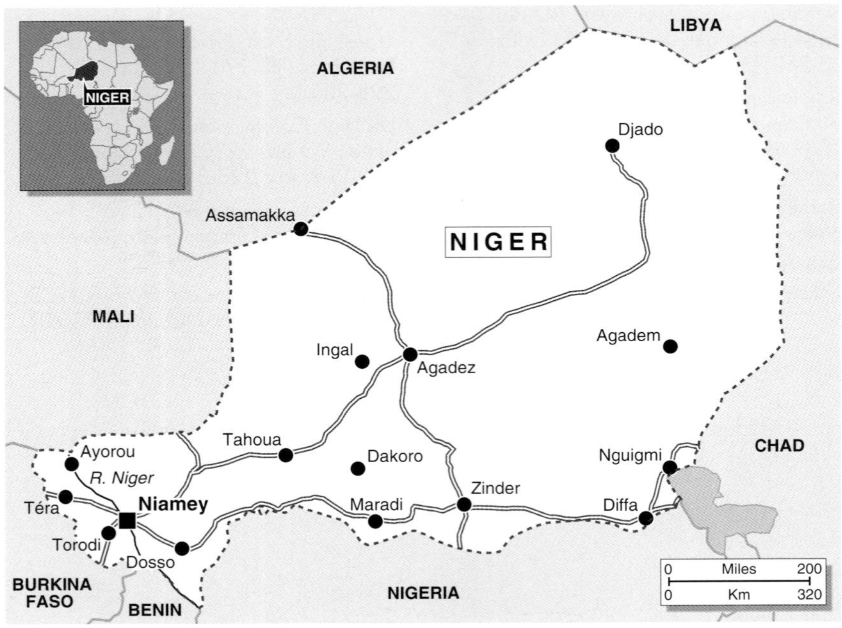

KEY FACTS

Official name: République du Niger (Republic of Niger)

Head of State: President Mamadou Tandja (MNSD) (elected Nov 1999; sworn in 22 Dec 1999)

Head of government: Prime Minister Hama Amadou (MNSD) (appointed 3 Jan 2000)

Ruling party: Mouvement National de la Société de Développement (MNSD) (National Movement for a Developing Society) (38 seats in Nov 1999 election; with its allies, MNSD has an absolute majority)

Area: 1,267,000 square km

Population: 11.20 million (2001)

Capital: Niamey

Official language: French

Currency: CFA franc (CFAf) = 100 centimes (Communauté Financière Africaine (African Financial Community) franc)

Exchange rate: CFAf622.85 per US$ (Jan 2003); CFAf655.95 per euro (pegged from Jan 1999)

GDP per capita: US$170 (2001)

GDP real growth: 7.60% (2001)

Inflation: 4.00% (2001); 0.5% (year-on-year, Feb 2002)

Balance of trade: -US$64.00 million (2001)

For the latest Key Facts, go to www.worldinformation.com

In 2001/02, Niger continued to fight against bankruptcy and struggled towards political stability and economic development. President Mamadou Tandja managed to preserve a tentative political stability and a good harvest kick-started the economy's growth, allowing the republic to meet its key target conditions for the continuance of foreign aid and debt relief. The government managed to arrest the famine that had plagued the country in 2000. Nevertheless, inefficient distribution of resources meant 16 per cent of the population continued to face food insecurity in 2002.

A fledgling democracy

Democracy is a relatively new concept in Niger. The country held its first free and open elections in 1993, 33 years after independence from France. Since then, there have been two military coups, in 1996 and 1999, the latter of which included the assassination of the president, Ibrahim Maïnassara Baré. Since a return to civilian rule and the consequent elections in 1999, the National Assembly has managed to work in accordance with the new constitution, which was also revised and approved by a national referendum in 1999.

During 2001 and 2002, the Mouvement National de la Société de Développement (MNSD) (National Movement for a Developing Society) administration of President Mamadou Tandja managed to remain in power, despite the continuing threat of a military coup and allegations of mismanagement and corruption made by opposition parties. The democratic regime of Niger continued to be dogged with controversy, particularly regarding the perceived inability of the MNSD to live up to the ideals of democracy.

Unrest

In 2001, at least ten students were detained, without trial, for several months after being arrested during the student riots in February 2001. By the beginning of 2002, two students remained incarcerated, including the secretary general of the Union des Étudiants Nigériens de l'Université de Niamey (Union of Nigerien Students at Niamey University). As a consequence of the troubles the university was closed down and further demonstrations were banned by the authorities. The decision was denounced as a serious violation of the constitution.

In August 2002, soldiers mutinied over pay and working conditions and took officials hostage in south-western Niger. In response, the government sent troops into the region, and quickly quashed the uprising.

Journalist jailbird

A further example of the government's lack of commitment to free speech and a fully democratic arena, was the repeated arrest in 2001 of Abdoulaye Tiémogo, a journalist who wrote several articles criticising government ministers. In June 2002, the journalist was arrested again after writing an article accusing Prime Minister Hama Amadou of seeking to bribe the National Assembly in order to retain his ministerial position. Media organisations and opposition parties called for the government to show its commitment to press freedom and debate. While recognising these shortfalls in Niger's supposed democracy, it should be noted that within the political arena of the National Assembly, political debate continued to tentatively follow the ideals of the constitution.

Fall of a sultan

Evidence of political infighting was highlighted in July 2001 when the Sultan of Zinder, the highest of Niger's traditional chiefs, was removed from his position by the government. Aboubacar Oumarou Sanda, who held the position of Sultan of Zinder for 20 consecutive years, was faced with a number of charges including plotting a coup, abduction, murder and cocaine trafficking. These charges were eventually dropped as the police could find no evidence to substantiate the accusations and the police report suggested that jealousy and political rivalry were the reasons behind the allegations. In September 2002, the Sultan was sentenced to two years in prison for fraud. It was a further blow to the traditional chieftains who, throughout 2001, had been vociferous in their opposition against the introduction of new local authorities, which they perceived to be a threat to their established authority and credibility.

Niger also had to struggle with the credibility of its constitution. Though the 1999 constitution aimed to be one of the foundations of Niger's fledgling democracy, it had to contain some dubious compromises in order to stand a chance of lasting. The most contentious issue was that of the amnesty given to those who were involved in human rights violations during the 1996 and 1999 military coups. This included impunity for those responsible for the murder of President Maïnassara. Unfortunately, while recognising the fact that this was not morally right, it could be viewed as being necessary in order to maintain a reasonable level of political stability, which was deemed to be one of the key fundamentals necessary for economic development.

Dependent development.

In the UN Development Programme's (UNDP) 2001 Human Development Report, Niger was ranked 161 out of 162 countries, making the republic the second least developed country in the world. The country was ranked low on all social indicators. In July 2001, it was estimated that only 13.6 per cent of Niger's 10.83 million population were literate, while 63 per cent of the population lived below the poverty line.

Since 2000, Niger's ambitious economic and financial programme has had ongoing support from the IMF under the Poverty Reduction and Growth Facility (PRGF). In December 2000, Niger qualified for debt relief under the Heavily Indebted Poor Countries Initiative (HIPC). Consequently, Niger benefited from additional assistance in 2001 amounting to 0.6 per cent of GDP or US$11.5 million. In August 2001, the IMF approved a further US$11 million and praised Niger's attempts to reduce poverty in the country. The money was used to implement a special poverty reduction programme, which included projects to increase literacy, to raise awareness about the threat of AIDS, and to introduce irrigation systems in drought-prone areas. The Japanese government also signed two agreements in 2002 worth CFAf2.5 billion (US$3.4 million) to aid further development of the republic's health system.

The financial assistance, particularly from the Bretton Woods institutions, came with stringent conditions, which included the privatisation of Niger's public enterprises for water, telecommunications, electricity and petroleum. The takeover of Niger's telecommunications company, Sonitel, by the Chinese telecommunications firm, ZTE, was viewed as a positive step towards Niger's debt repayment. The privatisation of the nation's water company, Société Nationale des Eaux (SNE), sent out a darker message, as clean water is not merely a commodity, but an essential ingredient to life that few of the poverty-stricken majority can afford.

Food for thought

Niger is extremely vulnerable to climatic conditions and is particularly susceptible to famines caused by recurring droughts. The year 2000 saw the country on the brink of bankruptcy and the people facing starvation. But 2001/02 showed the country's development in a more optimistic light. In July 2001, over US$6.5 million was donated by foreign sources in order to supply food to approximately four million Nigeriens who were suffering from starvation. By December 2001, it appeared that the threat of a prolonged famine had been averted as Niger harvested a cereal surplus of nearly 270,000 tonnes, following a season of satisfactory rainfall. The department of agriculture stated that no Nigerien district was experiencing food shortages because the harvest had produced enough cereal to be reserved as

KEY INDICATORS — Niger

	Unit	1996	1997	1998	1999	2000
Population	m	9.43	9.75	10.10	10.46	10.83
Gross domestic product (GDP)	US$bn	1.96	1.83	1.97	2.00	1.80
GDP per capita	US$	207	187	190	191	167
GDP real growth	%	3.4	2.8	10.4	-0.6	-1.4
Inflation	%	5.3	2.9	4.5	-2.3	2.9
Exports (fob) (goods)	US$m	166.3	158.5	175.6	287.0	253.0
Imports (fob) (goods)	US$m	229.3	228.4	250.2	317.0	298.0
Balance of trade	US$m	-63.0	-69.9	-74.6	-30.0	-45.0
Total reserves minus gold	US$m	78.5	53.3	53.1	39.2	80.3
Foreign exchange	US$m	64.3	41.5	40.8	26.1	69.1
Exchange rate	per US$	511.55	583.67	589.95	615.70	711.98

rural and urban security stocks. Though this was theoretically correct, the government's statement was based on the assumption that the supply was evenly distributed. Unfortunately, this assumption was contradicted by reports of numerous villages experiencing food shortages.

Niger's economic performance

Niger's vulnerability and dependency on climactic conditions was highlighted by the significant impact that the good harvest had on the economy. In 2001/02, the country still had a very limited economy, where economic development had been hindered by a long history of political and social instability. In 2001, it was estimated that 80 per cent of Nigeriens lived from subsistence agriculture. Agriculture and livestock accounted for 40 per cent of the country's economic output. The economy's export base is limited to cattle, agricultural products and uranium, which account for around 30 per cent of Niger's total exports.

Real GDP growth in 2001 was 5.1 per cent, which signified a vast improvement on the negative 1.4 per cent recorded in 2000. These favourable statistics were predominantly the result of good harvests. The external current account deficit (excluding official transfers) increased slightly to 8.5 per cent of GDP. This was understandable, given the continuing deterioration in the terms of trade.

As a result of the good harvests, the rural sector grew by more than 8 per cent, more than doubling official predictions of 4 per cent growth. Furthermore, the cereal surplus led to a decrease in food prices and lowered the inflation rate to 4 per cent in December 2001.

Though growth during the latter half of 2001 was encouraging, GDP growth fell to 2.9 per cent in 2002. Continued investment in the country's infrastructure should make the economy and its population less vulnerable to adverse weather conditions.

Nerves run high

The Tandja administration anxiously watched global events after the 11 September terrorist attacks in the US, the US-led war in Afghanistan, the October 2002 Bali bombing and the US's threat of war against Iraq. Niger, along with other developing countries, nervously considered the consequences of changing global priorities. Niger voiced concerns that these events would lead to a decrease in financial assistance, as industrial countries focused on other global regions.

Outlook

Throughout 2002, Niger's political stability and economic development generally looked more secure than it did in mid-2001. Bankruptcy no longer looks inevitable, as the government has shown its commitment to the development of Niger's infrastructure and economic growth. The interest of foreign companies in Niger's privatised enterprises is also an encouraging sign as it indicates that the business world recognises that Niger has the potential to evolve into an emerging economy.

Risk assessment

Economic	Poor
Political	Stable
Regional stability	Poor

COUNTRY PROFILE

Historical profile

Modern-day Niger was at one time occupied and ruled by, among others, the Songhai empire in the west, the Hausa kingdoms in the centre and the Kanam-Bournu empire around Lake Chad in the east.

1800s The British were the first Europeans to explore the area.

1891–1911 France colonised the region, although it did not gain full control until much later and even then resistance movements continued.

1960 Niger gained independence from France under the presidency of Hamani Diori.

1974 Diori was overthrown and replaced by Lieutenant General Seyni Kountche.

1987 Upon Kountche's death, Brigadier Ali Saibou became president.

1992 Following a year-long period of transitional rule, a referendum on 26 December gave overwhelming approval to a new multi-party constitution and nominated the interim prime minister and 10 other ministers to form a High Council of the Republic to run the country until the elections.

1993 Multi-party elections were held in March, resulting in an absolute majority for the Alliance of the Forces of Change (AFC); in presidential elections in February and March Mahamane Ousmane was elected.

1995 Early legislative elections held in January gave the opposition Mouvement National de la Société de Développement (MNSD) (National Movement for a Developing Society) and its allies a three-seat majority over AFC parties. A peace accord was signed.

1996 In January, Mahamane Ousmane was toppled in a coup and replaced by Ibrahim Maïnassara Baré. A military-backed civilian government was formed in February 1996 and Maïnassara won presidential elections in July.

1997 The government reached an agreement with northern Tuareg rebels of the Organisation of Armed Resistance on the re-integration of the ex-rebels into society.

1999 President Maïnassara was assassinated by one of his bodygards during a military coup in April. Major Daouda Mallam Wanké, the interim military ruler, signed a decree in August, promulgating a new constitution which balances power between the president, prime minister and the National Assembly. Mamadou Tandja won the November presidential election with just under 60 per cent of the votes.

2000 President Tandja appointed Hama Amadou as prime minister in January. Droughts lead to widespread food shortages. A meningitis outbreak resulted in over 1,000 deaths.

2001 In February, students staged a three-week uprising against tuition fees and campus conditions. Riots left one policeman dead. As a result of a poor harvest, food prices escalated leading to famine.

2002 In March, the EU granted Niger US$319.5 million for Niger's poverty reduction effort. The money will be used to fund a five-year programme (2002–07) to develop rural areas, food security and good governance.

Political structure

Constitution

The constitution was approved in 1993, and revised in 1996 and 1999. The 18 July 1999 constitution balanced power between the president, prime minister and National Assembly.

Voting: universal suffrage over 18 years. There are seven administrative divisions.

Form of state

Semi-presidential, unitary, multiparty republic.

The executive

Niger has a directly elected president, with a five-year term, renewable only once. The president is the head of state.

In June 1999, the prime minister was granted further power by the ruling military junta. He was named head of government with final responsibility for co-ordinating the actions of the executive branch of government. The president names the prime minister from a list of three candidates.

National legislature

An elected 83-member National Assembly with a maximum five-year term. The prime minister is head of government, which is accountable to the National Assembly.

Legal system

Based on French civil law system and customary law.

Last elections
17 October 1999 (first round presidential); 24 November 1999 (run-off presidential); 24 Nov (legislative).
Next elections
2004 (presidential and legislative).

Political parties
Ruling party
Mouvement National de la Société de Développement (MNSD) (National Movement for a Developing Society) (38 seats in Nov 1999 election; with its allies, MNSD has an absolute majority).
Main opposition party
Parti Nigerien pour la Démocratie et le Socialisme (PNDS) (Niger Party for Democracy and Socialism) (16 seats)

Population
10.83 million (2000), 11.82 million (2002).
Annual population growth rate: 3.4 per cent (1994–2000).
Population density: eight inhabitants per square km. Urban population: 21 per cent (1994–2000). Niger's population lives mostly in the southern and more fertile part of the country.
Ethnic make-up
Hausa (56 per cent), Djerma (22 per cent), Tuareg (8 per cent).
Religions
Islam (85 per cent), traditional beliefs (14.5 per cent), Christianity (0.5 per cent).

Education
Public expenditure on education is around 2 per cent of annual GDP. There are around 40 primary pupils per teacher. Adult illiteracy was 76.2 per cent in men and 91.6 per cent in women in 2000. It is estimated by Oxfam that 23 per cent of children age 6–11 will enrol for school by 2015.

Health
World Bank estimates during the period 1994 and 2000 showed that the average life expectancy was 46 years and the infant mortality rate stood at 116 per 1,000 live births. It is estimated that 50 per cent of children under the age of five were malnourished in the same period. The total fertility rate shows that 7.3 children are born per woman while the rate of contraception practices is estimated at 8 per cent among women aged 15–49. The maternal mortality rate is typically 590 deaths per 100,000 live births. World Bank estimates in 2000 showed that 59 per cent of the population had access to improved water sources. There are 2.4 physicians and 1.5 hospital beds typically available for 1,000 people.
According to World Bank estimates, government expenditure on healthcare averaged 2.6 per cent of GDP of which 1.2 per cent was public expenditure between 1990 and 1998. Expenditure on private healthcare (such as private household expenditure and insurance) averaged 1.4 per cent of GDP over the same period.
There are an estimated 64,000 people living with HIV/AIDS in Niger – 3,300 are under the age of 15 (2000). With infection rates at less than 1 per cent of the total population, Niger has so far escaped much of the African pandemic. However, with 25–35 per cent of sex workers testing positive in 1999, there is a chance that increased population mobility and a lack of condom use could make Niger vulnerable in the future.

Welfare
Around 61.4 per cent of the population live on less than US$1 per day and 85.3 per cent live on less than US$2 per day.
The distribution of wealth is highly unequal with a gini index of 50.5 and the richest 20 per cent of the population owning 53.3 per cent of the total wealth.

Main cities
Niamey (capital, estimated population 520,000 in 2002), Zinder, Tahoua, Maradi Agadez, Birni Nkonni.
Arlit, in the north-west, is a new town built for the local uranium mining industry.

Languages spoken
French is the universal language for documentation; others in daily use include Hausa, Djerma, Tamacheq, Fulani, Arabic, Kanauri, Courmantché and Toubou.
Official language/s
French

Media
Press
News bulletins include *Le Sahel* (daily), *Sahel Hebdo* (weekly) both in French, *Anfani* and *Le Republicain* covering issues of general interest. *Sahel Dimanche* is a privately owned Sunday newspaper and is renowned for its objective reporting. *Alternative* is a semi-monthly publication from Niamey.
Weeklies: *Sahel Dimanche* is the Sunday newspaper.
Broadcasting
Radio: The government operates La Voix du Sahel radio service in French and several Niger languages.
Television: Télé-Sahel broadcasts every day.

Economy
As one of the least developed countries in the world, Niger is heavily dependent on foreign aid and loans. Agriculture is the main source of income for most Nigerien households and subsistence farming predominates. However, uranium exports provide the largest amount of the country's foreign exchange, although mining only employs a small percentage of the workforce.
The IMF and the World Bank have agreed to support a reduction in the country's debt under the enhanced Heavily Indebted Poor Countries (HIPC) initiative. Total relief is worth about US$890 million or US$520 million in net present value terms, which is equivalent to 53.5 per cent of total debt outstanding. The IMF estimates that this will reduce debt service as a percentage of government revenue from 44 per cent in 2000 to 10.9 per cent in 2003 and average 4.3 per cent during 2010–19.
Niger's three-year Poverty Reduction and Growth Facility (PRGF) commits the government to reductions in the budget deficit through strengthening revenue, keeping wages down and reallocation of government expenditure. The IMF is also pushing for further privatisation measures. However, the onset of famine, declining terms of trade and continued dependency on foreign aid will restrict Niger's ability to meet IMF targets.

External trade
There are regular trade and current account deficits, partly financed by aid flows and foreign borrowing.
Exports
Principal exports are uranium concentrates, live animals, cowpeas, hides and skins, cotton (raw, yarn, fabrics), animal products.
Main destinations: France (typically 51 per cent of total), South Korea (34 per cent), UK (4 per cent), Nigeria (3 per cent).
Imports
Principal imports are consumer goods, raw materials and equipment, cereals, petroleum and products, food, textiles, paper, tobacco, rubber and products, pharmaceuticals.
Main sources: France (typically 17 per cent of total), Côte d'Ivoire (9 per cent), Germany (4 per cent), US (3 per cent).

Agriculture
Subsistence farming and stock rearing contribute around 40 per cent to GDP and employ 70 per cent of the workforce.
Less than 3 per cent of the total land area is cultivated.
Hides and skins and cotton account for around 20 per cent of export earnings.
The government is encouraging market gardening – galmi onions are an important cash crop.
Production of the two principal food crops, millet and sorghum, is generally insufficient to satisfy domestic needs and is supplemented by food aid. Other food crops include rice, cowpeas and green beans.
Recurrent drought and desertification have had a serious impact on livestock rearing

and have led to significant food shortages with disastrous consequences. An estimated 40 per cent of GDP is spent on anti-desertification schemes, and the government is encouraging animal husbandry.

Industry and manufacturing

The industrial sector is small-scale, contributing around 7 per cent to GDP and employing 5 per cent of the workforce.

Manufacturing is concentrated on the processing of agricultural commodities such as sugar refining, brewing, cotton ginning, tanning and flour/rice milling.

Other activities include small-scale production of cement and metals, textiles, plastics, soft drinks and construction materials.

Industrial development is handicapped by the shortage of capital and skilled labour and by the country's weak infrastructure.

Mining

The mining sector accounts for around 11 per cent of GDP and employs 5 per cent of the workforce.

Since the early 1970s uranium has been the country's principal export. Proven reserves total 280,000 tonnes with extraction undertaken mainly at two opencast mines, at Arlit and Akouta. Production stagnated at 3,000–3,200 tonnes for several years, after peaking at 4,360 tonnes in 1981. This stagnation was caused by a world slump in demand for uranium. The major export markets are France (about 2,000 tonnes), Japan, Spain, Germany and Egypt. Production has increased in recent years, but depressed prices on the world market have seen the value of uranium exports fall.

Other minerals exploited are the tin-bearing ore cassiterite, phosphates, molybdenum, salt and coal. There are also known reserves of iron ore.

Interest in gold mining is picking up. Etruscan of Canada is prospecting for gold at the Koma Bangou concession in west Niger; the area is thought to contain between 1 and 2 million troy ounces of gold. Imperial Metals is drilling for diamonds on the M'Banga concession.

Hydrocarbons

Niger is heavily dependent on imported petroleum.

Energy

Demand for electricity more than doubled during the 1980s owing to expansion of the uranium industry.

Domestic generation (mainly thermal) meets about 50 per cent of local needs, the deficit being imported from Nigeria.

Hydro potential is estimated at 250MW.

In July 2002, the African Development Fund approved a CFAf604.7 million grant to finance a study of the National Domestic Energy Strategy (SNED) for Niger, which should help reduce the use of fuel wood in households. It will involve preparing a 15-year action plan to implement the SNED.

Banking

Central bank

Banque Centrale des Etats de l'Afrique de l'Ouest.

Main financial centre

Niamey.

Time

GMT plus one hour

Geography

Niger is a land-locked country in western Africa, with Algeria and Libya to the north, Nigeria and Benin to the south, Mali and Burkina Faso to the west and Chad to the east.

Climate

Niger is very hot with temperatures ranging from 28–44 degrees Celsius. There is rain mainly in the south from June–September. Frequent Sahara dust storms occur from November–January. The dry season is from October–May.

Entry requirements

Passports

Required by all, except nationals of certain African countries with national ID card.

Visa

Required by all except nationals of Cuba, Finland, Morocco, Norway, Sweden and Tunisia. Visitors should carry a return ticket. All documents require a French translation.

Currency advice/regulations

No restriction of import on foreign currency subject to declaration. Declaration forms must be retained and all transactions recorded. Local currency import is unlimited. Export of local currency limited to CFAf25,000 (French nationals exempt).

Health (for visitors)

Mandatory precautions

Yellow fever vaccination certificate required if coming from an infected area.

Advisable precautions

Typhoid, hepatitis A, tetanus and polio vaccinations. Malaria prophylaxis should be taken as risk exists throughout the country. There is a rabies risk. Water precautions should be taken.

Personal medicines can be difficult to obtain.

Hotels

There are good hotels in Niamey. A 5 per cent service charge is usually added to bills.

Public holidays

Fixed dates

1 Jan (New Year's Day), 24 Apr (Concord Day), 1 May (Labour Day), 3 Aug (Independence Day), 18 Sep (Republic Day), 25 Dec (Christmas Day).

Variable dates

Easter Monday, Eid Al-Fitr, Eid Al-Adha (Tabaski), Prophet's Birthday, Islamic New Year.

Working hours

Banking

Mon–Fri: 0800–1100 and 1600–1700.

Business

Winter: Mon–Fri: 0730–1230, 1500–1800; Sat: 0730–1230.
Summer: Mon–Fri: 0730–1230, 1530–1830; Sat: 0730–1230.

Government

Oct–Feb: Mon–Fri: 0730–1230 and 1500–1800; Mar–Sep: Mon–Fri: 0730–1230 and 1530–1830.

Shops

Mon–Fri: 0800–1200, 1600–1900; Sat: 0800–1200.

Telecommunications

Telephone/fax

Dialling code for Niger: IDD access code + 227 followed by subscriber's number. There are no area codes.

Facilities mainly in Niamey. Good international links via Paris. Calls should be made via 'Linter Radio' Service.

Electricity supply

220/380V AC, 50 cycles.

Getting there

Air

National airline: Air Afrique (Niger is a shareholder).

International airport/s: Niamey International (Code: NIM), 12km south-east of city; bar, currency exchange, post office, shops, car hire, hotel courtesy coaches.

Airport tax: None.

Surface

Road: The Nigerian and Burkina Faso borders have been re-opened and road access is possible. Access from Algeria and Mali is difficult, but a surfaced road connects Benin with Niamey. Access from Chad is restricted.

Water: Ferries on the Niger River coming from Mali are dependent on the water level.

Getting about

National transport

Air: Charter flights are available in Niamey.

Road: Main highways link Tillabery with N'guigmi, Tahoua and Arlit. Petrol is not always available. Best months for road travel December–March. Visitors must report to police on arrival at main centres.

Buses: Services operate from Niamey to Zinder, Agadez, and other towns.

City transport

Taxis: Fixed rates apply for long-distance and urban services. Taxis in Niamey are cheap and widely available. Tipping is optional.

Taxi fare from airport to city centre CFAf2,000, journey time 10 minutes.

Car hire

Self-drive or chauffeur-driven cars are available in Niamey. Drivers compulsory outside the capital. International driving licence required. Petrol and spares in short supply.

BUSINESS DIRECTORY

Telephone area codes

Dialling code for Niger: IDD access code +227 followed by subscriber's number. There are no area codes.

Useful telephone numbers

Police: 17

Fire: 18

Chambers of Commerce

Chambre de Commerce, d'Agriculture et d'Industrie du Niger, BP 209, Niamey (tel: 732-210, 735-155).

Chambre de Commerce et d'Agriculture de Zinder, BP 83, Zinder (tel: 570-078).

Banking

Bank of Africa - Niger, (Head Office); BP 10 973, Immeuble Sonara II, Niamey (tel: 733-620, 733-621; fax: 733-818).

Banque Centrale des Etats de l'Afrique de l'Ouest (Agency); BP 487, Rond Point de la Poste, Niamey (tel: 722-491/92; fax: 734-743).

Banque Commerciale du Niger (Head Office); BP 11 363, Rond Point Maourey, Niamey (tel: 733-915, 733-331; fax: 732-163).

Banque Internationale pour l'Afrique au Niger (Head Office); BP 10350, Avenue de la Mairie, Niamey (tel: 733-101; fax: 733-595; e-mail: bia@intnet.ne).

Banque Islamique du Niger pour le Commerce et l'industrie (BINCI), BP 12754, Immeuble El-Nasr, Niamey (tel: 732-730, 732-740; fax: 734-735).

Caisse de Prêts aux Collectivités Territoriale, BP 730, Route Torodi, Rive droite, Niamey (tel: 723-412, 723-080).

Caisse Nationale d'Epargne, Avenue du Niger. BP 11778 Niamey (tel: 732-498, 732-499; fax: 735-812).

Crédit du Niger, BP 213, Blvd de la République, Niamey (tel: 722-701, 722-702; fax: 722-390).

Ecobank-Niger, BP 13804, Niamey (tel: 737-181, 901-052; fax: 737-204, 737-203).

Société Nigérienne de Banque, BP 891, Ave de la Mairie, Niamey (tel: 734-569, 734-643; fax: 734-693).

Central bank

Banque Centrale des Etats de l'Afrique de l'Ouest, PO Box 3108, Avenue Abdoulaye Fadiga, Dakar, Senegal (tel: 390-500; fax: 239-335).

Travel information

Niamey International Airport, ASECNA, BP 1096, Niamey (tel: 732-517/518/519, 732-381/382; fax: 735-512).

Office du Tourisme du Niger, BP 612, Niamey.

Other useful addresses

Centre for Investment Promotion, BP 12129, Niamey (tel: 736-836; fax: 736-772).

Conseil National de Développement, c/o Ministry of Planning, Niamey (tel: 722-233).

Direction des Statistiques, c/o Ministry of Planning, Niamey (tel: 722-799).

Niger Embassy (US), 2204 R Street, NW, Washington DC 20008 (tel: 483-4224; fax: 483-3169; e-mail: ambassadeniger@hotmail.com).).

Office Nationale des Ressources Minières (Onarem), BP 210, Niamey (tel: 723-935).

Société Nationale de Commerce et de Production du Niger, BP 615, Niamey.

Société Nigérienne de Produits Pétroliers (Sonidep), BP 2735, Niamey (tel: 733-335).

SONHOTEL (Société Nigerienne de Gestion des Hôtels de l'Etat) (tel: 732-387).

Syndicat des Commerçants, Importateurs et Exportateurs du Niger, BP 535, Niamey.

Internet sites

Africa Business Network: http://www.ifc.org/abn

AllAfrica.com: http://allafrica.com

African Development Bank: http://www.afdb.org

Africa Online: http://www.africaonline.com

Mbendi AfroPaedia (information on companies, countries, industries and stock exchanges in Africa): http://mbendi.co.za

Nigeria

Guy Arnold

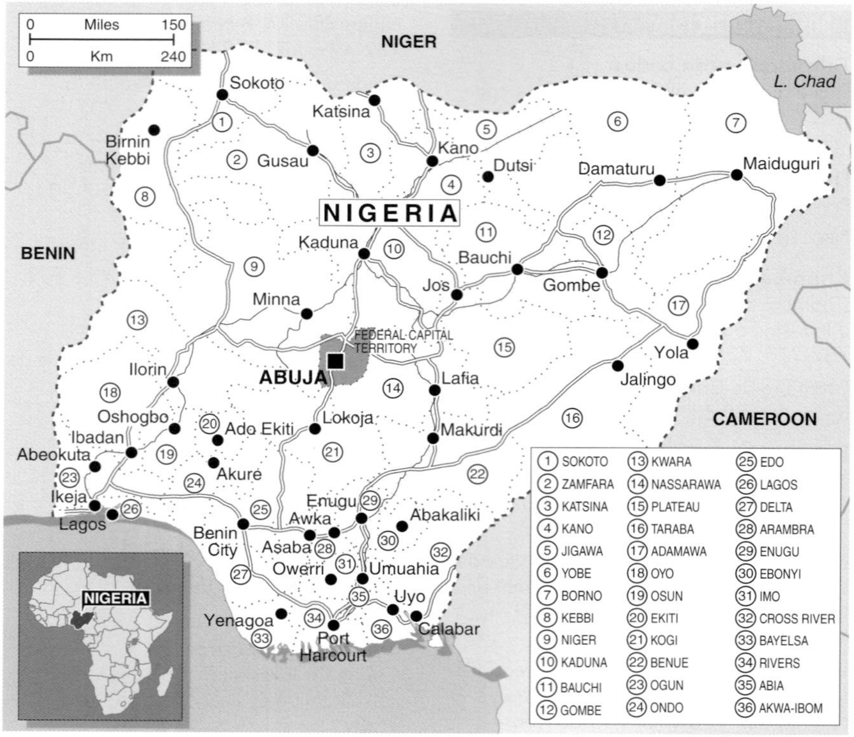

KEY FACTS

Official name: Federal Republic of Nigeria

Head of State: President General Olusegun Obasanjo (inaugurated 29 May 1999)

Head of government: President General Olusegun Obasanjo

Ruling party: People's Democratic Party (PDP)

Area: 923,768 square km

Population: 121.50 million (2002)

Capital: Abuja – federal capital since 1991; Lagos – commercial capital

Official language: English

Currency: Naira (N) = 100 kobo

Exchange rate: N128.80 per US$ (Jan 2003)

GDP per capita: US$331 (2001); US$316 (2002)*

GDP real growth: 2.90% (2001); -0.9% (2002)*

Labour force: 53.30 million (2001); 54.7 million (2002)*

Unemployment: 28.00% (2001)*

Inflation: 16.50% (2001); 13.8% (2002)*

Oil production: 2.15 million bpd (2001)

Balance of trade: US$3.16 billion (2001)

Foreign debt: US$32.13 billion (2001)

Annual FDI: US$1.80 billion (2001)

* estimated figure

For the latest Key Facts, go to www.worldinformation.com

President Olusegun Obasanjo has worked hard and with moderate success to improve Nigeria's international image. There has been a big shake-up in the key economic sectors and corruption has been brought under some measure of control. But Obasanjo's hope for a 'democracy dividend' that would follow 20 years of military dictatorship has yet to materialise. The majority of Nigerians still live well below the poverty line; the poor quality of life fuelled ethnic and religious tensions in 2002. Nigeria's paradox however, is that while millions are jobless and starving, the country has a great economic resource: oil. Given this country's oil prosperity, it is remarkable that so little of this wealth has fed through to the population.

A hotbed of violence

One of the most heated political debates in Nigeria is the issue of sharia (Islamic law). The governors of 12 predominantly Muslim northern states have succeeded in introducing sharia, albeit to different extents. This is giving the Islamic clergy unprecedented power over law-making and judicial decisions and, according to its critics, goes against the secular nature of the country's constitution. The Sharia penal code includes extreme measures such as flogging, stoning, amputation and capital punishment for criminal offences. In January 2002 Nigeria's first execution in the name of Sharia took place in the northern Islamic state of Katsina. A 27-year-old man, Sani Yakubu, was sentenced to death for the murder of a woman and her two children. Despite the promises made by Muslim leaders that sharia would not threaten the unity of Nigeria, the sizeable Christian minorities in the north are resistant to what they see as Islamicisation.

The growth in religious violence has also undermined Nigeria's image abroad. The government had hoped that the Miss World beauty pageant, held in November 2002, would improve foreign perceptions of Nigeria. Instead, it prompted widespread communal violence. Matters were made worse by the timing of the event, during the Muslim holy month of Ramadan, and an article in the *This Day* newspaper which suggested that the Prophet Muhammad would have approved of the pageant. Hundreds were killed in the riots and the Miss World competition was forced to relocate to the UK, a move that caused great embarrasment for the Nigerian authorities.

President Obasanjo has been unwilling to involve himself in the debate, fearing that to do so would make him seem partisan, thereby threatening the unity of Nigeria and the stability of its fragile democracy. Religious extremism among both Muslims and Christians as well as a rise in separatism has accompanied ethnic rivalry encouraged by opportunistic and corrupt politicians seeking to shore up their support locally. The competition between states is over control of oil wealth, with southern oil-producing states demanding a greater proportion of oil receipts and the power to raise revenue from oil production. While northern states have set up sharia courts, southern states have formed vigilante groups, the most notorious being the Bakassi Boys which have been implicated in the killing of hundreds of people. The groups have helped shore up the political position of many southern governors, who have voiced their support for complete independence from Nigeria.

Isolated president

The President's position at the federal level appeared increasingly isolated in 2002. Obasanjo's People's Democratic Party (PDP), which gained an absolute parliamentary majority in 1999, increasingly appeared to act as an opposition to the President. He managed to win the PDP's presidential nomination in January 2003 with over 75 per cent of the delegates backing him in the party's primary elections. His nearest rival, former vice president Alex Ekwueme, was left trailing with just 17 per cent of the vote. Ekwueme condemned the selection of Obasanjo as the PDP's presidential candidate as a 'charade', claiming delegates had been intimidated by the government. The lack of support for Obasanjo among two of Nigeria's three most powerful tribes, the Hausa and the Igbo, was certainly not mirrored by the high level of support accorded to the President at the party's convention. There had also been a high level of disenchantment among the Yoruba, who are seen as Obasanjo's natural constituency. Meanwhile, senior party members have urged the electorate to vote against him and in 2002 a number became embroiled in a plot to oust him from power. This raised the prospect of an open split within the ruling party. Ghali Na'Abba, the speaker of the House of Representatives, along with the PDP governors of the south-eastern Abia and Akwa-Ibom states and Senate president Pius Anyim, have threatened to break away from the PDP to form a new political party.

Obsanjo's detractors in the PDP claim he has abused his constitutional power, particularly over his refusal to pass the 2002 budget after it was amended by legislators who sought to increase spending by 20 per cent. Parliament has also criticised Obasanjo's alleged failure to implement budgets according to the appropriation law. The clash between the executive and the legislature over fiscal policy was highlighted in the National Assembly's delay in passing the 2002 budget, which took four months of deliberations before it was finally approved in March 2002.

Matters came to a head in August 2002, when the House of Representatives called on Obasanjo to resign or face impeachment. The Senate approved the lower house's impeachment threat. In September, both houses began working on a list of charges, including breaches of the constitution, imcompetence and abetting corruption, against Obasanjo and to prepare for an impeachment process. The President dismissed the move, which was backed by a majority of PDP members, as 'a joke taken too far' and defied parliament's request.

Bad management but rich returns

Nigeria has been criticised for the way its oil industry has been managed. The Nigerian economy is heavily dependent on oil and there has been little attempt to diversify. Oil accounts for 45 per cent of the country's GDP and 85 per cent of foreign exchange earnings. The reason that Nigeria has not been able to reap the benefits of its oil wealth is that the industry itself has not changed much since oil was discovered. Oil refineries are in a state of disrepair and the major oil-producing areas of the country have largely been ignored. Furthermore, years of ethnic and religious violence have diverted government attention from oil exploration. On top of this is the fact that most of the revenues from oil go straight into government pockets and not to needy communities.

Investment begins at home

An economic forum was held in Abuja during October 2001. It was attended by, among others, the US ambassador to Nigeria, Howard F Jeter, and the former British minister for overseas aid, Baroness Chalker, both of whom delivered similar messages to the forum. These were that corruption needed to be addressed and the high cost of doing business had to be reduced if Nigeria was to attract the investment it required. The US Ambassador said 'Nigerians have to invest more in Nigeria. You cannot expect many foreigners to invest their money when they see too many people who call Nigeria home taking their money away.' Home investment, he went on, was both economically important and

KEY INDICATORS — Nigeria

	Unit	1996	1997	1998	1999	2000
Population	m	101.41	103.90	106.41	108.95	111.50
Gross domestic product (GDP)	US$bn	30.80	39.90	41.40	43.10	41.10
GDP per capita	US$	267	337	341	345	319
GDP real growth	%	2.3	3.6	1.8	2.0	3.8
Inflation	%	29.3	8.2	10.3	6.6	6.9
Manufacturing output	1995=100	101.0	101.7	97.5	100.8	101.4
Oil output	'000 bpd	2,140.0	2,305.0	2,165.0	2,030.0	2,103.0
Natural gas output	bn cu m	5.4	5.1	5.1	5.7	11.0
Exports (fob) (goods)	US$m	16,120.0	15,210.0	8,970.0	12,880.0	20,441.0
Imports (fob) (goods)	US$m	6,440.0	9,500.0	9,210.0	8,590.0	13,696.0
Balance of trade	US$m	9,680.0	5,710.0	-240.0	4,290.0	6,745.0
Current account	US$m	3,510.0	550.0	-4,240.0	510.0	2,003.0
Foreign debt	US$bn	31.4	28.7	29.5	30.1	31.9
Exchange rate	per US$	21.88	21.89	21.89	92.34	101.70

a symbol of commitment to Nigeria's future.

Investors are being encouraged to participate in certain area development projects, particularly in the city of Abuja. A forum – the Abuja Investment-Development Forum and Exhibition (ABIDEV 2001) – was launched by the ministry of the federal capital territory (MFCT) as part of a government drive to attract investors. The city was still under construction in 2001 and required huge multi-sectoral intervention to meet the needs of its fast growing population. Foreign investors are offered a range of incentives including easy access to land and the provision of infrastructure, such as access roads, telecommunications and water as well as tax relief or exemptions and permission to repatriate a sizeable proportion of profits. While social, banking and housing developments have made good progress, not much industrial development has as yet been achieved, mainly because of lack of infrastructure and services.

Biting off more than they can chew?

At the end of October 2001, President Obasanjo presented a draft 2002 budget to the National Assembly for a total of N924 billion (US$8 billion) to consolidate the achievements of fiscal policies carried out in 2001. The budget was for 30 per cent less than projections in the 2001 budget, while revenue for the budget period was estimated at N1,156 billion (US$9.7 billion). This was based on an oil price of US$18 a barrel, with oil accounting for the bulk of the revenue. Emphasis was placed on power and steel development with N38.5 billion set aside to achieve uninterrupted power supply throughout the country (power shortages have long been a major problem). The sum of N32.9 billion (US$276 million) was allocated to the ministry of works and housing, in particular, in order to enable the ministry to carry out special highway projects that had been taken over from the defunct Petroleum (Special) Trust fund (PTF). Another N30.2 billion (US$254 million) was allocated to water resources development while the federal capital territory (FCT-Abuja) was allocated N22 billion (US$185 million).

The emphasis generally was on development of the infrastructure. In his speech, Obasanjo underlined the priority to be given to the improvement of education at all levels and said that both the Universal Basic Education (UBE) and Mass Literacy Programme (MLP) would be pushed in 2002. Sports and social development was allocated N15 billion (US$126 million). Another N10 billion (US$84 million) was assigned to the national identity card (NIC) project. This project has dragged on for two decades and has already cost N50 billion (US$420 million). Obasanjo explained the need to maintain internal order and security, especially in the light of violent conflict in some parts of the country. The project should be completed by 2003. Despite the emphasis placed upon the need to boost food production to feed the large population, the ministry of agriculture was only allocated N3.7 billion (US$31 million).

NITEL's failure

In November 2001, it appeared that Nigeria's giant state-owned telecommunications corporation, Nitel, was at last to be privatised. Investors International Limited (IIL), a consortium in partnership with telecommunications companies in several European countries, including Portugal and the Netherlands, was named as the preferred bidder for the 51 per cent government holding in Nitel. But IIL pulled out and in came the reserve bidder, Telnet. In early 2002, Korea's Telnet also pulled out signalling the complete failure of the government's privatisation plan. Poor investor confidence and ambiguous handling of the sale were cited as reasons why the privatisation failed to go ahead. This delay to Nitel's sale has hampered realisation of the government's economic objectives.

Sixteen companies from Asia, Europe, North America and the Middle East had originally taken part in the bid for the 51 per cent controlling interest in Nitel, which was heavily indebted. Criteria for bidders included the requirement that they had already operated a network of one million telephone lines and would commit themselves to installing a minimum of two million lines in Nigeria over the three years 2002–2005. Despite having received millions of dollars from the Nigerian taxpayer, Nitel only had 500,000 connected telephone lines after 40 years of operation for a population of 110 million.

Outlook

The controversy surrounding Obasanjo's election as the PDP's candidate and growing levels of violence will dog the President as the campaign gears up for the April presidential election. If Obasanjo wins the elections, his opponents are bound to question whether the elections were free and fair, leading to further political instability. The level of public distrust towards the government is heightened by a lack of confidence in the Independent National Electoral Commission (INEC), which bungled the voter registration exercise held in September 2002. At the time, INEC blamed unscrupulous members of its own organisation for hoarding and selling on registration forms, a situation that has not inspired confidence in the electoral system.

The increasing polarisation of Nigerian society will form the backdrop of an election which many anticipate will be among the most violent in the country's history. Obasanjo's main challenger is former military ruler Major-General Muhammadu Buhari, a northern Muslim selected to represent the All Nigeria People's Party (ANPP). Buhari is certain to attract the votes of Muslims disenchanted with Obasanjo's allegedly pro-Christian approach. This will mean that the elections will play out the country's north-south divisions, thereby heightening tension and eroding national unity.

Disputes will increasingly focus on the distribution of oil revenues, with Obasanjo's inability to solve the problem generating hostility from both the oil-producing Christian-dominated south and the militarily powerful Muslim north. Whoever wins the presidency will have to show firmer leadership and win support from all sections of Nigerian society. Otherwise Nigeria could return to military rule, a situation which will continue to set back the country's economic development.

Although Nigeria's most senior military officer, Chief of Defence Staff Admiral Ibrahim Ogohi, has ruled out a military take-over, he acknowledged that elements within the political system were using the political crisis as a pretext 'to incite the members of the armed forces against the constitutionally elected government'. The tensions within Nigeria and the growth of armed groups could also lead to a civil war. Evidence of mass killings indicates that Nigeria may already be in a period of political and social melt-down.

Risk assessment

Economic	Improving
Political	Improving
Regional stability	Improving
Stock market	Improving

COUNTRY PROFILE

Historical profile

Between the eleventh and fourteenth centuries a number of Islamic Hausa kingdoms flourished in the area of modern-day Nigeria, while in the fourteenth and fifteenth centuries the Yoruba empire developed into a regional power, and the Ibos, with a diffuse political structure, lived in the east. The Yoruba first made contact with Europeans (Portuguese) in the fifteenth century, who, along with other European nations, began trading in slaves from west Africa.

1914 The territory that is now Nigeria was taken over by the British.

1922 A legislative council was set up. Much local power was left in the hands of traditional chiefs.

1947 A constitution established a federal system of government which attempted to take into account the interests of the three main regions of the colony – the northern and mainly Muslim Hausa and Fulanis, the predominantly Catholic Ibo in the east and the mixed Anglican and Muslim Yoruba in the west.

1960 Nigeria became independent.

1963 The Federal Republic of Nigeria was proclaimed.

1967–70 The Ibo people of eastern Nigeria attempted to gain independence, leading to the Biafran War. Estimates for the death toll during the war range between 500,000 and two million.

1970s The oil boom led to Nigeria becoming one of Africa's wealthiest states until the price of oil plummeted in the early 1980s.

1985 After 25 years of political turbulence, General Ibrahim Babangida seized power, widely supported by intellectuals, the press, some former politicians and the business community. The General pledged to return Nigeria to civilian rule, but the handover date was repeatedly postponed.

1993 Elections were held in June but were later annulled. President Babangida stepped down from office on 23 August and Chief Ernest Shonekan was appointed head of the Interim National Government. On 17 November defence minister Sani Abacha staged a coup and became the country's ruler.

1995 General Abacha announced that the military government would remain in office until 1 October 1998. Ken Saro-Wiwa, Nigerian writer and champion of the cause of the Ogoni people in eastern Nigeria, and eight other minority rights activists were executed, leading to international outrage against the government and the Shell oil company, which had allegedly polluted Ogoni land.

1998 The death of General Sani Abacha on 6 June led to the appointment of General Abdulsalam Abubaker as head of state on 9 June. On 25 August, a full electoral timetable was announced for the first time. Local elections were held on 5 December.

1999 State legislative elections were held on 9 January, National Assembly elections on 20 February and presidential elections on 22 February. Olusegun Obasanjo was declared the winner in the presidential elections on 27 February, and inaugurated as president on 29 May.

2000 There were ethnic clashes in Lagos in October between Yoruba extremists and Hausas from the north. Equatorial Guinea and Nigeria signed a treaty in September agreeing to the demarcation of their maritime border.

2001 The heads of Nigeria's army, navy and air force all retired in April. Christians rebelled in Nassarawa state, in the centre of Nigeria, and Bauchi state, in the north, when an attempt was made in July to impose Islamic law in the town of Tafawa-balewa. In July, the government approved US$93 million spending towards the development of a national space programme, the National Space Research and Development Agency (NASRDA). A treaty establishing the Gulf of Guinea Commisssion was signed by five of the seven member states in July (Gabon, Congo, São Tomé and Príncipe, Nigeria and Angola). Cameroon and Equatorial Guinea did not sign, for which no reason was given.

2002 In January, a munitions depot in Lagos exploded killing 600 people. Legislation signed by President Obasanjo which would have banned new political parties from contesting presidential and legislative elections in 2003 was unanimously rejected by the House of Representatives.

Political structure

Constitution

The constitution of 5 May 1999, based on the 1979 constitution, devolves significant powers to the 36 states.

The political system is divided into three tiers: the federal or central level, the state level and local government.

Under the presidential system, the president, who is also the commander-in-chief of the armed forces, is vested with executive powers under the constitution of the federal republic. The president and his ministers form the federal executive council with the president as the chairman.

A similar structure exists in the states where the governor and his commissioners form the state executive councils. Each state has a legislature, executive and judiciary, although their legislative arm is unicameral.

Form of state

Federal republic comprising 36 states and the Federal Capital Territory (FCT, Abuja).

The executive

The executive is headed by an elected president who initiates the policies and programmes of the government and ensures that they are implemented after they have been passed into law by the legislature. The success or failure of any government depends largely on the incumbent president who combines the roles of the chief executive with those of the ceremonial head of state.

In accordance with the concept of separation of powers, the president is excluded from membership of both houses of the National Assembly.

The president cannot be removed from office except by death, impeachment or resignation.

Despite his wide-ranging power, the president has restrictions which include ratification of all his major appointments by the National Assembly. Although he is empowered to conduct foreign affairs, all treaties require the ratification of the Senate. Only the National Assembly can declare war and peace. While he appoints members of the judiciary, he cannot remove them.

National legislature

The legislative powers of the federal government are vested in a bicameral National Assembly consisting of two houses – a lower house, which is the House of Representatives and the upper house, the Senate.

At the state level, the legislature is a unicameral House of Assembly.

The National Assembly is made up of 109 Senators and 360 members of the House of Representatives elected for a term of four years, and always free to contest for re-election at subsequent polls. It has the ultimate say on the signing of international treaties and the declaration of war. Each of the states of the federation has a unicameral legislature.

Legal system

Nigeria's legal system is based on the English common law, Nigerian customs and tradition and Islamic Sharia. Sharia predominates in the northern Islamic states.

Last elections

20 February/7 March 1999 (parliamentary); 27 February 1999 (presidential).

Next elections

August 2002 (local elections, the first since military rule ended in 1999); April 2003 (presidential); 2003 (parliamentary).

Political parties

Ruling party

People's Democratic Party (PDP)

Main opposition party

The All People's Party (APP)

Population

111.5 million (2000); 116.9 million (2002). The population is expected to reach 278.8 million by 2050.

Annual population growth rate: 2.8 per cent (2002). About 52 per cent of the population is male and 48 per cent female. Approximately 47 per cent of the total population is under 15 years of age. Population density: 128 inhabitants per square km. Urban population: 44 per cent. Much of the population is concentrated in the southern part of the country as well and Kano in the north. There has been an expansion of a number of cities, spurred by development and rural–urban migration.

Ethnic make-up

Hausas (21 per cent), Yorubas (20 per cent), Igbos (17 per cent) and Fulani (9 per cent) comprise the four major tribes.

Religions

Islam (about 50 per cent), Christianity (about 40 per cent), traditional beliefs (about 10 per cent).

Education

In 2000 the adult illiteracy rate was estimated at 27.6 per cent and 44.2 per cent for men and women respectively. Primary schooling lasts for six years followed by secondary, academic, technical or vocational qualifications. The number of pupils per school teacher is typically 34. Typical enrolment in 1997 (indicating total enrolment regardless of age) of the relevant age group in education was 98 per cent for primary level, 33 per cent for secondary level and only 4 per cent for tertiary level. Public expenditure on education was equivalent to approximately 0.7 per cent of annual GNP in 1997 and included subsidies to private education at the primary, secondary and tertiary levels. In 2001, 7 per cent of the government's budget was allocated to education, compared with 18 per cent in 1997.

Health

In 2000, Nigeria had a birth and death rate of 39.69 births and 13.91 deaths per 1,000 population respectively. Life expectancy was 51 years and the infant mortality rate stood at 110 deaths per 1,000 live births. The fertility rate was high at 5.6 children born per adult woman while the maternal mortality rate was 1 per cent of live births. Nigeria has a large number of children under the age of five suffering from severe to moderate malnutrition, with an estimated 43 per cent of children suffering stunted growth. Nigeria has a growing problem of HIV/AIDS as well as a significant rise of other non-communicable diseases. The adult HIV rate was 5.8 per cent adults in 2002. In 2001, there were 9,496 deaths from AIDS.

The federal ministry of health (FMOH) provides policy and technical guidance to the 36 states and the federal capital territory (Abuja), co-ordinating state efforts towards the goals set by the national health policy. In 2001, health expenditure stood at 0.7 per cent of GDP, of which public expenditure was equivalent to 0.2 per cent of GDP and private expenditure was 0.5 per cent of GDP. Health expenditure per capita stood at US$23 in 2002. Approximately 2 physicians and 17 hospital beds per 10,000 people were available. Persistently low funding of healthcare facilities remains a major constraint for development. The primary healthcare network has seriously declined with low level coverage of services such as immunisation and supply of essential drugs. The Health System Fund is a major project implemented by the state and federal ministries of health aimed at institutional development, training and an essential drug programme. In 2001, Nigeria launched the National HIV/AIDS Emergency Action Plan (HEAP), a set of projects designed to combat the spread of the disease. The projects will be implemented from 2002–04. As part of the initiative the government is distributing free drugs to AIDS sufferers.

Welfare

The Nigerian public service schemes, the private sector self-administered and insured scheme, the National Provident Fund (NPF) and the Nigeria Social Insurance Trust Fund (NSITF) schemes, provide for old age, survivorship, invalidity and industrial injury benefits, gratuity and pension. The Workmen Compensation Act provides for industrial injury benefits. Despite the existence of these bodies, the social security system is virtually non-existent in Nigeria, partly due to the large informal sector.

In 2000, the government introduced reforms to the pay structure, minimum wage, salaries and allowances in the federal public service, at a time when the disposable income and purchasing power of Nigerian workers was ebbing. The payment of pensions and gratuity remained negligible. The government is under pressure to bridge the wide gap between the remuneration of workers in the public and private sectors. Currently pension schemes are fraught with many problems, often enmeshed in mismanagement and outright corrupt practices. Benefits are not only too low, but payment is often delayed. There is immediate need of capital mobilisation for rapid and sustained economic development and enhancing employee benefits.

Main cities

The seat of government is Abuja, Federal Capital Territory, in central Nigeria (estimated population two million).

Lagos is the former capital and main port (estimated population eight million in 2002).

Capitals of the 36 states are: Kaduna (state of Kaduna), Kano (Kano), Jos (Plateau), Sokoto (Sokoto), Maiduguri (Borno), Ilorin (Kogi – formerly Kwara), Ibadan (Oyo, estimated population 4.7 million), Port Harcourt (Rivers), Calabar (Cross River), Bauchi (Bauchi), Minna (Niger), Makurdi (Benue), Abeokuta (Ogun), Akure (Ondo), Ikeja (Lagos), Owerri (Imo), Katsina (Katsina), Uyo (Akwa Ibom), Benin City (Edo), Enugu (Enugu), Yola (Adamawa), Umuahia (Abia), Awka (Anambra), Asaba (Delta), Birnin Kebbi (Kebbi), Lokoja (Kogi), Yenogou (Bayelsa), Abakaliki (Eboniyi), Ado-Ekiti (Ekiti), Gombe (Gombe), Lafia (Nassaraw), Gusau (Zamfara), Osogbo (Osun), Jalingo (Taraba), Dutse (Jigawa), Damaturu (Yobe).

Languages spoken

English is used in business and public life. Hausa, Yoruba and Igbo are widely spoken.

Official language

English

Media

Press

The government controls the media through a media council, which has the power to discipline journalists and bar them from working. There are also strict laws of libel and an Official Secrets Act. However, the press is officially free and is often critical of the government. The News Agency of Nigeria (NAN), the country's only news agency, is government-owned but not official.

Dailies: At least 20 dailies circulate nationally. Three evening papers are published in Lagos and one in Ibadan. Principal dailies include the *Daily Times*, *National Concord*, *New Nigerian*, *The Guardian*, *Daily Sketch*, *The Punch*, *Vanguard*, *Daily Champion*, *Comet News*, *Post Express* and *The Tribune*. *Al Mizanr* is published in the local language Hausa.

Weeklies: There are several weekly news magazines, notably *Newswatch*, *African Concord*, *Abuja Mirror*, *Today* and *African Guardian*.

Business: *Policy* is a business and investment magazine.

Broadcasting

Radio: The government-controlled Federal Radio Corporation of Nigeria (FRCN) operates Nigeria's radio network. It operates an external service but reception outside Lagos is poor. Four regional zonal services broadcast in English and appropriate local languages from stations based in Lagos, Ibadan, Kaduna and Enugu. External services broadcast in English, French, Hausa, Arabic, German, Swahili. In addition to the national service, each state runs its own commercial radio station. FRCN is divided into five zones:

Lagos (English speaking);
Enugu (English, Ibo, Izon, Efik and Tiv);
Ibadan (English, Yoruba, Edo, Urhobo and Igala);
Kaduna (English, Hausa, Kanuri, Fulfulde, and Nupe).
External Services (English, French, Hausa, Arabic, German and Swahili)
Television: The Nigerian Television Authority (NTA) has 25 stations nationwide and claims an audience of 30 million people for its main network news bulletin at 2100. Several states also run their own stations. There are 14 companies operating private television stations.

Economy

Nigeria's economic decline since the 1980s has been one of the most spectacular in Africa, considering its size and potential. By 2000, the economy had become excessively dependent on oil, which supplied 85 per cent of trade earnings, yet still lacked the ability to attract the required foreign investment to allow the country's refineries to operate anywhere near their full capacity. The situation worsened in 2002, when Nigeria was forced to cut oil production in line with Opec's quota and did not benefit from the rise in international oil prices. The agricultural sector remained extensively subsistence based, while the manufacturing sector was dominated by light consumer industries and reliant on the government's inefficient import substitution policy and other subsidies. Foreign exchange shortages, low domestic demand and economic austerity have retarded the growth of all sections of the economy.
The most recent decline of the Nigerian economy is partly a result of the high level of corruption within the Abacha regime (1993–98), estimated to have siphoned as much as US$27 billion into private accounts. In 2001, the British government pledged to aid Nigeria to trace more than US$2 billion looted from the state by Abacha and his family. Other factors contributing to its decline are the economic costs of intense political conflict arranged around ethnic affiliations, poor management decisions, and the maintenance of a state-centred economy which hindered private investment and created excessive layers of bureaucracy.
In response to these failures, and goaded on by the relative success of regional rival Ghana in adopting structural adjustment, the Abacha government had tried to deregulate the economy after 1995. The government imposed tight monetary and fiscal constraints in an attempt to cut inflation, reduce budget deficits and establish a strong and stable currency. While the oil and gas sectors continued to grow, the non-oil domestic sector was hit hard by these policies, with retrenchments, lack of investment and reduced demand leading to poverty and crime. Much of the economy's infrastructure remain inadequate or crumbling as a result of insufficient capital renewal expenditure. According to the World Bank, around 70 per cent of Nigerians live on less than US$1 a day, despite the country being the world's sixth largest oil exporter.
Following the return of civilian rule, President Obasanjo has accelerated the pace of economic reform and sought to root out corruption. The country's economy is still blighted by the legacy of military dictatorship, with General Abubakar allegedly continuing to misappropriate funds right up to his handover of power in 1999. Meanwhile, the country has seen widespread violent protests against the oil and gas industries as well as a rumbling undercurrent of religious fundamentalism which has pitted the Muslim and Christian communities against each another.
The government missed its growth target of 3.4 per cent in 2000, with the economy registering only 3.0 per cent GDP growth. If the population growth of 2.7 per cent is taken into account, GDP per capita stayed relatively stagnant compared to the previous year. However, the government met its inflation target of 5.1 per cent. An extended one-year standby agreement allowing Nigeria to reschedule part of its US$22 billion debt to official creditors of the Paris Club expired in October 2001 after Nigeria failed to meet its economic targets for the previous year. In 2001, privatisation plans collapsed amid a period of serious social unrest. Economic growth however was maintained at 3.5 per cent, healthy for the West African region. In the long-term, Nigeria plans to diversify away from oil and concentrate on the energy sector as well as exploring its tourism potential. This can only be achieved however if the country is able to attract adequate foreign investment, which in the past has been a major challenge. The volatile domestic situation has succeeded in discouraging the inflow of foreign capital. Deregulation however, was the key theme at the start of 2002. Nigeria began the year by inviting international oil companies to bid to set up refineries in the country. Nigeria ended IMF monitoring of its economy in March 2002 and plans to implement, its own, home-grown economic programme.

External trade

Exports

Principal exports are oil (typically 90 per cent of total), cocoa, rubber, timber, manufactured goods.
Main destinations: US (44 per cent of 2000 total), EU (25.1 per cent), Spain (10.2 per cent), India (5.8 per cent), France (4.9 per cent).

Imports

Principal imports include fuel (because of the inefficiency of Nigeria's oil refineries), raw materials, machinery, spare parts, general merchandise, food, capital goods/aircraft and shipping vessels.
Main sources: US (50 per cent of 2000 total), EU (38 per cent), France (8 per cent), India (2 per cent), Spain (2 per cent).

Agriculture

The agriculture sector contributes between a quarter and a third of GDP and employs around half the workforce, but contributes just 3 per cent to exports.
The sector has suffered a relative decline because of the dominance of oil in the economy, but it is still the main area of employment and receives much official encouragement. Arable potential has been put at 25 per cent of total area, of which about 12 per cent is cultivated. The country suffers from soil degradation, deforestation and water pollution.
Key policies include food self-sufficiency and boosting non-food crops to meet demand from the agro-processing sector.
The sector is still dominated by unproductive smallholders raising subsistence crops such as sorghum, maize, cassava, yams, millet, rice and increasing quantities of wheat – up to 70 per cent of which is for their own consumption.
Plantations, sometimes owned by, or in partnership with, multinational corporations, are gaining ground in producing raw materials for company use (eg grain for breweries). Irrigation schemes, higher producer prices, the expansion of credit and improvements in the rural infrastructure are beginning to show positive results.
Cash crops include cocoa, rubber (nearly all exported), coffee, cotton and palm kernels. Cocoa is Nigeria's largest foreign exchange earner after oil, but the sector, which used to produce more than 308,000 tonnes in the 1970s, produces around 140,000–160,000 tonnes annually, about 6 per cent of the world supply. A lack of new planting has led to low yields, and disease is a problem. The palm oil sector which was a foreign exchange earner in the 1970s, is being redeveloped. Livestock farming is important, and poultry farming is rapidly increasing.

Industry and manufacturing

Production costs in industry are considerably increased by a lack of basic infrastructure, which compels every factory to have its own standby electricity plant and sometimes a water borehole. Companies also find it difficult to source vital components from abroad with uncertain supplies of foreign exchange, but this situation is gradually improving thanks to the liberalisation of the economy.

The most promising sub-sector is the textile industry, which has taken advantage of the country's production of raw materials, such as cotton. With growth in textiles, there has been substantial consolidation in the sector with many small operations being swallowed up by larger firms.

Environment

Drilling operations in the Niger Delta region have created huge pollution problems with over 4,000 oil spills since 1991. Oil spills and explosions caused by Shell's oil exploitation have been a fact of life for many people living in the Delta, particularly the Ogoni people. Shell has not shown significant response to the UN's recommendation that Shell clean up the environmental disaster created by the company's involvement in the region.

In June 2000, a Nigerian court ordered Shell to pay US$40 million for contaminating Ogoni land.

In 2001, there were fears of a cholera outbreak in the state of Ondo after water was contaminated by oil. Oil spills have left the water in the state unsafe to drink, forcing people to leave the area. Nigeria's pollution problems are exacerbated by the fact that the country does not have a pollution-control policy. The government was busy encouraging oil development activities in 2002, a focus which is likely to harm the environment even further. Analysts have reported that during oil prodution, Nigeria flares more natural gas than any other country in the world, contributing to global warming. The government hopes to end gas flaring by 2008. This is unlikely to be achieved since nothing has been implemented so far and the earlier target of 2004 was dropped.

Mining

Nigeria used to be one of the largest producers in the world of tin, with production based around the highland district of Jos. Production collapsed from an average of 10,000 tonnes per year (tpy) in the 1970s to 300 tonnes in 1995. Nigeria is now the smallest of the Association of Tin Producing Countries (ATPC). The country's only tin smelter is at Makeri. Tin reserves are estimated at 16,000 tonnes.

Independent estimates place iron ore reserves at 800 million tonnes, averaging 37 per cent metal content.

Deposits of uranium, lead, zinc, tungsten and gold are not yet exploited. There are 65 sites in Nigeria where gold has been located.

Hydrocarbons

The petroleum sector is the mainstay of the economy, contributing 20 per cent to annual GDP and 75 per cent to government revenues.

Oil

Nigeria contains proven oil reserves of 22.5 billion barrels, most of which is located along the Niger River Delta. Production averaged 2.14 million barrels per day (bpd) in 2000 and 2.23 million bpd for the first six months of 2001. At current production levels, reserves should last for approximately another 30 years. Nigeria hopes to increase production to four million bpd by 2010.

Oil production dominates the Nigerian economy, accounting for 85 per cent of foreign earnings. Nigeria is the sixth-largest exporter in the Organisation of the Petroleum Exporting Countries (OPEC). In April 2001, Nigeria agreed to a production quota of 1.99 million bpd.

Around 95 per cent of the country's crude production is through joint ventures (JVs) between the state-owned Nigerian National Petroleum Corporation (NNPC) and foreign oil companies. The NNPC takes a 50–60 per cent stake in the JVs, but many criticise it for not fulfilling its commitments. In the 2001 budget, the government allocated around US$3.5 billion for the NNPC's JV operations, an increase of US$1 billion. However, half of this increase was dedicated to settling outstanding arrears with contractors.

Oil companies sign a Production Sharing Contract (PSC), an arrangement whereby they are given a 10-year exploration period within which to locate oil. If the exercise is unsuccessful, their operating licences will be revoked. However, if oil is discovered the government pays production bonuses in US dollars equivalent to 0.2 per cent of the value of cumulative production up to 50 million barrels for deep offshore oil, and equivalent to 0.5 per cent of the value of cumulative production up to 20 million barrels of oil from inland basins.

The main catalyst for oil expansion is the rapid development taking place at four deepwater fields: Abo (block 316), Agbami (216), Bonga (212) and Erha (209). Together, these four fields have an estimated three billion barrels of recoverable reserves. Other offshore discoveries are made regularly. In 2001, Shell discovered a new field in block 212 southwest of Bonga Main and claimed that it was on a similar scale containing about 600 million barrels of oil. Shell produces 0.9 million bpd (45 per cent of Nigeria's output) and expects its share of output to rise to 1.4 million bpd by 2004. Unfortunately, most domestic companies are simply too small to be effective players. Despite the projected increase in output as Nigeria is a member of OPEC it may find that its quota will not be increased in line with its new discoveries and output.

A major development occurred in April 2002. Nigeria and Guinea agreed plans for oil exploration along the border separating the two countries. The two countries also plan to develop the Zafiro-Ekanga oil field which is thought to contain significant oil reserves.

Oil installations are frequently vandalised and company staff are taken hostage, resulting in major disruptions to oil production. Some of the attacks are politically motivated by people either opposed to the government of the day or those who resent the development of the oil industry and the uneven distribution of oil wealth to the federal rather than state governments. Illegal siphoning of fuel to supply the black market has resulted in a number of major explosions with hundreds of deaths each year. The government estimates that around 300,000bpd is illegally exported out of the country on the black market.

Gas

Proven and probable gas reserves stood at 124 trillion cubic feet (3.5 trillion cubic metres) in 2002, making Nigeria the second-largest African potential source of natural gas, after Algeria. Average annual production is 4.7 million tonnes. At this production rate, reserves could last for several hundred years.

Shell operates the Bonney Island Nigeria Liquefied Natural Gas (NLNG) plant, Nigeria's most ambitious LNG project and which supplies half the LNG output. The Bonny Island project involves taking advantage of the vast gas side-products previously flared off in most Nigerian oil production. By cutting gas emissions, the plant is also expected to improve air quality in the area. The plant is 49 per cent owned by the Nigerian Liquefied Natural Gas Corporation (NLNG) and 51 per cent by Royal Dutch/Shell, Agip and Elf. There are plans to add three LNG trains to the plant by 2005.

In February 2001, Nigeria and US ChevronTexaco, Conoco and ExxonMobil began feasibility studies for a new natural gas plant in the West Niger Delta. The plant is expected to come onstream by 2005.

Improved distribution could also expand the LNG industry. A pipeline from Ajaokuta-Abuja-Kaduna will supply natural gas to central and northern Nigeria. The Aba-Enugu-Gboko pipeline will supply gas to eastern Nigeria. The government of Lagos and the local gas company Gaslink Nigeria Limited (Gaslink) were developing a project in 2002 to supply nine residential areas in Lagos state.

Energy
Three hydroelectric stations and five thermal stations should provide around 5,900MW of installed electric generating capacity, although neglect and a lack of funding mean that actual capacity is only 2,000MW. The government's long-term objective is to increase capacity to 25,000MW.
Currently, it is estimated that only 10 per cent of rural households and 40 per cent of the total population have access to electricity. The government aims to increase total electricity coverage to 85 per cent by 2010 by building 16 new power plants and 15,000km of transmission lines. The development of hydro-electric power stations is hampered by persistent droughts ad funding difficulties. As a result the government is turning to developing a solar energy system to serve rural communities not served by the national grid.
In October 2001, the Electric Power Reform Bill was passed, allowing for the privatisation of the National Electric Power Authority (NEPA). The bill enables firms to takeover NEPA's functions and assets. It is hoped this will boost the energy industry and improve electricity distribution. In April 2002, Asea Brown and Boveri Limited (ABB), a Swiss-Swedish joint venture power company, won contracts worth US$44 million from NEPA for projects to upgrade Nigeria's electrical infrastructure.

Financial markets
The Nigerian Stock Exchange (NSE) was established in 1960 as the Lagos Stock Exchange and became NSE in December 1977. The NSE conducts its business on six trading floors spread across the country. It has branches in Lagos, Kaduna and Port Harcourt, with the bulk of business conducted in Lagos.
Most transactions are concentrated in the banking, conglomerates, breweries and food and drink sub-sectors. There were 194 companies listed on the NSE with a combined capitalisation of US$6 million in 2002.

Banking
Central bank
Central Bank of Nigeria (CBN)
Main financial centre
Lagos.

Time
GMT plus one hour

Geography
Nigeria is bounded to the west by Benin, to the north by Niger, to the north-east by Chad, to the east by Cameroon and to the south by the Bight of Benin (Atlantic Ocean). The main rivers, the Niger and Benue, merge in the centre of the country, dividing it into three main regions of north, south and east. The north consists of dry savannah, the south of dense jungle, with mangrove swamps nearer the coast, and the east of a plateau leading into the country's only major mountain range along the Cameroon border.

Climate
The climate varies from tropical on the coast to sub-tropical in the north. There are two main seasons, the rainy season from April to October and the dry season from November to March which is characterised by a cool dust haze from the Sahara known as the harmattan.
Average temperatures remain fairly constant throughout the year at 29 degrees Celsius (C) in the south. The average daytime temperature in the north is 42 degrees C, but the temperature can drop to as low as 6 degrees C at night.
Humidity is high in the south, with a maximum varying from 100 per cent to 80 per cent. Rainfall is heavy on the coast, ranging from about 180cm a year in the south-west to 430cm in the south east. Near temperate conditions are common on the central plateau and along the hilly north-eastern border with Cameroon.

Dress codes
Suits or traditional dress are worn for business meetings but otherwise dress is informal. Pure cotton, linen or feather-light wool are the best materials for the year-round hot and humid climate.
Women are advised to dress modestly, especially in the Islamic north.
For social occasions, dress as for a business meeting.

Entry requirements
Passports
Required by all. Passports must be valid for six months.
Visa
Required by all except nationals of Benin, Burkina Faso, Cameroon, Cape Verde, Chad, Côte d'Ivoire, The Gambia, Ghana, Guinea, Guinea Bissau, Liberia, Mali, Mauritania, Morocco, Niger, Senegal, Sierra Leone, Togo (all require an entry permit, however). Visas must be obtained in advance. A return or onward ticket is also required. Regulations regarding visas, transit etc should be checked carefully before travelling as they are liable to change at short notice.
Customs
Laws against exporting Nigerian antiquities are strictly enforced.
Prohibited imports
Sparkling wines are prohibited.

Health (for visitors)
Mandatory precautions
A yellow fever vaccination certificate is required if arriving from an infected area.
Advisable precautions
It is recommended to be 'in date' for the following immunisations: yellow fever (within 10 years), typhoid (within three years for injection; annually for oral capsule), tetanus, hepatitis A (within 10 years) and polio (within 10 years). Malaria prophylaxis is recommended.
Most visitors become ill through drinking unboiled and unfiltered tap water and after eating prepared food, particularly food sold in markets or by the roadsides, usually referred to as 'chop'. Food should be thoroughly washed before consumption, and only well-cooked meat, preferably hot, should be eaten. Dairy products made from local milk are to be avoided. Water precautions are essential outside of main towns.
Walking in bare feet, or even open sandals, can attract parasites, notably jikkers. Visitors should swim only in approved pools. Visitors should seek advice before accepting treatment involving hypodermic needles or blood transfusions. Medical insurance is essential and an adequate supply of personal medicines is urged.

Hotels
There is a wide range of hotels available, though rooms difficult to obtain and expensive in Lagos. Bills must be paid in foreign currency and a high deposit in advance is required to cover estimated length of stay. Most main hotels are air-conditioned.

Credit cards
Credit cards are not widely used.

Public holidays
Fixed dates
1 Jan (New Year's Day), 1 May, 1 Oct (National Day), 25 and 26 Dec (Christmas).
Variable dates
Eid Al-Fitr (End of Ramadan), Good Friday, Easter Monday, Eid Al-Adha (Feast of the Sacrifice), Mouloud (Prophet's Birthday).

Working hours
Banking
Mon: 0800–1500; Tue–Fri: 0800–1300 (some banks work until 1600 or 1700); Sat, some banks only: 1000–1500.
Business
Mon–Fri: 0800–1230 and 1400–1630. Some offices also Sat: 0800–1200.
Government
Mon–Fri: 0730–1530, some states also Sat: 0800–1300.
Shops
Mon–Fri: 0800–1200 and 1430–1800; Sat: 0800–1300.

Telecommunications

Telephone/fax

The service operated by NITEL is inadequate. The company has provided just 400,000 fixed lines for a population over 111 million.

Postal services

Internal services are unreliable. Air mail is slow.

Mobile phones

Mobile Telephone Network (MTN) Nigeria launched its service in Lagos in August 2001, extending its operations to Abuja and Port Harcourt in September.

Internet/e-mail

In 2002, it was estimated that Nigeria had 30,000 internet users. While this is low by international standards, Nigeria is one of the 11 African states to have over 20,000 subscribers. A number of internet bars have sprung up in the main towns.

Electricity supply

230V AC, 50 cycles.

Social customs/useful tips

Because of the prodigious traffic jams, called 'go–slows', which often grip Lagos, it is hard to be punctual, so both Nigerians and expatriates are generally tolerant of latecomers.

Handshaking is the common form of introduction. Smoking and excessive drinking are not part of the social norm. Gifts are welcomed but not essential, unless hospitality extends to accommodation and/or meals, in which case gifts are expected on departure.

Women enjoy significantly more freedom outside the Islamic north. There is considerable deference towards the old.

Appointments with government officials should be made in advance. With business executives, a more informal attitude prevails.

Gratuities are around 10 per cent. A service charge is usually added to restaurant and hotel bills. There is a custom of giving 'dash' or gratuities for other commercial services, which although officially discouraged, is widespread.

Security

Security remains a serious problem in several Nigerian cities, but chiefly in Lagos. During outbreaks of violence, the capital is likely to be dotted with checkpoints manned by armed police, where visitors should remain calm and courteous.

Getting there

Air

National airline: Nigeria Airways announced that it would resume London-Lagos flights from August 2002. The airline suspended air links with Britain in 1998 over security fears in Nigeria. The airline announced that it would add routes from Lagos to Jiddah, Saudi Arabia and Dubai.

Main airport: Abuja (Code: ABV), 35km from city; Kano-Malam Aminu (Code: KAN), 8km from city, duty-free shop, restaurant, bank, post office, shops, car hire; Lagos-Murtala Mohammed (Code: LOS), 22km from city, 2km from Ikeja, duty-free shop, restaurant, bar, buffet, bank, post office, car hire; Port Harcourt (Code: PHC), 24km from city.

It is advisable to be met at Lagos airport by someone you know. Do not give your passport to anyone but the immigration officer. Check in early for return flight because overbooking is common; British Airways allows passengers with luggage to check in at the airport from mid-day for night flights; those with hand luggage may check in early at its office in Victoria Island or at the Sheraton Hotel in Ikeja.

Airport tax: There is no airport departure tax.

Surface

Road: There are good roads linking Niger (Maradi, Zinder, Agadez, Niamey) to Kano, and from Benin; all-weather roads from Cameroon (Maroua, Mokolo) and Chad (N'Djamna). The southern road from Cameroon (Mamfe) to Enugu is not generally recommended.

Main ports: Apapa (Lagos), Port Harcourt, Calabar and the Delta Port complex including Warri, Sapele and Koko.

Getting about

National transport

Air: There are a number of local airlines providing intercity services. Routes and airlines frequently change.

If flying from Lagos, it is advisable to go to the airport and confirm that the aircraft is actually going to fly and that you have a definite confirmed seat before buying ticket. Beware of touts.

Road: A national road network system of 113,000km links all main centres. Principal main roads connect Lagos and Port Harcourt in the south with Kano and Katsina in the north.

Some secondary roads can become impassable during rainy season.

Buses: Coach services scheduled include: Kaduna-Jos; Lagos-Umuahia.

Rail: There are some 3,500km of railway, mostly single track.

There are two main rail lines: Lagos-Kano Express (via Ibadan and Minna) branches run to Baro, Kaura Namoda and Nguru, Plateau Express (Lagos-Jos); and Port Harcourt-Kano with branch to Jos and Maiduguri.

Water: Ferry services on the Benue and Niger Rivers, and along the southern coast.

City transport

Taxis: Taxis are widely available in Lagos and other main towns. The traditional taxis are usually yellow Peugeots in Lagos (these charge by distance), other colours elsewhere. Also numerous cars belonging to car hire companies. Taxi ranks are mainly found at the big hotels. Fare and tip should be agreed before starting journey. All drivers should have an Identity Card.

Journey time from Lagos Murtala Mohammed Airport to city centre is around 40 minutes.

Car hire

Available in most of the large towns through the main hotels. International driving licence and two passport-sized photographs required; chauffeur-driven services generally recommended.

BUSINESS DIRECTORY

Telephone area codes

The international direct dialling (IDD) code for Nigeria is +234, followed by area codes:

Abeokuta	39	Kaduna	62
Abuja	9	Kano	64
Akure	34	Katsina	65
Amuwo	1	Lagos	1
Bauchi	77	Maiduguri	76
Benin City	52	Makurdi	44
Birnin-Kebbi	68	Minna	66
Calabar	87	Owerri	83
Ebute-Metta	1	Oyo	38
Enugu	42	Port Harcourt	84
Ibadan	22	Shomolu	1
Ikeja	1	Sokoto	60
Ilorin	31	Yola	75
Jos	73	Zaria	69

Useful telephone numbers

Police: 199

Fire and ambulance: 999

Chambers of Commerce

Abuja Chamber of Commerce, Abuja (tel: 882-1555).

Enugu Chamber of Commerce and Industry, Trade Fair Complex, Abakaliki Road, PMB 734, Enugu (tel: 330-575).

Ibadan Chamber of Commerce and Industry, PMB 5168, Ibadan (tel: 710-021).

Kano Chamber of Commerce and Industry, 138 Ibrahim Taiwo Road, PMB 10, Kano (tel: 629-940, 620-165).

Lagos Chamber of Commerce and Industry, Commerce House, 1 Idowu Taylor Street, Victoria Island, PMB 109, Lagos (tel: 261-3898)

Nigerian Association of Chambers of Commerce, Industry, Mines & Agriculture, 15A Ikorodu Road, Maryland, PMB 12816, Lagos (tel: 496-4727, 496-4737).

Banking

Commercial Bank (Crédit Lyonnais Nigeria) Ltd, PMB 12829, Plot 146B Ligali Ayorinde, Victoria Island Annex, Lagos (tel: 262-5700; fax: 262-5699).

Ecobank Nigeria plc, 2 Ajose Adeogun St, Victoria Island, Lagos (tel: 262-0910/4; fax: 261-6568, 262-0920).

Investment Banking & Trust Co Ltd (IBTC), PMB 71707, IBTC Place, Walter Carrington Crescent, Victoria Island, Lagos (tel: 262-6520/40; fax: 262-6541/2; e-mail: IBTC@IBTCLagos.com).

Lion Bank of Nigeria plc, PMB 12852, 121/125 Broad St, Lagos (tel: 266-914).

Nigerian Industrial Development Bank Ltd (NIDB), PMB 2357, NIDB House, 63/71 Broad St, Lagos (tel: 266-3495; fax: 266-7074).

Savannah Bank of Nigeria plc, PMB 2317, 62/66 Broad Street, Lagos (tel: 260-0470/9; fax: 264-7332).

Central bank

Central Bank of Nigeria, PMB 0187, Zaria Street, Garki, Abuja, Federal Capital Territory, Nigeria (tel: 234-5333; fax: 234-5325).

Travel information

Nigeria Airways, PO Box 136, Murtala Muhammed Airport, Lagos (tel: 190-0470).

Ministry of tourism

Federal Ministry of Culture and Tourism, Area 1 Secretariat Complex, Garki, Abuja (tel: 234-2727).

National tourist organisation offices

Nigerian Tourism Developemnt Corporation, Old Secretariat, Area 1, Garki, PMB 167, Abuja (tel: 234-2764; fax: 234-2775; e-mail: information@nigeriatourism.net).

Ministries

Federal Ministry of Agriculture and Rural Development, Area 1 Secretariat Complex, Garki, Abuja (tel: 314-1185).

Federal Ministry of Aviation, New Federal Secretariat Complex, Shehu Shagari Way, Abuja (tel: 523-2112).

Federal Ministry of Commerce, Area 1 Secretariat Complex, Garki, Abuja (tel: 234-1884).

Federal Ministry of Communications, New Federal Secretariat Complex, Shehu Shagari Way, Abuja (tel: 523-7183).

Federal Ministry of Culture and Tourism, Area 1 Secretariat Complex, Garki, Abuja (tel: 234-2727).

Federal Ministry of Defence, Ship House, Central Area, Abuja (tel: 234-0534).

Federal Ministry of Education, New Federal Secretariat Complex, Shehu Shagari Way, Abuja (tel: 523-2800).

Federal Ministry for Federal Capital Territory, Area 11, Garki, Abuja (tel: 523-4014).

Federal Ministry of Finance, Garki, Abuja (tel: 234-4686).

Federal Ministry of Foreign Affairs, Maputo Street, Zone 3 Wuse District, Abuja (tel: 523-0576).

Federal Ministry of Health, New Federal Secretariat Complex, Shehu Shagari Way, Abuja, (tel: 523-0576).

Federal Ministry of Industries, Area 1 Secretariat Complex, Garki, Abuja (tel: 523-0576).

Federal Ministry of Information, Radio House, Herbert Macaulay Way, Garki, Abuja (tel: 234-6350).

Federal Ministry of Internal Affairs, Area 1 Secretariat Complex, Garki, Abuja (tel: 234-6884).

Federal Ministry of Justice, New Federal Secretariat Complex, Shehu Shagari Way, Abuja (tel: 523-5194).

Federal Ministry of Labour and Productivity, New Federal Secretariat Complex, Shehu Shagari Way, Abuja (tel: 523-5980).

Federal Ministry of Police Affairs, New Federal Secretariat Complex, Shehu Shagari Way, Abuja (tel: 523-0549).

Federal Ministry of Power and Steel, New Federal Secretariat Complex, Shehu Shagari Way, Abuja (tel: 523-7064).

Federal Ministry of Science and Technology, New Federal Secretariat Complex, Shehu Shagari Way, Abuja (tel: 523-3397).

Federal Ministry of Solid Minerals, New Federal Secretariat Complex, Shehu Shagari Way, Abuja (tel: 523-5830).

Federal Ministry of Sports and Social Development, New Federal Secretariat Complex, Shehu Shagari Way, Abuja (tel: 523-5905).

Federal Ministry of Transport, National Maritime Agency Building, Central Area, Abuja (tel: 523-7053).

Federal Ministry of Water Resources, Area 1 Secretariat Complex, Garki, Abuja (tel: 234-2376).

Federal Ministry of Women's Affairs and Youth Development, New Federal Secretariat Complex, Shehu Shegari Way, Abuja (tel: 523-7051).

Federal Ministry of Works and Housing, Mabushi Districti, Abuja (tel: 521-1622).

Other useful addresses

Economic Community of West African States (ECOWAS), 6 King George V Road, Lagos (tel: 260-0720/5).

Manufacturers' Association of Nigeria, 12th Floor, Unity House, 37 Marina, PO Box 3835, Lagos.

National Council on Privatisation, Secretariat, Bureau of Public Enterprises, 1 Osun Crescent, Off Ibrahim Babangida Way, Maitama District, PMB 442, Garki, Abuja (tel: 413-4660; fax: 413-4671; e-mail: bpegen@micro.com.ng).

National Maritime Authority, 4 Burma Road, Apapa, Lagos.

National Planning Commission, Federal Secretariat, Shehu Shagari Way, Abuja (tel: 523-6628; fax: 523-6625).

Nigeria Communications Commission, 72 Ahmadu Bello Way, :Benue Plaza, Abuja (tel: 234-2327; fax: 234-4593; e-mail: ncc@cyberspace.net.ng).

Nigeria Export Processing Zone Authority, 4th Floor, Radio House, Herbert Macauley Way (South), PMB 037, Garki-Abuja (tel: 234-3060; fax: 234-3061).

Internet sites

Africa Business Network: http://www.ifc.org/abn

AllAfrica.com: http://allafrica.com

African Development Bank: http://www.afdb.org

Africa News Online: http://www.allafrica.com

Africa Online: http://www.africaonline.com

Bureau of Public Enterprises: http://www.bpeng.org

Investment Banking & Trust Co Ltd (IBTC): http://www.IBTCLagos.com

Mbendi AfroPaedia (information on companies, countries, industries and stock exchanges in Africa): http://mbendi.co.za

Movement for the Survival of the Ogoni People: http://www.mosopcanada.org/index1.html

Nigerian Communications Commission: http://www.ncc.gov.ng

KEY FACTS

Official name: La Réunion

Head of State: President of France (Jacques Chirac)

Head of government: Prime Minister Lionel Jospin, represented by Préfét Gonthier Friederici (appointed Jun 2001)

Area: 2,512 square km

Population: 732,000 (2001)

Capital: Saint Denis

Official language: French

Currency: Euro ( ) = 100 cents (from 1 Jan 2002; previous currency French franc, locked at Ff6.56 per euro)

Exchange rate: 0.96 per US$ (Jan 2003)

GDP per capita: US$4,800 (2001)

GDP real growth: 3.80% (2001)

Unemployment: 35.70% (2001)

For the latest Key Facts, go to www.worldinformation.com

Réunion

COUNTRY PROFILE

Historical profile

The island was uninhabited until the beginning of the seventeenth century when Arab explorers called it Diva Margabin. The Portuguese renamed it Ilha Santa Apolonia, and the French settlers called it L'île Bourbon. After the French Revolution it was given its current name, Réunion.
1642 The island was first occupied by France and was ruled as a colony.
1946 La Réunion received full departmental status.
1974 It became an Overseas Department with the status of a region.
1992 Camille Sudre, a Frenchman, won the regional elections. The elections were annulled by the French and Sudre was banned from standing again.
1993 The Free-DOM party led by Camille Sudre's wife, Marguerite Sudre, won the elections.
1996 Unemployment reached 40 per cent.
1997 There were demonstrations due to social discontent.
1998 Paul Vergés was elected head of the Regional Council.
La Réunion is the headquarters of the French military forces in the Indian Ocean.
2001 Gonthier Friederici became Préfét in June.

Political structure

Réunion is an Overseas Department of France.
The French government is represented by an appointed prefect.
A Unicameral General Council is responsible for local legislation.
The 44-member General Council and 45-member Regional Council are elected for a six-year term by universal suffrage. There are five *arrondisements*. Five directly elected deputies are sent to the French National Assembly in Paris and three indirectly elected members to the Senate.

Political parties

Free-DOM (13 seats in the Regional Council); right-wing group (10); Parti Communiste de Réunion (PCR) (Réunion Communist Party) (nine); Rassemblement pour la République (RPR) (Gaullist Rally for the Republic) (seven); two factions of the Parti Socialiste (PS) (Socialist Party) (three each). The PS controls the General Council. The PCR, PS, RPR, Union pour la France (UPF) (Union for France), and Union pour la Démocratie Française-Centre Démocratique Sociale (UDF-CDS) (Union for French Democracy-Social Democratic Centre) each have one deputy in the French National Assembly.

Population

720,934 (2000)
In the decade 1986–96, the population increased by 20 per cent. The annual population growth rate was 1.63 per cent in 2000. Approximately 28 per cent of the population is under 15 years of age. Population density: 262 inhabitants per square km. Urban population: 69 per cent.

Ethnic make-up

The mixed population is of African (64 per cent), Indian (28 per cent), European (2.2 per cent) and Chinese (2.2 per cent) descent.

Religions

The majority of the population is Roman Catholic (94 per cent); there are also groups of Hindus, Muslims and Buddhists.

Health

Life expectancy was 73 years in 2000, with an infant mortality rate of nine per 1,000 live births.
Health services comply with French standards, with 1,268 doctors, 275 pharmacies, 17 hospitals and clinics (2001).

Main cities

Saint Denis (capital, population 131,557, March 1999 census), Saint Paul (87,712), Saint Pierre (68,915) Le Tampon (60,323), Saint Louis, Le Port, Saint André.

Languages spoken

French and Creole

Official language/s

French

Media

Press

Le Journal de L'Ile is a French daily published from St.Denis.

Broadcasting

The television service Antenne Réunion broadcasts on the island; Canal Réunion is a subscription television channel. Société Nationale de Radiodifussion et de Télévision pour l'Outre-Mer (RFO) relays radio and television services in French.

Economy

La Réunion is dependent on France for 75 per cent of its GNP.
Sugar-cane is the basis of the economy. It accounts for 70–75 per cent of export earnings.
Harvests are sporadically reduced by drought.

External trade

Exports

The main export is sugar (typically 75 per cent of total); other exports include molasses, rum, oil of geranium and crayfish. Main destinations are France and UK.

Imports

The main imports are agricultural, fishing and forestry products, processed agricultural products, fuels, intermediate goods, capital goods and consumer goods. Main sources are Bahrain, France, Germany, Italy, Japan and South Africa.

Agriculture

The agriculture sector contributes about 8 per cent to GDP and employs approximately 13 per cent of the workforce. Around 22 per cent of the land is cultivated.

Sugar-cane, the main crop, is grown on 30,900ha. Other crops include fruit, vegetables, maize, vanilla and tobacco. Ylang-ylang, vetiver and geraniums are used as components of aromatic essences. Other activities include rearing livestock, fishing and forestry.

Much of the island's food supply is imported.

Industry and manufacturing

The industrial sector contributes about 19 per cent to GDP and employs some 12 per cent of the workforce.

There are approximately 1,000 industrial enterprises of all kinds, but most industrial goods are imported.

The production of processed sugar and rum accounts for most industrial activity. The Ecopipe steel pipe mill (funded by the French government and South African private capital) started operations in 1997 at Le Port, on the west coast of Réunion. It has the capacity to produce 15,000 tonnes a year and employs 80 people.

Tourism

The number of tourists is increasing annually. There is a holiday village in Saint Gilles.

Energy

Approximately 66 per cent of the power is hydroelectric.

Banking

Central bank

Banque de France; European Central Bank (ECB).

Time

GMT plus four hours (winter); GMT plus three hours (summer).

Geography

Réunion is an island in the Indian Ocean, lying about 800km (500 miles) east of Madagascar. It is a volcanic, mountainous island.

Climate

The climate varies greatly according to altitude: at sea-level it is tropical, with average temperatures between 20 degrees Celsius (C) and 28 degrees C; in the uplands it is much cooler, with average temperatures between 8 degrees C and 19 degrees C. From July to November, temperature in high altitude places can drop to 10 degrees C during the day and to 6 degrees C at night. Rainfall is abundant, averaging 4,714mm annually in the uplands and 686mm at sea-level. The cyclone season lasts from December to April.

Summer runs from November to April with an average temperature of 27 degrees C. Winter stretches from May to October with an average temperature of 23 degrees C.

Dress codes

Generally light summer clothes are required, with some woollen garments for chilly evenings.

Entry requirements

Citizens of the EU can use a valid passport or identity card; all other citizens require a valid passport and a visa.

Health (for visitors)

There are no compulsory vaccinations. Passengers from endemic countries should be inoculated against yellow fever.

The drinking water is safe.

Credit cards

Major credit cards are accepted.

Public holidays

Fixed dates

1 Jan (New Year's Day), 1 May (Labour Day), 8 May (Victory Day), 14 July (National Day of France), 15 August (Assumption), 20 Dec (Abolition of Slavery Day), 25 Dec (Christmas Day).

Variable dates

Easter Monday, Whit Monday.

Working hours

Banking

Mon–Fri: 0800–1600

Business

Mon–Fri: 0800–1200; 1400–1800

Shops

Mon–Sat: 0830–1200; 1430–1800.

Some food stores are open on Sunday.

Telecommunications

Telephone/fax

The telephone network is entirely automatic and is linked to metropolitan France and the rest of the world via satellite.

Mobile phones

There is a cell phone network (SFR) and partnership agreements between cell phone companies. Most subscribers from outside countries can use their cell phones in Réunion (it is, however, advisable to check with the phone company).

Electricity supply

220V

Weights and measures

The metric system is in use.

Getting there

Air

National airline: Air Austral (Air France is a shareholder) operates scheduled services to Madagascar and the Comoros.

International airport/s: Roland-Garros airport, near Saint Denis (in the north), 5km from town.

The Pierrefonds airfield, near Saint Pierre (in the south) is being upgraded.

Airport tax: There is no airport departure tax.

Surface

Water: There are limited passenger services to the island. Cruise liners are more likely to call at Mauritius or the Seychelles.

Main port/s: Port de la Pointe des Galets (two ports: port Ouest and port Est).

Getting about

National transport

Road: A *route nationale* circles the island, following the coast and linking all the main towns, and another crosses the island from south-west to north-east linking Saint Pierre and Saint Benoît. There are 370km of main roads, 754km of secondary roads and nearly 1,600km of smaller secondary roads, all in good condition.

A French or international driver's licence is required to drive with the same highway code and right-hand driving as in France.

Buses: The island's bus service, called *Cars jaunes*, links most towns.

BUSINESS DIRECTORY

Telephone area codes

The international dialling code (IDD) for Réunion is +262; this is followed by another 262 and then the subscriber's number.

Useful telephone numbers

Available services for visiting cell phone users:

Emergency calls: 112 (free)
Telephone enquiries: 222 (call SFR for information)
Suberscriber services: 900 (local rate)

Chambers of Commerce

Chambre d'Agriculture, 24 Rue de la Source, BP 134, 97464 Saint Denis Cedex (tel: 212-588; fax: 210-617).

Chambre de Commerce et d'Industrie de la Réunion, 5 bis Rue de Paris, PO Box 120, 97463 Saint Denis Cedex (tel: 215-366; fax: 418-034).

Chambre des Métiers, 42 Rue Jean Cocteau, 97490 Sainte Clothilde (tel: 210-435; fax: 216-833).

Jeune Chambre Economique de Saint Denis de la Réunion, 25 Rue de Paris, BP 1151, 97483 Saint Denis.

Banking

Banque de la Réunion, 27 rue Jean-Chatel, 97711 Saint Denis, Cedex 9 (tel: 400-123; fax: 400-061).

Banque Nationale de Paris Intercontinentale (BNPI), 67 rue Juliette-Dodu, Saint Denis (tel: 403-030).

Banque Régionale d'Escompte et de Depot (BRED), 33 rue Victor-Mac-Auliffe, Saint Denis (tel: 901-560).

Caisse d'Epargne Ecureuil, 55 rue de Paris, Saint Denis (tel: 948-000).

Crédit Agricole, 18 rue Félix-Guyon, Saint Denis (tel: 909-100).

Banque Française Commerciale (BFC"OI"), 60 rue Alexis-de-Villeneuve, Saint Denis (tel: 405-555).

Central bank

Banque de France, 1 rue la Vrillière, 75001 Paris, Dept 75, France (tel: +33(1)4292-4292 fax: +33(1)4292-4500); European Central Bank (ECB), Kaiserstrasse 29, D-60311 Frankfurt am Main, Germany (tel: +49(69)13-440; fax: +49(69)1344-6000).

Travel information

Air Austral, 4 Rue de Nice, PO Box 611, 97473 Saint Denis Cedex (tel: 909-090, 488-020 (airport); fax: 909-091).

Air France Océan Indien, 7 Avenue de la Victoire, PO Box 845, 97477 Saint Denis Cedex (tel: 403-838, 488-086 (airport); fax: 403-840).

Air Liberté, 83 Rue Labourdonnais, Roland Garros Airport, 97400 Saint Denis (tel: 947-200, 488-384 (airport); fax: 416-800, 488-386).

AOM French Airlines, 7 Rue Jean Chatel, 97400 Saint Denis (tel: 947-777, 488-099 (airport); fax: 200-716).

Comité du Tourisme de la Réunion, Place du 20 Décembre 1848, PO Box 615, 97472 Saint Denis (tel: 210-041; fax: 202-593); representative in France: 90 Rue la Boétie, 75008 Paris, France (tel: +33 (1) 4075-0279; fax: +33 (1) 4075-0273).

La Maison de la Montagne, 10 Place Sarda Garriga, 97405 Saint Denis Cedex (tel: 907-878).

Office du Tourisme Syndicat d'Initiative de Saint Denis, 48 Rue Sainte Marie, 97400 Saint Denis (tel: 418-300; fax: 213-776; e-mail: ctr@la-reunion-tourisme.com).

Ministries

Direction Départementale des Affaires Sanitaires et Sociales, Rue Georges Brassens, BP 199, 97490 Sainte-Clothilde (tel: 486-060; fax: 486-008).

Direction Départementale du Travail et de l'Emploi, 24 Rue Maréchal Leclerc, 97488 Saint Denis Cedex (tel: 486-600; fax: 486-666).

Direction Régionale des Affaires Culturelles, 31 Rue Amiral Lacaze 97400 Saint Denis (tel: 219-171; fax: 416-193).

Direction Régionale de la Jeunesse et des Sports, 14 Allée des Saphirs, BP 297, 97487 Saint Denis Cedex (tel: 901-616; fax: 213-864).

Other useful addresses

Agence Nationale pour l'Emploi 10 Rue Champ Fleury, 97490 Sainte Clothilde (tel: 219-236; fax: 417-383).

Association of the Hotel Industry, Centhor – PO Box 6, 1 Route du Théatre, 97435 Saint Gilles les Hauts (tel: 553-730; fax: 553-729).

Association pour le Développement Industriel de la Réunion, 18 Rue Milius, 97468 Saint Denis Cedex (tel: 214-269; fax: 203-757).

British Consul, 94b Avenue Leconte Delisle, 97490 Sainte Clotilde (tel: 291-491; fax: 293-991).

Civil Aviation Management, 11 Avenue de la Victoire, 97489 Saint Denis Cedex (tel: 930-000; fax: 211-331).

Compagnie Générale Maritime (CGM), 2 Rue de l'Est, BP 2010, 97822 Le Port Cedex (tel: 420-088; fax: 432-304).

Conseil Général, Hôtel du Département, 2 Rue Source, 97400 Saint Denis (tel: 903-030; fax: 903-999).

Conseil Régional, Hôtel de la Région, Avenue René Cassin, Le Moufia, 97494 Sainte Clothilde Cedex (tel: 487-000; fax: 487-071).

Federation of Tourist Offices of Réunion Island (FROTSI), Résidence Saint Anne, 97400 Saint Denis Cedex (tel: 217-376; fax: 218-447).

Institut National de la Statistique et des Etudes Economiques, Service Régional de la Réunion, 15 Rue de l'Ecole, 97490 Sainte Clotilde (tel: 295-157).

Palais du Justice, 166 Rue Juliette Dodu, 97488 Saint Denis (tel: 405-858; fax: 219-532).

Préfecture de la Réunion, Délégation Régionale au Commerce, á l'Artisanat et au Tourisme, 2 Avenue de la Victoire, 97400 Saint Denis Cedex (tel: 407-758; fax: 407-701, 417-374).

Rectorat de la Réunion, 24 Avenue Georges, Brassens, 97702 Saint Denis, Messagerie Cedex 9 (tel: 481-010; fax: 481-366).

Société de Développement Economique de la Réunion (SODERE), 26 Rue Labourdonnais, 97469 Saint Denis (tel: 200-168; fax: 200-507).

Syndicat des Exportateurs d'Huiles Essentielles, Plantes Aromatiques et Medicinales de Bourbon, 38 bis Rue Labourdonnais, 97400 Saint Denis (tel: 201-023).

Syndicat des Fabricants de Sucre de la Réunion, BP 57, 97462 Saint Denis (tel: 216-700; fax: 412-413).

Syndicat des Producteurs de Rhum de la Réunion, BP 57, 97462 Saint Denis (tel: 216-700; fax: 412-413).

Syndicat Patronal du Bâtiment de la Réunion, BP 108, 97463 Saint Denis (tel: 210-381; fax: 215-507).

Internet sites

Africa Business Network: http://www.ifc.org/abn

AllAfrica.com: http://allafrica.com

African Development Bank: http://www.afdb.org

La Réunion tourist guide: http://www.la-reunion.web-france.com/

Mbendi AfroPaedia (information on companies, countries, industries and stock exchanges in Africa): http://mbendi.co.za

Rwanda

Guy Arnold

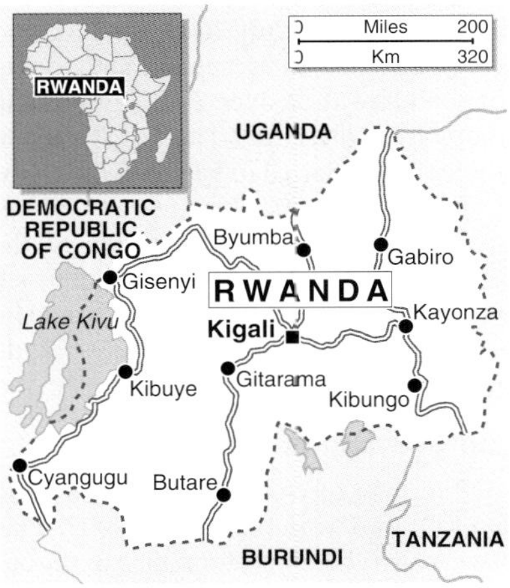

Returning the country to a semblance of political normality with local elections and the continuing aftermath of the genocide of 1994 formed the principal preoccupations of 2001/02. The pursuit of war criminals and trials should not become the overriding activity for any country, yet Rwanda has little choice if it is to exorcise the horrors of the past.

Local elections

The first local elections for 35 years were held in Rwanda on 6 March 2001. None of the total of 8,000 candidates contesting 154 district councils stood as members of political parties for fear of encouraging ethnic hatred. Instead, the candidates put themselves forward as independents and, according to officials, turnout was high. The elections marked the first step in a process of democratic transition, which should culminate in parliamentary and presidential elections in 2004. Human Rights Watch claimed that in 45 per cent of the districts, only one candidate stood for election and that some candidates were intimidated into standing for election against their will. These allegations were denied by the chairman of the National Election Commission (NEC), Protais Musoni, as well as Michel Moussalli, the special representative for the UN High Commissioner for Human Rights (UNHCR). Moussalli said that only 20 per cent of districts had just one candidate standing and claimed that the polls had been well conducted and that there was no evidence of intimidation.

On 16 May 2001, the government suggested that five political parties should be banned for 'having participated in inciting violence during the genocide and working illegally'. The parties were the Ecologist Party (Peco); the Rwandan Republican Party (Parerwa); the Rwandan Democratic Party (Pader), the Workers' Rally for Democracy (RTD) and the Progressive Party for Rwandan Youth (PPJR). In July, two other political parties – the National Revolutionary Movement for Development (MRND) and the Coalition for the Defence of the Republic (CDR) – were also banned for their involvement in the 1994 genocide. In August, President Paul Kagame carried out a minor cabinet reshuffle affecting four posts. In September the Transitional National Assembly voted to replace the former national anthem *Rwanda Rwacu* with a new one, *Rwanda Nzize*.

Pasteur Bizimungu

At the end of May 2001, the former president, Pasteur Bizimungu, was placed under house arrest when he was on the point of launching a new political party. However, he was released from house arrest in early June and in an interview claimed that he had been arrested in order to prevent him from forming a new political party, the Democratic Party for Rwanda. Three of the six founding members of the party had, meanwhile, defected, saying that 'promotion of ethnicity among Rwandans' was their reason for doing so.

Trials and prosecutions

The trial in Belgium of two Benedictine nuns, Consolata Mukangango and Julienne Mukabutera, on charges of aiding genocide in the southern Butare region in 1994 made headline news. The nuns, along with a professor, Vincent Ntezimana, and Alphonse Higaniro, a former industrialist and adviser to the late president Juvenal Habyarimana, were accused of taking part in the murder of 5,000 Tutsis. The nuns were alleged to have provided the Interahamwe militia with petrol,

KEY FACTS

Official name: Republika y'u Rwanda (The Republic of Rwanda)

Head of State: President Paul Kagame (RPF) (the first Tutsi to hold presidential office since Rwanda became independent in 1961; appointed interim president Mar 2000; officially elected president 17 Apr 2000)

Head of government: Prime Minister Bernard Makuza (MDR) (from Mar 2000)

Ruling party: Coalition: Front Patriotique Rwandais (FPR) (Rwanda Patriotic Front) (Tutsi-dominated); Mouvement Démocratique Républicain (MDR) (Republican Democratic Movement); Parti Social Démocrate (PSD) (Social Democratic Party); Parti Démocrate Chrétien (PDC) (Christian Democratic Party); Parti Libéral (PL) (Liberal Party)

Area: 26,338 square km

Population: 8.30 million (2001)

Capital: Kigali

Official language: Kinyarwanda, French, English

Currency: Rwanda franc (Rwf)

Exchange rate: Rwf507.25 per US$ (Jan 2003)

GDP per capita: US$206 (2001)

GDP real growth: 6.70% (2001); 6.0% (2002)*

Inflation: 3.40% (2001); 6.0% (2002)*

Balance of trade: -US$247.00 million (2001)

Foreign debt: US$1.32 billion (2001)

Annual FDI: US$4.00 million (2001)

* estimated figure

For the latest Key Facts, go to www.worldinformation.com

which was used to burn down a health centre where Tutsis had taken refuge, as well as handing over to the militia family members of Tutsi nuns. This was the first trial to use a 1993 Belgian law that allows charges to be brought for human rights violations committed abroad. On 8 June the two nuns were sentenced to 15 and 12 years respectively. Higaniro received a 20-year sentence and Ntezimana a 12-year sentence.

In April, the Rwandan government issued an international arrest warrant for Pierre-Celestin Rwigema on charges of involvement in the 1994 genocide, to be served in the US. Rwigema, who had been prime minister from 1995 to 2000, had been forced to resign amid charges of corruption and abuse of power, and had fled in June 2000 to claim political asylum in the US.

The war crimes issue would not go away. On 21 May 2001, the International Criminal Tribunal for Rwanda (ICTR) arrested one of its investigators whom it charged with genocide. Simon Nchamihigo had been working under a false name as a defence investigator but was identified by a witness at Arusha. He was wanted in Rwanda on charges as an organiser of genocide.

On 12 July, the chief prosecutor of the ICTR, Carla del Ponte, announced that three Rwandans had been arrested on genocide charges in three European countries. The men were Emmanuel Ndindababahizi, a former finance minister, who was arrested in Belgium, Emmanuel Rukunda, a former army chaplain, in Switzerland and Simon Bikindi, founder of the radio station *Mille Collines* which incited the massacres, in the Netherlands. Late in July, Protais Zigiranyiruza (the brother-in-law of the late President Habyarimana) was arrested in Belgium to face trial in Arusha. In September at the ICTR court in Arusha, the trial of the Rwandan clergyman Elizaphau Ntakirutimana opened. He was a senior pastor of the Seventh Day Adventist Church. His son Gerard was also charged on five counts of genocide. They were alleged to have set up safe havens for Tutsis and then invited Hutu death squads to butcher them.

In a move in early October 2001, Rwandans voted to elect traditional *Gacaca* 'justice on the grass' courts to deal with the huge backlog of people awaiting trial for alleged involvement in the genocide of 1994. Some 250,000 judges were to be elected to these courts to deal with lesser crimes such as looting and theft from 100,000 people in prison. The 10,000 alleged architects of genocide and rapists would continue to be dealt with by the normal legal system.

Hutu rebels

In late May and early June 2001, Hutu rebels from the DRC increased their incursions into north-western Rwanda. The government accused the DRC government of ordering these incursions. About 1,500 rebels, mainly youths, were killed or captured in the foothills of the Virunga mountains. A Hutu rebel leader, Pierre Habimana, was arrested in north-western Rwanda. A former major in the army, he was chief of staff of the rebel Army for the Liberation of Rwanda (ALIR) which had been carrying out attacks from bases in the DRC. It was possible that these rebels wished to return to Rwanda to avoid being disarmed during the DRC peace process.

Like its neighbour, Burundi, Rwanda was deeply implicated in events in the DRC. Developments there remained crucial to Rwanda. In July 2002, the DRC and Rwanda signed an agreement authorising the withdrawal of over 20,000 Rwandan troops from the DRC. The last Rwandan soldier was reported to have left the country in October 2002. It is feared that between 10,000 and 15,000 Hutus of the former Rwandan army may have returned to Rwanda, where their presence would be bound to destabilise an already fragile situation.

Improvement in the economy

GDP growth rose to 6.7 per cent in 2001 and followed a similar path in 2002. This was due to a better performance in the agriculture, construction and service sectors, and the government pursuing restrictive fiscal policies. The IMF has been assisting the Rwandan government to undertake economic reforms, primarily aimed at reducing the country's high current account deficit, which stood at US$6.8 million in 2000. In October 2001, the IMF provided Rwanda with a US$12 million arrangement under its Poverty Reduction and Growth Facility (PRGF) programme. Another US$5 million was approved in August 2002. Since 1998, Rwanda has drawn over US$67 million from the IMF to fund its economic reform programme.

In November 2001, the government announced in its 2002 budget that it would spend US$212 million on 166 economic projects, although the government stated that it would only contribute 12 per cent to the amount, hoping that the rest would be provided by international donors.

Outlook

President Paul Kagame remains highly dependent upon the new Rwandan army while his government is heavily dependent upon aid from the West. Further international aid will depend upon the continuing legal action against the perpetrators of genocide, maintaining a broad-based government and adopting a flexible policy towards the DRC. Kagame, therefore, walks a political tightrope between the extremes of maintaining a strong (autocratic) government that is able to deal with external threats from

KEY INDICATORS — **Rwanda**

	Unit	1996	1997	1998	1999	2000
Population	m	5.48	5.96	6.60	7.24	7.62
Gross domestic product (GDP)	US$bn	1.33	1.86	2.08	1.90	1.80
GDP per capita	US$	243	312	315	263	231
GDP real growth	%	12.0	10.9	10.0	5.9	5.2
Inflation	%	7.4	12.0	6.2	-2.4	3.9
Consumer prices	1995=100	107.4	120.3	127.8	124.7	129.6
Exports (fob) (goods)	US$m	61.7	93.2	64.5	63.3	69.1
Imports (fob) (goods)	US$m	218.5	278.2	262.6	249.7	222.3
Balance of trade	US$m	-156.8	-185.0	-198.1	-187.5	-153.2
Current account	US$m	-8.5	-62.2	-143.0	-72.2	-6.8
Foreign debt	US$bn	1.1	1.2	1.2	1.3	1.4
Total reserves minus gold	US$m	106.7	153.3	168.8	174.2	190.6
Foreign exchange	US$m	88.5	126.8	144.3	159.7	189.5
Exchange rate	per US$	306.82	301.53	312.31	333.94	389.70

Hutu extremists on its borders, balanced by a policy of reconciliation and national integration.

Risk assessment

Economy	Improving
Political	Poor
Regional stability	Poor

COUNTRY PROFILE

Historical profile

1899 Rwanda, which for a long time had been an independent monarchy, was absorbed into German East Africa.
1916 It was taken over by Belgium, along with what is now Burundi.
1918 After the First World War ended, the two became Ruanda-Urundi, a Belgian-administered trust territory of the League of Nations (later the UN).
1950s Belgian missionaries encouraged the formation of a modern Hutu identity.
1961 Rwanda's monarchy was abolished and a republic was proclaimed.
1962 Independence was granted.
1963 A massacre killed about 20,000 people, mostly Tutsis, causing many to emigrate to Uganda.
1973 Rwanda was run by President Gregoire Kayibanda, who was overthrown by Major General Juvenal Habyarimana.
1990 Some 10,000 guerrillas (Tutsi-dominated) entered Rwanda from Uganda and occupied several towns.
1994 The death of President Habyarimana in a plane crash in April, triggered the breakdown of civil society. About one million people may have died in the genocide of mostly the minority Tutsis by the majority Hutus.
In July, President Pasteur Bizimungu and a transitional coalition government were sworn in.
1998 In July, the United Nations Human Rights Field Office in Rwanda (HRFOR) was withdrawn when its mandate was not renewed.
1999 Local elections were held at the end of March. In June, the transitional government extended its term of office for another four years and the extension was approved by the cabinet in July. A draft constitution was promised.
2000 President Pasteur Bizimungu resigned in March and Paul Kagame was appointed interim president. He was officially elected president on 17 April in a joint vote of the Rwandan legislature and cabinet.
2001 A peace agreement was signed by Rwanda and Uganda in London on 6 November. A new national flag, emblem and anthem were unveiled on 31 December.

Political structure

Constitution

In June 1991, the amended constitution meant that Rwanda acquired a French-style political system with both a president and a prime minister.
The President is elected for five years and can stand for only two terms.
Rwanda is divided into 11 préfectures, each with a préfect appointed by the president. Préfectures are divided into sub-préfectures and then into 143 communes, each headed by a bourgmestre (administrator) who is also appointed by the president.

Form of state

Republic.

The executive

The president appoints the prime minister, who then appoints the cabinet; which approves decisions of the transitional government.

National legislature

Rwanda has a transitional coalition government until 2003, or until elections are held. The Assemblée Nationale du Transition (National Transition Assembly) has 74 appointed members (increased from 70 members in September 2000).

Last elections

March 1999 (local).

Next elections

2004 (parliamentary and presidential)

Political parties

Mouvement Révolutionnaire National pour le Démocratie et Développement (MRND) (National Republican Movement for Democracy and Development) (renamed former single party opposition) and its ally, the Coalition for the Defence of the Republic (CDR), were specifically excluded from the July 1994 government. The MRND and CDR were banned by the Court of First Instance on 5 July 2001, principally for their involvement in the 1994 genocide.

Ruling party

Coalition: Front Patriotique Rwandais (FPR) (Rwanda Patriotic Front) (Tutsi-dominated); Mouvement Démocratique Républicain (MDR) (Republican Democratic Movement); Parti Social Démocrate (PSD) (Social Democratic Party); Parti Démocrate Chrétien (PDC) (Christian Democratic Party); Parti Libéral (PL) (Liberal Party).

Population

7.62 million (2000)
Annual population growth rate: 5.2 per cent (1994–2000). About 41.5 per cent of the population is under 15 years.
Population density: 300 per square km.
Urban population: 6 per cent (1994–2000).

Ethnic make-up

Before the 1994 war, Rwanda was the most densely populated country in Africa, with a population growing at 3.4 per cent a year.
There are three ethnic groups: the Hutu (90 per cent) the Tutsi (9 per cent) and the Twa (1 per cent).
Some two million Rwandan Hutus became refugees in neighbouring Democratic Republic of Congo (DRC), Tanzania and Burundi, as they fled in fear of reprisal for the 1994 Hutu-led genocide of an estimated one million Tutsis. Mass repatriation efforts were complicated by screening operations, which were needed to identify genocide rebels from genuine refugees.

Religions

Traditional beliefs are still strong and operate alongside Christianity (Roman Catholic 85 per cent, Protestant 14 per cent) and Islam (1 per cent).

Main cities

Kigali (estimated population 390,000 in 1998), Butare, Gisenyi, Ruhengeri, Cyangugu.

Languages spoken

There are three official languages: Kinyarwanda (native Bantu language), French and English (adopted as the third official language in January 1996). KiSwahili is used among traders.

Official language

Kinyarwanda, French and English.

Media

Press

The government publishes the *Daily Bulletin (ARP)*, and weekly newspapers *La Relève* in French and *Imvaho* in Kinyarwanda. The church publishes the newspaper *Kinyamateka* and the children's newspaper *Hobe* in Kinyarwanda.

Broadcasting

Radio: Two SW and eight FM radio stations broadcast daily from 0500 to 0800 and from 1100 to 2300 in various languages including Kinyarwanda, French, KiSwahili and English.
Television: Rwanda Television is the only major broadcasting company in the country.

Economy

Most of the country's infrastructure was destroyed in the civil war and the number of people living below the poverty line grew from 40 per cent of the population to 70 per cent. The government estimated that the country required US$800 million to put the economy back together.
While growth has been strong following the end of the civil war, it slowed in 1999 and 2000 due to droughts, the high price of fuel imports and lower regional economic activity. However, GDP growth rose

from 5.2 per cent in 2000 to an estimated 6 per cent in 2001, due to increased economic activity in the agriculture, manufacturing and construction sectors. Rising fuel prices have been responsible for a hike in inflation.

By 2004, the government hopes to have reduced the fiscal deficit to 7.8 per cent of GDP. However, this depends on a reduction in the debt burden, improved government revenues and an improvement in the current account deficit.

The IMF withheld disbursements for the three-year recovery programme after the government's intervention in the civil war in the DRC. Donors delivered only US$30 million of US$56 million pledged and the IMF and the International Development Association (IDA) agreed to support a debt-reduction package under the enhanced Heavily Indebted Poor Countries (HIPC) Initiative in 2000. In October 2001, the IMF agreed to supply Rwanda with one US$12 million loan under its Poverty Reduction and Growth Facility (PRGF) programme. As part of the PRGF, the IMF is pushing the government to accelerate structural reforms to diversify the economy, professionalise the civil service and privatisation of telecommunications and electricity companies and tea estates.

The government's medium-term strategy has been to reduce the country's high current account deficits, tackle the burgeoning level of debt and integrate the Rwandan economy in regional and international markets. In the long-run, there is a need for diversification in a country where about 90 per cent of the population is engaged in mostly subsistence farming. Impressive growth statistics alone are not going to bring about full recovery in a country which has recently emerged from a genocidal civil war. Rwanda will continue to be the centre of international aid efforts for many years to come.

External trade

The external current account deficit widened from 15.3 per cent of GDP in 1999 to 16.8 per cent in 2000 due to weakening coffee export receipts, higher fuel and food import prices and a relaxation of monetary supply. On the advice of international financial institutions, the government is looking to restructure its economy to diversify exports while preventing excessive damage caused by fluctuating international commodity prices.

Exports

Principal exports: coffee (typically 70–80 per cent of total value), tea (10–13 per cent), tungsten and tin-ores and concentrates (5 per cent), quinquina, pyrethrum, cut flowers, fruit and vegetables.

Main destinations: Germany (17.8 per cent of 2000 total), Pakistan (7.9 per cent), Netherlands (7.2 per cent), US (5.4 per cent), Belgium (3.8 per cent).

Imports

Principal imports: food (typically 12–15 per cent of total value), machinery and tools (13–14 per cent), transport equipment (11–13 per cent), clothing (10–12 per cent), mineral fuels and lubricants (8–10 per cent), construction materials, semi-manufactures.

Main sources: Kenya (22.8 per cent of 2000 total), US (7.7 per cent), Belgium (7.1 per cent), Germany (3.8 per cent), Japan (3.8 per cent).

Agriculture

The agricultural sector contributes about 37 per cent to GDP and employs 82 per cent of the labour force.

The sector is the principal export earner. The main food crops are beans (17 per cent of cultivated land), sweet potatoes (14 per cent), sorghum (7 per cent), plantains, bananas, potatoes, cassava and maize.

Crop yields fluctuate due to drought, soil erosion and under-investment as well as social unrest.

Coffee is by far the most important export crop, mainly high quality arabica. Other export crops include tea (also of high quality), pyrethrum extract and quinquina.

Approximately 30 per cent of the land area is cultivated arable land, 31 per cent pasture and 9 per cent forest; tree planting programmes are under way to combat deforestation.

Coffee production 15,000 tonnes in 2000.

The Nile Basin Initiative (NBI) (signed by Egypt, Sudan, Tanzania, Kenya, Rwanda, Burundi, Uganda and Democratic Republic of Congo) is launching seven feasibility studies backed by US$140 million granted by the World Bank and donor governments in June 2001. It will also develop a parallel legal framework for shared water management. Ethiopia refused to sign and Eritrea's membership is pending.

Industry and manufacturing

The industrial sector contributes an estimated 19 per cent to GDP and employs 6 per cent of the workforce.

Industries include brewing, food processing, cigarette production, soaps, plastics, tin smelting and textiles. Growth of the sector is limited by the small domestic market, transport difficulties and irregular supply of imported fuels and raw materials which comprise 77 per cent of inputs.

Mining

The mining sector contributes 7 per cent to GDP and employs 1 per cent of the workforce.

Extraction of cassiterite (known reserves 90,000 tonnes) has been carried out since 1985, on an artisanal scale only.

Hydrocarbons

Rwanda has no upstream oil industry or refining plants and imports all its refined petroleum products from Kenya and Tanzania.

There are around 70 billion cubic metres of methane gas in Lake Kivu with a regenerative capacity of around 250 million cubic metres per annum. While the gas is being used by the Rwanda Brewery and Lemonade Company, South to South of Egypt has indicated it is willing to become involved in a multi-million dollar project to tap the gas.

Energy

The subsistence farming sector relies on wood and charcoal.

Urban areas and industry energy requirements are met by hydroelectricity generated by the Ntaruka, Mukungwa and Sebeya stations.

The Rusizi station has been developed with Burundi and DRC and generates more than 40 per cent of the energy used in Rwanda.

Plans are under way to exploit natural methane gas under Lake Kivu, which has reserves of more than 50 billion cu metres.

Banking

Central bank

Banque Nationale du Rwanda.

Main financial centre

Kigali.

Time

GMT plus two hours

Geography

Rwanda is a landlocked country in central Africa, just south of the Equator, bounded by the Democratic Republic of Congo to the west, by Uganda to the north, by Tanzania to the east and by Burundi to the south.

Climate

Warm, tempered by altitude. Rainfall is low and is concentrated in two seasons from mid-January to mid-May, and mid-October to mid-December. Average temperatures in Kigali range from 12–14 degrees Celsius (C) at night to 28–32 degrees C during the day. Cooler in the highland areas.

Entry requirements

Passports

Required by all. Passports must be valid for three months.

Visa

Required by all, except nationals of Tanzania and Uganda for a stay up to three months.

Currency advice/regulations
Import and export of local currency is limited to a maximum Rwf5,000. Import of foreign currency is unlimited but amounts should be declared on arrival, and export is only allowed up to the amount declared.

Health (for visitors)
Mandatory precautions
Yellow fever vaccination certificate is required by all.
Advisable precautions
Hepatitis A, tetanus, typhoid and polio vaccinations. Malaria prophylaxis is recommended. Water precautions should be taken. AIDS is prevalent. There is a rabies risk.

Hotels
Tend to be expensive in Kigali; cheaper in Butare, Gisenyi and Ruhengeri.

Public holidays
Fixed dates
1 Jan, 28 Jan (Democracy Day), 1 May, 1 Jul, 5 Jul, 1 Aug (Harvest Festival), 15 Aug, 25 Sep, 26 Oct, 1 Nov, 25 Dec.
Variable dates

Working hours
Banking
Mon–Fri: 0800–1200, 1400–1700; Sat: 0700–1300.
Business
Mon–Fri: 0800–1230, 1330–1700.
Government
Mon–Fri: 0800–1230, 1330–1700.
Shops
Dawn to dusk.

Telecommunications
RwandaTel remains the country's monopoly telecommunications operator.
Telephone/fax
The high quality digital telephone network has only limited penetration to areas outside the main cities.
Mobile phones
Rwandacell (SARL) provides GSM900 coverage, with investment from South African cellular operator MTN.
Internet/e-mail
With help from USAID, RwandaTel has established a full Internet service. ISDN and broadband services were being introduced in 2000.

Electricity supply
220V AC.

Security
At the start of 2002, the UK Foreign & Commonwealth Office (FCO) advised against non-essential travel to the north-west, and the border areas of the south-west, south and south-east of Rwanda. The threat of attack from rebel groups continues and despite the cease-fire in neighbouring DRC, the border regions are volatile. Local advice should be sought by those seeking to visit such areas, where a military escort may be necessary.

Getting there
Air
National airline: Air Rwanda
Main airport: Kigali-Kanombe (Code: KGL), 12km east of city.
Airport tax: There is no airport departure tax
Surface
Road: Roads from the Democratic Republic of Congo (Bukavu and Goma), Tanzania (Rusoma), Uganda (Cyanika, Katuna and Kagitumba) and Burundi (Akanyaru, Nemba, Ruhwa) affected by war

Getting about
National transport
Air: Air Rwanda operates internal services between Kigali, Gisenyi and Kamembe. It also operates to Entebbe (Uganda) and Bujumbura (Burundi).
Road: All cities are linked to the capital Kigali by paved roads, and the roads Ruhengeri-Cyanika and Kayonza-Kagitumba are paved. Other roads are poor with many being impassable in bad weather. There is danger of militia attacks and ambushes, particularly in the north-west and border areas to the south-west, south and south-east.
Buses: Reliable regular bus services are available from Kigali to the main cities and between some cities themselves. Private minibuses (belonging to an association called ATRACO) also operate between Kigali and other cities.
Water: Services run between Gisenyi and Cyangugu, on Lake Kivu.
City transport
Taxis: Available in the main towns. Fares should be agreed at the start of journey. Tipping is not necessary.
Car hire
Limited service is available in Kigali. International driving licence is required. All-weather roads are sparse and in poor condition.

BUSINESS DIRECTORY

Telephone area codes
Dialling code for Rwanda: IDD access code +250, followed by subscriber's number. There are no area codes.

Chambers of Commerce
Chambre de Commerce et d'Industrie du Rwanda, BP 319, Kigali (tel: 83-541, 83-537, 83-534; fax: 83-532).

Banking
Banque à la Confiance d'Or, BP 2059, Kigali (tel: 75780, 75763, 75761 fax: 75761).
Banque Commerciale du Rwanda SA, BP 354, Boulevard de la Revolution, Kigali (tel: 75591, 76117 fax: 73395.

Banque Continentale Africaine (Rwanda) SA, BP 331, 20 Kigali, Boulevard de la Revolution, Kigali (tel: 74456/7/8 fax: 73486.

Banque de Commerce, de Developpement et d'Industrie, BP 3268, Kigali (tel: 74143, 74132, 74427 fax: 73790, 74479).

Banque de Kigali SA, BP 175, 63 Avenue du Commerce, Kigali (tel:76931/2/3/4 fax: 73461, 75504).

Banque Rwandaise de Developpment, BP 1341, Kigali (tel: 75079, 75080 fax: 73569).

Campagne Generale de Banque, BP 5230, Kigali (tel: 86875 fax: 86876).

Union des Banques Populaires du Rwanda, BP 1348, Kigali (tel: 73564 fax: 73579).

Central bank
Banque Nationale du Rwanda, BP 531, Kigali, Rwanda (tel: 74282, 75249 fax: 72551).

Travel information
Office Rwandais du Tourisme et des Parcs Nationaux, BP 905, Kigali (tel: 76-514/5, 73-396; fax: 76-512; e-mail: Ortpn@rwandatel1.rwanda1.com).

Other useful addresses
Agence Rwandaise de Presse (ARP), 27 avenue du Commerce, BP 83, Kigali (tel: 75-665).

Economat Général (tobacco exports), BP 45, Ruhengeri.

L'Institut des Sciences Agronomiques du Rwanda, BP 138, Butare.

Office des Cafés, BP 104, Kigali (tel: 75-277).

Office du Pyrèthre au Rwanda, BP 79, Ruhengeri.

Office du Thé, BP 1344, Kigali (tel: 72-416).

Internet sites
Africa Business Network: http://www.ifc.org/abn

African Development Bank: http://www.afdb.org

Africa Online: http://www.africaonline.com

AllAfrica.com: http://allafrica.com

Harambee Afrika (UK business club for traders with east, central and southern Africa; includes annotated web resource list): http://www.harambee.co.uk

Mbendi AfroPaedia (information on companies, countries, industries and stock exchanges in Africa): http://mbendi.co.za

São Tomé and Príncipe

Nils P Mork

KEY FACTS

Official name: República Democrática de São Tomé e Príncipe (Democratic Republic of São Tomé and Príncipe)

Head of State: President Fradique Banderia Melo de Menezes (since 3 Sep 2001)

Head of government: Prime Minister Maria das Neves Ceita Baptista de Souza (from 7 Oct 2002)

Ruling party: Coalition government led by Movimiento de Libertaçao de São Tomé e Príncipe-Partido Social Democrático (MLSTP-PSD) (Movement for the Liberation of São Tomé and Príncipe-Social Democratic Party) (from 7 Oct 2002)

Area: 964 square km

Population: 160,000 (2001)

Capital: São Tomé

Official language: Portuguese

Currency: Dobra (Db) = 100 centavos

Exchange rate: Db9,019.70 per US$ (Jan 2003)

GDP per capita: US$313 (2001)

GDP real growth: 4.00% (2001)

Unemployment: 50.00% (2001)*

Inflation: 9.80% (2001)

Balance of trade: -US$18.00 million (2001)

Foreign debt: US$303.00 million (2001)

Annual FDI: US$4.00 million (2001)

* estimated figure

For the latest Key Facts, go to www.worldinformation.com

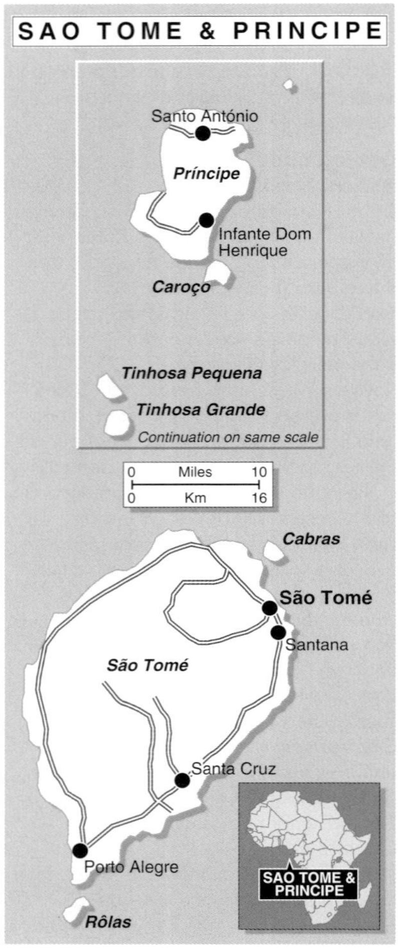

Democratic elections in July 2001 led to a prolonged political struggle in the tiny archipelago of São Tomé and Príncipe, but did not lead to social unrest. A new agenda of economic reform combined with prospects for future oil revenues herald the country's potential as an African 'tiger' economy, although the aid-dependent country's problems of corruption and mismanagement may undermine this aim.

Parties unite

It is often said that the real test of democracy is not elections, but a change of power. Accordingly, the presidential elections in July 2001 signified an apparent cementation of the country's dedication to democracy. Fradique de Menezes of the Açao Democrática Independente (ADI) (Independent Democratic Alliance), the party of the then president Miguel Trovoada, won an outright majority of 56.3 per cent. The result was a victory for those who favour a policy of openness for the former Portuguese colony in a mainly Francophone region. Widely seen as the embodiment of change in an otherwise conservative political landscape, Menezes is convinced that economic co-operation, trade liberalisation and structural reform are the keys to unlock São Tomé and Príncipe's potential.

President Menezes went on to consolidate his power, first by dissolving parliament in December 2001, on the grounds that it proved impossible to co-operate with the Movimiento de Libertaçao de São Tomé e Príncipe-Partido Social Democrático (MLSTP-PSD) (Movement for the Liberation of São Tomé and Príncipe-Social Democratic Party). President Menezes then dissociated himself with the ADI, still seen as a bastion of former president Trovoada, and formed the Movimento Democrático das Forças para a Mudança (MDFM) (Democratic Movement of Forces for Change) to run in coalition with the Partido de Convergência Democrática (PCD) (Party of Democratic Convergence). The election result was a draw between the MLSTP-PSD and the MDFM-PCD. In March 2002, the Supreme Court ruled that the MLSTP had won an extra seat. As a result, the president has come out of this power struggle with a broader mandate to effect change in this tiny island nation.

There were speculations of a regional agenda being played out under cover of the election. Angola, a traditional supporter of the MLSTP-PSD and would-be partner in the expanding oil developments of São Tomé and Príncipe, watched the elections closely and announced in June 2002 its intentions of closer military ties with the archipelago.

The prolonged political struggle temporarily disrupted the development of the oil resources found in waters adjacent to Nigeria. Relations with Nigeria grew closer in

February 2002 as it was announced that old border disputes were set aside in favour of the establishment of a Joint Development Zone, to the benefit of both countries. Under the accord, Nigeria will receive 60 per cent and São Tomé and Príncipe 40 per cent of the considerable revenues.

In August 2002, São Tomé and Príncipe announced that it had agreed to allow the US to establish a naval base on the island. It was reported that US and São Tomé and Príncipe officials had met in October 2002 to discuss enhancing defence and oil ties.

Eye of the tiger

President Menezes has remarked that oil opens more doors than chocolate, referring to the country's current major export commodity. The economy has struggled with a lack of economic diversification, depending on cocoa for 95 per cent of export earnings in an international environment of falling primary commodity prices. Combined with high debt servicing obligations and a history of poor macroeconomic management, the economy has been vulnerable to external and internal shocks. It has been highly dependent on external assistance, with up to 80 per cent of the national budget stemming from international aid.

A new government strategy aims at changing the situation. The cornerstone of a reform programme announced in February 2002 is the extraction of the country's black gold. The exploitation of oil is to be combined with the creation of export processing zones (EPZs) and new infrastructure developments to recreate São Tomé and Príncipe as a trading platform for the region. This is supposed to resemble the niche position held by 'tiger' economies such as Singapore and Taiwan, both of which offered their expertise and assistance to the government's scheme.

Already, international shipping companies have begun to deliver supplies to oil platforms in the Gulf of Guinea via the ports of São Tomé and Príncipe. Plans were announced in February 2002 for the construction of a much-needed deep sea port.

In June 2002, there were renewed efforts to combat corruption and improve transparency and economic governance. This was in response to criticism from the IMF in March 2002 that the archipelago's delays in structural reforms and public spending overshoots had derailed the country's economic plans.

Outlook

The most positive characteristic of São Tomé and Príncipe, and the reason why President Menezes' plans should not be lightly discarded, is its remarkable social stability – even in the face of political struggle such as from July 2001 to March 2002. Hopes for an oil boom – bidding for exploration of the reserves is expected to be held before the end of the 2002 – together with a recovery of the cocoa sector combine to create cautious optimism for the archipelago's future.

Risk assessment

Economic	Poor/improving
Political	Good
Regional Stability	Excellent

COUNTRY PROFILE

Historical profile

1469–72 The islands were first sighted by Portuguese sailors.
1485 The town of São Tomé was founded; Príncipe was not settled until 15 years later. The islands quickly became the largest sugar producing area in the world and used slave labour.
1700–1800 Coffee and cocoa plantations were set up using slave labour.
1875 Slavery was abolished, only to be replaced by a system of forced labour. The labour force consisted mainly of workers brought by the Portuguese from Angola, Mozambique and Cape Verde.
1974 The end of fascist rule in Portugal marked the beginning of freedom for its overseas colonies.
1975 The Democratic Republic of São Tomé and Príncipe gained independence from Portugal in July. The Portuguese had made no attempt to introduce education or health care systems for the local population; upon independence the literacy rate was 10 per cent and there was only one doctor in the entire country. The islands developed strong links with Cuba.
1990 The sole legal party was the Movimiento de Libertaçao de São Tomé e Príncipe-Partido Social Democrático (MLSTP-PSD) (Movement for the Liberation of São Tomé and Príncipe-Social Democratic Party) until a multi-party constitution was approved by referendum in August, allowing for direct and free elections for the presidency and legislature.
1991 At the country's first election the ruling MLSTP-PSD was defeated by the Partido da Convergencia Democrática-Grupo de Reflexão (PCD-GR) (Democratic Convergence Party-Reflection Group). The March presidential election resulted in Miguel Trovoada becoming president; he was an independent candidate supported by the PDC-GR.
1994 At the October elections the MLSTP-PSD was returned to office.
1995 President Trovoada's government survived a coup attempt by disaffected members of the military. The coup led to the formation of a coalition government of national unity which included members of the Ação Democrática Independente (ADI) (Independent Democratic Action), the Coligação Democrático da Oposição (CDO) (Democratic Opposition Coalition) and the Frente Democrática Crista (FDC) (Christian Democratic Font).
1996 President Trovoada was re-elected in July ahead of Manuel Pinto da Costa, the country's former Marxist ruler. In September, Prime Minister Armindo Vaz d'Almeida was replaced by Raul Bragança.
1998 Elections held on 8 November resulted in a victory for the centre-left MLSTP-PSD.
1999 In January, Guilherme Posser da Costa replaced Raul Bragança as prime minister.

KEY INDICATORS — São Tomé and Príncipe

	Unit	1996	1997	1998	1999	2000
Population	m	0.14	0.15	0.15	0.16	0.16
Gross domestic product (GDP)	US$bn	0.04	0.04	0.04	0.04	0.56
GDP per capita	US$	321	314	293	250	350
GDP real growth	%	1.5	2.5	2.5	2.5	3.0
Inflation	%	42.0	42.1	16.3	14.9	11.0
Exports (fob) (goods)	US$m	4.9	5.0	6.0	4.0	4.0
Imports (fob) (goods)	US$m	19.6	19.0	18.0	26.0	29.0
Balance of trade	US$m	-14.7	-14.0	-12.0	-22.0	-25.0
Foreign debt	US$bn	0.2	0.3	0.2	0.3	0.3
Total reserves minus gold	US$m	5.0	12.4	9.7	10.9	0.0
Foreign exchange	US$m	5.0	12.4	9.7	10.9	0.0
Exchange rate	per US$	2,203.20	4,552.50	6,883.20	7,119.00	7,978.20

2001 Fradique de Menezes won the July presidential election. A treaty establishing the Gulf of Guinea Commisssion was signed by five of the seven member states in July (Gabon, Congo, São Tomé and Príncipe, Nigeria and Angola).
2002 Preliminary results gave the two main parties – MLSTP-PSD and the Movimento Democrático das Forças para a Mudança-Partido de Convergência Democrática (MDFM-PCD) (Democratic Movement of Forces for Change-Party of Democratic Convergence) of President Fradique de Menezes, 23 seats each in the parliamentary election on 3 March; Uê Kédadji (UK) won nine seats. After a re-run, the Supreme Court ruled that the MLSTP had won an extra seat. In April, the MLSTP-PSD, MDFM-PCD and UK formed a coalition government.

Political structure

Form of state
Democratic republic

The executive
The president is elected for a five-year term.

National legislature
The Assembleia Popular Nacional (National People's Assembly) has 55 members elected by party list vote from 12 multi-seat constituencies, serving a four-year term.

Legal system
Portuguese legal system. The Supreme Court is appointed by the National People's Assembly.

Last elections
3 March 2002 (legislative); July 2001 (presidential)

Next elections
2006 (presidential)

Political parties

Ruling party
Movimiento de Libertaçao de São Tomé e Príncipe-Partido Social Democrático (MLSTP-PSD) (Movement for the Liberation of São Tomé and Príncipe-Social Democratic Party) (the two main parties, the MLSTP and the President's Movimento Democrático das Forças para a Mudança-Partido de Convergência Democrática (MDFM-PCD) (Democratic Movement of Forces for Change-Party of Democratic Convergence), each won 23 seats in the Mar 2002 election; after a re-run, the Supreme Court ruled the MLSTP-PSD had won an extra seat)

Population
160,000 (2000)
Annual population growth rate: 2.3 per cent (1994–2000). Approximately 39 per cent of the total population is under 15 years.
Population density: 151 inhabitants per square km. Urban population: 44 per cent (1994–2000). About 94 per cent of the total population live on São Tomé; around 8,000 people live on Príncipe.

Ethnic make-up
There are five groups among the islands' inhabitants: the Filhos da Terra are the descendants of imported slaves and Europeans (mostly Portuguese); the Angolares are descendants of former castaway slaves from Angola, now primarily fishermen; the Forros are descendants of slaves freed when slavery was abolished in 1875; the Servicios are migrant labourers, and the Ongas are their children, born on the islands.

Religions
Christianity (mostly Roman Catholic).

Health
Life expectancy: 65 years. Infant mortality rate: 65 per 1,000 live births (1994–2000). About 17 per cent of children were malnourished in the same period.

Main cities
São Tomé (population 42,000 in 1998) is the main population centre and capital.

Languages spoken
Fôrro and Crioulo are spoken.

Official language/s
Portuguese

Media

Press
There are two weekly newspapers including *Revolução* (official organ of Ministry of Information) and *Diário da República*. The weekend newspaper and magazine available is *Povo*.

Broadcasting
Radio: Approximately 25,000 receivers in use. Home service broadcast in Portuguese by Radio Nacional de São Tomé e Príncipe.
Television: There is no television service.

Economy
The country has one of the lowest per capita incomes and one of the highest debt ratios in the world. Primarily dependent on cocoa exports, the economy has struggled to diversify, particularly given the severe terms of trade shocks due to the fall in the global price of cocoa, the country's principal commodity export.
Construction activity related to the development of the oil, shipping and tourism sectors has helped buoy up GDP growth, which rose from 3 per cent in 2000 to 4 per cent in 2001. This has partly offset the effects of cocoa price fluctuations.
In the 1990s, the country struggled with high levels of inflation which nudged 81 per cent in 1997. However, by the end of 2001 estimated inflation had fallen to 9.3 per cent compared with 11 per cent in 2000. Under the country's IMF staff-monitored programme (SMP), inflation is targetted to fall to 7 per cent.
The country suffers from exchange rate instability, which is affected by the seasonal trade in cocoa, which typically represents 95 per cent of export earnings. The IMF estimated that the current account deficit, excluding official transfers, widened from 52.4 per cent of GDP in 2000 to 56.1 per cent in 2001. However, the deficit including official transfers narrowed from 20.5 per cent of GDP to 10.6 per cent.
The net present value of total outstanding external debt has fallen in recent years from 404.3 per cent of GDP in 1999 to 262 per cent in 2001 This has been due to the efforts made at debt reduction under the IMF and World Bank's enhanced Heavily Indebted Poor Countries (HIPC) initiative. Debt relief under HIPC is projected at 9 per cent of GDP between 2001–07. The IMF projects that debt service as a percentage of government revenue will be reduced to an average of 12 per cent during 1999–2009 from 44 per cent in 1999.
The discovery of vast oil reserves in the Gulf of Guinea is likely to fuel growth in the future, as the country's economy benefits from the development of the oil sector.

External trade
The balance of payments position depends on cocoa exports.

Exports
Principal exports are cocoa (typically 95 per cent of total), coffee, copra, palm kernels.
Main destinations: EU countries, particularly Germany and Spain.

Imports
Principal imports are consumer goods, food, fuel and machinery.
Main sources: Italy (typically 5 per cent of total), Portugal (23 per cent), US (10 per cent), France (7 per cent) and Japan.

Agriculture
Based on cocoa production (the islands were the world's largest cocoa producer at the beginning of the century). Prior to independence, production was in the hands of the Portuguese. Output slumped drastically after their departure in 1975, when 70 per cent of the plantations were nationalised.
There is a programme of returning cocoa-growing to the private sector, and government efforts to increase production are being intensified.
The second-largest export crop is coffee; other cash crops are copra, palm kernels, cinnamon, pepper and breadfruit. Priority is being given to the diversification of food crops in an effort to reduce the large food import bill. The country has mineral-rich farming lands due to its volcanic soil.

The country produces around 3,500 tonnes of cocoa and 18 tonnes of coffee every year.

Fishing

Fishing remains small-scale, but is being encouraged for local consumption and possible future export.

Industry and manufacturing

The industrial sector is limited to small-scale manufacturing concerns such as soap, soft drinks, timber processing, palm oil, bricks and textiles. The development of oil fields in the Gulf of Guinea is likely to increase industrial activity associated with the sector, particularly construction. In 2002, the government announced it was developing a number of export processing zones (EPZs) in order to exploit the country's position as a regional trading platform. These will give incentives to investors, with tax breaks and free movement of goods.

Tourism

The government has combined with the United Nations Development Programme (UNDP) and the World Bank to establish a tourism development strategy. Tourism is a growing part of the economy.

Hydrocarbons

Oil

The country's downstream industry is dependent on imported refined oil products. Oil-derived products supply 96 per cent of the islands' commercial energy requirements. Distribution and marketing of fuels is carried out by the state-owned oil company, Empresa Nacional de Combustiveis e Oleos (Enco).

In January 2002, Nigeria and São Tomé and Príncipe jointly established an authority to manage offshore oil exploration in the disputed Gulf of Guinea. The Gulf of Guinea, which lies between the two countries, is an oil-rich 180,000 square km area that has been contested by the two countries for years. Under the accord, Nigeria will receive 60 per cent of revenues and São Tomé and Príncipe 40 per cent. Both countries hope to offer between 20 to 25 blocks for exploration in 2002.

Energy

Installed electricity generating capacity is around 9MW. Blackouts are frequent.

Banking

Main financial centre

São Tomé.

Time

GMT.

Geography

São Tomé and Príncipe lies in the Gulf of Guinea, off the west coast of Africa. There are two main islands, São Tomé and Príncipe, and the country also includes the rocky islets of Caroço, Pedras and Tinhosas, off Príncipe, and Rôlas, off São Tomé

Climate

Equatorial with high temperatures and humidity. Average temperatures remain fairly constant throughout the year with a daily range from 20–32 degrees Celsius (C). Driest month July, wettest March

Entry requirements

Passports

Required by all.

Visa

Required by all.

Application should be made well in advance of visit.

Currency advice/regulations

There are no restrictions on the import of currency.

Health (for visitors)

Mandatory precautions

Yellow fever vaccination certificate is required by all.

Advisable precautions

Yellow fever, typhoid, tetanus, hepatitis A and polio vaccinations. Malaria prophylaxis should be taken.

Hotels

Very limited accommodation is available, mainly in the form of state-owned inns; there is one major international hotel – the 50-room Swiss-run Miramar.

Public holidays

Fixed dates

1 Jan, 1 May, 10 Jun, 15 Aug, 5 Oct, 1 Nov, [illegible] Dec, 25 Dec.

Variable dates

Shrove Tuesday, Good Friday, Easter Monday, Corpus Christi.

Working hours

Banking

Mon–Fri: 0730–1130, 1430–1630.

Business

Mon–Fri: 0730–1200, 1430–1800.

Government

Mon–Fri: 0800–1200, 1500–1800; Sat: 0800–1300.

Shops

Mon–Sat: 0800–1200, 1500–1900.

Telecommunications

Telephone/fax

Local telephone telegraph service described as good but international facilities are poor. 45 per cent automatic service.

Electricity supply

220V AC.

Social customs/useful tips

Business is conducted in Portuguese. Many executives speak French, and some speak English.

Getting there

Air

National airline: Linhas Aéreas de São Tomé.

International airport/s: São Tomé (Code: TMS), 5.5km from town.

Airport tax: Adult international departures tax includes an embarkation fee of US$20 and US$10 for children aged between one and 12 years, excluding infants only.

Surface

Main port/s: São Tomé (not deep water).

Getting about

National transport

Air: Restricted services link the two islands.

Road: There are only about 300km of roads, of which about two-thirds are asphalted, but the network is being improved.

Buses: Frequent, efficient service on São Tomé. Limited bus service on Príncipe.

City transport

Taxis: On São Tomé a minivan or collectivo shared taxi can be taken to anywhere on the island. There are no fixed schedules, they leave only when they are full.

BUSINESS DIRECTORY

Telephone area codes

The international dialling code (IDD) for São Tomé and Principe is +239, followed by subscriber's number. There are no area codes.

Banking

Banco Comercial do Equador, CP 361, Rua de Moçambique, São Tomé (tel: 21-898, 21-461, 23-761 fax: 21-989).

Banco Internacional de S Tomé e Príncipe, CP 536, Praça da Independência 3, São Tomé (tel: 22-991 fax: 22-427, 23462).

Central bank

Banco Central de São Tomé e Príncipe, CP 13, Praça da Independencia, São Tomé, São Tomé & Príncipe (tel: 21-966, 21-300, 21-269 fax: 22-501, 22-777).

Travel information

TAP–Air Portugal, Rua Patrice Lumumba, near Praça Indepêndencia (tel: 22-307, 21-432).

Internet sites

Africa Business Network: http://www.ifc.org/abn

AllAfrica.com: http://allafrica.com

African Development Bank: http://www.afdb.org

Africa Online: http://www.africaonline.com

Mbendi AfroPaedia (information on companies, countries, industries and stock exchanges in Africa): http://mbendi.co.za

Senegal

Vincent Foucher

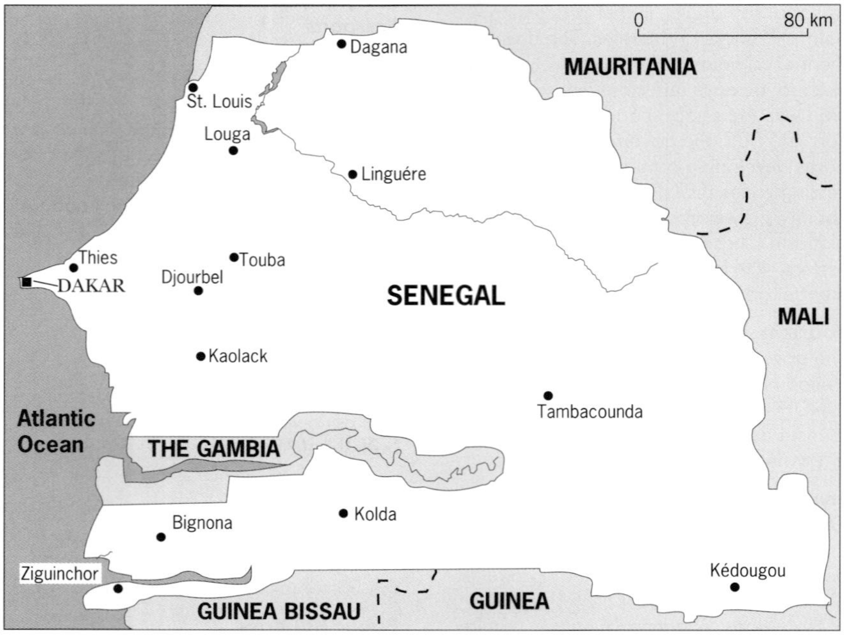

KEY FACTS

Official name: République du Sénégal (The Republic of Senegal)

Head of State: President Abdoulayé Wade (elected Feb/Mar 2000; sworn in Apr 2000)

Head of government: Prime Minister Idrissa Seck (appointed Nov 2002)

Ruling party: President Abdoulayé Wade's coalition, Sopi (Change), an alliance of 40 parties dominated by the Parti Démocratique Sénégalais (PDS) (Senegalese Democratic Party)

Area: 196,192 square km

Population: 9.80 million (2001)

Capital: Dakar

Official language: French

Currency: CFA franc (CFAf) = 100 centimes (Communauté Financière Africaine (African Financial Community) franc)

Exchange rate: CFAf629.73 per US$ (Jan 2003); CFAf655.95 per euro (pegged from Jan 1999)

GDP per capita: US$469 (2001)

GDP real growth: 5.70% (2001)

Inflation: 3.10% (2001); 0.7% (year-on-year, Feb 2002)

Balance of trade: -US$686.00 million (2001)

Foreign debt: US$3.50 billion (2001)

For the latest Key Facts, go to www.worldinformation.com

The local elections of May 2002, with a low turn-out and an increase in support for opposition parties, showed that the enthusiasm stirred by the 2000 election of Abdoulayé Wade as president was waning. Wade's party, the Parti Démocratique Sénégalais (PDS) (Senegalese Democratic Party) and its allies won a clear victory in the polls. However, the Cadre Permanent de Concertation (CPC) (Opposition Framework of Dialogue), the main opposition coalition which groups the former ruling Parti Socialiste Sénégalais (PS) (Socialist Party), Mustapha Niasse's Alliance des Forces du Progrès (AFP) (Alliance of Progressive Forces) and a number of smaller parties, managed to secure a third of rural and municipal councils and two of the nine regional councils.

Casamance: low-intensity chaos

The separatist Mouvement des Forces Démocratiques de Casamance (MFDC) (Democratic Forces of Casamance Movement) weakened in 2001, but this simply added to the complexity of the problem and made peace more elusive. In mid-2001, MFDC hardliners headed by Salif Sadio and Casamançais refugees were driven from the border with Guinea-Bissau. Meanwhile, Guinea-Bissau's President Kumba Yala formed an alliance with MFDC moderates, led by Father Augustin Diamacoune Senghor. Consequently, the southern region of Lower Casamance progressively went quiet, while troubles renewed north of the river, where partisans of Salif Sadio took refuge.

There are clear indications that bandits from northern Senegal, The Gambia and Guinea-Bissau also operate in Casamance. In the context of the poor security situation, armed banditry and drug-trafficking proliferated in 2001–02. The complexity of the military situation was made worse by the renewal of long-standing tensions between Father Diamacoune and Sidy Badji, former head of the military wing of the MFDC. In a MFDC conference in Banjul, The Gambia, in August 2001, Badji tried to marginalise Diamacoune, but his move failed. In November, Jean-Marie François Biagui, the secretary general, formed an alliance with Diamacoune and succeeded in thwarting Badji's bid for the MFDC leadership.

Localised security problems were also affected by the factionalism within the Casamance movement. The North Front, an MFDC splinter group led by Kamougué Diatta, resumed its military activities, carrying out massive assaults on Kafountine in March 2002 and Diouloulou in April 2002. This was in response to Senegalese troops pursuing MFDC partisans loyal to Sadio over land granted to the North Front. These attacks and the army's heavy-handed counter-attacks pushed thousands of refugees beyond the Gambian border.

War and regional affairs

The regionalised nature of the Casamance conflict has led to frictions with the neighbouring states of The Gambia and Guinea-Bissau, which it has accused of sponsoring MFDC rebels. Relations with Guinea-Bissau have improved since the election of President Kumba Yalla, who has helped scale down rebel activity in southern Casamance. However, arguments with The Gambia persist, with Senegal alleging that Gambian support for the MFDC has perpetuated conflict in northern Casamance. The Gambia is host to some 4,000 Senegalese refugees who have fled the Casamance conflict; hundreds of villagers from Casamance fled to The Gambia in mid-2002 following the military attacks on Kafountine and Diouloulou. The government's operations against the MFDC have inflamed tensions with The Gambia, with reports of frequent incursions by the Senegalese military on Gambian territory.

In November 2002, The Gambia and Senegal clashed over a decision by the Senegalese Transport Association to close the border between the two countries. The Senegalese government gave The Gambia a list of demands, including the construction of a bridge at Bambatenda-Yillitenda and a total review of the country's transport laws. As Senegal completely surrounds The Gambia (except for The Gambia's 80km coastline), the border dispute is having a detrimental effect on the Gambian economy and is likely to heighten tensions between the two countries.

Government capsizes

The political climate was stirred up following the capsizing of a Senegalese ferry, the MV Le Joola, off the coast of The Gambia in September 2002, killing over 1,000 people. The incident was described as Senegal's worst disaster in modern history and had serious political repercussions for the government. A commission of inquiry reported in November 2002 that a delay in the military's rescue efforts led to the death of many of the disaster's victims. Investigations also concluded that the ferry was over-loaded and that the crew failed to observe proper safety procedures.

President Wade sacked his entire government in November 2002 over its handling of the disaster, following Prime Minister Madior Boye's failure to accept government responsibility. Wade appointed Idrissa Seck as prime minister in a move that was seen as an attempt by Wade to tighten his control of the PDS-led coalition government. Before becoming prime minister, Seck was director of the president's office, minister without portfolio and deputy secretary-general of the PDS. His appointment as head of government appeared to confirm his position as Wade's hand-picked successor.

Wade's international activism

President Wade has been keen to portray himself as one of a new wave of African leaders committed to regional integration, economic reform and political liberalisation. He has played a leading role in the New Partnership for Africa's Development (Nepad), a programme signed by African leaders in October 2001. Nepad pledges IMF-style economic policies and democratisation in return for development aid from the G8 group of industrialised countries. Wade also intervened in the political crisis in Madagascar and in April 2002 he brokered a deal between Didier Ratsiraka and Marc Ravalomanana, who had both claimed the presidency.

Although the deal did not result in lasting peace, it did show Wade's intention to support peer review mechanisms within the African Union (AU). Under Wade, Senegal has maintained a high profile in West Africa's two main regional groupings: the Union Economique et Monetaire Ouest Africaine (UEMOA) (West African Economic and Monetary Union) and the Economic Community of West African States (Ecowas).

Stormy waters

Although President Wade is held in high esteem by the French government, particularly due to the links between the PDS and France's ruling Rassemblement pour la République (RPR) (Rally for the Republic) party, Senegal's relations with the EU were marred by a dispute over fishing rights. In January 2002, Senegal refused to extend a fishing rights accord which had allowed EU vessels to fish in Senegalese waters since 1997. The EU and Senegal clashed over which areas should be fished and the length of the rest periods, which are essential for fish stock recovery. The Senegalese authorities have raised the problem of over-fishing and illegal methods employed by EU trawlers, which is causing fish stocks to plummet and has put Senegalese fishermen's livelihoods at risk; around 600,000 people in Senegal depend on the fishing industry, the country's largest export earner, for an income. In June 2002, the EU agreed to pay Senegal 64 million (US$62 million) for the right to exploit its fishing grounds until 2006. The deal bans pelagic fishing, in which a net is dragged by two trawlers

KEY INDICATORS — Senegal

	Unit	1996	1997	1998	1999	2000
Population	m	8.80	9.04	9.28	9.28	9.52
Gross domestic product (GDP)	US$bn	4.68	4.43	4.65	4.70	4.40
GDP per capita	US$	530	540	520	511	462
GDP real growth	%	5.1	5.0	5.7	5.1	5.6
Inflation	%	2.8	1.7	1.1	0.8	0.7
Exports (fob) (goods)	US$m	986.0	932.0	956.0	1,027.1	997.0
Imports (fob) (goods)	US$m	1,268.0	1,196.0	1,238.0	1,372.8	1,500.0
Balance of trade	US$m	-282.0	-264.0	-282.0	-345.8	-503.0
Current account	US$m	-199.5	-184.8	-247.5	-320.2	-380.0
Foreign debt	US$bn	3.7	3.7	3.9	3.7	3.4
Total reserves minus gold	US$m	288.3	386.2	430.8	402.9	383.5
Foreign exchange	US$m	284.8	383.9	428.4	398.5	380.8
Exchange rate	per US$	511.55	583.67	589.95	615.70	711.98

resulting in significant wastage, and imposes a two-month rest period. Conservationists dismissed the deal, claiming it would continue to seriously undermine fish stocks and local livelihoods.

Restructuring the economy

Economic prospects for Senegal were good throughout 2001 and 2002. In 2001, Senegal registered GDP growth of 5.7 per cent and low inflation at 3 per cent. Despite renewed fears of a devaluation, the Communauté Financière Africaine (African Financial Community) franc (CFA franc) went unaffected by the adoption of the euro, with which it has been pegged at a rate of CFAf655.95 per since January 1999. The euro's gain in value against the US dollar during 2002 did not significantly affect Senegal's competitiveness in its external markets, which mainly consist of West African and European states.

Senegal has good relationships with international aid donors and receives more aid money than it can efficiently spend. The World Bank has consequently expressed its disappointment with Senegal. Even so, by mid-2002, Senegal was in the process of securing substantial loans under a three-year Poverty Reduction and Growth Facility (PRGF) with the IMF.

Under the Wade government, privatisation has gone ahead with mixed results. The national air company, Air Sénégal International, has done extremely well since its takeover by Royal Air Maroc in November 2000. Sonatel, the national phone company, controlled by France Télécom, has developed since its privatisation in 1997, particularly in the mobile phone sector. In 2001, there were more than 200,000 mobile phones operating in Senegal. On the other hand, the privatisation of Sénélec, the national electricity company, was delayed. An agreement signed with Vivendi in November 2001 was abandoned in February 2002 after the company failed to raise the necessary cash for the purchase due to falling confidence in infrastructural investments in Africa.

Unbalanced economy

Another sector where privatisation has been problematic is the marketing of groundnuts, Senegal's main cash crop. The dissolution of Sonagraines, the state-owned company that organised the collection and transportation of groundnuts, and the reorganisation of Sonacos, the country's groundnut oil processor, resulted in serious difficulties in the handling of the record groundnut production.

Groundnut production, which totalled 1.2 million tonnes in 2001/02, is no longer as dominant as it used to be and the Senegalese economy still depends on the phosphates, tourism and fishing sectors. Despite the war in Casamance, tourism has been booming in Senegal. There are plans to develop tourism from the present 500,000 tourists a year to more than 1.5 million. Phosphates, in which Indian companies are heavily involved, is another expanding sector and known reserves are abundant.

The key problem with the Senegalese economy is the lack of industrial development, although Senegal now enjoys a favourable international image. Standard and Poor's confirmed in 2002 its previous rating of B in the short-term and B+ in the long-term. There are some encouraging signs and private investments have come from, among others, Mauritian textile producers and South African mining companies in 2001/02.

Outlook

With a clear victory in the local elections, Abdoulayé Wade's mandate is secure. His problem will be to deliver the goods and to convince both the people and his international partners that Senegal can provide proper governance and economic welfare. Wade's position is bolstered by a favourable economic situation and an excellent international image. But he will have to check his own authoritarian tendencies, which have been tempered by his remarkable political opportunism.

The crisis in Casamance is another major liability and although the separatist cause has definitely lost its popular appeal, the rebels could keep fighting for a long time. The internal situation in both the Gambia and Guinea-Bissau will also remain major influences on the situation in Casamance.

Risk assessment

Economic	Good
Political	Good
Regional stability	Satisfactory

COUNTRY PROFILE

Historical profile

As a consequence of the fading of the Empire of Ghana which encompassed a large part of Senegal, many kingdoms developed and flourished from the thirteenth to the fourteenth centuries in Senegal's current territory: Djolof, Fouta, Cayor, Baol, Sine, Saloum. Portuguese traders made contact in the fifteenth century. They were displaced by the British, French and Dutch in the sixteenth century who all attempted to gain control of strategic points on the slave trade routes to America. By the end of the nineteenth century France controlled the whole of Senegal.

1960 Gained independence from France in June as part of the Federation of Mali, which collapsed due to misunderstandings between the political leaders of the two territories (former French Soudan and Senegal); independent Senegal was proclaimed in September 1960 under President Leopold Senghor.

1981 President Abdou Diouf first took office.

1982 Fighting commenced in Casamance between the Movement des Forces Démocratiques de Casamance (MFDC) (Democratic Forces of Casamance Móvement), a separatist movement, and the Senegalese government troops.

1983 Senegal's second multi-party elections (the previous election was held in 1978) saw the ruling Parti Socialiste Sénégalais (PS) (Senegal Socialist Party) returned to power with an overwhelming majority.

1993 Diouf was re-elected in February.

1998 The 24 May parliamentary elections resulted in a landslide victory for the PS.

2000 The February/March presidential elections were won by Abdoulayé Wade, ending Abdou Diouf's reign as head of state since 1981. Moustapha Niasse (AFP) was appointed prime minister by the president in April.

2001 More than 90 per cent voted for a new constitution which was adopted on 7 January. Moustapha Niasse was dismissed by the president in March and was replaced as prime minister by a judge, Madame Madior Boyé. President Abdoulayé Wade's coalition, Sopi (Change), won 90 of the 120 seats in the 29 April 2001elections. The PS which has dominated parliament since 1960, came third, with 10 seats.

2002 In June, the EU paid US$63 million to enable EU fishing trawlers to exploit Senegalese waters until 2006.

Political structure

Constitution

The 7 January 2001 constitution adopted by referendum allows for the formation of opposition parties, gives enhanced status to the prime minister and reduces the president's term of office from seven years to five. It also gives the president power to dissolve the reduced 120-seat National Assembly after it has served for two years.

Form of state

Republic

The executive

Executive power is vested in the president who is head of state, and commander-in-chief of the armed forces. The president is directly elected by universal

adult suffrage, for a five-year term (reduced from seven years in the 2001 constitution).
In the event of the presidency falling vacant, the president of the National Assembly automatically becomes head of state.

National legislature
Legislative power is held by the 120-member National Assembly. The prime minister is appointed by the president and the Council of Ministers is appointed by the prime minister in consultation with the president.

Legal system
The members of the Supreme Court of Justice are appointed by the president, on the advice of the Superior Court of Magistrates, which determines the constitutionality of laws. The High Court of Justice is appointed by the National Assembly from its members; it has power to impeach the president or members of the government.

Last elections
27 February/19 March 2000 (presidential); 29 April 2001 (parliamentary).

Next elections
2006 (parliamentary); 2005 (presidential).

Political parties

Ruling party
President Abdoulayé Wade's coalition, Sopi (Change), an alliance of 40 parties dominated by the Parti Démocratique Sénégalais (PDS) (Senegalese Democratic Party).

Main opposition party
Parti Socialiste Sénégalais (PS) (Socialist Party) (10 seats in the 29 April 2001 election).

Population
9.52 million (2000) 10.05 million (2002)
The annual population growth rate was 2.7 per cent during 1994–2000. Around 47 per cent of the total population is under 15 years of age.
Population density: 45 inhabitants per square km. Urban population: 45 per cent (1994–2000).

Ethnic make-up
Wolof (36 per cent), Fulani (17 per cent), Serer (17 per cent).

Religions
Muslim (92 per cent), Christian (mainly Roman Catholic) (5 per cent), indigenous beliefs (3 per cent).

Education
Adult illiteracy is 52.7 per cent for men and 72.3 per cent for women. The government is pursuing a broad based programme to eliminate illiteracy by 2010. Primary education is provided free of charge and is officially compulsory for children between the ages of six and 12. At the age of 13, children can choose between middle schools, which continue for four years, or higher schools, which take students on to the baccalauréat at age 18. Middle schools concentrate on technical subjects, particularly agriculture. Baccalauréat students can continue to Dakar University or the smaller university at Sanar near Saint Louis.

Health
World Bank estimates during the period 1994 and 2000 showed that the average life expectancy was 52 years and the infant mortality rate stood at 68 per 1,000 live births. It is estimated that 22 per cent of children under the age of five were malnourished in the same period World Bank estimates in 2000 showed that 78 per cent and 70 per cent of the population had access to improved water and sanitation facilities respectively. There are 0.1 physicians and 0.4 hospital beds typically available per 1,000 people.
There are an estimated 79,000 people suffering from HIV/AIDS, of which 3,300 are under the age of 15 years.
According to World Bank estimates, government expenditure on healthcare averaged 4.5 per cent of GDP of which 2.6 per cent was public expenditure between 1990 and 1998. Expenditure on private healthcare (such as private household expenditure and insurance) averaged 1.9 per cent of GDP over the same period.

Welfare
Most Senegalese are heavily indebted and poverty stricken. According to the World Bank, around 26 per cent of the population live below US$1 a day and around 68 per cent live on less than US$2 a day. The most heavily indebted are those between 55–59 years old. There is a state medical service and workers receive some maternity and family benefits.

Main cities
Dakar (capital, estimated population 2.3 million), Thiès (262,000), Kaolack (227,000), St Louis (147,000), Ziguinchor (206,000).

Languages spoken
The language group is Niger-Congo, West Atlantic; Wolof, Serer, Socé, Diola, Peulh and Toucouleur are spoken.
In business it is essential to speak French. Very few executives speak English There are interpreters who can be hired at short notice, but this can be expensive.

Official language/s
French

Media

Press
The press is subject to a Code de la Presse, adopted in March 1979, which stipulates that owners of national newspapers and magazines must be Senegalese. The same Code de la Presse provides for regulation and authorisation of journalists working in the national press, although there are no restrictions on the publication and distribution of the papers and magazines themselves.

Economy
President Wade inherited a legacy of financial mismanagement and uneven development. Despite relatively high levels of economic growth, averaging around 5 per cent throughout the 1990s, much of the wealth has been siphoned off by the political elite. Since 1979, Senegal has been the guinea-pig for structural adjustment policies, yet the country remains wedded to a peasant economy, enduring high levels of urban unemployment, despite being the most industrially advanced of the countries which once formed French West Africa.
Although a supporter of free market policies, President Wade is evidently not happy with programmes advocated by the World Bank. Instead, he plans to appeal to private investors for infrastructural projects and capital improvements. To attract sufficient private capital into his ambitious development programme, Wade plans to exploit the country's relative proximity to Europe, as well as its political and economic stability. Several factors have limited investment. The country's economy was beset by a drought cycle during the 1990s that diminished export growth. Moreover, the state struggles on the brink of bankruptcy due to the mismanagement and underfunding of state enterprises. As soon as he entered office, President Wade initiated an audit of state enterprises and found the country's former rulers had grossly misused funds from state assets. Wade claimed that Sotrac, the bus company, was over US$40 million in debt while the Post Office had a deficit of around US$24 million and the national lottery was nearly US$6 million in debt. The railways and ports were in a similar dire financial situation.
The state's efforts to liberalise the economy have not helped matters. Groundnuts, which once represented the country's main source of export income, have declined after the country reduced trade barriers to make the economy compete on a world commodity market that was drifting into depression. Education and social services have also deteriorated in recent years after the Diouf government engaged in spending cut-backs as part of its structural adjustment programme.
Although Senegal is better placed than other West African countries with a relatively advanced industrial sector that accounts for 25 per cent of GDP and employs over 17 per cent of the population, the likelihood that it can forge an independent development programme without development aid is doubtful over the medium-term.

Economic policy in 2002 is aimed at maintaining the rate of economic growth at 5 per cent and keeping inflation in check. The government also plans to speed up structural reforms and accelerate privatisation.

External trade

Senegal is part of the West African Economic and Monetary Union (WAEMU).

Exports

Principal exports are fish and fish products, groundnuts, phosphates, petroleum products, chemicals.

Main destinations: France (typically 20 per cent of total), Mali (12 per cent), Italy (8 per cent), Côte d'Ivoire (4 per cent), Guinea (4 per cent).

Imports

Principal imports are semi-finished goods, petroleum, food, capital goods.

Main sources: France (typically 37 per cent of total), Côte d'Ivoire (7 per cent), US (6 per cent), Thailand (5 per cent), Belgium/Luxembourg (4 per cent).

Agriculture

Agriculture contributes around 19 per cent to GDP and employs 70 per cent of the working population. Farming is carried out almost exclusively on smallholdings and is therefore relatively inefficient. Agricultural development has been hindered by poor transport infrastructure. Since 1984 Senegal has liberalised production by reducing state intervention in agriculture. As a result the distribution of fertilisers ceased to be a state monopoly and is now handled by private concerns. The government phased out subsidised credit for agricultural supplies but also established an agricultural development bank, the Caisse Nationale de Crédit Agricole. Marketing co-operatives were replaced by village co-operatives which enjoyed greater autonomy. The main subsistence crops are sorghum and millet, but production of rice is increasing. Horticultural output is also rising, supplying the domestic market and providing exports of out-of-season fruit and vegetables to the European markets. Cash crops include groundnuts, cotton and sugar. Sugar is the only sector with large plantations, which are operated by Compagnie Sucrière du Sénégal (CSS). Both groundnut and cotton output have been affected by the lack of farm credit. Cattle, sheep and goats are widespread and are kept for domestic use. Poultry numbers are showing a long-term increase and there has been a marked increase in the sheep population since the mid-1980s.

Fishing

The Senegalese government continues to support the development of marine fishing (tuna, oysters, prawns, lobsters). More than a quarter of foreign exchange earnings are from sea products. Fishing contributes around 2 per cent to GDP. Fishing is important in terms of the catch, export revenues from the fish processing and canning industries, and licence revenues from foreign ships operating in Senegalese waters. Fish and fish products are typically the largest single item in export earnings. The fisheries sector is targeted for expansion, with assistance being given to artisan fishermen, and the development of producer groups. Finance for this programme is partly derived from foreign fishing licence revenues.

A four-year fishing agreement (June 2002 to July 2006) was signed in 2002 with the EU. The EU agreed to pay US$63 million to Senegal to allow it to exploit its waters in this period. EU boats must process part of their catch at Senegalese ports.

Industry and manufacturing

The industrial sector contributes around 25 per cent to GDP, with the manufacturing sector contributing 17 per cent of GDP. Most industry is located inside the Dakar area of the Cap Vert peninsula. The only heavy export industries are an oil refinery at Dakar-Mbao, a sulphuric/phosphoric acid plant at Darou Khoudou and a fertiliser complex (Industries Chimiques du Sénégal) at Mbao.

The main industrial activity is light industry, transforming basic local commodities and import substitution goods to meet local demand. The government's industrial policy aims to make the economy more market-responsive and less centrally controlled. This entails a reduction in government participation in industry, price liberalisation and the encouragement of foreign investment (through a more favourable tax regime) and small businesses (through special incentives). It gives priority to high-value and export industries, especially chemicals, textiles, food processing and leather goods.

Light industry is mostly privately-owned and relies heavily on foreign capital and management skills. Most industrial enterprises are located in or around Dakar. Lack of adequate infrastructure has curtailed industrial development outside the capital.

Senegal's three major industries are food processing, textiles and chemicals. The food-processing sector and, to a lesser extent, textile manufacture, are influenced heavily by agricultural performance, as they rely mainly on locally-produced inputs. Therefore, industrial performance is affected by climatic conditions in a similar way to the agricultural sector.

Tourism

The state tourism agency is involved both in promoting the country in Europe (particularly in Italy and the UK), and in encouraging foreign investment in the development of further tourist facilities. The government sees tourism as a key, if neglected, foreign currency earner.

Mining

The mining sector contributes around 7 per cent to GDP and employs 3 per cent of the workforce.

Extraction of calcium and phosphates from open mines near Thiès are the most important. Workable deposits are around 130 million tonnes. Production (around 1.5 million tonnes per annum) is mainly for export, although it is also an important source of supply for the fertiliser complex at Mbao. Phosphates represent around 17 per cent of export earnings, although production declined by 30 per cent over the 1990s. The phosphate mine in the Matam area holds deposits of around 40.5 million tonnes.

Titanium, zircon and rutile are mined along the south coast of Cap Vert. Some 330 million tonnes of iron-ore deposits have been located at Falémé in the east of the country near the Mali border, but extraction is uneconomic at current market prices.

Hydrocarbons

Oil exploration has been undertaken since 1982 by Canada's Petrocanada International Assistance Corporation (PAIC) under an agreement with the state-owned Société Nationale des Petroles (Petrosen). The Dome Flore offshore field, discovered by French oil firm TotalFinaElf but now owned by Petrosen, has reserves estimated at over 50 million tonnes of heavy and light grades of crude. The low level of world oil prices in the 1980s and 1990s rendered exploitation of these deposits uneconomic.

Senegal and Guinea-Bissau established the Agence de Gestion et de Cooperation (AGC) in 1995 to co-operate on maritime matters, including oil prospecting, exploration and extraction. Under the terms of an AGC revision in August 2000, Senegal is granted an 80 per cent interest and Guinea-Bissau will receive 20 per cent of all oil resources in the territorial waters. Future offshore development in AGC waters would therefore give Senegal a sizeable chunk of the oil revenue.

Gas reserves are estimated at three billion cubic metres and are primarily located offshore (2001). Gas production is around 1.4 billion cubic metres (2001). Gas currently produced on the Diam Niadio East concession is supplied to Société Nationale d'Electricité (Senelec).

Energy

Electric power is supplied from six thermal stations, with a total installed capacity of

216MW. Virtually all commercial energy requirements are imported.
In rural areas, wood provides most fuel requirements, with consequent serious deforestation. A programme of reforestration is under way.
The government's 10-year energy plan aims to substitute 50 per cent of imported oil by local products, including oil/gas from the Dome Flore offshore field, peat deposits from Niayés and the expansion of hydropower from the Senegal and Gambia Rivers.
The Manantali dam on the Bafing river, which involves the South African company Eskom, should be fully operational by end-2002 and could help reduce the frequent power shortages which plague the Senegalese economy.

Banking

Central bank

Banque Centrale des Etats de l'Afrique de l'Ouest

Main financial centre

Dakar

Time

GMT

Geography

Senegal lies on the west coast of Africa, bordered to the north by Mauritania, to the east by Mali, and to the south by Guinea and Guinea-Bissau. Senegal surrounds the small state of The Gambia, which straddles the River Gambia in the south-west of Senegal, and forms a narrow enclave extending some 320 kilometres (200 miles) inland.
The country is low-lying and flat, and is situated in the savannah grasslands. Apart from the River Gambia and the Senegal River, which forms the northern boundary, most rivers are seasonal and dry up in the arid winter months.

Climate

The climate is tropical in the south (Casamance) and more temperate in the north.
During the dry season (December–May), temperatures range from 18–29 degrees Celsius. June–November suffers from occasional sand and dust storms, but is otherwise pleasant and represents the best time of the year to visit. Temperatures and rainfall are higher inland than on the coast.
The wet season is July–November, when the climate is hot and humid, and marked by frequent thunderstorms. Many businessmen take their annual leave during this period.

Dress codes

There is no restriction on clothing, although women are advised to dress modestly. In the dry season lightweight European clothing is suitable, and many government ministers wear lounge suits. Businessmen and other officials wear local dress – the *boubou*. Tropical clothing (not white) is necessary in the wet season.

Entry requirements

Passports

Required by all.

Visa

Required by all except nationals of the UK, US, EU and Japan and certain African countries. Return or onward travel ticket necessary for visa approval.

Currency advice/regulations

Local currency import is unlimited but export to countries outside the CFA franc zone is prohibited. Within the French Monetary Area, up to CFAf20,000 can be exported.
All foreign currency must be declared on arrival and departure. Amount taken out must not exceed the amount brought in. Visitors taking traveller's cheques are advised to take French francs or US dollars, as sterling is not widely accepted and there is a poor exchange rate for US dollars.

Health (for visitors)

There is no national health service, and medical assistance outside Dakar is minimal.

Mandatory precautions

A yellow fever certificate is required if arriving from an endemic area.

Advisable precautions

It is advisable to have immunisations for typhoid, polio, hepatitis 'A', tetanus and yellow fever. Malaria prophylaxis should be taken as risk exists throughout the country.

Public holidays

Fixed dates

1 Jan, 1 Feb (Confederation Day), 4 Apr (National Day), 1 May, 15 Aug (Assumption), 1 Nov (All Saints'), 25 Dec

Variable dates

Good Friday, Easter Monday, Ascension, Whit Monday, Eid Al-Fitr (Korité), Eid Al-Adha (Tabaski), Prophet's Birthday (Maouloud).

Working hours

Banking

Mon–Fri: 0800–1115, 1430–1630.

Business

Mon–Fri: 0800–1230, 1300–1600.

Government

Mon–Fri: 0800/0900–1200, 1500–1800; Sat: 0800/0900–1200.

Shops

Mon–Sat: 0800–1200, 1430–1800.

Telecommunications

Telephone/fax

Dial 15 for operator service
Outside Dakar there are few telephone lines.

Electricity supply

127/220V AC, 50 cycles. Plugs and sockets are mainly two-pin (round), and lampholders are mainly screw-type, but bayonet is also found.

Social customs/useful tips

Visitors should be punctual for appointments and visiting cards should be presented at business meetings. French-style formalities are observed. These include shaking hands when greeting and before departing.
Use the right hand when shaking hands and passing or receiving anything. Visits should be avoided during the Islamic month of Ramadan.
A service charge is normally added to the bill. Gratuities are not customary for taxis.
The minimum drinking age is 20 years.
Smoking is banned in some public places, including mosques.

Getting there

Air

National airline: Air Sénégal
International airport/s: Dakar-Leopold Sedar Senghor (Code: DKR), 17km north west of city; duty-free shop, bar, restaurant, buffet, bank, post office, shops, car hire, taxis.
Other airport/s: Other major airports at Saint-Louis, Ziguinchor and Tambacounda, in addition to about 12 small airfields.
Airport tax: There is no airport departure tax.

Surface

Road: Principal road routes are from the Gambia, Mali, Mauritania – those from Guinea and Guinea-Bissau are not generally recommended.
Rail: Twice weekly rail services operate between Dakar and Bamako (Mali) via Kaolack and Tambacounda.
Main port/s: Dakar is the second-largest port in West Africa and serves Senegal, Mauritania and the Gambia. The port has extensive facilities for fishing vessels and fish processing.

Getting about

National transport

Air: Air Sénégal links Dakar with all the main towns.
Small aircraft can be chartered from Africair Service.
Gambia Air Shuttle operates a twice-daily service between Dakar and Banjul in the Gambia.
Road: Tarred roads are mainly near the coast; inland areas are served by roads of variable quality. Main highways: Dakar to St. Louis, Rosso, Djourbel, Joal, Koalack and Ziguinchor.
Rail: The railway links Dakar with Tambacounda to the east, and with St. Louis and Linguère to the north-east.

Water: There is a ferry service from Dakar to Ziguinchor in the south, twice weekly. The Senegal river in the north is only navigable for parts of the year: for three months as far as Kayes (Mali); for six months as far as Kaedi (Mauritania); and all year as far as Rosso and Podor. Other rivers include the Saloun and the Casamance.

City transport

Taxis: Taxis are plentiful in Dakar. Most vehicles are licensed and fitted with meters. Tipping is not customary.

Buses, trams & metro: Regular flat-fare service is operated by SOTRAC (large green and yellow public buses).

Car hire

An international or national driving licence, insurance and car registration document (Carte Grise) are required. Vehicles coming from the right always have right of way.

BUSINESS DIRECTORY

Telephone area codes

The international dialling code (IDD) for Senegal is +221, followed by subscriber's number. There are no area codes.

Useful telephone numbers

Police: 823-7149, 823-2529, 823-8383.

Chambers of Commerce

Chambre de Commerce d'Industrie et d'Artisanat, Place de l'Indépendance, BP 118, Dakar (tel: 8237-189; fax: 8239-363).

Banking

Banque de l'Habitat du Sénégal, PO Box 229, 69 Boulevard Général de Gaulle, Dakar (tel: 8231-004; fax: 8238-043).

Banque Internationale pour le Commerce et l'Industrie du Sénégal SA, PO Box 392, 2 Avenue du Président L Senghor, Dakar (tel: 8390-390; fax: 8233-707).

Banque Islamique du Sénégal, PO Box 3381, Immeuble Abdallah Fayçal, Dakar (tel: 8496-262; fax: 8224-948) .

Banque Senegalo-Tunisienne (BST), PO Box 4111, Immeuble Kebe, 97 Avenue André Peytavin, Dakar (tel: 8237-576; fax: 8238-238).

Caisse Nationale de Crédit Agricole du Sénégal, PO Box 3890, 45 Avenue Albert Sarraut, Dakar (tel: 8222-300; fax: 8212-606).

Compagnie Bancaire de l'Afrique Occidentale, PO Box 129, 2 Place de l'Indépendance, Dakar (tel: 8231-000; fax: 8232-005).

Crédit Lyonnais Sénégal, PO Box 56, Boulevard El Hadji Djily Mbaye, angle Rue Huart, Dakar (tel: 8231-008; fax: 8238-430).

Société Générale de Banques au Sénégal SA, PO Box 323, 19 Avenue du Président L Senghor, Dakar (tel: 8395-500; fax: 8219-119).

Central bank

Banque Centrale des Etats de l'Afrique de l'Ouest, PO Box 3108, Avenue Abdoulaye Fadiga, Dakar (tel: 8231-042; fax: 8239-335).

Travel information

Ministry of tourism

Ministry of Tourism and Environment, 23 Rue Calmette, BP 4049, Dakar (tel: 8211-126; fax: 8229-413).

National tourist organisation offices

National Tourist Office, Ministry of Tourism and Air Transport, 23 Rue Calmette, PO Box 4049, Dakar (tel: 236-502).

Ministries

Ministry of Armed Forces, Batîment Administratif, Avenue Roume, Dakar (tel: 8231-216; fax: 8236-338).

Ministry of Commerce, Batîment Administratif, Avenue Roume, Dakar (tel: 8229-542; fax: 8219-132).

Ministry of the Habitat, Ex-Camp Lat-Dior, Dakar (tel: 8233-278; fax: 8236-245).

Ministry of the Interior, Place Washington, Dakar (tel: 8234-151; fax: 8210-542).

Ministry of Justice, Batîment Administratif, Avenue Roume, Dakar (tel: 8238-042; fax: 8232-727).

Ministry of Modernisation of the State, Rue Emile Zola, Dakar (tel: 8232-922; fax: 8229-764).

Ministry of National Education, Rue Calmette, Dakar (tel: 8224-123; fax: 8218-930).

Ministry of Tourism and Environment, 23 Rue Calmette, BP 4049, Dakar (tel: 8211-126; fax: 8229-413).

Ministry of Women, Children and the Family, Rue Beranger Ferraud, Dakar (tel: 8236-919; fax: 8236-673).

Prime Minister's Office, Batîment Administratif, Avenue Roume, Dakar (tel: 8224-917; fax: 8225-578).

Other useful addresses

Direction de la Statistique, BP 116, Dakar (tel: 8230-881).

Foire Internationale de Dakar (SOFIDAK), route de l'Aéroport, BP 3329, Dakar (tel: 8231-011).

Port Autonome de Dakar, 35 boulevard de la Libération, Dakar (tel: 8224-545, 8227-421).

Société de Développement Agricole et Industriel du Sénégal, 23 avenue Roume, PO Box 222, Dakar (tel: 8251-818).

Société Nationale d'Etudes et de Promotion Industrielle, BP 100, derrière Residence Seydou Nourou Tall, Dakar (tel: 8252-130).

Société Nationale des Télécommunications du Sénégal (SONATEL), 6 rue Wagane Diouf, BP 62, Dakar (tel: 8231-023, 8214-242).

Société Nouvelle des Etudes de Développement en Afrique, 36 rue Calmette, PO Box 2084, Dakar (tel: 8234-231).

Syndicat des Commerçants, Importateurs et Exportateurs de l'Ouest Africaine (Scimpex), angle rue Parent et avenue Abdoulaye Fadiga, PO Box 806, Dakar (tel: 8213-662).

Internet sites

Africa Business Network: http://www.ifc.org/abn

AllAfrica.com: http://allafrica.com

African Development Bank: http://www.afdb.org

Africa Online: http://www.africaonline.com

Mbendi AfroPaedia (information on companies, countries, industries and stock exchanges in Africa): http://mbendi.co.za

Seychelles

Nicole Goldin

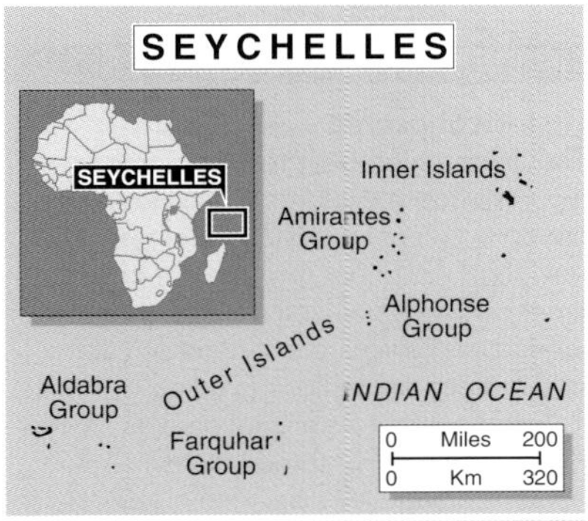

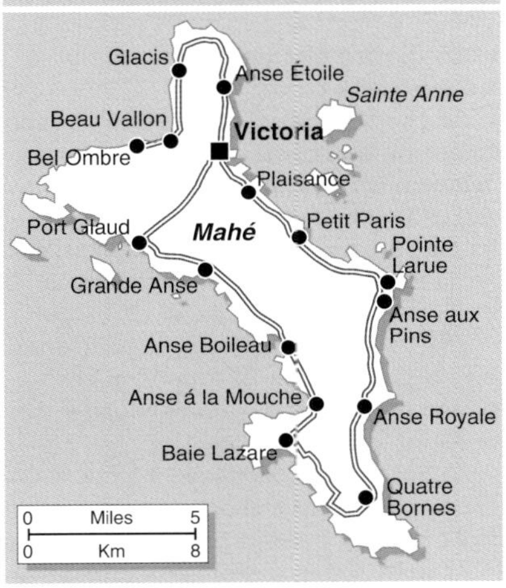

The sunny Seychelles are losing their shine. Political instability is looming following the September 2001 presidential election. Meanwhile, the country is suffering a decline in revenue from the all-important tourism sector due to the global economic downturn, the 11 September 2001 terrorist attacks in the US and the October 2002 Bali bombing.

Seeds of change

Despite France-Albert René's win in the Seychelles' third multi-party poll since the introduction of its constitution in 1993, his narrow margin of victory reflected rising discontent among the citizenry. He won just 54 per cent of the vote, compared with 67 per cent in the previous election in 1998. A mere 2,232 votes gave René the presidency, beating off a strong challenge from Wavel Ramkalawan, leader of the opposition Seychelles National Party (SNP). Ramkalawan picked up 45 per cent of the ballots, more than double his 1998 share of 19.5 per cent.

Evidence of the SNP's rising support was shown when Ramkalawan won a majority in nine of the country's twenty-five constituencies. Although declared essentially free and fair by the international community, the election did not pass without controversy. Claiming irregularities, the SNP petitioned the Constitutional Court to declare the result void. As anticipated, their petition was denied in January 2002, enhancing the likelihood of rising tensions in the run-up to the 2003 parliamentary elections.

Economic pressures

Since the early 1990s, in an effort to prop-up its quasi-socialist system, the government has reversed the liberalisation process of the 1980s and adopted an economic policy comprising a strict foreign exchange regime, price controls and heavy regulatory burden. Continuing the trend, the 2002 budget included a 42 per cent rise in subsidies to para-statals and a mere 4 per cent increase in ministerial spending. Equally disconcerting was the 14 per cent budget deficit. Foreign exchange reserves remained at just four weeks of import cover in early 2002, well below the internationally acceptable level of three months. The 2003 budget was announced in December 2002. Total expenditure is forecast at SR1.6 billion (US$284 million) while the budget deficit is expected to fall to 5.4 per cent of GDP.

Along with the interventionist policy regime, the global downfall in tourism, especially luxury tourism, contributed to the failure to generate more foreign exchange. The effects of the drop in tourism receipts spread throughout the economy, as the sector accounts for over 30 per cent of employment and 70 per cent of foreign exchange earnings. Rising fuel prices, increased security expenditure and soaring insurance costs – all knock-on effects of the 11 September attacks – led Air Seychelles to forecast losses of SR8–10 million (US$1.4–1.8 million) in the 2001/02 financial year. In 2002, Air Seychelles was making ambitious attempts to

KEY FACTS

Official name: Republic of Seychelles

Head of State: President France-Albert René (FPPS) (since 1977)

Head of government: President France-Albert René

Ruling party: Front Progressiste du Peuple Seychellois (FPPS) (Seychelles People's Progressive Front) (results of 4–6 Dec 2002 parliamentary elections: President France-Albert René's FPPS won 54.3 per cent of the vote (23 seats out of 34) and the Seychelles National Party (SNP) 42.6 per cent (11); turnout was 87 per cent)

Area: 453 square km

Population: 80,400 (2001)

Capital: Victoria

Official language: Creole, French and English

Currency: Seychelle rupee (SR) = 100 cents

Exchange rate: SR5.62 per US$ (Jan 2003)

GDP per capita: US$7,725 (2001)

GDP real growth: 1.00% (2001); 0.5% (2002)*

Inflation: 6.00% (2001); 6.0% (2002)*

Balance of trade: -US$244.00 million (2001)

Foreign debt: US$470.00 million (2001)

* estimated figure

For the latest Key Facts, go to www.worldinformation.com

overturn its losses by introducing a new 36-seat aircraft for regional flights and a new flight from Seychelles to Mumbai in India via the Maldives. Passenger confidence in the new flight may suffer following a hijacking attempt in September 2002. Fortunately, the man was overpowered by the crew, but the hijack attempt raised concerns about the airline's security arrangements since 11 September.

The fishing sector, the island's second most important contributor to GDP, also suffered in 2001/02. The outlook from the Indian Ocean Tuna Commission (IOTC) looks bleak. With catches of yellowfin and skipjack tuna below 2002 expectations, cannery-supporting vessels from Spain and France moved to Madagascan waters earlier than usual. This has led to rising fish prices, undermining Seychelles fish canning profit margins.

On a positive note, the manufacturing section of the state-owned the Seychelles Marketing Board (SMB) has performed better. In 2001, it introduced 14 new products and registered 8 per cent growth, contributing SR30 million (US$5.3 million) to foreign exchange reserves.

Hopeful international position

The Seychelles' international economic position is stronger than its domestic situation. Co-operation with India continues to deepen on several fronts: trade, investment and defence. The Seychelles was designated as a beneficiary of the US's African Growth and Opportunity Act (AGOA) which allows exports of certain products to the US on a tariff-free basis. In its 2002 report to Congress, the US Department of State reported that Seychellois duty-free exports to the US reached levels of US$4.2 million. The Seychelles also entered into a trade and investment protection act with Egypt.

With the highest GDP per capita in Africa, Seychelles has an important regional role and is a member of both the Southern Africa Development Community (SADC) and the Common Market for Eastern and Southern Africa (Comesa). However, tension between the open-minded Seychelles Chamber of Commerce (SCCI) and the control-oriented government has resulted in muted support for regional economic integration.

The Seychelles had pledged to cut all tariffs on intra-Comesa trade and commence participation in the free trade area (FTA) in June 2001, but by late 2002 it had yet to come into effect.

In 2001 and 2002, activity increased at the International Trade Zone (ITZ), where the Heinz Group has invested nearly US$8 million in a tuna canning plant. At least 12 applications for other ITZ projects have been submitted, ranging from re-exports to light manufacturing assembly. Perhaps the most significant external development came on 25 February 2002, when the EU made a five-year grant of 38 million (US$37 million) to support the country's structural adjustment reforms. While the Seychelles is enhancing its international presence through trade, it is barred from voting in the UN General Assembly since late January 2002 because of arrears.

Outlook

Only a victory for the SNP in the forthcoming legislative elections, which are constitutionally required to take place by May 2003, will lead to a rapid return to economic liberalisation. René looks poised to continue his restrictive regime and Seychelles will continue to be beset with a critical foreign exchange problem and limited growth. Vulnerable to political and social strife, the economic environment is rather unsteady.

KEY INDICATORS — Seychelles

	Unit	1996	1997	1998	1999	2000
Population	m	0.08	0.08	0.08	0.08	0.08
Gross domestic product (GDP)	US$bn	0.50	0.57	0.58	0.59	0.60
GDP per capita	US$	6,707	7,445	7,552	7,571	7,453
GDP real growth	%	4.7	4.3	2.3	-3.0	1.2
Inflation	%	-1.1	0.7	2.6	6.2	7.6
Exports (fob) (goods)	US$m	78.0	115.2	123.4	145.2	128.0
Imports (fob) (goods)	US$m	262.7	302.7	351.6	377.6	351.0
Balance of trade	US$m	-185.0	-188.0	-228.0	-232.0	-223.0
Current account	US$m	-56.5	-63.2	-124.6	-114.0	-62.0
Total reserves minus gold	US$m	21.8	26.3	21.6	30.4	43.8
Foreign exchange	US$m	20.6	25.2	21.6	30.3	43.7
Exchange rate	per US$	4.97	5.03	5.26	5.34	5.71

Risk assessment

Economic	Weak
Political	Vulnerable
Regional stability	Fair
Stock market	Fair

COUNTRY PROFILE

Historical profile

The uninhabited islands were sighted by the Portuguese explorer Vasco da Gama in the early sixteenth century, but it was not until the 1770s that any attempt to settle them was made when French farmers landed and introduced cinnamon, clove and nutmeg plantations (worked by slaves).

1794 The islands were taken over by the British and administered from Mauritius.

1903 The Seychelles became a separate colony.

1948 The first elections to the legislative assembly took place.

1964 The Seychelles' first political organisations were established – the Seychelles Democratic Party (SDP) led by James Mancham and the Front Progressiste du Peuple Seychellois (FPPS) (Seychelles People's Progressive Front) (formerly the SPUP) of France-Albert René.

1975 The Seychelles was granted internal self-government; the SDP and the FPPS formed a coalition government under the premiership of Mancham.

1976 Became an independent republic on 29 June. James Mancham became president and René became prime minister.

1977 René seized power in an armed coup in June and established a one-party state with the FPPS as the sole legal party.

1982 A mutiny in the army was put down by pro-government troops.

1991 René re-established a multi-party democracy.

1993 Multi-party presidential and legislative elections held on 23 July resulted in a landslide victory for both President René and the FPPS.

1998 Presidential and legislative elections held in March were won by President René and the FPPS.

2001 Presidential elections held on 31 August/2 September resulted in a victory for President René (54.2 per cent of the vote).

Political structure

Constitution

In a June 1993 referendum, a new constitution was approved, institutionalising multi-party politics and providing for the establishment of a National Assembly.

Form of state

Republic

The executive
Executive power rests with the president, elected for a five-year term; renewable three times.
National legislature
A National Assembly of 34 members, with 25 members directly elected on a constituency basis and the remaining nine allocated on a proportional basis. The term of the National Assembly is five years.
Last elections
31 August/2 September 2001 (presidential) (two years before the scheduled date and the first time that presidential elections were held separately from legislative elections); March 1998 (presidential and legislative).
Next elections
2003 (legislative); 2006 (presidential)

Political parties
Ruling party
Front Progressiste du Peuple Seychellois (FPPS) (Seychelles People's Progressive Front)
Main opposition party
Seychelles National Party (SNP) (known as the Opposition Unie (OU) (United Opposition) until 1998).

Population
80,260 (2000)
Annual population growth rate: 1.6 per cent (1994–2000). Approximately 34 per cent of the total population is under 15 years.
Population density: 178 inhabitants per square km. Urban population: 64 per cent (1994–2000).
Ethnic make-up
The islanders have a variety of ethnic origins – African, European, Indian and Chinese.
Religions
Practically the whole population is Christian, with 90 per cent belonging to the Roman Catholic faith.

Education
The literacy rate is well over 90 per cent with less gender disparities in education. The government provides free education and school is mandatory for every child under the age of 16 years. The school-going age population is largely concentrated on Mahe, the main island where most of the economic activities are concentrated. There are 13.8 pupils per primary school teacher according to estimates in 2000. Total expenditure in public education has grown in real terms. The pupil per capita cost in (public) primary schools is typically SR5,100.

Health
World Bank estimates during the period 1994–2000 showed that the average life expectancy was 72 years and the infant mortality rate stood at nine per 1,000 live births. About 6 per cent of children were malnourished in the same period. Health care is provided free of charge. The Victoria Hospital has about 445 beds and there are 56 in-patient admissions per bed per year.

Welfare
The social security law requires employers and employees to contribute to a national pension programme that gives retirees a modest pension. Self-employed persons contribute by paying 15 per cent of gross earnings. The government also provides low-cost housing and housing loans.
There is welfare provision for children and the disabled.

Main cities
Victoria, on Mahé island (capital, estimated population 30,000 in 1998).

Languages spoken
Creole is the local language, but English is used in business and government circles. French is also widely spoken.
Official language/s
Creole, French and English

Media
Press
Dailies: *Seychelles Nation* (http://www.seychelles-online.com.sc) is the online version of the daily government newspaper published from Monday to Saturday. There is one daily newspaper, *Nation*, which is government-owned.
Weeklies: *Seychelles Weekend Nation* is published on Saturdays.
Periodicals: *The People* is a monthly publication. A few periodicals are also published in English, French and Creole.
Broadcasting
Radio Television Seychelles (RTS) runs radio and television services in Creole, English and French. Reception is good on Mahé and the other main islands.

Economy
Seychelles has the highest standard of living in Africa, but economic diversification is necessary. The economy is reliant on tourism and suffers a foreign exchange problem partly due to government spending and high imports of food and equipment. Setbacks have been overcome in the recent past, suggesting that the economy is robust.
However, some islanders complain that foreign workers are filling positions that should be left open for native inhabitants. The opposition Democratic Party has warned that this could create racial tensions. There is also concern that the government is still running the country as a bureaucratic command economy, squashing free enterprise and inward investment. Others are concerned the government is doing little to protect and enhance local industry and that the country is overly dependent on food imports.
Beyond fishing and tourism, the country is looking to develop in areas such as telecommunications, financial services, light industry and international conferencing. This will require considerable foreign investment and the government will need to institute policies and adopt attitudes more compliant to investors.

External trade
The visible trade deficit is partially offset by earnings from tourism which is the main foreign exchange earner, plus foreign aid and investment, rental from a US satellite tracking station and a BBC relay station.
The Seychelles International Trade Zone (ITZ) is a business park for export-orientated activities. As an African, Caribbean and Pacific (ACP) country, it enjoys quota-free, duty free access to the EU under the Conotou convention; as a Comesa member, it enjoys the same trade benefits in Eastern and Southern Africa, although by mid-2002 it had yet to lift barriers to trade as agreed in June 2001.
Preferential import tariffs are granted to goods from Indian Ocean Commission (IOC) member countries – Mauritius, Comoros, Madagascar, Réunion. In return, Seychelles receives preferential export tariffs from IOC countries.
Exports
Principal exports are canned tuna, frozen and fresh fish, copra, re-exports of petroleum.
Main destinations: UK (30.4 per cent of 2000 total), France (16.3 per cent), Netherlands (10.1 per cent), Italy (10 per cent), Germany (8.2 per cent).
Imports
Principal imports are manufactured goods, machinery and transport equipment, food and live animals, fuel, chemicals.
Main sources: Saudi Arabia (13.1 per cent of 2000 total), South Africa (9.4 per cent), UK (9.2 per cent), Singapore (9 per cent), France (8.3 per cent).

Agriculture
The overall importance of the sector to the economy has declined with the expansion of the tourist industry, although it is still important as a source of foreign exchange and employment.
There is a shortage of cultivable land. Approximately 4 per cent of the total land area is agricultural, much of which is given over to copra and cinnamon – the islands' major export crops. The islands are faced with soil of low fertility but farming is traditionally organic and eco-friendly.
Small quantities of coconuts, vanilla, tea and limes are exported. Crops grown for local consumption include tropical fruits, cassava, sweet potatoes, yams, sugar-cane, bananas, tea and vegetables; but the country's staple food crop, rice, has to be imported. Seychelles is

self-sufficient in pork, chicken, fish and some vegetables. However, imported food, drink and tobacco account for about 17 per cent of GDP.
There are a number of large farms, 650 small farms and thousands of smallholdings, which the government hopes will reduce the island's dependency on imported foods.
Government reforms include privatisation of state farms, while setting up smaller co-operatives, a reafforestation project and new marketing structures; upgrading infrastructure and irrigation facilities for farms. An animal feed factory has been established by the Seychelles Marketing Board (SMB) to support production of meat and eggs.
About 98 per cent of milk is imported. The government is encouraging the production of bananas and mangoes.

Fishing

The fishing industry is a major foreign exchange earner for the Seychelles, accounting for about 90 per cent of domestically-produced goods exported. It is being expanded as part of the government policy of economic diversification, with foreign companies being encouraged to become involved.
The Seychelles sells fishing licences in its exclusive 1.3 million square km economic zone. However, despite the desire for a growth in capacity and productivity, artisanal fishing still represents about one-third of fishing exports. France and Italy are the main importers of Seychelles tuna, which is produced on an industrial basis with a cannery providing added value to tuna exports.

Industry and manufacturing

The industrial sector, including mining, manufacturing, construction and power, typically accounts for around 25 per cent of GDP.
There is a small-scale manufacturing sector. The main activities include the production of canned tuna, soft drinks, juices, jams, beer, cigarettes, paints, assembling of television sets and processing of cinnamon and coconuts.
Emphasis is on private-sector investment. The government aims to expand light industry in other areas such as artisanal products, packaging, assembly and services.
HJ Heinz acquired a 60 per cent majority stake in a Mahé-based tuna processing facility, which was renamed Indian Ocean Tuna (IOT). Heinz has invested nearly US$8 million in the plant, which operates in the country's International Trade Zone (ITZ).

Tourism

Tourism is the country's main economic sector, contributing 70 per cent of foreign exchange earnings and around 30 per cent of employment.
Seychelles is marketed as an exclusive, glamour destination due to tight building controls limiting accommodation. Most visitors come from European and African countries.
In 2001 and the first half of 2002, tourist numbers dropped substantially due to the effects of the global economic downturn and the 11 September terrorist attacks.

Mining

There is no mining on any large scale, but some granite is quarried for construction.

Hydrocarbons

Some gas reserves have been found offshore but as yet have not been exploited.
Seychelles National Oil Company (SNOC), a state-sponsored organisation, co-ordinates the search for hydrocarbons in the Exclusive Economic Zone (EEZ). The government has revised legal and fiscal regimes to encourage exploration activity.
The downstream oil industry is highly important, accounting for 25 per cent of imports and supplying 95 per cent of energy needs. Commercial consumption is around 160,000 tonnes per annum. Downstream activities are directed by the state-run Seychelles Petroleum Company.

Energy

Electricity is provided from petroleum and gas turbines. Annual generation of electricity amounts to around 83GW.

Banking

Central bank

Central Bank of Seychelles

Time

GMT plus four hours

Geography

The Republic of Seychelles comprises more than 100 islands, widely scattered over the western Indian Ocean. Apart from the Seychelles archipelago, the country contains several other island groups, the southernmost being about 210km (130 miles) north of Madagascar.

Climate

Tropical and humid. Average temperature 24–32 degrees Celsius throughout year. Hottest months December–May; wettest from December–March; cooler from June–November. Islands lie outside cyclone belt.

Entry requirements

Passports

Required by all. Passports must be valid for duration of stay.

Visa

A Visitor's Permit is issued on arrival, valid for one month (extensions are possible for three-month periods, fee SR200). All persons must hold onward or return tickets or pay a deposit equivalent to the value of a return ticket to the country of origin, and have confirmed accommodation and sufficient funds for the intended length of stay

Currency advice/regulations

Unlimited import/export of foreign currency is permitted. Only legal to exchange foreign exchange for Seychelles Rupees through a bank.
Travellers may take or send out of Seychelles up to SR100 of domestic currency.

Health (for visitors)

Mandatory precautions

Yellow fever certificate if arriving from infected area.

Advisable precautions

Hepatitis A, tetanus, typhoid and polio vaccinations. There is a rabies risk.

Hotels

Good standard and widely available. All the large hotels in Mahé are on the beach. Advisable to book and confirm reservation in advance, particularly at Christmas and during August. Government trades tax of 5 per cent is added to bill, and usually also a service charge. Tipping optional.

Credit cards

Major credit cards widely accepted.

Public holidays

Fixed dates

1/2 Jan (New Year), 1 May (Labour Day), 5 Jun (Liberation Day), 18 Jun (National Day), 15 Aug (Assumption/La Digue Festival), 1 Nov (All Saints' Day), 8 Dec (Immaculate Conception), 25 Dec (Christmas Day).

Variable dates

Good Friday, Easter Saturday, Corpus Christi.

Working hours

Banking

Mon–Fri: 0830–1300; Sat: 0800–1200.

Business

Mon–Fri: 0800–1200, 1300–1600.

Government

Mon–Fri: 0800–1200, 1300–1600.

Shops

Mon–Fri: 0800–1200, 1330–1700; Sat: 0800–1200; some open Sun morning.

Telecommunications

Telephone/fax

Direct dialling from Seychelles to most countries. As well as from hotels, calls can be made 24 hours a day from Cable and Wireless (Seychelles) Ltd, Francis Rachel Street, Victoria, Mahé. Fifty per cent of homes connected to digitalised network; 16 public telephone exchanges.

Electricity supply

240V AC, 50 cycles. Plugs are three-pin bayonet.

Getting there

Air

National airline: Air Seychelles.

International airport/s: Seychelles-Pointe Larue International (Code: SEZ), Mahé Island, 10km from Victoria; duty-free shop, bar, restaurant, buffet, bank, shops, car hire.
Airport tax: International departures include an embarkation tax of SR500 (residents), US$40 (non-residents, payable in foreign currency only), US$10 (transit passengers staying less than 24 hours); not applicable to children under 12 years.
Surface
Main port/s: Victoria, on Mahé island, has a deep harbour. The Government plans to make Victoria a major regional transshipment centre.
Privatisation of stevedoring operations has increased the productivity of the port.

Getting about
National transport
Air: Air Seychelles operates regular services from Mahé to Praslin, Desroches, Fregate, Bird and Dennis islands.
Aircraft charters are available to Assumption, Farquhar and Poivre.
Helicopter Seychelles provides services and charters from Mahé.
There are plans to expand the outer island airport at Praslin with World Bank funds. Airstrips exist on most of the outlying islands.
Road: The islands have 323km of roads, of which 231km are surfaced.
Mahé and Praslin are the only islands with appreciable surfaced roads. There are gravel roads elsewhere.
Buses: A cheap, regular bus service (provided by Seychelles Public Transport Corporation) operates to most areas of Mahé from Victoria. Services also operate on Praslin and La Digue.
Water: Regular ferry services connect Mahé and the islands of Praslin and La Digue.
The Marine Charter Association in Victoria assists with boat charters to other islands.
City transport
Taxis: Available on Mahé and Praslin. Fixed charges, tipping is optional.
Car hire
Available on Mahé and Praslin. Victoria and certain villages impose a speed limit of 40kph, elsewhere it is 65kph. Advance reservation advisable. Foreign or international driving licence required.

BUSINESS DIRECTORY

Telephone area codes
The international dialling code (IDD) for Seychelles is +248 followed by the customer's number.

Chambers of Commerce
Seychelles Chamber of Commerce & Industry, PO Box 599, Room 301, 38 Premier Building, Victoria (tel: 323-812; fax: 321-422).

Banking
Development Bank of Seychelles, PO Box 217, Independence Ave, Victoria (tel: 224471 fax: 224274)

Seychelles International Mercantile Banking Corporation Ltd; PO Box 241, Ground Floor, Victoria House, State House Avenue, Victoria (tel: 225011 fax: 224670).

Seychelles Savings Bank Limited, PO Box 531, Independence Ave, Victoria (tel: 225251 fax: 224713).

Central bank
Central Bank of Seychelles (CBS), Independence Avenue, PO Box 701, Victoria (tel: 225-200; fax: 224-958).

Travel information
Air Seychelles, Victoria House, PO Box 386, Victoria (tel: 225-300; fax: 225-159).

National Travel Agency, Kingsgate House, PO Box 611, Victoria (tel: 224-900; fax: 225-111).

Seychelles Tourism Marketing Authority, PO Box 1262, Victoria, Mahé (tel: 620-000; fax: 620-620).

Travel Services (Seychelles) Ltd., Victoria House, PO Box 356, Victoria (tel: 322-414; fax: 325-010).

Ministries
Investment Development Advisory Services (IDEAS), c/o Ministry of Finance and Communication, 3rd Floor, Central Bank Building, Box 313, Victoria (tel: 225-252; fax: 225-265).

Ministry of Administration and Manpower, National House, PO Box 56, Victoria (tel: 383-000; fax: 224-936).

Ministry of Agriculture and Marine Resources, Independence House, PO Box 166, Victoria (tel: 224-030; fax: 225-245).

Ministry of Community Development, Independence House, PO Box 199, Victoria (tel: 224-030; fax: 225-287).

Ministry of Education and Culture, Mont Fleuri (tel: 224-777; fax: 224-859).

Ministry of Finance and Communication, 3rd Floor, Central Bank Building, PO Box 313, Victoria (tel: 225-252; fax: 225-265).

Ministry of Foreign Affairs, Planning and Environment, Mont Fleuri (tel: 224-688; fax: 224-845).

Ministry of Health, PO Box 52, Mont Fleuri (tel: 388-000; fax: 224-792).

Ministry of Industry, Maison du Peuple, Victoria (tel: 224-030; fax: 225-086).

Ministry of Local Government Youth and Sports, Oceangate House, Victoria (tel: 225-477; fax: 225-262).

Ministry of Tourism and Transport, Independence House, PO Box 92, Victoria (tel: 225-313; fax: 225-131).

Other useful addresses
Island Development Company (IDC), PO Box 638, New Port, Victoria (tel: 224-640; fax: 224-467).

Public Utilities Corporation (PUC) Electricity: PO Box 174, Victoria (tel: 322-444; fax: 321-020).
Water: Unity House, PO Box 34, Victoria (tel: 322-444; fax: 322-127)..

Seychelles Agricultural Development Company Ltd., PO Box 172, Victoria (tel: 276-618).

Seychelles Broadcasting Corporation, Hermitage, PO Box 321, Victoria (tel: 224-161; fax: 224-641).

Seychelles Fishing Authority (SFA), PO Box 449, Victoria (tel: 224-521; fax: 224-508).

Seychelles Industrial Development Corporation (SIDEC), PO Box 537, Victoria (tel: 224-941; fax: 225-121).

Seychelles International Business Authority (SIBA), PO Box 991, Central Bank Building, Victoria (tel: 225-402; fax: 225-851).

Seychelles Licensing Authority, PO Box 3, Francis Rachel Street, Victoria (tel: 224-314; fax: 224-256).

Seychelles Marketing Board, PO Box 516, Victoria (tel: 224-444).

Seychelles Timber Company, Grand Anse, Mahe (tel: 278-343).

State Assurance Corporation ofSeychelles, Pirate's Arms Building, PO Box 636, Victoria (tel: 225-000; fax: 224-495).

Internet sites
Africa Business Network: http://www.ifc.org/abn

AllAfrica.com: http://allafrica.com

African Development Bank: http://www.afdb.org

Africa Online: http://www.africaonline.com

Harambee Afrika (UK business club for traders with east, central and southern Africa; includes annotated web resource list): http://www.harambee.co.uk

Mbendi AfroPaedia (information on companies, countries, industries and stock exchanges in Africa): http://mbendi.co.za

KEY FACTS

Official name: Republic of Sierra Leone

Head of State: President Ahmad Tejan Kabbah (SLPP) (elected 1996; re-elected 14 May 2002)

Head of government: President Ahmad Tejan Kabbah

Ruling party: Sierra Leone People's Party (SLPP) (elected 14 May 2002)

Area: 72,325 square km

Population: 5.10 million (2001)

Capital: Freetown

Official language: English

Currency: Leone (Le) = 100 cents

Exchange rate: Le2,010.00 per US$ (Jan 2003)

GDP per capita: US$133 (2001)

GDP real growth: 5.40% (2001)

Inflation: 2.10% (2001)

Balance of trade: -US$225.00 million (2001)

Foreign debt: US$1.17 billion (2001)

Annual FDI: US$2.00 million (2001)

For the latest Key Facts, go to www.worldinformation.com

Sierra Leone

Desmond Davies

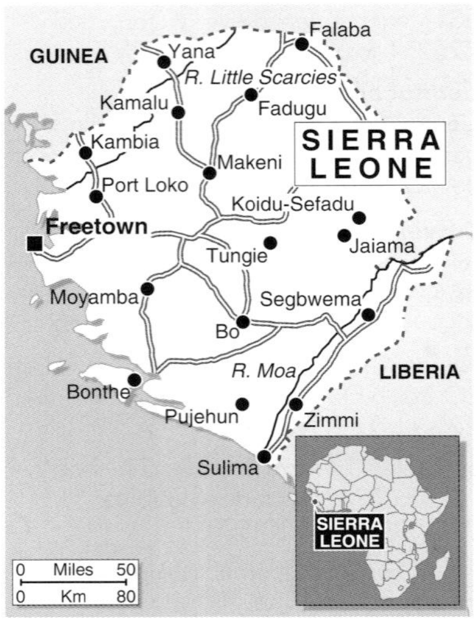

Presidential and parliamentary elections held on 14 and 16 May 2002 were seen by many Sierra Leoneans as a referendum on the performance of President Tejan Kabbah and his ruling Sierra Leone People's Party (SLPP), part of the Cabinet of National Unity. Since coming to power in 1996, Kabbah has had many challenges to his leadership, including a coup in 1997. Kabbah and the SLPP remained in power after the elections, largely due to his success at helping to bring the 10-year civil war to an end and because of disarray within the opposition camp.

A clean sweep?

Opposition parties had called for the elections to be postponed, arguing that the new district block system (DBS) of voting approved by the National Electoral Commission favoured the SLPP. The DBS proposal allowed for eight representatives from each of Sierra Leone's 14 districts to be elected to the 112-member House of Representatives (parliament), based on proportional representation. In addition, 12 paramount chiefs, each representing a district, also sit in parliament.

Kabbah was re-elected as president with 70.3 per cent of the vote against the All People's Congress' (APC) Ernest Koroma, who won 22.35 per cent. The SLPP won 83 of 112 seats in the 16 May parliamentary elections, with 27 seats going to the APC and two to the Peace and Liberation Party of the former junta leader, Major Johnny Paul Koroma.

Challengers to Kabbah

Kabbah's main challenger for the presindential nomination had been Charles Margai, who resigned as minister of safety and security in January 2002. Margai's hand was forced by Kabbah after months of rumours that as the son of the late Sir Albert, prime minister from 1964 to 1967, he was out to reclaim his family's leadership position in Sierra Leonean politics. Margai's uncle, Sir Milton, became Sierra Leone's first prime minister and led the country to independence in 1961.

Kabbah's team would not allow the president's position to be threatened. So Margai, who had actually left the SLPP in 1996 after Kabbah was chosen as the party's presidential candidate, was challenged in court to prove that he was still a registered member of the party. He failed to do so and when the SLPP's convention met in the southern town of Bo in March 2002, Kabbah was the sole presidential candidate. His running mate was Attorney General Solomon Berewa who defeated the incumbent vice president, Joe Demby.

The decision to select Berewa, who is in his late 60s, did not go down well with a large number of party members who believed that it was a retrograde step for the SLPP, which was supposed to be reaching out to its younger members. Kabbah, in his bid to retain the backing of the party, according to SLPP insiders, had promised that he would not serve his full five-year term if he won the election. In this light, it would mean that if he were to step down, Berewa would be in line for the presidency – and thus would be perpetuating the power of the older generation in the SLPP. The question being asked was, will Kabbah, being the astute politician he is, step down?

Special court for war crimes

While the politicians were busy preparing for the elections, the UN in March 2002 finally gave the go ahead for the Special

Court, which was due to be established by the end of 2002, to try Sierra Leonean war criminals. In the same month, the government lifted the state of emergency and charged rebel leader, Foday Sankoh, with the murder of 20 people outside his house in May 2000. The government had to take this action because, with the lifting of the state of emergency, it could no longer hold Sankoh, who had been in detention since May 2000, without charging him.

Unlike the Rwanda and Yugoslavia tribunals, the Court in Sierra Leone will be quite lean. The UN Security Council made it clear that it did not want the Court to be like those in Arusha and The Hague, with huge budgets and a slow pace of operation.

It is planned that the Special Court will run for three years with an annual budget of US$20 million. This is a far cry from the US$100 million the UN is spending each year on the tribunals in Arusha and The Hague. The Sierra Leone Special Court is not funded from the regular budget of the UN. The money was put up by voluntary contributions from about 20 donor states, including the US, Holland and the UK.

Economy still struggling

While peace was consolidated in Sierra Leone during 2002, creating a more stable political climate, the economic outlook was not as promising. For one thing, the government depended for 65 per cent of its budget from foreign donors, especially the European Union (EU) and the UK government, which has played a significant part in bringing peace to the country with the presence of British troops in Freetown. For another, the government was being financially squeezed as it made provisions for ex-combatants who were returning to society.

Thus, there was great pressure on the government's fiscal expenditure. The pressure was worsened by the huge payments the government had to make for imports, such as petroleum products, rice and building materials. As a result of these expenditures, the current account deficit widened from US$100 million in 2000 to US$107.8 million in 2001.

The country's external debt at the end of 2001 stood at US$1.2 billion. This was after the Paris Club agreed in October 2001 to restructure the country's debt following the IMF's approval of a three-year arrangement under the Poverty Reduction and Growth Facility (PRGF) for US$169 million to support the government's economic recovery programme. Debt relief led to the immediate cancellation of US$72 million and a reduction in debt service due to the Paris Club. The World Bank in December 2001 approved a second Economic Rehabilitation Recovery Credit of some US$45 million for the government. In March 2002, the IMF and World Bank also approved debt service relief of US$950 million under the Heavily Indebted Poor Countries (HIPC) Initiative.

Peace brings hope

With peace taking hold in the country, the government was planning to provide incentives for a post-conflict economy. New financial institutions sprang up in 2001 and 2002 to provide financial opportunities for entrepreneurs and ordinary citizens, the Home Finance Company being one of them. At the end of 2001, the Bank of Sierra Leone was considering applications for new banks and in 2002 the government planned to revamp rural banks. Crucially, the Bank of Sierra Leone and the Institute for Financial and Economic Management organised a workshop on capital markets in 2001. The government said it was considering the recommendations of this workshop with a view to establishing a stock exchange.

The government has placed great emphasis on the diamond industry to assist the country's economic recovery and has made attempts to gain access to mining areas that were previously in the hands of the rebel Revolutionary United Front (RUF). Once access had been gained and the diamond certification programme had been implemented, Finance Minister Peter Kuyembeh announced in his budget speech in December 2001 that the export sector had 'improved remarkably... on account of increased receipts from diamond exports'. There was no such good news for the agricultural sector, which, he said, was 'yet to contribute significantly to export revenues, as it remains sluggish'.

With a fully-fledged Maritime Administration in place, its head, Captain Abraham Macauley, announced in January 2002 that the government was planning to establish a ship registry. Although the cabinet approved the Merchant Shipping Bill, which will establish an open registration for shipowners, the legislation had not been sent to parliament for it to become law, before the it was dissolved for the May 2002 elections. The Maritime Administration is hoping that the new parliament would pass the bill and allow Sierra Leone to enter a potentially lucrative market.

Outlook

Sierra Leoneans have had almost two years of peace and are looking to finally pick up the pieces after 10 years of a brutal civil war. The presidential and parliamentary elections in May 2002 were expected to be part of the healing process. While the UK ended its military operation in Sierra Leone in July 2002, non-governmental organisations (NGOs), such as the International Crisis Group, are calling for caution. They argue that it was too early to declare the danger over and have warned that it is too early for the international community to take Sierra Leone off the international agenda.

The SLPP has become complacent, especially since its parliamentary election

KEY INDICATORS **Sierra Leone**

	Unit	1996	1997	1998	1999	2000
Population	m	4.29	4.42	4.57	4.72	4.82
Gross domestic product (GDP)	US$bn	0.91	0.82	0.92	0.67	0.64
GDP per capita	US$	200	160	190	142	133
GDP real growth	%	5.0	-20.2	14.8	-8.1	3.8
Inflation	%	23.1	14.9	35.5	34.1	-0.9
Exports (fob) (goods)	US$m	105.0	88.0	101.0	61.0	75.0
Imports (fob) (goods)	US$m	186.0	81.0	116.0	78.0	161.0
Balance of trade	US$m	-81.0	7.0	-15.0	-17.0	-86.0
Current account	US$m	-108.0	-18.0	2.0	-42.0	-100.0
Foreign debt	US$bn	1.0	1.0	1.0	1.3	1.3
Total reserves minus gold	US$m	26.6	38.5	44.1	39.5	50.9
Foreign exchange	US$m	18.9	27.3	33.7	18.6	45.6
Exchange rate	per US$	920.73	981.48	1,563.62	1,804.20	2,092.13

win. The presence of Berewa in such an influential position as that of vice president could alienate not only members of the SLPP, but ordinary Sierra Leoneans. He is known to be hawkish – this was one of the reasons why Kabbah preferred him instead of Septimus Kaikai, who was presidential spokesman before the May 2002 poll.

The government and the international community saw the elections as a return to normalcy in Sierra Leone. Sierra Leoneans will be hoping that the peace will not be shattered.

Risk assessment

Economic	Improving
Political	Improving
Regional stability	Improving

COUNTRY PROFILE

Historical profile

1787 The state was founded by the British as a homeland for freed slaves.
1808 Freetown became a British colony. Over the following 60 years around 70,000 ex-slaves arrived in the country, mainly in the Freetown area. The colonial authorities appointed non-indigenous Africans to the civil service and senior administrative positions, thus laying the foundation for future civil strife.
1954 Sierra Leone was allowed some degree of self-rule through a new local administration. Sir Milton Margai of the Sierra Leone People's Party (SLPP) was appointed the head of the newly-established administration .
1961 Sierra Leone gained independence from Britain in April, but remained part of the Commonwealth. Sir Milton Margai became the country's first prime minister.
1964 Following Sir Milton's death, his half-brother, Sir Albert Margai, was appointed as prime minister.
1967 After the All Peoples Congress (APC) won the parliamentary election and its leader, Siaka Stevens, was appointed as prime minister, Sierra Leonean military officers staged a coup.
1968 After an army revolt, Stevens and the APC returned to government.
1971 Sierra Leone became a republic. Stevens was appointed as the country's first president.
1978 A new constitution was introduced, which established one-party rule in the country.
1985 The APC appointed Major General Joseph Momoh as president.
1991 Fighting from the civil war in neighbouring Liberia spilled across into Sierra Leone. Taking advantage of this, rebel groups opposed to the government of Major General Joseph Momoh – principally the Revolutionary United Front (RUF) led by Foday Sankoh – launched a series of attacks which took much of the eastern part of the country.
1992 A coup at the end of April brought Captain Valentine Strasser to power. He presided over a military government, the National Provisional Ruling Council (NPRC), which suspended the constitution and ruled by decree.
1996 Strasser was deposed by his colleague Brigadier Julius Bio in January. Multi-party elections in February ended four years of military rule. Ahmed Tejan Kabbah of the SLPP won 59.49 per cent of the vote and became president.
1997 In May, Major Johnny-Paul Koroma led a coup and ousted President Kabbah. The Armed Forces Revolutionary Council (ARFC) was installed in government, backed by the RUF. The international community condemned the coup and imposed economic sanctions. The Economic Community of West African States (Ecowas) dispatched a peace-keeping force, the Ecowas Monitoring Group (Ecomog), to Sierra Leone in order to reinstate the government of President Kabbah. A peace accord was reached in October in which Koroma pledged to step down in April 1998.
1998 Ecomog launched a military offensive against the AFRC after Koroma showed no sign of implementing the October 1997 agreement. In March, Ecomog ejected the AFRC from Freetown and President Kabbah returned to Sierra Leone. The RUF remained in control of large areas outside the capital.
1999 In July, the government and the RUF signed a peace agreement, allowing for the deployment of UN peace-keeping forces. A Cabinet of National Unity was sworn in by President Kabbah in November.
2000 In February, British forces were deployed in Sierra Leone to provide emergency logistical and tactical support for the mainly third-world UN force. Foday Sankoh was arrested after peace with the RUF broke down.
2001 Legislative and presidential elections were postponed because of the unstable security situation in the country.
2002 The state of emergency was lifted in March. On 14 May, President Ahmad Tejan Kabbah (SLPP) was re-elected with 70.3 per cent of the vote against Ernest Koroma (All People's Congress) (APC) 22.35 per cent. The SLPP won 83 of 112 seats in the 16 May parliamentary elections, with 27 seats going to the APC and two to the Peace and Liberation Party of former junta leader, Johnny Paul Koroma. The former rebels, the RUF, failed to win a single seat.

Political structure

Constitution
A multi-party democratic constitution, based on the US system, was adopted in October 1991, following a referendum. On 25 January 2002, an amendment to the constitution was promulgated which introduced the District Block System (DBS) for voting.

Form of state
Multiparty republic

The executive
Executive power is vested in the president, who is directly elected for a five-term. Fifty-five per cent of the vote must be won for victory in the first round of the presidential election. The cabinet is composed of ministers of state who are appointed by and answerable to the president.

National legislature
The national legislature is the 112-member House of Representatives. Under the District Block System (DBS), eight representatives from each of Sierra Leone's 14 districts are elected by proportional representation. In addition, 12 paramount chiefs, each representing a district, also sit in paraliament.

Legal system
The legal system is based on English law and is composed of a Supreme Court, Appeals Court and a High Court. In April 2002, the UN announced the establishment of a Special Court to try Sierra Leonean war criminals. It will be functioning by the end of 2002 and will operate under Sierra Leonean law.

Last elections
14 May 2002 (presidential and parliamentary)

Next elections
2006 (legislative); 2007 (presidential)

Political parties

Ruling party
Sierra Leone People's Party (SLPP) (elected 14 May 2002)

Main opposition party
All People's Congress (27 seats)

Population

4.82 million (2000)
Annual population growth rate was 2.2 per cent per annum during 1994–2000. About 44 per cent of the total population is under 15 years.
Sierra Leone's civil war killed an estimated 10,000 people and displaced one-third of the population.
Population density: 66 inhabitants per square km. Urban population: 35 per cent (1994–2000).

Ethnic make-up
Temne (30 per cent), Mende (30 per cent), other (39 per cent)

Religions
Islam (60 per cent), indigenous beliefs (30 per cent), Christianity (10 per cent)

Education

It has been estimated by Oxfam that 42 per cent of children age 6–11 will enrol for school in 2015.

Health

Life expectancy at birth is 38 years (1998) and the infant mortality rate is 161 per 1,000 live births (1999).

AIDS has killed between two to three times more people in Sierra Leone than its bloody civil war, yet has received relatively little attention. Around 68,000 people are infected with HIV/AIDS in Sierra Leone, 3,300 of them are under 15-years-old. The adult infection rate is estimated at around 3 per cent (2000). Since the beginning of the epidemic, over 56,000 children have lost their mother or both parents to the disease (1999). There were an estimated 8,200 AIDS deaths in 1999. The spread of the disease is due to a low prevelance of condom use – only 4 per cent of the population uses any form of contraception.

Main cities

Freetown (capital, estimated population 80,000 – there were 800,000 inhabitants in 1995, but the civil war led to mass migration), Bo (39,000), Kenema (31,000), Makeni (26,000), Koidu-Sefadu.

Languages spoken

English is the official language and the main medium for business. Other major languages are Krio, Mende and Temne.

Official language/s

English

Media

Press

Dailies: Main daily newspapers are *The Pool Newspaper*, *Concord Times*, *Awoko*, *Independent Observer*, *Standard Times* and *Daily Mail*.

Weeklies: Weeklies include *New Sierra Leonean*, *Vision* and *Weekend Spark*.

Business: The Ministry of Information and Broadcasting publishes the quarterly *Sierra Leone Trade Journal*.

Broadcasting

Two commercial radio and one commercial TV stations (mainly received in Freetown area). Broadcasts in English, French and local languages.

Economy

Sierra Leone is an impoverished country – despite its extensive mineral resources. Economic performance has been severely affected by the brutal civil war, leading to a recession and tumbling per capita income. The country has also been wracked with hyperinflation, reaching 90 per cent in 2000. The war had an adverse impact on government finances, with the fiscal deficit rising every year since the start of the conflict from 7.5 per cent of GDP in 1997 to 21 per cent in 2000.

However, the situation improved as the government and the Revolutionary United Front (RUF) began negotiating and UN peace-keeping troops were mobilised within the country. GDP grew for the first time in years in 2000, at 3.8 per cent compared to a contraction of 8.1 per cent in the previous year. The current account deficit has widened considerably, despite an increase in international aid, from around 18 per cent of GDP in 2000 to 29 per cent in 2001. Foreign debt has risen and by the end of 2000 it was estimated at 206.6 per cent of GDP. In 2001, foreign debt totalled US$1.2 billion.

There is a tension between macroeconomic stabilisation, advocated by the IMF, and the desire to rehabilitate the economy and prevent an upsurge in violence, either from combatants or demobilised guerrillas pushed into banditry due to economic disadvantage. However, the impact of fiscal adjustment will be mitigated by transferring defence expenditure to priority sectors, such as health and welfare, as well as significant foreign aid. Donor support will have to be sustained over the long-term to cope with the demobilisation and reintegration programmes which are designed to give ex-combatants a chance to earn in a civilian life.

The IMF reported that in 2000 the government had successfully implemented a programme supported by the IMF under the emergency post-conflict assistance policy. In March 2002, the IMF agreed to provide Sierra Leone a US$12 million loan under its Poverty Reduction and Growth Facility (PRGF). In the same month, the IMF and World Bank agreed to provide the country US$950 million in debt relief under its Heavily Indebted Poor Countries (HIPC) initiative.

External trade

Exports

Principal exports are rutile (typically 44 per cent of the total), bauxite (26 per cent), diamonds (20 per cent), coffee (2 per cent), cocoa (1 per cent).

Main destinations: US (typically 31 per cent of total), Germany (12 per cent), UK (9 per cent), the Netherlands (4 per cent), other EU countries (22 per cent)

Imports

Principal imports are foodstuffs (typically 34 per cent of total value), machinery and transport equipment (19 per cent), manufactured goods (14 per cent), fuel (10 per cent).

Main sources: Nigeria, UK, Germany, Japan, the Netherlands

Agriculture

The civil war seriously disrupted agricultural activity. The agricultural sector contributes 25 per cent to GDP and employs 65 per cent of labour force.

Area under cultivation is approximately 25 per cent of the total land area. It is limited by a traditional land tenure system and is mostly in the hands of smallholders engaged in subsistence farming.

Major cash export crops are cocoa, coffee, palm kernels and ginger.

Rice is the country's staple foodstuff, but despite government efforts towards self-sufficiency, imports have risen. Other food crops include maize, cassava, sweet potatoes and sorghum.

Production has been hampered by a lack of incentives and a poor marketing/distribution system. However, producer prices have been substantially increased.

The fishing sector offers considerable potential and has been expanded with oyster and shrimp farming.

Industry and manufacturing

The industrial sector accounts for 12 per cent of GDP and employs 5 per cent of the workforce.

Mainly limited to light manufacturing of consumer goods such as cigarettes, alcoholic beverages, plastic footwear, nails, paint and confectionery. Emphasis is placed on import substitution industries, but attempts to establish heavy industry have met with only limited success.

Expansion is limited by weak local demand, power shortages, foreign exchange shortages and low investment.

Mining

The mining sector contributes around 35 per cent to GDP and employs 10 per cent of the workforce.

Foreign companies have suspended mining operations due to the civil war and all mining permissions were suspended in January 2000. As a result, the mining sector has been increasingly dominated by smuggling and 'conflict diamonds', which were sold to fund the RUF's war. Official diamond production has declined from 2.5 million carats in 1992 to 700,000 carats in 1999, although the war has seen an increase in unofficial artisinal mining.

In June 2001, diamond exports were US$14 million, well below government estimates. With the peace process and the deployment of UN peace-keeping troops in diamond mining areas, the government is gaining more control over the sector and foreign companies have begun to resume operations.

Bauxite mining is also an important sector with large reserves at Sieromco and Port Loko. However, the war stopped production and with local infrastructure now in a state of disrepair, a resumption of mining activities is unlikely in the foreseeable future.

Before the war, Sierra Leone's rutile production was the largest in the world. The Gbangbatok mine in the south west used to produce 25 per cent of the world's rutile. The owners of the country's sole producer, Sierra Rutile, are Nord Resources of the US and Consolidated Rutile of Australia. If they judge the mines can be reopened as a commercial venture, production could resume.

Hydrocarbons

Sierra Leone has no known oil reserves and imports all its oil requirements. Several companies have carried out exploratory surveys for domestic supplies. In August 2000, the government announced a project to prospect for potential reserves in the Liberian basin within the country's territorial waters. It disclosed substantial oil reserves in May 2001 following an offshore survey by US-based TGC. Norwegian company TGS Nopec is to handle the bidding round for the government, with production sharing contracts (PSCs) due to be signed by the end of 2002. The UK government, which had troops stationed in Sierra Leone as part of the UN peace-keeping force, has shown considerable interest in the oil finds, which will give it an interest in maintaining peace at all costs. Many critics have termed the newly found resource 'blood oil', implying that oil exploitation could fuel conflict, with politicians and military men squabbling over the revenues.
Downstream, a refinery with a capacity of 10,000 barrels per day (bpd) exists at Freetown, but has been mothballed since 1982.

Energy

Installed generation capacity is approximately 100MW (mostly oil-fired thermal power stations). The Sierra Leone Electricity Company (SLEC) oversees electricity generation and supply.
A US$300 million hydroelectric project is planned on the Seli River with a capacity of 53MW, in an attempt to reduce oil imports. Financing remains uncertain.
The serious energy shortage in Sierra Leone has forced many citizens to buy personal diesel generators; more than 86 per cent of the population use kerosene for lighting.

Banking

Central bank
Bank of Sierra Leone
Main financial centre
Freetown

Time

GMT

Geography

Sierra Leone lies on the west coast of Africa, with Guinea to the north and east and Liberia to the south.

Climate

Tropical, with high humidity and rainfall. Dry season November–April, wet season rest of year. Average temperature range of 21–32 degrees Celsius (C) remains fairly constant throughout the year.

Entry requirements

Passports
Passport required by all, and they must be valid for six months.
Visa
Required by all except nationals of certain African countries. Visitors are advised to check regulations carefully before travelling.
Currency advice/regulations
Local currency up to Le50,000 can be imported, and unlimited foreign currency, but it must be declared.
Export of local currency up to Le50,000 and foreign currency up to the amount imported and declared.
Customs
All visitors must complete a customs declaration form for presentation on entering country.

Health (for visitors)

Mandatory precautions
Yellow fever vaccination certificate required if arriving from an infected area.
Advisable precautions
Hepatitis A, tetanus, polio, yellow fever and typhoid vaccinations. Malaria prophylaxis should be taken. Water precautions should be taken. There is a rabies risk.

Hotels

Available in Freetown, especially at Lumley Beach, within easy taxi access of the centre of Freetown. Limited availability outside capital. Credit cards accepted only in major hotels and payment required in US dollars. A service charge is usually included in bill.

Credit cards

Public holidays

Fixed dates
1 Jan, 27 Apr (Independence Day), 25 Dec, 26 Dec.
Variable dates
Good Friday, Easter Monday, Eid Al-Fitr, Eid Al-Adha, Prophet's Birthday (Moulid An-Nabi).

Working hours

Banking
Mon–Thu: 0800–1330; Fri: 0800–1400.
Business
Mon–Fri: 0800–1200, 1400–1630.
Government
Mon–Fri: 0800–1230, 1330–1645; close 1500 on Fri.
Shops
Mon–Fri: 0800–1200, 1400–1630; shops open Sat.

Telecommunications

Sierra Leone Telecommunications Company Ltd (Sierratel) is the national telecommunications operator. Its networks have been badly damaged by recent conflict.
Telephone/fax
Dialling for Sierra Leone: IDD access code + 232 followed by area code (22 for Freetown), followed by subscriber's number.
Service can be unreliable. International connections can be difficult, except at the Sierra Leone External Telecommunications Office (SLET), where it may be necessary to wait.
Mobile phones
Celtel (SL) was licensed to provide GSM900 coverage in Freetown as of March 2000.
Internet/e-mail
Prior to the renewal of civil strife in 1999, Sierratel had plans to develop a 64kbps Internet access service with Global One of the US. Plans have now been put on hold. A number of Internet Service Providers (ISPs) were subsequently selected to provide retail Internet access, but many of these, including Securicom's Fidonet, have since halted operations.

Electricity supply

230/240V AC, 50 cycles. Voltage fluctuation and power cuts occur.

Security

In 2002, the UK Foreign & Commonwealth Office (FCO) still advised against all travel to Sierra Leone. If it is necessary to visit the country, travel after dark should be avoided. Avoid carrying valuables in public.

Getting there

Air
National airline: Sierra National Airlines (to Accra, Abidjan, Conakry and Lagos).
International airport/s: Freetown-Lungi International (Code: FNA), 20km north of city (other side of wide river with ferry links to central Freetown and Lumley Beach area); bar, currency exchange, post office, shops.
Other airport/s: Freetown Lungi International (FNA), 20km north of Freetown (on the other side of river).
Airport tax: International departures US$20; not applicable to infants and transit passengers.
Surface
Road: Possible from Guinea and Liberia but routes not generally recommended.

Water: Freetown is the main port.

Getting about

National transport

Freetown has been cut off from much of the rest of Sierra Leone by civil strife.

Road: Main roads include Freetown-Makeni-Kabala and Freetown-Bo-Kenema; other roads can be difficult particularly in the rainy season. The Bo-Tiama highway and the Masiaka highway were being rehabilitated as part of a seven-year US$100 million road re-habilitation programme funded mainly by the World Bank and the EU.

Buses: Buses in Freetown tend to be over-crowded and unreliable. Regular service Freetown-Kambia, Freetown-Pendembu, Freetown-Makeni-Kabala.

Rail: China has pledged help for resurrecting Sierra Leone's rail system, which was closed down in 1967 due to technical and financial constraints. More than US$90 million of aid was made available to redevelop the country's transportation network in the future.

City transport

Taxis: Available in main towns; cannot be summoned by phone; fares by negotiation; tipping is not usual.

Car hire

Car hire is available at relatively high rates. International driving licence required.

BUSINESS DIRECTORY

Telephone area codes

Dialling code for Sierra Leone: IDD access code +232, followed by area code (22 for Freetown), followed by subscriber's number.

Chambers of Commerce

Chamber of Commerce of Sierra Leone, Guma Building, Lamina Sankoh Street, PO Box 502, Freetown (tel: 26-305).

Banking

Bank of Sierra Leone, PO Box 30, Siaka Stevens Street, Freetown (tel: 226501 fax: 224764).

First Merchant Bank of Sierra Leone Ltd, Sparta Building, 12 Wilberforce Street, Freetown (tel: 228493 fax: 228318).

National Development Bank Ltd, 21/23 Siaka Stevens Street, Freetown (tel: 226791/2 fax: 224468).

Rokel Commercial Bank (Sierra Leone) Ltd, PO Box 12, 25-27 Stevens Street, Freetown (tel: 222501 fax: 222563).

SIERRA LEONE COMMERCIAL BANK LTD, 29-31 Siaka Stevens Street, Freetown (tel: 225264 fax: 225292).

Standard Chartered Bank Sierra Leone Ltd, PO Box 1155, 9-11 Lightfoot Boston Street, Freetown (tel: 225220, 225021 fax: 225760).

Union Trust Bank Ltd, 2 Howe Street, Freetown (tel: 222792, 226954 fax: 226214)

Central bank

Bank of Sierra Leone, PO Box 30, Siaka Stevens Street, Freetown. Sierra Leone (tel: 226501 fax: 224764)

Travel information

Sierra National Airlines, Leone House, PO Box 285, 25 Pultney Street, Freetown (tel: 2075, 6297; fax: 2026).

Ministries

Department of Finance, Secretariat Building, George Street, Freetown (tel 26-911, 22-211; fax: 23-355).

Ministry of Information and Broadcasting, Youyi Building, Brookfields, Freetown.

Ministry of Tourism and Culture, Wallace Johnson Street, Freetown (tel: 26-345, 24-776).

Ministry of Trade and Industry, Ministerial Building, George Street, Freetown (tel: 26-045, 22-755, 22-706; fax: 28-373).

Other useful addresses

Central Statistics Office, Tower Hill, Freetown (tel: 23-897, 24-267).

National Trading Co, Howe Street, Freetown (tel: 23-986, 26-179).

Sierra Leone Embassy (USA), 1701 19th Street, NW, Washington DC 20009 (tel: 939-9261; fax: 483-1793; e-mail: saloneweb@starpower.net).

Sierra Leone External Telecommunications (SLET) Office, Wallace Johnson Street, Freetown (tel: 22-801, 24-591).

Sierra Leone Ports Authority, PO Box 386, Freetown.

Internet sites

Africa Business Network: http://www.ifc.org/abn

African Development Bank: http://www.afdb.org

AllAfrica.com: http://allafrica.com

Africa Online: http://www.africaonline.com

Mbendi AfroPaedia (information on companies, countries, industries and stock exchanges in Africa): http://mbendi.co.za

Sierra Leone: http://www.sierra-leone.org

Somalia

Michael Fishpool

KEY FACTS

Official name: Jamhuriyadda ee Soomaaliya (Somali Republic)

Head of State: Interim President Abd Al-Qasim Salad Hassan (elected by transitional parliament Aug 2000; first civilian president since war broke out in 1990)

Head of government: Interim Prime Minister Hassan Abshir Farah (appointed 12 Nov 2001)

Ruling party: Transitional National Government (TNG) (from Aug 2000) (controls only parts of the capital and pockets of the rest of the country) (Somaliland presidential and parliamentary elections last week Jan 2003)

Area: 738,000 square km

Population: 10.40 million (2001)

Capital: Mogadishu

Official language: Somali, Arabic

Currency: Somali shilling (SoSh) = 100 centesimi

Exchange rate: SoSh2,620.00 per US$ (Jan 2003)

GDP per capita: US$140 (2001)

Inflation: 100.00% (2001)

Foreign debt: US$2.53 billion (2001)

For the latest Key Facts, go to www.worldinformation.com

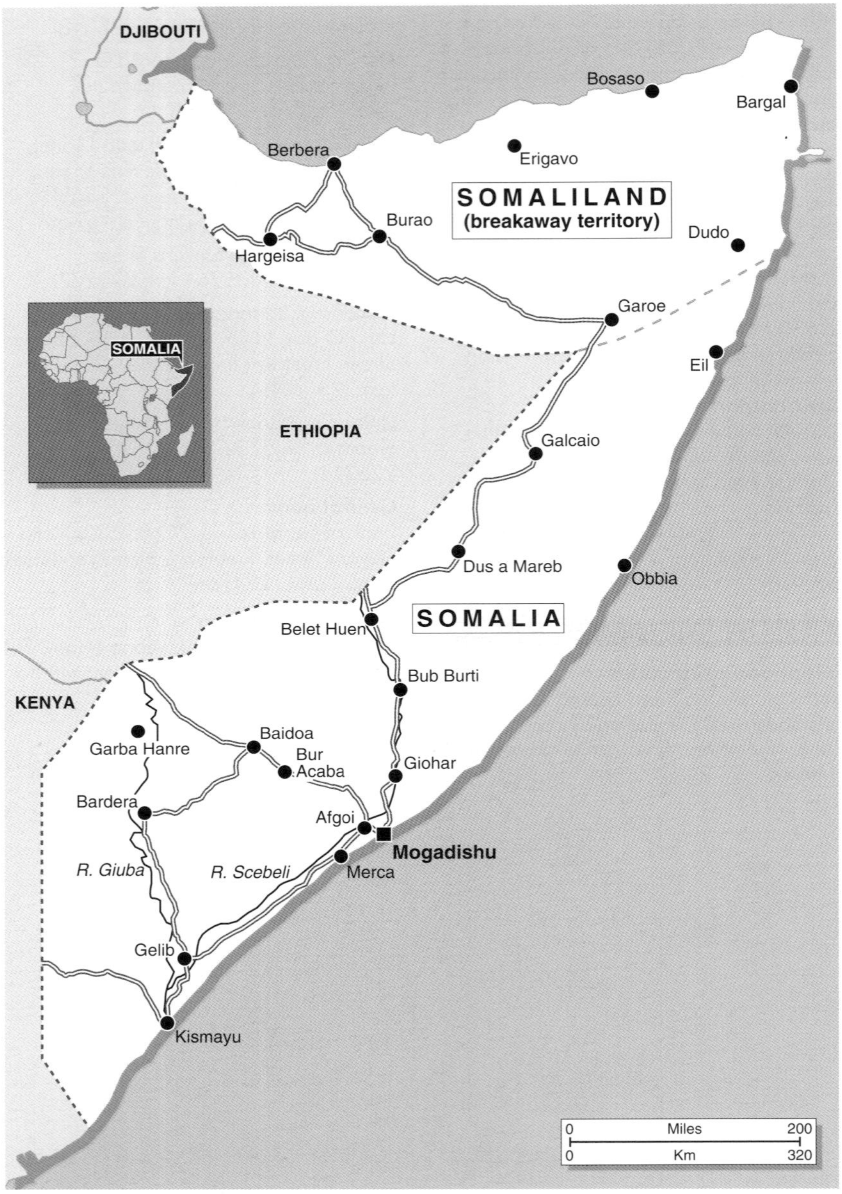

War and famine have destroyed Somalia, leaving a country in a complete state of anarchy and at the mercy of warlords. Attempts to bring peace and stability since 2000 by creating a Transitional National Government (TNG) and undertaking reconciliation talks between the warring militias have been slow. Opposition to the TNG, led by the Somali Reconstruction and Restoration Council (SRRC) – a coalition of warlords in southern Somalia – and Hussein Mohammed Aideed's United Somali Congress-Somali National Congress (USC-SNA), has reduced the effectiveness of the TNG. The TNG has continuously accused Ethiopia of interfering in Somalia's internal affairs by invading parts of the country and supporting opposition militias. In November 2001, divisions emerged within the TNG, leading the interim president, Abd Al-Qasim Salad Hassan, to appoint a new interim prime minister.

After the 11 September 2001 terrorist attacks in the US, Somalia returned to the international agenda with talk of a possible US attack on Somalia as part of the US's wider war on terrorism. International involvement in the Somali peace efforts was limited, causing long-term uncertainty and fuelling independence bids by self-proclaimed states in parts of the country.

Unsteady road

In October 2001, the interim prime minister, Ali Khalif Galaydh, was abruptly removed from office, following a vote of no confidence in the Transitional National Assembly (TNA). Interim President Hassan appointed former interior minister, Hassan Abshir Farah as the new interim prime minister in November 2001.

While Hassan Abshir Farahr is seen as a more popular figure in Somali politics and has promised to bring stability to the country, the new TNG faces an uphill struggle as it has little influence outside Mogadishu, where over 300,000 militiamen roam the countryside. In February 2002, the prime minister was provided with a stark warning of the problems in the country when unidentified Somalis threw hand grenades at his house in Mogadishu. The grenades exploded and injured two of his bodyguards. In October 2002, the TNG and 21 militias signed a cease-fire aimed at bringing the civil war to an end. It still remains to be seen whether the cease-fire will hold, especially as it was not signed by Somaliland and militias in control of central Somalia.

States within a state

Throughout 2001 and 2002, inter-clan violence continued unabated with the Rahanwein Resistance Army (RRA) engaged in fighting with rival militias in the central and south of the country. After deciding to formally break association with the TNG, in April 2002 the RRA announced the creation of a new state in south-western Somalia – South-West Somalia. The RRA's leader, Hassan Mohammed Nur Shatigadud, was appointed president and promised to increase the RRA control in Somalia. The self-proclaimed state is based around the RRA's strongholds of Bay and Bakol. This is the third part of Somalia to claim independence. Somaliland in north-western Somalia declared independence in 1991 and Puntland in the north-east in 1998.

Despite opposition from the TNG, Puntland and Ethiopia, Somaliland held a referendum on its constitution in May 2001. The referendum effectively re-confirmed Somaliland's desire for independence with voters overwhelmingly supporting the constitution. However, Somaliland's independence bid suffered from a serious setback in May 2002, when its president, Mohammed Egal, died from illness after undergoing treatment in South Africa. Vice President Dahir Riyale Kahin was appointed Egal's successor. As a member of the minority Gudabirsi clan rather than the majority Issak clan that Egal belonged to, there are fears that Kahin's appointment could lead to a political struggle which would jeopardise Somaliland's attempts for independence.

In July 2001, Puntland's leader, Abdullahi Yusaf, was sacked by tribal elders for attempting to overstay his elected term of office. When Jama Ali Jama was appointed as Yusaf's successor in mid-November 2001, Puntland looked close to civil war as fighting erupted between rival militias in Garowe, the capital of Puntland. It was alleged that Ethiopian troops were supporting militias loyal to Yusaf, although the accusation was quickly denied by the Ethiopian government.

On 21 November 2001, Yusaf's militias attacked and captured Garowe. Fighting in the surrounding area continued until May 2002, particularly around the towns of Qardho and Bosaso, the last stronghold of Jama's supporters. On 8 May, Yusaf's forces captured Bosaso, effectively returning Yusaf to the presidency. By regaining control, Yusaf has ensured Puntland's continued independence bid, at least until a peaceful and stable federal Somalian state can be achieved.

The next target?

After the fall of the Taliban in November 2001, the US became concerned that Bin Laden and Al-Qaeda members might try to escape to Somalia and stepped up surveillance of shipping in the Indian Ocean and off the Somali coast. In September 2001, the US named Somalia's Al-Itihaad Al-Islamiya (AIAI) (Unity of Islam) as having links with Al-Qaeda. AIAI was established in the late 1980s and wanted to turn Somalia into an Islamic state. The US believes that Al-Qaeda used AIAI bases to prepare for August 1998 attacks on its embassies in Kenya and Ethiopia. The US claims that after AIAI was driven out from southern Somalia and Puntland in the mid-1990s, its members dispersed into Somali villages, maintaining cells in Kenya and Tanzania, and financing local Islamic schools, courts and relief agencies. Following the US's allegation, the TNG claimed that the AIAI did not exist any longer and that Somalia was not involved in terrorism. Hussein Aideed accused the TNG of having links with AIAI and making Somalia a safe haven for terrorists.

In November 2001, the Al-Barakaat group of financial companies, which offered money-transfer facilities and international telephone service and was Somalia's largest employer, was named on a list of 62 organisations and individuals alleged to have provided funds to Al-Qaeda. Al-Barakaat's assets were frozen by the US, causing the company to cease operations. The company denied any link with Al-Qaeda and claimed that the US's action would affect ordinary Somalis as remittances from abroad are Somalia's largest source of foreign exchange, providing approximately US$500 million per year. Following Al-Barakaat's closure, Hormud Telecom purchased its assets for US$2 million in April 2002.

Need for peace

The ravages of war and famine have affected the Somali economy. High inflation of over 100 per cent in 2001 and the depreciation of the Somali shilling are also major barriers to Somalia's long-term economic recovery. Whereas many other

KEY INDICATORS — Somalia

	Unit	1996	1997	1998	1999	2000
Population	m	8.50	8.69	8.88	9.06	9.28
Gross domestic product (GDP)	US$bn	1.35	1.35	1.00	1.30	1.30
GDP per capita	US$	159	155	113	143	140
Foreign debt	US$bn	2.1	2.1	2.6	2.6	2.6
Exchange rate	per US$	2,620.00	2,620.00	2,620.00	2,586.00	2,587.58

unstable states have benefited from international loans as well as the presence of peace-keeping troops to help rebuild and bring stability, Somalia has had very little help. International attempts to bring some stability to Somalia during the early 1990s ended in failure when a US-led UN peace-keeping force unsuccessfully tried to capture the Somali warlord, General Farah Aideed.

The failure of the UN mission in the 1990s has made a return of a UN military force unlikely, although the TNG has constantly requested the presence of peace-keeping troops. In January 2001, the UN proposed to boost peace efforts by deploying a peace-building mission composed of political officers and aid agency workers. By February 2002, however, UN Secretary General Kofi Annan stated that Somalia was still too dangerous for the mission to deploy.

Without any stability in Somalia, international aid workers find it difficult and dangerous to work in the country. In March 2001, eleven aid workers from the UN and Médecins Sans Frontières (MSF) were abducted by militia in Mogadishu, but were later released. A rise in the number of kidnappings, where militias demand a ransom, has led aid agencies to continuously suspend aid operations.

Over 65 per cent of the population work on the land, but often face poor harvesting because of drought. Other factors also threaten farming, including the high cost of fuel, shortage of water and the high prices of local and imported food. In 2001, the rainy season failed to materialise on time, threatening famine in the south central regions of Somalia. The Gedo region was the worst hit and still did not experience any heavy rain when the rainy season arrived in May 2002. As a result, the World Food Programme (WFP) estimated that 600,000 Somalis needed at least 19,020 tonnes of food aid to survive during 2002.

Outlook

Without full international engagement in the reconciliation process in this war-torn country, Somalia's long-term prospects look bleak. Internal and regional attempts at peace have attempted to introduce a national government and improve relations between the various clans. This has had limited success, especially without financial aid to assist in the rebuilding of the country's economy. While talks of widening the US-led war on terrorism and attacking Somalia for alleged links with Al-Qaeda faded away by mid-2002, the US's involvement in Afghanistan could provide some hope for Somalia, by demonstrating that international engagement in a similar type of state can bring a chance of long-term peace after years of civil war.

Risk assessment

Economic	Poor
Political	Poor
Regional stability	Poor

COUNTRY PROFILE

Historical profile

Until the early sixteenth century, Somalia was part of the Arab-controlled Indian Ocean trading network.

The importance and prosperity of the Somali ports of Mogadishu and Brava were reduced once the Portuguese discovered a sea route to India via the Cape of Good Hope.

In the nineteenth century much of the Ogaden Desert – ethnically part of Somalia – was annexed by the Ethiopian empire of Menelik I; the area has remained part of Ethiopia ever since.

1900 Somalia was divided between Britain which controlled the northern region (the British Somaliland Protectorate) and Italy which controlled the southern region (Italian Somaliland – a UN Trust Territory under Italian administration between 1950–60).

1960 The northern and southern regions were united upon independence from Britain and Italy.

1969 Following the assassination of President Abdirashid Ali Shermarke, the army seized control and Mohammed Siad Barre became president. The country was renamed the Somali Democratic Republic, political parties were banned and the National Assembly dissolved.

1981 The Somali Salvation Front (which had staged an unsuccessful coup in 1978) joined forces with two other opposition groups to establish the Democratic Front for the Salvation of Somalia (DFSS).

1982 The DFSS linked up with the Somali National Movement (SNM) and with Ethiopian military support, invaded Somalia in July. Although the government repulsed the rebels, clashes continued throughout the 1980s.

1989 As the security situation worsened, President Barre offered to resign and hold free elections in 1990.

1991 On 28 January, President Siad Barre fled the country after rebels entered Mogadishu. Ali Mahdi Mohammed, leader of the Somali Salvation Council (SSC) was appointed interim president, but the coalition soon broke down and Mahdi was overthrown in November.

In May, Somaliland (in the north) broke away from war-torn Somalia. The self-styled Somaliland Republic, headed by Mohammed Ibrahim Egal, does not have international recognition.

1992 After a period of intense conflict between the numerous clans, the US sent a peace-keeping force to Somalia to protect the UN international humanitarian aid effort and restore order.

1993 A partial peace pact was signed in January. On 1 May, the UN began peace-keeping operations, taking over from the US Marines. From June through to October, the US launched a military offensive against General Aideed and the Somali National Alliance (SNA) in Mogadishu after US and UN troops were killed in an ambush.

1994 After an unsuccessful campaign, the US withdrew all of its forces from Somalia.

1995 Remainder of the UN peace-keeping force withdrew.

1996 General Aideed, leader of the USC and SNA, died from gunshot wounds in August. His son, Hussein Aideed, replaced him as head of the clan-based gang.

1997 On 22 December, 26 of Somalia's 28 factions signed the Cairo Declaration peace accord.

1998 The north-eastern region followed the example set by Somaliland and declared independence as Puntland under the leadership of Colonel Abdullahi Yussef Ahmed.

1999 Inter-clan violence continued in central and southern Somalia. In September, President Omar Guelleh of Djibouti announced an international peace plan based on the participation of Islamic and civil groups rather than warlords.

2000 In August, the four-month reconciliation conference in Djibouti ended when the transitional national government (TNG) elected the country's first civilian president since war broke out in 1990 – Abd Al-Qasim Salad Hassan, the interim president, appointed Ali Khalif Galaydh as interim prime minister in October. SNA chairman, Hussein Aideed, formed an opposition group to the TNG, the Somali Restoration and Reconciliation Council (SRRC).

2001 Fighting continued in the south of the country. In a referendum in May, a huge majority in Somaliland voted in favour of independence from the rest of Somalia.

On 25 July Yusuf Haji Nur was sworn in as president of the self-proclaimed autonomous region of Puntland in the north-east, replacing Colonel Ahmed Abdullahi Yusuf. The interim prime minister of the TNG, Ali Khalif Galaydh, and his cabinet lost a vote of no-confidence on 28 October. Hassan Abshir Farah was appointed interim prime minister on 11 November.

2002 The Rahanwin Resistance Army (RRA) declared the formation of a new state in south-western Somalia in April to rule six districts from its capital in Baidoa. The president of Somaliland, Muhammad Haji Ibrahim Egal, died on 4 May and was succeeded by the vice president, Dahir Riyale Kahin.

Political structure

The executive

The Transitional National Government (TNG), made up of different clan leaders, rules from Mogadishu. The self-styled republics of Somaliland and Puntland have their own elected governments (but are unrecognised internationally). In April 2002, a new state was declared in south-western Somalia.

National legislature

In July 2000, a charter for an interim government was agreed – a 225-member Transitional National Assembly (TNA), selected on a clan basis (25 seats reserved for women members), nominated by the peace conference delegates. The TNA nominated members of an interim three-year government and elected an interim president, who appointed a interim prime minister.

Legal system

There is no organised system of criminal justice in Somalia. Enforcement of criminal laws is haphazard.

Political parties

There are no formal political parties and warlords and their supporters wield most of the power. Political organisation largely reflects membership of clans and sub-clans. There are 28 main factions. The main groups include the Somali Reconstruction and Restoration Council (SRRC), United Somali Congress-Somali National Alliance (USC-SNA) and the Rahanwein Resistance Army (RRA).

Ruling party

Transitional National Government (TNG) (from Aug 2000) (controls only parts of the capital and pockets of the rest of the country)

Population

9.28 million (2000)

Annual population growth rate: 2.4 per cent (1994–2000). Approximately 47 per cent of the total population is under 14 years; 50 per cent 15–64; 3 per cent over 65. Population density: 15 inhabitants per square km. Urban population: 28 per cent (1994–2000).

Religions

Islam is the state religion (majority Sunni Muslims) (98 per cent), Christian minority (2 per cent).

Education

The UN Children's Fund (UNICEF) supports 352 primary schools in central and southern Somalia, out of 418 that are operational. Additionally, UNICEF has rehabilitated 35 schools, trained 2,300 teachers and initiated a school improvement programme. Several non-government organisations have concentrated on adult literacy programmes and civic education. Private education has recently been re-established in Somalia although school fees are proving to be out of reach of the ordinary Somali family. The adult literacy rate is estimated at 49.7 per cent for men and 25.8 per cent for women. The overall primary school enrolment is typically 13.8 per cent, with 14.9 per cent enrolment for boys and 12.1 per cent for girls. Somaliland expatriates residing in the United Arab Emirates (UAE) have initiated efforts to raise funds for the Amoud University. The University, established in 1997 in Boroma, is essentially a community project.

Health

The country's health services collapsed during the war and access to health care depends mostly on external assistance. UNICEF remains the key provider of essential medical services and supplies to 123 maternal and child health centres, 174 health posts, and 16 hospitals. World Bank estimates during the period 1994 and 2000 showed that the average life expectancy was 48 years and the infant mortality rate stood at 121 per 1,000 live births. Only 1.5 per cent of children between one- and two-years-old is vaccinated. The maternal mortality rate is typically 1,600 deaths per 100,000 live births. Somalia's nation-wide malnutrition rate of 23 per cent is one of the highest in the world. Surveys in areas with high concentrations of displaced families show malnutrition rates as high as 40 per cent. In addition, Somalia has the highest incidence of tuberculosis in the world, and cholera is endemic in most areas.

It is estimated that 31 per cent of the population have access to improved water facilities. There are 0.4 physicians and two nurses typically available per 100,000 people.

UN reports on food and nutrition in 2002 suggest that food insecurity experienced in Gedo (located west of the Somali capital, Mogadishu), coupled with drought and civil strife had resulted in the displacement of thousands of households and access to basic health care.

Welfare

In 2001, the worst drought in seven years displaced an estimated 25,000 people from their homes. Some 300,000 refugees and asylum seekers from Somalia lived in about two dozen countries at the end of 2001. An estimated 400,000 Somalis were internally displaced.

Although the World Food Program (WFP) supports the repatriation of refugees with a nine-month food supply or cash equivalent, more than 10 per cent of the population required emergency food assistance.

In 2001, UNICEF appealed to donor nations for US$23 million to support emergency operations in Somalia, of which only US$2 million was provided by mid-July 2001, forcing a rapid reduction in aid.

UN reports in May 2001 revealed that as the crisis in Gedo located west of the Somali capital, Mogadishu, continues to develop, humanitarian assistance has intensified to deliver basic services to Somali people on both sides of the Kenya/Somalia border. Insecurity continues to be the greatest threat to the lives and welfare of the population who are highly dependent on external assistance. International aid is jeopardised by widespread factional fighting, the kidnapping of aid workers and also by the mining of all major roads in Northern Gedo, the area most in need of food aid.

Main cities

Somalia: Mogadishu (capital, estimated population 980,000), Baidoa, Kismayu, Merca.

Somaliland: Hargeisa, Berbera, Burao, Boramo, Las Anod, Erigavo.

Puntland: Badhane, Bosaso, Garowe, Galkayo, Lasanod.

Languages spoken

English is often used for business and Italian is also in use.

Official language/s

Somali, Arabic

Media

Press

Dailies: Daily publications from Mogadishu include *Mogadishu Times*, *Quran* and *Xog-Ogaal*. *Jamhuurriya* is published from Hargeisa. There are internet daily news services from *Somali Press Online* (http://home.ica.net/~somalipress/) and *Dhambaal*.

Weeklies: Weeklies include *Dadka*, *Panorama*, *Republican* (Hargeisa), *Sanca* and *Xurmo*.

Periodicals: Periodicals are mainly monthly publications including *Ayaamaha* and *Himilo*.

Economy

Exports are dominated by livestock rearing, which is the country's principal foreign exchange earner. Since 70 per cent of the country lives on subsistence agriculture, with some working as nomadic herders, much of the economy is reliant on the weather. However, with periodic floods and droughts, harvests frequently produce fewer crops than the amount needed to sustain the population. This means that Somalia is dependent on foreign food aid. The permanent economic gloom has been heightened by civil war and famine, which

have destroyed Somalia's economy. Since hostilities began, the economy has been broken down under the jurisdiction of several regional leaders or clan leaders. The situation is complicated by the break-away Republic of Somaliland, which has become an autonomous zone with its own currency and government. Within the self-declared territory of Somaliland, there is also an autonomous region known as Puntland State of Somalia, which also has its own chaotic economic policy.
Somaliland represents the strongest local economy and has undergone something of a boom since it declared independence in 1991. In a situation of relative peace and without the tyranny of the central Somalian state, the autonomous region has undergone a modest transformation with infrastructural improvements and an emergent business elite. However, without international recognition, Somaliland cannot access funds from the IMF or World Bank or develop trade relations. The May 2001 referendum, which voted in favour of full independence from Somalia, could pave the way towards full statehood and therefore greater economic prosperity.
The Puntland State, where many Somalis wish to remain part of Somalia, faces many of the problems faced by Somalia proper – factional fighting and almost complete economic collapse.

External trade

The poor balance of trade reflects the continuing need for the large-scale import of fuels and food.

Exports

Principal exports are livestock and bananas. Saudi Arabia imposed a ban on the import of Somali sheep and goats in February 1998 after an outbreak of Rift Valley fever.
Main destinations: United Arab Emirates (34.2 per cent of 2000 total), Saudi Arabia (34.1 per cent), Yemen (16 per cent), Oman (7.3 per cent), Bahrain (1.6 per cent).

Imports

Principal imports are manufactures, non-fuel primary products, fuels, food, machinery and transport equipment, construction materials.
Main sources: Djibouti (26 per cent of 2000 total), Kenya (11.8 per cent), India (9.1 per cent), Thailand (6.9 per cent), Brazil (6 per cent).

Agriculture

The agricultural sector is the most important in the economy. It contributes about 65 per cent to GDP and employed 65 per cent of the working population. It is often badly affected by drought.
It is mostly a pastoral form of production. Before the civil war, land was owned by the state and leased by farmers.
Much of the land is desert or semi-desert and only 13 per cent is cultivated, making food security a constant concern. Some crops are grown on the fertile land in the Juba and Scebali valleys.
The grasslands are suitable for grazing livestock. Nomads (a very small sector), raise livestock, and are being encouraged to set up permanent agricultural or fishing communities.
Subsistence farmers grow maize and sorghum; wheat and rice are imported.
The most important cash crops are livestock, bananas, cotton and frankincense.

Industry and manufacturing

The industrial sector as a whole contributes about 9 per cent to GNP and employs 8 per cent of the working population.
The principal industries are meat and fish processing, sugar refining, fruit and vegetable canning, textiles and leather goods. Many factories are idle because foreign exchange shortages have cut off foreign inputs.

Tourism

There are no tourism facilities.

Mining

There are significant mineral resources, but they have not yet been commercially exploited. The most important regions include an area extending from the Ethiopian border to beyond Berbera in Somaliland and west of the River Scebali near Mogadishu. The former contains reserves of copper, gold, molybdenum and bismuth while the latter contains iron, gold and apatite.
The country also contains reserves of uranium, marble, manganese, tin, beryl and columbite. Salt and gypsum were extracted commercially before the civil war began.

Hydrocarbons

Potential oil and gas reserves have been found near Mogadishu and in the north, but the country still relies on imports for most of its fuel needs.
The Republic of Somaliland has invited international companies with exploration rights within its self-declared territories to return – including Agip, BP Amoco, Chevron and Conoco. It has also invited companies to take over the Berbera fuel distribution centre which contains the Republic's main port. This has attracted attention from TotalFinaElf and Royal/Dutch Shell. However, international investors appear to be waiting until Somaliland achieves full international recognition before resuming operations in this area.

Oil

Downstream, Somalia has a single oil refinery with a capacity of 10,000 barrels per day (bpd), although it has not been in use for some years and is probably in a state of disrepair.

Gas

Somalia has one natural gas field with reserves of around 6 billion cubic metres, although political and economic chaos have prevented exploitation.

Energy

Electricity generation (all thermal) amounts to under 100MW and is fuelled by diesel which has to be imported. A monopoly of electricity generation and supply is owned by the Ente Nazionale Energia Elettrica (ENEE).

Banking

Central bank

Central Bank of Somalia

Main financial centre

Mogadishu

Time

GMT plus three hours

Geography

Somalia lies on the east coast of Africa, with Ethiopia to the north-west and Kenya to the west. There is a short frontier with Djibouti. Somalia has a long coastline on the Indian Ocean and the Gulf of Aden, forming the Horn of Africa.

Climate

Tropical. Humid on coast, drier in north. Average temperatures 27–32 degrees Celsius (C) throughout year, but can reach 42 degrees C on coast. Dry seasons from January–February and August–September. Rainy seasons from March–June and October–December.

Dress codes

Lightweight clothes are required. Women should dress modestly.

Entry requirements

Passports

Required by all.

Visa

Required by all.

Currency advice/regulations

Import/export of only small amounts of local currency is allowed. Import of foreign currency is unlimited, but it must be declared on a form for which a small charge may be made. Currency transactions should be recorded at each exchange. Export of foreign currency is limited to the amount declared on arrival.
The Somali shilling is the unit of currency, except in Somaliland, which uses the Somaliland shilling. US dollars are accepted everywhere.

Health (for visitors)

Mandatory precautions

Yellow fever and cholera certificates are required if arriving from an infected area.

Advisable precautions

Yellow fever, cholera, typhoid and polio vaccinations are advisable. Malaria prophylaxis should be taken as risk exists throughout the country (two types of prophylaxis are recommended). The water system is poor so precautions are essential. There is a risk of meningitis in the north of the country.

During the first six months of 2002, there were some outbreaks of cholera in Mogadishu, Kismayu in the south and Puntland in the north-east.

Medical facilities in Somalia are limited and travellers should carry personal supplies of medicines and medications with them.

Hotels

Available in principal towns. Service charge of 10 per cent added to bills.

Credit cards

Credit cards are not accepted in Somalia.

Public holidays

Fixed dates

1 Jan, 1 May, 26 Jun (Independence), 1 Jul (National Day), 21–22 Oct (Anniversary of 1969 Revolution).

Variable dates

Eid Al-Fitr, Eid Al-Adha, Islamic New Year, Prophet's Birthday (Maulid An-Nabi), Ashoura.

Working hours

Banking

Sat–Thu: 0800–1130.

Business

Sat–Thu: 0800–1230, 1630–1900.

Government

Sat–Thu: 0800–1400.

Shops

Sat–Thu: 0900–1300, 1600–2000.

Telecommunications

An effective telecommunications system exists in major towns in Somalia.

Electricity supply

220V AC, 50 cycles. The electricity system is poor.

Social customs/useful tips

Islamic customs should be respected. It is the convention to use the right and not the left hand when shaking hands and passing or receiving anything. Muslims are not permitted to drink alcohol or eat pork. Do not smoke or drink in public during Ramadan. Refusal of offered refreshment is considered discourteous. Shoes should be removed on entry to mosques.

Security

Visitors are advised not to travel to southern Somalia or the northern-eastern autonomous region of Punt and in Somaliland.

Crimes are common, with kidnapping and armed robbery particularly occurring in Mogadishu and other areas in the south. It is advisable for visitors to check on conditions before travelling through the country.

Getting there

Air

Air Somalia, an airline launched in February 2001, privately owned by Somalis, flies between Mogadishu airport and Djibouti and the United Arab Emirates twice weekly. There is limited air travel to Mogadishu, Hargeisa (Somaliland), Galcayo and Bosaso (Puntland) from Addis Ababa (Ethiopia), Nairobi (Kenya) and Dubai (United Arab Emirates).

National airline: Somali Airlines (suspended operations from 1991).

International airport/s: Mogadishu International (Code: MGQ), 6.4km from city. Hargeisa airport (Somaliland) re-opened on 30 June 1997 after being closed for three years.

Surface

Road: There are road links with Kenya in the south and Djibouti in the north. Four-wheel drive vehicles are recommended.

Rail: There is no railway system in Somalia.

Main port/s: El Ma'an, Bassasso, Kismayu, Merca, Mogadishu.

Berbera is the economic lifeline for the self-declared Somaliland Republic.

Getting about

National transport

Air: Air Somalia, a private airline owned by Somalis, was launched in February 2001. It flies between Mogadishu and 10 towns throughout Somalia.

Road: Travel may be restricted outside Mogadishu. Local enquiries should be made. Driving is on the right. Travel to Hargeisa and Berbera is restricted because of insecurity.

Buses: The network outside Mogadishu is restricted.

Water: Coastal shipping of both freight and passengers is extensive. The number of incidents of piracy off the Somali coast has increased sharply in the last few years.

City transport

Taxis: Fares by negotiation; tipping is not usual. Can be hired on a time basis.

Car hire

Car hire is available in Mogadishu, with four-wheel drive vehicles obtainable from Marill (Somalia) Limited. There are no traffic lights in the country except in Hargeisa in Somaliland. The condition of the roads makes driving difficult and night driving is dangerous.

BUSINESS DIRECTORY

Telephone area codes

Dialling code for Somalia: IDD access code +252 followed by area code (1 for Mogadishu, 52 for Bosaso (Puntland), 21 for Hargeisa (Somaliland)), followed by subscriber's number.

Banking

Commercial and Savings Bank of Somalia, PO Box 203, Juley Street 1st, Mogadishu (tel: 22861, 22959, 25093, 20585).

Central bank

Central Bank of Somalia, PO Box 11, Corso Somalia 55, Mogadishu, Somalia (tel: 657733).

Travel information

Daallo Airlines, PO Box 1954, Djibouti-ville, Djibouti (tel: (+253) 353-401, 351-765; fax: (+253) 356-660).

Somali Airlines (operations suspended since 1991), PO Box 726, Via Medina, Mogadishu (tel: 81-533; fax: 80-489).

Other useful addresses

Agricultural Development Corporation, PO Box 930, Mogadishu.

Livestock Development Agency of Somalia, PO Box 1759, Mogadishu.

National Petroleum Agency of Somalia, PO Box 573, Mogadishu.

Somali Broadcasting Service, Ministry of Information and National Guidance, Private Bag, Mogadishu (tel: 2455).

Statistical Department, PO Box 1742, Mogadishu (tel: 80-385).

Internet sites

Africa Business Network: http://www.ifc.org/abn

African Development Bank: http://www.afdb.org

Africa Online: http://www.africaonline.com

AllAfrica.com: http://allafrica.com

Puntland State of Somalia: http://members.tripod.com/~Puntland/

Somalia News: http://www.somalianews.com

Somaliland official website: http://www.somalilandgov.com

United Nations Somalia: http://www.unsomalia.org

KEY FACTS

Official name: The Republic of South Africa

Head of State: President Thabo Mbeki (since Jun 1999)

Head of government: President Thabo Mbeki

Ruling party: African National Congress (ANC)

Area: 1,127,200 square km

Population: 44.40 million (2001)

Capital: Cape Town (legislative); Johannesburg (financial); Pretoria (administrative); Bloemfontein (judicial)

Official language: Afrikaans, English, Ndebele, Sesotho, Northern Sotho, SiSwati, Tsonga, Tswana, Venda, Xhosa, Zulu

Currency: Rand (R) = 100 cents

Exchange rate: R8.83 per US$ (Jan 2003)

GDP per capita: US$2,549 (2001); US$2,167 (2002)**

GDP real growth: 2.20% (2002); 2.6% (2002)** (revised)

Unemployment: 40.00% (2001)*

Inflation: 5.80% (2001); 7.1% (2002)**

Balance of trade: US$3.80 billion (2002)

Foreign debt: US$24.05 billion (2001)

* estimated figure

For the latest Key Facts, go to www.worldinformation.com

South Africa

Philip Alexander

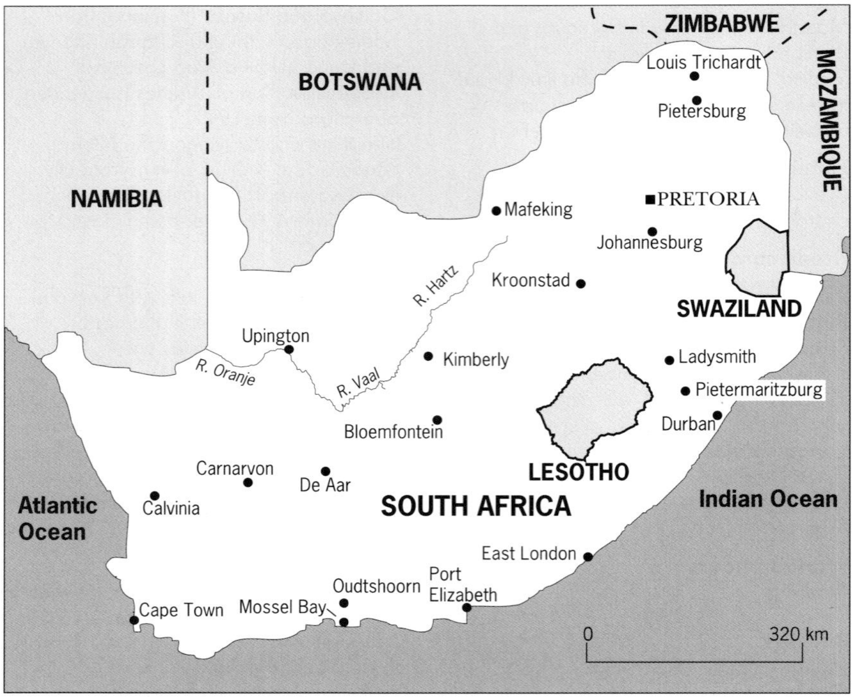

In many areas, 2002 was a year in which the progress made in South Africa since the end of the apartheid era continued relatively smoothly, but it was by no means without challenges for President Thabo Mbeki and his African National Congress (ANC) government. On the domestic side, the ANC collective conscience continued to wrestle with the competing needs of the party's revolutionary roots and the government's administration of one of Africa's most modern and open economies. Overseas, the financial crisis in Argentina and decline in trade, tourism and investment resulting from the terror attacks on the US on 11 September 2001 hit South Africa hard, especially due to its benchmark role in global metals and minerals markets. However, the most painful issue of all cut across foreign and domestic policy, to threaten the very beliefs at the heart of South Africa's post-apartheid multiracial democracy – the descent of Zimbabwe from one of Africa's most prosperous democracies into an impoverished, violent elected despotism.

The decline of the right

Since the end of the apartheid system in 1994, the ANC has consolidated its grip on South Africa and, faced with little organised opposition, appears virtually invincible. In the June 1999 elections, the ANC won 66.4 per cent of the vote, giving it 266 seats in the 400-seat assembly. The main opposition party is the centre-right, white-dominated Democratic Alliance (DA), which was formed by the Democratic Party, NNP and the tiny Federal Alliance after the parliamentary elections.

In October 2001, the NNP, the successor of the National Party which had introduced apartheid to South Africa, demerged from the DA and entered into a power-sharing agreement with the ANC. The deal between the erstwhile political foes gave the ANC control of Western Cape province, which had until then been the only province where the ANC had no involvement in government, while the NNP was given a number of posts at local, provincial and national level. The alliance strengthened the power of the ANC, which has already co-opted key opposition parties, including the Zulu-based Inkatha Freedom Party (IFP) and the pan-Africanist Azanian People's Organisation (Azapo). This leaves the DA, with just 10 per cent of the seats, as the only vocal opposition party in South Africa.

A one party state?

With such a broad support base, from the right-wing NNP to the left-wing South African Communist Party (SACP), the ANC appears to have turned South Africa into a one-party state. However, the ANC's shift to the right has alienated its traditional left-wing allies in the SACP and the Congress of South African Trade Unions (Cosatu). Political divisions threaten to destabilise Mbeki's power base within the ANC and shatter its apartheid-era alliance with the left and the trades unions.

Many of the problems stem from the President's uncompromising attitude, which many interpret as over-bearing arrogance and dogmatism. Mbeki likes to portray himself as a tough President who cannot be swayed from his long-term targets of macroeconomic stability and liberalisation. However, he has set himself up for damaging criticism on issues he need not have involved himself in, such as his claim that AIDS is not necessarily caused by the HIV virus. Meanwhile, he has faced condemnation of his failure to take a tougher line on other issues, notably the crisis in Zimbabwe.

Racial divisions are still apparent and threaten political stability, while arguments rage over the direction of economic policy, which has so far done little to alleviate the crushing poverty affecting millions of South Africa's poor. As tensions have grown, Mbeki appears to have become more autocratic and intolerant of criticism, which has made him deeply unpopular within parts of the coalition government.

The IFP leader, home affairs minister Chief Mangosuthu Buthelezi, has issued a number of threats to pull his party out of the coalition with the ANC. The ANC has opposed his proposal to relax immigration controls as part of an effort to ease the country's skills shortage. The IFP's national council has also reportedly discussed whether to expell the ANC from the provincial coalition that rules KwaZulu-Natal, the country's most populous province. Buthelezi has also clashed with Mbeki over his policy on HIV/AIDS and on the Zimbabwe issue, arguing that South Africa should take a tougher line against Zimbabwe's President Robert Mugabe. Buthelezi has instructed the premier of IFP-controlled KwaZulu-Natal, which has the highest incidence of HIV/AIDS in South Africa, to provide retroviral drugs free of charge to all HIV-infected pregnant women in a direct challenge to government policy

The SACP and Cosatu who fought alongside the ANC against the apartheid regime, are also in confrontation with Mbeki's economic restructuring programme, fuelled by public concern over unemployment which rose from 16 per cent in 1996 to around 40 per cent in 2001. Lower wage settlements coupled with rising costs of basic necessities – the cost of maize, the country's staple food, doubled in the year to June 2002 – have severely eroded quality of life and in 2002 a fifth of South African children showed signs of stunted growth due to malnutrition. The SACP and Cosatu also believe that state-owned companies should be used to even out the disparities caused by apartheid, whereas the government, under the auspices of the IMF, claims that greater private sector involvement in the economy is necessary to generate investment.

In July 2002, the SACP's general secretary, Jeremy Cronin, drew comparisons between the ANC and Zimbabwe's Zanu-PF, which had engaged in a campaign of repression against its opponents. The remarks were rejected by the ANC and Mbeki. Meanwhile, Cosatu has launched a number of strike actions over rising food prices and unemployment associated with the privatisation programme; the organisation, which represents nearly two million workers, claims that privatisation has resulted in over 100,000 job losses. Cosatu held two general strikes – in August 2001 and October 2002 – which achieved a mixed turn-out across the country, with most strikers employed in the public sector and the mining and textile industries. The ANC leadership condemned the strike action in 2002 as 'neither justified nor productive', indicating that it was unwilling to compromise with its alliance partners.

Aid for AIDS

The central issue which allowed Cosatu to diversify its activities was the continuing controversy surrounding ANC policy towards the HIV/AIDS pandemic in South Africa. More than 10 per cent of the population – over 4.5 million individuals – are thought to be infected, and as many as seven million are expected to have died from the disease by 2010. Mbeki has tried to distance himself from earlier comments that the disease was the product of poverty, rather than infection, but Cosatu has received support from figures of universal

KEY INDICATORS — South Africa

	Unit	1996	1997	1998	1999	2000
Population	m	40.34	41.23	42.13	43.05	44.70
Gross domestic product (GDP)	US$bn	0.00	148.50	134.50	130.20	125.50
GDP per capita	US$	3,568	3,590	3,188	3,029	2,863
GDP real growth	%	4.2	2.5	0.7	1.9	3.4
Inflation	%	7.4	8.6	6.9	5.2	5.4
Share prices	1995=100	116.1	120.1	107.1	103.8	116.5
Unemployment	%	5.1	5.4	5.6	37.5	*40.0
Manufacturing output	1995=100	101.5	104.3	101.1	101.4	105.9
Coal output	mtoe	109.3	116.5	119.1	116.7	118.8
Exports (fob) (goods)	US$m	30,263.0	31,171.0	29,234.0	28,361.0	31,434.0
Imports (fob) (goods)	US$m	27,569.0	28,848.0	27,216.0	24,611.0	27,202.0
Balance of trade	US$m	2,700.0	2,300.0	2,000.0	3,800.0	4,231.0
Current account	US$m	-1,900.0	-2,300.0	-1,900.0	-500.0	-469.0
Foreign debt	US$bn	21.2	23.7	24.2	24.2	24.9
Total reserves minus gold	US$m	942.0	4,799.0	4,357.0	6,353.0	6,083.0
Foreign exchange	US$m	940.0	4,790.0	4,171.0	6,065.0	5,793.0
Exchange rate	per US$	4.30	4.61	5.53	6.11	6.94

* estimated figure

appeal, such as Archbishop Desmond Tutu, for its complaints that the President remains too ambivalent on the issue. In particular, the 400 per cent increase in spending on combating HIV/AIDS over the next three years seems dominated by research and education priorities. While these preventative aims are in themselves laudable, the government appeared unwilling to confront the daunting task of treating those already infected.

A decision in April 2002 to offer anti-retroviral drug treatment to infected rape victims was seen as an important precedent, with moves to treat children who have contracted the disease from their mothers now on the cards. Questions will remain about how South Africa will be able to afford widespread treatment, but pressure on international pharmaceutical companies is beginning to pay dividends. In 2001, the US Congress granted permission for local companies to manufacture cheap generic versions of anti-retroviral drugs and several multinational manufacturers have offered to donate supplies as direct aid.

The Mugabe factor

The key to South Africa's success or failure in confronting HIV/AIDS would appear to be the strength of international goodwill towards the country. Unfortunately, President Robert Mugabe of Zimbabwe appeared during 2001/02 to be making strenuous efforts to undermine President Mbeki and his international standing. Since his defeat in a constitutional referendum in February 2000, which would have allowed him to extend his term of office without the elections tabled for March 2002, Mugabe has increasingly sought to control the country by terror. Above all, he unleashed his own personal force of storm troopers, the self-styled 'war veterans', many of whom were too young to have fought in Zimbabwe's war of independence in the 1970s, but were promised substantial inducements by the ruling Zanu-PF party. In particular, the group seized farms owned by the country's white minority, prompting international condemnation, and began systematic attacks on members of the opposition Movement for Democratic Change (MDC), which is led by Morgan Tsvangirai.

Tsvangirai and heads of government in a number of Commonwealth countries such as the UK and Australia looked to Mbeki to provide a lead in bringing Mugabe to heel. However, the South African President refused on a number of occasions during 2001 to condemn the conduct of the Zanu-PF administration explicitly. This was presented in part as a warning to the European former colonial masters that land and wealth distribution in southern Africa remained unequal, implying that the cause of 'war veteran' violence (if not the means) was legitimate. However, Mbeki's critics at home alleged that his real concern was because the MDC was a union-led movement, which therefore carried awkward echoes of the ANC's rocky relationship with Cosatu.

A tentative step forward was taken in September 2001, when Mbeki joined with President Olesegun Obasanjo of Nigeria to present a peace proposal, in which non-violent land redistribution would take place under the auspices, and with the financial aid, of the Commonwealth. Yet, in the wake of 11 September 2001, world attention focused elsewhere and momentum was lost. Additionally, in November, a group calling themselves the Pan-African Congress (PAC) attempted a series of war veteran-style land occupations in South Africa, and while they were removed promptly by the police, this development set alarm bells ringing, especially among the local business community.

Ultimately, Mugabe's determination to secure victory in the March 2002 presidential elections by any means fair or more especially foul doomed all attempts at conciliation. The election was marked by violence, the confiscation of ballots in MDC-supporting areas and deliberate moves to obstruct voters from going to the poll. Unsurprisingly, Mugabe was victorious. A more naked act of fraud would have been hard to imagine, prompting immediate condemnation from the EU and US. However, Mbeki initially claimed that the elections appeared to be free and fair. This provoked near panic in the South African press and markets, but at a meeting of the Commonwealth emergency committee, consisting of Mbeki, Obasanjo and Australian Prime Minister John Howard, the South African President finally agreed to act decisively and Zimbabwe was suspended from the organisation. Mbeki and Obasanjo subsequently sought to create a power-sharing agreement between Mugabe and Tsvangirai, but with Harare seeking to prosecute the MDC leader for treason, and Zanu-PF threatening to widen its land grab from the white minority to include the Asian community, the chances of success appear negligible.

Beyond prudence

His 'fruits of freedom' 2001 budget may have earned him the sobriquet 'Robin Hood', but by the time of his budget presentation in February 2002, Finance Minister Trevor Manuel seemingly proved that it is possible to please all of the people some of the time. In reality, Manuel's apparent largesse in 2001, including a pledge to increase total state expenditure by 4 per cent of GDP over three years, was built on solid foundations. Public external debt fell from US$36.86 billion in 2000 to around US$36.53 billion in 2001, while total government debt fell from 46.6 per cent of GDP to 45.3 per cent and GDP growth was sustained at around 2.8 per cent, despite poor international economic conditions.

Moreover, observers were generally increasingly impressed with the extent to which funds are actually reaching ground level, especially in public works projects such as water supplies and housing, which together with social services, account for half of all state expenditure. These areas saw a 16 per cent boost to spending in the 2002 budget, to R56.7 billion (US$5 billion), with an extra R6.7 billion (US$600 million) allocated to provincial governments for such projects. Additionally, the quality of revenue collection is improving rapidly, causing the 2001 budget deficit outcome to undershoot significantly, at 1.4 per cent of GDP, compared to a target of 2.3 per cent. This permitted tax relief of around R8.3 billion (US$740 million) for 2002, both in the form of improved benefits to poorer families, and in cuts on duties on the most popular consumer goods, which will assist business at the same time as easing household expenses. It is possible that higher state spending, together with the green shoots of recovery in the US and EU, will allow South African GDP growth to touch 3 per cent in 2002. The fiscal deficit target of 2.3 per cent of GDP looks realistic and Manuel's credibility should continue.

Privatisation remains something of a blot on the copybook, with the key sale of the state-owned fixed-line operator Telkom postponed for the second time, from November 2001, to fiscal year 2002/03 (in other words, March 2003 at the latest). In practice, the unhealthy conditions in the global telecommunications market in general imbued this move with a measure of common sense, a fact well demonstrated by the failed attempts of the respective governments to sell Nitel (Nigeria) and Kenya Telkom. Nonetheless, the delay was partly the result of ongoing difficulties over regulation in the sector, which landed Telkom directors and the Independent Communications Authority (ICASA) in court to settle their differences. Still, the government did successfully transfer a 20 per cent portion in mobile operator M-Cell to Dutch investor Ice Finance in January 2002, for US$475 million, which will act as an interim deal to tide over state coffers until a strategic investor is found to purchase a majority stake.

Telkom will be an important test of government commitment to allow private sector participation in the country's infrastructure. Pretoria perhaps has greater control over leading power generator Eskom, whose cheap running costs and exportable surplus capacity make it highly attractive to would-be purchasers. Cosatu was already angry in November 2001 about the possible employment impact of moves to deregulate the energy sector, but the state is in practice looking further afield for direction in its energy policy. Disastrous experiences in Brazil and California, both of which were faced with power shortages in 2001 after botched privatisations, raise questions about the wisdom of the Eskom sale and caution will therefore be well understood, with few political consequences.

Rand on the run

A successful career in the private sector behind him, the new governor of the South African Reserve Bank (SARB), Tito Mboweni, appointed in early 2001, brought a solid reputation to the post. Even so, he can hardly have wanted his first year in charge to end with an unparalleled exchange rate crisis, which saw the rand lose around 30 per cent of its value over three unnerving months, to trade as weakly as R13.50 per US$ at one stage in December 2001, from above R9.00 per US$ in October. Pressure on the rand fell in the first half of 2002, in response to the repatriation of export earnings, the weakening US dollar, the rising price of gold (one of South Africa's chief exports) and increased stability of emerging market currencies. In the second quarter, the rand appreciated from R11.28 per US$ in April to R9.74 in May. This helped producer price inflation, which fell from just under 18 per cent in April to 16 per cent in June.

From the end of the first half of 2002, the rand came under attack, falling from R9.74 per US$ in May to R10.42 by early October – at times the rand fell below R11 per US$. The main factors contributing to the fall in the second half included the country's poor inflation rates, uncertainty in the global economy, general anxieties about emerging markets and the deteriorating political situation in Zimbabwe. However, the most damaging development was the leaking of a draft mining code. This caused non-residents to sell R12 million worth of domestic securities in panic. The fall in the rand in 2001 and 2002 amplified the rise in international oil prices, which rose to the upper end of OPEC's target price range of US$22–28 per barrel from the second quarter of 2002.

Thabo Mbeki was sufficiently alarmed by the decline in the rand in 2001 to set up a special commission, under senior lawyer John Myburgh, in late February 2002, to investigate the causes of the crisis. This is with good reason as the substantial impact on the cost of imports caused CPIX inflation (the consumer price index excluding the cost of mortgages, the measure used by the SARB) to rise from just inside the monetary authority's 3–6 per cent target for 2001 to as high as 8 per cent year-on-year by March 2002. This forced Mboweni to end the monetary easing cycle by which he had assisted economic growth during 2001, raising the benchmark overnight repo rate from 9.5 per cent to 10.5 per cent in January 2002 and again to 11.5 per cent in March.

Yet, some elements on the left of the ANC appeared to see the Myburgh Commission as an opportunity to hit out at the perceived iniquities of globalisation, as embodied in the country's financial sector. Amid the recriminations, what is apparent is that speculation in fact played a relatively small part in the crisis. Negative international market sentiment, created by the collapse in Argentina, and chaos in Zimbabwe, formed a constant backdrop – with the impact of the latter made apparent by a renewed flurry in the exchange rate during the Zimbabwean presidential elections in March 2002.

However, a key structural element was the SARB's Net Open Forward Position (NOFP), four letters which may have meant little to most South Africans before late 2001, but which the whole country has now learned spells trouble. The NOFP consists of forward dollar obligations accumulated by the central bank as a result of capital movement restrictions operated during and immediately after the apartheid era, which imposed delays upon those looking to shift foreign currency out of South Africa. In effect, to repay dollars held temporarily in this way at a later date, the SARB had to sell its own currency short, creating a one-way market against the rand. Moreover, the persistence of some capital controls – contrary to the understanding of politicians calling for these to be reinforced – may have aggravated the slide, by creating an illiquid market. This meant that individual transactions of hundreds of millions of dollars, which had nothing to do with speculation (for example, South African industries buying equipment from overseas) could cause a noticeable blip in the exchange rate, triggering a snowball effect as the banking sector's complex automated hedging procedures kicked in to avoid losing money due to excessive exposure to the rand.

As a result, many leading bankers and economists testifying to the Myburgh Commission advised that, since confidence in the rand had been undermined in any case, the government should see this as a signal to remove capital controls altogether. This would cause a temporary slide in the currency, but prevent a repetition of a future crisis, since one-off transactions would have a smaller impact in a larger foreign exchange market. Although Mboweni is unlikely to be brave enough to undertake such a shift while events in Zimbabwe continue to cause jitters, he has moved to pay off the NOFP entirely by end-2002, by issuing bonds and borrowing from the treasury. These measures should be enough to underpin the rand after that time. Until then, the currency may not see much appreciation, even with a possible upturn in exports as world markets recover. As such, inflation could remain in an uptrend until the final quarter of 2002, and even though price pressures are largely imported (hence little affected by interest rates), the SARB seems likely to increase the repo rate by as much as a further 1.5 per cent during 2002, before the next cycle of monetary easing can begin.

Outlook

The growing rifts within the ANC have not so far affected Mbeki's position. In December 2002, the ANC's party convention re-elected him as party leader, automatically making him its candidate for president in 2004. His address to the convention disappointed many at the grassroots as it failed to talk about the HIV/AIDS pandemic, the growing instability in Zimbabwe or the rise in violent crime. Instead, Mbeki talked in broad terms about economic policy and racial equality, directing much of his fire at far-right Afrikaner terrorist groups. Mbeki is likely to win the June 2004 presidential elections and has secured the backing of Nelson Mandela, who is seen as the nation's king-maker.

Mbeki's determination to press ahead with his controversial economic policies raises the prospect that Cosatu and the SACP will quit the alliance, perhaps setting up a separate party of labour which would sit in opposition to the ANC. While this is unlikely to undermine the ANC's majority in the national assembly, it will signify a break-down of a relationship between the tripartite alliance members that once represented the resistance of the black masses to apartheid oppression. This would be psychologically damaging to the ANC, while it could mean a genuine step towards a pluralistic, non-racial multi-party democracy. With the opposition DA largely unable to gain ground and remaining politically ineffective, a left-wing opposition could be crucial in preventing the ANC from turning South Africa into a one-party state.

Risk assessment

Economic	Satisfactory and improving
Political	Good
Regional stability	Poor but improving
Stock market	Good

COUNTRY PROFILE

Historical profile

1652 The Dutch East India Company set up a station at Cape Town, supplying sailing ships to and from the Dutch East Indies (Indonesia).
1795 Britain took control of the Cape.
1806 The Cape Colony became British and settlement began in 1820.
1835 Mass treks by Afrikaners (Boers) who moved inland, fighting Ndebele and Zulu.
1899–1902 After many battles, the Boer War was eventually won by the British. With the signing of the Treaty of Vereeniging on the 31 May 1902, all Boers became British subjects.
1910 The Union of South Africa was established by the former British colonies of Cape and Natal and the Boer republics of Transvaal and Orange Free State. South Africa became a self-governing dominion led by former Boer generals.
1912 The Native National Congress, the precursor to the African National Congress (ANC), was founded.
1913 The Land Act was introduced to prevent blacks, except those in Cape province, from buying land outside reserves.
1914 The National Party was founded.
1919 South West Africa (Namibia), formerly a German colony, came under South African administration.
1948 Apartheid (separateness) laws excluding non-whites from political and economic influence were applied by successive National Party governments.
1950 The population was classified by race. The Group Areas Act was passed to segregate blacks and whites. The South African Communist Party (SACP) was banned. The ANC responded by a campaign of civil disobedience led by Nelson Mandela.
1960 Apartheid laws were brutally enforced; the most notorious incident was the Sharpeville massacre. The ANC became the main black political organisation opposing the government and consequently was banned.
1961 South Africa was declared a republic and left the Commonwealth. Mandela launched the ANC's military wing which began a campaign of disruption and sabotage.
1964 Nelson Mandela, leader of the ANC, was jailed for life. The UN imposed sanctions against South Africa.
1976 More than 600 people were killed in the Soweto uprising.
1983 Constitution established power-sharing of three population groups, effectively excluding participation of blacks.
1986 State of emergency was established during the township revolt.
1989 P W Botha (Prime Minister from 1978–83 and President from 1983–89) was replaced by F W de Klerk who began a reform programme which began dismantling apartheid.
1990 Nelson Mandela was released from prison. A peace accord was signed with the ANC and the state of emergency was lifted. Namibia became independent.
1991 International sanctions were lifted after the remaining apartheid laws were repealed. Fighting broke out between the ANC and the Inkatha movement which claimed to represent Zulu tribes.
1993 Parliament assented to the non-racial constitutional guidelines drawn up and adopted by a multi-racial negotiating forum. The three-chamber, racially-based parliament was adjourned and apartheid in the government essentially ended. A transitional Government of National Unity (GNU) was established.
1994 An interim constitution was adopted. Nelson Mandela was elected president and was inaugurated on 10 May. Commonwealth membership was restored, the remaining sanctions were lifted and South Africa took its seat in the UN General Assembly for the first time in 20 years.
1996 The constitution was adopted on 8 May. Some changes were made and an amended text of the constitution was adopted on 11 October. The Truth and Reconciliation Commission was set up, chaired by Archbishop Desmond Tutu. It began hearings on human rights abuse committed by both government and liberation movements under the apartheid regime. The National Party withdrew from the coalition government, claiming it was being ignored.
1998 The Truth and Reconciliation Commission branded apartheid a crime against humanity and held the ANC responsible for numerous human rights abuses. South Africa intervened militarily in Lesotho to prevent civil war breaking out in the kingdom.
1999 Thabo Mbeki became president in June, when in elections the ANC increased its share of the vote to 66.3 per cent from 62.6 per cent, and formed a coalition government with the mainly Zulu Inkatha Freedom Party (IFP).
2000 Despite President Mbeki's controversial views on AIDS, South Africa played host to the 13th World AIDS Conference in July. In August, the Democratic Party, the New National Party and the Federal Alliance merged to form the Democratic Alliance, which won a quarter of the vote in the December local elections.
2001 A legal action against the South African government by 39 mutli-national pharmaceutical companies over the production of generic AIDS drugs was dropped in April. This enabled South Africa and many other poor countries to import cheaper drugs to combat the epidemic. In October, the Democratic Alliance collapsed after the New National Party pulled out of the coalition. In November, the government was cleared of unlawful conduct by an independent tribunal over allegations of corruption surrounding an arms deal involving European firms. The High Court ruled that pregnant women must be given anti-retroviral drugs to prevent transmission of HIV to their babies.
2002 The name of Northern Province was changed to Limpopo Province.

Political structure

Constitution

The 1996 constitution was implemented from 4 February 1997.
The Republic of South Africa is a federal state, consisting of a central government and nine provincial governments. The head of a province is called a premier. The right to regional autonomy is enshrined in the constitution, subject to the principles of the national constitution.
Electoral system: list-system proportional representation based on universal adult suffrage.

Form of state

Federal state

The executive

Executive powers are vested in the presidency and the cabinet, which is appointed by the president. The president, who is both head of state and head of government, is elected by the National Assembly for a five-year term.

National legislature
The bicameral legislature is a 400-member National Assembly and a National Council of Provinces, serving five-year terms. The latter consists of 10 representatives from each of the nine provincial legislatures.
Elections to the National Assembly and provincial legislatures are conducted by proportional representation. Each of the nine provinces can determine its legislature, elected by proportional representation, and executive.
Legal system
Based on Roman-Dutch law and the 1996 constitution.
An anti-prejudice law was passed by the National Assembly on 26 January 2000.
Last elections
2 June 1999 (parliamentary and presidential)
Next elections
June 2004 (parliamentary and presidential)

Political parties

Ruling party
African National Congress (ANC)
Main opposition party
In 2000, the New National Party (NNP), which ruled South Africa from 1948 to 1994, merged with the Democratic Party (DP) and the Federal Alliance (FA) to form the Democratic Alliance (DA). However, in October 2001, the NNP suspended its participation in the DA.

Population

44.7 million (2000)
Annual population growth rate: 1.9 per cent (1994–2000). It is projected that the growth rate for the period 1999–2015 will be 0.5 per cent per annum. About 38 per cent of the total population is under 15 years.
Population density: 35 inhabitants per square km (2000). Urban population: 50 per cent of the total population (1994–2000).
It is estimated that about five million people stay illegally in South Africa.
Ethnic make-up
Black (77 per cent), white (12 per cent), coloured (8.5 per cent), Asian (2.5 per cent). There are around 2.6 million Afrikaners.
Religions
Christianity (77 per cent), Hinduism, Islam, Judaism and traditional beliefs.

Education

In 2000, the adult illiteracy rate was estimated at 14 per cent and 15.4 per cent for men and women respectively. Public expenditure on education typically amounted to 7.9 per cent of annual gross national income between 1994–97.
The government education system teaches almost a third of the total population and employs one in three civil servants.

Health

World Bank estimates during the period 1994–2000 showed that the average life expectancy was 55 years and the infant mortality rate was 51 per 1,000 live births. The fertility rate was 2.9 children born per adult woman.
Healthcare expenditure is equivalent to about 7.1 per cent of GDP, of which 3.3 is public expenditure and the remaining 3.8 per cent private according to surveys between 1990–1998.
Twenty-three per cent of the population were estimated to be HIV positive in 2000. Approximately 13 per cent of the population aged 15–49 years have HIV. The Government's five-year HIV/AIDS/STD Strategic Plan was released in June 2000. AIDS was revealed as the biggest killer in the Medical Research Council's 2001 report on South Africa's mortality rates.

Welfare

The social assistance programme of the Department of Social Development provides benefits to approximately three million people comprising the elderly, persons with disabilities and children under the age of seven years.

Main cities

Johannesburg (estimated population 4.1 million, financial capital), Durban (2.6 million), Cape Town (2.5 million, legislative capital), Pretoria (1.4 million, administrative capital), Port Elizabeth (1.3 million), Bloemfontein (583,903, judicial capital), East London (332,102), Pietermaritzburg (211,473).

Languages spoken

Official languages
Afrikaans, English, Ndebele, Sesotho, Northern Sotho, SiSwati, Tsonga, Tswana, Venda, Xhosa, Zulu.

Media

Press
Press freedom is guaranteed by the constitution.
Dailies: Major dailies include: *The Sowetan* (South Africa's largest selling daily with a circulation of over two million), *Beeld* (Afrikaans), *The Star*, *Daily News*, *Ilanga*, *Argus*, *The Citizen* and the *Cape Times*. *Die Burger* is a regional Afrikaans newspaper translated daily to English. *WOZA* (http://www.woza.co.za) is South Africa's daily online newspaper geared to covering the news and views of the business and policy-making community.
Weeklies: The *Daily Mail & Guardian* is South Africa's leading independent newspaper published weekly. The largest Sunday papers are *Sunday Times* (English), *The Sunday Star* (English), *Sunday Independent*, *Sunday Nation*, *City Press* (English) and *Rapport* (Afrikaans). Other weeklies mainly published from Johannesburgh and Cape Town include *New Nation*, *Die Afrikaner*, *Partriot*, *Post*, *The Southern Cross* and *Sowetan Sunday World*.
Business: Business publications include *Business Times*, *Business Day* and the *Financial Mail*. *Personal Finance* covering business issues is a South African Independent Newspapers publication.
Broadcasting
Radio: Commercial radio services broadcast throughout the country in various languages. The South African Broadcasting Corporation (SABC) is the national public service broadcaster.
Television: With the exception of the M-Net, television is state-influenced (SABC) comprising four networks.
Advertising
South Africa's sophisticated advertising industry boasts full-range services, and the presence of subsidaries of prominent international agencies. Television, radio, newspapers, magazines, outdoor advertisements, cinema and the Internet provide direct marketing opportunities.
Deregulation has brought further independent television channels and radio stations.
Anti-smoking legislation has affected agencies with tobacco accounts, and further regulation of comparable goods, including alcohol, is expected.

Economy

South Africa has a highly diversified economy and is classified as a middle-income country. The economy is largely based on the country's abundant mineral and energy resources. Manufacturing is underpinned by the mining sector while exports are dominated by gold and diamonds.
Foreign investors are attracted to the country's robust infrastructure, with developed transport, water and electricity networks. Dams have been built on the rivers and provide water for irrigation, industrial and household use. There are also developed professional services and one of the largest stock exchanges in the world.
Although white minority rule ended with the country's first free and fair elections in 1994, economic apartheid is very much alive and income disparities are among the largest in the world. Whites still own large tracts of fertile land and most of the industry and service sectors, while many blacks remain poor, landless and languishing in the country's shanty towns.
The government's economic programme, Growth, Employment and Redistribution (Gear), is wedded to monetarism,

privatisation, free trade and increasing foreign investment. Despite its promises of short-term sacrifices for long-term gains, unemployment remains high at around 40 per cent, workers are dissatisfied with their wage settlements, employers dislike the post-apartheid labour regulations and per capita income has plummeted with GDP growth unable to keep up with population growth.

Since 1998, South Africa has reversed poor growth rates and has now embarked on a period of sustained growth with low to moderate inflation, a manageable debt burden and a robust growth in exports. Even so, capital formation is still sluggish and the expected flood of foreign direct investment has still to materialise.

Diversification from the mining sector as the prime engine of growth continues to show progress although an alarming exodus of young, highly qualified whites is creating serious skilled manpower shortages. South Africa's tourism sector has expanded considerably since the end of the apartheid era but it still has a very long way to go before reaching its full potential.

The period 2001–04 could be a watershed for South Africa. The economy is now on a steady course, the rand showed signs of stabilisation in the first quarter of 2002, there is renewed confidence in the future and South African goods are making a stronger appearance on the quality end of the global market. However, social and equity problems remain and crime is still unacceptably high. Economic growth is expected to average 3.5 per cent between 2001–03, underpinned by a steady recovery of gross fixed capital formation and a robust trade performance. The highest level of growth is in tertiary sectors, such as financial services and telecommunications, although growth in the transport sub-sector was negligible due to high fuel prices and political and economic instability in Zimbabwe.

External trade

South Africa's trade pact with the EU, designed to liberalise 90 per cent of bilateral trade over a 12-year period, provisionally came into force on 1 January 2000. South Africa also trades heavily with the US and Japan. In May 2001, South Africa strengthened its trading relations with South-East Asia by signing a trade agreement with Thailand.

Exports

Principal exports are gold (typically 22 per cent of total), diamonds (12 per cent), metals and metal products (11 per cent), coal (7 per cent). South Africa is also a major exporter of granite, asbestos, iron, manganese, chrome and titanium ore.

Main destinations: UK (13.2 per cent of 2000 total), US (11.4 per cent), Japan (7.5 per cent), Germany (7.2 per cent), Netherlands (3.1 per cent).

Exports to the rest of Africa have increased by between 25–30 per cent a year since 1990. Africa is also the primary destination for South Africa's growing manufacturing export base.

Imports

Principal imports are capital goods, raw materials semi-manufactured goods (80 per cent of total trade imports) and consumer commodities.

Main sources: Germany (13.1 per cent of 2000 total), US (11.8 per cent), UK (8.7 per cent), Japan (7.9 per cent), France (4.2 per cent).

Agriculture

South Africa has achieved self-sufficiency in the agricultural production of staple grains, such as maize and wheat, and basic foodstuffs such as fresh milk and other dairy products, meat, vegetables and fruit. Since the late 1980s, two principles have become an established part of South Africa's agricultural policy: that farmers should take greater responsibility for production decisions and pricing and distribution should be opened up to market forces. The agricultural sector accounts for approximately 4.7 per cent of annual GDP and employs 14 per cent of the workforce.

South Africa has about 33 per cent of the southern hemisphere's deciduous fruit market in Europe. After minerals and metals, deciduous fruit is the country's largest export industry. In 1999, South African fruit exporters Unifruco and Outspan International merged to create Capespan, one of the top five fruit exporters in the world with annual turnover of around US$1 billion from sales of around 700,000 tonnes of produce.

Industry and manufacturing

In 2000, the industrial sector as a whole contributed about 31.0 per cent of GDP and employed 27.4 per cent of the workforce.

Most of the raw materials and semi-manufactured goods required by industry are available from local sources. Only clothing and textiles, furniture (hardwoods), chemicals and transport equipment (components) still rely to a lesser extent on imports of raw materials or intermediate goods. Output is dominated by engineering and metal products, especially steel. Leading South African steel companies include Iscor and Highveld Steel.

Other major growth areas are automobile production and the chemical industry. Although food and tobacco processing remain of great importance, their share of total output has fallen significantly. Food products, iron and steel and transport equipment together account for about a third of total gross manufacturing output. Other manufactures include paper and paper products, fabricated metal products, electrical and non-electrical machinery.

Tourism

The tourism sector contributes up to 5 per cent of GDP and is an important source of foreign exchange. Europe constitutes the greater part of the overseas market (typically 65 per cent), followed by Asia (11 per cent), North America (12 per cent), Australasia (5 per cent), the Middle East (2 per cent) and the Indian Ocean Islands (1 per cent).

South Africa's tourism sector has expanded considerably since the end of the apartheid era but it still has a very long way to go before reaching its full potential. The country, which receives 52 per cent of the 13.4 million visitors to southern Africa each year, is positioning itself as the hub of a region-wide 'tourism park' wherein visitors will be able to move from one southern African country to another without going through formal borders. By pooling their resources and attractions together, southern African countries hope to emulate the islands of the Caribbean and increase tourist numbers. In the meantime, South Africa is steadily moving towards becoming the most popular conference destination in Africa.

Mining

South Africa is one of the world's foremost producers of diamonds, platinum group metals (PGM) and ferroalloys, such as manganese and vanadium and an international leader in mining technology. At least 40 per cent of the world's total recoverable gold reserves are in South Africa. It is a major exporter of platinum group metals, iron ore, asbestos, manganese ore, ferro-chromium, chrome ore and granite. The mining sector employs 6 per cent of the country's labour force and contributes up to one-third of the export revenue. Mining accounted for only 6 per cent of GDP in 2001, a sign that South Africa is moving away from dependence on the domestic mining industry. The country continues to rely on gold exports, which make up one-fifth of its foreign exchange earnings.

Hydrocarbons

Oil

South Africa has proven oil reserves of 29.4 million barrels and produces 227,000 barrels per day (bpd), of which about 184,000bpd is synthetic (2000) and the rest is crude oil production. The country's oil refining capacity is over

466,000bpd, while oil consumption amounts to 471,000bpd (2000).
Net imports are 244,000bpd, with the main sources being primarily the Middle East, with Iran and Saudi Arabia as the chief suppliers. Refined products are both sold in the local market and exported to East Africa and the Indian sub-continent.
A joint venture by Sasol/Total is planning a US$123 million extension to its Natref refinery, increasing capacity by nearly 17,000bpd. The project was scheduled for completion by 2002, but a major fire at the refinery in June 2001 has delayed completion.

Energy

The bulk supply electricity company, Eskom, a self-financing utility agency, has an installed generating capacity of about 36.5GW. Largely through Eskom, South Africa supplies almost 60 per cent of the total electricity generated on the continent of Africa. However, only around 60 per cent of the country's population has access to the national grid. Eskom is the fourth-largest power company in the world by capacity and is being restructured with a view to eventual privatisation. The government is hoping to expand private sector involvement in the electrification drive, in the generation, transmission and distribution sectors.
Eskom produces about 97 per cent of South Africa's electricity needs, with the balance made up by mines, industries and municipalities with their own small stations. It operates 17 coal-fired power stations, two hydroelectric, two pumped storage schemes, two gas turbine stations and the country's only nuclear power plant at Koeberg. The 2,000MW nuclear power station, operated by Eskom and supervised by the Council for Nuclear Safety, is likely to remain the only nuclear facility for some time.
The extension of the electricity grid to less privileged, mainly rural, areas is a major priority of the government's energy policy. The emphasis is toward renewable energy resources such as solar energy and hydropower. The National Energy Council is investigating possibilities in this area. By 2001, renewable energy sources account for around 5 per cent of primary energy needs.
South Africa exports electricity to Botswana, Lesotho, Mozambique, Namibia, Swaziland and Zimbabwe. It also imports a small amount of electricity from neighbouring countries, mostly from Namibia, although the amount varies widely in accordance with the capacity of other countries to supply.

Financial markets

Stock exchange

After years of isolation, South Africa's financial markets have changed rapidly to adopt international standards and operate in a competitive global market. Since 1994, the Johannesburg Stock Exchange (JSE) has deregulated the market allowing the ownership of local brokers by foreign companies and banks. Anglo American dominates the JSE, with price changes in its stocks substantially affecting the market's indices. As such, the JSE is influenced to a significant extent by world gold prices. The South African Futures Exchange (Safex) was formally registered in 1990, but was taken over by the JSE in July 2001 in a R152 million (US$18 million) deal, following the approval of the country's competition regulators. This helps improve efficiency, security, transparency and cost-effectiveness of the country's financial markets.
Among projects to continue improving efficiency and competitiveness is the creation of a paperless financial exchange, known as Strate (share transactions totally electronic). Full dematerialisation of shares is expected by the end of 2002. Strate is 50 per cent owned by the JSE, but is open to all electronic settlements including those not listed as JSE securities. Such improvements are vital if South Africa's financial markets are to cope with rapidly rising volumes and with competition from other emerging markets. The market response to Strate has been strong and positive. However, the lower-than-expected daily trading volume (15,000 instead of the forecast 19,000) meant that Strate had to increase its fees for trades. In June 2002, the fee rose from a flat rate of R6 (US$0.55) to R10 (US$0.90) for transactions less than R200,000 (US$18,200), 0.005 per cent of the value of the transaction if it is between R200,000 and R1 million (US$18,200–91,000) and a flat rate of R50 (US$4.55) for transactions over R1 million (US$91,000).
The main issue facing the South African financial markets is the falling value of mining stocks, particularly gold and platinum. The terrorist attacks on the US in September 2001 fuelled a surge in international gold prices as investors sought to find a safe haven in volatile markets. This helped cushion the JSE from the impact of falls across the world's stock markets. A similar trend was observed after military strikes on Afghanistan, with gains recorded in the JSE's gold index as well as in the financials group.

Banking

The financial services sector has changed rapidly since South Africa re-entered the global economy in the 1990s, with domestic banks restructuring, foreign banks competing fiercely in the commercial sector and there has been a move towards mergers and diversification of the services offered by banks.
The South African Reserve Bank (SARB) (central bank) supervises the domestic and international activities of banks, discount houses and building societies. It is banker to the government and to other banking institutions, being custodian of the cash reserves which all registered banks are required to maintain with it. It provides facilities for the clearing and settlement of interbank claims and also acts as the lender of last resort. It issues the country's currency and is the custodian of South Africa's gold and foreign exchange reserves. It is responsible for the implementation of monetary policy which it formulates in conjunction with the finance ministry.
According to Deloitte and Touche Consulting Group, 13 per cent of the population is banked, 18 per cent is underbanked and the rest have monthly incomes too low for the banking industry. To overcome this, micro-finance (credit provision for deprived businesses and individuals) has become an increasingly relevant tool for low level capital mobilisation. NuBank, part of ABSA, provides microlending both to individual investors and other microfinanciers. The process, although embryonic, is believed to be an important way of redistributing investment to the 69 per cent of the population excluded from the traditional banking sector. The government has set up a special guarantor, Khula Enterprise Finance, to help bridge the gap between commercial lenders and the micromarket.

Central bank

South African Reserve Bank (SARB)

Main financial centre

Pretoria (renamed Tswane)

Time

GMT plus two hours

Geography

South Africa occupies the southern extremity of the African continent. It is bordered by Namibia to the north-west, by Botswana and Zimbabwe to the north, by Mozambique to the north-east, and by Swaziland to the east.

Climate

Sub-tropical, with regional variations. In Cape coastal area, summers, October–March, are warm with temperature averaging 25–28 degrees Celcius (C); average wet winter temperature 17–20 degrees C. In Pretoria and other high veld areas, winters are warm and dry, while most rain falls during the hot summer. On the Natal coast humidity can be high during the summer, while the winter is drier with temperatures around 22–24 degrees

C. Most rain falls during the summer months.

Entry requirements

Passports

Required by all.

Visa

In general required by all – except UK, German and Irish passport holders, business or holiday visitors from Switzerland and Liechtenstein.

Currency advice/regulations

Import and export of local currency is limited to R500 per person. Unlimited amount of foreign currency may be imported although amount must be declared, and re-export is limited to declared amount.

Customs

Licences required for certain imports, including consumer goods; all items need certificates of origin and value.

Health (for visitors)

Mandatory precautions

Yellow fever vaccination certificate required if travelling from infected or endemic area.

Advisable precautions

Malaria risk exists throughout the year in certain areas of northern Transvaal, eastern Lowveld and northern Natal – prophylaxis should be taken for visits to these areas. Water precautions should be taken in rural areas. AIDS is prevalent.

Hotels

Wide choice available in main commercial centres.

Public holidays

Fixed dates

1 Jan (New Year's Day), 21 Mar (Human Rights Day), 27 Apr (Freedom Day), 1 May (Workers' Day), 16 Jun (Youth Day), 9 Aug (National Women's Day), 24 Sep (Heritage Day), 16 Dec (Day of Reconciliation), 25 Dec (Christmas Day), 26 Dec (Goodwill Day).

Variable dates

Good Friday, Family Day (the Mon following Easter Sunday).

Working hours

Banking

Mon–Fri: 0900–1530; Sat: 0830–1100. Some banks have extended hours.

Business

Mon–Fri: 0730/0830–1600/1700. Some businesses have extended hours.

Government

Mon–Fri: 0730/0830–1600/1700.

Shops

Mon–Fri: 0830–1700; Sat: 0830–1300. Certain shops are open on Sundays.

Telecommunications

South Africa is the telecommunications leader on the African continent. The South African Regulatory Authority (Satra) oversees the industry

Mobile phones

MTN and Vodacom operate GSM900 networks. Data services (including mobile fax) carry additional charges.

Electricity supply

Usually 220/230V AC – but 220/250V in Port Elizabeth and 250V in Pretoria.

Social customs/useful tips

There are no particular taboos, but visitors should be mindful that in certain parts of the country strong racist attitudes still prevail. It is best not to get involved in political discussions.

Security

Visitors should avoid visiting black townships without guidance from reliable local residents and without a trustworthy companion.

Street crime is less of a problem in major urban areas, though care must be taken in central Johannesburg at night.

Getting there

Air

National airline: South African Airways

Main airport: The Airports Company South Africa (ACSA) operates nine state airports: JBM Hertzog at Bloemfontein; DF Malan at Cape Town; Louis Botha at Durban; BJ Schoeman at East London; P W Botha at George; Jan Smuts at Johannesburg; BJ Vorster at Kimberley; HF Verwoerd at Port Elizabeth; and Pierre van Ryneveld at Upington.

Airport tax: There is no airport departure tax.

Surface

Road: Possible from Botswana, Lesotho, Namibia, Swaziland, Zimbabwe (travellers are generally advised to check regulations and conditions regarding entry by road with the Automobile Association of South Africa).

The Maputo Corridor project includes a new road from the Atlantic coast at Namibia's Walvis Bay across the Kalahari desert to join the South African road network linking the western side of southern Africa with the Indian Ocean at Maputo, Mozambique. There is a toll road between Witbank in South Africa and the Mozambican capital.

Rail: There are services from Mozambique, Zimbabwe, Namibia and Botswana.

Getting about

National transport

Air: South African Airways operates frequent flights to all major centres. SA Airlink, British Airways/Comair, National Airlines, Inter Air and Sun Air also fly domestic routes.

Road: Extensive network of tarred roads, including 51,000km linking main centres. Also, 128,777km of untarred roads – some of the remoter sections can become impassable in wet weather.

Buses: Inter-city services are operated by Greyhound, Citiliner and other private companies.

Rail: Network of some 24,000km with good services throughout the country. Reservations for express trains should be made well in advance. Most long distance mainline trains have restaurant cars and all have sleeping accommodation (couchettes operated in both first and second class; bedding is charged).

Named services include: Blue Train world-famous five-star travel (Pretoria-Johannesburg-Cape Town); Trans Karoo (Cape Town-Johannesburg); Trans Orange (Durban-Cape Town); Trans Natal (Durban-Johannesburg).

City transport

Taxis: Widely available in all towns. Cannot be hailed in the street and must be called from a rank.

Buses, trams & metro: Bus services are operated in all main centres.

Car hire

Self-drive and chauffeur-driven cars are widely available. An international driving licence is required unless visitor's national licence carries the photograph and signature of the holder.

Driving is on the left.

BUSINESS DIRECTORY

Telephone area codes

The direct dialling code for South Africa is +27 followed by area code (Cape Town 21, Durban 31, Johannesburg 11, Pretoria 12, East London 431) followed by subscriber's number.

IDD access code from South Africa: 091.

Chambers of Commerce

Cape Chamber of Commerce and Industry, PO Box 204, Louis Gradner Street, Cape Town 8000 (tel: 418-4300; fax: 418-1800; e-mail: info@capechamber.co.za).

Durban Chamber of Commerce & Industry, PO Box 1506, 190 Stanger Street, Durban 4000 (tel: 335-1000; fax: 332-1288; e-mail: chamber@durbanchamber.co.za).

Johannesburg Metropolitan Chamber of Commerce and Industry, Private Bag 34, Cnr Empire Road and Owl Street, Auckland Park 2006 (tel: 726-5300; fax: 726-8421; e-mail: info@jcci.co.za).

Ladysmith Chamber of Commerce and Industry, PO Box 7, 21 Leeu Street, Ladysmith 3370 (tel: 631-0541; fax: 637-4407; e-mail: lcci@futurenet.co.za).

Orange Free State Chamber of Business, PO Box 87, Bloemfontein 9300 (tel: 447-3368; fax: 447-5064; e-mail:bcci@intekom.co.za).

Pietermaritzburg Chamber of Commerce and Industries, PO Box 11734, Dorpspruit 3206 (tel: 345-2747; fax: 394-4151; e-mail: pcci@futurenet.co.za).

Port Elizabeth Regional Chamber of Commerce and Industry, PO Box 2221, 22 Grahamstown Road, Port Elizabeth 6056 (tel: 484-4430; fax: 487-1851; e-mail: info@pechamber.org.za)

Pretoria Chamber of Commerce, PO Box 40653, Arcadia 0007 (tel: 342-3236; fax: 342-1486).

South African Chamber of Business, PO Box 91267, Milpark, Auckland Park 2006 (tel: 358-9700; fax: 358-9773).

Zululand Chamber of Commerce and Industries, PO Box 1133, Empangeni 3880 (tel: 922-335; fax: 922-487; e-mail: zcob@intekom.co.za).

Banking

Absa Bank Ltd, 2nd Floor, ABSA Towers North, 180 Commissioner Street, Johannesburg 2001 (tel: 350-4000; fax: 350-3768).

International Bank of Southern Africa Ltd, 3rd Floor, Sunnyside Ridge Bldg, 32 Princess of Wales Terrace, Parktown, Johannesburg 2193 (tel: 644-3300, 643-6740, 643-6743; fax: 643-1122).

Nedcor Bank Ltd, 135 Rivonia Rd, Sandown, Sandton, Johannesburg 2001 (tel: 294-4444; fax: 295-5555).

South African Bank of Athens Ltd, Bank of Athens Building, 116 Marshall Street, Johannesburg 2001 (tel: 832-1211; fax: 838-1001, 833-7976).

Standard Bank of South Africa Ltd, 5 Simmonds Street, Johannesburg 2001 (tel: 6369111 fax: 6363544).

Central bank

South African Reserve Bank, PO Box 427, Pretoria 0001 (tel: 313-3911; fax: 313-3197; e-mail: info@.resbank.co.za).

Travel information

Automobile Association of South Africa, Denis Paxton House, Alladale Road, Kyalami Midrand 1685; PO Box 596, Johannesburg 2000 (tel: 799-1000; fax: 799-1960; e-mail: aasa@aasa.co.za).

Blue Train Reservations, PO Box 2671, Joubert Park 2044 (tel: 334-8459; fax: 334-8464; e-mail: bluetrain@transnet.co.za).

Coach Services: Translux Express, PO Box 2383, Johannesburg 2000 (tel: 774-3333; fax: 774-3318); Greyhound Coach Lines, PO Box11229, Johannesburg 2000 (tel: 830-1301; fax: 830-1528); Intercape Mainliner, PO Box 618, Bellville 7535 (tel: 386-4400; fax: 386-2488).

Eastern Cape Tourism Board, PO Box 186, Bisho 5605 (tel: 635-2115; fax: 636-4019; e-mail info@ectourism.co.za).

Free State Department of Environmental Affairs and Tourism, PO Box 264, Bloemfontein 9300 (tel: 403-3435; fax: 448-8361).

Gauteng Tourism Authority, The Rosebank Mall, Rosebank 2196 (tel: 327-2000; fax: 327-7000; e-mail: tourism@gauteng.net).

KwaZulu-Natal Tourism Authority, PO Box 2516, Durban 4000 (tel: 304-7144; fax: 305-6693; e-mail: info@tourism-kzn.org).

Mpumalanga TourismAuthority, PO Box 679, Nelspruit 1200 (tel: 752-7001; fax: 759-5441; e-mail: mtarlpsa@cis.co.za).

Northern Cape Tourism Board, Private Bag X5017, Kimberley 8300 (tel: 832-2657; fax: 831-2937; e-mail: tourism@northerncape.org.za).

Northern Province Tourism Board, PO Box 1309, Pietersburg 0700 (tel: 288-0099; fax: 288-0094; e-mail: ceo@greatnorth.co.za).

North-West Parks and Tourism Council, PO Box 4488, Mmabatho 2735 (tel: 386-1225; fax: 386-1158; e-mail: nwptb@iafrica.com).

Rovos Rail Reservations, Victoria Hotel, PO Box 2837, Pretoria 0001 (tel 323-6052; fax: 323-0843).

South African Airways, Airways Towers, 39 Wolmarans Street, Bloemfontein; PO Box 7778, Johannesburg 2000 (tel: 356-2059; fax: 356-1795; e-mail: help@flysaa.com).

South African National Parks, 643 Leyds Street, Muckleneuk, Pretoria; PO Box 787, Pretoria 0001 (tel: 343-1991; fax: 343-0905; e-mail: reservations@parks-sa.co.za).

Western Cape Tourism Board, Private Bag X9108, Cape Town 8000 (tel: 426-5639; fax: 426-5640; e-mail: info@capetourism.org).

Ministry of tourism

Minisatry of Environmental Affairs and Tourism, Fedsure Forum Building, 315 Pretorius Street, Pretoria; Private Bag X447, Pretoria 0001 (tel: 310-3611; fax: 322-0082)

National tourist organisation offices

South African Tourism, 12 Rivonia Road, Illovo, Johannesburg 2196; Private Bag X10012, Sandton 2146 (tel: 778-8000; fax: 778-8001; e-mail: jhb@southafricantourism.com).

Ministries

N.B. For the following Ministry addresses: Pretoria (administrative), Cape Town (legislative).

Ministry of Agriculture and Land Affairs, Private Bag X250, Pretoria 0001 (tel: 319-6886; fax: 321-8558); Private Bag X9087, Cape Town 8000 (tel: 465-7690; fax: 465-6550).

Ministry of Arts, Culture, Science and Technology, Private Bag X727, Pretoria 0001 (tel: 337-8378; fax: 324-2687); Private Bag X9156, Cape Town 8000; (tel: 465-4850; fax: 461-1425).

Ministry of Communications, Private Bag X882, Pretoria 0001 (tel: 427-8111; fax: 362-6915); Private Bag X9151, Cape Town 8000 (tel: 462-1632; fax: 462-1646).

Ministry of Correctional Services, Private Bag X853, Pretoria 0001 (tel: 323-8803; fax: 323-4111); Private Bag X9131, Cape Town 8000 (tel: 462-2314; fax: 465-4375).

Ministry of Defence, Private Bag X427, Pretoria 0001 (tel: 355-6119; fax: 347-0118); PO Box 47, Cape Town 8000 (tel: 469-6070; fax: 465-5870).

Ministry of Education, Private Bag X603, Pretoria 0001 (tel: 312-5501; fax: 323-5989); Private Bag X9034, Cape Town 8000 (tel: 465-7350; fax: 461-4788).

Minisatry of Environmental Affairs and Tourism, Private Bag X447, Pretoria 0001 (tel: 310-3611; fax: 322-0082); Private Bag X9154, Capetown 8000 (tel: 465-7240; fax: 465-3216).

Ministry of Finance, Private Bag X115, Pretoria 0001 (tel: 323-8911; fax: 323-3262); PO Box 29, Cape Town 8000 (tel: 464-6100; fax: 461-2934).

Ministry of Foreign Affairs, Private Bag X152, Pretoria 0001 (tel: 351-0005; fax: 351-0253); 120 Plein St, Cape Town 8001 (tel: 464-3700; fax: 465-6548).

Ministry of Health, Private Bag X399, Pretoria 0001 (tel: 328-4773; fax: 325-5526); Private Bag X9070, Cape Town 8000 (tel: 465-7407; fax: 465-1575).

Ministry of Home Affairs, Private Bag X741, Pretoria 0001 (tel: 326-8081; fax: 321-6491); Private Bag X9102, Cape Town 8000 (tel: 461-5818; fax: 461-2359).

Ministry of Housing, Private Bag X645, Pretoria 0001 (tel: 421-1311; fax: 341-8513); Private Bag X9029, Cape Town 8000 (tel: 465-7295; fax: 465-3610).

Ministry of Intelligence Services, PO Box 56450, Arcadia 0007(tel: 338-1800; fax: 323-0718); PO Box 51278, Waterfront 8002 (tel: 401-1800; fax: 461-4644).

Ministry of Justice and Constitutional Development, Private Bag X276, Pretoria 0001 (tel: 323-8581; fax: 321-1708); Private Bag X256, Cape Town 8000 (tel: 465-7506; fax: 465-2783).

Ministry of Labour, Private Bag X499, Pretoria 0001 (tel: 322-6523; fax: 320-1942); Private Bag X9090, Cape Town 8000 (tel: 461-6030; fax: 462-2832).

Ministry of Minerals and Energy, Private Bag X646, Pretoria 0001 (tel: 322-8695; fax: 322-8699); Private Bag X9111, Cape Town 8000 (tel: 462-2310; fax: 461-0859).

Ministry of Provincial and Local Government, Private Bag X802, Pretoria 0001 (tel: 334-0705; fax: 326-4478); Private Bag X9123, Cape Town 8000 (tel: 462-1441; fax: 461-0851).

Ministry of Public Enterprises, Private Bag X15, Hatfield 0028 (tel: 431-1000; fax: 342-7224); Private Bag X9079, Cape Town 8000 (tel: 461-6376; fax: 465-2381).

Ministry of Public Service and Administration, Private Bag X884, Pretoria 0001 (tel: 314-7911; fax: 328-6529); Private Bag X9148, Cape Town 8000 (tel: 465-5491; fax: 465-5484).

Ministry of Public Works, Private Bag X890, Pretoria 0001 (tel: 324-1510; fax: 325-6380); Private Bag X9155, Cape Town 8000 (tel: 462-4184; fax: 461-6962).

Ministry of Safety and Security, Private Bag X463, Pretoria 0001 (tel: 339-2800; fax: 339-2819); Private Bag X9080, Cape Town 8000 (tel: 465-7400; fax: 461-2073).

Ministry of Social Development, Private Bag X885, Pretoria 0001 (tel: 312-7637; fax: 321-2658); Private Bag X9153, Cape Town 8000 (tel: 465-4011; fax: 465-4469).

Ministry of Sport and Recreation, Private Bag X869, Pretoria 0001 (tel: 334-3100; fax: 321-8493); Private Bag X9149, Cape Town 8000 (tel: 465-5506; fax: 465-4402).

Ministry of Trade and Industry, Private Bag X274, Pretoria 0001 (tel: 322-7677; fax: 322-7851); Private Bag X9047, Cape Town 8000 (tel: 461-7191; fax: 465-1291).

Ministry of Transport, Private Bag X193, Pretoria 0001 (tel: 309-3131; fax: 328-3194); Private Bag X9129, Cape Town 8000 (tel: 465-7260; fax: 461-6845).

Ministry of Water Affairs and Forestry, Private Bag X313, Pretoria 0001 (tel: 36-8733; fax: 328-4254); Private Bag X9052, Cape Town 8000 (tel: 464-1500; fax: 465-3362).

Office of the President, Private Bag X1000, Pretoria 0001 (tel: 337-5100; fax: 321-8870); Private Bag X1000, Cape Town 8000 (tel: 464-2100; fax: 464-2123).

Other useful addresses

Association of Advertising Agencies (AAA), PO Box 2289, Parklands 2121 (tel: 781-2772; fax: 781-2796; e-mail: aaa@gem.co.za).

Afrikaanse Handelsinstituut (AHI) (Afrikaans Trade Institute), Lynnwood Galleries, 354 Rosemary Street, Lynnwood 0081; PO Box 35100, Menlopark 00101 (tel: 348-5440; fax: 348-8771; e-mail: pta@ahi.co.za).

Association of Marketers (ASOM), 8 Sloane Street, Bryanston, Sandton; PO Box 98859, Sloane Park 2152, Bryanston (tel: 706-1633; fax: 706-4151; e-mail: asom@pixie.co.za).

Board on Tariffs and Trade, Fedlife Forum, Cnr Van der Walt and Pretorius Streets, Private Bag X753, Pretoria 0001 (tel: 322-8244; fax: 322-0149).

Chamber of Mines of South Africa, PO Box 61809, Marshalltown 2107 (tel: 498-7100; fax: 834-4251).

Chemical & Allied Industries Association, 15th Floor, Metal Box Centre, 25 Owl Street, Auckland Park 2006 (tel: 482-1671; fax: 726-8310).

Clothing Federation of South Africa, 42 van der Linde Street, Bedfordview 2008 (tel: 622-8125; fax: 622-8316).

Government Communications and Information System (GCIS), 356 Vermeulen Street, Pretoria; Private Bag X745, Pretoria 0001 (tel: 314-2127; 325-2030; e-mail: govcom@gcis.pwv.gov.za).

Industrial Development Corporation of South Africa, 19 Fredman Drive, Sandton 2146; PO Box 784055, Sandton 2146 (tel: 269-3000; fax: 269-3116; e-mail: callcentre@idc.co.za).

Iscor Limited, Roger Dyason Road, Pretoria West; PO Box 450, Pretoria 0001 (tel: 307-3000; fax: 307-4721; e-mail: webmaster@iscor.com).

JSE Securities Exchange (stock exchange), 1 Exchange Square, 2 Gwen Lane, Sandown, Sandton 2196; Private Bag X991174, Sandton 2146 (tel: 520-7000; fax: 520-8584; e-mail: miscellaneous@jse.co.za).

South African Association for the Conference Industry (SAACI), PO Box, Kloof 3640 (tel 764-6977; fax: 764-6974; e-mail: sec@saaci.co.za).

South African Business Initiative for Reconstruction and Development, 17th Floor, Metal Box Centre, 25 Owl Street, Auckland Park 2092 (tel: 482-5100; fax: 482-5507).

South African Diamond Board, 5th Floor, SA Diamond Centre, 240 Commissioner Street, Johannesburg 2001 (tel: 334-8980/6; fax: 334-8898; e-mail: mabombol@sadb.co.za).

South African Foreign Trade Organisation (SAFTO), Export House, 71 Maud Street, Sandton; PO Box 782706, Sandton 2146 (tel: 883-3737; fax: 883-6569; e-mail: safto@apollo.is.co.za).

South African Petroleum Industry Association, Trust Bank Centre, Adderley Street, Cape Town 8001; PO Box 7082, Roggebaai 8012 (tel: 419-8054; fax: 419-8058).

Statistics South Africa, Steyn's Building, 274 Schoeman Street, Pretoria 0002; Private Bag X44, Pretoria 0001 (tel: 310-8911; fax: 322-3374; e-mail: info@statssa.pwv.gov.za).

Trade and Investment South Africa, Rex Welsh House, Maud Street, Sandown, Sandton 2196; PO Box 782084, Sandton 2146 (tel: 884-2206; fax: 884-3236; e-mail: isa@isa.org.za).

Internet sites

African Development Bank: http://www.afdb.org

Africa Online: http://www.africaonline.com

AllAfrica.com: http://allafrica.com

Central Statistical Services: http://www.statssa.gov.za/

Harambee Afrika (UK business club for traders with east, central and southern Africa; includes annotated web resource list): http://www.harambee.co.uk

Johannesburg Stock Exchange: http://www.jse.co.za/

Maputo development corridor: http://www.dbsa.org/Development_Corridors/Corridors/Maputo

Mbendi AfroPaedia (information on companies, countries, industries and stock exchanges in Africa): http://mbendi.co.za

Province of the North West Tourist Board: http://www.tourismnorthwest.co.za/

South African Development Community (SADC): http://www.sadcreview.com

South African Futures Exchange: http://www.safex.co.za/

South African Airways: http://www.saap.vwv.com/

South African Tourism: http://www.south-african-tourism.org; http://www.southafrica.net

South African yellow pages: http://www.ipages.co.za/

Trade Web: http://www.trade.co.za/Africa Business Network: http://www.ifc.org/abn

Sudan

Anver Versi

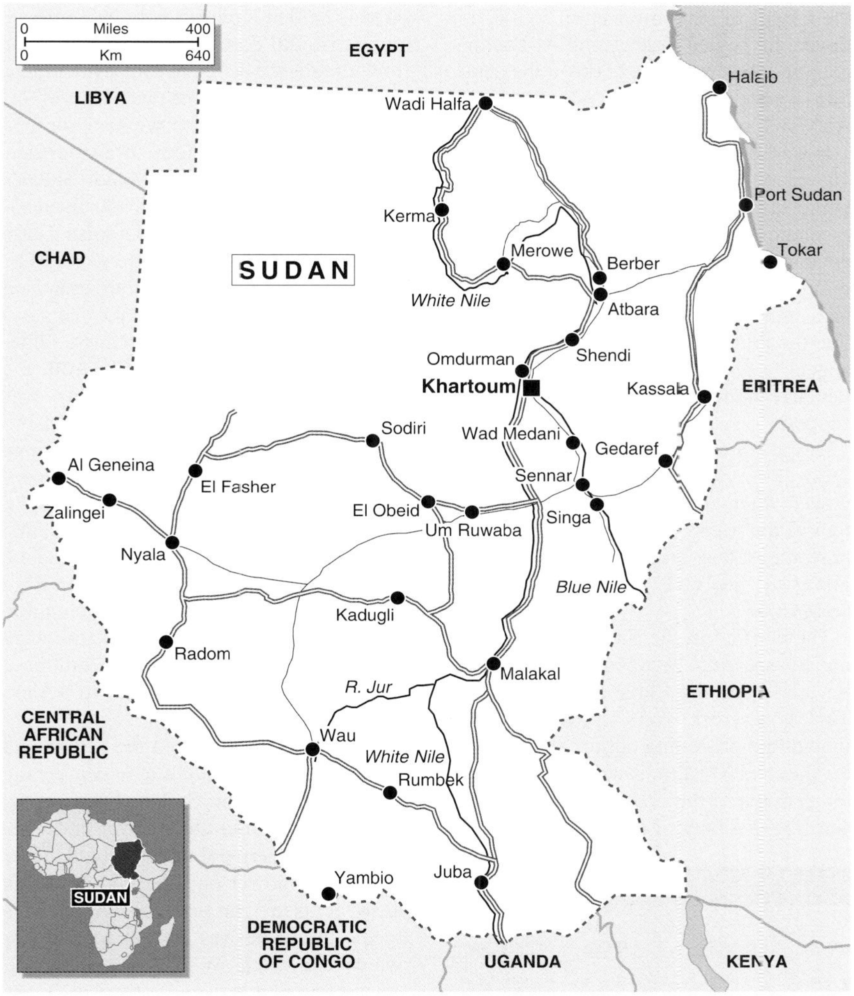

Since independence in 1956, Sudan's history has resembled a tragic drama in which the plot and characters remain the same, but some of the actors change. Short-lived civilian governments are replaced by military leaders, who in turn are replaced by short-lived civilian governments before the military takes over again. All this has happened against a backdrop of constant war interspersed with short periods of relative peace.

With a resounding victory in the one-sided elections of 2000, Omar Al-Bashir, no longer sporting the uniform which brought him to power in 1989, nevertheless took no chances with the likes of the mercurial religious hardliner, Hassan Al-Turabi, and extended the state of emergency he declared in 1999 to the end of 2002. He began a vigorous campaign of fence-mending with neighbours and erstwhile enemies, such as Uganda Ethiopia and Eritrea, and rewarded US Special Envoy, Senator John Danforth's peace initiative by declaring a six month cease-fire in the Nuba mountains.

With oil exports providing an additional US$500 million to the exchequer,

KEY FACTS

Official name: Jamhuryat es-Sudan (The Republic of Sudan)

Head of State: President Omar Hassan Ahmad Al-Bashir (NC) (re-elected Mar 1996 and Dec 2000)

Head of government: President Omar Hassan Ahmad Al-Bashir

Ruling party: National Congress Party (NCP) (elected Dec 2000) (in coalition with the Democratic Salvation Front, and from May 2001, including the Democratic Unionist Party (DUP) and the Muslim Brotherhood)

Area: 2,505,813 square km

Population: 31.1 million (2000)

Capital: Khartoum

Official language: Arabic

Currency: Sudanese dinar (SD) (worth 10 Sudanese pounds (S£)) was introduced 31 Jul 1999

Exchange rate: SD258.70 per US$ (Apr 2002)

GDP per capita: US$450 (2000); US$465 (2001)*

GDP real growth: 9.7% (2000); 5.3% (2001)

Inflation: 8.0% (2000); 5.0% (2001)

Balance of trade: US$606.7 million (2000)

Foreign debt: US$24.0 billion (2000); US$24.9 billion (2001)*

Aid flow: US$187.0 million (2001)*

* estimated figure

For the latest Key Facts, go to www.worldinformation.com

Al-Bashir sent his defence minister with a shopping list of new combat equipment to Russia and was able to post the first trade surplus in the country's modern history. He brandished olive branches in the direction of the veteran rebel leader, John Garang and his Sudan People's Liberation Movement (SPLM), but stepped up the bombardment of the rebel Sudan People's Liberation Army (SPLA) strongholds. By end-2002, Al-Bashir and his National Congress Party (NCP) were as much in control of Africa's biggest country as the previous military strongman turned civilian president, Jaafer Al-Nimieri, had been at the height of his powers in the 1970s.

Al-Bashir's strength led to limited political liberalisation, reflecting the government's self-confidence. In August 2002, Al-Bashir lifted a ban on political parties as a step towards establishing democratic institutions. This was a break from the days when Al-Turabi was the power behind the throne and political parties were banned with their leaders forced into exile. Nevertheless, Al-Bashir had already shored up his constitutional powers in March 2002 when he scrapped the two-term limitation for presidents, enabling him to stand for re-election in 2004. At the same time, he sought to eliminate the last vestiges of Al-Turabi's power by giving himself the power to choose state governors, which were formerly elected.

Al-Turabi's influence

Al-Turabi was the stormy petrel in Sudan's otherwise staid and traditional political groupings – the Umma Party (UP) led by Sadiq Al-Mahdi (the grandson of the Great Mahdi), the Democratic Unionist Party (DUP) (led by the rival Al-Mirghani family) and the Sudanese Communist Party (CPY), which has gone through several transformations but has retained its core leadership.

Al-Turabi commanded an almost fanatical devotion, especially from students at Khartoum University and the intelligentsia in Sudanese society. However, his National Islamic Front (NIF) remained on the fringes of real power until, so it is believed, he helped mastermind Al-Bashir's coup in 1989 and brought down the coalition government of which Sadiq Al-Mahdi was prime minister.

It was Al-Turabi who pushed a beleaguered Al-Nimieri to impose *Sharia* (Islamic law) in 1983, which triggered an escalation of the war in the south. *Sharia* gave Garang another cause for war and it brought several southern groups which had splintered away from the SPLM back into the fold. It also allowed the SPLM to appeal to far-right Christian groups, particularly in the US, for moral and material support.

Despite this attempt to use Islam as a rallying point, Al-Nimieri was toppled from power when thousands of professionals took to the streets – in a repeat of the demonstrations that brought the Abboud regime to an end – to demand his resignation.

The conflict in the Sudan is often portrayed as a battle between the Arab, Muslim north and the Christian, black south. This is a gross oversimplification. Although the prevailing culture in the north is Arab and Muslim, it would take a very long stretch of the imagination to call the startling diversity of peoples who inhabit these vast tracts as 'Arab'. The south, similarly, is anything but homogeneous. It is a collection of an equally wide variety of peoples who only roughly fall into the major ethnic categories – Dinka, Nuer and Equatorial. It is estimated that some 70 per cent of Sudanese are Muslim, with only around 5 per cent Christian. The experiment with autonomy in 1972 went disastrously wrong when the various southern groups battled it out for political, military and territorial dominance. The real cause of the war is the difference in development and cultures between the two halves of Sudan, a country the size of Western Europe.

The Sudanese Muslims, drawing their inspiration from the Great Mahdi, Sudan's nineteenth century Islamic leader, have always considered themselves a special case in the widely diverse Islamic world. The very moderate Sadiq Al-Mahdi, grandson of the Great Mahdi, was seen as the natural spiritual leader of the country. Sudanese Islam, borrowing heavily from the diversity of cultures within it, was easy-going and tolerant of other Muslim strains as well as other faiths. At the same time, groups of highly articulate, very well-educated and well-connected youth, with strong connections to the Islamic Brotherhood movements in Egypt and the Maghreb, wanted to uncouple Sudan from the myth of the Mahdi and make common cause with the wider Islamic and Arab worlds. Hasan Al-Turabi rose from these ranks and longed for a return to a 'pure state of Islam'.

Sadiq Al-Mahdi invited the SPLM and Garang to form part of a new democratic dispensation in the Sudan, but Garang, now heavily committed to war and worried that southern politicians would elbow him out of power once he laid down his arms, refused. This stretched Al-Mahdi's credibility as he was seen as too soft towards the south. With Al-Turabi's NIF growing in numbers and influence, it was not long before yet another coalition government went the way of former ones and this time Al-Bashir was the military strong man to step in. Al-Bashir, a rather stolid, uninspiring character, was the perfect medium for Al-Turabi to work through and push Sudan closer to his version of the Islamic ideal.

Al-Bashir breaks through

Under the Al-Bashir–Al-Turabi axis, the traditional parties were not only effectively silenced, but many of their leaders, including Al-Mahdi, went into exile. There was a steady exodus of some of the brightest professionals to the Gulf states,

KEY INDICATORS — Sudan

	Unit	1996	1997	1998	1999	2000
Population	m	28.57	29.18	29.79	30.42	31.10
Gross domestic product (GDP)	US$bn	8.30	10.60	10.30	10.00	11.90
GDP per capita	US$	304	384	363	348	450
GDP real growth	%	4.8	9.7	6.1	5.2	9.7
Inflation	%	132.8	46.7	17.1	16.0	8.0
Consumer prices	1995=100	232.8	341.4	399.8	463.8	0.0
Exports (fob) (goods)	US$m	620.0	594.0	596.0	780.1	1,806.7
Imports (fob) (goods)	US$m	1,315.0	1,543.0	1,636.0	1,256.0	1,200.0
Balance of trade	US$m	-719.2	-827.7	-1,319.0	-475.9	606.7
Current account	US$m	-826.8	-828.1	-2,000.0	-464.8	-556.8
Total reserves minus gold	US$m	106.8	81.6	90.6	188.7	0.0
Foreign exchange	US$m	106.8	81.6	90.6	188.7	0.0
Exchange rate	per US$	1,250.79	1,575.74	1,949.69	252.55	257.12

Europe and the US. Larger slices of the national budget went into the war effort, especially when it was clear that significant reserves of oil lay under the 'border' areas between north and south. The war took a nastier turn when the northern militia, armed and encouraged by Al-Bashir's government, set about depopulating oil-bearing areas. The SPLA in turn, supported and armed by hostile neighbours and fundamentalist Christian organisations in the US, caused havoc among communities it suspected of being sympathetic to Al-Bashir. Riek Macher, once Garang's deputy, broke from the movement accusing Garang of lacking vision and direction and, encouraged by Al-Turabi, went over to the government. Macher effectively kept the SPLA out of the oil-bearing areas around Benitiu long enough for production to begin in 1999.

With Al-Turabi's Islamic zeal drawing Sudan closer to extremist elements in the Middle East and further isolating it from the rest of the world, Al-Bashir seemed to understand public opinion and disengaged from Al-Turabi. By 1999, Al-Turabi was expelled from his own party; Al-Bashir declared a state of emergency to prevent him from regrouping and legitimised his own power by winning the 2000 elections. In March 2002, the ruling NCP announced it would table a motion scrapping the presidential two-term limitation statute in the constitution and also do away with elections for the country's 29 state governors. Instead, elective colleges would be created to submit a list of six possible governors and it would be up to the president to make the final choice. This would not only concentrate power in the presidency, it would allow the government to weed out remnants of Al-Turabi's influence.

Al-Turabi, who was placed under house arrest, formed a new party, the Popular National Congress (PNC), and has attempted to link up with the SPLA, but with little evident success.

Nuba mountains cease-fire

Following a week of negotiations in the Swiss resort of Bergenstock, US Special Envoy to the Sudan, John Danforth, managed to negotiate a limited cease-fire accord for a section of the Nuba area in January 2002. It was hoped that the cease-fire would allow humanitarian aid to reach millions of people facing starvation in the country's southern region.

By April 2002, the cease-fire was still holding. This was the first taste of peace for the area's beleaguered population in 19 years. The Nuba, who form a quarter of Sudan's estimated 4.5 million displaced people, are sandwiched between the north and the south and over the years have had a difficult time. The majority are Muslim and although they speak at least 50 local dialects, their main business language is Arabic. This has not prevented them coming under attack from government forces nor being press-ganged into military service by the SPLA.

With the imminent threat of starvation lifted by the cease-fire, the Nuba demanded a greater say in their future. They are worried by talks of southern secession and the ambitions of the more powerful Dinka and Equatorial ethnic groups, but are not prepared to be marginalised by the north either. A large portion of Sudan's oil fields lies in Nuba territory and both the north and the south want it included in their 'zones of control' should some sort of autonomy be granted to the south. The Nuba themselves would rather be in neither camp and the Nuba Alliance Party (NAP) called for wide-ranging talks in March 2002 with all parties concerned 'so that we can determine our fate before others do it for us'.

South still a problem

Expectations that the Nuba mountains cease-fire would be extended to other southern areas were dashed when John Garang, rejoined by Riak Macher in January 2002, said he would not stop attacks against oil companies operating in southern areas. In January 2002, the SPLA attacked Lundin Oil's operations and forced the Swedish company to 'temporarily' pull out of the area. The rebels also claimed that they had killed 190 government soldiers sent as reinforcements to Pultuni. Garang warned: 'We are determined to close down oil fields using whatever means we have at our disposal'.

Despite attempts by the international community to support negotiations between the government and rebels, conflicts continued to break out throughout 2002 with both sides ignoring truce agreements – a truce agreed by the government and the SPLA in October 2002 only lasted 10 minutes. The peace process is being conducted under the auspices of the Inter-Governmental Authority for Development (Igad), an initiative launched in 1993 which includes Kenya, Sudan, Ethiopia, Somalia, Djibouti, Uganda and Eritrea. Despite their public commitment to the Igad process, both the government and the SPLA have been unwilling to reach a compromise on the issue of self-determination for the south and the role of religion in public life. The governments of Egypt and Libya attempted to break the deadlock by issuing a joint memorandum, which called for the unity of Sudan, respect for human rights, democratic pluralism and an interim government. Although the SPLA and the government agreed to the Egypt-Libya initiative, the war has continued with government forces continuing to bomb civilians and relief centres in the south.

In the first half of 2002, the government prevented humanitarian organisations from accessing locations in southern Sudan and banned UN relief flights over two of Sudan's largest southern regions. The situation changed in October 2002 when the government and the SPLA agreed to allow unimpeded humanitarian access to war-ravaged areas for the duration of Igad peace talks, which were scheduled to finish by end-December 2002. Negotiations between the government and the SPLA are ongoing and in July 2002 Al-Bashir and SPLA leader John Garang held their first ever face-to-face meeting to sign a framework peace deal, the Machakos Declaration. The deal included a broad agreement to the right of self-determination for the south, albeit within a unified Sudanese state, and the separation of state and religion. It provided for a possible secession of the south after a referendum in 2008. Nevertheless, fighting continued, with the SPLA making significant advances in the second half of 2002, capturing the town of Torit near the border with Uganda.

Wires buzzing

Sudan's economy continued to improve during 2001. Oil exports, via the 1,600km pipeline from the Heglig and Unity fields to Port Sudan, added an estimated US$500 million to the exchequer and allowed Sudan to post its first-ever trade surplus in 2001. Liberalisation of the economy has attracted significant investments from the Gulf, the Far East, China and Russia. A host of new projects, including dams, irrigation schemes, water desalination plants and a water pipeline to serve Port Sudan, will ensure that Sudan's current growth rate of around 7 per cent will be maintained until around 2006.

Privatisation of some key services, such as the telecommunications and Internet monopoly Sudatel, has been more successful than expected. Sudatel was the first non-United Arab Emirate (UAE) company to be listed on the Abu Dhabi stock exchange and, after posting a profit of US$200 million in 2000, was also listed on the

Bahrain stock exchange. Emirates Telecommunications Corporation, encouraged by demand for its shares, bought a 9 per cent stake in Sudatel and was expected to bid for a larger stake in the future. Sudatel announced a profit of US$71 million for the first three-quarters of 2001.

Sudan's current production of 220,000 barrels per day (bpd) is expected to increase to 450,000bpd in 2004 as more wells come on-stream. The surge in oil and gas exports has led to plans to build another export terminal at Suakin, near Port Sudan. The refinery at Port Sudan has been renovated and capacity at the Khartoum refinery is expected to increase by 6,000bpd to 56,000bpd by end-2002.

The oil industry has great potential and many foreign investors are looking to stake a claim in what is likely to be an ever-expanding industry. For example, the Abu Jebra reserves (estimated at 1.7 billion barrels) has hardly been tapped. Companies from China, Malaysia, India and Russia are attempting to be the best placed for contracts before the US decides to lift its unilateral sanctions and the US giants begin to move in. The US sanctions were introduced in 1997 in response to alleged human rights abuses and Sudan's suspected involvement in an assassination attempt on the Egyptian president, Mohammed Hosni Mubarak. In September 2001, the UN lifted its sanctions against Sudan with the US's approval.

Canada's Talisman, which has come under concerted attack from the US and other Western countries for 'helping to fuel the war in the south', announced in April 2002 that it was prepared to sell its 25 per cent stake in the Greater Nile Petroleum Corporation (GNPC), the lead consortium exploiting and exporting Sudanese oil. There was no shortage of interested parties. Consortium partner Petronas of Malaysia was reported to be looking to increase its 30 per cent stake, as was the Sudanese government, which held 5 per cent. India's ONGC Videsh, the overseas arm of the Oil and Gas Corporation of India, had expressed interest but seemed daunted by Talisman's asking price of around US$1 billion.

Meanwhile, Slavneft, the joint Russo-Belarus oil and gas company, has successfully bought out the other Canadian operator, Mellut, by acquiring 93 per cent with the remaining 7 per cent going to the government. China National Petroleum Corporation (CPN), which already holds 40 per cent of GNPC, has signed a couple more exploration deals. The Qatar-based Gulf Petroleum Corporation has taken a 46 per cent stake in a 72,000 square km concession and Petronas has struck oil in the large Unity oil field. All this, industry insiders say, is only the beginning of an oil boom in Sudan.

According to reports, US oil giants are eagerly waiting for the green light from the US presidency to make their own move into Sudan. Now that lurid reports of a full-scale modern slave trade, involving Arab slavers and black slaves, has been exposed as little more than a get rich quick scam, the go-ahead might come sooner than earlier expected.

Power

Now that relations between Egypt and Sudan have improved, having been broken in 1995 because the Egyptian president believed Sudan was behind an attempt to assassinate him, the way is clear to begin preliminary work on the giant Merowe dam, below the confluence of the White and Blue Niles. The US$2 billion project, expected to be completed in 2008, will control seasonal floods and generate 1,250MW of electricity, more than trebling Sudan's current capacity. Arab funding institutions are believed to have already raised US$740 million, the government has committed US$400 million and the rest will be raised from international markets. A programme to build several smaller dams will boost the country's power supply in the meantime.

Outlook

There remain significant obstacles to a permanent settlement of the civil war: Al-Bashir's unwillingness to accept a compromise, a lack of unity among rebel groups, external interference and the issue of oil wealth distribution.

Firstly, in the past, Al-Bashir has shown that he is unwilling to tolerate the emergence of any opposition that could threaten his leadership. Al-Bashir is only willing to bring on board his opponents when they submit to his rule. A compromise with the SPLA would necessitate constitutional change, including power-sharing and devolution, and would entail a reduction of the president's executive powers. Consequently, Al-Bashir may try to derail any peace deal to maintain his grip on power.

Secondly, the rebel groups are disunited and unable to agree on a list of demands. While Al-Bashir has used these divisions to his advantage, there are growing signs of frustration within the government over the vacillations of the SPLA leadership with agreements being continually undermined by hardliners.

Thirdly, the process is being undermined by external interference, particularly by the US government, which is heavily influenced by right-wing Christian groups. Christian conservatives in the US are pressurising the Bush administration to back the SPLA against Al-Bashir, who they continue to portray as an ally of the Al-Qaeda terrorist group.

Lastly, one of the main stumbling blocks relates to the activities of foreign oil companies brought in by the central government. The SPLA has vowed that the fighting would not stop until there was 'a cessation of the exploration, development and export of oil'. Oil production has become politicised in the civil war, with the government displacing large numbers of civilians in the south to clear the way for oil exploration by multi-national corporations. The SPLA sees oil as the Khartoum government's economic life-line and a source of its power and has targetted oil installations in its military offensives. The heaviest fighting in 2002 was seen in the West Upper Nile region, which is the heart of the Sudanese oil industry. Any final agreement will involve a redistribution of oil wealth which would adversely affect the economic interests of the north and could prompt a rebellion within Al-Bashir's government. However, many claim that redistribution of oil wealth is Sudan's best hope for maintaining national unity in the long-term. Southerners will be less likely to accept secession in a referendum if they believe that economic development is assured under a unified government.

The crucial question is whether Al-Bashir will be able to break the cycle and actually accomplish what Al-Nimieri came so close to doing and bring civil war to an end. The prognosis in 2002 was not promising. Sudan is likely to enter a period of economic growth, civil liberties will gradually increase, the old political parties (most of which have returned from exile) will begin regrouping and, as in Al-Nimeiri's time, the south might be offered a measure of autonomy which would again set the various southern ethnic groups at each other's throats leading to a return to war.

Risk assessment

Economy	Improving
Political	Satisfactory
Regional stability	Satisfactory

COUNTRY PROFILE

Historical profile

2300 BC The Pharaonic kingdoms began extending south into modern-day Sudan. By 1000 BC the Nubia was an Egyptian colony. Further south, the independent kingdom of the Cush was developing. The Cush conquered Egypt in the ninth century BC before they were pushed south by the Assyrians in 666 BC.
400 AD The Cush kingdom fell to the Christian state of Axum in Ethiopia. A Christian kingdom grew up in Nubia.
651 The Nubians signed a peace treaty with the Arab armies which had seized Egypt from the Byzantine Empire in 641.
1250 The treaty lasted until Egypt came under the control of the Mamelukes; shortly afterwards the Nubians were conquered and an increasing number of Arabs moved into Sudan.
1821 The swamps of southern Sudan were unaffected by the Arab-controlled northern regions until the Turks defeated Egypt, conquered northern Sudan and opened the south to trade.
1869 After the opening of the Suez Canal the British became involved in Sudan.
1881 The Muslim Sudanese rebelled and massacred the British army at Khartoum. Sudan was ruled by the Great Mahdi (divine leader) for the next 17 years. The Mahdi united the tribes in a modern Islamic state.
1898 The Mahdi was defeated by the British and Anglo-Egyptian army.
1899 Sudan was ruled as an Anglo-Egyptian condominium from 1899 until it achieved independence as a parliamentary republic in 1956.
1945 At the end of the Second World War, political parties emerged: the Umma Party which was created by supporters of the Mahdi while the Ashiqqa Party was established by rivals of the Mahdi and eventually became the National Union Party (NUP).
1956 Sudan gained independence on 1 January. With southern calls for a federation or even secession rejected, a civil war broke out between the largely Muslim north and the south.
1958 A military coup led by General Ibrahim Abboud overthrew the government. Parliament was dismissed, martial law was declared and Abboud proclaimed himself prime minister.
1969 Colonel Jaafar Mohammed Al-Nimieri led a coup, installing a revolutionary council.
1972 Al-Nimieri became the country's first elected president and gave the southern provinces a degree of autonomy under the Addis Ababa agreement which reduced the level of fighting.
1983 The autonomy agreement was revoked and Sharia (Islamic law) was imposed across the country. The Sudan People's Liberation Movement (SPLM) was established, led by John Garang; its armed wing, the Sudan People's Liberation Army (SPLA) gained control of much of the south.
1985 Al-Nimieri was ousted in a bloodless coup in April and after a brief period of military rule Sadiq Al-Mahdi, the great-grandson of the Mahdi, became prime minister after elections in 1986.
1989 Sadiq Al-Mahdi was replaced following another bloodless coup; Omar Hassan Ahmad Al-Bashir became chairman of the Revolutionary Command Council for National Salvation (RCCNS).
1993 The RCCNS was abolished and Sudan returned to civilian rule, although the country was not strictly a democracy.
1996 The first presidential and legislative elections since 1989 were held in March. Al-Bashir was re-elected president with 75.7 per cent of the vote. Sanctions were imposed against Sudan by the UN for the country's failure to extradite three men suspected of involvement in the assassination attempt against Egyptian president, Mohammed Hosni Mubarak.
1997 The Khartoum Peace Agreement, signed in April, was ratified by the National Assembly in May. In July Sudan accepted a framework for negotiations clearing the way for a resumption in talks to end years of civil war. In October, peace talks between the SPLA and the government resumed in Nairobi. SPLA leader John Garang pressed for the Khartoum government to give way to a government of national unity and hold a referendum on self-determination by 2001.
1999 On 26 November the government and the opposition Umma Party (UP) reached agreement on a peace accord. In December, Al-Bashir imposed a state of emergency and dissolved the National Assembly.
2000 Al-Bashir replaced the cabinet, all state governors and his senior advisers in January. Most opposition parties boycotted the December elections and President Al-Bashir won the presidential election with 86.5 per cent of the vote and the ruling National Congress Party (NCP) won 355 seats in the elections to the National Assembly.
2001 The president issued a decree in January which led to a state of emergency until 2002. In September, the UN Security Council approved the lifting of sanctions.

Political structure

Constitution

A multi-party parliamentary system was introduced in 1986, comprising a five-member Supreme Council and a 360-member Majlis Watani (National Assembly).
In 1994, the government increased the number of states to 26. Each state has a *wali* (governor), legislative council and council of ministers. In March 2002, the government indicated that it would replace elections for the *walis* with a system of electoral colleges which would submit six possible candidates, giving the president the final decision on appointments.
A new constitution was promulgated on 1 January 1999, allowing opposition political associations to register prior to the elections. Eligibility for voting was reduced from 18 to 17 years on 3 January 1999.

Form of state

Federal republic

The executive

The president has inherited most of the powers of the now disbanded Revolutionary Command Council of National Salvation (RCCNS), which assumed unified powers in the 1989 military coup. These include the right to override constitutional elections to the 26 state governorships. Executive power at the operational level resides with the cabinet, which includes both civilian and military representatives. In March 2002, the ruling party proposed to scrap the two-term limitation to the presidency. The president is directly elected by universal suffrage.

National legislature

The Majlis Watani (National Assembly) was elected in December 2000, a year after it was suspended by presidential decree. Out of a total of 360 seats, 270 are directly elected for a four-year term in single-seat constituencies, 35 members represent women, 26 members represent university graduates and 29 are representatives of trade unions.

Legal system

Sharia (Islamic law) with an admixture of English common law operates officially at the federal level, although individual states choose whether or not it should apply at state level. In practice the legal system is split along political lines, with *sharia* imposed universally in the north, but ineffective in the rebel-held south. The judiciary is in theory politically independent under the constitution introduced at the beginning of 1999. However, military or paramilitary elements influence the judiciary or operate direct extra-judicial military rule throughout the country.

Last elections

December 2000 (parliamentary and presidential)

Next elections

2004 (parliamentary); 2005 (presidential).

Political parties
Ruling party
National Congress Party (NCP) (elected Dec 2000) (in coalition with the Democratic Salvation Front, and from May 2001, including the Democratic Unionist Party (DUP) and the Muslim Brotherhood)
Main opposition party
Umma Party (UP)

Population
31.10 million (2000)
Population estimates vary. Population growth stood at 2.6 per cent in 2000, compared with a 2.3 per cent average in the period 1980–97. Projections put the population at 50 million by 2030. Population under 15 years: 43 per cent; over 60 years: 3.8 per cent (2000).
Urban population: 32 per cent of the total population (2000). Around 7 per cent of the population are nomads.
Ethnic make-up
Black (52 per cent), Arab (39 per cent), Beja (6 per cent). In the north and central regions the population consists mainly of Muslim Arabs and Nubians. In the south the people are socially, culturally and historically related to the peoples of east Africa.
Religions
Islam (Sunni Muslim) in the north (70 per cent); in the south traditional beliefs (25 per cent) and Christianity (5 per cent).

Education
In 2000, the adult illiteracy rate was estimated at 30.2 per cent and 53.7 per cent for men and women respectively. Elementary education for those aged seven to 12 years is free. World Bank estimates show that the total primary school enrolment of the relevant age group typically stood at 55 per cent for boys and 47 per cent for girls (including repetition rates) between 1994 and 2000. The number of pupils per primary school teacher is typically 29. Intermediate education starts at the age of 13 and lasts three years. Secondary education starts at 16 years and also lasts for three years. Students completing secondary education are eligible for university. There are five universities, two in Khartoum (one is a branch of Cairo University), an Islamic university at Omdurman and universities at Juba and Wad Medani. Public expenditure on education typically amounted to 0.9 per cent of annual gross national income between 1994–97.

Health
World Bank estimates during the period 1994–2000 showed that the average life expectancy was 55 years and the infant mortality rate stood at 69 per 1,000 live births. The fertility rate shows that 4.5 children are born per adult woman. The rate of contraception practices is estimated at 10 per cent among women aged 15–49. The maternal mortality rate is typically 500 deaths per 100,000 live births. The HIV rate is increasing to nearly 0.99 per cent among adults. World Bank surveys in 2000 show that 75 per cent and 62 per cent of the population have access to improved water and sanitation facilities respectively. There are 0.1 physicians and 1.1 hospital beds typically available for 1,000 people.
World Bank estimates show that between 1990–98, health care expenditure was equivalent to about 3.4 per cent of GDP, of which 0.7 was public expenditure and the remaining 2.7 per cent private. Public health services are organised by the ministry of health. Some health care is provided free of charge.

Welfare
Social insurance in Sudan is not provided through the government. There is no social security budget.

Main cities
Khartoum (estimated population 2.7 million in 1998; 4.8 million including two million refugees in Omdurman and Khartoum North), Port Sudan, Wad Medani, Juba, Kassala, El Obeid, Atbara.

Languages spoken
African languages include Nilotic and Nilo-Hamitic. The government is considering eliminating the official teaching and the use of English as part of its Islamisation programme. However, English remains widely used in business.
Official language/s
Arabic

Media
The media are tightly constrained by censorship laws, statutory government ownership, harrassment by the security forces, and an unsurprising amount of corresponding self-censorship.
Press
Following the 1989 military coup, all press publications were banned except for the newspaper of the armed forces. Since 1997, press restrictions were eased with increasing discussion of some domestic and foreign policy issues. Ownership of publications by individuals or political groups is banned. The board and chairman of a publication must be government-appointed, and 26 per cent of the publisher's equity go to the government. The National Press and Publications Council (NPPC) has the power to suspend any publication. A wide variety of English and Arabic-language publications operate in the shadow of the government's information policy.
Dailies: There are nine daily newspapers published from Khartoum. Arabic language dailies include *Akhir Khabai* and *Al-Waan*. *Al-Rayaam* is a political newspaper. The main national dailies (state-controlled) are *Al Sudan al Hadith*, *Al-Ingaz Al-Wakari* and *Al-Quwait Al-Musalaha*. The Sudan News Agency (http://www.sunanews.net/) carries the latest news on Sudan from different English language sources. *Sudan Globe* (http://www.sudanglobe.com/) provides daily on-line news service. *Sudan.Net* (http://www.sudan.net/) provides daily news in both Arabic and English languages from various government and non-government organisations.
Weeklies: Weekly publications include *Akhbar Al Mujtama*, *Azzizati* (bi-weekly) and *Al Aliha* covering sports.
Periodicals: Periodicals include the Arabic political monthly magazine *Addaraweesh* and the political newspaper *Mehairah* covering current issues. The Sudanese Communist party publishes the monthly newspaper *Al-Midan*. There is a monthly English-language magazine, *Sudan Now*.
Broadcasting
Directly controlled by government, radio and television come under the purview of a special military censor. All broadcasting is controlled by the state-owned National Radio and Television Corporation based in Omdurman.
Radio: The Sudan Broadcasting Corporation broadcasts daily radio programmes in Amharic, Arabic, English, French, Somali and Tigrinya. The government does not jam foreign radio signals.
Television: The Sudan National Broadcasting Corporation is responsible for television programmes, which are broadcast for about 40 hours a week.
In February 2000, the government signed a contract to import a 25MW transmitter, to broadcast over Unity state, including the areas of Bentiu and Rubkona.
There are restrictions on satellite dish ownership, but satellite services are offered in tandem with domestic. A six-channel cable network offers CNN, Saudi Middle East Broadcasting Corporation (MEBC), Kuwait-TV and Dubai-TV.

Economy
Sudan's economy is predominantly agricultural. Subsistance farming is combined with cash crops such as gum arabic and cotton. However, recent economic growth is being fuelled by oil production. This has resulted in strong economic growth, while inflation has declined since the days of hyperinflation in the mid-1990s.
The liberalisation of trade and investment is a high priority for the Sudanese government. In 2000, it opened the Red Sea Free Trade Zone. The oil and gas sector is of great interest to foreign investors and Sudan stands to become one of the world's leading oil producers.

Sudan's improved relations with the IMF were evidenced with the publication of a report commending the government's handling of the macroeconomic environment. Sudan has won praise from the IMF amid circumstances which the Fund admits are 'very difficult'. In August 1999 the IMF lifted its declaration of non-co-operation and promised de-escalation of 'remedial measures' and by August 2000 it had lifted the suspension on Sudan's IMF voting rights. This is all the more impressive considering that in 1995 Sudan was on the verge of expulsion for defaulting on debt repayments.

In September 2001, the UN Security Council approved lifting sanctions imposed against Sudan in 1996.

External trade

Exports

Principal exports are oil and petroleum products, cotton, sesame, livestock, groundnuts, gum arabic and sugar.

Main destinations: China (37.6 per cent of 2000 total), Japan (15.8 per cent), Saudi Arabia (8.7 per cent), Republic of Korea (7.2 per cent), South Africa (4.5 per cent).

Imports

Principal imports are foodstuffs, manufactured goods, machinery and transport equipment, medicines and chemicals and textiles.

Main sources: China (12.1 per cent of 2000 total), Saudi Arabia (10 per cent), Germany (7.4 per cent), UK (6.7 per cent), France (5 per cent).

Agriculture

Sudan is a semi-arid country and a large part is desert. Irrigated farmland constitutes about one-fifth of the total cultivated area, but produces about 50 per cent of total crop production. The traditional farming areas are semi-arid and used for livestock rearing, while export crops are grown in the irrigated areas, mostly in the Gezira area between the Blue and White Niles. The country is often racked by drought and famine.

The rain-fed farming regions produce grains, oilseeds, gum arabic (tapped from acacia trees) and livestock (reared in semi-arid areas). Climatic risks are significant but intensification of agriculture could enhance productivity significantly. According to a study by the Arab Agricultural Organisation, Sudan has enough resources to feed the population six times over.

The principal food crops are sorghum (durra) (48 per cent of the cultivated land), millet (22 per cent), groundnuts (8 per cent), sugar-cane, dates, cassava, wheat and beans. Cotton is the main cash crop providing, followed by gum arabic and sesame. Cereal production increased slightly in 2001, but was still around 40 per cent lower than in 1998 and some regions faced serious food deficits as a result of drought.

Principal export crops are cotton, oil seeds (mainly groundnuts and sesame) and gum arabic (used in soft drinks, baking, cosmetics, pharmaceuticals and other industrial applications), of which Sudan is the world's largest producer. Main food crops include sorghum (dura) and millet. Cotton is the main cash crop providing 45 per cent of export earnings, followed by gum arabic and sesame (21 per cent). Livestock-raising is of considerable importance, employing about 40 per cent of the population. Sudan is aiming to become self-sufficient in rice and tea production. The Agricultural Bank of Sudan appears to have assumed the main responsibility for ensuring the growing, marketing and export of crops.

Farming

Sudan has attempted to tackle the problem of land usage. Government policy aims to increase the area of cultivable land (only about 10 per cent of the potential arable land is under cultivation) through the rehabilitation and expansion of existing irrigation schemes. A planting scheme has given precedence to food crops over land devoted to cotton production and export.

The Nile Basin Initiative (NBI) (signed by Egypt, Sudan, Tanzania, Kenya, Rwanda, Burundi, Uganda and Democratic Republic of Congo) is launching seven feasibility studies backed by US$140 million granted by the World Bank and donor governments in June 2001. It will also develop a parallel legal framework for shared water management. Ethiopia refused to sign and Eritrea's membership is pending.

Fishing

Sudan possesses vast freshwater and marine fishing potential, but the Nile fisheries are barely exploited. Fishing on the Red Sea coastline is being encouraged.

Industry and manufacturing

The industrial sector contributes around 10 per cent to GDP and employs 10 per cent of the workforce.

Activity is centred on the processing of agricultural products, particularly textiles, sugar, oilseeds, flour and footwear. Inadequate infrastructure, shortages of imported inputs, power cuts and lack of skilled manpower have thwarted government efforts at developing large-scale industries.

Mining

The mining sector has played a relatively insignificant role in the country's economic development, although experts indicate gold was mined in Sudan as long ago as 5,000 years. Several mineral deposits are known to exist, for example: zinc, lead, copper, talc, coal, nickel and tin, phosphate, uranium, chromite, gypsum, gold and iron ore, but only a few are exploited on a commercial basis (chromite, gypsum, gold and, more recently, iron ore). If financial and infrastructural problems can be overcome, this sector could make a significant contribution to the economy in the future.

Hydrocarbons

Sudan possesses commercially significant reserves of both oil and gas, but their exploitation has been hampered in the past by a combination of financing problems, civil war and US sanctions specifically intended to prevent petroleum investment by US companies. The exploitation of hydrocarbons should result in substantial foreign exchange savings on oil imports and would also allow for long-term expansion of electricity production.

Oil

Sudan has oil reserves of between 262.1 million and 1.7 billion barrels (2001) and has three oil refineries: the Khartoum Oil Refinery in the Jayli area (50,000 barrels per day (bpd)), Port Sudan (21,700bpd) and El Obeid (10,000bpd). Total oil production was estimated at 220,000bpd in 2001, while consumption was around 36,000bpd.

Sudan was granted observer status at Organisation of the Petroleum Exporting Countries (Opec) meetings in August 2001.

The development by Arakis of the Heglig and Unity fields began in 1996. In December 1996, Arakis entered into a consortium – the Greater Nile Petroleum Corporation (GNPC) (consisting of China National Petroleum Corportation (40 per cent), Petronas (30 per cent), Sudapet (5 per cent) and Arakis (25 per cent)) to construct the Greater Nile Oil Project (GNOP). Canada's Talisman later joined the project, but announced in April 2002 that it was selling its 25 per cent stake in the GNPC. This involved the construction of pipelines from the oil fields to an export terminal near Port Sudan. Pipeline capacity was 250,000bpd in 2001, but the consortium hopes to expand this to 450,000bpd reflecting the development of the Heglig and Unity fields. The GNOP infrastructure has come under attack by southern rebel groups which are determined to close down oil production operations.

The absence of competition from US oil majors has attracted investors despite the considerable political risk following from the activities of the SPLA guerrillas and other militias which have designated oil installations as legitimate military targets.

Gas
Total gas reserves are estimated at 85 billion cubic metres, but gas production is negligible.

Energy
Sudan has installed electricity generation capacity of 500MW. Generation, distribution and transmission are the responsibilities of the state-owned National Electricity Corporation.
Besides fuelwood and imported petroleum, hydroelectricity is the main source of energy providing 45 per cent of installed capacity (225MW). Power cuts are regular occurrences, particularly during the summer when drought impairs hydroelectric generation.
China and Malaysia are involved in the construction of the Kajbar and Merowe hydroelectric plants. Environmentalists have criticised the damage they would cause to the eco-system as well as the welfare of the Nubian people, who are being forcibly removed from the area.

Financial markets
Stock exchange
The first stock exchange opened in January 1995.

Banking
Commercial banks include: Bank of Khartoum, El Nilein Bank, Faisal Islamic Bank (Sudan), Tadamon Islamic Bank, Sudanese International Bank, Farmer's Commercial Bank, Sudanese French Bank and Unity Bank.
Development banks include: Agricultural Bank of Sudan (agricultural projects), Islamic Co-operative Development Bank (co-operative ventures), Sudanese Estates Bank (housing and mortgages), Industrial Bank of Sudan (industrial projects) and National Development Bank (economic, social projects).
Foreign banks include: Bank of Oman, Blue Nile Bank, Citibank, Habib Bank, Middle East Bank Limited and National Bank of Abu Dhabi.
Central bank
Bank of Sudan
Main financial centre
Khartoum

Time
GMT plus two hours

Geography
Sudan lies in northeastern Africa. Sudan is the largest country in Africa and the ninth largest in the world. It lies entirely within the tropics and is bordered by Egypt and Libya in the north, Ethiopia, Eritrea and the Red Sea in the east, Kenya, Uganda and the Democratic Republic of Congo in the south and the Central African Republic and Chad in the west.
The River Nile and its tributaries, the White and Blue Niles, are the country's most important physical features. The Blue Nile, in particular, plays a vital economic role, supporting 40 per cent of the current irrigated area and with the potential to support 70 per cent of future irrigated land. The Blue Nile is prone to serious seasonal flooding.

Climate
Tropical in the south, hot and dry in the north. In Khartoum, the hottest month is May (26–42 degrees Celsius (C)), the coldest is January (16–32 degrees C). The northern zone receives very little rainfall and is mainly desert. The south is mainly tropical while the central zone is semi-arid grassland.
From mid-April to the end of June the climate is extremely hot and dry. Sandstorms – *haboobs* – are frequent in desert areas between April and September. The rainy season extends from July to September. During this period road travel outside the cities is difficult. In Khartoum, the average temperature by day in the summer is 42 degrees C and 32 degrees C in the winter.

Dress codes
Formal clothing should be worn for business and social engagements. Lightweight clothing is essential at all times, although visitors should carry some warmer clothing if travelling to Sudan during the winter months (November to March). A light raincoat is needed during the months of July, August and September. Women should be aware of the fact that the north is predominantly Muslim and are advised to dress modestly.

Entry requirements
Passports
Required by all. Passports must be valid for six months from date of entry.
Visa
Visas are required by all nationalities and must be obtained in advance. They are valid for one month. Evidence of a previous visit to Israel will result in a visa refusal.
Travellers must obtain special permits to travel anywhere outside Khartoum. These are obtainable from the Passport and Immigration Office in Khartoum.
Visitors arriving in any town or city in Sudan must register with the police on their arrival and show the necessary paperwork.
Permits are required to visit archaeological or historical sites. These are fairly expensive and can be obtained from the Department of Antiquities in Khartoum.
Prohibited entry
Nationals of Israel and holders of passports with Israeli visas.
Currency advice/regulations
There are no restrictions on import of foreign exchange; export is allowed up to amount imported.
Import/export of local currency is prohibited.
Travellers cheques have limited acceptance.
Customs
Alcohol is strictly forbidden. Travellers arriving with alcoholic beverages are liable to immediate arrest.

Health (for visitors)
Mandatory precautions
Visitors travelling to the south of the country will need a valid certificate of vaccination against yellow fever. Travellers entering Egypt from the Sudan will need to produce either a certificate of vaccination against yellow fever or a location certificate showing that they have not been in a yellow fever area. A valid cholera certificate is required of travellers arriving from infected areas. Malaria, typhoid, rabies and polio are endemic. Bilharzia is also present and visitors should avoid swimming or paddling in fresh water.
Advisable precautions
Yellow fever, hepatitis A, tetanus, typhoid and polio vaccinations. Malaria prophylaxis is recommended as risk exists throughout the country. Water precautions are essential. Water and milk should be boiled. Local dairy products should be avoided as milk is unpasteurised. Vegetables should be cooked and meat and fish should be well cooked and eaten hot. Fruit should be peeled. Medical facilities are scarce outside Khartoum. Some health care is provided free of charge, but visitors are advised to take out health insurance which includes emergency repatriation in the event of illness.

Hotels
Accommodation can be difficult to obtain outside Khartoum and Port Sudan. Advisable to book in advance. Service charge of 10 per cent is usual. Hotel bills subject to 10 per cent sales tax.

Credit cards
Credit cards are generally accepted.

Public holidays
Fixed dates
1 Jan (Independence Day), 30 Jun (Revolution Day), 25 Dec (Christmas Day).
Variable dates
Sham Al-Naseem (Coptic Easter Monday), Eid Al-Fitr, Eid Al-Adha, Islamic New Year, Mouloud (Birth of the Prophet).

Working hours
Banking
Sat–Thu: 0830–1200.
Business
Sat–Thu: 0800–1430.

Government
Sat–Thu: 0800/0830–1330/1400.
Shops
Sat–Thu: 0800–1330, 1730–2000.

Telecommunications

Telephone/fax
Direct dialling to Sudan from Europe and the US – but frequent delays.
Dialling code for Sudan: IDD access code + 249 followed by area code (11 for Khartoum), followed by subscriber's number.
All other locations must be called through international operator.
There is direct telephone dialling to Europe and the US. Sudan has an earth satellite station operating on 36 channels at Umm Haraz. Sudan Telecommunications Company (Sudatel), the national carrier has set up a nationwide VSAT satellite network (Sudasat), with 30 earth stations in the provinces, and fibre-optic relays now link the major cities, with smaller cities connected to the Sudasat network by wireless loop. The system is large and well maintained, by African standards, and is improving as both domestic and external investment are released.
Postal services
Mail to the US takes about two weeks, but from the US mail can take up to four. Mail to and from Europe takes about a month, but is less reliable, with some correspondence lost. The post restante service is very unreliable even in the Khartoum area.
Mobile phones
Daewoo of Korea, in co-operation with native Sudatel, has agreed to set up a mobile phone service. GSM operator Mobitel was awarded a five-year franchise in 1996, while regional mobile satellite service provider Thuraya, in which Sudatel has a stake, plans to launch its satellite in 2000.
Internet/e-mail
In 1999, there was one Internet service provider in Khartoum, with about 300 subscribers.

Electricity supply

240V AC

Social customs/useful tips

Visitors should address Sudanese males using the form Sayed (meaning Mr) with the first name only. There are a large number of local traditions and most Muslim customs are observed. Politeness and patience are more important than punctuality. Women are often not present at business or social gatherings.
The Islamic legal and moral code, *Sharia*, was introduced in 1983, suspended in 1985 and reintroduced in the north in 1991. Much of the Christian south is controlled by the rebel Sudan People's Liberation Army (SPLA), which applies its own laws.
There is a ban on alcohol and gambling in the north.
Some souvenirs, such as cheetah skins, although available in the souks (markets) are banned by the Government.
Military establishments should not be photographed, nor should bridges, dams, rail and air transport facilities. Visitors should not attempt to photograph Sudanese people without permission or if they appear reluctant. Photography permits issued by the Tourist Information Office in Khartoum are often ignored by the authorities, who may confiscate your film and camera.
Most banks in Sudan are heavily fortified and resemble prisons as much as they do commercial institutions.

Security

Southern Sudan, the Nuba mountains, the Ethiopian and Eritrean borders and the Kassala area near the Eritrean border are all zones of military activity, including the laying of anti-personnel land mines, and are insecure. There is banditry in Darfa state. Travel in these areas should be avoided unless for essential relief work. In general, no land borders into or out of Sudan can be safely crossed, with the exception of the Wadi Halfa crossing into Egypt. The political situation in Sudan is not stable and visitors are advised to consult their embassy before travel, as well as brief themselves regularly regarding developments in the wider region. Demonstrations should be avoided and British and US citizens may wish to keep a low profile.

Getting there

Air
National airline: Sudan Airways.
International airport/s: Khartoum (Code: KRT), 4 km from city; duty-free shop, bar, buffet and restaurant.
Airport tax: International departures US$20, domestic departures SD600 excluding transit passengers and infants under two years (March 1999).
Domestic departures SD700; international departures SD700 (Egypt Air and Sudan Airways flights to Egypt), SD2500 (other international flights including flights to Egypt by other airlines); not applicable to 24-hour transit passengers.
Surface
Road: Roads link Sudan to Egypt, Libya, Chad, Uganda and the Central African Republic. The Ethiopia-Sudan highway was being refurbished in early 2000.
Drivers wishing to enter Sudan by road must apply for permission in Khartoum or from overseas representatives. Applicants must list vehicle and passenger details, with supporting documents from a recognised motorist society, or a guarantee from a bank or registered business.
Most border crossings remain dangerous, with the exception of the relatively secure border with Egypt via Wadi Halfa.
Rail: A rail link runs from Cairo to the Aswan High Dam in Egypt. Passengers can then take a river boat on to Wadi Halfa.
Water: Sudan's River Transport Corporation operates regular Nile cruises from Aswan in Egypt to Wadi Halfa. Ferry services to Sudan are available from Saudi Arabia and Yemen.
Main port/s: Port Sudan on the Red Sea and Suakin, served by passenger lines from the USA, Europe and several African countries, are the country's only sea ports.

Getting about

National transport
Before travelling, it is advisable to check the security situation in the area.
Air: Sudan Airways operates a regular service between Khartoum, Port Sudan and El Obeid. Small air taxi companies fly from Khartoum to main towns.
Road: Main tarred roads are the 1,186km route from Port Sudan to Khartoum, from Port Sudan to Kassala and on to Shavak, from Khartoum to Sennar and on to Malakal. Another 800km of tarred roads exist, but the rest of the country's 48,000km network is of very variable quality.
Buses: Scheduled coach services include Khartoum-Kosti, Khartoum-Omdurman, Khartoum-El Fasher, Juba-Nimule, Juba-Faradge.
Rail: A network links Khartoum with Port Sudan, Kassala, Wau, Nyala and Wadi Halfa, but not Juba. Services can be very slow.
Three-class service, with sleeping, dining and air-conditioned cars available.
Water: Ferries and steamers ply the Nile between Khartoum and Juba and on the Sobat and Jur Rivers.
City transport
Taxis: Easily available in Khartoum. Can be hailed, or taken from ranks. Official tariffs, but fares still subject to negotiation in advance of journey.
Car hire
Available in main centres but expensive. National or international driving licence required. There is not a reliable fuel station between Port Sudan and Khartoum, a distance of some 1,200km, and petrol is very difficult to obtain in Khartoum.

BUSINESS DIRECTORY

Telephone area codes

The international dialling code (IDD) for Sudan is +249 followed by area code (11 Khartoum; 31 Port Sudan City), followed by subscriber's number.

Chambers of Commerce
Sudan Chamber of Commerce, PO Box 81, Khartoum.

Banking
Bank of Khartoum, PO Box 1008, Khartoum (tel: 81-071; fax: 781-120).

Farmers Commercial Bank, PO Box 1116, Kasr Avenue, Khartoum (tel: 774-960; fax: 773-687).

Tadamon Islamic Bank, PO Box 3154, Baladia Avenue, Khartoum (tel: 785-481, 784-960; fax: 773-840).

Al-Baraka Bank, PO Box 3583, Al-Baraka Tower, Khartoum (tel: 782-964, 777-861; fax: 778-948).

El Nilein Industrial Development Bank, PO Box 466, 1722 United Nations Square, Khartoum (tel: 780-087, 771-586; fax: 785-811, 771-984).

Central bank
Bank of Sudan, PO Box 313, Khartoum, Sudan (tel: 774419, 780123, 783425, 772166, 778064 fax: 780273, 778547)

Travel information
Sudan Airways, SDC Building, Street 15, New Extension, PO Box 253, Khartoum (tel: 47-953, 452-359; fax: 47-978, 452-377).

Ministries
Ministry of Agriculture and Forests, Khartoum (tel: 780-951, 770-895).

Ministry of Animal Welfare, Khartoum (tel: 770-895).

Ministry of Aviation, Khartoum (tel: 776-894, 775-993).

Ministry of Culture and Information, Khartoum (tel: 771-967, 771-952).

Ministry of Defence, Khartoum (tel: 774-910).

Ministry of Education, Khartoum (tel: 770-016, 770-121).

Ministry of Energy and Mining, Khartoum (tel: 775-595, 781-043).

Ministry of the Environment and Tourism (tel: 462-604).

Ministry of Finance & National Economy, Khartoum (tel: 77-255).

Ministry of Foreign Affairs, Khartoum (tel: 773-101, 780-261, 780-286).

Ministry of Health, Khartoum (tel: 773-000, 771-110).

Ministry of Higher Education and Scientific Research, Khartoum (tel: 789-970).

Ministry of the Interior, Khartoum (tel: 776-554, 777-271).

Ministry of National Industry, Khartoum (tel: 777-770, 780-560).

Ministry of Public Services, Khartoum (tel: 779-892).

Ministry of Social Planning, Khartoum (tel: 779-008, 774-627).

Ministry of Trade, Khartoum (tel: 778-241, 779-157).

Ministry of Transport, Khartoum (tel: 775-290, 775-419).

Other useful addresses
Sudan Development Corporation, PO Box 710, Khartoum (tel: 79-536).

Sudanese Embassy (USA), 2210 Massachusetts Avenue, NW, Washington DC 20008 (tel: 338-8565; fax: 667-2406; e-mail: info@sudanembassyus.org).

Internet sites
Africa Business Network: http://www.ifc.org/abn

AllAfrica.com: http://allafrica.com

African Development Bank: http://www.afdb.org

Africa Online: http://www.africaonline.com

Mbendi AfroPaedia (information on companies, countries, industries and stock exchanges in Africa): http://mbendi.co.za

The Sudan Page: http://www.sudan.net/main1.html

Swaziland

Daniel Brett

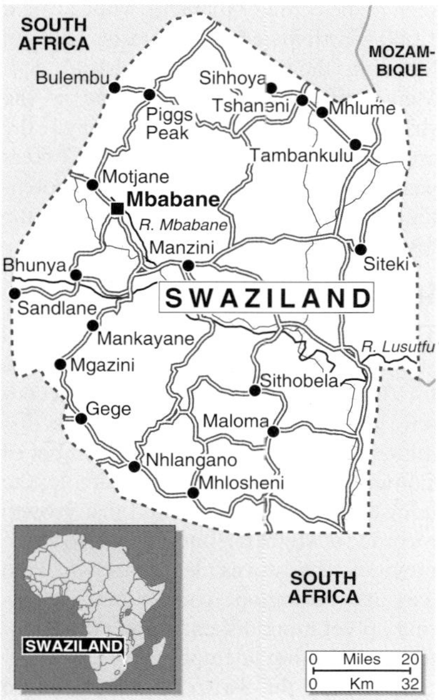

Big problems continued to blight one of Africa's smallest states throughout 2002. King Mswati III, Swaziland's irascible and dictatorial monarch, continues to maintain his grip on the throne by incarcerating anyone who questions his right to rule by decree. He has maintained his father's repressive state of emergency, which was imposed in 1973 along with the suspension of the constitution and the banning of political parties. The pro-democracy movement, independent media and trade unions have effectively been driven underground. This has stoked up yet more political confrontation that has frequently become violent.

Meanwhile, the King's subjects are plagued by the AIDS epidemic and severe food shortages in a country where life expectancy is plummeting and infant mortality is rocketing. By 2002, Swaziland had become isolated from international donors while its economy was collapsing.

Decree nasty

Constitutional government and human rights were put under further threat in 2001 and 2002. Decree 2 of 2001, introduced by Mswati in June, gave the monarch the power to overrule court decisions and set up state-sponsored kangaroo courts. It made it a seditious offence, punishable with a 10-year jail term, to 'impersonate, insult, ridicule or put into contempt' the King, tribal chiefs and state officials and allowed for the banning of publications without appeal.

The repressive move was the culmination of a long-running dispute between the King and the small independent press. The King had become incensed with the country's two leading independent newspapers, *The Nation* and the *Guardian*. After reporting that the King had been poisoned by one of his numerous wives and criticising the royal family's attempts to clamp down on civic organisations, the two papers were closed on the King's orders. However, after the US threatened to withdraw preferential trade benefits under the Africa Growth and Opportunities Act (AGOA), the King scrapped the decree in late June 2001 and lifted the ban on the two newspapers.

The secret trial of Masuku

Many optimists hailed the King's *volte-face*, claiming that the monarch was at last sensitive to international concerns over human rights violations. However, hopes of progress were dashed in October 2001 when Mario Masuku, the leader of the banned People's United Democratic Movement (Pudemo), was arrested for a minor breach of his bail conditions. Masuku was originally arrested in November 2000 after the police alleged he had called on Swazis to topple the monarchy through revolutionary means. It later emerged that the police had deliberately mistranslated the siSwati words spoken by Masuku, who was alleged to have said 'down with the King' during a series of demonstrations. Pudemo was keen to point out that 'even if the government's allegations were true, the worst that could be said is that he merely exercised his right of free speech'. Masuku was subsequently released on bail on the condition that he report daily to his local police station and refrain from addressing public rallies.

KEY FACTS

Official name: Umbuso weSwatini (Kingdom of Swaziland)

Head of State: King Mswati III

Head of government: Prime Minister Dr Barnabas Sibusiso Dlamini (since Jul 1996)

Ruling party: Political parties are banned under the 1978 constitution.

Area: 17,363 square km

Population: 1.10 million (2001)

Capital: Mbabane (Lobamba to become legislative capital)

Official language: English and siSwati

Currency: Lilangeni – plural Emalangeni (E) = 100 cents; at par with the South African Rand

Exchange rate: E8.83 per US$ (Jan 2003)

GDP per capita: US$1,087 (2001)

GDP real growth: 1.80% (2001); 2.1% (2002)*

Unemployment: 31.60% (2001)

Inflation: 7.50% (2001); 7.6% (2002)*

Balance of trade: -US$96.00 million (2001)

Foreign debt: US$308.00 million (2001)

* estimated figure

For the latest Key Facts, go to www.worldinformation.com

His failure to attend the police station one day in October 2001 for three days running while he attended a Pudemo annual conference in South Africa resulted in his re-arrest. Masuku claimed he 'had no option except to force my own arrest so that I get a speedy trial'. Kept in an over-crowded cell in a maximum security prison, Masuku was denied access to medical treatment for diabetes and hypertension. His sedition trial began in January 2002, but members of the public and press were barred from viewing the proceedings. The trial collapsed in the following month after it emerged that the presiding judge, Josiah Matsebula, was no longer legally employed as his contract had expired at the end of 2001 and had not been renewed by the King. Masuku was led away to custody, angrily exclaiming 'look how confused your government is'. The trial later resumed and Masuku was cleared of all charges and set free. The opposition leader remained defiant after his release, saying that the royal system of government could not be reformed and had to be 'wiped out'. He warned Mswati to 'open his ears as a great tide is coming. It will not spare him or anyone else, his wives and his brothers and sisters. The tide is so high; it is of the masses'. He has indicated that the king could retain his position as a ceremonial constitutional monarch, in the same mould as the monarchy in Lesotho. Masuku's stand against Mswati could see him re-arrested in 2003 as tensions grow over the lack of accountability in the political system.

Jet row

The issue of accountability became particularly important in the second half of 2002, when the government decided to purchase a US$45 million private jet for the King. The plan sparked condemnation from the opposition, trade union movement, members of parliament, church leaders, non-governmental organisations, foreign governments and even the IMF. With around a quarter of the population facing hunger and a quarter of adults infected with HIV/AIDS, many thought the move was irresponsible, particularly since the jet would cost more than the annual expenditure on healthcare. The government refused to bow to pressure and insisted that the jet was necessary both in terms of cost effectiveness and security for the monarch, who it claimed was vulnerable to terrorist attacks.

Controversy also surrounded Mswati's marriage to his tenth wife, whose mother claimed was abducted by royal courtiers. The engagement to the prospective queen in August 2002 occurred just two months after Mswati married wives number eight and nine, apparently in an attempt to beat his father's record of 125 wives recorded in his 61-year reign. The king's polygamy has been increasingly subject to criticism by women's rights groups and organisations trying to promote HIV/AIDS awareness. In November 2002, the King ordered the judges examining the allegations of kidnapping to cease their investigations or resign. The Director of Public Prosecutions, Lincoln Ng'arua, was also faced with the sack after he lodged sedition charges against the attorney general, Phesheya Dlamini, who he claimed was in breach of the constitution for demanding the resignation of judges. The affair put the monarch in direct conflict with the judiciary, which refused to back down over the case. It also pitted reformists against traditionalists.

The outcry over the jet issue and the controversy over Mswati's tenth wife prompted Pudemo and the trade unions to mount a general strike in December 2002. The 'stay-away' attracted little support, with only a few hundred demonstrators seen in the capital Mbabane, while around 1,000 participated in protests held in Manzini, the kingdom's industrial city. Many criticised the poor timing of the strike, which occurred during the pre-Christmas shopping period. Workers were unwilling to sacrifice pay and potentially lose their jobs in the run-up to the festival.

Starving growth

The government has been very guarded about releasing its GDP growth estimates for 2001. Its previous claim that the economy grew by 2.5 per cent in 2000 was dismissed as 'misleading' by the Chamber of Commerce. Although Majozi Sithole, the minister of finance, admitted that growth recorded a 'slight decline' compared to the previous year, it was clear that Swaziland was undergoing an economic crisis, stirring up yet more dissent among the country's burgeoning unemployed.

Up to half the Swazi population faced severe food shortages in early 2002 following serious food crop failures, mirroring the food crisis that is gripping the rest of southern Africa. In March 2002, the country's National Disaster Task Force called on the international community to donate at least 60,000 tonnes of maize, its staple food, in order to avert a famine. Maize reserves had dried out and neighbouring South Africa did not have enough stock left to export to Swaziland. However, the kingdom's efforts to secure food aid from potential overseas investors have largely failed, partly due to the diplomatic isolation of the regime and partly because the Swazi government did not heed the advice of its Early Warning Unit.

The food crisis, coupled with a sharp fall in the value of the lilangeni, drove up inflation and weakened the government's fiscal position in 2001. According to official statistics, by December 2001, inflation had risen to 10 per cent, compared to the average 7.5 per cent for the year. The government forecasts that inflation could rise to an average 12 per cent in 2002. Economic decline and a fall in donor assistance also put pressure on government finances, with an estimated budget deficit

KEY INDICATORS — Swaziland

	Unit	1996	1997	1998	1999	2000
Population	m	0.94	0.93	0.95	0.98	1.01
Gross domestic product (GDP)	US$bn	1.20	1.30	1.20	1.30	1.30
GDP per capita	US$	1,288	1,539	1,334	1,475	1,384
GDP real growth	%	3.6	3.7	4.7	3.5	2.5
Inflation	%	6.5	7.1	8.1	5.8	6.5
Consumer prices	1995=100	106.4	114.0	123.3	130.8	146.7
Exports (fob) (goods)	US$m	849.4	960.1	966.1	941.3	810.8
Imports (fob) (goods)	US$m	1,054.4	1,088.6	1,082.6	1,052.1	921.3
Balance of trade	US$m	-205.0	-128.5	-1,165.5	-110.8	-110.6
Current account	US$m	-53.1	9.0	-16.8	17.2	-40.1
Foreign debt	US$bn	0.2	0.2	0.2	0.2	0.3
Total reserves minus gold	US$m	254.0	294.8	358.6	375.9	351.8
Foreign exchange	US$m	241.2	282.8	346.0	363.6	340.1
Exchange rate	per US$	4.30	4.61	5.53	5.96	6.81

for 2001/02 of 6.1 per cent of GDP compared to the 4.8 per cent target. Meanwhile, depreciation increased the value of foreign debt, much of which is denominated in euros. The government is scrambling to revalue the debt in South African rands to offset the effects of depreciation. It is also seeking to reschedule short-term debt, which forms a relatively high proportion of the debt portfolio.

Outlook

Swazis are a generally conservative people, reluctant to ditch their King in favour of a western-style democracy, which is regarded as alien to their traditions. However, dissent is mounting as the economy heads towards disaster. One of the main issues in 2003 will be the introduction of a new constitution, which many believe will simply re-affirm the King's total control of Swaziland. The Internal Security Bill, enacted in June 2002, indicated that the government was clamping down on the opposition by making it illegal to display any sign of support for opposition groups, even wearing a Pudemo t-shirt. These moves towards greater authoritarianism could see Swaziland losing donor support and vital trade relations with the US, thereby fuelling the country's downward spiral.

Risk assessment

Economic	Poor
Political	Deteriorating
Regional stability	Poor

COUNTRY PROFILE

Historical profile

Many centuries ago an African people of Nguni descent (the ancestral root of the majority of South Africa's indigenous people) migrated southwards from central Africa and eventually, during the mid-eighteenth century, a group settled in the forested, mountainous area which is now Swaziland. These people, the Nkosi Dlamini, became known as the Swazis.

Swaziland first emerged as a separate nation in the 19th century when King Sobhuza I merged his own people with refugees fleeing from the violent expansion of the Zulus to establish a country capable of resisting the Zulu advance.

1903 After a period of rivalry between the British and the Boers, Swaziland became a British protectorate.

1963 Swaziland's first constitution was introduced.

1964 The first elections resulted in victory for the Imbokodvo National Movement (INM).

1967 Swaziland was granted internal self-government as a protected state. Sobhuza II was recognised as King and head of state; Prince Makhosini Dlamini, leader of the INM, was appointed prime minister.

1968 Independence was granted.

1973 The King revoked the Westminster-based constitution and banned political parties.

1978 The previous constitution was replaced with a system designed to accommodate both western and traditional styles of government. Political parties were banned.

1982 King Sobhuza II died.

1986 After a lengthy selection and training period, Crown Prince Makhosetive was chosen to succeed his father and he was crowned King Mswati III.

1992 Parliament was dissolved and Swaziland was governed by the *Liqoqo* (traditional tribal assembly).

1993 Democratic reforms led to the people directly electing some members of the *Liqoqo*.

1996 The King appointed a Constitutional Review Commission (CRC).

2000 Trade unions demonstrated against the government. In November, the government put five critics of the government under house arrest and banned trade union meetings. The Swaziland Federation of Trade Unions (SFTU) met in South Africa and drew up the Nelspruit Declaration demanding the formation of an interim government. The government amended the labour laws in December.

2001 Many people were forced into political exile in South Africa. Decree 2 was issued by King Mswati in June giving the monarch power to overrule court decisions. It was soon repealed after the US threatened to end the country's trade benefits under the Africa Growth and Opportunities act (AGOA).

2002 The Internal Security Bill was enacted in June which made it illegal to display support for any political party. In July, the Libyan leader Colonel Muammar Al-Qadafi visited Swaziland to give his support to the monarchy.

Political structure

The country is run on a dual system. The traditional structure of Swaziland is headed by the *Ingwenyama* (the King in a traditional setting) and administered through the chieftaincy system. The other is the western-style central government, headed by the King, acting together with parliament – cabinet and civil service.

Constitution

The constitution was promulgated in 1978.

Succession to the throne is governed by Swazi law and custom. Power lies in the hands of the *Ingwenyama* (the lion) (King), the *Ndlovukazi* (the she-elephant) (Queen Mother), and the more than 300 Chiefs who control the largely rural population. The kingdom is divided into four regions.

Form of state

Absolute monarchy

The executive

Under the 1978 constitution, considerable executive power is vested in the monarch and exercised through a cabinet of ministers (all appointed by the monarch).

National legislature

There is a bi-cameral *libandla* (legislature) consisting of the Senate (20 members appointed by the king; additional 10 members elected by the House of Assembly from among its own membership), and the *Liqoqo* (House of Assembly) (55 elective members, directly elected for the first time in 1993, with voters electing one representative from each of the *tinkhundla* (traditional assemblies); 10 further members appointed by the king).

Legal system

Decree 2 was issued by King Mswati in June 2001 giving the monarch power to overrule court decisions.

Next elections

Scheduled for 2003.

Political parties

Ruling party

Political parties are banned under the 1978 constitution.

Population

1.01 million (2000)

Annual population growth: 3 per cent (1994–2000). About 43 per cent of the population is under 14 years.

Population density: 59 inhabitants per square km. Urban population: 33 per cent (1994–2000).

Ethnic make-up

Africans (97 per cent), Europeans (3 per cent).

Religions

Christianity (60 per cent), traditional beliefs (40 per cent).

Education

Literacy in Swaziland is about 75 per cent although school attendance is not mandatory. Primary education is widely available and almost all children between the ages of six and 13 enrol. However, school drop-out rates for children of vulnerable households are increasing, as fees required for a quarter session are high and the equivalent of a month's food for a typical family. It is estimated that just over half the children in the secondary age group receive education.

In 2001, there were 728 schools in the country of which 549 were primary and 179 were secondary/high schools. The University of Swaziland provides higher education.

Although education is subsidised by government, public free education remains a distant goal.

Health

Life expectancy at birth was 37 years in 2001. Approximately 10 per cent of children were malnourished in the period 1994–2000.

Around 130,000 people suffer from HIV/AIDS and the adult infection rate is estimated at 25.25 per cent (2000). Around 50,000 children have lost their mother or both parents to AIDS (2001). UNAIDS estimates that the annual loss to GDP per capita due to AIDS will be 1.2 per cent by 2010.

Projections show that by 2010, Swaziland's population with be 25 per cent smaller than it should be on current population growth trends. By that time, life expectancy will be reduced to 27 years with an estimated 36 per cent of the population HIV positive. By 2001, King Mswati III had not developed or commissioned a national strategy on HIV/AIDS. However, some in the govern - ment have mooted the idea of concentration camps for AIDS sufferers where they will be isolated from the rest of the population to prevent the spread of infection.

Welfare

UN estimates show that 66 per cent of Swaziland's population live below the poverty line. The average unemployment rate is about 40 per cent, although this figure is higher in rural areas. According to the UN World Food Programme in early 2002, some 144,000 people will require food aid in Swaziland after a severe drop in agricultural production. The total food aid will amount to 17,720 tonnes.

Main cities

Mbabane (estimated population 50,000), Manzini (64,900), Nhlangano (5,900).

Languages spoken

English is widely spoken and official information and notices are published in English. Most Swazis are bi-lingual.

Official language/s

English and siSwati

Media

Press

Dailies: National daily and Sunday newspapers are *Times of Swaziland* and *The Swazi Observer* (closed by the government in 2000 and re-opened). *The Swazi News* (http://www.swazinews.co.sz) is the unofficial site of *Times of Swaziland*.

Weeklies: Weeklies include the *Swazi News* and *Weekend Observer* (http://www.swaziobserver.sz/) with on-line news updates. The Swaziland Solidarity Campaign runs an on-line news service on behalf of the political opposition (http://www.swazis.org.uk/~news).

Periodicals: The *Dzadze Family Magazine* caters to women and consumer interests.

Broadcasting

Radio: Programmes are broadcast by Swaziland Broadcasting and Information Service, Swaziland Commercial Radio Ltd and Trans World Radio. Broadcasts are in SiSwati and English.

Television: Government-owned Swaziland Television Broadcasting Corporation transmits colour services in English. Some programmes are in SiSwati.

Economy

In recent years, Swaziland's GDP has remained strong while inflation has remained in single-digit figures, indicating macroeconomic stability, although growth in GDP per capita is modest. Despite being classified as a middle-income country, the distribution of income is highly unequal and around 40 per cent of the population lives on less than US$230 per annum.

Swaziland's economic relations with South Africa remain close and the lilangeni is pegged to the rand. Company income taxes are in line with South Africa, although the rate on three-month treasury bills is generally 2 per cent lower.

The government's economic plans include the National Development Strategy which sought to ensure that by 2022 Swaziland would rank in the top 10 per cent of middle-income developing countries with sustainable economic development and political stability. However, a large drop in farm output in 2001/02 helped undermine economic growth and fuel inflation in 2002. Food prices rose while the cost of imported capital inputs soared due to the depreciation of the lilangeni.

External trade

Exports

Principal exports are sugar (typically 13 per cent of total), Coca-Cola syrup, woodpulp and canned/fresh fruit.

Main destinations: South Africa (typically 72 per cent of total), EU (14 per cent), Mozambique (4 per cent).

Imports

Principal imports are capital goods, manufactures, fuels, chemicals and food.

Main sources: South Africa (typically 89 per cent of total), EU (6 per cent).

Agriculture

The agricultural sector contributes around 19 per cent to GDP and employs half of the working population.

Sugar-cane is grown on 38,000 hectares of land. With yields of 100 tonnes per hectare, Swaziland is one of the world's seven most efficient sugar producers. All sugar-cane is grown under irrigation. The industry is regulated by the Swaziland Sugar Association (SSA). Sugar is Swaziland's highest export earner and accounts for 51 per cent of total agricultural production, 24 per cent of GDP, 13 per cent of total exports and 57 per cent of foreign exchange earnings.

Main food crops are maize, beans, groundnuts and sorghum.

Farming

Commercial farming, on the 40 per cent of the land owned by individual (mainly non-Swazi) freeholders, is centred on sugar, citrus (grown on large estates), pineapples, tobacco and cotton.

Most maize and cotton is grown by small-scale farmers on Swazi Nation Land (SNL) (60 per cent of the land).

Smallholders own 80 per cent of the livestock.

Production: Food self-sufficiency declined in the 1990s and efforts to expand local fruit and vegetable production by the National Agricultural Marketing Board (Namboard) has only had a limited impact.

In 2002, the country reached crisis point, with a yawning food deficit which required international food assistance to fill. Although the food crisis was related to drought, maize yields were generally low due to poor irrigation and a lack of capital inputs. Farmers have been unable to afford fertiliser and equipment due to the removal of government subsidies. With adequate investment in small-scale SNL farms, Swaziland has the potential to be self-sufficient in maize even during years of drought.

Forestry

Timber plantations cover 6 per cent of the total land area.

Industry and manufacturing

The industrial sector contributes around a third of GDP and employs over a fifth of the workforce. It is traditionally centred on the agro-industries: sugar refining, fruit canning and woodpulp processing. The forest products sector is one of the world's main sources of unbleached pulp.

Starting with textile production, the modern industrial sector is growing rapidly, with the South African market its main outlet. The US's Africa Growth and Opportunities Act (AGOA) has enabled Swazi textile producers to access lucrative US markets, although the US has threatened to withdraw these benefits unless the government undergoes democratic reform.

Other activities include brick manufacture and shoe production.

Tourism

Swaziland, which is often described as the Switzerland of Africa (due to its terrain), hopes to market itself jointly with other southern African countries through the Regional Tourism Association of Southern Africa (Retoso).

The Lubombo Spatial Initiative involves eastern Swaziland, the southern part of Mozambique's Maputo province and the north-east part of the KwaZulu Natal province of South Africa. It is a multimillion dollar project comprising new roads, lodges and hotels.

Mining

Mining activity has declined since 1997 due to the end of iron ore mining and the closure of the Bulembu asbestos mine. Most mining activity is focussed on the Maloma colliery and two aggregate quarries at Kwalini and Tonkwane. Mineral production accounts for around 2 per cent of GDP. The government is considering the commercial viability of mining tin and silica.

Hydrocarbons

There are no known oil or gas reserves. Swaziland imports its oil needs from South Africa. Coal is mined at Maloma to produce high-quality anthracite for overseas markets. Total production at Maloma in 2000 was 380,000 tonnes.

Energy

The Lupholohlo-Ezulwini hydroelectric project is often drought affected.
A 400KV feeder line from South Africa to Maputo, Mozambique, connecting Swaziland with the South African Power Pool will greatly improve the quality of electricity supply to the country.
The 15MW Komati hydroelectric station should reduce dependence on electricity imports from South Africa.

Financial markets

Stock exchange
The Swaziland Stock Exchange (SSE) began operating in 1990, and the Securities Market started in 1998. The SSE is one of the world's smallest bourses.

Banking

Central bank
Central Bank of Swaziland
Main financial centre
Mbabane

Time

GMT plus two hours

Geography

Swaziland lies between the Republic of South Africa and Mozambique. It is the smallest country in the southern hemisphere.
It is geographically unique, with ancient rock formations and four distinct areas, each with its own climate and characteristics. Altitudes vary from 400 to 1,800 metres above sea level.

Climate

Mbabane and the rest of the highveld are semi-temperate; drier in Manzini. Temperatures range from about 7–10 Celsius (with occasional frost) during April–September, to 20–30C during August–January. The wettest months are December and March.
The mountainous Highveld region to the north-west has a temperate climate with hot, wet summers and dry winters when the temperature rises during the day but with cold nights.
The adjacent Middleveld has a warm climate.
Further to the east lies the sub-tropical Lowveld.
The Lubombo region, adjacent to Mozambique, is also sub-tropical.

Entry requirements

Passports
Required by all.
Visa
Not required by UK and US nationals and nationals of a few European, Commonwealth and African countries.

Health (for visitors)

Mandatory precautions
A yellow fever certificate is required if arriving from an infected area.
Advisable precautions
Hepatitis A, polio, tetanus, typhoid vaccinations are advisable. Anti-malaria prophylaxis. There is an AIDS risk. Water precautions are essential.

Hotels

There is no official rating system. A 10 per cent government tax is added to the room rates.

Public holidays

Fixed dates
1 Jan, 19 Apr (Birthday of King Mswati III), 25 Apr (National Flag Day), 22 Jul (Birthday of the late King Sobhuza), 24 Aug (Umhlanga), 6 Sep (Independence), 24 Oct (United Nations Day), 25 Dec, 26 Dec.
Variable dates
Incwala, Good Friday, Easter Monday, Ascension Day, Commonwealth Day.

Working hours

Banking
Mon–Fri: 0830–1300/1430; Sat 0830–1100.
Business
Mon–Fri: 0800–1300, 1400–1700; Sat: 0815 or 0830–1230.
Government
Mon–Fri: 0800–1300, 1400–1700.

Electricity supply

230V AC, 50 cycles; 15 amp/round pin.

Getting there

Air
National airline: Royal Swazi National Airways
International airport/s: Manzini-Matsapa (Code: MTS), 5km south-west of Manzini, 40km from Mbabane; refreshments, currency exchange, car hire. No direct intercontinental flights to Swaziland. Regular services via South Africa, Kenya, Tanzania, Mozambique.
Airport tax: International departures include a passenger service charge of E20; not applicable to infants under three years and direct transit passengers.
Surface
Road: Tarred roads from Johannesburg and Durban and from Mozambique (Siteki-Lomahasha road). The Mbabanea-Ngwenye highway (the main road link to Johannesburg) is being upgraded to a dual-carriageway. Coach services from Maputo and Johannesburg are scheduled. Opening hours of border posts vary but the main border post with South Africa at Oshoek/Ngwenya is open to 2200hrs daily.

Getting about

National transport
Road: Extensive road improvement schemes are under way, between Mbabane-Manzine, between Mbabane and the border with South Africa at Ngwenya, and between Luyengo in the centre of the country and the South African border en route to Pietretief.
City transport
Taxis: Scarce. Best to order from hotel. A tip is usual.
Car hire
Self-drive cars are available at airport. A national driving licence is required; drive on left. General speed limit of 80kph.

BUSINESS DIRECTORY

Telephone area codes

Dialling code for Swaziland: IDD access code +268, followed by subscriber's number. There are no area codes.

Chambers of Commerce

Swaziland Chamber of Commerce, PO Box 72, Mbabane (tel: 44-408; fax: 45-442).

Banking

First National Bank of Swaziland Ltd, 2nd Floor, Sales House Building, Mbabane (tel: 45-401/2/3; fax: 44-735).

Nedbank (Swaziland) Limited, PO Box 68, Corner Plaza Mall Street and Bypass Road, Mbabane (tel: 43-351/5; fax: 44-060).

Standard Bank Swaziland Ltd, Standard House, Swazi Plaza, Mbabane (tel: 46-930/1/2 fax: 45-899).

Swaziland Development and Savings Bank, PO Box 336, Allister Miller Street, Mbabane (tel: 42-551/7; fax: 41-214).

Central bank
Central Bank of Swaziland, PO Box 546, Warner Street, Mbabane, Swaziland (tel: 43-221/2/3; fax: 48-530).

Travel information

Hotels and Tourism Association of Swaziland, PO Box 462, Mbabane (tel: 42-218; fax: 44-516).

Royal Swazi National Airways, PO Box 839, Matsapa Airport, Manzini (tel: 86-148; fax: 86-756).

Swaziland Government Tourist Office, PO Box 338, Mbabane (tel: 44-556).

Ministry of tourism

Ministry of Tourism & Communications, PO Box 58, Mbabane (tel: 46-420; fax: 46-438); Road Transport Board (tel: 46-420).

Ministries

Cabinet Office, PO Box 395, Mbabane (tel: 42-251; fax: 43-943).

Ministry of Agriculture, PO Box 162, Mbabane (tel: 42-731; fax: 44-700); Rural Development Areas Centre (tel: 23-014).

Ministry of Broadcasting, Information and Tourism, PO Box 338, Mbabane (tel: 42-761/9; fax: 42-774).

Ministry of Defence, PO Box 1928, Mbabane (tel: 42-809; fax: 42-483).

Ministry of Economic Planning and Development, PO Box 602, Mbabane (tel: 43-765; fax: 42-157); Statistics Section (tel: 42-151).

Ministry of Education, PO Box 39, Mbabane (tel: 42-491; fax: 43-880).

Ministry of Enterprise and Employment, PO Box 451, Mbabane (tel: 43-201; fax: 44-711); Trade Promotion Unit (tel: 45-180).

Ministry of Finance, PO Box 443, Mbabane (tel: 48-148; fax: 43-187).

Ministry of Foreign Affairs and Trade, PO Box 451, Mbabane (tel: 42-661; fax: 42-669).

Ministry of Health and Social Welfare, PO Box 5, Mbabane (tel: 42-431; fax: 42-092).

Ministry of Home Affairs, PO Box 432, Mbabane (tel: 42-941; fax: 44-303).

Ministry of Housing and Urban Development, PO Box 1832, Mbabane (tel: 46-035; fax: 44-085).

Ministry of Justice and Constitutional Development, PO Box 924, Mbabane (tel: 43-531; fax: 44-796); Attorney General's Chambers, PO Box 578, Mbabane (tel: 42-807).

Ministry of Natural Resources and Energy, PO Box 57, Mbabane (tel: 46-244; fax: 42-436); Geological Survey & Mines, PO Box 57, Mbabane (tel: 42-411). Rural Water Supply, PO Box 961, Mbabane (tel: 41-231).

Ministry of Public Service and Information, PO Box 338, Mbabane (tel: 42-761; fax: 42-774).

Ministry of Public Works and Transport, PO Box 58, Mbabane (tel: 42-321; fax: 42-364); Civil Aviation (tel: 42-420).

Prime Minister's Office, PO Box 395, Mbabane (tel: 42-251; fax: 43-943). Deputy Prime Minister's Office, PO Box A33 Swazi Plaza (tel: 42-723; fax: 44-085).

Other useful addresses

Central Co-operative Union, PO Box 551, Manzini (tel: 52-787; fax: 52-964).

Central Statistics Office, PO Box 456, Mbabane (tel: 42-151/4; fax: 42-157).

Central Transport Administration, PO Box 378, Mbabane (tel: 42-871; fax: 43-002).

Civil Service Board, PO Box 158, Mbabane (tel: 42-601).

Cotton Board, PO Box 230, Manzini (tel/fax: 52-775).

Dwaleni Investment Co (Pty) Ltd, PO Box 59, Nhlangano (tel: 78-484; fax: 78-055).

Federation of Swaziland Employers, PO Box 386, Manzini (tel: 22-768).

National Agricultural Marketing Board, PO Box 1713, Matsapha (tel: 85-211; fax: 84-088).

National Maize Corporation, PO Box 158, Manzini (tel: 52-265).

Parliament, King's Office (tel: 61-080). Parliament Offices (tel: 61-286).

Posts and Telecommunications Corporation, PO Box 125, Mbabane (tel: 42-341; fax: 43-130).

Small Enterprise Development Co Ltd, Mbabane Industrial Sites, PO Box A186, Swazi Plaza (tel: 42-811; fax: 40-723).

Statistics Department, PO Box 456, Mbabane (tel: 42-151; fax: 42-157).

Swazi Business Growth Trust, PO Box 78, Eveni (tel: 44-705, 55-116; fax: 44-783).

Swaziland Citrus Board, PO Box 343, Mbabane (tel: 43-547).

Swaziland Commercial Board, PO Box 509, Mbabane (tel: 42-930).

Swaziland Cotton Board, PO Box 230, Manzini (tel: 52-775).

Swaziland Dairy Board, PO Box 1789, Manzini (tel: 84-411; fax: 85-313).

Swaziland Electricity Board, PO Box 258, Mbabane (tel: 46-668; fax: 42-335).

Swaziland Industrial Development Company, PO Box 866, Mbabane (tel: 43-391; fax: 45-619).

Swaziland International Trade Fair, PO Box 877, Manzini (tel: 54-242; fax: 52-314).

Swaziland Meat Industries, PO Box 446, Manzini (tel: 84-165, 84-033; fax: 84-418).

Swaziland National Housing Board, PO Box 798, Mbabane (tel: 45-610; fax: 45-224).

Swaziland Railway, PO Box 475, Mbabane (tel: 42-486; fax: 45-009).

Swaziland Sugar Association, PO Box 445, Mbabane (tel: 42-646).

Swaziland Television Authority, PO Box A146, Swazi Plaza (tel: 43-036; fax: 42-093).

Tinkhundla Headquarters, PO Box A33, Swazi Plaza, Mbabane (tel: 42-723; fax: 44-058).

Water Services Corporation, PO Box 20 Mbabane (tel: 45-584; fax: 45-355).

Internet sites

Africa Business Network: http://www.ifc.org/abn

AllAfrica.com: http://allafrica.com

African Development Bank: http://www.afdb.org

Africa Online: http://www.africaonline.com

Harambee Afrika (UK business club for traders with east, central and southern Africa; includes annotated web resource list): http://www.harambee.co.uk

Mbendi AfroPaedia (information on companies, countries, industries and stock exchanges in Africa): http://mbendi.co.za

Simunye news service: http://www.swazis.org.uk/~news/

Swazi news: http://www.swazinews.co.sz/about.htm

Swazi Observer (closed by the government in 2000, re-opened 2001): http://www.swaziobserver.sz/

Swaziland Solidarity Campaign: http://www.swazis.org

Tanzania

Guy Arnold

With elections not due until the second half of 2005, members of the ruling Chama Cha Mapinduzi (CCM) (Party of the Revolution) began to engage in political infighting in 2002. This has raised the possibility that the CCM, which has presided over a one-party state since 1977, may split.

The breakdown in party unity has been encouraged by a lack of any credible opposition and the CCM's overwhelming majority; it controls 244 seats in the 269-seat Bunge (National Assembly). Meanwhile, the opposition Civic United Front (CUF) was brought into line following an agreement with the CCM to end hostilities between their supporters on the semi-autonomous Zanzibar islands.

Zanzibar tensions

Political instability has affected the islands since the October 2000 general elections, following accusations of vote-rigging orchestrated by the government. Violence has claimed the lives of hundreds of Zanzibaris since the elections. In October 2001, the CCM and the CUF agreed to reform the Zanzibar Electoral Commission (ZEC), establish a permanent voters' register and review Zanzibar's constitution and electoral law. By October 2002, the accord between the two parties appeared to be in danger of collapse as the CCM failed to make significant headway in implementing the agreement. The main bone of contention was a bill to amend the Zanzibar Election Act 1984, which was passed in the CCM-dominated Zanzibar

KEY FACTS

Official name: Jamhuri ya Muungano wa Tanzania (The United Republic of Tanzania)

Head of State: President Benjamin William Mkapa (leader of CCM) (since 1995; re-elected Oct 2000)

Head of government: Prime Minister Frederick Tluway Sumaye (since Nov 1995)

Ruling party: Chama Cha Mapinduzi (CCM) (Party of the Revolution) (re-elected 1995 and Oct/Nov 2000)

Area: 945,087 square km

Population: 34.50 million (2001)

Capital: Dar es Salaam; Dodoma (administrative capital)

Official language: KiSwahili, English

Currency: Tanzania shilling (Tsh) = 100 senti (made convertible Jul 1996 with currencies of Kenya and Uganda)

Exchange rate: Tsh993.00 per US$ (Jan 2003)

GDP per capita: US$264 (2001); US$253 (2002)*

GDP real growth: 5.60% (2001); 5.2% (2002)*

Labour force: 17.80 million (2001); 18.3 million (2002)*

Inflation: 4.90% (2001); 5.1% (2002)*

Balance of trade: -US$716.00 million (2001)

Foreign debt: US$6.18 billion (2001)

Annual FDI: US$203.00 million (2001)

* estimated figure

For the latest Key Facts, go to www.worldinformation.com

House of Representatives in October 2002, despite opposition from the CUF, which has refused to take up its seats in the local parliament.

The CUF is unhappy over the introduction of simple majority voting in presidential elections, as opposed to the old system where a candidate had to secure at least 51 per cent of the vote. Also, the CUF opposes the continued role of the *shehas* (local authorities) in the elections, which it regards as simply another arm of the CCM and contrary to the CUF-CCM accord. Another important issue is the role of CCM *wanagambo* (armed party militias) in human rights violations. The CUF alleges that the *wanagambo* are effectively working as paramilitary units, carrying out attacks on opposition activists with the help of the police and army. The accord's failure to meet the CUF's demands has resulted in infighting within the opposition party. In September 2002, a CUF faction calling itself G7 circulated leaflets accusing CUF Secretary General Seif Shariff Hamad of using the accord 'for personal gain' and betraying party members. It claimed that Hamad was favouring people from the island of Pemba and sidelining those originating from Unguja, Zanzibar's largest island.

Zanzibar's troubles are also fuelling a rise in religious violence between Muslims and Christians. The majority of Zanzibaris are Muslims, many of whom feel they have been politically and economically marginalised. Muslim and Christian fundamentalist organisations have sprung up, adopting an increasingly confrontational stance. Moderates and fundamentalists within the Muslim community have also engaged in street fighting as they vie for control of mosques in Zanzibar, Dar-es-Salam and other cities.

The budget and poverty

The 2002/03 budget pledged to continue to expand the tax base and improve the tax structure and administration. The government hopes to increase its revenue to 12.3 per cent GDP by the end of the fiscal year, although this is still well below the sub-Saharan average of 16.0 per cent GDP. One of the key concerns remains local government taxation. Although a cap was placed on local taxes in 2001/02, enforcement has been difficult and is stoking up problems for the agricultural sector, which pays land rent to local government. However, farmers have welcomed the writing off of land rent arrears accrued before July 2001 and the introduction of a new rate of TSh200 (US$0.20) per acre from July 2001, down from TSh600 (US$0.60) per acre.

Despite the improvements in fiscal performance, Tanzania's privatisation programme faced significant problems in 2002. One of the main criticisms levelled at the government is the lack of transparency in the privatisation process and the failure to involve trade unions in discussions. Also, investors are questioning whether involvement in Tanzania, which lacks a dynamic domestic market and suffers from under-capitalisation, is a safe investment opportunity.

The government's plan to privatise the Tanzanian Railway Corporation (TRC) appeared to come off the rails following a major train crash in June 2002, which killed around 300 people. The TRC's rolling stock consists of British-made trains from the colonial era, while the tracks, which the government hopes to lease to private operators, are worn out. This has left investors wary of becoming involved in Tanzania's out-dated and inefficient rail network. A lack of interest was also evident in the sale of a 49 per cent stake in Air Tanzania, which attracted only one bidder, South African Airways. Kenya Airways, which had qualified in the pre-bidding round, refused to participate, claiming that Air Tanzania would be a bad investment. The other bidder, South Africa's Nationwide, did not submit an offer. A further 26 per cent of the company is due to be sold off by the end of 2003. A row has also developed between the government and a European consortium which holds a 35 per cent stake in the Tanzania Telecommunications Company over shares which have not been paid for.

Always believing in gold

Tanzania hopes to become Africa's third largest producer of gold by 2004, after South Africa and Ghana. Output is expected to reach 1.4 million ounces when the four new western region projects – Geita, Nzesa, Golden Pride and Bulyanhula – become fully operational. Some 23 new gold mines opened in the first half of 2001. Other mineral deposits include commercial quantities of diamonds, rubies, iron ore, phosphates, tin, salt, uranium, nickel, cobalt, coal, gas and petroleum. Tanzanite, the 'blue diamond' which is unique to Tanzania is in demand all over the world. The new mining code has abolished export levies and, as a result, foreign investors have become more interested.

Mining has become the fastest growing sector in the economy and is led by rising gold sales. Mineral sales have risen from US$15 million in 1996 to US$185 million in 2001. Gold exports are expected to earn US$450 million in 2002. Mining has grown in proportion as state economic controls have been relaxed.

Down on the farm

The agricultural sector accounts for 50 per cent of GDP. However, the whole sector faces a number of difficulties and requires a radical overhaul. Poor roads, lack of implements and extension services are doing increasing harm to agriculture. Farmers are turning away from staples such as cotton, tea and coffee and, instead, are looking to flowers and vegetables, which are more lucrative products. Flowers, for

KEY INDICATORS — **Tanzania**

	Unit	1996	1997	1998	1999	2000
Population	m	29.09	29.98	32.10	32.79	33.64
Gross domestic product (GDP)	US$bn	4.82	6.92	7.50	8.07	9.00
GDP per capita	US$	158	220	250	246	268
GDP real growth	%	4.2	4.1	3.6	4.8	5.1
Inflation	%	21.0	16.1	12.8	6.3	5.9
Exports (fob) (goods)	US$m	764.1	715.3	589.5	543.3	665.7
Imports (fob) (goods)	US$m	1,213.0	1,164.0	1,365.0	1,368.0	1,339.8
Balance of trade	US$m	-449.0	-449.0	-776.0	-824.9	-674.1
Current account	US$m	-510.9	-629.8	-956.5	-765.4	-480.3
Foreign debt	US$bn	5.7	5.9	6.1	6.6	7.1
Total reserves minus gold	US$m	440.1	622.1	599.2	775.5	974.2
Foreign exchange	US$m	425.6	608.5	584.8	761.5	961.1
Exchange rate	per US$	579.98	612.12	664.67	744.76	800.41

example, give a return 700 times higher than maize. The government has neglected agriculture while it has been engaged in privatising parastatals and boosting the mining sector. The position of farmers has been made worse by the World Bank's and the IMF's insistence on the removal of subsidies that are vital to small farmers. However, it appears that the multilateral organisations are only interested in introducing more free market economy measures.

In June 2001, trade accounted for 25 per cent of investment, construction for 23 per cent, tourism 12.5 per cent, mining 10.4 per cent, communications 9.8 per cent, finance 7 per cent and agriculture, the largest sector of all, for a mere 5.4 per cent. According to Charles Keenja, the agriculture and food security minister, the sector attracted only 5 per cent of the Tanzania Investment Centre's 1,624 approved projects even though agriculture contributes half the country's GDP, accounts for 84 per cent of its foreign exchange earnings and employs 70 per cent of the work force. With a population of 32 million increasing at 2 per cent a year, Tanzania can no longer feed itself; nor can it find jobs for an additional 600,000 new job seekers every year. The average family has between one half and three hectares (ha) of land producing crops that vary between maize, bananas, cassava, cloves, rice, millet, sorghum, coffee, cashew nuts, tea, tobacco, fruit, vegetables and groundnuts. The liberalisation of agriculture was supposed to increase competition among buyers and so help farmers. In fact, buyers have formed cartels to keep prices down and farmers are no better off.

Other economic developments

Tax collection has been greatly improved and government revenues from taxation more than doubled over the years 1996–2000. The Dar es Salaam Stock Exchange (DSE) opened up the secondary market to foreign investment during 2002. In addition, it considered letting foreigners in at the initial public offering (IPO) stage as a means of solving the chronic liquidity shortage. The use of mobile phones increased rapidly through 2001, though with only 160,000 users the market potential is huge. There are now as many mobile phones as there are fixed lines.

Dar es Salaam is making major strides to becoming a modern city with an investment centre, new banks and a number of smart hotels. Kilimanjaro and Dar es Salaam International airports have been upgraded and Kilimanjaro is now able to handle Boeing 747s. It is the only fully privatised airport in Africa.

Tourism accounts for 14 per cent of GDP. The country possesses many superb tourist attractions, including Kilimanjaro, the beaches, Zanzibar (which can be reached by hydrofoil from Dar es Salaam), the Ngorogoro Crates and Selous Game Reserve. However, more attention needs to be given to tourist infrastructure.

There is a large illegal business in smuggling petroleum products throughout East Africa. Tanzania and the other members of the East African Community (EAC) have introduced what is known as BICODE fuel marketing technology for all petrol, diesel and kerosene that is sold locally. Fuel products destined for Rwanda, Burundi, Zambia, Malawi and the Democratic Republic of Congo (DRC) pass through Tanzania and much of this fuel has been diverted to the local market with no revenue being paid to the government. The government has commissioned the Société Générale de Surveillance (SGS) to implement the BICODE scheme. Wholesale suppliers must pay US$1.20 for the marking of each cubic metre of fuel. The scheme is projected to raise government fuel sales by 20 per cent. Other forms of smuggling remain a major problem: for example, the value of US imports of tanzanite over two years has been estimated as worth 10 times more than the minerals and energy ministry claims to have been exported worldwide, the difference being accounted for by smuggling.

Tanzanian investment

For the last 10 years, the UK has led the number and value of investment projects in Tanzania. According to the Tanzania Investment Centre (TIC), between 1990 and 2000 there were 255 British projects, 92 from Kenya, 60 India, 59 US, 54 Canada, 54 Germany, 50 Italy, 47 China and 41 The Netherlands. At a Commonwealth-Tanzania Investment Conference held in Dar es Salaam, Zanzibar's President Amani Karume announced lucrative packages for potential investors. He said that foreign investors would be allowed to establish business ventures with 100 per cent ownership. 'We shall continue to remove administrative and legislative barriers to foreign direct investment', he said, although he added that he hoped such investors would consider entering into partnership with domestic investors. He said that hotels, transport, agriculture, fishing and communications were the most viable sectors.

Outlook

The violence in Zanzibar is likely to worsen if the government does not put a halt to its campaign of intimidation and oppression on the islands. Moreover, the conflict could become an outright religious war with Muslim Zanzibaris pitted against the Christians who dominate the mainland. Muslims are aligning themselves with the CUF following unsubstantiated accusations by CCM leaders that the opposition party is Islamist. Tensions will be heightened if the educational and economic gap between Christians and Muslims grows with the breakdown of the education system due to lack of funds.

Already foreign governments are looking at the Mkapa administration with disdain over the Zanzibar issue and will undoubtedly put pressure on President Mkapa to find a peaceful solution to the conflict. However, public condemnation and intervention is unlikely due to the international community's reliance on the Tanzanian government as a regional peace-broker. Also, humanitarian agencies co-operating with the government to cope with the regional refugee crisis are unlikely to want to upset President Mkapa, who has tolerated the growing strain on his country's own resources and security.

In 2003, the government will be looking to increase foreign investment and improving its industrial capacity in an effort to compete with its partners in the East African Community (EAC) and elsewhere in Africa. This will mean improving the country's deteriorating transport infrastructure, reversing declining literacy rates, relaxing and simplifying trade and investment laws and reducing the country's dependence on exported commodities. These are tall orders when the government is also under pressure from international financial institutions to continue austerity measures. Coupled with the effect of crushing debt service repayments, the government has been forced into making large cuts in education and social services along with capital investment. The government has little room for manoeuvre in terms of fiscal policy and can only instigate economic change indirectly through careful management of interest rates and external tariff controls. Government steps towards widening the tax base and improving collection are unlikely to have any immediate effect and will not significantly reduce the country's dependence on foreign donors, who fund up to half the government's annual expenditure.

Risk assessment

Economic	Good
Political	Satisfactory
Regional stability	Poor
Stock market	Limited

COUNTRY PROFILE

Historical profile

1832 The increasing importance of Zanzibar as a spice and slave trading centre led the Sultan of Oman to transfer his capital there from Muscat. Around this time, the UK signed a number of agreements with Oman to limit the potential threat to Britain's colonies from France. Meanwhile, Germany signed a number of 'friendship' treaties with local chiefs – treaties which formed the basis of the German East Africa Company which was established to exploit and colonise what became Tanganyika.
1886 The UK and Germany signed an agreement which gave Germany control of mainland Tanzania and the UK control of Zanzibar.
1918 After Germany's defeat in the First World War, the League of Nations mandated the territory to Britain.
1961 Tanganyika gained independence under Julius Nyerere and the Tanganyika Africa National Union (TANU).
1964 The United Republic of Tanzania was formed following the union of Tanganyika and Zanzibar.
1965 Constitution established a one-party system for the country, but the state was governed by two different ruling parties, one from the mainland and one from Zanzibar. The 1977 constitution established a real one-party state for the whole of Tanzania after the two parties merged to create Chama Cha Mapinduzi (CCM) (Party of the Revolution).
1979 Tanzania invaded Uganda, forcing its dictator, Idi Amin to flee to Saudi Arabia.
1985 Nyerere stepped down as President and was replaced by Ali Hassan Mwinyi.
1992 In February, the CCM voted unanimously for the introduction of a multi-party system.
1995 The first multi-party elections took place in October. Benjamin William Mkapa (CCM) was elected president with 67.8 per cent of the vote and the CCM was re-elected to government. The Zanzibar opposition Civil United Front (CUF) refused to accept the election results in Zanzibar.
1999 On 7 June a reconciliation agreement was signed between the CCM and the CUF, bringing an end to four years of hostility. Julius Nyerere, the former president and founder figure of modern Tanzania, died on 14 October.
2000 President Benjamin Mkapa was re-elected for a second term in October. Because of unfair elections in Zanzibar, a re-run was held in 16 of its 50 constituencies; it was won by the ruling party, CCM.
2001 There were clashes in Zanzibar during January, between supporters of CUF and the police. On 10 October, the CCM and the opposition CUF signed a further agreement aimed at ending hostilities on Zanzibar.

Political structure

Constitution
The constitution was introduced in 1965 following the union of Zanzibar and Tanganyika in 1964. Zanzibar is partially autonomous, with 50 political constituencies.

Form of state
Republic

The executive
Executive power rests with the president, who is elected by direct popular vote for a five-year term. The president can serve a maximum of two terms.
One vice president is appointed by the president, as is the cabinet (in consultation with the prime minister), and the second vice president is the directly elected president of Zanzibar.

National legislature
The constitution, introduced in 1965, provides for legislative power to be held by a unicameral National Assembly with members serving a term of five years, and for universal adult suffrage. The legislative body, the Bunge, has 274 members with 232 elected for a five-year term in single-seat constituencies. The president allocates 37 special seats to women and five seats are dedicated to members of the Zanzibar House of Representatives.

Legal system
The legal system is based on English common law, the 1977 Union and 1985 Zanzibari constitutions, as amended. The judiciary is relatively independent. A permanent Commission of Enquiry has wide powers to investigate abuses of power. In Zanzibar, *Kadhis* (Islamic courts) have juridiction over certain areas of law.

Last elections
October/November 2000 (presidential and legislative).

Next elections
2005 (presidential and legislative).

Political parties

Ruling party
Chama Cha Mapinduzi (CCM) (Party of the Revolution) (re-elected 1995 and Oct/Nov 2000)

Main opposition party
Civic United Front (CUF)

Population

33.64 million (2000)
Annual population growth rate: 2.6 per cent (1994–2000). Projected annual growth rate for 1998–2015: 2 per cent; Approximately 47 per cent of the total population is under 15 years.
Urban population: 33 per cent (1994–2000).

Ethnic make-up
About 98 per cent of the population is of indigenous African or Arab (Zanzibar) origin, with the remainder mainly from the Indian sub-continent. Those of Indian, Pakistani and Goan descent tend to work in the towns, mainly dominating the trading environment, but also moving into the industrial sector. The small population of Arab descent is mainly engaged in trade. There are about 10,000 Europeans.
Over 120 tribal groups exist in Tanzania, the most important of which are Sukuma (12 per cent of total population), Makonde (4 per cent), Chagga (4 per cent), Haya (3 per cent), Nyamwezi (3 per cent), Ha (3 per cent), Gogo (3 per cent) and Hehe (3 per cent).

Religions
Islam and Christianity are the main organised religions. However, many people adhere to ancient tribal and animist religions. The religious make-up is believed to be Christianity: 33 per cent, Islam: 33 per cent, traditional beliefs: 33 per cent and Hinduism: 1 per cent.

Main cities

Dar es Salaam (capital, population 1.36 million, 1998 census), Dodoma (administrative capital, 250,000), Mwanza (223,000), Zanzibar, on the island of Unguja (300,000), Tanga (187,200), Arusha (145,000).

Languages spoken

KiSwahili is the first spoken language and some English is spoken by most people, especially in the main towns. English is the language most used in business.

Official language
KiSwahili, English

Media

The government allows private newspapers and private radio and television operators, although these organisations exercise a strong degree of self-censorship.

Press
Dailies: Shihata is the official news agency. Daily newspapers include the government-owned *Daily News* (English) and *Uhuru* (KiSwahili). Both are published in Dar es Salaam. Others are *The African*, *Daily Mail*, *Majira* and *Mtanzania*.
Weeklies: Weekly newspapers including Sunday papers are *Sunday News*, *Mzalendo* (KiSwahili), *Daily News on Saturday*, *East African*, *Express*, *Heko*, *Mfanyakazi*, *Shangwe*, *Sunday Mail*,

Sunday News, *Sunday observer*, *Sunday times* and *Taifa Letu*. The *Government Gazette* is a weekly, which lists official announcements.

Business: Business publications include the weekly publications *Business Times* and the *Financial Times*.

Periodicals: A wide range of periodicals is published in Tanzania. These include *The African Review*, published by the Department of Political Science of the University of Dar es Salaam; *Foreign Trade News Bulletin* published twice a year by the Ministry of Industry. Other popular periodicals are *Tantravel Magazine* (trade travel journal), *Mfanyakazi Magazine*, *Family Mirror*, *Moto Moto*, *Fahari*, *Radi*, *Michapo*, *Watu*, *Klongozi*, *Change*, *Mcheski*, *Mizani* and *Heko*.

Broadcasting

Radio: Radio Tanzania broadcasts internal service in KiSwahili and external services in English. The Voice of Tanzania and Zanzibar broadcasts on three wavelengths in KiSwahili.

Economy

The government's efforts to build an export-oriented economy were accompanied by a policy of economic stabilisation which entailed the devaluation of the exchange rate, austerity measures targetting inflation, and moves to cut state bureaucracy and loss-making public enterprises.

The IMF and World Bank are keen to promote Tanzania as a success story since the country adopted their liberalising agenda of rolling back the country's corrupt state bureaucracy, breaking protectionist barriers, privatising parastatals and instituting policies to attract foreign investment. Economic fundamentals seem to support this idea. During the years 1997–2000, the country achieved an average growth rate of 4.1 per cent as it developed its infrastructure and engaged in extensive infrastructural projects.

However, the level of growth, which was estimated at 5.0 per cent in 2001, has not been significant enough to have any noticable effects on the wider population, particularly the rural poor. The growth figures, measured in Tanzanian shillings, hide the stagnation of GDP in dollar terms due to currency depreciation. With a population growth rate of up to 3.0 per cent, GDP per capita actually declined from US$246 to US$240. The government's ability to commit funds for public services also diminished through trade liberalisation. While average tariff rates declined from 40 per cent in the mid-1980s to as low as 15 per cent by 2000, government revenue was also diminishing as it relied upon trade taxes for a large proportion of its income, further complicating its efforts to address its fiscal problems. Surveys suggest that poverty in rural areas increased between 1995 and 2001 under the structural adjustment programme while the international consumer products giant, Unilever, which is developing distribution networks in the country's poorer areas, claims there is little evidence of increased spending power as a result of liberalisation.

External trade

The government has sought to liberalise trade since the early 1990s to resolve the significant shortfall of foreign exchange created by restrictive trade policies. The country's Economic Recovery Programme (ERP), initiated in 1996, aimed to boost the export sector through a gradual elimination of trade barriers, including import and export taxes and non-tariff barriers such as import licenses.

However, the country has been reluctant to engage in trade liberalisation with its partners in the Common Market for Eastern and Southern Africa (Comesa) and the East African Community (EAC), which was launched in 1999. In 2000, Tanzania left Comesa, which planned to eliminate internal tariffs between its 20 member states by the end of the year. It has also slowed progress toward economic integration in the EAC, despite a commitment in its founding treaty to create a common customs and tariffs union by 2004.

The government is also concerned that Tanzania is at a competitive disadvantage within the tripartite EAC. The Confederation of Tanzanian Industries (CTI) has argued that costs of power, transport and labour were far higher than those incurred by their rivals in other EAC countries. Since efforts to open up the economy began in the mid-1990s, the CTI has complained that the government has failed to protect local industries against unfair competition from imported industrial products. Local sugar, textiles and batteries have been badly hit by cheap imports which are often smuggled in. The government is concerned that these trends will hamper the growth of the manufacturing sector, which currently provides a third of Tanzania's revenues. Local producers fear that the situation will be worsened if trade barriers within the EAC are reduced. They fear the local market will be swamped by Kenya which exports 20 times more to Tanzania than it imports. The government will need to be convinced that the growing trade deficit with Kenya will be reversed before it would be prepared to implement a common customs and tariffs union. However, bilateral trade between Tanzania and Uganda is skewed in favour of Tanzania, giving the government some encouragement in meeting the objectives of the EAC.

Exports

Main exports include coffee (14 per cent), cotton (5 per cent), minerals (13 per cent), tea (4 per cent), petroleum products (under 1 per cent), manufactured products (6 per cent), tobacco (8 per cent), cashew nuts (18 per cent), cloves, sisal (1 per cent), diamonds, live birds, honey and beeswax and other non-traditional products (48 per cent).

Main destinations: UK (20.2 per cent of 2000 total), India (13.4 per cent), Germany (9.1 per cent), Netherlands (6.3 per cent), Kenya (5.2 percent).

Imports

Principal imports are petroleum (6 per cent), machinery (21 per cent), transport equipment (18 per cent), metals, food (11 per cent), beverages and tobacco, textile products (suiting materials), pharmaceuticals, hospital equipment, clothes, shoes, books, paper and other stationery items.

Main sources: South Africa (11.5 per cent of 2000 total), Japan (9.3 per cent), UK (7 per cent), Australia (6.2 per cent), Kenya (6.1 per cent).

Agriculture

The agricultural sector is the mainstay of the economy. It contributes 50 per cent of GDP and 84 per cent of export earnings. Approximately 80 per cent of the population are peasant farmers.

Tanzania has more than 40 million hectares (ha) of arable land but only six million are cultivated. Only 15 per cent of the country has access to water, and the crops are almost totally dependent on the weather. Coffee, cotton, sisal, tobacco, cashew nuts and tea are the most important crops.

The export of Zanzibar cloves accounts for 90 per cent of the island's foreign exchange earnings; the island ranks number four in the world in terms of output, some 3,000 tonnes a year. Prices have plummeted due to oversupply of the spice on the world market. Roses are produced for export.

There has been a serious decline in production of most crops, which the government wishes to reverse. Coffee, cotton and sisal are among the crops which have declined and stagnated although some export crops are showing signs of growth, including tobacco, tea, cashew nuts and horticulture.

The cashew nut sector has benefited from a return to a system where smallholders deal directly with the buyers. Exports of raw cashew nuts have increased to about 130,000 tonnes per annum after dropping to less than 5,000 tonnes in 1990; Tanzania supplies more than one-quarter of the global market.

Industry and manufacturing

The industrial sector typically accounts for 7 per cent of GDP and employs 5 per cent of the workforce. Typically, less than a fifth of industrial production is exported. One of the country's stumbling blocks to industrial development is the dominance of parastal companies, although the sector opened up to private investment in 1993. Most production is geared towards import substitution and the government has traditionally directed public investment towards the sugar and textile industries, tanneries, pulp and paper mills, the fertiliser industry, cement factories, and sisal and cashew nut processing industries.

These are engaged in the processing of local minerals and agricultural raw materials for local consumption. Production also includes paper and pulp, cement, textiles and some light engineering.

Growth has been restricted by a lack of foreign exchange needed for the import of raw materials, spare parts and fuel. Foreign aid is aimed at rehabilitation of existing industries, but the government is slowly gearing production towards export markets. The high cost of credit inhibits the development of the private sector which is characterised by small enterprises. To help domestic producers offset the loss of revenue caused by the downturn in commodity prices, the government reduced duties on the import of manufacturing inputs in the late 1990s.

Tourism

The tourism potential of Tanzania in terms of game parks and unspoiled beaches has not been fully developed.

Upmarket tourist development is favoured in the underdeveloped 'southern circuit' to avoid heavy concentration in the north of Tanzania. It accounts for 14 per cent of GDP.

Tourist arrivals reached 777,000 in 2000, up from 627,000 in 1998 when the US embassy in Dar es Salaam was bombed. Earnings rose from US$570 million in 1998 to US$733 million in 1999.

Mining

The mining sector accounts for 14 per cent of GDP. There are considerable reserves of diamonds, gold, tanzanite (unique purple, semi-precious stone), iron, tin, gypsum and kaolin. There is a large phosphate mine at Minjingu, supplying a fertiliser plant at Tanga. Development is difficult due to the fragmented structure of industry and small-scale mining operations. With Africa's second largest gold reserves after South Africa, the Tanzanian gold mining sector has attracted considerable interest in gold exploration and development. As a result, the country now absorbs up to 15 per cent of Africa's exploration expenditure.

Diamonds, nickel and gemstones have also seen growth in recent years. Williamson, the country's sole diamond mine, is located at Mwadui near Mwanza and is owned by De Beers (70 per cent) and the Tanzanian government.

Hydrocarbons

Several companies are prospecting for onshore and offshore oil fields.

Natural gas reserves were estimated at 27.6 billion cubic metres (980 billion cubic feet) at the beginning of 2001. Offshore reserves have been recently discovered at Songo-Songo Island in the Indian Ocean, Kimbiji and Mnazi Bay near Mtwara. Ocelot and Trans Canada Pipelines (OTC), are developing the Songo-Songo reserves and plan to build a pipeline to deliver gas to Dar es Salaam.

There are proven coal reserves of 200 million tonnes in Mchuchuma in south-west Tanzania near the northern tip of Lake Nyasa, but the only developed colliery is at Songwe-Kiwara with capacity of 100,000 tonnes per year. Studies indicate the Mchuchuma coal deposits could provide fuel for 400MW generation capacity for up to 35–40 years. The coals are bituminous and with low sulphur content.

Energy

Tanzania has a heavy dependence on imports of oil and oil products (900,000 tonnes of crude oil per year), which may account for up to 50 per cent of export earnings, and can be in short supply due to a lack of foreign exchange reserves.

Total installed electricity generating capacity is about 590MW, of which about 379MW (64 per cent) is hydroelectric, and the remainder thermal (diesel and coal run). Only about 5 per cent of the hydro potential has been developed.

Electricity is only available to about 10 per cent of the population of Tanzania, mainly those who live in towns. Wood fuel is the major energy source in the country, which is having an adverse impact on the environment.

Tanzania has been implementing a rural electrification programme since 1967 but progress has been slow due to the very low population density and the high cost of supplying power to such a dispersed population.

Development plans are concentrated on further utilisation of the country's hydroelectric potential (estimated to be around 3,800MW), which is being developed with the aid of foreign investment. Mainly concentrated in south-west Tanzania and the Rufiji River basin.

The Kihansi 180MW hydroelectric project supplements supplies from Mtera hydropower station.

Independent Power Tanzania Ltd is building a 100MW plant at Tegeta, outside Dar es Salaam, at a cost of US$162 million; it will supply state-run electricity company Tanzania Electric Supply Co Ltd (Tanesco) with electricity.

Tanzania is a member of the South African Power Pool, enabling imports of electricity due to high costs of oil, and water shortages hampering its own production.

Financial markets

Stock exchange

The launch of Tanzania's stock exchange was delayed in 1997 because no companies were ready for official listing. The Dar es Salaam Stock Exchange (DSE) finally opened in 1998. By 2001, only four companies had registered, including Tanzania Breweries Ltd, Tanzania Cigarette Company, Tanzanian Tea Packers Ltd and Tanzania Oxygen Ltd (TOL).

The stock exchange is hampered by a lack of participation by foreign investors and the local investor community, which has few surplus funds and remains unconvinced of the value of investing in the stock market. Analysts have suggested that East Africa does not need three exchanges and proposed that Uganda and Tanzania merge their exchanges, especially after the creation of the EAC in late 1999.

Banking

The 35-branch National Bank of Commerce (NBC) was privatised in 1999.

Central bank

Bank of Tanzania.

Main financial centre

Dar es Salaam.

Time

GMT plus three hours

Geography

Tanzania consists of Tanganyika, on the African mainland, and the nearby islands of Zanzibar and Pemba. Tanganyika lies on the east coast of Africa, bordered by Uganda and Kenya to the north, by the Democratic Republic of Congo (DRC) to the west, and by Zambia, Malawi and Mozambique to the south. Zanzibar and Pemba are in the Indian Ocean about 40 km (25 miles) off the coast of Tanganyika, north of Dar es Salaam.

Tanzania is by far the largest country in east Africa. It is divided into three major regions: the coastal plains and river valleys, the central plateau and basin country, and the southern highlands.

The northern coastal area is humid and rainy, with some of the lushest vegetation in Tanzania. Further south the rainfall decreases and the vegetation develops into a drier savanna woodland. Tanzania's major rivers cut across the coastal plains, creating fertile alluvial fans where cotton,

sisal and tropical fruits are grown. A few miles inland from the ocean the vegetation switches to tropical savannah woodland.
The central plateau region occupies the major part of the country, wedged between the two rift valleys. The plateau is bordered by Lake Victoria in the north, the Rukwa Valley in the south, Lake Tanganyika and the Ruwenzori Mountains in the west, and the coastal plains in the east. The famous Serengeti Plains and the Masai Steppe are located in the north-east of this central region.
The southern highlands consist of a variety of mountain and hill formations and are sparsely populated.

Climate

Tropical, with variations according to altitude. Rainy seasons April–May and November–December. Warmer on coast, cooler in upland areas. Temperatures range from 23–30 degrees Celsius (C). Best time to visit June–September.
Climatically, Tanzania can be divided into two major zones, the wet and humid lowlands around Lake Victoria and the Indian Ocean, and the semi-arid plateau region. The coastal area is almost always hot and humid with a rainy season that extends for more than 10 months. The most uncomfortable period is December–April when the temperature sometimes exceeds 32 degrees C, with humidity over 90 per cent. The coolest time of the year, and the best time to visit, is June–September when the temperature drops to 15–21 degrees C with relatively low humidity.
The central plateau has distinct wet and dry seasons with great seasonal variations in temperature. Heavy rains fall in March–May and light rains in November–December.
In Dar es Salaam the rainy seasons are usually March–May and November–December, but these can vary from year to year.

Dress codes

Men should wear a lightweight/tropical suit and tie, and women a lightweight suit or formal dress, for business meetings. Women's dress should be modest. On safari it is considered best to avoid bright colours as they may irritate the animals. Visitors to the highlands are advised to take warm clothing. A light raincoat and umbrella are useful during the rainy season.

Entry requirements

Passports
Required by all.
Visa
Required by all except nationals of certain Commonwealth and Scandinavian countries. Visas are required for all business travellers and should be obtained in advance.
Currency advice/regulations
Foreign currency in cash or traveller's cheques may be exchanged at any bank and bureaux de change operating at international airports, major towns and border posts.
Import and export of local currency is prohibited (exception: if travelling between Tanzania, Uganda and Kenya by surface transport, local currency to the value of US$75 can be carried). Import and export of foreign currency is unlimited.
It is best to take US dollars which can be changed at varying rates.
Customs
Travellers have to go through customs again on arrival in Zanzibar.

Health (for visitors)

Visitors are likely to have difficulties at airports if they are not in possession of a valid certificate of vaccination for yellow fever.
The risk of catching malaria varies from place to place, with less risk in regions of high altitude. Visitors should seek medical advice on the type and frequency of dosage.
Dysentery is fairly prevalent and visitors are advised to avoid uncooked vegetables and salads, unless they have been properly prepared. It is advisable to make sure that drinking water has been boiled and filtered; water in better hotels is normally safe to drink.
Cholera, typhoid and para-typhoid 'A' and 'B' protection is not obligatory but visitors eating and drinking outside the major city hotels are advised to have protective vaccination. Rabies and bilharzia are present in Tanzania
The AIDS virus can be contracted through sexual contact or through medical treatment involving infected equipment. It may be advisable to carry a sterile needle kit, and where possible to seek the advice of the relevant embassy if medical treatment is required.
Mandatory precautions
A yellow fever vaccination certificate is required and must be shown again when entering Zanzibar.
Advisable precautions
Hepatitis 'A', tetanus, typhoid and polio vaccinations and malaria prophylaxis are recommended. Bottled water is readily available in Dar es Salaam. Water precautions should be taken – bilharzia risk exists.

Hotels

Accommodation tends to be expensive and can be difficult to obtain, especially in Dar es Salaam, so reservations should be made well in advance and confirmation obtained. Bills must be settled with foreign exchange.

Credit cards

Use restricted to a few shops and hotels, mainly in Dar es Salaam. Hotels mostly accept only American Express and Diners'. Limited use of MasterCard.

Public holidays

Fixed dates
1 Jan, 12 Jan (Zanzibar Revolution Day), 5 Feb (CCM Day), 26 Apr (Union Day), 1 May (Workers' Day), 7 Jul (Farmers' Day), 9 Dec (Independence Day), 25 Dec (Christmas).
Variable dates
Variable dates: Good Friday, Easter Monday, Eid Al-Fitr, Eid Al-Adha, Islamic New Year, Prophet's Birthday.

Working hours

Banking
Mon–Fri: 0830/0900–1530/1600; Sat: 0830/0900–1100/1130. In Dar es Salaam the Kariakoo, Temeke and Ubungo branches of the National Bank of Commerce open on Sundays from 0900–1300.
Business
Mon–Fri: 0900–1230, 1500–1700.
Government
Mon–Fri: 0800–1230, 1400–1600.

Telecommunications

Telecommunications services are provided by the state-owned Tanzania Posts and Telecommunications Corporation (TPTC). It is responsible to the Ministry of Communications and Public Works.
The main network consists of an east-west microwave system from Dar es Salaam to the Rwanda/Burundi border and a north-south system, with links to Malawi and Zambia in the south and Kenya in the north. Local links are mainly through open wire, although there are some VHF and HF radio links. In Zanzibar there is a Hitachi digital exchange.
There is an Intelsat standard B earth station working to the Indian Ocean satellite, and a standard A earth station working to the Atlantic Ocean satellite.
Tanzania has a GSM network, operated by TRI, which has 3,000 subscribers representing 0.01 per cent of the market.
Telephone/fax
There are four telephone mainlines per 1,000 people, with 28 mainlines per 1,000 in Dar es Salaam (1998). Each line generates an average of US$925 for operators.
Postal services
Internal services are slow but fairly reliable. It is advisable to despatch overseas mail by air.
Courier services
Air courier services are available.

Electricity supply
250V AC, 50 cycles. Usual industrial supply is 400V. Plugs are three square-pin variety.

Weights and measures
The metric system is in use but UK weights and measures are still used in many industries, for example, building.

Social customs/useful tips
Patience is required when doing business in Tanzania. Visitors should use cameras only in private settings and tourist resorts otherwise permission must be sought. Visitors should be aware that bridges, railway stations and public buildings are regarded as security installations and should not be photographed. There are no restrictions on alcohol. Almost all business executives speak English.
Where Muslim conventions apply, visitors should be perceptive to unfamiliar local customs.
Business visitors should address Tanzanians as Mr, Mrs or Ms. The term *Ndugu* is equivalent to comrade in English. The normal greeting when greeting an individual is *Jambo*. Handshaking is normal practice both on meeting and parting.
Tanzania has a large number of local traditions, although few will affect the business traveller or tourist. There are no particular taboos but visitors should be aware of religious customs. Muslims should not be offered pork or ham and many do not drink alcohol. During the Islamic holy month of Ramadan, Muslims do not eat or drink during daylight hours. Sikhs should not be offered anything to smoke.

Security
Street crime is a serious problem in Tanzania, especially in Dar es Salaam. Be attentive at all times. Passports, traveller's cheques, wristwatches and cash are regularly stolen. Use hotel safe deposit boxes and do not carry too much cash.

Getting there
Air
National airline: Air Tanzania, government-owned. Air Zanzibar.
Main airport: Dar es Salaam International (DAR), 15km south-west of city centre.
Airport tax: There is no airport departure tax.
Surface
Road: There is access from Zambia via a surfaced road between Lusaka and Dar es Salaam. There are also roads from Uganda, Rwanda (very poor quality), Kenya and Malawi.
Rail: The Tanzania–Zambia Railway Authority (Tazara), jointly owned and administered by the Tanzanian and Zambian governments, operates a 1,860km railway link between Dar es Salaam and New Kapiri Mposhi (copper belt) in Zambia.

Getting about
National transport
Travel by bus and train is possible but can be uncomfortable.
Air: Air Tanzania operates services between Dar es Salaam, Kilimanjaro, Mwanza, several other, small airports, Zanzibar and Pemba. Small private company, Precision Air, also operates scheduled domestic flights to the major cities. Gulf Air and Kenya Airways operate scheduled commercial flights to Zanzibar. Air Zanzibar also operates from mainland Tanzania, Kenya and Uganda using four small aircraft.
Charter companies operate to isolated airfields, national parks and numerous towns.
Water: Several passenger boats run to Zanzibar every day and cost from US$30 return.
City transport
Taxis: Taxis are available in main towns. Taxis from hotels have fixed rates for journeys within Dar es Salaam. Fares in any other taxis are by negotiation and should be fixed before the journey. Taxi drivers do not expect tips but 10 per cent would be acceptable.
Buses/trams: Shuttle buses run from the airport to city centre, journey time 30 minutes.
Car hire
Car hire can be arranged via the main hotels, but it is advisable to get a four-wheel-drive if going off the main roads.

BUSINESS DIRECTORY

Telephone area codes
Dialling code for Tanzania: IDD access code +255, followed by area code (from July 2000: (0)22 for Dar es Salaam; (0)28 for Mwanza; (0)27 for Arusha and Kilimanjaro; (0)24 for Zanzibar), followed by subscriber's number.

Chambers of Commerce
Dar es Salaam Chamber of Commerce, PO Box 41, Dar es Salaam (tel: 221-893).

Tanzania Chamber of Commerce and Agriculture (TCCIA), PO Box 9713, Dar es Salaam (tel: 237-3710, 211-3198).

Banking
Akiba Commercial Bank Limited, PO Box 669, TDFL Bldg (Phase II), Upanga Rd, Dar es Salaam (tel:118-340-4; fax: 114-173).

Azania Bancorp Ltd, PO Box 9271, Samora Ave, Dar es Salaam (tel: 118-026, 117-998; fax: 36-741).

Bank of Tanzania, PO Box 2939, 10 Mirambo Street, Dar es Salaam (tel: 211-0945/7, 211-0950/2; fax: 212-8151; 211-2671, 211-2573, 211-3325, 211-2537; e-mail: info@bot-tz.org).

Citibank (T) Limited, PO Box 71625, Ali Hassan Mwinyi Road, Dar es Salaam (tel: 117-575, 117-601; fax: 113-910, 117-576).

CRDB Limited, PO Box 268, Maktaba St, Dar es Salaam (tel: 117-442/7).

Diamond Trust Bank (T) Limited, PO Box 115, Jamhuri/Ali Hassan Mwinyi Rd, Dar es Salaam (tel: 114-888/892; fax: 114-210).

Eurafrican Bank (T) Limited, PO Box 3054, NDC Development House, Kivukoni/Ohio Street, Dar es Salaam (tel: 110-928, 111-229, 110-104; fax: 113-740).

Exim Bank (T) Limited, PO Box 6649, 9 Samora Avenue, Dar es Salaam (tel: 119-738; fax: 119-737).

Habib African Bank Limited, PO Box 70086, India St, Dar es Salaam (tel: 111-107/9).

International Bank of Malaysia (T) Limited, PO Box 9362, Haidery Plaza, Upanga/Kisutu St, Dar es Salaam (tel: 110-518, 110-520, 110-571; fax: 110-196).

Kenya Commercial Bank Ltd, PO Box 804, Audit House, 36 Upanga Road, Dar es Salaam (tel: 115-386/7/8; fax: 115-391).

Kenya Commercial Bank (T) Limited, PO Box 804, Peugot Hse, Dar es Salaam (tel: 115-386/7/8; fax: 115-391).

National Micro-Finance Bank Limited, PO Box 9213, Samora Ave, Dar es Salaam (tel: 116-925/9, 116-933, 110-900, 118-785; fax: 114-058).

NBC Limited, PO Box 1863, NBC House, Sokoine Drive, Dar es Salaam (tel: 113-914; fax: 112-887).

Stanbic Bank Tanzania Ltd, PO Box 72647, Sukari House, Ohio Street/Sokoine Drive, Dar es Salaam (tel: 112-195/200; fax: 113-.742)

Standard Chartered Bank Tanzania Ltd, PO Box 9011, Ohio/Sokoine Drive, Dar es Salaam (tel: 1173-50/52, 113-787, 117-377; fax: 113-770, 113-775).

Tanzania Investment Bank, PO Box 9373, Samora Avenue, Dar es Salaam (tel: 111-708/13; fax: 113-438) .

Tanzania Postal Bank, PO Box 9300, Mkwepu Street, Dar es Salaam (tel: 112-358/60, 112-385/9, 116-409, 117-748; fax: 38-212).

Central bank

Bank of Tanzania, 10 M'rambo Street, PO Box 2939, Dar es Salaam (tel: 211-0945/7, 211-0950/2, 211-0976/7; fax: 212-8151, 211-2573, 211-3325, 211-2702, 211-3941; e-mail: info@bot-tz.org; internet site: http://www.bot-tz.org).

Travel information

Air Tanzania, Tancot House, City drive, PO Box 543, Dar es Salaam (tel: 211-0245).

Air Zanzibar (tel: 223-1590).

Coastal Aviation (tel: 284-3033).

Dar es Salaam International Airport, PO Box 19043, Dar es Salaam (tel: 284-4610/19; fax: 284-4343, 284-3022, 284-4209).

Kilimanjaro International Airport, PO Box 995, Arusha (tel: 22-941; fax: 28-553).

Precisionair (tel: 211-3036).

Tanzanair, Azikiwe & Samora Ave/Airport International Terminal, PO Box 364, Dar es Salaam (tel: 230-232/4, 246-583; fax: 246-296).

Tanzania National Parks, PO Box 3134, Arusha (tel: 250-1930/1931; fax: 254-8216; e-mail: tanapa@yako.habari.co.tz; internet site: http://www.tanapa.com).

Zanzibar Tourist Corporation, PO Box 216, Zanzibar (tel: 232-344; fax: 233-430).

National tourist organisation offices

Tanzania Tourist Board, IPS Building, 3rd Floor, PO Box 2485, Dar es Salaam (tel: 211-1244/5; fax: 211-6420; e-mail: safari@ud.co.tz).

Ministries

Ministry of Agriculture and Irrigation, PO Box 9192, Dar es Salaam (tel: 286-2480).

Ministry of Energy and Minerals, PO Box 9153, Mkwepu Street, Dar es Salaam (tel: 211-7156).

Ministry of Industries and Commerce, PO Box 9503, Lumumba Street, Dar es Salaam (tel: 218-0049).

President's Office, State House, PO Box 9120, Dar es Salaam (tel: 46-261; fax: 46-913).

President of Zanzibar's Office, PO Box 776, Zanzibar (tel: 30-314; fax 33-722).

Prime Minister's Office, PO Box 980, Dodoma (tel: 23-320; fax: 46-232; PO Box 3021, Dar es Salaam (tel: 31-081; fax: 46-232).

Other useful addresses

Board of External Trade, PO Box 5402, Dar es Salaam (tel: 33-524).

Board of Internal Trade, PO Box 883, Dar es Salaam (tel: 28-301).

British High Commission, Hifadhi House, Samora Avenue, PO Box 9200, Dar es Salaam (tel: 117-659/665; fax: 112-951).

Cashew Nut Authority of Tanzania, PO Box 533, Mtwara (tel: 2310).

Coffee Authority of Tanzania, PO Box 732, Moshi (tel: 4011).

National Development Corporation, Development House, Kivukoni Front/Ohio Street, PO Box 2669, Dar es Salaam (tel: 211-2893, 211-1460/3; fax: 211-3618; e-mail: ndc@cats-net.com; internet site: http://www.ndctz.com).

National Insurance Corporation of Tanzania Ltd, PO Box 9264, Dar es Salaam (tel: 110-744, 113-052; fax: 113-403).

Presidential Parastatal Sector Reform Commission, 2nd Floor, Sukari House, Sokoine Drive/Ohio Street, PO Box 9252, Dar es Salaam (tel: 211-5482, 211-7988/9; fax: 211-3065/6, 212-2870; e-mail: info@psrctz.com).

Radio Tanzania, PO Box 9191, Dar es Salaam (tel: 38-011/6).

Sea Express Services Ltd, Dar es Salaam (tel: 37-049, 112-508); Zanzibar (tel: 33-002, 33-013).

Southern Paper Mills Co Ltd, (Marketing Dept) Tanzania Elimu Supplies Building, Bandari Road, Dar es Salaam (tel: 111-602, 32-113; fax: 113-233).

State Mining Corporation, PO Box 4958, Dar es Salaam (tel: 28-781).

Tanzania Electric Supply Company Ltd (TANESCO), PO Box 9024, Dar es Salaam (tel: 211-2891; fax: 211-3836; e-mail: mdtan@intafrica.com).

Tanzania Exporters' Association (TANEXA), c/o Sima International, PO Box 1175, Dar es Salaam (tel: 48-948; fax: 73-784).

Tanzania Harbours Authority, PO Box 9184, Dar es Salaam (tel: 21-212; fax: 32-066).

Tanzania National Parks, PO Box 3134, Arusha (tel: 250-1930/1931; fax: 254-8216; e-mail: tanapa@yako.habari.co.tz).

Tanzania Petroleum Development Corporation (TPDC), Managing Director, PO Box 2774, Dar es Salaam (tel: 181-407; fax: 180-047); Director of Exploration and Production, PO Box 5233, Dar es Salaam (tel: 36-086; fax: 29-663; e-mail: tpdcexploration@raha.com); Director of Research & Corporate Services, PO Box 2774, Dar es Salaam (tel: 152-019; fax: 152-017).

Tanzania Railways Corporation, PO Box 468, Dar es Salaam (tel: 26-241).

Tanzania Revenue Authority, PO Bnox 11491, Dar es Salaam (tel: 211-9591/4; fax: 212-8593; e-mail: trais@afsat.com).

Tanzanian Embassy (USA), 2139 R Street, NW, Washington DC 20008 (tel: 939-6129; fax: 797-7408; e-mail: tanz-us@clark.net).

Television Zanzibar, PO Box 314, Zanzibar (tel: 32-816).

US Embassy, Laibon Road, PO Box 9123, Dar es Salaam (tel: 37-501; fax: 37-408).

Internet sites

Africa Business Network: http://www.ifc.org/abn

AllAfrica.com: http://allafrica.com

African Development Bank: http://www.afdb.org

Africa Online: http://www.africaonline.com

Bank of Tanzania: http://www.bot-tz.org

Harambee Afrika (UK business club for traders with east, central and southern Africa; includes annotated web resource list): http://www.harambee.co.uk

Mbendi AfroPaedia (information on companies, countries, industries and stock exchanges in Africa): http://mbendi.co.za

Presidential Parastatal Sector Reform Commission: http://www.psrctz.com

Tanzania Harbours Authority: http://www.tanzaniaports.com

Tanzania National Parks: http://www.tanapa.com

Terres Australes

KEY FACTS

Official name: Le Territoire des Terres Australes et Antarctiques Françaises (French Southern and Antarctic Territories)

Head of State: President of France (Jacques Chirac)

Head of government: Prime Minister Lionel Jospin

Area: 439,797 square km consisting of: Kerguelen Archipelago 7,215 square km, Crozet Archipelago 515 square km, Amsterdam Island 60 square km, Saint Paul Island 7 square km, Adélie and Antarctica 432,000 square km

Population: 100 (2002)

Official language: French

Currency: Euro (eur) = 100 cents (from 1 Jan 2002; previous currency franc, locked at Ff6.56 per euro)

Exchange rate: eur0.96 per US$ (Jan 2003)

For the latest Key Facts, go to www.worldinformation.com

COUNTRY PROFILE

Historical profile

France possesses a number of islands at the southern extremity of the Indian Ocean that are grouped together with the French portion of the Antarctic continent into one administrative framework, 'Territoire.'

1552–59 Saint Paul and Amsterdam Islands were sighted by survivors of the Portuguese expedition led by Ferdinand Magellan.

1772 Captain Marion Dufresne and ship's mate Crozet saw the group of islands, which became known as the Crozet Archipelago.

1772 Yves de Kerguelen sighted another archipelago, later named after him.

1840 Adélie Land, on the Antarctic continent, was sighted.

1924 The French government decreed on 21 November to attach the islands to the general government of Madagascar (then a French colony).

1947 France arranged for the establishment of observation stations.

1955 Terres Australes et Antarctiques were accorded the status of a separate French territory in August.

Political structure

Le Territoire des Terres Australes et Antarctiques Françaises (French Southern and Antarctic Territories) is a French Térritoire d'Outre Mer (TOM) (Overseas Territory), but is administered under two different international laws. France exercises full sovereignty over the southern islands, unanimously recognised by all nations. However, Adélie Land is administered according to the Treaty of Washington. This is an international agreement which provides for broad scientific co-operation and demilitarisation of the Antarctic continent and freezes existing territorial claims without prejudicing the solution to the sovereignty problem.

The fully sovereign area is governed by one law and two main decrees. The law of 6 August 1955 confers administrative and financial autonomy on the TOM. The implementation decree of 13 January 1956 defines the TOM's financial system and the decree of 8 September 1956 provides for the TOM's administrative organisation.

The TOM is under the authority of a chief administrator (Brigitte Girardin since 1998) whose official residence is in Paris. The administrator is assisted by an advisory council, which meets twice a year and consists of seven members appointed for five-year terms. The council must be consulted on the TOM's draft budget and it is kept informed and consulted on any proposed new scientific missions or applications for concessions and commercial activities.

The TOM is divided into four districts, each under the authority of a district head appointed by the chief administrator.

Saint Paul and Amsterdam Islands: permanent settlement is Martin de Viviés.

Crozet Islands: settlement is Alfred Faure (Possession Island).

Kerguelen Islands: settlement is Port aux Français.

Adélie Land: settlement is Dumont D'Urville.

Population

100 (2002)

The population, which comprises members of scientific missions, fluctuates according to season – it is higher in the summer. Saint Paul Island is uninhabited.

Languages spoken

Official language

French

Economy

Scientific activities are supported and developed by the Institut Français pour la Récherché et la Technologie Polaires (IFRTP) (French Institute for Polar Research and Technology) and the administration of the TOM is in charge of the logistics. Most of the TOM's economic activities centre around supporting the IFRTP. Fishing is the main other economic activity; others are philately and tourist cruises. There was an attempt to start a lobster cannery on Saint Paul and an attempt to exploit elephant seals on the Kerguelen Islands, but both of these failed.

External trade

Crayfish and other fish are exported to France and Réunion.

Agriculture

Research has indicated the viability of largescale farming of giant brown macrocystis, a type of seaweed.

Fishing

French vessels fish for crayfish off Amsterdam and Saint Paul. There is an agreement between France and Ukraine to fish for icefish and toothfish.

A research programme which has been carried out since 1970, has shown that trout adapt well to a sub-antarctic environment and the result of sea-ranching salmon was also a biological success.

There are estimated to be 60 to 120 million tons of krill in the TOM's coastal waters. Around Saint Paul and Amsterdam Islands, there are plentiful supplies of bull head fish, false cod, crayfish and cape lobster.

Tourism

The French research vessel, *Marion Dufresne*, conducts tourist cruises.

Hydrocarbons

A limited amount of oil drilling has been carried out.

Banking

Central bank

European Central Bank (ECB)

Time

GMT plus five hours

Geography

The islands extend from the 37th south latitude all the way to the South Pole. The territory comprises Adélie Land, a narrow segment of the mainland of Antarctica, and several islands (Kerguelen and Crozet, St Paul and Amsterdam).

Climate

The climate of Saint Paul and Amsterdam Islands is oceanic, damp and mild. The temperature averages 15 degrees Celsius (C).

The climate is particularly extreme in the Crozet Archipelago – the islands lie at the centre of an area where tropical and antarctic air masses meet, causing deep depressions and cyclone-forming processes. The Kerguelen Islands have a cool, humid climate due to the proximity of the Antarctic continent. The summers last from December to March and are similar to those beyond the Arctic Circle. The winters from May to October are comparatively mild. The climate is unstable with constant winds, sometimes at a speed of 160kph. The temperature of the surrounding sea averages 4 degrees C.

Adélie Land's climate is harsh. The temperature of the coastal area never rises above 4 degrees C in summer and can fall to -37 degrees C in winter.

Weights and measures

The metric system is in use.

Getting there

Air

There are no air links with the bases.

Surface

Water: Relief ships bring new personnel and supplies. A charter vessel calls five times a year in the Antarctic islands and another calls twice a year in Adélie Land.

BUSINESS DIRECTORY

Banking

Central bank

European Central Bank (ECB), Kaiserstrasse 29, D-60311 Frankfurt am Main, Germany (tel: +49(69)13-440; fax: +49(69)1344-6000).

Other useful addresses

Institut Français pour la Recherche et la Technologie Polaires (IFRTP), Technopole Brest Iroise, BP 75, 29280 Plouzane, France (tel: (33-2) 9805-6500; fax: (33-2) 9805-6555).

Terres Australes et Antarctiques Françaises (TAAF), 34 Rue des Renaudes, 75017 Paris (tel: (33-1) 4053-4652; fax: (33-1) 4766-9123).

KEY FACTS

Official name: République Togolaise (Togolese Republic)

Head of State: President General Gnassingbé Eyadéma (RPT) (since 1967; re-elected Jun 1998; constitution amended Dec 2002 to allow for another term)

Head of government: Prime Minister Koffi Sama (appointed by the president, 27 Jun 2002)

Ruling party: Rassemblement du Peuple Togolais (RPT) (Rally of the Togolese People) (results of parliamentary elections 27 Oct 2002: RPT won 72 seats out of 81 in parliament; the nine remaining seats went to four minority parties close to the RPT; the main opposition parties called for a boycott of the elections and did not present candidates)

Area: 56,000 square km

Population: 4.70 million (2001)

Capital: Lomé

Official language: French

Currency: CFA franc (CFAf) = 100 centimes (Communauté Financière Africaine (African Financial Community) franc)

Exchange rate: CFAf629.73 per US$ (Jan 2003); CFAf655.95 per euro (pegged from Jan 1999)

GDP per capita: US$277 (2001)

GDP real growth: 2.70% (2001)

Inflation: 5.40% (2001); -0.9% (year-on-year, Feb 2002)

Balance of trade: -US$193.00 million (2001)

Foreign debt: US$1.41 billion (2001)

For the latest Key Facts, go to www.worldinformation.com

Togo

Jonathan Derrick

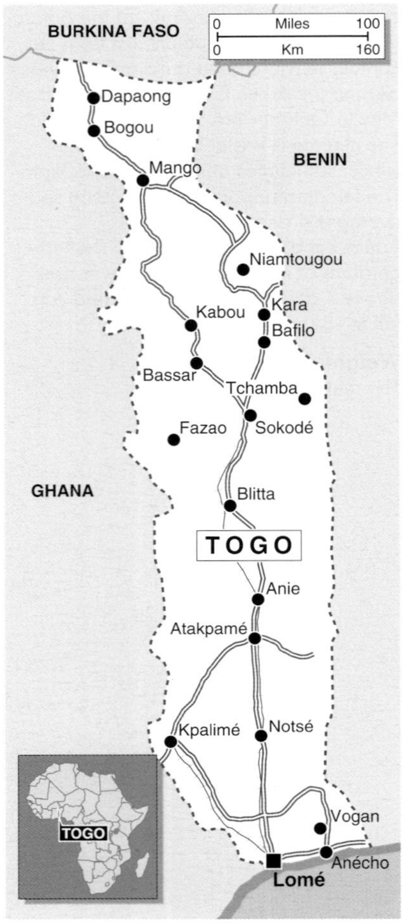

The running feud between President Gnassingbe Eyadéma and the opposition parties continued through 2001 and into 2002. While Western countries gave considerable backing to the opposition and continued to deny most aid because of the government's unfair conduct of elections and other dictatorial acts, Eyadéma remained in control, with African backing – he was Chairman of the Organisation of African Unity (OAU) until the Lusaka summit in June 2001 – and was able to a great extent to dictate progress under the agreement of 1999 with the opposition. He and the opposition parties continued to argue over details of the parliamentary elections to be held under that agreement. It was difficult for the four outside 'facilitators', representing France, Germany, the EU and the Francophonie organisation, to persuade the two sides to work together, such was their mutual suspicion.

Political divisions deepen

On 3 August 2001, Yaovi Agboyibo, leader of one of the two major opposition parties, the Comité d'Action pour le Renouveau (CAR) (Action Committee for Renewal) was sentenced to six months imprisonment for libelling Messan Agbeyome Kodjo, who had been prime minister since 2000. This worsened relations between the opposition and the President. Agbeyome Kodjo, who was reappointed at the head of a reshuffled government during the same month, declared on 30 August that General Eyadéma was seeking to amend the article of the constitution which would bar him from seeking re-election as president in 2003, at the end of his current term. This was quickly contradicted by the government and Eyadéma himself repeated that he would retire from office then – which was part of the deal worked out in 1999 to resolve the crisis following the unfair presidential election of 1998. In December 2002, parliament approved the constitutional changes, allowing Eyadéma to stay longer in his post.

Postponed until further notice

The parliamentary elections, already postponed, were due to be held on 14 and 28 October 2001. In September, they were postponed again. An official statement said the parties had agreed to a 'reasonable postponement' and it was reported that the National Independent Electoral Commission (CENI) had been unable to complete preparations in time. A UN mission at that time expressed doubts about the electoral code in force. On 19 September, the four facilitators finished a visit to Lomé without having persuaded the two sides to sit at the same table. In November, it was announced that the elections would take place in March 2002. However, the government and opposition remained far apart on several issues, including Agboyibo's imprisonment. The opposition also refused to resume talks within the Comité Paritaire de Suivi (CPS) – the joint government-opposition body set up to carry out the 1999 agreement – until he was released. On 10 January 2002, Agboyibo won an appeal against his conviction, but he had been charged on another count (of complicity with a criminal gang) in September, and he remained in custody on that charge.

Revision of the voters' register was completed in December 2001 and more than half the sum estimated by the government as needed to finance the elections had been raised by then. Other issues remained unresolved. The facilitators visited Togo again from 14–22 January 2002, but failed to bring the two sides together. The opposition wanted voting cards to be printed in France, while the president's side wanted to put the printing out to tender; Eyadéma argued that CENI members' terms of office had expired on 31 December and new members must be appointed. The facilitator's suggestion that the members appointed earlier should retain their posts until the elections was rejected by the government. On 3 January 2002, Eyadéma announced that a new law would be introduced banning candidates from standing who had not lived in the country for 12 months before the elections. This was clearly aimed at Gilchrist Olympio, leader of the Union des Forces du Changement (UFC) (Union of the Forces for Change) and Eyadéma's sworn enemy, who lived abroad fearing for his safety.

To complicate matters, as the date of elections on 10 and 24 March 2002 approached, the government decided unilaterally on 1 February to amend the electoral code. This led to strong protests from the EU, the US, the UN Secretary General and France, normally more friendly to Eyadéma. The French facilitator had blamed the government and the opposition equally for the deadlock in January, while the Germans blamed the government. On 8 February, the parliament, which is dominated by Eyadéma's party, the Rassemblement du Peuple Togolais (RPT) (Rally of the Togolese People) voted to reduce CENI membership from 20 to 10. On 20 February, opposition leaders met the president and insisted on the release of Agboyibo before opposition representatives joined CENI. On 5 March 2002, the government announced postponement of elections yet again. On 18 March, Eyadéma ordered the release of Agboyibo and the dropping of all charges against him.

Parliamentary elections finally took place on 27 October 2002. The RPT won 72 seats out of 81 in parliament while the remaining nine seats were shared by four minor parties, mostly allies of the RPT. The main opposition parties called for a boycott of the elections and did not present candidates. The president appointed a new cabinet on 3 December.

Debt problems

Deprived of most of the external aid it could have expected, the Togolese government was finding it increasingly difficult by early 2001 to service its debts and to meet ongoing expenditure. Full-scale resumption of aid depended on the holding of acceptable parliamentary elections; however, the government improved relations with the IMF and World Bank, concerned with economic more than political conditions for assistance.

In April 2001, the government agreed with the IMF on a six-month Staff Monitored Programme (SMP). It committed itself to clearing debt servicing arrears and increasing revenue, while an IMF-monitored cash flow system was supposed to control expenditure. Initially the government was far from being able to reduce the budget imbalance; revenue for 2001 was actually revised steeply downwards, from CFAf156 billion (US$210 million) to CFAf126 billion (US$169 million). Expenditure was revised slightly upwards, from CFAf172 billion (US$231 million) to CFAf173 billion (US$233 million). A joint mission of the IMF, World Bank and African Development Bank in late June 2001 commended the government for paying staff salaries on time and implementing most aspects of the structural reform programme.

Meanwhile, an anti-corruption commission and a debt collection commission were set up by the government in March 2001. The former took early action to clampdown on the unauthorised use of office telephones by officials and several people were publicly named and forced to return illicitly acquired money.

In August 2001, Togo repaid arrears of US$6.9 million owed to the World Bank meaning that the Bank's programmes in the country, suspended in November 2000, could now be resumed. The Bank had been aiding road transport, public and private enterprise restructuring, urban development and other projects and programmes in Togo. It also agreed to help the government proceed with the privatisation programme. There was progress by late 2001, in efforts to privatise four wholly or partially state-owned banks, despite the problem of those banks' huge bad debts. A consortium was appointed to value Togo Telecom and prepare it for sale, the cost of the whole process to be met by the World Bank.

The Office Togolais des Phosphates (OPT) remained in state ownership. Its output has been declining, particularly because of outdated equipment – 1.4 million tonnes in 2000, compared with 2.2 million in 1998 and the decline continued in 2001. The new managing agents – International Fertilizer Group-Togo (IFG-Togo), a 50: 50 joint venture of Brifco of France

KEY INDICATORS — **Togo**

	Unit	1996	1997	1998	1999	2000
Population	m	4.17	4.28	4.40	4.51	4.63
Gross domestic product (GDP)	US$bn	1.42	1.50	1.51	1.46	1.30
GDP per capita	US$	332	349	341	325	283
GDP real growth	%	9.1	4.7	4.9	3.5	-0.7
Inflation	%	4.7	8.3	1.0	-1.0	1.4
Wholesale prices	1995=100	104.7	0.0	0.0	0.0	0.0
Consumer prices	1995=100	104.7	113.3	114.4	114.3	116.5
Exports (fob) (goods)	US$m	441.0	423.0	420.0	385.0	346.0
Imports (fob) (goods)	US$m	568.0	531.0	554.0	589.0	406.0
Balance of trade	US$m	-127.0	-108.0	-133.0	-204.0	-60.0
Current account	US$m	-154.0	-177.0	-140.0	-127.1	-139.0
Foreign debt	US$bn	1.4	1.3	1.4	1.4	1.4
Total reserves minus gold	US$m	88.5	118.6	117.7	122.0	152.3
Foreign exchange	US$m	87.8	118.3	117.3	121.4	151.9
Exchange rate	per US$	511.55	583.67	589.95	615.70	711.98

and the Togolese government – announced plans in the latter part of 2001 to increase OTP output to 3 million tonnes per year over two years.

Sowing the seeds

Good cereal harvests in Togo were reported by the UN Food and Agricultural Organisation (FAO) for 2001 amounting to 685,000 tonnes, 13 per cent above average. The cotton crop was up as well, to 140,000 tonnes of seed according to an early estimate, in the 2001/02 cropping season, compared with 117,400 in 2000/01. GDP growth in 2001 was 2.7 per cent, showing a better situation than in 2000 when some estimates indicated a slight decline. Inflation in 2001 was 5.4 per cent and was higher than the 1.4 per cent registered in 2000. By 2002, GDP growth had risen to 2.9 per cent while inflation had fallen to 3.5 per cent. Despite these small favourable signs and even though some aid continued – French aid for health services and water supply, for example – Togo still had no early prospect of substantial aid.

Outlook

Despite experiencing some GDP growth in 2001 and 2002 due to an improved harvest and recovery in the cotton industry, Togo's economy shows little promise in the long-term without assistance from international donors. Until a government which is more acceptable to the West is in place, Togo will continue to experience long-term economic and political problems. Much will depend on whether Eyadéma does stand down as president in 2003 as he promised.

Risk assessment

Economic	Poor
Political	Poor
Regional stability	Good

COUNTRY PROFILE

Historical profile
1894 The country, then known as Togoland, became a German colony.
1914 Britain and France invaded and captured Togoland.
1922 Togoland was divided between Britain and France under a League of Nations mandate.
1930–50s The division of Togoland split the indigenous Ewe people, which led to the creation of a nationalist movement which demanded the unification of the two territories.
1956 British-ruled Togoland was incorporated into Ghana.
1960 The French section of Togoland gained independence under the leadership of Sylvanus Olympio and was declared a republic.
1962 A proposed referendum on unification with Ghana was blocked by President Olympio.
1963 Olympio was killed in a coup and replaced by Nicolas Grunitzky.
1967 Grunitzky was in turn ousted by Major General Gnassingbé Eyadéma.
1979 Eyadéma stood and won as the sole candidate in the presidential election.
1985 France intervened militarily to support the Eyadéma regime, following an attempted coup.
1991 President Eyadéma agreed to a national conference to pave the way for multi-party elections. The powers of the president were reduced. Joseph Koffigoh became prime minister and head of a transitional government.
1993 After a series of delays the country's first multi-party presidential elections were held in August. Eyadéma, standing for the Rassemblement du Peuple Togolais (RPT) (Rally of the Togolese People), was the only candidate and won 96 per cent of the vote.
1994 In legislative elections in February, the RPT won 37 seats, the RPT's and Comité d'Action pour le Renouveau (CAR) (Action Committee for Renewal) secured 33. The RPT's coalition partner, Union Togolaise pour la Démocratie (UTD) (Togolese Union for Democracy), won six seats.
1996 The RPT won three delayed by-elections, so increasing its representation to 40. These results meant that the RPT no longer required the support of the UTD to form a majority.
1998 Eyadéma won the June presidential election; the official results were contested by the opposition parties and by the UN.
1999 The March parliamentary elections were boycotted by all the opposition parties. In July, the president agreed to hold fresh legislative elections in 2000. The EU announced in November that it would assist in funding the elections.
On 29 July an independent electoral commission, Commission Electorale Indépendante (CENI), was formed, with equal representation of opposition and government.
2000 A vote of no-confidence in the government of Prime Minister Eugène Koffi Adogboli was passed in August. The president appointed Messan Agbeyome Kodjo prime minister. President Eyadéma confirmed in July that he intends to step down in 2003.
2001 Parliamentary elections that had been due to be held in October were postponed until March 2002, which were again postponed.

Political structure
Constitution
After 25 years of President Eyadéma's rule, in 1992, Togo promulgated a new constitution limiting future presidential terms to five years, renewable once only.
Form of state
Republic.
The executive
Executive power is vested in the president, who appoints and leads a council of ministers. The 1992 constitution limits the presidential term to five years, renewable once only.
National legislature
Legislative power is vested in the National Assembly.
Last elections
March 1999 (legislative)
Next elections
2002 (legislative) (postponed from March); 2003 (presidential).

Political parties
Ruling party
Rassemblement du Peuple Togolais (RPT) (Rally of the Togolese People)
Main opposition party
The main opposition parties are the Union Togolaise pour la Démocratie (UTD) (Togolese Union for Democracy); Comité d'Action pour le Renouveau (CAR) (Action Committee for Renewal); Co-ordination de la Force Nouvelle (CFN) (New Force Co-ordination); Alliance Togolaise pour la Démocratie (ATD) (Togolese Alliance for Democracy) and Union des Forces du Changement (UFC) (Union of the Forces of Change).

Population
4.63 million (2000)
Annual population growth rate: 2.6 per cent (1994–2000). Approximately 48 per cent of the total population is under 15 years.
Population density: 77 inhabitants per square km. Urban population: 33 per cent (1994–2000).
Ethnic make-up
African (99 per cent), European (1 per cent).
Religions
Traditional beliefs (50 per cent), Christianity (35 per cent) (mostly Roman Catholic), Islam (15 per cent).

Main cities
Lomé (estimated population 810,000), Sansanne-Mango (76,800), Sokodé (36,000), Kpalimé (30,000), Atakpamé (26,000), Anécho (15,000), Lama-Kara, Bassar, Dapaong.

Languages spoken
French is the official language, although Ewe and Kabyè are widely spoken.
Official language
French

Media

Press

The major news agencies include Afritel, Agence Togolaise de Presse and the Togolese News Agency. The main national state-owned newspaper is *Nouvelle Marche*. Other dailies include *La Tribune de Democrate*, *Le Mono*, *Togo Presse* and non-dailies include *Crocodile*, *Kpaka Desenchante* and *Le Temps*.

Broadcasting

Radio: State-operated Radiodiffusion Togolaise runs two radio stations broadcasting in French, English and African languages. There are also three privately-run radio stations.

Television: State-owned TV Télévision Togolaise broadcasts in French and national languages. Major hotels offer satellite TV.

Economy

Lack of aid, depressed cocoa prices and an energy crisis in 1998 has affected the Togolese economy. The economy begun to show signs of recovery with a growth rate of 3.5 per cent in 1999, but growth fell to an estimated -0.7 per cent in 2000. The economy is estimated to have grown by between 2.5 and 3 per cent in 2001, spurred on by recovery in the agricultural sector. Forecasts predict that if the country remains politically stable in 2002, the growth rate could rise to 5 per cent. This will bring welcome relief for the nation's burgeoning numbers of poor.

However, the political situation and human rights abuses has deprived Togo of potential foreign aid. The government is keen to appease foreign donors and has revitalised its privatisation programme. There is still some way to go before donors are convinced the country has turned the corner, but with President Eyadéma committed to ending his rule in 2003 the country is likely to come out of international isolation in the near future.

External trade

Exports

Principal exports are cotton, phosphates, coffee, cocoa, cement and manufactures.

Main destinations: Canada (typically 12 per cent of total), Zambia (8 per cent), Nigeria (7 per cent), Benin (6 per cent).

Imports

Principal imports are food, petroleum and petroleum products, machinery, construction materials, metals, transport equipment.

Main sources: China (21 per cent), France (11 per cent), Côte d'Ivoire (10 per cent), Thailand (9 per cent).

Agriculture

The agricultural sector contributes around 42 per cent to GDP and employs 60 per cent of the workforce.

Traditional methods of cultivation still prevail despite attempts at rapid modernisation.

Self-sufficiency in basic foodstuffs is generally maintained except during drought years.

The majority of farmers are smallholders who raise stock and grow maize, millet, yams, cassava, sorghum and rice.

Cotton, coffee and cocoa are the principal export earners.

A good cereal harvest in 2001 resulted in an increase of production by 13 per cent to 685,000 tonnes. Cotton production increased from 117,400 tonnes of cotton seed in 2000/01 to 140,000 tonnes in 2001/02.

Industry and manufacturing

The industrial sector contributes around 9 per cent to GDP and employs 10 per cent of the workforce.

It is small-scale but expanding. Activity is centred on the processing of agricultural commodities and the production of phosphoric acid, fertilisers and cement along with beverages, footwear, textiles and plastics.

Mining

The mining sector contributes around 12 per cent to GDP and employs 5 per cent of the workforce. Mining production is concentrated on phosphates, marble and limestone, although the country has potential for commercial extraction of diamonds, gold and base metals. There are also known reserves of iron ore, bauxite, dolomite and chromite.

Phosphate mining is the second principal export earner after cotton. Reserves are estimated at over 150 million tonnes, mainly located around Lake Togo. There are environmental concerns about the high level of cadmium in Togolese phosphate rock. The possible development of safer but lower-grade carbo-phosphates is being explored. There are 200 identified base metal deposits, including the lead zinc prospect at Pagala which is licensed out to Anglo American.

The government liberalised the sector with the passing of a Mining Code in 1995 which reformed the country's mining legislation to ensure it met international standards.

Hydrocarbons

There is no upstream oil industry, although the government is trying to attract foreign interest in offshore prospecting. The last exploration well was drilled in 1986 and foreign prospectors have generally ignored Togo. Bidding rounds for offshore blocks have received no applications, despite the regional oil rush. There is also no downstream oil industry and all petroleum products have to be imported in their refined form.

The US$260 million West African Gas Pipeline (WAGP) launched in 1999 is currently under way and will supply natural gas from Nigeria's Escravos field to Togo, Benin and Ghana by 2003. In 2000, an agreement was reached between the US company, Chevron, Anglo-Dutch Shell and the governments of Nigeria, Togo, Benin and Ghana on shareholding arrangements for WAGP.

Energy

Togo is heavily dependent on imported fuel. Electricity is imported from the Akosombo and Nkong hydroelectric dams in Ghana.

Banking

Central bank

Banque Centrale des Etats de l'Afrique de l'Ouest (Central Bank of West African States).

Main financial centre

Lomé.

Time

GMT.

Geography

Togo lies in West Africa, forming a narrow strip stretching north from a coastline of about 50km (30 miles) on the Gulf of Guinea. It is bordered by Ghana to the west, by Benin to the east, and by Burkina Faso, to the north.

Climate

Tropical, mean annual temperature 28 degrees Celsius (C). Drier in the north. Two rainy seasons between April–June and September–October.

Entry requirements

Passports

Required by all except certain African countries. Joint passports are not accepted. Passports must be valid for six months.

Visa

Required by all except nationals of some African countries. Multiple entry visas and extensions can be obtained within the country.

Currency advice/regulations

No restrictions on import of foreign currency. However, export of foreign currency must not exceed the amount declared on arrival.

No more than CFAf1 million may be taken in and no more than CFAf25,000 exported.

Health (for visitors)

Mandatory precautions

Yellow fever vaccination certificate required by all.

Advisable precautions

Hepatitis A, tetanus, typhoid and polio. Malaria prophylactic advisable. Drink bottled water. Rabies risk. There is an AIDS risk.

Hotels
High-standard hotels in Lomé, which should be booked well in advance. Ten per cent tip is usual.

Credit cards
Credit cards accepted.

Public holidays
Fixed dates
1 Jan, 13 Jan (National Liberation Day), 24 Jan (Sarakawa Day), 24 Apr (Victory Day), 27 Apr (Independence), 1 May (Labour day), 15 Aug (Assumption), 24 Sep (Anniversay of failed attack on Lomé), 1 Nov (All Saints'), 25 Dec.
Variable dates
Ascension Day, Whit Monday, Eid Al-Adha (Tabaski), Easter Monday, Eid al-Fitr.

Working hours
Banking
Mon–Fri: 0730–1130, 1430–1600.
Business
Mon–Fri: 0700–1200, 1430–1730.
Government
Mon–Fri: 0700–1200, 1430–1730.
Shops
Mon–Fri: 0800–1200, 1430–1730; Sat: 0730–1230.

Electricity supply
220V AC, 50 cycles.

Social customs/useful tips
Business is conducted in French.

Security
Togo is relatively trouble-free, although visitors should be wary of the occasional car-hijack. The coastal area is reported to be dangerous and visitors are advised to travel in groups throughout Togo, rather than alone.

Getting there
Air
Main airport: Lomé (Code: LFW), 4km from city; duty-free shop, bar, restaurant, buffet, bank, post office, shops, car hire.
Airport tax: International departures include an aeronautical development charge of CFAf5,000; not applicable to infants under two years and transit passengers.
Surface
Road: There is a well-surfaced coastal road connecting Accra (Ghana) and Lagos (Nigeria), which runs through Lomé. This route is also connected to Cotonou (Benin) and Ouagadougou (Burkina Faso).
The African Development Bank (ADB) agreed a loan in May 1999 for CFAf10.2 billion to refurbish the main highway (Route Nationale 1) linking Lomé with the northern states.
Main ports: Lomé

Getting about
National transport
Air: Air Togo flies between Lomé, Sokodé, Mango, Lama-Kara, Niamtougou and Dapaong.
Road: The main surfaced roads run to the borders of neighbouring countries; other roads may not be passable in the rainy season. The main route to the north is called 'Highway of Unity'.
Rail: The main lines run from Lomé to Blitta (midway between Atakpamé and Sokodé), and to Kpalimé.
Water: Coastal ferries operate between the southern ports.
City transport
Taxis: Readily available in Lomé, while shared taxis ply to other main towns; tipping is not usual.
Car hire
International driving licence required.

BUSINESS DIRECTORY

Telephone area codes
Dialling code for Togo: IDD access code +228, followed by subscriber's number. There are no area codes.

Chambers of Commerce
Chamber of Commerce, Agriculture & Industry of Togo, BP 360, Lomé (tel: 212-065).

Banking
Banque Centrale des Etats de l'Afrique de l'Ouest, BP 120, Avenue de Sarakawa, Lomé (tel: 212512, 215383/85 fax: 217602).

Banque Internationale pour l'Afrique au Togo SA, BP 346, 13 rue du Commerce, Lomé (tel: 213286, 212081 fax: 211019, 220238).

Banque Togolaise de Développement, BP 65, Place de L'Independance, Angle Avenue des Nîmes et Avenue Nicolas Grunitzky, Lomé (tel 213641/2 Fax: +228 214456).

Banque Togolaise pour le Commerce et l'Industrie, BP 363, 169 Boulevard du 13 Janvier, Lomé (tel: 214641/42 fax: 213265).

Ecobank-Togo, BP 3302, 20 Rue du Commerce, Lomé (tel: 217214 fax: 214237).

Société Inter Africaine de Banque, BP 4874, 14 rue du commerce, Lomé (tel: 212830, 211341 fax:215829).

Société Nationale d'Investissement et Fonds Annexes BP 2682, 11 Avenue du 24 Janvier, Lomé (tel: 216221 fax:216225).

Union Togolaise de Banques, BP 359, Place Van Vollen Hoven, Lomé (tel: 216411 fax: 212206).

Central bank
Banque Centrale des Etats de l'Afrique de l'Ouest, avenue de Sarakawa, BP 120, Lomé.

Travel information
National Tourist Board, BP 1177, Lomé.

Other useful addresses
British Honorary Consul, Lomé (tel: 264-606).

Direction de la Statistique, BP 118, Lomé (tel: 270-662).

Direction des Professions Touristiques, BP 1289, Lomé (tel: 215-662, 214-313).

Kpeme Port Authority, OTP BP 362, Lomé (tel: 213-901; fax: 217-105).

Office des Produits Agricoles du Togo, BP 1334, Lomé (agency dealing with marketing, export, development) (tel: 214-471).

OPTT-Post Office and Telecommunications of Togo, Lomé (tel: 213-737; fax: 210-373).

Togo Embassy (USA), 2208 Massachusetts Avenue, NW, Washington DC 20008 (tel: 234-4212; fax: 232-3190).

Internet sites
Africa Business Network: http://www.ifc.org/abn

AllAfrica.com: http://allafrica.com

African Development Bank: http://www.afdb.org

Africa Online: http://www.africaonline.com

Harambee Afrika (UK business club for traders with east, central and southern Africa; includes annotated web resource list): http://www.harambee.co.uk

Mbendi AfroPaedia (information on companies, countries, industries and stock exchanges in Africa): http://mbendi.co.za

Welcome to the Republic of Togo: http://www.afrika.com/togo/html

Tunisia

Daniel Brett

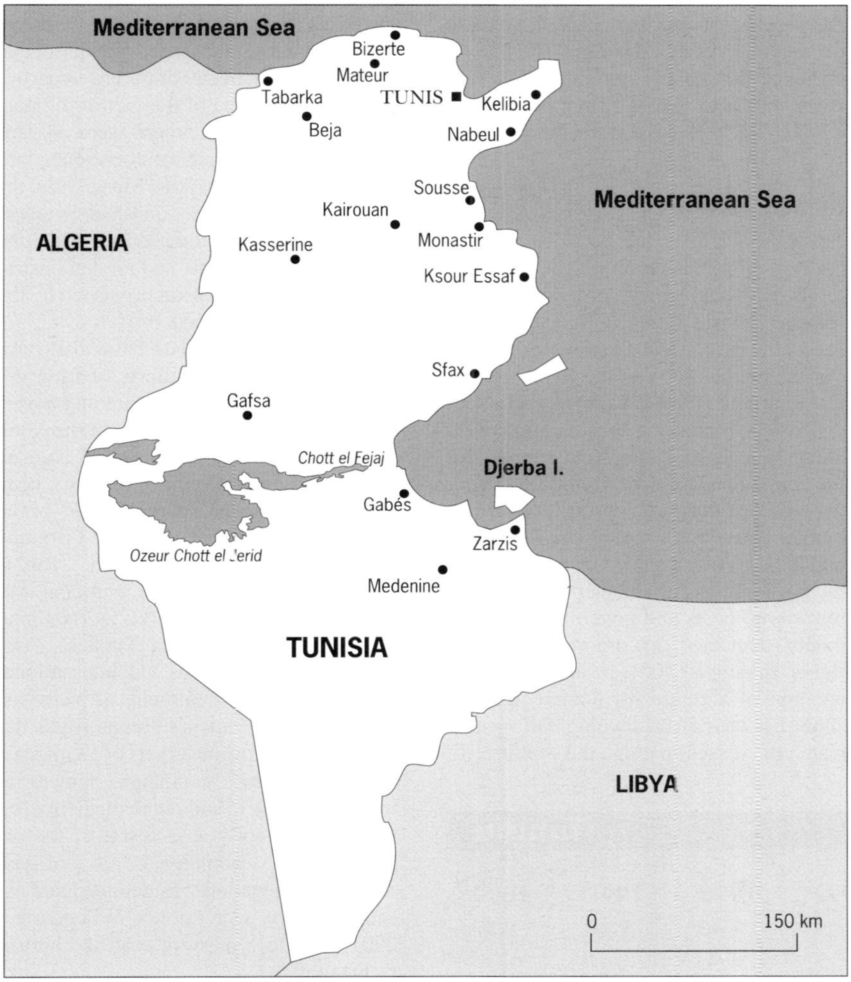

Tunisia's reputation as a stable and relatively prosperous country is tarnished by President Zine Al-Abidine Ben Ali's repressive leadership style. The global 'war on terrorism' discourse, which grew out of the 11 September 2001 attacks in the US, has enabled Ben Ali to brand his opponents as 'terrorists'. His allegations were strengthened by an Al-Qaeda attack on a synagogue in Djerba in April 2002 which killed 19 people, 15 of whom were European tourists. This has given the authorities the excuse to try political opponents in military, rather than civilian, courts which have consistently denied defendants the right to a fair trial. The move led to heightened repression in 2002, following a year which saw dozens of leading opponents rounded up and incarcerated. However, the international community has turned a blind eye to the government's excesses, since Ben Ali has successfully pioneered free market reform and positioned Tunisia as a bridge between the West and Islamist regimes in the Middle East.

Fourth term lucky

Tunisia's politics are dominated by the personality of Ben Ali, with the few legal

KEY FACTS

Official name: Jumhuriya At-Tunisiya (The Tunisian Republic)

Head of State: President Zine Al-Abidine Ben Ali (RCD) (since 1987; elected to a third and final five-year term Oct 1999) (May 2002 referendum: over 99 per cent voted to abolish the three-term limit for incumbent presidents and to raise the age limit to 75)

Head of government: Prime Minister Mohammed Ghannouchi (appointed Nov 1999)

Ruling party: Rassemblement Constitutionnel Démocratique (RCD) (Democratic Constitutional Rally) (re-elected Oct 1999)

Area: 164,150 square km

Population: 9.70 million (2001)

Capital: Tunis

Official language: Arabic

Currency: Dinar (D) = 1,000 millimes

Exchange rate: D1.32 per US$ (Jan 2003)

GDP per capita: US$2,064 (2001); US$1,182 (2002)*

GDP real growth: 5.00% (2001); 3.8% (2002)*

Labour force: 3.30 million (2001)*

Unemployment: 15.00% (2001); 15.2% (2002)*

Inflation: 1.90% (2001); 2.3% (2002)*

Oil production: 73,000 bpd (2001)

Balance of trade: -US$2.92 billion (2001)

Foreign debt: US$10.45 billion (2001)

* estimated figure

For the latest Key Facts, go to www.worldinformation.com

opposition parties in the National Assembly afraid to voice too many objections to his rule. A number of opposition parties have been banned by the government in recent years and there is a virtual media black-out on criticism of the President. Consequently, civil society has been marginalised, gagged and unable to organise any meaningful opposition to the regime.

Ben Ali is keen to cling to power at whatever cost. In the 1999 presidential elections, he won an overwhelming victory with almost 99 per cent of the vote, giving him a third term in office. However, the constitution barred him from seeking a fourth term in office. Instead of stepping down and allowing a new leader to emerge from the ranks of the ruling Rassemblement Constitutionnel Démocratique (RCD) (Democratic Constitutional Rally), Ben Ali decided to propose a change to the constitution to enable him to contest the 2004 presidential elections. The President proposed an the amendment to the constitution which was ratified in a referendum in May 2002. With most civic organisations in his clutches, Ben Ali knows it would be hard for his opponents to organise effectively to challenge him in 2004. The trade union movement, the mainstream media and the official opposition have rallied behind Ben Ali, thereby starving grass roots opposition of the oxygen of publicity. The rump of opponents who remain defiantly outspoken face arrest and imprisonment.

In June 2001, Mohammed Al-Mouadda, former leader of the opposition Mouvement des Démocrates Socialistes (MDS) (Movement of Democratic Socialists), was arrested and imprisoned for 11 years after he entered into a pact with the Islamic group Al-Nahda (Renaissance) to form a 'patriotic and democratic front based on the defence of public freedoms', which would oppose Ben Ali's candidacy in the 2004 elections. The 63-year-old was pardoned by the president in March 2002 following a hunger strike, but pledged to continue his battle to establish a more democratic system. Hamma Hammami, leader of the banned Communist Workers' Party, was also released from jail in September 2002 due to ill health, but vowed to continue his struggle.

Human wrongs

Throughout 2001, the president was at pains to stress his commitment to human rights and democracy, proclaiming that 'democracy and pluralism for me are an irreversible choice and an unavoidable process ... We believe that the foundation of the Republic relies on the protection of different opinions, the consolidation of dialogue and participation and support for the components of civil society to honour the rights of minority views'. The official human rights bureaucracy has flourished under Ben Ali's regime. In recent years, the president has established a plethora of ministerial posts and government departments dedicated to promoting human rights. In August 2001, he announced the creation of a centre for human rights to show he was 'strengthening the mechanism of disseminating the culture of human rights by providing necessary documentation services in this area'.

These efforts to promote Tunisia as a show-case for human rights in the Middle East are in stark contrast to the reality faced by those who attract the president's ire. Before Ben Ali seized power in a bloodless coup in 1987 against the ailing president, Habib Bourguiba, repression was targetted at Islamic groups. Since he has been in power, left-wing activists, trade unionists, the independent media, students and members of outlawed parties have become some of the victims of state repression. By 2001, there were an estimated 1,000 prisoners of conscience languishing in Tunisian jails. Meanwhile, the mainstream media has quashed criticism of the government, taking Ben Ali's line on almost every issue, and all demonstrations and mass rallies not organised by the government are banned.

Human rights activists have also been routinely arrested and imprisoned for 'defaming the Republic', 'threatening sovereignty' and 'spreading false information liable to disturb the public order'. Numerous human rights organisations have been effectively banned, including the Ligue Tunisienne des Droits de l'Homme (LTDH) (Tunisian Human Rights League) and the Conseil National des Libertés en Tunisie (CNLT) (National Council for Liberties in Tunisia). Amnesty International has led international criticism of the treatment of activists, claiming that 'Tunisia's human rights defenders are the prime targets of an increasingly relentless campaign aimed at intimidating them and reducing them to silence'. Apparently as a result of the organisation's campaign, an official Amnesty delegation was detained and assaulted by the secret police in September 2001 prior to a meeting with the human rights minister.

The overwhelming use of state oppression was denounced by Judge Mokhtar Yahiaoui in an open letter sent to Ben Ali in July 2001. In it, Yahiaoui alleged that judges 'render verdicts dictated to them by political authorities and enjoy no discretion to exercise any objectivity or critical scrutiny'. He was dismissed by a disciplinary council in December 2001 after he was accused of undermining the reputation of the judiciary, breaking his professional duty and breaching confidentiality. His remarks echoed those made by CNLT spokesperson Sihem Ben Sedrine on *Al-Mustakilla*, a London-based television channel, in June 2001. She was later arrested for 'defaming' the country and for

KEY INDICATORS — Tunisia

	Unit	1996	1997	1998	1999	2000
Population	m	9.09	9.21	9.33	9.46	9.57
Gross domestic product (GDP)	US$bn	19.60	18.94	19.80	20.90	19.58
GDP per capita	US$	2,155	2,052	2,127	2,214	2,046
GDP real growth	%	7.1	5.4	4.8	6.2	4.7
Inflation	%	3.7	3.7	3.2	2.7	2.9
Unemployment	%	15.5	15.4	15.2	15.3	15.3
Oil output	'000 bpd	90.0	80.0	85.0	85.0	80.0
Exports (fob) (goods)	US$m	5,519.0	5,559.0	5,724.0	5,873.0	5,840.0
Imports (fob) (goods)	US$m	7,280.0	7,514.0	7,875.0	8,014.0	8,092.0
Balance of trade	US$m	-1,761.0	-1,955.0	-2,152.0	-2,141.0	-2,252.0
Current account	US$m	-478.0	-595.0	-735.0	-503.0	-821.0
Foreign debt	US$bn	9.6	10.6	11.1	11.8	10.6
Total reserves minus gold	US$m	1,897.6	1,978.1	1,850.1	2,261.5	1,811.0
Foreign exchange	US$m	1,881.7	1,961.0	1,847.1	2,207.0	1,780.9
Exchange rate	per US$	0.97	1.11	1.14	1.19	1.37

criticising the judiciary for unfair treatment of political dissidents and the increasing use of military tribunals.

Tough decisions ahead

Regardless of the government's widespread use of repression, Tunisia continues to enjoy strong levels of growth. The success of the country's continued economic transformation was highlighted in a report published by the University of Tunis in 2001, which claimed that Tunisia had become a regional leader in economic development and that labour productivity was 35 per cent higher than the Maghreb average. Moreover, GDP per capita is 22 per cent higher than the regional average. However, there are wide income disparities, with a Gini index (the standard measure of income distribution) of 41.7 compared to lower levels of 35.3 in Algeria and 39.5 in Morocco. Official unemployment is over 15 per cent – actual unemployment is probably far higher – and a quarter of the rural population lives below the national poverty line.

Recurrent droughts and a contraction in the agricultural sector saw GDP growth fall from 4.7 per cent in 2000 to 4.0 per cent in 2001. However, the economy was buoyed by an influx of foreign investment, helped by the privatisation of over 40 state-owned companies, and a rise in tourism receipts related to the Mediterranean Games, which Tunisia hosted in September 2001. In 2001, inward investment exceeded US$1 billion for the first time, 85 per cent of which came from France, Italy and Germany. US investment represented just 2 per cent of the total, while Asian firms contributed less than 1 per cent.

Manufacturing growth was robust in 2001, led by continuing export growth which was largely immune from the effects of the global slowdown and a poor level of demand in the EU, Tunisia's main trading partner. Tunisia maintained its competitiveness with the depreciation of the dinar, which helped accelerate export growth. However, strong domestic demand ensured a growth in imports, leading to an increase in the current account deficit beyond the 4 per cent of GDP target and putting pressure on the country's foreign reserves. Despite this, external debt fell from 57 per cent of GDP in 2000 to 50 per cent in 2001 and, in the same period, the debt service to export ratio fell from 22.4 per cent to 15.0 per cent.

Strong growth and an increase in receipts from import tariffs saw tax revenue exceed budget estimates, enabling a reduction of the fiscal deficit to 2.3 per cent of GDP, which was below the government target of 2.9 per cent. A combination of tight fiscal policy and a more restrictive monetary policy in 2001 saw consumer price inflation drop below the 3 per cent target, while liquidity levels remained within government targets. The inflationary effects of depreciation were largely offset by a reduction in the rate of import tariffs which helped stabilise import prices.

Outlook

Growth may be curtailed by an expected fall in tourism receipts in 2002 as tourists will be mindful of the growing turbulence in the Middle East, even though Tunisia remains unaffected by terrorism. The 2002 budget aims to limit the deficit to 2.2 per cent of GDP, thereby helping to maintain a stable economy with low inflation and falling levels of external debt.

The government has a lot of work to do to meet its targets in the long-term. In order to reduce the fiscal deficit further, the government is faced with some hard choices over spending. There is considerable room for expenditure cuts, but these may conflict with the institutional interests that support Ben Ali. The large bureaucracy is resistant to deep personnel cuts and uneasy over further privatisation of key sectors, making cuts in the wage bill hard to achieve. On top of this, growing disenchantment with the government's economic liberalisation has the potential to bolster the political opposition, which has been forced underground by the Ben Ali regime. While this is not expected to foment any revolution, it could pose a significant challenge to Ben Ali if he contests the 2004 presidential elections.

The IMF has suggested a reduction in food subsidies, which soak up around a quarter of state revenue. However, this is politically contentious and could lead to widespread social unrest as seen in 2000, when the government last attempted to increase food prices. The cost of social security will also have to be tackled, particularly as the social security surplus is expected to be wiped out by end-2002 and funds in the private sector are likely to be in deficit by 2010. Although the IMF has criticised the rising cost of public sector pensions as a cause of the growing deficit, these costs are primarily associated with an increase in early retirement packages in an effort to reduce the burden of the public sector wage bill, which represented more than a third of government expenditure in 2001. Consequently, wage costs are being reduced while the pension burden is rising. As a result of increasing dependency and associated costs, the government is likely to consider an increase in social security contributions in 2002.

Another task facing the government is the reduction of import tariffs, which are scheduled to fall under the country's EU Association Agreement (EUAA), in which all customs barriers to EU imports have to be dismantled by 2010. In order to maintain government finances, the burden of taxation will have to be shifted, possibly to direct taxation such as income and corporate taxes. However, the government expects the country to reap the rewards of improved access to EU markets, which currently absorb around 80 per cent of Tunisian exports. This could potentially increase export growth further and stimulate the economy, ultimately leading to increased tax revenue.

Risk assessment

Economic	Good
Political	Good
Regional stability	Good

COUNTRY PROFILE

Historical profile

In the seventh century BC, after the Phoenician's defeat of the Assyrians, Carthage became the leading Phoenician city. The city-state of Carthage ruled the area of modern day Tunisia during the third century BC. During the following centuries Carthage was conquered by the Romans, the Vandals and the Byzantines.

670 The Arabs conquered Carthage.

1207–1574 After the Arab empire collapsed, Tunisia became part of the Moroccan empire of the Almohads before emerging as the independent Hafsid empire.

The Hafsids were defeated by the Ottomans who developed a system of rule by a local elite descended from the Turks, the Huseinid beys.

By the eighteenth century, Tunisia had become a national monarchy.

1881 France invaded from Algeria.

1883 Tunisia was declared a French protectorate.

1930s The Néo-Destour nationalist movement developed under Habib Bourguiba, who was jailed by the French.

1956 Tunisia gained independence from France under the leadership of Bourguiba.

1957 The Republic of Tunisia was declared.

1963 Evacuation of Bizerte. The last foreign soldier left Tunisia.

1987 On 7 November, in conformation with the constitution, Prime Minister Zine Al-Abidine Ben Ali succeeded President Bourguiba, who was declared by his

physicians unable to continue assuming the duties of the office.
1989 President Ben Ali won presidential elections in April.
1994 Ben Ali won a second term in office in the March elections.
1999 The first multi-party presidential elections were held in October, in which Ben Ali won over 90 per cent of the vote and entered a third and final five-year term as president.
2000 The ruling party won 94 per cent of the seats in municipal elections held in May.
2001 A number of high profile dissidents were arrested, including Mohamed Al-Mouadda, former leader of the opposition Mouvement des Démocrates Socialistes (MDS) (Movement of Democratic Socialists), who had formed a pact with the banned Islamist group Al-Nahda.
2002 Preliminary results of the May referendum: more than 99 per cent voted to abolish the three-term limit for incumbent presidents and to raise the age limit of a sitting president from 70 to 75.

Political structure

Constitution

The constitution was promulgated in 1959.
Parties must be officially recognised before they may contest elections.
An electoral law was passed in 1999 and guaranteed legal opposition parties a minimum of 34 seats in the unicameral parliament, compared to 19 in the previous parliament.

Form of state

Multi-party presidential republic.

The executive

Executive power is held by the president, elected by universal suffrage for a five-year term. The president appoints the prime minister and the Council of Ministers.
The head of state presides over the Council of Ministers. Should the Council of Ministers not receive the support of the National Assembly, it may be dissolved by the president and elections for a new Assembly held.

National legislature

Legislative power is vested in the 182-member unicameral National Assembly, elected for a five-year term, by universal adult suffrage.

Last elections

October 1999 (presidential and parliamentary)

Next elections

October 2004 (presidential and parliamentary)

Political parties

Ruling party

Rassemblement Constitutionnel Démocratique (RCD) (Democratic Constitutional Rally) (re-elected Oct 1999)

Main opposition party

Mouvement des Démocrates Socialistes (MDS) (Movement of Democratic Socialists)

Population

9.57 million (2000)
Annual population growth rate: 1.4 per cent (1994–2000). It is forecast to increase 1.2 per cent per annum between 1998 and 2015. About 34 per cent of the population is under 14 years; 61 per cent 15–64; 5 per cent over 65. Approximately 8 per cent of the population lives below the national poverty line.
Population density: 60 inhabitants per square km. Urban population: 66 per cent (1994–2000).

Ethnic make-up

Arab-Berber (98 per cent), European (1 per cent), Jewish (1 per cent).

Religions

Islam is the state religion – observance is strong (98 per cent); Christianity (1 per cent); Jewish (1 per cent).

Education

Education is free in Tunisia up to university level – the government typically spends as much as 20 per cent of its revenues on an extensive education system. Primary education begins at the age of six and lasts for six years. Secondary education begins at 12 and lasts seven years. Registration at primary schools is 95 per cent (100 per cent of boys and 89 per cent of girls) – the highest in north Africa and the Middle East. A compulsory schooling period of nine years has been introduced, although some children still leave school at the age of 12, especially in rural areas. A stronger emphasis has been placed on scientific and technical subjects at secondary level.

Health

Life expectancy: 73 years (1994–2000). Infant mortality rate: 24 per 1,000 live births (1994–2000). Around 9 per cent of children under five years suffer from malnutrition.
State health care is provided free of charge to the families of employees paying social security contributions and at least nominal tax. This covers an estimated 70 per cent of the population. Free state healthcare is also available for those with any kind of disability. The discrepancy between urban and rural access to healthcare diminished during the 1990s, with most rural areas having at least basic health clinics.
There is a well-developed private healthcare sector, with private clinics in towns providing substantially better facilities than state hospitals. Many healthcare professionals have carried out at least part of their training abroad, mostly in France.

Welfare

The social security system provides pensions for the elderly and disabled, and welfare for orphans and the needy. A total of 945,500 employees, or 47.7 per cent of the workforce, are insured under the social security system. The scheme is financed by compulsory levies from employers and employees. There are no contributions from the state budget. The main social security institution is the Caisse Nationale de la Sécurité Sociale (CNSS), which deals with about 45 per cent of outlay.
There is a graded scheme for contributions. The non-agricultural private sector pays most as a proportion of the employee's salary: 11.5 per cent paid by the employer and 6.25 per cent by the employee. In the public sector, where contributions are made to the Caisse Nationale de Retraite de la Prevoyance Sociale (CNRPS), the employer pays 8 per cent and the employee 7 per cent. State pensions are paid to CNSS and CNRPS contributors.

Main cities

Tunis (capital, estimated population 1.6 million), Sfax (230,900), Ariana (152,700), Ettadhamen (149,200), Sousse (125,000), Kairouan (102,600), Gabes (98,900), Bizerta (98,900), Bardo (72,700), Gafsa (71,100).

Languages spoken

Arabic and French are widely spoken. The number of Tunisians speaking English is increasing. French is the business language.

Official language

Arabic

Media

Tunis Afrique Press (TAP) is the official news agency and publishes in Arabic, French and English.

Press

The 1959 constitution guarantees freedom of expression, but the Press Code gives the government wide-ranging powers to ban publications. All opposition party publications have been suspended for varying periods under this code. However, there is no specific information ministry. The Press Code requires that publishers disclose their sources of funding, annual accounts and circulation figures. No group is allowed to control more than 30 per cent of total circulation. All imported publications must be submitted to government censors.
There are several independent newspapers and magazines, including two opposition party journals. The government relies upon direct and indirect methods to restrict press freedom and encourage a high degree of self-censorship. The

government uses the mandatory pre-screening of the print media and controls the advertising revenue to censor 'unacceptable' publications. This includes editions of foreign newspapers.

Dailies: National dailies in French include *Le Renouveau*, *La Presse*, *Le Temps* and (in Arabic) *As Sabah*, *Al-Nahda*, *Al Hurria*, *As-Sahafa* and *Ash-Shourouk*. *Al-Hurria* is the daily newspaper of the ruling party, RCD, while *As-Sabah* is financially independent and supports the opposition RSP. *Le Temps* is financially independent, unlike the RCD's *Le Renouveau*. International and foreign newspapers are available one day after publication in urban centres, although some issues may be withheld from public sale.

Weeklies: The main French-language weeklies are *Réalités*, *L'Observateur*, and *Tunis-Hebdo*. The main Arabic-language weekly is *Ar-Rai*. The weekly party publications are the Arabic-language *Al-Moustaqbal* and French-language *L'Avenir*, both belonging to the MDS. Others are *Dialogue*, *Al-Tariq Al-Jadid* (New Path) and *Al-Mauqif* . *Tunisia News* is the first English language weekly in the Maghreb, published on Saturdays.

Business: Economic information is available in the *Conjoncture Review*, edited monthly by the Ministry of Economic Affairs, and *L'Economiste Maghrebin* is published bi-monthly.

Periodicals: There are also over 140 periodicals and provincial newspapers which are published (91 in Arabic, 45 in French, six in Arabic and French and one in Italian). Another 450 foreign periodicals are also distributed.

Broadcasting

Radio: The national radio station broadcasts in Arabic, while the international station broadcasts mainly in French, with some programmes in Italian, English and German. There are two regional stations at Sfax and Monastir.

Television: The government-run Radiodiffusion Télévision Tunisienne, established in 1956, operates two television channels and four radio stations. Channel 1 television broadcasts in Arabic. Channel 2, established in 1983, broadcasts in French. Around 75 per cent of Channel 2's programmes are imported from France. The French network Antenne 2 broadcasts in Tunisia on Channel 2 for several hours per day. There are no commercial broadcasting stations.

Viewers in Tunis have long been able to receive television broadcasts from Rai, the Italian state company, which is considering extending coverage to other regions. Satellite television is becoming increasingly popular, with many households in the major towns having satellite dishes. Most hotels offer satellite television.

Advertising

Direct mail, outdoor and vehicle advertising, sponsorship of sporting events and print media offer opportunities for advertisers. Help is available from local marketing and media consultants, who can advise on the political acceptability of different aspects of an advertising campaign. References to religion are not acceptable. Press advertising tends to be governed by unwritten standards, determined by the publications' editorial policy. Foreign broadcast advertising is even more strictly regulated and advertising rates in the broadcast media are highly discriminatory, standing at three or four times rates for domestic advertisers.

Urban centres in Tunisia are thought to have a marketing profile similar to that of Europe.

Economy

Tunisia's economic growth is based on oil and gas, the development of the textile industry and the development of the tourism industry. The government is oriented toward a free market policy through reducing fiscal deficits, liberalising prices, trade and investment controls and decreasing the emphasis on the public sector to free up resources for the private sector.

Between 1995–2000, GDP growth averaged 5.2 per cent and although job creation was strong, unemployment remains at around 15 per cent. Adjustment and stabilisation programmes have helped to reduce the fiscal deficit and inflation.

The agricultural sector, in which official data include output from fisheries, constitutes less than 14 per cent of GDP, compared to 29 per cent for industry, of which manufacturing makes up 18 per cent. However, agriculture can still have a significant bearing on the economy. Mining makes up approximately 3 per cent of GDP. The remainder of the economy is made up by services which were opened to foreign competition in 2001. Tourism, traditionally the country's second-largest foreign exchange earner, is prominent in the service sector, typically contributing some 10 per cent of GDP. Remittances from over 600,000 Tunisians living abroad constitute a further important source of foreign exchange.

External trade

Tunisia has always run up a trade deficit, which is partly offset by earnings from tourism and remittances by emigrants. Tunisia belongs to the Arab Maghreb Union (AMU) with Algeria, Libya, Morocco and Mauritania. An EU agreement signed in July 1995, implemented from 1996, aims to create a non-agricultural free trade zone by 2008. In 1998, an EU Association Agreement (EUAA) with Tunisia came into force in 1998 and envisages a free trade area between the EU and Tunisia by 2010.

Exports

Textiles, mechanical goods, phosphates and chemicals, agricultural products, hydrocarbons.

Main destinations: France (26.3 per cent of 2000 total), Italy (22.5 per cent), Germany (12.3 per cent), Spain (5.3 per cent), Belgium (5 per cent).

Imports

Machinery and equipment, hydrocarbons, chemicals, food.

Main sources: France (26.6 per cent of 2000 total), Italy (19.1 per cent), Germany (9.5 per cent), US (4.6 per cent), Spain (4 per cent).

Agriculture

The agricultural sector employs approximately 30 per cent of the workforce. Around 30 per cent of the total land area is cultivable and only 3 per cent of arable land is irrigated. The main crops are wheat, barley, maize, sorghum, olives, dates and citrus fruit.

Imports of food and feedstock have shot up in recent years and now meet 40 per cent of domestic requirements. Rural depopulation, an inequitable land tenure system, soil erosion, over-grazing and low producer prices remain the major constraints to development. Moreover, Tunisia is losing at least 1 per cent of its forest annually through over-grazing by livestock and uncontrolled cutting for fuel. Water resource management also remains one of Tunisia's greatest challenges.

The 55 million olive trees occupy one third of all arable land and olive oil is Tunisia's most important agricultural export. Most seafood production is for domestic consumption and the sector is relatively undeveloped.

Industry and manufacturing

The industrial sector is based primarily on processing domestic raw materials, notably phosphates and agricultural commodities, and textiles, including clothing and leather products. An industrial restructuring programme launched in the mid-1990s has seen US$1 billion invested by the government in upgrading businesses' competitiveness, in preparation for the liberalisation of markets and European competition. The present strategy is to target specific types of products where relatively cheap labour, proximity to Europe and government incentives can combine to give Tunisia a price and quality advantage over other exporters. The programme has been particularly successful among small- and medium-sized enterprises (SMEs).

Tourism

The tourism sector accounts for around 10 per cent of GDP. One of the country's highest net earners of foreign exchange, it has been an increasingly important source of employment. Over 80 per cent of visitors come from EU countries.

During the 1990s, income from tourism more than doubled, although the sector may have grown too quickly. Capacity has doubled to 140,000 beds since 1980 and new hotels under construction and building permits saw that figure rise to 200,000 by the end of 2001. Prices have fallen sharply, to as low as US$20 per night for a five-star hotel room, raising doubts as to the viability of government plans for the sector.

Cheap intercontinental air fares have affected Tunisia's tourism revenue and some hotels are experiencing below 50 per cent occupancy.

Mining

The mining sector contributes 10 per cent of GDP and employs 4 per cent of the working population. Tunisia is the world's fifth-largest source of phosphates although the quality of the rock mined is poor. Extraction (largely in Metlaoui and Gafsa) is geared increasingly towards local phosphate processing rather than exporting it in a raw state. Other important minerals mined include iron ore, salt, fluorspar, barytes, lead and zinc (Bougrine in the north-west), potash and uranium. Foreign investment is being sought by the government for the mining industry.

Hydrocarbons

Oil

Oil was first discovered in the 1960s at Al-Borma in the far south and this remains by far the largest oil and gas field. The Al-Borma, Ashtart and Tazarka fields provide around 90 per cent of total oil output. The smaller Al-Baban field produces 5,000 barrels per day (bpd).

Total reserves stood at 300 million barrels in 2001; at current production levels these would last until 2013. Oil reserves are dwindling and by 2001, production had fallen rapidly from 110,000bpd to 82,000bpd. However, investment of US$400 million between 2000–02 is directed at boosting oil production and the government has awarded over 40 exploration permits to 25 companies. A number of other smaller fields, including the Al-Baban field, allowed a temporary reversal in the downward trend in 1998, when overall sectoral production rose by 3 per cent.

Al-Borma, the largest field, is operated by Société Italo-Tunisienne d'Exploitation Pétrolière (SITEP), a 50:50 joint venture between the Tunisian state oil company Entreprise Tunisienne des Activités Pétrolières (ETAP) and the Italian company Agip. The Ashtart field is operated by Société d'Exploitation et de Recherches Pétrolières en Tunisie (SEREPT), a similar joint venture between ETAP and the French company Elf Aquitaine, and the Tazarka field by ETAP, Shell and Agip. Because of the limited capacity at the only oil refinery in the northern town of Bizerte, Tunisia exports most of its crude oil and imports refined products.

Gas

To replace declining oil reserves, the government is promoting the natural gas sector; local production typically meets 80 per cent of domestic demand. The government receives gas in payment of transit fees by Algeria for the Trans-Mediterranean pipeline, which carries Algerian gas via Tunisia to Italy, and also buys gas from the pipeline. A national gas distribution network now encompasses just under 800km of pipeline.

The Miskar field near the town of Sfax, developed by British Gas, came on stream in the mid-1990s. The field, which is 120km offshore in the Gulf of Gabes, was discovered in the 1970s and has proven reserves of 169 billion cubic metres. The US$650 million project includes a gas processing plant and eight wells, as well as pipelines linking the towns of Msaken and Gabes to Miskar.

The government hopes to become self-sufficient in gas. It is hoped that production from the Miskar field will be augmented by reserves that exist at the Hasdrabul-3 field, 110km offshore from Tunisia's east coast. The field began production in 2000.

Energy

The state-owned electricity and gas company, Société Tunisienne de l'Electricité et du Gaz (STEG) monopoly on power generation has been scrapped, although the company retains its monopoly on distribution.

Emphasis is on expanding electricity production and distribution, and stepping up the oil and gas exploration programme. Demand for electricity is growing by 7 per cent per annum and around 95 per cent of homes have access to electricity. The government intends to add around 300MW of generating capacity every two to three years.

General Electric is to build a US$80 million, 240MW gas power station at Bir M'Cherga, bringing the STEG's capacity to 1,810MW, produced by five power stations (three gas and two thermal power). Tunisia's first build-own-operate-transfer (BOOT) generation contract was granted in 1997 to the US company, Community Energy Alternatives. A US$300 million 500MW plant will be constructed at Radés, near Tunis. Concession and financial contracts were signed in 1999. The final consortium involved included the Japanese company Marubeni. The plant came on-line in early 2002.

Libya and Tunisia agreed to work on linking their grids after a meeting of Arab energy ministers in April 2001.

Financial markets

Stock exchange

The Tunis Bourse became privately owned in 1995 and started trading on 20 November 1995. Legislation introduced in 1997 allows foreign investors to buy up to 49.9 per cent of the capital of enterprises on sale through the Bourse without authorisation and the remaining half with official approval. In 1998 the Bourse started operating a capitalisation-weighted index, which has gradually replaced the all-share average.

Despite increased investor interest, the Tunisian capital market is still mainly a retail market, with little activity from local financial institutions. While the number of stocks listed remains relatively few and in the absence of a secondary market, the stock exchange cannot become a major vehicle for raising capital.

Banking

Tunisia aims to become the regional financial centre and is keen to build on its status as the biggest African borrower with investment grade status. However, the banking sector is over-crowded, plagued by bad debts and dominated by the public sector.

The government is determined to rationalise the sector in advance of its anticipated full liberalisation by 2004, as stipulated by the World Trade Organisation (WTO) and EU agreements with Tunisia. With this in mind, the government engaged in a modernisation programme, including the privatisation and mergers. Consolidation in the sector meant that by 2001, there were 13 banks, eight development banks, eight offshore banks, two merchant banks and eight leasing institutions in Tunisia. The capital base of many banks has improved with the injection of government funds into state-owned banks and the restructuring of non-performing loans.

Offshore banking has developed rapidly since legislation was passed which aimed to attract banks leaving Beirut. Offshore banks are allowed to open savings accounts for residents, which may not exceed 1.5 per cent of their total deposits, and to participate in financing domestic projects. Offshore banks include Citibank, Union Tunisienne des Banques, Tunis International Bank, Loan and Investment Co (Link), Beit Ettamouil Saudi Tounsi (BEST), North African International Bank (NAIB), Tunis Arab African Bank (TAAB) and Al-Ubaf International Bank.

Those banks part-owned by foreign banks are the most highly rated in the sector.

These include Union Bancaire pour le Commerce et l'Industrie (UBCI), which is 50 per cent owned by French bank Banque Nationale de Paris Intercontinentale, and BIAT, which is 64 per cent owned by Amman-based Arab Bank.

Central bank

Banque Centrale de Tunisie

Main financial centre

Tunis

Time

GMT plus one hour

Geography

Tunisia is in North Africa, bordered by Algeria to the west and by Libya to the south-east. To the north and east, Tunisia has a coastline on the Mediterranean Sea.

Climate

Northern coastal area has Mediterranean climate with warm, rainy winters (December–March) and hot summers. Southern and inland area is hot and arid. Temperature in Tunis ranges from 6–14 degrees Celsius (C) in January to 21–33 degrees C in August. The wettest month is January and the driest is July.

Dress codes

Formal attire should be worn for business meetings. Women should wear clothes that cover most of the body, including shoulders and legs. However, beach wear can be worn at tourist resorts. In the countryside, western dress and customs are rare and dress should be modest.

Entry requirements

Passports

Required by all

Visa

Not required for UK citizens and most other western European citizens (exceptions Belgium, Luxembourg, Netherlands), US, Japan, Hong Kong citizens, and most Arab countries, for visits of less than 90 days.

Currency advice/regulations

Import/export of local currency is prohibited. No restrictions on amount of foreign currency which can be imported, although amounts over D1,000 should be declared to enable re-export. Note that reconversion of dinars into foreign exchange is limited to 30 per cent of any foreign currency previously converted, or D100, whichever is the greater. All currency forms should be retained.

Customs

Visitors may bring in one litre of spirits, two litres of wine, 400 cigarettes (or 100 cigars), a quarter litre of perfume, and one litre of eau de toilette, gifts to the value of D100.

Prohibited imports

Arms (except for hunting), explosives, drugs and all narcotic products, immoral or obscene illustrations and publications, forged books, walkie-talkies.

Health (for visitors)

Mandatory precautions

Yellow fever vaccination certificate required if arriving from an infected area.

Advisable precautions

Immunisation is recommended against diphtheria, hepatitis, polio, tetanus and typhoid. Rabies is present.

Hotels

In general hotels are cheap and easy to find. Classified into five categories. Government hotel tax added to bill. Hotel and restaurant staff expect 10 per cent tip.

Public holidays

Fixed dates

1 Jan (New Year's Day), 20 Mar (Independence Day), 21 Mar (Youth Day), 9 Apr (Martyrs' Day), 1 May (Labour Day), 25 Jul (Republic Day), 13 Aug (Women's Day), 7 Nov (Accession of President Ben Ali).

Variable dates

Aid El-Seghir (2 days, Eid Al-Fitr), Aid El-Kebir (2 days, Eid Al-Adha), Hejri (New Year's Day), Mouled (Prophet's Birthday).

Working hours

The weekly day of rest is Sunday, not Friday as is usual in the Muslim world. Tunis is virtually closed down during August.

Banking

Mon–Thu: 0800–1100, 1400–1600; Fri: 0800–1100, 1300–1530; mornings only in summer.

Business

Mon–Thu: 0800–1230, 1430–1800; (Fri–Sat) 0800–1200 in winter. Mon–Sat: 0700–1300 in summer.

Government

Mon–Thu: 0830–1300, 1500–1745; (Fri–Sat) 0830–1330; mornings only in summer.

Shops

There are no standard opening hours although the bigger department stores are usually open 0830–1200 and 1500–1800 in winter and 0800–1200 and 1600–1900 in summer.

Telecommunications

Telephone/fax

Internal automatic service covers nearly all of the country. The IDD access code from Tunisia is 00.

Postal services

The *Rapide Poste* office at Tunis-Carthage airport handles express postal services. Telegrams can be sent 24 hours a day from the Central Post Office.

Courier services

No commercial courier firms are allowed to operate.

Mobile phones

In addition to an older analogue service, the national telecommunications company operates Tunicell, a 900 megahertz GSM network.

Internet/e-mail

There are a number of Internet service providers. Tunisia enjoys an ISDN link with Germany.

Electricity supply

220V AC in tourist resorts

Social customs/useful tips

The legacy of French rule is considerable in the towns and a rather formal attitude to courtesy prevails. Senior government or company officials should be addressed as Monsieur and government ministers as Monsieur le Ministre.

Hospitality is important. It is appropriate to present a small gift in appreciation of hospitality.

Alcohol is freely available in towns, although less common in rural areas.

Hotel and restaurant staff usually receive a 10 per cent tip.

Getting there

Air

National airline: Tunisair.

Main airport: Tunis-Carthage (TUN), 8km from the city.

Airport tax: There is no airport departure tax.

Surface

Road: Access is by road from Algeria and Libya.

Rail: Access by rail from Algeria.

Main ports: Tunisia has six major ports, Tunis-La Goulette, Sfax, Bizerte, Gabes, Sousse and Zarzis. The largest are Tunis-Goulette and Sfax. There is also a special petroleum port at La Skhirra.

Passenger traffic comes mostly to Tunis-La Goulette.

Regular shipping services operate to Tunis from France, Italy and Malta.

Getting about

National transport

Air: Tuninter operates regular domestic services. The air taxi company, Tunisavia, also operates weekly flights to Sfax and some other towns.

Road: The road network extends for around 19,000km, of which main or national roads account for 10,800km. About 57 per cent of the network is paved. There is a 143km motorway between Tunis and Sousse.

Buses: The Société Nationale de Transports operates local buses on 153 routes.

Rail: A 2,200km network links the main towns.

Water: There are regular ferries from Sfaz-Iles Kerkenna and Jorf-Djerba island.

City transport

Taxis: Taxis are available in all main towns and are fairly easy to obtain. In louage taxis, the fare is shared by several passengers. Taxis are metered but be aware that some drivers will multiply the fare. Journey time is 15–20 minutes from airport to city centre.

Buses/trams: SNT service 35 and TUT service run every 30 minutes from airport to city centre, journey time 30 minutes.

Car hire

Cars are easy to hire at principal airports and hotels but are expensive and the condition of the cars vary. International or national driving licence required. Traffic drives on the right.

BUSINESS DIRECTORY

Telephone area codes

The international direct dialling (IDD) code for Tunisia is +216. From November 2001, '7' should be dialled before all area codes:

Bizerte	2	Monastir	3
Cathage	1	Sfax	4
Gabes	5	Sousse	3
Hammamet	2	Tunis	1
Marsa	1		

NB When using mobile phones, '8' (not '7') should be dialled before area codes.

Chambers of Commerce

Chambre de Commerce et d'Industrie du Centre, Rue Chedli Khaznadar, 4000 Sousse (tel: 225-044; fax: 224-227).

Chambre de Commerce et d'Industrie du Nord, 46 Rue Ibn Khaldoun, 7000 Bizerte (tel: 431-044, 432-445; fax: 439-033).

Chambre de Commerce et d'Industrie du Sud, 127 Rue Haffouz, 3000 Sfax (tel: 296-120; fax: 296-121).

Chambre de Commerce de Tunis, 1 Rue des Entrepreneurs, 1000 Tunis (tel: 242-810; fax: 354-744).

Banking

Alubaf International Bank – Tunis, PO Box 51, Rue 8007 Montplaisir, 1002 Tunis (tel: 783500 fax: 793905, 784343)

Amen Bank, Avenue Mohamed V, 1002 Tunis (tel: 340511 fax: 349909)

Banque Arabe Tuniso–Libyenne de Développment et de Commerce Extérieur, PO Box 102, 1002 Tunis (tel: 781500 fax: 782818)

Banque du Sud, 95 Avenue de la Liberté, 1002 Tunis (tel: 849400; fax: 782663)

Banque Internationale Arabe de Tunisie SA, PO Box 520, 70-72 Avenue Habib Bourguiba, 1080 Tunis Cedex (tel: 340733; fax: 340680).

Banque Nationale Agricole, Rue Hedi Nouira, 1001 Tunis (tel: 831000; fax: 835388)

Société Tunisienne de Banque SA, Rue Hedi Nouira, 1001 Tunis (tel: 340477; fax: 340009).

Tunis International Bank, PO Box 81, 18 Avenue des Etats Unis D'Amerique, 1002 Tunis (tel: 782411 fax: 789970)

Central bank

Banque Centrale de Tunisia, PO Box 777, 25 Rue Hédi Nouira, 1080 Tunis Cedex, Tunisia (tel: 340588, 254000 fax: 354214, 340615)

Travel information

National Tourist Office, 1 avenue Mohammed V, Tunis (tel: 341-077).

Tunisair, Boulevard 7 Novembre 1987, 2035 Tunis (tel: 700-100; fax: 700-897).

Tunisian Airports Office, BP 137 et 147, 1080 Tunis Cedex (tel: 754-000).

Tunisian National Railway Company, Gare de Tunis-Ville, Place de Barcelone, Tunis (tel: 244-440).

Ministries

Foreign Investment Promotion Agency, (tel: 792-144; fax: 782-971).

Ministry of Agriculture, 30 rue Alain Savery, 1002 Tunis Belvedere (tel: 287-133).

Ministry of Communication Technologies, Cabinet de Monsieur le Ministre, 3 bis, rue d'Angleterre, 1000 Tunis.

Ministry of Communications, Belvedere du 9 avril 1938, 1030 Tunis (tel: 336-409; fax: 354-628).

Ministry of Economic Development, Direction Générale de la Privatisation, Place Ali Zouaoui, 1000 Tunis (tel: 354-467; fax: 350-975).

Ministry of Defence, 1008 Montfleury, Tunis (tel: 560-244).

Ministry of Education, Boulevard Bab Bnat, Tunis (tel: 263-850; fax: 569-307).

Ministry of Equipment and Housing, Av H Cherita –Cite Jardin, 1002 Tunis (tel: 681-802).

Ministry of Higher Education, 28 rue de Sousse, 1030 Tunis (tel: 782-947).

Ministry of Public Health, Bab Saadoun, Tunis (tel: 260-727).

Ministry of Vocational Training and Employment, 21 rue de Lybie – Lafayette, 1002 Tunis (tel: 782-432).

Other useful addresses

Agence de Promotion de L'Industrie, 63 rue de Syrie, 1002 Tunis-Belvédère (tel: 792-144; fax: 782-482).

Agricultural Investment Promotion Agency, 62 rue Alain Savary, 1003 Tunis Khadra, Tunis (tel: 288-400; fax: 782-353).

CEPEX (non-profit government agency for promotion of exports), 28 rue v Gandhi, 1001 Tunis (tel: 350-043; fax: 353-683; e-mail: cepexedpuc@attmail.com).

Entreprise Tunisienne D'Activités Petrolières, 27 avenue Khéreddine Pacha, 1002 Tunis (tel: 782-288).

Export Promotion Centre, 28 rue Ghandi, 1001 Tunis (tel: 350-344; fax: 353-683).

Industrial Land Agency, 2 rue Badii Ezzamen, Cité Mahrajéne, 1002 Tunis-Belvédère, El Menza I (tel: 797-360, 800-616; fax: 782-303).

Institut National de Statistique, 27 rue de Liban, Tunis (tel: 282-500).

Maghreb Permanent Consultative Committee, 14 rue Yahia ibn Omar, Mutuelleville, Tunis.

National Sanitation Office, 32 rue Hedi Nouira, Tunis (tel: 704-000).

National Water Distribution Company, 67 rue Jawarhel ehru, Montfleury (tel: 493-700; fax: 390-561).

Office du Commerce de Tunisie, avenue Mohammed V, 1002 Tunis (tel: 288-673; fax: 788-974, 784-974).

Tunisian Electricity and Gas Company, 38 rue Kemal Ataturk, Tunis (tel: 341-311; fax: 349-981).

Tunisian External Communication Agency, 2 rue d'Algérie, 1001 Tunis (tel: 651-999, 350-202; fax: 341-902).

Union Tunisienne de l'Industrie, du Commerce et de l'Artisanat, 32 rue Charles de Gaulle, Tunis (tel: 243-711).

Internet sites

http://www.tunisiaonline.com

http://www.investintunisia.tn

http://www.tourismtunisia.com

http://www.tunisie.com

http://www.radiotunis.com

Africa Business Network: http://www.ifc.org/abn

AllAfrica.com: http://allafrica.com

African Development Bank: http://www.afdb.org

Mbendi AfroPaedia (information on companies, countries, industries and stock exchanges in Africa): http://mbendi.co.za

Uganda

Guy Arnold

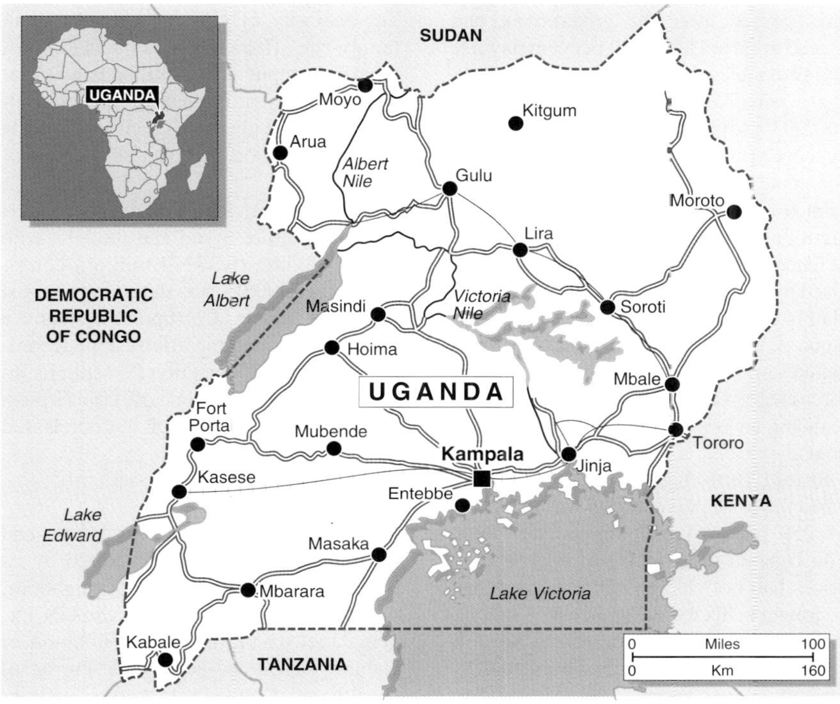

In the March 2001 presidential elections, Yoweri Museveni won a final five-year term of office. Uganda was accused by the UN of illegally exploiting the resources of its neighbour, the Democratic Republic of Congo (DRC): much of the wealth of the DRC's eastern regions was being extracted by Uganda, Burundi and Rwanda.

Elections held...

Museveni easily won the March 2001 elections, with 69.3 per cent of the vote, against his nearest rival, Kiza Besigye, with 28 per cent. International observers and donors expressed concern at electoral irregularities that were reported by the other candidates. Memgroup, a non-government election-monitoring group, noted serious irregularities in eight of the 56 electoral districts, mainly in favour of Museveni. Memgroup claimed that malpractices included multiple voting, the provision of pre-marked ballot papers, physical attacks on candidates' agents and the sale of vote registration cards. According to reports from its 17,000 observers, Memgroup claimed that between 5 and 15 per cent of the vote could have been compromised, though not enough to affect the result.

...and challenged

Kiza Besigye rejected the results and said that in 23 districts his agents had refused to accept the outcome. He said he would challenge the result through the courts. The campaign had been bitterly fought on both sides and on occasions, Museveni had called in the military to reinforce the police in areas where there was substantial support for Besigye. Museveni, who had earned respect for the way he had tackled AIDS, accused Besigye of 'carrying' the AIDS virus during the election campaign. After his election defeat, Besigye fled Uganda in August and went to the US, claiming that he had been harassed by the security forces. This, as well as the suggestion that Besigye had been placed

KEY FACTS

Official name: Republic of Uganda

Head of State: President Yoweri Kaguta Museveni (Movement) (since 1986 Revolution; elected May 1996; re-elected 12 Mar 2001)

Head of government: President Yoweri Kaguta Museveni; Prime Minister Apolo Nsimbabi heads the cabinet (re-appointed by the president in Jul 2001)

Ruling party: Non-party government (Movement)

Area: 236,036 square km

Population: 22.80 million (2001)

Capital: Kampala

Official language: English

Currency: Ugandan shilling (Ush) = 100 cents

Exchange rate: Ush1,867.00 per US$ (Jan 2003)

GDP per capita: US$255 (2001); US$250 (2002)*

GDP real growth: 5.40% (2001); 5.5% (2002)*

Labour force: 11.00 million (2001); 12.00 million (2002)*

Inflation: 2.00% (2001); -1.2% (2002)*

Balance of trade: -US$1.06 billion (2001)

Foreign debt: US$3.83 billion (2002)

Annual FDI: US$169.00 million (2001)

* estimated figure

For the latest Key Facts, go to www.worldinformation.com

under house arrest, was denied by the chief of military intelligence, Lieutenant Colonel Noble Mayombo. Violence marred the elections. Seven people were shot dead across the country on the day of the elections. Two bombs, which exploded in Kampala and Entebbe on 14 and 15 March respectively, were put down to dissatisfaction with the election result.

Legislative elections were held on 26 June and Museveni's 'No Party' Movement secured a majority in the seventh National Parliament. Speaking on 30 June, Museveni said the Movement had scored highly to win 230 seats. The National Parliament has a total of 292 members: 214 single seat constituencies (without party labels); 53 seats reserved for indirectly elected women candidates; 25 set aside for indirectly elected representatives of the armed forces (10), the disabled (5), youth (5) and workers (5).

President Museveni appointed a new cabinet, which was sworn in on 24 July. The incumbent prime minister, Apolo Nsimbabi, was reappointed. Speciosa Wandira Kazibwe had already been reappointed as vice president. There were seven new appointments to the cabinet and seven shuffles in a total of 23 posts. Uganda remained a 'no-party democracy'.

Money and coffee

The finance and economic planning minister, Gerald Ssendaula, said that the 2001/02 budget was intended to improve the falling economic growth rate and boost stagnating revenues. The budget aimed to deliver real GDP growth of 6 per cent. Growth for 2000/01 had fallen below the target of 7 per cent, reaching 5.4 per cent in 2001. The fiscal deficit rose to 12.6 per cent of GDP, compared to 10.6 per cent in the previous financial year and 12.2 per cent under the original budget. Including grants, the fiscal deficit amounted to 5.1 per cent of GDP, compared to 2.2 per cent in 2000/01 and 4.6 per cent under the original budget. The National Assembly finally approved the budget of US$152 million on 31 October; it was only passed after the government had agreed to award MPs a 40 per cent pay rise and provide each with US$11,286 to purchase personal vehicles. The budget for 2002/03 projects total spending of 22.8 per cent of GDP, with a fiscal deficit of 3.3 per cent, including grants. Spending for ministries will decrease by 23 per cent and the money saved will be used to increase defence spending, which has been criticised by the World Bank. The government claims that the defeat of the Lord's Resistance Army (LRA), which has been engaged in hostilities with government forces since the late 1980s, is essential to realising its long-term social development goals.

In mid 2001, Ugandans were shocked when the price of electricity was increased by 250 per cent with immediate effect. The Uganda Electrical Authority said its prices had not changed in nine years and no longer reflected the real cost of supplying power. Moreover, the energy sector's capital costs were mainly dominated by foreign exchange considerations. Changes, therefore, had to be pegged to fluctuations in foreign exchange. The new higher tariff was introduced to help pay for the Kitra power project and also help to improve service delivery and the extension of the grid. However, both industry leaders and the Uganda National Chamber of Commerce expressed their concern that such a big price rise might damage the economy.

The world fall in coffee prices had an adverse impact upon the Ugandan economy during 2001 and 2002. Uganda, with Côte d'Ivoire and Ethiopia, is one of Africa's three principal coffee producers. The majority of coffee farms are small family-run affairs. Uganda plans to boost its coffee output to five million bags a year under a five-year replanting scheme. Balancing the fall in coffee revenues, Uganda harvested a good tea crop as a result of better rainfall.

The West provided half Uganda's current expenditure in aid and the UK, with an £80 million (US$114 million) contribution for 2000/01, was the country's most important donor. Corruption remains a constant in economic affairs and, according to the 2001 Corruption Perceptions Index (CPI), Uganda is one of Africa's most corrupt countries, although it is outclassed by Nigeria.

Uganda and the DRC

Uganda's economic performance and other policies have been distorted by its intervention in the affairs of its neighbour, the DRC. On 16 April 2001, the UN Expert Panel on the Illegal Exploitation of Natural Resources and Other Forms of Wealth of Congo asked the Security Council to 'use strong measures, including sanctions' against Uganda, Rwanda and Burundi for looting the DRC's resources. The Panel claimed that there had been 'systematic looting', particularly by Uganda and Rwanda and President Museveni was criticised for allowing this to take place. The Panel urged the World Bank and the IMF to suspend cash payments to Uganda and Rwanda and the Security Council to ban gold, diamond and other mineral and timber exports from DRC. Uganda was singled out as responsible for timber extraction from the DRC's Orientale Province. Coltan, a rare mineral used for the high technology and aerospace industries, was also being taken illegally from the DRC. The Panel accused Uganda and the rebels it supported of creating new companies and businesses to handle these illegal activities. Export figures for gold from Uganda were consistently higher than the country's production values. The Bank of Uganda (BOU) was obliged to admit to IMF officials that the value of Ugandan gold exports did not reflect Ugandan production levels and that

KEY INDICATORS — Uganda

	Unit	1996	1997	1998	1999	2000
Population	m	19.85	20.44	21.03	21.62	22.19
Gross domestic product (GDP)	US$bn	6.05	6.30	6.78	6.00	5.70
GDP per capita	US$	305	308	322	278	257
GDP real growth	%	9.3	5.4	4.6	7.6	4.4
Inflation	%	7.2	6.9	0.0	6.4	6.3
Exports (fob) (goods)	US$m	639.0	576.0	466.0	515.0	439.0
Imports (fob) (goods)	US$m	987.0	1,043.0	1,393.0	1,344.0	1,513.0
Balance of trade	US$m	-348.0	-467.0	-927.0	-829.0	-1,070.0
Current account	US$m	-252.0	-388.0	-692.0	-746.0	-861.0
Foreign debt	US$bn	3.5	3.5	3.6	4.1	3.7
Total reserves minus gold	US$m	528.4	633.5	725.4	763.1	808.0
Foreign exchange	US$m	527.3	628.1	720.4	760.8	804.5
Exchange rate	per US$	1,046.10	1,083.00	1,240.30	1,454.80	1,644.50

some exports might be 'leaking over the borders' from the DRC. Similarly, diamond exports from Uganda were suspicious since the country has no known diamonds. These exports only commenced at the time Ugandan forces occupied parts of eastern DRC and their control of the rich diamond zone near Kisangani and Banalia. In addition, Uganda had become an exporter of niobium (a similar mineral to coltan), but had not produced this mineral prior to its 1997 involvement in the DRC. The DRC has been a source of illicit wealth, a cause of tension and sometimes fighting with Rwanda and an excuse to spend more money on the military.

UK Relations

In a letter to Clare Short, the UK overseas development minister, President Museveni first accused Rwanda of inciting enemies of his government inside Uganda and threatening war as a prelude to asking for understanding if Uganda's defence spending went over the prevailing 1.9 per cent of GDP. In a significant passage Museveni claimed: 'Given that Mr Kagame is turning the sister state of Rwanda into an enemy state to Uganda, we cannot go on with the hamstrung position of having a small, under-equipped army in such a volatile situation.' The letter was a prelude to a visit by Museveni and President Paul Kagame to the UK in November 2001 for talks with its prime minister, Tony Blair, and Clare Short. Museveni said that attacks upon civilians, and terrorism (incited by Rwanda), hurt tourism and stopped petroleum exploration and that this justified security spending as a primary economic investment. He suggested that between 2002 and 2005, Uganda would need an extra US$139 million in addition to the US$113 million that the country was already spending on defence. Museveni accused Kagame of planning open aggression against Uganda.

The publication of this letter on the Internet produced a heated debate. As one commentator said, 'Museveni's letter to Clare Short has once again exposed the fallacy of Uganda's independence. It has revealed who really is in control of Uganda, and has given credence to the arguments of one African political economist who wrote a few years ago that the real rulers of Uganda resided in Washington, London and other Western capitals. Rather troubling if truth must be told, but hard to argue with after reading the Museveni missive to Madam Short.'

In London on 6 November 2001, Presidents Museveni and Kagame signed a peace agreement in the hope of preventing fresh hostilities between their two countries. Former close allies, they had fallen out over their respective involvement in the DRC. Their meeting was chaired by Short and attended by Blair. The two African leaders agreed to crack down on cross-border support for dissidents and to allow a third country to monitor the agreement, including the inspection of alleged rebel training camps. Short warned that if they relapsed into hostilities they would jeopardise the provision of future British aid.

The fight against terrorism

In October 2001, Ugandan police arrested seven Pakistanis and one Zambian with false travel documents who were suspected of being linked to Osama Bin Laden. They had arrived in Uganda from Rwanda on their way to Europe. In mid-October, Kenya and Uganda agreed during a meeting at Kisumu on a joint strategy to combat terrorism. The two countries decided it was imperative to co-operate 'even more closely in the light of the terrorist attacks on New York and Washington on September 11'. They also discussed smuggling, the illegal drugs trade and arms trafficking on Lake Victoria.

Despite Museveni's overwhelming power, he has been unable to put down armed rebellion on the country's periphery. Attention is primarily fixed on the two principal guerrilla groups in Uganda – the LRA and the Allied Democratic Front (ADF). The government claims the LRA and its ally in Sudan, the West Bank Nile Front (WBNF), have used bases in southern Sudan as staging posts for attacks in Uganda. In July 2002, President Museveni agreed to engage in dialogue with the LRA, although the guerrillas had to stop abducting children and attacking government troops and regroup in designated areas in northern Uganda and southern Sudan. The president's offer was welcomed by Christian leaders, but the LRA appeared unwilling to call a truce.

In June 2002, the government and the rebel Uganda National Rescue Front II (UNRF-II) signed a formal ceasefire agreement with the aim of creating political dialogue in the West Nile region. The development followed a government amnesty in January 2001 for those rebels who renounced rebellion and surrendered to the Ugandan authorities. The UNRF-II was formed in 1996 by ex-soldiers of the Idi Amin regime after they broke away from the WBNF. Many of the UNRF-II's younger combatants are likely to be integrated into the UPDF.

Outlook

Uganda has been a troubled country since independence although, whatever criticisms can be levelled at Museveni's political system, the country has enjoyed a decade of relative stability. The elections ensured a final term for Museveni who received an overwhelming endorsement for his policies. However, the region itself is deeply unstable and Uganda's involvement in the DRC, apart from its doubtful legitimacy, has led to a growing rift with Rwanda that does not bode well for the future despite the rapprochement achieved at the UK meeting of Museveni and Kagame in 2001.

Risk assessment

Economy	Improving
Politics	Satisfactory
Regional stability	Poor
Stock market	Small, improving

COUNTRY PROFILE

Historical profile

By the eighteenth century, the territory was occupied by Nilotic peoples in the north – the Acholi and Langi – and by Bantus and Bagandas, from whom the country gets its name, in the south.

1886–1890 The UK colonised Uganda.

1900 Bugunda in western Uganda became an autonomous region with its own constitutional monarchy.

1958 The UK allowed Uganda self-government.

1962 Uganda became an independent state within the Commonwealth in October.

1963 Uganda became a republic. Sir Edward Mutesa II, the king of Bugunda, became Uganda's first president.

1966 Milton Obote, the defence minister, seized power with the help of Colonel Idi Amin, second-in-command of the army. Obote repressed Buganda and integrated it back into Uganda.

1967 The constitutional role of kings was abolished, along with federal system of government.

1971 Obote was ousted by Idi Amin, who expelled the large Asian (mainly Indian) community and carried out purges in which thousands died. Asians had owned 90 per cent of Uganda's businesses and the economy collapsed.

1979 Tanzania invaded Uganda, causing Amin to flee to Saudi Arabia. Yusufu Lule was briefly appointed president before being replaced by Godfrey Binaisa.

1980 Obote won the presidential election and started to pursue liberal economic policies to obtain aid from western donors, and the economy began to improve.
1985 Ethnic feuding resulted in a coup removing Obote from power.
1986 Yoweri Museveni came to power in January at the head of the National Resistance Movement (NRM), which had waged a guerrilla war since 1981. He banned multi-party politics, saying it led to ethnic fighting.
1996 President Museveni was elected for a five-year term.
1998 Uganda intervened in the Democratic Republic of Congo (DRC) on behalf of the rebels against the Kabila government.
2001 President Museveni was re-elected in March. In legislative elections held on 26 June, the supporters of the 'No Party' Movement secured a majority but over 50 MPs, including 10 ministers, lost their seats. A peace agreement was signed by Rwanda and Uganda in London on 6 November.

Political structure

In a referendum held on 29 June 2000, over 90 per cent of voters chose continuation of the 'No Party' Movement system in operation since 1986. Less than 10 per cent of the electorate voted. The Movement system allows parties to exist in name but not to function. All candidates in parliamentary elections run as individuals.

Constitution

An elected constituent assembly drafted a constitution which was promulgated on 8 October 1995. It retains the system of non-party government.

Form of state

Unitary republic.

The executive

The president is elected for a five-year term. The president appoints a prime minister and a cabinet composed of representatives of a number of political parties.

National legislature

The Ugandan parliament has 292 members including 214 elected constituency representatives, 53 district women representatives, 10 Uganda People's Defence Forces (UPDF) representatives, five youth representatives, five representatives of disabled people and five workers' representatives.
The Movement system allows parties to exist in name but not to function. All candidates in parliamentary elections run as individuals.

Legal system

The legal system is based on English common law and the 1995 constitution.

Last elections

6/14 March 2001 (presidential); 26 June 2001 (parliamentary).

Next elections

2006 (presidential and parliamentary).

Political parties

Political parties can exist, although public political activities like fund-raising and campaigning are banned.

Ruling party

Non-party government (Movement)

Population

22.19 million (2000)
The annual population growth rate was 3 per cent (1994–2000). Approximately 48 per cent of the total population is under 15 years of age.
Population density: 108 inhabitants per square km. Urban population: 13 per cent (1994–2000). There is a high rural density in the south, in a belt from east to west, with only 10 per cent of the population living in towns. The north is sparsely populated.

Ethnic make-up

There are over 20 ethnic groups of which the Baganda, Banyankole and Basoga are the largest. Approximately 99 per cent of the population is of African descent and 1 per cent European or Asian.

Religions

Christianity (71 per cent), traditional beliefs (13 per cent), Islam (5 per cent), others (11 per cent).

Education

Attendance at primary level rose from 50 per cent of the relevant age group in 1980 to 74 per cent in 1996; secondary level from 5 per cent in 1980 to 12 per cent in 1996, and tertiary level from 1 per cent in 1980 to 2 per cent in 1996. It has been estimated by Oxfam that 60 per cent of children age 6–11 will enrol for school in 2015.

Health

Life expectancy: 43 years (1998). Infant mortality rate: 99 per 1,000 live births (1997). Child malnutrition: 26 per cent of (1992–98). About 42 per cent of the total population have access to safe water. Government health expenditure was equivalent to 3.9 per cent of annual GDP 1990–97.

Main cities

Kampala (capital, estimated population 850,000 in 1998), Jinja (60,979), Mbale (53,634), Masaka (49,070), Gulu (42,841), Mbarara (40,385), Fort Portal (32,627).

Languages spoken

KiSwahili, Luganda and Luo are widely spoken.

Official language

English

Media

Press

Uganda has over 14 regularly published newspapers and periodicals, some of which are in local languages.
Dailies: *The Monitor* is the only daily independent newspaper. The other major daily is *The New Vision*, a government-owned newspaper. *Ngabo* is a national daily and Sunday newspaper.
Weeklies: Bi-weekly newspaper (Tue and Fri) *The Monitor*.
Periodicals: *Musizi* is a monthly publication containing religious and political information.

Broadcasting

Radio and television services are controlled by the government under the Ministry of Information and Broadcasting.
Radio: Radio Uganda is the only radio station in the country. It broadcasts on two channels: the Blue Channel and the Red Channel, in English, Kiswahili and 20 local languages.
Television: Uganda Television Service (UTS) is a state-owned commercial service, which broadcasts programmes mainly in English, KiSwahili and Luganda. Cable Sat Television (CTV) is a privately owned television network which is only received in areas within 50km from the Kololo television mast in Kampala.

Economy

Uganda's strategy to eradicate poverty is enshrined in two broad government initiatives: Vision 2025 and the Poverty Eradication Action Plan (Peap). The country has adopted an IMF-backed economic reform plan under its Poverty Reduction and Growth Facility (PRGF) agreed in 1997. This is directed towards achieving a consistently realistic exchange rate, reducing government expenditure, instigating trade liberalisation measures and reforming the civil service.
Vision 2025 represents the government's long-term aim while Peap serves as a policy framework to guide medium-term plans for all levels of government, including the budget process. Peap was revised in early 2000 to comply with the country's Poverty Reduction Strategy Paper (PRSP) demanded by the IMF. Peap's aim is to reduce poverty to less than 10 per cent of the population by 2017 with annual GDP growth at an average of 7 per cent and inflation contained at a maximum of 5 per cent.
GDP growth has risen from 4.4 per cent in 2000 to 5.4 per cent in 2001. Inflation fell from 6.3 per cent in 2000 to 4.6 per cent in 2001, following a food prices fall due to recovery in the agriculutural sector. However, the IMF has estimated that growth will continue to be hampered by a continuing decline in the terms of trade, which is estimated to have caused up to 2

per cent of GDP in lost income. While the economy could still reach the targets set by Peap, it is highly vulnerable to external shocks and the 2001 global economic slowdown could still prevent the economy from achieving these goals in the long-term.

The main problem concerns the country's reliance on coffee exports, accounting for 70 per cent of export revenues, which have declined in unit value due to the depressed world coffee market. Also, good macroeconomic indicators hide the fact that many Ugandans are not enjoying the fruits of growth, with a strong divide between the south east and the troubled north and south west. With monetary tools having a limited effect on macroeconomic indicators due to the effects of climate change and declining external markets on the economy, fiscal policy plays an important role in achieving economic goals. Despite the government's attempts at fiscal sustainability, it faces problems with revenue collection and over-spending which are largely linked to factors outside its control, such as droughts and depressed export prices.

External trade

The East African Community (EAC) pledges to work towards common action on the movement of labour and goods between Uganda, Kenya and Tanzania and the integration of transport, tourism and telecommunications. It has considerable economic potential as a regional bloc with a combined population of 80 million, a land area of 1.8 million square kilometres, common languages such as English and KiSwahili, and large amounts of natural resources, including minerals, water, energy, forestry and wildlife. However, the issue of tariffs is an obstacle for the Tanzanian government in particular which is concerned that complete free trade would heighten economic disparities within the EAC and undermine the country's struggling industrial sector.

Exports

Principal exports are coffee (typically 70 per cent of total), tea, fish, cocoa, spices, tobacco, cotton.

Main destinations: Germany (12 per cent of 2000 total), Netherlands (10.2 per cent), US (8.7 per cent), Spain (8 per cent), Italy (7.4 per cent), Australia (2.6 per cent).

Imports

Principal imports are capital goods (typically 19 per cent of total). manufactured goods, foodstuffs, fuels.

Main sources: Kenya (43.2 per cent of 2000 total), UK (7 per cent), India (6.8 per cent), South Africa (6.1 per cent), Colombia (0.2 per cent), Australia (0.2 per cent).

Re-exports

Gold, diamonds, coltan and niobium, mostly from neighbouring DRC.

Agriculture

The agricultural sector is the most important sector of the economy. However, its share of total productive output declined from 51 per cent in 1991/92 to 42 per cent in 1999/2000. Approximately 23 per cent of total land area is arable, 20 per cent pasture and 12 per cent forest. Agricultural development is hampered by shortages of vital inputs, damage caused by civil war, low producer prices and corrupt purchasing bodies.

Uganda's varied climate allows the production of a wide range of produce. Around 75 per cent of Uganda's agricultural output is made up of food crop production – two-thirds of this is used for subsistence. Maize is one of the main food crops and is grown around Lake Victoria as a cash crop. The fertility of Ugandan land could make it a bread basket for East Africa, particularly if the effects of periodic droughts are ameliorated by adequate irrigation techniques.

Coffee is the main cash crop, providing around 70 per cent of agricultural export earnings. However, most production is carried out on a small-scale basis with smaller economies of scale than the plantations in some of the larger Latin American countries. Rehabilitation of coffee holdings has been the main stimulus to economic growth in recent years. The government has encouraged planting of clone coffee which yields in a shorter period of around two years, is more disease resistant and gives higher yields.

The private sector controls over 90 per cent of the coffee trade in Uganda. Liberalisation of the coffee market has meant that producers can sell coffee on the open market to the highest bidder, although the dismantling of state marketing boards has meant that they are more vulnerable to price fluctuations and have to deal with often unscrupulous middlemen. However, the formation of co-operatives has become a basis for reducing the adverse effects of liberalisation.

Cotton was once an important cash crop, but due to its labour intensiveness, relatively high cost of production, poor marketing system, as well as security problems in the major growing zone in the early 1980s, farmers diverted to growing non-traditional cash crops which have a readily available market. However, cotton growing is being revived in some eastern areas, and production has been boosted by reforms in agricultural pricing and marketing regimes introduced in the early 1990s. Sugar is grown on several vast estates and production is creeping up after collapsing completely in the early 1980s. Tobacco and tea are also important cash crops

The Nile Basin Initiative (NBI) (signed by Egypt, Sudan, Tanzania, Kenya, Rwanda, Burundi, Uganda and Democratic Republic of Congo) launched seven feasibility studies backed by US$140 million granted by the World Bank and donor governments in June 2001. It will also develop a parallel legal framework for shared water management. Ethiopia refused to sign and Eritrea's membership is pending.

Fishing

Uganda's fishing industry (centred on Lake Victoria) is important, both for domestic consumption and export. The annual catch is typically around 220,000 tonnes, around 40 per cent of which is exported.

Industry and manufacturing

The industrial sector contributes about 8 per cent to GDP and employs 4 per cent of the workforce. Between 1991/92 and 1999/2000, industry's contribution to total output rose from 13 per cent to 20 per cent, reflecting a slow but steady process of industrialisation.

The industrial sector is mainly involved in import substitution. It has seen encouraging growth, particularly in food processing, tobacco, beverages, timber/paper and chemicals/soap. Under-utilisation of factory capacity and lack of foreign exchange continues to inhibit greater progress.

Other industries are textiles, cement, plastics, steel, metal products and brewing. Most of these are operating well below capacity mainly due to shortages of imported materials, spares and fuel, inadequate infrastructure and a lack of skilled manpower.

Despite this, industry has led growth over the past decade, remaining buoyant throughout 1999–2001 with growth of 7 per cent even though the economy suffered external shocks on the exchange rate. Manufacturing grew by 8.6 per cent while construction grew by 8.5 per cent. However, the strongest performance was in electricity, which grew by 11.1 per cent mainly due to the refurbishment and on-going upgrading of the Owen Falls Dam.

The building industry is hampered by a lack of finance and skilled manpower and most local building equipment factories still produce at only 50 per cent of their installed capacities. Consequently, many finished products, such as cement, sanitary ware, plumbing pipes and glass are imported.

Tourism

The government is promoting bird watching as a major draw for tourists. Safaris and gorilla watching tours are already popular.

Mining

Uganda has deposits of copper, cobalt and iron ore, as well as less viable fields of tungsten, beryl, columbo-tantalite, gold, bismuth, tin, limestone and phosphates. Copper was Uganda's second most important export, but output from the state-owned Kilembe mines, in south-west Uganda, was halted in 1982. The country's mineral potential remains untested due to very little exploration to date – the country has the potential for gold, tantalite, copper and cobalt production.

Hydrocarbons

Uganda has no known oil or gas resources. However, exploration of the Rift Valley led to favourable results in the late 1980s. Four foreign companies initially showed interest in exploration and an agreement was finally signed with Petrofina of Belgium for the exploration and development of oil in the western Rift Valley on the shores of Lake Albert. Petrofina will provide all the risk capital and will carry all the costs if no commercial discovery is made. However, if oil is found, Uganda stands to benefit significantly and notwithstanding proceeds from oil output, analysts estimate that investment could amount to US$60 million over 15 years.
The downstream industry is dependent on the importation of refined petroleum products and is the largest item of foreign exchange outflow. The development of the East African Community involving Uganda, Kenya and Tanzania will improve the pipeline infrastructure. Plans are afoot to extend the existing Mombasa-Nairobi-Eldoret pipeline to Kampala at a cost of US$90 million with a capacity of 16,500 barrels per day.

Energy

Uganda relies on imported oil for around 50 per cent of its energy needs, the balance being provided by hydroelectricity. Owen Falls Power Station, operating since the mid-1950s, has an installed capacity of 150MW, and exports 30MW to Kenya. Electricity is exported to western Kenya and Tanzania.

Financial markets

Stock exchange
The Kampala Stock Exchange (KSE) began trading in 1998.

Banking

Central bank
Bank of Uganda.

Time

GMT plus three hours

Geography

Uganda is a landlocked country in East Africa, bordered by Sudan to the north, the Democratic Republic of Congo to the west, Kenya to the east and Rwanda, Tanzania and Lake Victoria to the south.

Climate

Equatorial, tempered by high altitude. Temperatures are fairly constant throughout the year, hottest months December–February, June–August, with daytime range (in Kampala) of 27–29 degrees Celsius (C) compared with an annual average of 26 degrees C (night-time average 16 degrees C). Heaviest rainfall occurs March–May, October–November; April is wettest month (average fall for month 175 mm).

Dress codes

Lightweight clothing is advisable all year round. Senior officials tend to wear suits, local businessmen and government officials wear suits or safari suits. Light cotton dresses, skirts and blouses or lightweight suits are advised for women. A lightweight raincoat may be needed at any time of the year.

Entry requirements

Passports
Required by all. Passports must be valid for six months.
Visa
Not required for citizens of EU, US, Australia, New Zealand, Japan, Canada, Switzerland, Taiwan, Hong Kong, South Korea, Saudi Arabia, Kuwait, United Arab Emirates (UAE).
A return or onward ticket is required.
Currency advice/regulations
No restrictions on import of foreign currency. It is best to carry US dollars, euros or British pounds sterling.
When changing travellers' cheques a valid passport is required. Some agencies may ask for your sales advice slip.
Small denomination bills of US$1, 5, 10 and 20 are changed at substantially reduced rates, as are torn and soiled notes.
Customs
Baggage and property accompanying the passenger may be imported into the country duty-free, providing the goods are re-exported at the end of the visit.
Duty-free allowances are: one litre of spirits, wines and liqueurs; 500ml of perfume and toilet water; 250 grammes of cigarettes, cigars and tobacco.
Prohibited imports
Game trophies

Health (for visitors)

There is a risk of malaria, rabies and bilharzia and precautions should be taken against these diseases. Normal precautions for the tropics with regard to hygiene and drinking water should be taken.
Mandatory precautions
Valid international yellow fever vaccination certificate required.
Advisable precautions
Polio vaccination. Typhoid is comparatively rare and protection need only be sought by those intending to spend time living outside the main towns. Malaria prophylaxis should be taken as risk exists throughout the country.

Hotels

Private and government-owned, variable standard, but available in all main centres. Should be booked in advance.

Public holidays

Fixed dates
1 Jan (New Year's Day), 26 Jan (Liberation Day), 8 Mar (International Women's Day), 1 May (Labour Day), 3 Jun (Martyr's Day), 9 Oct (Independence Day), 25 and 26 Dec (Christmas).
Variable dates
Good Friday, Easter Monday, Eid Al-Fitr, Eid Al-Adha.

Working hours

Banking
Mon–Fri: 0900–1400. Some bureaux de change open Sat and Sun.
Business
Mon–Fri: 0830–1245, 1400–1700.
Government
Mon–Fri: 0830–1245, 1400–1700.
Shops
Mon–Fri: 0830–1700; Sat: 0900–1600.

Telecommunications

Telephone/fax
Uganda's telecommunications industry has been liberalised, breaking the former monopoly of the Uganda Posts and Telecommunications Corporation.
Postal services
Not very reliable.
Courier services
Air courier services available.

Electricity supply

240V AC, 50 cycles.

Social customs/useful tips

Appointments are essential for business meetings. Ugandans have a less urgent sense of time than Europeans, and appointments often run late, particularly if it is raining.
The customary form of greeting is to shake hands. Exchanging business cards is an established ritual.
Visitors should remember that an increasing number of Hindus and Muslims are engaged in commerce and local advice should be obtained if any entertainment is planned. There are many local traditions but few will affect business visitors and tourists.

Security

There are still areas of the country that are not under secure government control. Rebel activity occasionally targets tourists, and visitors are advised to check with local embassies if they intend to travel away from the main urban centres or main road and rail routes. The government has stepped up its campaign against lawlessness.

Due to rebel raids, including activity spilling over from neighbouring countries, visitors are warned against travelling to certain destinations, particularly the northern and south western regions, where the Mountains of the Moon and several game parks are located

Getting there

Air

National airline: Uganda Airlines

Main airport: Entebbe (Code: EBB), at Entebbe, 35km from Kampala; information desk, duty-free shop, restaurant, bank, post office, hotel reservations, car hire.

Airport tax: There is no airport departure tax.

Surface

Road: There is good road access from Kenya, although links with Rwanda may be disrupted by military activity.

Rail: It is possible to travel by train from Nairobi (Kenya) to Kampala via a connection at Tororo; this can be slow and uncomfortable.

Water: Water access is possible via Lake Victoria, from Mwanza (Tanzania) and Kisumu (Kenya).

Getting about

National transport

Air: Uganda Airlines operates irregular services to main centres (including Arua and Kasese) from Entebbe. Charter services are also available.

Road: Uganda has a road network of 27,540km. Main towns are connected by 2,096km of tarmac roads. Rehabilitation has started and many major roads are in good condition.

Buses: Regular services scheduled include Entebbe-Kampala (journey time: 30–45 minutes). There are services between most main centres but they tend to be crowded. An interstate bus service between Kampala and Kigali (Rwanda) is frequently suspended due to military activity. Akamba Bus regularly travels between Kampala and Nairobi (Kenya).

Rail: Approximately 1,200km of line exists, but only Kampala-Kasese and Kampala-Jinja-Mbale are functioning.

Water: Some freight and passenger transport is available on Lake Victoria.

City transport

Taxis: Available at airport and in Kampala at hotels, the railway station, main park and near major office blocks. The drive from Entebbe airport to Kampala city centre takes 45 minutes.

Matatus (public taxis) are available within Kampala, its suburbs and in all major towns.

Car hire

Car hire is expensive. Services are available, mainly with driver, from a number of rental firms, and through independent taxi drivers. Driving is on the left. A valid international driving licence is required.

BUSINESS DIRECTORY

Telephone area codes

The international direct dialling (IDD) code for Uganda is +256, followed by area code:

Entebbe	42
Fort Portal	483
Jinja	43
Kampala	41
Kasese	483
Lugazi	44
Masaka	481
Mbale	45
Mbarara	485
Tororo	45

Useful telephone numbers

Ambulance, fire, police: 999

Directory enquiries: 901

International hospital: 340-531, 345-768

Chambers of Commerce

Mbale Chamber of Commerce, PO Box 396, Mbale.

National Chamber of Commerce and Industry, 17-19 Jinja Road, PO Box 3809, Kampala (tel: 258-791).

Banking

Allied Bank International Uganda Ltd PO Box 2750, Plot 24 Jinja Road, Kampala (tel: 236-535/6; fax: 230-439).

Bank of Baroda (Uganda) Ltd PO Box 7197. 18 Kampala Road, Kampala (tel: 233-680/3; fax: 258-263).

Barclays Bank of Uganda Ltd, PO Box 2971, 16 Kampala Road, Kampala (tel: 230-972/6, 232-594/7; fax: 259-467).

Cairo International Bank Ltd, PO Box 7052, 1 Bombo Rd, Sure House, Kampala (tel: 230-130, fax: 230-135).

Centenary Rural Development Bank Ltd, PO Box 1872, 7 Entebbe Road, Kampala (tel: 251-276; fax: 251-273).

CitiBank (Uganda) Ltd, PO Box 7505, Centre Court, Ternan Avenue, Nakasero Plot 4, Kampala (tel: 340-625; fax: 340-624).

Crane Bank Limited, PO Box 22572, 38 Kampala Rd, Kampala (tel: 241-414/20; fax: 231-578).

Development Finance Company of Uganda Ltd, PO Box 2767, Rwenzori Hse, Plot 1 Lumumba Ave, Kampala (tel: 256-125, 232-212; fax: 259-435).

DFCU Bank Ltd, PO Box 70, Impala House, 13 Kimathi Avenue, Kampala (tel: 256-891/2/3, 231-784; fax: 231-687).

Diamond Trust Bank (U) Ltd, PO Box 7155, 17/19 Kampala Rd, Kampala (tel: 259-331; fax: 342-286).

East African Development Bank, PO Box 7128, East African Development Bank Building, 4 Nile Avenue, Kampala (tel: 230-021/5; fax: 259-763).

HSBC Equator Bank plc, PO Box 23232, Cargen Hse, 13/14 Parliament Ave, Kampala (tel: 347-699; fax: 347-701).

Nile Bank Ltd, PO Box 2834, Plot 22, Spear Hse, Jinja Rd, Kampala (tel: 346-904, 345-571/2, 226-110, 778-867/9; fax: 257-779).

Orient Bank Limited, PO Box 3072, Ground Floor, Plot 10, Uganda House, Kampala (tel: 236-012/5; fax: 236-066).

Stanbic Bank Uganda Ltd, PO Box 72647, 45 Kampala Road, Kampala (tel: 231-151, 230-811; fax: 231-116).

Standard Chartered Bank Uganda Ltd, PO Box 7111, 5 Speke Road, Kampala (tel: 258-211/7; fax: 231-473).

Trans Africa Bank Ltd, PO Box 1185, Udyam House, 4 Jinja Road, Kampala (tel: 234-554; fax: 234-575).

Tropical Africa Bank Ltd, PO Box 9485 or 7292, 27 Kampala Road, Kampala (tel: 232-857, 231-994; fax: 212-296).

Uganda Commercial Bank Ltd, PO Box 973, 12 Kampala Rd, Kampala (tel: 234-710, 258-012; fax: 259-012, 242-694).

Uganda Development Bank, PO Box 7210, 22 Hannington Rd, UDB Towers, Kampala (tel: 230-740/5; fax: 258-571).

Central bank

Bank of Uganda, PO Box 7120, 37–43 Kampala Rd, Kampala (tel: 258-441/6, 258-060/9; fax: 230-878, 233-818).

Travel information

Eagle Aviation (charter flights) (tel: 234-382).

Uganda Airlines Corporation, 6 Colville Street, PO Box 5740, Kampala (tel: 232-990/7; fax: 257-279); PO Box 187, Entebbe (tel: 20-456, 20-546, 21-058; fax: 20-355).

Uganda National Parks, Kanjokya Street, PO Box 3530, Kampala (tel: 530-158; fax: 530-159).

Uganda Tourist Board, PO Box 7211, Plot 13/15 Kimathi Avenue, Impala House, Kampala (tel: 342-196/7; fax: 342-188; e-mail: utb@starcom.co.ug; internet site: http://www.visituganda.co.ug).

Ministry of tourism

Ministry of Tourism, Wildlife and Antiquities, Parliament Avenue, PO Box 4241, Kampala (tel: 232-971/4; fax: 241-247).

National tourist organisation offices

Uganda Tourist Board, IPS Building, 9/11 Parliament Avenue, PO Box 7211, Kampala (tel: 242-196/7; fax: 242-188; e-mail: utb@starcom.com.ug).

Ministries

Ministry of Agriculture, Animal Industry and Fisheries, PO Box 102, Entebbe (tel: 20-981/9).

Ministry of Education and Sports, 17/19 Hannington Rd, PO Box 7063, Kampala (tel: 234-440/9).

Ministry of Energy, Minerals and Environment Protection, Amber House, 33 Kampala Rd, PO Box 7270, Kampala (tel: 230-070/415).

Ministry of Finance and Economic Planning (Finance), Apollo Kaggwa Rd, PO Box 8147, Kampala (tel: 234-700, 257-095).

Ministry of Finance and Economic Planning (Planning), Uganda House, 10 Kampala Rd, PO Box 7086, Kampala (tel: 235-051/4).

Ministry of Finance and Economic Planning (Statistics Department), PO Box 13, Entebbe.

Ministry of Foreign and Regional Affairs, Parliament Bldg, PO Box 7084, Kampala (tel: 257-525, 258-252; fax: 232-874, 256-722).

Ministry of Information and Broadcasting, Kampala.

Ministry of Land Housing and Urban Development, Jinja Rd, PO Box 7122, Kampala (tel: 242-931/4).

Ministry of Labour and Social Welfare, 1 Portal Ave, PO Box 7009, Kampala (tel: 254-964).

Ministry of Local Government, 10 Kampala Rd, PO Box 7037, Kamapal (tel: 241-279).

Ministry of Tourism, Trade and Industry, Farmers House, Plot 6/8 Parliament Avenue, PO Box 7103, Kampala (tel: 343-947; fax: 256-395; e-mail: uwa@uwa.or.ug).

Ministry of Women in Development, Youth and Culture, 4 Jinja Rd, PO BOx 7136, Kampala (tel: 254-881/8).

Ministry of Works, Transport and Communications, PO Box 10, Entebbe (tel: 20-101).

Prime Minister's Office, Nile Ave, PO Box 341, Kampala (tel: 232-222).

Other useful addresses

British High Commission, Commercial Section, 120/12 Parliament Avenue, PO Box 7070, Kampala (tel: 257-301/4, 257-054/9; fax: 257-304).

Central Tender Board (responsible for administering most government- and aid-funded tenders), PO Box 3925, Kampala.

Civil Aviation Authority, PO Box 5536, Kampala (tel: 256-874/5, 256-896; fax: 256-807).

Coffee Marketing Board Ltd, Plot 15 Kibira Rd, PO Box 7154, Kampala.

Commonwealth Development Corporation, Kampala (tel: 235-784).

Development Finance Company of Uganda, Kampala (tel: 256-125).

Export Policy Analysis and Development Unit (EPADU), Impala House, PO Box 10951, Kampala (tel: 231-390/363; fax: 231-329).

Immigration Department, PO Box 7165, Kampala.

Lint Marketing Board, PO Box 7018, Kampala.

National Housing and Construction Corporation, PO Box 659, Kampala.

Nile International Conference Centre, PO Box 3496, Kampala (tel: 258-619; fax: 259-130).

Privatisation Unit, Ministry of Finance and Economic Planning, IPS Building, 6th Floor, 14 Parliament Avenue, PO Box 10944, Kampala (tel: 256-467, 256-392; fax: 259-997, 242-403; e-mail: pmu@imul.com).

Public Enterprise Reform and Divestiture, IPS Building, 6-7 Floors, PO Box 10944, Kampala (tel: 256-467, 243-995, 259-997; fax: 259-997).

Radio Uganda, Nile Avenue, PO Box 2038, Kampala.

Statistics Department, PO Box 13, Entebbe (fax: 20-147).

Uganda Advisory Board of Trade, PO Box 6877, Kampala (tel: 233-311).

Uganda Development Corporation, UDC Building, Parliament Ave, PO Box 7042, Kampala (tel: 234-383, 241-588; fax: 241-588).

Uganda Export Promotion Council, Plot 17/19 Jinja Road, PO Box 5045, Kampala (tel: 259-779).

Uganda Industrial Development Corporation Ltd, PO Box 442, Kampala (tel: 234-281).

Uganda Investment Authority, Plot 28 Kampala Road, PO Box 7418, Kampala (tel: 251-562, 234-105; fax: 242-903; e-mail: info@ugandainvest.com; internet site: http://www.ugandainvest.com).

Uganda Manufacturers' Association, Kampala (tel: 220-285, 245-560).

Uganda News Agency (UNA), c/o Ministry of Information and Broadcasting, PO Box 7142, Kampala (tel: 254-461).

Uganda Railway Corporation, PO box 7150, Kampala (tel: 258-051; fax: 244-405).

Uganda Tea Corporation Ltd, Kasaku Estate, Jinja-Kampala Rd, PO Box 8955, Lugazi (tel: 48-230/45; fax: (041) 230-698).

Uganda Television Service, PO Box 4260, Kampala.

Ugandan Embassy (USA), 5911 16th Street, NW, Washington DC 20011 (tel: 726-7100; fax: 726-1727; e-mail: ugembassy@aol.com).

Internet sites

Africa Business Network: http://www.ifc.org/abn

African Development Bank: http://www.afdb.org

Africa Online: http://www.africaonline.com

AllAfrica.com: http://allafrica.com

Harambee Afrika (UK business club for traders with east, central and southern Africa; includes annotated web resource list): http://www.harambee.co.uk

Mbendi AfroPaedia (information on companies, countries, industries and stock exchanges in Africa): http://mbendi.co.za

Zambia

Anver Versi

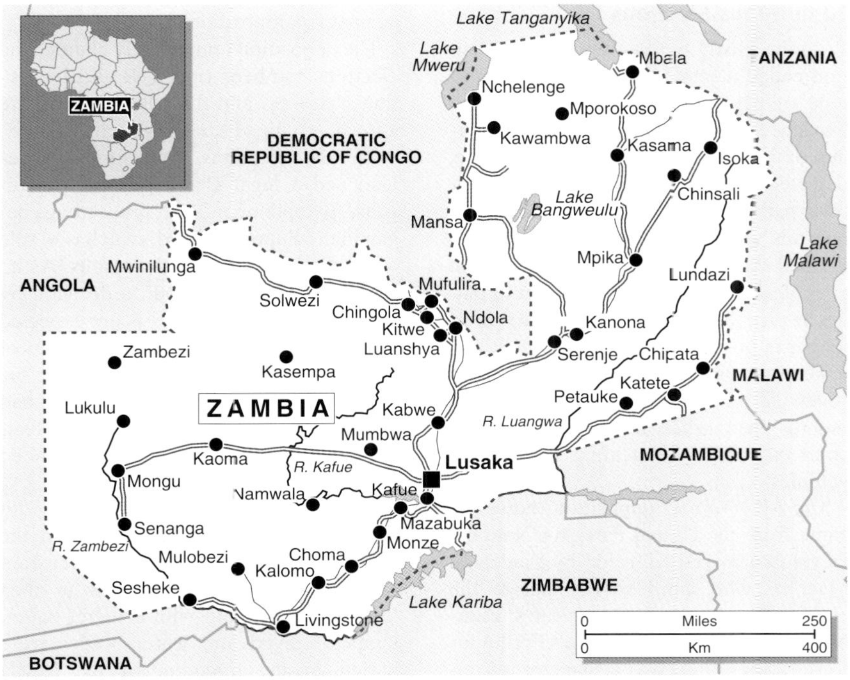

Yet again the gods seem to have taken a malicious delight in raising high expectations in Zambia before cruelly dashing them. As 2001 was drawing to a close, Zambia seemed poised to begin a new era of steady economic stability under a fresh and untainted political leadership. By end-2002, it was clear that these hopes had been dashed. The new president, Levy Mwanawasa, was locked in combat with his former supporters, including ex-president Frederick Chiluba. Anglo-American had pulled out of copper mining barely two years after buying in, and a large scale food shortage was staring the country in the face.

Chiluba's chum

The first signs that things were beginning to go seriously awry came during the December 2001 elections. Earlier in the year, President Chiluba had fought tooth and nail in an attempt to force changes to the constitution which would have allowed him to stand for a third term of office. Eventually, in April 2001, after a series of political manoeuvrings and skulduggery, he threw in the towel and quit the fight.

When the dust had settled, the ruling Movement for Multi-Party Democracy (MMD) found itself severely fractured with some of its leading lights, such as Christon Tembo and Brigadier General Godfrey Miyanda, firmly opposed to Chiluba and the party. As alliances were shuffled around and new parties began to sprout, Chiluba cast around within his own party to find a presidential candidate with 'saleable' qualities before electioneering began in earnest in the final quarter of 2001. He made it plain, however, that he had no intention of stepping down from the presidency of the party. This prompted concerns that he would rule the country 'by remote control'.

By appointing Enoch Kavindele as his vice president, Chiluba appeared to be promoting the person most likely to get the thumbs-up from the party as the MMD's presidential candidate. There were several other heavyweights waiting in the wings, men such as Chiluba's first

KEY FACTS

Official name: The Republic of Zambia

Head of State: President Levy Mwanawasa (MMD) (elected 27 Dec 2001; inaugurated 2 Jan 2002)

Head of government: President Levy Mwanawasa

Ruling party: Movement for Multi-party Democracy (MMD) (re-elected 27 Dec 2001)

Area: 752,614 square km

Population: 11.00 million (2001)

Capital: Lusaka

Official language: English

Currency: Kwacha (K) = 100 ngwee

Exchange rate: K4,870.00 per US$ (Jan 2003)

GDP per capita: US$333 (2001); US$328 (2002)*

GDP real growth: 4.00% (2001); 2.8% (2002)*

Labour force: 4.60 million (2001); 4.7 million (2002)*

Unemployment: 30.00% (2000)*

Inflation: 21.40% (2001); 22.1% (2002)*

Balance of trade: -US$382.00 million (2001)

Foreign debt: US$5.88 billion (2001)

Annual FDI: US$140.00 million (2001)

* estimated figure

For the latest Key Facts, go to www.worldinformation.com

finance minister, Emmanuel Kasonde, and the party's fiery national secretary, Michael 'King Cobra' Sata.

But when the party's national executive gathered to choose the heir apparent, matters took a dramatic turn. Levy Mwanawasa emerged from the dim and distant past to become the MMD presidential candidate.

Mwanawasa, a formidable lawyer with a penchant for 'lost' legal causes – including his famous 1989 defence of Christon Tembo and others charged with treason against the government of Dr Kenneth Kaunda – had been in the political wilderness since he had resigned the vice presidency from Chiluba's cabinet in 1994. At that time, following a serious row with Sata (then minister without portfolio), he left the government saying that doubts had been cast on his integrity and that his good name was worth more than any political office.

Although his nomination as the MMD's presidential candidate came as a shock to the public, it soon became clear that in fact, there had been no other choice. In a political system riddled with corruption, Mwanawasa's integrity shone out. The fact that the sum total of his political acumen could easily be contained on the head of a matchstick made him, in Chiluba's eyes at least, an even more desirable front man.

Opposition parties, for once, were stumped for lack of mud to throw at the MMD's candidate. Instead they expressed sorrow that a man of his calibre and standing had allowed himself to be used so blatantly by the 'Chiluba mafia'. With Mwanawasa running for president with the full machinery of MMD behind him, many claimed that Chiluba had assured himself of a 'third term as president'. Opposition slogans ran along the lines of: 'Mwanawasa will occupy the seat, but Chiluba will call the shots', 'a vote for Mwanawasa is a vote for Chiluba' and 'Mwanawasa is the acceptable face of Chiluba'.

Tumultuous elections

With the MMD fielding what the opposition called a 'puppet' candidate, a multitude of new political parties came into existence. Some MMD stalwarts, uncertain of their futures under the new regime, defected to the opposition or set up their own parties. Sata, perhaps recalling his quarrels with Mwanawasa back in 1994, jumped ship and set up the Patriotic Front to contest the elections. In the heat of battle, he presumably forgot that as he was no longer in government, he was not entitled to keep and use government vehicles. This 'oversight' caught up with him a few months later when he was hauled into court on charges of stealing government vehicles.

The MMD's real opposition, however, came from the United Party for National Development (UPND), led by Anderson Mazoka, who, until shortly before the elections, was Anglo-American's Zambian director. Christon Tembo's Forum for Democracy (FFD) was also a strong contender and had the two formed an alliance, the MMD would have had little chance of success.

The December 2001 elections, both for the presidency and parliament, were rowdy and ill-tempered. After much disputed counting, Levy Mwanawasa was declared the winner by one percentage point over Mazoka. Only 29 per cent of voters had cast their ballots for him which meant that some 70 per cent had voted against him. The MMD also scraped through, winning 69 out of the 150 contested parliamentary seats. Even with an extra eight seats nominated by the president, the MMD can only muster 77 seats against the opposition's 81.

The opposition immediately claimed the elections had been rigged. Both EU election observers and the US Carter Centre agreed, saying the results were 'unsafe'. After the elections, opposition parties launched a legal challenge over the results. In September 2002, proceedings began in the Supreme Court, which is to rule over whether to nullify the results. As no time limit was stipulatedl, a decision by the bench of seven judges is not expected until the second half of 2003. Few expect the verdict to succeed in over-turning the election results. The opposition had squandered a great opportunity of defeating MMD by failing to provide a united front, thereby splitting the vote.

Even in parliament the opposition could not make its majority count. When the MMD tried to replace the normal custom of electing the speaker through an open 'aye' and 'nay' vote with a secret ballot, tempers frayed and water bottles were hurled in the direction of the MMD benches. The opposition seemed determined to act together to prevent the MMD candidate and previous speaker, Amusaa Mwanamwambwe, from being re-elected. But, just before the vote, three opposition MPs defected and the MMD's man sailed in with 80 votes to 77 against.

His own man

During the election campaign, Mwanawasa was kept well away from the party's dirty tricks squad and it seems likely that he had no idea at all if any sort of rigging was involved. He seemed to relish the hurly-burly of electioneering and his odd sense of humour went down well with the public.

At his inauguration, he said he would pursue a policy of 'continuity with change' which many interpreted as 'Chiluba mark II'. But he also warned: 'I left in 1994 because of corruption in government, because I felt some people were being shielded and allowed to get away with plundering state resources. I return as president and pledge that no one shall be shielded, whether ministers or senior officials. I am going to run a clean government.'

KEY INDICATORS — Zambia

	Unit	1996	1997	1998	1999	2000
Population	m	9.45	9.78	10.10	10.41	10.72
Gross domestic product (GDP)	US$bn	3.30	3.90	3.40	3.50	3.60
GDP per capita	US$	348	398	337	332	336
GDP real growth	%	6.5	3.4	-1.9	2.2	3.6
Inflation	%	43.1	24.4	24.5	26.8	26.1
Exports (fob) (goods)	US$m	993.0	1,119.0	874.0	756.0	789.0
Imports (fob) (goods)	US$m	1,055.0	1,056.0	1,022.0	871.0	1,008.0
Balance of trade	US$m	-80.0	63.0	-148.0	-115.0	-219.0
Current account	US$m	-122.0	-252.0	-335.0	-195.0	-571.0
Foreign debt	US$bn	6.1	5.6	6.5	5.9	5.6
Total reserves minus gold	US$m	222.7	239.1	69.4	45.4	244.8
Foreign exchange	US$m	220.7	238.0	68.6	45.3	222.5
Exchange rate	per US$	1,207.90	1,314.50	1,862.07	2,388.02	3,110.84

To the consternation of a number of ministers, it became rapidly clear that Mwanawasa really meant what he said. Far from acting as Chiluba's hand-puppet as he was expected to do, he was turning out to be a dedicated anti-corruption missionary. Reports suggest that he tore up a list of ministerial nominees handed to him by Chiluba and drew up his own list. He brought the veteran Emmanuel Kasonde, one of the most polished finance ministers in Zambia's history, back into the fold, put Mundia Sikatana, an acknowledged Chiluba foe, in charge of agriculture and fired the formidable Vernon Mwanga from the ministry of information. Of the old guard, he retained Enoch Kavindele as vice president, but has increased the pressure on him by bringing the ministry of agriculture under his office at a time when serious food shortages face the country.

Chiluba in the sights

The most ruthless cut was reserved for Chiluba himself. The former president complained that Mwanawasa had done nothing to 'protect' him when the opposition took him to court over his end-of-service benefits. As part of his golden goodbye, Chiluba was entitled to a government-owned house, state security personnel, staff and a pension of around US$700,000 per year. Under the Former President's Act, past leaders can only enjoy their pensions and other privileges when they are no longer actively involved in politics. The opposition argued successfully that as president of MMD, Chiluba was still active in politics and therefore did not qualify for the benefits. As a result, he was forced to relinquish his official car, house and support staff. In July 2002, parliament voted unanimously to lift Chiluba's immunity against prosecution. Parliament's decision was approved by the High Court in September, after Chiluba supporters launched a legal bid to win back his immunity.

The move followed allegations by Mwanawasa that linked Chiluba and his close aides with high-level corruption. The president claimed that around US$20.5 million intended for arms purchases was diverted into accounts owned by Chiluba, his family and his close associates. Chiluba is also accused of bribing the former chief justice, Matthew Mgulube, while the former head of the Zambia Intelligence Security Services, Xavier Chunga, and the Zambian ambassador to the US, Attan Syasongwe, were arrested in connection with Chiluba's alleged corruption syndicate.

Copper come-down

In 2002, Zambia's economy was dominated by the implications of Anglo-American's decision to cut its losses and pull out of the Konkola Copper Mines (KCM) operations. The announcement, in late January, came just days after Levy Mwanawasa's inauguration as president.

Anglo-American's withdrawal came as a bitter blow to Zambians. There is little doubt that this is Africa's biggest privatisation failure and the ripples will extend far beyond Zambia's borders.

The impact of Anglo-American's withdrawal is not only confined to financial losses, but comes as a body blow to the nation's psyche. The revitalisation of copper mining had come to symbolise the revitalisation of the country's economy – a return of confidence in the future.

In response to Anglo-American's announcement, Mwanawasa said that 'Zambia was not for sale', echoing the sentiments of Kenneth Kaunda a generation ago. He said privatisation would continue, but 'at a pace that suits Zambia'. Therefore, it seems likely that the privatisation momentum, which ironically had been gathering pace over the past few years, will now be scaled down in a bid to protect jobs.

Anglo-American's decision also upset the World Bank and the Commonwealth Development Corporation (CDC), both of which held stakes in KCM and were deeply involved in the privatisation strategy. The World Bank's International Finance Corporation (IFC) and CDC Financial Services owned 7.5 per cent of KCM, with Zambia Copper Investments (ZCI) holding 65 per cent and the state-owned Zambia Consolidated Copper Mines (ZCCM) holding the remaining 20 per cent. Anglo-American holds a 50.9 per cent share in ZCI.

Anglo-American claimed that failure to raise external finance for the Konkola Deep Mine Project (KDMP), which was the centrepiece of their investment strategy, and the prevailing low prices for copper and cobalt had forced their hand. 'This has been a difficult and regrettable decision for all involved', said Tony Trahar, Anglo-American's chief executive officer. Simon Thompson, ZCI's chairman, was more forthright: 'The board, having taken financial advice, believes that there is no reasonable prospect of securing the required project financing. It is with deep regret that, without the prospect of KDMP, the board believes that further investment in the high cost, short life, loss making KCM cannot be justified.' Losses are estimated to be in the region of US$100 million since Anglo-American-controlled ZCI took a controlling stake in KCM in March 2000.

ZCI said it was considering several options, including the sale, transfer of assets or closure of KCM in a 'socially and environmentally responsible manner'. If a buyer cannot be found before early 2003, the most likely outcome will be the closure of KCM and an estimated job loss of 10,000 miners. The number of subsidiary and related jobs that could also go will be in the hundreds of thousands.

The government has said it will not close KCM, but this will take some doing. However, the World Bank and the IFC have pledged their support to Zambia 'through this difficult time'. The hope is that if the global economy puts on another spurt after the recent slowdown and prices for copper and cobalt pick up, buyers might be found for KDMP which has a projected life span of at least 30 years.

There was one ray of sunshine on an otherwise gloomy mining landscape. First Quantum Mineral Company of Canada began a full definition study on establishing a low-cost open pit mine at Kansanshi, west of the Zambia copper belt. The reserve is recognised as one of the premier undeveloped copper deposits in the world, hosting a near-surface resource of 242 million tonnes of copper and recoverable gold. The reserves convert into some 3.2 million tonnes of copper metal and 1.4 million ounces of gold. First Quantum holds an 80 per cent interest in the project with ZCCM holding the remaining 20 per cent. If the resource is eventually developed, the mine could produce up to 90,000 tonnes of copper metal per year. This would put Zambia into the big league of copper producers worldwide.

Outlook

The failure of the KCM privatisation and serious food shortages as the result of a two-year region-wide drought has put Zambia on the back foot. Grain reserves in Zimbabwe, Malawi and Zambia itself have long been run down. It was estimated that Zambia needed some additional 300,000 tonnes of grain to avoid starvation, particularly in the rural areas. As it is, the UN's Food and Agriculture Organisation (FAO) estimates that some 60 per cent of the population is chronically malnourished, rising to 80 per cent in rural areas.

There have also been several signs that Mwanawasa wants to rein in aspects of Zambia's liberal economic policies and reintroduce some measure of state intervention. The government has announced that it plans to introduce subsidised agricultural inputs and a state marketing body. Mwanawasa has demanded the repayment of millions of US dollars in loans made to government officials by the hopelessly out-of-touch Food Reserve Agency (FRA). The money will go towards creating a new crop marketing authority which will hopefully stabilise prices and provide the base for a strategic grain reserve.

The 10-year-old privatisation programme has been hailed by the World Bank as one of the most outstanding successes in Africa, but few if any of the benefits have reached the common man. Only in some instances has privatisation resulted in more jobs, greater output and more competitive prices.

President Levy Mwanawasa has set out on the near impossible task of changing the political culture of Zambia from one where the individual seeks to take from the nation to one where the individual seeks to give to the nation. He will first have to establish a strong base in the MMD itself and then bring in the best talent from the opposition benches to help in the national cause. But former president Chiluba, still smarting from being usurped by his protégé might have other plans in mind.

Risk assessment

Economic	Poor
Political	Poor
Regional stability	Poor

COUNTRY PROFILE

Historical profile

Shona people arrived in the area in the twelth century, establishing the empire of Mwene Mutapa, which included southern Zambia.

In the sixteenth century, people from the Luba and Lunda around the Congo set up small kingdoms in Zambia.

Portuguese explorers visited the region in the late eighteenth century.

Migration and slave-trading by the Portuguese and Arabs caused instability in the region.

1851 British missionary David Livingstone visited.

1880s British settlers followed Livingstone and the British South Africa Company, headed by British imperialist and financier, Cecil John Rhodes, opened its first copper mine at Broken Hill (later Kabwe) in 1908.

1924 The colony was put under direct British rule; white settlers soon began to call for integration with Southern Rhodesia.

1953–63 Northern Rhodesia (later Zambia) became part of the British-sponsored Federation of Rhodesia and Nyasaland.

1960 The United National Independence Party (UNIP) was formed by Kenneth Kaunda to campaign for independence and the dissolution of white minority rule.

1964 Zambia gained independence in October under the presidency of Kenneth Kaunda. The government supported Marxist rebels in Mozambique, independence movements in Zimbabwe and the African National Congress (ANC) in South Africa. This led to internal security problems and financial difficulties as Zambia's colonial neighbours attempted to destabilise the country.

1964–1970s Key enterprises and land were nationalised.

1972 Zambia became a one-party state with UNIP as the only legal party.

1975 The Tanzania-Zambia Railway Authority (Tazara) opened, linking the Zambia Copperbelt to the Tanzanian port of Dar es Salaam, reducing the country's dependence on Rhodesia and South Africa for port access.

1976 Zambia gave support for Rhodesia's bid for independence and its eventual transformation from white minority rule into Zimbabwe.

1989 Zambia began a programme of austerity measures to stabilise the economy following a long-term fall in the price of Zambia's chief export, copper.

1990 Food riots heightened calls for an end to one-party rule.

1991 Multi-party elections were held in which Kaunda was defeated by Frederick Chiluba and the Movement for Multi-party Democracy (MMD).

1996 At the November elections, the MMD and President Chiluba were re-elected in a landslide victory.

1999 In February, there was a spate of Angolan terrorist attacks in Lusaka. The oil refinery in Ndola was sabotaged in May.

2000 Kaunda resigned as leader of UNIP in April.

2001 Even though the MMD voted in May to change the constitution and allow the president to run for a third term in office, Chiluba announced he would not stand. In the December elections, which were said by the opposition to be flawed, the MMD was re-elected.

2002 Levy Mwanawasa (MMD) was inaugurated as president on 3 January although the opposition filed a petition to have the result of the presidential election nullified, alleging vote-rigging by the ruling party. The EU observer group declared that the results of the polls were flawed and that the electoral commission should publish the individual polling station results.

Political structure

Constitution

In November 1991 Zambia's one-party state was replaced by a multi-party democratic system based on a new constitution. In 1995 the ruling Movement for Multi-party Democracy (MMD) revised the constitution. The Zambia Law Association criticised the new constitution on the grounds that it allows parliament to make retrospective laws and that a president could be elected on receiving the highest number of votes cast even if these amounted to less than 50 per cent. It also condemned amendments to the Bill of Rights of the 1991 Constitution without a referendum. A controversial Bill passed by President Chiluba on 28 May 1996 made further amendments to the constitution: future presidential candidates must be second-generation Zambians.

Form of state

Republic

The executive

Executive power is held by the president elected by universal suffrage for a five-year term. The constitution provides for a cabinet appointed from within parliament and gives it extra powers; the president is not protected against prosecution and does not have the right to declare martial law. The president must obtain parliamentary approval to impose a state of emergency longer than seven days.

National legislature

Legislative power is held by a unicameral National Assembly. The National Assembly has 159 members, including 150 members elected in single seat constituencies for a five-year term, eight members appointed by the president and a speaker.

Legal system

The president appoints judges and nominates the chief justice. Courts include the Supreme Court of Zambia and the High Court.

Last elections

27 December 2001 (presidential and legislative)

Next elections

2006 (presidential and legislative)

Political parties

Ruling party

Movement for Multi-party Democracy (MMD) (re-elected 27 Dec 2001)

Main opposition party

United Party for National Development (UPND)

Population

10.72 million (2000)

Annual population growth rate: 2.4 per cent (1994–2000). The projected growth rate for the period 1999–2015 is 1.3 per cent per annum. Around 58 per cent of the total population is under 15 years of age.

Population density: 13 inhabitants per square km. Urban population: 44 per cent (1994–2000). The majority of people live in the northern Copperbelt towns and Lusaka.

Ethnic make-up

There are 73 ethnic groups in Zambia. The largest single group, comprising 34 per cent of the population, is the Bemba (north-east and Copperbelt areas). Other important groups include the Tonga of the southern province with 16 per cent of the population; the Nyanja of the eastern provinces (14 per cent) who are well represented in the capital, Lusaka; and the Lozi (9 per cent) of the west.

The European population live and work mostly in the urban areas, or on the farmlands along the railway lines. A high proportion of the Asian community is to be found on the Copperbelt and other urban centres.

Religions

Christian, Muslim and indigenous beliefs. Approximately 70 per cent of the population is Christian (mainly Roman Catholic and Protestant).

Labour market and unemployment

The workforce was estimated at 4.6 million people in 2001. The projected rate of growth of the labour force for the period 1999–2010 is 1.9 per cent per annum. Zambia has a high unemployment rate (30 per cent in 2000), although official figures are thought to underestimate vastly the real urban unemployment rate.

Education

The HIV/AIDS crisis in sub-Saharan Africa has not only undermined public investment in education but has also contributed to the shortage of trained teachers, declining literacy rates and low levels of school enrolment. The adult illiteracy rate in Zambia was estimated at 22 per cent over the period 1994–2000. Primary education is officially compulsory and lasts for seven years starting from the age of seven. World Bank estimates in 2000 show that the total primary school enrolment of the relevant age group typically stood at 92 per cent for boys and 86 per cent for girls. Enrolment rates for the richest households are more than one-third higher than for the poorest households. Secondary education begins at the age of 14 and lasts a further five years. There are two universities that provide higher education.

The government has developed a strong education sector reform through the Basic Education Sub-sector Investment Programme (Bessip), which has set the target of universal primary school enrolment for just under half a million children by 2005. Annual government expenditure during the first phase of the reform amounted to US$56 million, excluding contributions from international donors for the projects. The scheme aims to construct 2,000 additional classrooms and improve training in rural schools. Zambia spends typically less than 3 per cent of GDP on education.

Health

World Bank estimates show that the average life expectancy between 1994 and 2000 remained at 45 years and the infant mortality rate stood at 1‾4 per 1,000 live births. Malnutrition in children under the age of five has risen from one-third of the child population to more than half.

A report by the United Nations Development Programme (UNDP), released in Lusaka in 1998, stated that two-thirds of Zambians lived in poverty and there was chronic malnutrition. Approximately 64 per cent of the population had access to an improved water source in 2000.

Zambia has one of the highest rates of HIV in Africa. It is estimated that 42 per cent of hospital beds are occupied by HIV/AIDS sufferers. The World Bank reported that the AIDS epidemic would reduce the rate of population growth from 2.8 per cent annually in 1990–97 to 2.4 per cent by 2005.

The impact on households is severe, with children often kept from attending school in order to help with harvesting of subsistence crops. Households affected by HIV/AIDS have on average 30–35 per cent less income than those who are not affected. Around 60 per cent of families of AIDS sufferers endure food shortages and malnutrition as a direct result of the disease. Like healthcare, the education system is severely affected with a high rate of AIDS deaths among teachers. Studies show that around 55 per cent of households affected by HIV/AIDS are unable to pay school fees as a result. AIDS also poses a significant economic threat, with an estimated annual loss in GDP growth per capita of 1.15 per cent forecast for the period 2000–10. Government expenditure on care for AIDS sufferers is expected to reach US$21 million per annum by 2005 compared to US$12.9 million in 1995, posing an added burden on government expenditure.

Healthcare is provided free in state-funded hospitals and commercially in private sector clinics. Rural health care is rudimentary and frequently provided only by missionary hospitals and clinics. State funding cutbacks have led to severe shortages of medical equipment and staff. Many medical posts are unfilled for lack of funds. The government is keen to encourage private investment in hospitals and believes foreign investment provides the key to the redevelopment of the health sector.

Welfare

Zambia is one of the poorest countries in the world, with an estimated 80 per cent of its 10.7 million people living in desperate poverty. The government provides some basic welfare for pensioners, children and people affected by disasters.

The Pension Scheme Regulation Act of 1996 provides a regulatory framework for private pension schemes. The Zambia National Provident Fund (ZNPF) was successfully transformed into the National Pension Scheme Authority (Napsa) in early 2000. The weaknesses of ZNPF, which included poor benefits, delays in payment and ineffective record keeping were critically examined to overcome similar problems for the Napsa. The economic difficulties in Zambia and the low retirement age of 55 made it necessary for Napsa to begin with modest benefits. The scheme offers three principal benefits namely retirement, invalidity and survivors' benefits. Additionally, it provides a funeral grant.

The scheme is based on the principle of social insurance and requires compulsory financial contributions from both employees and their employers at a rate of 5 per cent each. Retirement benefit is paid on the basis of a minimum contributory period of 15 years. The scheme is basic to allow the development of private occupational pension schemes.

Main cities

Lusaka (capital, estimated population 1.3 million), Kitwe (600,000), Ndola (500,000), Mufulira (250,000), Chingola (200,000), Kabwe (170,000), Luanshya (160,000), Livingstone (150,000), Chililabombwe (100,000), Kalulushi (75,000)

Languages spoken

English is the usual medium for business. There are 73 identified African languages, all Bantu, of which seven are recognised as official vernaculars – Tonga, Lozi, Bemba, Kaonde, Luvale, Lunda and Nyanja. Zambian traders usually have a working knowledge of English.

Official language/s

English

Media

Press

Dailies: There are two principal national daily newspapers, *Times of Zambia* and the *Zambia Daily Mail*.

Weeklies: Major weeklies including Sunday papers are *Zambezi Times Weekly*, *Sunday Mail*, *Sunday Times*, *Sun*

, *Zambian Citizen*, *The Monitor* and *The Weekly Express*. *The Post* is Zambia's leading independent newspaper, published twice weekly.

Business: Business publications include *The Financial Review* and the *Financial Mail*.

Periodicals: Periodicals include the bi-monthly publication *National Mirror* and the monthly *New Age*. The Community Voice media, an organisation of young writers in Lusaka, launched the first community newspaper in March 1999 called the *Community Voice*.

Broadcasting

Radio: A domestic service, in English and seven local languages, is provided by Zambia National Broadcasting Corporation (three channels).

Television: There are services broadcast in English and seven vernacular languages by Zambia National Broadcasting Corporation in Lusaka, Livingstone and Copperbelt towns and all provincial towns, namely Karama, Chipata, Mongu, Solwezi, Mansa, Kabwe.

Economy

Zambia's main economic zone follows the rail-line southwards from the Copperbelt, around Ndola and Kitwe, through Lusaka the capital, to Victoria Falls. This area has been subject to urbanisation, although the rest of the country is relatively sparsely inhabited.

Approximately 43 per cent of GDP output is from the services sector, 39 per cent from industry and 18 per cent from agriculture.

The main economic activity is mining, copper making up almost 60 per cent of exports and cobalt around 20 per cent. The decline in the economy has mirrored the fall in both copper production and world copper prices. Economic restructuring since 1991 has focused on the development of non-copper sectors, which have subsequently recorded growth. However, this has not stopped falling incomes, increased poverty, rising unemployment, increased debt and a growing informal sector. The World Bank estimates that the formal sector employs only 10 per cent of the labour force, while the informal sector employs 60 per cent. Two-thirds of Zambians, mainly in rural areas, face expenditure limits well below the cost of their basic needs and over a third spend 85 per cent of their income on food. The country also faces high inflation and a widening current account deficit which are worsened with the continuing depreciation of the kwacha.

Economic policy is guided by the country's three-year Poverty Reduction and Growth Facility (PRGF), agreed with the IMF in 1999. The programme aims to achieve macroeconomic stability and high levels of growth. Additionally, Zambia is to receive debt service relief up until 2020 under the Enhanced Heavily Indebted Poor Countries Initiative (HIPC).

Full donor support and free market reform has had little impact on poverty and the economy still depends on the volatile price of copper while agricultural output is severely restricted by climatic change. The sharp fall in maize output in 2001 led to speculation that Zambia would not achieve its 5 per cent growth target. In early 2002, fears of an economic downturn were heightened when the Anglo-American mining conglomerate withdrew from the Konkola Copper Mines (KCM) venture. Analysts estimated that this could lead to 3 per cent of the workforce being made redundant, with adverse consequences for the entire economy. In March 2002, deputy finance minister Patrick Kalifungwa echoed these concerns, stating that 'unless another investor is found, there is going to be a serious threat to production, resulting in job losses and also loss in investor confidence in the whole economy'.

External trade

There are no restrictions on the importation of equipment.

Export formalities have been streamlined and exporters are free to trade in any currency at the current market rate.

Exports

Principal exports are copper (typically 58 per cent of total), cobalt (19 per cent), zinc, lead.

Main destinations: UK (25.3 per cent of 2000 total), South Africa (24.6 per cent), Switzerland (9.4 per cent), Malawi (7.5 per cent).

Imports

Principal imports are crude oil, fertilisers, electricity, machinery and transport equipment, basic manufactures, chemicals.

Main sources: South Africa (56.8 per cent of 2000 total), UK (8.3 per cent), Zimbabwe (6.3 per cent), US (5.0 per cent), Japan (3.2 per cent).

Agriculture

About 10 per cent of Zambia's 600 million hectares is arable land but only around 30 million hectares is under cultivation. The country has abundant perennial and underground water resources. Power generated by hydroelectric plants has been extended to some farming areas. In the wetter northern part of the country tea and coffee thrive at the higher altitudes, with maize and millet closer to sea level. The climate of the central province suits maize, soya beans, cotton and tobacco. The south and west are drier and suit sorghum, tobacco, cotton and groundnuts.

Agriculture accounts for approximately 18 per cent of GDP. Most of the 300,000 smallholders are subsistence farmers. Approximately 40 per cent of production originates from 500 commercial farms. Most state-run farms have been privatised. One problem that the industry faces is that much of the land is under tribal authority and difficult to access. To circumvent this problem, the government has set up areas of virgin land, such as the Tazara Corridor Services (Tazcor), which are open for investment.

Government policy has long been to achieve self-sufficiency in food production, increase exports and improve the supply of inputs to peasant farmers. Measures have included a wide range of production incentives, comprising preferential tax and loan rates, the encouragement of foreign investment and improvements in producer prices.

Agricultural reform during the 1990s was politically sensitive and socially painful. Most food prices were previously subsidised and state withdrawal from the market pushed up prices. Reform also hit productivity and profits. Deregulation has led to the collapse of the state farmer credit and marketing system and over one-third of Zambia's biggest farms ceased production as rising input prices made farming unprofitable. Wheat farmers find it difficult to compete with subsidised American flour imported from South Africa.

Official policy has also encouraged new crops for export which include coffee, flowers and exotic vegetables for European markets. In contrast to these successful new crops, cashew nut production has failed to penetrate European markets. Regional integration means that farmers are finding foreign competition difficult as high production costs, high taxation levels and cheap imports continue to undermine their competitiveness.

Zambian agriculture is barely sustaining its own producers, who are battling with an undervalued exchange rate, drought and an over-reliance on maize (a legacy of Kaunda's policies), which needs expensive fertilisers. Maize production has fallen drastically in recent years, leading to a worrying shortfall in the main staple food. Cotton is grown mainly in the eastern, central and southern provinces, where ginneries are operating. Output has fallen progressively since the late 1980s, although it showed signs of moderate revival in the late 1990s.

The Nakambala Estate was set up as a pilot project for the Zambia Sugar Company (ZSC) in 1964 by Tate and Lyle. It has a farm with 10,000 hectares and a refinery which processes its own cane as well as cane from other estates.

Nakambala has a capacity to produce 150,000 tonnes a year (tpy) of raw sugar, although production typically averages 135,000tpy. About 100,000tpy is needed for the domestic market, with the rest available for export.

Production of Virginia and Burley tobacco has increased since the mid-1980s on account of price rises. The most suitable areas for production are Mkushi and parts of the Eastern Province. Tobacco output is typically around 3,100tpy.

Farming

There are more than 300,000 smallholders, earning cash from growing mainly cotton and tobacco. About 500 highly mechanised commercial farms and estates account for 40 per cent of marketed crops and animal produce. There are vital shortages of input, but production has improved in recent years because of higher producer prices, higher spending on agricultural development and irrigation schemes.

In 2002, there was a food deficit caused by drought and floods in 2001. Starting in the second half of 2002, the government plans to resettle 15,000 farmers and provide them with free fertilisers and seeds, in an effort to boost maize production and diversify the economy.

Forestry

Half of Zambia's land area is covered by forest but there are only a few commercially exploitable tree species. Charcoal is a significant cooking and heating fuel in rural areas. In some regions, the trees are so decimated that unless the government encourages replanting there will be a severe shortage of charcoal.

Industry and manufacturing

The industrial sector typically contributes around 39 per cent to GDP and employs 8 per cent of the labour force.

Macroeconomic stabilisation and divestiture of state assets has led to a severe contraction in these sectors of the economy. The government is no longer willing to subsidise the industrial and manufacturing sector. This change contrasts vividly with policy in the 1960s and 1970s whereby vast copper profits were used to establish one of the largest parastatal economies in Africa.

Targeted sectors for development include agriculture derived processed products and non-traditional exports such as textiles, chemicals and engineering products.

Tourism

Tourism holds a lot of promise. The lunar eclipse and the Organisation of African Unity (OAU) summit in June and July 2001 attracted record numbers of visitors. International hotel chains have invested heavily in upgrading facilities. The Sun International resort complex in Livingstone (on the Zambian side of the Victoria Falls) which was opened in May 2001 and described as an African treasure, was built at a cost of US$38.5 million over 46 hectares of land. The complex expects 100,000 tourists a year, adding as much as 3 per cent to the country's GDP. The Zambian government has pledged to spend at least US$7 million on Livingstone airport to raise it to international standards capable of landing large-bodied passenger aircraft.

Mining

Zambia has enormous mineral wealth, with major deposits of copper, cobalt, lead, zinc, emeralds, aquamarine, amethyst and tourmaline. It also has small reserves of selenium, manganese, tin, nickel, iron, gold, silver and diamonds. The mining sector contributes around a fifth of GDP and employs around 10 per cent of the workforce. Copper and its by-products, mostly cobalt, account for around 90 per cent of mining production and mining exports. Zambia is also the second largest producer of cobalt after the Democratic Republic of Congo (DRC), with around a third of the world's reserves. The Zambia Consolidated Copper Mines (ZCCM) ranked fourth among market economies for mined copper production and sixth for refined copper in the early 1990's. Copper and cobalt production provide around 80 per cent of Zambia's foreign exchange and contribute to over 20 per cent of its GDP.

Substantial amounts of cobalt can be recovered from the copper slag heaps, for which Canada's Colossus Resources obtained a 25-year contract with ZCCM signed in 2000. MCM gained control of the Nkana and Mufulira cobalt mines and refineries in 2000, which are projected to produce 1,800 tonnes per year (tpy) of cobalt by 2004. The Nkana and Nchanga mines produce more than half of Zambia's copper and 70 per cent of its cobalt.

There is very little mining activity outside the Copperbelt although base metal exploration has continued in other regions. Zambia is prospecting for chromium, nickel, tin, tantalite and iron ore. The government allows private sector purchase and export of gemstones. Mining companies can retain 50 per cent of foreign exchange earnings.

In 2001, Zambian Copper Investments (ZCI), majority owned by South Africa's Anglo-American, withdrew its majority share-holding in the Konkola Copper Mines (KCM), also part-owned by the Commwealth Development Corporation (CDC) and the World Bank's International Finance Corporation (IFC). In early 2002, Anglo-American withdrew from ZCI. It claimed that the Konkola Deep Mine Project (KDMP), a central part of KCM's activities as well as being regarded as the main source of future growth in the Zambian mining sector, was unviable and it could not raise the necessary finance for the project. Unless another strategic partner can be found by 2003, KCM will be closed with an estimated loss of 10,000 jobs directly lost.

Zambia contains approximately a quarter of the world's gem emeralds and accounts for an estimated 20 per cent of output of rough emeralds. Other gemstones mined on a smaller scale include amethysts in the Southern Province near Lake Kariba and Kalomo. Deposits of aquamarine and tourmaline are mined for the jewellery trade. Production of gemstones is estimated to be worth US$200 million annually. The largest emerald mine, Kagem, is a joint venture between the state-owned Reserved Minerals Corporation (RMC) and an Indian/Israeli company, Hagura Limited. There are two large private mines and various smaller ones.

Hydrocarbons

Oil

Oil exploration has been completely neglected. The country is dependent on imported fuel supplies. The Tazara 1,710km pipeline from Dar es Salaam, Tanzania, supplies oil to a refinery at Ndola. Oil imports are significant, accounting for about one-fifth of the total import bill, although imports have been cut back steadily since the mid-1980s in order to save foreign exchange.

The Indeni oil refinery, which was destroyed by fire in May 1999, was due to be reopened in December 2000 following a US$14 million refurbishment. However, a second fire in December caused a further US$100,000 in damage and set back the reopening. The World Bank has advised the refinery be closed, claiming that importing crude for refining was more costly than importing refined products. In 2002, the government is to sell off its 50 per cent share in the Indeni refinery, while Agip plans to hold on to its 50 per cent stake.

Coal

Most coal is locally produced at the Maamba Collieries, which have reserves of over 50 million tonnes. Due to a variety of problems production has never exceeded 800,000 tonnes per year (tpy), compared with a rated capacity of 1.2 million tpy. The Maamba Collieries were privatised, with an 80 per cent share sold to Benicon Limited, in 1998.

Energy

Almost 70 per cent of total domestic energy needs are met by hydroelectricity, mostly from plants at Kafue Gorge, Kariba North and Livingstone, which, together with several smaller hydroelectric and diesel plants, have a capacity of 1,700MW. The national demand for power is about 1,000MW, of which 70 per cent is accounted for by the mining industry. However, only 10 per cent of the population has access to electricity.

The Zambian Electricity Supply Company (Zesco) is the national electricity authority responsible for transmission and distribution. It is up for privatisation, although divestment has been delayed due to ongoing political disputes and its lengthy reorganisation in preparation for privatisation. By 2002, the government had not set a date for privatisation.

Zambia also owns the Central African Power Corporation (CAPC) with Zimbabwe. CAPC operates the two Kariba power stations. The country is able to export power to Zimbabwe, Botswana, Namibia and Tanzania and is connected to the Democratic Republic of Congo (DRC) (from which Zambia has imported electricity) and South Africa.

Financial markets

Stock exchange

The Lusaka Stock Exchange (Luse) was launched in 1994. There was a slow response from foreign investors, despite Zambia's complete relaxation of controls on foreign exchange. However, South African institutions, including the Unity Trust group, expressed interest in the Chilanga Cement and Zambia Sugar Company shares. By the end of 2001, there were only nine companies listed on the stock exchange which has been dominated by Zambia Consolidated Copper Mines (ZCCM).

Banking

Zambia's banking sector has undergone a period of crisis and change. The liberalisation of the economy during the 1990s gave rise to the launch of a number of banks. Poor management and over-banking led to the closure of a number of these banks, prompting a wave of concern among investors and depositors who have lost money.

The main national commercial banks, Zambia National Commercial Bank and National Savings and Credit Bank of Zambia, are state-owned. The government hopes to complete the privatisation of the Zambia National Commercial Bank in 2002. African Commercial Bank, set up in 1984, is a private sector bank. The largest commercial banks, Barclays Bank of Zambia and Standard Chartered Bank Zambia, are foreign-owned. However, since January 1972 all foreign-owned banks have been required to incorporate locally.

There are several state-owned development banks and other financial institutions. The Development Bank of Zambia offers medium- and long-term loans and business consultancy services.The Agricultural Finance Company and Zambia Agricultural Development Bank were merged and renamed the Lima Bank. Zambia State Finance Company is a subsidiary of the government-owned Zambia State Insurance Corporation (ZSIC). Other development banks include the state-owned Zambia National Building Society and the Zambia Import and Export Bank.

In January 2002, President Mwanawasa pledged to revive the Co-operative Bank, which was closed in 1997. This is intended to extend lines of credit to farmers, who have suffered due to the closure of rural banking services and high interest rates.

Central bank

Bank of Zambia

Time

GMT plus two hours

Geography

Zambia is landlocked, bordered to the south by Zimbabwe and the Caprivi Strip (an extension of Namibia); to the south-east by Mozambique; to the east by Malawi; to the north-east by Tanzania; to the north and north-west by the Democratic Republic of Congo (DRC); and to the west by Angola.

About nine-tenths of the country is a high rolling plateau (900–1,200 metres above sea level) covered by savannah bush and woodland. The only relief from the monotony of the plateau is the Zambezi and Luangwa rift system. The Luapula River, part of the Congo River system, cuts into the northern part of the plateau.

Zambia takes its name from the Zambezi River. At 2,655km long, this is the third longest river in Africa.

Climate

Altitude governs Zambia's climate and it is generally cooler than its surrounding neighbours. There are three distinct seasons: cool and dry from May to August; hot and dry from September to October; and rainy from November to April. Rainfall varies widely across the country. The average temperature is 16 degrees Celsius (C) in the winter and 24 degrees C in summer.

The Zambezi and Luangwa river valleys can remain hot and humid all year, typical of tropical lowlands. They are particularly uncomfortable in the rainy season.

Dress codes

The contrast between morning, midday and evening temperatures means that a cardigan or pullover is often required in the early morning and after sunset between April and September. A light raincoat or umbrella is useful during the wet season from November to April.

Dress is generally informal. Lightweight suits can be worn for most of the year; during the hot season tropical suits are preferable. Tailored safari suits are popular. A hat and sunglasses are useful for protection against the sun.

Most women wear cotton or other lightweight dresses during the day and evening. Warm dresses and lightweight coats are needed during the coldest season, June to August.

Entry requirements

Passports

Required by all.

Visa

Citizens of the EU, except those from Ireland, require visas unless taking part in a pre-arranged organised tour in conjunction with a registered, Zambian-based tour operator. Visas are also required by citizens of the US but not by those of South Africa.

Copies of visa application forms may be obtained from internet site: http://www.zhcl.org.uk.

Currency advice/regulations

Foreign currency can be imported without limitation. It must be declared on arrival, and no amount over the declaration can be exported. Up to K100 in local currency may be imported or exported.

Health (for visitors)

Mandatory precautions

A yellow fever vaccination certificate is required if travelling from an infected area. Passengers travelling to Zambia by air should have a yellow fever vaccination certificate in case the aircraft is unavoidably detained in central Africa. A certificate of inoculation against cholera is required by travellers who have visited an infected area.

Advisable precautions

Malaria is present (especially the malignant falciparum strain which is resistant to chloroquine) from November to May throughout the country and all year in the Zambezi valley (both weekly nivaquine and daily paludrine should be taken). Rabies and bilharzia are also present, and visitors should avoid swimming or paddling in fresh water. There is a worsening HIV/AIDS epidemic in Zambia. Typhoid and typhus are rare. All water for drinking, brushing teeth or making ice should be sterilised. Milk is pasteurised and therefore safe. Vegetables should be cooked and fruit peeled.

Hotels

Several good quality hotels are available. Hotels are graded from one to five stars by the Hotels Board. A service charge of 10 per cent, plus 10 per cent sales tax are added to all bills. Room charges must be settled in foreign currency. Some hotels require a deposit to cover the room rate and an element for food and drink to be converted to Kwacha on arrival. Tipping not customary in Zambia but is acceptable.

Credit cards

Not widely accepted, except by hotels and duty-free shops.

Public holidays

Fixed dates

1 Jan (New Year's Day), 19 Mar (Youth Day), 1 May (Labour Day), 25 May (African Freedom Day, Anniversary of OAU's Foundation), 24 Oct (Independence Day), 25 Dec (Christmas Day).
Holidays which fall on a Saturday are not celebrated on another weekday.

Variable dates

Good Friday, Easter Saturday, first Mon of Jul (Heroes' Day), first Tue of Jul (Unity Day), first Mon of Aug (Farmers' Day).

Working hours

Banking

Mon–Fri: 0815–1430.

Business

Mon–Fri: 0800–1230, 1400–1630.

Government

Mon–Fri: 0800–1300, 1400–1700.

Shops

Privately owned: Mon–Fri: 0800–1700, Sat: 0800–1300; state-owned: Mon–Sat: 0800–1800, Sun: 0800–1200.
Note: There are wide variations outside city centres.

Telecommunications

Telephone/fax

The international dialling code is +260, followed by area codes: Lusaka 1, Ndola 2, Livingstone 3, Mbala 4, Solwezi 8. Domestic service is limited and expensive.

Electricity supply

230V AC

Social customs/useful tips

Visitors normally entertain business guests in hotels or restaurants, while residents prefer to entertain informally at home or at their clubs. Temporary membership of clubs can normally be obtained on an introduction from friends.

Security

The stealing of cheques has become a problem in Zambia. Visitors are advised to carry travellers' cheques in small denominations and to cash only sufficient for current needs. There has also been a rise in violent crime due to the economic decline and care must be taken when travelling after dark. It is not regarded as advisable to travel by car between Lusaka and the Copperbelt after dark.

Getting there

Air

National airline: There is no national airline.
International airport/s: Lusaka International (Code: LUN), 26km from city; duty-free shop, bar, restaurant, bank, shops, car hire.
Airport tax: Adult international departures (non-residents) US$20, payable in US dollar bills (no other form of payment is accepted), excluding transit passengers and infants under two years. International departure tax for nationals of Zambia and residents is K60,000 and domestic departures K15,000.

Surface

Road: There are tarred roads from Zimbabwe, Democratic Republic of Congo (DRC), Tanzania and Malawi; motorists should check border post hours at Kariba, Chembe, Chirundu, Mwami, Kasum-Balesa, Livingstone, Kazungula and Nakonde, and regulations concerning their vehicles. A customs bond may be required for the import of cars.
During rainy season many rural roads are impassable. It is not advisable to travel by car between Lusaka and the Copperbelt after dark.
Rail: The Tanzania Zambia Railway Authority (Tazara) railway links Zambia to Tanzania – the connection is at Kapiri Mposhi.
Zambia Railways Limited (ZRL) connects with Zimbabwe, Mozambique, South Africa, Botswana and DRC.
Water: Services include ferries from Botswana (Kazungula) and steamers from Kigoma, Tanzania across Lake Tanganyika to Mpulungu.

Getting about

National transport

Air: There are regular flights from Lusaka to Livingstone and to the Copperbelt in the north. There are several flights a week from Lusaka to other centres including Mfuwe in the Luangwa valley. There is also a scheduled service to Johannesburg. Eastern Air has connections with Livingstone, Mfuwe, Kasaba Bay, Ndola, Lusaka, Chipata, Mansa, Kasama and Mongu. Roan Air flies to tourist destinations. Charter companies also operate but are in heavy demand. There is a total of around 150 airfields and airstrips.
Road: The total network is almost 40,000km, of which about 6,500km are main roads. Surfaced roads link main centres. During the rainy season many rural roads are impassable.
Buses: Eagle Travel runs regular coach services to numerous locations including tourist sites. Non-tourist services can be irregular and crowded.
Rail: A passenger service called the Kafubu Express, run by Zambia Railways Limited (ZRL), links Lusaka with Ndola, Livingstone and Kitwe. The total network is over 2,000km.

City transport

Taxis: These are available between airports and hotels and within town centres. They are generally unmetered.
Buses, trams & metro: The United Bus Company of Zambia and other privately-owned companies run domestic services over a number of routes.

Car hire

The Zambia Tourist Board has authorised over 16 car-hire firms serving mainly Lusaka, Livingstone and the Copperbelt which are the major urban and tourist centres. Car hire is usually on a chauffeur-driven basis.

BUSINESS DIRECTORY

Telephone area codes

The international direct dialling (IDD) code for Zambia is +260, followed by the area code:

Chililabombwe	2	Lusaka	1
Chingola	2	Mansa	2
Chipata	62	Mazabuka	32
Itimpi (Garneton)	2	Mbala	4
Kabompo	8	Mufulira	2
Kabwe	2	Mungwi	4
Kasempa	8	Mwinilunga	8
Kitwe	2	Ndola	2
Livingstone	3	Solwezi	8
Luanshya	2		

Chambers of Commerce

Lusaka Chamber of Commerce, Gaudenzio Rossi, Ndeke Hotel, PO Box 30815, Lusaka (tel: 254-736/7).

Zambia Confederation of Industries and Chambers of Commerce (ZACCI), PO Box 30844, 10101 Lusaka.

Banking

Barclays Bank of Zambia, Cairo Rd, PO Box 31936, Lusaka (tel: 228-858/66; fax: 222-519, 226-185).

Cavmont Merchant Bank Ltd, Fourth Floor, Tazara House, Independence Avenue, PO Box 35476, Lusaka (tel: 225-853/6; fax: 224-304; e-mail: cavmont@zamnet.zm).

Citibank, Citibank House, PO Box 30037, Lusaka (tel: 229-025/6/7/8; fax: 226-264).

Credit Africa Bank, Anchor House, Cairo Rd, PO Box 36245, Lusaka (tel: 220-201/2/3/4; fax: 220-196).

Development Bank of Zambia, PO Box 33955, Lusaka (tel: 228-576, 224-072; fax: 222-426).

Finance Bank, PO Box 37102, Lusaka (tel: 229-789/742; fax: 227-544).

Indo Zambia Bank, 686 Cairo Rd, PO Box 35411, Lusaka (tel: 225-080, 222-622; fax: 225-090).

Stanbic Bank, Cairo Rd, Woodgate House, PO Box 31955, Lusaka (tel: 229-071/3, 229-285/6; fax: 221-152, 225-380).

Standard Chartered Bank, PO Box 32238, Lusaka (tel: 229-242; fax: 222-092).

Union Bank, Zimco House, PO Box 34940, Lusaka (tel: 229-397/8; fax: 221-866).

Zambia Export and Import Bank, PO Box 33046, Lusaka (tel: 229-504, 222-304, 229-486/88; fax: 222-313).

Zambia National Commercial Bank, Cairo Rd, PO Box 33611, Lusaka (tel: 228-979, 221-355; fax: 224-006).

Central bank

Bank of Zambia, Cairo Road, PO Box 30080, Lusaka 10101 (tel: 228-888, 229-885; fax: 226-844, 221-791).

Travel information

Tourism Council of Zambia, PO Box 36561, Lusaka (tel: 251-666; fax: 251-501; e-mail: tcz@zamnet.zm; internet: http://www.zambiatourism.com).

Ministry of tourism

Ministry of Tourism, PO Box 30575, Lusaka (tel: 227-645; fax: 225-174).

National tourist organisation offices

Zambia National Tourist Board (ZNTB), Tourist Centre, Mosi-oa-Tunya Road, PO Box 60342, Livingstone (tel: 321-404/5; fax: 321-487; e-mail: zntblive@zamnet.zm); Century House, Cairo Road, Lusaka Square, PO Box 30017, Lusaka (tel: 229-087/90; fax: 225-174; e-mail: zntb@zamnet.zm).

Zambian Airways, 5309 Dedan Kimathi Street, Mukuba Pension House, Lusaka (tel: 225-151; fax: 223-227; email: roanair@zamnet.zm).

Ministries

Ministry of Agriculture, Food and Fisheries, Mulungushi House, Box RW 50291, Lusaka (tel: 251-537/233; fax: 252-029).

Ministry of Commerce, Trade and Industry, Kwacha House Annex, PO Box 31968/34373, Lusaka (tel: 228-301, 221-184; fax: 226-673).

Ministry of Communication and Transport, PO Box 50065, Lusaka (tel: 251-444/938/740/759; fax: 002-601, 253-260).

Ministry of Community Development and Social Services, Fidelity House, PO Box 31958, Lusaka (tel: 227-840, 228-321; fax: 225-327).

Ministry of Defence, PO Box RW 17X, Lusaka (tel: 251-211, 254-667; fax: 254-670, 221-339, 253-875).

Ministry of Education, PO Box 50093, Lusaka (tel: 227-636; fax: 222-396).

Ministry of Energy and Water Development, Ministrial Headquarters, Lusaka (tel: 263-870; fax: 252-339).

Ministry of Environment and Natural Resources, Mulungushi House, PO Box 30055, Lusaka (tel: 252-711, 250-186; fax: 252-952).

Ministry of Finance, PO Box RW 50062, Lusaka (tel: 250-544, 227-668; fax: 250-501).

Ministry of Foreign Affairs, PO Box 50069, Lusaka (tel: 262-666; fax: 250-634/240, 252-867).

Ministry of Health, PO Box 30205, Lusaka (tel: 227-745, 223-435; fax: 223-435).

Ministry of Home Affairs, PO Box 50997, Lusaka (tel: 254-261/362; fax: 224-656, 254-669).

Ministry of Information and Broadcasting Services, PO Box 50200, Lusaka (tel: 251-766, 253-965; fax: 254-013, 252-391, 250-524).

Ministry of Labour and Social Security, PO Box 32186, Lusaka (tel: 227-640).

Ministry of Lands, Mulungushi House, PO Box 30069, Lusaka (tel: 252-288; fax: 250-130).

Ministry of Legal Affairs, PO Box 50106, Lusaka (tel: 251-588; fax: 253-695).

Ministry of Local Government and Housing, PO Box 34204, Lusaka (tel: 253-077; fax: 252-680).

Ministry of Mines and Minerals Development, PO Box 31969, Lusaka (tel: 252-990; fax: 251-224).

Ministry of Science, Technical Education and Vocational Training, PO Box 50464, Lusaka (tel: 229-673; fax: 252-951).

Ministry of Sports, Youth and Child Development, 4th Floor, Memaco House, Sapele Rd, Lusaka (tel: 227-168; fax: 223-996).

Ministry of Works and Supply, PO Box 50236, Lusaka (tel: 253-266; fax: 222-360).

Other useful addresses

Central Statistics Office, PO Box 31908, Lusaka.

Chilanga Cement plc, Kafue Road, PO Box 32639, Lusaka (tel: 225-2853, 701-297; fax: 252-853, 252-655).

Export Board of Zambia, PO Box 30064, Third Floor, State Lottery Building, Cairo Road, North End, Lusaka (tel: 228-106/7; fax: 222-509).

Lusaka Stock Exchange Ltd, Lusaka (tel: 228-594, 228-391; fax: 228-608, 225-969; e-mail: luse@zamnet.zm).

Metal Marketing Corp of Zambia, PO Box 35570, 10101 Lusaka (tel: 228-131/140).

National Commission for Development Planning, PO Box 50268, Lusaka.

National Import & Export Corporation, PO Box 30282, 10101 Lusaka (tel: 228-018).

Zambia Electricity Supply Corporation Ltd (Zesco), PO Box 33304, Stand 6949 Great East Road, Lusaka 10101 (tel: 223-970; fax: 223-971).

Zambian Embassy (USA), 2419 Massachusetts Avenue, NW, Washington DC 20008 (tel: 265-9717; fax: 332-0826; e-mail: info@zambiainfo.org).

Zambia Industrial & Commercial Copper Industry Service Bureau, PO Box 22100, Kitwe.

Zambia Investment Centre, 5th Floor, Ndeke House, Haile Selassie Avenue, PO Box 34580, Lusaka (tel: 252-130, 252-152; fax: 252-150; e-mail: invest@zamnet.zm).

Zambia National Broadcasting Corporation, PO Box 50015, 10101 Lusaka (tel: 229-648).

Zambia National Oil Company Limited (ZNOC), Lusaka (tel: 222-135; fax: 220-144, 221-265).

Zambia Privatisation Agency (ZPA), Privatisation House, Nasser Road, PO Box 30819, Lusaka (tel: 227-851, 223-859, 227-791; fax: 225-270; e-mail: zpa@zamnet.zm).

Zambia Railways Ltd (ZRL), PO Box 80935, Kabwe (tel: 223-822, 222-201/209; fax: 228-023/025).

Zambia Telecommunications Co Ltd, Lusaka (tel: 611-111, 612-399; fax: 613-055, 615-855).

Internet sites

Zambian Express: http://www.africa-insites.com

Africa Business Network: http://www.ifc.org/abn

AllAfrica.com: http://allafrica.com

African Development Bank: http://www.afdb.org

Africa Online: http://www.africaonline.com

Harambee Afrika (UK business club for traders with east, central and southern Africa; includes annotated web resource list): http://www.harambee.co.uk

Mbendi AfroPaedia (information on companies, countries, industries and stock exchanges in Africa): http://mbendi.co.za

Zimbabwe

Daniel Brett

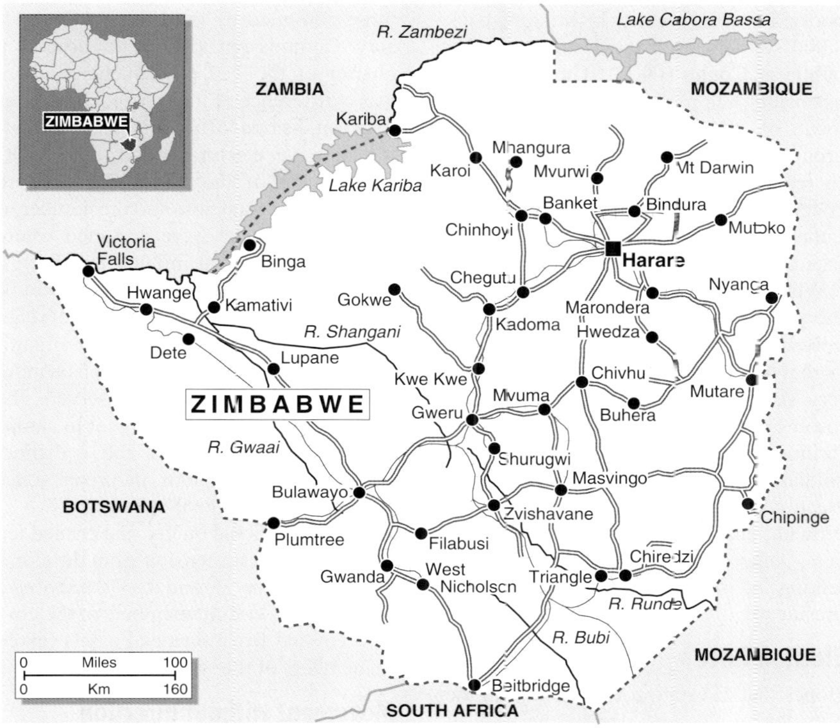

It is remarkable that President Robert Mugabe, an international pariah presiding over a country in ruins, managed to maintain his grip on power in 2001 and 2002. The opposition Movement for Democratic Change (MDC) was virtually driven underground by the ruling Zimbabwe African National Union-Patriotic Front (Zanu-PF) as Mugabe sought, and won, another term of office. Mugabe's victory led to a feeling of hopelessness among his embattled opponents, who were divided on how to proceed.

Meanwhile, the commercial farming sector, once the lynchpin of the economy, faced collapse with white farmers fleeing the notorious squads of self-styled 'war veterans', while over six million Zimbabweans faced starvation in 2002. Inflation was running at 114 per cent in April 2002 and the government was predicting another year of economic decline, with GDP forecast to contract by 10 per cent by end-2002. Mugabe's quest for power and wealth at all costs appears to have sealed Zimbabwe's fate as a deeply impoverished and isolated state

Silencing critics

In 2001 and 2002, the government stepped up its policy of intimidation against its opponents to seal Mugabe's victory in the 2002 presidential election. One of its targets was the independent media which faced harassment from the authorities and Mugabe's supporters as well as draconian legislation. The *Daily News*, Zimbabwe's main independent newspaper, faced threats of closure while its editor-in-chief, Geoffrey Nyarota, was frequently arrested by the police and its offices were fire-bombed by Zanu-PF supporters. The *Zimbabwe Independent* was also subjected to intimidation and its editor was placed under arrest following the elections, for investigating corruption linked to the president's family. Foreign journalists were also harassed, the BBC was

KEY FACTS

Official name: Republic of Zimbabwe

Head of State: President Robert Gabriel Mugabe (Zanu-PF) (since 1980)

Head of government: President Robert Gabriel Mugabe

Ruling party: Zimbabwe African National Union-Patriotic Front (Zanu-PF) (re-elected in Jun 2002 with 62 seats)

Area: 391,109 square km

Population: 12.30 million (2001)

Capital: Harare

Official language: English, Shona, Ndebele

Currency: Zimbabwe dollar (Z$) = 100 cents

Exchange rate: Z$55.45 per US$ (official rate) (Jan 2003)

GDP per capita: US$264 (2001); US$280 (2002)*

GDP real growth: -7.30% (2001); -5.6% (2002)*

Unemployment: 60.00% (Jun 2001)*

Inflation: 74.50% (2001); 138.1% (2002)*

Balance of trade: US$260.00 million (2001)

Foreign debt: US$3.78 billion (2001)

* estimated figure

For the latest Key Facts, go to www.worldinformation.com

banned and some correspondents for the foreign media were arrested.

A raft of new legislation has helped strengthen the government's hand over its political opponents and the private media. The Public Order and Security Bill, which came into law in January 2002, imposed prison sentences of up to five years for those who 'publish or communicate false statements prejudicial to the state', including criticism of the police or undermining the authority of the president. The police were given the power to close down and ban public meetings, making it virtually impossible for the MDC to organise election rallies. The bill was passed alongside the Electoral Act Amendment Bill, which gave the government the power to bar foreign and independent local election monitors. Despite being drastically watered down in parliament, the Access to Information and Protection of Privacy Bill, passed in February 2002, enabled officials to refuse access to information such as government policy.

The legislation, enacted just ahead of the election, stopped just short of completely closing the independent media down. It also changed the way the MDC fought the election. Instead of holding large demonstrations that would have attracted violence from the police and Zanu-PF gangs, Morgan Tsvangirai, leader of the MDC, opted to hold small private meetings and the MDC organised itself into small, secretive cells. Nevertheless, Mugabe's brigades continued to spread fear in the run-up to the election, with reports of beatings, abductions, torture, destruction of crops and property, death threats and the rape of female MDC supporters.

To insure himself against a *coup d'état*, Mugabe put the security forces on double pay from the beginning of January 2002. He had little to fear from the top brass, who are all Zanu-PF stalwarts, but the move ensured that the middle-ranks of the forces were pulled into line. He also boosted internal security by bringing back 8,000 soldiers from the Democratic Republic of Congo (DRC). They had been ostensibly helping to protect the government of Joseph Kabila against rebel groups and Ugandan and Rwandan forces. In reality, they were guarding diamond concessions given to Mugabe by Kabila's father, Laurent, before he was assassinated in January 2001.

While high ranking officers, along with the political elite, profited from the involvement of the Zimbabwe Defence Forces (ZDF) in DRC's civil war, the military venture has been unpopular among lower ranks. Not only did the arrival of returning troops help swell the numbers of soldiers available to assist with Mugabe's election campaign, but the move eased the growing disenchantment of junior officers, some of whom had been privately talking of staging a coup against the president.

Election farce

Hopes that Tsvangirai could still win the presidential elections despite the level of state violence used against his campaign were dashed after Mugabe secured a controversial election victory in the polls. The incumbent won by 55 per cent to the MDC leader's 42 per cent, but only after extensive rigging by the government. The MDC and the EU and Commonwealth observer missions challenged the legitimacy of the results.

There were huge discrepancies between the results announced by Registrar General Tobiah Mudede, a Mugabe ally, and those compiled by the Election Supervisory Commission (ESC). In around a quarter of the 120 constituencies, there was a difference of more than 5,000 votes between the two 'official' results, suggesting massive electoral fraud. The MDC claimed that if the ESC's figures were taken as the actual vote and the number of votes for Mugabe were deducted where the registrar general inflated the figures, Tsvangirai would have won the election.

Concerns were also raised by foreign governments, the MDC and civic organisations over the government's ban on independent domestic election observers, the location of polling stations next to camps housing Zanu-PF militia and a distinct lack of polling stations in urban areas, where the MDC vote is strongest.

The international outcry that ensued led to Zimbabwe's suspension from the Commonwealth. The EU and the US imposed a travel ban on leading members of the government and froze financial assets linked to members of the regime.

Movement without direction

The results threw the MDC into uncertainty. The opposition party is a relatively loose coalition of human rights activists, trade unionists, political activists and professionals; there is a significant possibility that, without any ideological coherence, it could disintegrate. After the elections, the South African government put pressure on the MDC and Zanu-PF to form a government of national unity. The proposal divided the MDC, which was already resentful at South African President Thabo Mbeki's failure to act against Mugabe's government. Some MDC moderates saw joining a coalition government as the only way to influence change within the government. They claimed that mass action on the streets would lead to a bloodbath, while legal action would ultimately fail due to doubts over the independence of the judiciary. They also saw a unity government as a way of re-engaging Zimbabwe in the international economy and reducing its diplomatic isolation. Those who objected to forming an alliance with Mugabe claimed it would simply give the

KEY INDICATORS — Zimbabwe

	Unit	1996	1997	1998	1999	2000
Population	m	11.91	12.29	12.68	13.08	12.63
Gross domestic product (GDP)	US$bn	8.60	8.50	6.10	5.60	7.20
GDP per capita	US$	722	692	481	428	570
GDP real growth	%	10.4	2.7	2.9	-0.7	-5.1
Inflation	%	21.5	18.8	31.7	58.5	55.9
Coal output	mtoe	3.3	3.3	3.4	3.5	2.6
Exports (fob) (goods)	US$m	2,500.0	2,424.0	1,925.0	1,924.0	1,801.0
Imports (fob) (goods)	US$m	2,210.0	2,654.0	1,675.0	1,675.0	1,500.0
Balance of trade	US$m	287.0	-154.0	250.0	249.0	301.0
Current account	US$m	-180.0	-827.0	-355.0	28.0	-143.0
Foreign debt	US$bn	4.6	5.0	4.7	4.6	3.9
Total reserves minus gold	US$m	598.8	160.1	130.8	268.0	193.1
Foreign exchange	US$m	588.9	159.6	130.1	266.5	192.5
Bank rate	%	27.0	31.5	39.5	74.4	57.8
Exchange rate	per US$	9.92	11.89	27.90	38.83	46.66

president legitimacy he does not deserve while it would fail to influence the policy of the dictatorial one-party state.

Tsvangirai and his top aides have rejected any unity agreement and have opted for a legal fight. This has disappointed not only the moderates, but also the radicals, many of whom are agitating for mass demonstrations, a boycott of parliament and even going into the bush and igniting a civil war. However, radical voices have been muted since the 'stay-away' called after the elections by the Zimbabwe Congress of Trade Unions (ZCTU), which failed to attract mass support. There is a growing feeling of disillusionment among the party's supporters in poor urban areas who are no longer interested in pursuing ultimately futile legal manouevres while they face starvation and state violence. The Zimbabwean Trotskyist party, the International Socialist Organisation (ISO), has accused MDC senior party figures of abandoning its grassroots.

Another threat to opposition unity comes from the possible imprisonment of Tsvangirai for treason. Shortly after the elections, the MDC leader and two other senior party leaders were accused of plotting to assassinate Mugabe at a meeting held with Canadian political consultants in December 2001. If the MDC leadership is imprisoned, there is a good chance that the party will disintegrate into factions due to lingering arguments over strategy.

In the end, the MDC leadership may have no control over events. Mass starvation caused by drought and Mugabe's disastrous land reform programme may provoke hungry youths to go on the rampage, particularly in the streets of the capital, Harare. In mid-2002, ZCTU Vice President Lucia Matibenga warned that civil unrest could spread to rural areas, which rely on remittances from relatives living in the city.

Farm fight

The most high-profile issue in the election campaign was the land reform programme. In the run-up, Zanu-PF tried to win support in its rural heartlands by speeding up the seizures of land owned by white commercial farmers. Mugabe called on the mythology of the *chimurenga*, the war of liberation against imperialism and white minority rule which he had helped to lead in the 1970s, to justify the land grab and rectify British imperial wrongdoing.

The unequal distribution of land between whites and blacks is a hang-over of colonialism, which had not been addressed in the years of black rule since 1980. Throughout the post-independence era, land redistribution was too expensive to carry out due to the high level of compensation demanded by white commercial farmers and the costs incurred after blacks are given the land. Mugabe was to a large extent to blame for these problems. He and his allies pocketed millions of US dollars in foreign donor aid which was intended to pay for land redistribution programmes. When donors stopped the flow of aid and Mugabe's popularity plummeted in the face of economic decline, the Zanu-PF sent in its strongarm squads to steal white-owned farms, regardless of whether they had inherited land under the colonial Rhodesian administration or bought it in post-independence Zimbabwe. Also, when the judiciary ruled in favour of white farmers in court cases in 2000 and 2001, judges were sacked and laws were either rewritten or ignored.

The election campaign saw a rise in violent land occupations. Mugabe's subsequent victory saw white farmers give up hope of maintaining ownership of their land and many left the country to buy farms in more stable countries, such as neighbouring Zambia and Mozambique or further afield in Australia. By mid-2002, the number of white commercial farmers had dwindled to under 2,900 from over 4,500 before the occupations began in 2000. Dismissing criticism from Western governments, the Mugabe regime made its final, devastating move against the white farming community in June 2002 and ordered them to abandon their land by 10 August or face imprisonment. Only 500 farms complied with another order to cease production immediately. The Commercial Farmers' Union (CFU), the representative body for white farmers, claimed that they did not want to leave their crops to rot in the fields while millions of Zimbabweans faced starvation. By end-August 2002, hundreds of white farmers took court action to challenge Mugabe's order that they stop farming. Calls also went out for government assistance for around 300,000 farm workers who had been made unemployed by the fast-track land reform. In September, 10 commercial farmers won a court challenge against their eviction. Farmers who had been arrested for failing to surrender their farms hoped this would set a precedent. By October, the government closed the loophole in the law which had given a reprieve to farmers on the basis that the bondholding bank had not been notified by the government over acquisition. Farmers leaving the land were also banned from moving their equipment outside Zimbabwe to where they may have acquired new land to farm.

Economic disaster zone

The land seizures have placed a heavy toll on the economy, with valuable crops left rotting in the fields following farm seizures, while capital flight has picked up pace. Productive fields that once produced bumper crops of maize and tobacco are now being farmed by peasant families using ox-drawn ploughs, who produce just enough to feed immediate relatives for a few months. Farm machinery has been left idle, while the production of cash crops for export, which are vital to the economy, has diminished. The UN's Food and Agriculture Organisation (FAO) reported that tobacco and maize output had each fallen by 23 per cent in 2001 compared to the previous year.

The land reform programme has helped throw the economy into reverse and exacerbate Zimbabwe's difficulties. Dwindling output of agro-exports and the lack of foreign currency reserves have destabilised the economy to an extent that it cannot afford sufficient commercial imports of staple grains to make up for the loss in domestic food output. With the economy in chaos, there is little hope that the rural *chimurenga* will lead to anything but disaster. Plots on redistributed land are too small to be productive and there is no money for inputs, and no skilled farmers while weather conditions are poor.

Mugabe's policies are also beginning to create disaster in the ailing industrial sector. Factories belonging to foreigners are being seized by Mugabe's allies and family members with the help of Zanu-PF gangs. The main targets are mining and manufacturing companies. In June 2002, Mugabe threatened to nationalise one of the country's largest companies, majority-owned by South Africa's Anglo-American Corporation. He accused the multinational company of manipulating food shortages to sabotage the economy. His comments came after National Foods, the country's largest food distributor, which is 34 per cent owned by Anglo- American, was accused of hoarding salt, which was in short supply in Zimbabwe. The police seized nearly 20 tonnes of salt from National Foods which they believed were going to be burnt 'in a suspected act of economic sabotage and political mischief'.

Outlook

The arbitrary and illegal seizure of private property by Zanu-PF is likely to continue as long as Mugabe is in power. This will result in further economic and political destabilisation along with increasingly desperate attempts by the government to crush the opposition and private media.

The continuation of this state of affairs can be partly blamed on the attitude of other African states towards Mugabe's rule. Apart from backing Zimbabwe's suspension from the Commonwealth, South Africa's mild condemnation of the regime and its scant and inconsistent attention to human rights concerns have fuelled polarisation both domestically and regionally. Meanwhile, Libya is bankrolling the Zanu-PF and supplying large amounts of cheap fuel to keep Mugabe's rule from collapsing. This has freed up resources for arms imports, including anti-riot tanks from Israel, for the inevitable showdown between the government and its opponents.

Unless and until the armed forces decide to remove Mugabe and install a more flexible and democratic government, there is a constant threat that the country's frustrated and angry urban working class will dismiss the MDC leadership's concerns and fight Zanu-PF and the security forces in the streets and in the bush. The result of such a confrontation will be disastrous, with a large loss of life and the possible disintegration of the MDC.

The crisis in Zimbabwe is having a deleterious effect on the regional economy and has helped drag down the value of the South African rand, upsetting trading relations within the Southern African Development Community (SADC). There may come a point where African governments will turn against the Zimbabwe leadership and adopt a more hardline approach, if only to protect their own interests.

Risk assessment

Economic	Very poor
Political	Very poor
Regional stability	Poor

COUNTRY PROFILE

Historical profile

In the eleventh century, the Shona people of Great Zimbabwe began trading with the Swahili traders on the Mozambique coast. Great Zimbabwe became southern Africa's richest and most powerful nation. In the 1500s, as Great Zimbabwe began to decline, the various Shona tribes broke up into autonomous states. Alliances between Shona states led to the formation of the Rozwi state.

1834 The Ndebele tribe invaded from the south, assassinated the leader of Rozwi and established the Ndebele state.

1870 Mzilikazi was succeeded by his son Lobengula. Around the same time Europeans, in particular Cecil John Rhodes, began exploring the regions.

1889 Rhodes formed the British South Africa Company and the territories that today comprise Zimbabwe became the British colony of Southern Rhodesia.

1922 The white minority of mostly British settlers voted to become a self-governing British dominion.

1953 Southern Rhodesia (Zimbabwe), Northern Rhodesia (Zambia) and Nyasaland (Malawi) were united in the Central African Federation (CAF).

The Zimbabwe African People's Union (Zapu) and the Zimbabwe African National Union (Zanu) were formed in the early 1960s as a result of growing black opposition.

1963 The CAF collapsed after Zambia and Malawi elected to become separate independent states.

1964 Ian Smith of the Rhodesian Front (RF) became prime minister. He called for full independence from Britain, with an electoral system that would preserve white minority rule.

1965 The RF made a unilateral declaration of independence (UDI). Despite international sanctions, Smith managed to keep his regime intact until 1980, with the support of apartheid South Africa and Portugal's colonialist regime in Mozambique. During this period both Zapu and Zanu began a campaign of guerrilla warfare.

1976 Although Zanu and Zapu formed the Patriotic Front (PF) alliance, co-operation between the two remained limited. The civil war continued and intensified towards the end of the 1970s.

1979 A new constitution, favourable to the PF, was drawn up at Lancaster House in London.

1980 Robert Mugabe's Zanu party won the general election and Zimbabwe gained independence from Britain. Mugabe became prime minister (and subsequently president). Conflict between Zanu (mainly Shona) and Zapu (mainly Ndebele) soon began, with Joshua Nkomo's Zapu largely destroyed by the North Korean-trained Fifth Brigade which Mugabe sent into Matabeleland. According to the Catholic church in Zimbabwe, a systematic campaign of terror was carried out against the rural population.

1985 Mugabe and Zanu were re-elected.

1987 Zanu and Zapu put their differences behind them and merged to form the Zimbabwe African National Union-Patriotic Front (Zanu-PF).

1990 Zanu-PF and Mugabe were re-elected.

1991 The Commonwealth issued its Harare Declaration at its summit in Zimbabwe, reaffirming its aims of fostering international peace and security, democracy, freedom of the individual and equal rights for all.

1995 Zanu-PF won the legislative election.

1996 Mugabe was re-elected.

1999 President Mugabe decided, without consulting parliament, to intervene in the war in Democratic Republic of Congo (DRC).

2000 On 12–13 February Zimbabweans voted against Mugabe's constitutional amendment in a referendum. Fifty-five per cent voted against a draft constitution that would have increased his powers and allowed him to stay in office for a further two terms. Zanu-PF won the parliamentary election in June, with 62 seats against the Movement for Democratic Change's (MDC) 57 seats. In October, there were riots in Harare in protest against rises in food prices and demanding Mugabe's resignation. The MDC began impeachment proceedings against the president.

2001 The Commonwealth ministerial team's proposed visit to look into the intimidation of Zimbabwe's judiciary and press was rejected by the government in March. Mugabe announced in April that he would stand for election in 2002. In April, President Mugabe's 'war veterans' occupied white-owned private businesses, demanding compensation for workers laid off in the recession. Zimbabwe assured the Committee of Commonwealth Foreign Ministers in Abuja, Nigeria, on 6 September, that it would carry out land reform fairly and legally in return for a pledge by the UK to pay for the programme. However, violence against farmers continued.

2002 New laws passed in January outlawed criticism of the president, made the carrying of ID cards mandatory and gave sweeping powers to the police to maintain public order. Penalties for offences are life imprisonment or death. The EU imposed sanctions on 20 members of the Zimbabwean government, including the president, after its team of observers was expelled. Controversial official results showed that Robert Mugabe was re-elected in the presidential elections held 9–11 March with 55 per cent of the vote, against 42 per cent for Morgan Tsvangirai, who was charged with treason. Following the elections, Zimbabwe was suspended from the Commonwealth. The opposition failed in a legal challenge over the election results.

Political structure

Constitution

From 1980 to 1987 Zimbabwe was bound by the Lancaster House Constitution drawn up in London in 1979. Amendments in 1987 resulted in the appointment of an executive president as head of state.

The election laws were amended in January 2002 to ban independent election monitors and deny voting rights to Zimbabweans living outside the country.

Form of state

Republic

The executive

Executive power is vested in the president (elected by universal suffrage every six years), vice presidents and cabinet. Both the vice presidents and cabinet are appointed by the president.

National legislature

Legislative power is vested in the parliament, comprising a 150-member House of Assembly made up of 120 directly elected members – 10 are nominated by the president. The remaining 20 are traditional chiefs' representatives and provincial governors. The Assembly is elected every five years.

Last elections

9–11 March 2002 (presidential); 24–25 June 2000 (parliamentary).

Next elections

2005 (parliamentary); 2008 (presidential).

Political parties

Ruling party

Zimbabwe African National Union-Patriotic Front (Zanu-PF)

Main opposition party

Movement for Democratic Change (MDC)

Population

12.63 million (2000)

The annual population growth rate was 2.6 per cent for the period 1994–2000 and is projected at 1.3 per cent per annum between 1997 and 2015. Around 45 per cent of the total population is under 15 years of age. Zimbabwe's young population, increasing at around 3 per cent year, represents a major strain on employment and the provision of social services.

Population density: 29 inhabitants per square km. Urban population: 31 per cent (1994–2000).

Over three-quarters of the population lived below the poverty line in June 2001.

Ethnic make-up

Shona (75 per cent) (including the Zezuru clan (18 per cent) and the Karanga clan (22 per cent); Ndebele (18 per cent); white (1 per cent). There are several minor ethnic groups, and a small number of inhabitants of Asian or mixed racial descent.

Religions

Dual Christian/indigenous beliefs (50 per cent), Christian (25 per cent), indigenous beliefs (24 per cent).

Education

Adult literacy: 88 per cent (1999).

Oxfam estimates that 85 per cent of Zimbabwean children age 6–11 will enrol for school by 2015. The educational system was one of the best in the region with universal primary school enrolment and secondary education reaching about 50 per cent of those eligible. However, with less than 30 per cent of school leavers able to find jobs, this creates a potentially volatile group of disenchanted citizens. The worsening public finances has put the country's education facilities at risk as the government rationalises non-military exenditure.

Health

World Bank estimates during the period 1994 and 2000 showed that the average life expectancy was 58 years and the infant mortality rate stood at 56 per 1,000 live births. It is estimated that 16 per cent of children under the age of five were malnourished in the same period. The total fertility rate shows that 3.6 children are born per woman while the rate of contraception practices is estimated at 48 per cent among women aged 15–49. The maternal mortality rate is typically 400 deaths per 100,000 live births. World Bank estimates in 2000 showed that 36 per cent of the population had access to improved water sources. There are 0.1 physicians and 0.5 hospital beds typically available for 1,000 people.

The state of Zimbabwe's healthcare was mixed in the 1990s. According to World Bank estimates, government expenditure on healthcare averaged 6.6 per cent of GDP of which 2.9 per cent was public expenditure between 1990 and 1998. Expenditure on private healthcare (such as private household expenditure and insurance) averaged 3.7 per cent of GDP over the same period.

HIV prevalence stands at around 26 per cent of the population aged 15–49 years, posing yet another serious barrier to Zimbabwe's imperiled development. Estimates in 2002 showed that 24 per cent of health workers' posts were vacant and 73 per cent of health facilities had no drugs.

Welfare

At present many companies operate some form of social security plan for their employees, which usually includes medical aid. Workers may individually contribute to private insurance and medical aid funds.

Main cities

Harare (capital, estimated population 1.5 million in 1998), Bulawayo (400,000), Gweru (80,000), Mutare (76,000), Kwekwe (65,000), Hwange (35,000).

Languages spoken

Official language/s

English, Shona, Ndebele

Media

The Zimbabwean government operates a highly repressive policy towards the media and members of the ruling party have occasionally bombed the offices of some newspapers. Criticism of President Mugabe was outlawed by the Public order and Security Bill passed in January 2002. On 1 February 2002, the Zimbabwe parliament passed the Access to Information Bill which made it an offence to report from Zimbabwe unless registered by a state-appointed commission. Only Zimbabwean citizens or residents of the country are eligible for registration. Foreign journalists can be allowed into the country to cover specific events only. A registration levy of US$12,000 was introduced in June 2002.

Press

Dailies: Major English-language dailies include *The Herald*, published in Harare, *The Chronicle*, *Zimbabwe Independent* and *The Daily News* (published by Associated Newspapers of Zimbabwe).

Weeklies: Weekly newspapers include *Zimbabwe Standard* and *The Gweru Times* (bi-lingual weekly in English and Shona). *Kwayedza* and *The Manica Post* cover current and political affairs. National Sunday newspapers are *The Sunday Mail* and *The Sunday News*.

Business: *The Financial Gazette* is the country's only wholly independent newspaper, published in Harare. *The Farmer* published weekly covers agricultural matters. Business news is also covered by *The Chronicle*, published in Bulawayo, the *Manica Post*, published in Mutare, and some regional publications.

Periodicals: *Journal of Social Development in Africa* is published twice annually featuring development issues. *Skyhost* covers travel and *Moto* current affairs.

Broadcasting

On 26 July 2001, the government suspended the press accreditation of the British Broadcasting Corporation (BBC).

Radio: There are radio services in English, Shona and Ndebele.

Television: Two television channels, broadcasting for about 45 hours per week, are transmitted by the Zimbabwe Broadcasting Corporation (ZBC).

Satellite systems are available.

Economy

Since the late 1990s, the Zimbabwean economy has experienced a sharp decline. In 2001, GDP contracted by 8.4 per cent and the government forecasts a further contraction of 10 per cent by end-2002. The IMF estimates that the cumulative decline in real GDP per capita from 1997 to 2001 was 23 per cent. Negative real interest rates and food shortages have helped create hyperinflation, which reached 114 per cent in April 2002. The government's land reform programme along with its threat to seize foreign-owned factories have undermined investor confidence. By the end of the third-quarter 2001, unemployment was estimated at 50 per cent. A lack of foreign exchange has led to import scarcities, thereby crippling the economy further and undermining the country's capital base. Unsustainable fiscal policies and political instability have also contributed to Zimbabwe's poor economic outlook.

The result of the political and economic turbulence has been Zimbabwe's increasing alienation from bilateral and multilateral donors. By 2002, the government was overwhelmingly reliant on aid from Libya, while relations with the developed world have broken down. In September 2001, the country was declared ineligible to draw on IMF funds and was barred from borrowing resources under the Poverty Reduction and Growth Facility (PRGF). In June 2002, the IMF adopted a declaration of non-co-operation with Zimbabwe due to the government's default on debt servicing repayments to the Fund. By mid-2002, Zimbabwe's total overdue obligations were around US$132 million. Without donor funds, Zimbabwe's situation remains extremely perilous.

External trade

Zimbabwe's competitiveness on international markets has been severely hampered by the country's currency, which has been set at an overvalued peg against the US dollar. This has led to a serious shortage of foreign exchange, the depletion of foreign reserves and rising levels of foreign debt arrears. Continued land invasions and political disruption has reduced output in Zimbabwe's key commercial farming sector, undermining export markets even further. President Mugabe appears reluctant or unable to reverse the situation and create stability in the export sector and this, coupled with declining foreign investment and a lack of hard currency, will lead to continuing significant problems for Zimbabwe's external trade situation in 2002.

Exports

The total value of exports fell from US$1.79 billion in 2000 to US$1.72 billion in 2001. Exports of commercial crops such as tobacco and cotton have declined in the wake of disruption to harvests due to the land occupations and deteriorating commodity prices. The overvalued currency peg has also made Zimbabwean exports less competitive. Tobacco farmers led the campaign for devaluation.

Principal exports include tobacco (approximately 35 per cent of 1999 total), gold (10 per cent), ferro-chrome (9 per cent), cotton, textiles and clothing, maize, sugar.

Main destinations: South Africa (13.1 per cent of 2000 total), UK (9.3 per cent), Japan (8.4 per cent), Germany (6.5 per cent), US (5.9 per cent).

Imports

The total value of imports fell from US$1.52 billion in 2000 to US$1.45 billion in 2001. This was largely related to the lack of currency reserves due to a legacy of economic mismanagement coupled with deteriorating commodity prices and a lack of foreign financing. As a result, the country has experienced a shortage of essential imports, particularly fuel.

Principal imports are machinery and transport (typically 38 per cent of the total), electricity (16 per cent), chemicals (16 per cent), semi-processed goods (15 per cent) and fuels and crude materials (6 per cent).

Main sources: South Africa (41.8 per cent of 2000 total), UK (7.1 per cent), Mozambique (3.9 per cent), US (3.2 per cent), Germany (2.6 per cent).

Agriculture

Farming

Agriculture is the dominant sector in the Zimbabwean economy, employing 70 per cent of the labour force. Maize is the staple food and tobacco, cotton and sugar are the main cash crops. Horticulture is a growth sector. The agricultural sector is still dominated by small scale and subsistence farming.

Since 2000, the government has appropriated white-owned farm property without compensation. The government maintains that as the first white settlers obtained their farmland mostly by expelling the indigenous black population, it is has no obligation to pay the commercial value of the seized farms. By mid-2002, there were less than 3,000 commercial farms operating in Zimbabwe, a fall of around 2,000 since mid-2000 when the often violent expropriation programme began. In June 2002, the government ordered commercial farmers to immediately halt production and abandon the land by 10 August or face imprisonment. The final destruction of the commercial farming sector is likely to severely undermine agricultural productivity and the export of commercial crops. The government has not sought to combine land transfers to poor black farmers with the necessary capital and expertise to run the farms, which has led to a crisis within the agricultural sector and widespread food shortages in 2002.

Many potential donors have refused to commit to help the land reform process, with the EU backing UK criticism of Mugabe's policy of allowing squatters to settle on white-owned land in defiance of High Court rulings. Even before the land crisis of 2000, critics noted that the land already acquired by the state often ended up in the hands of Zanu-PF leaders, who merely replaced white commercial farmers, instead of being used to alleviate overcrowding in rural black areas.

Forestry

Around half of Zimbabwe's land area is forested. In the period 1990–2000, Zimbabwe lost on average 1.54 per cent of forest cover every year, which is twice the African average. Forests are primarily used for fuelwood, which provides three quarters of domestic energy supplies. The country's main exported forest products are sandalwood and wood panels. In 2000, the export of forest products amounted to US$17.7 million while imports totalled US$34.3 million.

Industry and manufacturing

Zimbabwe's industrial sector was one of the most advanced and diversified in sub-Saharan Africa. By 2000, manufacturing accounted for around a third of the country's exports and included processing goods from the agricultural and mining sectors as well as brewing, chemicals and textiles.

However, the sector has been undermined by capital flight, a lack of foreign exchange, an overvalued exchange rate, severe fuel shortages and the constant threat of forced nationalisation. The largely liberalised textile sector is also struggling against competition from countries such as South Africa where subsidies and tariffs operate as barriers to free trade.

Other problems include a lack of capacity which can only be improved with increased foreign investment. With supporters of the Zanu-PF beginning to attack foreign companies operating in Zimbabwe, prospects for industrial expansion look dim.

Zimbabwe's heavy industries are also facing hard times, despite being targetted by the government as essential to developing import substitutes which would reduce the loss in foreign exchange. In recent years, the country has experienced an expansion in the chemicals and cement sectors.

Tourism

Tourism should be a growth area and the government is keen to promote high quality tourism. The Zimbabwe Tourism Authority (ZTA) claimed that arrivals were up by 6 per cent in January–September 2001 compared to the same period in the previous year. However, Zimbabwe Sun, the largest hotel operator in the country, claimed in 2001 that the country's poor political image abroad has led to a 'dramatic' drop in both regional and international tourists visiting the county. The worst affected are safari lodges, but all sectors are said to be facing collapse.

Mining

The mining sector accounts for around 8 per cent of GDP, and employs 5 per cent of the workforce. It generates between 35–45 per cent of export earnings.

Many minerals, including chromite, copper and nickel ores, iron ore, tin ore, gold ore, phosphate rock, limestone and iron pyrites are converted to downstream products. The main exceptions are coal, phosphate rock, pyrites and limestone, which, along with a substantial proportion of iron, steel, copper and asbestos production are sold on the domestic market. Import substitution is encouraged. However, increasing energy prices are the main source of cost increases to the industry, and has hampered mining development in recent years. Meanwhile, the over-valued exchange rate has undermined the mining sector's external competitiveness.

Zimbabwe has the potential to become a leading producer of platinum. In March 2001, Impala Platinum (Implats), the world's second-largest platinum producer, invested US$30 million in the purchase of 30 per cent of Zimbabwe Platinum Mines' (Zimplats) participation in the Ngezi opencast mine and the Hartley platinum joint venture company, which operates it. The Ngezi mine is expected to produce 2.2 million tonnes of ore annually. It is estimated that the US$264 million Hartley platinum mine project, 80km west of Harare, will provide some 3 per cent of world supply and annual export earnings of over US$100 million.

Gold is Zimbabwe's second export, after tobacco. The government gave gold producers a price subsidy of about 25 per cent above world bullion prices in 2001.

Hydrocarbons

Oil

There are no proven oil deposits in Zimbabwe. Zimbabwe has no refining capacity and imports all its oil from South Africa. The National Oil Company of Zimbabwe (Noczim) is responsible for supplying the country with oil, but due to a foreign currency crisis it is unable to pay its bills and oil supplies have been unreliable since 2000.

Gas

There are no proven natural gas deposits in Zimbabwe.

Coal

Coal is for domestic use only. Around 60 per cent of coal production is used for electricity generation. The Wankie Coal Company (WCC) is the country's only coal producer and is 40 per cent owned by the government. Annual production is typically around four million tonnes.

Energy

Coal meets 60 per cent of local electricity generation requirements with wood, oil and hydroelectric power providing the rest.

Emphasis is on developing local energy resources, particularly coal and hydropower. Projects under way involve expansion of the huge Hwange coal field, including two new thermal power stations, and the building of hydroelectric stations on the Zambezi River.

The Zimbabwe Electricity Supply Authority (Zesa), which oversees generation, transmission and distribution of electricity, has plans for a number of projects aimed at rehabilitating existing power generators as well as creating new ones. Zimbabwe is keen to co-operate with neighbouring states and will be largely helped by the growing ties within the Southern African Development Community (SADC). The government also plans to provide hundreds of rural districts with electricity through solar power to provide lighting as well as helping rural industries.

However, the country continues to face problems relating to the rising cost of oil and electricity imports. This has resulted in severe debts within the electricity sector and continual threats to power supply. This has dashed hopes of privatising Zesa, which is experiencing severe cash-flow problems and mounting debts.

Financial markets

Stock exchange

Although Zimbabwe's economy is shrinking rapidly, industrial share prices on the Zimbabwe Stock Exchange surged 68 per cent in the first six months of 2002, the explanation being that the escalating inflation had driven investors into equities.

Banking

Central bank

Reserve Bank of Zimbabwe

Main financial centre

Harare

Time

GMT plus two hours

Geography

Zimbabwe is a landlocked country in southern central Africa. It is bounded by the Limpopo river and South Africa to the south, by the Zambezi river and Zambia to the north, by Mozambique to the east and by Botswana to the west.

The country falls into three geographical areas: the Highveld, the Lowveld and the Eastern Highlands. The Highveld comprises the major part of the country extending across its central area and rising gradually from the south-west to the north-east, with an average altitude of 1,200 metres. The two main cities, Harare (altitude 1,472 metres) and Bulawayo (altitude 1,343 metres) lie in this area. The Lowveld comprises the Sabi-Limpopo valleys in the south (altitude 600 metres to 800 metres) and the Zambezi valley in the north (altitude 400 metres to 600 metres). The Eastern Highlands borders Mozambique and contains two ranges, the Chimanimani Mountains, with peaks reaching 2,436 metres, and the Inyanga Mountains, with peaks up to 2,595 metres.

A spectacular natural feature is the Victoria Falls on the Zambezi river, the border with Zambia, in the north-western corner of the country. Further east, the Zambezi is dammed for electricity generation at Kariba, forming a lake 250km long.

Climate

Most of the country is semi-tropical with day temperatures of 30 degrees Celsius (C), or slightly above on hot days in the rainy season, but falling as low as 0 degrees C at night in the dry winter season. Rainfall is largely confined to the months November to March and is subject to wide annual variations with considerable influence on agricultural production. Heavier rain falls in the Eastern Highlands.

Dress codes

Business dress is generally formal, suits or jacket with a tie and trousers for men. Many hotels and restaurants require smart casual attire, which excludes denim jeans, particularly in the evening with some insisting on jacket and tie. Women normally dress conservatively in a suit, dress or blouse and skirt; trouser suits are acceptable.

Entry requirements

Passports

Required by all.

Visa

Not required by citizens of most Commonwealth countries, EU, USA, Japan, Canada and some other countries. Visitors must have an onward or return ticket and 'sufficient' money for their stay.

Currency advice/regulations

No limit on foreign currency brought into country, but the amount must be declared and must not be exceeded by amount taken out at departure.

Health (for visitors)

Most areas, particularly the Highveld with the main cities of Harare and Bulawayo, have a comfortable climate.

Visitors have access to government emergency medical services, but these, and the services of private doctors, must be paid in full.

Mandatory precautions

Yellow fever vaccination certificate if travelling from an infected area.

Advisable precautions

Typhoid and polio vaccinations are recommended. Malaria risk exists in the Zambezi valley and other low-lying areas – anti-malaria tablets should be taken. Water precautions are necessary outside the main towns. Bilharzia is endemic, therefore avoid using lake or river water for drinking or swimming. Tap water and public and private swimming baths are safe. There is an AIDS risk: 10 per cent of the population is infected with HIV.

Hotels
Several hotels of various standards are available in the main cities, rated from one to five stars by the Tourist Board. Most of the larger ones are air-conditioned. The government imposes a bed tax per person per night, and it is usual to tip 10 per cent.

Public holidays
Fixed dates

1 Jan (New Year's Day), 18 Apr (Independence), 1 May (Workers' Day), 25 May (Africa Day), 11 Aug (Heroes' Day), 12 Aug (Defence Forces' Day), 25 and 26 Dec (Christmas).

Variable dates

Good Friday, Easter Monday.

Working hours
Banking

Mon–Fri: 0830–1500, (Wed) 0830–1300; Sat: 0830–1130.

Business

Mon–Fri: 0745/0830–1600/1700.

Government

Mon–Fri: 0745/0830–1600/1700.

Telecommunications
Telephone/fax

Dialling code for Zimbabwe: IDD access code + 263 followed by area code (Harare 4, Bulawayo 9, Gweru 54, Mutare (Umtali) 20, Victoria Falls 13), followed by subscriber's number.

Electricity supply
230V AC.

Social customs/useful tips
Zimbabweans generally rise early and go to bed early, particularly on weekdays. Punctuality is generally appreciated in business circles, though not uniformly reciprocated, particularly by members of the government. Hospitality, particularly for meals, is widely offered and may be freely reciprocated. The formal address (Mr, Mrs or Miss with surname) is usual and Christian-name terms are only adopted on closer acquaintance. The giving or receiving of gifts, other than between personal friends, is not customary. No particular proscriptions apply to eating, drinking or smoking and there are no particular religious observances or taboos. Tipping (for example, 10 per cent of a restaurant bill) is common.

It is unwise to photograph major government buildings, military personnel or equipment without prior official permission. Photographers should bring their own film as it is not generally available locally.

From January 2002, it is mandatory to carry ID cards.

Security
Crime is relatively low and urban areas are safe. However, particular care should be taken of cars, and valuables should not be left in them. Many hotels and restaurants provide guarded parking facilities, particularly at night.

Getting there
Air

National airline: Air Zimbabwe.

International airport/s: Bulawayo (Code: BUQ), 24km from city, restaurant; Harare (Code: HRE), 12km from city, duty-free shop, bar, buffet, restaurant, bank, post office, car hire; Victoria Falls (Code: VFA) 22km from city.

Other airport/s: Harare (HRE), 12km south-east of Harare.

Airport tax: International departures for non-residents US$20 payable in US dollar bills; nationals of Zimbabwe and alien residents Z$100; not applicable to transit passengers continuing their journey from the same airport within 24 hours and children under 12 years.

Surface

Road: Direct route from Lusaka (Zambia) to Harare, via Victoria Falls, Kariba and Chirundu. Entry from South Africa at Beitbridge and from Botswana at Plumtree. Most of the border posts are closed from 1800 to 0600 hours every day although specific hours vary.

Rail: Regular services from Zambia, via Victoria Falls, from Beira, from South Africa and from Maputo, Mozambique.

Getting about
National transport

Air: Regular inexpensive daily flights by Air Zimbabwe between Harare and Bulawayo, Buffalo Range, Gweru, Hwange, Kariba, Masvingo and Victoria Falls.

Road: Network of over 85,000 km, of which about one-quarter are classed as main or secondary roads and half are surfaced with gravel. Good roads connect major towns.

Buses: Express coach services from Harare to Bulawayo, Mutare, Kariba, Chipinge, Masvingo. Advisable to book in advance.

Rail: National Railways of Zimbabwe operate services between Harare and Gweru, Bulawayo, Victoria Falls, Mutare, Masvingo, Chinhoyi and intermediate towns.

City transport

Taxis: Not usually hailed in street. Available at ranks near main hotels. A 10 per cent tip is usual.

Buses, trams & metro: Urban services in some centres can be sporadic.

Car hire

Self-drive cars are available in main cities and at Harare airport. They can be a useful method of transport as most main intercity roads tend to be of good quality. Drive on the left. A foreign or international driving licence is acceptable for short visits.

BUSINESS DIRECTORY

Telephone area codes
The international direct dialling code (IDD) for Zimbabwe is + 263 followed by the area code:

Beitbridge	86	Kwekwe	55
Bulawayo	9	Marondera	79
Chipinge	27	Masvingo39	
Chitungwiza	70	Murambinda	21
Colleen Bawn	16	Mutare	20
Filabussi	17	Mvurwi	77
Glendale	758	Norton	62
Gweru	54	Plumtree	80
Harare	4	Ruwa	73
Hwange	81	Selous	628
Juliasdale	29	Victoria falls	13
Kadoma	68	Zvishavane	51
Kariba	61		

Chambers of Commerce
Zimbabwe National Chamber of Commerce, Bulawayo Branch, PO Box 1934, Bulawayo (tel: 69-769).

Zimbabwe National Chamber of Commerce, Harare Branch, PO Box 1934, Harare (tel: 708-611).

Banking
Barclays Bank of Zimbabwe Ltd, PO Box 1279, Barclay House, Jason Moyo Avenue/First Street, Harare (tel: 758280; fax: 752913).

First Merchant Bank of Zimbabwe, PO Box 2786, FMB House, 67 Samora Machel Avenue, Harare (tel: 703071; fax: 250682).

Merchant Bank of Central Africa, PO Box 3200, 14th Floor, Old Mutual Centre, Third Street, Jason Moyo Avenue, Harare (tel: 701636-52 fax: 708005).

NMB Bank, PO Box 2564, 1st Floor, Unity Court, Corner 1st Street/Union Avenue, Harare (tel: 759651; fax: 759648).

Stanbic Bank Zimbabwe Ltd, PO Box 300, Stanbic Bank Centre, 59 Samora Machel Avenue, Harare (tel: 759480; fax: 749030).

Standard Chartered Bank Zimbabwe Ltd, PO Box 373, John Boyne Hse, 38 Speke Ave, Harare (tel: 752864 fax: 758076).

Zimbabwe Banking Corp Ltd, PO Box 3198, Zimbank House, 46 Speke Avenue, Harare (tel:757471/94 fax: 757497).

Central bank

Reserve Bank of Zimbabwe, PO Box 1283, 80 Samora Machel Avenue, Harare, Zimbabwe (tel: 703000, 703111 fax: 405979, 705978/9, 707800).

Travel information

Air Zimbabwe, PO Box AP1. Harare Airport, Harare (tel: 575-111; fax: 575-068).

National tourist organisation offices

Zimbabwe Tourism Authority, 9th Floor, Kopje Plaza, 1 Jason Moyo Avenue, Cnr Jason Moyo/Rotten Row, PO Box CY286, Causeway, Harare (tel: 753-730/34; fax: 758-726/28; e-mail: mktg@ztazim.org; zta@africaonline.co.zw; internet site: http://www.tourismzimbabwe.co.zw).

Ministries

Ministry of Agriculture, Ngungunyana Building 1, Borrowdale Road, P.Bag 7701, Causeway, Harare (tel: 706-081, 700-596; fax: 734-646).

Ministry of Defence, Munhumutapa Building, Samora Machel Avenue, P.Bag 7713, Causeway, Harare (tel: 700-155, 728-271).

Ministry of Education, Ambassador House, Union Avenue, PO Box CY121, Causeway, Harare (tel: 734-051, 734-067; fax: 734-075).

Ministry of Environment and Tourism, 14th Floor Karigamombe Centre, 53 Samora Machel Avenue, P.Bag, 7753, Causeway, Harare (tel: 794-455, 704-701; fax: 794-450).

Ministry of Finance, Munhumutapa Building, Samora Machel Avenue, P.Bag, 7705, Causeway, Harare (tel: 794-571, 796-191; fax: 792-750).

Ministry of Foreign Affairs, Munhumutapa Building, Samora Machel Avenue, P.Box 4240, Harare (tel: 727-005, 794-681; fax: 706-293).

Ministry of Health and Child Welfare, Kaguvi Building, 4th Street, P.O. Box CY198, Causeway, Harare (tel: 730-011, 794-411; fax: 793-634).

Ministry of Higher Education: Old Mutual Centre, 1st Floor, 3rd Street/J.Moyo Avenue, PO Box UA 275, Union Avenue, Harare (tel: 702-361, 795-441; fax: 790-923, 728-730).

Ministry of Home Affairs, 11th Floor, Mukwati Building, P.Bag 505D, Harare (tel: 723-653, 703-642; fax: 728-768).

Ministry of Industry and Commerce, 13th Floor, Mukwati Building, 4th Street/ Livingston Avenue, P.Bag 7708, Causeway, Harare (tel: 702-731, 729-801).

Ministry of Information, Posts and Telecommunications, 8th-11th Floor, Linquenda House, Baker Avenue, PO Box CY1276 & CY825, Causeway, Harare (tel: 703-891, 706-891; fax: 735-640).

Ministry of Justice, Legal and Parliamentary Affairs, Corner House, Leopold Takawira Street, P.Bag 7704, Causeway, Harare (tel: 790-902; fax 790-901).

Ministry of Lands and Water Development, Ngungunyana Building, 1 Borrowdale Road, P.Bag 7701, Causeway, Harare (tel: 706-081, 700-596).

Ministry of Local Government, Rural and Urgan Development, 16th-20th Floors, Mukwati Building, P.Bag 7706, Causeway, Harare (tel: 790-601, 728-631).

Ministry of Mines, Zimre Centre, L.Takawira Street/Union Avenue, P.Bag 7709, Causeway, Harare (tel: 732-881, 732-885; fax: 790-704).

Ministry of National Affairs, Employment Creation and Co-operatives, Zanu PF Building, Rotten Row/S.Machel Avenue, PO Box 4530, Harare (tel: 734-691, 730-893; fax: 735-338).

Ministry of National Security, Chaminuka Building, 5th Street, Causeway, Harare (tel: 795-965).

Ministry of Public Construction and National Housing, Corner L.Takawira Street & H. Chitepo Avenue, PO Box CY441, Causeway, Harare (tel: 704-561, 704-021; fax: 702-271)

Ministry of Public Service, Labour and Social Welfare, 12th Floor Compensation House, Central Avenue/4th Street, P.Bag 7707, Causeway, Harare (tel: 790-871, 796-451).

Ministry of Sports Recreation and Culture, Pax House, 89 Union Avenue, Harare (tel: 707-411, 794-450; fax: 707-580).

Ministry of Transport and Energy, 4th Floor Atlas House, 62 Robert Mugabe Road, Private Bag 7742, Causeway, Harare (tel: 706-446; fax: 708-225).

Office of the President and Cabinet, Munhumutapa Building, Samora Machel Avenue/3rd Street, Private Bag 7700, Causeway, Harare (tel: 707-091, 707-098; fax: 734-644, 792-044).

Parliament of Zimbabwe, Baker Avenue Box 8055, Causeway, Harare (tel: 729-722, 795-548).

Other useful addresses

Agricultural Marketing Authority (AMA), Royal Mutual House, 45 Baker Avenue, PO Box 8094, Harare (tel: 730-944).

Attorney-General's Office, Corner House, Leopold Takawira Street, P.Bag 7704, Causeway, Harare (tel: 790-902, 790-905).

Chamber of Mines of Zimbabwe, 4 Central Avenue, PO Box 712, Harare (tel: 702-843; fax: 707-983).

Cold Storage Commission (CSC), Josiah Chinamano Road, Bulawayo (tel: 68-961; fax: 67-522).

Commercial Farmers' Union, Agriculture House, PO Box 1241, Leopold Takawira Street, Harare (tel: 791-881).

Confederation of Zimbabwe Industries, Industry House, 109 Rotten Row, PO Box 3794, Harare (tel: 739-833; fax: 702-873).

Cotton Marketing Board (CMB), Kurima House, 89 Baker Avenua, Harare (tel: 739-061; fax: 66-429).

Dairy Marketing Board (DMB), Dolphin House, Leopold Takawira Street, Harare (tel: 705-700).

Grain Marketing Board (GMB), Kurima House, 89 Baker Avenue, Harare (tel: 732-011; fax: 732-019).

Minerals Marketing Corporation of Zimbabwe, Globe House, 51 Jason Moyo Avenue, PO Box 2628, Harare (tel: 703-402, 705-862; fax: 722-441).

Parliament of Zimbabwe, Baker Avenue Box 8055, Causeway, Harare (tel: 729-722, 795-548).

Zimbabwe Broadcasting Corporation (ZBC), Broadcasting Centre, Pockets Hill, PO Box HG444, Highlands, Harare (tel: 486-670, 481-252/9; fax: 498-613).

Zimbabwe International Trade Fair, Zift, PO Famona, Bulawayo (tel: 64-911).

Zimbabwe Investment Centre, 109 Rotten Row, PO Box 5950, Harare (tel: 757-931/5; fax: 757-937).

Zimbabwe State Trading Corporation, Globe House, 51 Jason Moyo Avenue, Harare (tel: 729-353).

Zimbabwe Stock Exchange, PO Box UA234, 8th Floor, Southampton House, Union Avenue, Harare (tel: 736-861; fax: 791-045).

Zimbabwe Tourist Development Corporation, PO Box 8052, Causeway, Harare (tel: 793-666).

Internet sites

Africa Business Network: http://www.ifc.org/abn

AllAfrica.com: http://www.allafrica.com

African Development Bank: http://www.afdb.org

Africa Online: http://www.africaonline.com

Harambee Afrika (UK business club for traders with east, central and southern Africa; includes annotated web resource list): http://www.harambee.co.uk

Mbendi AfroPaedia (information on companies, countries, industries and stock exchanges in Africa): http://mbendi.co.za

World of Information Regional Reviews

Readable – reliable – relevant information on 228 countries

Knowledge is of two kinds. We know a subject ourselves, or we know where we can find information upon it'

Dr Samuel Johnson

Understanding world events is never easy. Quality information and analysis is essential for anyone with an active interest in world affairs. The World of Information series of 5 annual Reviews, now in its 27th year, provides the background essential to an understanding of global events. Each Review covers, country-by-country, its region's developments and challenges in a readable, uniform presentation.

Each year recognised experts are commissioned to give their objective assessment of the politics and economics of every country and territory in the world. This experience has made for Reviews a primary source for business people and academics, researchers, governments and diplomatic officials, international organisations and agencies.

Each of the 2003/04 editions also features a number of thought-provoking articles on key regional topics such as water, HIV/AIDS, terrorism, Islam, oil and international investment.

If doing business in the global economy, or explaining world events to others, forms part of your daily activities and responsibilities, the Reviews are an indispensable tool. No need to burn the midnight oil calculating North Korea's GDP or Iraq's inflation rate. The Reviews have done it for you. As they have year in and year out over the past 27 years.

			No of copies	Total Amount
Africa Review	Europe	£50/US$80/ 80		
	Rest of World	£80/US$120/ 120		
Americas Review	Europe	£50/US$80/ 80		
	Rest of World	£80/US$120/ 120		
Asia & Pacific Review	Europe	£50/US$80/ 80		
	Rest of World	£80/US$120/ 120		
Europe Review	Europe	£50/US$80/ 80		
	Rest of World	£80/US$120/ 120		
Middle East Review	Europe	£50/US$80/ 80		
	Rest of World	£80/US$120/ 120		
Set of 5 Reviews	Europe	£200/US$320/ 320		
	Rest of World	£320/US$480/ 480		

Name:

Title:

Company/Organisation

Address

Address

Address

City/Postal code

Country

Tel:

Fax:

E-mail

Please tick if you do not wish to receive mail from other companies

Total to pay £/US$/

Enclosed is my cheque for £/US$/
payable to Walden Publishing Ltd

I am paying by telegraphic transfer to Walden Publishing Ltd, a/c No 90906530, Barclays Bank plc, Saffron Walden Branch, Sort Code 20-74-05

Please charge my Visa/Amex/MasterCard/Diners

Account no

Expiry date

Signature